POLITICAL
PSYCHOLOGY

Key Readings in Social Psychology

General Editor: ARIE W. KRUGLANSKI, University of Maryland at College Park

The aim of this series is to make available to advanced undergraduate and graduate students key articles in each area of social psychology in an attractive, user-friendly format. Many professors want to encourage their students to engage directly with research in their fields, yet this can often be daunting for students coming to detailed study of a topic for the first time. Moreover, declining library budgets mean that articles are not always readily available, and course packs can be expensive and time-consuming to produce. **Key Readings in Social Psychology** aims to address this need by providing comprehensive volumes, each one of which will be edited by a senior and active researcher in the field. Articles will be carefully chosen to illustrate the way the field has developed historically as well as to define current issues and research directions. Each volume will have a similar structure, which will include:

- an overview chapter, as well as introductions to sections and articles
- questions for class discussion
- annotated bibliographies
- full author and subject indexes

Published Titles

The Self in Social Psychology	Roy F. Baumeister
Stereotypes and Prejudice	Charles Stangor
Motivational Science	E. Tory Higgins and Arie W. Kruglanski
Social Psychology and Human Sexuality	Roy F. Baumeister
Emotions in Social Psychology	W. Gerrod Parrott
Intergroup Relations	Michael A. Hogg and Dominic Abrams
The Social Psychology of Organizational Behavior	Leigh L. Thompson
Social Psychology: A General Reader	Arie W. Kruglanski and E. Tory Higgins
Social Psychology of Health	Peter Salovey and Alexander J. Rothman
The Interface of Social and Clinical Psychology	Robin M. Kowalski and Mark R. Leary
Political Psychology	John T. Jost and Jim Sidanius

Titles in Preparation

Attitudes	Richard E. Petty and Russell Fazio
Close Relationships	Harry Reis and Caryl Rusbult
Group Processes	John Levine and Richard Moreland
Language and Communication	Gün R. Semin
Persuasion	Richard E. Petty and Russell Fazio
Social Cognition	David L. Hamilton
Social Comparison	Diederik Stapel and Hart Blanton
Social Neuroscience	John T. Cacioppo and Gary Berntson

For contiually updated information about published and forthcoming titles in the Key Readings in Social Psychology series, please visit: www.keyreadings.com

POLITICAL PSYCHOLOGY
Key Readings

Edited by

John T. Jost
Department of Psychology
New York University

Jim Sidanius
Department of Psychology
University of California, Los Angeles

Routledge
Taylor & Francis Group

LONDON AND NEW YORK

First published 2004

Published 2016 by Routledge
2 Park Square, Milton Park, Abingdon, Oxon OX14 4RN
711 Third Avenue, New York, NY 10017, USA

Routledge is an imprint of the Taylor & Francis Group, an informa business

Copyright © 2004 by Taylor & Francis Books, Inc.

Transferred to Digital Printing 2005

Library of Congress Cataloging-in-Publication Data

    Political psychology : key readings / edited by John T. Jost and James Sidanius.
        p. cm. — (Key readings in social psychology)
    Includes index.
    ISBN 1-84169-069-4 (hbk) — ISBN 1-84169-070-8 (pbk.)
    1. Political psychology. I. Jost, John T. II. Sidanius, Jim. III. Series.
    JA74.5.P637 2003
    320'.0'9—dc21

                                      2003010695

ISBN-13: 9781841690704 (pbk)

Contents

About the Editors   ix
Acknowledgments   xi

Political Psychology: An Introduction   1
John T. Jost and Jim Sidanius

PART 1
Historical Introduction   19

READING 1
The Poly-Psy Relationship: Three Phases of a Long Affair   22
William J. McGuire

PART 2
Personality and Politics   33

A. Authoritarianism and Mass Psychology

READING 2
The Authoritarian Personality and the Organization of Attitudes   39
Roger Brown

READING 3
Threat and Authoritarianism in the United States: 1978–1987   69
Richard M. Doty, Bill E. Peterson, and David G. Winter

READING 4
The Other "Authoritarian Personality"   85
Bob Altemeyer

B. Political Elites and Leadership

READING 5
Can Personality and Politics Be Studied Systemically?   108
Fred I. Greenstein

READING 6
Leader Appeal, Leader Performance, and the Motive Profiles
of Leaders and Followers: A Study of American Presidents
and Elections   124
David G. Winter

PART 3
Mass Media and Candidate Perception   135

READING 7
Experimental Demonstrations of the "Not-So-Minimal"
Consequences of Television News Programs   139
Shanto Iyengar, Mark D. Peters, and Donald R. Kinder

READING 8
Altering the Foundations of Support for the President
Through Priming   150
Jon A. Krosnick and Donald R. Kinder

READING 9
Anxiety, Enthusiasm, and the Vote: The Emotional Underpinnings
of Learning and Involvement During Presidential Campaigns   163
George E. Marcus and Michael B. MacKuen

PART 4
Ideology and Public Opinion   177

A. Does Ideology Exist?

READING 10
The Nature of Belief Systems in Mass Publics   181
Philip E. Converse

READING 11
The Origins and Meaning of Liberal/Conservative
Self-Identifications   200
Pamela Johnston Conover and Stanley Feldman

B. Cognitive Style and Ideological Functioning

READING 12

The Fear of Equality 217

Robert E. Lane

READING 13

Cognitive Style and Political Belief Systems
in the British House of Commons 230

Philip E. Tetlock

PART 5
Challenges of Decision-Making 241

READING 14

Contrasting Rational and Psychological Analysis
of Political Choice 244

George A. Quattrone and Amos Tversky

READING 15

The Drunkard's Search 259

Robert Jervis

PART 6
Prejudice, Diversity, and Social Contact 271

A. Theories of Intergroup Relations in Society

READING 16

The Social Identity Theory of Intergroup Behavior 276

Henri Taifel and John C. Turner

READING 17

The Role of Stereotyping in System Justification and
the Production of False Consciousness 294

John T. Jost and Mahzarin R. Banaji

READING 18

Social Dominance Theory: A New Synthesis 315

Jim Sidanius and Felicia Pratto

B. The Enduring Problem of Racism

READING 19
Group Conflict, Prejudice and the Paradox
of Contemporary Racial Attitudes   333
Lawrence Bobo

READING 20
Is It Really Racism? The Origins of White Americans'
Opposition to Race-Targeted Policies   358
David O. Sears, Colette van Laar, Mary Carrillo, and Rick Kosterman

---

P A R T   7
Conflict, Violence, and Political Transformation   379

A. The Social Psychology of Wrongdoing and Harm

READING 21
Social Organization for the Production of Evil   383
John M. Darley

READING 22
The Psychology of Political Terrorism   411
Martha Crenshaw

B. Protest and Revolution

READING 23
Theoretical Approaches to Explaining Collective Political
Violence   432
Harry Eckstein

READING 24
Politicized Collective Identity   449
Bernd Simon and Bert Klandermans

Appendix: How to Read a Journal Article in Social Psychology   467
Christian H. Jordan and Mark P. Zanna

Author Index   477
Subject Index   489

About the Editors

John T. Jost received his Ph.D. in social and political psychology from Yale University. He is currently Associate Professor of Psychology at New York University and, until recently, he was Associate Professor of Organizational Behavior at Stanford University. He has been a visiting scholar at the University of California at Santa Barbara, the University of Bologna in Italy, and the Radcliffe Institute for Advanced Study at Harvard University. Jost has published dozens of scientific articles and book chapters on such topics as stereotyping, prejudice, ideology, justice, and intergroup relations. He is the editor of *Social Justice Research* and serves on the editorial boards of *Personality and Social Psychology Bulletin*, *Group Processes and Intergroup Relations,* and the *British Journal of Social Psychology.* His other books are *The Psychology of Legitimacy* (with B. Major) and *Perspectivism in Social Psychology: The Yin and Yang of Scientific Progress* (with M. Banaji and D. Prentice).

Jim Sidanius received his Ph.D. from the University of Stockholm, Sweden and has taught at several universities, including Carnegie-Mellon University, the University of Texas at Austin, New York University, Princeton University, the University of Stockholm, Sweden, and UCLA. He is author of some ninety scientific papers in the field of political psychology, largely dealing with the interface between political ideology and cognitive functioning, the political psychology of gender, and the evolutionary psychology of group conflict. His previous books include *Social Dominance: An Intergroup Theory of Social Hierarchy and Oppression* (with F. Pratto) and *Racialized Politics: Values, Ideology, and Prejudice in American Public Opinion* (with D. Sears and L. Bobo).

Acknowledgments

The editors and publishers are grateful to the following for permission to reproduce the articles in this book:

Reading 1: W. J. McGuire, The Poly-Psy Relationship: Three Phases of a Long Affair. In *Explorations in Political Psychology* [ed. by S. Iyengar & W. J. McGuire], pp. 9–35, 1993. Copyright © 1993 Duke University Press. All rights reserved. Reprinted/adapted with permission of the publisher.

Reading 2: R. Brown, The Authoritarian Personality and the Organization of Attitudes. From R. Brown (Ed.), *Social Psychology* (pp. 477–546). Copyright © 1965 The Free Press. Reprinted/adapted with permission.

Reading 3: R. M. Doty, B. E. Peterson and D. G. Winter, Threat and Authoritarianism in the United States: 1978-1987. *Journal of Personality and Social Psychology,* 61, 629–640. Copyright © 1991 by the American Psychological Association. Reprinted/adapted with permission.

Reading 4: B. Altemeyer, The Other "Authoritarian" Personality. *Advances in Experimantal Social Psychology,* 30, 47–91. Copyright © 1998. Reprinted with permission of the author.

Reading 5: F. Greenstein, Can Personality and Politics be Studied Systematically? *Political Psychology,* 13, 105–128. Copyright © 1992 Blackwell Publishers. Reprinted/adapted with permission.

Reading 6: D. G. Winter, Leader Appeal, Leader Performance, and the Motive Profiles of Leaders and Followers: A Study of American Presidents and Elections. *Journal of Personality and Social Psychology,* 52, 196–202. Copyright © 1987 by the American Psychological Association. Reprinted/adapted with permission.

Reading 7: S. Iyengar, M. Peters and D. Kinder, Experimental Demonstrations of the "No-So-Minimal" Consequences of Television News Programs. *American Political Science Review,* 81, 848–858. Copyright © 1982. Reprinted/adapted with the permission of Cambridge University Press.

Reading 8: J. A. Krosnick and D. R. Kinder, Altering the Foundations of Support for the President Through Priming. *American Political Science Review,* 84, 497–512. Copyright © 1990. Reprinted/adapted with the permission of Cambridge University Press.

Reading 9: G. E. Marcus and M. MacKuen, Anxiety, Enthusiasm, and the Vote: The Emotional Underpinnings of Learning and Involvement During Presidential Campaigns. *American Political Science Review,* 87, 672–685. Copyright © 1993. Reprinted with the permission of Cambridge University Press.

Reading 10: P. E. Converse, The Nature of Belief Systems in Mass Publics. In D. E. Apter (Ed.), *Ideology and Discontent* (pp. 206–226). Copyright

Reading 11: P. Conover and S. Feldman, The Origins and Meaning of Liberal-Conservative Self-Identification. *American Journal of Political Science,* 25, 617–645. Copyright © 1981 Blackwell Publishers. Reprinted with permission.

Reading 12: R. E. Lane, The Fear of Equality. *American Political Science Review,* 53, 35–51. Copyright © 1959. Reprinted/adapted with the permission of Cambridge University Press.

Reading 13: P.E. Tetlock, Cognitive Style and Political Belief Systems in the House of Commons. *Journal of Personality and Social Psychology,* 46, 365–375. Copyright © 1984 by the American Psychological Association. Reprinted/adapted with permission.

Reading 14: G.A. Quattrone and A. Tversky, Contrasting Rational and Psychological Analyses of Political Choice. *American Political Science Review,* 82, 716–736. Copyright © 1988. Reprinted/adapted with the permission of Cambridge University Press.

Reading 15: R. Jervis, The Drunkard's Search. In *Explorations in Political Psychology* [ed. by S. Iyengar & W. J. McGuire], pp. 338–360, 1993. Copyright © 1993 Duke University Press. All rights reserved. Reprinted with permission of the publisher.

Reading 16: H. Tajfel and J. C. Turner, The Social Identity Theory of Intergroup Behavior. From S. Worchel and W. G Austin (Eds), *Psychology of Intergroup Relations* (pp. 7–24). Copyright © 1986. Reprinted/adapted with permission of the authors.

Reading 17: J. T. Jost and M. R. Banaji, The Role of Stereotyping in System-Justification and the Production of False Consciousness. *British Journal of Social Psychology,* 33, 1–27. Copyright © 1994 by The British Psychological Society. Reprinted/adapted with permission.

Reading 18: J. Sidanius and R. Pratto, Social Dominance Theory: A New Synthesis. From J. Sidanius and R. Pratto, *Social Dominance: An Intergroup Theory of Social Hierarchy and Oppression.* Copyright © 1999. Reprinted with the permission of Cambridge University Press.

Reading 19: L. Bobo, Group Conflict, Prejudice and the Paradox of Contemporary Racial Attitudes. From P. A. Katz and D. A. Taylor (Eds), *Eliminating Racism: Profiles in Controversy* (pp. 85–116). Copyright © 1988 Kluwer Academic/Plenum Publishers. Reprinted with permission.

Reading 20: D. O Sears, C. van Laar, M. Carrillo and R. Kosterman, Is It Really Racism? The Origins of White Americans' Opposition to Race-Targeted Policies. *Public Opinion Quarterly,* 61, 16–53. Copyright © 1997 University of Chicago Press. Reprinted with permission.

Reading 21: J. M. Darley, Social Organization for the Production of Evil. *Psychological Inquiry,* 3, 199–218. Copyright © 1992 Lawrence Erlbaum Associates, Inc. Reprinted with permission.

Reading 22: M. Crenshaw, The Psychology of Political Terrorism. In M. Hermann (Ed), *Political Psychology: Contemporary Problems and Issues.* Copyright © 1986 Jossey-Bass. This material is reprinted/adapted by permission of John Wiley & Sons, Inc.

Reading 23: H. Eckstein, Theoretical Approaches to Explaining Collective Political Violence. From T. R. Gurr (Ed), *Handbook of Political Conflict: Theory and Research.* Copyright © 1980 by The Free Press. Reprinted and edited with the permission of The Free Press, a division of Simon & Schuster Adult Publishing Group.

Reading 24: B. Simon and B. Klandermans, Politicized Collective Identity. *American Psychologist,* 56, 319–331. Copyright © 2001 by the American Psychological Association. Reprinted/adapted with permission.

Editors' Acknowledgments

In addition to the many authors and publishers who granted us permission to reproduce the articles and chapters for this book, we are greatly indebted to a large group of people who provided us with invaluable assistance in the preparation of this book, including a number of anonymous reviewers for Psychology Press. We would especially like to thank those colleagues who gave so generously of their time in explicitly advising us on which selections to include and why. They are: Bob Altemeyer, Larry Bobo, Marilynn Brewer, John Duckitt, Betty Glad, Jack Glaser, Doris Graber, Fred Greenstein, Ted Robert Gurr, György Hunyady, Shanto Iyengar, M. Kent Jennings, Robert Jervis, Jon Krosnick, Robert Lane, Rick Lau, George Marcus, Sam McFarland, Tom Pettigrew, Wendy Rahn, Stanley Renshon, David Sears, Dean Keith Simonton, Charles Taber, Philip Tetlock, Charles Tilly, Judith Torney-Purta, Tom Tyler, David Winter, and Robert Zajonc.

We would also like to thank the series editor, Arie Kruglanski, as well as our development editors at Psychology Press, Stacy Malyil and Paul Dukes, for their support and encouragement. Finally, we gratefully acknowledge the help of Agnish Chakravarti, Cara Jolly, Golbie Kamarei, Lea Richards, Mike Unzueta, and Jojanneke van der Toorn in preparing the introductory chapter and linking material, generating discussion questions, and generally assisting with the administrative demands of the project.

Political Psychology: An Introduction

John T. Jost and Jim Sidanius

O n April 27, 1937, Nazi warplanes flew from Germany to the town of Guernica in the Basque region of Northern Spain and dropped bombs on the unsuspecting town for several hours. The town burned for 3 days, and most of the surrounding area was destroyed. More than 1,600 innocent civilians, one third of the local population, were killed. The obliteration of the Spanish town, little more than target practice for Hitler's incipient war machine, had been requested by a Spaniard, General Francisco Franco, the ultimately successful leader of a fascist coup to overthrow the democratically elected Spanish government. This horrible political event inspired Picasso's *Guernica,* the cover illustration for this book, a masterpiece that foreshadowed the Second World War. The painting symbolizes man's timeless struggle against tyranny, aggression, terrorism, war, corruption, nationalism, prejudice, and evil, and the image has been widely resurrected in the aftermath of September 11, 2001. *Guernica* captures ancient human themes that are among the core topics addressed by the science of political psychology.

What is Political Psychology?

Political psychology explores the border that runs between the intellectual nations of political science and psychology. It is a dynamic subfield that addresses the ways in which *political institutions* both affect and are affected by *human behavior*. Our understanding of the reciprocal relationship between politics and psychology (especially *social* psychology, which borders also on sociology) has been steadily evolving in recent years, making it a compelling and exciting area of study. To know everything there is to know about the world of politics in theory and in practice, one must be, among other things, an expert in psychology.

Political psychologists belong to a relatively young interdisciplinary community that not only draws on theories and methods from psychology and political science, but is also happy to borrow from neighboring fields such as international relations, anthropology, sociology, oganizational behavior, economics, history, and philosophy. The work of political psychologists can be quantitative and statistical, as with analyses of experimental effects on candidate perception or longitudinal studies of voting trends. Or their work can be qualitative and narrative, as with case studies of decision-making fiascoes or archival analyses of famous presidential speeches. There is no single way to do political psychology. In this book, you will learn many different approaches to the vast array of questions that emanate from this broad, exciting field of inquiry.

There are live controversies and unresolved issues—plenty of work for future generations of political psychologists to complete. One perennial question is whether drawing on one's own political values and ideological convictions can help to produce valid scientific insight, or whether this inevitably leads to distortion and bias. Tetlock (1994), for instance, argued that "the road to scientific hell is paved with good moral intentions" and complained that (predominantly liberal) social scientists have too often allowed their own personal views to influence their professional analyses of racism and other value-laden topics. To these charges, Sears (1994) replied that being explicit about one's theoretical and political preferences is "far healthier than cloaking our own feelings in a pretense of scientific objectivity, while ignoring a ream of scientific evidence we happen to find distasteful" (p. 555). To be sure, when moral and political values are at stake, perfect neutrality is elusive. But to what extent is it even desirable as an ideal goal? The reader will have to answer this thorny question for himself or herself.

It is important to realize that political psychology is part of a long, venerable, and often controversial cultural tradition that goes back many centuries in Europe. Our brief historical overview draws extensively on insightful summaries by Stone (1981), Van Ginneken (1988), Ward (2002), and Deutsch and Kinnvall (2002).

A Brief Historical Overview of Political Psychology

The advent of democracy as a political system in ancient Athens necessitated a philosophical consideration of the rights and responsibilities of the electorate, and Plato and Aristotle discussed these issues in light of their theories of human nature. Conceptions of the "political man" further evolved during the Medieval and Renaissance periods in Europe. One of the world's first political consultants, Niccolo Machiavelli (1469–1527), wrote a major work entitled *The Prince* (1513) about the qualities necessary for successful political leadership. In the intervening centuries, the author's name has become synonymous with a leadership style that is cynical, self-serving, and often successful.

In his major work, *The Leviathan* (1651), Thomas Hobbes (1588–1679) offered a pessimistic view of the life of political man as "nasty, brutish, and short." This view anticipated Sigmund Freud's (1865-1939) later writings on the nature of man and society, especially *Civilization and its Discontents* (1930), in which society is seen as imposing much-needed restraint on the individual's sexual and aggressive impulses. Jean Jacques Rousseau (1712–1778) argued, against Hobbes, that human nature was essentially good. Rousseau maintained that if man were left to his natural state he would be able to achieve inner harmony and positive relationships with other human beings and with nature. According to this perspective, man's inherent virtue is compromised through socialization and the demands of society.

John Locke (1632–1704), an Enlightenment thinker, rejected the idea that human nature has any fixed characteristics and posited instead that the individual is born as a *tabula rasa* onto which training and experience are inscribed. Locke's position foreshadowed J.B. Watson's (1878–1958) behaviorist movement in psychology, which emphasized the primacy of learned experience over "innate ideas" in determining behavior. Locke subscribed to a rational, collaborative view of society in which human affairs are driven by a social contract between the individual and society. According to this view, reason, moderation, and compromise are the virtues of human relationships; these ideas laid the groundwork for modern, liberal democratic philosophy.

Karl Marx (1818–1883) has had tremendous impact on the development of political thought in modern times, but his direct influence on psychology has been relatively slight. Marx stressed the economic or "material" foundations of society and politics, viewing culture and ideology as manifestations of economic systems like capitalism. He is most famous for his writings on revolution and political transformation, inciting the embattled "workers of the world" to organize and throw off the "chains" of their oppression. As the 20th century wore on, Marx's theories of ideology, which were used to explain why revolution was not forthcoming, were eventually merged with Freud's theory of psychoanalysis by members of the Frankfurt School, first in Germany and then in the United States. Wilhelm Reich (1897–1957) in *The Mass Psychology of Fascism* (1933) and Erich Fromm (1900–1980) in *Escape from Freedom* (1941) both addressed the question of what psychological characteristics led followers to flock to right-wing political movements. The theme that prejudice and anti-Semitism arose from unconscious personality needs was further developed by Adorno and his colleagues at UC Berkeley in one of the first major texts in political psychology: *The Authoritarian Personality* (1950).

Another pioneer in the modern effort to integrate psychology and politics was Graham Wallas (1859–1932), who argued that it was impossible to understand the nature of political affairs without considering the psychological nature of those conducting these affairs. In his book, *Human Nature in Politics* (1908), Wallas warned that it is dangerous for proponents of democracy to assume that "every human action is the result of an intellectual process." He believed that teaching people to become consciously aware of their own psychological processes would help them to defend against the exploitation of these processes by others and to better control their own behavior. The notion that consciousness-raising would be both personally and politically liberating was also consistent with the popular conjunction of Marxist and Freudian ideas.

Harold Lasswell (1902–1978) is considered by many to be the first American political psychologist. His epoch-making *Psychopathology and Politics* (1930) was based on his study of the clinical files of politically active people. Lasswell argued that political leaders often project their hidden, private conflicts onto public symbols and objects, rationalizing these specific concerns in terms of general public interests. Fascination with political persuasion and the uses of propaganda rose steeply during and immediately after World War II. Public opinion polling techniques were soon developed by George Gallup (1901–1984), Paul Lazarsfeld (1901-1976), and others, giving political psychologists significant credibility both inside and outside of the academy. Centers of research and training excellence were established at the University of Chicago, Columbia University, Yale University, and the University of Michigan. By the 1970's a critical mass of political psychologists finally existed. The International Society of Political Psychology (ISPP) was founded in 1977; its first annual convention was held in 1978; and its flagship journal, *Political Psychology*, was launched in 1979. Since then, thousands of students, educators, and practitioners have joined the emerging discipline.

An Introduction to this Volume

The chapters in this reader were written by leading scholars in the areas of political science and social psychology. The interdisciplinary fusion reflects the vast range of topics and issues at the forefront of each field, a range that this relatively limited set of readings can only begin to reveal. We have compiled both classic and contemporary articles to demonstrate the ever-changing nature of political psychology and to offer comprehensive coverage of several decades of psychological research into the processes that govern local and global affairs in the postmodern world. Topics include: the history of political psychology;

the personalities of political leaders and followers; mass media and candidate perception; ideology and public opinion; challenges of decision-making; prejudice, diversity, and social contact; and conflict, violence, and political transformation. We hope you will agree that section introductions, discussion questions, suggestions for further reading, and comprehensive indexing make this an ideal, accessible text for advanced undergraduate and graduate students in courses in political science and psychology.

History

The first reading we have selected, by William J. McGuire, provides an intellectual history of the symbiotic relationship between political science and psychology focusing on three separate eras during the late 20th century: the personality and culture era, the attitudes and voting behavior era, and the ideology era. This recent history of political psychology is most instructive because it represents the period in which basic assumptions were consolidated, the boundaries of the field were explicitly defined, consensus about methods emerged, and statistical advances improved measurement and analytical strategies.

Personality and Politics

The study of personality and politics is one of the oldest and most central topics in political psychology. Several of the most influential attempts to understand the role of personality in politics were inspired by Freudian *psychoanalytic theory*, which assumes that much of human behavior is driven by unconscious motivational forces. This is as true of research on the authoritarian personality and historical approaches to mass psychology as it is of any other area of political psychology (e.g., Adorno et al., 1950).

AUTHORITARIANISM AND MASS PSYCHOLOGY

Adorno and his colleagues set out to understand the psychological bases of fascism, anti-Semitism, and racial prejudice in the mass public. These researchers argued that economic hardship during the Great Depression led parents in Germany and elsewhere to adopt very strict styles of discipline, which in turn led their children to accumulate repressed hostility toward authority figures. Because the children, once grown, still could not express their anger toward their own parents, they developed exaggerated defensive tendencies to idealize authority figures and blame socially sanctioned scapegoats (like the Jews) for any personal setbacks. Relying on a combination of clinical interviews and structured attitude surveys, Adorno et al. proposed that ethnocentrism was one symptom of a broad underlying personality syndrome, which they labeled the *authoritarian personality*.

Despite its early success and influence, authoritarian personality theory was attacked on both theoretical and methodological grounds (e.g., Christie, 1954; Eysenck, 1954; Pettigrew, 1959; Rokeach, 1960; Shils, 1954). Objections to existing research included the use of nonrepresentative samples of respondents, high susceptibility to experimenter bias, the drawing of causal conclusions on the basis of correlational data, and the use of attitude scales that were susceptible to systematic measurement biases. In our second reading, Roger Brown discusses the significant strengths and weaknesses of early research on authoritarianism.

Neither the original authors nor subsequent researchers of that era were able to demonstrate conclusively the existence of an authoritarian syndrome or its origin in parent–child interaction. In response to growing evidence that many personality traits failed to exhibit cross-situational consistency (e.g., Mischel, 1968), psychologists during the 1970s and 1980s generally moved away from personality-based models of human behavior in favor of situational models emphasizing the immediate social and cultural context (e.g., Ross & Nisbett, 1991). Authoritarianism researchers, too, turned their attention to situational factors such as threat and system instability (e.g., Sales, 1972, 1973). This theme is the focus of our third reading by Doty, Peterson, and Winter, in which authoritarian attitudes in the United States during historical periods of high versus low societal threat are compared.

The accumulation of methodological concerns almost killed off the study of authoritarianism as a personality variable, but Robert Altemeyer (1981, 1988) single-handedly revitalized the topic by developing a new instrument called the *right-wing authoritarianism* (RWA) scale. The RWA scale was relatively free from problems of measurement bias and directly measured three components theorized to be part of the syndrome: authoritarian submission, conventionalism, and punitiveness toward deviants. As Altemeyer illustrates in Reading 4, respondents' scores on this newer measure of right-wing authoritarianism—especially in conjunction with scores on Pratto, Sidanius, Stallworth, and Malle's (1994) *social dominance orientation* (SDO) scale—significantly predict their degree of prejudice against immigrants, Blacks, Jews, foreigners, French-Canadians, and homosexuals, among other groups.

While political psychologists have not made much progress in determining the degree to which the authoritarian syndrome in particular is the result of family socialization processes, a great deal of research has addressed the degree to which political attitudes and behaviors in general are the result of socialization by parents, teachers, and peers. One major branch of political socialization research has focused on how social systems induce children to become good citizens of their respective societies (e.g., Easton & Dennis, 1969; Jennings & Niemi, 1974, 1981; Oppenheim, 1975). This work adopts what is referred to as a *system stability* focus. A second major branch has investigated how children come to adopt the specific sociopolitical attitudes and political party preferences that they hold, thereby taking a *partisanship* focus (e.g., Connell, 1972; Sidanius & Ekehammar, 1979).

At one time, almost all political psychologists began with the assumption that both parents and schools exert major impact on young people's support for the system and on their social and political attitudes, but research has consistently found that such effects are relatively small (Hess & Torney, 1967; Langton, 1969; Hyman, 1959; Sidanius & Ekehammar, 1979; Thomas & Stankiewicz, 1974). Although the strength of association between the attitudes of parents and children varies somewhat depending upon the type of attitudes being studied and the precise social characteristics of the families (Jennings & Niemi, 1974), the weakness of results contributed to a gradual decrease in attention devoted to the study of political socialization. While some have sought to resurrect this topic in recent years (Niemi, 1999; Watts, 1999; Westholm, 1999), the jury is still out on whether such efforts will yield strong support for the socialization thesis.

POLITICAL ELITES AND LEADERSHIP

In seeking to understand the personalities of political leaders and their followers, psychologists have had to confront controversies concerning the meaning of personality and its measurement. In the 1930s, the renowned personality theorist Gordon Allport catalogued 50 different definitions of the term "personality." Despite some level of persisting disagreement, three assumptions are common to most contemporary accounts of personality. First, most researchers agree that personality refers to a set of "organized dispositions" that an individual brings to any given situation. Second, it is widely assumed that for the individual this set of dispositions is relatively stable and consistent over time. Third, most theorists assume that individual differences in "behavioral expression" will emerge in specific situations, so that different people will react differently to the same situation. As Allport (1937) put it, "The same heat that melts the butter hardens the egg" (p. 351).

In addition to the definitional problem, Fred Greenstein (Reading 5) considers five other objections to studying the personality characteristics of political actors and responds constructively to each objection. Greenstein outlines the kind of scientific evidence that political psychologists must provide, addresses inferential limitations associated with different methods of personality assessment, and illustrates the interaction of personality, situational, and societal variables in producing observable political outcomes. Most research on personality and politics falls into one of three broad categories: (a) psychological case histories (or psychobiographies) of individual political actors, (b) typological studies focusing on the classification of political actors, and (c) aggregative analyses that examine the collective effects of individuals on the functioning of political institutions and vice versa (Greenstein, 1969).

Classic contributions of the first type include detailed psychological studies of public figures such as Martin Luther, the leader of the Protestant Reformation (e.g., Erikson, 1958), American presidents John Adams (e.g., McCullough, 2001), Woodrow Wilson (e.g., George & George, 1956), and Richard Nixon (e.g., Volkan, Itzkowitz, & Dod, 1999), and political revolutionaries like Lenin, Trotsky, and Gandhi (Wolfenstein, 1967). Some in-depth case studies have also investigated the personality characteristics of ordinary members of the general population (e.g., Lane, 1962; Smith, Bruner, & White, 1956). Groundbreaking typological contributions include Lasswell's (1930) division of political elites into "agitator," "administrator," and "theorist" categories, Adorno et al.'s (1950) work on authoritarian personality types, Rokeach's (1960) theory of *dogmatism*, Barber's (1965) taxonomic analysis of American legislators and presidents, and Christie and Geis' (1970) work in developing scales for measuring "Machiavellian" personality and leadership styles. Aggregative studies have often taken the form of portraits of "national character." Examples include Fromm's (1941) consideration of economic and religious factors in contributing to the authoritarian character of the German people, Benedict's (1946) ethnographic description of Japanese society, and Bettelheim's (1969) analysis of the Israeli Kibbutz and its effects on character development in children.

David Winter (Reading 6) blends aspects of these different research styles to shed light on the ways in which the personalities of specific political leaders interact with characteristics of the general population to predict the degree to which the leader is popular and, from a historical perspective, ultimately deemed to be successful. By comparing the motive profiles of American presidents from George Washington (1789) to Ronald Reagan (1981) with respect to power, affiliation, and achievement with the motivational themes that were found to dominate popular culture during the period in which they were elected, Winter was able to examine distinctive hypotheses about leadership style (personality) and leader-follower congruence (personality-situation interaction). He found that presidential popularity (but not presidential success) was significantly correlated with the degree of congruence between a leader and his followers. By contrast, historical success (but not presidential popularity) was significantly correlated with the personality characteristics of the leader, especially strong motivations for power, impact, and prestige. Other groundbreaking studies of presidential "greatness" have been carried out by Simonton (1981, 1988), who has investigated personality factors such as charisma and creativity and situational factors such as whether the country is at war and whether an assassination attempt has been made on the president's life.

Mass Media and Candidate Perception

The fates of political parties, leaders, and their policies are dependent on mass constituencies like voters, who are affected (whether they know it or not) by a wide range of social, cognitive, and motivational variables. Democracy, in other words, depends upon *persua-

sion, and whether a persuasive political message is successful depends upon several factors (Milburn, 1991; Popkin, 1991). Key variables include the characteristics of the audience and the channel or medium by which mass communication takes place (e.g., Cialdini, 2001; McGuire, 1985). The significance of these factors (especially the role of the mass media) was made especially clear by poll results following the presidential debate between Richard Nixon and John F. Kennedy in 1960. Pollsters found, surprisingly, that a majority of radio listeners believed that Nixon had won the debate, whereas most who had watched it on TV concluded that Kennedy had won. More than two decades later, a clever study by Mullen and his colleagues (1986) found that ABC news anchor Peter Jennings smiled more when reporting on stories involving Ronald Reagan in comparison with his presidential rival Walter Mondale and, furthermore, that people who watched ABC news reported more favorable attitudes toward Reagan than viewers of the other networks. Although the direction of causality is unclear from this study, there is accumulating evidence that exposure to media coverage of political events changes one's political attitudes. This fits with general conclusions drawn from heaps of social psychological research on the effects of conscious and nonconscious priming (or activation) of attitudes (e.g., Bargh & Chartrand, 1999).

A research program initiated by Iyengar, Peters, and Kinder (Reading 7) on *agenda setting* in the media has demonstrated, using experimental means, that television news coverage of a specific issue increases the degree to which people rate that issue as being personally significant, deserving of governmental attention, and an essential criterion for evaluating presidential performance. Krosnick and Kinder (Reading 8) built on this line of research, showing that media coverage of an embarrassing political event could erode support for an otherwise relatively popular leader. Most of the research on the effects of mass media on candidate and issue perception has focused on *cognitive* variables such as message framing, information processing, assimilation and contrast, priming and construct activation, and impression formation and organization (e.g., Bishop, Oldendick, & Tuchfarber, 1982; Fiske, 1986; Graber, 2001; Iyengar & Kinder, 1987; Lau & Sears, 1986; Lodge & McGraw, 1995; Lord, Ross, & Lepper, 1979; Rahn, Aldrich, Borgida, & Sullivan, 1990; Valentino, 1999). However, there is some work on the role of emotions in candidate perception and voting (e.g., Abelson, Kinder, Peters, & Fiske, 1982; Glaser & Salovey, 1998). Marcus and MacKuen (Reading 9) intriguingly find that anxiety stimulates attention and learning during a political election and that enthusiasm influences campaign involvement and candidate selection.

Ideology and Public Opinion

Milton Rokeach (1968) defined *ideology* as "an organization of beliefs and attitudes—religious, political, or philosophical in nature—that is more or less institutionalized or shared with others" (pp. 123–124). Most research on political ideology has focused on the left-right distinction, and although the distinction is far from airtight, it describes reasonably well many of the ideological conflicts that dominated the 20th century. But by defining ideology as a belief system that is internally consistent and logically coherent within the minds of *individuals*, political psychologists may have set the bar too high.

DOES IDEOLOGY EXIST?

As Converse (Reading 10) argued famously, it is only a reasonably small and well-educated percentage of the population that finds it necessary (or desirable or possible) to resolve inconsistencies among political beliefs or to organize their beliefs tightly around scholarly definitions of "left" and "right." Rather, the vast majority of the population would be hard-pressed to articulate ideological coherence. Since the publication of Converse's classic article in 1964, the reasons for being skeptical about the coherence of mass belief systems have accumulated. McGuire (1985, pp. 248–249) listed eight specific reasons for doubting that people are ideological: (a) They lack basic knowledge about political issues and tend to mistake the causes of their own preferences; (b) they frequently answer "no opinion" in response to issues of political significance; (c) their attitudes show little or no consistency over time; (d) their opinions differ in response to trivial changes in wording and ordering of items; (e) emotional evaluations correlate very weakly with cognitive judgments; (f) attitudes that are similar in terms of ideological content correlate very weakly with one another; (g) people often adopt positions that are contrary to their own self- or class-interest; and (h) their abstract policy preferences frequently contradict the judgments they make in specific situations. For all of these reasons, researchers have questioned whether the general public holds structured political opinions at all, let alone opinions that are structured around left and right or liberal and conservative dimensions.

Fortunately, these frustrations have not led contemporary researchers to abandon the study of political ideology altogether (e.g., Judd, Krosnick, & Milburn, 1981; Stone & Schaffner, 1988; Tetlock, 1983; Zaller, 1992). McGuire himself (1985) listed several strategies for salvaging the concept of ideology, including: (a) improving the statistical reliability of attitude measures; (b) sampling involved and educated respondents rather than uninvolved and uneducated respondents; (c) sampling political elites rather than the mass public; (d) conducting studies in countries that are more ideologically polarized and therefore more likely to yield meaningful ideological differences than in the United States; (e) investigating ideology in people of certain personality types, including analytical thinkers, high need for cognition types, political activists, and extremists; (f) focusing more on affect (or emotion) in political ideology; and (g) considering liberalism and conservatism as orthogonal dimensions, as Kerlinger (1984) has advocated.

Conover and Feldman (Reading 11) argued that ideological labels like *liberal* and *conservative* have symbolic, identity-based meanings, even if they lack philosophical coherence or fail to define opposite poles on a single dimension. To the extent that people identify with certain political groups, they also have positive or negative associations to other groups, such as capitalists or police officers or marijuana smokers or members of disadvantaged groups. Conover and Feldman found that people who identify with conservatives differ from liberals primarily in that they are more favorable toward groups that exemplify the *status quo*, groups that foster social control, and groups that are pro-business.

COGNITIVE STYLE AND IDEOLOGICAL FUNCTIONING

Assuming that people do hold ideological beliefs about political parties, the political system in general, specific groups in society, and the existence of inequality, there are further questions of why people hold the beliefs they do and how these beliefs function in their overall attempt to understand the world. In Reading 12, Robert Lane takes a motivational approach, concluding on the basis of structured interviews with relatively low-income blue-collar workers that disadvantageous economic inequality is personally threatening, especially in a society in which self-worth is linked to the amount of money that one earns. In order to live with the situation of inequality, Lane argued that people *rationalize* their own state of disadvantage, an assumption also made by system justification theorists (Jost & Banaji, 1994; Kay, Jimenez, & Jost, 2002).

A question that first arose in response to work on the authoritarian personality and dogmatism/intolerance of ambiguity is whether there are *general* differences in cognitive and motivational style between people who are left versus right of the political center. Philip Tetlock, the author of Reading 13, has probably done more than any other researcher to shed light on this question. He and his collaborators have developed coding schemes that can be used to classify archival material (like interviews, political speeches, legal verdicts, and autobiographical writings) as being either relatively high or low in cognitive complexity. Using these and other methods, researchers have investigated a number of possibilities, including the "rigidity of the right" hypothesis, the "extremist-as-ideologue" hypothesis, and the "contextual" hypothesis that political deviants are more sophisticated and knowledgeable than centrists (e.g., Gruenfeld, 1995; Sidanius, 1985, 1988; Tetlock, 1983; Wilson, 1973). A quantitative meta-analytic review by Jost, Glaser, Kruglanski, and Sulloway (2003) found that the most consistent evidence favors the "rigidity of the right" hypothesis that conservatives are significantly but modestly less cognitively complex than liberals in general.

Challenges of Decision-Making

It is safely assumed that elite decision-makers, including presidents, parliamentarians, and supreme court justices, strive to make good and wise decisions, but the reality is that they are human beings who are affected by emotional factors, conformity pressures, and information-processing limitations (e.g., Simon, 1985). To understand the psychological causes of common errors made by groups of decision-makers, Irving Janis (1972) studied a number of good and bad foreign policy decisions. He identified five major risk factors leading to poor decision outcomes, including a forceful leader whom others seek to impress, intense group cohesiveness, isolation and secrecy from others, a lack of clear decision-making procedures, and stress arising from a crisis mentality. According to Janis, these are the conditions that produce *groupthink*, which he described as a tendency for groups to suppress doubt and dissent, forego critical analysis, rush to judgment, and mindlessly follow the leader. This perspective dominated political psychologists' understanding of decision-making fiascoes for decades, but in recent years other researchers have failed to replicate some of Janis' key observations when applying the framework to new case studies (e.g., Ahlfinger & Esser, 2001; Choi & Ming, 1999; 't Hart, Stern, & Sundelius, 1997).

In economics and in political science, there is a strong tradition of *rational choice theory*, which emphasizes individual self-interest and the calculation of expected costs and benefits as normative criteria for evaluating judgment and decision-making (e.g., Downs, 1957; Green & Shapiro, 1994). Psychologists have generally regarded the assumptions of rational choice theory to be unrealistic in practice, and they have tended to take a *descriptive* (what people actually do) rather than *normative* (what people should do) approach. As Quattrone and Tversky demonstrate in Reading 14, there are a number of important ways in which actual decision-makers deviate from the strict standards of rationality. They offer *prospect theory* as a model for understanding a number of decision-making anomalies, especially preference reversals that arise from framing the same choice in terms of potential gains versus losses, and they discuss implications of the theory for incumbency effects in political elections. Robert Jervis (Reading 15) further analyzes a wide array of foreign policy and other political decisions in light of what psychological research teaches us with respect to the operation of cognitive and motivational biases under conditions of ambiguity and uncertainty.

Prejudice, Diversity, and Social Contact

Problems arising from hostility and conflict among racial, ethnic, religious, and cultural groups constitute some of the most serious and intractable problems facing the human species. Intergroup conflict is currently life-threatening in such diverse geographical contexts as the streets of Los Angeles, the mountain villages of Bosnia, and the forests of Uganda. While intergroup and interethnic violence has been a feature of human society for as long as anyone can remember, modern technological capacities for destructiveness mean that the understanding and control of aggressive impulses is imperative if our species is to survive. Given the practical significance of the topic, it is not surprising that intergroup conflict has been of central concern to political psychologists for several generations.

THEORIES OF INTERGROUP RELATIONS IN SOCIETY

As research on authoritarianism as a dispositional cause of prejudice waned throughout the 1960s and 1970s, highly influential theories of intergroup relations arose to take its place. According to *realistic conflict theory*, ethnocentrism and generalized forms of intergroup conflict resulted from the perception of zero-sum competition between groups over material resources such as territory and wealth (Campbell, 1965; Sherif et al., 1961). One of the most celebrated demonstrations of the power of competition to produce conflict was a field study conducted by Muzafer Sherif and his collaborators at a boys' summer camp in Robber's Cave, Oklahoma. By pitting two groups of boys against one another in a tournament competition, the experimenters elicited telltale signs of ethnocentrism and intergroup hostility, including strong preferences for ingroup members as friends, overevaluation of ingroup products and underevaluation of outgroup products, negative stereotyping of the outgroup, and outright aggression. Hostility between the two groups escalated to the point that the experimenters were forced to terminate the study prematurely in order to avoid physical injury. But before the study ended, Sherif and colleagues made two other important observations. First, they noted that intergroup competition increased morale, cohesiveness, and cooperation *within* each group, suggesting that intragroup cooperation and intergroup competition are two sides of the same coin (see replication by Blake & Mouton, 1962). Second, they found that creating a situation of interdependence by giving both groups a shared superordinate task (like fixing their broken down means of transportation) served to decrease competition and to increase cooperation across group boundaries. Just as competition creates conflict, cooperation breeds liking.

Social identity theorists such as Tajfel and Turner (Reading 16) found fault with both theories of authoritarianism and realistic group conflict as suitable explanations for ethnocentrism and outgroup hostility. They suggested that prejudice is neither the result of personality defects, as proposed by authoritarianism researchers, nor purely a consequence of competition for scarce resources, as claimed by realistic conflict theorists. Rather, Tajfel and Turner argued that people derive a sense of self-worth and social belongingness from their memberships in groups, and so they are motivated to draw favorable comparisons between their own group and other groups. In other words, social groups compete for symbolic resources such as status and prestige as well as material resources. This conclusion was derived from studies employing Tajfel's (1970) "minimal group paradigm," which demonstrated that merely *categorizing* people with no prior history of interaction into different groups was sufficient to trigger intergroup bias (see also Brewer, 1979). In recent years, social identity theory has increasingly found its way into the literature on political psychology (e.g., Conover, Mingst, & Sigelman, 1980; Gibson, & Gouws, 2000; Herring, Jankowski & Brown, 1999; Tyler & Degoey, 1995).

System justification theory (Jost & Banaji, 1994) and *social dominance theory* (Sidanius & Pratto, 1999) are the most recent additions to the list of theories dealing with the political psychology of intergroup discrimination. In contrast to earlier approaches, both deliberately approach issues of ideology, justice, and intergroup relations using multiple levels of analysis (see Jost & Major, 2001). System justification theory, for example, seeks to integrate the vast psychological literature on group stereotypes with classical theories from sociology and political science concerning the role of ideology and the concept of *false consciousness* (defined in this context as the holding of false beliefs that contribute to one's own subjugation). The goal of the theory is to use social, political, and psychological variables to understand the remarkable stability of hierarchically organized relationships among social groups (whether based on race, ethnicity, caste, class, gender, sexual orientation, religion, and so on). Jost and Banaji (Reading 17) argue that social stereotypes not only serve *ego-justifying* and *group-justifying* functions of defending and legitimizing the interests, positions, and actions of individuals and fellow ingroup members but also *system-justifying* functions of defending and legitimizing the *status quo*.

Social dominance theory, developed by Jim Sidanius and Felicia Pratto (1999), shares many similarities with system justification theory in that it also explores the manner in which consensually endorsed system-justifying ideologies (or legitimizing myths) contribute to the stability of oppressive and hierarchically organized social relations among groups. Social dominance theory is even more ambitious in embedding its explanations across multiple levels of analysis, including personality differences with regard to attitudes toward group-based inequality (or "social dominance orientation"), dispositional differences between males and females, and the dynamics of "hierarchy-enhancing" versus "hierarchy-attenuating" social institutions (see Reading 18). In contrast to most theories in political psychology, the social dominance perspective is also situated squarely within the emerging framework of evolutionary psychology (e.g., Barkow, Cosmides & Tooby, 1992; Sidanius & Kurzban, 2003; Sober & Wilson, 1998).

Although the influence of neo-Darwinian perspectives introduced by scholars such as Hamilton (1963), Trivers (1971), Williams (1966), and Wilson (1975) is still slight within political psychology, there are signs that it is increasing. Evolutionary psychologists argue not only that human behavior is the product of complex interactions between genetic predispositions and physical and cultural environments, but also that cultural environments are themselves subject to selective pressures. To date, the main applications of evolutionary thinking in political psychology have been in the areas of dominance and hierarchy (e.g., Somit & Peterson, 1997; Wiegele, 1979), the dynamics of intergroup conflict, and the political psychology of gender (e.g., Reynolds, Falger & Vine, 1987; Sidanius & Pratto, 1999).

THE ENDURING PROBLEM OF RACISM

On the subject of racism, political psychologists are in general agreement that racism still exists, but it has changed forms. Although some, like Bobo (Reading 19), believe that older theories such as *realistic conflict theory* are capable of explaining current racial attitudes in the United States and Europe, most believe that racism has gone "underground" and requires new theories and methods. The most influential approaches to the "new racism" include *modern racism theory* (McConahay, 1986), *symbolic racism theory* (Sears, 1988), *ambivalent racism theory* (Katz & Hass, 1988), *subtle racism theory* (Pettigrew & Meertens, 1995), *racial resentment theory* (Kinder & Sanders, 1996), and *aversive racism theory* (Dovidio & Gaertner, 1986, 1998). While there are important differences among these theoretical perspectives, all assume that old-fashioned, blatant racism is no longer the potent determinant of racial and political attitudes that it once was. Rather, the claim is that old-fashioned racism has been supplanted by a more subtle, insidious form of racial prejudice that is not always accessible to conscious awareness (see also, Ayres, 2001; Devine, 1989; Nosek, Banaji, & Greenwald, 2002).

Of the various "new racism" models, symbolic racism theory has been the most influential and controversial (e.g., Sears & Kinder, 1971; Sears, 1988). According to the theory, modern racial prejudice arises from a combination of traditional moral values (e.g., the Protestant work ethic and cultural norms of self-reliance) and negative affect directed at racial and ethnic outgroups. Sears and his colleagues have argued that symbolic racial attitudes are distinct from traditional racism and political conservatism and that they are the primary determinants of attitudes toward policies such as immigration, affirmative action, and minority aid. Symbolic racism theory has had more than its share of critics (e.g., Bobo, 1983; Colleau et al. 1990; Fazio et al. 1995; Miller, 1994; Raden, 1994; Sniderman & Tetlock, 1986; Weigel & Howes, 1985). Some of the most ardent critics have endorsed an alternative position, known as the *principled politics hypothesis*, which holds that European Americans' unfavorable attitudes towards racial policy initiatives (e.g., busing, affirmative action) are driven not by racism but by political convictions concerning the proper role of government and equity-based fairness norms (see Sniderman, Crosby & Howell, 2000; Sniderman & Piazza, 1993; Sniderman, Piazza, Tetlock & Kendrick, 1991). In Reading 20, Sears, van Laar, Carrillo, and Kosterman defend the symbolic racism perspective against these and other objections (see also Federico & Sidanius, 2002a, 2002b for a discussion of these issues).

Conflict, Violence, and Political Transformation

In the final section of this book, we explore the psychology of large-scale political conflict, violence, and political transformation within and among nation-states. There is ample evidence suggesting that the last century was the bloodiest in all of human history. More than 20 major wars were fought during the 20th century, claiming more than 100 million human lives; it is estimated that World War II alone caused 50 million deaths. To this awful tally, we must add the nearly 170 million people massacred during scores of genocidal campaigns (Rummel, 2001). In addition to the Nazi Holocaust, this list includes the Turkish mass murder of the Armenians, the killing fields of Cambodia, the slaying of more than 800,000 Rwandan Tutsis throughout the 1990s, and many thousands more killed in Bosnia and Herzegovina. Given the extravagant level of human suffering in the 20th century and the continued threat to human existence that genocide implies, one could argue that these are among the most pressing topics for social scientists to tackle. However, because it is ethically and practically impossible to study these phenomena in laboratory and other closely controlled contexts, hard scientific knowledge about political violence is limited. These challenges, however, have not prevented scholars from seeking to analyze cases of political violence, including war, genocide, terrorism, protest, and revolution (e.g., Kelman & Hamilton, 1988; Martin, Scully, & Levitt, 1990; Muller, 1980; Rejai & Phillips, 1988; Staub, 1989; Tilly, 1975).

THE SOCIAL PSYCHOLOGY OF WRONGDOING AND HARM

There is no more abhorrent form of political violence than the institutionalized mass murder of innocent men, women, and children. In an effort to bring the tools of experimental social psychology to bear on the question of how a catastrophe like the Holocaust could occur, Stanley Milgram's (1974) studies of "obedience to authority" demonstrated how easy it was to get normal people to administer painful and potentially lethal electric shocks to others when directed to do so by a legitimate authority figure. The results of these experiments, in conjunction with even more compelling and detailed historical analyses of the Holocaust and other genocides (e.g., Arendt, 1963), led political psychologists to an extremely uncomfortable conclusion. The evidence suggested that many, if not most, instances of genocide and mass murder, are not committed by people with depraved, deranged, or pathological personalities, but rather by quite ordinary people placed in extraordinary, yet "banal" bureaucratic situations (Kelman & Hamilton, 1988; Staub, 1989). This complex theme is developed in much more detail by John Darley (Reading 21).

The dramatic attacks of September 11, 2001 on New York and Washington, DC reminded the world that political violence is not restricted to instances of warfare and genocide but also includes the threat of terrorism. Because the subject of terrorism is inherently difficult to study and is easily susceptible to political bias (e.g., one person's "terrorist" is another's "freedom fighter"), genuine scientific insight into terrorism is hard to come by. Among the many seemingly intractable questions are: What precisely is terrorism? Are there different kinds of terrorism? What are the psychological characteristics of people who engage in terrorism? Under what circumstances is terrorism politically effective? And, finally, what are the most and least effective ways for governments to fight terrorism? While political psychologists are a long way from obtaining clear, unbiased answers to these questions, the chapter by Martha Crenshaw (Reading 22) should serve as a useful platform from which to start thinking about these vexing yet compelling questions more seriously and precisely.

PROTEST AND REVOLUTION

The issue of whether political violence is ever morally justifiable is made more complex by the fact that successful revolutions, including the French and American Revolutions of the 18th century, began as seemingly unjustifiable acts of mass violence. That they are now seen as legitimate protest movements is at least partially attributable to the fact that they were successful; these examples suggest that at least sometimes the ends do justify the means. But perhaps a better, more pragmatic question is whether social change and political transformation can ever be accomplished without the loss of life. The 20th century, despite its bloody legacy, gave us several examples of revolutionaries whose committed pacifism and methods of civil disobedience ultimately proved successful. Mahatma Gandhi, Martin Luther King, Vaclav Havel, and Nelson Mandela defeated, respectively, the British Empire in India, racial hegemony in the United States, Communist rule in the Czech Republic, and Apartheid in South Africa.

These historical events are relevant to a key question that social scientists have long confronted, namely whether political violence is natural and endemic to the human condition or whether it is the result of specific historical, social, and cultural conditions. If mass violence is part of human nature, then the best we can hope for is to uncover methods of intervention that will keep it to a minimum. If, on the other hand, organized aggression is the result of socially constructed forces, then it is at least theoretically plausible to imagine eliminating it altogether. We have selected two essays by Harry Eckstein (Reading 23) and Bernd Simon and Bert Klandermans (Reading 24) that address these and related issues concerning protest and revolution.

Suggestions for Further Reading

In this chapter, we have sought to provide an introduction both to the field of political psychology and to this book. While we can be reasonably confident of our success in relation to the latter goal, the former is much more difficult to accomplish in the space of a few pages. In writing this introduction, we have drawn on a number of secondary sources, some of which we would have liked to include in this book. We recommend these heartily as suggestions for further introductory reading in political psychology: Hermann (1986); Iyengar & McGuire (1993); Kinder (1998); Kinder & Sears (1985); Kressel (1993); Lau & Sears (1986); Lodge & McGraw (1995); Monroe (2002); Sears (1987); Sears, Huddy & Jervis (2003); and Stone & Schaffner (1988).

REFERENCES

Abelson, R. P., Kinder, D. R., Peters, M. D., & Fiske, S. T. (1982). Affective and semantic components in political person perception. *Journal of Personality and Social Psychology, 42*, 619–630.

Adorno, T. W., Frenkel-Brunswik, E., Levinson, D. J., & Sanford, R. N. (1950). *The authoritarian personality*. New York: Harper.

Ahlfinger, N. R., & Esser, J. K. (2001). Testing the groupthink model: Effects of promotional leadership and conformity predisposition. *Social Behavior & Personality, 29*, 31–41.

Allport, G. W. (1937). *Personality: A psychological interpretation*. New York: Holt.

Altemeyer, R. A. (1981). *Right-wing authoritarianism*. Winnipeg: University of Manitoba Press.

Altemeyer, R. A. (1988). *Enemies of freedom: Understanding right-wing authoritarianism*. San Francisco: Jossey-Bass Publishers.

Arendt, H. (1963). *Eichmann in Jerusalem: A report on the banality of evil*. New York: Viking Press.

Ayres, I. (2001). *Pervasive prejudice? Unconventional evidence of race and gender discrimination*. Chicago, IL: University of Chicago Press.

Barber, J. D. (1965). *The lawmakers*. New Haven, CT: Yale University Press.

Bargh, J. A., & Chartrand, T. L. (1999). The unbearable automaticity of being. *American Psychologist, 54*, 462–479.

Barkow, J. H., Cosmides, L., & Tooby, J. (1992). *The adapted mind: Evolutionary psychology and the generation of culture*. New York: Oxford University Press.

Bettelheim, B. (1969). *The children of the dream*. New York: Avon.

Bishop, G. F., Oldendick, R. W., & Tuchfarber, J. J. (1982). Political information processing: Question order and context effects. *Political Behavior, 4*, 177–200.

Blake, R. E., & Mouton, J. S. (1962). Overevaluation of own groups' product in ingroup competition. *Journal of Abnormal & Social Psychology, 64*, 237–238.

Bobo, L. (1983). Whites' opposition to busing: Symbolic racism or realistic group conflict? *Journal of Personality and Social Psychology, 45*, 1196–1210.

Brewer, M. B. (1979). In-group bias in the minimal intergroup situation: A cognitive-motivational analysis. *Psychological Bulletin, 86*, 307–24.

Campbell, D. T. (1965). Ethnocentrism and other altruistic motives. In D. Levine (Ed). *Nebraska symposium on motivation* (Vol. 13, pp. 282–311). Lincoln, NE: University of Nebraska Press.

Choi, J. N., & Ming, M. U. (1999). The organizational application of groupthink and its limitations in organizations. *Journal of Applied Psychology, 84*, 297-306.

Christie, R. (1954). Authoritarianism re-examined. In R. Christie & M. Jahoda (Eds.), *Studies in the scope and method of "The Authoritarian Personality"* (pp. 123–196). Glencoe, IL: Free Press.

Christie, R., & Geis, F. L. (1970). *Studies in Machiavellianism*. New York: Academic Press.

Cialdini, R. B. (2001). *Influence: Science and practice*. Boston: Allyn & Bacon.

Colleau, S. M., Glynn, K., Lybrand, S., Merelman, R. M., Mohan, P., & Wall, J. E. (1990). Symbolic racism in candidate evaluation: An experiment. *Political Behavior, 12*, 385–402.

Connell, R. W. (1972). Political socialization in the American family: The evidence re-examined. *Public Opinion Quarterly, 36*, 323–333.

Conover, P. J., Mingst, K. A., & Sigelman, L. (1980). Mirror images in Americans' perceptions of nations and leaders during the Iranian hostage crisis. *Journal of Peace Research, 17*, 325–337.

Converse, P. E. (1964). The nature of belief systems in mass publics. In D. Apter (Ed.), *Ideology and discontent*. New York: Free Press.

Deutsch, M., & Kinnvall, C. (2002). What is political psychology? In K. R. Monroe (Ed.), *Political psychology* (pp. 15–42). Mahwah, NJ: Erlbaum.

Dovidio, J. F., & Gaertner, S. L. (1986). *Prejudice, discrimination and racism*. New York: Academic Press.

Dovidio, J. F., & Gaertner, S. L. (1998). On the nature of contemporary prejudice: The causes, consequences, and challenges of aversive racism. In J. L. Eberhardt & S. T. Fiske (Eds.), *Confronting prejudice: The problem and the response* (pp. 3–32). Thousand Oaks, CA: Sage.

Downs, A. (1957). *An economic theory of democracy*. New York: Harper & Row.

Easton, D., & Dennis, J. (1969). *Children in the political system*. New York: McGraw-Hill.

Erikson, E. H. (1958). *Young man Luther: A study in psychoanalysis and history*. New York: Norton.

Eysenck, H. J. (1954). *The psychology of politics*. London: Routledge & Kegan Paul.

Fazio, R. H., Jackson, J. R., Dunton, B. C., & Williams, C. J. (1995). Variability in automatic activation as an unobtrusive measure of racial attitudes: A bona fide pipeline? *Journal of Personality and Social Psychology, 69*, 1013–1027.

Federico, C. M., & Sidanius, J. (2002a). Racism, ideology, and affirmative action, revisited: The antecedents and consequences of 'principled objections' to affirmative action. *Journal of Personality and Social Psychology 82*, 488–502.

Federico, C. M., & Sidanius, J. (2002b). Sophistication and the antecedents of Whites' racial-policy attitudes: Racism, ideology, and affirmative action in America. *Public Opinion Quarterly, 66*, 145–176.

Fiske, S. T. (1986). Scheme-based versus piecemeal politics: A patchwork quilt, but not a blanket of evidence. In R. R. Lau & D. O. Sears (Eds.), *Political cognition* (pp. 41–53). Hillsdale, NJ: Erlbaum.

Freud, S. (1930/1960). *Civilization and it discontents*. New York: Norton.

Fromm, E. (1941). *Escape from freedom*. New York: Holt.

George, A. L., & George, J. L. (1956). *Woodrow Wilson and Colonel House: A personality study*. New York: John Day.

Gibson, J. L., & Gouws, A. (2000). Social identities and political intolerance: Linkages within the South African mass public. *American Journal of Political Science, 44*, 278–292.

Glaser, J., & Salovey, P. (1998). Affect in electoral politics. *Personality and Social Psychology Review, 2*, 156–172.

Graber, D.A. (2001). *Processing politics: Learning from television in the Internet age*. Chicago, IL: University of Chicago Press.

Green, D. P., & Shapiro, I. (1994). *Pathologies of rational choice: A critique of applications in political science*. New Haven, CT: Yale University Press.

Greenstein, F. I. (1969). *Personality and politics.* Chicago: Markham Publishing Company.

Gruenfeld, D. H. (1995). Status, ideology, and integrative ideology on the U.S. Supreme Court: Rethinking the politics of political decision making. *Journal of Personality and Social Psychology, 68,* 5–20.

Hamilton, W. D. (1963). The evolution of altruistic behavior. *The American Naturalist, 97,* 354–356.

Hermann, M.G. (Ed.) (1986). *Political psychology: Contemporary problems and issues.* San Francisco: Jossey-Bass.

Herring, M. H., Jankowski, T. B., & Brown, R. E. (1999). Pro-Black doesn't mean anti-White: The structure of African-American group identity. *The Journal of Politics, 61,* 363–386.

Hess, R. D., & Torney, J. V. (1967). *The development of political attitudes in children.* Chicago: Aldine.

Hobbes, T. (1651/1946). *Leviathan.* Oxford: Clarendon.

Hobbes, T. (1651: 1947). *Leviathan.* New York: McMillan.

Hyman, H. H. (1959). *Political socialization: A study in the psychology of political behavior.* New York: Free Press.

Iyengar, S., & Kinder, D. (1987). *News that matters: Television and American opinion.* Chicago: University of Chicago Press.

Iyengar, S., & McGuire, W. J. (Eds.) (1993). *Explorations in political psychology.* Durham, NC: Duke University Press.

Janis, I. (1972). *Victims of groupthink.* Boston: Houghton Mifflin.

Jennings, K. M., & Niemi, R. G. (1974). *The political character of adolescence: The influence of families and schools.* Princeton, NJ: Princeton University Press.

Jennings, K. M., & Niemi, R. G. (1981). *Generations and politics: A panel study of young adults and their parents.* Princeton, NJ: Princeton University Press.

Jost, J. T., & Banaji, M. R. (1994). The role of stereotyping in system-justification and the production of false consciousness. *British Journal of Social Psychology, 33,* 1–27.

Jost, J. T., Glaser, J., Kruglanski, A. W., & Sulloway, F. (2003). Political conservatism as motivated social cognition. *Psychological Bulletin, 129,* 339–375.

Jost, J. T., & Major, B. (Eds.) (2001). *The psychology of legitimacy: Emerging perspectives on ideology, justice, and intergroup relations.* New York: Cambridge University Press.

Judd, C. M., Krosnick, J. A., & Milburn, M. A. (1981). Political involvement in attitude structure in the general public. *American Sociological Review, 46,* 660–669.

Katz, I. & Hass, R. G. (1988). Racial ambivalence and American value conflict: Correlational and priming studies of dual cognitive structures. *Journal of Personality and Social Psychology, 55,* 893–905.

Kay, A., Jimenez, M. C., & Jost, J. T. (2002). Sour grapes, sweet lemons, and the anticipatory rationalization of the status quo. *Personality and Social Psychology Bulletin, 28,* 1300–1312.

Kelman, H. C., & Hamilton, V. L. (1988). *Crimes of obedience: Towards a social psychology of authority and responsibility.* New Haven, CT: Yale University Press.

Kerlinger, F. N. (1984). *Liberalism and conservatism.* Hillsdale, NJ: Erlbaum.

Kinder, D. (1998). Opinion and action in the realm of politics. In G. Lindzey & E. Aronson (Eds.), *Handbook of social psychology* (4th ed., Vol. II, pp. 778–867). Boston: McGraw Hill.

Kinder, D. R., & Sanders, L. M. (1996). *Divided by color: Racial politics and democratic ideals.* Chicago, IL: University of Chicago Press.

Kinder, D. R., & Sears, D. O. (1985). Public opinion and political action. In G. Lindzey & E. Aronson (Eds.), *Handbook of social psychology* (3rd ed., Vol. II, pp. 714–726). New York: Random House.

Kressel, N. J. (Ed.) (1993). *Political psychology: Classic and contemporary readings.* New York: Paragon House.

Lane, R. E. (1962). *Political ideology: Why the American common man believes what he does.* New York: Free Press.

Langton, K. P. (1969). *Political socialization.* New York: Oxford University Press.

Lasswell. H. (1930). *Psychopathology and politics.* Chicago: University of Chicago Press.

Lau, R. R., & Sears, D. O. (Eds.) (1986). *Political cognition.* Hillsdale, NJ: Erlbaum.

Lodge, M., & McGraw, K. M. (Eds.) (1995). *Political judgment: Structure and process.* Ann Arbor, MI: University of Michigan Press.

Lord, C. G., Ross, L., & Lepper, M. (1979). Biased assimilation and attitude polarization: The effects of prior theories on subsequently considered evidence. *Journal of Personality and Social Psychology, 37,* 2098–2109.

Martin, J., Scully, M., & Levitt, B. (1990). Injustice and the legitimation of revolution: Damning the past, excusing the present, and neglecting the future. *Journal of Personality and Social Psychology, 59,* 281–290.

McCullough, D. (2001). *John Adams.* New York: Simon & Schuster.

McGuire, W. J. (1985). Attitudes and attitude change. In G. Lindzey & E. Aronson (Eds.), *Handbook of social psychology* (pp. 233–346). New York: Random House.

Milburn, M.A. (1991). *Persuasion and politics: The social psychology of public opinion.* Pacific Grove, CA: Brooks/Cole.

Milgram, S. (1974). *Obedience to authority: An experimental view.* New York: Harper & Sons.

Miller, A. H. (1994). Social groups as symbols in America's sense of democratic consensus. In A. H. Miller & B. E. Gronbeck (Eds.), *Presidential campaigns and American self images.* Boulder, CO: Westview.

Mischel, W. (1968). *Personality and assessment.* New York: Wiley.

Monroe, K.R. (Ed.) (2002). *Political psychology.* Mahwah, NJ: Erlbaum.

Mullen, B., Futrell, D., Stairs, D., Tice, D., Baumeister, R., Dawson, K., Riordan, C., Radloff, C., Goethals, G., Kennedy, J., & Rosenfeld, P. (1986). Newscasters' facial expressions and voting behavior of viewers: Can a smile elect a president? *Journal of Personality and Social Psychology, 51,* 291–295.

Muller, E. N. (1980). The psychology of political protest and violence. In *Political Conflict: Theory and Research* (pp. 69–99). New York: The Free Press.

Niemi, R. G. (1999). Editor's introduction. *Political Psychology, 20,* 471–476.

Oppenheim, A. N., Torney, J., & Farnen, R. (1975). *Civic education in ten countries.* New York: The Halstead Press.

Pettigrew, T. F. (1959). Regional differences in anti-Negro prejudice. *Journal of Abnormal and Social Psychology, 59,* 28–36.

Pettigrew, T. F., & Meertens, R. W. (1995). Subtle and blatant prejudice in Western Europe. *European Journal of Social Psychology, 25,* 57–75.

Popkin, S. L. (1991). *The reasoning voter: Communication and persuasion in presidential campaigns.* Chicago: University of Chicago Press.

Pratto, F., Sidanius, J., Stallworth, L. M., & Malle, B. F. (1994). Social dominance orientation: A personality variable predicting social and political attitudes. *Journal of Personality and Social Psychology, 67,* 741–763.

Raden, D. (1994). Are symbolic racism and traditional prejudice part of a contemporary authoritarian attitude syndrome? *Political Behavior, 16,* 365–384.

Rahn, W. M., Aldrich, J., Borgida, E., & Sullivan, J. (1990). A social-cognitive model of candidate appraisal. In J. Ferejohn & J. Kuklinski (Eds.), *Information and democratic process.* Chicago: University of Chicago Press.

Reich, W. (1946/1970). *The mass psychology of fascism* (Trans. V. R. Carfagno). New York: Farrar, Straus, & Giroux.

Rejai, M., & Phillips, K. (1988). *Loyalists and revolutionaries: Political leaders compared.* Praeger.

Reynolds, V., Falger, V., & Vine, I. (1987). *The sociobiology of ethnocentrism: Evolutionary dimensions of xenophobia, discrimination, racism and nationalism.* Beckenham, Kent: Croom Helm.

Rokeach, M. (1960). *The open and closed mind.* New York: Free Press.

Ross, L., & Nisbett, R. E. (1991). *The person and the situation: Perspectives of social psychology.* Philadelphia: Temple University Press.

Rummel, R. J. (2001). Freedom, democracy, peace; power, democide and war. http://www.mega.nu:8080/ampp/rummel/welcome.html.

Sales, S. M. (1972). Economic threat as a determinant of conversion rates in authoritarian and nonauthoritarian churches. *Journal of Personality and Social Psychology, 23,* 420–428.

Sales, S. M. (1973). Threat as a factor in authoritarianism: An analysis of archival data. *Journal of Personality and Social Psychology, 28,* 44–57.

Sears, D. O. (1987). Political psychology. *Annual Review of Psychology, 38,* 229–255.

Sears, D. O. (1988). Symbolic racism. In P. A. Katz & D. A. Taylor (Eds.), *Eliminating racism: Profiles in controversy.* (pp. 53–84). New York: Plenum.

Sears, D. O. (1994). Ideological bias in political psychology: The view from scientific hell. *Political Psychology, 15,* 547–556.

Sears, D. O., Huddy, L., & Jervis, R. (Eds.) (2003). *Handbook of political psychology.* New York: Oxford University Press.

Sears, D. O., & Kinder, D. R. (1971). Racial tensions and voting in Los Angeles. In W. Z. Hirsch (Ed.), *Los Angeles: Viability and prospects of metropolitan leadership.* New York: Praeger.

Sherif, M., Harvey, O. J., White, B. J., Hood, W. R., & Sherif, C. W. (1954/1961). *Intergroup conflict and cooperation: The Robber's Cave experiment.* Norman, OK: Oklahoma Book Exchange.

Shils, E. A. (1954). Authoritarianism: "right" and "left." In R. Christie & M. Jahoda (Eds.), *Studies in the scope and method of "The Authoritarian Personality"* (pp. 24–49). Glencoe, Illinois: Free Press.

Sidanius, J. (1985). Cognitive functioning and sociopolitical ideology revisited. *Political Psychology, 6,* 637–661.

Sidanius, J. (1988). Political sophistication and political deviance: A structural equation examination of context theory. *Journal of Personality and Social Psychology, 55,* 37–51.

Sidanius, J., & Ekehammar, B. (1979). Political socialization: A multivariate analysis of Swedish political attitudes and preference data. *European Journal of Social Psychology, 9,* 265–279.

Sidanius, J., & Kurzban, R. (2003). Evolutionary approaches to political psychology. In D.O. Sears, L. Huddy, & R. Jervis, R. *Handbook of Political Psychology.* New York: Oxford University Press.

Sidanius, J., & Pratto, F. (1999). *Social dominance: An intergroup theory of social hierarchy and oppression.* New York: Cambridge University Press.

Simon, H. A. (1985). Human nature in politics: The dialogue of psychology with political science. *The American Political Science Review, 79,* 293–304.

Smith, M., Bruner, J. S. M., & White, R. W. (1956). *Opinions and personality.* New York: Wiley.

Sniderman, P. M., & Tetlock, P. E. (1986). Symbolic racism: Problems of motive attribution in political analysis. *Journal of Social Issues, 42,* 129–150.

Sniderman, P. M., Crosby, G. C., & Howell, W. G. (2000). The politics of race. In D. O. Sears, J. Sidanius & L. Bobo (Eds.), *Racialized politics: Values, ideology, and prejudice in American public opinion* (pp. 236–279). Chicago: University of Chicago Press.

Sniderman, P. M., Piazza, T., Tetlock, P. E., & Kendrick, A. (1991). The new racism. *American Journal of Political Science, 35,* 423–447.

Sober, E., & Wilson, D. S. (1998). *Unto others: The evolution and psychology of unselfish behavior.* Cambridge, MA: Harvard University Press.

Somit, A., & Peterson, S. A. (1997). *Darwinism, dominance and democracy: The biological bases of authoritarianism.* Westport, CT: Praeger.

Staub, E. (1989). *The roots of evil: The psychological and cultural origins of genocide.* New York: Cambridge University Press.

Stone, W. F. (1980). The myth of left-wing authoritarianism. *Political Psychology, 2,* 3–19.

Stone, W. F. (1981). Political psychology: A Whig history. In S. L. Long (Ed.), *The handbook of political behavior* (Vol. 1, pp. 1–67). New York: Plenum.

Stone, W. F., & Schaffner, P. E. (1988). *The psychology of politics.* New York: Springer-Verlag.

't Hart, P., Stern, E. K., & Sundelius, B. (1997). *Beyond groupthink: Political group dynamics and foreign policymaking.* Ann Arbor, MI: University of Michigan Press.

Tajfel, H. (1970). Experiments in intergroup discrimination. *Scientific American, 223,* 96–102.

Tetlock, P. E. (1983). Cognitive style and political ideology. *Journal of Personality and Social Psychology, 45,* 118–126.

Tetlock, P. E. (1994). Political psychology or politicized psychology: Is the road to scientific hell paved with good moral intentions? *Political Psychology, 15,* 509–529.

Thomas, L. E., & Stankiewicz, J. F. (1974). Family correlates of parent-child attitude congruence: Is it time to throw in the towel? *Psychological Reports, 34,* 1038.

Tilly, C. (1975). Revolution and collective violence. In F.I. Greenstein, & W.P. Nelson (Eds.), *Handbook of political science: Macropolitical theory (Vol. 7).* Addison-Wesley.

Trivers, R. L. (1971). The evolution of reciprocal altruism. *Quarterly Review of Biology, 46,* 35–57.

Tyler, T. R., & Degoey, P. (1995). Collective restraint in social dilemmas: Procedural justice and social identification effects on support for authorities. *Journal of Personality and Social Psychology, 69,* 482–497.

Valentino, N.A. (1999). Crime news and the priming of racial attitudes during evaluations of the president. *Public Opinion Quarterly, 63,* 293–320.

Van Ginneken, J. (1988). Outline of a cultural history of political psychology. In W. F. Stone & P. Schaffner (Eds.), *The psychology of politics* (2nd ed., pp. 3–22). New York: Springer-Verlag.

Volkan, V. D., Itzkowitz, N., & Dod. A. W. (1999). *Richard Nixon: A psychobiography.* New York: Columbia University Press.

Wallas, G. (1908). *Human nature in politics.* London: A. Constable.

Ward, D. (2002). Political psychology: Origins and development. In K.R. Monroe (Ed.), *Political psychology* (pp. 61–78). Mahwah, NJ: Erlbaum.

Watts, M. W. (1999). Are there typical age curves in political behavior? The "age invariance" hypothesis and political socialization. *Political Psychology, 20,* 477–500.

Weigel, R. H., & Howes, P. W. (1985). Conceptions of racial prejudice: Symbolic racism reconsidered. *Journal of Social Issues, 41,* 117–138.

Westholm, A. (1999). The perceptual pathway: Tracing the mechanisms of political value transfer across generations. *Political Psychology, 20,* 525–552.

Wiegele, T. (1979). *Biopolitics: Search for a more humane political science.* Boulder, CO: Westview Press.

Williams, G. C. (1966). *Adaptation and natural selection.* Princeton, NJ: Princeton University Press.

Wilson, E. O. (1975). *Sociobiology: The new synthesis.* Cambridge, MA: Harvard University Press.

Wilson, G. D. (Ed.). (1973). *The psychology of conservatism.* San Diego, CA: Academic Press.

Zaller, J. R. (1992). *The nature and origins of mass opinion.* New York: Cambridge University Press.

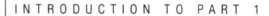

Historical Introduction

As we mentioned in the opening chapter, the historical origins of political psychology can be traced back many centuries to the philosophers of ancient Greece. Interest in the art and science of political rhetoric and the consequences of theories of human nature for the functioning of political systems continued throughout European intellectual history. It was not until the middle of the 20th century, however, that consensus first began to emerge about the theories and methods to be used in scientific investigations of political psychology.

The first reading is by William J. McGuire of Yale University, and it describes three eras of cooperation between psychology and political science throughout the 20th century. During the personality and culture era of the 1940s and 1950s, most researchers were *environmental determinists* who stressed nature over nurture in seeking to explain human behavior. Prevailing theories included Marxism, psychoanalysis, and stimulus-response behaviorism, and political psychologists struggled to understand the origins of fascism in the shadow of World War II. Work by Adorno, Horkheimer, Fromm, and others on the authoritarian personality—covered in Section II of this book—grew out of this important and defining period in political psychology.

As McGuire points out, the attitudes and voting behavior era of the 1960s and 1970s was dominated by rational choice theories inherited from the science of economics. Specifically, researchers assumed that people were subjective utility maximizers out to reap benefits and avoid costs through their political activities. Methodological innovations, particularly in the area of survey research, defined this period. The theoretical assumption that political actors (whether professional elites or mass members of the electorate) are primarily motivated by self-interest is one that still dominates many areas of political psychology even decades later (see Green & Shapiro, 1994). These and related issues are discussed in Sections III through V of this book.

The third historical period described by McGuire is the social cognition/political ideology era of the 1980s and 1990s. The influence of experimental social psychology was especially strong during these years, as several chapters in this book attest. Theoretical and methodological preoccupations focused on general mechanisms of information processing within the individual that had implications for political judgments and decisions, as covered in Sections IV and V. McGuire also speculates about a coming fourth era in political psychology, in which interpersonal and intergroup dynamics take on added urgency and interest. The readings we have selected for Sections VI and VII of this book suggest that this era has indeed begun.

Discussion Questions

1. To what extent do you see the historical eras of political psychology identified by McGuire as building on one another? Do you see the knowledge produced in political psychology as cumulative or as faddish?
2. Contrast *micro-scientific* and *macro-scientific* approaches to the question of why political leaders adopt the specific leadership styles that they do. Are these contradictory or complementary approaches to studying political behavior? Explain.
3. Historians have recently gained access to audiotapes recorded in the Lyndon Johnson White House during the Vietnam War era. How might *humanists* and *social scientists* differ in their use of these tapes for purposes of conducting research?
4. Suppose that the leader of an economically disadvantaged nation is perpetrating genocide on the people of a neighboring country. How would a researcher from the "personality and culture" era seek to explain such actions? Compare this type of explanation with one that might be offered by researchers from the "attitudes and voting behavior" and "political ideology" eras. Which type of explanation do you think you would find most convincing?

Suggested Readings

Deutsch, M., & Kinnvall, C. (2002). What is political psychology? In K.R. Monroe (Ed.), *Political psychology* (pp. 15–42). Mahwah, NJ: Erlbaum.

Green, D. P., & Shapiro, I. (1994). *Pathologies of rational choice: A critique of applications in political science.* New Haven, CT: Yale University Press.

Hermann, M. G. (Ed.) (1986). *Political psychology: Contemporary problems and issues.* San Francisco: Jossey-Bass.

Iyengar, S., & McGuire, W. J. (Eds.) (1993). *Explorations in political psychology.* Durham, NC: Duke University Press.

Kinder, D. (1998). Opinion and action in the realm of politics. In G. Lindzey & E. Aronson (Eds.), *Handbook of social psychology* (4th ed., Vol. II, pp. 778–867). Boston: McGraw Hill.

Kinder, D. R., & Sears, D. O. (1985). Public opinion and political action. In G. Lindzey & E. Aronson (Eds.), *Handbook of social psychology* (3rd ed., Vol. II, pp. 714–726). New York: Random House.

Kressel, N. J. (Ed.) (1993). *Political psychology: Classic and contemporary readings.* New York: Paragon House.

Lane, R .E. (1982). Government and self-esteem. *Political Theory, 10,* 5–31.

Lau, R. R., & Sears, D. O. (Eds.) (1986). *Political cognition.* Hillsdale, NJ: Erlbaum.

Lodge, M., & McGraw, K. M. (Eds.) (1995). *Political judgment: Structure and process.* Ann Arbor, MI: University of Michigan Press.

Long, S. L. (Ed.) (1981). *The handbook of political behavior (Vol. 1).* New York: Plenum.

Sears, D. O. (1987). Political psychology. *Annual Review of Psychology, 38,* 229–255.

Sidanius, J. (1985). Cognitive functioning and sociopolitical ideology revisited. *Political Psychology, 6,* 637–661.

Simon, H. A. (1985). Human nature in politics: The dialogue of psychology with political science. *The American Political Science Review, 79,* 293–304.

Stone, W. F. (1981). Political psychology: A Whig history. In S. L. Long (Ed.), *The handbook of political behavior* (Vol. 1, pp. 1–67). New York: Plenum.

Stone, W. F., & Schaffner, P. E. (1988). *The psychology of politics.* New York: Springer-Verlag.

Tetlock, P. E. (1983). Cognitive style and political ideology. *Journal of Personality and Social Psychology, 45,* 118–126.

Van Ginneken, J. (1988). Outline of a cultural history of political psychology. In W. F. Stone & P. Schaffner (Eds.), *The psychology of politics* (2nd ed., pp. 3–22). New York: Springer-Verlag.

Ward, D. (2002). Political psychology: Origins and development. In K. R. Monroe (Ed.), *Political psychology* (pp. 61–78). Mahwah, NJ: Erlbaum.

Winter, D. G. (2000). Power, sex, and violence: A psychological reconstruction of the 20th century and an intellectual agenda for political psychology. *Political Psychology, 21,* 383–404.

Wolf, R. P. (Ed.) (1966). *Political man and social man: Readings in political philosophy.* New York: Random House.

The Poly-Psy Relationship:
Three Phases of a Long Affair

William J. McGuire • Yale University

Interdisciplinary cross-fertilization, never above a modest level, has been as sustained between political science and psychology as between any two social sciences, which is surprising considering that each discipline has longer common borders with other fields—political science with history and economics, psychology with sociology and anthropology. The collaboration has persisted through three successive 20-year eras differing in preferred topics of study, theoretical explanations, and high-table approved methods. For clarifying uniformity, each era will be labeled here by its popular topics of study: Thus the first 1940s and 1950s interdisciplinary flourishing will be called the "personality and culture" era; the second, 1960s and 1970s wave, the "attitudes and voting behavior" era; and the third flourishing, which dominated the 1980s and 1990s, the "ideology and decision" era. Labeling each of the three by its preferred topic is convenient but should not obscure the fact that in some eras a shared theory or a shared method constituted a stronger bond than a shared topic.

Contributions were made during each of the three eras by both humanistic and scientific approaches, within each on both micro- and macrolevels. "Humanistic" research uses insights idiographically to account for peculiarities in the thick texture of complex concrete cases, whereas "scientific" research uses these insights nomothetically to study an abstract general relation as it manifests itself across a wide range of cases whose peculiarities tend to cancel each other out. The idiographic humanistic approach brings theory into confrontation with empirical observations better to understand the specific case; the nomothetic scientific approach confronts them better to develop the theory. Each has its uses. Within each approach some work is at the microlevel, investigating the variables of interest as they relate across individual persons as the units measured; other work is at the macrolevel, investigating these relations across collectives (e.g., nations, social classes, historical epochs) as the units measured.

Table 1.1 gives an overview of this half-century of interdisciplinary collaboration. Its three rows list the three successive 20-year eras focusing on personality, on attitudes, and on ideology, in turn. The seven columns define each era: The three leftmost columns give a connotative definition of each era in terms of its characteristic topics, theories, and methods; and the four rightmost columns provide a denotative definition of each era by citing some of its important contributions, partitioned first between the idiographic humanistic versus the nomothetic scientific approaches, these two each then subdivided between studies on the micro- versus macrolevels. My description is provocatively symmetrical, imposing sharp contours on an amorphous body of research that in actuality had more continuity and less direction than are represented here.

TABLE 1.1. Connotative Definitions (Distinguishing Features) and Denotative Definitions (Notable Examples) of the Three Successive Eras of Collaboration Between Political Science and Psychology

Connotative Definition: Distinguishing Characteristics

Eras	Preferred topics	Preferred Theories	Preferred methods
1. 1940s & 1950s	Political personality (in leaders and in masses)	Environmental determination (psychoanalysis, S-R behaviorism, Marxism)	Content analysis of records and interviews
2. 1960s & 1970s	Political attitudes and voting behavior	Rational person (subjective-utility maximizing, cognition → affects → action)	Questionnares in survey research; participant observation
3. 1980s & 1990s	Political ideology (content and processes of belief systems)	Information processing (cognitive heuristics, decision theories)	Experimental manipulation

Denotative Definition: Notable Contributions Within Each of Four Approaches

Humanistic approaches		Scientific approaches	
Micro	Macro	Micro	Macro
Psychohistory, psychobiography: Fromm (1941) Langer (1972) George & George (1956) Erikson (1958)	National character: Benedict (1946) Mead (1942) Gorer (1948) Riesman (1950)	Dollard et al. (1939) Adorno et al. (1950) Smith, Bruner, & White (1956) McClosky (1958)	Sorokin (1937–41) Kluckhohn & Murray (1948) HRAF (Murdock, Ford) Whiting & Child (1953)
Lane (1959, 1962) Goffman (1959, 1961)	Ariès (1960) *Annals* (Block) Foucault (1961, 1984)	Election studies Campbell et al. (1954, 1960, 1966) Roper Center	Lipset (1960) McClelland (1961) ICPSR (1962) Rokkan (1962) Almond & Verba (1963) Russett et al. (1964) Inkeles & Smith (1974)
George (1980) Larson (1985) Doise (1986)	Lebow (1981) Jervis et al. (1985, 1986) Radding (1985)	Tetlock (1981) Simonton (1984)	Archer & Gartner (1984) Tetlock (1985)

The 1940s–1950s Personality and Culture Era

In the first, personality and culture, era the main common ground among researchers was a shared theoretical enthusiasm for explaining political thoughts, feelings, and actions in terms of environmental (versus hereditary) determinants, using explanatory concepts drawn from psychoanalysis, behaviorism, and Marxism, in declining order of importance, often emphasizing childhood-experience determinants. I shall describe this personality and culture era, first connotatively in terms of its theoretical, topical, and methodological distinctive characteristics; then denotatively, in terms of significant research contributions in each of four approaches, the micro- and macrohumanistic and the micro- and macroscientific.

CONNOTATIVE DEFINITION OF THE 1940s–1950s PERSONALITY-CULTURE ERA: PREFERRED THEORIES

A unifying assumption behind this 1940s–1950s interdisciplinary flourishing is that political personality and the behavior of leaders and masses are formed by socialization experiences, especially those emphasized by the environmentalistic metatheorizing of psychoanalytic, behavioristic, and Marxist theorizing. The era's environmentalism was an exaggerated antigenetic reaction to the excesses of social Darwinism by Spencer and others earlier in the century, and held the hope of ameliorating the disturbed economic and political conditions left by World War I. Another shared ideological orientation was a loathing for the fascistic personality, a syndrome hard to define but (at least in those days) one knew it when one saw it. These revulsions against social Darwinism and fascism were probably related (Hofstadter, 1944; Stein, 1988).

Psychoanalytic theory had great impact on western European and North American social science during the middle part of the twentieth century. Behind the 1930s introjection of Freudianism by many students of politics looms the father figure of Harold Lasswell (1930, 1935), who popularized use of Freudian notions of unconscious erotic drives (but typically suppressing the thanatotic), of defense mechanisms that adaptively channel the expression of these drives, and of Freud's psychosexual developmental notions of how oral, anal, and phallic frustrations of early childhood shape the id, ego, and superego aspects of personality. These rich notions provoked a gold mine of hypotheses about the development and operation of politically relevant thoughts, feelings, and actions in public and in their leaders, although a few critics at the time (Bendix, 1952) objected to the reductionism of such psychologizing.

Environmental determinism in this 1940s–1950s political-personality theorizing derived also from Marxist historical materialism in attributing a society's political consciousness to its social and political institutions, shaped in turn by its modes and relationships of production, and these by physical realities. Marxists accepted Engels's (1884/1972) low opinion of the bourgeois family (the *Communist Manifesto* [1848] called for its abolition), but unlike the Freudians they did not detail the baleful effects of the early childhood home on adult political personality. S-R (stimulus-response) behaviorism or learning (reinforcement) theory also provided inspiration for the political-personality movement, particularly through the circle of interdisciplinary workers around Clark Hull at the Yale Institute of Human Relations. These theorists seasoned a "liberated" behaviorism with a generous sprinkling of psychoanalytic theory and a pinch of Marxism, as illustrated by their work on frustration and aggression, social learning, personality, and psychopathology (Dollard et al., 1939, 1950; Miller & Dollard, 1941).

PREFERRED TOPICS IN THE PERSONALITY AND CULTURE ERA

A secondary unifying focus of these interdisciplinary researchers in the 1940s and 1950s was a shared subject-matter interest in personality as a mediating explanatory variable, how it is affected by the individual's cultural experiences, and how it in turn affects the politically significant thoughts, feelings, and actions of the masses and their leaders. "Personality" was used broadly to include motivations and values, perceptions and stereotypes, cognitive and interpersonal styles, and characteristic modes of coping. Popular independent variables to account for these mediating personality variables were the culture's early childhood socialization experiences, singled out by psychoanalytic theory as crucial. Other popular independent-variable determinants, reflecting the behavioristic and Marxist materialism of the era's theorists, were the institutions of society in regard to the stimuli they presented, the response options they left available, the drives they aroused, and the schedules of reinforcement they administered. For example, the aggressive foreign policy of a national leader or the bellicosity of a population might be attributed: (a) to the culture's displacement of oedipal ambivalence regarding one's father to outgroup targets; or (b) to frustration caused by economic deprivation (absolute or relative to others' or to one's own rising expectations); or (c) to felt loss of control due to bureaucratization; or (d) to alienation of workers from the products of their labor; or (e) to social modeling and reinforcing of aggressive responses in childhood.

PREFERRED METHODS IN THE PERSONALITY AND CULTURE ERA

Researchers in this first era were not as self-conscious about methodologies as were workers in the next two eras. Scholars in its humanistic branch used secondary analysis of the textual record, occasionally supplemented by participant observation, interviews, and analysis of artifacts. These procedures continued to be popular in the humanist branch during the next two eras as well; methodological variations among the three eras are less pronounced in the humanistic than in the scientific approaches. Scientific workers in this first era characteristically used data from questionnaires or from content analyses of archival data. Their preferred descriptive statistics were measures of simple association, adequate for their purposes but inefficient for the study of nonmonotonic, mediational, and interactional relations.

DENOTATIVE DEFINITION OF THE 1940s–1950s PERSONALITY-CULTURE ERA: MICROHUMANISTIC STUDIES

The connotative definition given above of the culture and personality era in terms of its characteristic topics, theories, and methods can be supplemented by giving its denotative definition in terms of its major published contributions in each of four approaches, micro- and macrohumanistic and micro- and macroscientific. Political science, despite its name, has always depended largely on humanistic approaches, using "thick" descriptive analyses (Geertz, 1973, 1983) to demonstrate how some theory or combination of factors can account in depth for a concrete case. Humanistic studies on the microlevel use individual persons as the units of observation, and on the macrolevel use collectives (such as nations or historical epochs). The microhumanistic branch in this political-personality era has come to be known as "psychobiography" or "psychohistory," and its macro branch has been labeled "national character" study.

The master himself contributed one of the earliest microhumanistic psychobiographies in his analysis of Leonardo da Vinci (Freud, 1910). Psychobiographies are occasionally done on nonpolitical personages such as Martin Luther (Erikson, 1958), but political leaders have become the most popular subjects (Greenstein, 1969; Glad, 1973; Runyan, 1993). A seminal contribution was the George and George (1956) analysis of how Woodrow Wilson's boyhood experiences with a demanding father laid down a personality style that led to his fractious behavior in later authority situations, as illustrated by his recurring problems in dealing with the Princeton University trustees, the New Jersey legislature, and the U.S. Senate. Freud himself purportedly coauthored a Wilson

psychobiography, if the "Freud and" Bullitt (1967) hatchet job is authentic (Erikson & Hofstadter, 1967). Neo-Freudian, Marxist, and ego-psychological theorists contributed political psychobiographies of Hitler (Erikson, 1950; Fromm, 1973) and others. This movement gained status among policymakers by its World War II use, as illustrated on the micro side by Langer's (1972) psychobiography of Hitler and on the macro side by Benedict's (1946) analysis of the Japanese national character.

MACROHUMANISTIC NATIONAL CHARACTER STUDIES OF CULTURE AND PERSONALITY

The macro branch is illustrated by such influential studies as Benedict's (1946) depiction of Japanese national character and Riesman's (1950) depiction of personality orientation as evolving from tradition-directed, through inner-directed, to other-directed. Most of the 1940s national-character research in the macrohumanistic line was explicitly psychoanalytic. Psychoanalytically oriented theorists demonstrated that the Japanese national character was oral (Spitzer, 1947), and anal (LaBarre, 1945), and phallic (Silberpfennig, 1945), illustrating the protean quality, at once admirable and worrisome, of psychoanalytic theory. Concurrent analyses of American national character tended to be less Freudian (Mead, 1942; Gorer, 1948).

Notable work in the humanistic tradition has continued beyond its 1940s and 1950s prime, particularly in its micro, psychobiography branch, as reviewed by Runyan (1982, 1988, 1993) and Cocks and Crosby (1987). The challenge presented by Richard Nixon's personality (Brodie, 1981) by itself could have sufficed to revive the enterprise. The macro branch has been quiescent (Patai, 1973, 1977) after its 1940s and 1950s popularity, perhaps because ascribing distinctive characteristics to national or other groups can be politically dangerous, as illustrated by hostile reactions to Oscar Lewis's (1961) well-intentioned use of the "culture of poverty" concept. The shock to Europe and North America by the revolting youth in the late 1960s popularized macroanalyses of epoch personality of successive brief waves of youth cohorts, assigned acronyms and other picturesque labels such as "teddy boys," "skinheads," "beats," "flower children," "punks," "baby-boomers," "yuppies," "dincs," "yucas," and "Generation X," showing that the concept of adolescent political generations is a tenacious one (Mannheim, 1923/1952; Jennings & Niemi, 1981; Jennings, 1987).

MICROSCIENTIFIC STUDIES OF CULTURE AND PERSONALITY

Scientific approaches involve sampling cases from a designated universe to which one wishes to generalize and measuring each case both on the independent variable (in this first era, often on some psychoanalytically relevant dimension of early childhood experience) and on the dependent variable (here, usually some politically significant dimension of personality). Then the relation between distributions of scores on independent and dependent variables is calculated across cases (units of observation), which are individual persons on the microlevel and multiperson social composites (e.g., nations or epochs) on the macrolevel.

Both micro- and macroscientific examples are reported in the era-inaugurating Dollard et al. (1939) frustration-aggression volume with its Freudian underpinnings, although it does not fully exploit the richness of Freud's three theories of aggression (Stepansky, 1977). Microstudies in the Dollard et al. volume systematically manipulated the frustration levels of individual rats and then measured these rats' aggressiveness toward available targets not associated with their frustration; the volume's macrostudies (Hovland & Sears, 1939) correlated annual fluctuations in U.S. economic frustration (measured by gross national product or price of cotton) with annual scapegoating scores (measured by yearly numbers of lynchings in the United States).

A comparably important microscientific study in the political-personality era was the Adorno et al. (1950) authoritarian personality research deriving from Freudian and Marxist orientations, which postulated that the authoritarian (fascist) personality syndrome (characterized by hostility to Jews and other out-groups, along with idealization of high-power individuals and groups) resulted from an oedipal situation in which a boy's punitive father severely punished any hostility directed at him, resulting in the boy's growing up rigorously repressing aggressive feelings toward his father (and, by extension, to other authority fig-

ures) by the use of the reaction-formation mechanism of idealizing the father (and other authority figures) and releasing the pent-up hostility vicariously toward out-groups whose demographics or life-styles place them in opposition to, or at least outside, the Establishment's power structure. Other microscientific studies in the era included Almond's (1954) on the appeals of communism, Srole's (1956) on anomie and prejudice, Smith, Bruner, and White's (1956) on the functional bases of political attitudes, and McClosky's (1958) on political conservatism and personality.

MACROSCIENTIFIC STUDIES OF CULTURE AND PERSONALITY

Early scientific macrostudies (discussed later in this chapter) were Sorokin's (1937–41) formidable analysis of Western civilization over millennia and Richardson's (1960) posthumously published work on the statistics of deadly quarrels. These pioneers had to do Stakhanovite labor (before the availability of large research grants or computers or interuniversity data-bank consortia) to assemble personally, with a little help from their friends and students, large-scale historical data archives. Macroempirical research on personality was given a major impetus in the 1940s by the development of social-data archives, beginning when the Yale group set up the anthropological Human Relations Area Files of cross-cultural data (Kluckhohn & Murray, 1948; Whiting & Child, 1953).

In summary, this 1940s–1950s personality and culture era was an exciting time during which a small invisible college of interdisciplinary researchers, sharing overlapping explanatory targets, grew to a critical mass. Operating across disciplinary frontiers, using psychoanalytic (supplemented by behaviorist and Marxist) theorizing, they studied how a society's child-rearing practices or dominant socioeconomic institutions affect politically relevant personality syndromes, with politically significant consequences. Participants came from beyond psychology and political science (e.g., Benedict and Whiting were anthropologists and Adorno, a philosopher and musicologist). Cross-disciplinary research tends to be an exciting participatory sport, but it is a young person's game, drawing few spectators and fewer participants from the parent disciplines' established leaders who tend to be preoccupied by the traditional topics with which the discipline has become fairly comfortable. Because workers at interdisciplinary borders are relatively few, their focusing narrowly in any one era as regards topics, theories, and methods may be necessary if they are to attain a critical mass of mutually stimulating work. Such within-era narrowness tends to be corrected by sizable shifts of focus from one era to the next.

The 1960s–1970s Attitudes and Voting Behavior Era

In the second, 1960s and 1970s, interdisciplinary flourishing of political psychology, the topical focus shifted from political personality and behavioral pathology to political attitudes and voting behavior. As shown in the second row of Table 1.1, this second era, like the first, had its preferred topic, theory, and method, but the relative emphasis on the three characteristics reversed between the two eras. The primary commonality among these 1960s and 1970s political attitude workers was a shared methodological enthusiasm for survey research; a secondary bond was a shared topic preoccupation with political attitudes and voting behavior; while theory, in the form of a self-interest, rational-choice, subjective-expected-utility, benefits/costs maximizing view, supplied only a weak tertiary bond, often used only implicitly. I shall describe this second, political attitudes era first connotatively and then denotatively.

CONNOTATIVE CHARACTERISTICS OF THE 1960s–1970s ATTITUDES ERA: PREFERRED THEORIES

The interdisciplinary researchers in this political attitudes, second era were not doctrinaire about their own theoretical explanations, nor did they impute highly organized thought systems to the public (Converse, 1964), as befits an "end-of-ideology" era (Namier, 1955; Mills, 1959; Bell, 1960), even if it now appears that ideology was not dead but hiding out in Paris and Frankfurt (Skinner, 1985). Underlying much of the research was an implicit assumption that persons operate hedonistically in accord with the self-interest, subjective-utility maximizing model.

Supplementing this expected-utility conceptualization was another rationality assumption, the "cognitive→ affective→ conative" concept of the person as having beliefs that shape preferences that channel actions (Krech and Crutchfield, 1948). A third underlying assumption was the "reference group" consistency concept that the person maximizes in-group homogeneity and out-group contrast by adopting attitudes and behaviors normative and distinctive to his or her demographic or social groups (Newcomb, 1943). These three rationality postulates of the 1960s and 1970s political attitudes era went almost without saying, in contrast with the belligerent assertiveness of the psychoanalytic, behavioristic, and Marxist theorizing during the earlier 1940s and 1950s political personality era. An environmental determinism bridged both eras; the reawakening appreciation in the biological disciplines of the evolutionary and genetic contributions to human proclivities had as yet little influence on these researchers in politics and psychology.

PREFERRED TOPICS IN THE ATTITUDES/ VOTING ERA

At least as much as psychologists and political scientists, sociologists like Lazarsfeld at Columbia, Berelson at Chicago, and Lipset at Berkeley played major roles from the outset in studying how voting behavior and attitudes toward political issues, parties, and candidates are predictable from group memberships, personal interactions, and mass media. Before the 1930s depression political elections had been regarded as a great American game (Farley, 1938), an interesting, uncouth spectator sport like prizefighting and baseball. Upper class scholars, both in the academy (e.g., Frederick Jackson Turner) and outside it (e.g., Henry Adams), were willing to leave its practice to the upwardly mobile hinterland provincials and immigrant urban proletarians. As some of these outsiders shouldered or sidled their way into academic halls (Orren, 1985), and as the Great Depression and the prospect of international socialism and the terrors of National Socialism riveted scholars' attention on politics, the study of political attitudes and voting behavior became respectable in the relatively democratic nations. Turn-of-the-century political scientists (e.g., Acton, 1907) had found power distasteful, but by midcentury students of politics had become comfortable, even fascinated, with power and its study (Leighton, 1945; Lasswell, 1948; Hunter, 1953; Dahl, 1961; Winter, 1973; McClelland, 1975), perhaps because of seeing governmental power exercised both to perpetrate genocide and to defeat the perpetrators in a war that incidentally caged the big bad wolf of economic depression. Indeed, many of these post-1940 students of politics had played participatory Dr. Win-the-War roles.

PREFERRED METHODS IN THE ATTITUDES/ VOTING ERA

It was their shared "Do surveys; will travel" methodology that especially united these 1960s–1970s political attitudes and voting researchers, more than did their shared rational-person theoretical orientation, or even their shared topical interest in political attitudes and voting. They designed questionnaires asking a sample representative of some population about their demographics, media consumption, political information, or other personal characteristics (as independent variable measures) and about their political attitudes and voting intentions or behaviors (to measure political partisanship and participation as mediating and dependent variables). Such formal survey-research methods characterized the scientific branch of political attitudes work, while the humanistic branch often used less formalized depth interviews that allowed open-ended responses to general probes. Secondarily, participant observation passed from anthropology to sociology, with fertile use by Whyte (1943, 1949) in his studies of street-corner and restaurant societies, and by Goffman (1959, 1961) in his analyses of self-presentation in varied settings (e.g., gambling casinos and asylums).

DENOTATIVE MAPPING OF THE 1960s–1970s ATTITUDES ERA: THE MICRO-HUMANISTIC APPROACH

To provide a denotative definition of this 1960s and 1970s political attitudes and voting behavior era, prototypical contributions will be described in each of the four approaches. Throughout the century of progress following Henry Mayhew's (1861) microhumanistic interviews of the poor in early Victorian London, to the current sophisticated survey-research training programs at universities such as Michigan and Chicago, students of soci-

ety and mentality have made thoughtful use of the interview method, developing it from an art to a craft, if not yet quite a science. As an art, it calls for virtuosi such as Henry Mayhew and Studs Terkel (1967, 1970), who use intuitive techniques difficult to verbalize. Interviewing evolved to craft status as its experienced practitioners became able to articulate rules of thumb teachable to apprentices. It is only beginning to develop to the status of a science with an organized body of theory from which new testable relations can be derived and that can evolve by assimilating new findings. Robert E. Lane (1959, 1962) made early contributions of this type in his investigations of attitudes associated with political participation and then of the origins of these attitudes. Oral history archives promise to expand the collection and availability of useful bodies of interview materials for scholars in the future.

MACROHUMANISTIC STUDIES OF ATTITUDES

Precursory to macrohumanistic studies of collectives was Myrdal's (1944) analysis of an American dilemma, constituted by egalitarian attitudes at odds with racially discriminatory behavior. Regional studies, often centered on an archetypical community ("Jonesville," "Yankee City," "Middletown," etc.) depicted the political minds of the South, of New England, and of the American heartland; only the Far West was neglected (perhaps because in those pre-jet days academic researchers were loathe to travel three thousand miles from the ocean to make their observations). Paradoxically, this macrohumanistic research, originally preoccupied with the minutiae of overt behavior and objective physical data, metamorphosed into a depiction of modal group mentality. Participant observers such as Goffman recorded external gross behavior as data, but their interpretations often depict mentality more than do accounts by the survey researchers, even though the latter's verbal interview material promises more direct access to the subjective worlds of the respondents.

MICROSCIENTIFIC STUDIES OF ATTITUDES AND VOTING

Prototypical of the microscientific research on political attitudes were the early voting studies by Lazarsfeld, Berelson, and their colleagues

(Lazarsfeld et al., 1944; Berelson, Lazarsfeld, & McPhee, 1954) associated with Columbia University and the University of Chicago. The most sustained program of such research has been at the University of Michigan, involving A. Campbell, Converse, Miller, and their colleagues (Campbell et al., 1954, 1960, 1966). The 1960s and 1970s were the great decades of this microscientific research on political attitudes and voting, as summarized by Kinder and Sears (1985), but interest has remained high due to the practical importance of the topic.

MACROSCIENTIFIC STUDIES OF POLITICAL ATTITUDES

Macroscientific studies using conglomerates (nations, epochs, etc.) are rarer than microscientific studies. A macroscientific study transitional between the 1940s and 1950s political personality era and the 1960s and 1970s political attitudes era is McClelland's (1961) research on how societies' child-rearing practices affect and are affected by their citizens' achievement, power, and affiliation motivations, and how these in turn affect the rise and fall of the societies' political dominance, their cultural influence, and their economic affluence. McClelland's motivational mediators have elements both of the first era's personality and this second era's attitudinal mediators.

Because nations had been scored more frequently in regard to modal actions than modal attitudes, many macrostudies have focused on overt behaviors such as voting or violent acts rather than on the attitudes presumed to underlie them (although growing accumulations in social data archives are gradually facilitating work on the latter). Much of the macro work in the 1960s concentrated on politically disruptive behavior such as war, revolution, and crime (Davies, 1962; Feierabend & Feierabend, 1966; Gurr, 1970; Singer & Small, 1972; Naroll, Bullough, & Naroll, 1974). Other macroscientific studies focused on constructive characteristics, for example, Lipset's (1960) on political stability, Rokkan's (1962) and Almond and Verba's (1963) on cross-national differences in attitudes and political participation, Inkeles and Smith's (1974) on modernization attitudes, and Cantril's (1965) and Szalai and Andrews's (1980) on crossnational differences in felt quality of life and uses of leisure. The feasibility of such studies will increase as social data archives grow and multivariate, time-series causal analysis improves.

The 1980s–1990s Political Cognition and Decision Era

CHARACTERISTICS OF THE 1980s–1990s POLITICAL IDEOLOGY ERA

The preferred interdisciplinary border-crossing then shifted to a third frontier, political cognition, again with its distinguishing subject matter, method, and theory. It is best defined by its distinctive subject-matter focus, the content and operations of cognitive systems that affect decision-making in the political domain. Shared theoretical and methodological orientations provide only weak bonds in this third era, and are largely confined to using the computer as metaphor and tool. Depicting the person as an information-processing machine is a dominant theoretical model, with specifics drawn from cognitive science assumptions regarding how information is stored in memory and from decision theory assumptions regarding the heuristics of selective retrieval and weighing of information to arrive at a judgment (Axelrod, 1976; Tversky & Kahneman, 1983). Hastie (1986) summarizes aspects of cognitive science theorizing particularly pertinent to political psychology. Symptomatic of the computer inspiration of this third era is the use of computer flow charts to depict the person's ideology and decision processes (Janis, 1989).

The need to depict complex cognition systems and processes in this third era is likely to require more use of manipulational laboratory experimentation (Lodge & Hamill, 1986; Beer, Healy, Sinclair, & Bourne, 1987; Masters & Sullivan, 1993) than did the first two eras, but most data will continue to be collected in the natural political world (Tetlock, 1993). The complexity of using these natural-world data to clarify the structure and operation of ideology will require increasing use of path analysis, structural equation modeling (Hurwitz & Peffley, 1987), and computer simulations (Ostrom, 1988).

NOTABLE CONTRIBUTIONS IN THE 1980s–1990s POLITICAL IDEOLOGY ERA

It may be premature in the third, political ideology, era to define it denotatively by a definitive listing of its major monographic contributions, but illustrative contributions are discernible in each of the four approaches. As regards the micro-humanistic approach, noteworthy is Larson's (1985) use of cognitive heuristics to analyze the origins of the U.S. containment policy toward the Soviet Union during the early years of the cold war. George (1980) describes the effective use of information in presidential foreign-policy decisions. Purkitt and Dyson (1986) analyze the role of cognitive heuristics in affecting recent U.S. policy toward South Africa. Jervis (1986, 1993) analyzes how processes found in the laboratory (e.g., decision-makers ignoring base-rate information) may not operate in actual foreign-policy decision-making. Illustrative of the new cognitive psychobiography approach is Doise's (1986) analysis of how Mussolini's political ideology, derived from his study of Le Bon, Orano, and Sorel, affected his political policies and tactics. Depth interviewing is used to study the development of political consciousness and ideology in children by Coles (1986) and in adults by Reinarman (1987).

Macrohumanistic studies in the cognitive era, with nations as the units of observation, typically use case-history analyses such as those by Lebow (1981) on brinkmanship crises; by Jervis, Lebow, and Stein (1985) on the efficacy of a deterrence policy for averting war; and by Frei (1986) on cognitive barriers to disarmament. Popkin (1993) describes cognitive distortions that affect arms policies. Neustadt and May (1986) review the use of case histories by political decision-makers. A macrohumanistic study using epochs as the units of observation is Radding's (1985) application of Piaget's theory of cognitive development to account for a purported transformation toward abstractness in the mentality and society of western Europe from 400 to 1200 C.E.

The microscientific approach is illustrated by Suedfeld and Rank's (1976) and Tetlock's (1981, 1993) analyses of the kind of cognitive complexity required by revolutionary leaders if, like Fidel Castro, they are to avoid the classic Robespierrean trajectory of being consumed by their own revolution. These survivors need single-minded fanaticism to win the revolutionary struggle, but also flexibility to use compromise and accommodation in governing the postrevolutionary regime. Dean Keith Simonton has done intriguing microscien-

tific studies of social factors affecting the productivity and processes of political and cultural leaders.

Illustrative of the nation-as-unit macroscientific approach to political psychology are Archer and Gartner's (1984) account of crossnational differences in violence in terms of social conditions on the national level that affect the cognitive salience of aggression as a mode of coping; Reychler's (1979) analysis of national differences in patterns of diplomatic thinking; and Tetlock's (1985) discussion of complexity in Soviet and U.S. foreign-policy rhetoric. Peripherally related are Martindale's (1981) cross-epoch analysis of the evolution of stylistic consciousness in art and Reiss's (1986) cross-cultural analyses of societal-level factors affecting the conceptualization of sexuality.

Future Directions

The politics and psychology relationship has been lively and longlasting as interdisciplinary affairs go, its longevity fostered by frequent shiftings of its popular topics, methods, and theories. The fluidity has made participation both exciting and precarious, offering novelties that lure new recruits and facilitating the weeding out of tried-and-trivialized old constructs. The obverse of this tradition of novelty in interdisciplinary research is painfully rapid obsolescence. Earlier, the depth analysts of the political personality era were edged out of the fast lane by the survey researchers of the political attitudes era, well-funded to study U.S. presidential elections; now these second-era survey researchers are finding the third era's cognitive science mavens tailgating to edge them out of the passing lane into cyberspace.

PARTICIPANTS IN THIS INTERDISCIPLINARY WORK

Recruitment of workers for the successive eras has been accomplished more by replacement than by retooling. A few (e.g., Lasswell, George, Lane, Converse, etc.) have moved with the changing interests of successive eras. More typically, researchers who initially created each era have continued to do good work in that old line after the new generation has moved a replacement enthusiasm to center stage. Over the three eras the participating subdiscipline from within psychology and the auxiliary field have shifted from personality psychology and psychiatry, to social psychology and communication, to cognitive psychology and computer science; however, the political scientists in all three eras have come mainly from its politics subdiscipline, plus, recently, students of international relations (Sears & Funk, 1991).

There has been a shift across the three eras also in regard to which third, auxiliary disciplines have contributed most to this collaboration. In the first, the political personality era, outside help came primarily from psychiatrists and anthropologists (Stocking, 1987). In the second, the political attitudes and voting behavior, era, the main outside collaboration was from sociologists and communication theorists; indeed, the sociologists' contributions to the study of voting behavior may have exceeded that of the political scientists or the psychologists . . . but who's counting? In the third, the political ideology era, cognitive scientists and decision theorists are the main auxilary collaborators. Historians, particularly the quantitative branch not always welcomed by more orthodox humanistic historians (Barzun, 1974; Bogue, 1983), have also contributed substantially (McGuire, 1976c).

A POSSIBLE FOURTH ERA

Past trends allow projecting, at least through a glass darkly, a fourth flourishing of political science/psychology collaboration that might follow the 1980s and 1990s political ideology era. The past three eras have focused largely on intrapersonal topics (personality, attitudes, ideology), albeit as they are affected by social factors and as they in turn affect society. The fourth era is likely to switch, not again simply to another intrapersonal topic, but to interpersonal (and even intergroup) processes. The shift is adumbrated in the current work on how stereotypical perceptions and selective-information encoding affect international relations (Jervis, 1976), on jury decision-making (Hastie, Penrod, & Pennington, 1983), and on intergroup processes (Turner et al., 1987; Jervis, 1993; Sidanius, 1993).

If interest does move to interpersonal and intergroup processes, the union local of the psychological participants is likely to shift again, this time to group dynamics and organizational psychology; and participants from within political science are likely to come more often from foreign-policy and international relations as well as politics (Tetlock, 1986); the third-party collaboration is likely to come from historians and area specialists. Macroresearch is likely to grow relative to microresearch due to growing interest in intergroup issues. Both humanistic and scientific branches are likely to flourish: the humanistic, because the complexity of group processes invites the idiographic descriptive case-history approach; and the scientific, because increasing availability of social data archives and growing technical capacity for collecting and causally analyzing multivariate time-series data will make systems styles of research more possible. It would take more hubris than is pardonable to predict in fuller detail the shape of this fourth flourishing in the new millennium.

Personality and Politics

We have divided the readings on personality and politics into two subsections. First, we focus on the theory of authoritarianism and its consequences for understanding mass psychology. Second, we turn our attention to the personality structures of political leaders and other elites.

AUTHORITARIANISM AND MASS PSYCHOLOGY

A book published in 1950 by Adorno, Frenkel-Brunswik, Levinson, and Sanford entitled *The Authoritarian Personality* is probably the single most well-known work in all of political psychology. Christie and Cook (1958) found that in the first 7 years after the publication of this book, there were at least 230 published articles referring to it. It is a rare book in social science that stimulates *other* books to be written about *it*, but *The Authoritarian Personality* has received this honor more than once (e.g., Christie & Jahoda, 1954; Stone, Lederer, & Christie, 1993). At the time of writing the introduction to this section, a Google search of the Internet turned up 2,920 citations referring to the work by Adorno and his colleagues. These figures undoubtedly underestimate the degree of impact that this book has had, not only within political psychology and the social sciences in general, but especially on the lay public.

The work that resulted in the publication of *The Authoritarian Personality* was originally commissioned by the American Jewish Committee in 1944 and was aimed at deepening the scientific psychological understanding of anti-Semitism and the events leading to the Holocaust. In addition to the sheer scope and ambition of the project, *The Authoritarian Personality* was also unique because of its methodological creativity. It was the first study of its time to combine the relatively rigorous and empirically-oriented techniques of survey research with the use of psychoanalytically-oriented projective assessment techniques, including the Thematic Apperception Test (TAT) and clinical interviews. While the theory of authoritarianism had many contributors and had been in the works for years (e.g., Fromm, 1941; Horkheimer, 1936; Reich, 1946), the research by Adorno and his colleagues was the first attempt to investigate these ideas empirically.

As Roger Brown points out in the first reading we have selected for this section, some of the general ideas contained in *The Authoritarian Personality* had been independently explored by Nazi psychologists. Ernst R. Jaensch of the University of Marburg, for instance, wrote a (1938) book entitled *Der Gegentypus* (or *The Anti-Type*) in which he distinguished between two types of political personalities: (a) the S-type, which he believed was characterized by introversion, intelligence, femininity, passivity, lack of physical activity, and Jewish or mixed race ancestry; and (b) the J-type, which he believed was characterized by extraversion, strong reality constraints, masculinity, aggressiveness, interest in contact sports, Nazi attitudes, and Aryan ancestry. It is remarkable that such opposed theorists as Jaensch and the members of the Marxist-oriented Frankfurt School would propose parallel personality schemes linking general psychological characteristics to specific political belief systems. Whether there are in fact meaningful and measurable differences in the general cognitive and motivational styles of left-wingers vs. right-wingers remains a controversial issue to this day (Jost, Glaser, Kruglanski, & Sulloway, 2003).

According to Adorno and his colleagues, the authoritarian personality syndrome was theorized to include general ethnocentrism, ego-defensiveness (the inability to admit one's own fears or weaknesses combined with a lack of self-insight), mental rigidity and intolerance of ambiguity, projection and the idealization of authority figures, conformity and conventionalism, the expression of hostility and aggression towards deviants, and political-economic conservatism. The personality syndrome was assumed to result from oppressive, overly punitive and restrictive socialization practices within the family, arising from economic and other frustrations. The syndrome was measured with a survey instrument, called the *F*-Scale (or Fascism Scale), which was one of the most widely used scales in all of political psychology during the 1950s and 1960s.

Because Adorno et al. failed to write a succinct, thorough summary of their work, which was enormous in size (23 chapters and over 1,000 pages), we have chosen to introduce students to this tradition of research by reprinting Roger Brown's outstanding and influential (1965) review of the strengths and weaknesses of early research on the authoritarian personality. Criticisms of the work include all of the following: (a) the use of nonrepresentative samples in drawing general, far-reaching conclusions, (b) reliance on poorly constructed attitude surveys that allowed for the intrusion of response bias, (c) failure to establish controlled procedures for content analyses of the clinical interviews, and (d) reluctance to seriously consider alternative explanations for their empirical findings. For example, it seems plausible that correlations among authoritarianism, ethnocentrism, education, and socio-economic status could arise from cultural associations rather than personality dynamics per se (see Pettigrew, 1959). And even if one were to accept the validity of the authoritarian syndrome, the original researchers were never able to make a convincing case that it was caused by authoritarian child-rearing practices.

Despite numerous and serious methodological shortcomings of the original work by Adorno et al., many of their insights do stand the test of time. The second reading in this section by Richard Doty, Bill Peterson, and David Winter develops Fromm's (1941) ideas about the psychological causes of authoritarian behavior. Whereas Adorno et al. (1950) located the sources of authoritarianism in the family, Fromm put much greater emphasis on generalized threats caused by social, economic, and political instability. In testing this notion empirically, Doty and his colleagues demonstrate that various public manifestations of authoritarianism are increased during historical periods of relatively high threat. Similarly, with some interesting exceptions, authoritarianism appears to dip below baseline levels in periods of low threat.

The third reading in this section is by Bob Altemeyer, whose efforts to address the methodological shortcomings of classical measures of authoritarianism (such as the *F*-Scale) have contributed greatly to the revival of research interest in the construct of authoritarianism. As Brown recounts in Reading 2, the original Adorno et al. (1950) group had identified nine distinctive characteristics of authoritarians. After conducting a prodigious amount of research, Altemeyer (1981) concluded that this complicated typology could be more simply and accurately represented by as few as three distinctive components: (a) *authoritarian aggression*, defined as "a general aggressiveness, directed against various persons, which is perceived to be sanctioned by established authorities" (p. 148); (b) *authoritarian submission*, defined as "a high degree of submission to the authorities who are perceived to be established and legitimate in the society in which one lives" (p. 148); and (c) *conventionalism*, defined as a belief in conventional traditions preserved by established authority figures in society. Using these three components as a conceptual base, Altemeyer then developed a new measure of authoritarianism called *right-wing authoritarianism* (RWA). Subsequent research by Altemeyer and others has confirmed that measuring right-wing authoritarianism in this way is reliable and valid. Scores on the RWA scale predict racism, sexism, political conservatism, support for the death penalty, patriotism, religious fundamentalism, and militarism. In the Altemeyer article we have selected for inclusion, the author summarizes evidence that scores on RWA and *social dominance orientation* (SDO) are both uniquely predictive of social and political attitudes that are ethnocentric and reminiscent of the syndrome described more than 50 years ago by Adorno and the other members of the Frankfurt School.

POLITICAL ELITES AND LEADERSHIP

The remaining readings on personality and politics focus on understanding the behavior of individual political actors, especially professional politicians and other elite decision-makers. In Reading 5, Fred Greenstein directly confronts the most common major objections to studying personality in seeking to understand the dynamics of political events. These objections usually take one or more of the following forms: (a) Insofar as individual personality types are randomly distributed across different social roles, personality variables will "cancel out" and become irrelevant in comparison with the enactment of social roles; (b) Political behavior is determined much more by the specific political context than by the personality characteristics of individuals; (c) The psychodynamic aspects of personality that most political psychologists concern themselves with (e.g., ego-defense mechanisms) are not directly relevant to most political outcomes; (d) Social structural and demographic characteristics of political actors (e.g., race, social class, religion) have much greater political importance than do aspects of their "personalities;" and (e) Large-scale social forces, rather than individuals, are the real determinants of political events. Greenstein discusses the validity of each objection and suggests ways of overcoming them.

Our final article in this section is an excellent example of how researchers endeavor to investigate the personalities of political leaders "from a distance" in an effort to determine how personal and situational attributes might affect leadership success. Drawing on archival data concerning American presidents, David Winter assesses the evidence for and against three different models of successful political leadership: (a) the *leader characteristics* model, which assumes that successful leaders tend to share specific personality characteristics such as energy, decisiveness, and charisma; (b) a *leader-situation match* model, which proposes that the most successful leaders will be those with personal characteristics that are most appropriate for the immediate political context; and (c) a *leader-follower match* model, according to which the most successful political elites will be those whose personal characteristics are most consistent with the characteristics of the mass public. Winter's analysis suggests that when leadership success is defined in terms of electoral outcomes, the most successful presidents are those whose personal motives fit with the motives that are most prevalent and contemporary in society. However, when success is defined in terms of "presidential greatness" as judged by historical experts in retrospect, success is largely a function of the personal characteristics of the president and the degree of *in*congruence between the president and the society around him!

Discussion Questions

1. According to Brown, what are the most important contributions and the most serious methodological shortcomings of *The Authoritarian Personality*?
2. Assuming that various personality and attitudinal variables (e.g., intolerance of ambiguity, anti-Semitism, ethnocentrism) do correlate with one another in the manner that authoritarian researchers claim, what other theoretical explanations can you think of to account for such findings, in addition to explanations based on authoritarian personality theory?
3. What do Doty, Peterson, and Winter mean by the terms "dispositional authoritarians" and "situational authoritarians," and how are these concepts used to account for the conflicting results they obtained?
4. According to Altemeyer, what are the most important conceptual and empirical differences between the theoretical constructs of *right-wing authoritarianism* and *social dominance orientation*?
5. Greenstein discusses several objections that critics have raised concerning the potential usefulness of investigating the role of personality variables in leading to political action. What do you see as the most fruitful directions that political psychologists can take in responding to these objections?
6. What additional situational, cultural, and political factors can you identify that might moderate the validity of Winter's conclusions about the causes of success and failure in political leadership?

Suggested Readings

Adorno, T. W., Frenkel-Brunswik, E., Levinson, D. J., & Sanford, R. N. (1950). *The authoritarian personality*. New York: Norton.

Altemeyer, R. A. (1996). *The authoritarian specter*. Cambridge, MA: Harvard University Press.

Barber, J. D. (1985). *The Presidential character: Predicting performance in the White House* (3rd ed.). Englewood Cliffs, NJ: Prentice-Hall.

Christie, R. (1991). Authoritarianism and related constructs. In J. P. Robinson, P. R. Shaver, & L. S. Wrightsman (Eds.), *Measures of personality and social psychological attitudes* (pp. 501–571). San Diego, CA: Academic Press.

Duckitt, J. (1989). Authoritarianism and group identification: A new view of an old construct. *Political Psychology, 10*, 63–84.

Fromm, E. (1941). *Escape from freedom*. New York: Holt.

Jost, J. T., Glaser, J., Kruglanski, A. W., & Sulloway, F. (2003). Political conservatism as motivated social cognition. *Psychological Bulletin, 129*, 339–375.

McCann, S. J. H. (1997). Threatening times, "strong" presidential popular vote winners, and the victory margin, 1824–1964. *Journal of Personality and Social Psychology, 73*, 160–170.

Peterson, B. E., Doty, R. M., & Winter, D. G. (1993). Authoritarianism and attitudes toward contemporary social issues. *Personality and Social Psychology Bulletin, 19*, 174–184.

Pratto, F., Sidanius, J., Stallworth, L. M., & Malle, B. F. (1994). Social dominance orientation: A personality variable predicting social and political attitudes. *Journal of Personality and Social Psychology, 67,* 741–763.

Sales, S. M. (1972). Economic threat as a determinant of conversion rates in authoritarian and nonauthoritarian churches. *Journal of Personality and Social Psychology, 23,* 420–428.

Sales, S. M. (1973). Threat as a factor in authoritarianism: An analysis of archival data. *Journal of Personality and Social Psychology, 28,* 44–57.

Stone, W. F. (1980). The myth of left-wing authoritarianism. *Political Psychology, 2,* 3–19.

Stone, W. F., Lederer, G., & Christie, R. (Eds.) (1993). *Strength and weakness: The Authoritarian Personality today.* New York: Springer-Verlag.

Whitley, B. E. Jr. (1999). Right-wing authoritarianism, social dominance orientation, and prejudice. *Journal of Personality and Social Psychology, 77,* 126–134.

Wilson, G. D. (Ed.) (1973). *The psychology of conservatism.* London: Academic Press.

The Authoritarian Personality and the Organization of Attitudes

Roger Brown • formerly of Harvard University

In 1934 Hitler became chancellor of Germany. In 1938 E. R. Jaensch, a psychologist and also a Nazi, published the book *Der Gegentypus*. This book reported the discovery of a consistent human type—the *Gegentypus* or Anti-Type. The Anti-Type was also called the S-Type because Jaensch found that he was synaesthetic: one who enjoys concomitant sensation, a subjective experience from another sense than the one being stimulated, as in color hearing. Synaesthesia, which we are likely to regard as a poet's gift, seemed to Jaensch to be a kind of perceptual slovenliness, the qualities of one sense carelessly mixed with those of another. In other perceptual tasks Jaensch found the Anti-Type to be characterized by ambiguous and indefinite judgments and to be lacking in perseverance.

On the assumption that personalities manifest a *Stileinheit*, or "unity of style," Jaensch filled out his characterization of the S-Type more from imagination than evidence. The S would be a man with so-called "liberal" views; one who would think of environment and education as the determinants of behavior; one who would take a childish wanton pleasure in being eccentric, S would say "individualistic." S would be flaccid, weak, and effeminate. His general instability would be likely to stem from a racially mixed heredity. Jews are Anti-Types and "Parisians" and Orientals and communists.

The contrasting personality, an ideal for Jaensch, was the J-Type. J made definite, unambiguous perceptual judgments and persisted in them. He would recognize that human behavior is fixed by blood, soil, and national tradition. He would be tough, masculine, firm; a man you could rely on. His ancestors would have lived from time immemorial in the North German space and within the North German population; it would be these ancestors who had bequeathed him his admirable qualities. J made a good Nazi Party member.

In 1950, in the United States, *The Authoritarian Personality* was published. The research reported in this book undertook to discover the psychological roots of anti-Semitism. The anti-Semite in America turned out to be generally ethnocentric, generally antagonistic to groups other than his own because he thought of these groups as having various disagreeable innate qualities. Politically the anti-Semite tended to be conservative, a firm believer in "free enterprise," nationalistic, a friend of business, and an enemy of labor unions. A person with this combination of opinions sounded like a potential Fascist. The authoritarian type in his perception and thought appeared to be rigid and intolerant of ambiguity. He was, more or less, Jaensch's J-Type, but J, who was a hero to Nazi social science, was a villain to American social science. What Jaensch called "stability" we called "rigidity" and the flaccidity and eccentricity of Jaensch's despised Anti-Type were for us the flexibility and individualism of the democratic equalitarian. The typologies of Jaensch and of the authors of *The Authoritarian Personality* were much the same but the evaluations were different.

The Authoritarian Personality had the greatest possible relevance to the social issues of its day. The Soviet Union had been our ally in the war against fascism. American intellectuals generally accepted the Marxist interpretation of fascism as a movement of the extreme political right, as a conservatism driven to desperation by the economic problems of capitalism. The Equalitarian opposite to the Authoritarian held the leftish liberal views of a New Dealer in the 1930's. They were views common to humane liberals, to Henry Wallace's Progressive Party, to non-Stalinist communists, the authors of *The Authoritarian Personality*, and most American social psychologists. The Equalitarian was ourselves and the Authoritarian the man in our society whom we feared and disliked.

The research reported in *The Authoritarian Personality* was done at the University of California at Berkeley. The work was subsidized by the Department of Scientific Research of the American Jewish Committee. One of the authors of the book, a social psychologist with very great talent, was Else Frenkel-Brunswik. Mrs. Brunswik and her husband, the eminent psychologist Egon Brunswik, had been students and teachers at the University of Vienna during the period in which Hitler rose to power. They were Jews and well acquainted with anti-Semitism.

After the War, came the realignment of world powers into communist and democratic blocs. In this country the wartime solidarity with Russia was forgotten and Soviet Communism replaced German fascism as the principal villain in world affairs. American intellectuals were not as ready as the national majority to anathematize communists; the two fascist themes of prejudice and political reaction seemed worse evils to us. One of the first indications of general American anxiety about internal communism was the decision of the Regents of the University of California to require a loyalty oath of all its faculty members. This seemed to most of us an egregious infringement of academic freedom and we sympathized with those who refused to sign. We were generally alarmed by the communism phobia which at length led to

McCarthyism and to the stigmatization of liberal intellectuals as "eggheads."

Unquestionably there was some gratification for American social psychology during this period in the theory of the authoritarian personality which exposed the fear, the stupidity, and the sadism in nationalistic and reactionary politics. Was there perhaps also some distortion of truth in the service of values? If so, it was not so blatant as Jaensch's, not so obviously unsupported by evidence, not in the service of the state, perhaps not there at all. Still the authors of the 1950 study were not much interested in what has come to be called authoritarianism of the left. Interest in authoritarianism of the left apparently had to wait upon a change of the political climate, a time when disillusionment with communism was general among American intellectuals. It is not easy to do sound social psychological research on contemporary issues because any finding is, in these circumstances, a social force.

The Widening Circle of Covariation

Two kinds of behavior are said to covary when a change in one is associated in some regular way with a change in the other. The thousand pages of *The Authoritarian Personality* tell the story of behavior that covaries with attitudes toward Jews. The account moves from anti-Semitic attitudes to ethnocentric ideology to political and economic conservatism to implicit antidemocratic trends to needs and traits revealed in interviews, TAT stories, and answers to projective questions. It is all an account of covariation, of how one kind of behavior is associated with another.

In following the ever widening circle that centers on anti-Semitism we will cross one major methodological boundary. Anti-Semitism, ethnocentrism, political and economic conservatism, and implicit antidemocratic trends are all assessed with fixed-alternative questionnaires. In the remainder of the work, research methods are used which do not provide alternative responses but leave the subject free to construct his own answer; these include interviews, requests to tell stories about pictures, and requests to respond to projective questions. The fixed-alternative questionnaire item is like the multiple-choice examination question and the open-ended inquiry is like an essay question. Scoring the former is a mechanical process but the latter requires trained judgment and is handled by a method called content analysis.

The fixed-alternative questionnaire is primarily a method of survey research and the first part of the study is essentially an opinion survey. Interviews, TAT's, and projective questions are primarily methods of clinical psychology and the second part of the study is essentially a clinical investigation of a small number of persons. The subjects for the clinical inquiry were selected on the basis of their scores on the Ethnocentrism (E) Scale; they were high scorers and low scorers, ideological extremes. One of the innovations of *The Authoritarian Personality* was the combination in one study of the two kinds of method.

In addition to crossing a methodological boundary we will in this study cross a conceptual boundary; the two boundaries are related but not exactly coincident. The data are all verbal behavior, answers to questions of one kind or another. However, the authors of the Berkeley research conceptualized the data in two ways. They were, in the first place, concerned with ideology which they thought of as an organization of opinions, attitudes, and values, in political, economic, and religious spheres. They were in the second place concerned with personality which they thought of in the Freudian tradition, as an organization of needs varying in quality, intensity, and object; needs sometimes in harmony and sometimes in conflict. It was the effort to relate ideology to personality that made the California study strikingly original.

It is natural to anticipate that the survey part of the study which used questionnaire items would yield the data on ideology and that the clinical part of the study would yield the data on personality. In fact the coincidence is not quite that sharp. The Anti-Semitism (A-S) Scale, the Ethnocentrism (E) Scale, and the Political and Economic Conservatism (PEC) Scale are all concerned with explicit ideology. However, the F Scale is concerned with personality. It represents an attempt to assess by questionnaire the personality trends that are also assessed by interview and by projective methods. The methodological-conceptual coincidence is further blurred by the fact that the interview protocols and the TAT stories contain some material that is relevant to attitudes and ideologies. Apart from the present study, fixed-alternative questionnaires have very often been used to elicit person-

ality data and open-ended questions have come to be widely used in opinion surveys.

Covariation of Questioning Data

The investigators obtained most of their subjects by approaching organizations and asking to survey opinions in the entire membership. Among the subjects of these surveys were students from the University of California, from the University of Oregon, and from George Washington University. There were public school teachers, public health nurses, San Quentin Prison inmates, patients at the Langley Porter Psychiatric Clinic, veterans' groups, labor union groups, and Kiwanis clubs. More than two thousand persons took one or another of the attitude scales. Data from members of important minority groups were deliberately excluded. The majority of the subjects could be characterized as white, non-Jewish, native-born, middle-class Americans and the authors guessed that their findings would hold for this population.

All of the questionnaire items written for the survey portion of the research assumed the same form; they are called, in the terminology of attitude scaling, Likert-type items. Subjects were asked to mark each statement according to the degree of their agreement or disagreement with it by using the following scale:

+1: slight support, agreement   −1: slight opposition, disagreement

+2: moderate support, agreement   −2: moderate opposition, disagreement

+3: strong support, agreement   −3: strong opposition, disagreement

THE ANTI-SEMITISM (A-S) SCALE

The investigators' general conception of anti-Semitism was that it consists in "stereotyped negative opinions describing the Jews as threatening, immoral, and categorically different from non-Jews, and of hostile attitudes urging various forms of restriction, exclusion, and suppression as a means of solving the 'Jewish problem'" (Adorno, et al., 1950, p. 71). They wrote fifty-two questionnaire items to tap this attitude. The authors classified their fifty-two items under five subheadings: 1) *offensive* items described Jews as conceited, sensual, dirty, and the like; 2) *threatening* items described them as ruthless, competitive, radical, and the like; 3) *attitudes* items recommended various discriminative actions to be taken against the Jews; 4) *seclusive* items credited the "clannish" Jews with a desire to keep apart from gentiles; 5) *intrusive* items, on the other hand, attributed to Jews a desire to move in where they are not wanted.

All of the items were written so as to affirm an anti-Semitic opinion and so consistent agreement with items would produce a high A-S score. The authors discussed the possible objection to their procedure that a subject who was somehow "set" so as to agree with statements might mechanically produce a high score without in fact being intensely anti-Semitic. For various reasons they considered this unlikely but as we shall see, when we make a critique of the study, their decision was unwise. The items of all the subsequent scales, with the exception of the Political and Economic Conservatism (PEC) Scale, were also written so as to affirm the attitude in question.

The A-S Scale items were phrased so as to express a subtle hostility without seeming to offend the democratic values that most subjects would feel bound to support. Each item has a kind of fair-minded and reasonable veneer. It is sometimes rather difficult to find the sting. The following item is a good example: "The trouble with letting Jews into a nice neighborhood is that they gradually give it a typical Jewish atmosphere." How could it be otherwise? Surely Jews will produce a Jewish atmosphere. They will at any rate do so if one thinks of Jews as "categorically different from non-Jews." However it is just this saliency of "Jewishness" which the authors consider the beginning of anti-Semitism.

In the second place, if one thinks of "Jewishness" as a set of acquired traits which are subject to change then it is not inevitable that Jews should produce a characteristic neighborhood atmosphere. The atmosphere might chiefly depend on the occupation and education of the residents—Jewish or no. If however the ethnic category has innate ineluctable qualities then the "typical" atmosphere must always be there.

Notice next the use of the expression "letting into." One can only "let in" someone motivated to enter. If the outsider did not wish to come in he would have to be invited or urged or dragged in. How easily we assume that "letting into" is the only possible expression and yet by doing so we attribute to the ethnic category an "intrusive" impulse and that is part of the investigators' definition of an anti-Semitic frame of mind.

Finally there is hostility to this intrusive group in the clever use of the words "trouble" and "nice." Clearly the neighborhood is expected to be less "nice" if it acquires a typical Jewish atmosphere. The item, then, contains all the essentials of anti-Semitism, but they are so artfully expressed that the statement at first appears innocuous.

THE ETHNOCENTRISM (E) SCALE

We come now upon a very important fact: People who are antagonistic to Jews are likely also to be antagonistic to Negroes and to "Japs," "Okies," foreigners in general. "Of course," one says at first, but there is no logical necessity in the fact. If the reputation of an ethnic group with a particular man were dependent on that man's personal experience with members of the group it is not clear why a man who thinks ill of one minority would think ill of the others nor why a man who thinks well of one should think well of all. Because this is the case it seems likely that neither the behavior of minorities nor our acquaintance with a sample of that behavior is the critical determinant of our attitudes toward them.

Anti-Semitism most commonly appears as a single manifestation of ethnocentrism. The latter term was introduced by William Graham Sumner in his book *Folkways* (1906). Sumner defined ethnocentrism as a tendency to be rigid in the acceptance of the culturally alike and in the rejection of the culturally unlike.

The Berkeley investigators wrote thirty-four Likert-type items for the diagnosis of ethnocentrism. Some of these were concerned with Negroes, some with such other minorities as "Japs," "Okies," Filipinos, zootsuiters, foreigners, members of small political parties, criminals, and subnormals. In some items the emphasis was not so much on the odious qualities of minorities and outsiders as on the superior qualities of one's own family and the American Way.

Here are some sample items:

1. "Negroes have their rights, but it is best to keep them in their own districts and schools and to prevent too much contact with whites."

2. "America may not be perfect, but the American Way has brought us about as close as human beings can get to a perfect society."

The correlation of one half of the items in the Ethnocentrism Scale with the other half of the items, was .91. The correlation between Ethnocentrism and the original 52-item A-S Scale was .80. These results are evidence that antagonism to the culturally unlike is a generalized sentiment.

THE POLITICAL AND ECONOMIC CONSERVATISM (PEC) SCALE

By the end of the nineteenth century it was widely believed in both Europe and the United States that political views and political institutions could be ranged on a continuum from the radical left to the conservative right. The conservative right has believed in self-enrichment by personal exertion and in the rightness of the social and economic inequalities that follow from such individual competition; it has been opposed to such interferences with rugged individualism as social welfare legislation, state regulation of economic activity, and to the association of working men into labor unions. More generally conservatism has championed the *status quo*, religion, and tradition over science and humanitarianism. The radical left has chiefly stood for economic and social equality, for full suffrage, civil liberties, labor unions, welfare legislation, change, and science. Fascism, which emerged in the 1930's in Germany and Italy, was interpreted by Marxists and most intellectuals as a movement of extreme right conservatism and the Berkeley researchers made this same interpretation. German fascism was notably ethnocentric and anti-Semitic. The Berkeley group expected to find that its anti-Semitic and ethnocentric subjects would have the political and economic values of the American conservative right wing.

The Berkeley group took the definitive component of conservatism to be an attachment to "things as they are," a resistance to social change. Primary values for the American conservative seemed to include practicality, ambition, and financial success. "Most people get pretty much what they deserve," the conservative holds. The rich have earned their wealth and the poor their poverty. The radical or liberal sees poverty as a symptom of disorder in the political and economic system. He favors economic planning, strong labor unions, welfare legislation.

Here are some items written for the Political and Economic Conservatism (PEC) Scale:

1. "A child should learn early in life the value of a dollar and the importance of ambition, efficiency, and determination."
2. "The best way to solve social problems is to stick close to the middle of the road, to move slowly, and to avoid extremes."

The split-half reliabilities of the PEC scales are lower than the reliabilities of the A-S and the E scales; for PEC the average r = .73 while for A-S and E the correlations are between .8 and .9. This shows that the components of conservatism identified in this research cluster with some consistency but the consistency is less than in the case of the components of anti-Semitism or ethnocentrism.

Finally the scores of the PEC Scale did not correlate as highly with scores on the A-S Scale and the E Scale as did the scores on the latter two scales with one another. It is noteworthy that, of the thirty or so correlations calculated for different groups, none was negative. In short, neither ethnocentrism nor anti-Semitism ever showed a tendency to go with leftist liberal views; the conservative was always more ethnocentric and anti-Semitic but the association was not strong.

Conservatism and radicalism or liberalism do not, in these data, appear to be perfectly consistent ideologies. As an ideological continuum the conservative-liberal dimension is not closely aligned with either ethnocentrism or anti-Semitism but is in some degree aligned with them. Antagonism to minorities is more likely to be combined with conservative political views than with liberal views but the latter combination is also common and so, too, is a combination of conservatism with little antagonism to minorities.

THE IMPLICIT ANTIDEMOCRATIC TRENDS OR POTENTIALITY FOR FASCISM (F) SCALE

With the F Scale the Berkeley researchers believed that they were moving to the level of personality. While the scale items are statements of opinion and have the same form as items on the A-S, E, and PEC scales they do not make assertions about minority groups or about political and economic issues. The scale is intended to measure implicit authoritarian or antidemocratic trends in a personality, trends rendering the personality susceptible to explicit Fascist propaganda.

The thirty-eight items of the initial form of the F Scale are a greatly varied lot. In part they were suggested by fascist writings and by the speeches of anti-Semitic agitators. In part they were suggested by persistent themes in the interview protocols of ethnocentric subjects and in their TAT stories. For these data, which we have not yet described, had been collected and studied before the F Scale was written. Indeed the F Scale represents an effort to capture in a questionnaire the insights of the clinical studies.

The items are subclassified under nine general terms. These terms are supposed to constitute the antidemocratic or potentially fascistic syndrome. *Syndrome* is a word used in medicine for a collection of concurrent symptoms of a disease. The nine antidemocratic symptoms are not bound together by logic. If it turns out that they hang together empirically, that persons who have one tend to have all, then the explanation of this fact must be found in the disease process. In the present case that process is conceived as a system of personality dynamics.

Here now are the nine characteristics briefly defined and with two items to illustrate each one.

a. *Conventionalism*. A rigid adherence to conventional, middle-class values.

1. "Obedience and respect for authority are the most important virtues children should learn."
2. "The businessman and the manufacturer are much more important to society than the artist and the professor."

b. *Authoritarian Submission*. A submissive, uncritical attitude toward idealized moral authorities of the ingroup.

1. "Young people sometimes get rebellious ideas, but as they grow up they ought to get over them and settle down."
2. "Science has its place, but there are many important things that can never possibly be understood by the human mind."

c. *Authoritarian Aggression*. A tendency to be on the lookout for, and to condemn, reject, and punish people who violate conventional values.

1. "Sex crimes, such as rape and attacks on children, deserve more than mere imprisonment; such criminals ought to be publicly whipped, or worse."
2. "If people would talk less and work more, everybody would be better off."

d. *Anti-Intraception*. An opposition to the subjective, the imaginative, the tender-minded.

1. "When a person has a problem or worry, it is best for him not to think about it, but to keep busy with more cheerful things."
2. "Nowadays more and more people are prying into matters that should remain personal and private."

e. *Superstition and Stereotypy*. The belief in mystical determinants of the individual's fate, the disposition to think in rigid categories.

1. "Someday it will probably be shown that astrology can explain a lot of things."
2. "Some people are born with an urge to jump from high places."

f. *Power and "Toughness."* A preoccupation with the dominance-submission, strong-weak, leader-follower dimension; identification with power figures; overemphasis upon the conventionalized attributes of the ego; exaggerated assertion of strength and toughness.

1. "People can be divided into two distinct classes: the weak and the strong."
2. "Most people don't realize how much our lives are controlled by plots hatched in secret places."

g. *Destructiveness and Cynicism*. A generalized hostility, vilification of the human.

1. "Human nature being what it is, there will always be war and conflict."
2. "Familiarity breeds contempt."

h. *Projectivity*. The disposition to believe that wild and dangerous things go on in the world; the projection outwards of unconscious emotional impulses.

1. "Wars and social troubles may someday be ended by an earthquake or flood that will destroy the whole world."
2. "Nowadays when so many different kinds of people move around and mix together so much, a person has to protect himself especially care-

fully against catching an infection or disease from them."

i. *Sex*. Exaggerated concern with sexual "go-ings-on."

1. "The wild sex life of the old Greeks and Romans was tame compared to some of the go-ings-on in this country, even in places where people might least expect it."
2. "Homosexuals are hardly better than criminals and ought to be severely punished."

Do you know him—the Authoritarian, the Antidemocrat, the Pre-Fascist? It seems to me that I do. Item after item in the F Scale is something I have heard or very like something I have heard. Furthermore, the people I know who have made one of these statements have usually gone on to make others of them.

The items as a whole had something in common. The scores on each single item were correlated with total scores for the remaining items and the mean of these correlations was .33. At a later date the authors of the F Scale made their original data available to Melvin (1955) who did a factor analysis of it and found a very strong general factor running through all items (cited by Eysenck, 1954, p. 152). The Berkeley authors had found a superficially heterogeneous set of opinions that had, as a total set, some kind of psychological unity. However the items within a subscale were not more closely correlated with one another than they were with numerous items outside the subscale. The nine symptoms or characteristics (e.g., "conventionalism," "projectivity") were not, in short, shown to be psychologically real.

With the F Scale the Berkeley group hoped to identify a personality system that was potentially fascistic and so they expected F Scale scores to correlate with the explicit tenets of fascism expressed in the A-S, E, and PEC scales. This proved to be the case. For the first form of the scale the mean correlation with A-S was .53, with E it was .65, and with PEC, .54. The F Scale was revised several times by dropping items that did not correlate with total scores or that were not predictive of A-S and E scores. For the final version of the scale the mean correlation with an E Scale that included anti-Semitic items was .75; the correlation with PEC was only .57.

It was ethnocentrism, anti-Semitism, and potentiality for fascism that were most strongly interrelated. These attitudes and personality characteristics tended to be associated with conservatism in political and economic matters but not so strongly as they were associated with one another. This pattern suggests that there may have been quite a few ethnocentric and antidemocratic subjects who were leftish liberal in the political and economic sphere. That is a fact to remember because it is related to later developments.

Covariation of Interview and Projective Data

We are crossing the methodological line from fixed-alternative questionnaires to free-response interviews and projectives. It has been said that this is a line similar to that between multiple-choice examinations and essay examinations. Many teachers believe that the best way to sample a student's knowledge is to combine the two kinds of examination. Multiple-choice tests, and also questionnaire items, present a certain problem of communication: the student or subject must try to make out what the teacher or researcher means by the item. The greater burden of decoding is on the one who answers. Essay examinations, and also interview protocols and projective data, present the complementary problem of communication. The respondent is free to formulate his own answers, but the inquirer must try to figure out what he means by them. The greater burden of decoding is on the one who asks. The Berkeley investigators, like some teachers, seem to have believed that the best hope of discovering the truth lay in a combination of the two methods.

INTERVIEW COLLECTION AND CODING

The interview study dealt only with persons whose questionnaire responses identified them as ideologically extreme. There were eighty interviewees, of whom about half had placed in the highest quartile (25%) of the E Scale distribution and about half in the lowest quartile. Forty subjects were men and forty were women. You may remember that most subjects in the survey studies were recruited through some formal group. The researchers now wanted to select out particular interviewees but did not want to alarm them by saying that they had been picked because of the extremity of their attitudes. Consequently interviewees were told that they had been selected on the basis of age and regional origin. They were identified by birthdate only, in order to preserve anonymity.

High scorers are supposed to be anti-intraceptive and one item they are likely to have endorsed is: "Nowadays more and more people are prying into matters that should remain personal and private." Such subjects might, therefore, have been reluctant to submit to an intensive interview lasting one-and-a-half to three hours. Largely as an inducement to such interviewees the researchers offered a three-dollar fee; they report that this fee was helpful in obtaining their subjects.

The nature of the interview schedule used in this research must be appreciated if we are to make a sound evaluation of the results. There were six general areas to be covered: (1) Vocation; (2) Income; (3) Religion; (4) Clinical Data; (5) Politics; (6) Minorities and Race. There were subtopics in each area. Clinical data, for example, included: (4a) Family Background: Sociological Aspects; (4b) Family Figures: Personal Aspects; (4c) Childhood; (4d) Sex; (4e) Social Relationships; and (4f) School.

Within each subtopic the interviewer was to have in mind a set of critical underlying questions which were to be answerable from the talk of the interviewee. In the case of subtopic 4b (Family Figures: Personal Aspects) the underlying questions concerned the "Subject's Conception of Parent Figures" and the "Pattern of Power Relations between Father and Mother." These underlying questions were not to be asked in any direct form. One does not ask: "What was the power relation between your father and mother?" The interviewer's task was, instead, to ask more specific questions couched in familiar language and to continue asking such questions until he judged that material had been obtained which would enable a coder of the protocol to answer the underlying question. It was not for the interviewer himself to answer the underlying question. His job was simply to have those questions in mind and to keep asking about particulars until it seemed to him that there was material which would make it possible to answer the underlying questions.

For the particular direct questions to be used in probing for relevant material there was no required set and no required sequence but only a list of suggestions. For example, the interview schedule recommends the following inquiries as means of learning about the "Pattern of Power Relations between Father and Mother:"

How did your parents get along together?

In what ways were your parents most alike?

In what ways were they different from each other?

Who made the decisions usually? (Get specific information e.g., re. finances, recreation, discipline of children, residence, etc.)

Disagreements arise in every family from time to time; what bones of contention did your parents sometimes have? [Adorno, et al., 1950, p. 314]

Finally, interviewers were instructed to make a close study, in advance of the interview, of all the questionnaire responses of the interviewee. The Berkeley investigators believed that such advance knowledge would help the interviewer to focus on critical topics. They believed that there was no danger that the results would be biased by the interviewer's knowledge of his subject since the interviewers were not scheduled to code the data but only to collect it. The coders, of course, would not know anything about the questionnaire scores of the subjects since such knowledge could affect what they would "see" in a protocol. The priming of interviewers with knowledge of the questionnaire results is an aspect of the research procedure that was to be severely criticized.

Since the interviewers were oriented to a set of underlying questions it would be reasonable to anticipate that the coding of the data would simply have been a matter of sorting the answers to each underlying question into a set of mutually exclusive categories. Such is not the case. Consider, for example, the underlying question: "Pattern of Power Relations between Father and Mother." One might have guessed that there would be three response categories such as Father Dominant, Mother Dominant, and Parental Equality. Each subject would then be counted as having produced one of these three alternatives. This is not the way the investigators conceived of their questions and not the way they handled their data. The so-called "questions" are actually very general areas of inquiry and the inquiries produced complex multi-dimensional data which the authors coded in any way that promised to distinguish prejudiced subjects from unprejudiced subjects.

PROJECTIVE COLLECTION AND CODING

The work done with two other clinical instruments is very much like the interview study. The instruments were Murray's Thematic Apperception Test (TAT) and a set of projective questions. For the TAT, subjects are asked to tell a story about each of a standard set of pictures. In the present instance each subject saw ten pictures, some of them from Murray's standard set and some of them photographs selected for the study because they showed members of various minority groups. There were eight projective questions. Here are two of them:

1. "We all have times when we feel below par. What moods or feelings are the most unpleasant or disturbing to you?"
2. "We all have impulses and desires which are at times hard to control but which we try to keep in check. What desires do you often have difficulty in controlling?"

With both the TAT and the Projective Questions a comparison was made between subjects from the highest quartile of the E Scale results and subjects from the lowest quartile. Both sets of data were examined in search of High-Low contrasts before the Scoring Manuals were written. The scoring categories were defined so as to capture quantitatively the differences suspected to exist. In these respects the procedures were the same as in the case of the interview study.

TWO SPECIAL GROUPS OF SUBJECTS

Among the many groups of subjects who participated in the Berkeley study there were two of particular interest: 110 inmates of San Quentin Prison and 121 patients at the Langley-Porter Psychiatric Clinic. Both groups of subjects filled out the E, PEC, and F scales. The psychiatric patients were slightly but not significantly lower than the mean of all other groups tested on the E Scale. There was a tendency for neurosis to go with low scores and psychosis with moderately high scores.

The prisoners produced the highest mean scores of all groups tested on the E, PEC, and F scales. The criminal types represented in the San Quentin population were not, it seems, rebels against established authority. On the contrary, they were politically and economically conservative types,

highly patriotic, and filled with hatred for submerged ethnic groups.

Twelve of the prisoners were interviewed; of these, eight scored high on the E Scale and four scored relatively low. Among the high scorers there were three subjects whom the researchers characterize as "overt fascists." These three were not actually members of any self-styled fascist party and so their high scores on all scales cannot be taken as a validation of the characterization of these scales as measures of political fascism. The three subjects were labelled fascist by the authors because they explicitly endorsed the use of force to suppress minorities and to protect business against labor unions. They dispensed with the pseudo-democratic façade that was important to most prejudiced subjects.

The criminal interviews were not coded or treated quantitatively but they are quoted at length in *The Authoritarian Personality* to establish the authors' position that criminal authoritarianism had the same fundamental personality dynamics as did the authoritarianism that was within the law. Some of the quotations, especially those from the three prisoners who were labelled fascistic, are hair-raising. They suggest that we could find, in this country, willing recruits for a Gestapo. Concerning Negroes: "They're very closely linked with the jungle. They're built for it." Concerning Jews: "Most all of them Jews talk about sex mostly, or beatin' a guy out of his money." (This latter is from a man who had been arrested for sexually molesting his own children.) Concerning labor unions: "Take away their charters. . . . Abolish them." Concerning parents: ". . . always tried to teach me the right thing; being in prison is not my folks' fault." Concerning the determinants of human behavior. "If I ever did anything wrong, it was the Latin in me." And so on.

For the patients at the Langley-Porter Clinic the study centered on their first psychiatric interview—an interview concerned chiefly with the patient's description of his problems. These interviews were held by members of the regular clinic staff who had no knowledge of the research project and no expectation that the interviews would be studied by outsiders. This is an important fact because, as we shall later see, it exempts the present interview study from a very serious criticism that must be made of the major interview study.

The initial interviews for twenty-eight subjects

who scored high on the E Scale and thirty-one who scored low were coded for seven characteristics. Before the coding categories were defined all of the interviews were examined for content that seemed to distinguish prejudiced subjects from unprejudiced subjects. This again is an important fact because, as we shall see, it means that the study of the patient interviews was subject to one serious criticism that must also be made of all the other studies involving content analysis.

Most of the coding categories were similar to categories used in other parts of the study. For example, prejudiced subjects were expected to be anti-intraceptive and extrapunitive. Several categories adapt traits of ordinary authoritarians to the special case of psychiatric patients. Prejudiced subjects were expected chiefly to complain of somatic or physical ailments such as dizziness, tremor, fast heartbeat, and the like, while unprejudiced subjects were expected to complain of such psychological ailments as anxiety, conflict, and depression. In addition, prejudiced subjects were expected to blame their troubles on particular unlucky external events—an illness, a divorce, a death. Unprejudiced subjects would be more likely to see their symptoms as having been present in milder form for years, possibly since childhood.

All of the interviews were coded by two judges who were thoroughly familiar with the hypotheses and findings of the total research. In addition, however, there were seven control raters who were completely unacquainted with the research as a whole. Each control rater coded all interviews for *just one variable*. In the content analyses of the major interview study each rater coded all variables and that means that knowledge of one could easily have biased the coding of another. The study of psychiatric interviews was free of this flaw.

RESULTS

In all three sets of clinical data, in the interview protocols, the TAT stories, and the answers to the projective questions, the investigators found numerous statistically significant differences between prejudiced subjects and unprejudiced subjects. Some of the differences occur in content categories that are already familiar to us from the F Scale. "Anti-Intraceptive" is a content category for the analysis of interview protocols as well as a rubric under which certain F Scale items were classified.

In both sets of data it is the prejudiced subjects who are anti-intraceptive. Some of the distinctive content categories are very closely related to F Scale rubrics; the Pseudo- or Anti-Scientific category for interview analysis is very like the Superstition and Stereotypy of the F Scale. Again and again quotations from the subjects' freely composed responses echo the items of the F Scale. In considerable degree, then, the projective data confirm the covariation of implicit antidemocratic trends with prejudice which was demonstrated by the questionnaire data.

Analysis of the projective data also added many new items of behavior to the circle of covariation. Prejudiced subjects in interviews showed a tendency to separate sex and affection while unprejudiced subjects were likely to fuse the two. In the TAT stories of prejudiced subjects there was more primitive, impulsive aggression; the heroes of their stories were more often dependent on the demands and regulations of authority. In response to a projective question about the "worst crimes a person could commit" prejudiced subjects were likely to list crimes against the physical person while unprejudiced subjects were likely to list crimes against the personality—psychological cruelties and violations of trust.

All of these data are verbal, all of them roughly contemporaneous. They add up to a list, a very long one, of correlated differences. I have not the patience to write them all down and you would not find it interesting to read or possible to remember. But when the authors interpret the list it becomes a pattern, in more than one dimension, and the pattern is somewhat lifelike.

The transformation from list to personality is accomplished in the following way. Some of the things subjects said are assumed to have historical truth, to be realistic accounts of past events and so a genetic dimension is added. Some of the things subjects said are understood literally, others are interpreted as revelations of unconscious wishes and so a dimension of psychological "depth" is added. Some of the things subjects said are set alongside other things with which they are in conflict and so dynamic forces are added. The construction as a whole is guided by a general blueprint of human personality, the blueprint is psychoanalytic theory.

The widening circle of covariation has become too wide to keep in view and so we will stop describing uninterpreted data. The results of the studies of projective material are more interesting and memorable as parts of the intellectual construction called the authoritarian personality than as unpatterned fragments. The citation of data will be highly selective, chiefly from the interviews, but copious enough, I hope, so that you can judge the adequacy of the evidence.

Construction of the Personality

We can begin with findings which suggest that the prejudiced person has a more consistently favorable impression of himself than does the unprejudiced person. The most directly relevant contrast in the coding categories is: "Self-glorification" as opposed to "Objective self-appraisal." Prejudiced persons say such things as: "I have always tried to live according to His Ten Commandments" or "Think one of my best assets is my poise" or "I've always had a happy disposition, and I've always been honest with my family." From unprejudiced subjects come such appraisals as: "I'm rather shy, don't like competition" or "I don't mean I am in love with my mother, but I have a dependency complex . . . married a woman older than myself."

There are other interview categories which contribute to our impression that the prejudiced person has an exceptionally good opinion of himself. In describing their sexual experiences, for example, prejudiced men boast of their conquests and represent themselves as ideals of masculinity while women speak of having "scads of boyfriends." By contrast, an unprejudiced woman says: "I am avoided by the male sex perhaps because I am heavy" and a man reports that he has "always been rather inhibited about sex."

In addition to having a good opinion of themselves prejudiced persons have a good opinion of their parents. The most directly relevant interview categories are: "Conventional idealization of parents" vs. "Objective appraisal." Prejudiced subjects say of their fathers: "He is very sincere and very well liked by his friends and employees" and "He is exceptionally good looking, dresses well, has gray hair" and "I've always been very proud to be his son." Of their mothers they say: "Most terrific person in the world to me" and "She's friendly with everybody." The prejudiced person does not

have a father and a mother for parents; he has "Father's Day" and "Mother's Day."

Unprejudiced subjects said of their fathers: "Father tries to be rational but is not always so" and "I think he wanted a boy, so he paid little attention to me." Of their mothers they say: "She is practical and sensible, but she gets too much interested in fads" and "She gives me too much advice."

Very generally, prejudiced subjects do not describe themselves or their parents as fearful or dependent or slothful or aggressive against properly constituted authority or as having any of the traits of the other sex. Unprejudiced subjects are more likely to ascribe such faults and shortcomings to themselves and their parents. Here then are some new correlates of prejudice. We could stop here, with the simple listing, but instead we will attempt to figure out what the difference means, how it comes about.

One ought, in the first place, to consider the possibility that the two kinds of self and of parental appraisal are the simple truth. Prejudiced people and their parents may, in fact, be superior to the unprejudiced. As you might guess this was not the view of the Berkeley researchers. Their interpretation is actually revealed in the labelling of the categories: "Self-glorification" vs. "Objective appraisal" and "Conventional idealization of parents" against "Objective appraisal." These titles make it clear that the reports of unprejudiced subjects are presumed to be accurate or truthful ("objective") whereas the reports of prejudiced subjects are presumed to be inaccurate ("idealized" or "glorified"). What ground have they for treating the prejudiced as liars and the unprejudiced as truth tellers? Is this a prejudice of their own, a device to evade the unpalatable conclusion that prejudiced people are generally pleasanter people than the unprejudiced?

One might doubt the accuracy of the prejudiced subjects' glowing appraisal of himself and his parents on the ground of manifest improbability. People are simply not that good. Characters are always flawed by fearfulness or dependency or antagonism. People do not greatly differ in the degree to which they possess faults and shortcomings but only in their awareness of such unwelcome traits. Where character flaws are not explicitly confessed it must be because the subject does not want to be aware of them.

Ambivalent feelings are mixed feelings, positive and negative sentiments concentrated on the same object. As Freud always assumed, it is human nature to abhor ambivalence. Behind this abhorrence, I suspect, is the fact that ambivalence must tend to paralyze action. If one likes an object or person the thing to do is to approach and if one dislikes to retreat. Ambivalence must activate both tendencies but it is impossible to act on both.

While human beings do not welcome ambivalence there are ways of coping with it. One can differentiate the object for example, oneself or one's parents—into parts, some of them good and some bad. A mother can be practical and sensible but inclined to give too much advice; a father can be affectionate but not handsome or not practical. Ambivalence is resolved by cognitive complication, by making distinctions among the manifestations of an object, the traits of a person, or the members of a minority. The unprejudiced subject seems to cope with inevitable ambivalence by consciously recognizing both the good and bad parts.

On the presumption that some ambivalence of feeling for oneself and one's parents is inevitable it would seem that the prejudiced person is unable to cope with it by complicating his conceptions. He maintains the unity of the object of feeling and handles ambivalence by denying (perhaps repressing) one part of his feelings. Since it is important to think well of oneself and one's parents it is the negative feelings, the unfavorable judgments, that are denied. This argument holds that the person who reports only favorable judgments of himself and his parents is motivated to deny contrary judgments and the basis for that interpretation is the assumption that in any human life there must be grounds for such judgments. The prejudiced person keeps his consciousness clear and unambivalent by denying or repressing what is unwelcome.

This is not the whole story. Prejudiced subjects do not always give perfectly ideal portraits. There are in the interviews with prejudiced subjects some negative self-appraisals. "I have let myself slip, let my carnal self get away from me. . . ." "Except for my industriousness. That just doesn't exist." "I guess I just got that from the other side of the family." Concerning parents, too, there were some unfavorable remarks. "She [mother] was very nervous. Irritable only when overdoing." "He [father] has a hot temper." In the TAT stories and in the answers to projective questions there was additional evidence that many prejudiced subjects were

somewhat ambivalent about themselves and their parents.

So then we have direct evidence that prejudiced subjects hold some unfavorable feelings and we are not, after all, forced to posit the existence of such feelings on the grounds of simple probability. This is fine, but the drawback is that we appear to have lost the distinction we started with since both kinds of subjects are manifestly ambivalent. This is not the view of the California researchers. They and their coders judged that the negative feelings expressed by prejudiced subjects could be seen to have a quite different psychological status from the negative feelings of unprejudiced subjects. The criticisms of self and parents voiced by the prejudiced were, to use a psychoanalytic term, "ego-alien." The criticisms were not being consciously faced as such. They were foreign particles, excrescences, impositions from without.

How on earth could one tell whether a criticism is ego-alien? By any of several signs. The prejudiced subject said: "I have let my carnal self get away from me." The carnality is distinguishable from himself, it is not really he. Another subject said that his lack of industriousness was inherited from one side of his family. It was imposed on him, not something for which he himself could be held to account. In speaking of their parents prejudiced subjects frequently began with generalized glowing praise and then seemed to let slip some specific criticism. Such criticisms were often promptly retracted: "He forced some decisions on me" but "He allowed me to do as I pleased; arguments were about things he didn't want me to have" but "He never denied me anything I needed." There is an impression that the criticism pops out against the subject's intention and is then denied or blamed on an external cause or isolated from the essential self or parent.

In the TAT stories as well as the interview protocols it is said to be possible to recognize ego-alien negative feelings. What are the signs? One prejudiced subject told no stories in which the hero was aggressive against either a father or any sort of "father-figure." Since the storyteller is presumed to identify himself with the hero we might say that there was no consciously accepted aggression of this kind. However, aggression of this kind was exhibited by characters in the story whom the storyteller took pains to reject. The heroes identified themselves with authority but figures from whom the subjects dissociated themselves attacked authority. It is this kind of pattern that is taken to be evidence of ego-alien aggression.

Both prejudiced and unprejudiced subjects seem to have aggressive feelings about themselves and their parents but in the former subjects these feelings are ego-alien which means that they are repressed, denied, or isolated while in the latter subjects these feelings are integrated into objective conceptions. What difference does it make whether a feeling is ego-alien or integrated? Are there differential consequences? The first thing to note is that the subjects for whom negative feelings are ego-alien are the prejudiced subjects, the subjects who attribute undesirable characteristics to outgroups. The sins and weaknesses we miss in their self-descriptions and in their descriptions of their parents turn up in what they say about minority groups.

From the minorities section of the interviews come these assertions. "Jewish people are more *obsequious*." "Since the Negro has that feeling that he isn't up to par, he's always trying to show off. . . . Even though he can't afford it, he will buy an expensive car just to make a show." "The Jew is always crying." "They [Jews] suffer from every lust." "They [Negroes] all carry knives; if you do something they don't like, they will get even with you, they will slice you up." "But they [Jews] are so clannish and aggressive and loud that sometimes I can't stand them."

Let me summarize the case for the prosecution of authoritarians: Certain characteristics that are undesirable are not accepted as characteristic of the subject and his parents. However, there is reason to believe that these characteristics exist in the subject and his parents, leading a kind of covert, submerged life. Finally, these characteristics are confidently attributed to others, in this case to minority groups. This is exactly the pattern of evidence that Freud called projection. Something present in oneself but unwelcome, is projected outward. When we add that the unwelcome "somethings" are chiefly sex and aggression, the important drives in Freudian theory, then projection does indeed seem to be the word for it.

If you are a psychological functionalist it is not enough to label prejudice as projection. One must ask what is projection for? What is its utility for the prejudiced person? One answer is suggested by certain quotations from the interviews. A man who bought a fur coat for his mother from a Jewish salesman took advantage of the fact that the salesman misread the price tag and so quoted a price one hundred dollars below that on the tag. "That was a case where I out-Jewed a Jew." "I am not particularly sorry because of what the Germans did to the Jews. I feel the Jews would do the same type of thing to me." Finally, "I think the time will come when we will have to kill the bastards." The prejudiced person has aggressive impulses but he dare not direct them at members of the in-group. He can direct aggression against minorities if he believes the minorities are themselves aggressive and so deserve to be attacked.

Projection seems also to have a functional role in the southern white man's sexual use of Negro women. If one can believe that Negro women are inherently sensual and promiscuous, then one can believe that they seduce a man against his better impulses. On the other hand, if anything happens between a white woman and a Negro it must be rape since the woman could not desire the Negro while he is certain to desire her. History shows Negro men have often been lynched for rape when there was strong reason to believe that a white woman had acted provocatively.

By projecting his own unacceptable impulses to sex and aggression the prejudiced man is able to enjoy some direct expression of these impulses. The direct expression is justified by the supposed sexual and aggressive nature of his out-group targets. Since the beliefs which support the prejudiced man's actions are not the true causes of his actions they may be considered "rationalizations" as well as projections. From a set of static correlates the authors have inferred a dynamic sequence which is put in psychoanalytic terms. Repression of impulses leads to projection which functions as rationalization for an expression.

Why is it that some people are particularly bent on maintaining an idealized image of themselves and of those close to themselves? The evidence suggesting an answer is distributed across many categories coded from the interviews. It goes like this.

The prejudiced subject is exceptionally concerned with status and success and rather little concerned with solidarity and intimacy. He puts friendship, love, and marriage in the service of status-seeking. Anyone with whom he might become intimate or even acquainted is evaluated in terms of status points. The prejudiced man always asks: "What can he do for me?" Prejudiced men sometimes expressed a wish to marry a wealthy woman and usually said they wanted a wife who could help a man advance himself; a woman who would do a man credit. Since a woman's socio-economic status is largely derived from her husband, prejudiced women are more intent than are men on assessing the status potential of a possible spouse. "I'd like to marry someone, for instance, who is going into a profession—maybe a doctor." Speaking of a former boyfriend, a prejudiced woman said: "very wealthy family but he didn't have the drive and ambition that I want."

In speaking of the qualities they would hope to find in a spouse, unprejudiced subjects often mentioned beauty, sensuality, shared aspirations. They used the language of romantic love rather than the language of status calculation. Friends were not chosen because of their positions but because of their personal qualities. Desires for solidarity, intimacy, and love were strong in the unprejudiced.

The status and success that so much concern the prejudiced subject are conceived in a very external way. He speaks of money and material acquisitions and social esteem and power. "Every man has a certain ego that he has to satisfy. You like to be on top. If you're anybody at all, you don't like to be on the bottom." Another man said. "I never had any relations with anyone that didn't have money connected with it." Contrast the unprejudiced subjects: "Money has never meant much to me. . . . Maybe it is stupid and unrealistic. But it is the work itself that gives me satisfaction." And from another unprejudiced subject: "I like to work with young people . . . satisfaction of helping someone. . . . It doesn't pay financially, but . . . you are happier . . . makes good friends. . . ."

What is it that causes the prejudiced person to be so much concerned with status and success? The answer seems to be in the interview categories: "Family status-concerned" vs. "Family status-relaxed." Prejudiced subjects made the following observations "Well, they [parents] didn't want me to run with some kind of people—slummy women—always wanted me to associate with the higher class of people." "We lived in a nice house but really couldn't afford it. It was quite an effort to get into social circles." One man's father did

not want him to work as a boy because he thought "it was beneath me." An unprejudiced subject made the following remark: "My mother had and accepted a very simple way of life." Another said: "We had a sort of scorn for people who wanted too much."

It is easy to see that parents who are insecure about their own status may produce children who are bent on success. This is little more than a simple transmission of values. But what is the connection between status anxiety and prejudice? Parents who are anxious about their own status should be very concerned to see that their children are properly brought up; that they are children no one could confuse with the offspring of the lower classes. They will want little ladies and gentlemen, not dirty, brawling brats.

How does one create little ladies and gentlemen out of tiny primates? It is clearly a job for an animal trainer, someone who can "lay down the law in no uncertain terms." Status anxiety might cause parents to interpret the roles of parent and child in terms of authority and submission. Here are some things prejudiced subjects said about their parents as disciplinarians. "Well, my father was a very strict man. He wasn't religious, but strict in raising the youngsters. His word was law, and whenever he was disobeyed, there was punishment." Another man remarked: "Father had to give us one look and we knew what he meant."

The parents who were anxious about status probably set their authority firmly against weakness and passivity and unresponsibility. Probably too they firmly sex-typed behavior, requiring a stereotypical unmixed masculinity from their sons and femininity from their daughters. The exercise of so much authority would be bound to engender aggression but this seems to have been put down with a firm hand. A prejudiced woman says of her father: "You always did what he said, but it was right; there was no question about it." A man said: "We did what the elders told us to." (Ever question it?) "Well, I never questioned." A man speaks of overhearing, on the street, a child "sass" his mother and adds: "If I'd have said that to my mother, I wouldn't be able to sit down."

With the psychoanalytic concept of displacement we can make the connection to prejudice. Parental discipline frustrates the child and the frustration creates aggression. This aggression cannot be directed against its legitimate target, that would be insurrection against parental authority, and so the aggression is displaced to a less dangerous target—minority groups. Jews and Negroes and "Okies" and foreigners are inviting targets for displaced aggression because of historical circumstances that have caused them to be underprivileged and to have well-established bad reputations.

We see at last why the authors of *The Authoritarian Personality* have argued that the empirical clustering of beliefs that are not logically related argues for the existence of a dynamic psychological relationship. Why should people whose parents were anxious about status have an idealized image of themselves and of their parents and a very bad opinion of minorities and foreigners? It is because status anxiety produces authoritarian discipline which produces repression of faults and shortcomings and of aggression against authority. It is the fate of repressed faults and shortcomings to be projected to minorities and outsiders. It is the fate of the repressed aggression to be displaced from authority and directed against minorities and outsiders. Finally the projected faults and shortcomings rationalize the aggression. Prejudice plays an integral role in the total ideology but the role is psychological rather than logical.

Not all of the characteristics attributed to the authoritarian personality can be neatly fitted into the above construction but many can be; for example, the fact that the prejudiced person is anti-intraceptive. On the F Scale he agrees that there is too much prying into matters that ought to remain personal and private, that when one has a problem the best thing to do is not think about it and just keep busy. From the interviews it appears that he is not given to reflection or introspection. He does not strive for insight into his own psychological operations, he does not see their role in what happens to him. When things go wrong for the prejudiced person it is because of external forces. He is disposed to be "extrapunitive"—to blame others rather than himself. "She's mean and inconsiderate and doesn't give a darn about anyone else but herself."

Among the prejudiced subjects, even those who were patients at the Langley-Porter Psychiatric Clinic resisted psychological interpretations. In their initial interviews they stressed their somatic or physical symptoms—dizziness, tremor, fainting, breathlessness. As causes they favored particular external events—a death, an illness, a shock. They sometimes spoke of psychological illness as if it were a breakdown of a machine; as if some "part"—the nerves or the mind—had given way under external stress. Because the prejudiced man's psychic equilibrium is founded heavily on repression one would expect him to avoid introspection and psychological inquiries. And so anti-intraceptiveness fits in with the total construction. The unprejudiced subjects tended to construe human life much in the manner of modern psychology. A man is his own fate. Very much of what happens to him is a consequence of his character. For those of us who have become addicted to psychological inquiry there seems to be a dimension missing from the prejudiced person; he lives his life but does not examine it.

The Cognitive Style of the Authoritarian

We come now to the California researchers' independent discovery of Jaensch's typology. Among the coding categories applied to the interviews were two that are concerned with general cognitive style: Rigidity vs. Flexibility, and Intolerance of Ambiguity vs. Tolerance of Ambiguity. Prejudiced subjects were judged to be more rigid and also more intolerant of ambiguity than the unprejudiced.

By what reasoning did the authors arrive at their predictions in the sphere of cognitive style? Intolerance of ambiguity is a generalization of the prejudiced subject's intolerance of emotional ambivalence. Ambivalence exists when both love and hate are felt for the same person. The prejudiced man wants his loves and hates to be wholehearted; he idealizes himself and his parents and anathematizes out-groups. The unprejudiced person objectively appraises both, which means that he lives with a mixture of love and hate and so with uncertainties and conflicts that are not in the consciousness of the prejudiced.

Ambivalence is uncertainty of value and ambiguity is uncertainty of meaning. An ambiguous picture is one that might be either this or that; an ambiguous word is one that might signify either this or that. The prediction that prejudiced subjects will be generally intolerant of ambiguity derives from the assumption that personality manifests a unity of style. The intolerance of ambivalence which is motivated by status anxiety and the ban on aggression against authority is expected to spread into areas where it is not specifically motivated, to become a general style, the prejudiced person is expected to manifest intolerance of ambiguity in all perception and thought.

For the interview protocols it was suggested that the subject who is tolerant of ambiguity will make much use of limiting and qualifying language forms. The subject intolerant of ambiguity would take a more absolute tone. Of course the coders were free to consult the total protocol and so may simply have coded intolerance of ambiguity where there seemed to be intolerance of ambivalence or any of the other stigmata of authoritarianism. Consequently the interview results are not good evidence that prejudiced subjects were intolerant of ambiguity.

Rigidity is a term from common parlance with a root meaning that makes reference to the physical world. To produce changes of form in a substance a degree of resistance must be overcome. When this resistance exceeds our expectations—when a joint moves stiffly or a lump of clay is not malleable—we are likely to call the substance "rigid." Abstracting from the physical case we attribute rigidity to thought and behavior when they are exceptionally resistant to applied forces. An elderly person who cannot change his ideas with the changing times manifests rigidity; a patient in psychotherapy who does not relinquish his defenses, in spite of the therapist's insightful interpretations of them, manifests rigidity. The prejudiced person is supposed to show rigidity in his refusal to give up ethnic stereotypes which are presumably contradicted by common experience.

CRITIQUE OF THE AUTHORITARIAN PERSONALITY

It is probable that no work in social psychology has been given a more meticulous methodological and conceptual examination than has *The Authoritarian Personality*. There is even a follow-up volume of evaluative papers called *Studies in the Scope and Method of "The Authoritarian Personality"* (Christie & Jahoda, 1954). The definitive critique of method is the paper in that volume by Hyman and Sheatsley. We cannot review all of the criticisms that have been made but will cover vital ones.

Sampling and the Organization of Attitudes

While the authors of the Berkeley study guessed that their findings could be generalized to the population of white, non-Jewish, native-born, middle-class Americans they recognized that the sample of persons actually studied was not a representative or random sample of this population or of any other specifiable population. To mention only one restriction, the subjects were almost all members of at least one formal organization since the major method of recruiting subjects was through such organizations. It is known that people who belong to at least one formal organization are in very many respects different from people who belong to no organizations (Christie, 1954). The authors of the Berkeley study took the position that sampling considerations were not vital to their work because they were not interested in estimating the incidence of certain attitudes but rather in establishing relationships among attitudes.

Hyman and Sheatsley take issue with the notion that sampling does not matter in a study of relationships among variables: "Correlation coefficients, just like means or percentages, fluctuate from sample to sample and may well vary in different populations." It is conceivable that persons belonging to formal organizations, and this was the kind of person studied, are more concerned with the social issues that form the content of the A-S, E, and F scales than are persons who belong to no organizations. Concern with issues may create a high degree of organization (intercorrelation) among attitudes. Perhaps the conclusion that certain attitudes cohere into what may be called an antidemocratic ideology is only true of Americans who belong to organizations.

The record of related and subsequent researches on the intercorrelation of attitudes is instructive. These intercorrelations do indeed fluctuate from one sample to another and some of the fluctuations are interesting.

Whereas the magnitude of the correlations among A-S, E, and F fluctuates from sample to sample there is one impressive invariance—no negative correlations seem ever to have been reported (Christie, 1954). It does seem fairly safe therefore to conclude that A-S, E, and F were organized together for middle-class Americans in the 1940's and 1950's. The Berkeley researchers certainly were not justified in generalizing their conclusions as widely as they did, but they seem to have been lucky. They hit on a finding that is as highly reliable and highly general as they, on insufficient evidence, thought it was.

Acquiescence Response Set

The questionnaire items of the A-S, E, and F scales are all worded in such a way that agreement with the items represents, respectively, anti-Semitism, ethnocentrism, or potential fascism. The authors were aware that it is generally better practice in opinion-attitude scales to include both positive and negative items. In connection with the construction of the A-S Scale the authors set forth the considerations that persuaded them to write all the items of each scale as authoritarian assertions (Adorno, et al., 1950, p. 59). It is now clear that they made a mistake.

In a 1946 publication Cronbach discussed the problem of response sets in paper and pencil tests; for example, a subject might consistently tend to agree with assertions—regardless of their content. If all the items in a scale assert in the same direction a high score might be as much a manifestation of this sort of acquiescence response set as of agreement with the particular content of the assertions. Cohn (1953) was one of the first to propose that the F Scale was in part a measure of such acquiescent tendencies. He found a correlation of +.41 between agreement with a mixed lot of questions from a personality inventory (the MMPI) and a version of the F Scale. The storm really broke in 1955 when Bass composed reversed versions of the F Scale items and administered both the original scale and the reversed scale to the same subjects. If authoritarian content were the only determinant of responses then agreement with an F Scale item ought always to be associated with disagreement with that item's reversal. The resulting correlation between scores on the F Scale and the reverse scale should approximate −1.00. The obtained correlation was only −.20 and so it was evident that the degree of authoritarianism manifested on the F Scale was not usually matched by the degree of authoritarianism manifested on the reversed scale. Further analyses showed that some subjects consistently acquiesced with both authoritarian assertions and their reversals whereas some subjects consistently disagreed with both kinds of

assertions. The acquiescent subject, had he been given the F Scale alone, would have appeared to be authoritarian and the disagreeing subject would have appeared to be equalitarian. Indeed one treatment of his data (shown by Messick and Jackson in 1957 to be unwarranted) suggested to Bass that acquiescence was more important than authoritarianism as a determinant of F Scale scores.

The discovery of the role of acquiescence in the F Scale made uncertain the interpretation of many studies showing consistent correlations between F scores and scores on other paper and pencil tests. Many of these other tests were also written so that most items asserted in a single direction and so these tests like the F Scale were measures of acquiescence. Consequently many results that had been interpreted as manifestations of the generality of authoritarianism now appeared to be interpretable as manifestations of the generality of acquiescence. This unsettling possibility applied to the original correlations among A-S, E, and F scores since all of these scales were unbalanced. An assortment of researchers confirmed the importance of acquiescence as a determinant of F scores though, in general, it did not appear to be more important than authoritarianism as Bass had thought. In 1958 Christie and his associates added some depth to the discussion and also some superior data.

What does it mean to "reverse" an F Scale item? Consider the item: "Some people are born with an urge to jump from high places." One investigator constructed as its reverse: "No people are born with an urge to jump from high places." This latter is the logical contrary of the former and so agreement with both would suggest either a lapse of memory or extreme illogicality. However, disagreement with both would not be illogical. For while the two are contraries they do not between them exhaust the realm of possible opinions. One might hold that, in the absence of definite knowledge, the best view is that there may or may not be people who are born with an urge to jump from high places. An equalitarian who held this view would disagree with both the original F Scale item and its reversal.

It is fun to consider various reversals of F Scale items because in the process you discover some subtleties of linguistic meaning. Think back to our discussion of the A-S Scale and the item: "The trouble with letting Jews into a nice neighborhood is that they gradually give it a typical Jewish atmosphere." Suppose we try a psychological rather than a strictly logical reversal, substituting favorable terms for the unfavorable. "One delightful consequence of having Jews in a neighborhood is that they contribute a charming Jewish quality to the neighborhood atmosphere." It sounds like a gushy clubwoman overcompensating for a covert but especially vicious anti-Semitism. If she were speaking the sentence we would see her mouth give a wry twist and her voice break on "Jewish" in "charming Jewish quality." It is not an item that appeals to the equalitarian in spite of the intended reversal of sentiment.

It is probably not possible to write items that are perfect psychological contraries to the assertions of the F Scale. Each of these latter conveys a very complex pattern of connotations. To reverse that full pattern is not an easy trick. However, as Christie and his associates have shown (1958) the reversals can be better than those we have cited. Witness their: "An urge to jump from high places is probably the result of unhappy personal experiences rather than something inborn" and their "The findings of science may some day show that many of our most cherished beliefs are wrong." Even Christie's items are not invariably rejected when their reversals have been accepted, but the tendency across numerous subject samples has been in that direction. With these items it is possible to compose F Scales with equal numbers of authoritarian and equalitarian assertions.

Behavior that is consistent for one person over a range of situations and also different from one person to another is a personality characteristic. Response sets to agree or disagree first appeared as sources of error in personality inventories but we have come to realize that they are also personality characteristics in their own right; they may be characteristics of greater interest than most of those that the inventories were designed to measure. In 1960, Couch and Keniston gave names to the two personality types involved—"Yeasayers" and "Naysayers."

Couch and Keniston made a powerful demonstration of the existence of the two kinds of response set. They administered hundreds of items from a large and diversified collection of inventories and assigned each subject an "Over-all Agreement Score" (OAS). Subjects with a high OAS are the Yeasayers and subjects with a low OAS are the Naysayers. Yeasaying and Naysaying were demonstrated to be relatively stable and generalized traits by showing that subjects with a high OAS continued to agree with items from new tests of various kinds and subjects with low OAS continued to disagree. Clinical studies of extreme scorers on the OAS suggested that Yeasayers are individuals with weak ego controls who accept impulses without reservation whereas Naysayers are individuals who control and suppress impulses.

It had occurred to several investigators that Yeasaying, since it seems to be a matter of accepting authoritative statements, might itself be a manifestation of authoritarianism. However, Couch and Keniston demonstrated with pure measures of Yeasaying and of authoritarianism (using a balanced scale) that the two personality characteristics are completely independent.

In general summary, then, it seems to be certain that a tendency to acquiescence has been a factor in standard F Scale scores but not the major factor. Since acquiescence or Yeasaying is also a factor in many other personality inventories correlations between F Scale scores and other inventory scores may have been generated by acquiescence rather than authoritarianism. In the original Berkeley research the correlations demonstrating the generality of authoritarianism, the correlations among A-S, E, and F scores were probably somewhat elevated by the acquiescence set that was free to operate in all of them. It may be significant that the correlations of A-S, E, and F are somewhat lower with PEC (about .55) than with one another since the PEC scale was balanced with some items asserting conservative attitudes and some asserting liberal attitudes. It is equally certain that acquiescence is not a strong enough factor to have produced all of the correlation among A-S, E, and F and that significant evidence for the generality of authoritarianism remains intact. The results with interviews, TAT stories, and projective questions are exempt from the effects of response set, since with these methods one does not suggest an answer. The fact that the relations demonstrated in this work generally confirm the findings with questionnaires increases our confidence that the questionnaire findings were not entirely generated by response set. Future studies of authoritarianism should employ balanced F Scales, such as have been developed by Christie, and by Couch and

Keniston, in order to eliminate the effects of response set.

Criticisms of Content Analyses

Content analyses were made of the interviews of both normal subjects and psychiatric patients, as well as of projective sentence completions, and the TAT stories; in short for all data except the questionnaire responses. The methodological criticisms that must be made of these analyses are numerous and serious. The criticisms do not all apply to any one analysis but there was no analysis exempt from all criticism.

INTERVIEWER KNOWLEDGE OF QUESTIONNAIRE RESPONSES

In the main interview study forty highly prejudiced persons and forty unprejudiced persons served as subjects. "In each case the interview was preceded by the study, on the part of the interviewer, of the information gathered previously, especially a detailed study of the questionnaire responses" (Adorno, et al., 1950 p. 302). The investigators adopted this practice because the questionnaire responses could help to guide the interviewer in his probing for answers to the underlying questions of the interview schedule.

The coding of the interview protocols was to be done by persons not acquainted with a subject's questionnaire responses. It was perfectly clear to the investigators that if a coder knew he was dealing with the protocols of a prejudiced subject he might be more disposed to find "Rigidity" and "Intolerance of Ambiguity" and "Idealization of Parents" than if he knew he was dealing with the protocols of an unprejudiced subject. Blind coding was employed to obviate the possibility of inducing unreal associations between scale scores and the content of interview protocols. However, the danger warded off in the coding stage had already been welcomed aboard in the interviewing stage.

You may remember that the interview schedule left the interviewer free to determine the particular questions he would ask and the order of their asking. Is it not probable that when an interviewer knew he was dealing with a highly prejudiced subject he tried a little harder to obtain evidence of "Rigidity," "Idealization of Parents," and the like, than when he knew that he was dealing with an unprejudiced subject? Indeed there is fragmentary evidence in the interview quotations of the use of leading questions. Thus, when a respondent spoke of premarital sex relations, the interviewer asked, "All momentary relationships?" (Adorno, et al., 1950, p. 393) If bias did not enter into the questioning itself it may have done so in the interviewer's subsequent effort to make a verbatim record from his own shorthand notes. Expectations we know can have a selective effect on recall.

The "too knowledgeable" interviewer is a defect that occurred only in the major interview study. The interviews with psychiatric patients were taken by social workers and physicians who knew nothing about the authoritarian personality research. Interviews were not involved in the TAT study and the sentence completion study.

EXAMINATION OF DATA IN ADVANCE OF CODING

This is one criticism that applies to all four content analyses; the investigators invariably examined their data in search of contrasts between prejudiced and unprejudiced subjects before they made up a scoring manual. The coding categories were defined so as to capture the contrasts that seemed to be in the data. The blind coding from the manual is simply an effort to show that differences which appear to exist when one knows whether or not a subject is prejudiced can also be found when one does not know. And also, of course, to show that the content categories can be communicated from one person to another.

If one closely examines two sets of complex multidimensional data it will usually be possible to find some differences between the two that are consistent enough to be statistically significant. Suppose all of the conceivable dimensions of contrast were, in the full population of subjects, unrelated to the dimension that governs the division of our data into two sets. Suppose that across the whole population of middle class Americans none of the coding categories that might be used in an analysis is significantly related to being prejudiced or unprejudiced. It could nevertheless happen that in any small sample from this population some categories would be related to prejudice at such levels of significance as a p of .05 or .01. Consider what the .05 level of significance means: differences as great or greater than the one obtained would not occur more than five times out of a hundred in samples of this size if there were no difference in the population in question. If we had predicted our differences in advance and they were significant at this level we could be reasonably confident that these were not chance outcomes. However, if we permit ourselves to pick over the data until we find something significant then we may simply be seizing upon those few of the hundreds of conceivable contrasts which will in any particular sample fall by chance into a five-times-in-a-hundred pattern of contrast.

What ought to have been done? Probably the investigators needed to search at least one collection of data for contrasts between the prejudiced and unprejudiced. One would have thought, however, that one such free search would have sufficed to establish the personality dynamics we have described: Repression to Projection and Displacement and Anti-intraception to Aggression against Minorities. In subsequent studies the contrasts of content should have been predictable from this theory and these subsequent studies would then have tested the theory. Or, in any particular study, they might have examined only one-half of the data in advance and used the remaining half as a test of expectations generated in the first half. These things were not done in any study but, instead, the full collection of data was always examined in advance.

THE CODING OF MULTIPLE VARIABLES FROM THE SAME CONTENT

In the main interview study something like ninety variables were coded from each total protocol. Remember that the coders in this case were members of the research staff who were thoroughly familiar with the research hypotheses. These hypotheses suggest that one entire set of coded categories will hang together in the protocols of prejudiced subjects and another set in the protocols of unprejudiced subjects. Suppose now that in a given protocol a coder has found some quite unmistakable expressions of Anti-intraception and some clear indications of Extra-punitiveness and so has begun to think of the protocol as the production of a prejudiced person. Suppose it is now time to code for "Conventional Idealization of Parents" vs. "Objective Appraisal." What will he do with the following statement: "Mother was, of course, a very wonderful person. She was very nervous. Ir-

ritable only when overdoing" (Adorno, *et al.*, 1950 p. 342). It would seem as though the statement might be interpreted either as "Idealization" or as "Objective Appraisal." If the coder has already decided that he is working on the protocol of a prejudiced subject will he not be more likely to decide on "Idealization" which is a prejudiced category than if he has decided that he is working on the protocol of an unprejudiced subject? The statement in question was in fact coded as "Idealization."

It is to be expected in these circumstances that two coders, both acquainted with the research hypotheses, will make similar decisions and so show high scoring reliability. However, we cannot tell which of the ninety content categories are truly associated with prejudice and which only seem to be so associated because their scoring has been influenced by the scoring of other categories. The Berkeley investigators undertook to prevent this scoring bias (which they call a "halo effect") by instructing coders to adopt an analytic attitude—dealing with one category at a time in isolation from all others. Probably the coders tried very hard to do this. The difficulty is that we cannot be sure that they succeeded.

It was only the protocols from the main interview study that were coded for multiple variables by the same rater. The interviews with psychiatric patients were coded by seven control raters with each rater scoring *just one variable*. Consequently this smaller interview study is exempt from the present criticism. The TAT stories and responses to projective questions were shuffled so that the several productions of a subject could not be linked together. However, it was possible to score a single response—a story or an answer to a projective question—for more than one category and so there was the possibility of some halo effect. The scoring of one category on a story could influence the decision about another category. The analysis of these data was then somewhat less subject to the present criticism than was the analysis of the main interview protocols but it was not completely exempt.

THE REPORTING OF RELIABILITIES IN TERMS OF CODING CATEGORIES THAT ARE TOO GENERAL

For the main interview study nine protocols were coded by two raters. There were some ninety categories to be coded and these were put together as pairs such that one member was identified as a High Prejudice category and the other as a Low Prejudice category. We should like to know how well the authors agreed in their decisions for each pair even though there could only be nine items per pair. We are not given this information but instead *The Authoritarian Personality* reports for both raters the percentage of High categories scored in each total interview. For the most part these are closely similar but closely similar overall percentages do not guarantee closely similar decision patterns on particular categories. Both raters, for example, could have scored half of the pairs as High and half as Low but they might have exactly reversed one another in terms of the particular categories scored each way.

The reliability data reported suggest that coders can agree as to whether a total protocol is more likely to be the product of a prejudiced or an unprejudiced subject. But that reliability is not to the point since the discussion of the interviews chiefly concerns the particular content categories characteristic of the two kinds of subject. The study does not report the data that would tell us whether the individual categorical judgments can be made in a reliable fashion.

For the TAT and projective question studies, the judgments for which reliability coefficients are reported are not so crude as in the interview study but they are also not at the level of particular content categories which is the level of the discussion of results. For example, the first item among the projective questions asks subjects to say what moods they find particularly unpleasant or disturbing. The Low categories are: "Conscious conflict and guilt; Focal dependency and love-seeking; Open hostility, by self or others, toward love objects." The High categories are: "Violations of conventional values; Threatening or nonsupporting environment; Rumblings from below; and Omissions." The authors tell us that for answers to this question there was a mean agreement of 93 per cent as to whether an answer was High, Neutral, or Low. But two coders could agree that an answer was High and for one this might be because the response seemed to fall into the category "Violations of conventional values" while for the other it might seem to go in the category "Threatening or nonsupporting environment." We are not told how well coders agreed on particular content cat-

egories but conclusions are drawn in terms of these content categories.

It is only in the case of the psychiatric interviews that reliabilities are reported for coding judgments at the level of specificity appropriate to the treatment of results and to the theoretical discussion. Each variable was separately coded and the percentage agreements between a control rater and a principal rater are reported.

Authoritarianism and Education—IQ—SES

In *The Authoritarian Personality* there is a chapter that reports on the relations of ethnocentrism with IQ and with education. Table 2.1 presents one set of findings for IQ and Table 2.2 a set of findings for education. From one subject sample to another the correlations vary in size but they are invariably negative (E scores rise as IQ or years of education fall), generally significantly greater than zero but generally below .5. The authors conclude that there is a significant but not very large relation between ethnocentrism and the other two variables.

Hyman and Sheatsley (1954) in their critique of the Berkeley Study report data from a National Opinion Research Council survey showing the associations between five particular F Scale items and years of education. These are reproduced as Table 2.3 and they show a perfectly consistent decline of authoritarianism with increasing education. Hyman and Sheatsley also point to a number of differences between the prejudiced and unprejudiced, attributed to personality dynamics in the original study, that have a more obvious and plausible explanation in terms of education. For

TABLE 2.1. Mean Wechsler-Bellevue IQ Score for Each Quartile of the Ethnocentrism Scale (Psychiatric Clinic, Men and Women)

Form 45 E Scale quartiles	Range on E	N	Mean IQ
Low quartile	10–24	8	125.3
Low middle quartile	25–36	5	117.8
High middle quartile	37–50	13	113.9
High quartile	51–70	11	107.3
		37	114.9

(From *The Authoritarian Personality* by T. W. Adorno, et al. Copyright 1950 by The American Jewish Committee. Reprinted with the permission of Harper & Row, Publishers, Incorporated.)

TABLE 2.2. Mean Number of Years of Education for Each Quartile of the Ethnocentrism Scale (Psychiatric Clinic, Men and Women)

Form 45 E Scale quartiles	Range on E	N	Mean yrs. education
Low quartile	10–24	29	13.8
Low middle quartile	25–36	28	12.7
High middle quartile	37–50	27	11.8
High quartile	51–70	28	11.2
		112	12.4

(From *The Authoritarian Personality* by T. W. Adorno, et al. Copyright 1950 by The American Jewish Committee. Reprinted with the permission of Harper & Row, Publishers, Incorporated.)

example, one of the projective questions asked: "What great people do you admire most?" Unprejudiced subjects named Whitman, Pushkin, Beethoven, Voltaire, Comte, Freud, and Pestalozzi among others. Prejudiced subjects named General Marshall, General MacArthur, Lindbergh, the Pope, Henry Ford, and Bing Crosby among others. The researchers conceptualize the difference by saying that the unprejudiced value intellectual, scientific, aesthetic, and social achievements while the prejudiced value power, control, and conservative Americana. There is a simpler rubric: the names listed by the prejudiced are known to everybody in the United States while those listed by the unprejudiced are only known to the better educated.

IQ and years of education are, of course, positively correlated. In addition, years of education is one index of socioeconomic status (SES) and is somewhat correlated with such others as income and possessions. In addition there are certain less obvious correlates of the individual variables:

probably more schooling goes with being moderately young rather than elderly since the availability of education has increased in our lifetimes. Consequently we must suppose that ethnocentrism and authoritarianism are somewhat related to a great bundle of variables having something to do with socioeconomic status; the relationship seems to be negative.

How strong are the correlations between ethnocentrism and IQ, education, or other related variables? There have been a number of studies on this point, and Christie (1954), after reviewing them, estimates that the correlation between either IQ and F scores or years of education and F scores would, for a representative cross-sectional sample, range between $-.50$ and $-.60$. In the Berkeley studies the range of intelligence and education was, for the most part, quite restricted and restriction of range would operate to keep down the value of correlation coefficients. Christie found that in the various studies that have been reported the size of the correlation increased as the range increased. For this reason he argues that $-.50$ to $-.60$ is a reasonable estimate for correlations based on a full range on both IQ and F scores. IQ and years of education are themselves positively correlated. Christie estimates that with education partialed out the correlation between intelligence and F scores is only about $-.20$. It seems to be chiefly education or cultural sophistication, rather than intelligence *per se* that reduces authoritarianism.

What is the implication of the fact that the components of the authoritarian syndrome are correlated with education and SES? You remember that the Berkeley researchers held that the covariation

TABLE 2.3. Agreement with F Scale Items and Education

	College N = 217	High school N = 545	Grammar school N = 504
Agree that:			
The most important thing to teach children is absolute obedience to their parents	35%	60%	80%
Any good leader should be strict with people under him in order to gain their respect	36	51	66
Prison is too good for sex criminals. They should be publicly whipped or worse	18	31	45
There are two kinds of people in the world: the weak and the strong	30	53	71
No decent man can respect a woman who has had sex relations before marriage	14	26	39

of a mixed lot of attitudes and traits having no clear logical relationship argues for the existence of a unifying personality dynamic. Critics have contended that this position is destroyed by the demonstration of a correlation with education and SES. The numerous components of authoritarianism are found together in a person simply because they are the norms of his subculture—the little-educated, less bright, low SES subculture. To this we must respond by asking: Why does this subculture put its norms together as it does? Why should self-glorification, parent idealization, impunitiveness, anti-intraception, and prejudice cohere as a set of norms? The question is there whether you ask it for the individual or for the group.

It is possible, however, that low IQ, education, and SES can account for the syndrome without recourse to personality dynamics. Perhaps parents with low SES stamp out all aggression against authority in their children because it is likely to lead to delinquency and trouble with the police. Perhaps people with low SES are prejudiced against Negroes because it takes severe discrimination to keep the Negro beneath them in status. They may be prejudiced against Jews because the stereotype of the ruthless, clannish Jew accounts in an agreeable way for his occasional economic ascendance. Perhaps the person of low SES is not reflective or introspective because he is too busy hustling to earn a living. We can easily imagine plausible reasons for the association of each authoritarian trait with the cluster that includes low IQ, little education, and low SES and so the explanation of the covariation among the traits is simply their several particular ties to the same underlying factors.

In what way does the above account differ from the one offered by the Berkeley group? Both explain the covariation of traits but the question is whether those traits are a bundle or a system. If we account for their coherence entirely in terms of particular ties with income and education and the like, then the coherence is simply incidental to their common dependence on the same factors. The components hang together but are not interdependent. The Berkeley group contends, however, that the proscription of any aggression against authority requires ethnic prejudice because aggression must somehow be released. Proscription of aggression against authority in combination with ethnic prejudice requires that there be little introspection

or reflection because self-examination would disturb the system of repression, displacement, and rationalization. It is the view of the Berkeley group that the components of the authoritarian syndrome hang together because they are a working system. If it is true that these components are the norms of an underprivileged subculture then I think the contribution of the Berkeley research is to show that this combination of norms makes a viable pattern for human personalities. Norms are not put together at random or incidentally. When they stabilize into a particular combination it must be because that is a combination that works for human personalities.

In *The Authoritarian Personality* some importance is assigned to SES. It is status concern or anxiety that is presumed to cause certain parents to interpret their parental role in an authoritarian way and from this role-interpretation all the rest is supposed to follow. In 1954 Else Frenkel-Brunswik wrote a paper called *Further Explorations by a Contributor to "The Authoritarian Personality"* (Christie & Jahoda, 1954) in which she described an extensive study of prejudice in children and adolescents. In this work there were interviews with parents of children who were extremely high in prejudice and also with parents of children low in prejudice. Frenkel-Brunswik reports that the subjective feeling of socioeconomic "marginality" on the part of the parents rather than their objective SES was the crucial factor in ethnocentrism. A feeling of marginality is said to exist when there is a discrepancy between actual status and the status one aspires to. "Marginality" seems to be much the same as the status concern of the original study.

However, while marginality may be the crucial factor it is evident that Frenkel-Brunswik also found the familiar negative correlation between F scores and SES. She reports a "relatively high percentage of ethnocentric families among the workers . . ." (p. 233). It is easy to imagine a reconciliation of the two aspects of SES that seem to engender authoritarianism. Perhaps the feeling of marginality is the critical factor but feelings of marginality may be especially likely to arise at the lower end of the SES scale, among the working class. The latter part of this reconciliation does not sit well with the liberal intellectual since fascism is supposed to be a movement of the lower middle class rather than of the proletariat.

In summary, SES, intelligence, and education are all negatively related to F scores and the relationships are stronger than the Berkeley authors had realized. Of the various negative correlates it seems to be education that is strongest. Kornhauser, Sheppard and Mayer (1956) found that among men who were all auto workers, those with an eighth grade education or less were more authoritarian than those with a greater amount of education. Cohn and Carsch (1954) showed that among workers in a German cosmetics factory, those who had attended *Hochschule* had lower F scores than those with less education. Authoritarianism may be the world-view of the uneducated in western industrial societies. It may be that this world-view hangs together because of the dynamic inter-relations among the parts posited by the Berkeley research.

After the Critique

What of *The Authoritarian Personality* survives the many devastating criticisms of its methods? Hyman and Sheatsley (1954) summarize their masterful methodological critique by saying: "Our major criticisms lead us inevitably to conclude that the authors' theory has not been proved by the data they cite . . ." (p. 119). Notice the care with which this conclusion is formulated: the theory has not been proved by a particular set of data. A methodological critique cannot conclude that a theory is mistaken. Ultimately of course it is the correctness of the theory that we care about. What would be the best opinion on this important matter? By this time you have probably formed an opinion and so have I. How well do we agree?

There are really two sets of methodological criticisms dividing neatly into those that apply to the work with questionnaires and those that apply to the work with projective methods. The most serious defects in the questionnaire work are the inadequate sampling and the operation of response sets. Both criticisms are sound. In spite of their cogency it seems to me that there is a substantial residual probability that the chief conclusion of the questionnaire work is correct: attitudes of anti-Semitism, ethnocentrism, and authoritarianism do generally go together.

You remember that studies done since the original book, though never based on fully adequate samples, do very consistently find significant re-

lations among these attitudes. There seems never to have been a report of a negative relationship. Response set has certainly magnified the size of these relations but, from the evidence, the effects of response set are not great enough completely to wash out the relations. Finally, some of the findings of the questionnaire study were replicated in the projectives study and, while this latter work has its own deficiencies, some account must be taken of the convergence in the two sets of data.

Christie and Cook (1958) have published a bibliography of research relating to the authoritarian personality through 1956. They list 230 titles. In their summary of the work they write: "Although there are serious problems in evaluating research, the overall picture shows consistency of findings in many of the most intensively studied areas. The E and F Scales are found to be significantly correlated in a wide array of samples and predictions of relationships with attitudinal measures are almost invariably confirmed" (p. 189). I take this conclusion to be about the same as mine.

The flaws in the study of projectives are more serious: interviewer knowledge of the interviewees' questionnaire responses; derivation of scoring categories from prior examination of data; coding of multiple variables from the same data; inadequate reports of coding reliability. Each study of projective materials was flawed by at least one of these and so there are grounds for dismissing the evidence of each study. My own evaluation differs from that of Hyman and Sheatsley in that I should like to give some weight to the congruence of evidence across the main interviews, TATs, projective questions, and psychiatric interviews.

There is only one criticism that applies to all four studies: the derivation of scoring categories from prior examination of data. What the authors ought to have done in their first study is to examine a part of their data in search of discriminating categories and use the remainder to test. The four studies taken together suggest that the categories would have survived such a test. Suppose we consider one of the studies, for example the main interview study, as the preliminary examination of data in search of categories. Since the other studies employ some categories that are the same as or closely similar to those used with the main interviews it would seem that the authors could have used these studies as tests and need not have made preliminary examinations of data. The fact that they did make such examinations does not completely vitiate the force of the convergence in the findings.

Finally we can be more affirmative than Hyman and Sheatsley because we are not doing a critique of the Berkeley study but are trying to decide on the tenability of its conclusions in view of all the studies that have been done. Perhaps the least well-supported of all the findings in the Berkeley study are those concerning the genesis of authoritarianism in childhood. To begin with, the data were all obtained from adult recollections and such recollections can be grossly inaccurate. Secondly, the data were nearly all obtained in the main interview study and not directly checked in the projective materials; the main interview study had many methodological defects. However, Frenkel-Brunswik has directly studied prejudice in childhood and adolescence. She reports confirmation of most of the original findings.

"It was found that, at least after the age of ten, children's personalities tend to fall into patterns similar to those observed in the adults described in *The Authoritarian Personality*. Thus ethnocentric youngsters tend to display authoritarian aggression, rigidity, cruelty, superstition, externalization, and projectivity, denial of weakness, power orientation, and tend toward dichotomous conceptions of sex roles, of kinds of people, and of values" (Frenkel-Brunswik, 1954). In the homes of the ethnocentric children discipline was strict, rigid, and punitive. Unprejudiced children were more apt to see both positive and negative features in their parents; they were more able to accept feelings of love and hate for the same persons. Prejudiced children seemed compelled to see their parents as wholly good though there were indications that they also saw them, covertly, as wholly bad. Prejudiced children conceived it to be the chief business of both parents and teachers to discipline their charges and keep them in line. While Frenkel-Brunswik published several partial reports of this work (1949, 1953, 1954), she never made a complete report and that is unfortunate in view of its considerable importance.

On the level of covariation, of one variable correlated with another, the findings of *The Authoritarian Personality* seem to me to be quite well established. Anti-Semitism goes with ethnocentrism goes with anti-intraception goes with idealization of parents and self goes with authoritarian discipline in childhood goes with a rigid conception of sex roles, etc. Two of the presumptive correlates are not well established: status-concern or marginality and the cognitive style characterized by rigidity and intolerance of ambiguity.

On the level of interpretation, the level on which repression is supposed to lead to displacement, rationalization, and anti-intraception, things are less certain. These ideas about personality dynamics cannot be proved by correlation. Studies of an entirely different kind are needed. Is it the case, for example, that if an authoritarian somehow became able to tolerate ambivalence, to see faults in himself and his parents, that he would thereupon lose his prejudices or at any rate become able to adjust them to fact? One would have to find a way of bringing ambivalence into consciousness (psychotherapy? hypnosis?) without in any way directly attacking the prejudice. It would not be an easy kind of research to do and it has not been done.

The major alternative to the personality dynamic explanation of the covariation is the suggestion that the traits of the authoritarian cohere simply because they are the norms of people with little education and low SES. For each particular trait one could work out some plausible derivation from one or another aspect of SES. The dynamic explanation would make the coherence tighter by showing how one trait supports another, not logically but in terms of the needs and defenses postulated by psychoanalytic theory. It is likely that both sets of forces—the dynamic interrelations as well as the ties with status and education—cooperate to hold this mosaic together.

Is There an Authoritarian of the Left?

The best measure of authoritarianism is the F Scale. It is objective and quantitative and much easier to use than interview protocols or projective data. However, the F Scale was characterized by the authors in two ways: 1) As a means of identifying fascistic proclivities or an authoritarianism of the right; 2) as a means of identifying authoritarianism in general and this presumably could be of the left as well as of the right. The authors do not actually demonstrate a connection between F Scale scores and affiliation with fascistic political parties. The three inmates of San Quentin who were called fascists were so labelled by the researchers because of their violently antidemocratic views rather than because they were members of a fascist party. We shall first inquire whether the F Scale can identify genuine political fascists to see if it is a measure of authoritarianism of the right. If it is we shall then want to know whether it is only a measure of authoritarianism of the right or whether it can also identify authoritarians of the left—if such there be.

The F Scale Scores of Fascists and Communists

In the 1930's, more than a decade before the publication of *The Authoritarian Personality*, Stagner developed a scale for the assessment of fascistic attitudes. In German and Italian fascistic writings he identified seven characteristic content areas: 1) nationalism, 2) imperialism, 3) militarism, 4) racial antagonism, 5) anti-radicalism, 6) middle-class consciousness, and 7) a benevolent despot or strong-man philosophy of government. The first five of these areas suggest the content of the A-S and E scales and scores on these scales are highly correlated with F Scale scores. The last two seem to have been directly covered in the F Scale. Some of Stagner's items have near-matches in the F Scale; for example, from Stagner's scale we have: "America has plenty of plans—what it needs is strong men who are willing to work for recovery"; the F Scale includes: "What this country needs most, more than laws and political programs, is a few courageous, tireless devoted leaders in whom the people can put their faith." In sum, the ideological content found to be characteristic of fascism in Stagner's independent study (1936) is very similar to the content of the scales used to assess authoritarianism.

During World War II there were opportunities to investigate the personality characteristics of captured Nazis. Dicks (1950) conducted psychiatric interviews with 138 German POW's, some of whom were fanatical Nazis and some of whom were either politically uninvolved or else active anti-Nazis. At several points Dicks' description of the traits characteristic of the fanatical Nazis resembles the Berkeley characterization of the authoritarian. The fanatical Nazi was lacking in rebellion against his father; he showed sadism, projectivity, and a tabu on tenderness.

These fragments of indirect evidence are helpful but one waits for the decisive demonstration. What are the F Scale scores of members of fascist parties? Cohn and Carsch (1954) had the scale translated into German and they administered it in 1952 to 140 workers in a German cosmetics factory. The mean F score was 5.26 and the standard deviation was .86. This mean score was, at the time, the highest that had ever been reported; The San Quentin prisoners had the highest mean of the groups studied in the Berkeley research but that mean was only 4.73. If one makes the assumption that these German workers were former Nazis then the data support the validity of the claim that the F Scale measures fascistic tendencies. However, we do not know that the workers had all been Nazis. In addition, the sample was working class, and low SES groups everywhere have had high F scores. Further, some students of the F Scale (e.g., Peabody) doubt that it is possible strictly to "translate" the complex and subtle assertions of the scale from English into another language.

Can the scale be validated with English-speaking political fascists? The problem is to find them. In the immediate postwar period they could not be found in the United States. Today there are neo-Nazis but they have not been studied extensively. Luckily (from the research point of view) England has had an avowedly fascist group.

Coulter (1953) administered the F Scale to forty-three English Fascists, also to forty-three English Communists, and also to eighty-three English soldiers who did not belong to either political extreme. All subjects are said to have been of the working class. Coulter's research was done under the direction of H. J. Eysenck of London's Maudsley Hospital and we will, a little further on, discuss the several results of this study in connection with Eysenck's theory of the organization of attitudes.

The mean score of the Fascist men (Christie, 1956a, has calculated the means from Eysenck's report in *The Psychology of Politics*, 1954) was 5.30. The range of possible scores on the F Scale is from 1.0 to 7.0 with 4.0 the theoretical neutral point. American college students usually score in the range from 3.0 to 4.0. The highest group mean published before Coulter's study was the 5.26 reported by Cohn and Carsch (1954) for German workers. The Coulter result is therefore a strong confirmation of the claim that the F Scale measures fascistic trends.

The mean score of the forty-three working-class Communists (according to Christie, 1956a,) studied by Coulter was 3.13 and the score of the "politically neutral" soldiers was 2.50; the Communists were slightly above the soldiers but far below the Fascists. Eysenck draws from Coulter's data the truly extraordinary conclusion: ". . . we have found Communists to make almost as high scores on this scale as Fascists" (Eysenck, 1954, p. 149) and argues that the F Scale is not just a measure of fascistic tendencies but of authoritarianism in general. It would seem to be a more reasonable summary of the data to say that Communists scored slightly above neutrals but much below Fascists and so the F Scale is primarily a measure of authoritarianism of the right though slightly sensitive to the authoritarianism of the left. However, even this version must be questioned.

As Christie (1956a) has pointed out, Coulter's "neutral" soldiers were an extraordinarily equalitarian group. Their mean F Scale score is the lowest-but-one of the fifty or so group means known to Christie. It is well below the usual level of American college students and also well below some means obtained by Rokeach (1960) for samples of English college students. It looks as if Coulter's Communists are more authoritarian than the "neutrals" only because the neutrals are very exceptionally non-authoritarian.

The Communists' score of 3.13 falls in the lower part of the range of data available on American groups and on English college students. In absolute terms the mean is on the equalitarian side of the theoretical neutral point on the scale which falls at 4.0. Neither relatively nor absolutely is it clear that Coulter's Communists are authoritarian.

Among the subjects tested in the original Berkeley study there were nine who identified themselves as Communists and fifty-four who were attending the California Labor School, an organization designated by the Attorney General as under the domination of the Communist Party. The F Scale scores of these subjects unfortunately are not separated out in *The Authoritarian Personality*. However, Christie (1956a) has shown by some ingenious reasoning and comparing of tables of data that these scores must have been relatively low.

Finally, Rokeach (1960), visiting in Great Britain, obtained F Scale scores from thirteen Communist college students. Their mean was the lowest of five political groups studied and it was significantly lower than the means of Liberal Party students and Labor Party students of the Atleeite persuasion.

All of these Communist samples have been absurdly small and probably unrepresentative of total membership. Still the consistently low scores, always on the equalitarian side of neutrality and apparently near the bottom of the range for all groups tested, strongly indicate that Communists *in democratic countries* do not produce high scores on the authoritarianism scale. This can mean either of two things: 1) The F Scale only measures authoritarianism of the right or fascism; 2) the F Scale measures general authoritarianism, in some sense, but communists in democratic countries are not authoritarian. In any event the Berkeley researchers seem to have been correct in their belief that the F Scale is a measure of fascism.

In 1944 Edwards, in an article on fascism in America, quoted a Washington newspaper as follows: "Anyone whose opinion differs from our own is now known as fascist" (p. 301). For more recent times that statement could stand but with *communist* substituted for fascist. A great many of us have lived through both periods and have been "worked up" against both enemies. The F Scale and the research on the authoritarian personality provide a single dimension for the description of political ideologies and on this dimension our two ideological antagonists are opposite extremes. That is not a cognitively satisfying state of affairs. It makes it difficult, for instance, to find an attractive ideological stance for the United States; a rather empty moderation or neutrality is the only consistent position that will justify our antagonism to two extremes. Beyond that it is not satisfying, somehow, to feel that two villains are totally unlike. The human mind prefers to think of the evil things in this world as clustered together in opposition to the good things. There is an agreeable cognitive simplicity in dichotomous evaluation. It would be most satisfying to find that communism and fascism are somehow alike and that we have, all along, been consistently opposed to this quality they have in common. Perhaps it is this strain toward cognitive simplicity that caused Eysenck to see in Coulter's data the greater authoritarianism of both Fascists and Communists rather than the closeness of Communists to neutrals.

Of course there are some real similarities between the fascist and communist movements of our time. Shils (1954) has pointed out that Italian and German fascism were conservative or right wing in their concern with national traditions and the value they set on private property, but they were leftist (in nineteenth-century terms) in their governmental regulation of industry and in this respect similar to Soviet Communism. The latter movement has been leftist in its humanitarian social welfare plans and in its attitude to private property but it has resembled fascism in its suppression of civil liberties.

Throughout *The Authoritarian Personality* there are intimations that one dimension may not be adequate to the description of modern ideologies. The authors toy with a distinction between active, militant liberals and passive, inhibited liberals and with a distinction between "genuine conservatives" and "pseudoconservatives." Shils has taken them to task for not making more of these distinctions; he believes that the Berkeley group was oversold on a liberal-fascist dichotomy. There have been recent attempts to find more dimensions in the structure of attitudes and, in particular, a dimension that will put communism somewhere close to fascism.

Rokeach's Dogmatism

Rokeach (1960) has a suggestion of his own as to what is wrong with communists that is also wrong with fascists. He is convinced that the F Scale is a measure of right-authoritarianism rather than authoritarianism in general. A measure of general authoritarianism, he suggests, must be free of ideological content since it is to be found in people of every political persuasion as well as in Freudians, Unitarians, and art critics. In short, general authoritarianism is best conceived as a mode of thought rather than as a set of beliefs. In identifying intolerance of ambiguity and rigidity as characteristics of authoritarian thought the Berkeley investigators came nearer the identification of general authoritarianism than they did with the F Scale. Rokeach has chosen to call the cognitive style that is general authoritarianism by the name *dogmatism*. He provides an elaborate conceptualization of dogmatism, which is far from identical with popular understanding of that term, and then goes on to construct a questionnaire measure of the concept.

Rokeach does not report data on Fascists but he did manage to find some Communists in England,

all students and only thirteen of them. Both the F Scale and the Dogmatism Scale were given to five English groups. As we have seen the Communists obtained the most equalitarian mean score of all five groups and this mean was significantly lower than the means of Conservatives, Liberals, and Labor Party members. Only the left wing of the Labor Party was not significantly higher than the Communists. These results indicate that the F Scale is indeed a measure of authoritarianism of the right and Communists are not high on that measure. Are they high on Dogmatism, which is put forward as a measure of general authoritarianism?

On the Dogmatism Scale the Communists have the highest mean score of all five groups. However, none of the differences between the means attains a conventional level of statistical significance; the difference between Liberals and Communists comes close. No data are presented on the Dogmatism of explicit Fascists.

Conclusion

My conclusion, then, is that it has not been demonstrated that fascists and communists resemble one another in authoritarianism or in any other dimension of ideology. No one thus far has shown that there is an authoritarian of the left. Still the impression persists that such a type exists and that some communists belong to it. I believe that both Rokeach and the Berkeley authors have, at several points in their writings, hit upon a promising characterization of general authoritarianism but it is not the characterization they develop or use as the basis of their scales. Perhaps the authoritarian is a person who is best characterized by the kind of information that will induce him to change his attitudes. The authoritarian will reverse his evaluations on the simple say-so of an authority figure. If Stalin signs a pact with Berlin then Nazism becomes acceptable for the authoritarian Communist; if Khrushchev devaluates Stalin the Communist authoritarian does the same. The authoritarian liberal would change his views on Communism if Franklin Roosevelt had told him to do so. I would characterize the authoritarian in terms of the kind of information that is sufficient to induce a change of his attitudes.

The non-authoritarian will also change his attitudes but the requisite information is different. The endorsement of an authority will not be sufficient. Most generally he will need to see that the objects of his attitude are related to his more basic values in ways that he had not formerly realized. This is by no means a completely "logical" business and it is not clear that the contrast of authoritarian and non-authoritarian is on a dimension of rationality. I am simply proposing that it is a difference in the weight given to the unsupported opinions of an authority.

The proposed definition is dynamic rather than static. One could not diagnose authoritarianism from an inventory of beliefs but only from knowledge of the circumstances that will change belief. This means that the measurement problem is certain to be more difficult than when authoritarianism is defined in static terms and so one can understand a reluctance to accept such a definition.

By the proposed definitions not all communists will be authoritarian, not all fascists, and not all liberals. It is, however, possible that dynamic authoritarianism would be more often found in conjunction with some ideologies than with others. The focus on single, enduring, and very powerful authorities in fascist and communist states suggests that dynamic authoritarianism may be more common there than in democratic states. The apparent popular acceptance of radical transformations of attitude on little more than the say-so of dictators suggests that this is the case. When Russia invaded Hungary there were wholesale defections from European Communist parties which argues that many members were not dynamic authoritarians. On the other hand there were many who swallowed the Hungary treatment and also de-Stalinization and also the Soviet-German pact before the war.

The idea that all persons affiliated with an extremist political party should have the same personality characteristics is much too simpleminded. It is some improvement to recognize the kinds of personality differences among people adhering to a common ideology that are suggested by a dynamic conception of authoritarianism. But there are other differences that must exist. As Lasswell (1954) has argued an organization as complex as a political party must have a great variety of differentiated roles. The Nazi Party had use for a great many rigid, sadomasochistic, anti-intraceptive, anti-Semites of the kind described in the Berkeley study. But it also had need of clever propagandists, clear-thinking ministers, sensitive diplomats, and courageous military men. There may be some essential quality that occupants of all of these roles had to have in order to be Nazis but, in addition, they had to have distinctive characteristics. An institutionalized political movement could not have operated with personalities of a completely uniform type.

The Berkeley study of the authoritarian personality does not leave many people indifferent. Cool objectivity has not been the hallmark of this tradition. Most of those who have participated have cared deeply about the social issues involved. If it has been difficult for any one investigator to avoid ideological bias there have always been others of contrary bias to keep the argument moving in the direction of truth.

REFERENCES

Adorno, T. W., Frenkel-Brunswik, Else, Levinson, D. J., & Sanford, R. N. *The authoritarian personality*. New York: Harper, 1950.

Applezweig, Dee G. Some determinants of behavioral rigidity. *J. abnorm. soc. Psychol.*, 1954, **49**, 224–228.

Bass, B. M. Authoritarianism or acquiescence? *J. abnorm. soc. Psychol.*, 1955, **51**, 616–623.

Block, J., & Block, Jeanne. An investigation of the relationship between intolerance of ambiguity and ethnocentrism. *J. Pers.*, 1951, **19**, 303–311.

Brown, R. W. A determinant of the relationship between rigidity and authoritarianism. *J. abnorm. soc. Psychol.*, 1953, **48**, 469–476.

Christie, R. Authoritarianism re-examined. In R. Christie, & Marie Jahoda (Eds.), *Studies in the scope and method of "The authoritarian personality."* New York: Free Press, 1954.

Christie, R. Eysenck's treatment of the personality of Communists. *Psychol. Bull.*, 1956, **53**, 411–430. (a)

Christie, R. Some abuses of psychology. *Psychol. Bull.*, 1956, **53**, 439–451. (b)

Christie, R., & Cook, Peggy. A guide to published literature relating to the authoritarian personality through 1956. *J. Psychol.*, 1958, **45**, 171–199.

Christie, R., Havel, Joan, & Seidenberg, B. Is the F Scale irreversible? *J. abnorm. soc. Psychol.*, 1958, **56**, 143–159.

Christie, R., & Jahoda, Marie (Eds.), *Studies in the scope and method of "The authoritarian personality."* New York: Free Press, 1954.

Cohn, T. S. The relation of the F Scale to a response to answer positively. *Amer. Psychol.*, 1953, **8**, 335. (Abstract)

Cohn, T. S., & Carsch, H. Administration of the F Scale to a sample of Germans. *J. abnorm. soc. Psychol.*, 1954, **49**, 471.

Converse, P. E. The shifting role of class in political attitudes and behavior. In Eleanor E. Maccoby, T. M. Newcomb, & E. L. Hartley (Eds.), *Readings in social psychology*. (3rd ed.) New York: Holt, 1958.

Couch, A., & Keniston, K. Yeasayers and naysayers: Agreeing response set as a personality variable. *J. abnorm. soc. Psychol.*, 1960, **60**, 151–174.

Coulter, Thelma. An experimental and statistical study of the relationship of prejudice and certain personality variables. Unpublished doctoral dissertation. Univer. of London, 1953.

Cronbach, L. J. Response sets and test validity. *Educ. psychol. Measmt.*, 1946, **6**, 475–494.

Cronbach, L. J. *Essentials of psychological testing.* (2nd ed.) New York: Harper, 1960.

Davis, A. Socialization and adolescent personality. In T. M. Newcomb, & E. L. Hartley (Eds.), *Readings in social psychology.* New York: Holt, 1947.

Dicks, H. V. Personality traits and national socialist ideology. *Hum. Relat.*, 1950, **3**, 111–154.

Doob, L. W. The behavior of attitudes. *Psychol. Rev.*, 1947, **54**, 135–156.

Edwards, A. L. The signs of incipient fascism. *J. abnorm. soc. Psychol.*, 1944, **39**, 301–316.

Eysenck, H. J. General social attitudes. *J. soc. Psychol.*, 1944, **19**, 207–227.

Eysenck, H. J. Primary social attitudes as related to social class and political party. *Brit. J. Sociol.*, 1951, **2**, 198–209.

Eysenck, H. J. *The psychology of politics.* London: Routledge & Kegan Paul, 1954.

Eysenck, H. J. The psychology of politics: A reply. *Psychol. Bull.*, 1956, **53**, 177–182. (a)

Eysenck, H. J. The psychology of politics and the personality similarities between fascists and communists. *Psychol. Bull.* 1956, **53**, 431–438. (b)

Eysenck, H. J. *The dynamics of anxiety and hysteria.* New York: Praeger, 1957.

Eysenck, H. J. Classification and the problem of diagnosis. In H. J. Eysenck (Ed.), *Handbook of abnormal psychology: An experimental approach.* New York: Basic Books, 1961.

Ferguson, L. W. Primary social attitudes. *J. Psychol.*, 1939, **8**, 217–223.

Ferguson, L. W. The stability of the primary social attitudes: I. Religionism and humanitarianism. *J. Psychol.*, 1941, **12**, 283–288.

Fisher, S. Patterns of personality rigidity and some of their determinants. *Psychol. Monogr.*, 1950, **64**, No. 1 (Whole No. 307).

Franks, C. M. Conditioning and abnormal behaviour. In H. J. Eysenck (Ed.), *Handbook of abnormal psychology; An experimental approach.* New York: Basic Books, 1961.

Frenkel-Brunswik, Else. Intolerance of ambiguity as an emotional and perceptual personality variable. *J. Pers.*, 1949, **18**, 108–143.

Frenkel-Brunswik, Else. Further explorations by a contributor to "The authoritarian personality." In R. Christie, & Marie Jahoda (Eds.), *Studies in the scope and method of "The authoritarian personality."* New York: Free Press, 1954.

Frenkel-Brunswik, Else, & Havel, Joan. Prejudice in the interviews of children: I. Attitudes toward minority group. *J. genet. Psychol.*, 1953, **82**, 91–136.

Guildford, J. P. *Psychometric methods.* (2nd ed.) New York: McGraw-Hill, 1954.

Guildford, J. P. A revised structure of intellect. *Reports from the Psychological Laboratory of the University of Southern California*, 1957, No. 19.

Hilgard, E. R., & Marquis, D. G. *Conditioning and learning.* New York: Appleton-Century-Crofts, 1940.

Horowitz, E. L. Development of attitude toward Negroes. In T. M. Newcomb, & E. L. Hartley (Eds.), *Readings in social psychology* (1st ed.) New York: Holt, 1947.

Hyman, H. H., & Sheatsley, P. B. "The authoritarian personality"—A methodological critique. In R. Christie, & Marie Jahoda (Eds.), *Studies in the scope and method of "The authoritarian personality."* New York: Free Press, 1954. Pp. 50–122.

Jaensch, E. R. *Der Gegentypus.* Leipzig: Barth, 1938.

James, W. *Pragmatism.* New York: Longmans, Green, 1907.

Kimble, G. A. *Hilgard & Marquis' conditioning and learning.* (2nd ed.) New York: Appleton-Century-Crofts, 1961.

Kornhauser, A., Sheppard, H. L., & Mayer, A. J. *When labor votes.* New York: University Books, 1956.

Lasswell, H. D. The selective effect of personality on political participation. In R. Christie & Marie Jahoda (Eds.), *Studies in the scope and method of "The authoritarian personality."* New York: Free Press, 1954.

Luchins, A. R. Mechanization in problem-solving. *Psychol. Monogr.*, 1942, **54**, No. 6 (Whole No. 248).

MacKinnon, W. J., & Centers, R. Authoritarianism and urban stratification. *Amer. J. Sociol.*, 1956, **61**, 610–620.

Melvin, D. An experimental and statistical study of two primary social attitudes. Unpublished doctoral dissertation. Univer. of London, 1955.

Messick, S. J., & Jackson, D. N. Authoritarianism or acquiescence in Bass's data. *J. abnorm. soc. Psychol.*, 1957, **54**, 424–425.

Mowrer, O. H. *Learning theory and personality dynamics.* New York: Ronald, 1950.

Pavlov, I. P. *Conditioned reflexes and psychiatry.* Transl. and ed. by W. H. Gantt. New York: Int. Publishers, 1941.

Peabody, D. Attitude content and agreement set in scales of authoritarianism, dogmatism, anti-Semitism, and economic conservatism. *J. abnorm. soc. Psychol.*, 1961, **63**, 1–11.

Prothro, E. T. Ethnocentrism and anti-Negro attitudes in the deep south. *J. abnorm. soc. Psychol.*, 1952, **47**, 105–108.

Rokeach, M. Generalized mental rigidity as a factor in ethnocentrism. *J. abnorm. soc. Psychol.*, 1948, **43**, 259–278.

Rokeach, M. *The open and closed mind.* New York: Basic Books, 1960.

Rokeach, M., & Hanley, C. Eysenck's tender-mindedness dimension: A critique. *Psychol. Bull.*, 1956, **53**, 169–176.

Sartre, J. P. *Anti-Semite and Jew.* (*Réflexions sur la question Juive*, 1st ed., 1946.) Transl. by G. J. Becker. New York: Schocken, 1948.

Shils, E. A. Authoritarianism: "Right" and "left." In R. Christie, & Marie Jahoda (Eds.), *Studies in the scope and method of "The authoritarian personality."* New York: Free Press, 1954.

Skinner. B. F. *The behavior of organisms: An experimental analysis.* New York: Appleton-Century-Crofts, 1938.

Spearman, C. "General intelligence" objectively determined and measured. *Amer. J. Psychol.*, 1904, **15**, 201–293.

Stagner, R. Fascist attitudes: An exploratory study. *J. soc. Psychol.*, 1936, **7**, 309–319.

Sumner, W. G. *Folkways.* Boston: Ginn, 1906.

Thorndike, E. L. *Animal intelligence.* New York: Macmillan, 1911.

Thurstone, L. L. *Multiple factor analysis.* Chicago: Univer. of Chicago Press, 1947.

Thurstone, L. L. Primary mental abilities. *Psychometric Monogr.*, No. 1, 1938.

Threat and Authoritarianism in the United States, 1978-1987

Richard M. Doty, Bill E. Peterson, and David G. Winter

• University of Michigan

Studies at both the individual and collective levels have implicated threat as an important factor in authoritarianism. As a follow-up to Sales's (1973) study relating behavioral indicators of authoritarianism to levels of social threat, the present research analyzed archival data from the United States for high-threat (1978–1982) and low-threat (1983–1987) periods. Societal measures of most attitude and behavioral components of the authoritarian syndrome significantly decreased between the high-threat and the low-threat periods. These results support the threat–authoritarianism relationship but also suggest a more complicated theoretical model that links perceived social conditions, arousal of authoritarian sentiments, dispositional authoritarianism, and the nature of political appeals—particularly those that engage authoritarian aggression.

M any different lines of theory and research suggest that threat is an important antecedent of authoritarian beliefs and behaviors at both the individual and collective levels. Fromm (1941) explained the rise of fascism to be the result of threatening social and economic circumstances that increased people's sense of powerlessness and led them to "escape from freedom" and submit to authority. Lipset (1963) proposed that the higher levels of authoritarianism often observed among working class people reflect relatively higher levels of economic threat. Rokeach (1960) concluded that levels of dogmatism in Roman Catholic Church pronouncements were correlated with the degree of threat perceived by the church hierar-

chy. Studies of individuals, using the *F* scale or related measures, have implicated "threatening, traumatic, overwhelming discipline" from parents as an important factor in the development of the authoritarian personality (Adorno, Frenkel-Brunswik, Levinson, & Sanford, 1950, p. 372), although this psychoanalytic emphasis on parental influence has recently been challenged (see Altemeyer, 1988; Forbes, 1985). Finally, Sales and Friend (1973) found that experimentally induced threat of failure increased subjects' authoritarianism scores. Threat thus seems to produce similar effects on authoritarianism at both the individual and group levels.

Archival Studies of Threat and Authoritarianism

In a landmark study using archival data, Sales (1973) investigated the relationship between societal threat and the components of authoritarianism as articulated by Adorno et al. (1950). He compared social indicator measures of these components from two pairs of periods in United States history when there had been shifts from relatively low threat to much greater threat. Comparing the 1920s (a low-threat period) with the 1930s (a high-threat period) and 1959–1964 (low threat) with 1967–1970 (high threat), he found increases in most of the social indicator measures of authoritarianism. Other archival studies confirm this link (Jorgenson, 1975; McCann & Stewin, 1984, 1987, 1989; Padgett & Jorgenson, 1982; Sales, 1972).

Alternative explanations of Sales's (1973) study are possible. Because both of his low-threat periods preceded high-threat periods, perhaps the increases in threat and authoritarianism were both merely the result of population changes or other long-term secular trends or the result of improved record keeping in later time periods. A critical question, therefore, is what happens to the authoritarianism indicators when low threat follows high threat?

Furthermore, even if there is a relationship between threat and authoritarianism, does it hold across all levels of threat, including more moderate fluctuations of the business cycle and more limited foreign policy crises? Or is the authoritarian response confined to truly major, cataclysmic threats such as the Great Depression and the turmoil of the Vietnam era?

To clarify the relationship between environmental threat and societal levels of authoritarianism, we designed this study to replicate and extend Sales's (1973) study for the period 1978–1987, using the same social indicator measures of authoritarian syndrome components wherever possible, as well as some new measures. By selecting the years 1978–1987, however, we introduced two significant variations: (a) We examined a transition from high threat to low threat, whereas both of Sales's studies involved low threat to high threat and (b) we examined a period of milder threat, unlike the extreme threats used by Sales. These two variations make it possible to extend considerably the generality and precision of his findings.

Method

Identifying Periods of High and Low Threat

On the basis of the statistical indicators described below, we selected 1978–1982 as a period of high threat and 1983–1987 as a period of low threat. In making this decision, we took account of public opinion polling data as well as "objective" social and economic indicators. Although the mid-1980s were far from utopian, they were probably viewed by many Americans as a time when things were getting better, that is, when the sense of threat was diminishing.

Statistical Indicators. Sales (1973) defined *threat* to be high unemployment, low disposable income per capita, rises in the consumer price index, increased numbers of major crimes, high levels of civil disorder and work stoppages, and (less formally) increased likelihood of war or escalation of war, assassinations, and polling data about anxiety and fear (Sales, 1973, p. 51).

Data on several of these measures of societal threat for the periods 1978–1982 and 1983–1987 are presented in Table 3.1. By nearly all of Sales's objective measures, threat decreased between the first and the second period, and we saw similar trends reflected in our additional measures of the prime interest rate and the number of bombing incidents. Nevertheless, average levels of serious crimes were not significantly different between the two periods, and the unemployment rate was slightly (although not significantly) higher in 1983–1987. Note, however, that the unemployment rate had increased substantially throughout 1978–1982, rising from 5.8% in 1979 to 9.7% in 1982, and that whereas unemployment was high at the beginning of our low-threat period (9.6% in 1983), it fell to 7.5% the next year and to 6.2% by 1987. The average rate of increase of the unemployment rate was significantly higher in the high-threat period (8.9% in 1978–1982 vs. –8.2% in 1983–1987), $t(8) = 1.87$, $p < .05$, one-tailed. Thus, the changes in the unemployment rate do fit our characterization of threat levels in the two periods. Average rates of change for the other threat variables also tended to be in accord with our classification.

In summary, we found very strong support from our objective indicators for our categorization of 1978–1982 as a period of high threat and 1983–

TABLE 3.1. Indicators of Social, Economic, and Political Threat in 1978–1982 and 1983–1987

Social indicator	*M* for period of		Change		Significance	
	High threat (1978–1982)	Low threat (1983–1987)	Magnitude	Predicted direction?	*t*	*p*
Personal income[a]	9,756	10,583	827	Yes	4.22	<.005
Serious crimes[b]	12,653	12,629	−24	Yes	0.05	ns
Consumer Price Index[c]	9.78	3.32	−6.46	Yes	4.74	<.001
Work stoppages[d]	176.4	62.4	−114	Yes	4.38	<.005
Unemployment rate[e]	7.24	7.50	−0.26	No	0.29	ns
Prime interest rate[f]	14.14	9.86	−4.28	Yes	2.42	<.05
Bombing incidents[g]	972	661	−311	Yes	3.48	<.01

Note. Data in this table were taken from *Statistical Abstract of the United States*, 1989 (U.S. Bureau of the Census, 1979–1989) for personal income (Table 690), serious crimes (Table 277), Consumer Price Index (Table 749), work stoppages (Table 679), unemployment rate (Table 622, also *Statistical Abstract of the United States*, 1988, Table 607), and prime interest rate (Table 823). Data for bombing incidents were from *Sourcebook of Criminal Justice Statistics 1988* (Jamieson & Flanagan, 1989, Table 3.134). All tests of significance in this table are two-tailed.
[a]Per capita disposable income in constant 1982 dollars.
[b]Includes murder, forcible rape, robbery, aggravated assault, burglary, larceny–theft, and motor vehicle theft; number of crimes in thousands.
[c]Annual percentage change.
[d]Excludes those involving fewer than 1,000 workers or lasting less than 1 day.
[e]As percentage of labor force.
[f]Interest charged by banks, percentage per year.
[g]Actual detonations of explosive and incendiary bombs.

1987 as a period of low threat. Analysis of a composite measure of the seven indicators, in which each measure is standardized across the 10 years and then summed, yielded a highly significant difference between the two periods.

Polling Data. Further support for our choice of time periods comes from the Gallup poll results about anticipated future financial conditions (Gallup International, 1987, 1988b). Table 3.2 shows that pessimism about economic conditions

TABLE 3.2. Polling Data on Economic Outlook and Satisfaction With the United States From 1978–1987 (Per Year Average Percentage Responses)

Year	Expect financial conditions in next year to be			Attitude toward the way things are going		
	Better	Worse	Better − worse	Satisfied	Dissatisfied	Satisfied − dissatisfied
1978	41	21	20			
1979	36	29	8	19	77	−58
1980	38	28	10			
1981	43	24	19	26	69	−43
1982	40	27	13	25	72	−47
1983	43	19	24	35	59	−24
1984	52	12	40	50	44	6
1985	53	14	39	51	46	5
1986	56	17	39	57	39	18
1987	56	17	39	45	49	−4
Mean scores						
1978–1982 (high threat)	40	26	14	23	73	−50
1983–1987 (low threat)	52	16	36	48	47	1
Difference (high–low)	−12	10	−22[a]	−25	26	−51[b]

Note. Data in this table were taken from *Gallup Report* (1988c, p. 32; 1987, p. 26). Significance tests are one-tailed.
[a]*t* = 5.72, *p* < .001. [b]*t* = 5.97, *p* < .001.

was significantly higher during 1978–1982 than in the later years. Another Gallup poll series asking about more general satisfaction "with the way things are going in the U.S." also showed a clear trend of increasing satisfaction from 1979 to 1986 (Gallup International, 1987, 1988b).

Impressionistic Measures. Some indicators of societal threat do not lend themselves to quantification, yet deserve mention. The year 1979—perhaps the crest of the high-threat years—saw a near melt-down at the Three Mile Island nuclear power plant, the Soviet invasion of Afghanistan, anti-American revolutions in Nicaragua and Iran, and the seizure of the American embassy in Tehran. By January 1980, 40% of Americans believed that the United States would "become involved in a war during the next three years" ("Opinion Roundup," 1980).

Perhaps the most vivid example of the overall sense of threat was President Carter's July 1979 speech to the American people in which he spoke of an "erosion of confidence" and a "fundamental threat to American democracy" (Carter, 1980, p. 1237):

> The threat is nearly invisible in ordinary ways. It is a crisis of confidence. It is a crisis that strikes at the very heart and soul and spirit of our national will. We can see this crisis in the growing doubt about the meaning of our own lives and in the loss of unity of purpose for our nation. The erosion of our confidence in the future is threatening to destroy the social and the political fabric of America.

In retrospect, Carter's remarkable 1980 loss to the optimistic and "tough" Reagan seems to be largely the result of the threatening domestic and international conditions of the times. Although economic recession deepened in the early years of the Reagan administration, the recovery that began in 1983 was for many Americans a turning point in the transition to less threatening, more prosperous times.

COMPARISON WITH McCANN AND STEWIN'S MEASURES

Our designation of 1978–1982 and 1983–1987 as periods of high and low threat may be compared with the work of McCann and Stewin (1989), who recently developed an historical index of social, economic, and political threat (SEPT) in the United States for every year from 1920–1986 on the basis of a poll of American history professors. The average SEPT value for 1978–1982 was 3.76 and for 1983–1986 was 3.80, indicating no significant differences between the two periods. However, a summary composite measure of all 12 objective indicators used by McCann and Stewin to validate the professors' ratings showed significant differences for the two periods in accord with our prediction, $t(8) = 2.10$, $p < .05$.

Measures of Authoritarian Behavior

Following Sales's technique of exposition, we present each authoritarianism component separately, describing first our method and then our results. We then conclude with an integrated general discussion of our findings and their implications.

Measures of Level and Measures of Change. Two general points concerning the analysis of social indicators can be discussed here most conveniently. Sales (1973) analyzed differences in the average levels of indicators during the aggregated high-threat versus low-threat years but did not consider the year-to-year changes within periods or the average differences in such yearly changes between periods. We also examined trends and year-to-year fluctuations because an apparent *effect*, as indicated by significant differences in levels of an indicator, may actually be the result of long-term secular trends that are unrelated to threat. Moreover, political discourse and news media reporting often focus on change: trade and budget deficits, crime rates, inflation, and unemployment are usually discussed in relation to previous years' figures rather than in relation to absolute levels. Finally, some indicators may show changes in rates before they show changes in levels, especially because our contrasting high- and low-threat periods are contiguous and relatively brief.

LAG TIMES

Certain indicators were lagged 1 year to account for preparation and planning. As in Padgett and Jorgenson (1982), variables such as book publications and boxing matches in a given year were considered to have been conceived in the previous year; thus, books published or fights occurring in

1979 were counted as 1978 measures.

To summarize, we first looked at the average yearly levels of each indicator for the high- versus the low-threat periods. If these were significantly different (with one-tailed tests, because the direction of difference was predicted), we then checked whether the levels were higher in the early and mid-1970s than in 1978–1982, which would suggest an irrelevant long-term trend. If not, then we concluded that the significant difference in levels was an effect associated with threat. We also examined year-to-year changes in levels. If these were significantly different between periods, we concluded that there was an effect associated with threat. In this case, inertia or momentum may have kept levels high in the early part of our low-threat period, but the direction and magnitude of change reflected significant improvements during the period. In a few cases, large fluctuations (variance) kept the differences in both levels and changes from being statistically significant (given the small number of years in each group), and so we report actual yearly figures that suggest meaningful change. Because differences in both levels and changes of the indicators could be nonsignificant or even opposite to the hypothesized direction, our procedures do not capitalize excessively on chance. Rather, they attempt to rule out spurious effects and to take account of variations in societal manifestation among individual components of the authoritarian syndrome.

While we have analyzed our data in terms of the differences between two contiguous 5-year spans, we also report correlations between our composite threat index and the levels and changes of most indicators in the final summary table. These correlations give a more sensitive measure of year-to-year relationships, but at the cost of considering the differences between the grouped time spans and at the cost of considering the overall shift from high to low threat.

Threat and the Components of the Authoritarian Syndrome

Power and Toughness

To measure authoritarians' "preoccupation with the dominance-submission, strong-weak, leader-follower dimension" and "identification with power

figures" (Adorno et al., 1950, p. 256), Sales used three measures.

Dog Breeds. Sales found that the number of strong and powerful "attack" dogs (German shepherds, Doberman pinschers, and Great Danes) registered with the American Kennel Club in a given year rose significantly during a high-threat period, whereas the popularity of less powerful lapdogs (Pomeranians, Boston terriers, and Chihuahuas) decreased, a finding that is "quite consistent with the hypothesis that persons are more attracted to strength and power during times of stress" (Sales, 1973, p. 52).

According to the *World Almanac and Book of Facts* (1979–1989), a yearly average of 152,844 attack dogs was registered during the high-threat period, dropping to 113,358 in the low-threat period. On the other hand, the average number of lap dogs registered during our high-threat period was only 44,342 per year, rising to 54,758 for the low-threat period. Analysis of variance revealed a highly significant Breed × Period interaction, $F(1,16) = 28.77$, $p < .001$. A check of figures for the early 1970s indicated no consistent long-term trends among the six dog breeds. We conclude that in the 1978–1987 period, people tended to select (or at least register) dogs with a reputation for power and toughness during years of high threat and gentler breeds during times of low threat.

Boxing. Sales found that the number of heavyweight championship boxing matches rose during both his periods of high threat, and gate receipts and the number of people who box for a living showed trends in the expected direction. Using the *Information Please Sports Almanac 1990* (1989), we counted the number of world heavyweight boxing championship matches held in the U.S. during the high- and low-threat years. Lagging our data 1 year to account for time spent in the planning, training, advertisement, and promotion of the fight (i.e., fights occurring in 1979 were counted as 1978 fights), we found 21 matches during the high-threat years and 22 during years of low threat, which yields nonsignificant differences in level and year-to-year changes.

Fictional Characters. Sales coded comic strips and found that "fictional protagonists became more powerful during the threatening 1930s" (1973, p. 46). For the 1970s and 1980s, television shows seemed to be a more appropriate source of data than comic strips, and so we examined the yearly top 25 Nielsen-rated prime-time programs for 1978–1988. Capsule summaries of the programs (Brooks & Marsh, 1988) were rated for the presence or absence of characters who were "physically powerful or controlled great power" and had impact on others, such as police dramas or shows such as *Dallas* that emphasize wealth and status. This definition is similar to that of Sales's (1973, p. 46) and to the "overemphasis on the power motif in human relationships" discussed by Adorno et al. (1950, p. 237). All obvious identifying characteristics (e.g., character names or dates) were removed from each television show summary. (The first and second authors rated each plot summary with category agreement of .86; differences were resolved through discussion.) Because the television programming season begins in September and programming decisions rely on results of the previous spring's ratings, we did not use lag times. Thus, the shows in fall 1982 through spring 1983 were counted as a 1982 measure.

We counted an average of 6 "power" shows per season in our high-threat period and 6.6 shows in the low-threat period, a nonsignificant difference, $t(8) = 0.32$, $p = ns$. Analysis of the year-to-year changes, however, showed a rise in power shows (from 5 in 1978 to 10 in 1982) during the high-threat period (average increase of 0.8 per year) and

a decline (from 11 in 1983 to 3 in 1987) in the low-threat years (–1.4 per year), a trend that is just significant in the predicted direction, $t(8) = 1.64$, $p < .10$, as a replication of Sales's (1973) earlier comic strip findings. Overall, the "power and toughness" results give some support to the threat–authoritarianism hypothesis.

Cynicism

According to Adorno et al. (1950), the authoritarian character displays a "generalized hostility" and "vilification of the human" (p. 228)—in simpler words, destructiveness and cynicism. At the societal level, Sales (1973) cited previous content analysis and polling studies that showed a rise in cynicism during periods of high threat. We replicated this finding with polling data from yearly *Monitoring the Future* surveys (Bachman, Johnston, & O'Malley, 1976–1988), which showed declines in cynical attitudes toward social institutions from our high- to low-threat periods. Specifically, high school seniors were asked, "To what extent are there problems of dishonesty and immorality in the leadership of [selected institutions]?" In Table 3.3, the average responses for the classes of 1978–1982 and 1983–1987 are compared.

Significant declines occurred in cynical attitudes

TABLE 3.3. Cynicism: Survey Data on High School Seniors' Beliefs About Problems of Dishonesty and Immorality in U.S. Institutions

| Institution | Average % answering "considerable" or "great" to question[a] for classes of: | | | Significance | |
	1978–1982 (high threat)	1983–1987 (low threat)	Difference (high-low)	t	p
Large corporations	34.9	27.5	7.4	4.50	<.005
Congress	34.5	27.7	6.8	4.03	<.005
Police & law enforcement	31.5	28.6	2.9	3.68	<.005
Major labor unions	32.3	26.4	5.9	3.30	<.01
Presidency	32.2	28.5	3.7	1.87	<.05
Courts & justice system	23.5	22.7	0.8	1.58	ns
National news media	35.3	34.6	0.7	0.69	ns
Supreme court	22.0	22.1	–0.1	0.13	ns
Public schools	24.6	25.8	–1.2	1.29	ns
U.S. military	21.6	23.5	–1.9	2.15	ns
Colleges & universities	20.1	23.8	–3.7	2.58	<.05
Religious organizations	20.5	26.9	–6.4	3.97	<.01

Note. Data in this table were from the yearly *Monitoring the Future* surveys of the Institute for Social Research, University of Michigan, as reported in the *Sourcebook of Criminal Justice Statistics 1988* (U.S. Department of Justice, Bureau of Justice Statistics, 1989) Table 2.68. All tests of significance are one-tailed.
[a]The question was, "To what extent are there problems of dishonesty and immorality in the leadership of ...?"

toward 5 of the 12 institutions, with significant increases for only 2 institutions (universities and religious organizations). Whereas there is some evidence of a long-term decline in cynicism since the early 1970s, analysis of the year-to-year changes showed sharp increases in cynicism toward 4 of these 5 institutions between 1978 and 1979.

Distrust of governmental leadership also declined significantly in the low-threat period. The *Monitoring the Future* survey (Bachman et al., 1976–1988) also asked, "Do you think some of the people running the government are crooked or dishonest?" In 1978–1982, a yearly average of 13.1% replied, "Most of them are," but in 1983–1987, only an average of 9.5% made the reply, $t(8)$ = 3.30, $p < .01$. A sharp increase in distrust from 1977 to 1979 and 1980 suggests that this effect is not part of a long-term trend. The American National Election Study (Miller, 1978–1986) polls of the general population further support this threat–cynicism relationship. Responses to the question, "How much of the time can you trust the government in Washington to do what is right?" increased from an average of 30% "always" or "most of the time" in 1978–1982 years to an average of 42% in 1984–1986, $t(8) = 3.35$, $p < .05$.

Superstition

According to Adorno et al. (1950), people scoring high on the F scale believe in "mystical or fantastic external determinants of the individual's fate" and shift responsibility from within themselves onto uncontrollable outside forces (p. 236). As Sales (1973) did, we measured superstition by counting the number of astrology books and magazine articles written during high-and low-threat periods, allowing a 1-year time lag for publication delays for books but not magazine articles. On average, 23.4 astrology books were listed in the *Cumulative Book Index* (1975–1988) during each year of the high-threat period, versus 26 for the low-threat years, a nonsignificant difference, $t(8) = 0.50, p = ns$. Analysis of year-to-year changes also showed no differences between periods, $t(8)$ = 0.60.

Thus, we did not replicate Sales's results with astrology publications. One explanation may involve the New Age subculture of the 1980s, involving such things as crystals, holistic medicine, meditation, and astrological paraphernalia. In one sense they may be superstitious, yet New Age lifestyles seem more consistent with nonauthoritarian, postmaterialist values (see Inglehart, 1990) than with the classic authoritarian character.

Some polling data, however, do support the threat–astrology relationship. A *Gallup Report* (Gallup International, 1988a) found that the percentage of the public reporting belief in astrology fell from 29% in 1978 to 12% in 1988, whereas the number responding "don't believe" increased from 64% to 80% over the same period. Although the exact number of interviewees for the 1978 sample was not available, we assumed $Ns = 1,204$ (the sample size for the May 1988 poll) for both polls, which yields a highly significant decline in the belief in astrology, $c^2(1, N = 2,408) = 84.9$, $p < .001$.

Authoritarian Submission

The authoritarian personality displays an uncritical "exaggerated, all-out emotional need to submit" to "idealized moral authorities of the ingroup" (Adorno et al., 1950, pp. 228 and 231–232) because of a failure to develop an internal conscience or as a way of handling ambivalent feelings toward authority figures. At the societal level, Sales (1973) pointed to an increase in laws requiring loyalty oaths for schoolteachers during the threatening 1930s and to an increase in the circulation of the conservative periodical *Christian Beacon* in the late 1960s as indicative of "submission to the norms of the ingroup" (p. 53).

During 1978–1987, loyalty oaths were not an issue, and *Christian Beacon* circulation figures, gleaned from statements printed in the *Beacon*, were quite unstable. However, the conservative Moral Majority, an organization advocating submission to "divine" authority, did increase in popularity during the late 1970s and played a role in the victories of strongly right-wing candidates in the 1980 election. Thereafter, its influence ultimately declined, and in 1986 it changed its name to the *Liberty Federation*.

Censorship may also reflect submission to moral authorities. Information from the National Commission on Libraries and Information Science (1986) for the years 1975–1985 showed increases in the number of attempts at removing offensive materials in public and school libraries from 1979

(16 incidents) to 1982 (a peak of 57 incidents). The levels were rather stable at a lower level for the first part of the low-threat period (36 incidents in 1983 and 1984 and 39 in 1985). For the years 1986 and 1987, our own count of censorship attempts mentioned in issues of the *Newsletter on Intellectual Freedom* (American Library Association, 1986–1987) produced slight further declines to 35 and 26 incidents, respectively. Whereas the average levels of censorship attempts were not significantly different between high- and low-threat periods (32.2 vs. 34.4 incidents per year), $t(8) = 0.31$, $p = ns$, the average year-to-year changes showed a marginally significant trend in support of our hypothesis (average increase of 6.4 incidents in high-threat years vs. average decrease of 6.2 incidents in low-threat years, $t(8) = 1.76$, $p < .10$.

Anti-Intraception

Following Adorno et al. (1950), Sales reasoned that the "authoritarian individual is opposed to intraception and particularly to psychotherapy and psychiatry" (1973, p. 48). He found comparatively fewer popular magazine articles and books about psychoanalysis and psychotherapy published during the first, but not the second, high-threat period, and the number of undergraduate majors in psychology (presumably an intraceptive discipline) increased during the high-threat period of the late 1960s.

Assuming a 1-year lag, we found that average yearly *Cumulative Book Index* (1975–1988) listings of psychotherapy and psychoanalysis books increased from 55.6 during the high-threat years 1978–1982 to 74.4 books during the low-threat years 1983–1987, a significant difference in accord with our prediction, $t(8) = 2.13$, $p < .05$. Because the average number of books on these topics written during 1975–1977 was higher than in 1978–1982, there seems to have been no long-term upward trend.

Yearly average *Reader's Guide to Periodical Literature* (1978–1988) listings of popular magazine articles concerned with psychotherapy and psychoanalysis were 14.4 and 12.4 per year during the high- and low-threat eras, respectively, a nonsignificant difference, $t(8) = 0.61$. The difference in yearly changes was in accord with our hypothesis, although not significantly so (average yearly drop of 3.8 articles per year vs. average yearly gain of 0.6 articles during low threat), $t(8) = 1.21$.

These publication results only partly confirm our hypothesis. We may ask whether psychoanalysis and especially psychotherapy publications are always intraceptive. To develop a more accurate indicator, we analyzed trends in divisional membership in the American Psychological Association (APA), grouping Divisions 12 (clinical), 17 (counseling), 29 (psychotherapy), and 32 (humanistic) as intraceptive and Divisions 3 (experimental), 6 (physiological and comparative), 25 (experimental analysis of behavior), and 21 (applied experimental and engineering) as nonintraceptive. According to the *APA Membership Register* (APA, 1979–1987) and *Directory of the APA* (APA, 1978–1988), membership in the intraceptive divisions rose from a yearly mean of 12,295 during the high-threat years to 13,436 during the low-threat years. Membership in the nonintraceptive divisions, however, declined slightly from an average of 4,209 in the high-threat years to 4,183 during the low-threat years. A two-way analysis of variance with type of division and threat level as factors yielded a highly significant Division × Threat Level interaction, $F(1, 16) = 20.71$, $p < .001$, in support of our hypothesis. (Of course, long-term changes in the structure of the APA itself may somehow have contaminated this analysis.)

Authoritarian Aggression

Adorno et al. considered authoritarian aggression to be "the sadistic component of authoritarianism" concerned with the "desire to condemn, reject, and punish those who violate [conventional] values" (1950, p. 232). During periods of high social threat, therefore, one would expect greater aggression against outgroup members. Sales found relatively greater levels of state and local government expenditures for police departments (as compared with fire departments) during high-threat periods, as well as increased support for capital punishment during the 1967–1970 high-threat period.

Our replication produced mixed results. From the *Statistical Abstract of the United States* (U.S. Bureau of the Census, 1979–1989), we obtained the percentage of total budgets of state and local governments that was devoted to police and fire departments. There were no clear comparative differences in levels or trends evident for 1978–1982 versus 1983–1987. What about public support for capital punishment? There has been a long-term upward trend in support for the death penalty for murder, from 57% in 1972 to 79% in 1988 (*Gallup Report*, 1989, p. 29). In 1978 and 1981, an average of 64% favored and 26% opposed the death penalty, rising to an average 71% favoring and 21% opposing it in 1985 and 1986. The number of persons sentenced to death and the actual executions of prisoners also increased from our high- to low-threat periods (U.S. Bureau of the Census, 1979–1989). Thus, all of our results suggest a continuing long-term increase in punitive attitudes and behavior, with little or no inflection during times of low threat.

Sex

Sentences for Rape. The "concern with sexual goings on" component of the authoritarian syndrome presents some measurement problems. Citing the "concern with overt sexuality" and "willingness to punish severely [any] violation of sexual norms" identified by the original authoritarianism researchers, Sales measured "punitiveness toward sexual criminals" (1973, pp. 49–50) by comparing the average length of sentence for persons convicted of rape (as reflecting judicial and indirectly reflecting societal punitiveness toward sexual criminals) with average sentences for voluntary manslaughter (as a control for punitiveness toward crime in general).

Since the time of Sales's research, however, the influence of the women's movement (in particular Brownmiller's, 1975, landmark argument) has changed popular and judicial views of rape in ways that may now make Sales's measure invalid. First of all, rape is now more often understood to be a crime of violence rather than a crime of sex. Second, rape is more widely understood to be a serious crime that should be reported (by the victim), prosecuted (by law enforcement agencies), and punished (by the judicial system), rather than an unimportant offense brought on in part by the victim herself. These changes are arguably the result of increased feminist consciousness rather than increased authoritarianism, but the newer views might well have the same effect, increasing average sentences for rape.

With these differences in mind, we attempted to replicate Sales's measure by using yearly data from Michigan Department of Corrections records (1978–1988) on the distribution of minimum terms for first-degree criminal sexual conduct and (as a control) for manslaughter, grouped into the two categories of *5 years or less* and *longer than 5 years*. Results were in the direction opposite to those of Sales. Minimum sentences for first-degree criminal sexual conduct were significantly longer during the low-threat years than during the high-threat years (75% of 1,080 cases for 1983–1987 for longer than 5 years vs. 62% of 854 cases for 1978–1982, $t(8) = 3.91, p < .01$, whereas there was only a nonsignificant increase in length of sentence for manslaughter (48% of minimum sentences longer than 5 years for 1983–1987 vs. 43% for 1978–1982), $t(8) = 1.32, p = ns$.

Violent Pornography. Another aspect of sexuality that may engage authoritarian sentiments is the fusion of sex and aggression in violent pornography. Working from Rimmer's (1986) description of X-rated videotapes, Donovan, Stires, and Morrett (1988) coded the incidence of violence (that is, sex fused with violence, defined as "sadistic, violent and victimized sex," p. 2) in pornographic videotapes produced from 1967 through 1985. Using these figures, we found that during the high-threat years of 1978–1982, an average of 15.1% of all X-rated videotapes contained violent sex, whereas in the later low-threat years of 1983–1985, this yearly average dropped significantly to 4.7%, $t(8) = 2.16, p < .05$. (Consistent with this result is Slade's, 1984, pp. 159–161, estimate of higher levels of violence in pornographic films during Sales's two high-threat periods.) We conclude, therefore, that levels of societal threat are related to the incidence of themes of violent sexuality, at least in fantasy materials.

On the basis of these results, we suggest a slight alteration in our understanding of the part that sex plays in the authoritarian syndrome. For the authoritarian, sexuality is related to aggression (and perhaps vice versa). At the level of overt behavior, this cluster of impulses may be projected onto the offender, but at the level of fantasy it may be indulged. Sexuality itself is then seen as violent and aggressive; and punishment, as a "return of the repressed," takes on sexual overtones.

Conventionalism

Conventionalism, the "rigid adherence to conventional, middle-class values" (Adorno et al., 1950), is difficult to measure directly. Drawing on voting statistics, we developed a related measure of politico-economic conservatism, which is arguably one component of conventionalism. To avoid confounding by presidential charisma and the staggered Senate election cycle, we examined House of Representatives election returns (*World Almanac and Book of Facts*, 1972–1990) for 1978 (when threat levels were on the upswing) and 1986 (when threat levels had greatly receded). Did the higher and increasing threat of 1978 induce greater support for conservative candidates, compared with the low-threat election of 1986? In 1978, the Democrats won 277 seats in the House of Representatives, as compared with 258 in 1986, which argues against our hypothesis. However, these crude totals are affected by extraneous factors such as the "coattails" effect, incumbency, and differences in the candidates themselves. Moreover, party labels are not a very reliable guide to liberal-versus-conservative ideology. To control for these factors, we considered only cases in which the same incumbent stood for reelection in both 1978 and 1986. We chose incumbents from the two extremes of the ideological spectrum on the basis of overall ratings (from 1978–1986) by the liberal Americans for Democratic Action (ADA), the conservative Americans for Constitutional Action (ACA), and the American Conservative Union (ACU; Barone & Ujifusa, 1981, 1983–1987). Our final sample included the 30 most conservative (having the highest ACA or ACU minus ADA rating) and the 30 most liberal (having the highest ADA minus ACA or ACU rating) incumbent House candidates. From the election data reported in the same sources, we calculated the percentage margin of victory over the principal opponent in both 1978 and 1986 and then calculated the change in this margin between the two elections.

Conservative incumbents suffered an average loss of 2.4 percentage points (from an average 37.7% victory margin in 1978 to 35.3% in 1986), whereas liberals gained an average of 7.8 percentage points (from an average 39% victory margin in 1978 to 46.8% in 1986). The difference between these average changes in electoral margins—liberal gains and conservative losses—was significant, $t(58) = 2.33$, $p < .05$. Thus, incumbents who espoused conservative (and thus, arguably, conventional) values lost some appeal from high- to low-threat periods, whereas liberal incumbents who challenged conventionalism gained significantly with the transition. This pattern supports the hypothesized threat–authoritarianism relationship.

Prejudice

Beyond the replication of Sales's findings, we sought additional measures to track those components of the authoritarian personality he did not measure. For example, prejudice most thoroughly reflects the "tendency to be on the lookout for, and to condemn, reject, and punish people who violate [conventional] values" (Adorno et al., 1950, p. 228) and reflects other authoritarianism components such as stereotypy, destructiveness, and aggression as well. Indeed, anti-Semitic prejudice was the original impetus to the development of the *F* scale and has been among its most durable correlates.

ANTI-SEMITIC INCIDENTS

Because anti-Semitic ideology is such a basic element of the authoritarian syndrome, we used data published by the Anti-Defamation League of B'nai B'rith (1978–1988) on anti-Semitic incidents (such as vandalism of synagogues and painting of Nazi slogans and swastikas on Jewish property) for each year between 1978 and 1987. The data in Table 3.4 show a tremendous rise for each year 1978–1981, to a peak of 974 incidents, with some decline in later years. The difference between the average levels in high-threat years 1978–1982 (472 incidents) and low-threat years 1983–1987 (662 incidents) was not significant, $t(8) = 1.02$, $p = ns$, in part because of the enormous standard deviation ($SD = 414$) for the first time period. Analysis of the average yearly changes, however, did offer some support for our hypotheses: an average yearly increase of 157 incidents in the high-threat period, compared with an average yearly decrease of 27 incidents during the low-threat period. Although this difference was not quite significant, $t(8) = 1.36$, $p = .11$, it became so when expressed in percentage terms (average change of 102% in 1978–1982 vs. -2.7% in 1983–1987), $t(8) = 2.38$, $p < .05$. Thus, whereas authoritarian aggression and prejudice toward Jews were high in the threatening 1979–1981 years and remained high thereafter, there was some moderation during the low-threat period.

TABLE 3.4. Prejudice: Anti-Semitic Incidents of Vandalism, 1978–1987

Year	Incidents	Change from previous year	% change from previous year
1978	49	4[a]	8.9
1979	129	80	163.3
1980	377	248	192.2
1981	974	597	158.4
1982	829	−145	−14.9
1983	670	−159	−19.2
1984	715	45	6.7
1985	638	−77	−10.8
1986	594	−44	−6.9
1987	694	100	16.8
Mean 1978–1982 (high threat)	471.6	156.8	101.6
Mean 1983–1987 (low threat)	662.2	−27	−5.7
Difference (high-low)	−190.6	183.8	107.3
Significance	$t = 1.02$, $p = ns$	$t = 1.36$, $p = ns$	$t = 2.38$, $p < .05$

Note. Data in this table were from the annual *Audit of Anti-Semitic Incidents* of the Anti-Defamation League of B'nai Brith (1978–1988). Vandalism includes actual and attempted bombings and arson, cemetery desecrations, swastika daubings, and anti-Jewish graffiti. Tests of significance are one-tailed.
[a]Based on a reported average of 45 incidents per year for 1962–1977.

KU KLUX KLAN ACTIVITY

Because the Ku Klux Klan is an organization devoted to ethnic and racial hatred, we also predicted that Klan activity would rise during the high-threat years and then decline during times of lower threat. No direct statistics on Klan membership were available, but we counted the number of newspaper articles listed under *Ku Klux Klan* in the *New York Times Index* for each year from 1975–1988. By this indirect measure, Klan activity and impact produced a yearly average of 54.8 articles for 1978–1982, but only 15.4 for 1983–1987, $t(8) = 2.26$, $p < .05$, a significant difference in accord with our predictions. Much of this difference is attributable to the 1979 political killings by Klan members in Greensboro, North Carolina, and their subsequent trial, although such a blatant display of violence is scarcely an extraneous "contamination," but rather a striking instance of prejudice and aggression that (as predicted) occurred during a period of high societal threat. We found a yearly average of only 17 articles for the period 1975–1977 in the *New York Times Index* under the topic *Ku Klux Klan*, suggesting there was no general downward trend in reports on Klan activity.

SURVEY DATA ON PREJUDICE

One final measure of prejudice involved surveys of American high school seniors. Four items from the annual *Monitoring the Future* (Bachman, Johnston, & O'Malley, 1976–1988) surveys involve feelings about friendships and experiences with members of other races. The questions and average responses for the high- and low-threat periods are reproduced in Table 3.5. These data indicate that racial prejudice among high school students decreased significantly in the less threatening years. Although responses from 1975–1977 were higher than those of 1978–1982, there was no clear downward trend.

General Discussion

A summary of our findings and a comparison of them with Sales's original results are presented in Table 3.6 in terms of differences of levels or changes between the aggregated high- and low-threat years. The right-hand column also gives the correlation, across the 10 years, of each variable with the composite *threat index* made up of the seven independent variables of Table 3.1. As discussed at the end of the Method section, these correlations are an alternative test of the threat–authoritarianism hypothesis, although they ignore the overall shift from an era of high threat to an era of low threat.

Overall, our results confirm Fromm's (1941) original theory linking threat and authoritarianism.

TABLE 3.5. Prejudice: Survey Data on High School Seniors' Feelings About Friendships and Experiences With Members of Other Races

Question	Average % responding in "prejudiced" manner to question[a]		Difference (high-low)	Significance	
	1978–1982 (high threat)	1983–1987 (low threat)		t	p
Having close personal friends of another race?[b]	10.14	8.00	2.14	6.96	<.001
Having some of your (future) children's friends be of other races?[b]	12.90	11.46	1.44	3.56	<.005
Experiences you have had with people of other races?[a,c]	3.86	3.10	.76	4.66	<.005
How often do you do things with people of other races?[d]	11.74	9.56	2.18	2.50	<.05

Note. Data in this table were obtained from *Monitoring the Future* (Bachman, Johnston, & O'Malley, 1976–1988). Tests of significance are one-tailed.
[a]The first three questions were: "How would you feel about …?"
[b]Percentage responding "not at all acceptable" or "somewhat acceptable."
[c]Percentage responding "mostly bad" or "very bad."
[d]Percentage responding "not at all."

Thirteen out of 20 measures show significant differences (or near-significant trends) in levels or rates of change, far more than would be expected by chance. We found some supporting evidence for every authoritarianism component except authoritarian aggression. On the other hand, our results are not a strong confirmation of the particular measures used by Sales (1973): Only 4 of the 11 measures based on (or adapted from) his study showed significant or near-significant differences. Why were Sales's measures less effective? In some cases, the social context and meaning of the measure has changed, as for sentences for rape and perhaps for interest in boxing and astrology. In other cases, such as police budgets and support for the death penalty, factors other than authoritarianism, such as actual crime rates, municipal labor agreements, or political persuasion, may exert effects on the measures, perhaps maintaining them at high levels. For these reasons of changing historical context and effects of other variables, then, isolated individual measures are likely to have limited historical generality. The researcher's task is to identify and construct measures that may be functionally equivalent across time and social change. We believe that we have done so in the present case, so that even though our results offer only limited confirmation of Sales's measures, they offer substantial confirmation of his general theory.

Yet the present study is much more than a mere replication of Sales's methodology applied to recent times. Our modifications and extension shed light on more subtle interactions among the components of the authoritarian syndrome and their unique associations with changing societal conditions. Whereas both of Sales's studies analyzed the transition from periods of low threat to periods of high threat and found increases in levels of authoritarian behavior, our study examined the reverse sequence and found decreases in authoritarian attitudes and behavior. This strengthens the argument in favor of a causal link between societal threat and authoritarianism by helping to rule out the possibility that societal measures of authoritarianism simply increase over time because of expanding population, economic growth, or other secular trends unrelated to threat levels. Furthermore, we examined time periods that were shorter and also less extreme than those used by Sales.

What about our negative results? Some of them may be due to continuing mild levels of threat in 1983–1987. Although our threat indicators reversed their trends between 1982 and 1983, the differences were not always sharply defined. Unemployment continued to be quite high in 1983, and the prime interest rate was above 10% until 1985. Most important, perhaps, were the continuing high levels of crime, increasing again after 1984. A more detailed analysis of the interactions among the separate threat variables and the separate authoritarianism indicators might reveal additional, complex relationships. For example, does economic threat differ from threats of war and terrorist violence abroad or crime at home? How do

TABLE 3.6. Summary of Findings and Comparison With Sales's Study

| Component and measure | Type of difference | Significantly related to threat levels? | | | Year-by-year correlation with threat index |
		Present study: 1978–1982 vs. 1983–1987	Sales 1:[a] 1920s vs. 1930s	Sales 2: 1959–1964 vs. 1967–1970	
Power and toughness					
Interest in boxing	Levels	ns	Yes	Trend	−.27
	Change	ns			.16
Dog registrations[b]	Levels	Yes	−	Yes	.81**
Fictional characters	Levels	ns	Yes[c]	−	.04
	Change	Trend			.64*
Cynicism					
Polls of students		Yes	−	Yes[d]	
Polls of general public		Yes	−	−	
Superstition					
Astrology books	Levels	ns	Yes	Yes	−.31
Astrology articles	Levels	ns	Trend	Yes	−.42
Polls of general public		Yes	−	−	
Authoritarian submission—					
censorship incidents	Levels	ns	−	−	−.04
	Change	Trend			.55*
Anti-intraception					
Psychoanalysis books	Levels	Yes	Yes	Yes	−.66*
Psychoanalysis articles	Levels	ns	Yes	ns	−.10
APA division membership[e]	Levels	Yes	−	−	−.87**
Authoritarian aggression					
Police budgets		ns	Yes	Yes	−.72
Support for death penalty		No	−	Yes	
Sex					
Sentences for sex offenders		No	Yes	Yes	−.60
Violent pornography	Levels	Yes	−	−	.36
Conventionalism—					
congressional victory margins		Yes	−	−	
Prejudice					
Anti-Semitic incidents	Levels	ns	−	−	−.11
	Change	Yes			.80**
Ku Klux Klan activity	Levels	Yes	−	−	.80**
Polls on racial prejudice		Yes	−	−	

Note. Table reflects one-tailed tests of significance; *no* indicates results were significantly opposite to the predicted direction.
[a]Results from Sales, 1973. Dash indicates Sales did not use the measure.
[b]Standardized attack versus lapdog registrations.
[c]Sales analyzed comic strips: we examined television programs.
[d]Sales cited polls of college students; our surveys involved high school seniors.
[e]Standardized intraceptive vs. nonintraceptive division membership.
*$p < .05$.
**$p < .01$.

emerging threats such as the AIDS epidemic, global warming, or toxic waste contamination of the environment affect authoritarian beliefs and behaviors? Are tangible, personal experiences of threat or abstract impressions of threat dramatized by the media more important in arousing authoritarianism? What factors in society contribute to maintaining high levels of some authoritarian behaviors despite declines in actual threat?

Authoritarian Aggression: A Ratchet?

The variables that most clearly ran counter to our predictions were those involving authoritarian aggression. Why? Perhaps authoritarian aggression, once aroused by threat, remains at a high level in spite of a decline in the overall level of societal threat. Such a ratchet effect might involve differential reactions by two distinct groups of people. Perhaps aggression and punitiveness on the part of more authoritarian people (dispositional authoritarians) may be more easily tolerated or condoned by the less authoritarian general population during high-threat periods. The extremist organization and activity of dispositional authoritarians, evoked and encouraged during threatening times, may continue at high levels even after the societal threat recedes, whereas the nonauthoritarian majority adjust their beliefs and behavior in accord with diminishing perceptions of threat.

In contrast to the dispositional authoritarians, then, mildly authoritarian and nonauthoritarian people may put on and take off aggression according to the climate of threat. During high-threat times they buy powerful dogs; they become more cynical, more anti-intraceptive, and perhaps more superstitious; they embrace more conventional values, and so forth; but as threat diminishes, they return to their customary outlooks and behavior. They are, in short, "situational authoritarians" in response to threat. Signs of an enduring punitiveness toward criminals are an exception even to this generalization, however. Perhaps the appointments of more conservative federal judges is a legacy or ratchet of the conservative political victories of 1980, yet we must also account for the growth in support of capital punishment among the general public. This punitiveness toward a criminal outgroup may be maintained in part by prominent and graphic portrayals of crime in the news and entertainment media and the repeated emphasis on the threat of crime in the political appeals by candidates for public office. Whereas the lessening of economic and foreign policy threats may moderate the general authoritarian tendencies of the nation, the threat of crime seems to remain high, thereby eliciting high levels of specifically anticriminal authoritarian aggression in the American people.

Political Leaders and Political Climate

More generally, how does the political process, including the time lag between an election and the implementation of the agenda of a newly elected administration, interact with the perception of threat and society's expression of authoritarianism? There seems to be little doubt that the Reagan landslide of 1980 was given impetus by perceptions of high threat, when Reagan's image as being tough on crime, the Soviet "Evil Empire," and the Iranian hostage takers appealed to a nation eager for strong authority. Perhaps the mere election of this perceived strong leader—someone who would reduce threat—reduced the sense of threat among situational authoritarians, while at the same time fueling the energies of dispositional authoritarians.

By 1984, threat was lower. Compared with his platform in 1980, Reagan's reelection appeal sounded a different trumpet, that is, his success in returning the nation to less threatening and more prosperous times, in contrast to an earlier emphasis on the failures of the past and the perils of the present. Thus, in his second inaugural speech in January 1985, Reagan's (1988) tone became distinctly nonauthoritarian:

> With heart and hand, let us stand as one today . . . to be heroes who heal our sick, feed the hungry, protect peace among nations, and leave the world a better place.

Did Reagan and his advisers also change substantive policies along the specific lines suggested by decreased threat and lower authoritarian sentiments during his second term? This question could be explored through a detailed study of policy changes and pronouncements by the administration, guided by the overall theory of authoritarianism and the results of the present study.

Needed Future Research

Integrating the study of individuals with the study of social processes is essential for obtaining comprehensive, useful theories of human behavior. We have applied the model of Adorno et al.'s (1950) authoritarian personality to the nation as a whole, but it would also be valuable to consider intermediate-sized groups such as states, cities, and even smaller communities. At finer levels of analysis, we might better isolate antecedent conditions of threat and more accurately measure associated levels of authoritarianism. We could also begin to separate the authoritarianism components of different types of threat (economic, crime, foreign affairs, terrorism, racial violence, etc.), as well as determine whether the relationships reported in this article vary as a function of people's race, class, gender, or other demographic groups. If threats continue to be with us, then there is a continuing need for an increased understanding of the authoritarian syndrome in all its manifestations.

REFERENCES

Adorno, T. W., Frenkel-Brunswik, E., Levinson, D. J., & Sanford, R. N. (1950). *The authoritarian personality*. New York: Harper.

Altemeyer, B. (1988). *Enemies of freedom*. San Francisco: Jossey-Bass.

American Library Association. (1986–1987). *Newsletter on intellectual freedom*. Chicago: Author.

American Psychological Association. (1979–1987). *APA membership register*. Washington, DC: Author.

American Psychological Association. (1978–1988). *Directory of the APA*. Washington, DC: Author.

Anti-Defamation League of B'nai B'rith. (1978–1988). *Audit of anti-Semitic incidents*. New York: Author.

Bachman, J. G., Johnston, L. D., & O'Malley, P. M. (1976–1988). *Monitoring the future*. Ann Arbor, MI: Institute for Social Research.

Barone, M., & Ujifusa, G. (1981). *Almanac of American politics 1982*. Washington, DC: Barone & Company.

Barone, M., & Ujifusa, G. (1983–1987). *Almanac of American politics (1984–1988)*. Washington: National Journal.

Brooks, T., & Marsh, E. (1988). *The complete directory of prime time network TV shows*. New York: Ballantine.

Brownmiller, S. (1975). *Against our will: Men, women, and rape*. New York: Simon & Schuster.

Carter, J. (1980). Energy and national goals, address to the nation, July 15, 1979. In *Jimmy Carter: 1979* (Public papers of the presidents of the United States, pp. 1235–1241). Washington, DC: U.S. Government Printing Office.

Cumulative book index. (1975–1988). New York: Wilson.

Donovan, R. L., Stires, L. K., & Morrett, D. C. (1988, April). *Has violent pornography increased?* Paper presented at the Eastern Psychological Association convention, Buffalo, NY.

Forbes, H. A. (1985). *Nationalism, ethnocentrism, and personality*. Chicago: University of Chicago Press.

Fromm, E. (1941). *Escape from freedom*. New York: Holt, Rinehart & Winston.

Gallup International. (1987). Satisfaction: Public mood shows no sign of brightening. In *Gallup Report* (No. 266, pp. 25–27). Princeton, NJ: Author.

Gallup International. (1988a). Nancy Reagan and astrology: Confidence in president, first lady shaken by astrology controversy. In *Gallup Report* (No. 272, pp. 2–7). Princeton, NJ: Author.

Gallup International. (1988b). The economy: Consumer optimism rises sharply; unsurpassed in Reagan's tenure. In *Gallup Report* (No. 272, pp. 25–29). Princeton, NJ: Author.

Gallup International. (1988c). The economy: Consumer outlook is brightest in 12-year Gallup trend. In *Gallup Report* (No. 277, pp. 28–32). Princeton, NJ: Author.

Gallup International. (1989). Death penalty: Public support for death penalty is highest in Gallup annuals. In *Gallup Report* (No. 280, pp. 27–29). Princeton, NJ: Author.

Information please sports almanac 1990. (1989). Boston: Houghton Mifflin.

Inglehart, R. (1990). *Culture shift in advanced industrial society*. Princeton, NJ: Princeton University Press.

Jamieson, K. M., & Flanagan, T. J. (Eds.). (1989). *Sourcebook of criminal justice statistics 1988*. U.S. Department of Justice, Bureau of Justice Statistics. Washington, DC: U.S. Government Printing Office.

Jorgenson, D. O. (1975). Economic threat and authoritarianism in television programs: 1950–1974. *Psychological Reports, 37*, 1153–1154.

Lipset, S. M. (1963). *Political man*. New York: Anchor Books.

McCann, S. J. H., & Stewin, L. L. (1984). Environmental threat and parapsychological contributions to the psychological literature. *Journal of Social Psychology, 122*, 227–235.

McCann, S. J. H., & Stewin, L. L. (1987). Threat, authoritarianism, and the power of U.S. presidents. *Journal of Psychology, 121*, 149–157.

McCann, S. J. H., & Stewin, L. L. (1989, August). *"Good" and "bad" years: An index of American social, economic, and political threat (SEPT) 1920–1986*. Paper presented at the annual meeting of the American Psychological Association, New Orleans, LA.

Michigan Department of Corrections. (1978–1988). *Statistical presentation*. Lansing, MI: Michigan Department of Corrections, Bureau of Administrative Services, Data Processing Division.

Miller, W. E. (1978–1986). *American national election study, 1978–1986* [Machine-readable data file]. Ann Arbor: University of Michigan, Center for Political Studies.

National Commission on Libraries and Information Science. (1986). *Censorship activities in public and public school libraries, 1975–1985: A report to the Senate subcommittee on appropriations for the Departments of Labor, Health and Human Services, and Education and related agencies*. Washington, DC: Author. (ERIC Document Reproduction Service No. ED 270 125)

New York Times index. (1975–1988). New York: New York Times Co. Opinion roundup: The international cauldron. (1980). *Public Opinion, 3*(2), 21.

Padgett, V. R., & Jorgenson, D. O. (1982). Superstition and economic threat: Germany, 1918–1940. *Personality and Social Psychology Bulletin, 8*, 736–741.

Reader's guide to periodical literature. (1978–1988). New York: Wilson.

Reagan, R. W. (1988). Inaugural address, January 21, 1985. In *Ronald Reagan: 1985* (Public papers of the presidents of the United States, pp. 55–58). Washington, DC: Government Printing Office.

Rimmer, R. H. (1986). *The X-rated videotape guide*. New York: Harmony Books.

Rokeach, M. (1960). *The open and closed mind*. New York: Basic Books.

Sales, S. M. (1972). Economic threat as a determinant of conversion rates to authoritarian and nonauthoritarian churches. *Journal of Personality and Social Psychology, 23*, 420–428.

Sales, S. M. (1973). Threat as a factor in authoritarianism: An analysis of archival data. *Journal of Personality and Social Psychology, 28*, 44–57.

Sales, S. M., & Friend, K. E. (1973). Success and failure as determinants of level of authoritarianism. *Behavioral Science, 18,* 163–172.

Sharp, J. M. (1988). *The directory of congressional voting scores and interest group ratings.* New York: Facts on File.

Slade, J. W. (1984). Violence in the hard-core pornographic film: A historical survey. *Journal of Communication, 34,* 148–163.

State of Michigan. (1981). *State of Michigan compiled laws 1979.* Lansing, MI: Michigan Legislative Council.

U.S. Bureau of the Census. (1979–1989). *Statistical abstract of the United States (1981–1989).* Washington, DC: U. S. Government Printing Office.

U.S. Department of Justice, Bureau of Justice Statistics. (1989). *Sourcebook of criminal justice statistics 1988.* Washington, DC: U.S. Government Printing Office.

World almanac and book of facts. (1972–1990). New York: Newspaper Enterprise Association.

The Other "Authoritarian Personality"

Bob Altemeyer • University of Manitoba, Winnipeg, Canada

Pull up from your memories those haunting, spectacular scenes of the Nuremberg rallies. A huge crowd of ardent Nazis fills the stadium on Party Day, while on the podium Adolf Hitler feasts on their adoration. "To see the films of the Nuremberg rallies even today is to be recaptured by the hypnotic effect of thousands of men marching in perfect order. The music of the massed bands, the forest of standards and flags . . . the sense of power, of force, of unity was irresistible" (Bullock 1962, p. 379).

A decade after all that power, force, and unity awed the world, the worst war in history and a Holocaust later, many of the Nazi leaders stood trial in Nuremberg for crimes against humanity. As the world learned of the horrors ravaged upon Europe by the Third Reich, people trying to grasp the barbarity and the millions of deaths asked, "Why?"

A psychoanalyst, Erich Fromm (1941), had already given an answer. He argued that the Nazi regime arose from a sickness in the German people. The leaders on the podium at the Nuremberg rallies and the vast crowds of faithful followers before them allegedly manifested the two faces of the sadistic–masochistic personality. This one illness drove both groups, Fromm proposed, locking them into a dominance–submissive authoritarian embrace.

This explanation and psychoanalytic theory in general helped shape the famous "Berkeley" research program on authoritarianism (Adorno, Frenkel-Brunswik, Levinson, & Sanford, 1950).

While Sanford and his team did not include an "authoritarian *domination*" trait in their model of the prefascist personality to complement the "authoritarian submission" trait that *did* appear, it is clear from several items on the Fascism Scale that the research team thought the authoritarian personality would both submit *and* dominate. Adorno's still-cited metaphor of the bicycle rider who bows from the waist up and kicks from the waist down sums it up (if you overlook the fact that one does not kick at anything when pedaling a bicycle).

I. The Submissive Personality

But a funny thing happened to research on authoritarianism after 1950. It almost never studied domination, but instead focused on the many people in our society who seem ready to submit to a Hitler. This focus makes sense in that wanna-be tyrants in a democracy are just comical figures on soapboxes when they have no following. So the real fascist threat lay coiled in parts of the population itself, it was thought, ready someday to catapult the next Hitler to power with their votes. So investigators studied the submitters.

Research has since painted a fairly clear picture of those most vulnerable to the appeal of "a man on horseback." As measured by the Right-Wing Authoritarianism (RWA) scale (Altemeyer, 1981, 1988, 1996; see Exhibit 1 for the latest version), right-wing authoritarians believe strongly in submission to established authorities and the social norms these authorities endorse. They also believe in aggressing against whomever these authorities target. This personality structure, observable by early adulthood and better explained by social learning than by psychoanalytic theory, is thought to develop during adolescence from earlier training in obedience, conventionalism, and aggression, as modified by the individual's subsequent experiences.

Adult authoritarians tend to be highly ethnocentric and heavy users of the "consensual validation pill" (Newcomb, 1961). They travel in tight circles of like-minded people so much, they often think their views are commonly held in society, that they are the "Moral Majority" or the "Silent Majority." It has been hard to miss the evidence

that certain kinds of religious training have sometimes helped produce their ethnocentrism and authoritarianism.

High RWAs' thinking, based more on memorization of what authorities have told them than on independent, critical appraisal, tends to be unintegrated, highly compartmentalized, and rife with inconsistencies. Authoritarians harbor many double standards and hypocrisies—seemingly without realizing it—which lead them to "speak out of both sides of their mouths" from one situation to another. For example, they will proclaim their patriotism and love of democracy at the drop of a hat. But they also seem ready to chuck most of the Bill of Rights, and no matter how many times they say the Pledge of Allegiance, they never seem to notice its coda, "with liberty and justice for all."

EXHIBIT 1. The 1997 Right-Wing Authoritarianism Scale

This survey is part of an investigation of general public opinion concerning a variety of social issues. You will probably find that you *agree* with some of the statements, and *disagree* with others, to varying extents. Please indicate your reaction to each statement by blackening a bubble on the bubble sheet, according to the following scale:

Blacken the bubble labeled   −4 if you *very strongly disagree* with the statement.
                             −3 if you *strongly disagree* with the statement.
                             −2 if you *moderately disagree* with the statement.
                             −1 if you *slightly disagree* with the statement.
Blacken the bubble labeled   +1 if you *slightly agree* with the statement.
                             +2 if you *moderately agree* with the statement.
                             +3 if you *strongly agree* with the statement.
                             +4 if you *very strongly agree* with the statement.

If you feel exactly and precisely *neutral* about an item, blacken the "0" bubble.

You may find that you sometimes have different reactions to different parts of a statement. For example, you might very strongly disagree (-4) with one idea in a statement, but slightly agree (+1) with another idea in the same item. When this happens, please combine your reactions, and write down how you feel "on balance" (i.e., a -3 in this case).

1. The established authorities generally turn out to be right about things, while the radicals and protectors are usually just "loud mouths" showing off their ignorance.
2. Women should have to promise to obey their husbands when they get married.
3. Our country desperately needs a mighty leader who will do what has to be done to destroy the radical new ways and sinfulness that are ruining us.
4. Gays and lesbians are just as healthy and moral as anybody else.*
5. It is always better to trust the judgment of the proper authorities in government and religion than to listen to the noisy rabble-rousers in our society who are trying to create doubt in people's minds.
6. Atheists and others who have rebelled against the established religions are no doubt every bit as good and virtuous as those who attend church regularly.*

7. The only way our country can get through the crisis ahead is to get back to our traditional values, put some tough leaders in power, and silence the troublemakers spreading bad ideas.
8. There is absolutely nothing wrong with nudist camps.*
9. Our country *needs* free thinkers who will have the courage to defy traditional ways, even if this upsets many people.*
10. Our country will be destroyed someday if we do not smash the perversions eating away at our moral fiber and traditional beliefs.
11. Everyone should have their own lifestyle, religious beliefs, and sexual preferences, even if it makes them different from everyone else.*
12. The "old-fashioned ways" and "old-fashioned values" still show the best way to live.
13. You have to admire those who challenged the law and

the majority's view by protesting for women's abortion rights, for animal rights, or to abolish school prayer.*

14. What our country really needs is a strong, determined leader who will crush evil, and take us back to our true path.

15. Some of the best people in our country are those who are challenging our government, criticizing religion, and ignoring the "normal way things are supposed to be done."*

16. God's laws about abortion, pornography, and marriage must be strictly followed before it is too late, and those who break them must be strongly punished.

17. It would be best for everyone if the proper authorities censored magazines so that people could not get their hands on trashy and disgusting material.

18. There is nothing wrong with premarital sexual intercourse.*

19. Our country will be great if we honor the ways of our forefathers, do what the authorities tell us to do, and get rid of the "rotten apples" who are ruining everything.

20. There is no "ONE right way" to live life; everybody has to create their *own* way.*

21. Homosexuals and feminists should be praised for being brave enough to defy "traditional family values."*

22. This country would work a lot better if certain groups of troublemakers would just shut up and accept their group's traditional place in society.

23. There are many radical, immoral people in our country today, who are trying to ruin it for their own godless purposes, whom the authorities should put out of action.

24. People should pay less attention to the Bible and the other old forms of religious guidance, and instead develop their own personal standards of what is moral and immoral.*

25. What our country needs *most* is discipline, with everyone following our leaders in unity.

26. It's better to have trashy magazines and radical pamphlets in our communities than to let the government have the power to censor them.*

27. The facts on crime, sexual immorality, and the recent public disorders all show we have to crack down harder on deviant groups and troublemakers if we are going to save our moral standards and preserve law and order.

28. A lot of our rules regarding modesty and sexual behavior are just customs which are not necessarily any better or holier than those which other people follow.*

29. The situation in our country is getting so serious, the strongest methods would be justified if they eliminated the troublemakers and got us back to our true path.

30. A "woman's place" should be wherever she wants to be. The days when women are submissive to their husbands and social conventions belong strictly in the past.*

31. It is wonderful that young people today have greater freedom to protest against things they don't like, and to make their own "rules" to govern their behavior.*

32. Once our government leaders give us the "go ahead," it will be the duty of every patriotic citizen to help stomp out the rot that is poisoning our country from within.

Note. Only items 3–32 are scored. Items 1 and 2 are "table-setters" to help familiarize the respondent with the subject matter and the –4 to +4 response format.

*indicates a con-trait item, for which the 1–9 scoring key is reversed.

Right-wing authoritarians also have plenty of "kick" in them. They are hostile toward so many minorities, they seem to be equal opportunity bigots. But they do not usually realize they are relatively ethnocentric. Nor do they want to find out. They will often say that if they score highly on a measure of prejudice, they do not want to learn they did.

High RWAs kick in other directions, too. When asked to play judge and pass sentence on convicted criminals, they tend to lower the boom, just as they deliver more powerful shocks when serving as a teacher in a mini-Milgram experiment. They are relatively ready to help the government persecute almost any group you can think of—including themselves! Furthermore, Walker and Quinsey (1991) and Walker, Rowe, and Quinsey (1993) found that High RWA males were more likely to have sexually assaulted women.

One can hypothesize many psychological roots of right-wing authoritarian aggression. But two factors have been blessed more than others by experiments. First, high RWAs are scared. They see the world as a dangerous place, as society teeters on the brink of self-destruction from evil and violence. This fear appears to *instigate* aggression in them. Second, right-wing authoritarians tend to be highly self-righteous. They think themselves much more moral and upstanding than others—a self-perception considerably aided by self-deception, their religious training, and some very efficient guilt evaporators (such as going to confession). This self-righteousness *disinhibits* their aggressive impulses, and releases them to act out their fear-induced hostilities as "God's Designated Hitters."

When I call right-wing authoritarians *right-wing* authoritarians, I am using the phrase in a social psychological sense based on their submission to the perceived established authorities in society. But it turns out the phrase applies in its economic/political contexts, too. High RWAs tend to hold "conservative" economic attitudes, and they tend to be concentrated on the political "right." In fact, studies of most of the legislatures in Canada and nearly all the state legislatures in the United States have found that Canadian Conservative/Canadian Reform/Republican politicians, like their supporters in the voting booths, zoom higher on the RWA Scale than Canadian New Democrats/Canadian Liberals/Democrats do.

High RWA lawmakers also score higher in prejudice, and wish they could pass laws limiting freedom of speech, freedom of the press, the right of assembly, and other freedoms guaranteed in the Bill of Rights. They want to impose strict limitations on abortion, they favor capital punishment, and they oppose tougher gun control laws. Finally, politicians answer the RWA Scale with such extraordinary levels of internal consistency, it appears the scale provides our most powerful measure of the liberal–conservative dimension in politics.

II. The Dominant Personality

Like the Fascism Scale before it, the RWA Scale contains items that both submissive *and* dominant persons could endorse: for example, "It is always better to trust the judgment of the proper authorities in government. . . ." So we cannot be surprised that some lawmakers—not at all submissive individuals, one imagines—concur with such views; after all, they are "proper authorities in government." But the RWA Scale has never been a good measure of authoritarian dominance; it was constructed more to capture the psychology of the submissive crowd. The trouble is, nothing else has provided a good measure of such dominance either.

Enter Felicia Pratto and Jim Sidanius. Pratto, Sidanius, Stallworth, and Malle (1994) created the Social Dominance Orientation (SDO) scale (Exhibit 2) to tap "a general attitudinal orientation toward intergroup relations, reflecting whether one generally prefers such relations to be equal, versus hierarchical" (p. 742). Carefully developed over 12 student studies, the SDO scale was built to tap something different from both authoritarianism *and* interpersonal dominance. Accordingly, the SDO and RWA scales correlated only .14 in the one sample that answered both (not statistically significant with 95 *df*). SDO scores also rendered *r*s less than .25, usually nonsignificant, with the Dominance scales from both the California Personality Inventory (Gough, 1987) and the Jackson Personality Research Form (Jackson, 1965).

On the other hand, the test rang up some very impressive correlations (usually over .50) with measures of nationalism, patriotism, cultural elitism, a rejection of noblesse oblige, and anti-Black racism. Connections with other relevant attitudes (e.g., social policies regarding the poor, racial policies, women's rights, support of the Gulf War, support of capital punishment, and various measures of political–economic conservatism) proved almost as high.

Thanks to the energy of its inventors, the SDO scale has already been used in many studies. In particular, SDO relationships with ethnic preju-

---

EXHIBIT 2. The Fourteen-Item Social Dominance Orientation (SDO) Scale

1. Some groups of people are simply not the equals of others.
2. Some people are just more worthy than others.
3. This country would be better off if we cared less about how equal all people were.
4. Some people are just more deserving than others.
5. It is not a problem if some people have more of a chance in life than others.
6. Some people are just inferior to others.
7. To get ahead in life, it is sometimes necessary to step on others.
8. Increased economic equality.*
9. Increased social equality.*
10. Equality.*
11. If people were treated more equally we would have fewer problems in this country.*

12. In an ideal world, all nations would be equal.*
13. We should try to treat one another as equals as much as possible. (All humans should be treated equally.)*
14. It is important that we treat other countries as equals.*

Notes. * indicates a con-trait item, for which the scoring key is reversed. In my studies I intermixed the pro-trait and con-trait items. I also used, as Items 1 and 2 "table-setters," two statements from Pratto et al.'s (1994) item pool that were eventually dropped: "As a country's wealth increases, more of its resources should be channeled to the poor," and "This country would be better off if inferior groups stayed in their place."

The items are reprinted with permission of the American Psychological Association.

dice, sexism, militarism, punitiveness, and conservatism usually appeared as predicted when the scale was tested in Canada, China, Israel, Mexico, New Zealand, and Taiwan (Pratto, Liu, Levin, Sidanius, Shih, & Bachrach, 1996). In another study, persons riding commuter trains were cleverly involved in an experiment that confirmed student-based findings that people would hire High SDOs for positions that serve the interests of privileged groups, and Low SDOs for jobs that serve oppressed groups. Independently of this, subjects also tended to hire men for the "hierarchy-enhancing" roles, and shunted women into hierarchy-diminishing positions (Pratto, Stallworth, Sidanius, & Siers, 1997). Many studies have found that men score higher than women on the SDO scale in almost every culture tested thus far.

Because Felicia Pratto shared some of her preliminary results with me, I quickly discovered that the SDO scale dominated the RWA Scale when it came to explaining prejudice. In a March 1993 study involving 187 undergraduates at my school, RWA correlated .48 with answers to the Manitoba Ethnocentrism scale—a 20-item instrument measuring hostility toward aboriginals, Arabs, Asians, Blacks, Francophones, Jews, and so on, that I con-

sider my best measure of general prejudice among "white" Manitobans (Exhibit 3). But an early 18-item version of the SDO scale banged out an eye-popping .71 with the sum of such prejudices! RWA and SDO correlated .38. Put in my place and impressed—if not stunned—I never considered what the two scales could do *together*.

A. The McFarland and Adelson (1996) Study

Enter Sam McFarland and Sherman Adelson, who employed 438 Kentucky students and 283 nonstudent adults in a grand pitting experiment featuring 22 different psychological measures. Three of these assessed prejudice against Blacks, women, and homosexuals, and a fourth scale tapped patriotic attitudes. Abbreviated versions of 18 personality tests that had shown some connection with prejudice, including the RWA and SDO scales, composed the rest of the longish booklet. The researchers wanted to see how much of the "target" prejudice/patriotism scores could be explained by these personality tests.

EXHIBIT 3. The 1997 Manitoba Ethnocentrism Scale

1. If we don't watch out, Asians will control our economy and we'll be the "coolies."
2. We should take in more refugees fleeing political persecution by repressive governments.*
3. Arabs are too emotional, and they don't fit in well in our country.
4. If Sikhs who join the RCMP want to wear turbans instead of the usual hat, that's fine.*
5. It is good to live in a country where there ae so many minority groups present, such as Blacks, Asians, and aboriginals.*
6. There are entirely too many people from the wrong sorts of places being admitted into Canada now.
7. "Foreign" religions like Buddhism, Hinduism, and Islam are just as good as Christianity, all things considered.*
8. As a group aboriginal people are naturally lazy, dishonest, and lawless.
9. The more we let people from all over the world into our country, the better.*
10. Black people are, by their nature, more violent and "primitive" than others.
11. Jews can be trusted as much as everyone else.*
12. The people from India who have recently come to Canada

have mainly brought disease, ignorance, and crime with them.
13. Every person we let in from overseas means either another Canadian won't be able to find a job, or another foreigner will go on welfare here.
14. Canada should guarantee that French language rights exist across the country.*
15. It is a waste of time to train certain races for good jobs; they simply don't have the drive and determination it takes to learn a complicated skill.
16. Canada has much to fear from the Japanese, who are as cruel as they are ambitious.
17. There is nothing wrong with intermarriage among the races.*
18. Aboriginal people should keep protesting and demonstrating until they get just treatment in Canada.*
19. Many minorities are spoiled; if they really wanted to improve their lives, they would get jobs and get off welfare.
20. It is a sad fact that many minorities have been persecuted in our country, and some are still treated very unfairly.*

*Note.** indicates a con-trait item, for which the scoring key is reversed.

The results which could have been quite gnarly proved utterly simple in both samples. SDO scores correlated about .50 with McFarland and Adelson's index of overall prejudice, while RWA answers notched a .47. The two tests barely interconnected (.21 and .07), so when you plunked them into a regression analysis, they explained different segments of overall prejudice and served up a multiple r of .64 in each sample. *None of the other personality tests mattered much once these two scales had their say.* In fact, gender entered the equation next among the students, ahead of all the remaining scales (with males being more prejudiced than females).

B. The September 1996 Manitoba Student Study

Fascinated, I quickly involved 354 Manitoba introductory psychology students in a two-session experiment during which they answered the full versions of most of the tests McFarland and Adelson had used, plus a few others. In the first session the booklet began with a Religious Fundamentalism scale (Altemeyer & Hunsberger, 1992), followed by the 1996 version of the RWA scale and the SDO measure. Then Rubin and Peplau's (1973) Just World scale appeared, and all 56 of the items in Schwartz's (1992) measure of "value types." Schaller, Boyd, Yohannes, and O'Brien's (1995) Need for Structure scale followed, then Rosenberg's (1965) Self-Esteem instrument. Eysenck and Eysenck's (1976) Psychoticism measure ended the booklet. With instructions, it took most students 50–60 minutes to answer all these tests.

The second booklet, completed two days later, began with a survey of environmental attitudes unrelated to our concerns here. Then students answered a revision of my Dangerous World Scale and my measure of self-righteousness (Altemeyer, 1988, pp. 195–196, 157–160). Luhtanen and Crocker's (1992) Collective Self-Esteem instrument followed, as did Fletcher, Danilovacs, Fernandez, Peterson, and Reeder's (1986) Attributional Complexity scale. Then came the four target variables: McFarland's measures of prejudice against homosexuals, Blacks, and women, and his patriotism scale. The 1996 Manitoba Ethnocentrism scale (Altemeyer, 1996,

pp. 24–25) and homegrown measures of attitudes toward aboriginals and Quebec followed these, to test for further relevance. Srole's (1956) Anomie scale and a demographic survey ended the booklet. With minimal need for instructions, it took most students 40–50 minutes to answer this booklet.

All of the tests were answered on a -4 to +4 basis except the value type scales, which solicited 0 to 9 responses, and the self-righteousness measure, which requested 0 to 6 replies. The students, identified only by a "secret number" of their own choosing, served in groups of about 150 in a lecture hall during an afternoon 75-minute slot in the university timetable. As usual, the students answered virtually everything. The largest data loss occurred with the Psychoticism Scale, which two participants failed to complete.

Results

Table 4.1 presents the psychometric properties of the measures used, and the relationships of central interest. Most of the scales posted good interitem correlations, the exceptions being the Just World and Psychoticism scales, and the target measure of patriotism. Reliability alphas, which reflect the length of a test as well as its internal consistency, bounced about quite a bit.

As for explaining prejudice with personality measures, the results strongly replicated McFarland and Adelson's findings. The SDO scores had the best overall relationships with the four target measures, leaving the RWA scale some distance behind. A regression analysis of the sum of Sam McFarland's four tests ("Sum of Sam"), after standardizing the scores to control for unequal means and variances, found that SDO and RWA *as a package* accounted for 50% of overall prejudice. (That is, their multiple r equaled .71.) Subject's sex came in third, with males again showing more prejudice than females. Gender raised the multiple r to .76. The remaining scales could add only pennies to this accounting.

If you broaden the basis for generalization by adding the standardized Ethnocentrism, Aboriginal, and Quebec scores to the targets, and drop Patriotism with its questionable validity in this sample, you get the same results for the "Sum of Six." First came SDO, then RWA. Their multiple r of .70 again explained most of the reliable variance. Gender boosted the coefficient to .75.

TABLE 4.1. Results of the September 1996 Study

Scales	Psychometric properties			Prejudice toward				"Sum of Sam"	"Sum of Six"	Corr. with social dom.	Corr. with RWA
	No. of items	Mean inter-item corr.	Alpha	Homosex.	Blacks	Women	Patriotism				
Social Dominance Orientation	14	.29	.84	.42	.52	.49	.28	.59	.59	—	.22
Right-Wing Authoritarianism	30	.29	.92	.61	.30	.38	.14	.51	.49	.22	—
Just World	16	.08	.59	-.05	-.07	-.08	.07	-.03	-.03	-.02	.12
Need for Structure	12	.31	.84	.11	.09	-.01	.04	.10	.10	.06	.34
Self-Esteem	10	.37	.84	.04	-.05	.07	.07	.05	.08	.07	.01
Psychoticism	25	.10	.72	.28	.35	.43	.03	.38	.38	.34	-.01
Collective Self-Esteem	16	.29	.86	-.07	-.20	-.17	.12	-.12	-.14	-.08	.04
Attributional Complexity	28	.26	.91	-.23	-.27	-.31	-.17	-.33	-.31	-.19	-.17
Value:											
Conformity	4	.42	.74	.08	.02	-.04	.02	.03	.04	.00	.40
Security	7	.23	.66	-.04	.00	-.11	.14	-.01	.03	.02	.17
Power	5	.44	.80	.22	.26	.21	.29	.34	.33	.43	.09
Achievement	6	.37	.77	-.08	.00	-.08	.07	-.03	-.03	.00	.01
Hedonism	2	.48	.64	-.11	.07	-.01	.21	.06	.07	.17	-.25
Stimulation	3	.48	.73	.00	.06	.06	.10	.07	.09	.10	-.09
Self-Direction	6	.32	.73	-.28	-.09	-.18	-.06	-.21	-.19	-.13	-.27
Universalism	8	.32	.79	-.35	-.17	-.32	-.16	-.34	-.33	-.31	-.17
Benevolence	7	.42	.83	-.10	-.10	-.21	-.10	-.18	-.17	-.20	.19
Traditionalism	5	.35	.72	.16	.15	.05	-.02	.13	.12	.04	.51
Spirituality	4	.26	.56	.04	-.02	-.01	-.12	-.02	-.02	-.08	.26
Religious Fundamentalism	20	.35	.92	.44	.18	.22	-.04	.28	.26	.04	.77
Dangerous World	14	.29	.85	.24	.08	.03	-.05	.10	.17	.00	.49
Self-Righteousness	8	.46	.87	.47	.19	.23	.11	.34	.34	.13	.63
Anomie	5	.24	.60	.15	.22	.09	-.06	.13	.21	.01	.20
Subject's Sex	—	—	—	.42	.24	.54	.10	.45	.45	.29	.09
Prejudice toward Homosexuals	10	.62	.94							.42	.61
Blacks	8	.29	.74							.52	.30
Women	8	.42	.85							.49	.38
Patriotism	10	.15	.63							.28	.14
Ethnocentrism	20	.33	.90							.58	.30
Attitudes toward Aboriginals	20	.42	.94							.45	.28
Attitudes toward Quebec	14	.28	.85							.19	.20

Notes. "Sum of Sam" = sum of standardized scores on Prejudice toward Homosexuals, Blacks, Women, and Patriotism scales. "Sum of Six" = sum of standardized scores on Prejudice toward Homosexuals, Blacks, Women, Ethnocentrism, Aboriginals, and Quebec scales. Subject's sex was coded 0 = female, 1 = male.

The implications of McFarland and Adelson's discovery, should it reappear in other populations and with other measures, overpower one. For if you want to explain the many kinds of prejudice exposed in this situation, *they are largely matters of personality. And only two kinds of personality are basically involved*: the social dominator and the right-wing authoritarian.

C. Who Are the High Social Dominators?

I shared these results with the directly interested parties, and then tried to figure out who high Social Dominators *are*. One hypothesis, for which you have been primed, leapt to mind. When you think of the persons who have most advocated inequality between groups, to the point of genocide, whom do you think of first? The figures on the podium at Nuremberg, right? Go back to Exhibit 2, and answer the SDO scale as you imagine Hitler would have. Just about SDO to the max, right?

Keeping this prototype in mind, does it not seem probable that high SDOs would also be high in *interpersonal* dominance? True, Pratto et al. (1994) found no SDO connections with dominance scales from two personality omnibuses. But one of the items on the SDO scale ("To get ahead in life, it is sometimes necessary to step on others") suggests that interpersonal dominance *is* involved.

You get more than a suggestion if you look at the SDO correlations with the other personality measures in Table 4.1. Note the .43 coefficient with valuing Power—assessed by such items as "SOCIAL POWER (control over others, dominance)" and "AUTHORITY (the right to lead and command)." In turn, the .34 correlation with the nebulous Psychoticism Scale was mostly based on SDO connections with such items as "Would you like other people to be afraid of you?" and "Do you enjoy practical jokes that can sometimes really hurt people?"

"Compare and Contrast . . ."

We shall go galloping down these trails later, but first let us stand social dominators and authoritarians side by side and size them up. Besides having in common uncommon levels of prejudice, High SDOs also resemble High RWAs in being politically conservative. The students in this study who favored the Reform Party of Canada averaged 48.0 on the Social Dominance Scale, and those who supported the Conservatives had a mean of 43.9, while the Liberal and NDP enthusiasts averaged 39.2 and 40.0, respectively.

[Similar findings with social dominance were obtained in two 1994 studies of Canadian legislators using statements from Pratto et al.'s (1994) initial SDO pool. Tory members of the Alberta legislature scored significantly higher than Liberals ($r = .47$), and Reform Party members of the federal parliament showed a significantly darker "SDO streak" than NDP members ($r = .50$), with Liberal lawmakers in between.]

Their similarities in prejudice and political conservatism aside, however, you can see from Table 4.1 that social dominators and right-wing authoritarians hardly resemble peas in a pod. Most notably, high SDOs are not particularly religious, but high RWAs usually are. Similarly, high scorers on the SDO scale do not claim to be benevolent, but high RWAs do. In contrast, social dominators have a wisp of hedonism about them, but authoritarians disavow such. The former do not need structure nor value conformity and traditions, but the latter do. Social dominators tend to be men; right-wing authoritarians do not. And quite strikingly, high SDOs do not see the world being nearly as dangerous as authoritarians do, nor do they appear to be nearly as self-righteous—implying their prejudice does not have the same psychological roots that previous studies have unearthed in right-wing authoritarians.

Which is not to say the two traits are completely unrelated. Their correlation of .22 in this study easily reached statistical significance; three times as many High RWAs (33) as Lows (11) (i.e., the top and bottom quartiles of the RWA distribution) placed in the top quartile on the SDO scale. Still, *most* social dominators do not belong to the "RWA Club." Why not? When you examine their answers to the RWA scale, you find they liked items that flashed some hostility (e.g., Nos. 14, 23, 29, and 32 in Exhibit 1), and they were turned off by statements advocating tolerance (e.g., Nos. 4, 8, and 11). But otherwise they did not answer the test distinctively. So, unlike high *RWAs*, high SDOs do not particularly endorse kowtowing to authorities, nor do they show marked degrees of conventionalism. Therefore, SDO–RWA correlations will usually be weak.

D. The October 1996 Student Study

With these findings in hand, I administered another set of surveys under "secret number" conditions to 116 more Manitoba students. The booklet began with the Religious Fundamentalism scale, then the RWA and SDO measures. My Attitudes toward Homosexuals, and Economic Philosophy (Exhibit 4) scales followed. Then students encountered the 1996 Manitoba Ethnocentrism scale, a Religious Emphasis (while growing up) measure, my Parental Anger (while young) scale, and a question about how often they had been physically punished as youngsters. Some items probing for a hypothesized drive for personal power, meanness, and domination, and a demographic survey ended my inquiries.

Results

First of all, the key findings from the earlier studies held a reunion. SDO and RWA correlated only .08, but both predicted ethnocentrism (.55 and .27, respectively) and hostility toward homosexuals (.28 and .70). Together they explained 56% of the variance of the sum of standardized scores from these two prejudice scales, with RWA taking the lead because of its strong relationship with attitudes toward homosexuals. (This is not surprising, as it mentions homosexuals in several items, whereas the SDO scale piles up its correlations without naming any particular group.) Social dominance orientation did not correlate with religious fundamentalism (−.04) nor with emphasis placed on religion while growing up (−.17), but RWA did, .65 and .58. Once again, social dominance cropped up more among guys (.30), but authoritarianism did not (.11).

Past studies have shown that introductory

EXHIBIT 4. The Economic Philosophy Scale

1. Anything that government agencies can do, private enterprise can do better because competition has made it much more efficient.
2. Labor unions should be encouraged. They have established the rights of workers and raised their standard of living in a way that the whole country has benefitted.*
3. Governments should run a debt when necessary to create jobs and protect our social programs.*
4. The more government interferes with private enterprise and tries to regulate it, the worse things will get in our country.
5. The government should intervene in our economy to produce greater equality for disadvantaged groups in our country.*
6. Public agencies should be run like businesses: no waste, no "bleeding hearts," and no deficits.
7. There should be *higher* taxes on businesses in this country.*
8. Governments should sell all their operations ("privatize") that businesses want to run.
9. The wealth of our country should be spread out much more evenly; right now, too much is owned by too few.*
10. Governments should be forced by law to have balanced budgets. Otherwise they just throw money away on worthless causes.
11. Government-created jobs are usually "do nothing" jobs that cost the taxpayers millions.
12. People who say we should run governments the way businesses are run forget how many companies fail. The private sector makes as many mistakes as public officials do.*
13. The best way to solve the government's deficit problem is to cut back on our expensive social programs, which spend money as if it grows on trees.
14. We should run governments, as always, as public institutions, not like businesses. Governments have to be fair, merciful, and concerned with everyone's welfare.*
15. Only business can create wealth. Governments just spend what others have earned.
16. If we let private enterprise take over ("privatize") lots of government programs, the poor and the public will be the big losers. Companies do not care about the public good.*
17. People should be willing to pay higher taxes to protect our medical programs, education, and the unemployed.*
18. Labor unions only hold us back, making us less efficient.
19. "Do-gooders" must stop trying to increase equality in our country by making governments interfere with the natural forces of the economy. Such attempts are doomed to failure.
20. Government agencies can do many jobs better than private enterprise can.*

Notes. * indicates a con-trait item, for which the scoring key is reversed. Whenever possible I begin the scale with the following "table-setters": "Public agencies only mess things up when they get involved in the economy, and spend money like drunken sailors," and "Balanced budget laws will greatly hurt the economy. There are situations when it is wise for the government to run a deficit."

psychology students do not usually have well-organized economic opinions. In this instance responses to the Economic Philosophy items intercorrelated only .12 on the average, producing a meager alpha of .73. Economic Philosophy scores still fetched rs of .42 with SDO and .22 with RWA, .45 with ethnocentrism and .20 with hostility toward homosexuals. Item analyses revealed these relationships sprung mostly from those who favored the business sector, privatization, and balanced budgets, while disliking labor unions, social programs, and a more even distribution of wealth.

My searches for a "personal power, meanness, and dominance" drive in High SDOs hit pay dirt here and there. Social dominance correlated significantly if modestly (.21 to .43), which is usual for single-item assessments, with relatively affirmative answers to "Would you be mean and revengeful, it that's what it took to reach your goals?," "Do money, wealth, and luxuries mean a lot to you?," "Do you enjoy having the power to hurt people when they anger or disappoint you?," "Winning is not the first thing; it's the *only* thing," and "Do you enjoy taking charge of things and making people do things your way?" Social dominators were also relatively likely to say *no* to "Would you like to be a kind and helpful person to those in need?"

The efforts to find childhood antecedents of a social dominance orientation proved less successful. Students responded to the question about physical punishment by checking one of seven categories running from "Never" to "Practically every day." The median response was "Three, four, or five times," and SDO scores proved unrelated to these answers. High SDOs also did not seem to have had angrier parents than low SDOs did (−.06). [High *RWAs* also did not report having been physically punished a lot, nor having especially angry parents (.07).]

E. The October 1995 Parent Study

I had, with no foresight whatsoever, done an earlier study on the issues now before us by including the SDO scale in a booklet answered anonymously by 501 parents of Manitoba students in the fall of 1995. This booklet also contained the RWA scale and two measures of prejudice, the Manitoba Ethnocentrism scale and Spence and Helmreich's (1978) Attitudes toward Women scale. Social dominance correlated .61 and .47 with these, compared with authoritarianism's .45 and .55. SDO and RWA interconnected .28, and together they explained 58% of the variance of the sum of the standardized prejudice scores.

Some small demographic relationships appeared. As usual, men racked up higher SDO scores than women did ($r = .22$), but no such difference appeared with the RWA scale (.00). The age of the parents proved unrelated to either variable. But (for the upteenth time) RWA scores came in significantly higher among the less educated (−.25) and poorer (−.21) parents. SDO had no relationship with education or income. Finally, high RWAs (for the zillionth time) went to church more than most (.35); high SDOs did not (−.13).

F. The October 1996 Parent Study

1. Booklet A

I was ready to do some heavy comparisons of social dominators with right-wing authoritarians when I sent questionnaires to the parents of about 400 introductory psychology students in October 1996. Half the homes got a booklet, to be answered anonymously, featuring measures of authoritarian aggression. It began with the RWA, SDO, and Economic Philosophy scales. Then the Left-Wing Authoritarianism Scale appeared. This test measures submission to *revolutionary* authorities dedicated to overthrowing "the Establishment," aggression in their name, and adherence to the conventions of such a movement. The Attitudes toward Homosexuals and my Posse-after-Radicals measures followed. Then came the Ethnocentrism scale, at the end of which the respondent was asked to estimate (on a −4 to +4 basis) how prejudiced he or she would turn out to be compared with the other parents answering the booklet. I then poked and probed with more personal power, meanness, and dominance items, and asked for reactions to a letter to the editor that urged the repeal of Canada's Charter of Rights and Freedoms because "it gives rights to everyone" including pornographers, criminals, and abortionists (Altemeyer, 1996, p. 20). Next, the parents were asked what sentences they would impose on criminals convicted of spitting on a premier, of muggings, and of heroin dealing. Burt's (1980) Rape Myth Acceptance Scale and a demographic survey ended the booklet.

Results. The SDO and RWA scores of the 239 parents who answered Booklet A correlated .50 and .41, respectively, with ethnocentrism, and .41 and .57 with hostility toward homosexuals. Interconnecting .17, they accounted for 51% of the variance of the combined standardized prejudice scores. As in earlier studies, High RWAs did not think they would prove more prejudiced than others (r = .02). But high SDOs, to some extent, knew they *would* (.28).

What about the other measures? Social dominance and authoritarianism correlated .20 and .35 with willingness to help persecute "radicals," .12 and .32 with sentences handed out in the Trials situation, .24 and .32 with acceptance of myths about rape, and .20 and .57 with willingness to repeal Canada's Bill of Rights. While all these pointed in the expected direction, the RWA relationships emerged significantly stronger in all cases except Rape Myth. Let's put that in the back of our minds for a moment, along with the relationships with the remaining variables in this questionnaire, and go on to the second booklet.

2. Booklet B

Answered by 243 parents, Booklet B began with the Religious Fundamentalism, RWA, SDO, Eco-nomic Philosophy, and Left-Wing Authoritarianism Scales. Next came an anti-Semitic "Militia" scale, which I developed after the Oklahoma City bombing (Exhibit 5). I tried out some other personal power, meanness, and domination items. Then I presented four situations in which High RWAs had shown double standards in the past: abuse of power during an election by a left-wing or a right-wing provincial government (Altemeyer, 1981, p. 323), Quebec's right to leave Canada versus Montreal's right to leave a seceding Quebec, sentencing a prohomosexual or an antihomosexual activist who led an attack upon opponent demonstrators, and sentencing either a panhandler or an accountant who attacked the other after a sidewalk argument. (Accordingly, two versions of Booklet B were distributed to homes. In one, parents judged the seriousness of a conservative government abusing its power, Quebec's right to leave Canada, an antihomosexual who led an attack on homosexuals, and a panhandler who attacked an accountant; in the other version of Booklet B parents judged the opposite cases.) The booklet ended with the Religious Emphasis scale and the question about being physically punished while growing up. A demographic survey wrapped up the task.

Results. Mean responses to the 12 Militia items indicated these parents put little stock overall in the premise of a Jewish-led conspiracy in the federal government to take away everyone's guns and impose a left-wing dictatorship on the country. But

---

EXHIBIT 5. The Militia Attitudes Scale

1. Highly placed people in the national government are planning to impose a Communist-type dictatorship soon.
2. The federal government is *NOT* plotting to destroy freedom in our country.*
3. Our country is basically controlled by Jewish-owned financial institutions.
4. If people knew the truth, they'd know that Jews are causing most of the corruption and suffering in our country.
5. The federal government is *NOT* taking away our rights, nor is it conspiring to destroy democracy in our country.*
6. There is an international Jewish conspiracy that is trying to dominate the world through control of banks, the news media, the movie industry, and so on.
7. It is ridiculous to think that some group of Jews or anyone else is planning on selling our country out to the United Nations or some mythical "world conspiracy."*

8. Jews are not trying to take over the world. That is simply a myth spread by bigots to make people fear and hate Jews.*
9. Our national government has been taken over by homosexuals, radical feminists, atheistic Communist-types, and, especially, by Jews.
10. Our country is a much better place because of the Jews who live in it.*
11. Powerful elements of our government, led by Jews, want to take all the guns and spirit from the people so they can enslave us.
12. We have more freedom than almost anybody else on earth, and no group of Jews or feminists or "left-wingers" is plotting to take it away from us.*

Note. * indicates a con-trait item, for which the scoring key is reversed.

some people believed this, and responses to the items in Exhibit 5 intercorrelated .39 on the average, producing an alpha = .88. The "believers" slightly tended to be males (.11) with low income (−.22). Religious fundamentalists were also disposed to accept the premise (.29). But the strongest relationships loomed with social dominance orientation (.31), *right*-wing authoritarianism (.43), and especially *left*-wing authoritarianism (.62). (We shall make sense of this seeming contradiction in a bit.)

As for the four double-standard situations, neither high RWAs nor high SDOs showed significant inconsistency in the abuse-of-political-power scenario—a failure to replicate for the RWA Scale. Both high and low RWA parents thought Montreal had more of a right to secede from a breakaway Quebec than Quebec had to secede from Canada; but the double standard erupted larger among high RWAs (a replication of previous results). Both low and high *Social Dominators* showed the same double standard regarding secession, but equally and *less* than that found in the high RWAs. Right-wing authoritarians displayed the predictable double standard in sentencing a homosexual instigator versus an antihomosexual one in the attack over gay rights. But high SDOs harbored no such double standard. Finally, high RWAs also sentenced the panhandler to a longer prison term than they did an accountant found guilty of the same crime. But high SDOs did not.

The correlations with religious variables reinforced previous findings. Right-wing authoritarians tended to come from strong religious backgrounds (.45), and they were quite inclined toward religious fundamentalism (.71). But the same comparisons for Social Dominance Orientation equaled .08 and .18.

These parents reported having been physically punished slightly more as children than the students in the October 1996 study did. But neither High RWA nor High SDO parents were seemingly spanked or otherwise struck more than others.

3. Scales Present on Both Booklets

SDO and RWA scores correlated .18 over all 482 respondents. Economic attitudes proved better organized among parents than among students (an old finding), the average intercorrelation of .21 producing an alpha of .84. Holding conservative economic opinions correlated .18 with RWA and .43 with SDO scale scores (and .34 with ethnocentrism and .29 with hostility toward homosexuals in Booklet A). Left-wing authoritarianism had associations of .17 and .11, respectively, with RWA and SDO. High RWAs went to church more than low RWAs did (.37); SDO scores proved unconnected (−.07) with church attendance.

The explorations of the personal power, meanness, and dominance hypothesis confirmed previous findings and added a few new ones. Compared with others in the sample, high social dominators said yes to "Do you like other people to be afraid of you?" and agreed "It's a dog-eat-dog world where you have to be ruthless at times." They did *not* think "the best way to lead a group under your supervision is to show them kindness, consideration, and treat them as fellow workers, not as inferiors" [which reminds me of McGregor's (1960) "Theory X" managers]. Nor did they "hate practical jokes that can sometimes really hurt people." They said it would *not* particularly bother them "if people thought you were mean and pitiless." (Item correlations with SDO ranged from .21 to .26.)

As for demographics males again tended to be more socially dominant than females (.19), but not more right-wing authoritarian (.01). No connection appeared between education and scores on either scale in this study. High RWAs tended to be poorer (−.22), but SDO again proved unrelated (−.01) to income. Finally, right-wing authoritarians tended to live a little more in rural areas.

4. Discussion

I designed this study primarily to see how much social dominators acted like right-wing authoritarians. Mostly, I think they did not.

Take our central concern, prejudice. High RWAs often grew up in a religious environment. Usually they were taught that prejudice against the minorities they fear and dislike is morally wrong, and this teaching tempers the answers they give to the Ethnocentrism scale. But their self-righteousness and "tight circles" inflict a certain self-blindness, and they do not realize how ethnocentric they remain compared to most people. On the other hand, religious teachings that God hates homosexuality allow them to go hog-wild on the Attitudes toward Homosexuals scale; and high RWAs *know* they dislike homosexuals more than most people do (Altemeyer. 1988, p. 188).

But high SDOs do not typically have religious reasons for "low balling" their answers to the Ethnocentrism scale, nor to pump up their dislike of homosexuals. Nor do they seem highly self-righteous. So they *do* know to a certain extent that they are more prejudiced than most. They just do not care, apparently.

For another contrast, high RWAs showed more hostility on the Posse and Trials measures than high SDOs did. Again, I think this reflects the different roots of aggression in the "submissive" and the "dominating." In the Posse and Trials situations established authority sanctioned punishment, and that means a lot more to authoritarians than it does to social dominators.

High RWAs also agreed significantly more to abolishing constitutional guarantees of civil rights because pornographers, criminals, and abortionists were "hiding behind them." But high SDOs do not get as excited about these issues.

Even when the two scales correlated similarly, you will recall, with the Rape Myth measure, they did so for somewhat different reasons. High RWAs most bought into myths that condemned rape victims on *moral* grounds: "When women go around braless or wearing short skirts and tight tops, they are just asking for trouble" and "If a girl engages in necking or petting and she lets things get out of hand, it is her own fault if her partner forces sex on her." But high SDOs blamed rape victims more for letting themselves fall into the *power* of the attacker: "A woman who goes to the home or apartment of a man on their first date implies that she is willing to have sex" and "Women who get raped while hitchhiking get what they deserve."

I attribute high RWAs' frequent use of double standards to the way they acquired many of their ideas: by copying authorities. Being dogmatically certain of their beliefs (Altemeyer, 1996, Chapter 8), they do not spend much time checking them for internal consistency. But high *SDOs* showed almost no double standards, strengthening the perception that right-wing authoritarians and social dominators usually differ in many ways.

5. The Militia Scale

I call persons who reject the normal established authorities in society *right-wing* authoritarians when they believe the "real" established authority (e.g., their reading of God's will, or the Constitution) has been usurped by left-wing Jews, feminists, homosexuals, and so on (Altemeyer 1996, p. 9). And indeed, RWA scores correlated solidly with Militia scale responses in this study. But some social dominators also held militia sentiments, and *left-wing* authoritarianism scores roared out the mightiest relationship of all. What in the name of holy conspiracy theories is going on here?

I developed the LWA Scale to test Shils's (1954) hypothesis that Communist-types as well as fascist-types could be authoritarian. Accordingly, I tried hard to create this frame of reference for respondents by developing a preamble to the LWA Scale that reads: "In the items that follow, the 'Establishment' refers to the people in our country who have traditionally had the most power, the greatest control over the economy. That is, the wealthiest people, the large corporations and banks who are often called the RIGHT-WING forces in Canada. Whereas a 'revolutionary movement' denotes a LEFT-WING movement dedicated to overthrowing the Establishment, and taking away its power."

I hoped that calling the Establishment "right-wing," and the revolutionaries "left-wing" would keep people who thought the Establishment was controlled by left-wing Jews, Communists, and so on from scoring highly on the LWA Scale—while coaxing all of Shils's left-wing authoritarians into view. To nail down this frame of reference, I put two "table-setters" at the beginning of the LWA Scale that gave proper names to the "revolutionary movement" under discussion: "Communism has its flaws, but the basic idea of overthrowing the right-wing Establishment and giving its wealth to the poor is still a very good one"; and "Socialism will never work, so people should treat left-wing revolutionaries as the dangerous troublemakers they are."

I have yet to find a single "socialist/Communist-type" who scores highly on absolute terms on the LWA Scale. Shils may have been right about his era, but the "authoritarian on the left" has been as scarce as hens' teeth in my samples. On the other hand, a mysterious group of "high–highs" consistently appeared in my studies who landed in the top quartile on *both* the RWA and LWA scales. These seemingly contradictory people proved to be highly prejudiced, and quite hostile in general.

I called these puzzling people "Wild-Card Authoritarians," and the Militia scale provides the key to understanding many of them.

The present study indicates most Wild-Card Authoritarians have anti-Semitic militialike sentiments. Of the 25 high RWAs–high LWAs in the sample that answered Booklet B, 17 (68%) also scored in the top quartile on the Militia scale. So most of these "wild-cards" seem to be right-wing authoritarians who overrode the preamble and table-setters to the LWA Scale because they "know" the Establishment is composed of Jews and their accomplices who control an oppressive, plotting, gun-grabbing government. Accordingly, the LWA scale's scan for revolutionary authoritarianism uncovered such authoritarianism in the anti-Semitic militia-oriented High RWAs.

Moving beyond the mystery of the Wild-Card Authoritarians, which seems more understandable now, who overall harbors anti-Semitic militia sentiments? Of the 60 respondents who scored in the top quartile on the Militia scale, 20 were High RWAs, 14 were High SDOs, and an additional 10 were both. So right-wing authoritarianism and social dominance—the two major consorts of prejudice in our society it seems—provided 73% of the anti-Semitic Militia types in this study.

G. The November 1996 Student Studies

Both the parent studies indicated that SDO–RWA results obtained with student samples had broader validity. So I prepared another booklet for some yet-unsurveyed Manitoba introductory psychology students, which 185 of them completed in November under "secret number" conditions. However, circumstances dictated that this questionnaire had to be answered on a 48-hour "take-home" basis. As this can produce sloppy responding, I attached a slip of paper to each booklet that read, "It is a condition of this study that you will answer carefully and honestly. So do not participate if you cannot do a conscientious job." I stressed this precondition when describing the experiment in the students' class.

The booklet began with the Religious Fundamentalism, Right-Wing Authoritarianism, and Social Dominance Orientation scales. Then Christie and Geis's (1970) Machiavellianism ("Mach IV") scale appeared, followed by some

"Mach-type" items of my own invention. An updated version of the Manitoba Ethnocentrism scale once again provided a broad-band measure of prejudice; it ended by asking respondents how prejudiced they thought they would be compared with the rest of the sample. I then presented my choicest assortment of personal power, meanness, and dominance items. A demographic survey ended the task.

The results proved considerably stronger than I had any right to expect, so I gave essentially the same booklet to another untested class on the same take-home basis. Their 177 sets of answers simmered down the earlier findings when stirred in, and I shall present the results from the merged samples.

Results: Old Tricks and New Tricks

SDO and RWA correlated .11 with each other, but .67 and .40, respectively, with Ethnocentrism. Together they explained 54% of the prejudice scores—obviously due mostly to the social dominance measure. As usual, high RWA students seldom realized they would prove more prejudiced than average (–.02), but high SDOs usually knew they would (.44). As before, right-wing authoritarians tended to be religious fundamentalists (.80), to accept the teachings of their home religion (.52), and to attend church (.53). But high SDOs had no such leanings (–.02, –.15, –.08). Males popped up more often than females among the socially dominant (.39) but not among the high RWAs (.03).

Now for some new tricks. The Machiavellianism scale had a low mean interitem correlation of .11 and an alpha = .72. Whatever its items measure, its summed score correlated .54 with SDO and –.18 with RWA. The hefty relationship with social dominance got its heft from such "Mach" items as "The biggest difference between most criminals and other people is that criminals are stupid enough to get caught"; "The best way to handle people is to tell them what they want to hear"; "Never tell anyone the real reason you did something unless it is useful to do so"; and "All in all, it is better to be humble and honest than important and dishonest" (with which High SDOs disagree).

The suspicion that high social dominators tend to be Machiavellian (in the generic sense) was reinforced by the Mach-type items I wrote, nearly all of which correlated with SDO scores. The strongest relationships (all over .40) sprouted with "One of the most useful skills a person should develop is how to look someone straight in the eye and lie convincingly"; "Basically, people are objects to be quietly and coolly manipulated for your own benefit"; "There really is no such thing as 'right' and 'wrong.' It all boils down to what you can get away with"; "You know most people are out to 'screw you,' so you just have to get them first when you get the chance"; and "Deceit and cheating can be justified if they get you what you really want."

My probing attempts to discover "What makes SDOs run?" beget, by the end of these studies, the entirely ad hoc Personal Power, Meanness, and Dominance ("PP-MAD") scale shown in Exhibit 6. Its items interconnected, .21 on the average, generating an alpha of .82. Summed PP-MAD scores correlated an unambiguous .61 with SDO, -.08 with RWA, .52 with Ethnocentrism, and .42 with gender.

H. Connecting the Dots

Examination of the statements in Exhibit 6 reveals a fair amount about social dominators, compared to others. As we surmised earlier, they not only believe some people were meant to dominate others, they personally want to do the dominating. Winning is the only thing for them. They want power and relish using it, to the point of being relatively ruthless, cold blooded, and vengeful. They enjoy making other people afraid of them, and worried about what they might do next. They would not mind being considered mean and pitiless. More than most people, they say they will destroy anyone who deliberately blocks their plans.

I think these revelations expose the separate roots of RWA and SDO prejudice. Right-wing authoritarians, who do *not* score high on PP-MAD, seem to be highly prejudiced mainly because they were raised to travel in tight, ethnocentric circles; and they fear that authority and conventions are crumbling so quickly that civilization will collapse and they will be eaten in the resulting jungle. In contrast, high SDOs *already* see life as "dog eat dog" and—compared with most people—are determined to do the eating. High *RWAs* also see themselves as "righteous dudes," to the point of being quite self-righteous, and this disinhibits their aggression. But we have seen that high SDOs do not need this release, and we can now see why.

EXHIBIT 6. The Personal Power, Meanness, and Dominance Scale

1. It's a mistake to interfere with the "law of the jungle." Some people were meant to dominate others.
2. Would you like to be a kind and helpful person to those in need?*
3. "Winning is not the first thing; it's the *only* thing."
4. The best way to lead a group under your supervision is to show them kindness, consideration, and treat them as fellow workers, not as inferiors.*
5. If you have power in a situation, you should use it however you have to get your way.
6. Would you be cold blooded and vengeful, if that's what it took to reach your goals?
7. Life is NOT governed by the "survival of the fittest." We should let compassion and moral laws be our guide.*
8. Do money, wealth, and luxuries mean a lot to you?
9. It is much better to be loved than to be feared.*
10. Do you enjoy having the power to hurt people when they anger or disappoint you?
11. It is much more important in life to have integrity in your dealings with others than to have money and power.*
12. It's a dog-eat-dog world where you have to be ruthless at times.
13. Charity (i.e., giving somebody something for nothing) is admirable, *not* stupid.*
14. Would you like to be known as a gentle and forgiving person?*
15. Do you enjoy taking charge of things and making people do things your way?
16. Would it bother you if other people thought you were mean and pitiless?*
17. Do you like other people to be afraid of you?
18. Do you hate to play practical jokes that can sometimes really hurt people?*
19. It would bother me if I intimidated people, and they worried about what I might do next.*
20. I will do my best to destroy anyone who deliberately blocks my plans and goals.

Notes. * indicates a con-trait item, for which the keying is reversed. Later studies indicated that the internal consistency of the PP-MAD scale improves if Items 8, 14, and 18 are replaced by "You have to be tough to get ahead in life; sentimentality and sympathy are for 'losers' "; "I prefer to work with others in an equal partnership: I do *not* try to 'get the edge' on the other guy"; and "People on 'power trips' are headed down a deadend road. It's better to work cooperatively with people as equals than to try to be the 'boss' controlling things."

Righteousness itself means little to someone who rejects being guided by moral laws, who instead believes, more than most people, "There really is no such thing as 'right' and 'wrong.' It all boils down to what you can get away with."

So is there any mystery as to why so many social dominators are prejudiced? Weak minorities provide easy targets for exerting power, for being mean, and for dominating others. For that matter, is there any mystery as to why many Social Dominators *are* social dominators? They reject equality on the SDO scale more than most people do because they tend to reject equality in general. It is antithetical to their outlook on life, and their personal motivation.

I. The January 1997 Parent Study

As soon as students returned from their 1996 Christmas holidays I flung questionnaires far and wide to challenge and pursue the findings captured thus far. For example, 331 parents obligingly answered a booklet containing the Economic Philosophy, RWA, SDO, Ethnocentrism, and PP-MAD scales. In addition, a balanced 16-item Sexual Harassment scale (mainly composed of items presented in Mazer and Percival (1989) was tucked in, along with an ad hoc Exploitive Manipulative Amoral Dishonesty (EMAD) scale I had worked up from Machiavellianism and "Mach-type" items used earlier.

Once more, Social Dominance Orientation (.61) and Right-Wing Authoritarianism (.46) correlated substantially with Ethnocentrism, and together explained 48% of its variance. (The two predictors had an r of .24 in this sample; in general, SDO and RWA correlate a little higher among parents than among students.) Parents holding conservative economic attitudes again proved likely to be prejudiced (.40), due in part to their tendency to be high SDOs (.33) and high RWAs (.20).

The PP-MAD items intermeshed .29 on the average, creating an alpha of .88. The strong PP-MAD relationship with SDO obtained with students reappeared among these parents (.59). But again, RWA scores were minimally connected to being power hungry, mean, and domineering (.15). PPMAD predicted ethnocentrism (.45), chiefly through its relationship with social dominance orientation. But the PP-MAD association with

gender proved more subdued among the parents (.17).

The sexual harassment items (e.g., "It is only natural for a man to make sexual advances to a woman he finds attractive"; "Sexual intimidation is a serious social problem"—a con-trait) interconnected .22 on the average, yielding an alpha = .82. Besides the expected correlation with gender (.29), persons who minimized sexual harassment issues tended to be ethnocentric (.51), high SDOs (.49), PP-MADs (.55), economic conservatives (.28), and RWAs (.25). These sexual harassment relationships harmonize with the Spence and Helmreich (1978) Attitudes toward Women and the Rape Myth Acceptance data we saw earlier.

If you sense that scores on the new Exploitive Manipulative Amoral Dishonesty scale (Exhibit 7) are going to slip neatly into place in this intertwining nest of traits, you are right. Responses to its 20 items intercorrelated .29 on the average, giving an alpha of .88. High E-MAD parents were usually PP-MAD as well, the Mad–Mad correlation being .71. Such parents also scored higher on SDO (.53), pooh-poohed sexual harassment issues (.53), and proved more ethnocentric (.39). But again, they were *not* likely to be high RWAs (.11).

J. The January 1997 Student Studies

I conducted three more student studies in January 1997, revisiting classes that had answered my autumn surveys. All three investigations used the "two-day, take-home" format with the participants serving anonymously.

The first booklet, answered by 214 students supposedly as part of a "test–retest reliability study of the scales involved," re-presented the RWA, SDO, Ethnocentrism, and PP-MAD measures. But spaced among them were two tests previously used only with parents, the anti-Semitic Militia and E-MAD scales.

There is no point in scrutinizing the new editions of relationships already established with these students, such as SDO and RWA connections with prejudice. Generally they proved stronger in January than in the fall, but that usually happens when people answer surveys a second time (Altemeyer, 1988, pp. 42–45).

Can one find traces of an anti-Semitic "militia mentality" among university students? The 12

Militia items intercorrelated .39 and had an alpha of .88—the same values obtained with parents in October. Militia scores connected .35 with RWA, .42 with SDO, .62 with Ethnocentrism, and .30 with PP-MAD responses. As with the parents, a solid majority (65%) of the 54 students who landed in the top quartile of Militia scores were either High RWAs (11), High SDOs (14), or both (10).

The 20 E-MAD items served up a mean interitem correlation of .35 and an alpha of .91— somewhat loftier than the parent results. E-MAD relationships with our other measures also vaulted somewhat higher: .78 with PP-MAD, .61 with SDO, and .42 with Ethnocentrism. High *RWAs* proved significantly *unlikely* to display E-MAD sentiments (-.19). "Militiatypes" proved mildly E-MADish (.29).

To summarize, just as the January parent survey reinforced earlier student results, this study backed up parent-based outcomes. While it may bore one to watch findings from these different populations continually vouching for one another, they do assure the scarred investigator that he is not picking at some extremely tiny nit.

My second student study in January 1997 arose from my earlier-stated opinion that Hitler was a very high SDO type. To test whether others saw him the same way, I invited students in an introductory psychology class to answer a booklet containing the RWA, SDO, PP-MAD, and E-MAD scales as they thought Adolf Hitler would, "if he were to tell the truth about how he really felt."

Hitler's *RWA* scale answers, as role-played by 50 responding students, equaled 233.0. That amounts to 86% of the maximum possible total of 270 (which no one to my knowledge has ever scored). The students thought Hitler would be even more Social Dominance Oriented, giving him a mean of 116.2 (or 92% of the maximum of 126). Hitler was also seen as being highly PP-MAD, averaging 108.7 or 91% of the maximum 120. His inferred answers to the E-MAD scale also approached the limit, being 153.2 or 85% of the maximum 180.

So Adolf Hitler's image produced a definite "profile" on these four measures: Extraordinarily High. This supports these scales' validity, for Hitler seems to have been an extremely right-wing au-

---

EXHIBIT 7. The Exploitive Manipulative Amoral Dishonesty (E-MAD) Scale

1. You know that most people are out to "screw" you, so you have to get them first when you get the chance.
2. All in all, it is better to be humble and honest than important and dishonest.*
3. There really is no such thing as "right" and "wrong." It all boils down to what you can get away with.
4. Do unto others as you would have them do unto you, and never do anything unfair to someone else.*
5. One of the most useful skills a person should develop is how to look someone straight in the eye and lie convincingly.
6. It gains a person nothing if he uses deceit and treachery to get power and riches.*
7. Basically, people are objects to be quietly and coolly manipulated for your own benefit.
8. Deceit and cheating are justified when they get you what you really want.
9. One should give others the benefit of the doubt. Most people are trustworthy if you have faith in them.*
10. The best skill one can have is knowing the "right move at the right time": when to "soft-sell" someone, when to be tough, when to flatter, when to threaten, when to bribe, etc.
11. Honesty is the best policy in all cases.*
12. The best reason for belonging to a church is to project a good image and have contact with some of the important people in your community.
13. No one should do evil acts, even when they can "get away with them" and make lots of money.*
14. There's a sucker born every minute, and smart people learn how to take advantage of them.
15. The end does NOT justify the means. If you can only get something by unfairness, lying, or hurting others, then give up trying.*
16. Our lives should be governed by high ethical principles and religious morals, not by power and greed.*
17. It is more important to create a good image of yourself in the minds of others than to actually be the person others think you are.
18. There's no excuse for lying to someone else.*
19. One of the best ways to handle people is to tell them what they want to hear.
20. The truly smart person knows that honesty is the best policy, not manipulation and deceit.*

Note. * indicates a con-trait item, for which the scoring key is reversed.

thoritarian (yes, fascist), dictatorial, power-driven, mean, personally domineering, exploitive, manipulative, amoral, and dishonest person.

The third January student study was prompted by John Duckitt, who wondered if the "nest" of SDO correlations was actually assembled by social desirability effects. Suppose some people are willing to admit bad things about themselves on a survey, but others are relatively reluctant to admit such, or are even unaware of them. If so, then responses to a collection of scales that raise sensitive issues will be glued together to some extent by this "willing-to-look-bad versus try-to-look-good" response style, whether the traits involved really are related. In this light, high SDOs may *not* be more prejudiced than others, nor more PP-Mad, E-MAD, accepting of rape myths, and so on, but merely less defensive.

Since all of my respondents served anonymously, no one could have been trying to shape a public persona. So this alternate interpretation has to be couched in terms of self-deception. Do people answering surveys sometimes sugar-coat their responses because they do not like to admit bad things about themselves *to themselves*? I suspect we do. The trouble is, how do we measure this tendency in people? Ask them about it on a questionnaire?

The usual approach has been to develop surveys that assess people's tendencies to say "goody-goody" things about themselves and deny "nasty-nasties." The 33-item Marlowe–Crowne scale (Crowne & Marlowe, 1964) comes to mind, and Paulhus (e.g., Paulhus & Reid, 1991) has developed 20-item measures of Impression Management, Self-Deceptive Enhancement, and Denial. However, High RWAs, who *ought* to rack up big numbers on measures of social desirability because of their conventionalism, and who we know *from experiments* are highly defensive and reluctant to admit bad news about themselves to themselves have never scored highly on such instruments.

Nevertheless, I distributed a booklet containing the RWA, SDO, Marlowe–Crowne, and Paulhus's three measures (Form 60A) to 206 students. The Marlowe–Crowne had poor internal consistency (mean interitem correlation = .13). Impression Management did better (.19), but Self-Deceptive Enhancement (.09) and Denial (.14) fell discouragingly short. The alphas of the four measures equaled .82, .82, .66, and .77, respectively.

Once again, none of the four measures correlated well with RWA, the *r*s being .05, .17, −.02, and .13. Three had significant negative correlations with social dominance orientation: Marlowe–Crowne (−.25), Impression Management (−.21), and Denial (−.23). But the supposedly most relevant Self-Deceptive Enhancement correlated only −.03 with SDO. So even if you believe these scales are valid, despite their failure to connect with the demonstrably relevant RWA dimension, the "SDO nest" does *not* appear to be much of a social desirability artifact.

K. Summing Up What We Have Learned in these Studies about the Social Dominator

Looking back, what do the nine studies reported in this paper tell us about High SDOs? First, social dominators outpointed even the High RWAs in prejudice. But they did *not* act as aggressively as right-wing authoritarians in the Trials or Posse situations. So however prejudiced they may be, we cannot color them dark, dark *authoritarian* aggressive.

What about religion? A few social dominators appear quite religious, but usually they seem pretty indifferent. It would not astound me if high SDOs who attend church tend to fall among the "extrinsically oriented" people whom Gordon Allport (1966) thought he spotted in the pews, whose religion was "strictly utilitarian; useful to the self in granting safety, social standing, solace and endorsement for one's chosen way of life (p. 455)."

If high SDOs are relatively "principle challenged," how did they pass the double standards test? Do they strive for personal integrity after all, their answers to the E-MAD scale notwithstanding? Possibly. But were their own irons, or feet, in the fire in any of those cases? No. So I would predict that social dominators will use double standards quite freely when necessary to achieve their own ends—and do so fairly knowingly and nonchalantly, just as they often know that they are relatively prejudiced, but do not care.

Do high SDOs threaten democracy? In their defense, they proved much less inclined than right-wing authoritarians to overturn constitutional guarantees of liberty. But they proved just as likely to hold anti-Semitic "militia sentiments." And can one view persons prejudiced against women, aboriginals, Blacks, Arabs, homosexuals, people of Asian ancestry, Latin-Americans, Quebecois, and others as model citizens? High SDOs, by virtue of their answers to the SDO scale itself, seem opposed to one of democracy's central values: equality.

Economic Orientation

This opposition finds expression in their economic philosophy. The persons most advocating privatization, reduction in social spending, weakening of unions, balanced budgets, lower taxes for businesses and the rich, less government involvement in the economy, and so on generally scored high in social dominance. They also admit they *oppose* a more even distribution of wealth in their country. Economic rationales are frequently offered for these stands. But if you think social dominators care an awful lot about their *own* well-being, it seems likely that their economic views are powerfully driven by their own drive for power.

Incidentally, the SDO–Economic Philosophy connection explains another group that, along with "Wild-Card Authoritarians," displayed a ton of hostility in many of my earlier studies. I frequently have asked respondents to indicate the nature of their most important outlook in life. Among the nine alternatives, I offer "A *capitalist* social perspective; a capitalist theory of how society should operate." (Other possibilities include "a religious outlook," "a scientific outlook," a "socialist outlook," and so on.) Self-declared capitalists consistently racked up such high scores on the Ethnocentrism, Attitudes toward Homosexuals, and Posse-Radical measures that in 1996 I wrote, "The capitalists would have won the gold medal in all three tests if this had been the Authoritarian Hostility Olympics" (p. 213).

I slipped the "most important outlook" question into the demographic survey used in several of the present investigations. In the October 1995 parent study, "capitalists" scored higher than any other group on the Social Dominance Orientation and Ethnocentrism scales. In the 1996 student-based replication of McFarland and Adelson (1996), capitalists outpointed all others on SDO again, and scored highest on *every one* of the six measures of prejudice. Similarly, the capitalists in the October 1996 parent study topped all others in social dominance, ethnocentrism, and hostility toward homosexuals.

Political Orientation

Moving from economic to political orientation, every study I have done with the SDO scale has found that persons who favored the Reform Party of Canada scored higher in social dominance than any other party's supporters. Those who liked the Conservatives always scored next highest. Then came the Liberals and NDPers, usually in that order.

You find the same rank ordering when you look at right-wing authoritarianism, and that leads to a rather striking analysis of what kind of people prefer the programs of the different political parties. Combining the parents who served in the October 1995 and 1996 and January 1997 studies ($N = 1314$), 84 of them favored the Reform Party on the federal level. Of these, 22 placed in the top quartile of the RWA distribution, 18 were High SDOs, and 14 more were both. So altogether (54/84 =) 64% of the Reform Party supporters could be characterized as high right-wing authoritarians or high social dominators, or both. Of the 316 who favored the Conservatives, 46% were high RWAs or high SDOs, or both. The figure for the 356 Liberals equaled 39%, and that for the 107 NDP supporters was 29%. (The rest of the sample were Independents, or had no interest in politics.)

If you do the same analysis for the 832 students who served in the fall 1996 experiments, 65% of the Reformers, 64% of the Tories, 46% of the Liberals, and 31% of the NDPers turned out to be high right-wing authoritarians or high social dominators, or both. Similarly, study after study has found that Reform Party enthusiasts are more *prejudiced* than any others, followed by the Conservative supporters, Liberals, and NDPers.

One supposes that relatively authoritarian, dominance-oriented, and prejudiced people prefer the Reform and Conservative parties because they sense these parties' leaders share their outlooks. And so they do. Reform and Tory *politicians* also tend to be more right-wing authoritarian, socially dominant, and prejudiced than Liberal and NDP politicians.

L. Origins of Social Dominance Orientation

Where do high SDOs come from? The smart money will bet on the interaction of genes and environment. We should take the genetic prospects quite seriously. Virtually all animal societies are built around dominance systems and humans have been able to breed aggressive, dominant behavior in some species, and greatly reduce it in others. Hence cock and bull fights; hence our docile lab rats.

But social learning almost certainly plays a strong hand, too, even if we have had to release for the moment one of the usual suspects—being physically punished while a child—for lack of evidence. We have known since Bandura, Ross, and Ross (1963) that children find social power attractive, and imitate those who have it. And few things can be as reinforcing as holding power, because it means you have the Law of Effect in a hammer lock. Reduced to its essence, having power means getting more of the rewards in life, and fewer of the punishments.

Although it tells us nothing about nature versus nurture scripting, an "SDO inheritance" can be traced from one generation to the next in my studies. I asked the students whose parents answered the October 1996 survey to put their own "secret number" on their parents' bubble sheets. This led to matchups for 104 students with 89 of their mothers and 95 of their fathers. Daughters' ($N = 60$) social dominance correlated .16 with their mothers' social dominance, and .37 with their fathers'. For sons ($N = 44$) the respective coefficients came in at .11 and .45. Combining the offsprung, fathers' SDO proved significantly more predictive of their children's SDO (.40) than did the mothers' (.13). Pairs of mothers and fathers displayed similar levels of social dominance, by the way (.45), but as usual, the males had higher levels overall.

By comparison, students' *right-wing authoritarianism* has correlated about .40 with their parents' RWA scores over many studies (Altemeyer, 1988, p. 64), with neither parent appearing more influential. In this study the mother–child RWA hand-me-down was .40, and the father–child RWA resemblance equaled .36.

To focus on the "nurture" side of the issue, we have identified many *experiences* that make people more or less right-wing authoritarian as they go through life. Accordingly, I asked the students who served in my last November 1996 survey, at the end of the booklet, "Why do you think you are as competitive, personally ambitious, and 'determined to beat the other fellow' as you are? How did you get that way? Can you name two or three experiences you had that were particularly important in getting you to want power over others in life? Do you have a model like this that you want to be like? Or does none of this apply to you?"

Comparing the answers of the High SDOs with the other students, social dominators more often said such things as "This is the way the world works; people want to get ahead of others"; "Everyone is taught that you have to be competitive to be in control of your future in today's society"; and "This is the only way you will ever achieve in this world." So social dominators certainly picked up these cultural messages clearly. They also seemed to have engaged in competitive sports more often than most people, where they described the thrill of victory and (especially) the agony of defeat: "It's because of the rush I get every time I win"; and "I really get off when my team wins"; "I like the feeling of winning and maybe more importantly I hate losing"; "I hate losing"; "I detest losing"; "I will do anything to not lose"; and "I absolutely hate losing." High SDOs often said both parents had encouraged their drives to be Number One; but fathers were mentioned more often as their "pushers," and as the role models they followed.

M. Some Further Observations

One can get excited about Pratto et al.'s (1994) social dominance construct for many reasons. It has produced an extraordinary measure of prejudice. Indeed, with some help from the RWA scale this test explains most of the prejudice in the samples studied thus far. That amazes me. Also the SDO scale provides the best measure we have of the missing link in the domination–submission authoritarian social system—a link I never realized was missing. Furthermore, high SDOs certainly grip one, and merit study in their own right. And finally, social dominance orientation helps explain most of the confusing findings that have popped up thus far in research using the RWA Scale.

For example, Richard Christie and I were surprised that RWA did not associate highly with scores on his Machiavellianism scale. In fact, it usually correlated negatively. Now I see that we were "carriers" of a misconception that goes back to Erich Fromm. We expected just one kind of personality to play a role in authoritarianism, when in fact the Machiavellianism associated with dictatorial behavior appears to come from high SDOs, not high RWAs.

David Winter and I were similarly mystified when his TAT-based measure of need-Power (Winter, 1973, 1988) proved uncorrelated with RWA. Want to bet I was not again confusing dominators with submitters? High RWAs may usually be content to bow to those above them, but high SDOs are driving to rise in the ranks.

For a final Ancient Mystery of the RWA Scale, the positive correlation between left-wing and right-wing authoritarianism also surprised me. Now it appears that the "Wild-Card Authoritarians" detected in those data were mainly hostile high RWA and high SDO "militia-types" who interpreted the Establishment as Jews, homosexuals, feminists, and other "left-wingers."

N. Are High SDOs "Authoritarians"?

This paper is entitled "The Other 'Authoritarian Personality.'" Why the qualification? Are not high SDOs authoritarians? Yes and no. I would say they are in the sense that "authoritarian" connotes "dictatorial." I think you can count on high SDOs dictating to others when they have the social authority to do so.

But social authority probably does not *produce* dominance in high SDOs, the way it triggers submission in high RWAs. Instead, high SDOs will probably try to dominate others in general, legitimately or otherwise. If some group landed in a *Lord of the Flies* wilderness and social authority evaporated, I think the high SDOs would quickly start snarling and scheming to become the alpha animal. So I would not call social dominators "authoritarians, pure and simple." They do not have the reverence for established authority that right-wing authoritarians have, aside from its being a means to their end. They are social dominators, pure and simple. But they will produce authoritarian social *systems* with the support of high RWAs

if they become legitimate authorities.

Why then do high SDOs tend to end up on the "high RWA end" on many social issues? I can offer three reasons. First, social dominators tend to hold conservative economic and political philosophies. Second, experiments have shown that high *RWAs* (but not lows) will trust untrustworthy people who tell them what they want to hear. So if—no offense intended—you believe that "one of the most useful skills a person should develop is how to look someone straight in the eye and lie convincingly," where will you find your easiest sell on the political spectrum? Whom do you sidle on up to and praise the Lord? The right-wing authoritarians.

Third, some social dominators could express strong belief in submitting to the established authorities on the RWA scale if they consider themselves (now or someday) the authorities *others* should submit to. Hitler would seem to have been such a person, and the students who role-played his beliefs produced extremely high scores on *both* the SDO and RWA scales. Such "High SDO–High RWAs" are somewhat rare, as the correlation between the two measures only comes in around .20. But about 8% of my samples did score in the upper quartiles of both the RWA and SDO distributions. These "dominating right-wing authoritarians" proved distinctive in another way. In every study, they had the highest prejudice scores of any group in the sample. They are thus the most worrisome persons I have found in my investigations.

O. Improving the Social Dominance Orientation Scale

Just as I constantly tinker with my own measures, I have tried to improve the internal consistency of the SDO scale. Adding the following 6 statements to the 14 original ones shown in Exhibit 2 raises the mean interitem correlation (and the test's relationship with prejudice) a small but useful amount: "Some people are just much better than everyone else, and deserve to have power and control over others"; "This country would be better off if inferior groups stayed in their place"; "The best people should *not* be expected to accept others as 'equals'"; "We should strive with our mightiest efforts to increase equality and social justice in our country" (con-trait); "The poor and the weak deserve the pleasures of life just as much as the rich and powerful people do" (con-trait); and "There should be much more equal opportunity for everyone from birth, regardless of who their parents are" (con-trait).

I am not proposing that the SDO scale be modified at this point. But I hope that others will test my conclusions in their own populations, and also try out these new social dominance items. The results should be forwarded to the inventors of the SDO scale, should they want to revise their measure someday.

One may find a certain symmetry in this paper's closing with an appeal for replication, for it began with a repeating of McFarland and Adelson's extraordinary study of the sources of personal prejudice. As well, the paper illustrates the replication-based nature of the scientific quest, in which far-flung researchers test old findings and add new ones in the cooperative development of insight. Indeed, this quest began over 50 years ago in the fertile mind of the late Nevitt Sanford.

Finally, we should remember that we are questing to *avoid* repeating some of the darkest moments of human history. I think we understand the people on the podium a bit better now, just as we have developed an understanding of the adoring crowd before them. May this double our protection against the calamity that can result when these mutually attracting forces find one another, and embrace in lethal union.

REFERENCES

Adorno, T. W., Frenkel-Brunswik, E., Levinson, D. J., & Sanford, R. N. (1950). *The authoritarian personality*. New York: Harper.

Allport, G. W. (1966). The religious context of prejudice. *Journal for the Scientific Study of Religion*, 5, 447–457.

Altemeyer, B. (1981). *Right-wing authoritarianism*. Winnipeg: University of Manitoba Press.

Altemeyer, B. (1988). *Enemies of freedom*. San Francisco: Jossey-Bass.

Altemeyer, B. (1996). *The authoritarian specter*. Cambridge, MA: Harvard University Press.

Altemeyer, B., and Hunsberger, B. (1992). Authoritarianism, religious fundamentalism, quest, and prejudice. *International Journal for the Psychology of Religion*, 2, 113–133.

Bandura, A., Ross, D., & Ross, S. (1963). A comparative test of the status envy, social power, and secondary reinforcement theories of identificatory learning. *Journal of Abnormal and Social Psychology*, 67, 527–534.

Bullock, A. (1962). *Hitler: A study in tyranny*. Harmondsworth, Middlesex, England: Pelican Books.

Burt, M. R. (1980). Cultural myths and supports for rape. *Journal of Personality and Social Psychology*, 38, 217–230.

Buss, A. H., & Durkee, A. (1957). An inventory for assessing different kinds of hostility. *Journal of Consulting Psychology*, 21, 343–349.

Christie, R., & Geis, F. (1970). *Studies in Machiavellianism*. New York: Academic Press.

Crowne, D. P., & Marlowe, D. (1964). *The approval motive*. New York: Wiley.

Eysenck, H. J., & Eysenck, S. B. (1969). *Personality structure and measurement*. San Diego: Knapp.

Eysenck, H. J., & Eysenck, S. B. (1976). *Psychoticism as a dimension of personality*. New York: Crane, Russak, & Company.

Fletcher, G. J. O., Danilovacs, P., Fernandez, G., Peterson, D., & Reeder, G. D. (1986). Attributional complexity: An individual differences measure. *Journal of Personality and Social Psychology*, 51, 875–884.

Fromm, E. (1941). *Escape from freedom*. New York: Holt, Rinehart, & Winston.

Gough, H. (1987). *California psychological inventory: Administrator's guide*. Palo Alto, CA: Consulting Psychologists Press.

Jackson, D. N. (1965). *Personality research form*. Goshen, NY: Research Psychologists Press.

Luhtanen, R., & Crocker, J. (1992). A collective self-esteem scale: Self-evaluation of one's social identity. *Personality and Social Psychology Bulletin*, 18, 302–318.

Mazer, D. B., & Percival, E. F. (1989). Ideology or experience? The relationships among perceptions, attitudes, and experiences of sexual harassment in university students. *Sex Roles*, 20, 135–151.

McFarland, S. G., & Adelson, S. (1996). *An omnibus study of personality, values, and prejudice*. Paper presented at the annual meeting of the International Society for Political Psychology, Vancouver, British Columbia.

McGregor, D. (1960). *The human side of enterprise*. New York: McGraw-Hill.

Newcomb, T. M. (1961). *The acquaintance process*. New York: Holt, Rinehart, & Winston.

Paulhus, D. L. (1984). Two-component models of socially desirable responding. *Journal of Personality and Social Psychology*, 46, 598–609.

Paulhus, D. L., & Reid, D. B. (1991). Enhancement and denial in socially desirable responding. *Journal of Personality and Social Psychology*, 60, 307–317.

Pratto, F., Liu, J. H., Levin, S., Sidanius, J., Shih, M., & Bachrach, H. (1996). *Social Dominance Orientation and legitimization of inequality across cultures*.

Pratto, F., Sidanius, J., Stallworth, L. M., & Malle, B. F. (1994). Social Dominance Orientation: A personality variable predicting social and political attitudes. *Journal of Personality and Social Psychology*, 67, 741–763.

Pratto, F., Stallworth, L. M., Sidanius, J., & Siers, B. (1997). The gender gap in occupational role attainment: A social dominance approach. *Journal of Personality and Social Psychology*, 72, 37–53.

Rosenberg, M. (1965). *Society and the adolescent self-image*. Princeton, NJ: Princeton University Press.

Rubin, Z., & Peplau, A. (1973). Belief in a just world and reactions to another's lot: A study of participants in the national draft lottery. *Journal of Social Issues*, 29, 73–93.

Schaller, M., Boyd, C., Yohannes, J., & O'Brien, M. (1995). The prejudiced personality revisited: Personal need for structure and the formation of erroneous group stereotypes. *Journal of Personality and Social Psychology, 68,* 544–555.

Schwartz, S. H. (1992). Universals in the content of structure and values: Theoretical advances and empirical tests in 20 countries. *Advances in Experimental Social Psychology* (Vol. 25). New York: Academic Press.

Shils, E. A. (1954). Authoritarianism: Right and left. In R. Christie & M. Jahoda (Eds.), *Studies in the scope and method of "The Authoritarian Personality."* Glencoe, IL: Free Press.

Spence, J. T., & Helmreich, R. L. (1978). *Masculinity and femininity: Their psychological dimensions, correlates, and antecedents.* Austin: University of Texas Press.

Srole, L. (1956). Social integration and certain corollaries: An exploratory study. *American Sociological Review, 21,* 709–716.

Walker, W. D., and Quinsey, V. L. (1991). *Authoritarianism, attitudes toward women, and sexual aggression.* Unpublished manuscript, Queens University, Kingston, Ontario.

Walker, W. D., Rowe, R. C., & Quinsey, V. L. (1993). Authoritarianism and sexual aggression. *Journal of Personality and Social Psychology, 65,* 1036–1045.

Winter, D. (1973). *The power motive.* New York: The Free Press.

Winter, D. (1988). The power motive in women—and men. *Journal of Personality and Social Psychology, 54,* 510–519.

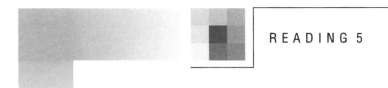

Can Personality and Politics Be Studied Systematically?

Fred I. Greenstein • Princeton University

The study of personality and politics is possible and desirable, but systematic intellectual progress is possible only if there is careful attention to problems of evidence, inference, and conceptualization. This essay reviews such problems, setting forth a conceptualization that takes account of, and builds on, many of the recurring reservations that are advanced about the utility of studying the personalities of political actors. In doing so, it takes selective account of the classical literature on political psychology and more recent developments in the field.

Introduction

The personalities of political actors impinge on political affairs in countless ways, often with great consequences. Political life regularly generates such contrary-to-fact conditionals as "If Kennedy had lived, such-and-such would or would not have happened." Counterfactual propositions are not directly testable, but many of them are so compelling that even the most cautious historian would find them persuasive. Most historians would agree, for example, that if the assassin's bullet aimed at President-Elect Franklin D. Roosevelt in February 1933 had found its mark, there would have been no New Deal, or if the Politburo had chosen another Leonid Brezhnev, Konstantin Chernenko, or Yuri Andropov rather than Mikhail Gorbachev as General Secretary of the Communist Party of the Soviet Union in 1985, the epochal changes of the late 1980s would not have occurred, at least not at the same time and in the same way.

The seemingly self-evident effects of many changes in leadership, including changes of a much lesser order in lesser entities than the national governments of the United States and the Soviet Union, along with the innumerable other events in the political world that are difficult to account for without taking cognizance of the actors' personal peculiarities, lead the bulk of nonacademic observers of politics, including journalists, to take it for granted that personality is an important determinant of political behavior. It may seem truistic to those members of the scholarly community whose interests direct them to read a journal entitled *Political Psychology* that such lay political observers are correct and that there is need for systematic study of personality and politics. Yet it is rare in the larger scholarly community for specialists in the study of politics to make personality and politics a principal focus of investigation. Instead, they tend to concentrate on impersonal determinants of political events and outcomes, even those in which the participants themselves believe personality to have been significant. Or, if they do treat individual action as important, they posit rationality, defining away personal characteristics and presuming that the behavior of actors can be deduced from the logic of their situations (cf. Simon, 1985).

My argument in this paper is that the study of personality and politics is possible and desirable, but that systematic intellectual progress is possible only if there is self-conscious attention to evidence, inference, and conceptualization. In setting that argument forth, I build on, augment, and modify my previous writings on problems of explanation in political psychology (Greenstein, 1969, 1975), selectively incorporating later scholarship, particularly the extensive work in recent years on political cognition. My formulation builds on the very controversies that often impede the study of personality and politics.

The study of personality and politics sometimes appears to have more critics than practitioners. Some of the controversy is no more than the usual methodological and empirical disagreements within the ranks of those who seek to unravel a complex and varied real-world phenomenon, but the most important disagreements for the purposes of this essay are over whether in principle there *is* a need for the study of personality and politics, and, if so, what the scope of such study might be.

Reservations have been expressed about the utility of studying the personalities of political actors on the grounds that (1) political actors are randomly distributed in roles and therefore their personalities "cancel out"; (2) political action is determined more by the actors' political environments than by their own characteristics; (3) the particular stratum of the psyche many political scientists equate with *personality*, psychodynamics, and the ego defenses, does not have much of a political impact; (4) the social characteristics of political actors are more important than their psychological characteristics; and (5) individuals are typically unable to have much effect on political outcomes. On analysis, each of these reservations or disagreements proves to have important conceptual implications for the study of personality and politics. The debate about scope has roots in the definitional ambiguity of the basic terms *personality* and *politics* and is best dealt with before the objec-

tions and their positive implications for systematic inquiry.

Definitional Questions

Narrowly construed, the term *politics* in *personality and politics* refers to the politics most often studied by political scientists—that of civil government and of the extra-governmental processes that more or less directly impinge upon government, such as political parties and interest groups. Broadly construed, it refers to politics in all of its manifestations, whether in government or any other institution, including many that are rarely studied by political scientists—for example, the family, school, and workplace. By this broader construction, the common denominator is the various referents of *politics*, including the exercise of influence and authority and the diverse arts of interpersonal maneuver, such as bargaining and persuasion, connoted by the word *politicking*, none of which are monopolized by government.

Personality also admits of narrow and broad definitions. In the narrow usage typical of political science, it excludes political attitudes and opinions and often other kinds of subjective states that are of a political nature (for example, the ideational content associated with political skill) and applies only to non-political personal differences, or even to the subset of psychopathological differences that are the preoccupation of clinical psychology. In psychology, on the other hand, the term has a much broader referent—in the phrase of the personality theorist Henry Murray (1968), it "is the most comprehensive term we have in psychology." Thus, in their influential study of *Opinions and Personality*, the psychologists M. Brewster Smith, Jerome Bruner, and Robert White (1956, p. 1) use a locution one would not expect from political scientists, describing opinions as "an integral part of personality."

Although usage is a matter of convention and both the narrow and the broad definitions encompass phenomena worthy of study, this seemingly semantic controversy has a significant bearing on what scholars study. As Lasswell (1930, p. 42–45) argued long ago, there are distinct advantages to adopting the broader definition. A perspective that transcends governmental politics encourages study of comparable phenomena, some of which may happen to be part of the formal institutions of governance and some of which may not. Browning and Jacobs (1964), for example, compared the needs for power, achievement, and affiliation of businessmen and public officials in highly diverse positions that imposed sharply divergent demands. They found that the public officials were by no means all cut from the same psychological cloth, but that there were important similarities between certain of the public officials and businessmen. The underlying principle appears to be that personality tends to be consistent with the specific demands of roles, whether because of preselection of the role incumbents or because of in-role socialization.

The Distribution of Individuals in Roles

Even if the first of the reservations sometimes expressed about the value of studying personality and politics—the claim that individuals are randomly distributed in political roles and therefore their impact is somewhat neutralized—is empirically sound, it is by no means a reason not to study personality and politics. If one visualizes political processes as analogous to intricately wired computers, political actors can be viewed as key junctures in the wiring, for example circuit breakers. If anything, it would be *more*, not less, urgent to know the performance characteristics of the circuit breakers if their operating properties were random, with some capable of tripping at inappropriate times, losing valuable information, and others failing to trip, exposing the system to the danger of meltdown.

In the real political world, events sometimes do more or less randomly assign individuals with unanticipated personal styles and proclivities to political roles, often with significant consequences. This was the case of two of the national leaders referred to in the opening of the article: neither Franklin Roosevelt's or Mikhail Gorbachev's contemporaries anticipated the innovative leadership they displayed in office. As the Browning and Jacobs study suggests, however, people do not appear to be randomly distributed in political roles, though the patterns of their distribution appear to be complex and elusive. Ascertaining them, examining their political consequences and determin-

ing the "fit" between role and personality are important parts of the intellectual agenda for the study of personality and politics (George, 1974).

Personality and Environment

The second reservation about the study of personality and politics—that environment has more impact than personality on behavior—and the other three reservations need to be considered in the context of a general clarification of the types of variables that in principle can affect personality and politics and their possible interconnections. An important example of such a clarification is M. Brewster Smith's (1968) well-known "map for the study of personality and politics." (See also Stone and Schaffner's [1988, p. 33] depiction of "political life space.") The representation that I will employ (Greenstein, 1975) is introduced in segments in Figs. 5.1 and 5.2 and set forth in its entirety in Fig. 5.3.

The most fundamental distinction in the map is the rudimentary one that, as Kurt Lewin (1936, pp. 11–12) put it, "behavior or any kind of mental event . . . depends on the state of the person and at the same time on the environment." Figure 5.1 depicts the links between the two broad classes of behavioral antecedent Lewin refers to and behavior itself, using the terminology of Lasswell and Kaplan (1950, pp. 4–6), who ground an entire conceptual framework for the analysis of politics on the equation that human response (R) is a function of the respondent's environment (E) and predispositions (P): $E \rightarrow P \rightarrow R$. Here again, terminology is a matter of convenience. Instead of *predispositions*, it would have been possible to use many other of the 80 terms Donald Campbell (1963) enumerates in his account of the logic of studying "acquired behavioral dispositions." Such terms as *situation*, *context*, and *stimulus* are common alternative labels for all or part of the environment of human action.

The $E \rightarrow P \rightarrow R$ formula provides a convenient way of visualizing the fallacy in the claim that behavior is so much a function of environments that individuals' predispositions need not be studied (reservation two). In fact, environments are always mediated by the individuals on whom they act; environments cannot shape behavior directly, and much politically important action is not reactive to immediate stimuli. Indeed, the capacity to be *proactive* (Murray, 1968) and transcend existing perceptions of what the environment dictates is at the core of effective leadership. But the debate about whether environments determine political behavior is a reminder of the endless interplay of individuals and the political contexts in which they find or place themselves.

Some contexts are indeed associated with the kind of behavior that leads social determinists to be skeptical about the need to study personality. Informed of the impending collapse of a building, everyone—irrespective of temperament and personality type—will seek to leave it. Other contexts illustrate Gordon Allport's (1937, p. 325) aphorism that "the same heat that hardens the egg, melts the butter." Still others are virtual ink blots, leading individuals with varying characteristics to project their inner dispositions onto them. The connection between personality and context is so integral that this relationship has become the basis of an important approach to personality theory known as interactionism (Endler, 1981; Magnusson & Endler, 1977; Pervin & Lewis, 1978). By systematically analyzing personality and politics in interactional terms, the analyst is sensitized to the kinds of contingent relationships that make the links between personality and politics elusive.

A good example of a contingent relationship in which the impact of personality is mediated by the environment is to be found in the work of Katz and Benjamin (1960) on the effects of authoritarianism in biracial work groups in the North and the South. Katz and Benjamin compared white undergraduates in the two regions who scored low and high on one of the various authoritarian personality measures to see how they comported themselves in interracial problem-solving groups. They found that in the South authoritarianism (which previous studies showed to be associated with race prejudice) was associated with attempts of white students to dominate their black counterparts, but that in the North the authoritarians were more likely than the nonauthoritarians to be *deferential* to blacks. The investigators' conclusion was that the sociopolitical environment of the Southern authoritarians enabled them to give direct vent to their impulses, but that the liberal environment of the Northern university led students with similar proclivities to go out of their way to avoid coming in conflict with the prevailing norms.

The relative effect of environment and personality on political behavior varies. Ambiguous environments—for example, new situations and political roles that are only sketchily defined by formal rules (Budner, 1962; Greenstein, 1969, pp. 50–57)—provide great latitude for actors' personalities to shape their behavior. Structured environments—for example, bureaucratized settings and contexts in which there are well-developed and widely known and accepted norms—tend to constrain behavior. The environment also is likely to account for much of the variance in political behavior when strong sanctions are attached to certain possible courses of action.

The dramatic reduction of political repression in the Soviet Union and Eastern Europe in the late 1980s led to an outpouring of political action. Just as the absence of authoritarian rule leads individuals in the aggregate to express their personal political proclivities, its presence magnifies the effects of leaders, assuming that the authoritarian system is one in which the individual or individuals at the top have more or less absolute power (Tucker, 1965). The striking capacity of leaders' personalities to shape events in an authoritarian system was evident in the leeway Gorbachev appears to have had at the time of the initiation of glasnost and perestroika, if not later when the forces of pluralism began to bedevil him.

Just as environments vary in the extent to which they foster the expression of individual variability, so also do predispositions themselves vary. There is an extensive literature on the tendency of people to subordinate themselves to groups and consciously or unconsciously suppress their own views when they are in the company of others. But some individuals are remarkably resistant to such inhibitions and others have compliant tendencies (Allen, 1975; Asch, 1956; Janis, 1982). The intensity of psychological predispositions promotes expression of them. Most people suppress their impulses to challenge the regimes of authoritarian systems, but those with passionate convictions and strong character-based needs for self-expression or rebellion are more likely to oppose such regimes. (In doing so, they alter the environment, providing social support for their more compliant fellows to join them.)

Psychopathological and Other Political Motivation

One of the ways in which humans vary is in the extent to which they manifest emotional disturbance and ego defensiveness. Equating all of personality with the psychological stratum that traditionally concerns clinical psychologists, some students of politics voice the third of the reservations about the study of personality and politics, arguing that the links between psychopathology and politics are rare and unimportant. A specific exploration of the general question of whether ego-defense motivation is common in politics can be found in the extensive empirical literature on the student political protest movements of the 1960s. Some research findings appeared to indicate that protest was rooted in "healthy" character traits, such as inner strength to stand by one's convictions and the cognitive capacity to cut through propaganda, whereas other reports suggested the possible influence of the kinds of neurotic needs that might, for example, arise from repressed resentment of parents or other everyday-life authority figures.

In order to consider the general issue of the role of psychopathology in politics and the specific issue of the roots of protest, it is necessary to elaborate the E → P → R formula. Figure 5.2 expands the personality panel in Fig. 5.1. The panel is constructed so as to suggest, in a metaphor common in personality theory (Hall and Lindzey, 1970), "levels" of psychic functioning. The level closest to the surface and most directly "in touch" with the environment is the perceptual. Perceptions can be thought of as a cognitive screen that shapes and structures environmental stimuli, sometimes dis-

torting them, sometimes reflecting them with considerable verisimilitude. In the 1970s and 1980s there was burgeoning inquiry into political perception and cognitive psychology more generally (Jervis, 1976; Jervis *et al.*, 1985; Lau & Sears, 1986; Vertzberger, 1990). Also at the surface, in the sense that they are conscious or accessible to consciousness, are political orientations such as attitudes, beliefs, and convictions. Psychologists commonly conceive of dispositions at this level as composites of the more basic processes of cognition (thought), affect (emotion), and conation (proclivities toward action).

The subpanel of Fig. 5.2 labeled "functional bases of conscious orientations" and, more or less synonymously, "basic personality structures," represents the level of psychic activity that political scientists often have in mind when they speak of personality. Different personality theorists emphasize the importance of different underlying personality structures, but most of them distinguish (in varied terminology) three broad classes of inner processes—those bearing on thought and perception, on emotions and their management (including feelings of which the individual may have little conscious understanding), and on the relation of the self to significant others. The terms used for these processes in Fig. 5.2 are *cognition, ego defense,* and *mediation of self–other relations.* Figure 5.2 also includes a subpanel identifying the genetic and acquired physical states that contribute to personality and diffuse into political behavior (Masters, 1989; Park, 1986).

Both the broad question of whether psychopathology manifests itself in political behavior and the narrow question of what motivates political rebels can be illuminated by reference to Fig. 5.2. One way of thinking about political attitudes and behavior is in terms of the functions they serve for the personality (Pratkanis et al., 1989; Smith et al., 1956)—hence the use of the phrase "functional

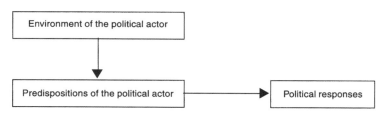

FIGURE 5.1 ■ Basic antecedents of political behavior: $E \rightarrow P \rightarrow R$.

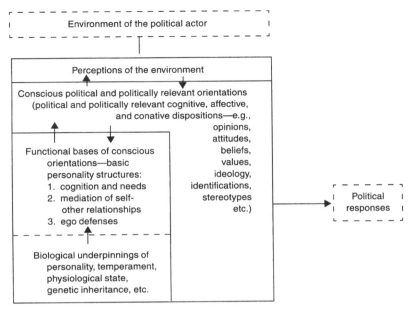

FIGURE 5.2 ■ Predispositions of the political actor.

bases of conscious orientations." What might on the surface seem to be the same belief or class of action, may serve different functions in the motivational economies of different people. For one individual a certain view—for example, a positive or negative racial stereotype—may result from the available information in the environment, mainly serving needs for cognitive closure. For another, the view might be rooted in a need to take cues from (or be different from) significant others. For a third, it might serve the ego-defensive function of venting unacknowledged aggressive impulses. (More often than not, a political behavior is likely to be fueled by more than one motivation but with varying mixes from individual to individual.)

The incidence of psychopathological and other motivational bases of political orientations needs to be established by empirical inquiry. Just as some environmental contexts leave room for the play of personality in general, some are especially conducive to the expression of ego defenses. These include stimuli that appeal to the powerful emotional impulses that people are socialized to deny but that remain potent beneath the surface. There is an especially steamy quality to political contention over issues that bear on sexuality like abortion and pornography. Nationalistic issues such as

flag burning and matters of religious doctrine also channel political passions (Davies, 1980), for reasons that have not been adequately explained. Extreme forms of behavior are also likely (though not certain) to have a pathological basis, as in the behavior of American presidential assassins such as Ronald Reagan's would-be killer, John Hinckley, Jr. (Clarke, 1990).

The circumstances under which psychopathology and its lesser variants find their way into politics are of great interest, as are those under which the other motivational bases of political behavior come into play. Depending upon the basic personality systems to which a given aspect of political performance is linked, differences can be expected in the conditions under which it will be aroused and changed, as well as in the detailed way it will manifest itself. Opinions and actions based in cognitive needs will be responsive to new information. Those based on social needs will respond to changes in the behavior and signals provided by significant others. Those based on ego defenses may be intractable, or only subject to change by extensive efforts to bring about self-insight, or by certain manipulative strategies such as suggestion by authority figures (Katz, 1960).

The functional approach to the study of political orientations provides a useful framework for determining whether and under what circumstances political protest has motivational sources in ego-defensive needs. There is much evidence bearing on this issue, at least as it applies to student protest. A remarkable number of empirical studies were done of student protest activity of the late 1960s and early 1970s in the United States and elsewhere, no doubt because that activity occurred in contexts where numerous social scientists were available to conduct research. A huge literature ensued, abounding in seemingly contradictory findings, many of which, however, appear to fit into a quite plausible larger pattern, once one takes account of the diversity of the institutions in which protest was studied and of the particular periods in the cycle of late-1960s and early 1970s student protest in which the various studies were conducted.

The earliest student protests of the 1960s occurred in colleges and universities with meritocratic admissions policies and upper-middle-class student bodies. The first studies of this period, those by Flacks (1967) of University of Chicago students, suggested that student protest was largely a cognitive manifestation—the response of able students to the perceived iniquities of their political environment. Later analyses of data collected in the same period on similar populations (students at the University of California, Berkeley) suggested a more complex pattern in which some of the activists did seem to have the cognitive strengths and preoccupations that Flacks had argued were the mark of *all* of them, but others appeared to be channeling ego-defensive needs (based in troubled parent-child relations) into their protest behavior. The students whom the later analysts concluded had ego-defensive motivations and those who they concluded were acting out of cognitive needs showed different patterns of protest behavior, the first directing their activity only on the issues of national and international politics, the second taking part in local reform activities (Block et al., 1969).

The psychological correlates of student activism changed over time in the United States, as activism became transformed from the activity of a few students in the "elite" universities to a widespread form of behavior, which at the time of the Nixon administration's incursion into Cambodia and the killing of student protesters at Kent Sate

University manifested itself on virtually every American college and university campus. Studies conducted at that time found little evidence that protesters had distinctive distinguishing characteristics (Dunlap, 1970; Peterson & Bilorusky, 1971).

Personality, Historical Context, and Social Background

Variation according to historical context and change over time are so important in determining how personality becomes linked with politics that the map around which this article is organized needs to be expanded, as it is in Fig. 5.3, which encompasses the time dimension and differentiates the immediate and remote features of the political environment. Figure 5.3 suggests that the fourth reservation about the utility of studying personality and politics—the claim that social backgrounds are more important than psychological characteristics—is grounded in a confusion which can be readily dissolved. The social backgrounds of political actors (panel 2 of Fig. 5.3) influence their actions but only as mediated by the individual's developing predispositions (panel 3) and the different levels of personality they shape (panels 4, 5, and 6). Thus, to take a final example from the literature on student protest in the 1960s, it was (as Block et al., 1969, pointed out at the time) fallacious for Lipset (1968) to argue that because so many student activists were young, middle-class Jews, personality was not an important determinant of activism. To the extent that Jewish background was connected with activism, it had to be part of a causal sequence in which developmental experiences specific to Jews contributed to their psychological orientations. The latter, not Jewish background per se, would have been the mediator of behavior.

The study of how ethnicity, class, and other of the so-called background characteristics affect political behavior is important and highly relevant to (but no substitute for) the study of personality and politics. To the extent that a characteristic becomes part of an actor's personal make-up, it is no longer "background"—it is an element of the psyche. But evidence about whether background experience distinguishes members of one social group from those of others is grist for political psychologists. Lipset may have been correct in

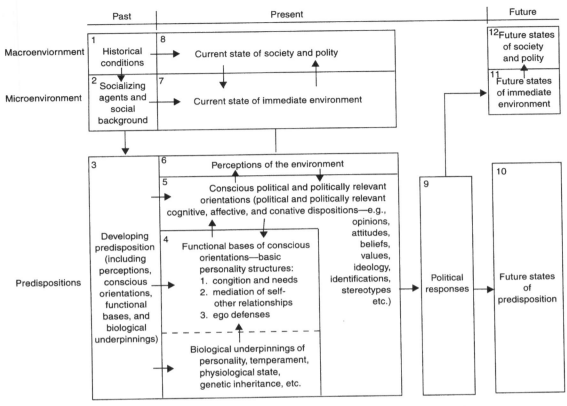

FIGURE 5.3 ■ A comprehensive map for the analysis of personality and politics.

sensing that Jewish political activists of the 1960s had some distinctive qualities that were important for their behavior. The observation that many student protesters were Jewish not only fails to prove this, but also forecloses systematic inquiry.

An appropriate program of inquiry into Lipset's claim would entail specifying the precise psychological dynamics that ostensibly make Jewish protesters distinctive and comparing Jewish and non-Jewish protesters with comparable nonprotesters in order to determine whether the imputed patterns existed. If they did, one would want to know whether they resulted from particular developmental histories, whether they had predictable consequences for political behavior, and why some Jews protested and some did not. Whether a distinctly Jewish psychology of political protest exists is an empirical question and is part of a broader set of questions that can be asked about how group membership affects personality and political behavior.

The Impact of Personality on Events

The last of the reservations about the study of personality and politics derives from the view that individuals are not likely to have much impact on events. Such a premise underlies many theories of history. In the 19th century the question of whether historical actors have an impact on events was the basis of a fruitless grand controversy, with such social determinists as Herbert Spencer denying the efficacy of historical actors and such Great Man theorists as Thomas Carlyle proclaiming their overriding importance (Kellerman, 1986, pp. 3–57). Contemporary leadership theorists typically describe themselves as interactionists, emphasizing the interdependence of leaders and their environments and the contingent nature of the leader's impact on larger events (Burns, 1978; Tucker, 1981).

The debate about whether actors can shape

events concerns the causal chain from personality (panels 4–6 of Fig. 5.3), through political response (panel 9), to future states of the immediate and more remote political and social environment (panels 11 and 12). Claims that a particular actor's personality did or did not affect a particular historical outcome usually prove to be claims about *action dispensability* and *actor dispensability* (Greenstein, 1969, pp. 40–46)—that is, about whether the outcome in question would have taken place in the absence of that individual's actions and whether the actions in question were ones that any similarly placed actor would have taken. The second issue is one I have already explored under the heading of personality and environment. The first requires clarification.

The capacity of actors to shape events is a variable not a constant. The sources of variation are parallel to the determinants of success in the game of pool. The number of balls a player will be able to sink is in part a function of the location of the balls on the table. The parallel in politics is the malleability of the political environment (Burke & Greenstein, 1989, p. 24). The second determinant of success in the pool room is the position of the cue ball. This is analogous to the actor's position in the relevant political context. Roosevelt and Gorbachev could not have had an impact from lower-level administrative positions. The third class of variable has the same labels in the games of pool and politics—skill, self-confidence, and the other personal requisites of effective performance.

Personality Theory, Role, and Culture

The distinctions summarized in Fig. 5.3 represent many of the basic categories in the multitude of personality theories that offer partial visions of psychic structure and function. The seeming Babel of competing personality theories and alternative nomenclatures conceals basic commonalities: all theories necessarily take cognizance that humans are thinking, feeling creatures who exist in social environments and have inner qualities that shape their response to those environments.

Beyond that, personality theories differ from one another in what they emphasize. The various personality theorists—Freud, Jung, Allport, Murray, and the many others—differ in the extent to which

they emphasize one class of motivation over another, in their sensitivity to the individual's environment, in the weight they put on biology, in the extent to which they view personality to be structured and in many other respects. For the present purposes it is not appropriate to recommend a particular personality theory. The advice Hall and Lindzey (1970, p. 602) offer all students of personality is equally sound for students of personality and politics. After becoming broadly acquainted with the field of personality, become immersed in a particular personality theory and "wallow in it, revel in it, absorb it, learn it thoroughly, and think that it is the best possible way to conceive of behavior," but "reserve in one small corner of [the] mind the reservation that the final crucible for any theory is the world of reality studied under controlled conditions." Then "set about the cold hard business of investigation."

Figure 5.3 does not make explicit provision for two important concepts for the student of political psychology—role and culture. What is their conceptual standing? The first of these terms has already appeared with some regularity in this paper. It is difficult to envisage an extended discussion of political psychology that does not take account of the way political actors perform their roles, and of the fit between role and personality and related matters. Yet, as Levinson (1959) shows, the referents of *role* are systematically ambiguous. Sometimes the term is used to refer to political behavior itself (Figure 5.3, panel 9), as in "His role in the Cuban Missile Crisis was critical." Sometimes it refers to the expectations in an individual's environment about what behavior is appropriate for someone filling that individual's position, in which case the referent would be mapped in panels 7 and 8 of Fig. 5.3. And sometimes the term refers to the role-incumbent's own assumptions about what the role entails (panel 5). As long as the referent is specified, an investigator may use the term in any of these senses, depending on his or her theoretical assumptions and concerns. Indeed, the mere act of recognizing the diversity of meaning may suggest fruitful hypotheses—for example, about whether and to what extent incumbents in particular roles and the individuals with whom they interact have shared conceptions of what the roles entail.

If the term role is ambiguous, culture is ambiguity run riot (Kroeber & Kluckhohn, 1952;

Merelman, 1984). A simple solution would be to conceive of the term as the counterpart at the collective level to personality at the individual level. If personality is used as an omnibus term to encompass the various elements of an individual's subjectivity, culture then would be used to encompass those elements at the collective level for societies, polities, and lesser entities. In Fig. 5.3, the referent would be the environmental panels (7 and 8). Such a usage, however, would leave no referent for terms like "acculturate," which refer to the individual's incorporation of cultural norms and assumptions. And it would bypass the issues that make culture such a protean term to begin with—for example, the debates about whether cultures are marked by structure and about what kinds of orientations are and are not parts of a culture. (If the term is simply synonymous with public opinion, it is redundant.) As with role, there seems to be no single usage that will command agreement. Because the various usages refer to different (and, in many cases, potentially interesting) phenomena, it is essential for investigators to specify the sense in which they are using the term.

Kinds of Personality and Politics Analysis

Every human being is in certain ways like all other human beings, in certain ways more like some human beings than others, and in certain ways unique (Kluckhohn & Murray, 1953). Each of these resemblances is reflected in an analytically distinct kind of personality-and-politics analysis. The universality of human qualities is explored in writings that seek in some broad way to make the connection stated in the title of Graham Wallas' *Human Nature and Politics* (1908). Sigmund Freud's *Civilization and its Discontents* (1930), Fromm's *Escape from Freedom* (1941), Norman O. Brown's *Life Against Death* (1959) and Herbert Marcuse's *Eros and Civilization* (1966) are notable contributions to this tradition. At their best such works provide fascinating and provocative perspectives on the human condition. Many of them are rich in insights that suggest testable hypotheses.

Because they seek to explain the variable phenomena of political behavior with a constant, such efforts are not themselves subject to confirmation or disconfirmation. In contrast, it *is* possible to conduct systematic, replicable inquiries into political actors' unique qualities (*single-case analysis*) and the qualities that make them more like some individuals than others (*typological analysis*). The ways in which individual and typical political psychology affects the performance of political processes and institutions (*aggregation*) can also be studied systematically.

Single-case personality analysis is more important in the field of personality and politics than it has come to be in personality psychology generally because students of politics are concerned with the performance of specific leaders and their impact on events. There have been noteworthy personality-and-politics studies of leaders as diverse in time, culture and circumstances of their leadership as Martin Luther (Erikson, 1958), Louis XII (Marvick, 1986), Woodrow Wilson (George & George, 1964), Kemal Ataturk (Volkan & Itzkowitz, 1984), and Josef Stalin (Tucker, 1973), as well as many others. There also have been valuable single-case psychological analyses of figures whose political importance derives from their impact on leaders—for example, George and George's analysis (1964) of the influence of Colonel Edward House on Woodrow Wilson and Kull's (1988) of defense policy advisers. In addition, there is a tradition in the field of personality and politics of single-case analyses of "faces in the crowd"—people who are without policy influence but who illustrate in depth the psychological process that can only be examined more superficially in surveys (Riesman & Glazer, 1952; Smith *et al.*, 1956; Lane, 1962).

Typological study of political and other actors is of potentially great importance: if political actors fall into types with known characteristics and propensities, the laborious task of analyzing them *de novo* can be obviated, and uncertainty is reduced about how they will perform in particular circumstances. The notion of a psychological *type* can be stretched to include all efforts to categorize and compare the psychology of political actors, even straightforward classifications of the members of a population in terms of whether they are high or low on some trait such as ego strength, self-esteem, or tolerance of ambiguity. The more full-blown political psychology typologies parallel diagnostic categories in medicine and psychiatry. They identify syndromes—patterns of observable characteristics that reflect identifiable underlying conditions, result from distinctive developmental histories, and have predictable consequences.

Of the many studies that employ the first, simpler kind of psychological categorization, the studies by Herbert McClosky and his students are particularly valuable because of their theoretical and methodological sophistication and the importance of the issues they address (e.g., Di Palma & McClosky, 1970; McClosky, 1967; McClosky & Zaller, 1984; Sniderman, 1974). Political personality typologies of the second, more comprehensive variety go back at least to Plato's account in the eighth and ninth books of *The Republic* of the aristocrat, the democrat, the timocrat, and the tyrant—political types that Plato believed were shaped in an intergenerational dialectic of rebellion of sons against their fathers' perceived shortcomings. (For a gloss on Plato's account, see Lasswell [1960].) Latter-day typologies that have generated important bodies of literature are the authoritarian, dogmatic, and Machiavellian personality classifications (Adorno *et al.*, 1950; Christie & Geis, 1970; Rokeach, 1960).

Within political science, the best-known personality typology has been James David Barber's (1985) classification of the character structures of American presidents. Within psychology, the best-known has been that of the authoritarian personality. Both typologies have engendered methodological controversies that for a time, at least, threatened to submerge the insights in the works in which they were originally set forth (George, 1974; Kirscht & Dillehay, 1967), but both contain important insights and may eventually stimulate cumulative bodies of scholarship.

This can occur even after a long dormant period, as can be seen by the tangled history of studies of authoritarianism. By the late 1960s, the massive literature exploring the implications of that construct appeared to be at a dead end. But in the 1980s an ingenious and rigorous program of inquiry by Altemeyer (1981, 1988) furnished persuasive empirical evidence that the original authoritarian construct was an approximation of an important political–psychological regularity—the existence in some individuals of an inner makeup that disposes them to defer to authority figures.

Single-case and typological studies alike make inferences about the inner quality of human beings (panels 4, 5, and 6) from outer manifestations—their past and present environments (panels 1, 2, 7, and 8) and the pattern over time of their political responses (panel 9). They then use those inferred constructs to account for the same kind of phenomena from which they were inferred—responses in situational contexts. The danger of circularity is obvious, but tautology can be avoided by reconstructing personality from some response patterns and using the reconstruction to explain others.

The failure of some investigators to take such pains contributes to the controversial status of the personality-and-politics literature, as does the prevalence of certain other practices. Some biographers, for example, impose diagnostic labels on their subject, rather than presenting a systematic account of the subject's behavior in disparate circumstances (George, 1971). Some typological analysts categorize their subjects without providing the detailed criteria and justifications for doing so. Some analysts of individuals as well as of types have engaged in the fallacy of observing a pattern of behavior and simply attributing it to a particular developmental pattern, without documenting causality, and perhaps even without providing evidence that the pattern existed. Finally, some analysts commit what might be called the psychologizing and clinical fallacies: they explain behavior in terms of personality without considering possible situational determinants, or conclude that it is driven by psychopathology without considering other psychological determinants, such as cognition. Both fallacies were evident in a body of literature attributing the high scores of poor blacks and other minorities on the paranoia scale of the Minnesota Multiphasic Personality Inventory (MMPI) to emotional disturbance. The scores appear actually to have reflected cognitively based responses to the vicissitudes of the ghetto environment (Gynther, 1972; Newhill, 1990).

It is not surprising that some personality-and-politics studies are marked by methodological shortcomings. Certain of the inferences mapped in Figure 5.3 pose intrinsic difficulties. Claims about the determinants of personality characteristics (that is, of the connections between panels 1 and 2 and panels 3–6) are unlikely to be conclusive. Characterizations of personality structures themselves are never wholly persuasive, if only because of the absence of uniformly accepted personality theories with agreed-upon terminologies.

Fortunately, the variables depicted in Figure 5.3 that *can* be characterized with great confidence are those closest to and therefore most predictive of behavior: the environments in which political action occurs (panels 7 and 8) and the patterns that action manifests over time (panels 9, 10, etc.). Those patterns are themselves variables, and they can be treated as indicators of an important further dimension of personality and politics—*political style.*

Two examples of political biographies that provide impressively comprehensive accounts of the precise patterns of their subjects' behavior are Walter's study of Australian Prime Minister Gough Whitlam (1980) and Landis's (1987) of Senator Joseph McCarthy. Richard Christie's (Christie & Geis, 1970) studies of the types of people who manifest the Machiavellian syndrome—the characterological proclivity to manipulate others—provide a model of careful measurement and theoretically sophisticated analysis in which contingent relationships are carefully explored. People who score high on tests of Machiavellianism do not differ in their behavior from non-Machiavellians in all contexts, only in contexts in which their manipulative impulses can be effective—for example, in situations that permit improvisation and in situations requiring face-to-face interaction.

Personality is likely to interest most political scientists only if it has aggregate consequences for political institutions, processes, and outcomes. The literature on the aggregate effects of personality on politics is varied because the processes of aggregation are varied. Broadly speaking, political psychology affects the performance of political systems and processes through the activities of members of the public and the deliberations and decision-making of leaders. The impact of mass publics on politics, except through elections and severe perturbations of public opinion, is partial and often elusive. On the other hand, the political impact of leaders and others in the active political stratum, more generally is direct, readily evident, and potentially momentous in its repercussions.

The first efforts to understand the psychology of mass populations go back to the accounts by writers in the ancient world, such as Tacitus, of the character of the inhabitants of remote tribes and nations. Such disquisitions are an antecedent of the vexed post-World War II national character literature in which often ill-documented ethno-graphic reports and cultural artifacts such as child-rearing manuals, films, and popular fiction were used to draw sweeping conclusions about modal national character traits. That literature came therefore to be known to students of politics mainly for its methodological shortcomings, but it anticipated later, more systematic studies of political culture (Inkeles & Levinson, 1967; Inkeles, 1983).

By the 1950s, there was broad scholarly consensus that it is inappropriate simply to attribute psychological characteristics to mass populations on the basis of anecdotal or indirect evidence. Direct assessment of publics through survey research became the dominant mode of studying mass populations. Studies like those of McClosky and his associates provide survey data on basic personality processes such as ego-defenses and cognitive styles and how they affect political opinion. But basic personality processes have not been persuasively linked to the aspect of mass behavior that most clearly and observably has an impact on political institutions and processes—electoral choice. Most members of the general public appear to be too weakly involved in electoral politics for their voting choices to tap deeper psychological roots, and many of those who are involved appear to take their cues from party identifications formed in their early years and short-run situational stimuli.

If what is commonly thought of as personality is not linked to electoral choice, attitudinal political psychology most definitely is. The literature on electoral choice (Niemi & Weisberg, 1984) is too vast to begin to review here, but the research of Kelley (1983) is of particular interest in that it is explicitly aggregative; it reveals the precise distributions of attitudes and beliefs about issues and candidates that were associated with post-World War II American election outcomes. So is the research of Converse and Pierce (1986), who have convincingly linked certain attributes of the French political system to the distinctive ways members of that nation's electorate orient themselves to political parties.

In contrast to the ambiguous links between mass publics and political outcomes other than elections, the connections between political decision-makers and political outcomes are direct and palpable. Nevertheless, many historical reconstructions of political decision-making are insufficiently specific about which actors in what precise contexts took which actions with what consequences.

Sometimes the historical record does not contain the appropriate data. Often, however, the difficulty is not with the record but with the way it has been analyzed.

The questions the analyst needs to ask of an historical record are suggested by two of the analytic distinctions introduced above—*action dispensibility* and *actor dispensibility*. Establishing whether an individual's actions were necessary for a particular outcome to have taken place calls for reconstructing the determinants of the outcome, asking whether it would have occurred if the actions of the individual in question had not occurred. Establishing whether that individual's personality shaped the outcome calls for a different and more complex reconstruction that asks whether the situation of the actor in question would have imposed the same course of action on anyone who might plausibly have occupied that individual's position. This calls for examining not only the psychology of the individual in question, but also the historical context, including the other significant actors and their claims, demands, perceptions, and personal qualities.

A good example of an historical reconstruction that addresses both issues is the analysis by George and George (1956) of Woodrow Wilson's role in the crisis over ratification of the Versailles Treaty. The intense, uncompromising qualities of Wilson the man, at least in certain kinds of conflicts, are an essential part of any account of the ratification fight. There is abundant evidence that the political context did not impose a course of action on Wilson that would have kept him from achieving his goal of ratification. All that was required was that he accept certain nominal compromises that his supporters urged upon him, pointing out that they had no practical significance. Moreover, Wilson's actions are necessary to explain the outcome. Wilson's supporters were lined up for a favorable ratification vote, but were unprepared to act unless he authorized them to accept mild qualifying language. This he refused to do.

The explanatory logic of propositions about whether an individual's actions and characteristics were consequential in some episode is that of counter-factual reasoning. This is the only available alternative in analyses of single events to the quantitative analysis that would be called for if data existed on large numbers of comparable episodes. Counter-factual reasoning is not falsifiable, but it can be systematic. To be so it must be explicit and addressed to bounded questions—not conundrums about remote contingencies. "Was Lyndon Johnson's action necessary for the 1965 American escalation in Vietnam to have occurred?" is an example of a question that is susceptible to investigation (Burke & Greenstein, 1989). "If Cleopatra's nose had been an inch longer, how would world history have been changed?" is an example of one that is not.

Personality and political psychology more generally affect political processes not only through the actions taken by leaders more or less on their own, but also through group processes such as the collective suspension of reality testing manifested in what Irving Janis (1983) has characterized as groupthink. Groupthink occurs in highly cohesive decision-making groups. The members of such groups sometimes become so committed to their colleagues they more or less unconsciously suspend their own critical faculties in order to preserve group harmony. Janis, who is scrupulous about setting forth the criteria for establishing whether a group has engaged in groupthink, analyzes a number of historical episodes (the most striking example being the Bay of Pigs) in which a defective decision-making process appears to have led able policy-makers to make decisions on the basis of flawed assumptions and defective information. To the extent that groupthink is a purely collective phenomenon, emerging from group interaction, it is a manifestation of social psychology rather than personality psychology. But, as Janis suggests, personality probably contributes to groupthink in that some personalities are more likely than others to suspend their critical capacities in group settings.

Concluding Remarks

Political institutions and processes operate through human agency. It would be remarkable if they were *not* influenced by the properties that distinguish one individual from another. In examining that influence, I have emphasized the logic of inquiry. In doing so I have not attempted a comprehensive review of the literature. For a variety of useful reviews and compendia, readers should consult Greenstein and Lerner (1971), Knutson (1973), Stone (1981), Hermann (1986), and Simonton (1990).

To the extent that this article brings out possible pitfalls in studies of personality and politics, its message to cautious scholars may *seem* to be the following: Find pastures that can be more easily cultivated. Even daring scholars might conclude that the prospects for the systematic study of personality and politics are too remote to justify the investment of scholarly time and effort. Nothing in this article is meant to support such conclusions. In a parable on the shortcomings of scientific opportunism, Kaplan (1964, pp. 11, 16–17) relates the story of a drunkard who lost his keys in a dark alley and is found searching for them under a street lamp, declaring, "It's lighter here." The drunkard's search is a poor model. If the connections between the personalities of political actors and their political behavior are obscure, all the more reason to illuminate them.

REFERENCES

Adorno, T. W., Frenkel-Brunswick, E., Levinson, D. J., & Sanford, R. N. (1950). *The authoritarian personality.* New York: Harper.

Allen, V. L. (1975). Social support for nonconformity. *Advances in Experimental Social Psychology 8*, 1–43.

Allport, G. W. (1937). *Personality: A psychological interpretation.* New York: Holt.

Altemeyer, B. (1981). *Right-wing authoritarianism.* Winnipeg: University of Manitoba Press.

Altemeyer, B. (1988). *Enemies of freedom: Understanding right-wing authoritarianism.* San Francisco: Jossey-Bass.

Asch, S. E. (1956). Studies of independence and conformity: A minority of one versus a unanimous majority. *Psychological Monographs 70*, 9, Whole No. 406.

Barber, J. D. (1985). *The presidential character: Predicting performance in the White House*, 3rd ed., Englewood Cliffs, NJ: Prentice-Hall.

Brown, N. O. (1959). *Life against death.* Middletown, CT: Wesleyan University Press.

Browning, R. P., & Jacobs, H. (1964). Power motivation and the political personality. *Public Opinion Quarterly 24*, 75–90.

Block, J. H., Haan, N., and Smith, M. B. (1969). Socialization correlates of student activism. *Journal of Social Issues 25*, 143–77.

Budner, S. (1962). Intolerance of ambiguity as a personality variable. *Journal of Personality 30*, 22–50.

Burns, J. M. (1978). *Leadership.* New York: Harper and Row.

Burke, J. P., & Greenstein, F. I. (1989). *How presidents test reality: Decisions on Vietnam, 1954 and 1965.* New York: Russell Sage Foundation.

Campbell, D. T. (1963). Social attitudes and other acquired behavioral dispositions. In S. Koch, (Ed.), *Psychology: A study of a science*, Vol. 6 (pp. 94–172). New York: McGraw Hill.

Christie, R., & Geis, F. L. (1970). *Studies in Machiavellianism.* New York: Academic Press.

Clarke, J. W. (1990). *On being mad or merely angry: John W. Hinckley Jr. and other dangerous people.* Princeton, NJ: Princeton University Press.

Converse, P. E., & Pierce, R. (1986). *Political representation in France.* Cambridge, MA: Harvard University Press.

Davies, A. F. (1980). *Skills, outlooks and passions: A psychoanalytic contribution to the study of politics.* Cambridge, MA: Cambridge University Press.

Di Palma, G., & McClosky, H. (1970). Personality and conformity: The learning of political attitudes. *American Political Science Review 64*, 1054–1073.

Dunlap, R. (1970). Radical and conservative student activists: A comparison of family backgrounds. *Pacific Sociological Review 13*, 171–181.

Endler, N. S. (1981). Persons, situations, and their interactions. In A. I. Rabin, J. Aronoff, A. M. Barclay, & R. A. Zucker (Eds.), *Further explorations in personality* (pp. 114–151). New York: Wiley

Erikson, E. H. (1958). *Young man Luther: A Study in psychoanalysis and history.* New York: Norton.

Flacks, R. (1967). The liberated generation: An exploration of the roots of student protest. *Journal of Social Issues 25*, 52–75.

Freud, S. (1930). Civilization and its discontents. In J. Stratchey (Ed.), *The standard edition of the complete psychological works of Sigmund Freud*, Vol. 17. London: Hogarth.

Fromm, E. (1941). *Escape from freedom.* New York: Rinehart.

George, A. L. (1971). Some uses of dynamic psychology in political biography: Case materials on Woodrow Wilson. In Fred I. Greenstein, & Michael Lemer (Eds.), *A source book for the study of personality and politics.* Chicago: Markham. [Reprinted in Cocks, G., & Crosby, T. L. (Eds.), *Psycho/history: Readings in the method of psychology, psychoanalysis and history.* New Haven, CT: Yale University Press, 1987, pp. 132–156.]

George, A. L. (1974). Assessing presidential character. *World Politics 26*, 234–282.

George, A. L. (1980). *Presidential decisionmaking in foreign policy: The effective use of advice and information.* Boulder, CO: Westview Press.

George, A. L., & George, J. L. (1956). *Woodrow Wilson and Colonel House: A personality study.* New York: John Day (Reprinted by Dover 1964).

Greenstein, F. I. (1969). *Personality and politics: Problems of evidence, inference and conceptualization.* Chicago: Markham (Current edition Princeton University Press, 1987).

Greenstein, F. I. (1975). Personality and politics. In F. I. Greenstein, & N. W. Polsby (Eds.), *The handbook of political science: Micropolitical theory.* Vol. 2 (pp. 1–92). Reading, MA: Addison-Wesley

Greenstein, F. I. (1991). Personality and politics. In M. Hawkesworth, & M. K. Kogan (Eds.), *Routledge encyclopedia of government and politics.* In press.

Greenstein, F. I., & Lerner, M. (1971). *A source book for the study of personality and politics.* Chicago: Markham.

Gynther, M. (1972). White norms and black MMPIs: A prescription for discrimination. *Psychological Bulletin 78*, 386–402.

Hall, C. S., & Lindzey, G. (Eds.) (1970). *Theories of personality.* 2nd ed., New York: Wiley.

Hermann, M. G. (Ed.) (1986). *Political psychology*. San Francisco: Jossey-Bass.

Inkeles, I. (1983). *Exploring individual modernity*. New York: Columbia University Press.

Inkeles, I., & Levinson, D. J. (1967). National character: The study of modal personality. In Lindzey, G., & Aronson, E. (Eds.), *The handbook of social psychology*. Vol. 4, 2nd ed., Reading, MA: Addison-Wesley.

Janis, I. L. (1982). *Groupthink: Psychological studies of policy decisions and fiascos*, 2nd ed., Boston, MA: Houghton, Mifflin.

Jervis, R. (1976). *Perception and misperception in international politics*. Princeton. NJ: Princeton University Press.

Jervis, R., Lebow, R. N., & Stein, J. (1985) *Psychology and deterrence*. Baltimore, MD: Johns Hopkins University Press.

Kaplan, A. (1964). *The conduct of inquiry: Methodology for behavioral sciences*. San Francisco: Chandler.

Katz, D. (1960). The functional approach to the study of attitudes. *Public Opinion Quarterly 24*, 163–204.

Katz, I., & Benjamin, L. (1960). The effects of authoritarianism on biracial work groups. *Journal of Abnormal and Social Psychology 61*, 448–456.

Kellerman, B. (Ed.) (1986). *Political leadership: A source book*. Pittsburgh. PA: University of Pittsburgh Press.

Kelley, S. K., Jr. (1983). *Interpreting elections*. Princeton, NJ: Princeton University Press.

Kirscht, J. P., & Dillehay, J. P. (1967). *Dimensions of authoritarianism*. Lexington, KY: University of Kentucky Press.

Kluckhohn, C., & Murray, H. A. (1953). Personality formation: The determinants. In C. Kluckhohn. & H. A. Murray (Eds.), *Personality in nature, society and culture*, 2nd Ed. (pp. 53–67). New York: Knopf.

Knutson, J. N. (1973). *Handbook of political psychology*. San Francisco: Jossey-Bass.

Kroeber, A. L., & Kluckhohn, C. (1952). Culture: A critical review of concepts and definitions. In *Papers of the Peabody Museum of American Archaeology and Ethnology 47*, I, Harvard University, Cambridge, MA.

Kull, S. (1988). *Minds at war: Nuclear reality and the inner conflict of defense policymakers*. New York: Basic Books.

Landis, M. (1987). *Joseph McCarthy: The politics of chaos*. Cranbury, NJ: Associated Universities Presses.

Lane, R. E. (1962). *Political ideology: Why the common man believes what he does*. New York: The Free Press of Glencoe.

Lasswell, H. D. (1930). *Psychopathology and politics*. Chicago: University of Chicago Press, (University of Chicago Press Midway Reprint, 1986).

Lasswell, H. D. (1960). Political character and constitution. *Psychoanalysis and Psychoanalytic Review 46*, 1–18.

Lasswell, H. D., & Kaplan, A. (1950). *Power and society: A framework for political inquiry*, New Haven, CT: Yale University Press.

Lau, R. R., & Sears, D. O. (Eds.) (1986). *Political cognition*. Hillsdale, NJ: Lawrence Erlbaum Associates.

Levinson, D. J. (1959). Role, personality, and social structure in the organizational setting. *Journal of Abnormal and Social Psychology 58*, 170–180.

Lewin, K. (1935). *Principles of topological psychology*. New York: McGraw-Hill.

Lipset, S. M. (1968). The activists: A profile. In Daniel Bell, & Irving Kristol (Eds.), *Confrontation: The student rebellion and the universities* (pp. 44–57). New York: Basic Books.

Magnusson, D., & Endler, N. S. (Eds.) (1977). *Personality at the crossroads: Current issues in interactional psychology*, Hillsdale, NJ: Lawrence Erlbaum Associates.

Marcuse, H. (1966). *Eros and civilization* (revised edition). Boston, MA: Beacon.

Marvick, E. W. (1986). *Louis XIII: The making of a king*. New Haven, CT: Yale University Press.

Masters, R. D. (1989). *The nature of politics*. New Haven, CT: Yale University Press.

McClosky, H. (1967). Personality and attitude correlates of foreign policy orientations. In J. N. Rosenau (Ed.), *Domestic sources of foreign policy* (pp. 51–109). New York: The Free Press of Glencoe.

McClosky, H., and Zaller, J. (1984). *The American ethos: Public attitudes toward capitalism and democracy*. Cambridge, MA: Harvard University Press.

Merelman, R. M. (1984). *Making something of ourselves: On culture and politics in the United States*. Berkeley, CA: University of California Press.

Murray, H. A. (1968). Personality: contemporary viewpoints: Components of an evolving personological system. *International encyclopedia of the social sciences* Vol. 12. New York: Macmillan.

Newhill, C. E. (1990). The role of culture in the development of paranoid symptomatology. *American Journal of Orthopsychiatry 60*, 176–85.

Niemi, R., & Weisberg, H. E. (1984). *Controversies in voting behavior*, 2nd Ed., Washington, DC: Congressional Quarterly Press.

Park, B. E. (1986). *The impact of illness on world leaders*. Philadelphia, PA: University of Pennsylvania Press.

Pervin. L. A., & Lewis, M. (Eds.) (1978). *Perspectives on interactional psychology*. New York: Plenum.

Peterson. R. E., & Bilorusky, J. A. (1971). *May 1970: The campus aftermath of Cambodia and Kent State*. New York: The Carnegie Foundation for the Advancement of Teaching.

Pratkanis, A. R., Breckler, S. J., & Greenwald, A. G. (Eds.) (1989). *Attitude structure and function*. Hillsdale, NJ: Lawrence Erlbaum Associates.

Riesman, D., & Glazer, N. (1952). *Faces in the crowd: Individual studies of character and politics*. New Haven, CT: Yale University Press.

Rokeach, M. (1960). *The open and the closed mind: Investigations into the nature of belief systems and personality systems*. New York: Basic Books.

Simon, H. A. (1985). Human nature in politics: The dialogue of psychology with political science. *American Political Science Review 79*, 293–304.

Simonton, D. K. (1990). Personality and politics. In L. A. Pervin (Ed.), *Handbook of personality: Theory and research* (pp. 670–692). New York: Guilford.

Smith, M. B. (1968). A map for the study of personality and politics. *Journal of Social Issues 24*, 15–28.

Smith, M. B., Bruner, J. S., & White, R. W. (1956). *Opinions and personality*. New York: Wiley.

Sniderman, P. M. (1974). *Personality and democratic politics*. Berkeley, CA: University of California Press.

Stone, W. F. (1981). Political psychology: A Whig history. In S. L. Long (Ed.), *The handbook of political behavior*, Vol. 1, New York: Plenum.

Stone, W. F., & Schaffner, P. E. (1988). *The psychology of politics*, 2nd Ed., New York: Springer Verlag.

Tucker, R. C. (1965). The dictator and totalitarianism. *World Politics 17*, 555–583.

Tucker, R. C. (1973). *Stalin as revolutionary, 1879–1929: A short study in history and personality.* New York: Norton.

Tucker, R. C. (1981). *Politics as leadership.* Columbia, MO: University of Missouri Press.

Vertzberger, Y. Y. I. (1990). *The world in their minds: Information processing, cognition, and perception in foreign policy decisionmaking.* Stanford, CA: Stanford University Press.

Volkan, V. D., and Itzkowitz, N. (1984). *The immortal Ataturk: A psychobiography.* Chicago: University of Chicago Press.

Wallas, G. (1908). *Human nature and politics*, 3rd Ed. New York: Crofts.

Walter, J. (1980). *The leader: A political biography of Gough Whitlam.* St. Lucia, Queensland: University of Queensland Press.

Leader Appeal, Leader Performance, and the Motive Profiles of Leaders and Followers: A Study of American Presidents and Elections

David G. Winter • Wesleyan University

Three leader trait and leader–follower interaction models of leader appeal and leader performance are evaluated with data about the motive profiles of American presidents and American society, in both cases measured at a distance. Presidential appeal, defined in terms of electoral success, is significantly correlated with the congruence or match between the president's motive profile and that of his contemporary society. In contrast, presidential greatness, as rated by historians, as well as several important outcomes involving war and peace are associated with certain of the president's motives by themselves, but not with president–society congruence.

What is a great leader? What is a popular leader? Are they the same? Are they the result of the same or different factors? Our naive belief in the "great person" theory of leadership, that the person shapes events and the leader creates his or her own greatness, has long been challenged by scholars from diverse disciplines who analyze leadership appeal and performance into broad impersonal forces and social-structural factors. Yet in the real world of politics, the factor of personal appeal or having (in the language of the Harris poll) "an attractive, forceful personality" is of enormous concern to campaign strategists and journalists (even if it is largely treated as error

variance by voting analysts; see Nie, Verba, & Petrocik, 1979; Sears, 1969). And in the real world of history, successful leaders such as Abraham Lincoln or Franklin D. Roosevelt display such a blend of wisdom, flexibility, and good tactics that we conclude their greatness must be based, at least in part, on personal characteristics (e.g., see Burns, 1956; Haley, 1969; Vidal, 1984).

Can these phenomena of greatness and appeal among political leaders be analyzed in psychological terms? Several classic theories and a good deal of contemporary social psychological research suggest a variety of models for a leader's appeal and performance. This article presents data on the psychological characteristics of one kind of leader—American presidents—and one series of followers—American society from the 1780s through the 1960s—as an empirical commentary on (not a test of) these theories and issues.

Theories and Models of Leader Appeal

Leader Characteristics

Max Weber's concept of charisma (or the "gift of grace") as one base of the legitimacy of authority is obviously related to the leader's personal appeal and performance when structural and traditional factors are held constant. To Weber, the charismatic leader possesses "a certain quality of personality by virtue of which he is set apart from ordinary men and treated as endowed with supernatural, superhuman, or at least specifically exceptional powers or qualities." Followers obey out of duty rather than choice or calculation; as Weber put it, "No prophet has ever regarded his quality [of charisma] as dependent on the attributes of the masses around him." Of course Weber did acknowledge that in the long run the followers' needs and satisfactions are important. "If [the leader] is for long unsuccessful, above all if his leadership fails to benefit his followers, it is likely that his charismatic authority will disappear" (1947, pp. 358–360).

Although Freud analyzed the dynamics of group formation in terms of the followers' identification in their ego ideal or superego with the leader, he emphasized the characteristics of the successful leader in facilitating these identifications. "The leader himself need love no one else, he may be of a masterful nature, absolutely narcissistic, self-confident, and independent" (1921/1955, pp. 123–124).

Thus one psychological model of political leaders' appeal and success focuses on relatively enduring personal characteristics (e.g., narcissism, energy, self-direction) that some leaders simply happen to possess. Although the great-person theory of leadership implicit in this model is now in some disrepute (see Gibb, 1969; Hollander, 1964), many experimental studies do show the modest positive correlations between leadership and self-esteem, self-confidence, and related variables (see Bass, 1981, pp. 74–92) that would be predicted from the Weber–Freud model.

Leader–Situation Match

Nowadays many theorists and most experimentalists would argue that the leader's appeal and success depend on the situation, so that the personality characteristics required for successful, appealing leadership will vary with the situation. Recently Bem and Funder (1978) and Bem and Lord (1979) have expressed this notion more formally in the concept of the degree of match between a person and the *template* (required characteristics) of the situation, and they have gone on to suggest ways of measuring situational demands.

Barber's (1980) recent cyclical model of American elections is an application of the notion of leader–situation template matching or congruence in a political context. According to Barber, American presidential elections follow a regular course: first, a focus on *conflict* of forces; then, a concern for *conscience*; and finally, a need for *conciliation* to bring all parties together again. This leads, in turn, to a renewed conflict orientation. From election to election the requirements for personal appeal and success in office might vary in a corresponding fashion: In a "conflict" year, the candidate who is the best fighter will be appealing and victorious, but when the concern is with conciliation, the candidate who promises to "bring us together" will gain popular appeal. Barber believed that these three issues are derived from the most basic social-political aspects of human nature; that the cyclical dynamic has a force of its own. Thus his theory involves a kind of match between leader and situation, but the situation is conceived in terms of abstract, impersonal forces rather than in terms of particular personal characteristics of the followers.

Leader–Follower Match

In contrast to the impersonal cycle of Barber's theory, Erikson offered a theory of the relation between leaders and their societies that is explicitly focused on the relation between leaders' and followers' characteristics. On the basis of several studies of "inspiring and effective [men] of action" such as Hitler, Luther, and Gandhi (Erikson, 1950,

1958, and 1969, respectively), Erikson concluded that leaders, with their own identities, conflicts, and needs, are "found and chosen by contemporaries possessed of analogous conflicts and corresponding needs" (1964, p. 204). In other words, the success of such leaders depends on a match between their own personal characteristics and the historically conditioned characteristics of their potential followers. Phrased in this way Erikson's theory is supported by the extensive experimental literature relating leadership success to a kind of congruence between leaders' characteristics and followers' characteristics (see Bass, 1981, pp. 31–33). Erikson also mentioned some transsituational abilities of the leader, but they are not formally incorporated into his theory: "An unusual energy of body, a rare concentration of mind, and a total devotion of soul. . . . Intuitive grasp of the actualities of the led . . . [and] ability to introduce himself into that actuality as a new, vital factor (personality, image, style)" (1964, pp. 203, 208).

Taken together, these theories suggest several different kinds of factors that may account for the personal appeal and greatness of political leaders: (a) leader characteristics independent of the situation, (b) leader characteristics that match systematically changing situational demands, and (c) leader characteristics that match characteristics of followers or of the population in general, whatever the determinants of these latter characteristics may be.

The several explanations of leadership are quite parallel to familiar psychological explanations of other behaviors: an initial person or "trait" explanation (e.g., Allport, 1937), later debunked for a time (e.g., Mischel, 1968), and followed by a focus on the interaction of person and situation (e.g., Magnusson & Endler, 1977). The rest of this article will explore the usefulness of these models by analyzing American presidents and presidential elections. Some questions to be asked include: What is the psychological basis of presidential appeal? Does it involve leader characteristics or some kind of leader–situation match? What is the psychological basis of presidential greatness? Are the leaders who appeal the most to the electorate also the greatest or best leaders? In some sense, this last question reaches down to the foundations of democratic political theory. (See Simonton, 1981, for a study of other, nonpsychological determinants of presidential greatness.)

Empirical Studies of Presidents and Elections

The American presidency is an excellent source of material for studying the appeal and performance of political leaders. Although the size of the population is rather small, the efforts of historians, political scientists, and archivists have accumulated an enormous amount of data. In recent years, many scholars have begun to analyze the presidency with the quantitative and statistical methods familiar to the behavioral sciences (e.g., Maranell, 1970; Murray & Blessing, 1983; Simonton, 1981). Recent advances in the technology for assessing the personalities of key political actors at a distance (cf. Hermann, 1977) and measuring the modal personality of groups of followers over time through coding cultural documents (e.g., McClelland, 1961, 1975, especially Appendix IV) have made it possible to study, in psychological terms, the leadership appeal and performance of American presidents in their society.

For both leaders and followers, this study focuses on three important human social motives: (a) the achievement motive, a concern for excellence, which is associated with moderate risk taking, using feedback, and entrepreneurial success (McClelland, 1961); (b) the affiliation–intimacy motive, a concern for close relations with others, which is associated with interpersonal warmth, self-disclosure, and good overall adaptation to life (McAdams, 1982); and (c) the power motive, a concern for impact and prestige, which is associated with getting formal social power and also profligate impulsive actions such as aggression, drinking, and taking extreme risks (Winter, 1973; Winter & Stewart, 1978).

Motivation focuses on the broad classes of people's goals and goal-directed actions, and so it is a component of personality that is especially important to the relations between leaders and followers. These particular motives are drawn from Murray's comprehensive taxonomy. Although they are not the only human motives, several lines of evidence do suggest that they are major motives involving the most important common human concerns. Power and affiliation, for example, repeatedly emerge as the two fundamental dimensions of social behavior (see Brown, 1965, chapter 2) and interpersonal traits (Conte & Plutchik, 1981; Wiggins, 1980). Achievement reflects the dimension of evaluation that is consistently the most important factor of connotative meaning (Snider & Osgood, 1969). These three motives are closely matched to the three dimensions used by Bales (1970) to describe group functioning (forward–backward, positive–negative, and upward–downward, respectively).

Winter and Stewart (1977) have demonstrated that these three motives are relevant to several important kinds of political action and outcomes. Whereas the motives were originally measured in individuals by content analysis of Thematic Apperception Test (TAT) responses, the new integrated scoring system, developed by Winter (1983) for scoring motive imagery in any kind of verbal material, makes it possible to score presidents at a distance. Thus, both leaders and followers are assessed by means of the same methods and scoring techniques. This makes it possible to describe the characteristics of leaders and situations (or followers) in terms that are both psychologically meaningful and also commensurate with each other. (See Winter, 1973, 1983, for a general description of the psychometric characteristics, including reliability, of the motive measures.)

Method

Sources of Data

For each president from Washington through Reagan, the first inaugural address was scored for achievement, affiliation–intimacy, and power motive imagery.[1] (Presidents Tyler, Fillmore, Andrew Johnson, Arthur, and Ford were never elected and inaugurated in their own right and, therefore, are not included.) Although some speeches had been scored in the past by Donley and Winter (1970) and Winter and Stewart (1977), for the present study all speeches were mixed together and newly scored by two trained and reliable scorers (demonstrated category agreement with expert scoring over .85), who discussed and resolved any disagreements that had occurred. Raw scores were expressed in terms of images per 1,000 words and then standardized with an overall mean of 50 and a standard deviation of 10 for each motive. Motive imagery scores for each president, in standardized and raw form, are presented in Table 6.1.

Motive scores for American society were adapted from the work of McClelland (1975, chap-

ter 9), who collected three kinds of standard cultural documents dating from each decade from the 1790s through the 1960s: popular novels, children's readers, and hymns. A few details of McClelland's procedure should be mentioned at this point. For each kind of document in each decade, selected pages (readers) or 10-line page segments (novels and hymns) were scored for achievement, affiliation, and power motive imagery. The results were expressed in terms of proportion of pages (or 10-line segments) scored for a particular motive. These scores were then standardized across all decades, separately for each motive. Separate scores from each type of document were then averaged (see McClelland, 1975, pp. 330–332, 403–410, for further methodological information). For the present study, these average decade scores were then restandardized, also with an overall mean of 50 and a standard deviation of 10 for each motive. Thus the motive levels of the presidents and of American society at the time of each president's election are measured in comparable ways and expressed in comparable terms.

Definitions of Variables

Several characteristics that are important to leader appeal and leader performance in the theories of Freud and Weber, such as energy, impact, prestige, and even narcissism, are closely related to the known action characteristics of the power motive. For example, power-motivated people tend to be energetic, in terms of both self-report and physiological arousal, especially in power-related situations (Steele, 1977). They seek impact on others and are concerned about prestige, while maintaining their own autonomy and self-direction (Winter, 1973; Winter & Stewart, 1978). Their own estimates of their influence, as well as their responses to ingratiation by subordinates, suggest a considerable narcissism (Fodor & Farrow, 1979). Thus power motivation is a leader characteristic of great interest in its own right. Some recent studies of organizations further suggest that the combination of high-power motivation and low affiliation–intimacy motivation—the so-called leadership motive pattern—predicts successful leadership among managers and high morale among followers (McClelland, 1975, chapter 8; McClelland & Boyatzis, 1982; McClelland & Burnham, 1976). In the present case, this motive

TABLE 6.1. Motive Imagery Scores of American Presidents' Inaugural Addresses, 1789–1981

President	Date	Motive scores					
		Standardized			Raw		
		Ach	Aff	Pow	Ach	Aff	Pow
Washington, George	1789	39	54	41	3.85	3.85	4.62
Adams, John	1797	39	49	42	3.89	3.03	4.76
Jefferson, Thomas	1801	49	51	51	5.65	3.30	6.59
Madison, James	1809	55	51	57	6.84	3.42	7.69
Monroe, James	1817	57	46	51	7.22	2.41	6.62
Adams, John Quincy	1825	48	51	37	5.43	3.40	3.74
Jackson, Andrew	1829	43	47	45	4.48	2.69	5.38
Van Buren, Martin	1837	42	48	40	4.38	2.83	4.38
Harrison, William Henry	1841	32	41	40	2.56	1.52	4.31
Polk, James	1845	33	41	50	2.65	1.43	6.32
Taylor, Zachary	1849	53	53	41	6.39	3.65	4.56
Pierce, Franklin	1853	49	44	50	5.72	2.11	6.33
Buchanan, James	1857	46	47	42	5.05	2.53	4.69
Lincoln, Abraham	1861	36	45	53	3.34	2.23	6.97
Grant, Ulysses	1869	56	47	36	7.02	2.63	3.51
Hayes, Rutherford	1877	51	48	48	6.07	2.83	6.07
Garfield, James	1881	46	35	49	5.09	0.34	6.10
Cleveland, Grover	1885	53	46	63	6.52	2.37	8.89
Harrison, Benjamin	1889	37	45	45	3.49	2.18	5.45
McKinley, William	1897	47	41	46	5.30	1.51	5.55
Roosevelt, Theodore	1905	62	38	38	8.14	1.02	4.07
Taft, William Howard	1909	44	38	58	4.79	0.92	7.93
Wilson, Woodrow	1913	66	49	53	8.83	2.94	7.06
Harding, Warren	1921	48	57	42	5.41	4.51	4.81
Coolidge, Calvin	1925	44	46	45	4.69	2.47	5.43
Hoover, Herbert	1929	68	45	48	9.18	2.16	5.94
Roosevelt, Franklin	1933	53	44	61	6.37	2.12	8.50
Truman, Harry	1949	56	65	78	6.91	5.99	11.98
Eisenhower, Dwight	1953	43	57	49	4.50	4.50	6.14
Kennedy, John	1961	50	85	77	5.90	9.59	11.81
Johnson, Lyndon	1965	55	59	49	6.77	4.74	6.09
Nixon, Richard	1969	66	76	53	8.94	8.00	7.06
Carter, Jimmy	1977	75	59	59	10.60	4.89	8.16
Reagan, Ronald	1981	60	51	63	7.78	3.28	9.01

Note. Ach = achievement. Aff = affiliation. Pow = power.

combination was defined as the difference between standard-scored power motive imagery and standard-scored affiliation–intimacy imagery.

How can Barber's cyclical theory be operationalized with the motive measures? Barber's three issues seem closely related to the three motives: Conflict suggests power, conciliation suggests affiliation, and (more loosely) conscience may involve achievement. A variable reflecting the cycle-appropriate motive was therefore defined as follows: the power motive score for presidents chosen in the conflict elections (1912, 1924, 1948, 1960); the affiliation–intimacy score for presidents taking office in conciliation years (1908, 1920, 1932, 1968); and the achievement score for the winners of conscience elections (1904, 1928, 1952, 1964, 1976).

To determine the extent of congruence between a president and American society at the time of his election, the absolute values of the discrepancies between presidential score and society score for each motive were summed to yield a total discrepancy score. With sign reversed, this was used as a measure of president–society motive congruence.

Dependent variables reflecting presidential appeal and presidential performance were taken from several sources. Presidential appeal was measured by the percentage of popular votes received in their first election to the presidency and by the margin of votes over the second-place candidate. (These two measures intercorrelated +.71, but diverged in years such as 1860, 1912, 1968, and 1980 when there were three or more major candidates.) The four cases where the winning candidate was a former vice president who had taken office on the death of the president (Theodore Roosevelt, Coolidge, Truman, and Lyndon Johnson) were eliminated because these men had not initially gained the presidency in their own right. They had no real first election and first inaugural address to study and score. One other measure of presidential appeal, this time involving not only initial popular appeal but also popular reaction to all 4 years of an administration, is whether the president was reelected. Two separate measures were used to measure reelection; one considered each president as a single case (including the four vice presidents mentioned earlier), and the other treated each attempted reelection as a separate case. Obviously those presidents who died during their first term were not included here.

Next, the total national percentage of votes for the House of Representatives candidates of the president's party was taken as a measure of the appeal of the president's *party* as distinguished from the appeal of the president as a *person*. (Alternatively, this is a measure of the *coattails* effect.) Data for these election variables were taken from the *Historical Statistics of the United States* (Bureau of the Census, 1984).

Generating popular appeal is one kind of political skill, but working successfully with Congress is also important. Although it is difficult to give each president an overall score on his relations with Congress, there are some objective measures that might reflect that relationship, including the number of rejections of court and cabinet appointments (taken from Kane, 1956) and the percentage of vetoes overridden (taken from U.S. Senate Library, 1976). A final aspect of a president's political skill involves his party's election success at the midterm elections 2 years after the inauguration. Normally, the president's party loses seats. In the House of Representatives, the percentage of seats lost varied inversely with the percentage size of

the initial majority ($r = -.29$ for 24 midterm elections; percentages rather than raw changes in seats were necessary because of the changing size of the U.S. House of Representatives over time). When the effects of this negative correlation were removed by subtracting the expected loss from the actual loss, the result was an adjusted measure of the performance of the president's party.

Of the many things that can happen in a presidential administration, war and peace are surely among the two most important. In the present study, war entry was defined in terms of the list developed by Richardson (1960), with his definitions used for the years before 1820 and after 1945. (Because of the difficulty of demarcating separate wars and the uncertainty of casualty figures, all Indian conflicts are excluded. Thus in the present context, *war* really means *interstate war*.) Not every crisis necessarily results in war, however. Small (1980), for example, listed 19 crises that could easily have escalated into war but that were in fact settled peacefully. Some examples include the dispute with England about violations of American neutrality (1791), the Oregon boundary dispute (1845), the *Panay* incident (1937), and the Cuban Missile Crisis (1962). These are labeled *war avoidance* in the present study. Another aspect of peacemaking involves the limitation of arms. Starting with the first arms limitation conference at The Hague during McKinley's administration, historical sources were used to identify presidents who concluded treaties with at least one other major power for the limitation or banning of one or more specific weapons systems.

What is presidential greatness? Perhaps it is impossible to define. First, we can never know all the facts about a president's actions and what independent effects these actions had on historical outcomes. Even with these facts, moreover, any ratings of greatness will mostly reflect the values attached by the rater to these outcomes. For example, raters who value military greatness will tend to rate highly presidents who involved the United States in victorious wars. Second, presidential greatness probably has many separate (and uncorrelated) components. How can these be weighed and synthesized into a single rating?

One approach to measuring presidential greatness is to rely on the judgments of scholars of American history. Although their judgments are undoubtedly affected by their values, historians are presumably in possession of more facts than are most people and are in a better position to make objective evaluations and comparative ratings. Over the past 35 years, historians have often been polled on presidential greatness. In one of the most extensive polls, Maranell (1970) asked 571 historians of the United States to rate the presidents on several dimensions, including general prestige, strength of action, presidential activeness, and accomplishments of the administration. Because these four dimensions were highly intercorrelated, they were standardized and summed to produce a consensus on the relative greatness of the presidents from Washington to Lyndon Johnson. Washington and Lincoln, for example, were the highest rated presidents, whereas Grant and Harding were at the bottom. In a sense, these ratings are only another aspect of presidential appeal, to historians rather than to voters. In fact, though, the correlations between the summed Maranell study ratings and the percentage of vote and margin of victory measures were essentially zero. At the very least, then, rated greatness is different from voter appeal. Another facet of presidential greatness involves making decisions that have historic impact on the country and world, as compiled and judged by Morris (1967). Some examples of "great" presidential decisions include the purchase of Louisiana (by Jefferson), the abolition of central banking (by Jackson), and the attack on business trusts (by Theodore Roosevelt).

Results

Table 6.2 presents the relations between each of the four major variables assessing presidential motives or president–situation motive match and the dependent variables reflecting presidential appeal, political skill, and presidential performance. Presidential appeal, as measured by success at both election and re-election, is a straightforward function of how congruent the president's motive levels were with those of the American society of the time. The much lower correlation with the total percentage of House of Representatives vote for candidates of the president's party suggests that this motive congruence predicts the specific personal appeal of the president (percentage of votes cast, margin, reelection), rather than the national support for the president's party (or the coattails effect). In general, the summed discrepancy/congruence score gave results more significant than those for the discrepancy scores on any individual motive, suggesting that discrepancies on *each* motive contributed to most overall effects. Algebraically signed discrepancy scores gave no significant results. This suggests that what is important is the *discrepancy* between president and society, rather than whether the president or the society is higher on any particular motive.

Neither presidential power motivation nor power minus affiliation–intimacy, by itself, was related to any aspect of political appeal. The *cyclically appropriate motive* measure, drawn from Barber's theory, actually reversed and was negatively correlated with most of the appeal measures. For political appeal, as reflected in the size of the personal electoral mandate, then, Erikson's theory of leader–follower personality congruence was the theory most strongly supported by the results.

None of the measures of political skill in office was significantly associated with any of the presidential or congruence motive measures. Probably veto overrides and appointment rejections are fragmentary measures that do not adequately reflect presidential political skill and are much affected by particular historical circumstances.

Presidential outcomes showed a very different pattern. Power motivation was strongly related to war entry, as expected on the basis of numerous other findings (e.g., Winter, 1980). It was also related, almost at a significant level, to *avoiding* war in a crisis situation. This suggests that the power motive is a leader characteristic associated with dramatic, crisis-oriented, perhaps confrontational foreign policy, which may end peacefully but which can easily end in war (see Hermann, 1980). Power motivation by itself was also associated with both measures of greatness, more strongly so than power minus affiliation–intimacy or the leadership motive pattern. This latter variable was negatively associated with arms reduction, largely because of the strong positive relation between affiliation–intimacy imagery and arms limitation agreements ($r = .43$). The cycle-appropriate motive measure also showed low, nonsignificant correlations in the same direction as those for the power motive. Congruence between president and society, in contrast, was significantly negatively associated with both measures of greatness as well as war avoidance. It seems those presidents who matched the country's

TABLE 6.2. Correlations of Variables Assessing Aspects of Presidential Appeal and Performance With Presidential Characteristics and President–Situation Match

Variable	Presidential characteristics		President–situation match	
	Power motive	Power minus affiliation–intimacy	Cycle-appropriate motive	President–society congruence
Electoral appeal				
Vote percentage[a]				
r	−.04	.10	−.38	.60****
n	25	25	9	23
Margin of victory[a]				
r	−.07	.05	−.52	.46**
n	25	25	9	23
Reelected				
r	.06	−.05	−.40	.37
n	25	25	9	25
Reelected, all instances[b]				
r	.27	.16	−.40	.44**
n	30	30	9	30
Percentage vote for party's House candidates				
r	.13	.20	−.11	.21
n	30	30	9	28
Political skills in office				
Court/cabinet rejections				
r	−.19	−.20	−.12	.23
n	24	31	13	23
Percentage vetoes overridden				
r	.01	−.04	.24	-.01
n	27	27	13	26
Adjusted midterm House loss				
r	−.23	.03	−.19	.09
n	24	24	13	23
Presidential outcomes				
War entry				
r	.52***	.36*	.13	−.05
n	31	31	13	30
War avoidance				
r	.34*	.16	.26	−.39**
n	29	29	11	29
Arms limitation				
r	−.05	−.55**	.44	.03
n	14	14	13	13
Consensus of greatness				
r	.40**	.35	.23	−.46**
n	29	29	11	29
Great decisions cited				
r	.51***	.27	.31	−.37**
n	29	29	11	29

[a]Excluding all vice presidents who assumed office on the death of the president.
[b]Including all attempts at reelection.
*$p < .10$, two-tailed.
**$p < .05$, two-tailed.
***$p < .01$, two-tailed.
****$p < .001$, two-tailed.

motives at the time were in the end among the least great of the presidents, at least in the judgment of historians.

Discussion

These results suggest two conclusions. First, among American presidents at least, leader appeal is a function of how well the leader's own motives fit the motive imagery profile of the times. Presidential leadership performance, however, is a very different matter. Both rated performance and several of the most significant outcomes were functions more of leader attributes (especially power motivation) than of leader–situation match. Indeed, among American presidents it appears that the greatest presidents were those who were least congruent with the followers of their society.

Some examples will illustrate these two conclusions. Abraham Lincoln is generally considered to be one of the two greatest American presidents. Yet he was one of four major candidates in 1860, elected with only a minority of the total popular vote. His motive profile was highly discrepant with that of American society in the 1860s; in fact, he is among the half dozen most discrepant presidents. Some others with motive profiles highly discrepant from their times include: Washington, Theodore Roosevelt, Truman, and Kennedy—all highly rated by historians. And some congruent presidents include Buchanan, Grant, Harding, and Coolidge—three of whom are considered to be failures if not outright disasters. (To be fair, it must also be noted that Franklin Roosevelt was highly congruent and Nixon highly discrepant.)

These results diverge somewhat from those obtained by Simonton (1981) in his study of presidential greatness (summed ratings along five dimensions, from Maranell) and presidential performance (duration of administration, war years, assassination attempt, and scandal). Simonton found that personality traits, including specifically achievement and power motivation scores, made little predictive contribution to presidential greatness or performance. How can this conclusion be reconciled with the results of the present study? First, there are differences in the motive scores used. Simonton used scores originally reported by Donley and Winter (1970), based on an informal adaptation of the original scoring

systems, for the 12 presidents from 1905 to 1969. When the final codified version of the integrated scoring system was developed (Winter, 1983), the first inaugurals of all presidents were mixed together and scored. This resulted in some changed scores for speeches scored earlier, most notably for Theodore Roosevelt and William Howard Taft. The later scorings, shown in Table 6.1, should be taken as definitive. Thus the present study involved slightly different motive data and used a much larger group of presidents. Second, Simonton used some presidential performance variables that were different from those of the present study and others that were defined differently. For example, Simonton did not measure war avoidance, arms limitation, or great decisions; and the definitions of one overlapping variable—war—seem to be different in the two studies. Finally, Simonton analyzed the effect of motives "within a multivariate framework" (1981, p. 321), which seems to mean hierarchical regression (cf. p. 314), although this is not clear. No doubt different researchers would make different judgments about whether, in predicting performance and greatness, personality variables should be entered before or after variables reflecting other biographical information or administration events. Simonton did not investigate the relation between presidential and societal motives. Overall, then, the differences in the results of these two studies suggest the need for careful definition of variables and explicit theory about the relation of leader motivation to other kinds of variables.

Although the present results are based on a small population of leaders and measures that involve several assumptions, they do suggest some interesting hypotheses about leadership in the real world of politics: (a) Leader *appeal* seems to involve a person–situation (or leader–follower) match on psychological characteristics. (b) Leader *performance* (historically rated greatness and some major outcomes), when it is more than a function of circumstances, may involve more enduring and less situationally defined psychological characteristics of the leader.

Why do these conclusions diverge from much of the experimental social psychological research on leadership? The timebound constraints of the laboratory often lead researchers to rely on group member sociometric ratings of leadership; that is, leader appeal. Not surprisingly, the results often involve some kind of complex leader–situation interaction. But factors that predict leadership that is sociometrically defined in this way may not necessarily predict long-term effective leader performance and evaluation, which of course is hard to study in the time-foreshortened laboratory microcosm. This divergence of leader appeal and leader performance should underline the importance of studying leadership in the real world, using archival, at-a-distance measures.

The conclusions of the present study are also relevant to the basic philosophical assumptions of democratic political theory. We may vote for the candidate who feels most "comfortable" or congruent to us, who fits our dimly perceived hierarchies of motives and goals. At best, though, such leader appeal has little to do with leader effectiveness. And often enough the "uncomfortable" leader, discrepant in motive from the larger society of the times, turns out to be regarded as the great leader.

NOTES

1. When formal prepared speeches are scored, it is natural to ask whether the results reflect the motives of the president or those of the speechwriters. There are, however, several reasons for believing that this is not an important problem. First, any good speechwriter knows how to produce words and images that feel appropriate and comfortable to the presidential client. Second, before a speech as important as the first inaugural address, presidents spend a good deal of time reviewing and changing the text, paying special attention to the kinds of images that are coded in the motive-scoring systems. For example, the various drafts of President Kennedy's inaugural address show insertions and deletions of storable imagery, in Kennedy's own handwriting. Many speeches in the Eisenhower Library archives show the same. Thus, although the words may have originated from many sources, in the end an inaugural address probably says almost exactly what the president wants it to say. The final justification of these scores, of course, is their validity in terms of predicting presidential actions and outcomes, as shown in this article and in other studies using the scores.

REFERENCES

Allport, G. W. (1937). *Personality: A psychological interpretation*. New York: Holt.

Bales, R. F. (1970). *Personality and interpersonal behavior*. New York: Holt, Rinehart & Winston.

Barber, J. D. (1980). *The pulse of politics: Electing presidents in the media age*. New York: Norton.

Bass, B. M. (1981). *Stogdill's handbook of leadership* (rev. ed.). New York: Free Press.

Bem, D. J., & Funder, D. C. (1978). Predicting more of the people more of the time: Assessing the personality of situations. *Psychological Review, 85*, 485–501.

Bem, D. J., & Lord, C. G. (1979). Template-matching: A proposal for probing the ecological validity of experimental settings in social psychology, *Journal of Personality and Social Psychology, 37*, 833–846.

Brown, R. W. (1965). *Social psychology*. New York: Free Press.

Bureau of the Census. (1984). *Historical statistics of the United States*. Washington, DC: U.S. Government Printing Office.

Burns, J. M. (1956). *Roosevelt: The lion and the fox*. New York: Harcourt, Brace.

Conte, H. R., & Plutchik, R. (1981). A circumplex model for interpersonal personality traits. *Journal of Personality and Social Psychology, 40*, 701–711.

Donley, R. E., & Winter, D. G. (1970). Measuring the motives of public officials at a distance: An exploratory study of American presidents. *Behavioral Science, 15*, 227–236.

Erikson, E. H. (1950). *Childhood and society*. New York: Norton.

Erikson, E. H. (1958). *Young man Luther*. New York: Norton.

Erikson, E. H. (1964). *Insight and responsibility*. New York: Norton.

Erikson, E. H. (1969). *Gandhi's truth*. New York: Norton.

Fodor, E. M., & Farrow, D. L. (1979). The power motive as an influence on use of power. *Journal of Personality and Social Psychology, 37*, 2091–2097.

Freud, S. (1955). Group psychology and the analysis of the ego. In J. Strachey (Ed.), *The standard edition of the complete psychological works of Sigmund Freud* (Vol. 18, pp. 67–143). London: Hogarth. (Original work published 1921)

Gibb, C. A. (1969). Leadership. In G. Lindzey & E. Aronson (Eds.), *Handbook of social psychology* (rev. ed.). Reading, MA: Addison-Wesley.

Haley, J. (1969). *The power tactics of Jesus Christ and other essays*. New York: Grossman.

Hermann, M. G. (Ed.). (1977). *A psychological examination of political leaders*. New York: Free Press.

Hermann, M. G. (1980). Explaining foreign policy using personal characteristics of political leaders. *International Studies Quarterly, 24*, 7–46.

Hollander, E. P. (1964). *Leaders, groups and influence*. New York: Oxford University Press.

Kane, J. N. (1956). *Facts about the presidents* (3rd ed.). New York: H. W. Wilson.

Magnusson, D. & Endler, N. S. (Eds.). (1977). *Personality at the crossroads: Current issues in interactional psychology*. Hillsdale, NJ: Erlbaum.

Maranell, G. (1970). The evaluation of presidents: An extension of the Schlesinger poll. *Journal of American History, 57*, 104–113.

McAdams, D. P. (1982). Intimacy motivation. In A. J. Stewart (Ed.), *Motivation and society*. San Francisco: Jossey-Bass.

McClelland, D. C. (1961). *The achieving society*. Princeton, NJ: Van Nostrand.

McClelland, D. C. (1975). *Power: The inner experience*. New York: Irvington.

McClelland, D. C., & Boyatzis, R. E. (1982). Leadership motive pattern and long-term success in management. *Journal of Applied Psychology, 67*, 737–743.

McClelland, D. C., & Burnham, D. (1976). Power is the great

motivator. *Harvard Business Review, 54*, 100–111.

Mischel, W. (1968). *Personality and assessment.* New York: Wiley.

Morris, R. B. (1967). *Great presidential decisions: State papers that changed the course of history* (rev. ed.). Philadelphia: Lippincott.

Murray, R. K., & Blessing, T. H. (1983). The presidential performance study: A progress report. *Journal of American History, 70*, 535–555.

Nie, N. H., Verba, S., & Petrocik, J. R. (1979). *The changing American voter* (enlarged ed.). Cambridge, MA: Harvard University Press.

Richardson, L. (1960). *Statistics of deadly quarrels.* Pittsburgh, PA: Boxwood Press.

Sears, D. O. (1969). Political behavior. In G. Lindzey & E. Aronson (Eds.), *Handbook of social psychology* (Rev. ed., Vol. 5, pp. 315–458). Reading, MA: Addison-Wesley.

Simonton, D. (1981). Presidential greatness and performance: Can we predict leadership in the White House? *Journal of Personality, 49*, 306–323.

Small, M. (1980). *Was war necessary? National security and United States entry into war.* Beverly Hills, CA: Sage.

Snider, J. G., & Osgood, C. E. (Eds.). (1969). *Semantic differential technique: A sourcebook* Chicago: Aldine.

Steele, R. S. (1977). Power motivation, activation, and inspi-

rational speeches. *Journal of Personality, 45*, 53–64.

U.S. Senate Libary. (1976). *Presidential vetoes, 1789–1976.* Washington, DC: U.S. Government Printing Office.

Vidal, G. (1984). *Lincoln.* New York: Random House.

Weber, M. (1947). *The theory of social and economic organization.* New York: Free Press.

Wiggins, J. S. (1980). Circumplex models of interpersonal behavior. In L. Wheeler (Ed.), *Review of personality and social psychology* (Vol. 1, pp. 265–294). Beverly Hills, CA: Sage.

Winter, D. G. (1973). *The power motive.* New York: Free Press.

Winter, D. G. (1980). Measuring the motives of southern Africa political leaders at a distance. *Political Psychology, 2*(2), 75–85.

Winter, D. G. (1983). *Development of an integrated system for scoring motives in verbal running text.* Unpublished manuscript, Wesleyan University, Middletown, CT.

Winter, D. G., & Stewart, A. J. (1977). Content analysis as a method of studying political leaders. In M. G. Hermann (Ed.), *A psychological examination of political leaders* (pp. 27–61). New York: Free Press.

Winter, D. G., & Stewart, A. J. (1978). Power motivation. In H. London & J. Exner (Eds.), *Dimensions of personality* (pp. 391–447). New York: Wiley.

Mass Media and Candidate Perception

Winston Churchill, the British Prime Minister from 1940–1945, famously observed: "It has been said that democracy is the worst form of government except all the others that have been tried." In seeking to underscore the close relationship between politics and persuasion, the social psychologist William J. McGuire (1985) alluded to Churchill's remark in writing that "persuasion is the worst possible mode of social mobilization and conflict resolution – except for all the others" (p. 235). In today's world, one could say that politics *is* a mass-mediated persuasive campaign designed to form and change impressions of candidates and issues. For better or for worse, there is no longer any clear boundary between democratic politics and product marketing. Indeed, politicians and political parties in the West frequently hire advertising specialists to serve as expert campaign advisors.

What are the factors that determine whether a given candidate or policy argument will be looked upon favorably by a mass audience? This is one of the central questions of social psychology (e.g., Cialdini, 2001; Eagly & Chaiken, 1993; Petty & Cacioppo, 1986; Pratkanis & Aronson, 1991). McGuire (1985) identified several classes of variables that determine the degree to which persuasive communications are effective, including the personality and other characteristics of the communication source, the quality and other characteristics of the message itself, the channel or medium through which the message is communicated, demographic and other characteristics of the audience or receiver, and the goal or target of the communication attempt. A huge amount of research on the effects of the mass media on political issue and candidate perception has resulted from investigation of these important variables (e.g., Graber, 2001; Iyengar & Kinder, 1987; Milburn, 1991; Mullen et al., 1986; Popkin, 1991).

In our first reading in this section, Iyengar, Peters, and Kinder take an experimental approach to measuring the effects of television news coverage on audience members' ratings of issue importance. They find that, whether or not viewers are persuaded by the specific opinions represented on a news program, they are indeed influenced by the degree to which certain issues are covered. Specifically, people weigh issues that have been featured prominently in the news more heavily than issues that have not been prominently featured, and these subjective weights do influence political judgments and evaluations. Studies of *agenda setting* by Iyengar, Kinder, and their colleagues have been extremely influential in political psychology, in part because they have successfully applied the virtues of experimental methods to real-world political contexts and in part because they have managed to reawaken a long dormant disciplinary interest in the effects of the mass media in political science.

One of the most solid, well-supported conclusions reached by experimental social and cognitive psychologists over the past two decades is that people are automatically (unconsciously) influenced by the presentation of environmental stimuli, including words, pictures, and persuasive messages (e.g., Bargh & Chartrand, 1999). The process

of making concepts or ideas more accessible to an individual, without necessarily making the individual aware of the increased accessibility, is known as *priming*. Although most of the evidence concerning the effects of priming has come from tightly controlled laboratory studies, Krosnick and Kinder have explored the consequences of priming (again through repeated media coverage) in a more naturalistic setting. Their research led to the publication of an article that we have selected for this book's eighth reading. In the article, Krosnick and Kinder demonstrate that, because of heightened accessibility brought on by media priming, embarrassing news coverage of a political scandal can in fact alter the foundations of support for the president.

Because interest in information-processing mechanisms and social cognition has so dominated political psychology and neighboring fields for the last 20 years or more (e.g., Fiske & Taylor, 1991), the role of affect and emotion has been given relatively short shrift in research on candidate perception and voting behavior (but see Abelson, Kinder, Peters, & Fiske, 1982; Glaser & Salovey, 1998). Our final reading in this section, by Marcus and MacKuen (1993), helps to fill this gap. These researchers address the emotional underpinnings of people's responses to political election campaigns. They find that campaigns do stir up emotions and that these emotions are highly consequential for individual and political outcomes. Specifically, Marcus and MacKuen demonstrate that *anxiety* stimulates people's attention and learning, whereas *enthusiasm* affects their degree of involvement and candidate preferences.

Discussion Questions

1. What are the major psychological processes that allow the news media to influence our political attitudes?
2. Would you expect media agenda-setting to differentially impact political experts and novices? Why or why not?
3. Consider the dramatic decline in former President George H.W. Bush's approval ratings from the Persian Gulf War to the 1992 presidential elections. How might the media have played a role in this decline?
4. Do you believe that partisan political advertisements have the same capacity as news programs to influence political attitudes? Why or why not?
5. Marcus and MacKuen propose and test a two-dimensional model of emotional responses to political campaigns. Are there other emotional dimensions (in addition to anxiety and enthusiasm) that you feel should be considered? Explain.

Suggested Readings

Abelson, R. P., Kinder, D. R., Peters, M. D., & Fiske, S. T. (1982). Affective and semantic components in political person perception. *Journal of Personality and Social Psychology, 42*, 619–630.

Cialdini, R. B. (2001). *Influence: Science and practice*. Boston: Allyn & Bacon.

Eagly, A. H., & Chaiken, S. (1993). *The psychology of attitudes*. Philadelphia: Harcourt, Brace Jovanovich.

Fiske, S. T. (1986). Schema-based versus piecemeal politics: A patchwork quilt, but not a blanket of evidence. In R. R. Lau, & D. O. Sears (Eds.) *Political cognition* (pp. 41–53). Hillsdale, NJ: Erlbaum.

Fiske, S. T., & Taylor, S. E. (1991). *Social cognition* (2nd ed). New York: McGraw-Hill.

Gilliam, F. D., Jr. & Iyengar, S. (2000). Prime suspects: The influence of local television news on the viewing public. *American Journal of Political Science, 44*, 560–573.

Glaser, J., & Salovey, P. (1998). Affect in electoral politics. *Personality and Social Psychology Review, 2*, 156–172.

Graber, D. A. (2001). *Processing politics: Learning from television in the Internet age*. Chicago, IL: University of Chicago Press.

Iyengar, S., & Kinder, D. (1987). *News that matters: Television and American opinion*. Chicago: University of Chicago Press.

Iyengar, S., & McGuire, W. J. (Eds.) (1993). *Explorations in political psychology*. Durham, NC: Duke University Press.

Kinder, D., & Palfrey, T. (1993). *Experimental foundations of political science*. Ann Arbor, MI: University of Michigan Press.

Lau, R. R., & Sears, D. O. (Eds.) (1986). *Political cognition*. Hillsdale, NJ: Erlbaum.

Lodge, M., & McGraw, K. M. (Eds.) (1995). *Political judgment: Structure and process*. Ann Arbor, MI: University of Michigan Press.

Lord, C. G., Ross, L. & Lepper, M. (1979). Biased assimilation and attitude polarization: The effects of prior theories on subsequently considered evidence. *Journal of Personality and Social Psychology, 37*, 2098–2109.

McDermott, M. (1997). Voting cues in low-information elections: Candidate gender as a social information variable in contemporary United States elections. *American Journal of Political Science, 41*, 270–283.

McGuire, W. J. (1985). The nature of attitudes and attitude change. In G. Lindzey & E. Aronson (Eds.), *Handbook of social psychology* (3rd ed., Vol. 2, pp. 233–346). New York: Random House.

Milburn, M. A. (1991). *Persuasion and politics: The social psychology of public opinion.* Pacific Grove, CA.

Mullen, B., Futrell, D., Stairs, D., Tice, D., Baumeister, R., Dawson, K., Riordan, C., Radloff, C., Goethals, G., Kennedy, J., & Rosenfeld, P. (1986). Newscasters' facial expressions and voting behavior of viewers: Can a smile elect a president? *Journal of Personality and Social Psychology, 51*, 291–295.

Petty, R. E., & Cacioppo, J. T. (1986). *Communication and persuasion: Central and peripheral routes to attitude change.* New York: Springer-Verlag.

Popkin, S. L. (1991). *The reasoning voter: Communication and persuasion in presidential campaigns.* Chicago: University of Chicago Press.

Pratkanis, A., & Aronson, E. (1991). *Age of propaganda: The everyday use and abuse of persuasion.* New York: W.H. Freeman.

Rahn, W. M., Aldrich, J., Borgida, E., & Sullivan, J. (1990). A social-cognitive model of candidate appraisal. In J. Ferejohn & J. Kuklinski (Eds.), *Information and democratic process* (pp. 136–159). Chicago, IL: University of Chicago Press.

Valentino, N. A. (1999). Crime news and the priming of racial attitudes during evaluations of the president. *Public Opinion Quarterly, 63,* 293–320.

Experimental Demonstrations of the "Not-So-Minimal" Consequences of Television News Programs

Shanto Iyengar and Mark D. Peters • Yale University
Donald R. Kinder • University of Michigan

Two experiments sustain Lippmann's suspicion, advanced more than a half century ago, that media provide compelling descriptions of a public world that people cannot directly experience. More precisely, the experiments show that television news programs profoundly affect which problems viewers take to be important. The experiments also demonstrate that those problems prominently positioned in the evening news are accorded greater weight in viewers' evaluations of presidential performance. We note the political implications of these results, suggest their psychological foundations, and argue for a revival of experimentation in the study of political communication.

[The press] is like the beam of a searchlight that moves restlessly about, bringing one episode and then another out of the darkness into vision.

W. Lippmann (1922)

Four decades ago, spurred by the cancer of fascism abroad and the wide reach of radio at home, American social scientists inaugurated the study of what was expected to be the sinister workings of propaganda in a free society. What they found surprised them. Instead of a people easily led astray, they discovered a people that seemed quite immune to political persuasion. The "minimal effects" reported by Hovland and Lazarsfeld did much to dispel naive apprehensions of a gullible public (Lazarsfeld, Berelson, & Gaudet, 1944; Hovland, Lumsdaine, & Sheffield, 1949). Moreover, later research on persuasion drove home the

point repeatedly: propaganda reinforces the public's preferences; seldom does it alter them (e.g., Katz & Feldman, 1962; Patterson & McClure, 1976; Sears & Chaffee, 1978).

Although politically reassuring, the steady stream of minimal effects eventually proved dispiriting to behavioral scientists. Research eventually turned elsewhere, away from persuasion, to the equally sinister possibility, noted first by Lippmann (1922), that media might determine what the public takes to be important. In contemporary parlance, this is known as agenda setting. Cohen put it this way:

the mass media may not be successful much of the time in telling people what to think, but the media are stunningly successful in telling their audience what to think about (1962, p. 16).

Do journalists in fact exert this kind of influence? Are they "stunningly successful" in instructing us what to think about? So far the evidence is mixed. In a pioneering study that others quickly copied, McCombs and Shaw (1972) found that the political problems voters thought most important were indeed those given greatest attention in their media. This apparently successful demonstration, based on a cross-sectional comparison between the media's priorities and the aggregated priorities of uncommitted voters in one community, set off a torrent of research. The cumulative result has been considerable confusion. Opinion divides over whether media effects have been demonstrated at all; over the relative power of television versus newspapers in setting the public's agenda; and over the causal direction of the relation between the public's judgments and the media's priorities. A telling indication of this confusion is that the most sophisticated cross-sectional study of agenda setting could do no more than uncover modest and mysteriously context-dependent effects (Erbring, Goldenberg, & Miller, 1980). In short, "stunningly successful" overstates the evidence considerably.

But the problem may rest with the evidence, not the hypothesis. Along with Erbring and his colleagues, we believe that much of the confusion is the result of the disjuncture between cross-sectional comparisons favored by most agenda setting researchers, on the one hand, and the agenda setting hypothesis, which implies a dynamic process, on the other. If problems appear and disappear—if they follow Downs's (1972) "issue-attention cycle"—then to look for agenda setting effects cross-sectionally invites confusion. If they are to be detected, agenda setting effects must be investigated over time.

Though few in number, dynamic tests of agenda setting do fare better than their cross-sectional counterparts. Funkhouser (1973), for example, found substantial concurrence between the amount and timing of attention paid to various problems in the national press between 1960 and 1970 and the importance accorded problems by the American public. These results were fortified by MacKuen's more sophisticated and more genuinely dynamic analysis (MacKuen & Coombs, 1981). MacKuen discovered that over the past two decades fluctuations in public concern for problems like civil rights, Vietnam, crime, and inflation closely reflected changes over time in the attention paid to them by the national media.

For essentially the same reasons that motivate dynamic analysis, we have undertaken a pair of experimental investigations of media agenda setting. Experiments, like dynamic analysis, are well equipped to monitor processes like agenda setting, which take place over time. Experiments also possess important advantages. Most notably, they enable authoritative conclusions about cause (Cook & Campbell, 1978). In our experiments in particular, we systematically manipulated the attention that network news programs devoted to various national problems. We did this by unobtrusively inserting into news broadcasts stories provided by the Vanderbilt Television News Archive. Participants in our experiments were led to believe that they were simply watching the evening news. In fact, some participants viewed news programs dotted with stories about energy shortages; other participants saw nothing about energy at all. By experimentally manipulating the media's agenda, we can decisively test Lippmann's assertion that the problems that media decide are important become so in the minds of the public.

Our experimental approach also permits us to examine a different though equally consequential version of agenda setting. By attending to some problems and ignoring others, media may also alter the standards by which people evaluate government. We call this "priming." Consider, for example, that early in a presidential primary season, the national press becomes fascinated by a dramatic international crisis, at the expense of covering worsening economic problems at home. One consequence may be that the public will worry more about the foreign crisis and less about economic woes: classical agenda setting. But in addition, the public's evaluation of the president may now be dominated by his apparent success in the handling of the crisis; his management (or mismanagement) of the economy may now count for rather little. Our point here is simply that fluctuations in the importance of evaluational standards may well depend on fluctuations in the attention each receives in the press.

Another advantage of experimentation is the opportunity it offers to examine individual-level processes that might account for agenda setting. Here we explore two. According to the first, more news coverage of a problem leads to the acquisition and retention of more information about the problem, which in turn leads to the judgment of the problem as more important. According to the second, news coverage of a problem provokes the viewer to consider the claims being advanced; depending on the character of these ruminations, agenda setting will be more or less powerful.

In sum, we will: (a) provide authoritative experimental evidence on the degree to which the priorities of the evening newscasts affect the public's agenda; (b) examine whether network news' priorities also affect the importance the public attaches to various standards in its presidential evaluations; and (c) further exploit the virtues of experimentation by exploring individual cognitive processes that might underlie agenda setting.

Method

Overview

Residents of the New Haven, Connecticut area participated in one of two experiments, each of which spanned six consecutive days. The first experiment was designed to assess the feasibility of our approach and took place in November 1980, shortly after the presidential election. Experiment 2, a more elaborate and expanded replication of Experiment 1, took place in late February 1981.

In both experiments, participants came to two converted Yale University offices to take part in a study of television newscasts. On the first day, participants completed a questionnaire that covered a wide range of political topics, including the importance of various national problems. Over the next four days participants viewed what were represented to be videotape recordings of the preceding evening's network newscast. Unknown to the participants, portions of the newscasts had been altered to provide sustained coverage of a certain national problem. On the final day of the experiment (24 hours after the last broadcast), participants completed a second questionnaire that again included the measures of problem importance.

Experiment 1 focused on alleged weaknesses in U.S. defense capability and employed two conditions. One group of participants (N = 13) saw several stories about inadequacies in American defense preparedness (four stories totalling 18

minutes over four days). Participants in the control group saw newscasts with no defense-related stories (N = 15). In Experiment 2, we expanded the test of agenda setting and examined three problems, requiring three conditions. In one group (N = 15), participants viewed newscasts emphasizing (as in Experiment 1) inadequacies in U.S. defense preparedness (five stories, 17 minutes). The second group (N = 14) saw newscasts emphasizing pollution of the environment (five stories, 15 minutes). The third group (N = 15) saw newscasts with steady coverage of inflation (eight stories, 21 minutes). Each condition in Experiment 2 was characterized not only by a concentration of stories on the appropriate target problem, but also by deliberate omission of stories dealing with the two other problems under examination.

Participants

Participants in both experiments responded by telephone to classified advertisements promising payment ($20) in return for taking part in research on television. As hoped, this procedure produced a heterogeneous pool of participants, roughly representative of the New Haven population. Participants ranged in age from 19 to 63, averaging 26 in Experiment 1 and 35 in Experiment 2. They were drawn primarily from blue collar and clerical occupations. Approximately 30 percent were temporarily out of work or unemployed. Blacks made up 25 percent and women, 54 percent of the participants in Experiment 1 and 10 percent and 61 percent, respectively, in Experiment 2.

Participants were first scheduled for one of several daily sessions. Each of these sessions, with between five and ten individuals, was then randomly assigned to one of the two conditions in Experiment 1, or one of the three conditions in Experiment 2. Random assignment was successful. Participants in the defense condition in Experiment 1 did not differ at all in their demographic characteristics, in their political orientations, or in their political involvement from their counterparts in the control condition, according to day 1 assessments. The sole exception to this pattern—the control group had a significantly larger proportion of black participants (38 vs. 15 percent, $p < .05$)—is innocuous, since race is unrelated to the dependent variables. And in Experiment 2, across many demographic and attitudinal pretreatment comparisons, only two statistically significant differences emerged: participants in the defense condition reported watching television news somewhat more often ($p < .05$), and participants in the pollution condition were somewhat less Democratic ($p < .03$). To correct for this, party identification has been included as a control variable, where appropriate, in the analyses reported below.

Manipulating the Networks' Agenda

On the evening before each day's session, the evening national newscast of either ABC or NBC was recorded. For each of the conditions being prepared, this broadcast was then copied, but with condition-inappropriate stories deleted and condition-appropriate stories inserted. Inserted stories were actual news stories previously broadcast by ABC or NBC that were acquired from the Vanderbilt Television News Archive (VTNA). In practice, the actual newscast was left substantially intact except for the insertion of a news story from the VTNA pool, with a condition-irrelevant story normally deleted in compensation. All insertions and deletions were made in the middle portion of the newscast and were spread evenly across experimental days. In Experiment 1 the first newscast was left unaltered in order to allay any suspicions on the part of the participants, and for the next three days a single news story describing inadequacies in U.S. military preparedness was inserted into the broadcasts. Similar procedures were followed in Experiment 2, except that we added material to all four newscasts. The stories comprising the treatments in both experiments are listed and described in the Appendix.[1]

Avoiding Experimental Artifacts

In both experiments we undertook precautions to guard against "demand characteristics" (Orne, 1962)—cues in the experimental setting that communicate to participants what is expected of them. In the first place, we initially presented to participants a diverting but wholly plausible account of our purpose: namely, to understand better how the public evaluates news programs. Participants were told that it was necessary for them to watch the news at Yale to ensure that everyone watched the same newscast under uniform conditions. Second,

editing was performed with sophisticated video equipment that permitted the cutting, adding, and rearranging of news stories without interrupting the newscast's coherence. Third, though key questionnaire items were repeated from pretest to posttest, they were embedded within a host of questions dealing with political affairs, thus reducing their prominence. The success of these precautions is suggested by postexperimental discussions. Not a single participant expressed any skepticism about either experiment's real purpose.

We also tried to minimize the participants' sense that they were being tested. We never implied that they should pay special attention to the broadcasts. Indeed, we deliberately arranged a setting that was casual and informal and encouraged participants to watch the news just as they did at home. They viewed the broadcasts in small groups, occasionally chatted with their neighbors, and seemed to pay only sporadic attention to each day's broadcast. Although we cannot be certain, our experimental setting appeared to recreate the natural context quite faithfully.

Results

Setting the Public Agenda

We measured problem importance with four questions that appeared in both the pretreatment and posttreatment questionnaires. For each of eight national problems, participants rated the problem's importance, the need for more government action, their personal concern, and the extent to which they discussed each with friends. Because responses were strongly intercorrelated across the four items, we formed simple additive indices for each problem. In principle, each ranges from four (low importance) to twenty (high importance).[2]

The agenda-setting hypothesis demands that viewers adjust their beliefs about the importance of problems in response to the amount of coverage problems receive in the media. In our experiments, the hypothesis was tested by computing adjusted change scores for the importance indices and then making comparisons across conditions. Adjusted change scores measure the extent to which pretest responses underpredict or overpredict using Ordinary Least Squares (OLS) regression posttest responses (Kessler, 1978). Participants whose posttest scores exceeded that predicted by their pretest scores received positive scores on the adjusted change measure; those whose posttest scores fell short of that predicted received negative scores.

Table 7.1 presents the adjusted change scores for each of the eight problems inquired about in Experiment 1. In keeping with the agenda-setting hypothesis, for defense preparedness *but for no other problem*, the experimental treatment exerted a statistically significant effect ($p < .05$). Participants whose news programs were dotted with stories alleging the vulnerability of U.S. defense capability grew more concerned about defense over the experiment's 6 days. The effect is significant substantively as well as statistically. On the first day of the experiment, viewers in the experimental group ranked defense sixth out of eight problems, behind inflation, pollution, unemployment, energy, and civil rights. After exposure to the newscasts, however, defense ranked second, trailing only inflation. (Among viewers in the control group, meanwhile, the relative position of defense remained stable.)

Experiment 2 contributes further support to classical agenda setting. As in Experiment 1, participants were randomly assigned to a condition—this time to one of three conditions, corresponding to an emphasis upon defense preparedness, pollution, or inflation. Changes in the importance of defense, pollution, and inflation are shown in Table 7.2. There the classical agenda setting hypothesis is supported in two of three comparisons. Participants exposed to a steady stream of news about defense or about pollution came to believe that defense or pollution were more consequential problems. In each case, the shifts surpassed statistical signifi-

TABLE 7.2. Adjusted Change Scores for Problem Importance: Experiment 2

Problem	Condition		
	Pollution	Inflation	Defense
Pollution	1.53**	−.71	−.23
Inflation	−.11	.11	−.06
Defense	−.44	−.34	.76*

*$p < .05$.
**$p < .01$.

cance. No agenda setting effects were found for inflation, however. With the special clarity of hindsight, we attribute this single failure to the very great importance participants assigned to inflation before the experiment. Where twenty represents the maximum score, participants began Experiment 2 with an average importance score for inflation of 18.5!

As in Experiment 1, the impact of the media agenda could also be discerned in changes in the rank ordering of problems. Among participants in the defense condition, defense moved from sixth to fourth, whereas pollution rose from fifth to second among viewers in that treatment group. Within the pooled control groups, in the meantime, the importance ranks of the two problems did not budge.

Taken together, the evidence from the two experiments strongly supports the classical agenda-setting hypothesis. With a single and, we think, forgivable exception, viewers exposed to news devoted to a particular problem become more convinced of its importance. Network news programs seem to possess a powerful capacity to shape the public's agenda.

Priming and Presidential Evaluations

Next we take up the question of whether the media's agenda also alters the standards people use in evaluating their president. This requires measures of ratings of presidential performance in the designated problem areas—national defense in Experiment 1, defense, pollution, and inflation in Experiment 2—as well as measures of overall appraisal of the president. For the first, participants rated Carter's performance from "very good" to "very poor" on each of eight problems including "maintaining a strong military," "protecting the

TABLE 7.1. Adjusted Change Scores for Problem Importance: Experiment 1

Problem	Condition	
	Defense	Control
Defense*	.90	−.79
Inflation	−.49	.23
Energy	−.40	.22
Drug addiction	−.19	−.48
Corruption	−.67	.05
Pollution	−.58	.60
Unemployment	.28	.54
Civil rights	−.27	−.27

*$p < .05$, one-tailed t-test.

environment from pollution," and "managing the economy." We measured overall evaluation of President Carter in three ways: a single five-point rating of Carter's "*overall performance* as president"; an additive index based on three separate ratings of Carter's *competence*; and an additive index based on three separate ratings of Carter's *integrity*.[3]

In both Experiments 1 and 2, within each condition, we then correlated judgments of President Carter's performance on a particular problem with rating of his overall performance, his competence, and his integrity. (In fact these are partial correlations. Given the powerful effects of partisanship on political evaluations of the kind under examination here, we thought it prudent to partial out the effects of party identification. Party identification was measured in both experiments by the standard seven-point measure, collapsed for the purpose of analysis into three categories.)

At the outset, we expected these partial correlations to conform to two predictions. First, when evaluating the president, participants will weigh evidence partly as a function of the agenda set by their news programs. Participants exposed to stories that question U.S. defense capability will take Carter's performance on defense into greater account in evaluating Carter overall than will participants whose attention is directed elsewhere; that is, the partial correlations should vary according to the broadcasts' preoccupations, in keeping with the priming hypothesis. Second, the priming effect will follow a semantic gradient. Specifically, priming is expected to be most pronounced in judgments of Carter's overall performance as president, somewhat less apparent in judgments of his competence, a personal trait relevant to performance; and to be least discernible in judgments of his integrity, a personal trait irrelevant to performance.

Experiment 1 treated our two predictions unevenly. As Table 7.3 indicates, the first prediction is corroborated in two of three comparisons. Steady coverage of defense did strengthen the relationship between judgments of Carter's defense performance and evaluations of his overall job performance, and between judgments of Carter's defense performance and integrity, as predicted. However, the relationship reverses on judgments of Carter's competence. And as for our second prediction, Experiment 1 provides only the faintest encouragement.

TABLE 7.3. Correlations Between Overall Evaluations of Carter and Judgments of Carter's Performance on Defense as a Function of News Coverage: Experiment 1

	Coverage emphasizes defense	Coverage neglects defense
Carter's overall performance	.59	.38
Carter's competence	.03	.58
Carter's integrity	.31	.11

Table entries are first-order Pearson partial correlations, with party identification held constant.

More encouraging is the evidence provided by Experiment 2. As Table 7.4 indicates, our first prediction is upheld in eight of nine comparisons, usually handsomely, and as predicted, the effects are most striking for evaluations of Carter's overall performance, intermediate (and somewhat irregular) for judgments of his competence, and fade away altogether for judgments of his integrity.

In sum, Experiments 1 and 2 furnish considerable, if imperfect, evidence for priming. The media's agenda does seem to alter the standards people use in evaluating the president. Although

TABLE 7.4. Correlations Between Overall Evaluations of Carter and Judgments of Carter's Performance on Specific Problems as a Function of News Coverage: Experiment 2

	Coverage emphasizes defense	Coverage neglects defense
Carter's overall performance	.88	.53
Carter's competence	.79	.58
Carter's integrity	.13	−.17

	Coverage emphasizes pollution	Coverage neglects pollution
Carter's overall performance	.63	.42
Carter's competence	.47	.56
Carter's integrity	.33	.15

	Coverage emphasizes inflation	Coverage neglects inflation
Carter's overall performance	.63	.39
Carter's competence	.71	.38
Carter's integrity	.07	.08

Table entries are first-order Pearson partial correlations, with party identification held constant.

the patterns are not as regular as we would like, priming also appears to follow the anticipated pattern. A president's overall reputation, and, to a lesser extent, his apparent competence, both depend on the presentations of network news programs.

Mediation of Agenda Setting

Having established the consequences of the media's priorities, we turn finally to an investigation of their mediation. One strong possibility is information recall. More news coverage of a problem leads to the acquisition and retention of more information. More information, in turn, leads individuals to conclude that the problem is important.

Participants in both experiments were asked to describe "what the news story was about" and "how the story was presented" for each story they could recall something about. We coded both the number of stories as well as the volume of information participants were able to recall. We then correlated recall with participants' posttest beliefs about the importance of the target problem, controlling for their pretest beliefs.

In Experiment 1 the partial correlation using the number of defense stories recalled was −.13 (ns); in the case of volume of defense information recalled it was even tinier (−.03). The recall hypothesis also failed in Experiment 2. Here, for reasons of parsimony, we pooled the importance and recall data across the three conditions. The appropriate partial correlation between the number of news stories recalled and posttest importance, controlling for pretest importance was -.20 (ns). Recall of information seems a most unlikely mediator of agenda setting.

The failure of the recall hypothesis led us to consider a second possibility, that agenda setting might be mediated by covert evaluations triggered by the news stories. This hunch is consistent with a growing body of experimental research in which people are invited to record their thoughts as a persuasive message is presented. These thoughts are later classified as unfavorable, favorable, or as neutral to the persuasive message. It turns out that attitude change is predicted powerfully by the intensity and direction of such covert evaluations: the greater the number of unfavorable reactions, the lower the level of attitude change and vice versa. (For a detailed review of these experiments see Petty, Ostrom, & Brock, 1980.)

This result extends with little effort to agenda setting. Viewers less able or willing to counterargue with a news presentation should be more vulnerable to agenda setting. To test this hypothesis, participants in Experiment 2 were asked to list "any thoughts, reactions, or feelings" about each news story they recalled. These responses were then scored for the number of counterarguments, with an average inter-coder correlation across the three treatment problems of .86. Consistent with the covert evaluation hypothesis, such counterarguing was inversely related to increases in problem importance. The partial correlation between the number of counterarguments (concerning news stories about the treatment problem) and posttest importance, controlling for initial importance was −.49 ($p < .05$) in the defense treatment group; −.35 (ns) in the inflation treatment group; and −.56 ($p < .05$) in the pollution treatment group. Pooled across conditions, the partial correlation was −.40 ($p < .05$).[4]

And who are the counterarguers? They are the politically involved: those who claimed to follow public affairs closely, who reported a higher level of political activity, and who possessed more political knowledge. Of these three factors, political knowledge appeared to be the most consequential. In a regression analysis, pooling across the experimental groups, counterarguing was strongly predicted only by political knowledge (Beta = .43, $p < .05$).

To summarize, agenda setting is strengthened to the degree audience members fail to counterargue. Agenda setting appears to be mediated, not by the information viewers recall, but by the covert evaluations triggered by the news presentations. Those with little political information to begin with are most vulnerable to agenda setting. The well informed resist agenda setting through effective counterarguing, a maneuver not so available to the less informed.[5]

Conclusion

Fifty years and much inconclusive empirical fussing later, our experiments decisively sustain Lippmann's suspicion that media provide compelling descriptions of a public world that people cannot directly experience. We have shown that by ignoring some problems and attending to others, television news programs profoundly affect which problems viewers take seriously. This is so especially among the politically naive, who seem unable to challenge the pictures and narrations that appear on their television sets. We have also discovered another pathway of media influence: priming. Problems prominently positioned in television broadcasts loom large in evaluations of presidential performance.[6]

How long do these experimental effects persist? We cannot say with certainty. Our results are generally consistent with MacKuen's time-series analysis of agenda setting, which finds news media to exert persisting effects on the judgments the public makes regarding the country's most important problems (MacKuen & Combs, 1981). We also know that our experimental effects survive at substantial levels for at least 24 hours, since posttests in both experiments were administered a full day after the final broadcast. This is a crucial interval. The dissemination of television news is of course periodic, typically following cycles of 24 hours or less. The regularity and frequency of broadcasts mean that classical agenda setting and priming are, for most people, continuous processes. When news presentations develop priorities, even if rather subtle ones as in our experiments, viewers' beliefs are affected—and affected again as new priorities arise.

Political Implications

We do not mean our results to be taken as an indication of political mischief at the networks. In deciding what to cover, editors and journalists are influenced most by organizational routines, internal power struggles, and commercial imperatives (Epstein, 1973; Hirsch, 1975). This leaves little room for political motives.

Unintentional though they are, the political consequences of the media's priorities seem enormous. Policy makers may never notice, may choose to ignore, or may postpone indefinitely consideration of problems that have little standing among the public. In a parallel way, candidates for political office not taken seriously by news organizations quickly discover that neither are they taken seriously by anybody else. And the ramifications of priming, finally, are most unlikely to be politically evenhanded. Some presidents, at some moments, will be advantaged; others will be undone.

Psychological Foundations

On the psychological side, the classical agenda setting effect may be a particular manifestation of a general inclination in human inference—an inclination to overvalue "salient" evidence. Extensive experimental research indicates that under diverse settings, the judgments people make are swayed inordinately by evidence that is incidentally salient. Conspicuous evidence is generally accorded importance exceeding its inferential value; logically consequential but perceptually innocuous evidence is accorded less (for reviews of this research, see Taylor & Fiske, 1978; Nisbett & Ross, 1980).

The analogy with agenda setting is very close. As in experimental investigations of salience, television newscasts direct viewers to consider some features of public life and to ignore others. As in research on salience, viewers' recall of information seems to have little to do with shifts in their beliefs (Fiske, Kenny, & Taylor, 1982). Although this analogy provides reassurance that classic agenda setting is not psychologically peculiar, it also suggests an account of agenda setting that is unsettling in its particulars. Taylor and Fiske (1978) characterize the process underlying salience effects as "automatic." Perceptually prominent information captures attention; greater attention, in turn, leads automatically to greater influence.

Judgments are not always reached so casually, however; according to their retrospective accounts, our participants occasionally quarreled with the newscasts and occasionally actively agreed with them. Counterarguing was especially common among the politically informed. Expertise seems to provide viewers with an internal means for competing with the networks. Agenda setting may reflect a mix of processes therefore: automatic imprinting among the politically naive; critical deliberation among the politically expert.

Alterations in the standards by which presidents are evaluated, our second major finding, may also reflect an automatic process, but of a different kind. Several recent psychological experiments have shown that the criteria by which complex stimuli are judged can be profoundly altered by their prior (and seemingly incidental) activation. (For an excellent summary, see Higgins & King, 1981.) As do these results, our findings support Collins and Loftus's (1975) "spreading-activation" hypothesis.

According to Collins and Loftus, when a concept is activated—as by extended media coverage—other linked concepts are made automatically accessible. Hence when participants were asked to evaluate President Carter after a week's worth of stories exposing weaknesses in American defense capability, defense performance as a general category was automatically accessible and therefore relatively powerful in determining ratings of President Carter.

Methodological Pluralism

Over 20 years ago, Carl Hovland urged that the study of communication be based on field *and* experimental research (Hovland, 1959; also see Converse, 1970). We agree. Of course, experimentation has problems of its own, which our studies do not fully escape. That our participants represent no identifiable population, that our research setting departs in innumerable small ways from the natural communication environment, that the news programs we created might distort what would actually be seen on network newscasts—each raises questions about the external validity of our results. Do our findings generalize to other settings, treatments, and populations—and to the American public's consumption of evening news particularly? We think they do. We took care to avoid a standard pitfall of experimentation—the so-called college sophomore problem—by encouraging diversity in experimental participants. We undertook extra precautions to recreate the natural communication environment: participants watched the broadcasts in small groups in an informal and relaxed setting. And we were careful not to tamper with standard network practice in constituting our experimental presentations.

Limitations of experimentation—worries about external validity especially—correspond of course to strengths in survey-based communication research. This complementarity argues for methodological pluralism. We hope our results contribute to a revitalization of Hovland's dialogue between experimental and survey-based inquiries into political communication.

NOTES

1. Had participants viewed the actual newscasts each evening and compared them to the version presented on the subse-

quent day, they might well have discovered our alterations. This possibility was circumvented by instructing participants not to view the national network newscasts at home during the week of the study.

2. The wording of these items is given below:
Please indicate how important you consider these problems to be.
Should the federal government do more to develop solutions to these problems, even if it means raising taxes?
How much do you yourself care about these problems?
These days how much do you talk about these problems?
Index reliability was assessed with Cronbach's Alpha. In Experiment 1, the obtained values for the defense importance indices were .77 and .79. In Experiment 2, the alpha values ranged from .69 to .89.

3. On the importance of and distinction between competence and integrity, consult Kinder, Abelson, and Peters 1981. The specific trait terms were smart, weak, knowledgeable (competence), and immoral, power-hungry, dishonest (integrity). The terms were presented as follows: How well do the following terms describe former President Carter: extremely well, quite well, not too well, or not well at all? The average intercorrelation among the competence traits was .43 in Experiment 1 and .62 in Experiment 2. For the integrity traits the correlations were .60 and .30.

4. Typical counterarguments were: in the defense condition a viewer reacted to a story depicting Soviet superiority over the U.S. in the realm of chemical warfare by saying, "The story was very one sided and made me feel even more strongly that the military is overfunded." In the pollution condition, a viewer reacted to a story on the evils of toxic waste: "Overdone—reporter admitted no evidence to link this with lung disease." Counterarguments with respect to inflation news were comparatively rare. Most came in the form of remarks critical of President Reagan's proposed cuts in social programs.

5. These results work against the claim that the classical agenda setting and priming effects are special products of artificially high levels of attention induced by our experimental setting. In the first place, as we argued earlier, attention did not seem to be artificially high. Second, the information recall results imply the greater the attention, the *less* (marginally) beliefs are changed. Third, the counterarguing results imply, similarly, that the more "alert" viewers are, the *more* able they are to defend themselves against the media's priorities. All this suggests that our experimental setting, if anything, *underestimates* the influence of network news.

6. In a pair of experiments conducted since the two reported here, we found additional strong support both for classical agenda setting and for priming. The new experiments demonstrated also that priming depends not only on making certain evidence prominent but also on its relevance; priming was augmented when news presentations portrayed the president as responsible for a problem (Iyengar, Kinder, & Peters, 1982).

REFERENCES

Becker, L. B., McCombs, M. C., and McCleod, J. 1975. The development of political cognitions. In *Political communi-*

cation: issues and strategies for research. ed. S. H. Chaffee, Beverly Hills: Sage.

Cohen, B. 1963. *The press and foreign policy.* Princeton: Princeton University Press.

Collins, A. M., and Loftus, E. F. 1975. A spreading-activation theory of semantic processing. *Psychological Review* 82:407–28.

Converse, P. E. 1970. Attitudes and non-attitudes: continuation of a dialogue. In *The quantitative analysis of social problems.* ed. E. R. Tufte, Reading, Mass.: Addison-Wesley.

Cook, T. D., and Campbell, D. T. 1978. *Quasi-experimentation.* Chicago: Rand-McNally.

Downs, A. 1972. Up and down with ecology—the "issue attention cycle." *Public Interest* 28:38–50.

Epstein, E. J. 1973. *News from nowhere.* New York: Random House.

Erbring, L., Goldenberg, E. N., and Miller, A. H. 1980. Front-page news and real-world cues: a new look at agenda setting by the media. *American Journal of Political Science* 24:16–49.

Fiske, S. T., Kenny, D. A., and Taylor, S. E. 1982. Structural models for the mediation of salience effects on attribution. *Journal of Experimental Social Psychology* 18:105–27.

Funkhouser, G. R. 1973. The issues of the sixties: an exploratory study of the dynamics of public opinion. *Public Opinion Quarterly* 37:62–75.

Higgins, E. T., and King, G. 1981. Category accessibility and information-processing: consequences of individual and contextual variability. In *Personality, cognition, and social interaction,* ed. N. Cantor and J. Kihlstrom. Hillsdale: Lawrence Erlbaum.

Hirsch, P. M. 1975. Occupational, organizational and institutional models in mass media research. In *Strategies for communication research.* ed. P. Hirsch et al., Beverly Hills: Sage.

Hovland, C. I. 1959. Reconciling conflicting results derived from experimental and survey studies of attitude change. *American Psychologist* 14:8–17.

Hovland, C. I., Lumsdaine, A., and Sheffield, F. 1949. *Experiments on mass communication.* Princeton: Princeton University Press.

Iyengar, S., Kinder, D. R., and Peters, M. D. 1982. The evening news and presidential evaluations. Unpublished manuscript.

Katz, E., and Feldman, J. 1962. The debates in the light of research: a survey of surveys. In *The great debates.* ed. S. Krauss, Bloomongton: Indiana University Press.

Kessler, R. 1978. The use of change scores as criteria in longitudinal research. *Quality and Quantity* 11:43–66.

Kinder, D. R., Abelson, R. P., and Peters, M. D. 1981. Appraising presidential candidates: personality and affect in the 1980 campaign. Paper delivered at the Annual Meeting of the American Political Science Association, New York City, September.

Lazarsfeld, P., Berelson, B., and Gaudet, H. 1944. *The people's choice.* New York: Columbia University Press.

Lippmann, W. 1922. *Public opinion.* New York: Harcourt, Brace.

MacKuen, M. J., and Coombs, S. L. 1981. *More than news: media power in public affairs.* Beverly Hills: Sage.

McCombs, M. C., and Shaw, D. 1972. The agenda setting function of the mass media. *Public Opinion Quarterly* 36:176–87.

Nisbett, R. E., and Ross L. 1980. *Human inference: strategies and short-comings of social judgment.* Englewood Cliffs, N.J.: Prentice-Hall.

Orne, M. T. 1962. On the social psychology of the psychology experiment. *American Psychologist* 17:776–783.

Patterson, T. E., and McClure, R. D. 1976. *The unseeing eye: the myth of television power in national elections.* New York: G. P. Putnam.

Petty, R. E., Ostrom, T. M., and Brock, T. C. 1981. *Cognitive responses in persuasion.* Hillsdale: Lawrence Erlbaum.

Robinson, M. J. 1976. Public affairs television and the growth of political malaise. *American Political Science Review* 70:409–32.

Sears, D. O., and Chaffee, S. H. 1979. Uses and effects of the 1976 debates: an overview of empirical studies. In *The great debates, 1976: Ford vs. Carter.* ed. S. Krauss, Bloomington: Indiana University Press.

Taylor, S. E., and Fiske, S. T. 1978. Salience, attention and attribution: top of the head phenomena. In *Advances in experimental social psychology, Vol. 11.* ed. L. Berkowitz, New York: Academic Press.

APPENDIX

Day	Network	Length (min)	Content
			Experiment 1
1	ABC	1.40*	Increases in defense spending to be proposed by the incoming Reagan Administration.
2	ABC	4.40	Special assignment report on the declining role of the U.S. as the "arsenal of democracy." Story notes the declining level of weapons production since the early seventies and points out the consequences on U.S. ability to respond militarily.
3	NBC	4.40	Special segment report on U.S. military options in the event of Soviet aggression in the Persian Gulf region. Story highlights Soviet superiority in conventional forces and tanks and suggests that a U.S. "rapid deployment force," if used, would be overwhelmed.
4	ABC	1.10*	Air crash in Egypt during joint U.S.-Egyptian military exercises.
		4.30	Special assignment report on the low level of education among incoming military recruits. Describes resulting difficulty in the use of advanced equipment and shows remedial education programs in place.

Day	Network	Length (min)	Content
			Experiment 2

Defense

Day	Network	Length (min)	Content
1	ABC	4.40	Declining role of the U.S. as the "arsenal of democracy" (see above).
2	NBC	4.00	Special report on the readiness of the National Guard. Notes dilapidated equipment being used and lack of training among members.
3	NBC	3.00*	Growing U.S. involvement in El Salvador; draws parallel with Vietnam.
4	ABC	2.00	Deteriorating U.S.-USSR relations over El Salvador.
4	ABC	4.00	Special report on U.S. capability to withstand a chemical attack. Story highlights the disparity in the production of nerve gases between the U.S. and USSR and notes the vulnerability of U.S. forces to chemical weapons.

Pollution

Day	Network	Length (min)	Content
1	ABC	2.20	Congressional hearings on toxic waste in Memphis.
		2.10	Report on asbestos pollution in the soil and resulting dangers to health for residents of the area.
2	ABC	2.40	Toxic dumping in a Massachusetts community and the high rate of leukemia among the town's children.
3	NBC	2.10*	Underground coal fire in Pennsylvania; carbon monoxide fumes entering residents' homes.
4	ABC	5.10	Special feature on the growing dangers from toxic waste disposal sites across the nation. Sites shown in Michigan, Missouri, Louisiana, and California.

Inflation

Day	Network	Length (min)	Content
1	ABC	2.30*	Reagan's approach to inflation to concentrate on government spending reductions. Results of a public opinion poll concerning cuts in government spending reported.
		2.20*	Taxpayers in Michigan protest the high level of taxes.
2	ABC	2.20*	Reagan's plans to deal with inflation discussed.
		4.10	Special report on supply-side economics as a means of controlling inflation; views of various economists presented.
3	NBC	3.00*	Latest cost of living statistics announced in Washington and reaction from the Administration and Congress.
		1.20*	Reaganomics discussed at a House committee hearing.
4	ABC	3.00	Special report on economic problems in the U.S. and the prospects for improvement under the Reagan Administration.
		2.30*	Democrats attack the proposed cuts in social services and programs.

*Story appeared live in original newscast.

Altering the Foundations of Support for the President through Priming

Jon A. Krosnick • Ohio State University
Donald R. Kinder • University of Michigan

The disclosure that high officials within the Reagan administration had covertly diverted to the Nicaraguan Contras funds obtained from the secret sale of weapons to Iran provides us with a splendid opportunity to examine how the foundations of popular support shift when dramatic events occur. According to our theory of priming, the more attention media pay to a particular domain—the more the public is primed with it—the more citizens will incorporate what they know about that domain into their overall judgment of the president. Data from the 1986 National Election Study confirm that intervention in Central America loomed larger in the public's assessment of President Reagan's performance after the Iran-Contra disclosure than before. Priming was most pronounced for aspects of public opinion most directly implicated by the news coverage, more apparent in political novices' judgments than political experts', and stronger in the evaluations of Reagan's overall performance than in assessments of his character.

Presidents who are popular in the country tend to have their way in Washington. Popularity is a vital political resource, perhaps the president's single most important base of power (Neustadt, 1960; Ostrom & Simon, 1985; Rivers & Rose, 1985). Popularity, in turn, depends on the prevailing economic, social, and political conditions of the times. Unemployment, inflation, economic growth, flagrant violations of public trust, the human toll of war, sharply focused international crises, dramatic displays of presidential authority—all affect the president's standing with the public at large (Hibbs, Rivers, & Vasilatos, 1982a, 1982b; Kernell, 1978; MacKuen, 1983; Ostrom & Simon, 1985). A president's popularity (and therefore his power) is shaped by large events played on a national and international stage.

Our purpose here is to illuminate in greater detail the foundations of public support for the U.S. president by taking an approach different from, but complementary to, the one that now dominates research. In the dominant approach, time series statistical methods are applied to aggregated public opinion data. The typical model includes a handful of macroeconomic measures, an indicator or two to reflect the costs of war, and a miscellaneous set of measures to stand for crises, scandals, domestic unrest, presidential initiatives, and more. Although this approach can point with authority to the important national and international events that drive change in popular support in the aggregate, it cannot tell us about the dynamics of *individual* change. The aggregate time series results may tell us that scandal weakens the president's support with the public but not how scandal affects the thinking of individual citizens. Other than making the analytically convenient but highly unrealistic claim of homogeneity (that all citizens react in exactly the same way), the time series work is silent on what, exactly, citizens are doing. It does not and cannot tell us what is happening at the individual level.[1]

Our approach is to examine processes of change in popular support for a president at the level of the individual citizen, with the goal of informing and enriching aggregate studies of presidential popularity. We pursue this ambition by looking closely at citizens' responses to a single event—the highly publicized and dramatic revelation, on 25 November 1986, that funds received by the United States from the sale of arms to Iran had been secretly channeled by members of President Reagan's National Security Council to the Nicaraguan Contras. We treat the Iran-Contra revelation as a critical test for a theory—which we call *priming*—that claims to provide a comprehensive and psychologically plausible account of how citizens formulate and revise their views of presidential performance.

The Iran-Contra Connection

The Iran-Contra drama began to unfold on 3 November 1986, when a Lebanese magazine reported

that Robert C. McFarlane, the President's National Security Advisor, had secretly visited Tehran and that the United States had subsequently sent arms to Iran. In the face of mounting pressure from the news media, President Reagan went public on 13 November, disclosing that a "diplomatic initiative" with Iran had in fact been under way for some 18 months. The purpose of the initiative, he said, was to forge a new relationship with Iran, to bring an honorable end to the Iran-Iraq war, to eliminate state-sponsored terrorism, and to secure the safe return of the U.S. hostages held in Lebanon. Reagan went on to say that as part of this diplomatic initiative, he had authorized "the transfer of small amounts of defensive weapons and spare parts." He assailed the "wildly speculative false stories about arms for hostages and alleged ransom payments" and concluded with the emphatic declaration, "We did not—repeat, did not—trade weapons or anything else for hostages nor will we," a claim he repeated in a nationally televised news conference on 19 November.

On 25 November, the focus of the brewing scandal shifted abruptly away from Iran and the arms-for-hostages question. At noon that day, Attorney General Meese announced to a national television audience that funds obtained from the secret sale of weapons to Iran had been channeled to the Contras fighting to overthrow the Sandinista government in Nicaragua. The diversion of funds had been accomplished through a covert operation

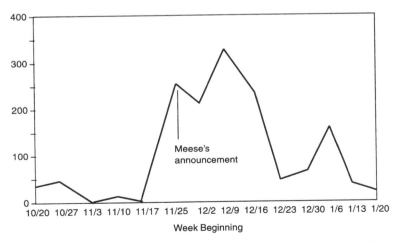

FIGURE 8.1 ■ ■ Average Number of Lines per Day Devoted to the Nicaraguan Contras on the Front Page of the *New York Times*

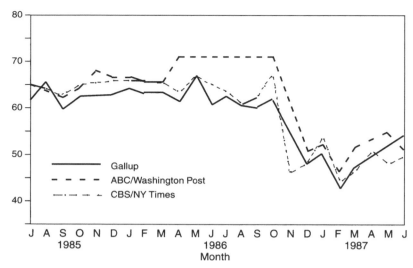

FIGURE 8.2 ■ Proportion of the American Public Approving of President Reagan's Job Performance

managed by members of the president's National Security Council (NSC). President Reagan then disclosed that Vice Admiral John Poindexter, director of the NSC, had resigned and that staff member Oliver North had been dismissed.

These remarkable revelations immediately took over the national news: suddenly, and dramatically, Nicaragua and aid to the Contras were the focus of front-page stories (see Figure 8.1).[2] Such news was not good for President Reagan's popularity. Figure 8.2 presents results from polls conducted by Gallup, ABC with the *Washington Post*, and CBS with the *New York Times*. All three register sharp declines in public support for President Reagan's performance, roughly coincident with the Iran-Contra revelation. It is impossible to estimate from these data how much of the decline in Reagan's popularity should be traced directly to disclosure of the Iran-Contra connection alone, but it is clear that the events of November significantly shook citizens' confidence in their president.

A Theory of Priming

Equipped with our theory of priming, we believe that Reagan's declining popularity can be explained, in part, by the conjunction of two facts: (1) the media's newfound fascination with covert aid to the Contras and (2) the public's opposition to intervention in Central America. According to the priming theory, when faced with a judgment or choice, people ordinarily do not take all plausible considerations into account, carefully examine and weigh all their implications, and then integrate them all into a summary decision. People typically forgo such exhaustive analysis and instead employ intuitive shortcuts and simple rules of thumb (Kahneman, Slovic, & Tversky, 1982). One such heuristic is to rely upon information that is most *accessible* in memory, information that comes to mind spontaneously and effortlessly when a judgment must be made (Fischhoff, Slovic, & Lichtenstein, 1980; Higgins & King, 1981; Taylor, 1982; Tversky & Kahneman, 1981). When asked to evaluate a president's performance, U.S. citizens generally focus only on the aspects of their knowledge that happen to be most accessible at the time of judgment.

In turn, what information is accessible for presidential evaluations is determined by the prevailing economic, social, and political conditions of the times. For their knowledge about such conditions, most citizens of course rely on information and analysis provided by mass media. This means that the standards citizens use to judge a president may be substantially determined by which stories media choose to cover and, consequently, which considerations are made accessible. The more attention the news pays to a particular domain—the more frequently it is primed—the more citizens will, according to the theory, incorporate what they know about that domain into their overall judgment of the president. Hence, by calling attention to some matters while ignoring others, news media may alter the foundations of public opinion toward the president.

This central claim of priming has been supported handsomely in a series of realistic experimental tests (Iyengar & Kinder, 1987; Iyengar et al., 1984; Iyengar, Peters, & Kinder, 1982). When primed by television news stories focusing on national defense, people judge the president largely by how well he has provided, as they see it, for the nation's defense. When primed by stories about inflation, people evaluate the president by how he has managed, in their view, to keep prices down. The empirical support for priming is strong; but so far it comes entirely from experimental studies. While experiments have genuine advantages, they also suffer inescapable limitations. Dependable conclusions about priming—or anything else—are based most securely in corroboration across different methods. So a demonstration of priming in a natural and politically consequential setting, free of the limitations of the experimental laboratory, would considerably bolster confidence in the phenomenon.

Priming and the Iran-Contra Connection

The Iran-Contra disclosure provided us with a perfect opportunity to undertake such a test. We do so by exploiting the serendipitous fact that as the attorney general was making his announcement on 25 November, Survey Research Center interviewers were busy questioning citizens all across the country as part of the 1986 National Election Study. That the attorney general's announcement came roughly midway through the 1986 study enables us to see whether, as the theory of priming requires, citizens who happened to be interviewed after the Iran-Contra disclosure evaluated President Reagan more in line with their views on U.S. intervention in Central America than did those (otherwise comparable) citizens who happened to be interviewed before the story broke. If public assessments of the president's performance do indeed depend upon which pieces of political memory come most readily to mind, surely the

Iran-Contra disclosure should have enhanced the impact of Central American policy on the public's view of Reagan.

In addition to testing this general hypothesis, we also evaluated three more detailed claims. The first pertains to the degree of correspondence between the news stories that constitute the prime and the opinions that are the target of priming. Several experimental results suggest a specificity to priming—that news coverage influences only the aspects of public opinion that are directly and immediately implicated by the story (e.g., Iyengar & Kinder, 1987). In the Iran-Contra context we would expect priming to be most pronounced on the questions of aid to the Contras and U.S. intervention in Central America, less evident on the abstract principle of whether the United States should generally intervene in other countries, still less apparent on judgments of U.S. power and prestige in the world, and invisible on matters completely unconnected to the Iran-Contra disclosure, such as the health of the national economy or the desirability of federal programs that assist blacks.

We also used the Iran-Contra revelation to examine whether some citizens are more susceptible to priming than others. We focused in particular on *expertise*. Compared to novices, experts know more about a particular domain; and their knowledge is better organized (Fiske & Kinder, 1981). Political experts and novices may react differently to changes in the media's agenda for a number of reasons: (1) because their knowledge is denser and better organized, experts possess a greater and more flexible ability to deal with new information and to interpret it in ways consistent with their prior convictions (Fiske, Kinder, & Larter, 1983); (2) because experts possess more informational support for their beliefs, they may be harder to budge; and (3) drawing attention to a particular aspect of national life may only remind experts of what they already know. In a pair of early experiments, experts were indeed relatively immune to priming by television news (Iyengar et al., 1984). But in subsequent experiments (reported in Iyengar & Kinder, 1987) this result disappeared, so the significance of expertise in conditioning the impact of news coverage is presently unclear. Here we will see whether novices were more primed by the Iran-Contra revelations than were experts.

Finally, we examined whether news coverage altered the foundations of the public's judgments of President Reagan's *character*, particularly judgments of his competence and integrity in addition to judgments of his performance. The experimental results suggest that the impact of priming on judgments of presidential performance is greater than on judgments of presidential character but that judgments of character also seem to depend to some degree on which aspects of national life news media choose to cover. Because the 1986 National Election Study included questions measuring the public's view of President Reagan's competence and integrity, we can pursue these results in the context of the Iran-Contra affair.

Data

Our investigation draws on the 1986 National Election Study (NES) carried out by the Center for Political Studies of the Institute for Social Research at the University of Michigan. Following the November national election, face-to-face interviews were conducted with a national probability sample of 2,176 U.S. citizens of voting age. We confined our analysis to the 1,086 individuals who received Form A of the questionnaire, which included an elaborate assessment of views of President Reagan and a rich battery of questions on foreign affairs in addition to standard questions about the campaign, the candidates, the parties, serious national problems and pressing policy choices, and registration and voting.

In order to test priming, we partitioned the Form A sample into two groups: the first was comprised of the respondents who happened to have been interviewed before the 25 November revelations (N = 714); the second was made up of those who happened to have been interviewed afterward (N = 349). Respondents interviewed on 25 November were excluded. Initial comparisons revealed that the pre-revelation and postrevelation groups were essentially indistinguishable across a variety of demographic and political comparisons, including education, race, age, gender, employment status, family income, partisanship, interest in politics, and ideological self-identification. This means that whatever differences between groups we might detect in public opinion toward President Reagan can reasonably be attributed to the Iran-Contra revelations.

We focused on three related but distinct aspects

of the public's support for President Reagan: evaluations of his overall performance as president, assessments of his competence, and assessments of his integrity. Table 8.1 shows that after the Iran-Contra revelations, public support for President Reagan declined across all three. These results are in rough accordance with those reported in various commercial polls bracketing this period (see Figure 8.2).

Our special interest in these public troubles of President Reagan has to do, of course, with whether such troubles can be connected—in the way specified by the theory of priming—to the Iran-Contra revelations and the avalanche of pictures and stories that they precipitated. Did the revelations enhance the political importance of foreign affairs for the public's assessment of the president? In operational terms, we measured foreign affairs opinions with four questions: (1) whether federal spending on aid to the Contras in Nicaragua should be increased, decreased, or kept about the same; (2) whether the United States should become more or less involved in the internal affairs of Central American countries; (3) whether the United States would be better off not getting involved in the affairs of other nations; and (4) whether the United States' position in the world had grown weaker, stronger, or stayed about the same during the previous year.

Table 8.1 reveals that public opinion on these matters changed hardly at all in response to the Iran-Contra revelation. Isolationism as a broad stance, attitudes toward U.S. involvement in Central America in general, and willingness to support more assistance to the Contras were all apparently unaffected by news of the diversion of funds, although more citizens than before claimed afterward that the United States' position in the world was weakening (45.1% vs. 37.6%, $p < .02$). This one shift probably has less to do with the Iran-Contra disclosure than with the wide-spread perception in the public that the Reagan administration had undertaken an arms-for-hostages deal with Iran.

Results

To examine priming empirically, we must first specify a model of public support for the president relevant to the case at hand. In formal terms, the model is given by the following equation:

TABLE 8.1. Assessments of President Reagan and Opinions on Foreign Affairs Before and After the Iran-Contra Revelation (%)

Assessment	Prerevelation	Postrevelation
1. Reagan's job performance		
Approve strongly	37.9	32.9
Approve not so strongly	30.0	26.9
Disapprove not so strongly	10.8	13.8
Disapprove strongly	21.2	26.3
2. Reagan's competence		
Intelligent		
Extremely well[a]	22.7	17.5
Quite well	51.2	53.2
Not too well	20.2	20.5
Not well at all	5.9	8.8
Knowledgeable		
Extremely well[a]	29.0	23.4
Quite well	43.8	43.3
Not too well	19.4	21.7
Not well at all	7.7	11.6
3. Reagan's integrity		
Moral		
Extremely well[a]	31.0	28.5
Quite well	52.4	46.5
Not too well	12.8	18.3
Not well at all	3.8	6.6
Decent		
Extremely well[a]	38.5	33.9
Quite well	51.0	49.6
Not too well	8.2	11.2
Not well at all	2.3	5.3
4. Aid to Contras in Nicaragua		
Increase support	9.1	7.0
Same	23.6	21.6
Decrease support	67.3	71.4
5. U.S. involvement in Central America		
Much more involved	5.2 ⎫	6.4 ⎫
	5.5 ⎬ 20.8	7.1 ⎬ 22.9
	10.1 ⎭	9.4 ⎭
In between	23.4	25.6
	17.2 ⎫	17.8 ⎫
	17.2 ⎬ 55.7	16.5 ⎬ 51.5
Much less involved	21.3 ⎭	17.2 ⎭
6. Isolationism		
Agree (U.S. should stay home)	30.8	29.2
Disagree (U.S. should not stay home)	69.2	70.8
7. U.S. position in the world		
Stronger	21.9	14.6
Same	40.5	40.3
Weaker	37.6	45.1
Number of cases	714	349

Source: 1986 National Election Study.
[a]The question asked how well the words *intelligent, knowledgeable, moral,* and *decent* described Reagan.

Overall Performance $= b_0 + b_1$ (Contras and Central America) $+ b_2$ (isolationism) $+ b_3$ (U.S. strength) $+ b_4$ (national economic assessments) $+ b_5$ (aid to blacks) $+ b_6 - b_{15}$ (control variables). (1)

Notice that Equation 1 includes three variables to represent the domain of foreign affairs, not four. In preliminary analyses, we found that attitudes toward U.S. involvement in Central America and attitudes toward aid to the Contras were highly correlated. People who opposed aid to the Contras were likely to oppose U.S. involvement in Central America, and those who favored aid to the Contras were likely to favor U.S. involvement in Central America ($r = .42$). These two attitudes correlated more weakly with views on isolationism and on U.S. strength ($.10 < r < .25$), and these latter two attitudes were uncorrelated with each other ($r = .04$). Therefore, in the analysis of priming, we averaged attitudes toward aid to the Contras and toward U.S. intervention in Central America into a single measure.

In addition to the three measures of opinion on foreign affairs, Equation 1 also includes a measure of the citizen's assessment of national economic conditions (an average of the citizen's perception of change over the past year in unemployment, inflation, and the general economy) and a measure of the citizen's opinion regarding the desirability of federal programs that provide assistance to blacks (averaged across two questions). We included national economic assessments and race policy views because both are highly relevant to presidential evaluations (e.g., Fiorina, 1981; Kinder, Adams, & Gronke, 1989; Rosenstone,

1983) and because they are utterly unrelated to the Iran-Contra revelation. We expected that the impact of national economic assessments and race policy views on evaluations of President Reagan should either be unaffected by the revelation or should decline, a reflection of the media's sudden preoccupation with Central America. Finally, Equation 1 also includes a standard set of background variables important for control purposes though of little substantive interest in their own right: employment status, age, race, gender, region, education, income, and party identification.[3]

To test the basic claim of priming, we estimated Equation 1 twice, first based on respondents in the prerevelation group, then based on respondents in the postrevelation group. Priming insists first of all that the impact on assessments of President Reagan's performance due to foreign affairs opinions—indexed in Equation 1 by b_1, b_2, and b_3—be greater in the postrevelation group than in the prerevelation group. Priming also requires that the impact of economic assessments and racial attitudes on evaluations of Reagan—indexed by b_4 and b_5—should remain the same or decline across the two groups.

The results of estimating Equation 1 with Ordinary Least Squares (OLS) regression are presented in Table 8.2. To interpret the coefficients shown there, keep in mind that all variables were coded to range from 0 to 1, with 1 indicating (a) favorable evaluations of Reagan's performance, (b) support for the Contras and for U.S. involvement in Central America, (c) support for interventionist foreign policy in general, (d) the view that the U.S. had grown stronger in the world, (e) belief that national economic conditions had improved over

Table 8.2. Estimated Impact of Public Opinion on Assessments of President Reagan's Performance, Before and After the Iran-Contra Revelation (Unstandardized OLS Regression Coefficients)

Opinion Domain	Prerevelation	Postrevelation	Difference	Significance of Difference[a]
Contras-Central America	.18*	.29*	.11	.17
Isolationism	.02	.10*	.08	.02
U.S. strength	.14*	.15*	.01	.45
Economic assessments	.33*	.35*	.02	.36
Aid to blacks	.22*	.00	−.22	.05
Number of cases	607	296	–	–

Source: 1986 National Election Study.
[a]Entries in this column are one-tailed p values.
*$p < .05$ (one-tailed).

the previous year, and (f) opposition to federal aid to blacks, respectively. As Table 8.2 reveals, public opinion on foreign affairs did indeed become more important for assessments of the president's performance in the immediate aftermath of the Iran-Contra disclosures. Foreign affairs attitudes were relatively unimportant to the public's view of Reagan's performance prior to 25 November (see Table 8.2, col. 1). After 25 November, however, the story is very different—foreign affairs loomed rather large in the public's presidential assessment (see Table 8.2, col. 2).

Moreover, the sharpest increases in Table 8.2 appear for the aspects of public opinion on foreign affairs most immediately implicated by the revelations. The importance of public opinion on the question of assistance to the Contras and U.S. intervention in Central America increased substantially from the prerevelation period to the postrevelation period (the unstandardized regression coefficient went from .18 to .29), as did the importance of the public's view of the general choice between intervention and isolationism (from .02 to .10). Meanwhile, the public's view of the strength of the United States around the world was evidently unaffected by the revelation (.14 vs. .15). This pattern of results corroborates the experimental findings noted earlier. Both suggest that priming requires a close correspondence between the news stories that do the priming and the opinions that are primed.[4]

The theory of priming predicts not only that public opinion on foreign affairs will become more important for presidential assessments after the Iran-Contra disclosure, but also that aspects of public opinion relevant to the president's success but unrelated to the disclosure will not become more important. The results in Table 8.2 confirm this prediction as well. First, citizens' assessments of national economic conditions contributed sizably to their view of President Reagan's performance—but did so equally before and after 25 November (.33 vs. .35). Second, citizens' views on race policy were evidently shunted aside (if momentarily) by the media's sudden preoccupation with Central America. Prior to 25 November, citizens who opposed federal programs designed to help blacks were more likely than citizens who supported them to support President Reagan. After 25 November, however, this political difference over race no longer contributed to public differ-

ences over the president's performance (.22 vs. .00). It would appear that the disclosure of 25 November altered the foundation of support for the president both by bringing certain aspects of public life to center stage and by pushing other aspects of public life off the stage altogether.

In order to illustrate the magnitude of the priming effects documented in Table 8.2, we generated predicted evaluations of Reagan, first using the prerevelation group's regression coefficients and then using the coefficients estimated with the postrevelation group. This required us to specify values of all the predictor variables in Equation 1. For this purpose we chose to represent an average, middle-of-the-road U.S. citizen: a white, female, forty-year-old high school graduate from the Midwest with an annual family income of $22,000, a political independent, who believed that national economic conditions had changed little over the previous year and who neither favored nor opposed federal programs for blacks. We carried out this exercise twice: once assuming that our hypothetical average citizen held views on foreign affairs that would predispose her to support Reagan (favored aid to the Contras and U.S. involvement in Central America, favored international interventionism generally, and believed the United States was maintaining its international strength) and once assuming she held views on these issues that would move her in the opposite direction (opposed aid to the Contras and U.S. intervention in Central America, favored isolationism, and believed that the U.S. had lost international strength).

The results of this simulation suggest that the consequences of priming for presidential support are contingent on the citizen's prior views. Among (typical) citizens predisposed to support Reagan on foreign policy grounds, the effects of priming were negligible. Equation 1 predicts evaluation of President Reagan's performance by such people to be .73 (on the zero-to-one scale) prior to the Iran-Contra revelation and .75 afterward. But among typical citizens predisposed to *oppose* Reagan on foreign policy grounds, the story is very different: Equation 1 now predicts a Reagan evaluation of .53 before the revelation and only .38 after, a steep falloff in support. Thus, the effect of priming was to reduce assessments of President Reagan's performance among critics of U.S. policy in Central America substantially.

In the 1986 NES data, the prerevelation group's

average evaluation of Reagan (on the zero-to-one scale) was .60 whereas the postrevelation group's was .55. How much of this .05 decrease can be attributed to priming? We used each of the 1986 NES respondents' actual demographics and attitudes to generate two predicted Reagan evaluations: one using the prerevelation regression weights, the other using the postrevelation regression weights. The average predicted prerevelation evaluation was .53 and the average predicted postrevelation evaluation was .50, a difference of .03. Thus, almost two-thirds of the decrease in this sample's Reagan approval ratings can be attributed to priming.

Our next move was to investigate whether political novices were more susceptible to priming than political experts. We assessed expertise using measures of objective knowledge about political affairs. In particular, we partitioned the 1986 NES respondents according to their success at identifying six political figures: George Bush, Caspar Weinberger, William Rehnquist, Paul Volker, Robert Dole, and Tip O'Neill. The 65% who correctly identified three or fewer were considered novices, and the 35% who correctly identified four or more were considered experts. Then we simply repeated the analysis summarized in Table 8.2, separately within each group.[5]

Among political novices, the Iran-Contra revelation had a substantial priming effect (see the upper panel of Table 8.3). Opinions on foreign affairs were more important in novices' assessments of Reagan's performance after the revelation than before, whereas national economic assessments were no more important, and opinions on federal programs to aid blacks were less important. Particularly noteworthy was the dramatically enhanced prominence of Central American policy in novices' presidential evaluations after 25 November (the regression coefficient nearly tripled, from .12 to .35). As a general matter, the pattern of priming effects noted for the public as a whole is maintained and sharpened among novices alone.

Meanwhile, priming was less apparent in the assessments of President Reagan's performance offered by political experts (see the lower panel of Table 8.3). Indeed, priming among experts seems confined to a single aspect of opinion. In the wake of the Iran-Contra disclosure, experts were more likely to evaluate President Reagan according to their general views on U.S. intervention in international affairs (.06 vs. .20). It is interesting both that experts seem generally less susceptible to priming and that the character of priming among experts is different. Novices ap-

Table 8.3. Estimated Impact of Public Opinion on Assessments of President Reagan's Performance Before and After the Iran-Contra Revelation, Separately for Political "Novices" and Political "Experts" (Unstandardized OLS Regression Coefficients)

Opinion Domain	Prerevelation	Postrevelation	Difference	Significance of Difference[a]
Among Political "Novices"				
Contras-Central America	.12*	.35*	.23	.06
Isolationism	.01	.08*	.07	.09
U.S. strength	.14*	.18*	.04	.32
Economic assessments	.29*	.39*	.10	.19
Aid to blacks	.20*	.03	−.17	.05
Number of cases	383	191	—	—
Among Political "Experts"				
Contras-Central America	.22*	.28*	.06	.43
Isolationism	.06	.20*	.14	.05
U.S. strength	.16*	.06	−.10	.29
Economic assessments	.39*	.41*	.02	.41
Aid to blacks	.20*	.07	−.13	.37
Number of cases	222	105	—	—

Source: 1986 National Election Study.
[a]Entries in this column are one-tailed ps.
*p < .05 (one-tailed).

pear to be primed on those aspects most directly and concretely implicated by the news coverage while experts, insofar as they are primed at all, are influenced at a more abstract level.[6]

The distinction between novices and experts apparent in Table 8.3 is consistent with our experimental results (reported in Iyengar et al., 1984) and with other aspects of the NES survey data as well. In particular, the decline in support for President Reagan's performance in the immediate aftermath of the attorney general's disclosures registered in the public as a whole was greater among novices than among experts. Of the novices, 64.8% approved of Reagan's performance prior to the Iran-Contra revelations while just 57.4% did so afterward, a net change of 7.4 percentage points. Meanwhile, 67.6% of the experts approved of Reagan's performance before the revelations, and 65% did so afterward, a net change of 2.6 percentage points. Novices were more likely than experts to be swept away by the avalanche of stories and pictures set in motion by the 25 November revelations.

Finally, we examined whether media coverage of the Iran-Contra connection altered the foundations of the public's assessments of President Reagan's character. To do so, we reestimated Equa-

tion 1, first with assessments of Reagan's competence, then with assessments of his integrity, as the dependent variable.[7] The results shown in Table 8.4 replicate, in a somewhat attenuated fashion, those reported earlier regarding the public's assessments of President Reagan's performance. For judgments of character, as for judgments of performance, opinions on Central American policy became more important after the Iran-Contra revelation than before while assessments of national economic conditions and views on government race policy became, if anything, less important. The effects of priming were a bit more pronounced in the public's judgments of Reagan's competence than in judgments of his integrity. Indeed, apart from the increased importance of views on Central American policy, the public's assessment of Reagan's integrity appears quite unmoved by the Iran-Contra revelation. The greater susceptibility of competence assessments apparent in Table 8.4 may reflect, in part, how the news media began to frame the Iran-Contra story, namely, as exposing Reagan's disengagement from U.S. foreign policy. Framed in this way, the Iran-Contra story naturally implicated the president's competence more than his integrity.

Table 8.4. Estimated Impact of Public Opinion on Assessments of President Reagan's Character Before and After the Iran-Contra Revelation (Unstandardized OLS Regression Coefficients)

Opinion Domain	Prerevelation	Postrevelation	Difference	Significance of Difference[a]
Assessing Reagan's Competence				
Contras–Central America	.09**	.20**	.11	.15
Isolationism	.04**	.09**	.05	.04
U.S. strength	.12**	.06*	−.06	.06
Economic assessments	.10**	.07	−.03	.07
Aid to blacks	.14**	.12**	−.02	.41
Number of cases	632	304	–	–
Assessing Reagan's Integrity				
Contras-Central America	.03	.12**	.09	.14
Isolationism	.05**	.06**	.01	.21
U.S. strength	.07**	.07**	.00	.47
Economic assessments	.13**	.13**	.00	.39
Aid to blacks	.05*	.04	−.01	.28
Number of cases	629	303	–	–

Source: 1986 National Election Study.
[a]Entries in this column are one-tailed ps.
*p < .10 (one-tailed).
**p < .05 (one-tailed).

Discussion

The disclosure in the fall of 1986 that funds received from the sale of arms to Iran had been secretly channeled to the Nicaraguan Contras provides an excellent opportunity to test the theory of priming in a politically consequential setting. By and large, the theory stands up well to this examination. Citizens questioned after the revelations held President Reagan to an altered set of standards, and these alterations can be directly traced to the changes in the media's agenda provoked by the Iran-Contra revelations. As expected, priming was particularly pronounced for the aspects of public opinion most directly implicated by the news coverage (aid to the Contras and involvement in Central America), was more apparent in the judgments of political novices than in the judgments of political experts, and showed up more clearly in the public's evaluations of President Reagan's overall performance than in assessments of his character. Taken together, these results strongly support the theory of priming and are important not least because they escape the artificiality that inevitably accompanies experimental laboratory research, which had provided priming's sole empirical support up until now. Our confidence in priming is fortified by the close convergence between previous experimental results on the one hand and the results reported here, based on personal interviews with a national sample of citizens responding to a real crisis, on the other.

The comparative advantages of the present investigation—representative sampling, professional interviewers, careful and elaborate pretesting, the serendipitous intrusion of a dramatic and heavily covered event—are real enough; but we should also acknowledge some comparative disadvantages as well. As we noted earlier, the prerevelation group closely resembles the postrevelation group in terms of basic demographic and political characteristics. However, the two groups could still differ from one another in consequential ways that we missed. Given the present design, we cannot be certain that the differences we observed between the prerevelation and postrevelation groups in their assessments of President Reagan were actually due to priming and not to some preexisting and unmeasured difference or to some event other than the Iran-Contra revelation. Notice that this worry is swept aside by the procedure of random assignment that is the heart of the experimental method. It is the convergence of results across different methods of testing that is crucial in science in general and crucial to the standing of the theory of priming in particular.

Priming provides an empirically grounded, psychologically plausible account of how individuals form and revise their views of presidential performance. Priming therefore aspires to complement the dominant tradition in research on support for the president, which applies time series methods to estimate the impact of national and international events on change in the public support. This research has been enormously informative about the aggregate effects of such events while revealing little about the diversity among citizens' reactions that seem certain to underlie change and stability in the aggregate. From such research we know a great deal about how the public as a whole will respond to a change in unemployment or to a dramatic international crisis but virtually nothing about which citizens are most likely to increase their support for the president, which are likely to decrease their support, and which are likely to be unmoved. The literature is even less prepared to tell us *why* different citizens respond differently to the same event. Priming provides a general framework to answer such questions.

Priming also carries an implication for the study of political change more generally. Most quantitative studies of this sort assume that the effects of economic and social change are constant over time—that, say, the impact of a one-percentage-point change in the unemployment rate on the incumbent's reelection chances is invariant across history (or, less dramatically, the length of the time series). Priming collides head-on with this assumption. According to priming, shifts in news media content alter the political importance that the public attaches to the flow of events. If priming is pervasive, the assumption of constant effects seems dubious. This does not mean that the typical time series analysis of political change is worthless, only that such analysis would be enhanced by incorporating the fundamental insight of priming— that through its monopoly over the immediate telling of political history, media possess the power to influence what the public considers and what it ignores.

A final implication of our findings involves stepping back and taking a normative stance on the matter of political change. Exposure to political information through mass media varies enormously across the U.S. public. Some citizens are constantly preoccupied with the flow of political news while others are utterly indifferent to it. Not surprisingly, those who are most heavily exposed to political news also accumulate the most political knowledge. The devoted viewer, listener, and reader becomes society's political expert. With this in mind, we might expect that it would be the expert who would be most influenced by changes in the media's agenda. In the case of the Iran-Contra affair, the news media's daily updating would presumably have the greatest impact on citizens who absorbed the complete story and the least impact on those exposed only to fragments of it. Our results suggest just the opposite. Citizens with the least knowledge (and presumably the least exposure) manifested the largest priming effects. Thus, change in support for the president in response to the Iran-Contra revelations appears to have been dominated by the least-informed, a result that has troubling implications for the exercise of power in Washington. Presidents who enjoy popular support typically have success in shaping the political agenda of the nation (Kernell, 1986; Rivers & Rose, 1985). Our findings suggest that change over time in popular approval—and thus the waxing and waning of presidential power—may depend the most on the citizens who know the least.

NOTES

1. Most, but not quite all, the time series work presumes that citizens respond uniformly to whatever is happening in the country. The conspicuous and excellent exception is provided by Hibbs, Rivers, and Vasilatos (1982a), who found that citizens' reactions to events were conditioned by their class affiliations and partisan attachments.
2. Figure 8.1 displays the number of front page column-lines (text, headlines, and pictures) mentioning the Nicaraguan rebels, Nicaragua, or the Contras.
3. Employment status was coded 0 for respondents who were looking for work and 1 for respondents who were not. Age and educational attainment were coded in years. Income was coded 1 to 22, representing 22 separate income categories. Race was coded 1 for whites and 2 for nonwhites. Gender was coded 1 for males and 2 for females. Party identification was represented by two dummy variables: the first was coded 1 for Democrats and 0 for all other respondents; the second was coded 1 for Republicans and 0 for all other respondents. Region was represented by three dummy variables: the first was coded 1 for residents of central states and 0 for all others; the second was coded 1 for residents of southern states and 0 for all others; and the

third was coded 1 for residents of western states and 0 for all others.
4. To test the statistical significance of the changes in the coefficients across the pre- and postrevelation groups, we estimated an enhanced version of Equation 1. In particular, we added the following variables to it: (pre-post), (pre-post)(Contras–Central America), (pre-post)(isolationism), (pre-post)(U.S. strength), (pre-post)(national economic assessments), (pre-post)(aid to blacks). Pre-post is a dummy variable coded zero for the prerevelation group and one for the postrevelation group. Thus, the coefficients associated with each of the multiplicative terms tests whether the impact of each aspect of public opinion on evaluation of Reagan's performance differs from the prerevelation group to the postrevelation group. The significance levels of these coefficients appear in the text and in the far righthand column of Table 8.2.
5. We set the dividing line between experts and novices in this fashion because it generated as close to equal-sized groups as possible while making the experts more rare than the novices, a distribution that suits current wisdom about the distribution of political expertise (see Kinder & Sears, 1985). Operationalizing expertise in terms of general knowledge about politics differs from the way we have operationalized it in our previous studies of priming. There, we used measures of domain-specific knowledge (e.g., Iyengar & Kinder, 1987; Iyengar et al., 1984). In the present case, we would have preferred to use measures of knowledge about Central American affairs or about Nicaragua in particular, had such measures been included in the 1986 NES.
6. To assess the statistical significance of the differences associated with expertise, we estimated an enhanced version of the equation described in n. 4. To that equation we added six new terms: (expertise), (expertise)(pre-post)(Contras/Central America), (expertise)(pre-post)(isolationism), (expertise)(pre-post)(U.S. strength), (expertise)(pre-post)(national economic assessments), (expertise)(pre-post)(aid to blacks). Here we treated political expertise as a continuous variable defined as the proportion of the six political figures correctly identified. The coefficients associated with the multiplicative terms then assess whether the magnitude of the pre- to postrevelation difference in each attitude's impact depends upon expertise. When we estimated this enhanced equation, we found that the three-way interaction involving attitudes toward Central American policy and that involving views on isolationism were both marginally significant ($p = .09$ and $.14$ respectively) but that the remaining three three-way interactions were not ($p > .25$ in each case).
7. The measure of competence is an average of respondents' judgments of how well the terms *intelligent* and *knowledgeable* describe Reagan; the measure of integrity is an average of comparable judgments regarding *moral* and *decent*.

REFERENCES

Fiorina, Morris. 1981. *Retrospective Voting in American National Elections*. New Haven: Yale University Press.
Fischhoff, Baruch, Paul Slovic, and Sarah Lichtenstein. 1980. "Knowing What You Want: Measuring Labile Values." In

Cognitive Processes in Choice and Decision Behavior, ed. Thomas Wallsten. Hillsdale, NJ: Erlbaum.

Fiske, Susan T., and Donald R. Kinder. 1981. "Involvement, Expertise, and Schema Use: Evidence from Political Cognition." In *Personality, Cognition, and Social Interaction*, ed. Nancy Cantor and John Kihlstrom. Hillsdale, NJ: Erlbaum.

Fiske, Susan T., Donald R. Kinder, and W. Michael Larter. 1983. "The Novice and the Expert: Knowledge-based Strategies in Political Cognition." *Journal of Experimental Social Psychology* 19:381–400.

Hibbs, Douglas A., Jr., Douglas Rivers, and Nicholas Vasilatos. 1982a. "On the Demand for Economic Outcomes: Macroeconomic Performance and Mass Political Support in the United States, Great Britain, and Germany." *Journal of Politics* 44:426–62.

Hibbs, Douglas A., Jr., Douglas Rivers, and Nicholas Vasilatos. 1982b. "The Dynamics of Political Support for American Presidents among Occupational and Partisan Groups." *American Journal of Political Science* 26:312–32.

Higgins, E. Tory, and Gary King. 1981. "Accessibility of Social Constructs: Information-processing Consequences of Individual and Contextual Variability." In *Personality, Cognition, and Social Interactions*, ed. Nancy Cantor and John Kihlstrom. Hillsdale, NJ: Erlbaum.

Iyengar, Shanto, and Donald R. Kinder. 1987. *News That Matters*. Chicago: University of Chicago Press.

Iyengar, Shanto, Mark D. Peters, Donald R. Kinder, and Jon A. Krosnick. 1984. "The Evening News and Presidential Evaluations." *Journal of Personality and Social Psychology* 46:778–87.

Iyengar, Shanto, Mark D. Peters, and Donald R. Kinder. 1982. "Experimental Demonstrations of the Not-So-Minimal Political Consequences of Mass Media." *American Political Science Review* 76:848–58.

Kahneman, Daniel, Paul Slovic, and Amos Tversky. 1982. *Judgment under Uncertainty: Heuristics and Biases*. New York: Cambridge University Press.

Kernell, Samuel. 1978. "Explaining Presidential Popularity." *American Political Science Review* 72:506–22.

Kernell, Samuel. 1986. *Going Public*. Washington: Congressional Quarterly.

Kinder, Donald R., Gordon S. Adams, and Paul W. Gronke. 1989. "Economics and Politics in the 1984 American Presidential Election." *American Journal of Political Science* 33:491–515.

Kinder, Donald R., and Thomas R. Palfrey. 1989. "On Behalf of Experimentation." University of Michigan, Ann Arbor. Typescript.

Kinder, Donald R., and David O. Sears. 1985. "Public Opinion and Political Behavior." In *Handbook of Social Psychology*, 3d ed., Vol. 2, ed., Gardner Lindzey and Elliot Aronson. New York: Random House.

MacKuen, Michael. 1983. "Political Drama, Economic Conditions, and the Dynamics of Presidential Popularity." *American Journal of Political Science* 27:165–92.

Nuestadt, Richard E. 1960. *Presidential Power; The Politics of Leadership*. New York: Wiley.

Ostrom, Charles W., and Dennis M. Simon. 1985. "Promise and Performance: A Dynamic Model of Presidential Popularity." *American Political Science Review* 79:334–58.

Rivers, Douglas, and Nancy L. Rose. 1985. "Passing the President's Program: Public Opinion and Presidential Influence in Congress." *American Journal of Political Science* 29:183–96.

Rosenstone, Steven J. 1983. *Forecasting Presidential Elections*. New Haven: Yale University Press.

Taylor, Shelley E. 1982. "The Availability Bias in Social Perception and Interaction." In *Judgment under Uncertainty: Heuristics and Biases*, ed. Daniel Kahneman, Paul Slovic, and Amos Tversky. New York: Cambridge University Press.

Tversky, Amos, and Daniel Kahneman. 1981. "The Framing of Decisions and the Psychology of Choice." *Science* 211:453–58.

Zaller, John. 1990. "Political Awareness, Elite Opinion Leadership, and the Mass Survey Response." *Social Cognition* 8:125–153.

Anxiety, Enthusiasm, and the Vote: The Emotional Underpinnings of Learning and Involvement During Presidential Campaigns

George E. Marcus • Williams College

Michael B. MacKuen • University of Missouri, St. Louis

By incorporating emotionality, we propose to enrich information-processing models of citizens' behavior during election campaigns. We demonstrate that two distinct dynamic emotional responses play influential roles during election campaigns: anxiety and enthusiasm. Anxiety, responding to threat and novelty, stimulates attention toward the campaign and political learning and discourages reliance on habitual cues for voting. Enthusiasm powerfully influences candidate preferences and stimulates interest and involvement in the campaign. The findings support a theoretical perspective that regards cognitive and emotional processes as mutually engaged and mutually supportive rather than as antagonistic. We suggest that the democratic process may not be undermined by emotionality as is generally presupposed. Instead, we believe that people use emotions as tools for efficient information processing and thus enhance their abilities to engage in meaningful political deliberation.

Fear is associated with the expectation that something destructive will happen to us. . . . People do not believe this when they are, or think they are, in the midst of great prosperity, and are in consequence insolent, contemptuous, and reckless . . . nor yet when they have experienced every kind of horror already and have grown callous about the future [for] there must be some faint expectation of escape.

. . . Fear sets us thinking what can be done, which of course nobody does when things are hopeless. Consequently, when it is advisable that the audience should be frightened, the orator must make them feel that they are really in danger.

—Aristotle, *Rhetoric* 2.5.1383

We would like to suggest that emotion is a catalyst for political learning. In particular, the analyses we shall present argue that threat powerfully motivates citizens to learn about politics. On the face of it, our proposition makes too much sense to ignore. Generally inattentive to political matters, citizens may require sharp notice before they become motivated to learn anything new. And at least at the intuitive level, threat seems as good a spur to action as any. In addition, we suggest that the ability of political leaders to generate enthusiasm stimulates political involvement. This second claim has a long-standing and long recognized status (e.g., Schattschneider, 1960). More deeply, we believe that a mounting body of evidence in neurophysiology, psychology, and political science points toward the distinctive roles that different emotions play in stimulating political attentiveness. We offer a view that shows how emotionality aids, rather than disrupts, political reasoning and enhances, rather than diminishes, the quality of democratic life.

We shall report a series of empirical tests that establish the importance of anxiety and enthusiasm for political learning and involvement, respectively. First, we demonstrate that fear (anxiety) and enthusiasm are distinctive emotional responses to political candidates and thereby eliminate a simple "valence" view of emotions. Second, we observe that people's anxiety and enthusiasm varies with political events and is not a permanent feature of individual personalities. Third, we consider evidence that anxiety and enthusiasm play distinctive parts in the voting decision. Fourth, we show explicitly that anxiety, rather than enthusiasm, moves people to learn policy-related information about candidates. More generally, we argue that anxiety works cooperatively with learning to shift attention to political matters and to diminish reliance on habit in voting decisions. Finally, in a parallel analysis, we show that enthusiasm, rather than anxiety, has a distinct effect on political involvement.

Theoretical Background

The idea of threat as an attention-getting device makes common sense. Hit it over the head with a two-by-four and you can get the attention of even a mule. Nothing focuses the mind so well as the prospect of one's own hanging. And so on.

Anxiety also occupies a prominent place in the contemporary psychology of emotions. Over the past decade, psychologists have developed a two-dimensional typology of emotional response that clearly distinguishes anxiety from such emotions as depression (e.g., Ax, 1953; Diener & Emmons, 1985; Plutchik, 1980; Russell, 1980; Tellegen, 1985; Watson & Tellegen, 1985; Zevon & Tellegen, 1982). At the same time, the two-dimensional character of emotional response has proven a powerful schema for the analysis of citizen response to political candidates (Abelson et al., 1982; Marcus, 1988b; Masters & Sullivan, 1989; Sullivan & Masters, 1988).

Parallel evidence lies in current neurophysiology. It is now widely understood that the human brain's limbic system has two subsystems, each of which generates distinctive emotional responses (Eccles, 1989; Fonberg, 1986; Gray, 1981, 1987a, 1987b). One subsystem generates emotions that fall in the class of excitement, elation, and enthusiasm; the other subsystem generates emotions that fall in the class of anxiety, stress, and fear. The combined outputs of these systems generate the mood state (forming what is most often described as a *circumplex*). It is important to emphasize that this model describes mood—and changes in mood—as two-dimensional. Mood states are an *amalgam* formed by two distinct physiologically based systems of arousal, each of which influences specific gradations of mood that we readily recognize and to which we assign everyday labels (Storm & Storm, 1987).

Especially intriguing is the neurophysiological work on the strategic functions played by distinct emotional responses. Each of the two systems—that of anxiety and that of enthusiasm—appears linked to behaviorally different sorts of psychological orientation.

Consider first the threat-attendant system that generates moods ranging from safety to anxiety. Feeling calm, placid, and secure indicates the absence of threat; feeling apprehensive, fearful, or in dread indicates the presence of threat. According to Gray's (1987b) model of anxiety, this system operates to interrupt ongoing activity. It does not control subsequent behavior; rather, it arrests ongoing activity and enables other control systems—cognitive and emotional—to respond (cf. Simon, 1967). More specifically, the *behavioral inhibition system* continually matches incoming sensory stimuli against contemporary plans and expectations. As long as the comparisons continue to confirm the safety of the environment, moods of calmness and safety prevail and ongoing actions are left undisturbed. However, if a "mismatch" occurs, then ongoing activity is inhibited, attention is shifted toward the intrusive source, and increased arousal occurs. Put more plainly, the appearance of a novel or threatening intrusion causes us to stop, look, listen, and get ready for action.

Anxiety, as we use the term, is not the sort of primitive emotion that underlies the fight/flight system (Gray 1987b). In the realm of electoral politics, candidates and parties may anger, disgust, and threaten fundamental values and beliefs of voters. Yet they do not present physical dangers that engage the instinctive, reptile-brain-centered responses that operate independent of cognition. Instead, these threats endanger symbolic worlds, environs of values and beliefs, the stuff of contemporary mass politics (Edelman, 1964). Thus, the emotional responses that we label "anxiety" reflect mechanisms that join cognitions with emotions.

Experiments in cognitive psychology demonstrate that negative events increase attention and that emotional reactions are crucial to the stimulation of attention (Derryberry, 1991; Pratto & John, 1991). Thus, current work in psychology and in neurophysiology supports a theoretical view about how people come to learn about politics: they abandon complacency and start to pay attention when the world signals that something is not right.

The second class of emotional arousal monitors current behavior. This system generates moods of enthusiasm or elation as our personal tasks and social activity succeed and generates moods of melancholy or depression as we experience failure. The *behavioral approach system* provides active feedback of our ongoing behavior and marshals the physical and mental resources necessary for success. These moods are essential for the proper performance of learned behavior. The variance in moods generated by the behavioral approach system provides an important marker for the strengthening or wavering of motivation. Thus, for politics, we ought to find that variations in enthusiasm ought to predict variations in political involvement. More precisely, during political campaigns, candidates must generate enthusiasm for themselves among voters in order to gain their support and to create active interest in the election. When voters respond to a candidate with enthusiasm, they are not merely evincing passive sympathetic reactions but sharing convictions and commitment to common endeavors. Rather than stopping, looking, and listening, enthusiasts throw themselves into the cause.

We suggest that people rely on their feelings to provide them with important strategic information. More than coloring cognitions with values, changes in mood constitute a critical part of information-processing mechanisms (Cacioppo et al., 1986). We aim to demonstrate that this particular view (which emphasizes the role of *anxiety* in information processing) uniquely contributes to our understanding of political matters. We shall develop and test hypotheses about political information processing that depend crucially on emotional response.

Two Types of Emotional Response

The empirical work in both mood psychology and neurophysiology indicates that we should expect two types of emotional response, which we call "anxiety" and "enthusiasm." Our first empirical steps show that political candidates elicit these two sorts of responses in the mass public. Here we extend work already done (Abelson et al., 1982; Marcus, 1988b) by adding two new twists. First, we observe that the "dual-system" view of emotional response stands up under different measurement techniques. In so doing, we eliminate the alternative "valence" hypothesis about the structure of emotional response. Second, we observe that this dual system is not stable but instead reacts to the psychic pressure of the campaign. Thus we support an understanding that emotional responses are functionally focused, with one system alert to intrusive signals of novelty and threat and the other system monitoring the success of current behavior.

In order to test the dimensionality and the dynamics of emotional response, we examine two data sets. The first is the familiar American National Election Studies (ANES) panel of 1980, with interviews taken in January, June, and October. The second, a commercial survey, represents the views of Missourians during the 1988 presidential campaign in a series of three cross sections taken during June, July, and October. We are fortunate in that the ANES staff included seven emotional response items in the 1980 panel, eliciting a variety of emotional responses. In each wave, respondents were asked: "I am going to name a political figure, and I want you to tell me whether that person, or something he has done has made you have certain feelings like 'anger' or 'pride,' or others I will mention. Think about Jimmy Carter. Now, has Carter—because of the kind of person he is, or because of something he has done—ever made you feel: angry?" The respondent was then asked whether Carter had made him or her feel "hopeful," "afraid of him," "proud," "disgusted," "sympathetic toward him," and "uneasy." The same sequence was repeated for Reagan (and then other candidates). While "anxiety" is not included as one of the response items, we expect that the terms *afraid*, *uneasy*, *anger* and *disgust* will serve as appropriate markers. Similarly, though "enthusiasm" is not included, we expect that the terms *proud*, *hope*, and *sympathy* will be appropriate markers for this dimension.

We begin our work by examining how people reacted to the candidates. If our dual-system understanding of emotional response is correct, then we should see some evidence of the candidates' stimulating a *combination* of emotional responses. On the other hand, if the conventional "valence" understanding is correct, then the candidates

should produce a single emotional response (like vs. dislike). Thus, we want to see if Carter and Reagan got people to experience (a) a *combination* of enthusiasm and anxiety or (b) a sense of enthusiasm as *opposed* to anxiety.

A factor analysis of the seven items moves us forward in two ways. First, it permits us to see whether the enthusiasm items hang together and the anxiety items hang together. This is a measurement issue, a matter of fundamental importance. Second, the factor analysis provides a weak test of the valence versus dual-system view of emotional response. The valence model predicts that the enthusiasm and anxiety items will line up in polar opposites; the dual-system model predicts that enthusiasm and anxiety need not be—and are unlikely to be—polar opposites.

A straightforward factor analysis of the seven items (here from the January reading, i.e., before the campaign began) suggests the plausibility of a two-dimensional view. Figure 9.1 presents the factor space. The data clearly sustain our measurement requirement that the enthusiasm items and the anxiety items separate into distinctive clusters. Further, the pattern clearly defeats the valence theoretical view: the enthusiasm and anxiety clusters do not line up as polar opposites.

Yet the nature of the 1980 ANES survey questions does not allow us to eliminate an alternative understanding. The data could still prove consistent with the valence model under a subtle but plau-

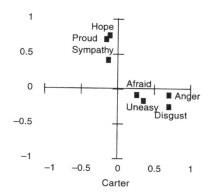

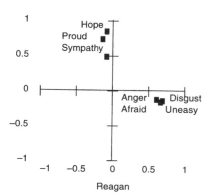

FIGURE 9.1 ■ Factor Space of Seven Affect Terms Used To Map Emotional Responses to the 1980 Presidential Candidates

Source: 1980 ANES data.

Note: The figures represent a varimax rotation of a principal factor solution for the correlation matrix among the seven items for each candidate. The dimensionality of a factor space is not, of course, a simple statistical inference. Here, it appears that two dimensions capture the bulk of the common variance. The eigenvalues for Carter are 1.48, .74, and .14. For Reagan, the eigenvalues are 2.07, 1.03, and .35.

sible interpretation. It is possible that individuals respond in conventional valence terms (positive opposed to negative) while the second dimension represents the intensity of the emotional response (see Larsen, Diener, & Cropanzano, 1987; MacKuen, 1987; Russell, 1980).

In order to bring evidence to bear on this matter, we designed a special-purpose question wording to tap each of the two dimensions. We chose appropriate word markers to elicit responses most closely associated with each of the two dimensions (Watson, Clark, & Tellegen, 1988). Importantly, we ensure that a respondent can report (a) an absence of emotional response toward a candidate on one or both dimensions of emotionality and (b) intermediate degrees of response, for example, a sense that the candidate was somewhat (or very) calming or boring.

We presented the respondent with a modified feeling thermometer anchored by pairs of words connoting anxiety versus safety or, alternatively, enthusiasm versus depression. In order to obtain a minimal validation test, we chose two pairs for each dimension. The enthusiasm pairs were (*enthusiastic* vs. *unenthusiastic*) and (*interested* vs. *indifferent*) and the anxiety pairs were (*upset* vs. *comfortable*) and (*anxious* vs. *safe*). For an enthusiasm example, consider the following:

When we talk to people about the major Presidential candidates, they use different words to describe how they feel about them. For both Vice

President Bush and Governor Dukakis, I'd like to read you some pairs of words. For each pair, let's use one [1] for the lowest possible rating and 100 as the highest possible rating.

Let's start with Vice President Bush. Would you say you feel "unenthusiastic" or "enthusiastic" about him? One [1] would be the most unenthusiastic rating and 100 would be the most enthusiastic rating.

We then piggybacked our emotion-thermometer items onto a commercial poll in the state of Missouri during three periods of the 1988 presidential campaign. The first wave, in June, followed the Missouri primary by three months and represents a period of relative calm in the local environment. The second wave, in July, immediately followed the Democratic National Convention and represents the high point for the Dukakis campaign. Finally, the third wave, in late October, measures emotional response at the end of the national campaign.

A similar factor analysis (here for the relatively quiet June period) of the four new items produces Figure 9.2. Note that the two item pairs fall neatly into two distinct clusters: anxiety and enthusiasm. Further, the distinctiveness of the emotions is apparent. Were anxiety and enthusiasm antipodes, the four items would line up along one dimension, with *enthusiasm* and *interest* at one end and *anxious* and *upset* at the other end. This is obviously not so since the enthusiastic-unenthusiastic and

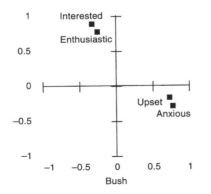

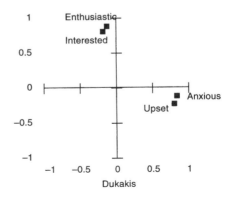

FIGURE 9.2 ■ Factor Space of Four Affect Terms Used To Map Emotional Response to the 1988 Presidential Candidates
Source: 1988 Missouri Data.
Note: The figures represent a varimax rotation of a principal factor solution for the correlation matrix among the four items for each candidate. Again, it appears that two dimensions capture the bulk of the common variance. The eigenvalues for Bush are 2.09, .74, and .04. For Dukakis, the eigenvalues are 1.96, .94, and .02.

interested-indifferent ratings are nearly orthogonal to the upset-comfortable and anxious-safe ratings. Thus in these new measures, the enthusiasm and anxiety measures are not mere opposites, as the valence view of emotional response would predict; instead, they appear to be separate entities, as the dual-system view expects.

In the end, the factor-structural evidence rejects the hypothesis of a single valence dimension and instead supports the current view that anxiety and enthusiasm are distinctive emotional responses. Yet this evidence should not persuade. So far, we observe only static correlation, a matter of *which* emotional responses go together, rather than evidence of theoretical function. More persuasive evidence would require that we demonstrate that each dimension of emotional arousal has systematic and distinct behavioral consequences congruent with the dual-system theory. That requires that we show that one distinct behavior, learning, is influenced by changes over time in moods of anxiety and that another distinct behavior, political involvement in the campaign, is influenced by changes over time in moods of enthusiasm. We turn to the dynamic relationships between political events, mood responses, political learning, and political involvement.

The Dynamics of Emotional Response

People's emotional responses react to the ongoing campaign. As the winds of the campaign shift one way and the next, so do emotional responses. The evidence on dynamics is crucial for testing the validity of our theoretical view. We posit that

emotions enhance people's ability to interact with the environment. To be effective, these emotions cannot be permanent features of an individual's personality or of a candidate's image. Only when emotions reliably react to changes in the informational environment (i.e., to campaign news) can they encourage citizens to become engaged with their favorite candidate's prospects or, more interestingly, interrupt citizens' ordinary political activity and spur information processing.

Table 9.1 shows how the public's emotional reactions reflected the events of the 1980 and 1988 campaigns. Each entry is the amount of anxiety or enthusiasm that each candidate (the column heads) elicited from the public. For example, in January 1980, about 40% of the public volunteered terms such as *uneasy* or *disgusted* to describe their reactions to Carter. Following severe failures in both economic and foreign policy (a spectacular inflation scare, rising unemployment, the enduring hostage crisis), this portion climbed to 53% by June and maintained that level for October. Reagan avoided such reactions through June and only began to generate uneasiness when brought under attack during the fall campaign. We observe a similarly transparent pattern in 1988: the July survey, taken directly after the Democratic National Convention, shows a high level of anxiety about Bush. By October the anxiety about Bush has receded, while the survey reveals the public's disquietude about Dukakis after that fall's pointedly "negative" campaign.

None of this is entirely remarkable by itself. Instead, it demonstrates that a sense of anxiety is not a permanent feature of the political landscape but a dynamic one, closely linked to prominent

TABLE 9.1. Aggregated Means of Emotional Response over the 1980 Presidential Campaigns

Time of Survey	Enthusiasm	Anxiety	Enthusiasm	Anxiety
1980 Presidential Campaign[a]	Carter		Reagan	
January	.65	.40	.29	.20
June	.58	.53	.38	.25
October	.52	.50	.39	.39
1988 Presidential Campaign[b]	Bush		Dukakis	
June	.40	.52	.49	.48
July	.27	.55	.53	.45
October	.50	.43	.42	.56

[a]*Source*: 1980 ANES.
[b]*Source*: 1988 Missouri data.

external events. It is, however, weak evidence at best; it merely indicates that the two emotional systems operate independently. We next turn to more crucial and demanding tests.

Emotional Response and the Voting Decision

Understanding that anxiety and enthusiasm represent structurally and dynamically distinctive emotional responses carries us only part way. We shall show that anxiety and enthusiasm play importantly different roles in the voting decision. In particular, the data indicate that enthusiasm directly affects voting preference (reflecting something very close to the voting decision itself), while anxiety has practically no direct impact on choice. Equally important for our point of view, anxiety appears to give voters pause—to get voters to base their decision on candidate characteristics or campaign information rather than merely stick with their "standing choice."

Consider first the relative power of enthusiasm and anxiety on voting preferences. The standard "valence" view of emotion would predict that emotions will affect voting preference directly. More to the point, this view expects enthusiasm and anxiety to affect those preferences equally. Our theoretical position, that anxiety focuses attention while enthusiasm moves psychological involvement, suggests that enthusiasm will directly affect the voting decision while anxiety's role will be muted. Thus, an evaluation of voting preference as a function of the two distinctive emotions will tell the tale. If both emotions play about equal parts, then the standard view prevails. If enthusiasm is more important than anxiety, then the dual-system view stands stronger.

Table 9.2 presents simple voting equations, one for each of the three waves in 1988. A quick look tells the story. Enthusiasm matters enormously, anxiety not at all. For all three waves, the parameter for enthusiasm is both substantial and statistically significant. For all three waves, the parameter for anxiety is invisible. Clearly, enthusiasm leads the way in guiding vote choice. Importantly, the data substantiate the pattern of results in a similar (though more elaborate) analysis of voting in the 1984 election (Marcus, 1988b). This, of course, does not by itself indicate that the dual-system view prevails. We have merely shown that anxiety plays a decisively different role than does enthusiasm. If our view is correct, then we should expect that the voting calculus will differ for those who perceive threat in the environment than for those who remain calm.

The behavioral inhibition system is rarely intrusive, because we are infrequently confronted by threat or sudden surprise. The effect of the anxi-

TABLE 9.2. Estimating Presidential Preference 1988 During Three Waves: Multivariate Model

Independent Variables	Regression Coefficients and Standard Errors		
	June	July	October
Comparative enthusiasm	1.16*	1.04*	1.07*
	(.10)	(.09)	(.10)
Comparative anxiety	−.00	−.10	−.05
	(.10)	(.09)	(.09)
Partisanship	.35*	.31*	.35*
	(.07)	(.06)	(.08)
Constant	−.29*	−.15	−.26*
	(.09)	(.08)	(.09)
Number of cases	253	247	246
Adjusted R^2	.59	.68	.64
Root Mean Square Error	.29	.25	.28

Source: 1988 Missouri Data.
Note: Voting preference indicates Dukakis or Bush supporters (scored 1 and 0), "leaners" (.75 or .25), and undecided (.50). All variables are scored to a common range of 0–1. The entries are unstandardized regression coefficients with standard errors in parentheses.
*$p \le .05$, two-tailed test.

ety system will be manifest only when a threatening stimulus is apprehended. This suggests that the influence of negative affect is sporadic, not constant. When threat is low, the behavioral approach system governs action: we go forward when our enthusiasm increases and withdraw when we sense frustration and exhaustion. However, when we feel threatened, we set aside habits and focus attention on the problematic.

Because a political campaign is a struggle between competing partisans, some citizens, though not all, experience the cut-and-thrust of politics as threatening. People unaroused will safely vote their standing choice while those pricked by anxiety will perk up, gather new information, and perhaps abandon their old habits.

For evidence, look at Table 9.3. Here we model vote preference as a function of comparative enthusiasm and partisanship (as in Table 9.2) as well as anxiety's effect on the role of comparative enthusiasm and partisanship. In this equation, we introduce the respondent's total anxiety meaned over both candidates (as opposed to the comparative anxiety measure in Table 9.2) to measure the amount of environmental threat. (Note that someone greatly, but equally, uneasy about both candidates will produce a comparative anxiety score of zero but, properly, a high total anxiety score.) Because the behavioral inhibition system responds to threat, our dual-system theory predicts that the

presence of anxiety will cause people to drop partisanship as a sure guide to candidate choice and to turn to candidate-specific information for judgment.

We estimate the direct effects and the crucial conditional effects when we write explicit interaction terms (in rows 2 and 4). We see that the presence of anxiety increases the importance of comparative enthusiasm (.62) and diminishes the role of partisanship (-.60). In fact, high anxiety almost eliminates partisanship as a consideration. As the dual-system theory predicts, a rise in anxiety *weakens* the reliance on partisanship and *strengthens* the reliance on contemporary emotional reactions to the candidates. A drop in anxiety (i.e., an increase in complaisance) strengthens the impact of partisan identification and weakens reliance on concurrent feelings of enthusiasm toward the candidates.

Thus, the two emotions matter for voting but matter in different ways. Comparative enthusiasm affects how closely people are willing to embrace either candidate. Anxiety plays a very different role: it stimulates peoples' attention and releases them from their standing decisions.

Direct Evidence on Learning

The evidence suggests that threat stimulates learning. Yet, it is circumstantial evidence. All we have established to this point is that anxious voters are less reliant on habit. For a more direct test, we need to observe how people's political knowledge changes over time. We turn to the 1980 ANES panel.

Over the course of any campaign, citizens acquire and develop views about candidates. From January to October in 1980, the public developed an increasingly rich portrait of the challenger, Reagan. The portion claiming to know something about him rose from 86% to 95%, the portion willing to evaluate his personal characteristics rose from about 60% to 90%, and the portion identifying his position on policy questions rose more modestly from about 50% to 70%. All these gains made Reagan almost, but not quite, as familiar as the incumbent Carter (see also Markus, 1982; Miller & Shanks, 1982).

Yet cognitive elaboration is not the same thing as learning. Hence, we need a measure of what

TABLE 9.3. Estimating Presidential Preference 1988: Anxiety's Effect on the Role of Enthusiasm and Partisanship

Independent Variables	Coefficients	Standard Errors
Comparative enthusiasm	.79*	(.12)
Anxiety * comparative enthusiasm	.62*	(.22)
Partisanship	.64*	(.11)
Anxiety * partisanship	−.60*	(.21)
Constant	−.25*	(.02)
Sample size	746	
Adjusted R²	.65	
Root Mean Square Error	.27	

Source: 1988 Missouri Data.
Note: For comparability, all variables are scored to a common range of 0 to 1. Voting preference indicates Dukakis or Bush supporters (scored 1 and 0), "leaners" (.75 or .25) and undecided (.50). The anxiety interactions (in rows two and four) represent multiplicative interactions. Anxiety is the voter's mean anxiety (over both candidates). The values are unstandardized regression coefficients with standard errors in parentheses.
*p ≤ .05, two-tailed test.

people know about politics and, more decisively, a measure of what they know that is relevant for their vote choice. Here, we use a device, used elsewhere, that concentrates on what is deemed to be objectively true. To be brief, we measure knowledge by the respondent's ability to say that Ronald Reagan is more conservative than Jimmy Carter. Each individual obtains a "knowledge" score that counts the number of times, on a set of seven-point issue scales, that the individual placed Reagan to the right of Carter.

As measures of political learning, these policy-related cognitions have several useful features. First, they are relatively unambiguous. Compared with prompts about candidate traits or open-ended responses about political objects, respondents who manufacture cognitions can be found out. Second, they represent important and easily available political facts. Information that Reagan was more conservative than Carter could be easily obtained from either the mass media or from conversations with political knowledgeables. The public, when aggregated, had little trouble seeing that Reagan was well to the right of Carter on every one of these issues. Finally, such elementary policy-related knowledge is crucial in the link between voting and public policy. In fact, it is hard to imagine that anyone who paid attention to the 1980 campaign could have escaped this information.

Of course, many did. Table 9.4 displays the proportion, corrected for guessing, of the public who positioned Reagan to the right of Carter on three central policy questions as well as on the liberal–conservative continuum. The proportions are given for samples taken in January, June, and October of 1980. First, observe the overall levels; substantial numbers of the electorate, even in the end, remained unaware of the candidates' policy differences.

In learning terms, however, note that the public began to see the policy distinctions more and more clearly as the campaign progressed. Most striking, when the campaign began only 13% saw Reagan as more committed to defense spending, but when the season turned to fall, fully 51% realized what was going on. The public similarly gained understanding about the candidates' stances on the spending-and-social-welfare and détente issues as well on the ideological spectrum. The row of numbers across the bottom shows a composite measure, the means for proper placements on the three issues and for ideology. Overall, it looks as though the campaigners' efforts to "inform" the electorate had a salutary, though modest, effect.

Our question is whether this learning was motivated by emotions. After all, other plausible learning mechanisms abound. To proceed, we shall control for powerful alternative hypotheses when we estimate the amount of learning that might be attributed to anxiety.

Start with a cognitive model. As ever, education matters. Surely college-educated, rather than grade-school-educated, people can better extract issue-oriented information from the hurly-burly of campaign rhetoric. To education, add interest. We now understand that the already well informed and motivated will be most likely to learn (Neuman, 1986; Tichenor, Donohue, & Olien, 1970). Having a knowledge base both marks a more permanent interest in, and capacity for, politics as well as provides the framework in which new information can be integrated to produce increments in knowledge. After all, information about presidential candidates fills the air: learning requires not a search for information but instead an inclination to pay attention to, and make sense of, what is readily available.

Next, add in partisanship. Strong partisan attachments should enable individuals to make correct inferences about the political world that might otherwise be impossible. Brady and Sniderman (1985) show that individuals use an affect-heuristic that assumes that friends (liked social and political groups) have compatible political views

TABLE 9.4. Knowledge About Candidate Policies over Time

Policy Area	Corrected Proportion Saying Reagan More Conservative Than Carter[a]		
	January	June	October
Defense spending	.13	.34	.51
Détente with Soviets	.21	.28	.37
Cut spending/social programs	.29	.29	.34
Liberal–conservative continuum	.19	.35	.34
Summary measure[b]	.21	.32	.39

Source: ANES 1980 Data.
[a]Proportion placing Reagan to the right of Carter minus the proportion placing Carter to the right of Reagan.
[b]The mean score for all items.

while opponents (disliked others) have different political views. Understanding candidate stances is, for the most part, a matter of inference rather than knowledge. The Brady-Sniderman hypothesis, in a way familiar to "new look" psychology of the 1940s and 1950s (e.g., Heider, 1958; Rosenberg & Abelson, 1960), suggests that citizens process information in ways consistent with emotional attachments. Thus, strong partisans, Democratic or Republican, should better be able to make inferences about the candidates' policy positions. They simply "balance" their inferences with their own policy preferences and their partisan attachments (e.g., Brent & Granberg, 1982; Granberg & Brent, 1974; Kinder, 1978). To the extent that the world makes easy sense (i.e., Democrats liberal, Republicans conservative), this heuristic will aid learning.

Finally, consider emotion. Again, theoretically, we expect that the presence of threat in the environment will spur political learning while enthusiasm will not. An initial answer lies in Table 9.5, columns 1–2. The estimation equations (each represented by a column) include a "lagged dependent variable"—the respondents' level of knowledge at the previous survey—to control for "regression to the mean" types of effects. Substantively, three variables represent cognition: education (for capacity), campaign interest (for cognitive motivation), and strength of partisanship (for the affect-heuristic model). As much previous work predicts, education helps learning. The difference between a college-educated and a grade-school-educated citizen is .21 and .16 (for January–June and June–October, respectively), a substantial learning differential. Similarly, the difference in learning for the uninterested and the avidly interested is .06 and .14. The partisan-guided-learning hypothesis, however, fails. The strength-of-partisanship variable is statistically insignificant and in any case, it has the wrong sign (−.03 and −.05).

More to the point, examine the coefficients for emotional response. Our expectations are clearly met. In both sequences, a gain in knowledge is strongly associated with prior anxiety and not at all with prior enthusiasm. The gains associated with enthusiasm are minimal and statistically invisible. In power, anxiety measures up well against

TABLE 9.5. Learning and Campaign Involvement as a Function of Emotion and Cognition During the 1980 Presidential Campaign

Independent Variables	Learning Model[a]		Campaign Involvement Model[b]	
	January–June	June–October	January–June	June–October
Enthusiasm$_{(t-1)c}$	−.00	−.01	.08	.13*
	(.04)	(.04)	(.05)	(.04)
Anxiety$_{(t-1)}$	.12*	.12*	.06	.03
	(.05)	(.05)	(.05)	(.05)
Strength of partisanship$_{(t-1)}$	−.03	−.05	.15*	.08
	(.04)	(.04)	(.04)	(.04)
Education	.21*	.16*	.03	−.03
	(.04)	(.04)	(.04)	(.04)
Knowledge$_{(t-1)}$	−.42*	−.43*	.14*	−.11*
	(.04)	(.03)	(.04)	(.03)
Campaign interest$_{(t-1)}$	.06*	.14*	−.52*	−.50*
	(.03)	(.03)	(.03)	(.03)
Constant	.02	.03	.11*	.18*
	(.03)	(.04)	(.04)	(.04)
Number of cases	644	639	643	623
Root Mean Square Error	.27	.28	.29	.27
Adjusted R²	.18	.19	.26	.27

Source: 1980 ANES Data.
Note: The entries are unstandardized regression coefficients with standard errors in parentheses.
[a]Learning is measured by the change in knowledge from one time to the next: [knowledge$_{(t)}$ − knowledge$_{(t-1)}$].
[b]Campaign involvement is measured by the change in campaign interest from one time to the next: [interest$_{(t)}$ − interest$_{(t-1)}$].
[c]For comparability, all variables are scored to a common range of 0–1.
*$p \leq .05$, two-tailed test.

(though it does not dominate) the cognitive portion of the model. The difference in learning due to anxiety is about .12 (for both the early and late periods), or about the average amount of learning that took place in the campaign. The numbers are both statistically significant and substantively important. Further, the pattern is theoretically correct. Anxiety is positively associated with learning, and enthusiasm is not. The dual-system model is again confirmed.

The duality of emotional response is made even clearer by turning our attention from political learning to political involvement, from citizens' acquiring new information to their engagement in the campaign. Our theory leads us to expect that for matters of already-learned behavior, for getting involved in an ongoing campaign, the key should lie in the positive-feedback mechanisms associated with enthusiasm rather than the attention-interrupt mechanisms of anxiety. Thus, the empirical pattern of the learning model in Table 9.5 should be reversed when we change our focus to the campaign involvement model.

Our theory predicts that involvement, measured by a change in campaign interest, will vary as a function of changes in enthusiasm (while controlling for previous education, partisan intensity, and candidate knowledge). The expectation is confirmed. The empirical equations for the campaign involvement model are presented in Table 9.5. The key coefficients lie in Table 9.5, columns 3–4. During the spring primaries (January–June), the emotions are minimally—statistically insignificantly—associated with change in campaign involvement. If anything, partisanship is dominant. It is only during the fall campaign that candidate-induced emotional response spurs involvement. Crucially, the dominant factor becomes enthusiasm, not anxiety.

Discussion

Our empirical work thus sustains a view that emotionality affects how people approach politics. Clearly, emotions are complex and subtle. Just as obviously, the simple valence model of political emotions can no longer stand. At the very least, mood states represent an amalgam of underlying feelings. Of this we are confident.

Our analyses also indicate that we gain theoretical leverage by turning to a dual-system model that produces complex emotions as a mixture of two distinct types: enthusiasm and anxiety. The first, associated with an ongoing emotional monitoring system, governs how far people allow themselves to engage with candidates and with politics more generally. The second, a manifestation of the behavioral inhibition system, spurs people to pay closer and more conscious attention to political matters and to act accordingly.

Our evidence carries weight because it confirms and extends an already-established theoretical view. We here rely on survey interviews about presidential candidates, a data source with well-known strengths and weaknesses. The data allow neither experimental control over the emotional stimuli nor subtle analyses of cause and effect. At best, we know the broad outlines and too little of the details or complexities. Yet we are able to show that a theory grounded in neurophysiology and in psychology can be usefully applied in the realm of politics. While we are in no way certain about the mechanisms that translate elementary processes (the stuff of neural transmitters, etc.) into political emotions and cognitions, we are now encouraged to think that further study will reward. Moreover, we *can* safely conclude that the emotional significance of information clearly affects to what, when, and how we react.

In short, enthusiasm increases campaign involvement and anxiety enhances learning. Of course, matters are never so simple. Our data reveal subtle relationships among enthusiasm, anxiety, involvement, and learning. Nevertheless, we believe that the main story lies along these lines: when politics makes people anxious, people sharpen their eyes and pay careful attention; when politics drums up enthusiasm, people immerse themselves in the symbolic festival.

Understanding this enlarges our view of emotion's role in politics. We may be fairly sure that emotion matters not only in how it colors people's voting choices but also in how it affects the way they regard the electoral contest. This much is important enough. However, this new understanding has implications for how we, as social scientists, think about elections and political life.

First, finding that people's approach to politics depends on their emotional state tells us that the fundamental "voter" model should include a conditional component. That is to say, voters act differently under different conditions; they afford politics closer scrutiny when they are anxious than when they are enthusiastic. By introducing this conditionality, we can combine two views of citizen political involvement. The first divides the public by *stable trait*: active versus passive, attentive versus inattentive (classically, Converse, 1962; Luskin, 1987; Milbrath & Goel, 1977; Neuman, 1986; Verba & Nie, 1972). The second view suggests that there are *variable states* that people can, at any given moment, fall into, say spectator versus participant (Marcus, 1988a; Schattschneider, 1960). We here propose a dynamic model of political learning that combines trait and state explanations to produce a richer view of how citizens inform their electoral choice. In states of anxiety, citizens activate their political consciousness; in states of enthusiasm, they engage their hearts in political affairs.

This emphasis on state-conditionality further points the way toward resolving a long-standing controversy about the basic character of citizen voting. Loosely speaking, a "public choice" school emphasizes the rational calculus of policy alternatives, while a "symbolic politics" school emphasizes the power of deeply ingrained normative commitments, such as partisanship, to shape voter preferences. The extent to which one or the other of these views characterizes voting is of obvious importance for democratic theory and has been the subject of years of intellectual debate and empirical investigation (e.g., Downs, 1957; Enelow & Hinich, 1984; Kinder & Kiewiet, 1979; Markus & Converse, 1979; Miller, 1991; Miller et al., 1976; Rabinowitz & MacDonald, 1989; Sears, 1990; Sears, Hensler, & Speer, 1979; Sears et al., 1980). While we do not hope to settle the matter, we believe that putting these "models" in competition may mislead.

Our understanding about anxiety and enthusiasm suggests that voters' emphasis on conscious rational choice (as opposed to long-standing commitment) will be conditioned on their emotional state. Voters can, and often will, vote their "standing decisions." However, they also rely on their internal emotional states to signal when to abandon their predispositions and begin conscious political choice. Emotionality thus empowers voters to confront their circumstances and react efficiently and appropriately. In the absence of anxiety, vot-

ers safely rely on preexisting partisan dispositions and the greater enthusiasm generated by the favored candidate; however, when disturbed by their emotional signals, voters pay more attention to the issues and no longer defer to established dispositions. Rather than being antagonistic or detrimental to citizenship, emotion enhances the ability of voters to perform their citizenly duties.

Because individual voters thus act differently under different conditions, we can expect that the quality of the entire electorate's behavior will vary when the macropolitical scene offers different blends of anxiety and enthusiasm. For example, consider conventional wisdom about positive and negative campaigns. Contemporary popular debate has almost universally condemned campaigns that seem to rely heavily on "attack" commercials while, implicitly, endorsing "positive" themes— odd. Our data indicate that positive campaigns, ones that emphasize visionary goals or candidate accomplishments, should do little for conscious deliberation. Instead, they seem best viewed as mobilization or activation—devices that yield a citizen involvement free from the burden of choice. On the other hand, campaigns that spur concern about the current state of affairs would seem much more likely to motivate people to pay closer attention to public affairs, to engage their full capacities, and to make rational decisions.

More generally, the deliberative content of elections depends on the extent to which citizens feel comfortable or uneasy with the contemporary political situation. Partly, this comfort or discomfort will be a product of politicians' tactics. More interesting, though, is the likelihood that the public's emotional state will arise from social, economic, and political reality. Periods of economic depression (with the accompanying job losses and threats aimed at large numbers of families) will certainly activate people's emotional triggers and motivate their political attention. Economic booms, on the other hand, may induce enthusiasm and, thus, political involvement without deliberation. Similarly, failure during war-time should spur close attention while success should lead to grand parades in the collective fantasy. Because deliberation seems, at least in part, a function of emotionality, the nature of democratic government thus depends on how emotions get linked to political circumstances and how that link varies over time.

In the end, it appears that exploring the connection between emotions and political consciousness should yield much. We shall begin to appreciate how democracy handles changing social, economic, and political circumstances. At the very least, we shall begin to understand that the politics of emotion and rationality are closely intertwined.

REFERENCES

Abelson, Robert P., Donald R. Kinder, Mark D. Peters, and Susan T. Fiske. 1982. "Affective and Semantic Components in Political Personal Perception." *Journal of Personality and Social Psychology* 42:619–30.

Ax, Albert. 1953. "The Physiological Differentiation between Fear and Anger in Humans." *Psychosomatic Medicine* 15:433–22.

Brady, Henry, and Paul Sniderman. 1985. "Attitude Attribution: A Group Basis for Political Reasoning." *American Political Science Review* 79:1061–78.

Brent, E., and D. Granberg. 1982. "Subjective Agreement with the Presidential Candidates of 1976 and 1980." *Journal of Personality and Social Psychology* 42:393–403.

Bruce, John M. 1991. "Emotion and Evaluation in Nomination Politics." Presented at the annual meeting of the American Political Science Association, Washington.

Cacioppo, John T., Richard E. Petty, Mary E. Losch and Haisook Kim. 1986. "Electromyographic Activity over Facial Muscle Regions Can Differentiate the Valence and Intensity of Affective Reactions." *Journal of Personality and Social Psychology* 50:260–68.

Converse, Philip E. 1962. "Information Flow and the Stability of Partisan Attitudes." *Public Opinion Quarterly* 26:578–99.

Derryberry, Douglas. 1991. "The Immediate Effects of Positive and Negative Feedback Signals." *Journal of Personality and Social Psychology* 61:267–78.

Diener, Ed, and Robert A. Emmons. 1985. "The Independence of Positive and Negative Affect." *Journal of Personality and Social Psychology* 47:1105–17.

Downs, Anthony. 1957. *An Economic Theory of Democracy.* New York: Harper & Row.

Eccles, John C. 1989. *Evolution of the Brain: Creation of the Self.* London: Routledge.

Edelman, Murray. 1964. *The Symbolic Uses of Politics.* Urbana: University of Illinois Press.

Enelow, James M., and Melvin J. Hinich. 1984. *The Spatial Theory of Voting: An Introduction.* New York: Cambridge University Press.

Fonberg, Elzbieta. 1986. "Amygdala, Emotions, Motivation, and Depressive States." In *Emotion: Theory, Research, and Experience*, ed. R. Plutchik and H. Kellerman. London: Academic.

Fowles, Don C. 1980. "The Three Arousal Model: Implications of Gray's Two-Factor Learning Theory for Heart Rate, Electrodermal Activity, and Psychopathy." *Psychophysiology* 17:87–104.

Granberg, D., and E. Brent. 1974. "Dove-Hawk Placements in the 1968 Election: Application of Social Judgment and Balance Theories." *Journal of Personality and Social Psychology* 29:687–95.

Gray, Jeffrey A. 1981. "The Psychophysiology of Anxiety." In *Dimensions of Personality*, ed. R. Lynn. New York: Pergamon.

Gray, Jeffrey A. 1987a. "The Neuropsychology of Emotion and Personality." In *Cognitive Neurochemistry*, ed. S. M. Stahl, S. D. Iversen, and E. C. Goodman. Oxford: Oxford University Press.

Gray, Jeffrey A. 1987b. *The Psychology of Fear and Stress.* 2nd ed. Cambridge: Cambridge University Press.

Heider, Fritz. 1958. *The Psychology of Interpersonal Relations.* New York: Wiley.

Kinder, Donald R. 1978. "Political Person Perception: The Asymmetrical Influence of Sentiment and Choice on Perceptions of Presidential Candidates." *Journal of Personality and Social Psychology* 36:859–71.

Kinder, Donald R., and D. R. Kiewiet. 1979. "Economic Grievances and Political Behavior: The Role of Personal Discontents and Collective Judgements in Congressional Voting." *American Journal of Political Science* 23:495–527.

Kinder, Donald R., Mark D. Peters, Robert R. Abelson, and Susan T. Fiske. 1980. "Presidential Prototypes." *Political Behavior* 2:315–38.

King, Gary. 1986. "How Not To Lie with Statistics: Avoiding Common Mistakes in Quantitative Political Science." *American Journal of Political Science* 30:666–87.

Larsen, Randy, Ed Diener, and Russell Cropanzano. 1987. "Cognitive Operations Associated with Individual Differences in Affect Intensity." *Journal of Personality and Social Psychology* 53:767–74.

Lazarus, Richard. 1982. "Thoughts on the Relations of Emotion and Cognition." *American Psychologist* 37:1019–24.

Lazarus, Richard. 1984. "On the Primacy of Cognition." *American Psychologist* 39:124–29.

Lazarus, Richard, Edward Opton, Markellos Nomikos, and Neil Rankin. 1965. "The Principle of Short-circuiting of Threat: Further Evidence." *Journal of Personality* 33:622–35.

Lewicki, Pawel. 1986. *Nonconscious Social Information Processing.* New York: Academic.

Luskin, Robert C. 1987. "Measuring Political Sophistication." *American Journal of Political Science* 31:856–99.

Luskin, Robert C. 1991. "*Abusus non tollit usum*: Standardized Coefficients, Correlations, and R²s." *American Journal of Political Science* 35:1032–46.

MacKuen, Michael. 1987. "Political Emotion and the Structuring of Political Cognition." Presented at the annual meeting of the American Political Science Association, Chicago.

Marcus, George E. 1988a. "Democratic Theories and the Study of Public Opinion." *Polity* 21:25–44.

Marcus, George E. 1988b. "The Structure of Emotional Response: 1984 Presidential Candidates." *American Political Science Review* 82:735–61.

Marcus, George E. 1991. "Emotions and Politics: Hot Cognitions and the Rediscovery of Passion." *Social Science Information* 30:195–232.

Marcus, George E., Michael MacKuen, and Andrew D. Glassberg. 1989. "The Role of Emotional Response in Presidential Campaign Dynamics: Excitement and Threat." Presented at the annual meeting of the American Political Science Association, Atlanta.

Marcus, George E., and Wendy Rahn. 1990. "Emotions and

Democratic Politics." In *Research in Micropolitics*, ed. S. Long. JAI Press.

Markus, Gregory B. 1982. "Political Attitudes during an Election Year: A Report on the 1980 NES Panel Study." *American Political Science Review* 76:538–60.

Markus, Gregory B. 1986. "Stability and Change in Political Attitudes: Observed, Recalled, and 'Explained.' " *Political Behavior* 8:21–44.

Markus, Gregory B., and Philip E. Converse. 1979. "A Dynamic Simultaneous Equations Model of Electoral Choice." *American Political Science Review* 73:1055–70.

Masters, Roger D., and Denis G. Sullivan. 1989. "Nonverbal Displays and Political Leadership in France and the United States." *Political Behavior* 11:123–56.

Mayer, John D., and Yvonne N. Gaschke. 1988. "The Experience and Meta-experience of Mood." *Journal of Personality and Social Psychology* 55:102–11.

Mayer, John D., Peter Salovey, Susan Gomberg-Kaufman, and Kathleen Blainey. 1991. "A Broader Conception of Mood Experience." *Journal of Personality and Social Psychology* 60:100–11.

Milbrath, Lester W., and M. L. Goel. 1977. *Political Participation*, 2nd ed. Chicago: Rand McNally.

Miller, Arthur H., Warren E. Miller, Alden S. Raine, and Thad A. Brown. 1976. "A Majority Party in Disarray: Policy Polarization and the 1972 Presidential Election." *American Political Science Review* 70:753–78.

Miller, Warren E. 1991. "Party Identification, Realignment, and Party Voting: Back to the Basics." *American Political Science Review* 85:557–68.

Miller, Warren E., and J. Merrill Shanks. 1982. "Policy Directions and Presidential Leadership: Alternative Interpretations of the 1980 Presidential Election." *British Journal of Political Science* 12:299–356.

Neuman, Russell. 1986. *The Paradox of Mass Politics: Knowledge and Opinion in the American Electorate*. Cambridge: Harvard University Press.

Nie, Norman H., Sidney Verba, and John R. Petrocik. 1976. *The Changing American Voter*. Cambridge: Harvard University Press.

Plutchik, Robert. 1980. *Emotion: A Psychoevolutionary Synthesis*. New York: Harper & Row.

Pratto, Felicia, and Oliver P. John. 1991. "Automatic Vigilance: The Attention-grabbing Power of Negative Social Information." *Journal of Personality and Social Psychology* 61:380–91.

Rabinowitz, George, and Stuart Elaine MacDonald. 1989. "A Directional Theory of Issue Voting." *American Political Science Review* 83:93–121.

Rosenberg, Milton J., and Robert P. Abelson. 1960. "An Analysis of Cognitive Balancing." In *Attitude Organization and Change*, ed. M. J. Rosenberg, R. P. Abelson, and J. W. Brehm. New Haven: Yale University Press.

Russell, James A. 1980. "A Circumplex Model of Affect." *Journal of Personality and Social Psychology* 39:1161–78.

Schattschneider, E. E. 1960. *The Semi-sovereign People*. New York: Holt, Rinehart, & Winston.

Sears, David O. 1990. "Symbolic Politics: A Socio-psychological Analysis." Presented at the annual scientific meetings of the International Society of Political Psychology, Washington.

Sears, David O., Carl Hensler, and Leslie Speer. 1979. "Whites' Opposition to 'Busing': Self-Interest or Symbolic Politics?" *American Political Science Review* 73:369–85.

Sears, David O., Richard R. Lau, Tom R. Tyler, and Harris M. Allen, Jr. 1980. "Self-Interest Versus Symbolic Politics in Policy Attitudes and Presidential Voting." *American Political Science Review* 74:670–84.

Simon, Herbert. 1967. "Motivational and Emotional Controls of Cognition." *Psychological Review* 74:29–39.

Storm, Christine, and Tom Storm. 1987. "A Taxonomic Study of the Vocabulary of Emotions." *Journal of Personality and Social Psychology* 53:805–16.

Sullivan, Dennis, and Roger Masters. 1988. "Happy Warriors: Leaders' Facial Displays, Viewers Emotions, and Political Support." *American Journal of Political Science* 32:345–68.

Taylor, Shelley E. 1991. "Asymmetrical Effects of Positive and Negative Events: The Mobilization-Minimization Hypothesis." *Psychological Bulletin* 110:67–85.

Tellegen, Auke. 1985. "Structures of Mood and Personality and Their Relevance to Assessing Anxiety, with an Emphasis on Self-Report." In *Anxiety and the Anxiety Disorders*, ed. A. H. Tuma and J. D. Maser. Hillsdale, NJ: Lawrence Erlbaum Associates.

Tichenor, P. J., G. A. Donohue, and C. N. Olien. 1970. "Mass Media Flow and Differential Growth in Knowledge." *Public Opinion Quarterly* 34:159–70.

Verba, Sidney, and Norman H. Nie. 1972. *Participation in American: Political Democracy and Social Equality*. New York: Harper & Row.

Watson, David, Lee Anna Clark, and Auke Tellegen. 1988. "Development and Validation of Brief Measures of Positive and Negative Affect: The PANAS Scales." *Journal of Personality and Social Psychology* 54:1063–70.

Watson, David, and Auke Tellegen. 1985. "Toward a Consensual Structure of Mood." *Psychological Bulletin* 98:219–35.

Zajonc, Robert B. 1980. "Feeling and Thinking: Preferences Need No Inferences." *American Psychologist* 39:151–75.

Zajonc, Robert B. 1982. "On the Primacy of Affect." *American Psychologist* 39:117–23.

Zevon, Michael, and Auke Tellegen. 1982. "The Structure of Mood Change: An Ideographic/Nomothetic Analysis." *Journal of Personality and Social Psychology* 43:111–22.

Ideology and Public Opinion

Two of the biggest scientific controversies in modern political psychology concern the study of ideology and public opinion. The first of these has to do with whether or not people possess internally coherent belief systems that can be located definitively on a left-right dimension. Bucking received wisdom, Bell (1960) famously claimed that the world had witnessed the "end of ideology" in the aftermath of World War II. This contrarian position stimulated intense debates in the social sciences in general (e.g., Rejai, 1971; Waxman, 1968; Zaller, 1992) and in social psychology in particular (e.g., Judd, Krosnick, & Milburn, 1981; Kerlinger, 1984; McGuire, 1985).

The second controversy, which depends in some sense upon the resolution of the first, was initiated by critics of *The Authoritarian Personality* (e.g., Eysenck, 1954; Rokeach, 1960; Shils, 1954). It pertained to the question of whether there are in fact general psychological differences between liberals and conservatives in terms of cognitive and motivational style (e.g., McClosky & Chong, 1985; Sidanius, 1985, 1988; Stone, 1980; Tetlock, 1983; Wilson, 1973). This debate has raged on right up until the present day (Greenberg & Jonas, 2003; Jost, Glaser, Kruglanski, & Sulloway, 2003a, 2003b).

DOES IDEOLOGY EXIST?

In our first reading in this section, Converse cleverly weighs in on the "end of ideology" debate by arguing for the necessity of distinguishing between the belief systems of political elites and ordinary citizens. On the basis of survey data, Converse concludes that only a small percentage of voters (approximately 15%) should be classified as "ideologues" or "near-ideologues" and that more than a third of the population cannot accurately define even such basic political terms as *liberal* and *conservative*. This does not mean, however, that the left-right distinction is meaningless or inconsequential. Elite politicians—whose belief systems are far more constrained by social and psychological forces than are the belief systems of mass publics—do use conventional ideological dimensions to organize their political attitudes.

In Reading 11, Conover and Feldman (1981) propose that ideological labels like *liberal* and *conservative* are important to people as social identities, even if the common usage of these terms lacks philosophical coherence. Insofar as people value their affiliations with certain political groups, they can be expected to hold positive and negative attitudes toward other political groups. Conover and Feldman demonstrate, for example, that self-identified conservatives have more positive attitudes than do liberals toward groups that uphold the status quo, serve social control functions, and are procapitalist. Self-identified liberals, by contrast, have more positive attitudes than do conservatives toward groups that question the status quo and seek social reform.

COGNITIVE STYLE AND IDEOLOGICAL FUNCTIONING

If we accept that at least some people do hold internally coherent political belief systems that correspond to the left-right ideological distinction, then it makes sense to ask whether other psychological differences accompany ideological differences. Researchers have generally focused on a set of interrelated cognitive and motivational variables, including cognitive complexity, need for structure, intolerance of ambiguity, and uncertainty avoidance. A substantial body of research now suggests that, as a general rule, conservatives are somewhat lower in cognitive complexity, higher in need for structure, and more likely to experience ambiguity and uncertainty as aversive, in comparison with liberals (see Jost et al., 2003a, 2003b). These findings generally vindicate the assumptions of authoritarian personality researchers that general differences in mental rigidity exist between adherents of left-wing and right-wing ideology.

Robert Lane in Reading 12 (1959) focuses specifically on ideological attitudes toward economic inequality. He argues, on the basis of survey interviews with low-income workers, that the presence of inequality in the workplace requires explanation and, in some cases, rationalization. Drawing on such diverse theoretical backgrounds as Marxism, psychoanalysis, authoritarianism, and cognitive dissonance theory, Lane investigates specific forms of rationalization for inequality, including "poor but happy" and "poor but honest" variants. These ideas have been taken up again in recent research by Kay and Jost (2003).

Philip Tetlock in Reading 13 (1984) employs content analytic methods to compare the degree of cognitive complexity inherent in the ideological reasoning of political elites, in this case British parliamentarians, as a function of political orientation. The British context is a useful one for distinguishing between the "rigidity-of-the-right hypothesis" and the "ideologue hypothesis," because it contains a wider range of ideological opinion than is generally present in, for example, American politics. Tetlock's results indicate that moderate socialists exhibited more cognitive complexity than did extreme socialists, moderate conservatives, and extreme conservatives (who exhibited the least cognitive complexity). This general pattern of findings was replicated in a number of other archival studies conducted by Tetlock and his colleagues (e.g., Tetlock, Bernzweig, & Gallant, 1985; Tetlock, Hannum, & Micheletti, 1984).

Discussion Questions

1. What are Converse's reasons for suggesting that political elites and the mass public do not share the same ideological patterns of belief? What data does he use to support this claim?

2. How, according to Conover and Feldman, is it possible for self-identified liberals and conservatives to have such drastically different understandings of these ideological labels? What are the implications, if any, of these differences on research that treats liberalism and conservatism as opposite poles on an ideological continuum?

3. Conover and Feldman join Converse in arguing that major shifts in the distribution of the public's support for different political parties need not reflect core changes in people's political beliefs. What explanations would these authors favor? In what ways are these explanations similar and in what ways are they different?

4. Lane proposes that low-income workers can tolerate their circumstances better to the extent that they "can believe that the rich are not receiving a happiness income commensurate with their money income." What kinds of beliefs do you think might help high-income workers to assuage feelings of guilt that might arise from their privileged circumstances?

5. Which findings from Tetlock's research are inconsistent with the "rigidity-of-the-right hypothesis," and which are inconsistent with the "ideologue hypothesis"? Do you believe that the value pluralism model provides a better explanation of the results? Why or why not?

Suggested Readings

Bell, D. (1960). *The end of ideology*. Glencoe, IL: Free Press.

Eysenck, H. J. (1954/1999). *The psychology of politics*. New Brunswick, NJ: Transaction Publishers.

Greenberg, J., & Jonas, E. (2003). Psychological motives and political orientation—The left, the right, and the rigid: Comment on Jost et al. (2003). *Psychological Bulletin, 129*, 376–382.

Jost, J. T., & Banaji, M. R. (1994). The role of stereotyping in system-justification and the production of false consciousness. *British Journal of Social Psychology, 33*, 1–27.

Jost, J. T., Glaser, J., Kruglanski, A. W., & Sulloway, F. (2003a). Political conservatism as motivated social cognition. *Psychological Bulletin, 129*, 339–375.

Jost, J. T., Glaser, J., Kruglanski, A. W., & Sulloway, F. (2003b). Exceptions that prove the rule—Using a theory of motivated social cognition to account for ideological incongruities and political anomalies: Reply to Greenberg and Jonas (2003). *Psychological Bulletin, 129*, 383–393.

Judd, C. M., Krosnick, J. A., & Milburn, M. A. (1981). Political involvement in attitude structure in the general public. *American Sociological Review, 46*, 660–669.

Kay, A. C., & Jost, J. T. (2003). Complementary justice: Effects of "poor but happy" and "poor but honest" stereotype exemplars on system justification and implicit activation of the justice motive. *Journal of Personality and Social Psychology,* in press.

Kerlinger, F. M. (1984). *Liberalism and conservatism: The nature and structure of social attitudes.* Hillsdale, NJ: Erlbaum.

McGuire, W. J. (1985). The nature of attitudes and attitude change. In G. Lindzey & E. Aronson (Eds.), *Handbook of social psychology* (3rd ed., Vol. 2, pp. 233–346). New York: Random House.

McClosky, H., & Chong, D. (1985). Similarities and differences between left-wing and right-wing radicals. *British Journal of Political Science, 15*, 329–363.

Rejai, M. (Ed.) (1971) *Decline of ideology?* Chicago: Aldine/Atherton.

Rokeach, M. (1960). *The open and closed mind.* New York: Free Press.

Shils, E. A. (1954). Authoritarianism: "right" and "left." In R. Christie & M. Jahoda (Eds.), *Studies in the scope and method of "The Authoritarian Personality"* (pp. 24–49). Glencoe, IL: Free Press.

Sidanius, J. (1985). Cognitive functioning and sociopolitical ideology revisited. *Political Psychology, 6*, 637-661.

Sidanius, J. (1988). Political sophistication and political deviance: A structural equation examination of context theory. *Journal of Personality and Social Psychology, 55*, 37–51.

Stone, W. F. (1980). The myth of left-wing authoritarianism. *Political Psychology, 2*, 3–19.

Taylor, I. A. (1960). Similarities in the structure of extreme social attitudes. *Psychological Monographs, 74*, 1–36.

Tetlock, P. E. (1983). Cognitive style and political ideology. *Journal of Personality and Social Psychology, 45*, 118–126.

Tetlock, P. E., Bernzweig, J., & Gallant, J. L. (1985). Supreme Court decision making: Cognitive style as a predictor of ideological consistency of voting. *Journal of Personality and Social Psychology, 48*, 1227–1239.

Tetlock, P. E., Hannum, K. A., & Micheletti, P. M. (1984). Stability and change in the complexity of senatorial debate: Testing the cognitive versus rhetorical style hypotheses. *Journal of Personality and Social Psychology, 46*, 979–990.

Waxman, C. I. (Ed.) (1968). *The end of ideology debate.* New York: Funk & Wagnalls.

Wilson, G. D. (Ed.) (1973). *The psychology of conservatism.* London: Academic Press.

Zaller, J. R. (1992). *The nature and origins of mass opinion.* New York: Cambridge University Press.

The Nature of Belief Systems in Mass Publics

Philip E. Converse • University of Michigan

Belief systems have never surrendered easily to empirical study or quantification. Indeed, they have often served as primary exhibits for the doctrine that what is important to study cannot be measured and that what can be measured is not important to study. In an earlier period, the behaviorist decree that subjective states lie beyond the realm of proper measurement gave Mannheim a justification for turning his back on measurement, for he had an unqualified interest in discussing belief systems.[1] Even as Mannheim was writing, however, behaviorism was undergoing stiff challenges, and early studies of attitudes were attaining a degree of measurement reliability that had been deemed impossible. This fragment of history, along with many others, serves to remind us that no intellectual position is likely to become obsolete quite so rapidly as one that takes current empirical capability as the limit of the possible in a more absolute sense. Nevertheless, while rapid strides in the measurement of "subjective states" have been achieved in recent decades, few would claim that Mannheim could now find all of the tools that were lacking to him many years ago.

This article makes no pretense of surpassing such limitations. At the same time, our substantive concern forces upon us an unusual concern with measurement strategies, not simply because we propose to deal with belief systems or ideologies, but also because of the specific questions that we shall raise about them. Our focus in this article is upon differences in the nature of belief systems held on the one hand by elite political actors and, on the other, by the masses that appear to be "numbered" within the spheres of influence of these belief systems. It is our thesis that there are important and predictable differences in ideational worlds as we progress downward through such "belief strata" and that these differences, while obvious at one level, are easily overlooked and not infrequently miscalculated. The fact that these ideational worlds differ in character poses problems of adequate representation and measurement.

I. Some Clarification of Terms

A term like "ideology" has been thoroughly muddied by diverse uses.[2] We shall depend instead upon the term "belief system," although there is an obvious overlap between the two. We define a *belief system* as a configuration of ideas and attitudes in which the elements are bound together by some form of constraint or functional interdependence.[3] In the static case, "constraint" may be taken to mean the success we would have in predicting, given initial knowledge that an individual holds a specified attitude, that he holds certain further ideas and attitudes. We depend implicitly upon such notions of constraint in judging, for example, that, if a person is opposed to the expansion of social security, he is probably a conservative and is probably opposed as well to any nationalization of private industries, federal aid to education, sharply progressive income taxation, and so forth. Most discussions of ideologies make relatively elaborate assumptions about such constraints. Constraint must be treated, of course, as a matter of degree, and this degree can be measured quite readily, at least as an average among individuals.

In the dynamic case, "constraint" or "interdependence" refers to the probability that a change in the perceived status (truth, desirability, and so forth) of one idea-element would *psychologically* require, from the point of view of the actor, some compensating change(s) in the status of idea-elements elsewhere in the configuration. The most obvious form of such constraint (although in some ways the most trivial) is exemplified by a structure of propositions in logic, in which a change in the truth-value of one proposition necessitates changes in truth-value elsewhere within the set of related propositions. Psychologically, of course, there may be equally strong constraint among idea-elements that would not be apparent to logical analysis at all, as we shall see.

We might characterize either the idea-elements themselves or entire belief systems in terms of many other dimensions. Only two will interest us here. First, the idea-elements within a belief system vary in a property we shall call *centrality*, according to the role that they play in the belief system as a whole. That is, when new information changes the status of one idea-element in a belief system, by postulate some other change must occur as well. There are usually, however, several possible changes in status elsewhere in the system, any one of which would compensate for the initial change. Let us imagine, for example, that a person strongly favors a particular policy; is very favorably inclined toward a given political party; and recognizes with gratification that the party's stand and his own are congruent. (If he were unaware of the party's stand on the issue, these elements could not in any direct sense be constrained within the same belief system.) Let us further imagine that the party then changes its position to the opposing side of the issue. Once the information about the change reaching the actor has become so unequivocal that he can no longer deny that the change has occurred, he has several further choices. Two of the more important ones involve either a change in attitude toward the party or a change in position on the issue. In such an instance, the element more likely to change is defined as less central to the belief system than the element that, so to speak, has its stability ensured by the change in the first element.

Whole belief systems may also be compared in a rough way with respect to the *range* of objects that are referents for the ideas and attitudes in the system. Some belief systems, while they may be internally quite complex and may involve large numbers of cognitive elements, are rather narrow in range: Belief systems concerning "proper" baptism rituals or the effects of changes in weather on health may serve as cases in point. Such other belief systems as, for example, one that links control of the means of production with the social functions of religion and a doctrine of aesthetics all in one more or less neat package have extreme ranges.

By and large, our attention will be focused upon belief systems that have relatively wide ranges, and that allow some centrality to political objects, for they can be presumed to have some relevance to political behavior. This focus brings us close to what are broadly called *ideologies*, and we shall use the term for aesthetic relief where it seems most appropriate.

II. Sources of Constraint of Idea-Elements

It seems clear that, however logically coherent a belief system may seem to the holder, the sources of constraint are much less logical in the classical sense than they are psychological—and less psychological than social. This point is of sufficient importance to dwell upon.

Logical Sources of Constraint

Within very narrow portions of belief systems, certain constraints may be purely logical. For example, government revenues, government expenditures, and budget balance are three idea-elements that suggest some purely logical constraints. One cannot believe that government expenditures should be increased, that government revenues should be decreased, and that a more favorable balance of the budget should be achieved all at the same time. Of course, the presence of such objectively logical constraints does not ensure that subjective constraints will be felt by the actor. They will be felt only if these idea-elements are brought together in the same belief system, and there is no guarantee that they need be. Indeed, it is true that, among adult American citizens, those who favor the expansion of government welfare services tend to be those who are more insistent upon reducing taxes "even if it means putting off some important things that need to be done."[4]

Where such purely logical constraint is concerned, McGuire has reported a fascinating experiment in which propositions from a few syllogisms were scattered thinly across a long questionnaire applied to a student population. The fact that logical contingencies bound certain questions together was never brought to the attention of the students by the investigator. Yet one week later the questionnaire was applied again, and changes of response to the syllogistic propositions reduced significantly the measurable level of logical inconsistency. The conclusion was that merely "activating" these objectively related ideas in some rough temporal contiguity was sufficient to sensitize the holders to inconsistency and therefore to occasion readjustment of their beliefs.[5]

On a broader canvas, such findings suggest that simple "thinking about" a domain of idea-elements serves both to weld a broader range of such elements into a functioning belief system and to eliminate strictly logical inconsistencies defined from an objective point of view. Since there can be no doubt that educated elites in general, and political elites in particular, "think about" elements involved in political belief systems with a frequency far greater than that characteristic of mass publics, we could conservatively expect that strict logical inconsistencies (objectively definable) would be far more prevalent in a broad public.

Furthermore, if a legislator is noted for his insistence upon budget-balancing and tax-cutting, we can predict with a fair degree of success that he will also tend to oppose expansion of government welfare activities. If, however, a voter becomes numbered within his sphere of influence by virtue of having cast a vote for him directly out of enthusiasm for his tax-cutting policies, we cannot predict that the voter is opposed as well to expansion of government welfare services. Indeed,

if an empirical prediction is possible, it may run in an opposing direction, although the level of constraint is so feeble that any comment is trivial. Yet we know that many historical observations rest directly upon the assumption that constraint among idea-elements visible at an elite level is mirrored by the same lines of constraint in the belief systems of their less visible "supporters." It is our argument that this assumption not only can be, but is very likely to be, fallacious.

Psychological Sources of Constraint

Whatever may be learned through the use of strict logic as a type of constraint, it seems obvious that few belief systems of any range at all depend for their constraint upon logic in this classical sense. Perhaps, with a great deal of labor, parts of a relatively tight belief system like that fashioned by Karl Marx could be made to resemble a structure of logical propositions. It goes without saying, however, that many sophisticated people have been swept away by the "iron logic" of Marxism without any such recasting. There is a broad gulf between strict logic and the quasi-logic of cogent argument. And where the elements in the belief system of a population represent looser cultural accumulations, the question of logical consistency is even less appropriate. Indeed, were one to survey a limited set of ideas on which many belief systems have registered opposite postures, it would be interesting to see how many permutations of positions have been held at one time or another by someone somewhere.

Such diversity is testimony to an absence of any strict logical constraints among such idea-elements, if any be needed. What is important is that the elites familiar with the total shapes of these belief systems have *experienced* them as logically constrained clusters of ideas, within which one part necessarily follows from another. Often such constraint is quasi-logically argued on the basis of an appeal to some superordinate value or posture toward man and society, involving premises about the nature of social justice, social change, "natural law," and the like. Thus a few crowning postures—like premises about survival of the fittest in the spirit of social Darwinism—serve as a sort of glue to bind together many more specific attitudes and beliefs, and these postures are of prime centrality in the belief system as a whole.

Social Sources of Constraint

The social sources of constraint are twofold and are familiar from an extensive literature in the past century. In the first place, were we to survey the combinations of idea-elements that have occurred historically, we should undoubtedly find that certain postures tend to co-occur and that this co-occurrence has obvious roots in the configuration of interests and information that characterize particular niches in the social structure. For example, if we were informed that dissension was rising within the Roman Catholic Church over innovations designed to bring the priest more intimately into the *milieu* of the modern worker, we could predict with a high degree of success that such a movement would have the bulk of its support among the *bas-clergé* and would encounter indifference or hostility at the higher status levels of the hierarchy.

Of course, such predictions are in no sense free from error, and surprises are numerous. The middle-class temperance movement in America, for example, which now seems "logically" allied with the small-town Republican right, had important alliances in the 19th century with the urban social left, on grounds equally well argued from temperance doctrines.[6] Nonetheless, there are some highly reliable correlations of this sort, and these correlations can be linked with social structure in the most direct way. The idea-elements go together not simply because both are in the interest of the person holding a particular status but for more abstract and quasi-logical reasons developed from a coherent world view as well. It is this type of constraint that is closest to the classic meaning of the term "ideology."

The second source of social constraint lies in two simple facts about the creation and diffusion of belief systems. First, the shaping of belief systems of any range into apparently logical wholes that are credible to large numbers of people is an act of creative synthesis characteristic of only a miniscule proportion of any population. Second, to the extent that multiple idea-elements of a belief system are socially diffused from such creative sources, they tend to be diffused in "packages," which consumers come to see as "natural" wholes, for they are presented in such terms ("If you believe this, then you will also believe that, for it follows in such-and-such ways").

Where transmission of information is at stake, it becomes important to distinguish between two classes of information. Simply put, these two levels are what goes with what and why. Such levels of information logically stand in a scalar relationship to one another, in the sense that one can hardly arrive at an understanding of why two ideas go together without being aware that they are supposed to go together. On the other hand, it is easy to know that two ideas go together without knowing why. For example, we can expect that a very large majority of the American public would somehow have absorbed the notion that "Communists are atheists." What is important is that this perceived correlation would for most people represent nothing more than a fact of existence, with the same status as the fact that oranges are orange and most apples are red. If we were to go and explore with these people their grasp of the "why" of the relationship, we would be surprised if more than a quarter of the population even attempted responses (setting aside such inevitable replies as "those Communists are for everything wicked"), and, among the responses received, we could be sure that the majority would be incoherent or irrelevant.

The first level of information, then, is simple and straightforward. The second involves much more complex and abstract information, very close to what Downs has called the "contextual knowledge" relevant to a body of information.[7] A well-informed person who has received sufficient information about a system of beliefs to understand the "whys" involved in several of the constraints between idea-elements is in a better position to make good guesses about the nature of other constraints; he can deduce with fair success, for example, how a true believer will respond to certain situations. Our first interest in distinguishing between these types of information, however, flows from our interest in the relative success of information transmission. The general premise is that the first type of information will be diffused much more readily than the second because it is less complex.

It is well established that differences in information held in a cross-section population are simply staggering, running from vast treasuries of well organized information among elites interested in the particular subject to fragments that could virtually be measured as a few "bits" in the technical sense. These differences are a static tribute to the extreme imperfections in the transmission of information "downward" through the system: Very little information "trickles down" very far.

Consequences of Declining Information for Belief Systems

It is our primary thesis that, as one moves from elite sources of belief systems downwards on such an information scale, several important things occur. First, the contextual grasp of "standard" political belief systems fades out very rapidly, almost before one has passed beyond the percentage of the American population that has completed standard college training. Increasingly, simpler forms of information about "what goes with what" (or even information about the simple identity of objects) turn up missing. The net result, as one moves downward, is that constraint declines across the universe of idea-elements, and that the range of relevant belief systems becomes narrower and narrower. Instead of a few wide-ranging belief systems that organize large amounts of specific information, one would expect to find a proliferation of clusters of ideas among which little constraint is felt, even, quite often, in instances of sheer logical constraint.

For example, "limited horizons," "foreshortened time perspectives," and "concrete thinking" have been singled out as notable characteristics of the ideational world of the poorly educated. Such observations have impressed even those investigators who are dealing with subject matter rather close to the individual's immediate world: his family budgeting, what he thinks of people more wealthy than he, his attitudes toward leisure time, work regulations, and the like. But most of the stuff of politics—particularly that played on a national or international stage—is, in the nature of things, remote and abstract. Where politics is concerned, therefore, such ideational changes begin to occur rapidly below the extremely thin stratum of the electorate that ever has occasion to make public pronouncements on political affairs.

This seems to be consistently misunderstood by the sophisticated analysts who comment in one vein or another on the meaning of mass politics. There are some rather obvious "optical illusions" that are bound to operate here. A member of that tiny elite that comments publicly about political

currents (probably some fraction of 1% of a population) spends most of his time in informal communication about politics with others in the same select group. He rarely encounters a conversation in which his assumptions of shared contextual grasp of political ideas are challenged. Intellectually, he has learned that the level of information in the mass public is low, but he may dismiss this knowledge as true of only 10 to 20% of the voters, who affect the course of mass political events in insignificant ways if at all. It is largely from his informal communications that he learns how "public opinion" is changing and what the change signifies, and he generalizes facilely from these observations to the bulk of the broader public.

III. Active Use of Ideological Dimensions of Judgment

Economy and constraint are companion concepts, for the more highly constrained a system of multiple elements, the more economically it may be described and understood. From the point of view of the actor, the idea organization that leads to constraint permits him to locate and make sense of a wider range of information from a particular domain than he would find possible without such organization. One judgmental dimension or "yardstick" that has been highly serviceable for simplifying and organizing events in most Western politics for the past century has been the liberal-conservative continuum, on which parties, political leaders, legislation, court decisions, and a number of other primary objects of politics could be more—or less—adequately located.

The efficiency of such a yardstick in the evaluation of events is quite obvious. Under certain appropriate circumstances, the single word "conservative" used to describe a piece of proposed legislation can convey a tremendous amount of more specific information about the bill—who probably proposed it and toward what ends, who is likely to resist it, its chances of passage, its long-term social consequences, and, most important, how the actor himself should expect to evaluate it if he were to expend further energy to look into its details. The circumstances under which such tremendous amounts of information are conveyed by the single word are, however, twofold. First, the actor must bring a good deal of meaning to the term, which is to say that he must understand the constraints surrounding it. The more impoverished his understanding of the term, the less information it conveys. In the limiting case—if he does not know at all what the term means—it conveys no information at all. Second, the system of beliefs and actors referred to must in fact be relatively constrained: To the degree that constraint is lacking, uncertainty is less reduced by the label, and less information is conveyed.

The economies inherent in the liberal-conservative continuum were exploited in traditional fashion in the early 1950s to describe political changes in the United States as a swing toward conservatism or a "revolt of the moderates." At one level, this description was unquestionably apt. That is, a man whose belief system was relatively conservative (Dwight D. Eisenhower) had supplanted in the White House a man whose belief system was relatively liberal (Harry Truman). Furthermore, for a brief period at least, the composition of Congress was more heavily Republican as well, and this shift meant on balance a greater proportion of relatively conservative legislators. Since the administration and Congress were the elites responsible for the development and execution of policies, the flavor of governmental action did indeed take a turn in a conservative direction.

The causes underlying these changes in leadership, however, obviously lay with the mass public, which had changed its voting patterns sufficiently to bring the Republican elites into power. And this change in mass voting was frequently interpreted as a shift in public mood from liberal to conservative, a mass desire for a period of respite and consolidation after the rapid liberal innovations of the 1930s and 1940s. Such an account presumes, once again, that constraints visible at an elite level are mirrored in the mass public and that a person choosing to vote Republican after a decade or two of Democratic voting saw himself *in some sense or other* as giving up a more liberal choice in favor of a more conservative one.

On the basis of some familiarity with attitudinal surveys drawn from cross-section samples of the electorate, this assumption seems thoroughly implausible. It suggests in the first instance a neatness of organization in perceived political worlds, which, while accurate enough for elites, is a poor fit for the perceptions of the common public. Second, the yardstick that such an account takes for

granted—the liberal-conservative continuum—is a rather elegant high-order abstraction, and such abstractions are not typical conceptual tools for the "man in the street." Fortunately, our interview protocols collected from this period permitted us to examine this hypothesis more closely, for they include not only "structured" attitude materials (which merely require the respondent to choose between prefabricated alternatives) but also lengthy "open-ended" materials, which provided us with the respondent's current evaluations of the political scene in his own words. They therefore provide some indication of the evaluative dimensions that tend to be spontaneously applied to politics by such a national sample. We knew that respondents who were highly educated or strongly involved in politics would fall naturally into the verbal shorthand of "too conservative," "more radical," and the like in these evaluations.

It soon became apparent, however, that such respondents were in a very small minority, as their unusual education or involvement would suggest. At this point, we broadened the inquiry to an assessment of the evaluative dimensions of policy significance (relating to political issues, rather than to the way a candidate dresses, smiles, or behaves in his private life) that seemed to be employed *in lieu of* such efficient yardsticks as the liberal-conservative continuum. The interviews themselves suggested several strata of classification, which were hierarchically ordered as "levels of conceptualization" on the basis of *a priori* judgments about the breadth of contextual grasp of the political system that each seemed to represent.

In the first or top level were placed those respondents who did indeed rely in some active way on a relatively abstract and far-reaching conceptual dimension as a yardstick against which political objects and their shifting policy significance over time were evaluated. We did not require that this dimension be the liberal-conservative continuum itself, but it was almost the only dimension of the sort that occurred empirically. In a second stratum were placed those respondents who mentioned such a dimension in a peripheral way but did not appear to place much evaluative dependence upon it or who used such concepts in a fashion that raised doubt about the breadth of their understanding of the meaning of the term. The first stratum was loosely labeled "ideologue" and the second "near-ideologue."

In the third level were placed respondents who failed to rely upon any such overarching dimensions yet evaluated parties and candidates in terms of their expected favorable or unfavorable treatment of different social groupings in the population. The Democratic Party might be disliked because "it's trying to help the Blacks too much," or the Republican Party might be endorsed because farm prices would be better with the Republicans in office. The more sophisticated of these group-interest responses reflected an awareness of conflict in interest between "big business" or "rich people," on the one hand, and "labor" or the "working man," on the other, and parties and candidates were located accordingly.

It is often asked why these latter respondents are not considered full "ideologues," for their perceptions run to the more tangible core of what has traditionally been viewed as ideological conflict. It is quite true that such a syndrome is closer to the upper levels of conceptualization than are any of the other types to be described. As we originally foresaw, however, there turn out to be rather marked differences, not only in social origin and flavor of judgmental processes but in overt political reactions as well, between people of this type and those in the upper levels. These people have a clear image of politics as an arena of group interests and, provided that they have been properly advised on where their own group interests lie, they are relatively likely to follow such advice. Unless an issue directly concerns their grouping in an obviously rewarding or punishing way, however, they lack the contextual grasp of the system to recognize how they should respond to it without being told by elites who hold their confidence. Furthermore, their interest in politics is not sufficiently strong that they pay much attention to such communications. If a communication gets through and they absorb it, they are most willing to behave "ideologically" in ways that will further the interests of their group. If they fail to receive such communication, which is most unusual, knowledge of their group memberships may be of little help in predicting their responses. This syndrome we came to call "ideology by proxy."

The difference between such narrow group interest and the broader perceptions of the ideologue may be clarified by an extreme case. One respondent whom we encountered classified himself as a strong Socialist. He was a Socialist because he knew that Socialists stood four-square for the working man against the rich, and he was a working man. When asked, however, whether or not the federal government in Washington "should leave things like electric power and housing for private businessmen to handle," he felt strongly that private enterprise should have its way, and responses to other structured issue questions were simply uncorrelated with standard socialist doctrine. It seems quite clear that, if our question had pointed out explicitly to this man that "good Socialists" would demand government intervention over private enterprise or that such a posture had traditionally been viewed as benefiting the working man, his answer would have been different. But since he had something less than a college education and was not generally interested enough in politics to struggle through such niceties, he simply lacked the contextual grasp of the political system or of his chosen "ideology" to know what the appropriate response might be. This case illustrates well what we mean by constraint between idea-elements and how such constraint depends upon a store of relevant information. For this man, "Socialists," "the working man," "non-Socialists" and "the rich" with their appropriate valences formed a tightly constrained belief system. But, for lack of information, the belief system more or less began and ended there. It strikes us as valid to distinguish such a belief system from that of the doctrinaire socialist. We, as sophisticated observers, could only class this man as a full "ideologue" by assuming that he shares with us the complex undergirding of information that his concrete group perceptions call up in our own minds. In this instance, a very little probing makes clear that this assumption of shared information is once again false.

The fourth level was, to some degree, a residual category, intended to include those respondents who invoked some policy considerations in their evaluations yet employed none of the references meriting location in any of the first three levels. Two main modes of policy evaluation were characteristic of this level. The first we came to think of as a "nature of the times" response, since parties or candidates were praised or blamed primarily because of their temporal association in the past with broad societal states of war or peace, prosperity or depression. There was no hint in these responses that any groupings in the society suffered differentially from disaster or profited excessively in more pleasant times: These fortunes or misfortunes were those that one party or the other had decided (in some cases, apparently, on whim) to visit upon the nation as a whole. The second type included those respondents whose only approach to an issue reference involved some single narrow policy for which they felt personal gratitude or indignation toward a party or candidate (like social security or a conservation program). In these responses, there was no indication that the speakers saw programs as representative of the broader policy postures of the parties.

The fifth level included those respondents whose evaluations of the political scene had no shred of policy significance whatever. Some of these responses were from people who felt loyal to one party or the other but confessed that they had no idea what the party stood for. Others devoted their attention to personal qualities of the candidates, indicating disinterest in parties more generally. Still others confessed that they paid too little attention to either the parties or the current candidates to be able to say anything about them.

The ranking of the levels performed on *a priori* grounds was corroborated by further analyses, which demonstrated that independent measures of political information, education, and political involvement all showed sharp and monotonic declines as one passed downward through the levels in the order suggested. Furthermore, these correlations were strong enough so that each maintained some residual life when the other two items were controlled despite the strong underlying relationship between education, information, and involvement.

The distribution of the American electorate within these levels of conceptualization is summarized in Table 10.1. The array is instructive as a portrait of a mass electorate, to be laid against the common elite assumption that all or a significant majority of the public conceptualizes the main lines of politics after the manner of the most highly educated. Where the specific hypothesis of the "revolt of the moderates" in the early 1950s is concerned, the distribution does not seem on the face of it to lend much support to the key assumption. This disconfirmation may be examined further, however.

Since the resurgence of the Republicans in the Eisenhower period depended primarily upon crossing of party lines by people who normally considered themselves Democrats, we were able to isolate these people to see from what levels of conceptualization they had been recruited. We found that such key defections had occurred among Democrats in the two bottom levels at a rate very significantly greater than the comparable rate in the group-interest or more ideological levels. In other words, the stirrings in the mass electorate that had led to a change in administration and in "ruling ideology" were primarily the handiwork of the very people for whom assumptions of any liberal-conservative dimensions of judgment were most farfetched.

In short, then, the supposition of changing ideological moods in the mass public as a means of understanding the exchange of partisan elites in 1952 seems to have had little relevance to what was actually going on at the mass level. And once again, the sources of the optical illusion are self-evident. While it may be taken for granted among well educated and politically involved people that a shift from a Democratic preference to a Republican one probably represents a change in option from liberal to conservative, the assumption cannot be extended very far into the electorate as a whole.

IV. Recognition of Ideological Dimensions of Judgment

It is a commonplace in psychology that recognition, recall, and habitual use of cognized objects or concepts are rather different. We are capable of *recognizing* many more objects (or concepts) if they are directly presented to us than we could readily *recall* on the basis of more indirect cues; and we are capable of recalling on the basis of

TABLE 10.1. Distribution of a Total Cross-Section Sample of the American Electorate and of 1956 Voters, by Levels of Conceptualization

	Proportion of total sample	Proportion of voters
I. Ideologues	2½%	3½%
II. Near-ideologues	9	12
III. Group interest	42	45
IV. Nature of the times	24	22
V. No issue content	22½	17½
	100%	100%

such hints many more objects (or concepts) than might be *active* or *salient* for us in a given context without special prompting. In coding the levels of conceptualization from free-answer material, our interest had been entirely focused upon concepts with the last status (activation or salience). It had been our assumption that such activation would be apparent in the responses of any person with a belief system in which these organizing dimensions had high centrality. Nevertheless, we could be sure at the same time that if we presented the terms "liberal" and "conservative" directly to our respondents, a much larger number would recognize them and be able to attribute to them some kind of meaning.

In a 1960 reinterview of the original sample whose 1956 responses had been assigned to our levels of conceptualization, we therefore asked in the context of the differences in "what the parties stand for," "Would you say that either one of the parties is more *conservative* or more *liberal* than the other?" (It was the first time we had ever introduced these terms in our interviewing of this sample.) If the answer was affirmative, we asked which party seemed the more conservative and then, "What do you have in mind when you say that the Republicans (Democrats) are more conservative than the Democrats (Republicans)?" When the respondent said that he did not see differences of this kind between the two parties, we were anxious to distinguish between those who were actually cynical about meaningful party differences and those who took this route to avoid admitting that they did not know what the terms signified. We therefore went on to ask this group, "Do you think that people generally consider the Democrats or the Republicans more conservative, or wouldn't you want to guess about that?" At this point, we were willing to assume that if a person had no idea of the rather standard assumptions, he probably had no idea of what the terms meant; and indeed, those who did try to guess which party other people thought more conservative made a very poor showing when we went on to ask them (paralleling our "meaning" question for the first group), "What do people have in mind when they say that the Republicans (Democrats) are more conservative than the Democrats (Republicans)?"

The responses were classified in a code inspired by the original work on levels of conceptualization, although it was considerably more detailed. Within this code, top priority was given to explanations that called upon broad philosophical differences. These explanations included mentions of such things as *posture toward change* (acceptance of or resistance to new ideas, speed or caution in responding to new problems, protection of or challenge to the *status quo*, aggressive posture towards problems versus a *laissez-faire* approach, orientation toward the future or lack of it, and so forth); *posture toward the welfare state, socialism, free enterprise, or capitalism* (including mention of differential sensitivity to social problems, approaches to social-welfare programs, governmental interference with private enterprise, and so forth); *posture toward the expanding power of federal government* (issues of centralization, states' rights, local autonomy, and paternalism); and *relationship of the government to the individual* (questions of individual dignity, initiative, needs, rights, and so forth). While any mention of comparably broad philosophical differences associated with the liberal-conservative distinction was categorized in this top level, these four were the most frequent types of reference, as they had been for the full "ideologues" in the earlier open-ended materials.

The simple distributional results were as follows. Roughly three respondents in eight (37%) could supply no meaning for the liberal-conservative distinction, including 8% who attempted to say which party was the more conservative but who gave up on the part of the sequence dealing with meaning. Between those who could supply no meaning for the terms and those who clearly did, there was naturally an intermediate group that answered all the questions but showed varying degrees of uncertainty or confusion. The situation required that one of two polar labels (conservative or liberal) be properly associated with one of two polar clusters of connotations and with one of two parties. Once the respondent had decided to explain what "more conservative" or "more liberal" signified, there were four possible patterns by which the other two dichotomies might be associated with the first. Of course, all four were represented in at least some interviews. For example, a respondent might indicate that the Democrats were the more conservative because they stood up for the working man against big business. In such a case, there seemed to be a simple error consisting in reversal of the ideological labels. Or a respondent might say that the Republicans were more liberal because they were pushing new and progressive social legislation. Here the match between label and meaning seems proper, but the party perception is, by normal standards, erroneous.

People making these confused responses might or might not *feel* confused in making their assessments. Even if they knew that they were confused, it is unlikely that they would be less confused in encountering such terms in reading or listening to political communications, which is the important point where transmission of information is concerned. If, on the other hand, they were wrong without realizing it, then they would be capable of hearing that Senator Goldwater, for example, was an extreme conservative and believing that it meant that he was for increased federal spending (or whatever other more specific meaning they might bring to the term). In either case, it seems reasonable to distinguish between the people who belong in this confused group at the border of understanding and those who demonstrate greater clarity about the terms. And after the confused group is set aside, we are left with a proportion of the sample that is slightly more than 50%. This figure can be taken as a maximum estimate of reasonable recognition.

V. Constraints Among Idea-Elements

In our estimation, the use of such basic dimensions of judgment as the liberal-conservative continuum betokens a contextual grasp of politics that permits a wide range of more specific idea-elements to be organized into more tightly constrained wholes. We feel, furthermore, that there are many crucial consequences of such organization: With it, for example, new political events have more meaning, retention of political information from the past is far more adequate, and political behavior increasingly approximates that of sophisticated "rational" models, which assume relatively full information.

It is often argued, however, that abstract dimensions like the liberal-conservative continuum are superficial if not meaningless indicators: All that they show is that poorly educated people are inarticulate and have difficulty expressing verbally the more abstract lines along which their specific political beliefs are organized. To expect these people to be able to express what they know and feel, the critic goes on, is comparable to the fallacy of assuming that people can say in an accurate way why they behave as they do. When it comes down to specific attitudes and behaviors, the organization is there nonetheless, and it is this organization that matters, not the capacity for discourse in sophisticated language.

If it were true that such organization does exist for most people, apart from their capacities to be articulate about it, we would agree out of hand that the question of articulation is quite trivial. As a cold empirical matter, however, this claim does not seem to be valid. Indeed, it is for this reason that we have cast the argument in terms of constraint, for constraint and organization are very nearly the same thing. Therefore when we hypothesize that constraint among political idea-elements begins to lose its range very rapidly once we move from the most sophisticated few toward the "grass roots," we are contending that the organization of more specific attitudes into wide-ranging belief systems is absent as well.

Table 10.2 gives us an opportunity to see the differences in levels of constraint among beliefs on a range of specific issues in an elite population and in a mass population. The elite population happens to be candidates for the United States Congress in the off-year elections of 1958, and the cross-section sample represents the national electorate in the same year. The assortment of issues represented is simply a purposive sampling of some of the more salient political controversies at the time of the study, covering both domestic and foreign policy. The questions posed to the two samples were quite comparable, apart from adjustments necessary in view of the backgrounds of the two populations involved.

Where constraint is concerned, the absolute value of the coefficients in Table 10.2 is the significant datum. The first thing the table conveys is the fact that, for both populations, there is some falling off of constraint *between* the domains of domestic and foreign policy, relative to the high level of constraint *within* each domain. This result is to be expected: Such lowered values signify boundaries between belief systems that are relatively independent. If we take averages of appropriate sets of coefficients entered in Table 10.2 however, we see that the strongest constraint *within*

TABLE 10.2. Constraint between Specific Issue Beliefs for an Elite Sample and a Cross-Section Sample, 1958[a]

	Domestic			Foreign			Party preference
	Employment	Education	Housing	Economic	Military[b]	Isolationism	
Congressional candidates							
Employment	–	.62	.59	.26	.06	.17	.68
Aid to education		–	.61	.50	.06	.35	.55
Federal housing			–	.41	–.03	.30	.68
Economic aid				–	.19	.59	.25
Military aid					–	.32	–.18
Isolationism						–	.05
Party preference							–
Cross-Section Sample							
Employment	–	.45	.08	–.04	.10	–.22	.20
Aid to education		–	.12	.06	.14	–.17	.16
Federal housing			–	–.06	.02	.07	.18
Economic aid				–	.16	.33	–.07
Soldiers abroad[b]					–	.21	.12
Isolationism						–	–.03
Party preference							–

[a]Entries are tau-gamma coefficients, a statistic proposed by Leo A. Goodman and William H. Kruskal in "Measures of Association for Cross Classifications," *Journal of the American Statistical Association*, 49 (Dec., 1954), No. 268, 749. The coefficient was chosen because of its sensitivity to constraint of the scalar as well as the correlational type.
[b]For this category, the cross-section sample was asked a question about keeping American soldiers abroad, rather than about military aid in general.

a domain for the mass public is less than that *between* domestic and foreign domains for the elite sample. Furthermore, for the public, in sharp contrast to the elite, party preference seems by and large to be set off in a belief system of its own, relatively unconnected to issue positions (Table 10.3).

It should be remembered throughout, of course, that the *mass* sample of Tables 10.2 and 10.3 does not exclude college-educated ideologues or the politically sophisticated. But they are grossly outnumbered, as they are in the active electorate. The general point is that the matrix of correlations for the elite sample is of the sort that would be appropriate for factor analysis, the statistical technique designed to reduce a number of correlated variables to a more limited set of organizing dimensions. The matrix representing the mass public,

however, despite its realistic complement of ideologues, is exactly the type that textbooks advise against using for factor analysis on the simple grounds that through inspection it is clear that there is virtually nothing in the way of organization to be discovered.

VI. Social Groupings as Central Objects in Belief Systems

While for any unbiased sampling of controversial belief items we would predict that the relevant elite would show a higher level of internal constraint among elements than those shown by their publics, we would predict at the same time that it would be possible to bias a choice of issues in such

TABLE 10.3. Summary of Differences in Level of Constraint within and between Domains, Public and Elite (based on Table 10.2)

	Average Coefficients			
	Within domestic issues	Between domestic and foreign	Within foreign issues	Between issues and party
Elite	.53	.25	.37	.39
Mass	.23	.11	.23	.11

a way that the level of constraint in the public could surpass that among the elites. This possibility exists because of the role that visible social groupings come to play as objects of high centrality in the belief systems of the less well informed. Such a reversal of the constraint prediction could be attained by choosing items that made it clear that a particular grouping, within the population and visible to most respondents, would be helped or hurt by the alternative in question.

All groups, including those that become important politically, vary in their visibility. Groups delimited by physical characteristics "in the skin" (racial groups) are highly visible, if specimens are present for inspection or if the individual has been informed in some rather vivid way of their existence. Similarly, groups that have buildings, meetings, and officers (church, congregation, and clergy for example) are more visible than groups, like social classes, that do not, although the salience of any "official" group *qua* group may vary widely according to the individual's contact with its formal manifestations.

Some groups—even among those to which an individual can be said to "belong"—are much less visible. Two important examples are the social class and the nation. Where social class is concerned, virtually all members of a population are likely to have absorbed the fact that some people have more means or status than others, and most presumably experience some satisfaction or envy on this score from time to time. Such perceptions may, however, remain at the same level as reactions to the simple fact of life that some people are born handsome and others homely; or, as Marx knew, they may proceed to cognitions of some more "real" and bounded groups. The difference is important.

Much the same kind of observation may be made of the nation as group object. On the basis of our analysis, it might be deduced that nationalist ideologies stand a much better chance of penetrating a mass population than would, for example, the single-tax ideology of the physiocrats, for nationalist ideologies hinge upon a simple group object in a way that single-tax notions do not. This kind of deduction is perfectly warranted, particularly if one has in mind those Western nations with systems of primary education devoted to carving the shape of a nation in young minds as a "real" entity. But Znaniecki has observed, for example, that

the vast majority of peasants in 19th-century Tsarist Russia was "utterly unconscious that they were supposed to belong to a Russian society united by a common culture." Again he reports that a 1934–1935 study in the Pripet marshes showed that nearly half of those inhabitants who were ethnically White Ruthenian had no idea that such a nationality existed and regarded themselves as belonging at most to local communities.[8] The nation as a bounded, integral group object is difficult to experience in any direct way, and its psychological existence for the individual depends upon the social transmission of certain kinds of information. What is deceptive here, as elsewhere, is that decades or even centuries after the *literati* have come to take a nation concept for granted, there may be substantial proportions of the member population who have never heard of such a thing.

While cognitions of certain groups are not always present, the much more typical case is one in which the interstitial or contextual information giving the group a clear political relevance is lacking. For example, a substantial proportion of voters in the United States is unable to predict that any particular party preference will emerge in the votes of different class groupings, and this inability is particularly noticeable among the least involved citizens, whose partisan behavior is itself essentially random with respect to social class.

VII. The Stability of Belief Elements Over Time

All of our data up to this point have used correlations calculated on aggregates as evidence of greater or lesser constraint among elements in belief systems. While we believe these correlations to be informative indicators, they do depend for their form upon cumulations among individuals and therefore can never be seen as commenting incisively upon the belief structures of individuals.

A longitudinal study of the American electorate over a four-year period has permitted us to ask the same questions of the same people a number of times, usually separated by close to two-year intervals. Analysis of the stability of responses to the "basic" policy questions of the type presented in Table 10.2 yields remarkable results. Faced with the typical item of this kind, only about thirteen people out of twenty manage to locate themselves even on the same *side* of the controversy in successive interrogations, when ten out of twenty could have done so by chance alone.

While we have no comparable longitudinal data for an elite sample, the degree of fit between answers to our issue items and congressional roll calls is strong enough to suggest that time correlations for individual congressmen in roll-call choice on comparable bills would provide a fair estimate of the stability of an elite population in beliefs of this sort. It is probably no exaggeration to deduce that, in sharp contrast to a mass sample, eighteen out of twenty congressmen would be likely to take the same positions on the same attitude items after a two-year interval. In short, then, we feel very confident that elite-mass differences in levels of constraint among beliefs are mirrored in elite-mass differences in the temporal stability of belief elements for individuals.

We observed much earlier that the centrality of a specific belief in a larger belief system and the relative stability of that belief over time should be highly related. From our other propositions about the role of groups as central objects in the belief systems of the mass public, we can therefore arrive at two further predictions. The first is simply that pure affect toward visible population groupings should be highly stable over time, even in a mass public, much more so in fact than beliefs on policy matters that more or less explicitly bear on the fortunes of these groupings. Second, policy items that do bear more rather than less explicitly upon their group interest should show less stability than affect towards the group *qua* group but more than those items for which contextual information is required.

Figure 10.1 gives strong confirmation of these hypotheses. First, the only question applied longitudinally that touches on pure affect toward a visible population grouping is the one about party loyalties or identifications. As the figure indicates, the stability of these group feelings for individuals over time (measured by the correlation between individual positions in two successive readings) registers in a completely different range from that characterizing even the most stable of the issue items employed. This contrast is particularly ironic, for in theory of course the party usually has little rationale for its existence save as an instrument to further particular policy preferences of the sort that show less stability in Figure 10.2.

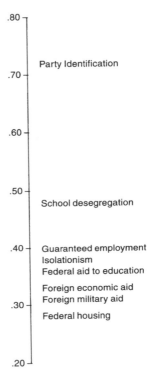

FIGURE 10.1 ■ Temporal Stability of Different Belief Elements for Individuals, 1958–60.[a]
[a]The measure of stability is a rank-order correlation (tau-beta) between individuals' positions in 1958 and in 1960 on the same items.

The policy is the end, and the party is the means, and ends are conceived to be more stable and central in belief systems than means. The reversal for the mass public is of course a rather dramatic special case of one of our primary generalizations: The party and the affect toward it are more central within the political belief systems of the mass public than are the policy ends that the parties are designed to pursue.

Figure 10.1 also shows that, within the set of issues, the items that stand out as most stable are those that have obvious bearing on the welfare of a population grouping—the Blacks—although the item concerning federal job guarantees is very nearly as stable. In general, we may say that stability declines as the referents of the attitude items become increasingly remote, from jobs, which are significant objects to all, and Blacks, who are attitude objects for most, to items involving ways and means of handling foreign policy.

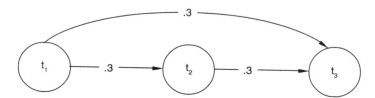

FIGURE 10.2 ■ Pattern of Turnover Correlations Between Different Time Points.

Although most of the less stable items involve foreign policy, the greatest instability is shown for a domestic issue concerning the relative role of government and private enterprise in areas like those of housing and utilities. Interestingly enough, this issue would probably be chosen by sophisticated judges as the most classically "ideological" item in the set, and indeed Table 10.2 shows that the counterpart for this question in the elite sample is central to the primary organizing dimension visible in the matrix. Since the item refers to visible population groupings—"government" and "private business" —we might ask why it is not geared into more stable affect toward these groups. We do believe that measures of affect toward something like "private business" (or better, perhaps, "big business") as an object would show reasonable stability for a mass public, although probably less than those for more clearly bounded and visible groups like Blacks and Catholics. The question, however, is not worded in a way that makes clear which party—government or private business— will profit from which arrangement. Lacking such cues, the citizen innocent of "ideology" is likely to make rather capricious constructions, since the issue is probably one that he has never thought about before and will never think about again except when being interviewed.

In short, all these longitudinal data offer eloquent proof that signs of low constraint among belief elements in the mass public are not products of well knit but highly idiosyncratic belief systems, for these beliefs are extremely labile for individuals over time. Great instability in itself is *prima facie* evidence that the belief has extremely low centrality for the believer.

The fact that we have asked these questions at more than two points in time provides a good deal of leverage in analyzing the processes of change that generate aggregate instability and helps us to

illuminate the character of this instability. For example, in Figure 10.2 we discover, in comparing our indicators of the degree of instability associated with any particular belief as they register between t_2 and t_3 with the same figures for t_1 and t_2, that estimates are essentially the same. This result is an important one, for it assures us that within a medium time range (4 years), differences among issues in degree of response stability are highly reliable.

Far more fascinating, however, is another property that emerges. Quite generally, we can predict t_3 issue positions of individuals fully as well from a knowledge of their t_1 positions alone as we can from a knowledge of their t_2 positions alone. In other words, the turnover correlations between different time points for these issues tend to fit the scheme shown in Figure 10.2.

It can be shown that there is no single meaningful process of change shared by all respondents that would generate this configuration of data. In fact, even if we assume that there is a relatively limited number of change processes present in the population, we find that only two such models could generate these observations. The first of these models posits that some of the respondents managed in a deliberate way to locate themselves from one measurement to another on the opposite side of an issue from the one they had selected at the preceding measurement. It would have to be assumed that a person who chose a leftish alternative on a certain issue in the first measure would be motivated to remember to seek out the rightish alternative two years later, the leftish again 2 years after that, and so on. Naturally, an assumption that this behavior characterizes one member of the population is sufficiently nonsensical for us to reject it out of hand.

Once this possibility is set aside, however, there is only one other model involving a mixture of two types of process of change that fits the observed data. This model is somewhat surprising but not totally implausible. It posits a very sharp dichotomy within the population according to processes of change that are polar opposites. There is first a "hard core" of opinion on a given issue, which is well crystallized and perfectly stable over time. For the remainder of the population, response sequences over time are statistically random.

As another check on the question of reliability, we decided to examine the temporal stability of belief elements of this sort among very limited sets of people whose broader interviews gave us independent reasons to believe they had particular interest in narrower belief areas (like the Black question). We took advantage once again of interviews with a good deal of open-ended material, sifting through this voluntary commentary to find people who had shown "self-starting" concern about particular controversies. Then we went back to the relevant structured issue questions to examine the stability of these belief elements for these people over time. The turnover correlations for these limited subpopulations did increase substantially, beginning to approach the levels of stability shown for party identification (see Figure 10.1). Once again, the evidence seemed clear that extreme instability is associated with absence of information, or at least of interest, and that item reliability is adequate for people with pre-existing concern about any given matter.

The substantive conclusion imposed by these technical maneuvers is simply that large portions of an electorate do not have meaningful beliefs, even on issues that have formed the basis for intense political controversy among elites for substantial periods of time. If this conclusion seems self-evident, it is worth reflecting on the constancy with which it is ignored and on the fact that virtually none of the common modes of dealing empirically with public beliefs attempts to take it into account. Instead, it is assumed that a location must be found for all members of a population on all dimensions of controversy that are measured. Our data argue that, where any single dimension is concerned, very substantial portions of the public simply do not belong on the dimension at all. They should be set aside as not forming any part of that particular *issue public*. And since it is only among "members" of any given issue public that the political effects of a controversy are felt (where such

"effects" include activated public opinion expressed in the writing of letters to the editor, the changing of votes, and the like), we come a step closer to reality when we recognize the fragmentation of the mass public into a plethora of narrower issue publics.

VIII. Issue Publics

Our longitudinal data on eight specific political issues permit us to sketch crudely the boundaries of a sampling of eight issue publics. While details of specific publics are not appropriate here, the general picture that emerges provides some final confirming glimpses into the character of political belief systems in a mass public.

First, of course, these publics vary in size, although none embraces any clear majority of the electorate. As would be expected, relative size is almost perfectly correlated with the ranking of issue stability (Figure 10.1), and the smallest issue public (that associated with the "ideological" private-enterprise issue) includes less than 20% of the electorate.

Since all members of the same population fall either within or outside eight different issue publics, a second analytic question involves the structure that would be revealed were we to map several issue publics at once. What proportions of the electorate would fall at the intersection of two, three, or even more issue publics? One logically possible outcome of such mapping would be a set of concentric rings, suggesting that these issue concerns are cumulative.

The reality does not approach such neatness, however. Memberships and overlapping memberships in issue publics are quite dispersed phenomena, although distribution is not entirely random. The departure from a cumulative structure is extreme, and the simple conclusion seems to be that different controversies excite different people to the point of real opinion formation. One man takes an interest in policies bearing on race and is relatively indifferent to or ignorant about controversies in other areas. His neighbor may have few crystallized opinions on the race issue, but he may find the subject of foreign aid very important. Such sharp divisions of interest are part of what the term "issue public" is intended to convey.

IX. Summary

Our discussion of issue publics has brought us full circle, for there is an obvious relationship among the divisions of the common citizenry into relatively narrow and fragmented issue publics, the feeble levels of constraint registered among specific belief elements of any range, and the absence of recognition or understanding of overarching ideological frames of reference that served as our point of departure. For the truly involved citizen, the development of political sophistication means the absorption of contextual information that makes clear to him the connections of the policy area of his initial interest with policy differences in other areas; and that these broader configurations of policy positions are describable quite economically in the basic abstractions of ideology. Most members of the mass public, however, fail to proceed so far. Certain rather concrete issues may capture their respective individual attentions and lead to some politically relevant opinion formation. This engagement of attention remains narrow however: Other issue concerns that any sophisticated observer would see as "ideologically" related to the initial concern tend not to be thus associated in any breadth or number. The common citizen fails to develop more global points of view about politics. A realistic picture of political belief systems in the mass public, then, is not one that omits issues and policy demands completely nor one that presumes widespread ideological coherence; it is rather one that captures with some fidelity the fragmentation, narrowness, and diversity of these demands.

Such a description is not particularly economical, and the investigator is confronted by the fact that, in coping with a poorly constrained system, he must choose between parsimony and explanatory power. This dilemma confronts him only in the degree that he insists upon dealing with the issue or ideological base of mass politics. That is, the very diffusion of this issue base at the mass level means that many of the threads cancel themselves out and can be ignored at one level of description. With good information on basic party loyalties in a population, with knowledge of sudden disruptions of economic expectations, and with freedom to treat other short-term perturbations in mass political behavior in terms of such inelegant factors as candidate popularity, there is no reason

to feel that mass political phenomena are difficult to understand or predict in relatively economical terms. But such accounts do not probe to the level that supplies for many the fundamental "why" of politics—its issue or ideological base.

Whatever problems are posed for description by the diffuseness of the issue base of mass politics, the most important insights are to be gained from the fact that ideological constraints in belief systems decline with decreasing political information, which is to say that they are present among elites at the "top" of political systems, or subsystems and disappear rather rapidly as one moves "downward" into their mass clienteles. We see the importance of this fact in a number of standard phenomena of both routine and crisis politics.

Perhaps the simplest and most obvious consequences are those that depend on the fact that reduced constraint with reduced information means in turn that ideologically constrained belief systems are necessarily more common in upper than in lower social strata. This fact in turn means that upper social strata across history have much more predictably supported conservative or rightist parties and movements than lower strata have supported leftist parties and movements.

These facts have further bearing on a number of asymmetries in political strategy, which typically arise between elites of rightist and leftist parties. These elites operate under rather standard ideological assumptions, and therefore recognize their "natural" clienteles in the upper and lower strata of the society respectively. The cultural definitions that separate upper and lower in most if not all modern societies are such that the lower clientele numerically outweighs the upper. The net result of these circumstances is that the elites of leftist parties enjoy a "natural" numerical superiority, yet they are cursed with a clientele that is less dependable or solid in its support. The rightist elite has a natural clientele that is more limited but more dependable.

Abolition and the Rise of the Republican Party

Historians have devoted a great deal of prose to the rise of abolitionist ferment in the North after 1820. Popular sentiment against slavery seems to have gathered momentum in the relatively unbroken line that is so typical of *successful* reform movements, from the persistent agitations of Lundy and William Lloyd Garrison through the formation of antislavery societies in the 1830s, the development of the underground railroad, the birth of the Republican Party in the name of abolition, and its final electoral triumph in a popular majority for Lincoln outside the South in 1860. A number of figures are commonly cited to express the deep penetration of the ferment into the consciousness of the general public, including the membership of 200,000 attracted by the American Anti-Slavery Society in the seven short years after 1833 and the truly remarkable sales of *Uncle Tom's Cabin* in 1852 and after.

We obviously do not challenge the mountains of evidence concerning the high pitch of this controversy. We assume from the outset that this ferment among the elites and near-elites was in point of fact most noteworthy and has been accurately described. If we take the figures at face value, for example, we can compute that the Anti-Slavery Society's membership amounted to between 3% and 4% of the adult population outside of the South at that time. Against what we have considered to be the commonly "visible" part of the political public (5% to 15% of the total adult public), this figure does indeed represent a vigorous development of antislavery sentiment. What interests us instead is the gap between the figure of 4% indicative of a sturdy ideological movement, and the 46% of the nonsouthern popular presidential vote won by the Republican Party two years after its conception in Wisconsin and birth in Michigan under the pure banner of abolition. The question is: Essentially what part did beliefs in abolition play in attracting the votes of the mass base that made the Republican Party a political success?

The question seems particularly worth asking, for among events or causes that have commonly been assumed to have had some substantial resonance among the mass public in American history, few would strike us as less plausible than abolition. But it is hard to imagine that the ordinary nonsoutherner in 1855 would have had reason to be concerned about the plight of his "black brother" in a land several days' journey away—certainly not reason sufficient to make any visible contribution to his political responses. Indeed, we are tempted to the heresy that there were very substantial portions of the nonsouthern population in

that period who were only dimly aware that slavery or a controversy about it existed.

If this latter statement seems dubious in the light of the torrents of literature poured out on the subject in the 1850s, the reader might reflect upon the feeble impact registered in the mass public by "the communist hysteria" of the McCarthy era in the early 1950s. At an elite level, the controversy was bitter and all-pervasive for a considerable period of time. Yet, during the nationally televised hearings that climaxed the affair, Stouffer found that 30% of a cross-section public could not think of any senator or congressman investigating internal communism, and the low salience of the whole controversy for most of the public was clearly demonstrated in other ways as well.[9] In the 1952 presidential campaign, the Republican charges against the Democratic Party were summed up in the handy slogan "Corruption, Korea and Communism." Our materials drawn at the time from a mass electorate showed a strong spontaneous response to the issues of corruption and Korea (although there was little understanding of the "Great Debate" that was in full swing over how the Korean conflict should be terminated) but almost no response at all to the third item, even though it referred to a controversy that, like abolition in the 1850s, has tended to remain in elite minds as the principal struggle of its period.[10] The controversy over internal communism provides a classic example of a mortal struggle among elites that passed almost unwitnessed by an astonishing portion of the mass public. Quite clearly, there is no necessary connection between the noise, acrimony, or duration of an elite debate and the mass penetration of the controversy, however automatically the equation is made.

The Mass Base of the Nazi Party

The rise of the Nazi Party in Germany between the two World Wars entrained such a tragic sequence of events that the experience has provoked diagnoses from every school of thought concerned with people, politics, or societies. Typically, the question has been: How could the German people have lent support to a movement with an ideology as brutal and authoritarian as that of the Nazis? Some years ago, Bendix argued that it was important to differentiate between the top Nazi leaders, the party members, and the masses whose sudden surge of support at the polls converted the National Socialists from simply another extremist fringe group of the sort that many societies harbor much of the time to a prominence that permitted them to become masters of Germany soon after 1932.[11]

Who was particularly attracted to this mass base? Once again, there is fair agreement among analysts that there was a significant connection between the marked increase in voter turnout and the sudden surge in Nazi votes that marked the 1928–1932 period. Bendix noted that the staggering increase of 5½ million votes picked up by the Nazi Party in 1930 over its 1928 totals coincided with a rapid influx into the active electorate of nearly 2½ million adults who had failed to vote in 1928. These figures for new voters are exclusive of the estimated 1,760,000 young people who became eligible and voted for the first time, and there is reason to believe that these young people flocked to the Nazis in disproportionate numbers.[12] In addition, there is convincing evidence from Heberle and others that, among older voters, the most dramatic shifts from other parties to the Nazi Party occurred in rural areas and especially among peasants.[13] We conclude therefore that, whatever the social backgrounds or motivations of the activist cadre of the Nazis, its mass base was disproportionately recruited from among customary nonvoters, the young and the peasantry.

Of course, chronic nonvoters would lie at the bottom of any scale of political sophistication or ideological comprehension. As we have noted, too, the young are the most politically unsophisticated age grade, despite their higher average education. Finally, for American data at least, it is clear that political information and political involvement decline systematically with declining mean education from urban areas to increasingly rural areas. Even taken as a whole, farmers in modern America are more remote from and comprehend less of the normal political process than do the lower echelons of the urban occupational hierarchy.[14] Furthermore, the Heberle data for Germany suggest that, among farmers, it was the most isolated and the poorest educated who shifted in the most dramatic proportions to the Nazi ticket in the crucial years. In sum it shows the mass base of the Nazi movement represented one of the more unrelievedly ill-informed clienteles that a major political party has assembled in a modern state.

Even had the clientele of the Nazi Party been of average education and political sophistication, there would be strong reason to doubt the degree to which prior awareness of Nazi ideology among its voters could be claimed. In view of the actual peculiarities of its mass base, the question verges on the absurd. The Nazis promised changes in a system that was near collapse. Under comparable stresses, it is likely that large numbers of citizens in any society (and particularly those without any long-term affective ties to more traditional parties) would gladly support *ad hoc* promises of change without any great concern about ideological implications. And typically, they would lack the contextual information necessary to assess these implications, even if some stray details were absorbed. We believe this response would be true of any mass public and not only those that, like Germany, had experienced only a brief democratic tradition.

X. Conclusion

In this paper, we have attempted to make some systematic comments on the kind of phenomena that seem crucial to any understanding of elite and mass belief systems. We have tried to show the character of the "continental shelf" between elites and masses and to locate the sources of differences in their belief systems in some simple characteristics of information and its social transmission.

The broad contours of elite decisions over time can depend in a vital way upon currents in what is loosely called "the history of ideas." These decisions in turn have effects upon the mass of more common citizens. But, of any direct participation in this history of ideas and the behavior it shapes, the mass is remarkably innocent. We do not disclaim the existence of entities that might best be called "folk ideologies," nor do we deny for a moment that strong differentiations in a variety of narrower values may be found within subcultures of less educated people. Yet for the familiar belief systems that, in view of their historical importance, tend most to attract the sophisticated observer, it is likely that an adequate mapping of a society (or, for that matter, the world) would provide a jumbled cluster of pyramids or a mountain range, with sharp delineation and differentiation in beliefs from elite apex to elite apex but with the mass bases of the pyramids overlapping in such profusion that it would be impossible to decide where one pyramid ended and another began.

NOTES

1. Karl Mannheim, *Ideology and Utopia* (New York, 1946), especially pp. 39 ff.
2. See David W. Minar, "Ideology and Political Behavior," *Midwest Journal of Political Science*, V (November, 1961), No. 4, 317–31.
3. Garner uses the term "constraint" to mean "the amount of interrelatedness of structure of a system of variables" when measured by degree of uncertainty reduction. Wendell R. Garner, *Uncertainty and Structure as Psychological Concepts* (New York, 1962), pp. 142ff. We use the term a bit more broadly as relief from such polysyllables as "interrelatedness" and "interdependence."
4. See A. Campbell, P. E. Converse, W. Miller, and D. Stokes, *The American Voter* (New York, 1960), pp. 204–9.
5. William J. McGuire, "A Syllogistic Analysis of Cognitive Relationships," in Milton J. Rosenberg, Carl I. Hovland, William J. McGuire, Robert P. Abelson, and Jack W. Brehm, *Attitude Organization and Change*, Yale Studies in Attitude and Communication, Vol. 3 (New Haven, 1960), pp. 65–111.
6. Joseph R. Gusfield, "Status Conflicts and the Changing Ideologies of the American Temperance Movement," in Pittman and Snyder, eds., *Society, Culture and Drinking Patterns* (New York, 1962).
7. Anthony Downs, *An Economic Theory of Democracy* (New York, 1957), p. 79.
8. Florian Znaniecki, *Modern Nationalities* (Urbana, 1952), pp. 81–2.
9. S. A. Stouffer, *Communism, Conformity and Civil Liberties* (New York, 1955).
10. Campbell, *et al.*, *op. cit.*, pp. 50–51.
11. Reinhard Bendix. "Social Stratification and Political Power," in Bendix and S. M. Lipset, eds., *Class, Status and Power* (New York, 1953), pp. 596–609.
12. Bendix, *ibid.*, pp. 604–5.
13. Rudolf Heberle, *From Democracy to Nazism* (Baton Rouge, 1945). See also Charles P. Loomis and J. Allen Beegle, "The Spread of German Nazism to Rural Areas," *American Sociological Review*, 11 (December, 1946), 724–34.
14. See Campbell *et al.*, *op. cit.*, Chap. 15. The above remarks on the Nazi movement are a condensation of a case study originally written as part of this chapter.

The Origins and Meaning of Liberal/Conservative Self-Identifications

Pamela Johnston Conover and Stanley Feldman
• University of Kentucky

Although over the past few decades liberal/conservative self-identifications have often played a part in studies of belief systems, they have seldom been the focus of research. Recently, however, several studies have suggested that such identifications play a significant role in voting behavior and political perception. Implicit in this research, however, are two tenuous assumptions: that liberal/conservative identifications are bipolar in meaning and that underlying this bipolarity is cognitive meaning based on political issues. In this paper, we develop a model of ideological identifications that emphasizes their symbolic and nondimensional origins and nature. Based on the 1976 and 1978 National Election Studies, our empirical analysis reveals strong support for the model. Specifically, ideological identifications are found to have largely symbolic meanings, a fact that helps to explain some of the findings concerning the relationship of the liberal/conservative continuum to political perception and behavior.

One of the enduring questions characterizing the study of mass electorates has been whether or not there is ideological thinking in terms of the liberal/conservative continuum. Curiously, though research on this question has been both abundant and controversial, it has tended to ignore—or perhaps take for granted—the meaning of liberal/conservative self-identifications and their impact on political behavior. Typically, it has been assumed that the logical links between ideological self-identifications, on the one hand, and general political orientations and specific issue positions, on the other hand, do in fact exist. Only in the past few years have researchers begun to probe the wisdom of such traditional reasoning. Notably, Levitin and Miller (1979, p. 751) recently explored "the use of the terms 'liberal' and 'conservative' as they are applied by citizens to describe themselves, the political parties, presidential candidates, and positions on issues of public policy." Along similar lines, Holm and Robinson (1978) have compared the impact of partisan and ideological identifications on voting behavior. Finally, from a cross-national perspective, Klingemann (1979a, 1979b) has studied both the use and meaning of the terms "left" and "right."

Generally, these researchers have concluded that, although many members of the public may lack a complete understanding of such ideological terms as traditionally conceptualized, these labels and related self-identifications nonetheless have considerable impact on political perceptions and behavior. Thus, these studies have succeeded in establishing the political significance of ideological labels and identifications. At the same time, however, they have left in doubt the dynamics of the process underlying the influence of such identifications. In particular, in order to understand why liberal/conservative identifications are as influential as recent researchers have claimed, it is necessary to explore the meaning they hold for members of the public, a task which is undertaken in this paper. In so doing, we attempt to bridge the gap between the more traditional research on mass belief systems and the recent work on the political impact of ideological labels.

The Meaning of Ideological Labels

It is our contention that in order to understand fully the nature of ideological self-identifications, it is first necessary to uncover the meaning of the "liberal" and "conservative" labels. In this regard, implicit in much of the mass belief system's literature are two questionable assumptions: (a) that the meaning of ideological labels is structured in dimensional terms; and (b) that the content of such meaning is largely issue oriented. Clearly, these assumptions are not unreasonable given the predominant direction of research on mass belief systems. Nonetheless, there is substantial reason to doubt their validity.

The Structure of Meaning

Traditionally, it was assumed that the meaning of ideological labels and self-identifications could be easily summarized in terms of a single dimension: the liberal/conservative continuum. In recent years, however, this viewpoint has undergone some modification. The decade of the 1970s ushered in a variety of "social" issues—abortion, marijuana use, the Equal Rights Amendment (ERA)—which did not fit easily into the traditional liberal/conserva-

tive spectrum. Because of this, many researchers now posit that the meaning of ideological labels and self-identifications must be interpreted within the context of two liberal/conservative dimensions: one economic and one social (Asher, 1980; Miller & Miller, 1977; Weisberg & Rusk, 1970).

Whether one assumes the presence of a single or several liberal/conservative dimensions does not fundamentally alter our argument. From our perspective, what is critical is the assumption of bipolarity which is common to *both* dimensional interpretations. That is, both the single- and two-dimensional conceptualizations assume that with regard to a particular dimension of meaning the liberal perspective is simply the opposite of the conservative one. In effect, liberals and conservatives are depicted as sharing the same perceptual framework(s); all that differs is that their view is from opposite sides of the field. Because of such shared meaning, voters ought to be able to compare candidates, issues, and parties, and subsequently evaluate such objects using their own identification as an anchoring point. But, recent works reveal that many voters are unable to make accurate comparisons of candidates and issues in liberal/conservative terms (Erikson et al., 1980; Levitin & Miller, 1979). Furthermore, this tendency is especially pronounced in the case of issues, where, based on traditional conceptualizations, one might logically expect to find the clearest liberal/conservative distinctions. For example, Erikson et al. (1980, p. 57) note a Harris poll which revealed that only 50% of the electorate was able to "correctly identify the liberal and conservative sides of major political issues." Similarly, Levitin and Miller (1979) found that on some issues even so-called ideologues had difficulty in distinguishing the liberal position from the conservative one. One interpretation of such findings is that most members of the electorate attribute relatively little meaning to the terms "liberal" and "conservative." An alternate interpretation, however, is that researchers have erred in their basic assumption that the meaning of ideological terms is necessarily structured in dimensional terms. Both empirical findings and theoretical arguments suggest that the latter interpretation is the more valid one.

To begin with, those studies (Asher, 1980; Weisberg & Rusk, 1970) which posit the existence of two liberal/conservative dimensions raise a possibility which paradoxically conflicts with a dimensional interpretation of the meaning of ideological terms. Namely, for some voters, one dimension might be significantly more salient than the other in determining the meaning associated with such terms. Some people, for example, might define ideological labels almost exclusively in terms of social issues while, at the same time, others may base their interpretation entirely on economic issues. Were this to occur, different groups of people would have fundamentally different, rather than opposing or bipolar, ideological perspectives. More generally, several studies have found that people organize their beliefs in a multidimensional fashion, with the nature and number of dimensions often varying from individual to individual (Brown, 1970; Conover & Feldman, 1980; Coveyou & Piereson, 1977; Herzon, 1980; Jackson & Marcus, 1975; Lane, 1962, 1973; and Marcus et al., 1974). As a critical by-product of such multidimensionality, the salience of specific beliefs is likely to vary among people, thus creating different frames of reference from which they interpret the meaning of ideological labels (Brown & Taylor, 1973). As a consequence, the ways in which self-defined liberals and conservatives understand those labels may differ in important respects.

Several studies support this hypothesis. Warr et al. (1969), for example, discovered that the political judgements of left-wing, center, and right-wing British respondents were based on different sets of cognitive dimensions. Along somewhat similar lines, Brown and Taylor (1973) found that a group of students differed considerably in how they conceptualized the term "conservatism." Some focused on the "lack of change" which they felt was inherent in the philosophy, while others concentrated on what they perceived to be the "elitist" aspect of conservatism. But, perhaps most relevant to our argument is Kerlinger's (1967, 1972) theory of "criterial referents." Kerlinger posits that attitudes differ in terms of their "referents," or focus; referents that are "criterial" or central to one attitude may be irrelevant to another. With respect to the social attitudes composing political belief systems, Kerlinger (1967, p. 112) suggests that "liberal is not just the opposite of conservative"; rather than representing endpoints on the same continuum, liberalism and conservatism constitute relatively distinct attitude systems based on different criterial

referents. Kerlinger's thesis received strong support from his factor analysis which revealed that predesignated "liberal" and "conservative" referents did load on different dimensions, and that there were few negative loadings. Taken together, such findings indicate a distinct lack of bipolarity in the beliefs defining liberalism and conservatism. Thus, based on such evidence it seems quite plausible that the meaning of ideological labels is not structured in bipolar terms. Instead, different referents or concepts may be critical to defining the terms "liberal" and "conservative."[1]

The Content of Meaning

The assumption that the meaning of ideological labels is bipolar typically has been accompanied by a second assumption about the content of that meaning. Specifically, as Levitin and Miller (1979) note, it is traditionally assumed that ideology is based on issue preferences, and consequently that ideological labels are largely issue oriented in meaning. Yet, the findings of several recent studies suggest that the mass public must associate considerable nonissue-based meanings with labels like "liberal/conservative" and "left/right," and that ideological self-identifications may not be determined entirely, or even primarily, by issue stances (Klingemann, 1979a, 1979b; Levitin & Miller, 1979).

If not issue oriented, then what is the meaning associated with ideological labels? Clearly, to some degree such meaning may be partisan in nature, if not origin. Both Levitin and Miller (1979) and Holm and Robinson (1978) note a substantial relationship between partisan and ideological self-identifications; as the former explains, "when people describe themselves as having an ideological position, they also seem to be saying something about their positions on the parties, quite apart from their issue or policy stands" (Levitin & Miller, 1979, p. 768). But, it is unlikely that party identification accounts for all the meaning lent ideological terms, especially given Levitin and Miller's (1979) normal-vote analysis which indicates that liberal/conservative self-placements have an impact on vote choice independent of that of party identification. In any case, to say simply that partisan and ideological labels share some common meaning begs the question in that the nature of that shared meaning remains unspecified. Consequently, we will return to this question once we have explored the meaning of ideological labels.

Our approach to unraveling the meaning associated with ideological labels begins with the assumption that such terms are powerful, political symbols to many members of the public.[2] As symbols, the meaning which people attach to ideological labels, such as "liberal" and "conservative," may be of two types: (a) cognitive—the "objective information or substantive content associated with the symbol," and (b) evaluative—the affect elicited by the symbol (Cobb & Elder, 1973, p. 313). From this perspective, then, much of the previous research has focused on the cognitive content of ideological labels. But, if for many people ideological labels have sparse cognitive meaning, as research seems to suggest, then the symbolic power of such terms most likely stems from their evaluative content: their ability to generate strong positive or negative feelings.

Logically, then, the next step is to focus on the origins of the evaluative meaning of ideological labels. One source may actually be the cognitive content, however little, that is associated with the label. In effect, not only may issue-oriented factors directly define the cognitive content of ideological terms, but they also indirectly influence the evaluation of such terms. For example, an individual may react positively to the term "liberal" because he or she associates favorably evaluated issue positions with it. Alternatively, when cognitive sources of meaning are lacking, ideological labels may derive their affect from other, related symbols whose own evaluations may be influenced by long-standing predispositions. To illustrate, deeply ingrained racial prejudices may prompt a strong negative reaction to the *symbol* of busing

(Sears et al., 1979); subsequently, linking that symbol with the "liberal" label should trigger a negative reaction to the latter.

Political symbols differ, however, in their basic nature, and consequently some are more likely than others to be related to ideological symbols such as the terms "liberal" and "conservative." Cobb and Elder (1972, 1973) have argued that political symbols may pertain to four different sorts of political objects: the political community, regime norms, formal political positions, and situational settings involving nongovernmental actors or specific political issues. These various types of symbols play different roles in society; some serve as a foundation for social solidarity while others act as a basis for social differentiation and conflict. For example, symbols of the community (i.e., democracy, freedom) and the regime (majority rule, due process) tend to be sources of consensus and unity in society. In contrast, certain groups (i.e., the Black Panthers, women's liberation) and political issues (i.e., busing, end the war) are symbolic of the lines of conflict in society. Within this context, the traditional nature of ideological concerns suggests that ideological labels should act as a basis for social differentiation. Thus, in the absence of substantial cognitive content, ideological symbols or labels are expected to derive their affect from their association with other symbols of social conflict such as various groups and issues.

A Model of Ideological Self-Identification

Having discarded the assumptions that the meaning of ideological labels is largely bipolar and issue oriented, a different model of the nature and

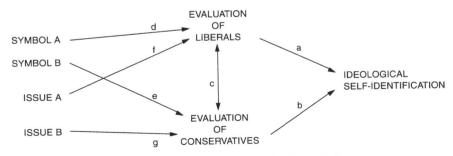

FIGURE 11.1 ■ Model 1 of Ideological Self-Identification

origins of ideological self-identifications may be outlined (see Figure 11.1). A critical element in this model is the specification of the relationship between ideological labels and self-identifications. Based on our earlier discussion, we argue that it is the *evaluative* meaning of ideological labels that is most closely related to self-placement. In effect, it is assumed that identification with an ideological label is associated with a positive evaluation of it. Having made this assumption, we are left with the difficult task of untangling the direction of causality in the relationship. In addressing this problem, two factors govern our thinking: the presumed lack of bipolarity in the meaning of ideological labels and our conceptualization of self-identification. A presumption of bipolarity is implicit in any causal model in which a single factor, such as ideological identification, is depicted as determining evaluations of both liberals and conservatives. In contrast, a causal ordering in which evaluations of ideological labels influence self-identification requires no assumption about bipolarity or its absence, and is thus consistent with our theoretical argument.

Our conceptualization of self-identification leads us to the same conclusion. If ideological self-placements are thought of merely as acts of social categorization, then considerable research suggests that the.more reasonable causal ordering is one in which self-placement stimulates a positive evaluation of the ideological label identified with (for a review, see Hamilton, 1976). If, on the other hand, the act of self-identification is treated as a statement of group consciousness—a declaration of group loyalty—then the reverse causal ordering is more appropriate; that is, a positive evaluation of an ideological group should enhance identification with it (Miller et al., 1978). For our part, we follow the latter line of reasoning by adopting a conceptualization of ideological identification that closely parallels that commonly associated with party identification. Specifically, like Levitin and Miller (1979), we assume that ideological self-placement reflects a "psychological attachment" to a particular group.

In summary, the basic premise underlying our model is that ideological self-placement is determined directly by the individual's evaluation of the two major ideological labels or groups—liberals and conservatives. This relative comparison of evaluations is indicated in the model by parameters a and b. Furthermore, in the absence of a bipolar structure of meaning, liberals will not necessarily evaluate conservatives negatively and vice versa. Thus, parameter c should approach zero, rather than being strongly negative. The direct relationship between ideological self-placement and the evaluation of ideological labels suggests that the meaning of such identifications derives from the meaning of the labels themselves. With respect to the structure of meaning, it was argued earlier that, in the aggregate, liberal and conservative labels have meanings which are not structured in a bipolar or dimensional fashion. Instead, those concepts associated with a positive evaluation of one term are likely to differ considerably from those central to determining a positive evaluation of the other. This lack of bipolar meaning assumes a special significance when considered in conjunction with individual self-identifications. Specifically, it implies that individuals who label themselves as liberals do so for very different reasons than those who call themselves conservatives, in the sense that different concepts or referents are critical in determining their positive evaluations of their respective ideological labels. In essence, then, it is posited that liberals and conservatives view the political world not from different sides of the same coin, but rather, if you will, from the perspective of entirely different currencies. In the model this is indicated by the fact that each of the symbols and issues are linked with evaluations of either liberals *or* conservatives, but not both.

Turning to the content of meaning, both cognitive factors and political symbols can influence attitudes towards liberals and conservatives, and thus ideological self-identifications. In the model this linkage is represented by paths d through g. Individuals may vary, however, in the degree to which they derive their evaluations of ideological labels from cognitive sources such as issue preferences or emotional sources such as political symbols. For some members of the electorate, ideological labels may hold substantial cognitive meaning which complements that derived from various symbols, so that the two sources interact in a consistent fashion to produce the affect associated with the label. Alternatively, lacking issue-oriented information about ideological labels, other individuals are expected to base their evaluations largely on the affective relationship of the label with other political symbols. In both cases, people may attach significant symbolic meaning to ideological labels, and although the sources of the meaning differ, its impact on self-identification, and subsequently behavior, may not.

To summarize, our model specifies a set of causal processes underlying liberal/conservative self-identifications that goes against much of the common wisdom on the subject. As with any model, it is not possible to *prove* that it has been specified correctly. Instead, final judgments about it depend on the theoretical justification of the processes specified, the fit of the model to the data, and the explanatory power of the model. Since we believe that we have established a sound theoretical basis for the model, let us turn now to an empirical assessment of it.

Data and Methods

In testing this model, we had the option of two different research strategies. By focusing on a relatively small group of people, the meaning of ideological self-identifications could be examined on an individual by individual basis. Alternatively, we could take a larger, representative sample and assess the common, or shared meaning of ideological labels. Although individual variations in meaning are important, we have chosen the second route for several reasons. First, this follows the general approach of those studies noted earlier which have raised many of the problems we wish to address. Second, since ideological labels like "liberal" and "conservative" are in large part societally defined, there should be an important component to such identifications that is shared by many people. And finally, looking at the common meaning of such labels provides a basis for assessing their ability to aggregate individual patterns of belief and symbolism. Thus, this approach provides a good first test for the model and ultimately a base line against which group differences may be assessed.

Given this, the data employed in the test of our model are taken from the 1976 National Election Study conducted by the Center for Political Studies. In order to test the model properly, it is necessary to operationalize three categories of variables: (a) ideological self-identification, (b) evaluations of ideological labels, and (c) the cognitive and symbolic sources of the meaning of ideological labels. Let us consider each of these.

Ideological Self-Identification

Ideological self-identification was measured in terms of a standard CPS question which focuses on *political* liberal/conservative identification. Specifically, respondents were asked to place themselves on a seven-point scale whose values ranged from "people whose political views" are "extremely liberal" on one end, to "moderate" in the middle, to "extremely conservative" on the other end. The higher the score, the more conservative the self-identification.

Evaluation of Ideological Labels

Evaluations of the two major ideological labels—liberal and conservative—were measured in terms of "feeling thermometer" ratings. In particular, respondents were asked to rate on a scale from 0 to 100 degrees how warm or cold they felt toward "liberals" and "conservatives"; high scores on each item indicate a positive evaluation of the ideological label.

Cognitive and Symbolic Sources of Meaning

In assessing the cognitive and symbolic sources of the meaning of ideological labels, we were faced with a critical measurement dilemma: whether to employ closed-ended or open-ended questions as the basis for our measures. On the one hand, responses to closed-ended questions dealing with peoples' issue orientations and their attitudes towards various political symbols could be correlated with evaluations of ideological labels in order to identify the meaning of the labels. While this constitutes something of an indirect approach, such closed-ended questions are a relatively clear-cut way of getting at the shared, or aggregate, meaning of ideological labels. In contrast, open-ended questions—such as those asking respondents what the terms "liberal" and "conservative" mean—are a much more direct method of establishing the meaning of ideological labels. However, verbal abilities play a large role in determining whether responses to such questions accurately reflect the meaning associated with ideological labels. Those respondents with lower levels of education may be hampered by the question format so that their responses are not good indicators of the real meaning which ideological labels hold for them. Similarly, because open-ended questions allow for greater individual expression, they make it more difficult to identify patterns of aggregate meaning than is the case with close-ended measures. All this, taken together with our interest in the shared patterns of meaning, led us to employ closed-ended questions as the primary means of establishing the cognitive and symbolic sources of meaning of ideological labels.

Cognitive Sources. Our assessment of the cognitive sources of meaning is based on the respondents' specific issue positions. In adopting this approach, we acknowledge that measuring the meaning of ideological labels in terms of specific issue positions becomes problematic once we abandon the assumption that belief systems are structured unidimensionally (Coveyou & Piereson, 1977; Jackson & Marcus, 1975; Marcus et al., 1974). In particular, a measure of issue orientation based on a series of issue positions aggregated according to their relationship to a liberal/conservative continuum runs the risk of penalizing those respondents who, in fact, do not structure their attitudes along that dimension. Nonetheless, given that previous research has strongly emphasized the role of issues in determining the meaning of ideological labels and the nature of self-identifications, we considered it necessary to employ specific issue positions in our measure of cognitive meaning, even though in doing so some bias may have been introduced into our analysis.

With that caveat in mind, the respondents' specific issue positions were used to construct three summated rating scales which represent the major domains of domestic policy: economic concerns, social issues, and racial questions (Knoke, 1979). Listed below are the three scales and the issues used in their construction.

I_1: Economic Issues—health insurance, guaranteed jobs and standard of living, and taxation policy

I_2: Racial Issues—busing, school desegregation, and aid to minorities

I_3: Social Issues—marijuana use, abortion, ERA, and sex roles

In constructing the scales, all the issues were first put in standardized form (mean = 0; standard deviation = 1) and then summed to produce an overall score for the respondent on that scale. In each case, high scores indicate more conservative issue positions.

SYMBOLIC SOURCES

As noted earlier, to the degree that evaluations of ideological labels are based upon their association with other political symbols, these are likely to be symbols of social differentiation and conflict rather than consensus. Consequently, in measuring the symbolic sources of ideological meaning we focused upon nongovernmental actors or groups that might constitute symbolic representations of various cleavages in American society. Specifically, the respondents' feeling-thermometer ratings of 27 different groups in society were factor analyzed. This analysis produced six factors with eigenvalues greater than one. The interpretation of these factors was based on the assumption that factor loadings of .5 or greater were substantively significant. Based on this criteria, six additive scales

TABLE 11.1. Six Symbolic Meaning Scales and Their Components

S_1: STATUS QUO	S_2: RADICAL LEFT
Protestants	Radical Students
Working Men	Women's Liberation
Whites	Marijuana Users
Men	Black Militants
Middle-Class People	(reliability = .73)
(reliability = .89)	
S_3: CAPITALISM	**S_4: REFORMIST LEFT**
Big Business	Blacks
Republicans	Chicanos
Businessmen	People on Welfare
(reliability = .77)	Jews
	Civil Rights Leaders
	(reliability = .77)
S_5: DISADVANTAGED	**S_6: SOCIAL CONTROL**
Poor People	Police
Older People	Military
Women	(reliability = .69)
Young People	
(reliability = .74)	

All reliabilities are coefficient alpha.

were formed from the feeling-thermometer ratings; positive scores on each scale indicate positive feelings towards the groups composing it.

As indicated in Table 11.1, each of the six scales is composed of a distinct cluster of groups which symbolically represent major cleavages in society. The first scale represents the "status quo" and is composed of mainstream groups traditionally associated with the "protestant ethic" and "middle America." The second scale deals with the "radical left": groups symbolic of revolutionary or rapid change such as "black militants" and "radical students." The third scale is symbolic of "capitalism." The "reformist left" is represented by the fourth scale which concerns groups or minorities related to moderate social change. The symbolic meaning associated with the "disadvantaged" segments of society is captured by the fifth scale which pertains to relatively powerless groups such as the "poor" and "older people." Finally, the last scale deals with symbols of "social control" such as the police and military. It is important to recognize that, taken together, these scales symbolically tap the various dimensions of meaning traditionally associated with the liberal/conservative continuum (Converse, 1964; Klingemann, 1979a). Yet, at the same time, these scales also act as a symbolic representation of some of the new social issues, which emerged in the late 1960s, centered around the agents of social control and the evolution of a counterculture (Miller & Levitin, 1976).

Findings

SELF-IDENTIFICATION AND THE EVALUATION OF IDEOLOGICAL LABELS

First, our model suggests that ideological self-placement should reflect evaluations of the two major ideological groups—liberals and conservatives. Our findings confirm this relationship as indicated by the form of the regression equation:

Self-Identification = .309 evaluations of
    conservatives −.422 evaluations of liberals
(coefficients are beta weights)

Taken together, evaluations of liberals and conservatives explain 36 percent of the variance in ideological self-placement (multiple Pearson's R

= .60). Furthermore, it is interesting to note that evaluations of liberals have a somewhat stronger impact on self-identification than do evaluations of conservatives. This pattern may reflect the nature of the political environment in the 1960s and 1970s, when the "New Left" and the social issues which it championed tended to dominate political discourse in the United States. As a consequence, the "liberal" label may have become more salient and reactions to it more emotionally charged than in the case of the "conservative" label, thus accounting for the relatively stronger impact of the "liberal" label on self-identification. However, with the current emergence of the "New Right" and the concomitant ascendancy of the "conservative" label, evaluations of conservatives may come to have a stronger impact on self-identifications in future years.

The finding that ideological self-identification is strongly influenced by evaluations of liberals and conservatives takes on added significance when considered in conjunction with the following finding: though evaluations of liberals and conservatives are both strongly related to self-identification, they have only a weak negative relationship with one another; Pearson's r equals −.17 for those respondents having an ideological self-identification. This finding runs counter to the argument that the aggregate meaning of ideological labels is bipolar in its structure. Instead, it suggests that evaluations of ideological symbols are relatively independent. In essence, a positive evaluation of liberals does not guarantee a negative attitude towards conservatives, though it does not preclude it either. In more general terms, this finding parallels a pattern uncovered in the study of attitudes towards political parties. Several researchers (Maggiotto & Piereson, 1977; Weisberg, 1980) have found that evaluations of Democrats and Republicans are relatively independent of one another. Taken together, these two sets of findings suggest that the dimensional models so typical in the study of political attitudes be approached with some caution.

Next, our model posits not only that evaluations of ideological labels influence self-identification, but also that they mediate the impact of all other sources of meaning. To test this argument, two regressions were run. In the first, ideological self-placement was regressed on the three issue-posi-

TABLE 11.2. Regressions of Liberal/Conservative Self-Placements on the Issue-Position Scales, the Symbolic-Meaning Variables, and Evaluations of Liberals and Conservatives[a]

Independent Variables	Regression 1		Regression 2	
I. *Symbolic-Meaning Variables*				
S_1: Status Quo	−.019	(−.0004)	−.018	(−.0008)
S_2: Radical Left	−.113	(−.0027)*	−.037	(−.0009)
S_3: Capitalism	.252	(.0079)*	.067	(.0027)
S_4: Reformist Left	−.232	(.0052)*	−.071	(−.0018)
S_5: Disadvantaged	.009	(.0003)	.009	(.0003)
S_6: Social Control	.095	(.0042)	.076	(.0034)
II. *Issue-Position Scales*				
I_1: Economic	.189	(.131)*	.099	(.069)*
I_2: Racial	.019	(.011)	−.006	(−.003)
I_3: Social	.152	(.070)*	.085	(.031)
III. *Evaluations*				
Of Conservatives	−		.259	(.019)*
Of Liberals	−		−.385	(−.027)*
	(*R* = .56)		(*R* = .65)	

[a]Unparenthesized entries are beta weights; parenthesized entries are unstandardized regression coefficients.
*$p < .05$ level.

tion scales (economic, racial, and social) and the six symbolic-meaning scales. In the second regression, ideological self-placement was regressed on the three issue-position scales, the six symbolic-meaning scales, *and* the evaluations of the two ideological labels (see Table 11.2). A comparison of the two regressions reveals that, with only one exception, all those variables having a significant impact in the first regression had no influence once liberal and conservative evaluations were entered into the regression; only evaluations of liberals and conservatives, and economic issues remained significant in the second regression. Furthermore, although economic issues continued to have some direct effect on self-identification, it is important to note that evaluations of liberals and conservatives had a much stronger impact. Thus, although there remains a weak vestige of what once might have been a strong direct link between New Deal economic issues and ideological identification, by and large our prediction is borne out; both cognitive and symbolic sources of meaning influence ideological self-placement primarily through their contribution to the evaluative meaning associated with ideological labels.

Thus, to this point several key findings have supported our argument that evaluations of liberals and conservatives are the most immediate determinants of ideological self-identification. De-

spite this, in order for our interpretation to be fully convincing we must consider two major alternatives to our model, both of which seriously question the validity of our causal ordering of the evaluation of ideological labels and self-identification. As illustrated in Figure 11.2, the first alternative, model 2, reverses our causal ordering so that self-identification is depicted as influencing evaluations rather than vice versa. Another alternative conceptualization is represented by model 3 which is based on the assumption that evaluations of both the "liberal" and "conservative" labels, as well as ideological self-placement, are simply multiple indicators of the same underlying construct, rather than measures of different constructs, as we have assumed. Such a model would be most consistent with the measurement strategy adopted by Levitin and Miller (1979) in their recent examination of ideological identifications.

Both of these alternative conceptualizations lead to certain predictions which can be tested. In particular, model 2 predicts that once ideological self-placement—the intervening variable—is held constant then the symbolic variables and the issue scales should have little or no direct impact on evaluations of liberals and conservatives. This prediction was tested in the following two regressions (coefficients are beta weights and starred coefficients are significant):

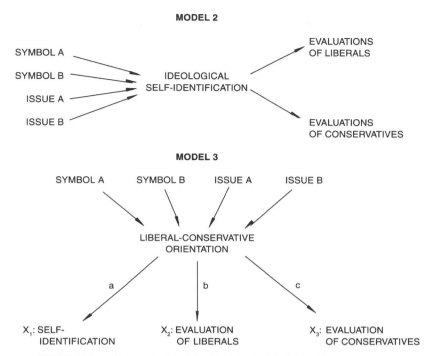

FIGURE 11.2 ■ Alternative Models of Ideological Self-Identification

Evaluations of Liberals = $.07S_1 + .21*S_2 - .09S_3 + .17*S_4 - .01S_5 + .09S_6 - .15*I_1 + .04I_2 - .06I_3 - .33*$ Self-placement ($R = .69$)

Evaluations of Conservatives = $.11*S_1 + .06S_2 + .42*S_3 - .02S_4 + .02S_5 + .14*S_6 + .00I_1 + .17*I_2 - .03I_3 + .22*$ Self-placement ($R = .71$)

As the estimates show, although self-placement did have an impact on evaluations, the model is clearly misspecified in this form; both the symbolic variables and the issue scales had a substantial direct impact on the evaluations even with self-placement included in the regression. Thus, based on this test, model 2 is not as strongly supported as the original model.

Our test of the third model focuses on the relationship between the theoretical construct of a general liberal/conservative orientation and its three hypothesized indicators—self-placement, and evaluations of liberals and conservatives. In this model, there are three unknowns: the epistemic correlations (a, b, and c) which represent the relationships between the theoretical construct and its indicators. There are also three known quantities:

the observed correlations (r_{12}, r_{13}, and r_{23}) among the indicators. Since there are three unknown and three known quantities, the model is just identified. Consequently, although we can solve for the three epistemic correlations, there is no excess information to test for goodness of fit. Instead, the only weak condition that must be met in order for the model to hold is that the estimates of a, b and c not exceed ±1, since they are effectively correlations (Duncan, 1972).[3] But, as the following estimates demonstrate, the model fails even this relatively simple test: $a = 1.21$, $b = -.44$, and $c = .39$. Since the estimate for parameter a exceeds one, model 3 cannot be accepted in its present form. In essence, self-identification and evaluations of liberals and conservatives cannot be considered to be indicators of the same theoretical construct.

Thus, in their present forms neither model 2 nor model 3 fits the data very well. Such a relatively poor showing by both of these alternative models bolsters our confidence in our own conceptualization of the nature of the relationship between evaluations of ideological labels and self-identification. Nonetheless, the choice between these various models ultimately must be made on theoretical grounds; no amount of empirical testing can establish the appropriate causal ordering in the absence of a sound theoretical basis (Duncan, 1975). From such a theoretical perspective, any specification of the causal relationship between ideological self-placement and evaluations must be consistent with one's understanding of the nature of those evaluations and their determinants. In this regard, our conceptualization differs critically from the alternative models in our treatment of the question of bipolarity. Because we posit a lack of bipolarity in the meaning of ideological labels, we necessarily must hypothesize structurally *distinct* determinants of the evaluations of such labels. In contrast, the other two models assume bipolarity and therefore are theoretically compatible with the idea of structurally *identical* determinants. This suggests that our judgment as to the appropriate causal ordering between ideological self-identification and evaluations should not be divorced from our assessment of the validity of our broader theoretical framework, particularly our argument concerning bipolarity. Therefore, the next step is to examine the sources of the evaluations of ideological terms.

Sources of the Evaluation of Ideological Labels

As noted earlier, two general types of factors are considered as possible sources of an individual's attitudes towards liberals and conservatives: specific issue positions and other political symbols. To test the relative contribution of each of these types of factors, evaluations of liberals and conservatives were separately regressed on the three issue-position scales and the six symbolic-meaning scales. The results are presented in Table 11.3.

Considering first the content of meaning, symbolic factors clearly played a more important role than issue positions in determining the evaluation of ideological labels. Attitudes towards liberals and conservatives were each significantly influenced by four variables; yet, in both cases only one of these was an issue-position scale. Furthermore, for both liberals and conservatives the most important determinants were symbolic in nature. Specifically, positive attitudes towards liberals were primarily a function of positive feelings towards the symbols of the radical and reformist left. Negative sentiments towards the symbol of capitalism and a traditional liberal perspective on economic issues were also significant, though less important, determinants of attitudes towards liberals. In contrast, positive evaluations of conservatives were most heavily influenced by a positive affect towards the symbol of capitalism. In addition, a positive affect towards the status quo and social control symbols, and a conservative stance on racial issues also contributed to a positive evaluation of conservatives.

Turning now to a consideration of the structure of the meaning of underlying the evaluation of ideological symbols, we find ample support for

Table 11.3. Regression of Evaluations of Liberals and Conservatives on Issue Positions and the Symbolic-Meaning Variables[a]

Independent Variables	Evaluation of Liberals	Evaluation of Conservatives
I. *Symbolic-Meaning Variables*		
S_1: Status Quo	.078 (.019)	.125 (.032)*
S_2: Radical Left	.305 (.073)*	−.022 (−.008)
S_3: Capitalism	−.154 (−.063)*	.473 (.169)*
S_4: Reformist Left	.246 (.080)*	.015 (.004)
S_5: Disadvantaged	−.037 (−.013)	.051 (.016)
S_6: Social Control	.052 (.028)	.192 (.088)*
II. *Issue Positions*		
I_1: Economic	−.132(−1.28)*	.042 (.326)
I_2: Racial	.029 (.207)	.167 (1.00)*
I_3: Social	−.075 (−.337)	.016 (.083)
	(R = .61)	(R = .69)

[a]Unparenthesized entries are beta weights; parenthesized entries are unstandardized regression coefficients.
*p < .05 level.

our hypothesis that the structure is not bipolar. Specifically, with only one exception, different referents were central to defining the meaning of the terms liberal and conservative. The one shared referent, the symbol of capitalism, was associated positively with evaluations of conservatives and negatively with those of liberals (see Table 11.3). But, while the capitalism symbol was the most critical determinant of attitudes towards conservatives, it was one of the least important determinants of evaluations of liberals. Thus, for the most part, the aggregate pattern of meaning associated with ideological terms was not bipolar. Rather, the two labels derived their meaning largely from different sources, primarily of a symbolic nature.

The implications of such findings for our understanding of ideological self-identifications are diagrammatically outlined in the path model shown in Figure 11.3. While our findings by no means render the liberal/conservative classification meaningless, they do fundamentally challenge the traditional understanding of this distinction. In par-

ticular, our findings indicate that the meaning of ideological labels is largely symbolic in content and nondimensional in structure. Furthermore, our finding of a predominant lack of bipolarity also allows us to discount further the viability of the alternative models considered in the last section, since neither of those models is theoretically consistent with such a pattern. Thus, instead of all people viewing the political world from the same perspective, our model suggests that individuals vary in the affect and salience which they attach to political symbols, and this is reflected in how they label themselves ideologically. For the most part, it is likely that conservatives identify themselves as conservatives for quite different reasons than liberals label themselves liberals.

Meaning of Ideological Labels

Even though direct open-ended questions were rejected as a way of initially identifying the mean-

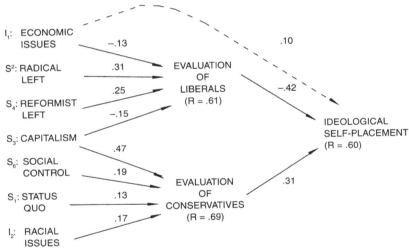

FIGURE 11.3 Path Model Relating Symbolic Meaning Variables and Issue Positions to Evaluations of Liberals and Conservatives, and Ideological Self-Placement
NOTE: Coefficients are standardized regression weights; all are significant at the .05 level. Only significant paths are shown.
The correlations among the seven exogenous variables are:

	S_2	S_3	S_3	S_6	I_1	I_2
S_1	.14	.43	.42	.46	.00	.07
S_2		.03	.47	−.08	−.21	−.31
S_3			.22	.44	.23	.13
S_4				.25	−.30	−.48
S_6					.09	.18
I_1						.39

ing of ideological labels, they are nonetheless useful in further testing the viability of our model. If conservatives and liberals really do view politics from different perspectives there should be some evidence of this in their self-definitions of ideological labels. To test this possibility, we examined the responses given to the following two questions:

> People have different things in mind when they say that someone's political views are liberal or conservative. . . . What sorts of things do you have in mind when you say that someone's political views are liberal? And, what do you have in mind when you say that someone's political views are conservative?

For each question, up to three answers were coded for every respondent. The original coding scheme for these answers was reduced to 13 categories.[4] The percentage of all respondents, of self-identified liberals, and of self-identified conservatives using each category is presented in Table 11.4; because some respondents gave more than one answer to each question, the column totals exceed 100 percent.

To begin, the percentage of respondents using various categories provides one way of assessing whether or not the aggregate meaning of ideological terms has a bipolar structure. As shown in Table 11.4, the ideological labels had some shared mean-

ing for liberals and conservatives. Both groups tended to define both labels with reference to "change," "fiscal policies," and "New Deal policies." *At the same time, however, liberals and conservatives clearly emphasized different categories in their definitions*; there were significant differences between the two groups in their use of all but one category of meaning—minority groups. Thus, as expected, liberals and conservatives did have distinct perspectives on politics which were reflected in the structure of the meaning they lent ideological labels.

Furthermore, the content of the meaning of ideological labels revealed by this analysis accords nicely with our earlier analysis. First, in their definition of ideological labels, liberals made relatively greater use of four categories: "change," "recent social issues," "equality," and "concern with problems." Especially noteworthy is the finding that the liberal viewpoint was dominated by a concern with change; proportionately twice as many liberals as conservatives made reference to "change" and "recent social issues" such as abortion and ERA. This is quite consistent with our earlier finding that a positive reaction to liberals was a function of an attachment to the groups associated with rapid and moderate change in society—the symbols of the radical and reformist left. At the same time, liberals made some use of the various eco-

TABLE 11.4. Frequency Distribution of the Self-Defined Meaning of Ideological Labels[a]

Category	Meaning of "Liberal"			Meaning of "Conservative"		
	All	Liberals	Conservatives	All	Liberals	Conservatives
Change	34.9%	52.3%**	23.5%	43.2%	56.8%**	35.5%
Recent Social Issues	7.6	12.7**	6.3	3.0	6.1**	2.4
Equality	4.1	7.5**	2.1	1.6	2.7**	.5
Concern with Problems	4.4	7.5**	3.4	3.1	4.8*	2.1
Group References	4.8	6.6*	3.7	3.9	3.2	3.7
Fiscal Policies	22.7	9.3	33.5**	28.2	12.2	41.8**
Socialism/Capitalism	9.4	7.5	14.7**	11.9	11.3	15.5*
New Deal Issues	14.4	10.9	22.1**	5.5	3.4	9.0**
Foreign Policy	4.0	2.3	7.1**	6.3	4.5	8.7**
Big Government	5.6	5.4	7.6	4.6	4.3	8.1*
Law & Order	3.3	2.3	5.3*	2.2	2.0	3.5
Ideological Terms	2.9	1.1	3.1*	2.7	1.8	2.4
Minority Groups	7.3	7.9	8.5	1.7	2.7	1.6
N =	1673	442	620	1673	442	620

[a]Entries are the percentage of respondents mentioning that category; percentages total to greater than 100 percent because some respondents gave more than one answer to the question.
**The difference between liberals and conservatives is significant at the .01 level, for that category and label.
*The difference between liberals and conservatives is significant at the .05 level, for that category and label.

nomic categories—"fiscal policies," "socialism/ capitalism," and "New Deal issues"—thus, supporting our claim that the symbol of capitalism also influences the evaluations of liberals. But, it is critical to note that liberals made relatively much less use of such categories than conservatives: a finding that confirms our earlier conclusion that capitalism is considerably more important in defining the conservative, as opposed to liberal, perspective.

Turning to the conservatives, we find that they made relatively more references to four categories of meaning: "fiscal policies," "socialism/capitalism," "New Deal issues," and "foreign policy." In particular, the conservative viewpoint was heavily influenced by a strong focus on economic matters; proportionately three times as many conservatives as liberals made reference to "fiscal policies," and twice as many conservatives mentioned "New Deal issues" such as minimum wages and social security. This is consistent with our finding that an attachment to the symbol of capitalism is the most critical factor in producing positive evaluations of conservatives. Similarly, the conservatives' relatively greater use of the "foreign policy" and "law and order" categories supports our contention that the symbols of social control—the military and the police—are relatively more important in defining the conservative, as compared to the liberal, perspective. In summary, our examination of liberals' and conservatives' self-definition of the two major ideological labels strongly supports the conclusion of our earlier analysis. For the most part, liberals and conservatives do have distinct political perspectives which are not simply mirror images of one another.

Conclusions

In summary, in three important respects, our data analysis has provided support for our specification of the processes underlying the development of ideological self-identifications. First, although there may be some reciprocal effects between the two, the data are consistent with our assumption that causality runs primarily from evaluations of ideological labels to self-identification. Not only do such evaluations have a strong impact on self-identification, but they also mediate almost all of the impact which issues and symbols have on such

identifications. Furthermore, neither of the two major alternative models of the relationship between self-identifications and evaluations fits the data very well, nor are either of them theoretically consistent with a lack of bipolarity. Second, and related to our first point, three key findings run contrary to the traditional bipolar conception of ideological identifications: the absence of any strong negative correlation between evaluations of liberals and conservatives; the relationships of different symbols and issue stances to those evaluations; and the different emphasis which liberals and conservatives placed on various categories in their definitions of ideological terms. Finally, our analysis indicates that ideological labels, and consequently self-identifications, have largely symbolic, nonissue-oriented meaning to the mass public.

Several methodological implications stem from our finding that the meaning of ideological labels is largely based on symbols rather than issues. Specifically, this finding suggests that the common method of using the liberal and conservative labels as stimuli to measure ideological or issue-oriented thinking may be misleading. For the same reason, we should also be cautious of interpretations of political change which rely on shifts in ideological identifications as an empirical indicator of changes in basic issue positions. Our findings imply that major shifts in the distribution of the public's ideological identifications are indicative of fundamental alterations in the symbolic meaning of politics, rather than major changes in issue orientations.

Our model and findings also have several theoretical implications. In particular, one of the major puzzles suggested by both the Levitin and Miller (1979) and Holm and Robinson (1978) studies is why ideological identifications have such an impact on vote choice, even though most voters encounter a great deal of difficulty in labeling which side of an issue is conservative and which is liberal. This is, perhaps, even more curious in a "nonideological" election like 1976 in which voters perceived more of a difference between Ford and Carter in their ideological identifications than on any specific issue position (Page, 1978, p. 98). From our perspective, the symbolic meaning underlying liberal/conservative identifications is the key to understanding these phenomenon. Specifically, even when information about candidates' issue positions is absent or very costly (Page, 1978), the symbolic cues associated with various groups and "easy issues" (Carmines and Stimson, 1980) should still be available. To the degree such symbols are linked to ideological identifications, voters may readily make inferences about the candidates which subsequently influence their evaluations and ultimately their vote choice. Thus, as traditionally argued and empirically confirmed, ideological identifications should act as cues or reference points in the evaluation of candidates. But, contrary to traditional expectations, the basis for these comparisons is largely symbolic, rather than issue oriented, and therefore, may occur in the absence of any true ideological conflict or debate between the candidates.

Similarly, our findings help to unravel the nature of the shared meaning binding together ideological and party identifications. Recall that Levitin and Miller (1979) suggested that such identifications share considerable meaning which, to a large extent, may not be issue based. Given our understanding of the nature of ideological identifications, we can now posit that such shared meaning is primarily symbolic in content. In effect, both party and ideological identifications may represent symbolic ties to the political world which overlap in their meaning. Some insight into the specific nature of this overlap is gained by reviewing the symbolic determinants of evaluations of liberals and conservatives. Specifically, evaluations of Republicans were a component of the capitalism scale—the symbol having the greatest impact on evaluations of conservatives. This suggests that positive evaluations of the conservative label are related to positive evaluations of Republicans, and thus there may be some tendency for self-identified Republicans to also identify themselves as conservatives. At the same time, evaluations of Democrats did not fit into any of our symbolic-meaning scales. Consequently, with no direct symbolic link between evaluations of Democrats and evaluations of either liberals or conservatives, one might expect greater variation in the ideological identifications of Democrats. In fact, this is precisely what Levitin and Miller (1979) found: "Republicans were more homogeneous than Democrats in their ideological self-placement, and they were also much more often unqualified in their ideological commitments" (p. 757). Thus, based on our preliminary findings, we would argue that

party and ideological identifications share a common meaning which centers around the symbol of capitalism.

Finally, one criticism of our empirical analysis is likely to be that the results are time bound: the symbolic meaning associated with the "liberal" and "conservative" terms is a consequence only of the conflicts and events of the 1960s. But, a closer look at our empirical analysis reveals a basis for drawing more general conclusions concerning the meaning of these terms. The nature of the major symbolic referents that defined each label— the reformist and radical left for liberals, and capitalism, social control, and the status quo for conservatives—indicates that the core symbolic meaning of these labels revolves around elements of "change vs. the preservation of traditional values." In general, liberals seem to favor change and progress even at the expense of government involvement; conservatives, on the other hand, wish to preserve traditional arrangements particularly those threatened by government involvement. This interpretation is somewhat broader than Converse's (1964) "spend-save" characterization of the differences between liberals and conservatives, although there are certainly elements of such a distinction in our analysis. Similarly, Robinson and Holm's (1980) recent description of liberals as being "pro-change" and conservatives as "antigovernment" is compatible with the broad lines of our own characterization.

Given this interpretation of the fundamental differences between liberals and conservatives, it can be argued that at any one point in time the major symbols of change and progress become associated with evaluations of liberals, while the symbols associated with the preservation of traditional values determine evaluations of conservatives. If this is in fact the case, then liberal/conservative identifications should always reflect in symbolic terms the dominant cleavages in society. This would account for the observed changes in the meaning of these terms over time (Erikson et al., 1980); as the cleavages evolve and change so do the symbolic referents associated with each term. Ideological self-identifications, therefore, may serve an important function for the public by providing a symbolic framework which simplifies societal conflicts. Furthermore, these core meanings of change and the preservation of traditional values do capture symbolically the general, more ideological definitions typically associated with these terms. Thus, our analysis suggests that the public's usage of ideological labels is more a simplification than a distortion of reality, and that ideological identifications constitute more a symbolic than issue-oriented link to the political world.

REFERENCES

Asher, Herbert B. 1980. *Presidential elections and American politics*, 2nd ed. Homewood, Ill.: Dorsey Press.

Brown, Steven R. 1970. Consistency and the persistence of ideology: some experimental results. *Public Opinion Quarterly*, 34 (Spring 1970): 60–68.

Brown, Steven R., and Richard W. Taylor. 1973. Frames of reference and the observation of behavior. *Social Science Quarterly*, 54 (June 1973): 29–40.

———. 1972. Perspectives in concept formation. *Social Science Quarterly*, 52 (March 1972): 852–860.

Carmines, Edward G., and James A. Stimson. 1980. The two faces of issue voting. *American Political Science Review*, 74 (March 1980): 78–91.

Cobb, Roger W., and Charles D. Elder. 1973. The political uses of symbolism. *American Politics Quarterly*, 1 (July 1973): 305–339.

———. 1972. Individual orientations in the study of political symbolism. *Social Science Quarterly*, 53 (1972): 79–90.

Conover, Pamela Johnston, and Stanley Feldman. 1980. Belief system organization in the American electorate. In John Pierce and John L. Sullivan, eds., *The electorate reconsidered*. Beverly Hills, Calif.: Sage.

Converse, Philip E. 1964. The nature of belief systems in mass publics. In David Apter, ed., *Ideology and discontent*. New York: Free Press.

Coveyou, Michael R., and James Piereson. 1977. Ideological perceptions and political judgment: Some problems of concept and measurement. *Political Methodology*, 4 (Winter 1977): 77–102.

Duncan, Otis D. 1975. *Introduction to structural equation models*. New York: Academic Press.

———. 1972. Unmeasured variables in linear models for panel analysis. In Herbert L. Costner, ed., *Sociological methodology*. San Francisco: Jossey-Bass.

Edelman, Murray. 1964. *The symbolic uses of politics*. Urbana: University of Illinois Press.

Erikson, Robert S., Norman R. Luttbeg, and Kent L. Tedin. 1980. *American public opinion: Its origins, content and impact*. New York: Wiley.

Hamilton, David L. 1976. Cognitive biases in the perception of social groups. In John S. Carroll and John W. Payne, eds., *Cognition and social behavior*. Potomac, Md.: Erhlbaum.

Herzon, Frederick D. 1980. Ideology, constraint, and public opinion: The case of lawyers. *American Journal of Political Science*, 24 (May 1980): 232–258.

Hicks, Jack M., and John H. Wright. 1970. Convergent-discriminant validation and factor analysis of five scales of liberalism-conservatism. *Journal of Personality and Social Psychology*, 14 (February 1970): 114–120.

Holm, John D., and John P. Robinson. 1978. Ideological identification and the American voter. *Public Opinion Quarterly*, 42 (Summer 1978): 235–246.

Jackson, Thomas H., and George Marcus. 1975. Political competence and ideological constraint. *Social Science Research*, 4 (June 1975): 93–111.

Kerlinger, Fred N. 1972. The structure and content of social attitude referents: A preliminary study. *Educational and Psychological Measurement*, 32 (1972): 613–630.

———. 1967. Social attitudes and their criterial referents: A structural theory. *Psychological Review*, 74 (March 1967): 110–122.

Klingemann, Hans D. 1979a. Measuring ideological conceptualizations. In Samuel H. Barnes et al., eds., *Political action: Mass participation in five western democracies*. Beverly Hills, Calif.: Sage.

———. 1979b. Ideological conceptualization and political action. In Samuel Barnes et al., eds., *Political action: Mass participation in five western democracies*. Beverly Hills, Calif.: Sage.

Knoke, David. 1979. Stratification and the dimensions of American political orientations. *American Journal of Political Science*, 23 (November 1979): 772–791.

Lane, Robert E. 1973. Patterns of political belief. In Jeanne Knutson, ed., *Handbook of political psychology*. San Francisco, Calif.: Jossey-Bass.

———. 1962. *Political ideology*. New York: Free Press.

Levitin, Teresa E., and Warren E. Miller. 1979. Ideological interpretations of presidential elections. *American Political Science Review*, 73 (September 1979): 751–771.

Luttbeg, Norman. 1968. The structure of beliefs among leaders and the public. *Public Opinion Quarterly*, 32 (Fall 1968): 398–409.

Maggiotto, Michael A., and James E. Piereson. 1977. Partisan identification and electoral choice: The hostility hypothesis. *American Journal of Political Science*, 21 (November 1977): 745–768.

Marcus, George, David Tabb, and John L. Sullivan. 1974. The application of individual differences scaling to the measurement of political ideology. *American Journal of Political Science*, 18 (May 1974): 405–420.

Miller, Arthur, Patricia Gurin, and Gerald Gurin. 1978. Electoral implications of group identification and consciousness: The reintroduction of a concept. Paper delivered at the 1978 annual meeting of the American Political Science Association, New York, August 31-September 3, 1978.

Miller, Arthur H., and Warren E. Miller. 1977. Partisanship and performance: "Rational" choice in the 1976 presidential election. Paper presented at the annual meeting of the American Political Science Association, 1977, Washington, D.C.

Miller, Warren E., and Teresa E. Levitin. 1976. *Leadership and change: Presidential Elections from 1952–1976*. Cambridge, Mass.: Winthrop.

Page, Benjamin I. 1978. *Choices and echoes in presidential elections: Rational man and electoral democracy*. Chicago: University of Chicago Press.

Robinson, John, and John Holm. 1980. Ideological voting is alive and well. *Public Opinion*, 3 (April/May 1980): 52–58.

Sears, David O., Carl P. Hensler, and Leslie K. Speer. 1979. Whites' opposition to "busing": Self-interest or symbolic politics? *American Political Science Review*, 73 (June 1979): 369–384.

Warr, Peter B., H. M. Schroder, and S. Blackman. 1969. The structure of political judgment. *British Journal of Social and Clinical Psychology*, 8 (February 1969): 32–43.

Weisberg, Herbert F. 1980. A multidimensional conceptualization of party identification. *Political Behavior*, 2 (No. 1, 1980): 33–60.

———, and Jerrold G. Rusk. 1970. Dimensions of candidate evaluation. *American Political Science Review, 64 (December 1970): 1167–1185.*

NOTES

1. Our examination of the structure of the meaning of ideological labels focuses primarily on their aggregate or shared meaning. In effect, we are suggesting that the public as a whole, does not have a dimensional conception of the two terms. We do not mean to suggest as a general rule that individuals fail to see these terms as opposites, though in some instances there may be a lack of bipolarity at the individual level as well.

2. For a discussion of the various types of symbols, see Edelman (1977).

3. In order to estimate the parameters, each correlation is first expressed in terms of the three parameters: $r_{12} = ab$, $r_{13} = ac$, and $r_{23} = bc$. These three equations can then be solved for each unknown, with the following results:

$$a = \sqrt{\frac{r_{12} \times r_{13}}{r_{23}}} \quad b = \sqrt{\frac{r_{12} \times r_{23}}{r_{13}}} \quad c = \sqrt{\frac{r_{13} \times r_{23}}{r_{12}}}$$

For the calculations noted in the text: $r_{12} = -.53$, $r_{13} = .47$ and $r_{23} = -17$.

4. We found that 91.2 percent of all the responses on the "liberal" question and 93.9 percent of all the responses on the "conservative" question were codable within these 13 categories. The rest of the responses were either uninterpretable or were very infrequently cited reasons. The following constitutes a representative sample of the CPS codes for each category:

(1) CHANGE—acceptance/resistance to change, new ideas; slow/rash responses to problems; cautious, irresponsible;

(2) RECENT SOCIAL ISSUES—abortion; birth control; women's rights; Equal Rights Amendment;

(3) EQUALITY—equal rights; elitist; special privileges;

(4) CONCERN WITH PROBLEMS—sensitive to social problems, reform; interested/not interested in improving conditions;

(5) GROUP REFERENCES—all people, working people, common people, middle class;

(6) FISCAL POLICIES—government spending; too much spending; tight economic policies; sound money;

(7) SOCIALISM/CAPITALISM—socialistic, welfare state; free enterprise, capitalism; big business; rich people;

(8) NEW DEAL ISSUES—minimum wage; social security; health insurance; control of utilities; social welfare; poverty programs;

(9) FOREIGN POLICY/NATIONAL SECURITY—peace/war; internationalist/isolationist; national defense;

(10) BIG GOVERNMENT—centralized government; local government; local initiative;

(11) LAW AND ORDER—hard line/soft line on law and order;

(12) IDEOLOGICAL TERMS—radical; extreme; reactionary; far right; and

(13) MINORITY GROUPS—minorities, black, racist, civil rights.

The Fear of Equality

Robert E. Lane • Yale University

Since the writings of Marx in 1848, it has been assumed that the drive for a more equalitarian society, its effective social force, would come from the stratum of society with the most to gain, the working classes. This was thought to be the revolutionary force in the world—the demand of workers for a classless society sparked by their hostility to the owning classes. It was to be the elite among the workers, not the *lumpenproletariat*, not the "scum," who were to advance this movement. Just as "liberty" was the central slogan of the bourgeois revolution, so "equality" was the central concept in the working class movement. Hence it was natural to assume that whatever gains have been made in equalizing the income and status of men in our society came about largely from working class pressure.

But on closer investigation the demands for greater liberty or "freedom" turn out to have been of an ambiguous nature. The middle classes sought freedom of speech and action in large part for the economic gains that this would give them, and moralized their action with the theology of freedom. But the freedom that they gained was frightening, for it deprived them of the solidary social relationships and the ideological certainty which often gave order and meaning to their lives. On occasion, then, they sought to "escape from freedom."[1] The older unfree order had a value which the earlier social commentators did not appreciate.

There is a parallel here with the movement toward a more equalitarian society. The upper working class, and the lower middle class, support specific measures embraced in the formula "welfare state," which have equalitarian consequences. But, so I shall argue, many members of the working classes do not want equality. They are afraid of it. In some ways they already seek to escape from it. Equality for the working classes, like freedom for the middle classes, is a worrisome, partially rejected, by-product of the demand for more specific measures. Inequality has values to them which have been overlooked. It is these attitudes on status and equality that I shall explore here.

I. Extended Interviews with Fifteen Men

This discussion is based upon extended interviews of from 10 to 15 hours each (in from four to seven sessions) with a sample of American urban male voters. The sample is a random selection from the white members on a list of 220 registered voters in a moderate income (not low income) housing development where income is permitted to range between $4,000 and $6,500, according to the number of dependents in the family. Out of fifteen asked to participate, fifteen agreed, for a modest cash consideration. The characteristics of the sample, then, are as follows:

> They are all men, white, married, fathers, urban, Eastern seaboard.
> Their incomes range from $2,400 to $6,300 (except for one who had just moved from the project. His income was $10,000 in 1957.)

Ten had working class (blue collar) occupations such as painter, plumber, railroad fireman, policeman, machine operator.

Five had white collar occupations such as salesman, bookkeeper, supply clerk.

Their ages ranged from 25 to 54; most are in their thirties.

Twelve are Catholic, two are Protestants, one is Jewish.

All are native born; their nationality backgrounds are: six Italian, five Irish, one Polish, one Swedish, one Russian, one Yankee. Most are second- or third-generation Americans.

All were employed at the time of the interviews.

Their educational distribution was: three had only grammar school education; eight had some high school; two finished high school; one had some college; one completed graduate training.

The interviews with these men were taped, with the permission of the interviewees, and transcribed. They were conducted by means of a schedule of questions and topics followed by conversational improvised probes to discover the underlying meanings of the answers given. The kinds of questions employed to uncover the material to be reported are illustrated by the following: "What do you think the phrase 'All men are created equal' means?" "How would you feel if everyone received the same income no matter what his job?" "Sometimes one hears the term 'social class'—as in working class or middle class. What do you think this term 'social class' means?" "What class do you belong to?" "How do you feel about it?" There were also a number of questions dealing with status, private utopias, feelings of privilege or lack of privilege, and other topics, throughout the interview schedule which sometimes elicited responses bearing on the question of social and economic equality.[2]

II. How to Account for One's Own Status

It is my thesis that attitudes toward equality rest in the first instance upon one's attitude towards one's own status. Like a large number of social beliefs, attitudes towards equality take their direction from beliefs about the self, the status of the self, and one's self-esteem or lack thereof. It is necessary, therefore, first to explore how people see themselves in American hierarchical society.

The American culture and the democratic dogma have given to the American public the notion that "all men are created equal." Even more insistently, the American culture tells its members: "achieve," "compete," "be better, smarter, quicker, richer than your fellow men"; in short, "be unequal." The men I interviewed had received these inequalitarian messages, some eagerly, some with foreboding. Having heard them, they must account for their status, higher than some, lower than others. They must ask themselves, for example, "Why didn't I rise out of the working class, or out of the 'housing project class,' or out of the underpaid office help class?" And, on the other hand, "Why am I better off than my parents? or than the fellows down the road in the low rental project? or the fellows on relief?" Men confronted with these questions adopt a variety of interesting answers.

Is It Up to Me?

The problem of accounting for status is personally important for these men only if they think that their decisions, effort, and energy make a difference in their position in life. Most of my subjects accepted the view that America opens up opportunity to all people; if not in equal proportions, then at least enough so that a person must assume responsibility for his own status. Thus O'Hara, a maintenance oiler in a factory, in a typical response, comments that the rich man's son and the poor man's son "have equal opportunity to be President . . . if they've got the education and the know how." But, he goes on to say, "some of them have a little more help than others." This is the constant theme: "all men can better themselves," the circumstances of American life do not imprison men in their class or station—if there is such a prison, the iron bars are within each man.

There were a few, of course, who stressed the differences of opportunity at birth, the mockery of the phrase "all men are created equal." Here, as only rarely in the interviews, a head of steam builds up which might feed radical social movements—but this is true for only a few of the sample. Three or four angry young or middle aged men deny the Jeffersonian phrase. Rapuano, an auto parts supply man, says:

How could you say we were born equal when, for instance, when I was born, I was born in a family that were pretty poor. You get another baby born in a family that has millions.

And Kuchinsky, a house painter, says:

Are we created equal? I don't believe we are, because everybody's got much more than one another and it's not right, I think. Of course, ah, we have no choice. I mean we can't do nothing about it. So we're not as equal as the next party, that's for sure.

And Ferrera, a salesman, says:

All men created equal? Ah, very hypocritical, cause all men are not created equal—and— I don't know—you really pick some beauties don't you? ... The birth of an individual in a [social] class sort of disputes this.

To these men, then, subordination and life position is attributable not so much to the efforts of the individual, something for which he must assume responsibility, as to the circumstances of birth, over which he has no control. Yet for each of those men the channels of advancement were seen as only partly blocked. Rapuano, for example, says elsewhere that income is generally proportionate to ability. Like the theme of "moral equality," the theme of differential life chances from birth is easily available. What is surprising is not that it is used at all, but rather that it is used so infrequently.

III. Reducing the Importance of the Struggle

When something is painful to examine, people look away, or, if they look at it, they see only the parts they want to see. They deny that it is an important something. So is it often with a person's class status when the reference is upward, when people must account not for the strength of their position, but for its weakness. How do they do this?

In the first place they may *insulate themselves*, limit their outlook and range of comparisons. Ferrera, an insurance salesman, who says, "It's pretty hard for me to think there is anyone in the upper class and I'm not in the upper class," slides into a prepared position of insulated defense:

I think a lot of people place a lot of stress on the importance of social classes [but] I feel that I have a job to do, I have my own little unit to take care of. If I can do it to the best ability that is instilled in me at birth or progress through the years, I feel that I rightly deserve the highest classification you can get. I don't particularly like the headings, "upper, middle, working, and lower."

It is a resentful narrowing of focus in this case: two years at an inferior college may have led to ambitions which life then failed to fulfill. Contrast this to Woodside, a policeman with a Middlewestern rural background, who accepts the "categories" of social class rather willingly. He says, after dealing with the moral and intangible aspects of equality:

["Are there any people whom you regard as not equal to you?"] Well, that is a tough question. Well, in fairness, I'd say all people are equal to one another in his own category. When I say category, I mean you couldn't exactly expect a person that had very little knowledge to be, we'll say, should have a position where a person with a lot more education had it.

Equality must be treated within classes, not between them, to be meaningful—and in this way the problem of placing oneself becomes tolerable, or sometimes rather gratifying.

A second device for reducing the importance of class position is to *deny its importance*. This is not to deny the importance of getting ahead, but to limit this to the problem of job classification, or occupational choice—nothing so damaging to the self-esteem as an ordering of persons on a class scale. Rapuano, resisting the class concept, says:

I don't think it [social class] is important, I mean whenever I went and asked for a job, the boss never asked me what class I was in. They just wanted to know if I knew my business. Oh yes, and I don't think in politics it makes any difference.

Others maintain that for other countries social class is important, but not for Americans. There are rich and poor, perhaps, but not status, class, or deference levels to be accounted for.

A third device for reducing the significance of the struggle for status and "success" is *resignation*, a reluctant acceptance of one's fate. When some men assume this posture of resignation one senses a pose; their secret hopes and ambitions will not down. For others it rings true. When Dempsey, a factory operative, speaks of his situation at the age of 54, one believes him:

> It's hard, very hard. We seem to be struggling along now, as it is, right here, to try and get above our level, to get out of the rut, as you might say, that we're probably in right now. ... [But] After you get to a certain age, there, you stop—and you say, "Well, I can't go any further." I think I've gotten to that point now.

But when Sokolsky reports that he is contented with his station in life, it does not seem authentic:

> Being in the average group [He wouldn't assign himself a class status] doesn't bother me. I know I make a living—as long as I make a living, and I'm happy and I have what I want —try to give my family what they want. It doesn't bother me— no. I'm satisfied.

But then he adds: "I hope to God my children will do better than their father did."

Contrast these views with those of Johnson, a plumber, who says, "I feel someday I'll be better off. I feel that way because I believe I have it within me to do it"; and with Flynn, a white collar worker, who answers:

> No, I'm nowhere near satisfied. It seems to me every time I start to move up a little bit, all the levels move up one step ahead of me. I can't ever get out of this area. I have a certain desire and willingness to do something extra.

IV. The Working Class Gets Its Share

When comparing their status with those lower on the scale, however each man may define it, it is easy to point with pride to achievement, material well-being, standing in the community. But satisfaction with one's self and one's friends depends on seeing some advantage in one's situation vis-a-vis those who live and work on a higher status level. At first, this seems to be a difficult task, but in many simple ways it can be easily done. Our sample, for example, found ways of ascribing greater happiness, power, and even income to the

working class than would be found in the upper class.

The equality of happiness is a fruitful vein. Lower income and status is more tolerable when one can believe that the rich are not receiving a happiness income commensurate with their money income. "Are the rich happier than people who are just average?" O'Hara does not think so:

> I think lots of times they're never happy, because one thing is, the majority of them that are rich have got more worries. You see a lot more of them sick than you do, I think, the average. I think a lot of your mental strain is a lot greater in the higher class—in the rich class—than in the other.

And Johnson, a maintenance plumber, says:

> Well, even though this rich man can go places and do things that others can't afford, there's only certain things in life that I think make people happy. For instance, having children, and having a place to live—no matter where it is, it's your home ... the majority of these big men—I don't think they devote as much time and get a thrill out of the little things in life that the average guy gets, which I think is a lot of thrills.

Indeed, hardly a man thought the rich were happier. And yet, O'Hara says, on another occasion, "What is the most important thing that money can buy? Happiness, when you come down to it." Perhaps he means that money buys happiness for the average man, but not for the rich. But more likely he means ["I can take care of a gnawing and illegitimate envy by appropriating happiness for me and my kind."][3]

Power, like happiness, is awarded to the working (or lower middle) class. The sheer fact of numbers gives a sense of strength and importance. Costa, a factory operative, says, for example, "People like you [the interviewer] are the minority and people like me are the majority, so we get taken care of in the long run." Whether a person sees himself as middle class or working class, he is likely to believe that most people belong to his class. This being true, his class, people like him, become the most important force in electoral decisions. O'Hara puts it this way:

> The biggest part of the people in this country are working class. And I think they've got the most to do with—they've got a big part to do with run-

ning this country—because the lower class, a lot of them don't vote, when you come down to it, they don't have the education to vote, and your upper class isn't that much—isn't as great as the other, so really when you come down to it, it's your working class that's deciding one way or the other.

Not only do they "have the biggest part to do with running the country," they are crucial for the economy. This is not only as producers—indeed no one mentioned the theme which romantic writers on the laboring man and the immigrant have often employed—"they cleared the land and built the cities." Rather it is because of their power to shatter the economy and their power to survive in a depression that they are important. Kuchinsky explains this as follows:

I think the lower class of people are the important people. I think so because of the business end of it. Without us, I don't think the businessman could survive. I mean if we don't work—of course, they have the money, but, ah, a lot of times during the crash which was an awful thing, too, I think a lot of 'em lived so high that they couldn't stand it any more when they went broke, and they committed a lot of suicides there. But we were used to living that way, it didn't bother us.

Today, as perhaps never before, the working class man can see his status loss compared to white collar workers compensated by income advantages. Thus, De Angelo, a factory operative and shop steward, reports:

You got people working in offices, they might consider themselves upper class, y'know, a little better than the working man. But nine times out of ten the working man is making more money than he is.

And in the same vein, Rapuano says:

I certainly would hate like hell to be a white collar worker in the middle class and making the money that the white collar worker does. I would rather be a worker in the lower class, and making their money, see?

Of course, this assignment of income advantages to the working class hinges upon a narrowing of the range of competition—but this is the range that makes a difference for these men.

V. Moral Equality

Another device for dealing with subordination in a society where invidious comparison with others is constantly invited represents, in effect, a borrowing from an older classical or religious tradition—an emphasis upon the intangible and immeasurable (and therefore comfortingly vague) spiritual and moral qualities. The only clearly adequate expression of this religious view was given by McNamara, a gentle and compassionate bookkeeper, who said "All men are created equal? That's our belief as Catholics," implying some sort of religious equality, perhaps such an idea as is captured in the phrase "equality of the soul." Woodside, a Protestant policeman, takes, in a way, a secular 18th Century version of this view when he says that men are equal "not financially, not in influence, but equal to one another as to being a person." Being a person, then, is enough to qualify for equal claims of some undefined kind.

But it seems probable that when men assert their own equality in this vague sense, typically phrased in something like O'Hara's terms: "I think I'm just as good as anybody else. I don't think there's any of them that I would say are better," something other than moral or spiritual equality is at issue. These moral qualities are what the educated commentator reads into the statement, but O'Hara means, if I may put words in his mouth ["Don't put on airs around me," "I'm trying to preserve my self-respect in a world that challenges it; I therefore assert my equality with all." "I won't be pushed around." "I know my rights," and, to the interviewer: "Just because you're a professor and I'm an oiler, it doesn't mean you can patronize me."] And when Sokolsky, a machine operator and part-time janitor, says, in the interview, "The rich guy—because he's got money he's no better than I am. I mean that's the way I feel," he is not talking about moral or spiritual qualities. He is saying, in effect to his prosperous older brother and his snobbish wife, ["Don't look down on me,"] and to the world at large: ["I may be small, but I will protect my self-esteem."] These men are posting notices similar to the motto on the early American colonies' flags: "Don't tread on me."

Speaking of moral virtues, we must observe how easy it would have been to take the view that the morality of the middle levels of society was superior because the rich received their wealth illegitimately. None of my clients did this. Nor did they stress the immoral lives of the wealthy classes, as did Merton's sample[4] some thirteen years ago—a commentary, perhaps, upon changing attitudes toward the upper classes taking place over this period. The psychic defenses against subordination available in stressing moral equality or superiority were used—but only rarely.

VI. People Deserve Their Status

If one accepts the view that this is a land of opportunity in which merit will find a way, one is encouraged to accept the status differences of society. But it is more than logic which impels our men to accept these differences. There are satisfactions of identification with the going social order; it is easier to accept differences which one calls "just" than those that appear "unjust"; there are the very substantial self-congratulatory satisfactions of comparison with those lower on the scale. Thus this theme of "just desserts" applies to one's own group, those higher, and those lower.

So Kuchinsky says: "If you're a professor, I think you're entitled to get what you deserve. I'm a painter and I shouldn't be getting what you're getting." Furthermore, confidence in the general equity of the social order suggests that the rewards of one's own life are proportionate to ability, effort, and the wisdom of previous decisions. On ability, Costa, a machine operator, says:

I believe anybody that has the potential to become a scientific man, or a professor, or a lawyer, or a doctor, should have the opportunity to pursue it, but there's a lot of us that are just made to run a machine in a factory. No matter what opportunities some of us might have had, we would never have reached the point where we could become people of that kind. I mean everybody isn't Joe DiMaggio.

And on the wisdom of earlier decisions, Johnson, a plumber, says:

I don't consider myself the lower class. In between someplace. But I could have been a lot better off but through my own foolishness, I'm not. [Here he refers back to an earlier account of his life.] What causes poverty? Foolishness. When I came out of the service, my wife had saved a

few dollars and I had a few bucks. I wanted to have a good time. I'm throwing money away like water. Believe me, had I used my head right, I could have had a house. I don't feel sorry for myself—what happened, happened, you know. Of course you pay for it.

But the most usual mistake or deficiency accounting for the relatively humble position is failure to continue one's education due to lack of family pressure ("they should have made me"), or youthful indiscretion, or the demands of the family for money, or the depression of the 1930s.

THE UPPER CLASSES
DESERVE TO BE UPPER

Just as they regard their own status as deserved, so also do they regard the status of the more eminently successful as appropriate to their talents. Rapuano, an auto parts supply man, reports:

Your income—if you're smart, and your ability calls for a certain income, that's what you should earn. If your ability is so low, why hell, then you should earn the low income. ["Do you think income is proportionate to ability now?"] I would say so. Yes.

But there is a suggestion in many of the interviews that even if the income is divorced from talent and effort, in some sense it is appropriate. Consider Sokolsky again, a machine operator and part-time janitor, discussing the tax situation:

Personally, I think taxes are too hard. I mean a man makes, let's say $150,000. Well, my God, he has to give up half of that to the government—which I don't think is right. For instance if a man is fortunate enough to win the Irish Sweepstakes, he gets $150,000—I think he has about $45,000 left. I don't think that's right.

Even if life is a lottery, the winner should keep his winnings. And De Angelo, a machine operator, comes spontaneously to the same conclusion:

I think everybody needs a little [tax] relief. I mean, I know one thing, if I made a million dollars and the government took nine-tenths of it—boy, I'd cry the blues. I can't see that. If a man is smart enough to make that much, damn it, he's got a right to holler. I'm with the guy all the way.

Because he is "smart enough" to make the money, it is rightfully his. Surely, beyond the grave, there is a spectre haunting Marx.

The concept of "education" is the key to much of the thinking on social class and personal status. In a sense, it is a "natural" because it fits so neatly into the American myth of opportunity and equality, and provides a rationale for success and failure which does minimum damage to the souls of those who did not go to college. Thus in justifying their own positions, sometimes with reference to the interview situation, my clients imply, "If I had gone to college (like you) I would be higher up in this world." Costa, a machine operator, speaks this theme:

> Now what would be the advantage of you going 20 years to school so you wind up making $10,000 a year, and me going 8 years to school, making $10,000. You would be teaching the young men of tomorrow, the leaders of tomorrow, and I would be running a machine. You would have a lot more responsibility to the country as a whole than I would have. Why shouldn't you be rewarded in proportion.

McNamara, a mild mannered bookkeeper who went to night school to get his training in accounting and bookkeeping, emphasizes education in response to the question: "Do you think it's easy or hard to get from one class to another?"

> Well, I think it's hard because . . . not because of the class itself, or what the influence they have on you, but you just seem to reach a certain point, and if you don't have it, you just don't—you don't make the grade. I've found that to be true. I always seem to be one step away from a good spot. And it's no one's fault—it's my fault. I just don't have the education—just don't—just don't have what it takes to take that step.

And Sokolsky, a machine operator and part-time janitor, says, in his justification of income differences:

> A man that gets out of eighth grade—I don't think he would have the ability to do the job as a man that got out of college.

But later, he says, of politicians and businessmen:

> If a man with more education has been in politics, he should get the job, but if there's a man

that, let's say, just got out of high school, and he's been around in politics all his life, I think he should have a chance too. It's how good he is. There's some big business people who just haven't got it. [But] there could be some men with a gift of gab—maybe just out of eighth grade—they could sell anything.

What is it about education that justifies differences in income? In the above interviews it is clear that education is thought to increase skills which should be suitably rewarded. Furthermore, it appears that the time necessary for educational preparation deserves some reward—a recurrent theme. With education goes responsibility—and responsibility should be rewarded. But there is also some suggestion in the interview material that the pain and hard (unpleasant) work associated with going to school deserves compensation. People who did not like school themselves may be paying homage to those who could stick it out. It is a question whether O'Hara, a maintenance oiler, implies this when he says:

> I think a person that is educated deserves more than somebody that isn't. Somebody who really works for his money really deserves it more than somebody that's lazy and just wants to hang around.

In this and other ways, education serves as a peg on which to hang status; and, like "blood," whether a person got the education or not is not his "fault," or at least it is only the fault of an irresponsible youth, not a grown man.[5]

The Lower Classes Deserve No Better Than They Get

By and large those in the lower orders are those who are paid daily (not weekly) or are on relief; they live in slums or in public housing projects (but not middle income projects); they do not live respectable lives; they have only grammar school education; they may have no regular jobs. Closer to home, those slightly lower in status are people like "The lady next door who has a little less than I have," the man who can't afford to take care of his kids properly in the project, people who spend their money on liquor, the person with less skill in the same line of work.

The rationale for their lower status turns chiefly

on two things: their lack of education and therefore failure to know what they want or failure to understand lifesmanship, and their general indifference. It is particularly this "not caring" which seems so salient in the upper working class mind. This is consonant with the general view that success is a triumph of the will and a reflection of ability. Poverty is for lazy people, just as middle status is for struggling people. Thus Ruggiero, an office building maintenance man, accounts for poverty by saying: "There's laziness, you'll always have lazy people." De Angelo, a factory operative, sees it this way:

> A guy gets married and, you know, he's not educated too well, he doesn't have a good job and he gets a large family and he's in bad shape, y'know what I mean. It's tough; he's got to live in a lousy rent—he can't afford anything better.

But De Angelo takes away some of this sympathy the next moment when he goes on to say:

> But then you get a lot of people who don't want to work; you got welfare. People will go on living on that welfare—they're happier than hell. Why should they work if the city will support them?

In general, there is little sympathy given to those lower in the scale, little reference to the overpowering forces of circumstance, only rare mention of sickness, death of a breadwinner, senility, factories moving out of town, and so forth. The only major cause of poverty to which no moral blame attaches is economic depression or "unemployment"—but this is not considered a strikingly important cause in the minds of my clients. They are Christian in the sense that they believe "The poor ye have with you always," but there is no trace of a belief that the poor are in any way "blessed."

VII. What if There were Greater Equality of Opportunity and Income?

We have examined here the working (and lower middle) class defenses of the present order. They are well organized and solidly built. By and large these people believe that the field is open, merit will tell. They may then deprecate the importance of class, limit their perspectives, accept their situ-

ation reluctantly or with satisfaction. They may see the benefits of society flowing to their own class, however they define it. They tend to believe that each person's status is in some way deserved.

How would these lower middle and working class men feel about a change in the social order such that they and their friends might suddenly be equal to others now higher or lower in the social order? Most of them wouldn't like it. They would fear and resent this kind of equality.

ABANDONMENT OF A RATIONALE

Changing ideas is a strain not to be lightly incurred, particularly when these ideas are intimately related to one's self-esteem. The less education one has, the harder it is to change such ideas. Painfully these men have elaborated an explanation for their situation in life; it helps explain things to their wives who take their status from them; it permits their growing children to account for relative social status in school; it offers to each man the satisfactions of social identity and a measure of social worth. Their rationales are endowed with moral qualities; the distribution of values in the society is seen as just and natural. While it gives satisfactions of an obvious kind to those who contemplate those beneath them, it also gives order and a kind of reassurance, oddly enough, to those who glance upwards towards "society" or "the four hundred." This reassurance is not unlike the reassurance provided by the belief in a Just God while injustices rain upon one's head. The feudal serf, the Polish peasant, the Mexican peon believed that theirs was a moral and a "natural order"—so also the American working man.

THE PROBLEM OF SOCIAL ADJUSTMENT

Equality would pose problems of social adjustments, of manners, of how to behave. Here is Sokolsky, unprepossessing, uneducated, and nervous, with a more prosperous brother in the same town. "I'm not going to go over there," he says, "because every time I go there I feel uncomfortable." On the question of rising from one social class to another, his views reflect this personal situation:

> I think it's hard. Let's say—let's take me, for instance. Supposing I came into a lot of money, and I moved into a nice neighborhood—class—maybe

I wouldn't know how to act then. I think it's very hard, because people know that you just—word gets around that you . . . never had it before you got it now. Well, maybe they wouldn't like you . . . maybe you don't know how to act.

The kind of equality with others which would mean a rapid rise in his own status is a matter of concern, mixed, of course, with pleasant anticipation at the thought of "telling off" his brother.

Consider the possibility of social equality including genuine fraternization, without economic equality. Sullivan, a railroad fireman, deals with this in graphic terms:

> What is the basis of social class? Well, things that people have in common . . . Money is one, for instance, like I wouldn't feel very comfortable going around with a millionaire, we'll say . . . He could do a lot and say a lot—mention places he'd been and so on—I mean I wouldn't be able to keep up with him . . . and he wouldn't have to watch his money, and I'd have to be pinching mine to see if I had enough for another beer, or something.

And, along the lines of Sokolsky's comments, Sullivan believes that moving upwards in the social scale is easier if one moves to a new place where one has not been known in the old connection. Flynn holds that having the right interests and conversational topics for the new and higher social group will make it possible—but otherwise it could be painful. Kuchinsky, the house painter, says "I suppose it would feel funny to get into a higher class, but I don't believe I would change. I wouldn't just disregard my friends if I came into any money." Clinging to old friends would give some security in that dazzling new world.

De Angelo, a factory operative, also considers the question of whether the higher status people will accept the *arriviste*, but for himself, he dismisses it:

> I wouldn't worry much about whether they would accept or they wouldn't accept. I would move into another class. I mean—I mean—I don't worry much about that stuff. If people don't want to bother with me, I don't bother with them, that's all.

These fears, while plausible and all too human on the face of it, emerged unexpectedly from the interview material designed to capture ideas and emotions on other aspects of class status. They highlight a resistance to equalitarian movements that might bring the working class and this rejecting superior class—whether it is imaginary or not—in close association. If these were revolutionaries, one might phrase their anxieties: "Will my victims accept me?" But they are not revolutionaries.

These are problems of rising in status to meet the upper classes face to face. But there is another risk in opening the gates so that those of moderate circumstances can rise to higher status. Equality of opportunity, it appears, is inherently dangerous in this respect: There is the risk that friends, neighbors, or subordinates will surpass one in status. O'Hara has this on his mind. Some of the people who rise in status are nice, but:

> You get other ones, the minute they get a little, they get big-headed and they think they're better than the other ones—where they're still—to me they're worse than the middle class. I mean, they should get down, because they're just showing their illiteracy—that's all they're doing.

Sokolsky worries about this possibility, too, having been exposed to the slights of his brother's family. But the worry over being passed by is not important, not salient. It is only rarely mentioned.

Deprivation of a Meritorious Elite

It is comforting to have the "natural leaders" of a society well entrenched in their proper place. If there were equality there would no longer be such an elite to supervise and take care of people—especially "me." Thus Woodside, our policeman, reports:

> I think anybody that has money—I think their interest is much wider than the regular working man. . . . And therefore I think that the man with the money is a little bit more educated; for the simple reason he has the money, and he has a much wider view of life—because he's in the knowledge of it all the time.

Here and elsewhere in the interview, one senses that Woodside is glad to have such educated, broad-gauged men in eminent positions. He certainly opposes the notion of equality of income. Something similar creeps into Johnson's discussion of social classes. He feels that the upper classes, who "seem to be very nice people," are "willing to lend a helping hand—to listen to you. I would say they'd help you out more than the middle class [man] would help you out even if he was in a position to help you out." Equality, then, would deprive society, and oneself, of a group of friendly, wise, and helpful people who occupy the social eminences.

THE LOSS OF THE GOALS OF LIFE

But most important of all, equality, at least equality of income, would deprive people of the goals of life. Every one of the 15 clients with whom I spent my evenings for seven months believed that equality of income would deprive men of their incentive to work, achieve, and develop their skills. These answers ranged, in their sophistication and approach, across a broad field. The most highly educated man in the sample, Farrel, answers the question "How would you feel if everyone received the same income in our society?" by saying:

> I think it would be kind of silly . . . Society, by using income as a reward technique, can often insure that the individuals will put forth their best efforts.

He does not believe, for himself, that status or income are central to motivation—but for others, they are. Woodside, our policeman, whose main concern is not the vistas of wealth and opportunity of the American dream, but rather whether he can get a good pension if he should have to retire early, comes forward as follows:

> I'd say that [equal income]—that is something that's pretty—I think it would be a dull thing, because life would be accepted—or it would— rather we'd go stale. There would be no initiative to be a little different, or go ahead.

Like Woodside, Flynn, a white collar worker, responds with a feeling of personal loss—the idea of such an equality of income would make him feel "very mad." Costa, whose ambitions in life are most modest, holds that equality of income "would eliminate the basic thing about the wonderful opportunity you have in this country." Then, for a moment the notion of his income equaling

that of the professional man passes pleasantly through his mind: "don't misunderstand me—I like the idea"; then again, "I think it eliminates the main reason why people become engineers and professors and doctors."

Rapuano, whose worries have given him ulcers, projects himself into a situation where everyone receives the same income, in this case a high one:

> If everyone had the same income of a man that's earning $50,000 a year, and he went to, let's say 10 years of college to do that, why hell, I'd just as soon sit on my ass as go to college and wait till I could earn $50,000 a year, too. Of course, what the hell am I going to do to earn $50,000 a year— now that's another question.

But however the question is answered, he is clear that guaranteed equal incomes would encourage people to sit around on their anatomy and wait for their pay checks. But he would like to see some levelling, particularly if doctors, whom he hates, were to have their fees and incomes substantially reduced.

THAT THESE SACRIFICES
SHALL NOT HAVE BEEN IN VAIN

The men I talked to were not at the bottom of the scale; not at all. They were stable breadwinners, churchgoers, voters, family men. They achieved this position in life through hard work and sometimes bitter sacrifices. They are distinguished from the lower classes through their initiative, zeal, and responsibility, their willingness and ability to postpone pleasures or to forego them entirely. In their control of impulse and desire they have absorbed the Protestant ethic. At least six of them have two jobs and almost no leisure. In answering questions on "the last time you remember having a specially good time" some of them must go back ten to fifteen years. Nor are their good times remarkable for their spontaneous fun and enjoyment of life. Many of them do not like their jobs, but stick to them because of their family responsibilities—and they do not know what else they would rather do. In short, they have sacrificed their hedonistic inclinations, given up good times, expended their energy and resources in order to achieve and maintain their present tenuous hold on respectability and middle status.

Now in such a situation to suggest that men be equalized and the lower orders raised and one's own hard-earned status given to them as a right and not a reward for effort, seems to them desperately wrong. In the words of my research assistant, David Sears, "Suppose the Marshall Plan had provided a block and tackle for Sisyphus after all these years. How do you think he would have felt?" Sokolsky, Woodside, and Dempsey have rolled the stone to the top of the hill so long, they despise the suggestion that it might have been in vain. Or even worse, that their neighbors at the foot of the hill might have the use of a block and tackle.

THE WORLD WOULD COLLAPSE

As a corollary to the view that life would lose its vigor and its savor with equality of income, there is the image of an equalitarian society as a world running down, a chaotic and disorganized place to live. The professions would be decimated: "People pursue the higher educational levels for a reason—there's a lot of rewards, either financial or social," says Costa. Sullivan says, "Why should people take the headaches of responsible jobs if the pay didn't meet the responsibilities?" For the general society, Flynn, a white collar man, believes that "if there were no monetary incentive involved, I think there'd be a complete loss. It would stop all development—there's no doubt about it." McNamara, a bookkeeper, sees people then reduced to a dead level of worth: with equal income "the efforts would be equal and pretty soon we would be worth the same thing." In two contrasting views, both suggesting economic disorganization, Woodside believes "I think you'd find too many men digging ditches, and no doctors," while Rapuano believes men would fail to dig ditches or sewers "and where the hell would we be when we wanted to go to the toilet?"

Only a few took up the possible inference that this was an attractive, but impractical ideal—and almost none followed up the suggestion that some equalization of income, if not complete equality, would be desirable. The fact of the matter is that these men, by and large, prefer an inequalitarian society, and even prefer a society graced by some men of great wealth. As they look out upon the social scene, they feel that an equalitarian society would present them with too many problems of moral adjustment, interpersonal social adjustment,

and motivational adjustment which they fear and dislike. But perhaps, most important, their life goals are structured around achievement and success in monetary terms. If these were taken away, life would be a desert. These men view the possibility of an equalitarian world as a paraphrased version of Swinburne's lines on Jesus Christ, "Thou hast conquered, oh pale equalitarian, and the world has grown gray with thy breath."

VIII. Some Theoretical Implications

Like any findings on the nature of men's social attitudes and beliefs, even in such a culture-bound inquiry as this one, the new information implies certain theoretical propositions which may be incorporated into the main body of political theory. Let us consider seven such propositions growing more or less directly out of our findings on the fear of equality:

1. The greater the emphasis in a society upon the availability of "equal opportunity for all," the greater the need for members of that society to develop an acceptable rationalization for their own social status.
2. The greater the strain on a person's self-esteem implied by a relatively low status in an open society, the greater the necessity to explain this status as "natural" and "proper" in the social order. Lower status people generally find it less punishing to think of themselves as correctly placed by a just society than to think of themselves as exploited, or victimized by an unjust society.
3. The greater the emphasis in a society upon equality of opportunity, the greater the tendency for those of marginal status to denigrate those lower than themselves. This view seems to such people to have the factual or even moral justification that if the lower classes "cared" enough they could be better off. It has a psychological "justification" in that it draws attention to one's own relatively better status and one's own relatively greater initiative and virtue.
4. People tend to care less about *equality* of opportunity than about the availability of *some* opportunity. Men do not need the same life chances as everybody else, indeed they usually care very little about that. They need only

chances (preferably with unknown odds) for a slightly better life than they now have. Thus: Popular satisfaction with one's own status is related less to equality of opportunity than to the breadth of distribution of some opportunity for all, however unequal this distribution may be. A man who can improve his position one rung does not resent the man who starts on a different ladder half way up.

These propositions are conservative in their implications. The psychological roots of this conservatism must be explored elsewhere, as must the many exceptions which may be observed when the fabric of a social order is so torn that the leaders, the rich and powerful, are seen as illegitimate—and hence "appropriately" interpreted as exploiters of the poor. I maintain, however, that these propositions hold generally for the American culture over most of its history—and also, that the propositions hold for most of the world most of the time. This is so even though they fly in the face of much social theory—theory often generalized from more specialized studies of radicalism and revolution. Incidentally, one must observe that it is as important to explain why revolutions and radical social movements do *not* happen as it is to explain why they do.

The more I observed the psychological and physical drain placed upon my sample by the pressures to consume—and therefore to scratch in the corners of the economy for extra income—the more it appeared that competitive consumption was not a stimulus to class conflict, as might have been expected, but was a substitute for or a sublimation of it. Thus we would say:

5. The more emphasis a society places upon consumption—through advertising, development of new products, and easy installment buying—the more will social dissatisfaction be channeled into intra-class consumption rivalry instead of inter-class resentment and conflict. The Great American Medicine Show creates consumer unrest, working wives, and dual-job-holding, not antagonism toward the "owning classes."

6. As a corollary of this view: The more emphasis a society places upon consumption, the more will labor unions focus upon the "bread and butter" aspects of unionism, as contrasted to

its ideological elements.

We come, finally, to a hypothesis which arises from this inquiry into the fear of equality but goes much beyond the focus of the present study. I mention it here in a speculative frame of mind, undogmatically, and even regretfully:

7. The ideals of the French Revolution, liberty and equality, have been advanced because of the accidental correspondence between these ideals and needs of the bourgeoisie for freedom of economic action and the demands of the working class, very simply, for "more." Ideas have an autonomy of their own, however, in the sense that once moralized they persist even if the social forces which brought them to the fore decline in strength. They become "myths"—but myths erode without support from some major social stratum. Neither the commercial classes nor the working classes, the historical beneficiaries of these two moralized ideas (ideals or myths), have much affection for the ideals in their universal forms. On the other hand, the professional classes, particularly the lawyers, ministers, and teachers of a society, very often do have such an affection. It is they, in the democratic West, who serve as the "hard core" of democratic defenders, in so far as there is one. It is they, more frequently than others, who are supportive of the generalized application of the ideals of freedom and equality to all men. This is not virtue, but rather a different organization of interests and a different training. Whatever the reason, however, it is not to "The People," not to the business class, not to the working class, that we must look for the consistent and relatively unqualified defense of freedom and equality. The professional class, at least in the American culture, serves as the staunchest defender of democracy's two greatest ideals.

NOTES

1. Erich Fromm, *Escape from Freedom* (New York: Rinehart, 1941).
2. One way of finding out whether these working class men reported their "true feelings"—the ones which form the basis of their relevant behavior and thought—to the listening professor, is to find out how they talk to each other. Fortunately, we have some evidence on this in the tran-

scribed protocols of discussions where two groups of three men each, selected from the fifteen reported on here, argued with each other, without an interviewer present, on the job performance of certain public officials. In these discussions the main themes reported on below are apparent. Illustrative of one of these themes is Costa's remark to Woodside and O'Hara: "If you're the business man and I'm the working man, I don't care if you make a hundred million dollars a year, as long as I make a living. In other words, you got your money invested. You're supposed to make money." And O'Hara then chimes in "That's right."

3. Brackets are used here and below to distinguish inferred meanings or imputed statements from direct quotations.

4. Robert K. Merton, *Mass Persuasion; The Social Psychology of a War Bond Drive* (New York: Harper, 1946).

5. Contrast de Tocqueville: "I never met in America a citizen so poor as not to cast a glance of hope and envy on the enjoyments of the rich or whose imagination did not possess itself by anticipation of those good things that fate still obstinately withheld from him." *Democracy in America* (New York: Vintage ed.), Vol. II, p. 137.

Cognitive Style and Political Belief Systems in the British House of Commons

Philip E. Tetlock • University of California, Berkeley

This study used the integrative complexity coding system to analyze confidential interviews with 89 members of the British House of Commons. The primary goal was to explore the interrelation between cognitive style and political ideology in this elite political sample. The results indicated that moderate socialists interpreted policy issues in more integratively complex or multidimensional terms than did moderate conservatives who, in turn, interpreted issues in more complex terms than extreme conservatives and extreme socialists. The latter two groups did not differ significantly from each other. These relations between integrative complexity and political ideology remained significant after controlling for a variety of belief and attitudinal variables. The results are interpreted in terms of a value pluralism model that draws on Rokeach's two-value analysis of political ideology and basic principles of cognitive consistency theory.

Individuals obviously vary widely in the political views that they endorse. Less obviously, people also differ in their styles of thinking about political issues. For instance, some people rely on a few broad principles or generalizations in interpreting events, reject inconsistent evidence, and have little tolerance for alternative viewpoints. Others interpret events in more flexible, multidimensional ways and attempt to develop perspectives that integrate a wide range of information and values specific to the problem at hand (cf. Lasswell, 1948; Putnam, 1971; Rokeach, 1960; Sidanius, 1978; Suedfeld & Rank, 1976; Taylor, 1960; Tetlock, 1981a, 1981b).

Researchers have shown substantial interest in the interrelations between content and stylistic dimensions of political thought. The key question has been: Do persons who differ in cognitive style (i.e., their characteristic ways of organizing and processing information) also differ in the political views they typically endorse? Two hypotheses have dominated psychological speculation on this topic: the "rigidity-of-the-right" and ideologue hypotheses.

The rigidity-of-the-right hypothesis is derived largely from the well-known studies of the authoritarian personality (Adorno, Frenkel-Brunswik, Levinson, & Sanford, 1950; Sanford, 1973). According to authoritarian personality theory, people often develop extremely conservative political-economic opinions as means of coping with deep-rooted psychodynamic conflicts that can be traced to early childhood. Conservative attitudes in this view frequently serve ego-defensive functions. Individuals who identify with the sociopolitical right are therefore more likely than persons who identify with the sociopolitical center and left to feel threatened by ambiguous or belief-challenging events. One result is that extreme conservatives, in their attempts to maintain psychological equilibrium, are especially prone to view issues in rigid, dichotomous (good vs. bad) terms. Other investigators, working from different theoretical assumptions, have reached similar conclusions (e.g., McClosky, 1967; Wilson, 1973).

Advocates of the ideologue hypothesis were quick to note, however, the insensitivity of this analysis to "authoritarianism of the left" (Rokeach, 1956; Shils, 1956; Taylor, 1960). According to the ideologue hypothesis, adherents of movements of the left and right are much more similar to each other in cognitive style than they are to individuals near the center of the political spectrum. Differences in the content of left-wing and right-wing belief systems should not be allowed to obscure fundamental similarities in how ideologues organize and process political information. "True believers" (regardless of their cause) are more likely to view issues in rigid, dichotomous terms than are individuals who take less extreme or polarized political positions.

Most empirical work on this topic has involved the mass administration of personality and attitude scales to survey respondents or college students. Stone (1980) has concluded in a recent review of this literature that the preponderance of the evidence is consistent with the rigidity-of-the-right hypothesis and inconsistent with the ideologue hypothesis. He noted that across a variety of measurement instruments and subject populations, right-wing respondents usually appear to be more dogmatic, intolerant of ambiguity, and cognitively simple than their left-wing or moderate counterparts (e.g., Barker, 1963; McClosky, 1967; Neuman, 1981; Sidanius, 1978; Wilson, 1973). These findings do not, of course, indicate that there is no authoritarianism of the left (Eysenck, 1981). They indicate only that in 20th-century Western democracies (e.g., Britain, United States, Sweden) certain cognitive stylistic traits occur more frequently among members of the public conventionally classified as being on the sociopolitical right.

In the last few years, investigators have also begun to explore the relation between cognitive style and ideology in samples of political elites or leaders. One approach to this issue has been to develop research methods such as content analysis that permit the assessment of political leaders "at a distance" (Hermann, 1977; Suedfeld & Rank,

1976; Tetlock, 1981a, 1983b; Winter & Stewart, 1977). For instance, Tetlock (1983a) used the integrative complexity coding system to explore the relation between cognitive style and ideology in the United States Senate. This coding system, originally developed for scoring open-ended responses to a semiprojective test designed to measure individual differences in integrative complexity (Schroder, Driver, & Streufert, 1967), has proven to be a flexible methodological tool that can be adapted to analyze a wide range of archival documents, including the letters, diaries, and speeches of political elites (e.g., Levi & Tetlock, 1980; Suedfeld & Rank, 1976; Suedfeld & Tetlock, 1977; Tetlock, 1979, 1981a, 1981b).

The actual coding rules define integrative complexity in terms of two cognitive structural variables: differentiation and integration (see Schroder et al., 1967; Streufert & Streufert, 1978; Tetlock, 1979, 1981a; 1981b). Individuals at the simple end of the complexity continuum tend to rely on fixed, one-dimensional evaluative rules in interpreting events and to make decisions on the basis of only a few salient items of information. Individuals at the complex end tend to interpret events in multidimensional terms and to integrate a variety of evidence in making decisions. (See the Method section for more detail.)

Tetlock (1983a) attempted to test the rigidity-of-the-right and ideologue hypotheses by assessing the integrative complexity of speeches given by United States senators with extremely liberal, moderate, or extremely conservative voting records. He found that senators with extremely conservative voting records in the 94th Congress made less integratively complex policy statements than their moderate or liberal colleagues. This finding remained significant after controlling for the influence of a number of potential confounding variables, including political party affiliation, education, age, years of service in the Senate, and types of issues discussed.

Although these results converge impressively with previous work on non-elite samples that supports the rigidity-of-the-right hypothesis, two problems complicate interpretation of the findings. The first problem stems from relying on public statements for inferring the cognitive styles of senators. Public policy statements may shed more light on how senators seek to influence other political actors (colleagues, the executive branch of government, the press, special interest groups) than on how senators actually think about policy issues. In short, conservatives may differ from liberals and moderates in rhetorical style, not cognitive style.

The second problem stems from the limited ideological range of positions represented in the United States Senate. A defender of the ideologue hypothesis could argue that there were not enough representatives of the ideological left to provide a fair test of the hypothesis (i.e., there is no influential socialist or communist party in the United States). This line of argument, however, gains force only to the extent its advocates can offer an explicit and defensible (as opposed to ad hoc) rationale for why the ideologue hypothesis applies only to the far left. How far must one go to the sociopolitical left and why?

Tetlock (1983a) offered a theoretical model of the relation between cognitive style and ideology that addresses this key issue. The model draws on Rokeach's (1973, 1979) two-value analysis of political ideology as well as Abelson's (1959) work on modes of resolving cognitive inconsistency. Following Rokeach (1973), the model assumes that the major ideological movements of the 20th century—communism, democratic socialism, laissez-faire or conservative capitalism, and fascism—vary in the importance they attach to the basic and often conflicting values of individual freedom and social equality. Briefly, laissez-faire capitalists and democratic socialists value freedom highly, whereas communists and fascists do not. In contrast, communists and democratic socialists value equality highly, but capitalists and fascists do not.

Following Abelson (1959), the model also assumes that people prefer simple or least-effort modes of resolving cognitive inconsistency whenever feasible. Simple modes of resolving inconsistency are feasible when competing values such as freedom and equality are of unequal strength. It is then easy to deny the importance of one of the competing values or to bolster the importance of the other value. In contrast, when competing values are of approximately equal strength, denial and bolstering are much less plausible modes of inconsistency reduction. People must turn to more complex and effort-demanding strategies such as differentiation (e.g., distinguishing the impact of policies on the two competing values) and integration or transcendence (e.g., developing rules for coping with conflicts between values). Because

there is often a tension or trade-off between equality and freedom (especially economic freedom) in policy debates, advocates of ideologies (liberals, social democrats) that attach relatively high importance to both values should feel much greater pressure to rely on integratively complex modes of inconsistency reduction than advocates of ideologies (communists, laissez-faire capitalists, fascists) that attach high importance to only one or neither of these values. In short, the value pluralism of an ideology may determine both the frequency with which people experience cognitive inconsistency and the complexity of the strategies they typically use to cope with inconsistency.

This value pluralism model of the relation between cognitive style and ideology has two noteworthy advantages. First, it explains why several studies have found that advocates of moderate left-wing causes interpret issues in more flexible, multidimensional ways than advocates of conservative or right-wing causes. The traditional ideologue hypothesis, which emphasizes deviation from a vaguely defined political center, is hard pressed to explain these findings. Second, the value pluralism model specifies how far to the sociopolitical left one must go for integrative complexity to fall off: to the point at which concern for equality consistently dominates concern for individual rights and liberties (radical socialists, communists).

The current study provides a stronger test of the relation between cognitive style and ideology in an elite sample than the earlier Tetlock study of senators. The data consist of verbatim transcripts of confidential interviews that the political scientist Putnam (1971) conducted with members of the British House of Commons. There is good reason to believe that political impression management motives exerted much less influence on what the politicians said in this setting than in more public settings such as press conferences or the House of Commons. The politicians interviewed were willing on several occasions to criticize their own party and even themselves in the course of the discussions. In addition, the politicians examined in this study represented a wider variety of ideological positions than exists in the United States Senate. The parliamentarians included "extreme socialists" (who favored the nationalization of all major businesses and industries), "moderate socialists" (who favored limited expansion of public control of the economy), "moderate conservatives" (who favored limited denationalization of industry), and "extreme conservatives" (who opposed any government intervention in the economy).

The primary goal of this study was to test alternative (although not mutually exclusive) hypotheses on the relation between cognitive style and ideology by assessing the integrative complexity of the parliamentarians in the Putnam sample. For instance, the rigidity-of-the-right hypothesis leads us to expect that extremely conservative members of Parliament will be less integratively complex than their moderate conservative and socialist colleagues. The ideologue hypothesis leads us to expect that extreme conservatives and extreme socialists will be less integratively complex than their moderate conservative and moderate socialist colleagues. Finally, the value pluralism model leads us to expect that moderate socialists (who, according to Rokeach [1973], place approximately equal importance on freedom and equality) will be more integratively complex than members of all three other ideological groups (who either value freedom over equality, like conservatives, or value equality over freedom, like extreme socialists). In addition, the value pluralism model predicts that moderate conservatives will be more integratively complex than extreme conservatives (because moderate conservatives attach closer to equal importance to freedom and equality than do extreme conservatives).

The study reported here also had other theoretical objectives. These included (a) assessing the stability or consistency of parliamentarians' integrative complexity scores derived from the interviews (How reliable is our measure of individual differences in integrative complexity?), and (b) exploring the relations among ideology, integrative complexity, and a variety of measures of political beliefs and attitudes that Putnam developed.

Method

Background to the Study

The study is based on analyses of transcripts of interviews that Putnam (1971) conducted with members of the British House of Commons in 1967. Of an initial randomly drawn sample of 110 parliamentarians, 93 (85%) were interviewed. Putnam reported that the individuals interviewed faithfully reflected the composition of the entire Parliament (635 members) over a wide range of characteristics (e.g., party affiliation, age, education, social class, parliamentary seniority, and political importance).

Putnam and two assistants performed the interviews. Before each session, the interviewers informed respondents of the purpose of the study (a cross-cultural investigation of elite political culture) and assured them of the absolute confidentiality of their responses. The interviewers relied primarily on open-ended questions (in part, because the parliamentarians balked at the forced-choice format typically used in survey research). Although the interviewers tried (generally successfully) to keep questioning as constant as possible across sessions, they permitted some flexibility to "maintain the tone of a genuine conversation" (Putnam 1971, p. 19). The interviews always began with questions concerning the personal background of the respondent—his or her career path, likes and dislikes of political life, and general view of problems facing Great Britain. Respondents then discussed two current policy issues and the policymaking process. At this point, the interview turned to a variety of additional topics, including the "essential characteristics" of democracy, the differences between the two major political parties, the nature of social and political conflict, and the type of society the respondent desired for the future. The average interview lasted for 75 min. Interviews were audiotaped and transcribed verbatim.

Integrative Complexity Coding

We randomly sampled 10 paragraph-sized statements for integrative complexity scoring from the interview protocols of each of 89 parliamentarians. The estimated average length of the paragraphs sampled was 80 words. There were no significant differences in the length of material sampled from the different ideological groups of parliamentarians.

All material was coded for integrative complexity on a 7-point scale (Schroder et al., 1967). The scale defines integrative complexity in terms of two variables: differentiation and integration. Differentiation refers to the number of characteristics or dimensions of a problem that are taken into account in decision making. For instance, a decision maker might analyze policy issues in an undifferentiated way by placing options into one of two value-laden categories: the "good socialist policies," which promote redistribution of wealth, and the "bad capitalist policies," which preserve or exacerbate inequality. A highly differentiated approach would recognize that different policies can have multiple, sometimes contradictory, effects that cannot be readily classified on a single evaluative dimension of judgment—for example, effects on the size of the government deficit, interest rates, inflation, unemployment, the balance of trade, and a host of other economic and political variables. Integration refers to the development of complex connections among differentiated characteristics. (Differentiation is thus a prerequisite for integration.) The complexity of integration depends on whether the decision maker perceives the differentiated characteristics as operating in isolation (low integration), in first-order or simple interactions (the effects of A on B depend on levels of C, moderate integration), or in multiple, contingent patterns (high integration).

Scores of 1 reflect low differentiation and low integration. For instance:

> The key problem is that we [the British] have been living way beyond our means for far too long. We have to tighten our belts. Nobody likes to face this unpleasant truth, but that's the way it is. Our standard of living will inevitably fall. It is as straightforward as that. I don't think anyone in touch with current economic reality can deny that.

Scores of 3 reflect moderate or high differentiation and low integration. For instance:

> In politics, of course, it is not only a question of doing what is right or best for the country. It's also a question of what you can carry. An incomes policy [limits on wage increases] is needed to get our economic house in order. But it would be political suicide to go whole hog and impose a straight-jacket policy.

Scores of 5 reflect moderate or high differentiation and moderate integration. For instance:

> The Opposition responded in two seemingly contradictory ways to the steel bill [to nationalize the industry]. They had to go through some ritual posturing to show the colonels in their constituencies they were doing a good job. But they also had some serious suggestions for improving the bill which they knew full well was going to pass.

So they behaved constructively in committee working on technical details, but were strident opponents when more in the public eye.

Scores of 7 reflect high differentiation and high integration. For instance:

> We always have to deal with competing priorities in making up the budget. Most basically, we face the tension between the need to fund social welfare programs to which we are committed and the need to stimulate private sector expansion. But there is no simple rule to resolve that tension. A lot depends on factors that are to some extent beyond our control: the state of the pound, our trade balance, unemployment, and those sorts of things. Usually no one is very satisfied: we end up with different priorities in different years and wind up looking rather inconsistent.

Scores of 2, 4, and 6 represent transition points between adjacent levels.

It should be emphasized that the complexity coding system focuses on the cognitive structure, not the content, of expressed beliefs and is therefore not biased for or against any particular philosophy. One can be simple or complex in the advocacy of a wide range of political positions. For instance, Karl Marx and Adam Smith developed highly integratively complex arguments to support polar opposite positions on fundamental issues of economic policy (communism vs. capitalism). A corollary of the above point is that there is no necessary relation between integrative complexity and the correctness of the positions taken by individuals (Tetlock, 1983a).

Statements were coded for integrative complexity by three trained scorers who were unaware of the hypotheses to be tested and the sources of the material. Substantial agreement existed among coders (mean interrater $r = .84$). Disagreements were resolved by discussion among coders and, when necessary, between the coders and the author.

ASSESSING POLITICAL ORIENTATION

Two types of information were used to classify political orientation: (a) party membership (Labour vs. Conservative) and (b) ratings of parliamentarians' responses to a question concerning their views on the proper role of government in regulating the economy and providing social welfare (traditionally divisive issues in British politics). Coders in the Putnam research team rated politicians on a 5-point continuum in which 1 represented an extreme socialist position (support for state control of all major means of production), 2 a moderate socialist position (limited expansion of state control of the economy), 3 a centrist position (for the status quo), 4 a moderate conservative position (reduced state control of the economy), and 5 an extreme conservative position (minimal state control of the economy or classic market capitalism). We classified parliamentarians as extreme socialists if they were members of the Labour Party and favored state control of all major means of production, as moderate socialists if they were members of the Labour Party and favored limited expansion of state control of the economy or the status quo, as moderate conservatives if they were members of the Conservative Party and favored limited reduction of state control of the economy or the status quo and as extreme conservatives if they were members of the Conservative Party and favored virtually total dismantling of state control of the economy. According to these criteria, 12 parliamentarians were classified as extreme socialists, 41 as moderate socialists, 24 as moderate conservatives, and 12 as extreme conservatives.

ADDITIONAL RELEVANT VARIABLES EXAMINED IN THE PUTNAM RESEARCH

The Putnam research team coded the interviews with the parliamentarians for a number of variables that it was reasonable to suspect might be related to integrative complexity. We explored the following possible correlates of integrative complexity:

1. The ideological style index. This index (derived from factor analysis) consists of four interrelated variables: (a) *generalizer-particularizer*, the tendency to discuss issues in terms of abstract principles or in terms of specific details of the problem; (b) *deductive-inductive thinking*, the tendency to deduce positions on issues from abstract theory or to reason inductively from available evidence; (c) *reference to a named ideology*, the tendency to refer to a specific ideology or doctrine such as free enterprise or socialism; and (d) *reference to a future utopia* as a standard for judging policy. The Putnam research team rated each interview for the presence of each variable on 3-point scales. In computing the ideological style index, we stan-

dardized scores on each of the four variables and then gave equal weight to each variable. An individual received a high score on the ideological style index to the extent he or she was a generalizer, exhibited deductive thinking, and referred to a named ideology and a future utopia in evaluating policy alternatives.

2. Use of historical context in discussing issues. Putnam assessed the importance of historical context to a respondent's thinking on a 3-point scale (1 indicating that historical context was a central element in the discussion, 2 indicating that historical context was referred to in passing or vaguely, and 3 indicating that historical context was not important).

3. Moralizing. Putnam assessed the tendency to assign blame for current problems on a 3-point scale (1 indicating that the assignment of blame was a central element in the discussion, 2 indicating that the assignment of blame was referred to in passing, and 3 indicating that blame was not assigned).

4. Extent of party differences. To measure this variable, Putnam coded responses to the question, "All in all, do you think there is a great deal of difference between the parties, some difference, or not much difference?" He used an 8-point scale (1 indicating "very great differences," 4 indicating important differences except for a "limited group which is closer," and 8 indicating not much difference).

5. Tolerance of opposing opinions. Putnam assessed this variable on a 3-point scale (1 indicating the respondent was very intolerant or very unwilling to entertain ideas different from his or her own, 2 indicating the respondent was "somewhat intolerant," and 3 indicating the respondent was tolerant or not at all reluctant to consider opposing ideas).

Results

Figure 13.1 presents the mean integrative complexity of the interview protocols of parliamentarians classified as extreme and moderate conservatives and socialists. We performed a single-factor (ideological classification) analysis of variance on the mean integrative complexity scores of the parliamentarians. This analysis revealed highly significant differences in the integrative complexity of the four

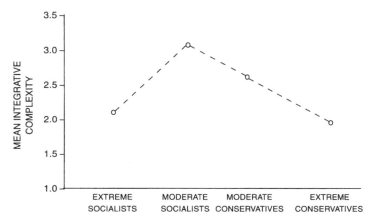

FIGURE 13.1 ■ Mean integrative complexity of members of the British House of Commons.

ideological groups, $F(3.85) = 26.95$, $p < .001$. As the value pluralism model of the relation between cognitive style and ideology predicted, moderate socialists discussed issues in more integratively complex ways than did extreme socialists, moderate conservatives, and extreme conservatives (all comparisons based on the Tukey honestly significant difference test, Winer, 1971). Two other pairwise comparisons were also significant: moderate conservatives were more integratively complex than extreme conservatives, and extreme socialists. There was no difference in the complexity of extreme conservatives and extreme socialists.

An interesting portrait of the integratively complex politician emerges from the correlations between integrative complexity and several belief and attitudinal variables assessed in the Putnam research. The integratively complex politician tended (a) to be politically left of center, $r(87) = -.30$, $p < .01$ (although, as we have seen, the relation between the left-right continuum and complexity is curvilinear); (b) to de-emphasize the differences between the major political parties, $r(87) = .29$, $p < .01$; (c) to be tolerant of opposing viewpoints, $r(87) = .52$, $p < .001$; (d) to think about issues in nonideological terms, $r(87) = .20$, $p = .05$; and (e) to be unconcerned with assigning blame for societal problems, $r(82) = .18$, $p = .05$. In short, integrative complexity is associated with a pragmatic, open-minded, and nonpartisan world view.

We used analysis of covariance to assess whether the relation between integrative complexity and ideology remained significant after controlling for

these belief and attitudinal variables. Three variables emerged as significant covariates: the ideological style index, $F(1, 83) = 3.87$, $p = .05$; tolerance for opposing viewpoints, $F(1, 84) = 54.13$, $p < .001$; and perceptions of the magnitude of the differences between the major political parties, $F(1, 84) = 13.47$, $p < .01$. Interestingly though, none of these analyses substantially altered the conclusions of the earlier analysis of variance. The relation between ideology and integrative complexity continued to be highly significant, and the pattern of mean ideological differences across groups remained essentially unchanged.[1]

Finally, we explored the stability of individual differences among parliamentarians in integrative complexity. One way of viewing the integrative complexity scores assigned to the paragraphs sampled from each of the interview protocols is as items in a test designed to assess the "trait" of integrative complexity. From this perspective, it is appropriate to assess the reliability or internal consistency of the complexity scores. The coefficient alpha of .67 indicates that, although room for improvement certainly exists, the integrative complexity index derived from the protocols has a degree of internal consistency comparable to many self-report measures of traits and attitudes.

Discussion

The results indicated that moderate socialists viewed issues in more integratively complex ways than extreme socialists and moderate and extreme conservatives. Moderate conservatives were, in turn, more integratively complex than extreme conservatives and extreme socialists who were not significantly different from each other. This basic pattern of results held up, moreover, after controlling for a variety of belief and attitudinal variables that Putnam (1971) assessed.

The rigidity-of-the-right hypothesis is hard pressed to explain all of these findings. It can explain why complexity of thought fell as one moved from moderate socialists to moderate conservatives to extreme conservatives (a progression toward increasingly "authoritarian" positions) but not why complexity fell as one moved from moderate to extreme socialists, or why extreme conservatives and extreme socialists interpreted issues in equally integratively simple ways. These latter findings are difficult to explain in terms of a theoretical position that posits a special affinity between support for right-wing causes and rigid, dichotomous thought.

The ideologue hypothesis is in a better position to explain why extreme socialists and conservatives were less complex than their moderate socialist and conservative colleagues. Supporters of this position have long maintained that fundamental cognitive stylistic similarities exist between persons on the far left and the far right. However, the ideologue hypothesis is unable to explain another aspect of the results: the tendency for moderate socialists to be more integratively complex than moderate conservatives. As in earlier studies of United States senators (Tetlock, 1983a) and of non-elite samples (Neuman, 1981; Stone, 1980), why was the point of maximum complexity displaced to the left of center?

The value pluralism model is in the best position to explain these findings. Advocates of ideologies that value both freedom and equality highly are under greater pressure to think about policy issues in integratively complex terms than advocates of ideologies that place much greater weight on one value than the other. Since advocates of moderate socialist causes are most likely to value both freedom and equality highly (Rokeach, 1973), these individuals were more integratively complex than extreme socialists (who valued equality more than freedom) or moderate or extreme conservatives (who valued freedom more than equality). Using similar logic, one can also explain why

moderate conservatives were more complex than extreme conservatives and extreme socialists. A good case can be made that moderate conservatives (by our operational definition, individuals who favored a mixed capitalist economy) attached closer to equal importance to the values of equality and freedom than did extreme conservatives (who supported pure or classic market capitalism) and extreme socialists (who supported virtually total state control of the economy).

Although the value pluralism model fits the data well, we should not overlook possible alternative explanations. One interesting alternative is Eysenck's (1954) two-dimensional model of social attitudes. According to Eysenck, social attitudes are structured around two orthogonal dimensions: radicalism vs. conservatism and tough-mindedness vs. tender-mindedness. Radicalism-conservatism is similar to the familiar left-right continuum. The tough-minded vs. tender-minded dimension is based on William James's analysis of these concepts. The tough-minded person is intolerant of opposition, suspicious, hard-headed, and egotistical; the tender-minded person is tolerant, idealistic, and altruistic. There are reasons for suspecting that variation on this personality trait may partly explain the differences in integrative complexity among ideological groups. For instance, Eysenck and Coulter (1972) found that extremists of the left and right were more tough-minded than moderates. In addition, some studies have found that tough-mindedness is positively correlated with rigidity, dogmatism, and intolerance of ambiguity (Eysenck & Wilson, 1978). This pattern of evidence suggests that the lower integrative complexity of extremists in the current sample is a reflection of their greater tough-mindedness. We cannot completely rule out this possibility; however, two findings cast doubt on the proposition that the tough-minded-tender-minded distinction is sufficient to account for all the data on the relation between ideology and integrative complexity. First, Putnam's measure of tolerance for opposing viewpoints appears to tap a central component of the tough-minded-tender-minded distinction. Analysis of covariance indicated that even though this variable did explain a substantial amount of the variance in the relation between integrative complexity and ideology, highly significant differences continued to exist in the integrative complexity of moderates and extremists. Second, the tough-minded-tender-minded distinction is theoretically orthogonal to radicalism-conservatism (Eysenck & Wilson, 1978). It is therefore difficult to explain why moderate socialists were more integratively complex than moderate conservatives—two groups that, according to Eysenck, should be equally tender-minded.

Another explanation that merits consideration emphasizes the impact of political role on complexity of thought. Previous work on United States presidents and senators suggests that politicians in opposition roles make more simplistic public statements than politicians in policymaking roles (Tetlock, 1981a; Tetlock, Hannum, & Micheletti, 1984). It has been argued that the opposition role grants politicians the rhetorical license to present issues in sharp, black-white ("us against them") terms: the major goal is to rally support for the cause of "throwing the rascals out." In contrast, the policymaking role imposes more reality constraints on rhetoric: politicians must explain and justify unpopular trade-off decisions that inevitably arise in managing complex economic and social systems (cf. Katz & Kahn, 1978). Since the Labour Party was in power during the interviews (1967), an advocate of the political role hypothesis could argue that moderate socialists appeared most complex because they happened to control the government at the time. Again, we cannot completely rule out this possibility; however, there are two reasons to doubt the adequacy of the political role hypothesis. First, the interviews with the parliamentarians were confidential and off the record. Although one can never be sure that respondents were being completely candid and not trying to project a desired social or political image (Putnam, 1971), impression management goals almost certainly exerted less influence on these private interview responses than on the public statements analyzed in earlier studies. Second, the political role hypothesis leaves too many questions unanswered. For instance, why did significant differences in complexity exist between moderate and extreme members of the opposition Conservative Party and moderate and extreme members of the governing Labour Party? Perhaps even more difficult to explain in terms of political role, why were moderate conservatives (in an opposition role) more integratively complex than extreme socialists (at least nominally in a policymaking role)?

Given that the value pluralism model provides the most viable explanation for the current findings, it is appropriate to consider directions that future research might take to refine the model or subject it to further test. One interesting implication of the model is that a reciprocal causal relation exists between cognitive style and political ideology. On the one hand, the value pluralism of a person's ideology may shape how he or she typically thinks about policy issues. Ideologies with one value of overriding importance (monistic ideologies) may encourage adherents to view issues in simple, black-white terms, whereas multivalue ideologies may sensitize adherents to the need to balance competing objectives, often in different ways in different situations. On the other hand, one's cognitive style may shape the value content of one's ideology. Individuals who dislike ambiguity and cognitive inconsistency may be more attracted to monistic than pluralistic ideologies. Such individuals are likely to grow quickly impatient with the difficult trade-offs that pluralistic ideologies require. Detailed longitudinal data are obviously needed to test these hypotheses on the reciprocal effects of cognitive style and ideology on each other.

The value pluralism model also suggests that we should not confidently assume that certain ideological groups will always be more integratively complex than other groups, regardless of the issue being discussed. Ideology-by-issue interactions probably occur in integrative complexity. Interpreted at the most abstract level, the model asserts that people are likely to think about policy issues in complex ways to the degree that two or more approximately equally important values imply contradictory courses of action. For a conservative, this might occur when concern for individual freedom clashes with concern for national security (e.g., domestic C.I.A. operations, compulsory military service). For a liberal or social democrat, this might occur when concern for economic efficiency and growth clashes with concern for equality (e.g., redistributive income policies). A promising avenue for future work is to explore ideology-by-issue variations in complexity of this type.

In conclusion, we raise an issue that all researchers in this area inevitably confront: the issue of whether our own political beliefs and ideals contaminate our research. The authors of *The Authori-*

tarian Personality have been accused of bias against the sociopolitical right; advocates of the ideologue hypothesis have been accused of a centrist bias (against extremism of the left and right). We are potentially vulnerable to the same type of criticism. If one assumes that being integratively complex is always better than being integratively simple (a dubious assumption), we presumably appear biased against monistic and in favor of pluralistic ideologies. For this reason, we shall close with a disclaimer. The research reported here offers no empirical justification for positing a positive or negative relation between integrative complexity of thought and the soundness of the policies advocated. We do not yet understand how integrative complexity is related to the "effectiveness" of high-level policymaking, and, given the difficulty of defining what exactly is sound or effective policymaking, there is little reason to expect the issue to be easily or quickly resolved.

NOTES

1. We also used analysis of covariance to control for the potential confounding influences of age and education. Neither variable was a significant covariate.

REFERENCES

Abelson, R. P. (1959). Modes of resolution of belief dilemmas. *Journal of Conflict Resolution, 3,* 343–352.

Adorno, T., Frenkel-Brunswik, E., Levinson, D., & Sanford, N. (1950). *The authoritarian personality.* New York: Harper.

Barker, E. N. (1963). Authoritarianism of the political right, center and left. *Journal of Social Issues, 19,* 63–74.

Baumeister, R. (1982). A self-presentational view of social phenomena. *Psychological Bulletin, 91,* 3–26.

Eysenck, H. J. (1954). *The psychology of politics.* London: Routledge and Kegan Paul.

Eysenck, H. J. (1981). Left-wing authoritarianism: Myth or reality? *Political Psychology, 3,* 234–239.

Eysenck, H. J., & Coulter, T. T. (1972). The personality and attitudes of working class fascists. *Journal of Social Psychology, 87,* 59–73.

Eysenck, H. J., & Wilson, G. D. (1978). *The psychological sources of ideology.* Lancaster, England: MTP Press.

Hermann, M. G. (1977). *The psychological examination of political leaders.* New York: Free Press.

Katz, D., & Kahn, R. L. (1978). *The social psychology of organizations* (2nd ed.). New York: Wiley.

Lasswell, H. (1948). *Power and personality.* New York: Viking.

Levi, A., & Tetlock, P. E. (1980). A cognitive analysis of Japan's 1941 decision for war. *Journal of Conflict Resolution, 24,* 195–211.

McClosky, H. (1967). Personality and attitude correlates of foreign policy orientation. In J. N. Rosenau (Ed.), *Domestic sources of foreign policy* (pp. 51–109). New York: The Free Press.

Neuman, W. R. (1981). Differentiation and integration in political thinking. *American Journal of Sociology, 86,* 1236–1268.

Putnam, R. (1971). Studying elite culture: The case of ideology. *American Political Science Review, 65,* 651–681.

Rokeach, M. (1956). Political and religious dogmatism: An alternative to the authoritarian personality. *Psychological Monographs, 70* (No. 18, Whole No. 425).

Rokeach, M. (1960). *The open and closed mind: Investigations into the nature of belief systems and personality systems.* New York: Basic Books.

Rokeach, M. (1973). *The nature of human values.* New York: The Free Press.

Rokeach, M. (1979). *Understanding human values: Individual and social.* New York: The Free Press.

Sanford, N. (1973). The authoritarian personality in contemporary perspective. In J. Knutson (Ed.), *Handbook of political psychology.* San Francisco: Jossey-Bass.

Schroder, H. M., Driver, M., & Streufert, S. (1967). *Human information processing.* New York: Holt, Rinehart & Winston.

Shils, E. (1956). Ideology and civility: On the politics of the intellectual. *Sewanee Review, 66,* 450–480.

Sidanius, J. (1978). Intolerance of ambiguity and socio-politico ideology: A multidimensional analysis. *European Journal of Social Psychology, 8,* 215–235.

Stone, W. F. (1980). The myth of left-wing authoritarianism. *Political Psychology, 2,* 3–20.

Streufert, S., & Streufert, S. (1978). *Behavior in the complex environment.* Washington, DC: V. H. Winston.

Suedfeld, P., & Rank, A. D. (1976). Revolutionary leaders: Long-term success as a function of changes in conceptual complexity. *Journal of Personality and Social Psychology, 34,* 169–178.

Suedfeld, P., & Tetlock, P. E. (1977). Integrative complexity of communications in international crises. *Journal of Conflict Resolution, 21,* 169–184.

Taylor, I. A. (1960). Similarities in the structure of extreme attitudes. *Psychological Monographs, 74* (2, Whole No. 489).

Tetlock, P. E. (1979). Identifying victims of groupthink from the public statements of decision makers. *Journal of Personality and Social Psychology, 37,* 1314–1324.

Tetlock, P. E. (1981a). Pre- to postelection shifts in presidential rhetoric: Impression management or cognitive adjustment? *Journal of Personality and Social Psychology, 41,* 207–212.

Tetlock, P. E. (1981b). Personality and isolationism: Content analysis of senatorial speeches. *Journal of Personality and Social Psychology, 41,* 737–743.

Tetlock, P. E. (1983a). Cognitive style and political ideology. *Journal of Personality and Social Psychology, 45,* 118–126.

Tetlock, P. E. (1983b). Psychological research on foreign policy: A methodological overview. In L. Wheeler (Ed.), *Review of personality and social psychology* (Vol. 4, pp. 45–78). Beverly Hills, CA: Sage.

Tetlock, P. E., Hannum, K. A., & Micheletti, P. M. (1984). Stability and change in the complexity of senatorial debate: Testing the cognitive versus rhetorical style hypotheses. *Journal of Personality and Social Psychology, 46,* 979–990.

Thurow, L., (1975). *Generating inequality: Mechanisms of distribution in the U.S. economy.* New York: Basic Books.

Wilson, G. D. (1973). *The psychology of conservatism.* New York: Academic Press.

Winer, B. J. (1971). *Statistical principles of experimental design* (2nd ed.). New York: McGraw-Hill.

Winter, D., & Stewart, A. J. (1977). Content analysis as a technique for assessing political leaders. In M. Hermann (Ed.), *The psychological examination of political leaders* (pp. 27–61). New York: The Free Press.

Challenges of Decision-Making

The work of political psychologists has the capacity to improve decision-making procedures and outcomes in political domains such as domestic affairs and foreign policy (e.g., Renshon & Larson, 2003; Tetlock, 1986; Tyler, 1990). Progress comes in part from analyzing past mistakes, such as the Kennedy administration's mishandling of the Cuban Missile Crisis or the Nixon administration's decision to authorize a burglary of the Watergate offices of the Democratic National Committee (e.g., Cialdini, 2001; Janis, 1982). Because political psychologists study the vices and virtues of human reasoning, they are in a good position to consider implications for how difficult and complex decision-making tasks should be structured and executed by individuals and groups (e.g., Dawes, 1998; Jervis, 1976; Sniderman, Brody, & Tetlock, 1991; Stein, 1988).

Approaches to decision-making typically focus either on *normative* considerations about what people *should do* or on *descriptive* considerations of what people *actually do* (e.g., Simon, 1985). Rational choice theorists in political science borrow cost-benefit analyses of human behavior from economists and apply them to cases of political decision-making (e.g., Arrow, 1951; Downs, 1957; Olson, 1965; see also Green & Shapiro, 1994 for a critique). In doing so, rational choice theorists generally opt for the normative approach (e.g., Coleman & Fararo, 1992; Monroe, 1991). By contrast, most psychologists prefer a descriptive approach and seem to delight in demonstrating all of the ways in which real people (including political decision-makers) deviate from normative standards of rationality (Dawes, 1998; Gilovich, Griffin, & Kahneman, 2002; Kahneman, Slovic, & Tversky, 1982; Thaler, 1994).

Our first reading in this section is by Quattrone and Tversky, who do a fine job of summarizing the major differences between these two approaches. They draw on Kahneman and Tversky's (1979) *prospect theory* to explain the effects of outcome framing (in terms of potential gains vs. losses) on decision-making under risk and incumbency effects in political elections. Quattrone and Tversky join many other researchers in arguing that a descriptive approach that takes into account subjective (psychological) utility functions is better at accounting for actual human decisions than a normative approach that takes into account objective (economic) utility functions.

Robert Jervis, whose earlier (1976) work on misperception in international relations broke new ground in political psychology, is the author of Reading 15. In this chapter, he draws important lessons from social psychological research on the role of cognitive and motivational biases in decision-making under conditions of uncertainty and ambiguity (e.g., Fiske & Taylor, 1991; Nisbett & Ross, 1980). Specifically, Jervis illustrates the ways in which several common biases, including oversimplification, availability, egocentricity, and expectancy confirmation, dangerously affected foreign policy decision-making during World War II and the Cold War. In order to minimize psychological sources of error such as these, Tetlock (1986) has recommended that policymakers be sensitized to their own potential for bias and that procedures such as formal decision analysis and cognitive mapping of implicit and explicit assumptions be implemented as part of a system of checks and balances in the decision-making arena.

Discussion Questions

1. Do you see normative and descriptive analyses as inherently opposed to one another, or can you conceive of ways in which they might be integrated?
2. How would you go about testing Quattrone and Tversky's hypothesized explanation for political incumbency effects by using archival data?
3. Which of the cognitive and motivational biases discussed by Jervis do you think would be minimized by increasing the public accountability of the decision-maker, and which biases do you think would be unaffected (or even made worse) by increased accountability?

Suggested Readings

Arrow, K. J. (1951). *Social choice and individual values*. New Haven, CT: Yale University Press.

Cialdini, R. B. (2001). *Influence: Science and practice*. Boston: Allyn & Bacon.

Coleman, J. S., & Fararo, T. J. (1992). *Rational choice theory: Advocacy and critique*. Newbury Park, CA: Sage.

Dawes, R. M. (1998). Behavioral decision making and judgment. In D. T. Gilbert, S. T. Fiske, & G. Lindzey (Eds.), *The handbook of social psychology* (Vol. 1, pp. 497–548). Boston, MA: McGraw-Hill.

Downs, A. (1957). *An economic theory of democracy*. New York: Harper & Row.

Fiske, S. T., & Taylor, S. E. (1991). *Social cognition* (2nd ed.). New York: McGraw-Hill.

Gilovich, T., Griffin, D., & Kahneman, D. (Eds.) (2002). *Heuristics and biases: The psychology of intuitive judgment*. New York: Cambridge University Press.

Green, D. P., & Shapiro, I. (1994). *Pathologies of rational choice: A critique of applications in political science*. New Haven, CT: Yale University Press.

Janis, I. L. (1982). *Groupthink: Psychological studies of policy decisions and fiascoes* (2nd ed.). Boston: Houghton Mifflin.

Jervis, R. (1976). *Perception and misperception in international politics*. Princeton, NJ: Princeton University Press.

Kahneman, D., Slovic, P., & Tversky, A. (Eds.) (1982). *Judgment under uncertainty: Heuristics and biases*. Cambridge: Cambridge University Press.

Kahneman, D., & Tversky, A. (1979). Prospect theory: An analysis of decision under risk. *Econometrica, 47*, 263-291.

Lebow, R. N. (1981). *Between peace and war: The nature of international crisis*. Baltimore: Johns Hopkins University Press.

Monroe, K. R. (Ed.) (1991). *The economic approach to politics*. New York: Harpers Collins.

Nisbett, R. E., & Ross, L. (1980). *Human inference: Strategies and shortcomings of social judgment*. Englewood Cliffs, NJ: Prentice-Hall.

Olson, M. (1965). *The logic of collective action*. Cambridge, MA: Harvard University Press.

Renshon, S. A., & Larson, D. W. (Eds.) (2003). *Good judgment in foreign policy: Theory and application*. Boulder, CO: Rowman and Littlefield.

Simon, H. A. (1985). Human nature in politics: The dialogue of psychology with political science. *The American Political Science Review, 79*, 293–304.

Sniderman, P. M., Brody, R. A., & Tetlock, P. (1991). *Reasoning and choice*. Cambridge, UK: Cambridge University Press.

Stein, J. G. (1988). Building politics into psychology: The misperception of threat. *Political Psychology, 9*, 245–271.

Tetlock, P. E. (1986). Psychological advice on foreign policy: What do we have to contribute? *American Psychologist, 41*, 555–567.

Thaler, R. H. (1994). *Quasi-rational economics*. New York: Russell Sage Foundation.

Tyler, T. R. (1990). *Why people obey the law*. New Haven, CT: Yale University Press.

Contrasting Rational and Psychological Analyses of Political Choice

George A. Quattrone and Amos Tversky • Stanford University

We contrast the rational theory of choice in the form of expected utility theory with descriptive psychological analysis in the form of prospect theory, using problems involving the choice between political candidates and public referendum issues. The results showed that the assumptions underlying the classical theory of risky choice are systematically violated in the manner predicted by prospect theory. In particular, our respondents exhibited risk aversion in the domain of gains, risk seeking in the domain of losses, and a greater sensitivity to losses than to gains. This is consistent with the advantage of the incumbent under normal conditions and the potential advantage of the challenger in bad times. The results further show how a shift in the reference point could lead to reversals of preferences in the evaluation of political and economic options, contrary to the assumption of invariance. Finally, we contrast the normative and descriptive analyses of uncertainty in choice and address the rationality of voting.

The assumption of individual rationality plays a central role in the social sciences, especially in economics and political science. Indeed, it is commonly assumed that most if not all economic and political agents obey the maxims of consistency and coherence leading to the maximization of utility. This notion has been captured by several models that constitute the rational theory of choice including the expected utility model for decision making under risk, the riskless theory of choice among commodity bundles, and the Bayesian theory for the updating of belief. These models employ different assumptions about the nature of the options and the information available to the decision maker, but they all adopt the principles of coherence and invariance that underlie the prevailing notion of rationality.

The rational theory of choice has been used to prescribe action as well as to describe the behavior of consumers, entrepreneurs, voters, and politicians. The use of the rational theory as a descriptive model has been defended on the grounds that people are generally effective in pursuing their goals, that the axioms underlying the theory are intuitively compelling, and that evolution and competition favor rational individuals over less rational ones. The objections to the rationality assumption were primarily psychological. The human animal, it has been argued, is often controlled by emotions and desires that do not fit the model of calculating rationality. More recent objections to the maximization doctrine have been cognitive rather than motivational. Following the seminal work of Herbert Simon (1955, 1978) and the emergence of cognitive psychology, it has become evident that human rationality is bounded by limitations on memory and computational capabilities. Furthermore, the experimental analysis of inference and choice has revealed that the cognitive machinery underlying human judgment and decision making is often inconsistent with the maxims of rationality. These observations have led to the development of a descriptive analysis of judgment and choice that departs from the rational theory in many significant respects (see, e.g., Abelson & Levi, 1985; Dawes, 1988; Kahneman, Slovic, & Tversky, 1982; Tversky & Kahneman, 1986).

We contrast the rational theory of choice with a descriptive psychological analysis, using a series of questions involving political candidates and public referenda. These problems are used to illustrate the differences between rational and descriptive theories of choice and to test their predictions. Some of the questions probed our respondents' views about familiar political issues, such as the Equal Rights Amendment and the prevalence of crime in Black neighborhoods compared to White neighborhoods. In other cases involving the test of general hypotheses, such as risk aversion, we introduced hypothetical problems in order to achieve experimental control and eliminate the influence of irrelevant factors. The use of hypothetical problems raises obvious questions regarding the generality and the applicability of the finding. Nevertheless, we believe that the use of carefully worded questions can address key issues regarding people's values and beliefs so long as respondents take the questions seriously and have no particular reason to disguise or misrepresent their true preferences. Under these conditions hypothetical questions can be used to compare alternative theories of political choice that cannot be readily tested using available survey and voting data. Our results, of course, do not provide definitive conclusions about political decision making, but they may shed light on the formation of political judgment and stimulate new hypotheses that can be tested in national election surveys in the years to come.

We focus on expected utility theory, which is the major normative theory of decision making under risk (von Neumann & Morgenstern, 1947; Raiffa, 1968; Savage, 1954). This model is contrasted with prospect theory, a descriptive analysis developed by Kahneman and Tversky (1979, 1984). The first section deals with the role of the reference point and its impact on the choice between political candidates. In the second section we test the assumption of invariance and contrast it with a psychophysical analysis of numerical scales. The third section deals with the perception and the weighting of chance events, and the role of uncertainty in choice. The fourth section addresses the classical issue of the rationality of voting. It contrasts, again, a rational analysis based on the probability of casting a decisive vote with a less rational analysis that incorporates an element of self-deception. The implications of the present analysis are discussed in the fifth and final section.

Reference Effects, Risk Attitudes, and Loss Aversion

The standard utility function, derived from the expected utility model, has two essential characteristics. First, it is defined by wealth, or final asset position. Thus, a person with wealth W accepts an even chance to win $1,000 or lose $500 if the difference between the utility of $W + $1,000 and the utility of W (the upside) exceeds the difference between the utility of W and the utility of $W - $500 (the downside). Second, the utility function is concave; that is, the subjective value of an additional dollar diminishes with the total amount of money one has. The first assumption (asset integration) is necessitated by basic considerations of coherence. The second assumption (concavity) was introduced by Bernoulli (1954) to accommodate the common observations of risk aversion, and it has played an essential role in economics. A person is risk-averse if he or she prefers a sure outcome over a risky prospect that has an equal or greater expected value. For example, most people prefer $100 for sure over an even chance to win $200 or nothing. Risk aversion is implied by the concavity of the utility scale because the utility of $2x$ is less than twice the utility of x.

Although risk aversion is quite common, particularly for prospects with positive outcomes, risk seeking is also prevalent, particularly for prospects with negative outcomes. For example, most people find a sure loss of $100 more aversive than an even chance to lose $200 or nothing. To explain the combination of risk aversion and risk seeking, prospect theory replaces the traditional concave utility function for wealth by an S-shaped function for changes of wealth. In this theory, therefore, the carriers of values are positive or negative changes (i.e., gains and losses) defined relative to a neutral reference point. Furthermore, the value function is assumed to be concave above the reference point and convex below it, giving rise to risk aversion in the domain of gains and risk seeking in the domain of losses. As in the classical theory, it is assumed that the difference between $100 and $200 is subjectively larger than the (numerically equivalent) difference between $1,100 and $1,200. Unlike the classical theory, however, it is assumed that the difference between a loss of $100 and a loss of $200 is subjectively larger than the numerically equivalent difference between a loss of $1,100 and a loss of $1,200. Thus, the value function of prospect theory is steepest at the origin and it gets shallower as one moves away from the reference point in either direction. An important property of the value function —called loss aversion—is that the downside is considerably steeper than the upside; that is, losses loom larger than the corresponding gains. A typical value function with these characteristics is given in Figure 14.1.

Attitudes Towards Risk

Expected utility theory and prospect theory yield different predictions. The classical theory predicts risk aversion independent of the reference point,

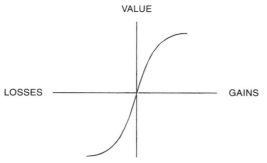

FIGURE 14.1 ■ A hypothetical value function

whereas prospect theory predicts risk aversion in the domain of gains and risk seeking in the domain of losses (except for small probabilities). Furthermore, prospect theory implies that shifts in the reference point induced by the framing of the problem will have predictable effects on people's risk preferences. These phenomena are illustrated in the following four problems, each involving a choice between alternative political prospects.

The respondents to these and other problems reported in this article were undergraduates at Stanford University or at the University of California at Berkeley. The problems were presented in a questionnaire in a classroom setting. Each problem involved a simple choice between two candidates or positions on a public referendum. The respondents were asked to imagine actually facing the choice described, and they were assured that the responses were anonymous and that there were no correct or incorrect answers. The number of respondents in this and all subsequent problems is denoted by N, and the percentage who chose each outcome is given in parentheses.

Problem 1 ($N = 89$)

Suppose there is a continent consisting of five nations, Alpha, Beta, Gamma, Delta, and Epsilon. The nations all have very similar systems of government and economics, are members of a continental common market, and are therefore expected to produce very similar standards of living and rates of inflation. Imagine you are a citizen of Alpha, which is about to hold its presidential election. The two presidential candidates, Brown and Green, differ from each other primarily in the policies they are known to favor and are sure to implement. These policies were studied by Alpha's two leading economists, who are of equal expertise and are impartial as to the result of the election. After studying the policies advocated by Brown and Green and the policies currently being pursued by the other four nations, each economist made a forecast. The forecast consisted of three predictions about the expected standard of living index (SLI). The SLI measures the goods and services consumed (directly or indirectly) by the average citizen yearly. It is expressed in dollars per capita so that the higher the SLI the higher the level of economic prosperity. The three projections concerned.

1. the average SLI to be expected among the nations Beta, Gamma, Delta, and Epsilon
2. the SLI to be expected by following Brown's policy
3. the SLI to be expected by following Green's policy

The forecasts made by each economist are summarized in the following table:

	Projected SLI in Dollars per Capita		
	Other Four Nations	Brown's Policy	Green's Policy
Economist 1	$43,000	$65,000	$51,000
Economist 2	$45,000	$43,000	$53,000

Suppose that as a citizen of Alpha, you were asked to cast your vote for Brown or Green. On the basis of the information provided, whom would you vote for? [Brown, 28%; Green, 72%]

A second group of respondents received the same cover story as in Problem 1, but the economists' forecasts about the other four nations were altered. The forecasts made about the candidates remained the same.

Problem 2 (*N* = 96)

	Projected SLI in Dollars per Capita		
	Other Four Nations	Brown's Policy	Green's Policy
Economist 1	$63,000	$65,000	$51,000
Economist 2	$65,000	$43,000	$53,000

Suppose that as a citizen of Alpha, you were asked to cast your vote for Brown or Green. On the basis of the information provided, whom would you vote for? [Brown, 50%; Green, 50%]

Comparing the responses to problems 1 and 2 shows that the choice between Brown and Green was influenced by the projected SLI in other countries. This effect can be explained in terms of the value function of prospect theory. Because the two economists were said to be impartial and of equal expertise, we assume that respondents gave equal weight to their projections. Hence, the actuarial expected value of Brown's policy ($54,000) is about the same as that of Green's policy ($52,000). However, Brown is riskier than Green in the sense that the outcomes projected for Brown have greater spread than those projected for Green. Therefore, Brown would profit from risk seeking and Green from risk aversion. According to prospect theory,

an individual's attitude towards risk depends on whether the outcomes are perceived as gains or losses, relative to the reference point.

In Problems 1 and 2 it seems reasonable to adopt the average SLI projected for the other nations as a point of reference, because all five nations were said to have comparable standards of living. The reference point then will be about $44,000 in problem 1 and $64,000 in problem 2. Outcomes projected for Brown and Green would, therefore, be treated as gains in the first problem and as losses in the second. As a consequence, the value function entails more risk aversion in problem 1 than in problem 2. In fact, significantly more respondents opted for the relatively risk-free Green in problem 1 (72%) than in problem 2 (50%). Another factor that may have contributed to the finding is a tendency for people to discount the highly discrepant projection for the risky candidate, Brown (i.e., the one made by Economist 1 in problem 1 and by Economist 2 in problem 2). Although this consideration may have played a role in the present case, the same shift in attitudes towards risk have been observed in many other problems in which this account does not apply (Tversky & Kahneman, 1986).

To address whether the predictions based on the value function apply to other attributes besides money, we included in the same questionnaire one of two problems in which the rate of inflation was the outcome of the choice.

Problem 3 (*N* = 76)

Now imagine that several years have passed and that there is another presidential contest between two new candidates, Frank and Carl. The same two economists studied the candidates' preferred policies and made a projection. This time, however, the forecast concerned the projected rate of inflation. The forecasts made by each economist are summarized in the following table:

	Projected Rate of Inflation (%)		
	Other Four Nations	Frank's Policy	Carl's Policy
Economist 1	24	16	4
Economist 2	26	14	26

Suppose that as a citizen of Alpha, you were asked to cast your vote for Frank or Carl. On the basis of the information provided, whom would you vote for? [Frank, 74%; Carl, 26%]

A second group of respondents received the same cover story as in problem 3, but the economists' forecasts about the other four nations were altered. The forecasts made about the candidates remained the same.

Problem 4 (*N* = 75)

	Projected Rate of Inflation (%)		
	Other Four Nations	Frank's Policy	Carl's Policy
Economist 1	4	16	4
Economist 2	6	14	26

Suppose that as a citizen of Alpha, you were asked to cast your vote for Frank or Carl. On the basis of the information provided, whom would you vote for? [Frank, 52%; Carl, 48%]

The analysis of problems 3 and 4 closely follows that of problems 1 and 2. The expected rate of inflation was 15% for both candidates. However, this value was below the expected continental rate of 25% in problem 3 and above the expected continental rate of 5% in problem 4. Because high inflation is undesirable, values below reference are likely to be viewed as gains, whereas values above reference are likely to be viewed as losses. Assuming that the continental rate of inflation was taken as a point of reference, the results confirmed the prediction of prospect theory that the more risky candidate (Carl) would obtain more votes in problem 4 (48%) than in problem 3 (26%).

Together, the responses to problems 1–4 confirm the prediction of prospect theory that people are risk-averse in the domain of gains and risk-seeking in the domain of losses, where gains and losses were defined relative to the outcomes projected for other countries. These results may shed light on the so-called incumbency-oriented voting hypothesis. Numerous investigators have shown that the evaluation of an incumbent party is responsive to fluctuations in the national economy. In general, incumbent presidents and congressional candidates of the same party benefit at the polls from improving economic conditions whereas they suffer from deteriorating conditions (Kramer, 1971). These results can be understood, in part, as a consequence of the divergent attitudes towards risks for outcomes involving gains and losses. Following Shepsle (1972),

we maintain that incumbents are usually regarded by voters as less risky than the challengers, who are often unknowns and whose policies could drastically alter the current trends, for better or for worse. If people are risk-averse for gains and risk-seeking for losses, the less risky incumbent should fare better when conditions are good than when they are bad. This analysis assumes that the re-election of the incumbent is perceived by voters as a continuation of the current trends, which is attractive when times are good. In contrast, the election of the challenger offers a political gamble that is worth taking when "four more years" of the incumbent is viewed as an unsatisfactory state.

It is important to distinguish this analysis of incumbency-oriented voting from the more common explanation that "when times are bad you throw the rascals out." In the latter account, voters are thought to regard a credible challenger as having to be better than the incumbent, who "got us into this mess to begin with." The present account, in contrast, is based on the notion that the challenger is *riskier* than the incumbent, not necessarily better overall. In problems 2 and 4, the risky candidates profit from hard times even though their expected value was no better than that of the relatively riskless candidates. Obviously, however, a challenger whose expected value is substantially below the incumbent's is unlikely to be elected even in the presence of substantial risk seeking.

In light of this discussion, it is interesting to share an unsolicited response given by one of our participants, who received problem 4 in the winter of 1981. This respondent penciled in *Carter* over Frank, the less risky candidate, and *Reagan* over Carl, the riskier candidate. Recall that in this problem the outcomes were less desirable than the reference point. Evidently, our respondent—who voted for Carl—believed that the erstwhile incumbent Carter would have guaranteed the continuation of unacceptable economic conditions, while the erstwhile challenger Reagan, with his risky "new" theories, might have made matters twice as bad as they were or might have been able to restore conditions to a satisfactory level. Because economic and global conditions were widely regarded as unacceptable in 1980, the convexity of the value function for losses may have contributed to the election of a risky presidential prospect, namely Reagan.

Loss Aversion

A significant feature of the value function is that losses loom larger than gains. For example, the displeasure associated with losing a sum of money is generally greater than the pleasure associated with winning the same amount. This property, called *loss aversion*, is depicted in Figure 1 by the steeper slope for outcomes below the reference point than for those above.

An important consequence of loss aversion is a preference for the status quo over alternatives with the same expected value. For example, most people are reluctant to accept a bet that offers equal odds of winning and losing x number of dollars. This reluctance is consistent with loss aversion, which implies that the pain associated with the loss would exceed the pleasure associated with the gain, or $v(x) < -u(-x)$. This observation, however, is also consistent with the concavity of the utility function, which implies that the status quo (i.e., the prospect yielding one's current level of wealth with certainty) is preferred to any risky prospect with the same expected value. These accounts can be discriminated from each other because in utility theory the greater impact of losses than of gains is tied to the presence of risk. In the present analysis, however, loss aversion also applies to riskless choice. Consider the following example: Let $x = (x_i, x_u)$ and $y = (y_i, y_u)$ denote two economic policies that produce inflation rates of x_i and y_i and unemployment rates of x_u and y_u. Suppose $x_i > y_i$ but $x_u < y_u$; that is, y produces a lower rate of inflation than x but at the price of a higher rate of unemployment. If people evaluate such policies as positive or negative changes relative to a neutral multiattribute reference point and if the (multiattribute) value function exhibits loss aversion, people will exhibit a reluctance to trade; that is, if at position x (the status quo) people are indifferent between x and y, then at position y they would not be willing to switch to x (Kahneman & Tversky, 1984). We test this prediction in the following pair of problems.

Problem 5 (*N* = 91)

Imagine there were a presidential contest between two candidates, Frank and Carl. Frank wishes to keep the level of inflation and unemployment at its current level. The rate of inflation is currently at 42%, and the rate of unemployment is currently at 15%. Carl proposes a policy that would decrease the rate of inflation by 19% while increasing the rate of unemployment by 7%. Suppose that as a citizen of Alpha, you were asked to cast your vote for either Frank or Carl. Please indicate your vote. [Frank, 65%; Carl, 35%]

Problem 6 (*N* = 89)

Imagine there were a presidential contest between two candidates, Frank and Carl. Carl wishes to keep the rate of inflation and unemployment at its current level. The rate of inflation is currently at 23%, and the rate of unemployment is currently at 22%. Frank proposes a policy that would increase the rate of inflation by 19% while decreasing the rate of unemployment by 7%. Suppose that as a citizen of Alpha you were asked to cast your vote for either Frank or Carl. Please indicate your vote. [Frank, 39%; Carl, 61%]

It is easy to see that problems 5 and 6 offer the same choice between Frank's policy (42%, 15%) and Carl's policy (23%, 22%). The problems differ only in the location of the status quo, which coincides with Frank's policy in problem 5 and with Carl's policy in problem 6. As implied by the notion of multiattribute loss aversion, the majority choice in both problems favored the status quo. The reluctance to trade is in this instance incompatible with standard utility theory, in which the preference between two policies should not depend on whether one or the other is designated as the status quo. In terms of a two-dimensional value function, defined on changes in inflation and unemployment, the present results imply that both $v(19, -7)$ and $v(-19, 7)$ are less than $v(0,0) = 0$.

We have seen that the combination of risk aversion for gains and risk seeking for losses is consistent with incumbency-oriented voting: incumbents profit from good times, and challengers from bad times. We wish to point out that loss aversion is consistent with another widely accepted generalization, namely that the incumbent enjoys a distinct advantage over the challenger. This effect is frequently attributed to such advantages of holding office as that of obtaining free publicity while doing one's job and being perceived by voters as more experienced and effective at raising funds

(Kiewiet, 1982). To these considerations, the present analysis of choice adds the consequences of the value function. Because it is natural to take the incumbent's policy as the status quo—the reference point to which the challenger's policy is compared—and because losses loom larger than gains, it follows that the incumbent enjoys a distinct advantage. As we argued earlier, the introduction of risk or uncertainty also tends to favor the incumbent under conditions that enhance risk aversion; that is, when the general conditions are good or even acceptable, voters are likely to play it safe and opt for the relatively riskless incumbent. Only when conditions become unacceptable will the risky challenger capture an edge. Hence, the properties of the value function are consistent with the generally observed incumbency effects, as well as with the exceptions that are found during hard times.

Loss aversion may play an important role in bargaining and negotiation. The process of making compromises and concessions may be hindered by loss aversion, because each party may view its own concessions as losses that loom larger than the gains achieved by the concessions of the adversary (Bazerman, 1983; Tversky & Kahneman, 1986). In negotiating over missiles, for example, each superpower may sense a greater loss in security from the dismantling of its own missiles than it senses a gain in security from a comparable reduction made by the other side. This difficulty is further compounded by the fact, noted by several writers (e.g., Lebow & Stein, 1987; Ross, 1986), that the very willingness of one side to make a particular concession (e.g., eliminate missiles from a particular location) immediately reduces the perceived value of this concession.

An interesting example of the role of the reference point in the formation of public opinion was brought to our attention by the actor Alan Alda. The objective of the Equal Rights Amendment (ERA) can be framed in two essentially equivalent ways. On the one hand, the ERA can be presented as an attempt to eliminate discrimination against women. In this formulation, attention is drawn to the argument that equal rights for women are not currently guaranteed by the constitution, a negative state that the ERA is designed to undo. On the other hand, the ERA can be framed as legislation designed to improve women's status in society. This frame emphasizes what is to be gained from the amendment, namely, better status and equal rights for women. If losses loom larger than gains, then support for the ERA should be greater among those who are exposed to the frame that emphasizes the elimination of discrimination than the improvement of women's rights. To test Alda's hypothesis, we presented two groups of respondents with the following question. The questions presented to the two groups differed only in the statement appearing on either side of the slash within the brackets.

Problem 7 ($N = 149$)

> As you know, the Equal Rights Amendment to the Constitution is currently being debated across the country. It says, "Equality of rights under law shall not be denied or abridged by the United States or by any state on account of sex." Supporters of the amendment say that it will [help eliminate discrimination against women/improve the rights of women] in job opportunities, salary, and social security benefits. Opponents of the amendment say that it will have a negative effect by denying women protection offered by special laws. Do you favor or oppose the Equal Rights Amendment? (check one)

Not surprisingly, a large majority of our sample of Stanford undergraduates indicated support for the ERA (74%). However, this support was greater when the problem was framed in terms of eliminating discrimination (78%) than in terms of improving women's rights (69%).

Just as the formulation of the issue may affect the attitude of the target audience, so might the prior attitude of the audience have an effect on the preferred formulation of the issue. Another group of respondents first indicated their opinion on the ERA, either pro or con. They then responded to the following question.

Problem 8 ($N = 421$)

> The status and rights of women have been addressed in two different ways, which have different social and legal implications. Some people view it primarily as a problem of eliminating inequity and discrimination against women in jobs, salary, etc. Other people view it primarily as a problem of improving or strengthening the rights of women in different areas of modern society.

How do you see the problem of women's rights? (check one only)

Of those who indicated support of the ERA, 72% chose to frame the issue in terms of eliminating inequity, whereas only 60% of those who opposed the ERA chose this frame. This finding is consistent with the common observation regarding the political significance of how issues are labeled. A familiar example involves abortion, whose opponents call themselves prolife, not antichoice.

Invariance, Framing, and the Ratio-Difference Principle

Perhaps the most fundamental principle of rational choice is the assumption of invariance. This assumption, which is rarely stated explicitly, requires that the preference order among prospects should not depend on how their outcomes and probabilities are described and thus that two alternative formulations of the same problem should yield the same choice. The responses to problems 7 and 8 above may be construed as a failure of invariance. In the present section, we present sharper tests of invariance in which the two versions of a given choice problem are unquestionably equivalent. Under these conditions, violations of invariance cannot be justified on normative grounds. To illustrate such failures of invariance and motivate the psychological analysis, consider the following pair of problems.

Problem 9 (N = 126)

Political decision making often involves a considerable number of trade-offs. A program that benefits one segment of the population may work to the disadvantage of another segment. Policies designed to lead to higher rates of employment frequently have an adverse effect on inflation. Imagine you were faced with the decision of adopting one of two economic policies.

If program J is adopted, 10% of the work force would be unemployed, while the rate of inflation would be 12%. If program K is adopted, 5% of the work force would be unemployed, while the rate of inflation would be 17%. The following table summarizes the alternative policies and their likely consequences:

Policy	Work Force Unemployed (%)	Rate of Inflation (%)
Program J	10	12
Program K	5	17

Imagine you were faced with the decision of adopting program J or program K. Which would you select? [program J, 36%; program K, 64%]

A second group of respondents received the same cover story about trade-offs with the following description of the alternative policies:

Problem 10 (N = 133)

Policy	Work Force Employed (%)	Rate of Inflation (%)
Program J	90	12
Program K	95	17

Imagine you were faced with the decision of adopting program J or program K. Which would you select? [program J, 54%; program K, 46%]

The modal response was program K in problem 9 and program J in problem 10. These choices constitute a violation of invariance in that each program produces the same outcomes in both problems. After all, to say that 10% or 5% of the work force will be unemployed is to say, respectively, that 90% or 95% of the work force will be employed. Yet respondents showed more sensitivity to the outcomes when these were described as rates of unemployment than as rates of employment. These results illustrate a "psychophysical" effect that we call the *ratio-difference principle.*

Psychophysics is the study of the functional relation between the physical and the psychological value of attributes such as size, brightness, or loudness. A utility function for money, therefore, can also be viewed as a psychophysical scale relating the objective to the subjective value of money. Recall that a concave value function for gains of the form depicted in Figure 14.1 implies that a difference between $100 and $200 looms larger than the objectively equal difference between $200 and $300. More generally, the ratio-difference principle says that the impact of any fixed positive difference between two amounts increases with their ratio. Thus the difference between $200 and $100 yields a ratio of 2, whereas the difference between $300 and $200 yields a ratio of 1.5.

The ratio-difference principle applies to many perceptual attributes. Increasing the illumination of a room by adding one candle has a much larger impact when the initial illumination is poor than when it is good. The same pattern is observed for many sensory attributes, and it appears that the same psychophysical principle is applicable to the perception of numerical differences as well.

Unlike perceptual dimensions, however, numerical scales can be framed in different ways. The labor statistics, for example, can be described in terms of employment or unemployment, yielding the same difference with very different ratios. If the ratio-difference principle applies to such scales, then the change from an unemployment rate of 10% to 5%, yielding a ratio of 2, should have more impact than the objectively equal change from an employment rate of 90% to 95%, yielding a ratio that is very close to unity. As a consequence, program K would be more popular in problem 9 and program J in problem 10. This reversal in preference was obtained, although the only difference between the two problems was the use of unemployment data in problem 9 and employment data in problem 10.

The ratio-difference principle has numerous applications to political behavior. For example, many political choices involve the allocation of limited funds to various sectors of the population. The following two problems demonstrate how the framing of official statistics can effect the perceived need for public assistance.

Problem 11 (*N* = 125)

The country of Delta is interested in reducing the crime rate among its immigrant groups. The Department of Justice has been allocated $100 million ($100M) for establishing a crime prevention program aimed at immigrant youths. The program would provide the youths with job opportunities and recreational facilities, inasmuch as criminal acts tend to be committed by unemployed youths who have little to do with their time. A decision must be made between two programs currently being considered. The programs differ from each other primarily in how the $100M would be distributed between Delta's two largest immigrant communities, the Alphans and the Betans. There are roughly the same number of Alphans and Betans in Delta. Statistics have shown that by the age of 25, 3.7% of all Alphans have a criminal

record, whereas 1.2% of all Betans have a criminal record.

The following two programs are being considered. Program J would allocate to the Alphan community $55M and to the Betan community $45M. Program K would allocate $65M to the Alphan community and to the Betan community $35M. The following table summarizes these alternative programs:

Program	To Alphan Community	To Betan Community
Program J	$55M	$45M
Program K	$65M	$35M

Imagine you were faced with the decision between program J and program K. In light of the available crime statistics, which would you select? [program J, 41%; program K, 59%]

A second group of respondents received the same cover story and program description as in problem 11, with the criminal statistics framed as follows:

Problem 12 (*N* = 126)

Statistics have shown that by the age of 25, 96.3% of all Alphans have no criminal record whereas 98.8% of all Betans have no criminal record. . . . In light of the available crime statistics, which would you select? [program J, 71%; program K, 29%]

It should be apparent that the crime statistics on which respondents were to base their choice were the same across the two problems. Because of the ratio-difference principle, however, the Alphans are perceived as much more criminal than the Betans in problem 11—roughly three times as criminal—but they are seen as only slightly less noncriminal than the Betans in problem 12. As hypothesized, respondents selected that program in which differences in allocations between the groups matched as closely as possible differences in perceived criminality, resulting in a large reversal of preference.

The preceding two problems illustrate an important social problem concerning the perception of crime rates among minority and nonminority segments of the population. It is generally believed that the members of minority groups, such as blacks, have much higher crime rates than do the members of nonminority groups, such as whites (Tursky et al., 1976). Indeed, according to the actual crime statistics compiled by the FBI in 1982, 2.76% of black citizens were arrested for a serious crime compared to .68% of white Americans. The between group difference does appear quite large. Problems 11 and 12 suggest, however, that judgments about the divergent crime rates in the two communities may be altered by how the data are framed. The apparently large difference between crime rates of 2.76% and .68% can be reframed as a relatively small difference between law-obedience rates of 97.24% and 99.32%.

Quattrone and Warren (1985) showed a sample of Stanford undergraduates the 1982 crime statistics, framed either in terms of the percentages of blacks and whites who were arrested for crime or the percentages who were not. Other respondents were not exposed to these data. As implied by the ratio-difference principle, the respondents who were exposed to the crime commission statistics considered the crime rate to be substantially higher in black communities than in white communities, whereas those exposed to the law-obedience statistics considered the communities to be more at par in crime. Furthermore, the subjects who were not shown the FBI crime data gave responses that were virtually indistinguishable from those given by subjects exposed to the crime commission statistics. This comparison suggests that people may generally formulate beliefs about the proportions of blacks and whites who commit crime, not the proportions who abide by the law.

In another question the subjects who had consulted the FBI statistics were asked to allocate $100M targeted for the prevention of crime between the two racial communities. It was observed that subjects exposed to the crime commission statistics allocated more money to the black community (mean = $58.4M) than did the subjects exposed to the law obedience statistics (mean = $47.2M). Hence, the basic results of this section were replicated for nonhypothetical groups. Moreover, a second study by Quattrone and Warren demonstrated that the same reversals due to framing are obtained when racial differences in crime must be inferred from a set of photographs rather than being explicitly pointed out in a neat statistical table. Taken as a whole, the results suggest that the decision of how to frame the data can have significant political consequences for individuals as well as for entire social groups. We suspect that the more successful practitioners of the art of persuasion commonly employ such framing effects to their personal advantage.

The Weighting of Chance Events

A cornerstone of the rational theory of choice is the expectation principle. In the expected utility model, the decision maker selects that option with the highest expected utility that equals the sum of the utilities of the outcomes, each weighted by its probability. The following example of Zeckhauser illustrates a violation of this rule. Consider a game of Russian roulette where you are allowed to purchase the removal of one bullet. Would you be willing to pay the same amount to reduce the number of bullets from four to three as you would to reduce the number from one to zero? Most people say that they would pay more to reduce the probability of death from one-sixth to zero, thereby eliminating the risk altogether, than to reduce the probability of death from four-sixths to three-sixths. This response, however, is incompatible with the expectation principle, according to which the former reduction from a possibility (one bullet) to a certainty (no bullets) cannot be more valuable than the latter reduction (from four to three bullets). To accommodate this and other violations of the expectation principle, the value of each outcome in prospect theory is multiplied by a decision weight that is a monotonic but nonlinear function of its probability.

Consider a simple prospect that yields outcome x with probability p, outcome y with probability q, and the status quo with probability $1 - p - q$. With the reference point set at the status quo, the outcomes are assigned values $\upsilon(x)$ and $\upsilon(y)$, and the probabilities are assigned *decision weights*, $\pi(p)$ and $\pi(q)$. The overall value of the prospect is

$$\pi(p)\upsilon(x) + \pi(q)\upsilon(y).$$

As shown in Figure 14.2, π is a monotonic nonlinear function of p with the following properties:

1. Impossible events are discarded, that is, $\pi(0) = 0$, and the scale is normalized so that $\pi(1) = 1$. The function is not well behaved at the endpoints though, for people sometimes treat highly likely events as certain and highly unlikely events as impossible.

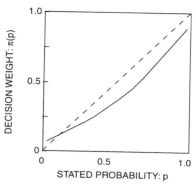

FIGURE 14.2 ■ A hypothetical weighting function

2. Low probabilities are overweighted, giving rise to some risk seeking in the domain of gains. For example, many people prefer one chance in a thousand to win $3,000 over $3 for sure. This implies

$$\pi(.001)\upsilon(\$3,000) > \upsilon(\$3),$$

hence

$$\pi(.001) > \upsilon(\$3)/\upsilon(\$3,000) > .001$$

by the concavity of υ for gains.

3. Although for low probabilities, $\pi(p) > p$, in general, $\pi(p) + \pi(1 - p) < 1$. Thus low probabilities are overweighted, moderate and high probabilities are underweighted, and the latter effect is more pronounced than the former.

4. For all $0 < p, q, r < 1$, $\pi(pq)/\pi(p) < \pi(pqr)/\pi(pr)$; that is, for any ratio of probabilities q, the ratio of decision weights is closer to unity when the probabilities are small than when they are large; for example, $\pi(.4)/\pi(.8) < \pi(.1)/\pi(.2)$. This property implies the common response to the Russian roulette problem because $\pi(1/6) - \pi(0) > \pi(4/6) - \pi(3/6)$.

Although the description of π has involved stated numerical probabilities, it can be extended to events whose probabilities are subjectively assessed or verbally implied. In these situations, however, the decision weights may also be affected by the vagueness or other details of the choice.

Certainty and Pseudocertainty

Many public policies involve the allocation of funds for projects whose outcomes cannot be known with certainty. The following problems illustrate how preferences among risky projects may be affected by the properties of p, and the results are contrasted with those predicted by the expected utility model.

Problem 13 (*N* = 88)

The state of Epsilon is interested in developing clean and safe alternative sources of energy. Its Department of Natural Resources is considering two programs for establishing solar energy within the state. If program X is adopted, then it is virtually certain that over the next four years the state will save $20 million ($20M) in energy expenditures. If program Y is adopted, then there is an 80% chance that the state will save $30M in energy expenditures over the next 4 years and a 20% chance that because of cost overruns, the program will produce no savings in energy expenditures at all. The following table summarizes the alternative policies and their probable consequences.

Policy	Savings in Energy Expenditures
Program X	$20M savings, with certainty
Program Y	80% chance of saving $30M, 20% chance of no savings

Imagine you were faced with the decision of adopting program X or program Y. Which would you select? [program X, 74%; program Y, 26%]

The same respondents who received problem 13 also received the following problem. Order of presenting the two problems was counterbalanced across booklets.

Problem 14 (*N* = 88)

The state of Gamma is also interested in developing clean and safe alternative sources of energy. Its Department of Natural Resources is considering two programs for establishing solar energy within the state. If program A is adopted, then there is a 25% chance that over the next 4 years the state will save $20 million ($20M) in energy expenditures and a 75% chance that because of cost overruns, the program will produce no savings in energy expenditures at all. If program B is adopted, there is a 20% chance that the state will save $30M in energy expenditures and an 80% chance that because of cost overruns, the program will produce no savings in energy expenditures at all. The following table summarizes the alternative policies and their probable consequences:

Policy	Savings in Energy Expenditures
Program A	25% chance of saving $20M, 75% chance of no savings
Program B	20% chance of saving $30M, 80% chance of no savings

Imagine you were faced with the decision of adopting program A or program B. Which would you select? [program A, 39%; program B, 61%]

Because the same respondents completed both problems 13 and 14, we can examine the number who selected each of the four possible pairs of programs: X and A, X and B, Y and A, Y and B. These data are shown in below.

	Problem 14	
Problem 13	Program A	Program B
Program X	27	38
Program Y	7	16

The pair most frequently selected is X and B, which corresponds to the modal choices of each problem considered individually. These modal choices pose a problem for the expected utility model. Setting $u(0) = 0$, the preference for X over Y in problem 13 implies that $u(\$20M) > (4/5)u(\$30M)$, or that $u(\$20M)/u(\$30M) > 4/5$. This inequality is inconsistent with that implied by problem 14, because the preference for A over B implies that $(1/4)u(\$20M) < (1/5)u(\$30M)$, or that $u(\$20M)/u(\$30M) < 4/5$. Note that programs A and B (in problem 14) can be obtained from programs X and Y (in problem 13), respectively, by multiplying the probability of nonnull outcomes by one-fourth. The substitution axiom of expected utility theory says that if X is preferred to Y, then a probability mixture that yields X with probability p and 0 otherwise should be preferred to a mixture that yields Y with probability p and 0 otherwise. If $p = 1/4$, this axiom implies that X is preferred to Y if and only if A is preferred to B. From the above table it is evident that more than half of our respondents (45 or 88) violated this axiom.

The modal choices, X and B, however, are consistent with prospect theory. Applying the equation of prospect theory to the modal choice of problem 13 yields $\pi(1)\upsilon(\$20M) > \pi(.8)\upsilon(\$30M)$, hence $\upsilon(\$20M)/\pi(\$30M) > \pi(.8)/\pi(1)$. Applied to problem 14, the equation yields $\pi(.2)/\pi(.25) > \upsilon(\$20M)/\upsilon(\$30M)$. Taken together, these inequalities imply the observed violation of the substitu-

tion axiom for those individuals for which $\pi(.8)/p(1) < \upsilon(\$20M)/\upsilon(\$30M) < \pi(.2)/\pi(.25)$. Recall that for any ratio of probabilities $q < 1$, the ratio of decision weights is closer to unity when the probabilities are small than when they are large. In particular, $\pi(.8)/\pi(1) < \pi(.2)/\pi(.25)$. Indeed, 38 of the 45 pairs of choices that deviate from expected utility theory fit the above pattern, $p < .001$ by sign test.

It should be noted that prospect theory does not predict that all respondents will prefer X to Y and B to A. This pattern will be found only among those respondents for whom the value ratio, $\upsilon(\$20M)/\upsilon(\$30M)$, lies between the ratios of decision weights, $\pi(.8)/\pi(1)$ and $\pi(.2)/\pi(.25)$. The theory requires only that individuals who are indifferent between X and Y will prefer B to A and those who are indifferent between A and B will prefer X to Y. For group data, the theory does predict the observed shift in modal preferences. The only pair of choices *not* consistent with prospect theory is Y and A, for this pair implies that $\pi(.2)/\pi(.25) < \pi(.8)/\pi(1)$. This pair was in fact selected least often.

The modal preferences exhibited in the preceding two problems illustrate a phenomenon first reported by Allais (1953) that is referred to in prospect theory as the *certainty effect:* reducing the probability of an outcome by a constant factor has a greater impact when the outcome was initially certain than when it was merely possible. The Russian roulette game discussed earlier is a variant of the certainty effect.

Causal Versus Diagnostic Contingencies

A classical problem in the analysis of political behavior concerns the rationality of voting and abstaining. According to Downs (1957), it may not be rational for an individual to register and vote in large elections because of the very low probability that the individual would cast a decisive vote coupled with the costs of registering and going to the polls. Objections to Downs's view were raised by Riker and Ordeshook (1968), who argued that an individual may derive from voting other benefits besides the possibility of casting a decisive ballot. These additional benefits are collectively referred to as *citizen's duty,* or D, and they include affirming one's allegiance to the democratic system, complying with a powerful ethic, participating in a common social ritual, as well as "standing up and being counted." To these rational consequences of voting, we suggest adding a somewhat less rational component.

Elsewhere (Quattrone & Tversky, 1984) we have shown that people often fail to distinguish between causal contingencies (acts that produce an outcome) and diagnostic contingencies (acts that are merely correlated with an outcome). For example, there is a widespread belief that attitudes are correlated with actions. Therefore, some people may reason that if they decide to vote, that decision would imply that others with similar political attitudes would also decide to vote. Similarly, they may reason that if they decide to abstain, others who share their political attitudes will also abstain. Because the preferred candidates can defeat the opposition only if politically like-minded citizens vote in greater numbers than do politically unlikeminded citizens, the individual may infer that he or she had better vote; that is, each citizen may regard his or her single vote as diagnostic of *millions* of votes, which would substantially inflate the subjective probability of one's vote making a difference.

To test this hypothesis, which we call the *voter's illusion*, we had a sample of 315 Stanford undergraduates read about an imaginary country named Delta. Participants were to imagine that they supported party *A*, opposed party *B*, and that there were roughly four million supporters of each party in Delta as well as four million nonaligned voters. Subjects imagined that they were deliberating over whether to vote in the upcoming presidential election, having learned that voting in Delta can be costly in time and effort. To facilitate their decision, they were to consult one of two prevailing theories concerning the group of voters who would determine the electoral outcome.

Some subjects considered the *party supporter's theory*. According to this theory, the nonaligned voters would split their vote fairly equally across the two parties. The electoral outcome would be determined by whether the supporters of party *A* or party *B* became more involved in the election. The political experts were split as to whether the supporters of *A* or *B* would become more involved, but all agreed that the party whose members did become more involved would win by a margin of roughly 200 thousand to 400 thousand votes. Other subjects received the *non-aligned voter's theory*,

which held that the supporters of each party would vote in equal numbers. The electoral outcome would in this account be determined by whether the nonaligned voters would swing their support primarily to party *A* or party *B*. The experts were split as to which party would capture the majority of the nonaligned voters, but all agreed that the fortunate party would win by a margin of at least 200 thousand votes.

Note that the consequences of voting included in the rational analysis are held constant across the two theories. In both, the "utility difference" between the two parties, the "probability" of casting a decisive vote, the costs of voting, and citizen's duty are the same. But according to the party supporter's theory, there is a correlation between political orientation and participation; that is, either the supporters of party *A* will vote in greater numbers than will the supporters of party *B*, or vice versa. In contrast, the non-aligned voter's theory holds that political orientation is independent of participation because party supporters will turn out in equal numbers. Therefore, only subjects presented with the former theory could infer that their decision to vote or to abstain would be diagnostic of what their politically like-minded peers would decide. If being able to make this inference is conducive to voting, then a larger "turnout" should be found among subjects presented with the party supporter's theory than among those presented with the non-aligned voter's theory. In fact, when asked, "Would you vote if the theory were true and voting in Delta were costly," significantly more subjects responded *no* under the party supporter's theory (16%) than under the nonaligned voter's theory (7%) ($p < .05$ by sign test).

An additional finding corroborated the analysis that this difference in turnout was attributable to the perceived diagnosticity of voting. Respondents were asked to indicate how likely it was that the supporters of party *A* would vote in greater numbers than the supporters of party *B* "given that you decided to vote" and "given that you decided to abstain." Responses to these two questions were made on nine-point scales with verbal labels ranging from "extremely likely" to "extremely unlikely." Subjects were informed that their decision to vote or abstain could not be communicated to others. Nonetheless, subjects exposed to the party supporter's theory thought that their individual choice would have a greater "effect" on what others decided to do than did subjects exposed to the nonaligned voter's theory. Similar effects were observed in responses to a question probing how likely party A was to defeat party B "given that you decided to vote" and "given that you decided to abstain." This latter difference was obtained despite subject's knowing that they could cast but one vote and that the likely margin of victory was about 200 thousand votes.

The observed differences between respondents exposed to the party supporter's and nonaligned voter's theory cannot be readily justified from a normative perspective (cf. Meehl, 1977). The present analysis of causal versus diagnostic contingencies recalls the tragedy of the commons and it applies to other phenomena in which collective action dwarfs the causal significance of a single individual's contribution. The outcomes of most wars would not have changed had one fewer draftee been inducted, and the success or failure of most charity drives do not ordinarily depend on the dollars of an individual donor. These collective actions defy a routine rational analysis for the individual because if each citizen, draftee, or donor "rationally" refrains from making his or her paltry contribution, then the outcomes would be drastically affected. For this reason, exhortations to vote, to fight, and to help those less fortunate than oneself are usually framed, "If you don't vote/fight/contribute, think of what would happen if *everyone* felt the same way." This argument is compelling. Still, just how *does* an individual's private decision materially affect the decisions made by countless other persons?

Concluding Remarks

We contrasted the rational analysis of political decision making with a psychological account based on descriptive considerations. Although there is no universally accepted definition of rationality, most social scientists agree that rational choice should conform to a few elementary requirements. Foremost among these is the criterion of invariance (or extensionality [Arrow, 1982]), which holds that the preference order among prospects should not depend on how they are described. Hence, no acceptable rational theory would allow reversals of preference to come about as a consequence of whether the choice is based on rates of employment or rates of unemployment, crime commission statistics or law obedience statistics. These alternate formulations of the problems convey the same information, and the problems differ from each other in no other way. We have seen, however, that these alternate frames led to predictable reversals in preference.

Whether our studies paint a humbling or flattering picture of human intellectual performance depends on the background from which they are viewed. The proponent of the rational theory of choice may find that we have focused on human limitations and have overlooked its many accomplishments. The motivational psychologist, accustomed to finding the root of all folly in deep-seated emotional needs, may find our approach much too rational and cognitive. Many readers are no doubt familiar with the versions of these opposing viewpoints found in political science. *The Authoritarian Personality* (Adorno et al., 1950), for example, well illustrates the use of motivational assumptions to explain the appeal of a particular ideology to certain elements of the population.

The descriptive failure of normative principles, such as invariance and coherence, does not mean that people are unintelligent or irrational. The failure merely indicates that judgment and choice—like perception and memory—are prone to distortion and error. The significance of the results stems from the observation that the errors are common and systematic, rather than idiosyncratic or random, hence they cannot be dismissed as noise. Accordingly, there is little hope for a theory of choice that is both normatively acceptable and descriptively adequate. A compelling analysis of the uses and abuses of rationality in theories of political behavior has been presented by Converse (1975), who has detailed the often arbitrary and inconsistent criteria by which rationality has been defined. Our intention was not to reopen the discussion about the meaning of rationality but rather to enrich the set of concepts and principles that could be used to analyze, explain, and predict the decisions made by individuals in their private lives, in the marketplace, and in the political arena.

REFERENCES

Abelson, Robert, and Ariel Levi. 1985. Decision Making and Decision Theory. In *The Handbook of Social Psychology*, 3d ed., ed. Gardner Lindzey and Elliot Aronson. Hillsdale, NJ: Lawrence Erlbaum.

Adorno, Theodor, Else Frenkel-Brunswik, Daniel Levinson, and R. Nevitt Sanford. 1950. *The Authoritarian Personality*. New York: Harper.

Allais, Maurice. 1953. Le comportement de l'homme rationnel devant le risque: Critique des postulates et axiomes de l'école americaine. *Econometrica* 21:503–46.

Arrow, Kenneth J. 1982. Risk Perception in Psychology and Economics. *Economic Inquiry* 20: 1–9.

Bazerman, Max H. 1983. Negotiator Judgment. *American Behavioral Scientist* 27:211–28.

Bernoulli, Daniel. 1954. Exposition of a New Theory on the Measurement of Risk. *Econometrica* 22:23–36. 23–36.

Converse, Philip. 1975. Public Opinion and Voting Behavior. In *Handbook of Political Science*, vol. 4, ed. Fred Greenstein and Nelson Polsby. Reading, MA: Addison-Wesley.

Dawes, Robyn. 1988. *Rational Choice in an Uncertain World*. New York: Harcourt, Brace, Jovanovich.

Downs, Anthony. 1957. *An Economic Theory of Democracy*. New York: Harper & Row.

Kahneman, Daniel, Paul Slovic, and Amos Tversky. 1982. *Judgment under Uncertainty: Heuristics and Biases*. New York: Cambridge University Press.

Kahneman, Daniel, and Amos Tversky. 1979. Prospect Theory: An Analysis of Decision under Risk. *Econometrica* 47:263–91.

Kahneman, Daniel, and Amos Tversky. 1984. Choices, Values, and Frames. *American Psychologist* 39:341–50.

Kiewiet, D. Roderick. 1982. The Rationality of Candidates Who Challenge Incumbents in Congressional Elections. Social Science Working Paper no. 436, California Institute of Technology.

Kramer, Gerald H. 1971. Short-Term Fluctuations in U.S. Voting Behavior, 1896–1964. *American Political Science Review* 65:131–43.

Lebow, Richard N., and Janice G. Stein. 1987. Beyond Deterrence. *Journal of Social Issues* 43: 5–71.

Meehl, Paul. 1977. The Selfish Voter Paradox and the Thrown-away Vote Argument. *American Political Science Review* 71:11–30.

Quattrone, George A., and Amos Tversky. 1984. Causal versus Diagnostic Contingencies: On Self-Deception and on the Voter's Illusion. *Journal of Personality and Social Psychology* 46: 237–48.

Quattrone, George A., and Diann Warren. 1985. The Ratio-Difference Principle and the Perception of Group Differences. Stanford University. Typescript.

Raiffa, Howard. 1968. *Decision Analysis: Introductory Lectures on Choices under Uncertainty*. Reading, MA: Addison-Wesley.

Riker, William, and Peter Ordeshook. 1968. A Theory of the Calculus of Voting. *American Political Science Review* 10:25–42.

Ross, Lee. 1986. Conflict Notes. Stanford University. Typescript.

Savage, Leonard. 1954. *The Foundations of Statistics*. New York: John Wiley & Sons.

Shepsle, Kenneth. 1972. The Strategy of Ambiguity: Uncertainty and Electoral Competition. *American Political Science Review* 66:555–68.

Simon, Herbert. 1955. A Behavioral Model of Rational Choice. *Quarterly Journal of Economics* 69:99–118.

Simon, Herbert. 1978. Rationality As Process and As Product of Thought. *American Economic Review* (*Papers and Proceedings*) 68:1–16.

Tursky, Bernard, Milton Lodge, Mary Ann Foley, Richard Reeder, and Hugh Foley. 1976. Evaluation of the Cognitive Component of Political Issues by Use of Classical Conditioning. *Journal of Personality and Social Psychology* 34:865–73.

Tversky, Amos, and Daniel Kahneman. 1986. Rational Choice and the Framing of Decisions. *The Journal of Business* 59:251–78.

Von Neumann, John, and Oskar Morgenstern. 1947. *Theory of Games and Economic Behavior*, 2d ed. Princeton, NJ: Princeton University Press.

The Drunkard's Search

Robert Jervis • Columbia University

Just like the drunk who looked for his keys not where he dropped them, but under the lamppost where the light was better, people often seek inadequate information that is readily available, use misleading measures because they are simple, and employ methods of calculation whose main virtue is ease. For example, in 1949 when Senator Joseph O'Mahoney tried to convince his colleagues not to cut the Air Force budget, he argued: "We do not need details here. All we need to know is that this . . . is a reduction from a 58-group air force to a 48-group air force. In my judgment, a 58-group air force would be too little" (Schilling, 1962, p. 129). This argument is straightforward and makes minimal demands on one's ability to find and process information. But it is not satisfactory. Even a person who believed that the Air Force should be larger than 58 groups still should want to know the costs and effectiveness of smaller forces. If a much larger force was beyond reach, one could prefer a force of 48 groups to one that was 10 groups larger if the gap in effectiveness was relatively slight and the cost difference very great. Furthermore, the most important consideration might not be the size of the Air Force, but its composition, training, state of readiness, and supplies. It is also possible that expansion might profitably be delayed a few years if changes in technology were in the offing.

Of course, information and decision costs must be considered when judging the availability of a decision-making procedure, and methods that seem irrational when these factors are ignored can become rational once they are weighed (for example, see Downs, 1957; Jervis, 1989a; Riker & Ordeshook, 1973; Stigler, 1961). But there is more to it than this. In many cases, searching further or looking at less obvious criteria could significantly increase the chance of a better decision at a manageable cost. Without being able to specify exactly how much effort would be optimal, it seems likely that people seize on easier ways of processing and calculating information than they would if they were fully aware of what they were doing.

Ways of Decreasing the Burden of Cognition

Simple Models and Decision Rules

The propensity to conserve cognitive resources in seeking and processing information manifests itself in several forms. First, people prefer simple decision rules and unitary causal accounts to ones that posit a multiplicity of factors and causal paths. In areas in which they are expert, people may reject an explanation as too simple, but even here there may be more lip service than actual avoiding of simplicity. In some contexts, simplicity is valued for well-thought-out reasons: parsimony is a criteria for a good scientific theory not only because it increases the theory's power (i.e., the ability to explain a lot with relatively few independent variables), but because at least some scientists believe that the phenomena they are trying to capture are themselves parsimonious. But finding parsimony at the end of data collection and analysis is one thing; assuming it from the start is another.

Two linked manifestations of the preference for seeing a minimum of causal factors are the propensity of people to believe conspiracy theories and the hesitancy of even sophisticated observers to give full credit to the role of chance and confusion. Conspiracies are complicated in one sense— they involve a large number of activities that may seem bewildering. But the underlying causation is simple: Everything is knit together into a coherent plan. The drive to see conspiracies varies across personalities and cultures, but a general cognitive bias also is important. Even those who reject one or another of these theories often sense the attractiveness of an explanation that ties so many odd bits of behavior together. It sometimes takes a great deal of training and experience to produce a reaction against this kind of explanation as being "too neat to be true."

If the belief in conspiracies is common, the resistance to accepting a large role for chance is almost universal. People see order even in random data. They seek parsimony even when it is not present. Thus, they are slow to explain the policies of states in terms of a multiplicity of bureaucratic factors or a multiplicity of changing motives; other states are seen as coordinated and Machiavellian when in fact they may be blundering and incoherent (Jervis, 1976).

A similar pattern is displayed when people are asked to report how many kinds of evidence they used to arrive at a decision (e.g., on which stocks to buy, on what disease a patient has, on whether to admit an applicant to graduate school). People claim to use a large number of cues, but statistical analysis of the pattern of their choices indicates that they rely on only very few. People also report that they look for complex interactive patterns (i.e., they would buy a stock if indicator A were high and B were low or if B were low and A were high, but not if both were either high or low) when in fact they treat the same variables in a simple additive manner (see Dawes & Corrigan, 1981). In the same way, when people search for the solution to puzzles in experimental settings, they focus on rules with only one element. They are slow to explore the possibility that the required answer is conjunctive (i.e., the presence of two or more ele-

ments) and even slower to think of possibilities that are disjunctive (i.e., one element present but another absent). This was a clear result of Bruner, Goodnow, and Austin's *A Study of Thinking* in which subjects were asked to reconstruct the rule by which an item was determined to belong to a category established by the experimenter. The task was relatively easy if having an attribute was both a necessary and sufficient cause for inclusion in the category; it was more difficult if having such an attribute was necessary but not sufficient; it was beyond most people's reach when there were several sufficient conditions.

In much the same way, people avoid value trade-offs (Jervis, 1976). That is, they often reach a decision based on how the alternative policies are likely to affect one value although several are at stake. Furthermore, people generally fail to realize that this is what they are doing; instead, they think they have looked at several value dimensions and conveniently found that the preferred course of action is best on all counts. This would imply that the world is simply and benignly arranged, a belief that most people would reject if it were explicitly posed. But people act as though the world were so arranged in part because making trade-offs, especially when values of very different kinds are involved, places strain on cognitive abilities. To take the example of buying a house, how would one go about balancing cost, size, proximity to public transportation, noise, estimated future value, and other considerations? How would these different values be measured by a common yardstick? Although people hesitate to acknowledge that they do not go through the sort of trade-offs that full rationality would call for, they must concentrate on one or two values.

Certainty

The preference for simple calculations also is revealed by people's tendency to think in terms of certainties and, when they must employ probabilities, to use round numbers, especially 50 percent. Cognitive resources are conserved by declaring that many alternatives are simply impossible. Sometimes a more sophisticated formulation is called up: "The chance that X will occur is so unlikely that it is not worth thinking about." But conditions can change that increase the likelihood of X without triggering further consideration for it.

The preference for absolutes also is found in experiments: people who are shown statements of the form "Some X are Y" and "All (or No) X are Y" are more likely to remember the former as being the latter than vice versa (Dawes, 1966).

A related device is for the person to refuse to consider complicating factors. Thus, during the Cold War it seems that the American intelligence community paid little attention to the possibility of extensive deception and that analysts who raised this problem were not taken seriously. Because this stance was not limited to those with a benign view of the USSR, the best explanation is the need to keep one's task manageable. It was hard enough to try to estimate Soviet capabilities and intentions; to constantly have had to doubt much of the information that one was using would have made the problem intolerably complex. All of one's time and intellectual energy would have been taken up by trying to tell what information was deceptive, and very little time would have been left for the main job. So it is not surprising that analysts often ignored a great deal of evidence that in retrospect clearly indicated deception. The Germans in World War II similarly failed to grasp any of the innumerable clues that their spy network in England had been "turned" and taken over by the British. Although the British blatantly used the network to deceive the Germans on the location of the invasion of the Continent, even after D-Day the Germans continued to take the reports from their "agents" at face value, much to the amazement of the British.

Benchmarks and Analogies

The burdens of calculation are further reduced by the use of benchmarks to guide decisions. Round numbers often serve this function. Thus, Herbert York (1970) explained that the Atlas missile was designed to be able to carry a 1-megaton warhead in large part because, having 10 fingers, we build our number system on the base of 10. Similarly, although considerations of both strategy and domestic politics were important in determining the rough number of Minuteman missiles President Kennedy decided to procure in the early 1960s, the advantage of the figure 1,000 as compared with, say, 875 or 1,163 was that it was a round number. The other side of this coin is that when a person wants others to believe that a figure she has selected was the result of complex and detailed calculations, she will pick a number that is *not* round.

Benchmarks also can be provided by other people's behavior. States often compare their performance with other states, even when this comparison is not fully appropriate. Or an actor will copy another actor believing (or acting as though he believes) that the two of them are in such similar positions and have such similar interests that they can save themselves a lot of cognitive work simply by following the other's lead. It would be hard to otherwise explain the call for an American Fractional Orbiting Bombardment System after the Soviets had tested one, or NATO's drive to match the Soviet's ss-20.

When people try to determine whether a policy has succeeded, they often use two related measuring rods. First, if the situation is competitive, they ask who won and who lost. This is appropriate if the situation is zero-sum, but it will be misleading if both sides could be better off (or worse off) than they would have been had alternative courses of action been followed. Even when misleading, the question often is asked because it is easier to answer than a more complex one would be. Under some circumstances, actors ask whether they are gaining (or losing) more than another, and doing so is sensible when the nature of the interaction makes relative position or standing crucial, as is often the case when power or status are involved. But use of this measure does not seem to be restricted to situations where it fits.

The second benchmark is to compare the result of the interaction to the result of previous ones. Doing better than before is equated with winning, which in turn is equated with success. A good example is provided by the way that observers—at least American observers—judged American policy in 1986 after the Soviets arrested Nicholas Daniloff and the United States gained the reporter's freedom by a complex trade. Politicians and reporters alike compared this exchange to similar cases in the past, often arguing that the United States "lost" because Soviet spies previously had been kept in jail longer and more dissidents had been released in similar trades. Setting aside the difficulties in deciding whether the circumstances of earlier cases really were the same, what is crucial here is that many people jumped from the judgment that the Soviets did better this time to the conclusion that they "won"—that is, "set a precedent that would make Western governments think twice about arresting Soviet spy suspects."[1] But even if this trade was more palatable to the Soviets than earlier ones, it may not have been so attractive as to tempt them to repeat the adventure. By the same token, the terms of the trade could have been worse than in previous cases without being excessively costly. But the baseline of the past establishes our expectations, and so we concentrate on deviations from it, even if logically they do not carry much meaning.

Other benchmarks are more ad hoc, rising out of the prominent features of the environment. For example, when President Johnson "began to search for the elusive point at which the costs of Vietnam would become unacceptable to the American people, he always settled upon mobilization, the point at which reserves would have to be called up to support a war that was becoming increasingly distasteful to the American public" (Schandler, 1977, p. 56). Although Johnson's view may have been correct, he neither sought a way around the ceiling nor considered whether a shorter war with mobilization might have been more acceptable than a longer and inconclusive one fought with fewer men. Instead, the ceiling was taken as an absolute prohibition. In the same way, when a person is considering a major purchase, he may well set an upper limit on what he is willing to spend and not consider going higher even for something of greater value. As these examples show, benchmarks can be used by the actor to restrain himself. In moments of calm, he can construct barriers that are difficult for him to break through under circumstances of temptation. Furthermore, as Thomas Schelling (1960) has shown, benchmarks can be particularly useful when several people are involved; they can provide a way for people to coordinate their behavior and can guide bargaining. But these functions also depend in part on the fact that benchmarks are artificially attractive.

Using Common Dimensions

People also can ease their burden of calculation by comparing alternatives only on the dimension that they have in common. This is fully rational if that dimension is the most important one: but the method will be employed whether or not this is the case, as is brought out by an experiment in which subjects are asked to compare pairs of stu-

dents. For each student there were scores on two dimensions; one was common to both of them and was different for each. For example, one student might have scores for English skills and need for achievement, while the other would have scores on English skills and aptitude for quantitative analysis. In their evaluations, subjects weighed the common dimensions more heavily: the student with the higher English skill was likely to be rated as superior overall, even if the gap on this dimension was slight, and the student who lagged here did extremely well on the unique dimension. Furthermore, neither cautioning subjects about the effect nor giving them feedback as to the "correct" answers changed their method. Interestingly, when the subjects were questioned after the experiment, they denied that they had given extra weight to the common dimension (Slovic, 1975; Slovic & MacPhillmay, 1974). This discredits one obvious explanation that would undermine my argument: People could give extra weight to any dimension that was held in common on the not unreasonable grounds that the very fact that it was common indicates that it was important.

Few foreign policy cases are as clear as this experiment, although the way in which states compare each others' military strength (discussed below) fits this pattern. In other cases as well, it seems at least plausible that a policy which is believed to be superior to the alternatives on the one dimension that is shared by all will have a major advantage. Although the noncognitive explanation of the importance of the common dimension cannot be dismissed—any policy proposal will have to speak to the concern that is most deeply felt—ease of comparison is still likely to play a role.

In a related manifestation of the same impulse, one reason why the American armed services after World War II were a bit slower to see the Soviet Union as a threat than were the other parts of government was that each branch of the services tended to examine the single dimension that concerned it the most. When they looked into the future, each military service saw its potential enemies as those states that had, or could develop, extensive capabilities that resembled theirs or that could be countered by their service. "Air Force planners eyed a renascent Germany or Japan as the most probable enemies because both possessed the technology to develop strategic air power. Certain that only nations with a strategic bombing capability would dare wage war in the future, they dismissed the Soviet Union as a foe because it failed to develop a strategic force during the war and appeared to lack both technology and doctrine to do so for at least 20 or 30 years. The navy also minimized the Russian threat, since the Soviets demonstrated no more flair for battleships than for bombers" (Sherry, 1977, p. 168; also see Davis, 1966; Smith, 1970). Of course, the Soviet Union had a large army, but because it could not be used to attack the United States, it did not alarm the army's planners. Bureaucratic politics cannot explain this way of thinking because each service had an interest in detecting Soviet threats; judging the Soviet Union on the most salient military dimension was such a powerful cognitive shortcut that it was employed even though doing so would not maximize the military's role or budget.

Using Only the Most Readily Available Information

To ease calculations, people concentrate on questions about which they have a good deal of information, pay most attention to the factors on which they are best-informed, and attribute the causes to variables with which they are familiar. Of course, outside the laboratory it is hard to tell which way causality runs (and it may be reciprocal); people seek information about factors that they believe are important. But this is not the entire story, as Tversky and Kahneman's research on availability shows. Tversky and Kahneman have found that ease of recall strongly influences judgments in ways that cannot be explained by the rational seeking and using of information. For example, if a person is asked whether the number of words beginning with a particular letter is greater than the number of words in which the letter appears third, he is likely to answer in the affirmative because it is easier to recall the first letters of words. But this ease of recall is not a good measure of frequency. The fact that it is hard for us to call to mind words with a given third letter does not mean that such words are uncommon (Tversky & Kahneman, 1973).

As with the other effects we have discussed, the impact of readily available information often is not conscious. Thus, experiments have shown that if the salience of a factor is increased, people will treat that factor as of greater importance, even

though they do not understand the manipulation and probably would deny that the manipulation had any effect on them (Fiske & Taylor, 1991). For example, while actors usually attribute their own behavior to the stimuli they confront, and observers attribute the behavior to the actor's internal characteristics, if videotapes are used to change the actors' and the observers' perspectives, the attributions change correspondingly (see Arkin & Duval, 1975; Regan & Toten, 1975; Storms, 1973). Similarly, differences in interpretation of events often can be traced to differences in the information that is salient, with each person attributing greater importance to the factors with which he is most familiar.

For many of the same reasons, "individuals tend to accept more responsibility for a joint project than other contributors attribute to them" (Ross & Sicoly, 1979, p. 322). This is true for couples' beliefs about how much each of them contributes to routine household chores and major decisions; it also is the case for subjects in problem-solving experiments. That the effect is present, although attenuated, when the group product is criticized shows that ego gratification cannot entirely explain the bias. Further evidence that what is at work is the propensity for people to attribute primary responsibility to factors about which they are most aware—which is usually things they have said or done—is supplied by an experimental manipulation. If the experimenter heightens the subject's recollection of the other person's actions, the subject will accord the other person a greater share of the responsibility for the outcome.

In foreign policy as well, the degree to which a factor is seen as influential depends in part on the amount of information that the decision-maker has about it. What the decision-maker is most likely to know about are his own worries and plans, thus contributing to the egocentric nature of inference. This bias is not necessarily a self-serving one— the actor does not always see himself in a favorable light. Rather, people place themselves at the center of others' attention, believing that others are reacting to them or trying to affect them. Since the decision-maker knows about his state's policy in great detail, it will be relatively easy for him to find some element in it that could have been the cause or the object of the other state's actions. By contrast, many of the other possible causes of the other state's behavior are seen only in dim outline.

It was to correct this propensity and to better understand Soviet behavior in the Strategic Arms Limitation Treaty (SALT) negotiations that Marshall Shulman, as Secretary of State Cyrus Vance's assistant, kept a chart of what he called "correlated activities" (Talbott, 1979, pp. 80, 120, 146), which showed all the events that were likely to be affecting the Russians, not only those which were of primary interest to the United States. Of course, people can draw inferences only when they have some information to work with. But rarely are they aware of the degree to which hidden factors could be more powerful than those about which they are informed. They implicitly assume that factors not in their purview are unimportant.[2]

It also is easier to see how a new technology fits into one's own plans than it is to see how an adversary might use it. The difficult task of discerning the implications of new developments can be made easier by using a framework that the person already understands well—most often his nation's capacities and intentions. He will have much less information on how the other side might employ the new device and so will pay less attention to this problem or, when he studies it, will implicitly assume that the other side will see it as he does. This was the pattern in many of the Royal Navy's attempts to grasp the implications of new technologies before World War I. When trying to understand how the torpedo boat would change warfare, both those who urged its adoption and those who denied its importance paid most attention to how it could be used in the close blockade that the Royal Navy planned to institute in the event of war. Little thought was given to how England's enemies might use torpedo boats to thwart the blockade, a mission that they could in fact perform well (Cowpe, 1977). Similarly, most of the discussion of submarines was in terms of their utility to the British, which was slight. Only a few people shared Lord Balfour's insight: "The question that really troubles me is not whether *our* submarines could render the enemy's position intolerable, but whether *their* submarines could render our position untenable" (Kennedy, 1977). Some of this effect may be explained by the tendency of military commanders to think in terms of taking the initiative rather than having to react to what the adversary is doing. But probably at least as important is the fact that they can make the problem of judging new weapons less intractable by

concentrating on how they could use them rather than trying to guess how the other side might do so, a question about which there is less information and whose answer requires the use of a less familiar mental framework.

In a variant of this pattern, states assume that other states will use their weapons in the same way that the state is planning. This makes some sense because a great deal of thought presumably went into developing the state's own plans and, if the problems and outlook of other states are similar, they are likely to come up with similar answers. But even if these conditions do not hold, the simplifications that are permitted by assuming that they do hold exert such a strong attraction that decision-makers are not likely to abandon them. Thus, in the 1930s the British believed that the Germans planned to use air power in the same way that the British did—that is, in strategic attacks on the adversary's homeland. There was little in German military doctrine to lead to this conclusion and German airplanes were not suited to this mission, but those factors were not sufficient to destroy the illusion of symmetry (see Jervis, 1982).

Until shortly before the outbreak of World War II, the British Air Ministry made the same kind of assumption the basis for its estimates of the size of the German air force. It thought that "the best criteria for judging Germany's rate of expansion were those which governed the rate at which the RAF could itself form efficient units" (Hinsley et al., 1979, p. 299). Up to the mid 1970s, the United States thought that Soviet nuclear doctrine resembled American views even though Soviet history, context, and civilian-military relations were very different. Beliefs about how the Soviets would use specific weapons similarly proceeded on the assumption that they would adopt the American pattern, and it took several years before U.S. analysts realized the Soviets' large missiles were not targeted as we would have used them, but instead were aimed at the U.S. command and control structure (Steinbruner, 1981).

Consequences

Inertia

The first consequence of the need to simplify calculations is that incrementalism is encouraged.

Decision-making is made much easier if the person searches only for alternatives when the current policy is failing badly, limits the search to policies that are only marginally different from the current one, concentrates on the particular value dimension that is causing trouble, evaluates only a few alternatives, and adopts the first alternative that puts the person above an acceptable level of satisfaction. Furthermore, some of these processes operate at the perceptual level as well as at later and more conscious levels of decision-making. Thus, people engage in "perceptual satisficing"—i.e., rather than waiting, collecting more information, and comparing several accounts, each of which is at least minimally satisfactory, they accept the first image or belief that makes minimal sense out of data. Once an initial belief is formed, even if the person means it to be tentative, it will tend to become solidified because all but the most discrepant evidence will be assimilated to it; people will not search for new beliefs or images as long as the ones that they hold are not clearly inadequate (for further discussion, see Jervis, 1976).

Linked to this characteristic is the tendency for a policy to continue even as the rationales for it shift. In the case of nations, many explanations for inertia stem from bureaucratic, domestic, and international politics; vested internal interests often support continuity, and their policies constitute commitments that are hard to break. But in many cases this phenomenon has a cognitive component as well. Once a person has worked through the arguments that led him to a conclusion, he is likely to conserve his resources by not reexamining it unless he has to. As the reasons that originally led to the policy erode, they often are gradually replaced by new and sometimes incompatible ones. Thus, an experience-induced belief can persevere even when the person is told that the evidence which established it is false (see Jervis, 1976; Ross, Lepper, & Hubbard, 1975).

Ignoring Interaction Effects

A second consequence of the need to keep calculation manageably simple is that problems which involve many interrelated elements often are analyzed as though each element were separate (Dawes, 1971; Dawes & Corrigan, 1981; Einhorn, 1972; Jervis, 1991). While people think they are using interactive models and complex methods of calculation, in fact they implicitly assume additivity. People are better at seeing what variables are important than they are at combining them. This is consistent with Cyert and March's (1963) finding that organizations deal with complexity by dividing up problems into smaller ones and seeking separate solutions for each part of them ("factored problems—factored solutions").

The same patterns appear in political decision-making. Interactive models place enormous strain on our cognitive abilities and, even when we know they are appropriate, we shy away from using them. Thus, the flaw in the Royal Navy's analysis of the threat posed by air power to battleships in the interwar period: "Although specific problems ... such as the effect of underwater explosives were occasionally analyzed in depth, there was little continuing research into the ... problem as a whole" (Till, 1977, p. 119). Taken one at a time, the problems might be manageable, but when combined the threat could be overwhelming. The German analysis in late 1916 and early 1917 employed the same shortcut and similarly produced erroneous results. In deciding whether to adopt unrestricted submarine warfare, the Germans estimated the amount of goods that Britain needed to maintain her position and the numbers of ships that the Germans thought they could sink. The conclusion was that they could quickly reduce the flow of material coming into Britain to below the minimum level; thus, Britain would sue for peace before the impact of U.S. entry into the war could be felt. While the specific calculations were accurate, the influence of one of the factors on the others was neglected. That is, once the United States entered the war, the British were willing to suffer what earlier would have been an intolerable loss of shipping because they realized that if they held on a bit longer the tide would turn (Ikle, 1971).

The pattern of dividing up problems and examining each solution in isolation contributes to the propensity for states to follow policies that embody conflicting elements. To say that the right hand does not know what the left hand is doing is not quite accurate: rather the right hand does not pay any attention to the implications of the left hand's activities. Thus, in the interwar period Japan acted as though its policies toward China would not influence the prospects for relations with the West (Iriye, 1969). Similarly, in 1918 the French ministry of war supported Japanese intervention in Siberia but "tended to ignore the obvious consequences of this policy on [French] relations with the Bolsheviks, or preferred to treat European Russia and Siberia as two separate theaters of action" (Carley, 1976, p. 432).

Net Assessment

The drunkard's search is illustrated by the way that the British judged German air power in the 1930s and American analysts compared Soviet and American nuclear strength throughout the cold war. In both cases, the basic question asked was "Who is ahead?" not "Do we have sufficient military force to support our foreign policy?" A glance at almost any article on what is called nuclear or strategic balance shows a preoccupation with the question of whether or not the United States trails the Soviet Union. Similarly, in the interwar period both Neville Chamberlain and Winston Churchill focused on the question of whether the United Kingdom had what they called "air parity" with Germany.

But this approach, while simple, is highly misleading. Most obviously, the United States and the USSR could have had equal numbers of strategic forces, but the weapons could have been configured in such ways that both sides had first-strike capability, thus creating tremendous instability. While everyone knew of this danger, it sometimes was lost sight of in comparing the size of the two sides' forces. Even less frequently recognized was the fact that depending on the task and context, a state could have more military power than its adversary and still not have enough, or that it could be inferior and still have more than it needed. In the interwar period, air parity might have been sufficient to deter a direct attack on England, but not enough for "extended deterrence" against German expansion to the east. Similarly, the analysis of many hawks during the cold war implied that a significant margin of superiority—perhaps what Herman Kahn called a "not-incredible first strike capability"—was needed if the American commitment to NATO was to be credible (Kahn, 1960). The implication of the arguments of many doves was that significantly less than parity was needed, certainly to protect the United States, and probably to protect vital European interests as well. But the logic of both positions was abandoned when much of the debate focused on the question of who was ahead, which is a much more manageable question than estimating how much was enough to deter the Soviets and how various configurations of forces could have contributed to terminating a war in the least possible unfavorable way.

In general, it is very difficult to estimate what would happen in the event of a war—the "outputs" of the weapons. The interaction of what each side will do is terribly complex. It is much easier to measure the "inputs"—what weapons each side has—even though the relationship between these and the outputs is tenuous. So, just as the drunk looks under the lamppost, so it is that analysts use inputs to judge military balance.

Little attention was paid to the composition of the forces on both sides, and numbers of planes often were compared without separating fighters from bombers. On some occasions, the British fighter force was compared to the German one and the bombers were compared to those of the adversary. But while fighters would sometimes meet in an air battle, bombers never would. What was really needed was some way of judging how many German bombers could penetrate British defenses on a sustained basis and how much damage they could do. Similarly, one wanted to know how much the British bombers could damage German targets. So comparing each side's bombers with the other's fighters and antiaircraft guns would have made some sense. Even this would have omitted many crucial factors, such as the ability of defenders to disperse or hide and the ability of the attackers to navigate across hostile terrain in good weather and in bad—in the first year of the war, few British bombers could find their way to their targets. But at least such a measure would have been closer to what would affect the outcome of a war than the simple comparison that was used.

Furthermore, in looking at inputs people have a preference for absolutes, for examining what is most easily quantified, and for stressing what they have most information on. Thus, in the 1930s the British judged comparative air strength by counting the number of planes each side had. Sometimes they distinguished the total number from what they called "first-line" aircraft—planes of the most modern design—but even this degree of complexity was often dropped (Gilbert, 1967). This was not because the British treated the whole question of the comparison casually. There were long debates over how to calculate first-line strength (Gilbert, 1967), but the attempts to push beyond this measure were few and desultory.

Quality of the aircraft was omitted from most calculations. For example, the British official history notes that in looking at the effectiveness of a planned expansion of their bombers, the British took "no account of the fact that paper plans were . . . actively being made within the Air Ministry to incorporate the new heavy four-engined machines into the bomber force" (Gibbs, 1976, p. 569). Government critics like Churchill who called for a rapid expansion of the RAF also generally ignored the linked questions of what aircraft were ready for production and whether it would have been better to postpone increased procurement until a new generation of planes was available.

Quality of personnel likewise was given short shrift. Although the Germans suffered from the "teething problems" associated with a young and expanding force, questions of training, morale, and maintenance were generally ignored. Similarly, emphasis on numbers of planes usually excluded consideration of each side's production capacity, which was vital for sustaining and increasing its force in wartime. A country might be stronger with a somewhat smaller standing air force supported by large and flexible production facilities than it would be with a larger force that would not be maintained in the face of wartime losses. But production facilities remained marginal to the British estimates of the military balance.

This pattern of assessment was not limited to air power. In judging their naval strength before World War I, the British also relied exclusively on numerical comparisons without consideration of quality. As the battles showed, seamanship, strength of armor, accuracy of fire, ship design, and the effectiveness of shells were extremely important, and the German superiority in the latter two categories cost the British dearly. The impact of factors such as these also shows up in ground combat. In 1940, French tanks were superior to German tanks in numbers and roughly equal in quality. Tactics, training, morale, coordination, and political will made all the difference. But even had planners been aware of their importance, it is doubtful whether they could have developed sufficient understanding of them to have usefully employed them in their analysis.

In summary, British decision makers concentrated on what was relatively easy to measure at the expense of trying to develop more complex, but more revealing, measures of relative strength. By implicitly assuming that both sides were planning to use their airplanes in the same way, which they could have learned was not correct, they were able to concentrate on only one dimension, just as the experimental subjects did. The yardstick they employed was distinguished only by the extent to which it facilitated comparisons and decisions. It gave them manageable simplicity, summary numbers they could hold in their minds and easily use.

The same pattern was apparent during the Cold War. Heavy reliance was placed on "static indicators"—numbers of missiles and warheads, the amount of throw-weight, and the extent of the damage that each side could do to the other. (The indicators of latter capability were themselves derived from highly oversimplified calculations.) Although there was some discussion of "counter-balancing asymmetries," arguments often were couched in terms of which side was ahead on any of these dimensions. For example, in the fall of 1981 many officials in the United States were disturbed by reports that Soviet missiles had become more accurate than American missiles, just as in other periods there was fear that the Soviets were developing better bombers than the United States possessed. Calculations are facilitated by such comparison, but this conservation of cognitive resources is purchased at the price of answering questions that make no sense. The accuracy of each side's missiles or the quality of its bombers were significant, but the direct comparison of these factors was not. Each weapons system should have been evaluated in terms of its ability to carry out its mission; an increase in, say, the quality of Soviet bombers may have had important implications for U.S. air defense, but it said nothing about the utility of American bombers. There may have been reasons to be disturbed if Soviet missiles were extremely accurate, but comparison with the accuracy of American missiles says nothing about the ability of either side's forces to carry out useful missions.

At first glance, numbers of bombers and missiles (or their destructive capabilities) would seem to make more sense. But they do not. As noted earlier, whether the state is ahead or behind its adversary in strategic weaponry says little about the question of whether the state's military force is adequate for its foreign policy. Furthermore, in a counterforce war in which strategic forces are to be attacked, what is crucial is the match between the numbers and characteristics of the weapons (particularly accuracy) on the one hand and the numbers and characteristics of the targets on the other. This complex matter is not illuminated by comparing the two sides' weapon systems themselves. One side could have more weapons, warheads, throw-weight, or even hard-target kill capability than the other yet be less able to wage a counterforce war than the adversary because the latter's forces are more protected than the former's. To come closer to what we want to know, we need to consider the state's ability to locate the adversary's forces and communicate with its own, but here again knowing—or estimating—which side is "ahead" in this regard does not tell us which side's forces, if either, could complete their required missions.

Arms control negotiations show the same concern with equality of static indicators, especially numbers of missiles and warheads. Indeed, the Jackson amendment passed in the wake of SALT 1 agreements required that future treaties should "not limit the United States to levels of intercontinental strategic forces inferior to the limits provided for the Soviet Union" (Wolfe, 1979, p. 301). In the months that followed its passage, this somewhat vague prescription hardened into a mandate for a force of the same size as that of the USSR, and Henry Kissinger's attempts to gain agreement within the United States on proposals embodying "offsetting asymmetries" failed because opponents were able to rally forces in and outside of government to the misleading standard of equality. Furthermore, even more sophisticated analysts, who saw that there was no magic in equality, generally argued that lower numbers of weapons would make the world safer and paid surprisingly little attention to the goal of stability that arms control was initially designed to reach and whose relationship to reduced numbers was only problematical (Schelling, 1985).

Similar intellectual shortcuts are revealed by the tendency to compare how well American forces would have done in a first strike with how well the USSR would have done if struck first. In fact, while both of these estimates were significant, it does not matter who was "ahead" in this regard.

Both sides cannot simultaneously strike first, and these capabilities can never be matched against each other. The degree of first-strike capability that the United States needed was not a function of the damage that the Soviets could have done if they had struck first.

When output is measured in terms of civilian rather than military damage, a parallel flaw often appears. One of Nixon's criteria for "essential equivalence" was that the Soviet Union not be able to do more damage to the United States than the United States could do to it. Winston Churchill made the same point in 1934: "I believe that if we maintain at all times in the future an air power sufficient to enable us to inflict as much damage upon the most probable assailant, upon the most likely potential aggressor, as he can inflict upon us, we may shield our people effectually in our times from all those horrors that I have ventured to describe" (Gilbert, 1967, p. 574). But in neither case was such a simple yardstick appropriate. States do not decide to go to war on the basis of comparisons between how much they will suffer and how much harm will come to their adversaries. If decision makers are even minimally rational, they compare their estimates of the probable gains and losses of going to war with what the state expects the situation to be if it does not attack. Thus an aggressor could be deterred even if a state thought it could inflict more damage than it would receive or, in other circumstances, could attack even if it thought this balance was reversed. Such assessments of damage also fit the drunkard's search metaphor in their omission of many factors whose importance is matched only by the difficulty of measuring them, such as long-term casualties and environmental effects of nuclear war.

There is little dispute on these points: all analysts agree that it is better to use "dynamic indicators" that attempt to capture the likely courses of wars fought under various conditions. But such measures are much more expensive in terms of time and cognitive resources and do not yield simple and straightforward summary numbers. Because they involve a large number of variables of widely different kinds and are highly sensitive to conditions and context—e.g., how the war starts, what each side's targeting strategy is, how well the weapons work, etc.—they do not lend themselves to easy comparison over time or between two adversaries. Thus, it is not surprising that static indicators remained popular; for all their inadequacies, they are relatively easy to develop and use.

Even dynamic indicators pay little attention to factors that, while crucial, are particularly difficult to capture, such as command, control, and communications. The survival and efficiency of these systems would have an enormous impact on the way that any war could be fought and terminated—indeed a significant advantage on this dimension would more than outweigh a major disadvantage in numbers of missiles. But we know so little about how these systems would function in wartime that they do not figure in our assessments.

In the same way, political factors that would have influenced the outcome of a limited war were left out of most analyses of the strategic balance. We hardly need to be reminded that the victor in Vietnam was incomparably weaker than its adversary on all standard military indicators. The outcome of any war that ends through negotiations will be strongly influenced by the stakes each side has in the conflict, each side's willingness to bear pain, each side's fear that the war will continue and grow even more destructive, and each side's perception of how the other side stands on these dimensions (see Jervis, 1984). But since these factors—which may be highly situation-specific—are so hard to estimate and complicate analysis enormously, they too are neglected.

Most attempts to assess the strategic balance also conformed to our model in that they pretended to greater certainty than the information actually permitted. They did not deal adequately with the large number of unknowns that characterize the complex weapons systems that have never been used. Would missiles have been as accurate when fired over the North Pole as they were on test ranges? Could a large number of missiles have been fired simultaneously? How vulnerable were various targets? How would nuclear explosions have affected communications systems? What would be the environmental effects of a war? This list could be readily expanded even if we ignored questions about human behavior. Indeed, there may be crucial questions that we do not even know enough to ask—only in the past decade did people think about the effects of explosions on world climate.

These uncertainties are so enormous that they present insurmountable obstacles to a complete and thorough analysis. But what is striking from the standpoint of common sense, but expected by the model of the drunkard's search, is that few discussions contained any sensitivity analysis. That is, they did not explain how the results would have differed if the assumptions on which they were based were altered. Instead, most analyses of the effects of various strikes presented misleadingly firm conclusions about the expected consequences of nuclear war. One used to read, for example, that a Soviet first strike would probably destroy all but 50 U.S. ICBMS. But while this claim might have been based on the best estimate, what was generally ignored was that the number of ICBMS might have been much higher or lower. In other words, this number represented some sort of average of the uncertainties and concealed the extent to which the result could have been wildly different if any of the assumptions were incorrect. It matters a great deal how likely it is that an outcome will be radically different from the best estimate—e.g., whether all missiles in a first strike might miss their targets. Only occasionally did one get some of this information in the form of a range of 50%, 75%, or 90% within which the analysts were certain that the outcome would fall. In the overwhelming majority of cases, the prediction came in the form of a misleadingly precise estimate of the likely outcome rather than in a presentation of the range of outcomes within which the actual result was likely to occur. It often will turn out that if one wants 90% certainty, the range will be so wide that the analysis is extremely difficult to use. At bottom is the problem that to dwell on the unknowns could render the calculations unmanageable, as perhaps the problems themselves are.

In both the 1930s and the Cold War, one can argue that it made sense for the actors to use illogical but simple measures because others whom the actors wanted to influence considered them accurate measures of strategic power. A self-fulfilling prophecy was then at work. For example, the British were under pressure to build a "shop window" force (one that had no reserves), because the Germans would count only these planes, and so deterrence would be maximized. As the minutes of a British cabinet meeting paraphrased the secretary of state for air's explanation

of his proposed bomber expansion program, he pointed to the crux of the matter, that military considerations as such really had little to do with the issue; . . . arguing that "the policy now being considered was designed largely as a gesture to check Herr Hitler's continual demands. . . ." The program that resulted [from these deliberations] had no function other than to produce the same size front line as Germany was expected to have in April 1937. No notion of wartime use of such a force [or of the fact that Britain was more vulnerable than Germany and had more alliance commitments] . . . entered into the considerations. (Smith, 1986, pp. 156–57)

Similarly, during the Cold War the United States had to be concerned with the throw-weight balance or the warhead balance because the Soviets, NATO allies, and neutrals believed that the side that was ahead on these dimensions was more likely to stand firm and prevail in disputes. A full discussion of this question would take us off the track (see Jervis, 1989b), but it should be noted that this consideration cannot be the entire explanation for the phenomenon. Not only is there no direct evidence to support the claim that others see the strategic military balance in this way—the Germans did not in the 1930s and the Soviets probably did not during the Cold War—but purely military analyses that are not concerned with second-order political implications display the same pattern of using only easily available information. What is in control, I think, is the pressure to simplify in order to conserve our time, energy, and cognitive resources.

Summary

We find the story of the drunkard's search humorous because we recognize that it is not entirely fictitious: people do look where the light is brightest. Nor is it entirely foolish: the costs of gathering and processing information need to be taken into account by any intelligent decision maker. But the pattern cannot be entirely explained by the rational search for and use of information. The data that analysts and decision makers use are often more distinguished by their ready availability than by their relation to the questions being asked. Like people in their everyday lives, statesmen tend to see a minimum of causal factors at work, minimize uncertainty, use simple benchmarks and analogies, and make comparisons that are manageable but inappropriate. Intellectual resources are conserved, but at a high price.

NOTES

1. Serge Schemann, "A Limited Success for Gorbachev," *New York Times*, October 1, 1986.
2. Thus telling someone about a possible factor is likely to increase the weight he or she will give to it. See Fischhoff, Slovic, and Lichtenstein, 1978.

Challenges of Decision-making

The work of political psychologists has the capacity to improve decision-making procedures and outcomes in political domains such as domestic affairs and foreign policy (e.g., Renshon & Larson, 2003; Tetlock, 1986; Tyler, 1990). Progress comes in part from analyzing past mistakes, such as range of cultural and historical contexts. Second, we take a look at the specific problem of racism as a political issue, mainly but not exclusively within the context of the United States.

THEORIES OF INTERGROUP RELATIONS IN SOCIETY

Although authoritarian personality theory (e.g., Adorno et al., 1950; Brown, 1965; Fromm, 1941) and realistic conflict theory (e.g., Campbell, 1965; Sherif et al., 1961) dominated the study of intergroup conflict in the middle of the 20th century, these perspectives were challenged by the emergence of social identity theory in the 1970s (e.g., Tajfel, 1978, 1981). The most cogent and compact description of this approach was published by the late Henri Tajfel and John Turner in 1986, and it is the first reading in this section. Tajfel and Turner argue that intergroup conflict arises from psychological processes of perceptual categorization, social comparison, and identity enhancement. This theory has generated a tremendous amount of research on phenomena such as ingroup favoritism and discrimination against outgroups.

The second reading in this section summarizes one of the more recent approaches to the political psychology of stereotyping and intergroup relations. This approach is called system justification theory and was introduced by John Jost and Mahzarin Banaji in 1994. Briefly, Jost and Banaji argue that group stereotypes serve an ideological *system justification* function in addition to two other cognitive-motivational functions long recognized by psychologists, namely *ego justification* (the tendency to defend and justify one's own actions, interests, and self-esteem) and *group justification* (the tendency to defend and justify the actions, interests, and esteem of fellow ingroup members). By recognizing that people seek to defend and justify the status quo—even when it seems to conflict with personal and group interests, system justification theory helps to understand why many members of disadvantaged groups accept and even perpetuate stereotypes that provide moral and intellectual justification for the overarching social system and for their own state of disadvantage.

The third reading in this section gives a brief description of social dominance theory and is taken from the second chapter of Sidanius and Pratto's (1999) book entitled *Social Dominance: An Intergroup Theory of Social Hierarchy and Oppression.* Social dominance theory shares several similarities with system justification theory; it is also an integrative theory, combining several different disciplinary approaches to explore consensually endorsed stereotypes, norms, and ideologies (or *legitimizing myths*). One important focus of the theory is on individual differences in social dominance orientation (e.g., Pratto et al., 1994). Social dominance theory embeds its analysis of group-based social hierarchy and

oppression within the framework of modern evolutionary psychology (e.g., Barkow, Cosmides, & Tooby, 1992).

THE ENDURING PROBLEM OF RACISM

Despite the successful passage of civil rights legislation in the United States securing basic political and human rights for African Americans and other ethnic minorities, despite the fact that blatant racism is no longer acceptable in public discourse and policy debates, and despite the fact that European Americans now broadly endorse general principles of racial equality, the fact is that whites generally oppose specific policies that promote equality in actual practice. This apparent contradiction in public opinion has become known as the *principle-implementation gap*. It has manifested itself in a number of areas, including opposition to busing to achieve racial integration in the schools, resistance to strong enforcement of anti-discrimination laws in housing and employment, and the widespread rejection of affirmative action policies.

One of the most prominent scholars to investigate this issue is Lawrence Bobo of Harvard University. In a (1988) chapter that we have reprinted, Bobo uses a variation of realistic conflict theory to argue that—in addition to racial prejudice and other "irrational hostilities" that whites might harbor against blacks—much of whites' resistance to redistributive racial policies (such as affirmative action) stems from their desire to maintain a privileged position at the top of American society. Thus, collective action and political mobilization on the part of African Americans and on their behalf is (quite "rationally") perceived as a threat to European Americans.

Another group of researchers has proposed alternatively that the racial attitudes of European Americans are best understood as reflecting a qualitatively new kind of racial prejudice. While different researchers have chosen different labels for this "new racism" (e.g., *aversive racism, ambivalent racism, modern racism, symbolic racism,* and *subtle racism*), they are in basic agreement that the new racism plays a significant role in the outcome of political events, including elections, legislation, and policy attitudes held by the mass public. One of the most influential proponents of this school of thought is David O. Sears of UCLA. Sears and his collaborators have argued that the civil rights movement of the 1960s was largely successful in eliminating traditional, "old-fashioned" racism from American society, but that it has been replaced by a new, insidious form of *symbolic racism.* Symbolic racism is defined as the conjunction of anti-black affect and the holding of traditional American values such as self-reliance, individualism, and the Protestant Work Ethic.

While symbolic racism theory has been very influential in political science and social psychology, it has also come under intense criticism (e.g., Sniderman & Tetlock, 1986; Sniderman, Piazza, Tetlock, & Kendrick, 1991; Weigel & Howes, 1985). Five major criticisms have been leveled against symbolic racism theory: (a) symbolic racism is simply "old wine in a new bottle," (b) in terms of measurement and conceptualization, symbolic racism captures a hodgepodge of heterogeneous beliefs rather than a coherent, homogenous single dimension, (c) symbolic racism is just another name for political conservatism, (d) symbolic racism simply refers to a variant of authoritarianism, and (e) the strong relationship that has been observed between symbolic racism and opposition to racial policies such as affirmative action is due to conceptual overlap between the measurement of symbolic racism and the racial policy attitudes that it is meant to predict.

In the final article included in this section, Sears and his colleagues make the most ambitious attempt yet to address the various criticisms that have been leveled at symbolic racism theory. One of their most important empirical arguments is that symbolic racial attitudes explain considerable variation in Whites' opposition to race-targeted policies across a wide range of policy issues, even after statistically controlling for factors such as political conservatism, authoritarianism, and endorsement of individualistic norms. Sears and his colleagues argue furthermore that symbolic racism has considerably more predictive power than traditional measures of racial prejudice. The issues raised by this relatively small collection of papers on intergroup relations and racism are among the most influential statements in recent times. Of course, many of the most controversial issues are far from having been settled in any definitive sense and will most likely rage on for several years to come.

Discussion Questions

1. What are the most important similarities and differences among social identity theory, system justification theory, social dominance theory, realistic conflict theory, and symbolic racism theory?
2. Do you think that ingroup favoritism and outgroup derogation are universal human motives? Why or why not?
3. The focus of the American debate on "race" has shifted dramatically over the last 30 years. What is the nature of this shift and what are the primary theoretical arguments concerning race that scholars are now engaged in?
4. Using existing theory and research from political psychology, what are at least three promising ways of understanding the *principle-implementation gap*?
5. In the debate between theorists of symbolic racism and their critics, which side do you take on each of the key issues and why?

Suggested Readings

Bobo, L., & Hutchings, V.L. (1996). Perception of racial group competition: Extending Blumer's theory of group position to a multiracial social context. *American Sociological Review, 61,* 951-973.

Brewer, M. B. (1979). In-group bias in the minimal intergroup situation: A cognitive-motivational analysis. *Psychological Bulletin, 86,* 307–324.

Carmines, E. G., & Merriman, W.R., Jr. (1993). The changing American dilemma: Liberal values and racial policies. In P. M. Sniderman, P. E. Tetlock, & E.G. Carmines (Eds.), *Prejudice, politics, and the American dilemma* (pp. 237–255). Stanford, CA: Stanford University Press.

Conover, P. J., Mingst, K. A., & Sigelman, L. (1980). Mirror images in Americans' perceptions of nations and leaders during the Iranian hostage crisis. *Journal of Peace Research, 17,* 325–337.

Dovidio, J. F., & Gaertner, S.L. (1998). On the nature of contemporary prejudice: The causes, consequences, and challenges of aversive racism. In J. L. Eberhart & S. T. Fiske (Eds.), *Confronting prejudice: The problem and the response* (pp. 3–32). Thousand Oaks, CA: Sage.

Edsall, T. B., & Edsall, M. D. (1991, May). When the official subject is Presidential politics, taxes, welfare, crime, rights, or values . . . the real subject is race. *Atlantic Monthly,* pp. 53–86.

Federico, C. M., & Sidanius, J. (2002). Sophistication and the antecedents of Whites' racial-policy attitudes: Racism, ideology, and affirmative action in America. *Public Opinion Quarterly, 66,* 145–176.

Herring, M. H., Jankowski, T. B., & Brown, R. E. (1999). Pro-Black doesn't mean anti-White: The structure of African-American group identity. *The Journal of Politics, 61,* 363–386.

Hochschild, J. L. (1995). *Facing up to the American dream: Race, class, and the soul of the nation.* Princeton, NJ: Princeton University Press.

Hogg, M. A., & Abrams, D. (1988). *Social identifications: A social psychology of intergroup relations and group processes.* London: Routledge.

Jackman, M. (1994). *The velvet glove: Paternalism and conflict in gender, class and race relations*. Berkeley: University of California Press.

Jackman, M. R. & Muha, M. J. (1984). Education and intergroup attitudes: Moral enlightenment, superficial democratic commitment, or ideological refinement? *American Sociological Review, 49,* 751–769.

Jost, J. T., & Major, B. (2001). *The psychology of legitimacy: Emerging perspectives on ideology, justice and intergroup relation*. Cambridge, UK: Cambridge University Press.

Kinder, D. R., & Sanders, L. M. (1996). *Divided by color: Racial politics and democratic ideals*. Chicago: University of Chicago Press.

Klinkner, P. A., & Smith, R. M. (1999). *The unsteady march: The rise and decline of racial equality in America*. Chicago: University of Chicago Press.

McConahay, J. B. (1986). Modern racism, ambivalence, and the modern racism scale. In S. L. Gaertner & J. F. Dovidio (Eds.), *Prejudice, discrimination, and racism: Theory and research* (pp. 91–125). New York: Academic Press.

Mendelberg, Tali (2001). *The race card: Campaign strategy, implicit messages, and the norm of equality*. Princeton: Princeton University Press.

Sears, D. O. (1988). Symbolic racism. In P. A. Katz & D. A. Taylor (Eds.), *Eliminating racism: Profiles in controversy* (pp. 53–84). New York: Plenum.

Sears, D. O., & Henry, P. J. (2002). The symbolic racism 2000 scale. *Political Psychology, 23,* 253–283.

Sears, D. O., Sidanius, J., & Bobo, L. (2000). *Racialized politics: The debate about racism in America*. Chicago: University of Chicago Press.

Sidanius, J. & Pratto, F. (1999). *Social dominance: An intergroup theory of social hierarchy and oppression*. New York: Cambridge University Press.

Sidanius, J., Pratto, F., & Bobo, L. (1996). Racism, conservatism, affirmative action and intellectual sophistication: A matter of principled conservatism or group dominance? *Journal of Personality and Social Psychology, 70,* 476–490.

Sniderman, P. M., & Piazza, T. (1993). *The scar of race*. Cambridge, MA: Harvard University Press.

Sniderman, P. M., & Tetlock, P. E. (1986). Symbolic racism: Problems of motive attribution in political analysis. *Journal of Social Issues, 42,* 129–150.

Sniderman, P., Piazza, T., Tetlock, P. E., & Kendrick, A. (1991). The new racism. *American Journal of Political Science, 35,* 423–447.

Thernstrom, S., & Thernstrom, A. (1997). *America in black and white: One nation, indivisible*. New York, NY: Simon & Schuster.

Turner, J. C., Hogg, M. A., Oakes, P. J., Reicher, S., & Wetherell, M. S. (1987). *Rediscovering the social group: A self-categorization theory*. Oxford: Basil Blackwell.

The Social Identity Theory of Intergroup Behavior

Henri Tajfel • Formerly of the University of Bristol, England
John C. Turner • Macquarie University, Australia

Introduction

The aim of this chapter is to present an outline of a theory of intergroup conflict and some preliminary data relating to the theory. First, however, this approach to intergroup behavior and intergroup conflict must be set in context, in relation to other approaches to the same problem.

Much of the work on the social psychology of intergroup relations has focused on patterns of individual prejudices and discrimination and on the motivational sequences of interpersonal interaction. Outstanding examples of these approaches can be found, respectively, in the theory of authoritarian personality (Adorno et al., 1950) and in the various versions and modifications of the theory of frustration, aggression, and displacement (such as Berkowitz, 1962, 1969, 1974). The common denominator of most of this work has been the stress on the intraindividual or interpersonal psychological processes leading to prejudiced attitudes or discriminatory behavior. The complex interweaving of individual or interpersonal behavior with the contextual social processes of intergroup conflict and their psychological effects has not been in the focus of the social psychologist's preoccupations (see Tajfel, 1981, pp. 13–56, and Turner & Giles, 1981, for more detailed discussions).

The alternative to these approaches has been represented by the work of Muzafer Sherif and his associates and has been referred to by D. T. Campbell (1965) as the "realistic group conflict theory" (RCT). Its point of departure for the explanation of intergroup behavior is in what Sherif (1967) has called the functional relations between social groups. Its central hypothesis—"real conflict of group interests causes intergroup conflict"—is deceptively simple, intuitively convincing, and has received strong empirical support (including Avigdor, 1953; Bass & Dunteman, 1963; Blake & Mouton, 1961, 1962; Diab, 1970; Harvey, 1956; Johnson, 1967; Sherif et al., 1961; Sherif & Sherif, 1953).

RCT was pioneered in social psychology by the Sherifs, who provided both an etiology of intergroup hostility and a theory of competition as realistic and instrumental in character, motivated by rewards which, in principle, are extrinsic to the intergroup situation (see Deutsch, 1949; Julian, 1968). Opposed group interests in obtaining scarce resources promote competition, and positively interdependent (superordinate) goals facilitate cooperation. Conflicting interests develop, through competition, into overt social conflict. It appears, too, that intergroup competition enhances intragroup morale, cohesiveness, and cooperation (Fiedler, 1967; Kalin & Marlowe, 1968; Vinacke,

1964). Thus, real conflicts of group interests not only create antagonistic intergroup relations but also heighten identification with, and positive attachment to, the in-group.

This identification with the in-group, however, has been given relatively little prominence in RCT as a theoretical problem in its own right. The development of in-group identifications is seen in RCT almost as an epiphenomenon of intergroup conflict. As treated by RCT, these identifications are associated with certain patterns of intergroup relations, but the theory does not focus either upon the processes underlying the development and maintenance of group identity nor upon the possibly autonomous effects upon the in-group and intergroup behavior of these "subjective" aspects of group membership. It is our contention that the relative neglect of these processes in RCT is responsible for some inconsistencies between the empirical data and the theory in its "classical" form. In this sense, the theoretical orientation to be outlined here is intended not to replace RCT, but to supplement it in some respects that seem to us essential for an adequate social psychology of intergroup conflict—particularly as the understanding of the psychological aspects of social change cannot be achieved without an appropriate analysis of the social psychology of social conflict.

The Social Context of Intergroup Behavior

Our point of departure for the discussion to follow will be an a priori distinction between two extremes of social behavior, corresponding to what we shall call interpersonal versus intergroup behavior. At one extreme (which most probably is found in its pure form only rarely in real life) is the interaction between two or more individuals that is fully determined by their interpersonal relationships and individual characteristics, and not at all affected by various social groups or categories to which they respectively belong. The other extreme consists of interactions between two or more individuals (or groups of individuals) that are fully determined by their respective memberships in various social groups or categories, and not at all affected by the interindividual personal relationships between the people involved. Here

again, it is probable that pure forms of this extreme are found only infrequently in real social situations. Examples that might normally tend to be near the interpersonal extreme would be the relations between wife and husband or between old friends. Examples that would normally approach the intergroup extreme are the behavior of soldiers from opposing armies during a battle, or the behavior at a negotiating table of members representing two parties in an intense intergroup conflict.

Some of the theoretical issues concerning this continuum are discussed by Turner (1982, 1984), Brown & Turner (1981), and Stephenson (1981); the main empirical questions concern the conditions that determine the adoption of forms of social behavior nearing one or the other extreme. The first—and obvious—answer concerns intergroup conflict. It can be assumed, in accordance with our common experience, that the more intense is an intergroup conflict, the more likely it is that the individuals who are members of the opposite groups will behave toward each other as a function of their respective group memberships, rather than in terms of their individual characteristics or interindividual relationships. This was precisely why Sherif (1967, for example) was able to abolish so easily the interindividual friendships formed in the preliminary stages of some of his field studies when, subsequently, the individuals who had become friends were assigned to opposing groups.

An institutionalized or explicit conflict of objective interests between groups, however, does not provide a fully adequate basis, either theoretically or empirically, to account for many situations in which the social behavior of individuals belonging to distinct groups can be observed to approach the "group" extreme of our continuum. The conflict in Sherif's studies was "institutionalized" in that it was officially arranged by the holiday camp authorities; it was "explicit" in that it dominated the life of the groups; and it was "objective" in the sense that, given the terms of the competition, one of the groups had to be the winner and the other group the loser. And yet, there is evidence from Sherif's own studies and from other research that the institutionalization, explicitness, and objectivity of an intergroup conflict are not necessary conditions for behavior in terms of the "group" extreme, although they will often prove to be sufficient conditions. One clear example is provided by our earlier experiments (Tajfel, 1970; Tajfel et al., 1971), which we shall discuss briefly below, in which it was found that intergroup discrimination existed in conditions of minimal in group affiliation, anonymity of group membership, absence of conflicts of interest, and absence of previous hostility between the groups.

Other social and behavioral continua are associated with the interpersonal-intergroup continuum. One of them may serve to summarize a quasi-ideological dimension of attitudes, values, and beliefs that may be plausibly hypothesized to play a causal role in relation to it. This dimension will also be characterized by its two extremes, which we shall refer to as "social mobility" and "social change." These terms are not used here in their sociological sense. They refer instead to individuals' belief systems about the nature and the structure of the relations between social groups in their society. The belief system of "social mobility" is based on the general assumption that the society in which the individuals live is a flexible and permeable one, so that if they are not satisfied, for whatever reason, with the conditions imposed upon their lives by membership in social groups or social categories to which they belong, it is possible for them (be it through talent, hard work, good luck, or whatever other means) to move individually into another group that suits them better. A good example of this system of beliefs, built into the explicit cultural and ideological traditions of a society, is provided in the following passage from Hirschman (1970):

> The traditional American idea of success confirms the hold which exit has had on the national imagination. Success—or, what amounts to the same thing, upward social mobility—has long been conceived in terms of evolutionary individualism. The successful individual who starts out at a low rung of the social ladder, necessarily leaves his own group as he rises; he "passes" into, or is "accepted" by, the next higher group. He takes his immediate family along, but hardly anyone else. (pp. 108–109)

At the other extreme, the belief system of "social change" implies that the nature and structure of the relations between social groups in the society is characterized by marked stratification, making it impossible or very difficult for individuals,

as individuals, to divest themselves of an unsatisfactory, underprivileged, or stigmatized group membership. The economic or social realities of a society may be such (as, for example, in the case of the millions of unemployed during the Depression of the 1930s) that the impossibility of "getting out" on one's own, as an individual, becomes an everyday reality that determines many forms of intergroup social behavior. But even this example is still relatively extreme. Many social intergroup situations that contain, for whatever reasons, strong elements of stratification perceived as such may tend to move social behavior away from the pole of interpersonal patterns toward the pole of intergroup patterns. This is as true of groups that are "superior" in a social system as of those that are "inferior" in it. The major characteristic of social behavior related to this belief is that, in the relevant intergroup situations, individuals will not interact *as* individuals, on the basis of their individual characteristics or interpersonal relationships, but as members of their groups standing in certain defined relationships to members of other groups.

Obviously, one must expect a marked correlation between the degree of objective stratification in a social system (however measured) and the social diffusion and intensity of the belief system of "social change." This, however, cannot be a one-to-one relationship for a number of reasons, some of which will be discussed below, although we cannot in this chapter go into the details of the many social-psychological conditions that may determine the transition in certain social groups from an acceptance of stratification to behavior characteristic of the intergroup pole of our first continuum—that is, to the creation of social movements aiming to change (or to preserve) the status quo (see Tajfel, 1978a; Giles & Johnson, 1981, provide a thorough discussion of this issue in the context of seeking to predict the conditions under which ethnic groups will accentuate their distinctive languages, dialects, or accents).

It may be interesting, however, to point to the close relationship that exists between an explicit intergroup conflict of interests, on the one hand, and the "social change" system of beliefs on the other. One of the main features of this belief system is the perception by the individuals concerned that it is impossible or extremely difficult to move individually from their own group to another group. This is precisely the situation in an intense conflict of interests, in which it is extremely difficult for an individual to conceive of the possibility of "betraying" his or her own group by moving to the opposing group. Although this does happen on occasion, sanctions for such a move are, on the whole, powerful, and the value systems (at least in our cultures) are in flagrant opposition to it. To use an example from social-psychological research, it seems hardly possible that one of the boys in Sherif's holiday camps would decide to change sides, even though some of his previously contracted friendships overlapped group boundaries.

The intensity of explicit intergroup conflicts of interests is closely related in our cultures to the degree of opprobrium attached to the notion of "renegade" or "traitor." This is why the belief systems corresponding to the "social change" extreme of our continuum are associated with intense intergroup conflicts. These conflicts can be conceived, therefore, as creating a subclass or a subcategory of the subjective intergroup dichotomization characteristic of that extreme of the belief continuum. They share the basic feature of the "social change" system of beliefs, in the sense that the multigroup structure is perceived as characterized by the extreme difficulty or impossibility of an individual's moving from one group to another.

The continuum of systems of beliefs discussed so far represents one conjecture as to one important set of subjective conditions that may shift social behavior toward members of out-groups between the poles of "interpersonal" and "intergroup" behavior within particular situations and societies. To conclude this part of our preliminary discussion, we must characterize briefly two further and overlapping continua, which can be considered as encompassing the major consequences of social behavior that approaches one or the other end of the interpersonal-intergroup continuum. They both have to do with the variability or uniformity within a group of behavior and attitudes concerning the relevant out-groups. The first may be described as follows: The nearer members of a group are to the "social change" extreme of the belief-systems continuum and the intergroup extreme of the behavioral continuum, the more uniformity they will show in their behavior toward members of the relevant out-group; an approach toward the opposite extremes of both these continua will be correspondingly associated with greater in-group variability of behavior toward

members of the out-group. The second statement is closely related to the first: the nearer members of a group are to the "social change" and the "intergroup" extremes, the more they will tend to treat members of the out-group as undifferentiated items in a unified social category, rather than in terms of their individual characteristics. The vast literature in social psychology on the functioning of group stereotypes in situations of intense intergroup tensions is no more than an example of this general statement.

Thus, this preliminary conceptualization represents an approach to the social psychology of intergroup relations that takes into account social realities as well as their reflection in social behavior through the mediation of socially shared systems of beliefs. This convergence occurs at both ends of the sequence just discussed; at the beginning, because it can be assumed without much difficulty that the "social change" belief system is likely to reflect either an existing and marked social stratification or an intense intergroup conflict of interests, or both; at the end, because the consequences of the systems of beliefs arising from the social situations just mentioned are likely to appear in the form of unified group actions—that is, in the form of social movements aiming either to create social change or to preserve the status quo. We shall return later to an elaboration of the kinds of hypotheses that can be put forward concerning the creation of change versus the preservation of status quo. But before this is done, the realistic group conflict theory must be considered against this general background.

The implications of this conceptualization for intergroup relations in stratified societies and institutions are both evident and direct. Whenever social stratification is based upon an unequal division of scarce resources—such as power, prestige, or wealth—and hence there is a real conflict of interests between social groups, the social situation should be characterized by pervasive ethnocentrism and out-group antagonism between the over- and underprivileged groups (Oberschall, 1973, p. 33). However, decades of research into ethnic-group relations suggest that ethnocentrism among stratified groups is, or at least it has been, very much a one-way street. Milner (1975, 1981) and Giles and Powesland (1975) summarize a great deal of evidence that minority or subordinate group members—such as the American Blacks, the

French Canadians, the New Zealand Maoris, or the South African Bantus—have frequently tended to derogate the in-group and display positive attitudes toward the dominant out-group. In other words, deprived groups are not always ethnocentric in the simple meaning of the term; they may, in fact, be positively oriented toward the depriving out-group. Data of this kind are not consistent with a simple application of RCT. (Recent detailed reviews of other field and laboratory data relevant to assessing the validity of the theory are provided by Brewer, 1979, Stephenson, 1981, and Turner, 1981.)

Some writers (including Gregor & McPherson, 1966; Milner, 1975, 1981; Morland, 1969) have argued that the status relations between dominant and subordinate groups determine the latter's identity problems. (By social status we mean a ranking or hierarchy of perceived prestige.) Subordinate groups often seem to internalize a wider social evaluation of themselves as "inferior" or "second class," and this consensual inferiority is reproduced as relative self-derogation on a number of indices that have been used in the various studies. Consensual status itself—where subjective and accorded prestige are identical—is problematic for RCT, which conceptualizes prestige as a scarce resource, like wealth or power. Status differences between groups, like other inequalities, should tend to accentuate the intergroup conflict of interests. Therefore, according to RCT, the impact of low status upon a subordinate group should be to intensify its antagonism toward the high-status group (Thibaut, 1950). Yet, under some conditions at least, low social status seems to be correlated with an enhancement, rather than a lessening, of positive out-group attitudes.

It could be argued that only conflicts of interest perceived as such create hostility. This requires that groups must compare their respective situations. And, according to some views, it is only relatively similar groups that engage in mutual comparisons; therefore, many forms of status differences will reduce perceived similarity (see Festinger, 1954; Kidder & Stewart, 1975). It follows that status systems may reduce social conflict by restricting the range of meaningful comparisons available to any given group. This hypothesis may be a useful tool to account for some of the determinants of social stability; but if it is taken to its logical conclusion, it can account for no more than that. It

fails to account for social change (in the sense of changes in the mutual relations, behavior, and attitudes of large-scale human groups that have been distinctly different in status in the past), particularly when the processes of change become very rapid. Status differences between groups often do not remain unilaterally associated with low levels of intergroup conflict. For example, the generalization made above—that certain forms of political, economic, and social subordination of a social group tend to eliminate or even reverse its ethnocentrism—is already dated. Research conducted over the last two decades reveals a changing pattern in intergroup relations. American Blacks (Brigham, 1971; Friedman, 1969; Harris & Braun, 1971; Hraba & Grant, 1970), French Canadians (Berry, Kalin & Taylor, 1977), New Zealand Maoris (Vaughan, 1978) and the Welsh (Bourhis, Giles & Tajfel, 1973; Giles & Powesland, 1975), for instance, now seem to be rejecting (or have already rejected) their previously negative in-group evaluations and developing a positive ethnocentric group identity. (Milner, 1981, and Tajfel, 1982b, argue that these new data are likely to be a genuine reflection of social change.) This construction of positive in-group attitudes has often been accompanied by a new militancy over political and economic objectives (see Tomlinson, 1970).

But these developments do not rescue RCT in its original form. The very suddenness with which the scene has changed effectively rules out objective deprivation and therefore *new* conflicting group interests as sufficient conditions for the "subordinate" group ethnocentrism. On the contrary, there has often been less objective deprivation than there was in the past. An active and new search for a positive group identity seems to have been one of the critical factors responsible for the reawakening of these groups' claims to scarce resources (Dizard, 1970).

In summary, RCT states that opposing claims to scarce resources, such as power, prestige, or wealth, generate ethnocentrism and antagonism between groups. Therefore, low status should tend to intensify out-group hostility in groups that are politically, economically, or socially subordinate. The evidence suggests, however, that where social-structural differences in the distribution of resources have been institutionalized, legitimized, and justified through a consensually accepted status system (or at least a status system that is sufficiently firm and pervasive to prevent the creation of cognitive alternatives to it), the result has been less and not more ethnocentrism in the different status groups. The price of this has often been the subordinate group's self-esteem. On the other hand, whenever a subordinate group begins, for whatever reasons, to question or deny its presumed characteristics associated with its low status, this seems to facilitate the reawakening of a previously dormant conflict over objective resources. At the same time, it is likely that one of the counter-reactions from the dominant groups in such situations will be to work for the preservation of the previously existing "subjective" and "objective" differentiations.

A tentative hypothesis about intergroup conflict in stratified societies can now be offered: An unequal distribution of objective resources promotes antagonism between dominant and subordinate groups, provided that the latter group rejects its previously accepted and consensually negative self-image, and with it the status quo, and starts working toward the development of a positive group identity. The dominant group may react to these developments either by doing everything possible to maintain and justify the status quo or by attempting to find and create new differentiations in its own favor, or both. A more detailed specification of some of the strategies and "solutions" that can be adopted in this situation can be found in Tajfel (1978a); we shall return later to a discussion of some of them. For the present, it will be sufficient to state that, whether valid or not, the hypothesis raises some important theoretical problems that need to be considered. The first question is: What social-psychological processes are involved in the development of positive group identity? The second question concerns the conditions under which the status differences between social groups are likely to enhance or to reduce intergroup conflict. In order to continue the discussion of these questions, we must now abandon speculation and consider some relevant data.

Social Categorization and Intergroup Discrimination

The initial stimulus for the theorizing presented here was provided by certain experimental investigations of intergroup behavior. The laboratory analogue of real-world ethnocentrism is in-group bias—that is, the tendency to favor the in-group over the out-group in evaluations and behavior. Not only are incompatible group interests not always sufficient to generate conflict (as concluded in the last section), but there is a good deal of experimental evidence that these conditions are not always necessary for the development of competition and discrimination between groups (Brewer, 1979; Turner, 1981), although this does not mean, of course, that in-group bias is not influenced by the goal relations between the groups.

All this evidence implies that in-group bias is a remarkably omnipresent feature of intergroup relations. The phenomenon in its extreme form has been investigated by Tajfel and his associates. There have now been in addition to the original studies (Tajfel, 1970; Tajfel et al., 1971) a large number of other experiments employing a similar procedure (methodological and conceptual issues concerning the experimental paradigm are discussed by Aschenbrenner & Schaefer, 1980; Bornstein et al., 1983a; Bornstein et al., 1983b; Branthwaite, Doyle, & Lightbown, 1979; Brown, Tajfel, & Turner, 1980; Turner, 1980, 1983a, 1983b; and the results of the relevant studies are summarized most recently by Turner, 1983a, and in a wider theoretical and empirical context by Brewer, 1979; Brown & Turner, 1981; Turner, 1981, 1982), all showing that the mere perception of belonging to two distinct groups—that is, social categorization per se—is sufficient to trigger intergroup discrimination favoring the in-group. In other words, the mere awareness of the presence of an out-group is sufficient to provoke intergroup competitive or discriminatory responses on the part of the in-group.

In the basic paradigm the subjects (both children and adults have acted as subjects in the various studies) are randomly classified as members of two nonoverlapping groups—ostensibly on the basis of some trivial performance criterion. They then make "decisions," awarding amounts of money to pairs of other subjects (excluding self) in specially designed booklets. The recipients are anonymous, except for their individual code numbers and their group membership (for example, member number 51 of the X group and member number 33 of the Y group). The subjects, who know their own group membership, award the amounts individually and anonymously. The response format of the booklets does not force the subjects to act in terms of group membership.

In this situation, there is neither a conflict of interests nor previously existing hostility between the "groups." No social interaction takes place between the subjects, nor is there any rational link between economic self-interest and the strategy of in-group favoritism. Thus, these groups are purely cognitive and can be referred to as "minimal."

The basic and highly reliable finding is that the trivial, ad hoc intergroup categorization leads to in-group favoritism and discrimination against the out-group. Fairness is also an influential strategy. There is also a good deal of evidence that, within the pattern of responding in terms of in-group favoritism, maximum difference (MD) is more important to the subjects than maximum in-group profit (MIP). Thus, they seem to be competing with the out-group, rather than following a strategy of simple economic gain for members of the in-group. Other data from several experiments also show that the subjects' decisions were significantly nearer to the maximum joint payoff (MJP) point when these decisions applied to the division of money between two anonymous members of the in-group than when they applied to two members of the out-group; that is, relatively less was given to the out-group, even when giving more would not have affected the amounts for the in-group. Billig and Tajfel (1973) have found the same results even when the assignment to groups was made explicitly random. This eliminated the similarity on the performance criterion within the in-group as an alternative explanation of the results. An explicitly random classification into groups proved in this study to be a more potent determinant of discrimination than perceived interpersonal similarities and dissimilarities not associated with categorization into groups. Billig (1973), Brewer and Silver (1978), Locksley, Ortiz and Hepburn (1980), and Turner, Sachder and Hogg (1983) have all replicated this finding that even explicitly arbitrary social categorizations are sufficient for discrimination, and Allen and Wilder (1975) have provided additional evidence for the importance of group classification compared to similarities between people without such classification.

The question that arises is whether in-group bias in these minimal situations is produced by some form of the experimenter effect or of the demand characteristics of the experimental situation—in other words, whether explicit references to group membership communicate to the subjects that they are expected to, or ought to, discriminate. The first point to be made about this interpretation of the results is that explicit references to group membership are logically necessary for operationalizing in these minimal situations the major independent variable—that is, social categorization per se. This requires not merely that the subjects perceive themselves as similar to or different from others as individuals, but that they are members of discrete and discontinuous categories—that is, "groups." Second, a detailed analysis of the subjects' postsession reports (Billig, 1972; Turner, 1975a) shows that they do not share any common conception of the "appropriate" or "obvious" way to behave, that only a tiny minority have some idea of the hypothesis, and that this minority does not always conform to it. Thirdly, the relevant experimental data do not support this interpretation. St. Claire and Turner (1982) exposed observer-subjects to exactly the same experimental cues as normal categorized subjects; the former were required to predict the responses of the latter in the standard decision booklets. The categorized subjects did discriminate significantly, but the observers failed to predict it and in fact expected significantly more fairness than was actually displayed.

The more general theoretical problem has been referred to elsewhere by one of us as follows:

> Simply and briefly stated, the argument (e.g., Gerard and Hoyt, 1974) amounts to the following: the subjects acted in terms of the intergroup categorization provided or imposed by the experimenters, not necessarily because this has been successful in inducing any genuine awareness of membership in separate and distinct groups, but probably because they felt that this kind of behavior was expected of them by the experimenters, and therefore they conformed to this expectation. The first question to ask is why should the subjects be expecting the experimenters to expect of them this kind of behavior? The Gerard and Hoyt answer to this is that the experimental situation was rigged to cause this kind of expectation in the subjects. This answer retains its plausibility only if we assume that what was no more than a hint from the experimenters about the notion of "groups" being relevant to the subjects' behavior had been sufficient to determine, powerfully and consistently, *a particular form* of in-

tergroup behavior. In turn, if we assume this—and the assumption is by no means unreasonable—we must also assume that this particular form of intergroup behavior is one which is capable of being induced by the experimenters much more easily than other forms (such as cooperation between the groups in extorting the maximum total amount of money from the experimenters, or a fair division of the spoils between the groups, or simply random responding). And this last assumption must be backed up in its turn by another presupposition: namely, that for some reasons (whatever they may be) competitive behavior between groups, at least in our culture, is extraordinarily easy to trigger off—at which point we are back where we started from. The problem then must be restated in terms of the need to specify why a certain *kind* of intergroup behavior can be elicited so much more easily than other kinds; and this specification is certainly not made if we rest content with the explanation that the behavior occurred because it was very easy for the experimenters to make it occur. (Tajfel, 1978a, pp. 35–36)

Two points stand out: first, minimal intergroup discrimination is not based on incompatible group interests; second, the baseline conditions for intergroup competition seem indeed so minimal as to cause the suspicion that we are dealing here with some factor or process inherent in the intergroup situation itself. Our theoretical orientation was developed initially in response to these clues from our earlier experiments. We shall not trace the history of its development, however, but shall describe its present form.

Social Identity and Social Comparison

Many orthodox definitions of "social groups" are unduly restrictive when applied to the context of intergroup relations. For example, when members of two national or ethnic categories interact on the basis of their reciprocal beliefs about their respective categories and of the general relations between them, this is clearly intergroup behavior in the everyday sense of the term. The "groups" to which the interactants belong need not depend upon the frequency of intermember interaction, systems of role relationships, or interdependent goals. From the social-psychological perspective, the essential criteria for group membership, as they apply to

large-scale social categories, are that the individuals concerned define themselves and are defined by others as members of a group.

We can conceptualize a group, in this sense, as a collection of individuals who perceive themselves to be members of the same social category, share some emotional involvement in this common definition of themselves, and achieve some degree of social consensus about the evaluation of their group and of their membership in it. Following from this, our definition of intergroup behavior is basically identical to that of Sherif (1967, p. 62): any behavior displayed by one or more actors toward one or more others that is based on the actors' identification of themselves and the others as belonging to different social categories.

Social categorizations are conceived here as cognitive tools that segment, classify, and order the social environment, and thus enable the individual to undertake many forms of social action. But they do not merely systematize the social world; they also provide a system of orientation for *self-reference*: they create and define the individual's place in society. Social groups, understood in this sense, provide their members with an identification of themselves in social terms. These identifications are to a very large extent relational and comparative: they define the individual as similar to or different from, as "better" or "worse" than, members of other groups. It is in a strictly limited sense, arising from these considerations, that we use the term *social identity*. It consists, for the purposes of the present discussion, of those aspects of an individual's self-image that derive from the social categories to which he perceives himself as belonging. With this limited concept of social identity in mind, our argument is based on the following general assumptions:

1. Individuals strive to maintain or enhance their self-esteem: they strive for a positive self-concept.
2. Social groups or categories and the membership of them are associated with positive or negative value connotations. Hence, social identity may be positive or negative according to the evaluations (which tend to be socially consensual, either within or across groups) of those groups that contribute to an individual's social identity.
3. The evaluation of one's own group is deter-

mined with reference to specific other groups through social comparisons in terms of value-laden attributes and characteristics. Positively discrepant comparisons between in-group and out-group produce high prestige; negatively discrepant comparisons between in-group and out-group result in low prestige.

From these assumptions, some related theoretical principles can be derived:

1. Individuals strive to achieve or to maintain positive social identity.
2. Positive social identity is based to a large extent on favorable comparisons that can be made between the in-group and some relevant out-groups: the in-group must be perceived as positively differentiated or distinct from the relevant out-groups.
3. When social identity is unsatisfactory, individuals will strive either to leave their existing group and join some more positively distinct group and/or to make their existing group more positively distinct.

The basic hypothesis, then, is that pressures to evaluate one's own group positively through in-group/out-group comparisons lead social groups to attempt to differentiate themselves from each other (Tajfel, 1978a; Turner, 1975b). There are at least three classes of variables that should influence intergroup differentiation in concrete social situations. First, individuals must have internalized their group membership as an aspect of their self-concept: they must be subjectively identified with the relevant in-group. It is not enough that the others define them as a group, although consensual definitions by others can become, in the long run, one of the most powerful causal factors determining a group's self-definition. Second, the social situation must be such as to allow for intergroup comparisons that enable the selection and evaluation of the relevant relational attributes. Not all between-group differences have evaluative significance (Tajfel, 1959), and those that do vary from group to group. Skin color, for instance, is apparently a more salient attribute in the United States than in Hong Kong (Morland, 1969); whereas language seems to be an especially salient dimension of separate identity in French Canada, Wales, and Belgium (Giles & Johnson,

1981; Giles & Powesland, 1975). Third, in-groups do not compare themselves with every cognitively available out-group: the out-group must be perceived as a relevant comparison group. Similarity, proximity, and situational salience are among the variables that determine out-group comparability, and pressures toward in-group distinctiveness should increase as a function of this comparability. It is important to state at this point that, in many social situations, comparability reaches a much wider range than a simply conceived "similarity" between the groups.

The aim of differentiation is to maintain or achieve superiority over an out-group on some dimensions. Any such act, therefore, is essentially competitive. Fully reciprocal competition between groups requires a situation of mutual comparison and differentiation on a shared value dimension. In these conditions, intergroup competition, which may be unrelated to the objective goal relations between the groups, can be predicted to occur. Turner (1975b) has distinguished between social and instrumental or "realistic" competition. The former is motivated by self-evaluation and takes place through social comparison, whereas the latter is based on "realistic" self-interest and represents embryonic conflict. Incompatible group goals are necessary for realistic competition, but mutual intergroup comparisons are necessary, and often sufficient, for social competition. The latter point is consistent with the data from the minimal group experiments that mere awareness of an out-group is sufficient to stimulate in-group favoritism, and the observations (Doise & Weinberger, 1973; Ferguson & Kelley, 1964; Rabbie & Wilkens, 1971) that the possibility of social comparison generates "spontaneous" intergroup competition.

Social and realistic competition also differ in the predictions that can be made about the consequences for subsequent intergroup behavior of winning or losing. After realistic competition, the losing groups should be hostile to the out-group victors, both because they have been deprived of a reward and because their interaction has been exclusively conflictual. However, when winning and losing establish shared group evaluations concerning comparative superiority and inferiority, then, so long as the terms of the competition are perceived as legitimate and the competition itself as fair according to these terms, the losing group may acquiesce in the superiority of the winning out-group. This acquiescence by a group considering itself as legitimately "inferior" has been shown in studies by Caddick (1980, 1982), Commins and Lockwood, (1979) and Turner and Brown (1978). Several other studies report findings that are in line with this interpretation: losing in-groups do not always derogate, but sometimes upgrade, their evaluations of the winning out-groups (for example, Bass & Dunteman, 1963; Wilson & Miller, 1961).

Retrospectively, at least, the social-identity/social-comparison theory is consistent with many of the studies mentioned in the preceding section of this chapter. In particular, in the paradigm of the minimal group experiments, the intergroup discrimination can be conceived as being due not to conflict over monetary gains, but to differentiations based on comparisons made in terms of monetary rewards. Money functioned as a dimension of comparison (the only one available within the experimental design), and the data suggest that larger absolute gains that did not establish a difference in favor of the in-group were sacrificed for smaller comparative gains, when the two kinds of gains were made to conflict.

There is further evidence (Turner, 1978a) that the social-competitive pattern of intergroup behavior holds even when it conflicts with obvious self-interest. In this study, the distribution of either monetary rewards or "points" was made, within the minimal intergroup paradigm, between self and an anonymous other, who was either in the in-group or in the out-group. As long as minimal conditions existed for in-group identification, the subjects were prepared to give relatively less to themselves when the award (either in points or in money) was to be divided between self and an anonymous member of the in-group, as compared with dividing with an anonymous member of the out-group. These results seem particularly important, since the category of "self," which is by no means minimal or ad hoc, was set here against a truly minimal in-group category, identical to those used in the earlier experiments. Despite this stark asymmetry, the minimal group affiliation affected the responses.

The theoretical predictions were taken outside of the minimal categorization paradigm in a further study by Turner (1978b). He used face-to-face groups working on a discussion task. In each ses-sion, two three-person groups discussed an identical issue, supposedly to gain an assessment of their verbal intelligence, and then briefly compared their respective performance. The subjects were 144 male undergraduates. The criterion for intergroup differentiation was the magnitude of in-group bias shown in the ratings of the groups' work. Half the triads, composed of Arts students, believed that verbal intelligence was important for them (High Importance); half, composed of Science students, did not (Low Importance). Half the sessions involved two Arts or two Science groups (Similar Out-group), and half involved one Arts and one Science group (Dissimilar Out-group). Finally, in the Stable Difference condition, subjects were instructed that Arts students were definitely superior and Science students definitely inferior in verbal intelligence; in the Unstable Difference condition, there was no explicit statement that one category was better than the other. These variables were manipulated in a $2 \times 2 \times 2$ factorial design.

The results showed that the Arts (High Importance) groups were more biased than the Science (Low Importance) groups, that similar groups differentiated more than dissimilar groups in the Stable condition, but that they were no more biased (and sometimes even less so) in the Unstable condition; and that, on some of the measures, there was a significant main effect for out-group similarity: in-group bias increased against a similar out-group. Although these data are relatively complex, they do support some of our theoretical expectations and provide an illustration that variations in in-group bias can be systematically predicted from the social-identity/social-comparison theory.

We have argued that social and realistic competition are conceptually distinct, although most often they are empirically associated in "real life." In an experiment by Turner, Brown, and Tajfel (1979) an attempt was made to isolate the effects on intergroup behavior of the postulated autonomous processes attributed to a search for positive social identity. Children were used as subjects, and the manipulations involved decisions by the subjects about the distribution of payments for participation in the experiment, to be shared equally by the in-group, between the in-group and the out-groups that were made relevant or irrelevant to comparisons with the in-group's performance. Monetary self-interest (of a magnitude previously ascertained to be of genuine significance to the subjects) would have produced no difference in the distribution decisions involving the two kinds of out-group; it would also have led to decisions tending toward maximum in-group profit (MIP) rather than toward maximum difference (MD).

MD was the most influential strategy in the choices. Furthermore, when the subjects could choose in-group favoritism (MD + MIP) and/or a fairness strategy, they were both more discriminatory and less fair toward the relevant than the irrelevant comparison group. Other measures of in-group favoritism produced an interaction between reward level and type of out-group: more discrimination against the relevant than the irrelevant group with high rewards, and less with low rewards. Whatever may be other explanations for this interaction, we can at least conclude that when reward levels are more meaningful, in-group favoritism is enhanced against a more comparable out-group, independently of the group members' economic interests. Indeed, insofar as the subjects used the MD strategy, they sacrificed "objective" personal and group gain for the sake of positive in-group distinctiveness.

A study by Oakes and Turner (1982) also deserves mention here since it seems to provide some direct evidence for the social competition interpretation of the minimal group experiments. They simply compared the self-esteem of subjects categorized as in Tajfel et al. (1971) but who were not asked to complete the decision booklets with subjects who were categorized and also discriminated in the normal manner. The latter subjects were found to have higher self-esteem than the former—in line with the idea that discrimination serves to achieve a positive social identity. Needless to say, work is progressing to replicate and explore this finding.

On the whole, the above studies provide some confirmation for the basic social-identity/social-comparison hypothesis. Further studies testing the theory in both field and laboratory settings and discussions of its application to the analysis of specific social contexts (e.g., male-female relations, linguistic conflict, Protestant-Catholic conflict in Northern Ireland, prejudice and black identity, etc.) are to be found or are reviewed in Tajfel (1978b, 1982a, 1982b) and Turner and Giles (1981). We shall now attempt to outline in general terms the analysis of inter-group behavior in strati-

fied societies implied by the theory when it is applied to some of the problems raised in the second section.

Status Hierarchies and Social Change

The reconceptualization of social status attempted earlier needs now to be made more explicit. Status is not considered here as a scarce resource or commodity, such as power or wealth; it is the *outcome* of intergroup comparison. It reflects a group's relative position on some evaluative dimensions of comparison. Low subjective status does not promote inter-group competition directly; its effects on inter-group behavior are mediated by social identity processes. The lower is a group's subjective status position in relation to relevant comparison groups, the less is the contribution it can make to positive social identity. The variety of reactions to negative or threatened social identity to be discussed below are an elaboration of the principles outlined earlier in this chapter.

1. INDIVIDUAL MOBILITY

Individuals may try to leave, or dissociate themselves from, their erstwhile group. This is probably more likely the more they approach the "social mobility" pole of the continuum of belief-systems described previously. This strategy usually implies attempts, on an individual basis, to achieve upward social mobility, to pass from a lower- to a higher-status group. In a four-group hierarchy, Ross (1979) found a direct linear relationship between low status and the desire to pass upward into another group. Many earlier studies report the existence of strong forces for upward social movement in status hierarchies. Tendencies to dissociate oneself psychologically from fellow members of low-prestige categories are known to many of us from everyday experience: they have been noted more systematically by Jahoda (1961) and Klineberg and Zavalloni (1969), among others, and indirectly by the whole literature on racial identification and preference. The most important feature of individual mobility is that the low status of one's own group is not thereby changed: it is an individualist approach designed, at least in the short run, to achieve a personal, not a group, solution. Thus, individual mobility implies a disidentification with the erstwhile in-group.

2. SOCIAL CREATIVITY

The group members may seek positive distinctiveness for the in-group by redefining or altering the elements of the comparative situation. This need not involve any change in the group's actual social position or access to objective resources in relation to the out-group. It is a group rather than an individualistic strategy that may focus upon:

(a) Comparing the in-group to the out-group on some new dimension. Lemaine (1966) found, for example, that children's groups that could not compare themselves favorably with others in terms of constructing a hut—because they had been assigned poorer building materials than the out-group—tended to seek out other dimensions of comparison involving new constructions in the hut's surroundings. The problems that obviously arise here are those of legitimizing the value assigned to the new social products—first in the in-group and then in the other groups involved. To the extent that this legitimization may threaten the out-group's superior distinctiveness, an increase in intergroup tension can be predicted.

(b) Changing the values assigned to the attributes of the group, so that comparisons which were previously negative are now perceived as positive. The classic example is "black is beautiful." The salient dimension—skin color—remains the same, but the prevailing value system concerning it is rejected and reversed. The same process may underlie Peabody's (1968) finding that even when various groups agree about their respective characteristics, the trait is evaluated more positively by the group that possesses it.

(c) Changing the out-group (or selecting the out-group) with which the in-group is compared—in particular, ceasing or avoiding to use the high-status out-group as a comparative frame of reference. Where comparisons are not made with the high-status out-group, the relevant inferiority should decrease in salience, and self-esteem should recover. Hyman's (1942)

classic paper on the psychology of status suggested that discontent among low-status-group members is lessened to the degree that intraclass rather than intergroup comparisons are made. More recently, Rosenberg and Simmons (1972) found that self-esteem was higher among blacks who made self-comparisons with other blacks rather than whites. Other work also suggests (see Katz, 1964; Lefcourt & Ladwig, 1965) that, in certain circumstances, black performance was adversely affected by the low self-esteem induced by the presence of the members of the dominant out-group. It follows that self-esteem can be enhanced by comparing with other lower-status groups rather than with those of higher status. This is consistent with the fact that competition between subordinate groups is sometimes more intense than between subordinate and dominant groups—hence, for example, lower-class or "poor white" racism.

3. SOCIAL COMPETITION

The group members may seek positive distinctiveness through direct competition with the out-group. They may try to reverse the relative positions of the in-group and the out-group on salient dimensions. To the degree that this may involve comparisons related to the social structure, it implies changes in the groups' objective social locations. We can hypothesize, therefore, following RCT, that this strategy will generate conflict and antagonism between subordinate and dominant groups insofar as it focuses on the distribution of scarce resources. Data relevant to this strategy have been referred to earlier in this chapter.

Let us assume as an ideal case some stratification of social groups in which the social hierarchy is reasonably correlated with an unequal division of objective resources and a corresponding status system (based on the outcomes of comparisons in terms of those resources). Under what conditions will this *not* lead to intergroup conflict—or, more precisely, to the development of competitive ethnocentrism on the part of the subordinate group?

First, to the extent that the objective and the subjective prohibitions to "passing" are weak (see our earlier discussion of the "social mobility" system of beliefs), low status may tend, in conditions of unsatisfactory social identity, to promote the widespread adoption of individual mobility strategies, or at least initial attempts to make use of these strategies. Insofar as individual mobility implies disidentification, it will tend to loosen the cohesiveness of the subordinate group. This weakening of subjective attachment to the in-group among its members will tend: (a) to blur the perception of distinct group interests corresponding to the distinct group identity; and (b) to create obstacles to mobilizing group members for collective action over their common interests. Thus, the low morale that follows from negative social identity can set in motion disintegrative processes that, in the long run, may hinder a change in the group status.

Second, assuming that the barriers (objective, moral, and ideological prohibitions) to leaving one's group are strong, unsatisfactory social identity may stimulate social creativity that tends to reduce the salience of the subordinate/dominant group conflict of interest. Strategy 2(c) mentioned above is likely to be crucial here since, in general, access to resources such as housing, jobs, income, or education is sufficiently central to the fate of any group that the relevant comparisons are not easily changed or devalued. Few underprivileged groups would accept poverty as a virtue, but it may appear more tolerable to the degree that comparisons are made with even poorer groups rather than with those that are better off (see Runciman, 1966).

As noted above, some writers (Festinger, 1954; Kidder & Stewart, 1975) imply that strategy 2(c) is a dominant response to status differences between groups. The assumption is that intergroup comparability decreases as a direct function of perceived dissimilarity. If this were the whole story, then, somewhat paradoxically, the creation of a consensual status system would protect social identity from invidious comparisons. The causal sequence would be as follows: similar groups compare with each other; the outcome determines their relative prestige; the perceived status difference reduces their similarity and hence comparability; intergroup comparisons cease to be made; subjective superiority and inferiority decrease in salience; correspondingly, the groups' respective self-esteems return to their original point. There may be occasions when this social-psychological recipe for the maintenance of the status quo can be observed in something like its pure form. However,

we shall argue presently that there are many status differences that do not reduce comparability.

For the moment, we can note that both individual mobility and some forms of social creativity can work to reduce intergroup conflict over scarce resources—though with different implications. The former is destructive of subordinate-group solidarity and provides no antidote to negative social identity at a group level. The latter may restore or create a positive self-image but, it can be surmised, at the price either of a collective repression of objective deprivation or, perhaps, of spurious rivalry with some other deprived group. It is interesting in this context that the French Canadians, having recently gained a more assertive identity, are now apparently more disparaging of other minority groups than are the English Canadians (Berry et al., 1977).

By reversing the conditions under which social stratification does not produce intergroup conflict, we can hypothesize that negative social identity promotes subordinate-group competitiveness toward the dominant group to the degree that: (a) subjective identification with the subordinate group is maintained; and (b) the dominant group continues or begins to be perceived as a relevant comparison group. As a great deal of work has been done in social psychology on the determinants of cohesiveness and loyalty within groups— Hogg (1983), Turner et al. (1983), and Turner, Sachdev & Hogg (1983) have recently looked in particular at the problem of how groups that are associated with costs and deprivations (such as subordinate ones) are able to maintain their cohesiveness—we shall concentrate on the second condition.

Our hypothesis is that a status difference between groups does not reduce the meaningfulness of comparison between them providing that there is a perception that *it can be changed*. For example, consider two football (or any other) teams that at the end of their season may have come first and second in their league respectively. There is no argument about which has the higher status, but alternative comparative outcomes were and, in the future, still will be possible. When the new season begins, the teams will be as comparable and competitive as they had been before. This example illustrates Tajfel's (1978a) distinction between *secure* and *insecure* intergroup comparisons. The crucial factor in this distinction is whether *cogni-*

tive alternatives to the actual outcome are available—whether other outcomes are conceivable. Status differences between social groups in social systems showing various degrees of stratification can be distinguished in the same way. Where status relations are perceived as immutable, a part of the fixed order of things, then social identity is secure. It becomes insecure when the existing state of affairs begins to be questioned. An important corollary to this argument is that the dominant or high-status groups, too, can experience insecure social identity. Any threat to the distinctively superior position of a group implies a potential loss of positive comparisons and possible negative comparisons, which must be guarded against. Such a threat may derive from the activity of the low-status group or from a conflict between the high-status group's own value system (for example, the sociopolitical morality) and the actual foundations of its superiority. Like low-status groups, the high-status groups will react to insecure social identity by searching for enhanced group distinctiveness.

In brief, then, it is true that clear-cut status differences may lead to a quiescent social system in which neither the "inferior" nor the "superior" groups will show much ethnocentrism. But this "ideal type" situation must be considered in relation to the perceived stability and legitimacy of the system. Perceived illegitimacy and/or instability provide new dimensions of comparability that are directly relevant to the attitudes and behavior of the social groups involved, whatever their position in the system. This is the social-psychological counterpart to what is widely known today as "the revolution of rising expectations." Providing that individual mobility is unavailable or undesirable, consensual inferiority will be rejected most rapidly when the situation is perceived as both unstable and illegitimate. This is (or was) probably the set of conditions underlying the development of ethnocentrism among black Americans, French Canadians, and New Zealand Maoris, for instance. Vaughan (1978) reports that the perceived feasibility of social change (probably including, in this instance, the perceived illegitimacy of the present situation) is an important predictor of the developing Maori ethnocentrism; Friedman (1969) argues that what we may term the "cognitive alternative" of black nationalism in the developing countries was influential in enhancing black American social identity.

On the other hand, when the dominant group or sections of it perceive their superiority as legitimate, they will probably react in an intensely discriminatory fashion to any attempt by the subordinate group to change the intergroup situation. Such perhaps was the postbellum situation in the southern United States: the whites, threatened by those who had been their slaves, rapidly abandoned their paternalistic stereotypes of the blacks as "childlike" in favor of openly hostile and derogatory ones (Van der Berghe, 1967). The reactions of illegitimately superior groups are more complex (Turner & Brown, 1978). It seems that conflicts of values are reduced by greater discrimination when superiority is assured, but by less discrimination when it is unstable. This calls to mind some Prisoner Dilemma studies in which white discrimination against black opponents increased the more cooperative was the opponent, but decreased the more competitive he was (Baxter, 1973; Cederblom & Diers, 1970). Baxter suggested in the title of his article ("Prejudiced Liberals?") that a conflict of values may underlie his data. Research on the different effects of secure and insecure status differences is reported in Tajfel (1978b, 1982a, 1982b; see also Caddick, 1980 and Skevington, 1980).

Many of the points and hypotheses we have advanced in this chapter are not, in themselves, new (see, for instance, Sherif, 1967; Runciman, 1966; Milner, 1975; Billig, 1976). What is new, we think, is the integration of the three processes of social categorization, self-evaluation through social identity, and intergroup social comparison, into a coherent and testable framework for contributing to the explanation of various forms of intergroup behavior, social conflict, and social change. This framework contains possibilities of further development, and to this extent, we hope that it may stimulate theoretically directed research in areas that have not been considered here.

But some cautionary points should be made. The equation of social competition and intergroup conflict made above rests on the assumptions concerning an "ideal type" of social stratification in which the salient dimensions of intergroup differentiation are those involving scarce resources. In this respect, we have simply borrowed the central tenet of RCT. There is no reason, in fact, to assume that intergroup differentiation is inherently conflictual. Some experimental work already points clearly to the conclusion that evaluative derogation of an out-group is conceptually and empirically distinct from out-group hostility (Turner et al., 1979). On the other hand, social-identity processes may provide a source of inter-group conflict (in addition to the cases outlined above) to the degree that the groups develop conflicting interests with respect to the maintenance of the comparative situation as a whole. It seems plausible to hypothesize that, when a group's action for positive distinctiveness is frustrated, impeded, or in any way actively prevented by an out-group, this will promote overt conflict and hostility between the groups. This prediction, like many others, still remains to be tested.

'Objective' and 'Subjective' Conflicts

None of the arguments outlined in this chapter must be understood as implying that the social-psychological or "subjective" type of conflict is being considered here as having priority or a more important causal function in social reality than the "objective" determinants of social conflict of which the basic analysis must be sought in the social, economic, political, and historical structures of a society. The major aim of the present discussion has been to determine what are the points of insertion of social-psychological variables into the causal spiral; and its argument has been that, just as the effects of these variables are powerfully determined by the previous social, economic, and political processes, so they may also acquire, in turn, an *autonomous* function that enables them to deflect in one direction or another the subsequent functioning of these processes.

It is nearly impossible in most natural social situations to distinguish between discriminatory intergroup behavior based on real or perceived conflict of objective interests between the groups and discrimination based on attempts to establish a positively valued distinctiveness for one's own group. However, as we have argued, the two can be distinguished theoretically, since the goals of actions aimed at the achievement of positively valued in-group distinctiveness often retain no value outside of the context of intergroup comparisons. An example would be a group that does not necessarily wish to increase the level of its own salaries but acts to prevent other groups from get-

ting nearer to this level so that differentials are not eroded. But the difficulty with this example—as with many other similar examples—is that, in this case, the preservation of salary differentials is probably associated with all kinds of objective advantages that cannot be defined in terms of money alone. In turn, some of these advantages will again make sense only in the comparative framework of intergroup competition. Despite this confusing network of mutual feedbacks and inter-actions, the distinctions made here are important because they help us to understand some aspects of intergroup behavior that have often been neglected in the past.

A further distinction must be made between explicit and implicit conflicts—a distinction that has to do with conflicts that are "objective" in a different sense. A conflict may be "objective" despite the fact that the goals the groups are aiming for have no value outside of the context of inter-group comparison in that it may be institutional-ized and legitimized by rules and norms (of whatever origin) accepted by the groups themselves. This was the case in Sherif's studies in their phase of competition between the groups; and it also is the case in any football match and in countless other social activities. The behavior toward out-groups in this kind of explicit conflict can be classified, in turn, into two categories, one of which can be referred to as *instrumental* and the other as *noninstrumental*. The instrumental category consists of all those actions that can be directly related to causing the group to win the competition. The noninstrumental category, which could be referred to as "gratuitous" discrimination against the out-group, includes the creation of negative stereotypes and all other aspects of the "irrelevant" in-group/out-group differentiations so well described, for example, in Sherif's studies. The first category of actions is both commonsensically and theoretically accounted for by assuming nothing more than the group's desire to win the competition—although this poses all the theoretical "comparison" problems discussed in this chapter; the second category of actions can be directly and parsimoniously accounted for in terms of the so-cial-comparison/social-identity/positive-in-group-distinctiveness sequence described here.

The implicit conflicts are those that can be shown to exist despite the absence of explicit in-stitutionalization or even an informal normative acceptance of their existence by the groups involved. The proof of their existence is to be found in the large number of studies (and also everyday occurrences in real life) in which differentiations of all kinds are made between groups by their members although, on the face of it, there are no "reasons" for these differentiations to occur. Examples of this have been provided in several studies mentioned in this chapter in which the introduction by the subjects of various intergroup differentiations directly decreased the objective rewards that could otherwise have been gained by the in-group, or even directly by the individual. Findings of this kind, which can be generalized widely to many natural social situations, provide a clear example of the need to introduce into the complex spiral of social causation the social-psychological variables of the "relational" and "comparative" kind discussed in this chapter.

REFERENCES

Adorno, T. W., Frenkel-Brunswik, E., Levinson, D. J., & Sanford, R. N. (1950). *The authoritarian personality*. New York: Harper.1950.

Allen, V. L., & Wilder, D. A. (1975). Categorization, belief similarity, and intergroup discrimination. *Journal of Personality & Social Psychology, 32*(6), 971–977.

Aschenbrenner, K. M., & Schaefer, R. E. (1980). Minimal intergroup situations: Comments on a mathematical model and on the research paradigm. *European Journal of Social Psychology, 10*, 389–398.

Bass, B. M., & Dunteman, G. (1963). Biases in the evaluation of one's own group, its allies, and opponents. *Journal of Conflict Resolution, 2*, 67–77.

Baxter, G. W. (1973). Prejudiced liberals? Race and information effects in a two-person game. *Journal of Conflict Resolution, 17*, 131–161.

Berkowitz, L. (1962). *Aggression: A social psychological analysis*. New York: McGraw-Hill.

Berkowitz, L. (1969). The frustration-aggression hypothesis revisited. In L. Berkowitz (Ed.), *Roots of aggression: A reexamination of the frustration-aggression hypothesis*. New York: Atherton Press.

Berkowitz, L. (1974). Some determinants of impulsive aggression: Role of mediated associations with reinforcements for aggression. *Psychological Review, 81*, 165–176.

Berry, J. W., Kalin, R., & Taylor, D. M. (1976). *Multiculturalism and ethnic attitudes in Canada*. Kingston, Ontario: Queen's University.

Billig, M. (1972). *Social categorization in intergroup relations*. University of Bristol, Bristol.

Billig, M. (1973). Normative communication in a minimal intergroup situation. *European Journal of Social Psychology, 3*(3), 339–343.

Billig, M. (1976). *Social psychology and intergroup relations* (Vol. 9). London: Academic Press.

Billig, M., & Tajfel, H. (1973). Social categorization and simi-

larity in intergroup behaviour. *European Journal of Social Psychology, Vol. 3*(1), 27–52.

Blake, R. R., & Mouton, J. S. (1961). Competition, communication and conformity. In I. A. Berg & B. M. Berg (Eds.), *Conformity and deviation*. New York: Harper.

Blake, R. R., & Mouton, J. S. (1962). The intergroup dynamics of win-lose conflict and problem-solving collaboration in union-management relations. In M. Sherif (Ed.), *Intergroup relations and leadership*. New York: Wiley.

Bornstein, G., Crum, L., Wittenbraker, J., Harring, K., Insko, C. A., & Thibaut, J. (1983a). On the measurement of social orientation in the minimal group paradigm. *European Journal of Social Psychology, 13*, 321–350.

Bornstein, G., Crum, L., Wittenbraker, J., Harring, K., Insko, C. A., & Thibaut, J. (1983b). Reply to Turner's comments. *European Journal of Social Psychology, 13*, 360–381.

Bourhis, R. Y., Giles, H., & Tajfel, H. (1973). Language as a determinant of Welsh identity. *European Journal of Social Psychology, 3*, 447–460.

Brantwaite, A., Doyle, S., & Lightbown, N. (1979). The balance between fairness and discrimination. *European Journal of Social Psychology, 9*, 149–163.

Brewer, M. B. (1979). In-group bias in the minimal intergroup situation: A cognitive-motivational analysis. *Psychological Bulletin, 86*(2), 307–324.

Brewer, M. B., & Silver, M. (1978). Ingroup bias as a function of task characteristics. *European Journal of Social Psychology, 8*(3), 393–400.

Brigham, J. C. (1971). *Views of White and Black schoolchildren concerning racial differences*. Paper presented at the Midwestern Psychological Association, Detroit, Michigan.

Brown, R. J., Tajfel, H., & Turner, J. C. (1980). Minimal group situations and intergroup discrimination: Comments on the paper by Aschenbrenner and Schaefer. *European Journal of Social Psychology, 10*(4), 399–414.

Brown, R. J., & Turner, J. C. (1981). Interpersonal and intergroup behaviour. In J. C. Turner & H. Giles (Eds.), *Intergroup behaviour*. Oxford: Basil Blackwell.

Caddick, B. (1980). Equity theory, social entity and intergroup relations. *Review of Personality and Social Psychology, 1*, 219–245.

Caddick, B. (1982). Perceived illegitimacy and intergroup relations. In H. Tajfel (Ed.), *Social identity and intergroup relations*. Cambridge: Cambridge University Press.

Campbell, D. T. (1965). Ethnocentric and other altruistic motives. In D. Levine (Ed.), *Nebraska Symposium on Motivation* (pp. 283–311). Lincoln: Nebraska: University of Nebraska Press.

Cederblom, D., & Diers, C. J. (1970). Effects of race and strategy in the prisoner's dilemma. *Journal of Social Psychology, 81*, 275–276.

Commins, B., & Lockwood, J. (1979). The effects of status differences, favoured treatment, and equity on intergroup comparisons. *European Journal of Social Psychology, 9*, 281–290.

Deutsch, M. (1949). A theory of cooperation and competition. *Human Relations, 2*, 129–151.

Diab, L. (1970). A study of intragroup and intergroup relations among experimentally produced small groups. *Genetic Psychology Monographs, 82*, 49–82.

Dizard, J. E. (1970). Black identity, social class, and Black power. *Psychiatry, 33*, 195–207.

Doise, W., & Weinberger, M. (1973). Représentations masculines dans differentes situations de rencontres mixtes. *Bulletin de Psychologie, 26,* 649–657.

Ferguson, C. K., & Kelley, H. H. (1964). Significant factors in overevaluation of own group's products. *Journal of Abnormal & Social Psychology, 69,* 223–228.

Festinger, L. (1954). A theory of social comparison processes. *Human Relations, 7,* 117–140.

Fiedler, F. E. (1967). The effect of inter-group competition on group member adjustment. *Personnel Psychology, 20*(1), 33–44.

Friedman, N. (1969). Africa and the Afro-Americans: The changing Negro identity. *Psychiatry, 32*(2), 127–136.

Giles, H., & Johnson, P. (1981). The role of language in ethnic group relations. In J. C. Turner & H. Giles (Eds.), *Intergroup behavior.* Oxford: Basil Blackwell.

Giles, H., & Powesland, P. E. (1976). *Speech style and social evaluations.* London: Academic Press, European Monographs in Social Psychology.

Gregor, A. J., & McPherson, D. A. (1966). Racial preference and ego identity among White and Bantu children in the Republic of South Africa. *Genetic Psychology Monographs, 73,* 217–254.

Harris, S., & Braun, J. R. (1971). Self-esteem and racial preferences in Black children. *Proceedings of the 79th Annual Convention of the American Psychological Association, 6.*

Harvey, O. J. (1956). An experimental investigation of negative and positive relations between small groups through judgmental indices. *Sociometry, 19,* 201–209.

Hirschman, A. O. (1970). *Exit, voice and loyalty: Responses to decline in firms, organizations and states.* Cambridge, MA: Harvard University Press.

Hogg, M. A. (1983). *The social psychology of group-formation: A cognitive perspective.* Unpublished doctoral dissertation, University of Bristol.

Hraba, J., & Grant, G. (1970). Black is beautiful: A reexamination of racial preference and identification. *Journal of Personality & Social Psychology, 16*(3), 398–402.

Jahoda, G. (1961). *White man.* Oxford, England: Oxford University Press.

Johnson, D. W. (1967). Use of role reversal in intergroup competition. *Journal of Personality & Social Psychology, 7*(2), 135–141.

Julian, J. W. (1968). The study of competition. In W. E. Vinacke (Ed.), *Readings in general psychology.* New York: American Book Company.

Kalin, R., & Marlowe, D. (1968). The effects of intergroup competition, personal drinking habits and frustration in intra-group cooperation. *Proceedings of the American Psychological Association, 3,* 405–406.

Katz, I. (1964). Review of evidence relating to effects of desegregation on the intellectual performance of Negroes. *American Psychologist, 19*(6), 381–399.

Kidder, L. H., & Stewart, V. M. (1975). *The psychology of intergroup relations.* New York: McGraw-Hill.

Klineberg, O., & Zavalloni, M. (1969). *Nationalism and tribalism among African students.* The Hague and Paris: Mouton.

Lefcourt, H. M., & Ladwig, G. (1965). The effect of reference group upon Negroes' task persistence in a biracial competitive game. *Journal of Personality and Social Psychology, 1,* 688–671.

Lemaine, G. (1966). Inegalité, comparison et incomparabilité:

Esquisse d'une theorie de l'originalité socialite. *Bulletin de Psychologie, 252*(20), 1–2,1–9.

Locksley, A., Ortiz, V., & Hepburn, C. (1980). Social categorization and discrimination behaviour: Extinguishing the minimal intergroup discrimination effect. *Journal of Personality and Social Psychology, 39,* 773–783.

Milner, D. (1975). *Children and race.* Harmondsworth, Middlesex: Penguin.

Milner, D. (1981). Racial prejudice. In J. C. Turner & H. Giles (Eds.), *Intergroup behavior.* Oxford: Basil Blackwell.

Morland, J. K. (1969). Race awareness among American and Hong Kong Chinese children. *American Journal of Sociology, 75*(360–374).

Oakes, P. J., & Turner, J. C. (1982). Social categorization and intergroup behaviour: Does minimal intergroup discrimination make social identity more positive? *European Journal of Social Psychology, 10,* 295–301.

Oberschall, A. (1973). *Social conflict and social movements.* New York: Prentice-Hall.

Peabody, D. (1968). Group judgments in the Philippines: Evaluative and descriptive aspects. *Journal of Personality and Social Psychology, 10,* 290–300.

Rabbie, J. M., & Wilkens, C. (1971). Intergroup competition and its effects on intra- and intergroup relations. *European Journal of Social Psychology, 1,* 215–234.

Rosenberg, M., & Simmons, R. G. (1972). *Black and White self-esteem: The urban school child.* Unpublished manuscript.

Ross, G. F. (1979). *Multiple group membership, social mobility and intergroup relations.* Unpublished doctoral dissertation, University of Bristol.

Runciman, W. G. (1966). *Relative deprivation and social justice.* London: Routledge and Keegan Paul.

Sherif, M. (1967). *Social interaction: Process and products.*

Sherif, M., Harvey, O. J., White, B. J., Hood, W. R., & Sherif, C. W. (1961). *Intergroup cooperation and competition: The Robber's Cave experiment.* Norman, OK: University Book Exchange.

Sherif, M., & Sherif, C. W. (1953). *Groups in harmony and tension; an integration of studies of intergroup relations.* New York: Harper.

Skevington, S. M. (1980). Intergroup relations and social change within a nursing context. *British Journal of Social & Clinical Psychology, 19,* 201–213.

St Claire, L., & Turner, J. C. (1982). The role of demand characteristics in the social categorization paradigm. *European Journal of Social Psychology, 12*(3), 307–314.

Stephenson, G. M. (1981). Intergroup bargaining and negotiation. In J. C. Turner & H. Giles (Eds.), *Intergroup behavior.* Oxford: Basil Blackwell.

Tajfel, H. (1959). A note on Lambert's "Evaluational reactions to spoken languages." *Canadian Journal of Psychology, 13,* 86–92.

Tajfel, H. (1970). Experiments in intergroup discrimination. *Scientific American, 223*(5), 96–102.

Tajfel, H. (1972a). Experiments in a vacuum. In J. Israel & H. Tajfel (Eds.), *The context of social psychology: A critical assessment.* London: Academic Press, European Monographs in Social Psychology.

Tajfel, H. (1972b). La catégorisation sociale. In M. S (Ed.), *Introduction à la psychologie sociale* (Vol. 1). Paris: Larousse.

Tajfel, H. (1974a). *Intergroup behavior, social comparison and social change.* Paper presented at the Katz-Newcomb Lectures, University of Michigan, Ann Arbor.

Tajfel, H. (1974b). Social identity and intergroup behaviour. *Social Science Information, 13*(2), 65–93.

Tajfel, H. (1975). The exit of social mobility and the voice of social change: Notes on the social psychology of intergroup relations. *Social Science Information, 14*(2), 101–118.

Tajfel, H. (1978a). The achievement of group differentiation, *Differentiation between social groups: Studies in the social psychology of intergroup relations.* London: Academic Press.

Tajfel, H. (1978b). The psychological structure of intergroup relations. In H. Tajfel (Ed.), *Differentiation between social groups: Studies in the social psychology of intergroup relations.* London: Academic Press.

Tajfel, H. (1981). *Human groups and social categories.* Cambridge, UK: Cambridge University Press.

Tajfel, H. (1982a). Social psychology of intergroup relations. *Annual Review of Psychology, 33*, 1–39.

Tajfel, H. (Ed.). (1982b). *Social identity and intergroup relations.* Cambridge: Cambridge University Press.

Tajfel, H., & Billig, M. (1974). Familiarity and categorization in intergroup behavior. *Journal of Experimental Social Psychology, Vol. 10*(2), 159–170.

Tajfel, H., Billig, M. G., Bundy, R. P., & Flament, C. (1971). Social categorization and intergroup behaviour. *European Journal of Social Psychology, Vol. 1*(2), 149–178.

Thibaut, J. (1950). An experimental study of the cohesiveness of underpriviledged groups. *Human Relations, 3,* 251–278.

Tomlinson, T. M. (1970). Contributing factors in Black politics. *Psychiatry, 33*(2), 137–281.

Turner, J. C. (1975a). *Social categorization of social comparison in intergroup relations.* Unpublished doctoral dissertation, University of Bristol.

Turner, J. C. (1975b). Social comparison and social identity: Some prospects for intergroup behaviour. *European Journal of Social Psychology, 5*(1), 5–34.

Turner, J. C. (1978a). Social categorization and social discrimination in the minimal group paradigm. In H. Tajfel (Ed.), *Differentiation between social groups: Studies in the social psychology of intergroup relations* (pp. 101–140). London: Academic Press.

Turner, J. C. (1978b). Social comparison, similarity and ingroup favoritism. In H. Tajfel (Ed.), *Differentiation between social groups: Studies in the social psychology of intergroup relations* (pp. 235–250). London: Academic Press.

Turner, J. C. (1980). Fairness or discrimination in intergroup behavior? A reply to Branthwaite, Doyle and Lightbown. *European Journal of Social Psychology, 10*(2), 131–147.

Turner, J. C. (1981). The experimental social psychology of intergroup behavior. In J. C. Turner & H. Giles (Eds.), *Intergroup behavior.* Oxford: Basil Blackwell.

Turner, J. C. (1982). Towards a cognitive redefinition of the social group. In H. Tajfel (Ed.), *Social identity and intergroup relations* (pp. 15–40). New York: Cambridge University Press.

Turner, J. C. (1983a). A second reply to Bornstein, Crum, Wittenbraker, Harring, Insko and Thibaut on the measurement of social orientations. *European Journal of Social Psychology, 13*(4), 383–387.

Turner, J. C. (1983b). Some comments on . . . "the measurement of social orientations in the minimal group paradigm." *European Journal of Social Psychology, 13*(4), 351–367.

Turner, J. C. (1984). Social identification and psychological group formation. In H. Tajfel (Ed.), *The social dimension: European developments in social psychology.* New York: Cambridge University Press.

Turner, J. C., & Brown, R. (1978). Social status, cognitive alternatives and intergroup relations. In H. Tajfel (Ed.), *Differentiation between social groups: Studies in the social psychology of intergroup relations* (pp. 201–234). New York: Academic Press.

Turner, J. C., & Brown, R. J. (1976). Social status, cognitive alternatives and intergroup relations. In H. Tajfel (Ed.), *Differentiation between social groups: Studies in the social psychology of intergroup relations.* London: Academic Press.

Turner, J. C., Brown, R. J., & Tajfel, H. (1979). Social comparison and group interest in ingroup favouritism. *European Journal of Social Psychology, 9*(2), 187–204.

Turner, J. C., & Giles, H. (Eds.) (1981). *Intergroup behavior.* Oxford: Basil Blackwell.

Turner, J. C., Sachdev, I., & Hogg, M. A. (1983). Social categorization, interpersonal attraction and group formation. *British Journal of Social Psychology, 22*(3), 227–239.

Van Den Berghe, P. L. (1967). *Race and racism.* New York: Wiley.

Vaughan, G. M. (1978). Social change and intergroup preferences in New Zealand. *European Journal of Social Psychology, 8,* 297–314.

Vinacke, W. E. (1964). Intra-group power differences, strategy, and decisions in inter-triad competition. *Sociometry, 27,* 27–40.

Wilson, W., & Miller, N. (1961). Shifts in evaluations of participants following intergroup competition. *Journal of Abnormal & Social Psychology, 63,* 428–431.

The Role of Stereotyping in System-Justification and the Production of False Consciousness

John T. Jost and Mahzarin R. Banaji • Yale University

Although the concept of justification has played a significant role in many social psychological theories, its presence in recent examinations of stereotyping has been minimal. We describe and evaluate previous notions of stereotyping as ego-justification and group-justification and propose an additional account, that of system-justification, which refers to psychological processes contributing to the preservation of existing social arrangements even at the expense of personal and group interest. It is argued that the notion of system-justification is necessary to account for previously unexplained phenomena, most notably the participation by disadvantaged individuals and groups in negative stereotypes of themselves, and the consensual nature of stereotypic beliefs despite differences in social relations within and between social groups. We offer a selective review of existing research that demonstrates the role of stereotypes in the production of false consciousness and develop the implications of a system-justification approach.

[T]he rationalizing and justifying function of a stereotype exceeds its function as a reflector of group attributes—G. W. Allport (1954, p. 196).

The concept of justification, in the sense of an idea being used to provide legitimacy or support for another idea or for some form of behavior, has played a prominent role in social psychological theorizing. The notion that people will justify some state of affairs, to themselves and to others, has been explicit or implicit in psychoanalytic theory (Freud, 1946), social comparison theory (e.g. Festinger, 1954; Suls & Wills, 1991),

cognitive dissonance theory (Festinger, 1957; Wicklund & Brehm, 1976), self-perception theory (Bem, 1972), attribution theory (e.g. Heider, 1958; Jones, Kanouse, Kelley, Nisbett, Valins & Weiner, 1972; Kelley, 1967), self-presentation theory (e.g. Jones, 1964; Schlenker, 1980), theories of human reasoning (e.g. Nisbett & Ross, 1980; Tversky & Kahneman, 1974), just-world theory (Lerner, 1980), social identity theory (e.g. Hogg & Abrams, 1988; Tajfel, 1978; Tajfel & Turner, 1979, 1986), and self-affirmation theory (Steele, 1988). Empirical research has demonstrated that people seek explanations or justifications for, *inter alia*:

1. social events (e.g. Brickman, 1987; Hastie, 1984; Hewstone, 1989; McClure, 1991; McLaughlin, Cody & Read, 1992; Tajfel, 1981a, b)
2. their own thoughts, feelings, and behaviors (e.g., Aronson & Mills, 1959; Festinger & Carlsmith, 1959; Greenwald, 1980; Marshall & Zimbardo, 1979; Monson & Snyder, 1977; Schachter & Singer, 1962; Schwarz & Clore, 1988, Scott & Lyman, 1968; Zanna & Rempel, 1988; Zillman, 1978)
3. aggressive or discriminatory behaviors (e.g. Bandura, 1983; Bar-Tal, 1989, 1990; Brock & Buss, 1964; Lifton, 1986; Martin, Scully, & Levitt, 1990; Scully & Marolla, 1984; Staub, 1989; Sykes & Matza, 1957).
4. their status or position (e.g. Chaikin & Darley, 1973; Gerard, 1957; Janoff-Bulman, 1992; Kipnis, 1976; Miller & Porter, 1983; Ross, Amabile, & Steinmetz, 1977; Sampson, 1969; Sidanius, 1993).
5. the status or position of others (e.g. Cialdini, Kenrick & Hoerig, 1976; Darley & Gross, 1983; Eagly, 1987; Eagly & Steffen, 1984; Hoffmann & Hurst, 1990; Howard, 1984; Lerner, 1980; Pepitone, 1950; Ross et al., 1977; Ryan, 1971; Sampson, 1969; Sidanius, 1993; Stotland, 1959)
6. the aggressive or discriminatory acts of other in-group members (e.g. Bar-Tal, 1989, 1990; Hogg & Abrams, 1988; LaPiere, 1936; LaViolette & Silvert, 1951; Struch & Schwartz, 1989; Tajfel, 1978, 1981a, b)
7. prevailing social conditions (e.g. Bem & Bem, 1970; Blumenthal, Kahn, Andrews & Head, 1972; Campbell & LeVine, 1968; Howard & Pike, 1986; Kahn, 1972; Kluegel & Smith, 1986; Lerner, 1980; Samuelson & Zeckhauser, 1987; Sidanius, 1993; Sidanius & Pratto, 1993; Tetlock, 1992; Tyler, 1990; Tyler & McGraw, 1986).

Indeed, the second half of the 20th century in social psychology may well be remembered as an era of research on justification. We point out the extensive attention to the concept of justification in order to note its striking absence in theory and particularly in research on stereotyping.

In this paper, we review previous work on ego-justification and group-justification and build on them to propose a third category of justification which we term system-justification. Briefly stated, ego-justification refers to the notion that stereotypes develop in order to protect the position or behavior of the self (e.g. Adorno, Frenkel-Brunswik, Levinson, & Sanford, 1950; Katz & Braly, 1935; Lippmann, 1922). Group-justification views assume that stereotyping emerges in the service of protecting not just the individual ego, but the status or conduct of the social group as a whole (e.g. Hogg & Abrams, 1988; Huici, 1984; Tajfel, 1981a, b). While both views are important and useful, they each leave some key issues unaddressed. Chief among these is the phenomenon of negative stereotyping of the self or the in-group, and the degree to which stereotypes are widely shared across individuals and social groups. In response to these issues, we propose that the concept of system-justification is necessary to address adequately the social functions of stereotyping (cf. Sidanius & Pratto, 1993).

System-justification is the psychological process by which existing social arrangements are legitimized, even at the expense of personal and group interest. In this paper, the concept of system-justification is meant to bring into prominence the degree to which stereotypes emerge and are used to explain some existing state of affairs, such as social or economic systems, status or power hierarchies, distributions of resources, divisions of social roles, and the like (cf. Ashmore & Del Boca, 1981; Eagly & Steffen, 1984; Hoffman & Hurst, 1990; Schaff, 1984; Snyder & Miene, 1994; Sunar, 1978). Stereotypes, which are widespread beliefs about social groups, are hypothesized to accompany any system characterized by the separation of people into roles, classes, positions, or statuses, because such arrangements tend to be explained and perceived as justifiable by those who participate in them.

Central to this discussion is the concept of false consciousness, defined here as the holding of beliefs that are contrary to one's personal or group interest and which thereby contribute to the maintenance of the disadvantaged position of the self or the group (cf. Cunningham, 1987; Eagleton, 1991; Elster, 1982; Meyerson, 1991). Examples might include "accommodation to material insecurity or deprivation" (Parkin, 1971, p. 90), developing "needs which perpetuate toil, aggressiveness, misery, and injustice" (Marcuse, 1964, p. 5), deriving a "kind of comfort from believing that [one's] sufferings are unavoidable or deserved" (Wood, 1988, p. 359), and thinking that "whatever rank is held by individuals in the social order represents their intrinsic worth" (McMurtry, 1978, p. 149). By drawing on the concept of false consciousness, we postulate a system-justification function for stereotyping in addition to the previously recognized functions of ego- and group-justification. More specifically, it is argued that under some circumstances, stereotypes that serve to justify an existing state of affairs will operate even at the expense of individual or collective self-interest.

The purpose of this paper is to address the relationship between stereotyping and false consciousness. After identifying the contributions and limitations of the ego- and group-justification approaches, we review support for the system-justification view. From experimental social psychology we select evidence to show that individuals generate beliefs about themselves and stereotypes about social groups in such a way that existing situations are justified. From recent research on the unconscious modus operandi of stereotyping (cf. Banaji & Greenwald, 1994), we discuss the possibility that stereotypic justifications may operate implicitly. The unconscious nature of system-justification may allow existing ideologies to be exercised without the awareness of perceivers or targets.

The Ego-Justification Approach

Walter Lippmann (1922) is generally credited with importing the term "stereotype" into the social sciences (e.g., Ashmore & Del Boca, 1981; Brigham, 1971; Fishman, 1956; LaViolette & Silvert, 1951). While Lippmann (1922) emphasized the cognitive functions of simplification and categorization which are served by the stereotype, he also posited a motivational function:

> There is another reason, besides economy of effort, why we so often hold to our stereotypes when we might pursue a more disinterested vision. The systems of stereotypes may be the core of our personal tradition, the defenses of our position in society (p. 95, emphasis added).

In other words, Lippmann argued that individuals stereotype because it justifies their personal sta-

tus or conduct in relation to others. This assumption that stereotypes serve to justify the behavior of individuals figured prominently in the early social psychological literature (e.g. Adorno et al., 1950; Allport, 1954; Katz & Braly, 1933, 1935). For instance, Katz & Braly (1935, p. 182) wrote that: "Group prejudices are rationalizations by which the individual maintains his self-esteem and advances his economic and other interests." Similarly, Allport (1958, p. 187) claimed that the main function of the stereotype is "to justify (rationalize) our conduct in relation to" other social categories. What is common to all of these accounts (and, we argue, partially responsible for their failure) is the suggestion that stereotyping is employed for exploitative purposes and, in particular, as a personal defense or rationalization of exploitation.

The notion that stereotypes serve ego-justification functions continued to influence researchers adopting a "functional approach," especially those influenced by psychoanalytic perspectives on stereotyping and prejudice (e.g. Adorno et al., 1950; Bettelheim & Janowitz, 1964; Katz, 1960; Myrdal, 1944; Smith, Bruner, & White, 1956). Following Freud (1946), these writers proposed that stereotyping served as a "defense mechanism" whereby internal conflicts were projected onto societal scapegoats. Although many such accounts reconciled the Freudian view with sociological approaches (e.g. Adorno et al., 1950), the ego-defensive hypothesis with respect to stereotyping was criticized for its "far-reaching lack of interest in the influence of the social environment on the individual" (Bettelheim & Janowitz, 1964, p. 50). The function of ego-justification, however alluring, failed to produce satisfactory empirical evidence and was rejected along with social psychology's rejection of psychoanalysis more generally (see Sherif & Cantril, 1947) even before modern alternatives to conceptualizing attitude and stereotype function became available.

While researchers have returned to the study of the functions of attitudes, and to a much lesser extent, of stereotypes (e.g., Herek, 1984, 1986; Shavitt, 1989; Snyder & DeBono, 1989; Snyder & Miene, 1994), ego-justification remains among the least studied of the functions. Nevertheless, there are occasional findings which support Lippmann's (1922) hypothesis that stereotypes are used by the advantaged as "defenses of [their] position in society" (p. 95). For instance, Ashmore & McConahay (1975) report that the probability of stereotyping poor people as lazy and therefore deserving of their plight is correlated positively with one's socio-economic status, which suggests that those occupying high positions in society need to justify themselves by derogating others who are less fortunate. It has also been observed that aggressive actors may justify their own behavior through a stereotypic process of "delegitimization" whereby their victims are denied human status, as when soldiers refer to the enemy as "savages" or "'satanic" (e.g., Bar-Tal, 1989, 1990). Indeed, functional theorists continue to address the motivational gains made by stereotypers in their efforts to justify their own status and behavior (e.g., Herek, 1986; Snyder & Miene, 1994; Sunar, 1978), and some Marxist theorists also have suggested that ego-justification may be "required to explain how people doggedly sustain such superficial and anti-human views as racism and sexism" (cf. Adorno et al., 1950; Cunningham, 1987, p. 259). By contrast, we argue for a system-justification view of stereotyping whereby the attribution of role-specific traits arises not out of individual motivations but results from information processing in an ideological environment.

There are several ways in which the ego-justification hypothesis is incomplete. First, and perhaps most importantly from our standpoint, ego-justification cannot account for the many documented cases of negative self-stereotyping whereby disadvantaged group members subscribe to stigmatizing stereotypes about their own group and about themselves (e.g. Allport, 1954; Bettelheim & Janowitz, 1964; Brown, 1986; Clark & Clark, 1947; Gergen, 1969; Giles & Powesland, 1975; Gregor & McPherson, 1966; Lambert, Hodgson, Gardner, & Fillenbaum, 1960; Lewin, 1941; McNaught, 1983; Millet, 1970; Pettigrew, 1964; Sarnoff, 1951; Williams & Morland, 1979). While the phenomenon of "self-hate" has a checkered past in the social sciences, and many methodological and empirical challenges have been raised against it (e.g., Banks, 1976; Crocker & Major, 1989; Greenwald & Oppenheim, 1968; Hraba & Grant, 1970; Katz & Zalk, 1974; Porter & Washington, 1989; Rosenberg, 1989; Turner & Brown, 1978), researchers continue to observe negative self-stereotyping among many low-status groups whose opportunities for effective collective advancement are severely limited (e.g. Aboud, 1988; Bernat & Balch, 1979; Broverman, Vogel, Broverman, Clarkson, & Rosenkrantz,

1972; Fine & Bowers, 1984; Jahoda, Thompson, & Bhatt, 1972; Milner, 1981; Peterson & Ramirez, 1971; Tajfel, 1982; Vaughan, 1978). Clearly, if such evidence can be trusted to demonstrate the frequent if not ubiquitous character of negative self-stereotyping, it would seem to exhaust the explanatory capacities of ego-justification theories, since it hardly seems self-serving to derogate oneself on stereotypic dimensions.

A second, related weakness of ego-justification approaches is that often people stereotype in the absence of any personal behavior or status requiring justification. For instance, many people subscribe to negative stereotypes of groups with whom they have never interacted and therefore would have no conduct to rationalize (e.g., Diab, 1962; Katz & Braly, 1933; Prothro, 1954). Similarly, disadvantaged groups frequently have negative stereotypes of one another, although neither is in a relative position of high status that would seem to require defense, as in the case of "working-class racism" (e.g. Willhelm, 1980).

Thirdly, stereotypes are characterized by their consensuality, the fact that they are shared by large segments of society (e.g., Allport, 1954; Ehrlich, 1973; Fishman, 1956; Katz & Braly, 1933; Tajfel, 1981a, b). For example, Triandis, Lisansky, Setiadi, Chang, Marin, and Betancourt (1982) found that Hispanics and Blacks had approximately the same stereotypes of one another that Whites had of them. If the contents of stereotypes arose out of processes of individual justification, as the ego-justification hypothesis suggests, it seems unlikely that they would be so uniformly shared, because individuals should vary on the dimension in need of rationalization. We will return to this issue of consensuality in our discussion of the group-justification approach to stereotyping.

The Group-Justification Approach

Tajfel (1981b) is well known for having argued that stereotyping ought to be considered in the context of group interests and social identity. More specifically, he postulated that stereotypes serve to justify actions of the in-group, "committed or planned," against outgroups. In other words, Tajfel expanded the initial ego-justification hypothesis to the level of intergroup relations, an endeavor that was begun by Allport (1954) and others (e.g., Cox, 1948; LaPiere, 1936, LaViolette & Silvert,

1951; Sherif & Sherif, 1956). Similar group-based functions have been proposed by others under the rubrics of "social integration" (e.g., Schaff, 1984) and "social adjustment" (Katz 1960; Smith, Bruner & White, 1956; Sunar, 1978), terms that are meant to emphasize the degree to which the in-group consolidates itself in order to distinguish itself from other groups.

The work of Tajfel and colleagues may be viewed as initiating a second wave of attention to the "justification" function of stereotypes, culminating in the insight that stereotypes serve intergroup functions of rationalizing or justifying the in-group's treatment of the out-group (e.g. Condor, 1990; Hogg & Abrams, 1988; Huici, 1984; Tajfel, 1981a, b). Furthermore, in-group members are expected to employ negative stereotypes of the outgroup in an attempt to differentiate their group from others, that is, by making comparative social judgements that benefit the in-group relative to the out-group (e.g. Tajfel, 1978; Tajfel & Turner, 1979, 1986; Turner, 1975). Social identity theory is referred to as a "conflict theory" because it assumes that groups in society must compete with one another for symbolic and material resources, and that they will develop stereotypes of other groups in an effort to justify their competition (Billig, 1976; Hogg & Abrams, 1988). Experiments cited on behalf of the notion that groups use stereotypes to positively differentiate themselves from other groups include Hewstone, Jaspars, and Lalljee (1982), Wagner, Lampen, and Syllwasschy (1986), and Spears and Manstead (1989), although the support is not as strong as one might expect. Nevertheless, virtually every recent review of the literature has accepted Tajfel's assumption that people are motivated to hold positive stereotypes of the in-group and negative stereotypes of the out-group (e.g., Ashmore & Del Boca, 1981; Bar-Tal, 1989; Bar-Tal, Graumann, Kruglanski, & Stroebe, 1989; Brewer & Kramer, 1985; Dovidio & Gaertner, 1986; Hamilton, 1981; Hamilton & Trolier, 1986; Hewstone & Giles, 1986; Hogg & Abrams, 1988; Howard & Rothbart, 1980; Huici, 1984; Jussim, Coleman, & Lerch, 1987; Maass & Schaller, 1991; Messick & Mackie, 1989; Mullen, Brown, & Smith, 1992; Stephan, 1985; Wilder, 1986; Worchel & Austin, 1986).

By expanding the concept of ego-justification from protection of the self to include protection of the extended self, Tajfel's group-justification

view overcomes several difficulties faced by Lippmann, Katz, Allport, and others. For instance, an individual may subscribe to certain stereotypes not necessarily to justify some personal conduct or social position, but as a way of defending the actions of others with whom he or she shares a social identification. Thus, people could possess stereotypes of groups whom they as individuals had never encountered, but whom other members of their group had encountered (cf. Gergen, 1969). In addition, social identity theory's emphasis on competition between groups helps to explain why disadvantaged groups would promulgate negative stereotypes of one another. Although neither group could be said to occupy a privileged position in need of defense or justification, as Lippmann, Katz and Braly, and others emphasized, both groups may make psychological gains by comparing themselves favorably to other groups near in status to them (e.g., Tajfel, 1978).

The notion that stereotypes emerge within the context of group behavior also helps to explain why stereotype contents are more uniform than would be predicted on the basis of the ego-justification hypothesis alone. According to Hogg and Abrams (1988, p. 75), the "sharedness is due to a social process of social influence which causes conformity to group norms." In other words, social identity theory states that stereotypes are consensual because all members of the social group are expected to follow them so as to establish collective justifications for intergroup behavior. However, this does not explain why stereotypes are consensual across groups—why members of different social groups often possess the same stereotypes of a certain group, despite the fact that their intergroup relationships are not the same. For example, it has been found that men and women subscribe to similar gender stereotypes (e.g. Ashmore & Del Boca, 1986; Banaji & Greenwald, 1994; Banaji, Hardin, & Rothman, 1993; Basow, 1986; Broverman et al., 1972; Howard, 1984; McKee & Sherriffs, 1956), and Whites and Blacks also possess similar racial stereotypes (e.g. Bayton, McAlister, & Hamer, 1956; Katz & Braly, 1933; Sagar & Schofield, 1980). In addition, Triandis et al. (1982) reported that Whites, Blacks, and Hispanics did not differ in the stereotypes that they had of one another, despite the significant status differences among these groups in the United States. One of the earliest and most dramatic conclusions of the stereotyping literature was that stereotypes of specific nationalities were widely shared by different groups, even across cultures (e.g., Diab, 1962; Gergen, 1969; Katz & Braly, 1933; Prothro, 1954). Researchers, too, have reported considerable cross-cultural generality with regard to gender stereotypes (e.g., Basow, 1986; Ward, 1985; Williams & Best, 1982).

Condor (1990, pp. 236–237) criticizes social identity theorists for taking the consensuality of stereotypes to be an "a priori assumption" without saying why different groups should subscribe to the same stereotypes. We argue that social identity theory's ability to account for phenomena such as the societal (or cross-societal) consensuality of stereotype contents is indeed limited. A complete theory would need to address the concept of ideological domination (to explain the social processes by which knowledge is created and disseminated by those in power) and evidence from psychological accounts of false consciousness (to explain the cognitive mechanisms by which such knowledge is learned and used) in order to understand why members of disadvantaged groups adhere to norms and justifications that are not in their interest.

While the social identity perspective does accommodate the phenomenon of self-stereotyping, defined as the tendency of an individual to categorize himself or herself in terms of group membership (e.g. Hogg & Turner, 1987; Lorenzi-Cioldi, 1991; Oakes & Turner, 1990; Turner, Hogg, Oakes, Reicher, & Wetherell, 1987; Turner, Oakes, Haslam, & McCarthy, 1992), it does not account for the phenomenon of negative self-stereotyping, which we raised in the discussion of ego-justification approaches. For example, the female subjects in the Broverman et al. (1972) study actually evaluated their own group negatively by endorsing stereotypic items such as "irrational," "passive," and "incompetent" (but see Widiger & Settle, 1987). While Eagly and Mladinic (1994) and others are correct to point out that stereotypes of women are positive in many respects, it is important to recognize that negative stereotypes of the in-group (and positive stereotypes of the out-group) are at odds with the function of group-justification.

There is also some evidence for in-group devaluation on stereotypic dimensions provided by studies using social identity theory's own empirical paradigm. Spears and Manstead (1989), for instance, found that students from Manchester University rated the typical Oxford University student to be more "hard-working," "self-assured," "articulate," and "intellectually minded" than the typical Manchester student. Even if such differences were validated by objective criteria such as grades and test scores or if they were widely believed by most of society, one might expect subjects to defend the in-group "at all costs," in the words of Hogg and Abrams (1988, p. 76).

In a recent meta-analytic review by Mullen et al. (1992) including 77 laboratory tests of the hypothesis that experimental or ad hoc groups would evaluate the in-group more favorably than the out-group, the authors conclude that there is a statistically reliable but moderately sized tendency to favor the in-group. Although Mullen et al. make little mention of out-group favoritism among low-status groups, Jost (1993) reorganized the studies they cited according to the type of bias exhibited (in-group, out-group, or none) and found that a full 85 per cent of low-status groups made trait evaluations favoring the higher-status out-group, while none of the high-status groups showed out-group favoritism. The paper by Mullen et al. (1992) therefore underestimates the degree to which low-status group members express preferences for the out-group in experimental situations, possibly reflecting a type of false consciousness. While the signs of out-group favoritism disappear in the review by Mullen et al. of the data for "real"-world groups, who manifest in-group bias more generally, such groups can provide only imprecise evidence about the operation of theoretically specified variables. The reasons for the "interaction" between status and type of group (laboratory or "real") are far from clear, perhaps reflecting greater patterns of social desirability among real-world respondents.

A growing number of writers have noted that social identity theory currently does not account for the phenomenon of "out-group favoritism" (e.g. Apfelbaum, 1979; Dittmarr, 1992; Hewstone & Jaspars, 1984; Hinkle & Brown, 1990; Jost, 1993; Kalmuss, Gurin, & Townsend, 1981; Sidanius, 1993; Sidanius & Pratto, 1993). Hinkle and Brown (1990), for instance, argue that:

> Out-group favouritism per se does not fit with [social identity theory's] view that group members create and maintain positive social identi-

ties by engaging in in-group favouring processes of intergroup comparison. (p. 49)[1]

Social identity theory alone does not possess a ready account of phenomena such as negative stereotyping of the in-group, although issues relevant to it have been discussed in the literature (e.g., Tajfel, 1982; Tajfel & Turner, 1979, 1986; Turner & Brown 1978; van Knippenberg, 1978, 1984).

At times, the social identity or self-categorization perspective clearly seems to suggest that the individual is motivated to form positive stereotypes of the in-group (e.g. Hogg & Abrams, 1988; Turner et al., 1987), and at other times that stereotypes of the in-group will reflect the group's position in society, whether positive or negative (e.g. Hogg and Turner, 1987; Tajfel & Turner, 1979, 1986). For example, Hogg and Abrams (1988, p. 76) write that "there is a vested interest in preserving the evaluative superiority of the ingroup at all costs," whereas Hogg and Turner (1987, p. 31) state that "the precise form taken by the self-stereotyping [ethnocentric, ambivalent, or deprecatory] will only be predictable from knowledge of the relations" between the groups. This ambiguity can perhaps be traced to social identity theory's on-again/off-again relationship to concepts of ideology and false consciousness (cf. Apfelbaum, 1979; Condor, 1990). The theory seems to acknowledge that powerless groups will often internalize the norms of powerful outgroups, but it also predicts that the powerless groups will develop their own norms in order to achieve positive distinctiveness. Even if social identity theory is not incompatible with phenomena such as negative self-stereotyping and out-group favoritism (e.g. Tajfel & Turner, 1986; Turner & Brown, 1978), it does not seem to possess a mechanism to account for them in the way that a need for positive social comparison is capable of accounting for positive stereotyping of the in-group and negative stereotyping of out-groups (e.g. Hinkle & Brown, 1990; Hogg & Abrams, 1988).

Social identity theorists attempt to resolve the ambiguity between the hypothesis of group-justification and the finding of out-group favoritism among disadvantaged groups under the rubric of perceived "legitimacy" and "stability" of the system, or the extent to which group members are able to conceive of "cognitive alternatives" to the current state of affairs (Tajfel, 1982; Tajfel & Turner, 1979, 1986; Turner & Brown, 1978). With

respect to social stereotyping, this factor has been conceptualized as the "consensuality" of the stereotype, that is, the degree to which its content is undisputed or widely accepted as valid (e.g., Spears & Manstead, 1989; van Knippenberg, 1984). In other words, social identity theory supposes that when negative images of the in-group are seen as both legitimate and unlikely to change, disadvantaged groups may internalize harmful stereotypes of themselves; when these stereotypes, however, are perceived as unfair or open to change, in-group favoritism will prevail once again and negative stereotyping of the in-group will disappear (e.g. Tajfel & Turner, 1986). Thus, Spears and Manstead (1989) found that Manchester students acknowledged the superiority of Oxford students on consensually accepted dimensions such as "hard-working" and "intellectually minded," but evaluated the in-group more positively than the out-group on traits such as "practically minded," "easygoing," and "aware of trends in music and fashion." The system-justification approach would suggest that the traits on which subordinate groups positively differentiate themselves actually may serve to reinforce the status quo, by creating stereotypes whereby less advantaged groups are seen by themselves and others as accommodating or content ("easygoing") or not particularly concerned with achievement ("interested in music and fashion"). Perceptions concerning the stability and legitimacy of the status quo or the consensuality and validity of stereotypes may be symptoms of what we call "system-justification."

We argue that justification of the status quo frequently appears to outweigh the individual's defense of group interests. In cases such as these, negative stereotyping of the in-group seems to serve the function of justifying an unequal state of affairs, even at the expense of personal and group interest (cf. Sidanius & Pratto, 1993). For this reason and others, we postulate a third system-justifying function for the stereotype which is consistent with the idea of false consciousness and is supported by theory and data from experimental social psychology.

The System-Justification Approach

The time is at hand for social psychology to address a third view of justification whereby stereotypes are documented as serving ideological functions in addition to or, better, frequently in opposition to, motivational functions associated with personal or group defense. In postulating that stereotypes serve the function of "system-justification," we do not seek to displace previous theories of justification, but rather to build on them in order to account for ignored or unexplained phenomena. Just as Turner and his colleagues argue that the individual may move back and forth from personal categorization to group categorization (e.g., Oakes & Turner, 1990; Turner et al., 1987; 1992), we suggest that the individual will sometimes adopt a "system-justifying" stance whereby an existing state of affairs is preserved "at all costs." Incidentally, we do not claim that system-justification accounts for the formation and maintenance of all stereotypes, only that many stereotypes serve for their adherents the function of preserving the status quo.

We seek to develop the argument that stereotypes serve ideological functions, in particular that they justify the exploitation of certain groups over others, and that they explain the poverty or powerlessness of some groups and the success of others in ways that make these differences seem legitimate and even natural. This position is consistent with a large body of social psychological research which finds that "one of the most commonly observed characteristics of social existence is that people imbue social regularities with an 'ought' quality" (Lerner, 1980, p. 10). Based on theories of and data on self-perception, attribution, cognitive conservatism, the division of social roles, behavioral confirmation, and the belief in a just world, we stipulate a process whereby stereotypes are used to explain the existing social system and the positions and actions of self and others. This notion, as we have said, is not new. The resistance-to-change view underlies broadscale social philosophies such as Marxism and feminism as well as psychological accounts of cognitive conservatism, confirmation biases, and implicit stereotyping.

Because the ideas of the dominant tend to become the ideas of the dominated (e.g. Kluegel & Smith, 1986; MacKinnon, 1989; Marcuse, 1964; Marx & Engels, 1846; Mason, 1971), system-justifying stereotypes may be advanced by even those who stand to lose from them. The system-justification approach addresses issues of false consciousness more directly than approaches emphasizing ego- or group-justification, since the former stipulates that under certain conditions people will justify the status quo at all costs, above and beyond the desire to justify their own interests or the interests of other group members. Theorists adopting a social dominance perspective (e.g. Sidanius, 1993; Sidanius & Pratto, 1993) have drawn attention to these same ideological processes in terms of "legitimizing myths" that serve to justify the oppression of some groups by others. While Sidanius and Pratto also claim that unequal social systems tend to be justified consensually through stereotypes and other belief systems, they posit a sociobiological explanation which leads to the conclusion that oppression is "inevitable" (Sidanius & Pratto, 1993). Our social cognitive approach to the study of false consciousness, on the other hand, may suggest ways of ultimately changing the social and political conditions that give rise to it (see Cunningham, 1987; MacKinnon, 1989).

System-justification refers to the psychological process whereby an individual perceives, understands, and explains an existing situation or arrangement with the result that the situation or arrangement is maintained. Unlike ego-justification or group-justification views that postulate a psychologically adaptive mechanism (protection of the ego or the extended collective ego), system-justification does not offer an equivalent function that operates in the service of protecting the interests of the self or the group. In fact, system-justification refers to the psychological process by which existing social arrangements are preserved in spite of the obvious psychological and material harm they entail for disadvantaged individuals and groups. It is this emphasis on the production of false consciousness that contrasts the system-justification view most sharply with previous views. We submit that an explanation of this scope may be required to explain, among other things, negative in-group stereotyping among disadvantaged groups and the societal or cross-societal consensuality of some stereotypes.

Evidence for Stereotyping as System-Justification

Our purpose in this section is to review a series of social psychological findings demonstrating that people will develop ideas about the characteristics of the self and others on the basis of some social arrangement, like a division of social roles or responsibilities, or an outcome such as a legal decision or victimization by assault. In such domains, it has been found that people will ascribe to themselves and others traits that are consonant with their social position, whether positive or negative, rather than question the order or legitimacy of the system that produced such an arrangement or outcome. These tendencies toward system-justification occur even when subjects know that the arrangements or outcomes were arrived at arbitrarily and result in negative consequences for them. Stereotyping in such circumstances may result in false consciousness, the holding of "false beliefs that sustain one's own oppression" (Cunningham, 1987, p. 255).

For example, random assignment in an experiment leads one individual to play the role of "contestant" and another to play the role of "questioner"; historical events lead Africans to serve as slaves and Europeans to serve as masters; and evolutionary events lead to the ability of females, but not males, to bear offspring. Then, an experimental division of roles leads contestant and observer to identify the questioner as more knowledgeable (Ross et al., 1977); assignment to the role of slave leads both master and slave to view the slave as "child-like" and "subservient" (e.g., Ashmore & Del Boca, 1981); and assignment to the role of childbearer leads women and men to see women as "nurturing" and men as "autonomous" (e.g., Eagly & Steffen, 1984; Hoffman & Hurst, 1990). Once a set of events produces certain social arrangements, whether by historical accident or human intention, the resulting arrangements tend to be explained and justified simply because they exist. Stereotyping, as it operates in such contexts, appears to be a psychological vehicle for system-justification.

The concept of "system" here is an admittedly vague term, intended to cover a wide variety of cases. We mean to include social arrangements such as those found in families, institutions, organizations, social groups, governments, and nature. System-justification refers to the psychological process whereby prevailing conditions, be they social, political, economic, sexual, or legal, are accepted, explained, and justified simply because they exist. As Mason (1971) writes, the disadvantaged come to "believe that the system is part of the order of nature and that things will always be like this" (p. 11). We argue that stereotypes often

are used to serve this ideological function. The research literature we review is that of experimental social psychology, although work in many other disciplines is relevant to our thesis. It is no accident that most of the experiments supporting our position involve an inequality in the division of roles or outcomes, insofar as inequality between individuals or groups needs to be justified in order for it to be maintained.

Our view is well-suited to account for the myriad of results indicating that stereotypes based on social class are pervasive and system-justifying (e.g. Ashmore & McConahay, 1975; Darley & Gross, 1983; Dittmarr, 1992; Feldman, 1972; Howard & Pike, 1986; Jones, 1991). We emphasize the tendency for people to infer stereotypic attributes directly from information about status or position, mainly in order to justify differences in status or position. Thus, stereotypes of the working class as unintelligent, incompetent, dirty, and unreliable may serve the ideological function of rationalizing their economic plight. Similarities between stereotypes of the lower class and those of African Americans have led some to suggest that racial stereotypes were inferred from economic disadvantage (e.g. Bayton et al., 1956; Jussim et al., 1987; Smedley & Bayton, 1978; Triandis, 1977), a point that is congenial to our perspective.

The work of Eagly and her colleagues (Eagly, 1987; Eagly & Steffen, 1984, 1986; Eagly & Wood, 1982) is important because it demonstrates that stereotypes emerge in order to explain or justify existing divisions of labor. For example, Eagly and Steffen (1984) found that gender stereotypes are derived from assumptions about men and women occupying different roles. In particular, it was demonstrated that people judge women to be "communal" because it is consistent with their assumed "homemaker" role, and they judge men to be "agentic" because it is consistent with their assumed role of "employee." Thus, male homemakers were rated to be as communal as female homemakers and more communal than females whose occupation was unspecified, while female employees were seen as more agentic than male employees and males with no occupational description given. Eagly and Steffen (1986) extended these results by demonstrating that part-time female employees were stereotyped as more communal and less agentic than full-time female employees, and part-time male employees were judged to be less agentic than full-time male employees. The authors argued that "the proximal cause of gender stereotypes is the differing distributions of women and men into social roles" (Eagly & Steffen, 1984, p. 752), because people's stereotypes were mediated by their beliefs about the targets' occupations. Stereotyping may therefore arise from efforts to explain and justify why men and women typically occupy different social roles.

Hoffman and Hurst (1990) similarly stress the importance of social roles in determining the contents of stereotypes. Following Eagly, they argue that gender stereotypes "originate in an attempt to rationalize the division of labor by attributing to each sex those qualities deemed necessary for performance of the assigned functions" (pp. 206–207). By asking subjects to complete trait ratings of two fictional groups, "Orinthians" and "Ackmians," whose occupations were listed as "childraisers" and "city workers," respectively, Hoffman and Hurst demonstrate that people spontaneously stereotype the groups in ways that justify their alleged division into separate roles in society. Specifically, childraisers were judged to be more patient, kind, and understanding than city workers, who were judged to be self-confident and forceful. Furthermore, stereotyping in general was more prevalent when subjects were first asked to explain why the groups occupied different roles, lending support to the notion that stereotypes are created by a demand to justify an existing arrangement. A second experiment replicated the basic finding for two other social roles, "business persons" and "academics," who were stereotyped as "extraverted/ambitious" and "introverted/intellectual" respectively.

Because subjects in the Hoffman and Hurst studies were judging fictional groups on another planet, they had no personal or group conduct in need of justification. Nevertheless, they attributed traits to each of the groups in such a way that the existing state of affairs was reinforced. Hoffman and Hurst (1990) write that gender "stereotypes are largely an attempt to rationalize, justify, or explain the sexual division of labor" (p. 199), a conclusion that forms the basis of our system-justification approach.

Skrypnek and Snyder (1982) establish a further link between stereotyping and system-justification by showing that subjects' gender stereotypes bring about divisions of labor that are consistent with the stereotypes. Specifically, stereotypic expectations led females who were believed by others to be male to choose to perform stereotypically "masculine tasks" such as fixing a light switch or attaching bait to a fishing hook, while females who were believed to be female opted for "feminine tasks" such as decorating a birthday cake and ironing a shirt (see Geis, 1993, for a more complete discussion of expectancy confirmation with respect to gender stereotypes). Taking the studies by Eagly and Steffen (1984, 1986), Hoffman and Hurst (1990), and Skrypnek and Snyder (1982) together, it seems that gender stereotypes both reflect and reproduce the division of social roles. The system-justification view holds that stereotypes follow from social and political systems in that certain systems lead people to stereotype themselves and others in such a way that their status, role, and the system in general are explained and justified. In this way, stereotypic beliefs both reflect and justify existing social arrangements.

A number of studies have demonstrated that people will ascribe traits to themselves as well as other people in such a way that the status or role that they occupy is justified. For example, in a singularly important demonstration, Ross et al. (1977) showed the ease with which a social situation creates justification for beliefs about the self and others. The researchers randomly assigned subjects to play either the role of contestant or questioner in a variant of the game of "Jeopardy," which tests players' aptitude for general knowledge. Results were that people attributed greater knowledge to questioners than contestants simply because the latter were in a far more challenging position, despite the fact that assignment to these roles was explicitly random, and that any differences that emerged were due purely to the position subjects found themselves occupying. These false attributions persisted even when subjects judged their own abilities: people judged themselves to be less knowledgeable when they were assigned to the contestant role than when they were assigned to the questioner role. Ross et al. acknowledge the relevance of their findings for what we refer to as false consciousness:

> People are apt to underestimate the extent to which seemingly positive attributes of the powerful simply reflect the advantages of social control. Indeed, this distortion in social judgment

could provide a particularly insidious brake upon social mobility, whereby the disadvantaged and powerless overestimate the capabilities of the powerful who, in turn, inappropriately deem members of their own caste well-suited to their particular leadership tasks (p. 494).

The result, of course, is that the powerful are stereotyped, even by the powerless, in such a way that their success is explained or justified; meanwhile, the powerless are stereotyped (and self-stereotyped) in such a way that their plight is well-deserved and similarly justified. The process may be self-perpetuating in that people who are stereotyped tend to choose social roles for themselves that are consistent with the stereotypic expectations others have of them (e.g., Geis, 1993; Skrypnek & Snyder, 1982; Swann, 1983). To the extent that stigmatized groups can be made to believe in their own inferiority, they may be prevented from achieving positive outcomes (e.g., Steele, 1992).

Another body of evidence suggesting that people will form negative ideas about themselves in order to make sense of social reality comes from Lerner's (1980) work on the just-world theory. Lerner argues that people are motivated to subscribe to a "belief in a just world" in which people "get what they deserve," since it is only in such a world that people can have control over outcomes (e.g., Lerner, 1980; Lerner & Miller, 1978). The theory accounts for the phenomenon of self-blame among victims of violence (e.g., Janoff-Bulman, 1992; Miller & Porter, 1983; Wortman, 1976), which we take to be analogous to the problem of negative self-stereotyping among the disadvantaged, by postulating that victims would rather blame themselves for their plight than admit that the world in which they live is "capricious and unfair" (Miller & Porter, 1983, p. 140; but see Crocker & Major, 1989).

Consistent with the notion that people engage in blaming the self or the in-group for negative consequences in order to maintain their belief that people get what they deserve, Howard (1984) reported that females as well as males tend to blame female victims of physical assault more than male victims. The author concludes that these results are difficult to account for in terms of ego-defense (and, we would add, group-defense). In situations such as this, people seem to be more interested in justifying a system that condones terrifying outcomes than in defending the innocence of its victims, even when they are members of the in-group. Cunningham (1987) cites "false blame" as one of the main types of false consciousness. From perspectives such as Marxism and feminism, it is indeed false for members of disadvantaged groups to blame themselves or each other for their misfortune (e.g. Cunningham, 1987; MacKinnon, 1989).

Just-world theory is compatible with the Marxist/feminist view of stereotyping as ideology, insofar as both views hold that attributions about groups of people are made in such a way that the apparent integrity and rationality of the social world is sustained, even at the expense of personal or group interest. The difference, perhaps, is that Lerner (1980) sees the "belief in a just world" as a natural, universal motivation, whereas critical theorists might interpret the need for ideological justification as a requirement particular to exceedingly exploitative systems such as capitalism, totalitarianism, or patriarchy. Our expectation is that system-justification will vary widely according to social, historical, cultural, and economic contexts (cf. Billig, 1985).

Although not directly related to stereotyping, Tyler and colleagues have sought to understand why people maintain loyalty to legal and political institutions even when such institutions produce unfavorable outcomes for them (e.g., Lind & Tyler, 1988; Tyler, 1990; Tyler & McGraw, 1986). We see this problem as analogous to the one we consider here, namely why people subscribe to stereotypes that justify the existing system of arrangements at the psychological expense of the self and the group. For instance, it has been found that people are satisfied with procedural systems as long as they are provided with an opportunity to participate in the process, even if their participation has no effect over relevant outcomes (Lind & Tyler, 1988; Tyler, 1990). Tyler and McGraw (1986) make explicit the connection here to the concept of false consciousness, concluding that "the disadvantaged are led to focus upon aspects of their situation that are ineffective in inducing a sense of injustice and, hence, lead to political quiescence" (p. 126). Similarly, we propose that disadvantaged groups subscribe to stigmatizing stereotypes of themselves and others and thereby justify the system that produces the oppression. The result, of course, is that the existing arrangements are perpetuated.

Greenwald (1980; see also Janoff-Bulman, 1992) has reviewed considerable evidence for "cognitive conservatism," a disposition to preserve existing systems of knowledge and beliefs at the cost of accuracy in information processing. Greenwald argues that people tend to resist changing their attitudes and beliefs by selectively attending to and generating attitude-consistent information and by misremembering past experiences in order to cohere with current perceptions (see also Ross, 1989). Decision-making theorists, too, have identified a "status quo effect" such that people express strong preferences for the current state of affairs, whatever it is, even if new options would be more desirable (e.g., Samuelson & Zeckhauser, 1987; Tetlock, 1992). We suggest that cognitive conservatism and the tendency to prefer choices of inaction to action may contribute to system-justification, because maintaining the legitimacy of existing social arrangements would eliminate the need for attitude and behavioral change.

While Greenwald (1980) sees only an analogy between the practices of conservative systems of government and the cognitive tendency to avoid change, we suggest a more direct link: political systems that seek to preserve the status quo at all costs may produce people whose minds work to preserve the status quo at all costs. We assume that biases such as "cognitive conservatism" (e.g., Greenwald, 1980; Janoff-Bulman, 1992) acquire the particular effects they do because they operate in the context of unequal social systems requiring substantial ideological justification, as suggested by critical aspects of feminist and Marxist philosophies.

Recent theoretical and empirical advances on the "cognitive unconscious" (e.g. Greenwald, 1992; Jacoby, Lindsay, & Toth, 1992; Kihlstrom, 1990) may help to explain how and why people subscribe to beliefs that harm them. A number of studies have demonstrated the unconscious nature of stereotyping (Banaji, Hardin, & Rothman, 1993; Devine, 1989; Gaertner & McLaughlin, 1983; Gilbert & Hixon, 1991), and discussions have focused on implications for theory and practical issues concerning awareness and intentionality (Banaji & Greenwald, 1994; Crosby, Bromley, & Saxe, 1980; Fiske, 1989). The findings from this research are important for our discussion of stereotyping and false consciousness for at least two reasons. First and foremost, they demonstrate that

prior exposure to stereotype-related information can influence judgements and actions even when perceivers are unaware of it. For example, Banaji and Greenwald (1994) found that subjects unconsciously misattributed fame to males more often than females. Banaji, Hardin, and Rothman (1993) showed that word primes associated with a female stereotype (dependence) or a male stereotype (aggression) were used implicitly but selectively in judgements of targets whose gender fit the social category of the primed stereotype. Devine (1989) found that subliminal presentations of racial stereotypes of Black Americans later influenced Whites' judgements of an ambiguously described person. Gilbert and Hixon (1991) identified the limiting conditions of cognitive load under which subjects are more or less likely to use an unconsciously activated racial stereotype on tasks of word-fragment completion.

While research of this type has demonstrated the effects of perceivers' unawareness of stereotype use, these studies have not examined the effects of implicit stereotyping on targets. We suggest that stereotyped groups and individuals similarly may be unaware of the operation of some stereotypes. Males and females, for example, have been found to be equally unaware of the influence of gender priming on judgements of fame (Banaji & Greenwald, 1994). If this is the case, then implicit stereotyping would not allow stigmatized groups to engage in self-protective (or ego-justifying) strategies as suggested by Crocker and Major (1989). In other words, targets who are unaware that a stereotyped judgement has occurred will not attribute that judgment to perceivers' prejudice toward their social group. Nevertheless, it is quite possible that the effects of such judgements may register unconsciously in affect, cognition, and behavior. System-justification, especially if it conflicts with personal or group interest, may be more likely when it occurs outside of conscious awareness.

A second way in which research on implicit stereotyping may contribute to an understanding of false consciousness is by demonstrating dissociations between consciously and unconsciously expressed beliefs. For example, Devine (1989) showed that even people who explicitly reject prejudicial attitudes were influenced by previously seen racial primes in judging the aggressiveness of a target. Banaji and Greenwald (1993) found that the bias of assigning males greater fame than females when no such credit was due held irrespective of subjects' conscious beliefs about gender equality. Taken as a whole, the data on implicit stereotyping present an additional challenge for views of stereotyping derived solely from ego- or group-justification because unconscious stereotyping occurs independent of group membership or individual differences with respect to prejudicial attitudes.

While our aim has been to suggest the importance of system-justification, we recognize that people do not always (consciously or unconsciously) subscribe to beliefs that reinforce the status quo. That is, we do not claim that system-justification always takes place, or that false consciousness is unavoidable in the face of inequality. We do think, however, that psychologists in general and stereotyping researchers in particular have underemphasized the degree to which people persist in explaining and justifying social systems that disadvantage them.

In order for the concept of system-justification to be useful, future research would need to identify conditions that produce responses of system-justification as opposed to responses of ego- and group-justification. One potential trigger of the system-justification response might be the absence of a revolutionary "class consciousness" (e.g., Gramsci, 1971; Gurin, Miller, & Gurin, 1980; Kalmuss, Gurin, & Townsend, 1981; Lukács, 1971; Mészáros, 1971; Meyerson, 1991). Similarly, isolation of disadvantaged group members from one another or low degrees of group identification among them in general may result in increased system-justification (e.g., Archibald, 1989; Tajfel & Turner, 1986; Vaughan, 1978). The relationship between group identification and group consciousness needs to be clarified, as does the question of whether achieving group consciousness (as opposed to what we have been calling false consciousness) requires that one advance negative stereotypes about out-groups in general. A third issue bearing on the operation of system-justification involves a somewhat different use of the concept of "consciousness" (e.g., Banaji & Greenwald, 1994; Devine, 1989; Greenwald, 1992; Kihlstrom, 1990). System-justification may occur more frequently when judgements are made implicitly or out of conscious awareness. By focusing attention explicitly on issues pertaining to the system of

social arrangements, it may be possible to avoid the consequences of system-justification, as researchers have found with respect to stereotyping in general (Greenwald & Banaji, 1993). A fifth and final factor which may make system-justification more likely is the insidiousness of the system. Somewhat paradoxically, it may be that the more painful, humiliating, or unfair a system is, the more it evokes the system-justification response, as cognitive dissonance researchers found when investigating the effects of initiation rites (e.g.. Aronson & Mills, 1959; Gerard & Mathewson, 1966).

Implications of the System-Justification Approach for the Content of Stereotypes

There is obviously not space here, in the first presentation of our view, to develop fully the many implications and predictions of the system-justification approach for the process of stereotyping and the content of stereotypes. As important as it would be to identify the specific sociological and psychological mechanisms involved in system-justification, we have only pointed out that the phenomenon occurs. The scope of this paper prohibits a more detailed analysis of the ways in which system-justifying stereotypes are developed and spread. Nevertheless, because the foregoing has emphasized processes of justification associated with stereotyping, it seems useful to list some of the main consequences of bringing our perspective to bear on issues of the content of stereotypes. Such consequences include the possibilities that contents of stereotypes are derived from prevailing systems of social arrangements, that changes to the existing system of arrangements will produce changes in the contents of stereotypes, that stereotypes of subordinate groups may be similar across different systems, and that their contents need not originate from a "kernel of truth." In addition, we propose that system-justifying stereotypes of disadvantaged groups need not be unfavorable and those of advantaged groups need not be favorable in content. All of these implications, of course, are offered speculatively as hypotheses and would need to be supported by empirical research before being accepted.

The system-justification view assumes that specific contents of stereotypes may be predicted on the basis of objective, material factors such as status or position in society. Tajfel (1978, 1981a) was fond of quoting Robert LeVine, who made the following challenge: "Describe to me the economic intergroup situation, and I shall predict the content of the stereotypes." Our own position is not one of economic reductionism, because it is necessary to understand inequalities due to gender, race, ethnicity, religion, sexual orientation, and other noneconomic grounds. At the same time, however, we do conceive of stereotypes as arising from objective, material factors including divisions of labor and social practice rather than, for example, as ideas prior to or independent of material forces in society (see MacKinnon, 1989; Marx & Engels, 1846).

Once in place, stereotypes may reproduce the same old state of affairs by eliciting behavioral confirmation on the part of stereotyped actors (e.g. Geis, 1993; Snyder, 1981). In other words, stigmatized groups may begin to act in such a way that other people's negative expectancies of them are supported, thereby ensuring their continued subordination. For example, Word, Zanna, and Cooper (1974) found that White interviewers' stereotypic expectations about Black job applicants evoked nervous behavior and poor performance on the part of black respondents, an outcome that is likely to reinforce rather than supplant racial inequalities. Similarly, Skrypnek and Snyder (1982) demonstrated that subjects' beliefs about the sex of their interaction partner determined the latter's behavior; partners whom the other believed to be male chose to perform stereotypically male roles, while partners believed to be female chose stereotypically female roles. Thus, stereotyped groups and individuals implicitly may come to deliver what is expected of them, and this may be one way in which stereotypes derived on the basis of social status, position, or role may allow powerless groups to engage in a form of passive resistance (Sunar, 1978) or otherwise perpetuate the target's occupation of that status, position, or role (see Geis, 1993).

A second implication of the system-justification approach which follows from the first is that a most expedient way of changing stereotypes is to change material reality (see Banaji & Greenwald, 1994; Eagly & Steffen, 1984; Hoffman & Hurst, 1990; MacKinnon, 1989), an assumption that is even more basic to our view than to

social identity theory. We take evidence presented by social identity theorists (e.g. Haslam, Turner, Oakes, McGarty, & Hayes, 1992) that stereotypes change in accordance with alterations in the social structure of relations between groups to be supportive of the position defended here, which is that stereotypes rationalize systems of social, economic, and sexual relations. In many ways, our thesis is similar to one advanced by Campbell and LeVine (1968, p. 561) whose merging of cognitive dissonance theory and anthropological data resulted in the proposition that changes in the system of relations between groups are met by corresponding changes in "group labels and stereotypes."

A third prediction of our view is that the stereotype contents of different but also disadvantaged groups may be more similar than would be predicted on the basis of ego-justification or group-justification. Therefore, a somewhat surprising consequence of the system-justification approach is that different groups across cultures should share essentially the same stereotype contents if they share the same relative status in their respective societies. In fact, Tajfel (1970) made just this observation:

> I remember presenting some years ago to students in Oxford a set of adjectives mentioned to me at the time by Jezernik as typical of the Slovene characterizations of immigrant Bosnians. When the students were asked where these descriptions came from and to whom they applied, the unanimous guess was that they were the stereotypes used about coloured immigrants in England (p. 130).

Our system-justification view would predict some commonalities among the stereotypes of different groups who occupy similar statuses in societies, insofar as the ideological justifications needed for these specific situations would be much the same (cf., Sunar, 1978). In order to make a similar point, Millet (1970) considered the similarities between stereotypes of blacks and women and concluded that:

> common opinion associates the same traits with both: inferior intelligence, an instinctual or sensual gratification, an emotional nature both primitive and childlike, an imagined prowess in or affinity for sexuality, a contentment with their own

lot which is in accord with a proof of its appropriateness, a wily habit of deceit, and concealment of feeling (p. 57).

We have thus arrived at a peculiar possibility: research on the contents of stereotypes may turn out to be characterized not so much by "tremendous variations in the specific forms which prejudice assumes," as Katz and Braly (1935, p. 183) reasonably expected, as by regularities in the contents of stereotypes of different groups which may emerge by virtue of their similar positions in society. An informal review by Sunar (1978) supports such a prediction, as does the historical work of Myrdal (1944), although more systematic research is obviously needed. The system-justification approach at any rate offers the possibility that the contents of stereotypes may be predicted as well as described (e.g., Hoffman & Hurst, 1990).

A fourth implication of our view is that stereotypes need not arise from a "kernel of truth," as psychologists and laypersons have frequently assumed (e.g., see Allport, 1954; Brigham, 1971; Fishman, 1956). If the kernel of truth view holds that each stereotype must originate on the basis of some valid observation of differences between groups, then we disagree with it. Insofar as stereotypes arise in order to justify some system of social arrangements, they may arise out of false as well as "true" consciousness; the justification used may bear no relation to actual characteristics of the group. This was the case in the experiments conducted by Hoffman and Hurst (1990), who showed that stereotypes about childraisers and city workers develop not from observed differences in attributes or behaviors, but from a rationalization of the division of social roles.

However, it has become customary to take demonstrations of the self-fulfilling nature of stereotypic expectancies as supporting the "kernel of truth" position. In other words, stereotypes that were false to begin with may acquire a kind of accuracy because stereotyped individuals and groups conform to others' expectations of them (e.g., Geis, 1993). If this is what is meant by the kernel of truth view, then it is compatible with the system-justification view. We agree that some group differences may become validated through processes of behavioral confirmation or material deprivation, but this validity is indeed a specious one.

It is important to note that the system-justification view does not assume that disadvantaged groups will be stereotyped in negative terms, only that they will be stereotyped in ways that justify their occupation of a particular status or role. For instance, Saunders (1972) finds that blacks in Brazil are stereotyped as "faithful" and "humble," because these attributes justify their use as servants for whites. In contrast to earlier studies by McKee and Sherriffs (1956) and Broverman et al. (1972), Eagly and her colleagues have suggested that stereotypes of women are actually more favorable than stereotypes of men (Eagly & Mladinic, 1989; Eagly, Mladinic, & Otto, 1991). It would be useful to determine whether positive stereotypes of women actually serve to perpetuate their disadvantaged position in society (e.g., Hoffman & Hurst, 1990). While evidence for the favorability of female stereotypes is undoubtedly important (see Eagly & Mladinic, 1994, for a review), it is difficult to rule out demand characteristics associated with subjects' unwillingness to express unpopular negative attitudes about stigmatized groups. Furthermore, people may hold racist or sexist beliefs that are "aversive" to them and therefore are expressed only indirectly (e.g., Dovidio & Gaertner, 1986), and people's explicitly avowed stereotypical beliefs may bear no relation to their implicit beliefs about out-group members (e.g. Devine, 1989).

Just as the system-justification perspective does not assume that underprivileged groups will be stereotyped negatively, neither does it assume that privileged groups will always be stereotyped in positive terms. It has been suggested that dominant groups will occasionally evaluate subordinate groups more favorably than their own group in an effort to lend legitimacy to the status quo (e.g., van Knippenberg, 1978), although the evidence for out-group favoritism among high-status groups does not seem to be very strong in the experimental literature on intergroup relations (see Jost, 1993). Nevertheless, both men and women seem to hold stereotypes of men that include socially undesirable traits such as "aggressive," "selfish," "competitive," and "hostile" (e.g., Eagly & Mladinic, 1994; Spence, Helmreich, & Holahan, 1979; Widiger & Settle, 1987). According to the system-justification view, even negative stereotypes of dominant groups may serve the function of system-justification, as long as they indicate that the group is somehow well-suited for its status or role. Thus, men's relative success in a competitive social or economic system may be justified by attributing to them a high endowment of competitive qualities.

Conclusion

We have argued that system-justification may override motives to justify the positions or actions of the self or group, thus leading to negative stereotyping of the self or in-group and the high degree of consensuality of stereotypes. The review of selected evidence indicates that people often will make sense of existing states of affairs by assigning attributes to the self and others that are consonant with the roles or positions occupied by individuals and groups. Stereotypes appear to serve a system-justification function for their adherents such that prevailing systems of social arrangements are justified and reproduced. By acknowledging the importance of stereotyping as justification, we can begin to address the psychological basis of false consciousness.

NOTE

1. It is interesting to note that Tajfel & Turner (1979, 1986) originally raised the phenomenon of out-group favoritism among subordinate groups in order to criticize "realistic conflict theory" as defended by Sherif, Campbell, and others. Social identity theory was offered in order to account for negative social identity among disadvantaged groups, but mainly to propose that there are psychological pressures for these groups to improve their situation by challenging established hierarchies. The theory holds that disadvantaged individuals are highly motivated to overcome the effects of the existing social system and that they are frequently successful at it (e.g. Hogg & Abrams, 1988; Tajfel & Turner, 1979, 1986; Turner & Brown, 1978). This view may underestimate the extent to which ideological domination is possible and the degree to which members of disadvantaged groups persist in explaining and justifying the social order that creates their oppression.

REFERENCES

Aboud, F. E. (1988). *Children and Prejudice*. New York: Basil Blackwell.

Adorno, T. W., Frenkel-Brunswik, E., Levinson, D. J. & Sanford, R. N. (1950). *The Authoritarian Personality*. New York: Harper.

Allport, G. W. (1954/1958). *The Nature of Prejudice*. Cambridge, MA: Addison-Wesley.

Apfelbaum, E. (1979). Relations of domination and movements for liberation: An analysis of power between groups. In W. G. Austin & S. Worchel (Eds), *The Social Psychology of Intergroup Relations*. Monterey, CA: Brooks/Cole.

Archibald, W. P. (1989). *Marx and the Missing Link: "Human Nature."* Atlantic Highlands, NJ: Humanities Press International.

Aronson, E. & Mills, J. (1959). The effects of severity of initiation on liking for a group. *Journal of Abnormal and Social Psychology, 59,* 177–181.

Ashmore, R. D. & Del Boca, F. K. (1981). Conceptual approaches to stereotypes and stereotyping. In D. L. Hamilton (Ed.), *Cognitive Processes in Stereotyping and Intergroup Behavior.* Hillsdale, NJ: Erlbaum.

Ashmore, R. D. & Del Boca, F. K. (1986). *The Social Psychology of Female-Male Relations: A Critical Analysis of Central Concepts.* New York: Academic Press.

Ashmore, R. D. & McConahay, J. B. (1975). *Psychology and America's Urban Dilemmas.* New York: McGraw-Hill.

Banaji, M. R. & Greenwald, A. G. (1993). Implicit gender stereotyping in judgements of fame. Unpublished manuscript, Yale University.

Banaji, M. R. & Greenwald, A. G. (1994). Implicit stereotyping and prejudice. In M. P. Zanna & J. M. Olson (Eds), *The Psychology of Prejudice/The Ontario Symposium, vol. 7.* Hillsdale, NJ: Erlbaum.

Banaji, M. R., Hardin, C. D., & Rothman, A. J. (1993). Implicit stereotyping in person judgement. *Journal of Personality and Social Psychology, 65,* 272–281.

Bandura, A. (1983). Psychological mechanisms of aggression. In R. G. Geen & E. I. Donnersten (Eds), *Aggression: Theoretical and Empirical Reviews, vol. 1.* New York: Academic Press.

Banks, W. C. (1976). White preference in blacks: A paradigm in search of a phenomenon. *Psychological Bulletin, 83,* 1179–1186.

Bar-Tal, D. (1989). Delegitimization: The extreme case of stereotyping and prejudice. In D. Bar-Tal, C. F. Graumann, A. W. Kruglanski, & W. Stroebe (Eds), *Stereotyping and Prejudice: Changing Conceptions.* New York: Springer-Verlag.

Bar-Tal, D. (1990). *Group Beliefs: A Conception for Analyzing Group Structure, Processes, and Behavior.* New York: Springer-Verlag.

Bar-Tal, D., Graumann, C., Kruglanski, A. W., & Stroebe, W. (1989). *Changing Conceptions of Stereotyping and Prejudice.* New York: Springer-Verlag.

Basow, S. A. (1986). *Gender Stereotypes: Traditions and Alternatives.* Monterey, CA: Brooks/Cole.

Bayton, J. A., McAlister, L. B., & Hamer, J. (1956). Race-class stereotypes. *Journal of Negro Education, 41,* 75–78.

Bem, D. J. (1972). Self perception theory. In L. Berkowitz (Ed.), *Advances in Experimental Social Psychology, vol. 6.* New York: Academic Press.

Bem, S. L., & Bem, D. J. (1970). Case study of a nonconscious ideology: Training the woman to know her place. In D. J. Bem (Ed.), *Beliefs, Attitudes, and Human Affairs.* Belmont, CA: Brooks/Cole.

Bernat, G., & Balch, P. (1979). The Chicano Racial Attitude Measure (CRAM): Results of an initial investigation. *American Journal of Community Psychology, 7,* 137–146.

Bettelheim, B. & Janowitz, M. (1964). *Social Change and Prejudice.* New York: Free Press.

Billig, M. (1976). *Social Psychology and Intergroup Relations*. London: Academic Press.

Billig, M. (1985). Prejudice, categorization and particularization: From a perceptual to a rhetorical approach. *European Journal of Social Psychology, 15*, 79–103.

Blumenthal, M. D., Kahn, R. L., Andrews, F. M., & Head, K. B. (1972). *Justifying Violence: Attitudes of American Men*. Ann Arbor, MI: Institute for Social Research.

Brewer, M. B. & Kramer, R. M. (1985). The psychology of intergroup attitudes and behavior. *Annual Review of Psychology, 36*, 219–243.

Brickman, P. (1987). *Commitment, Conflict, and Caring*. Englewood Cliffs, NJ: Prentice-Hall.

Brigham, J. C. (1971). Ethnic stereotypes. *Psychological Bulletin, 76*, 15–33.

Brock, T. C., & Buss, A. H. (1964). Effects of justification for aggression and communication with the victim on postaggression dissonance. *Journal of Abnormal and Social Psychology, 68*, 403–412.

Broverman, I., Vogel, S. R., Broverman, D. M., Clarkson, F. E., & Rosenkrantz, P. S. (1972). Sex-role stereotypes: A current appraisal. *Journal of Social Issues, 28*, 59–78.

Brown, R. (1986). *Social Psychology (2nd ed)*. New York: Free Press.

Campbell, D. T., & LeVine, R. A. (1968). Ethnocentrism and intergroup relations. In R. P. Abelson, E. Aronson, W. J. McGuire, T. M. Newcomb, M. J. Rosenberg, & P. H. Tannenbaum (Eds), *Theories of Cognitive Consistency: A Sourcebook*. Chicago: Rand McNally.

Chaikin, A. L., & Darley, J. M. (1973). Victim or perpetrator? Defensive attribution of responsibility and the need for order and justice. *Journal of Personality and Social Psychology, 25*, 268–275.

Cialdini, R. B., Henrick, D. T. & Hoerig, J. (1976). Victim derogation in the Lerner paradigm: Just world or just justification. *Journal of Personality and Social Psychology, 33*, 719–724.

Clark, K. B., & Clark, M. P. (1947). Racial identification and preferences in Negro children. In T. M. Newcomb & E. L. Hartley (Eds), *Readings in Social Psychology*. New York: Holt.

Condor, S. (1990). Social stereotypes and social identity. In D. Abrams & M. A. Hogg (Eds), *Social Identity Theory: Constructive and Critical Advances*. Hemel Hempstead: Harvester.

Cox, O. C. (1948/1959). *Caste, Class and Race: A Study in Social Dynamics*. New York: Monthly Review Press.

Crocker, J. & Major, B. (1989). Social stigma and self-esteem: The self-protective properties of stigma. *Psychological Review, 96*, 608–630.

Crosby, F., Bromley, S., & Saxe, L. (1980). Recent unobtrusive studies of black and white discrimination and prejudice: A literature review. *Psychological Bulletin, 87*, 546–563.

Cunningham, F. (1987). *Democratic Theory and Socialism*. Cambridge: Cambridge University Press.

Darley, J. M., & Gross, R. H. (1983). A hypothesis-confirming bias in labeling effects. *Journal of Personality and Social Psychology, 44*, 20–33.

Devine, P. G. (1989). Stereotypes and prejudice: Their automatic and controlled components. *Journal of Personality and Social Psychology, 56*, 5–18.

Diab, L. (1962). National stereotypes and the "reference group" concept. *Journal of Social Psychology, 57*, 339–351.

Dittmarr, H. (1992). Perceived material wealth and first impressions. *British Journal of Social Psychology, 31*, 379–391.

Dovidio, J. F., & Gaertner, S. L. (1986). *Prejudice, Discrimination, and Racism*. Orlando, FL: Academic Press.

Eagleton, T. (1991). *Ideology*. London: Verso.

Eagly, A. H. (1987). *Sex Differences in Social Behaviour: A Social-Role Interpretation*. Hillsdale, NJ: Erlbaum.

Eagly, A. H., & Mladinic, A. (1989). Gender stereotypes and attitudes toward women and men. *Personality and Social Psychology Bulletin, 15*, 543–558.

Eagly, A. H., & Mladinic, A. (1994). Are people prejudiced against women? Some answers from research on attitudes, gender stereotypes and judgements of competence. In W. Stroebe & M. Hewstone (Eds), *European Review of Social Psychology, vol. 5*. New York: Wiley.

Eagly, A. H., Mladinic, A. & Otto, S. (1991). Are women evaluated more favourably than men? *Psychology of Women Quarterly, 15*, 203–216.

Eagly, A. H., & Steffen, V. J. (1984). Gender stereoypes stem from the distribution of women and men into social roles. *Journal of Personality and Social Psychology, 46*, 735–754.

Eagly, A. H., & Steffen, V. J. (1986). Gender stereotypes, occupational roles, and beliefs about part-time employees. *Psychology of Women Quarterly, 10*, 252–262.

Eagly, A. H., & Wood, W. (1982). Inferred sex differences in status as a determinant of gender stereotypes about social influence. *Journal of Personality and Social Psychology, 43*, 915–928.

Ehrlich, H. J. (1973). *The Social Psychology of Prejudice*. New York: Wiley.

Elster, J. (1982). Belief, bias, and ideology. In M. Hollis & S. Lukes (Eds), *Rationality and Relativism*. Oxford: Basil Blackwell.

Feldman, J. M. (1972). Stimulus characteristics and subject prejudice as determinants of stereotype attribution. *Journal of Personality and Social Psychology, 21*, 333–340.

Festinger, L. (1954). A theory of social comparison processes. *Human Relations, 7*, 117–140.

Festinger, L. (1957). *A Theory of Cognitive Dissonance*. Stanford: Stanford University Press.

Festinger, L. & Carlsmith, J. M. (1959). Cognitive consequences of forced compliance. *Journal of Abnormal and Social Psychology, 58*, 203–210.

Fine, M., & Bowers, C. (1984). Racial self-identification: The effects of social history and gender. *Journal of Applied Social Psychology, 58*, 203–210.

Fishman, J. A. (1956). An examination of the process and function of social stereotyping. *Journal of Social Psychology, 43*, 27–64.

Fiske, S. T. (1989). Examining the role of intent: Toward understanding its role in stereotyping and prejudice. In J. S. Uleman & J. A. Bargh (Eds.), *Unintended Thought*. New York: Guilford Press.

Freud, S. (1946). *The Ego and Mechanisms of Defense*. New York: International University Press.

Gaertner, S. L. & McLaughlin, J. P. (1983). Racial stereotypes: Associations and ascriptions of positive and negative characteristics. *Social Psychology Quarterly, 46*, 23–30.

Geis, F. L. (1993). Self-fulfilling prophecies: A social psychological view of gender. In A. E. Beall & R. J. Sternberg (Eds.), *Perspectives on the Psychology of Gender.* New York: Guilford

Gerard, H. B. (1957). Some effects of status, role clarity and group goal clarity upon individuals' relation to group process. *Journal of Personality, 25,* 475–488.

Gerard, H. B., & Mathewson, G. C. (1966). The effects of severity of initiation on liking for a group: A replication. *Journal of Experimental Social Psychology, 2,* 278–287.

Gergen, K. J. (1969). The significance of skin color in human relations. *Daedalus,* 390–406.

Gilbert, D. T. & Hixon, J. G. (1991). The trouble of thinking: Activation and application of stereotypic beliefs. *Journal of Personality and Social Psychology, 60,* 509–517.

Giles, H., & Powesland, P. F. (1975). *Speech Style and Social Evaluation.* London: Academic Press.

Gramsci, A. (1971). *Selections From the Prison Notebooks.* New York: International Publishers.

Greenwald, A. G. (1980). The totalitarian ego: Fabrication and revision of personal history. *American Psychologist, 35,* 603–618.

Greenwald, A. G. (1992). New look 3: Unconscious cognition reclaimed. *American Psychologist, 47,* 766–779.

Greenwald, A. G., & Banaji, M. R. (1993). A theory of implicit social cognition: Attitudes, stereotypes, self, and prejudice. Unpublished manuscript, University of Washington.

Greenwald, H. J., & Oppenheim, D. B. (1968). Reported magnitude of self-identification among Negro children: Artifact? *Journal of Personality and Social Psychology, 8,* 49–52.

Gregor, A. J., & McPherson, D. A. (1966). Racial preference and ego-identity among white and Bantu children in the republic of South Africa. *Genetic Psychology Monographs, 73,* 217–253.

Gurin, P., Miller, A. H., & Gurin, G. (1980). Stratum identification and consciousness. *Social Psychology Quarterly, 43,* 30–47.

Hamilton, D. L. (1981). *Cognitive Processes in Stereotyping and Intergroup Behavior.* Hillsdale, NJ: Erlbaum.

Hamilton, D. L., & Trolier, T. K. (1986). Stereotypes and stereotyping: An overview of the cognitive approach. In J. F. Dovidio & S. L. Gaertner (Eds.), *Prejudice, Discrimination, and Racism.* Orlando, FL: Academic Press.

Haslam, S. A., Turner, J. C., Oakes, P. J., McGarty, C. & Hayes, B. K. (1992). Context-dependent variation in social stereotyping 1: The effects of intergroup relations as mediated by social change and frame of reference. *European Journal of Social Psychology, 22,* 3–20.

Hastie, R. (1984). Causes and effects of causal attribution. *Journal of Personality and Social Psychology, 46,* 44–56.

Heider, F. (1958). *The Psychology of Interpersonal Relations.* New York: Wiley.

Herek, G. (1984). Beyond "homophobias": A social psychological perspective on attitudes toward lesbians and gay men. *Journal of Homosexuality, 10,* 1–21.

Herek, G. (1986). The instrumentality of attitudes: Toward a neofunctional theory. *Journal of Social Issues, 42,* 99–114.

Hewstone, M. (1989). *Causal Attribution.* Oxford: Basil Blackwell.

Hewstone, M., & Giles, H. (1986). Social groups and social stereotypes in intergroup communication: A review and model of intergroup communication breakdown. In W. B.

Gudykunst (Ed.), *Intergroup Communication.* London: Arnold.

Hewstone, M., & Jaspars, J. (1984). Social dimensions of attribution. In H. Tajfel (Ed.), *The Social Dimension: European Developments in Social Psychology, vol. 2.* Cambridge: Cambridge University Press.

Hewstone, M., Jaspars, J., & Lalljee, M. (1982). Social representations, social attribution and social identity: The intergroup images of "public" and "comprehensive" schoolboys. *European Journal of Social Psychology, 12,* 241–269.

Hinkle, S., & Brown, R. (1990). Intergroup comparisons and social identity: Some links and lacunae. In D. Abrams & M. A. Hogg (Eds), *Social Identity Theory: Constructive and Critical Advances.* Hemel Hempstead: Harvester.

Hoffman, C. & Hurst, N. (1990). Gender stereotypes: Perception or rationalization? *Journal of Personality and Social Psychology, 58,* 197–208.

Hogg, M. A. & Abrams, D. (1988). *Social identifications: A social psychology of intergroup relations and group processes.* London: Routledge.

Hogg, M. A., & Turner, J. C. (1987). Intergroup behavior, self-stereotyping and the salience of social categories. *British Journal of Social Psychology, 26,* 325–340.

Howard, J. A. (1984). Societal influences on attribution: Blaming some victims more than others. *Journal of Personality and Social Psychology, 47,* 494–505.

Howard, J. A. & Pike, K. C. (1986). Ideological investment in cognitive processing: The influence of social statuses on attribution. *Social Psychology Quarterly, 49,* 154–167.

Howard, J. & Rothbart, M. (1980). Social categorization and memory for in-group and out-group behavior. *Journal of Personality and Social Psychology, 38,* 301–310.

Hraba, J., & Grant, G. (1970). Black is beautiful: A reexamination of racial preference and identification. *Journal of Personality and Social Psychology, 16,* 398–402.

Huici, C. (1984). The individual and social functions of sex role stereotypes. In H. Tajfel (Ed.), *The social dimension, vol. 2.* Cambridge: Cambridge University Press.

Jacoby, L. L., Lindsay, D. S., & Toth, J. P. (1992). Unconscious processes revealed: A question of control. *American Psychologist, 47,* 802–809.

Jahoda, G., Thompson, S. S. & Bhatt, S. (1972). Ethnic identity and preferences among Asian immigrant children in Glasgow. *European Journal of Social Psychology, 2,* 19–32.

Janoff-Bulman, R. (1992). *Shattered assumptions: Toward a new psychology of trauma.* New York: Free Press.

Jones, E. E. (1964). *Ingratiation.* New York: Appleton-Century-Crofts.

Jones, E. E., Kanouse, D. E., Kelley, H. H., Nisbett, R. E., Valins, S. & Weiner, B. (1972). *Attribution: Perceiving the causes of behavior.* Morristown, NJ: General Learning Press.

Jones, M. (1991). Stereotyping Hispanics and Whites: Perceived differences in social roles as a determinant of ethnic stereotypes. *Journal of Social Psychology, 131,* 469–476.

Jost, J. T. (1993). Is it time for a theory of outgroup favoritism? A comment on the paper by Mullen, Brown & Smith. Unpublished manuscript, Yale University.

Jussim, L., Coleman, L. M., & Lerch, L. (1987). The nature of stereotypes: A comparison and integration of three theories. *Journal of Personality and Social Psychology, 52,* 536–546.

Kahn, R. L. (1972). The justification of violence: Social problems and social solutions. *Journal of Social Issues, 28,* 155–175.

Kalmuss, D., Gurin, P., & Townsend, A. L. (1981). Feminist and sympathetic feminist consciousness. *European Journal of Social Psychology, 11,* 131–147.

Katz, D. (1960). The functional approach to the study of attitudes. *Public Opinion Quarterly, 24,* 163–204.

Katz, D., & Braly, K. (1933). Racial stereotypes in one hundred college students. *Journal of Abnormal and Social Psychology, 28,* 280–290.

Katz, D., & Braly, K. (1935). Racial prejudice and racial stereotypes. *Journal of Abnormal and Social Psychology, 30,* 175–193.

Katz, P. A., & Zalk, S. R. (1974). Doll preferences: An index of racial attitudes? *Journal of Educational Psychology, 66,* 663–668.

Kelley, H. H. (1967). Attribution theory in social psychology. In D. Levine (Ed.), *Nebraska Symposium on Motivation, vol. 15.* Lincoln: University of Nebraska Press.

Kihlstrom, J. F. (1990). The psychological unconscious. In L. A. Pervin (Ed.), *Handbook of Personality: Theory and Research.* New York: Guilford Press.

Kipnis, D. (1976). *The Powerholders.* Chicago: University of Chicago Press.

Kluegel, J. R. & Smith, E. R. (1986). *Beliefs about inequality: Americans' views of what is and what ought to be.* New York: Aldine de Gruyter.

Lambert, W. E., Hodgson, R. C., Gardner, R. C. & Fillenbaum, S. (1960). Evaluational reactions to spoken languages. *Journal of Abnormal and Social Psychology, 60,* 44–51.

LaPiere, R. T. (1936). Type-rationalizations of group antipathy. *Social Forces, 15,* 232–237.

LaViolette, F. & Silvert, K. H. (1951). A theory of stereotypes. *Social Forces, 29,* 257–262.

Lerner, M. J. (1980). *The belief in a just world: A fundamental delusion.* New York: Plenum Press.

Lerner, M. J. ,& Miller, D. T. (1978). Just world research and the attribution process: Looking back and ahead. *Psychological Bulletin, 85,* 1030–1051.

Lewin, K. (1941). Self-hatred among Jews. *Contemporary Jewish Record,* June, 461–474.

Lifton, R. J. (1986). *The Nazi doctors: Medical killing and the psychology of genocide.* New York: Basic Books.

Lind, E. A. & Tyler, T. R. (1988). *The social psychology of procedural justice.* New York: Plenum Press.

Lippmann, W. (1922). *Public Opinion.* New York: Macmillan.

Lorenzi-Cioldi, F. (1991). Self-stereotyping and self-enhancement in gender groups. *European Journal of Social Psychology, 21,* 403–417.

Lukács, G. (1971). *History and class consciousness.* Cambridge, MA: MIT Press.

Maass, A., & Schaller, M. (1991). Intergroup biases and the cognitive dynamics of stereotype formation. In W. Stroebe & M. Hewstone (Eds.), *European Review of Social Psychology, vol. 2.* New York: Wiley.

MacKinnon, C. A. (1989). *Toward a Feminist Theory of the State.* Cambridge, MA: Harvard University Press.

Marcuse, H. (1964). *One-dimensional man.* Boston: Beacon Press.

Marshall, G. D., & Zimbardo, P. G. (1979). Affective consequences of inadequately explained physiological arousal.

Journal of Personality and Social Psychology, 37, 970–988.

Martin, J., Scully, M., & Levitt, B. (1990). Injustice and the legitimation of revolution: Damning the past, excusing the present, and neglecting the future. *Journal of Personality and Social Psychology, 59,* 281–290.

Marx, K. & Engels, F. (1846/1970). *The German ideology* (Ed. C. J. Arthur). New York: International Publishers.

Mason, P. (1971). *Patterns of dominance.* London: Oxford University Press.

McClure, J. (1991). *Explanations, accounts and illusions: A critical analysis.* Cambridge: Cambridge University Press.

McKee, J. P. & Sherriffs, A. C. (1956). The differential evaluation of males and females. *Journal of Personality, 25,* 356–371.

McLaughlin, M. L., Cody, M. J., & Read, S. (1992). *Explaining one's self to others: Reason-giving in a social context.* Hillsdale, NJ: Erlbaum.

McMurtry, J. (1978). *The Structure of Marx's world-view.* Princeton: Princeton University Press.

McNaught, B. R. (1983). Overcoming self-hate in gays. In G. W. Albee, J. M. Joffe & L. A. Dusenbury (Eds.), *Prevention, powerlessness, and politics: Readings on social change.* Newbury Park, CA: Sage.

Messick, D. M. & Mackie, D. (1989) Intergroup relations. *Annual Review of Psychology, 40,* 45–81.

Mészáros, I. (1971). *Aspects of history and class consciousness.* London: Routledge & Kegan Paul.

Meyerson, D. (1991). *False consciousness.* Oxford: Clarendon Press.

Miller, D. T. & Porter, C. A. (1983). Self-blame in victims of violence. *Journal of Social Issues, 39,* 139–152.

Millet, K. (1970). *Sexual politics.* New York: Avon Books.

Milner, D. (1981). Racial prejudice. In J. C. Turner & H. Giles (Eds.), *Intergroup Behavior.* Chicago, IL: University of Chicago Press.

Monson, T. C., & Snyder, M. (1977). Actors, observers and the attribution process: Toward a reconceptualization. *Journal of Experimental Social Psychology, 13,* 89–111.

Mullen, B., Brown, R. J. & Smith, C. (1992). Ingroup bias as a function of salience, relevance, and status: An integration. *European Journal of Social Psychology, 22,* 103–122.

Myrdal, G. (1944). *An American dilemma.* New York: Harper & Row.

Nisbett, R. E. & Ross, L. D. (1980). *Human inference: Strategies and shortcomings of social judgement.* Englewood Cliffs, NJ: Prentice-Hall.

Oakes, P. J., & Turner, J. C. (1990). Is limited information processing capacity the cause of social stereotyping? In W. Stroebe & M. Hewstone (Eds.), *European Review of Social Psychology, vol. 1.* New York: Wiley.

Parkin, F. (1971). *Class inequality and political order.* New York: Praeger.

Pepitone, A. (1950). Motivational effects in social perception. *Human Relations, 3,* 57–76.

Peterson, B., & Ramirez, M. (1971). Real, ideal-self disparity in Negro and Mexican-American children. *Psychology, 8,* 22–26.

Pettigrew, T. (1964). *A profile of the Negro American.* Princeton: Van Nostrand.

Porter, J. R. & Washington, R. E. (1989). Developments in research on black identity and self-esteem: 1979–1988.

Revue Internationale de Psychologie Sociale, 2, 341–353.

Prothro, E. T. (1954). Cross-cultural patterns of national stereotypes. *Journal of Social Psychology, 40,* 53–59.

Rosenberg, M. (1989). Old myths die hard: The case of black self-esteem. *Revue Internationale de Psychologie Sociale, 2,* 357–365.

Ross, L. D., Amabile, T. M. & Steinmetz, J. L. (1977). Social role, social control, and biases in social-perception processes. *Journal of Personality and Social Psychology, 35,* 485–494.

Ross, M. (1989). Relation of implicit theories to the construction of personal histories. *Psychological Review, 96,* 341–357.

Ryan, W. (1971). *Blaming the victim.* New York: Pantheon Books.

Sagar, H. A., & Schofield, J. W. (1980). Racial and behavioral cues in Black and White children's perceptions of ambiguously aggressive acts. *Journal of Personality and Social Psychology, 39,* 590–598.

Sampson, E. E. (1969). Studies of status congruence. In L. Berkowitz (Ed.), *Advances in Experimental Social Psychology, vol. 2.* New York: Academic Press.

Samuelson, W. & Zeckhauser, R. (1987). Status quo bias in decision making. *Journal of Risk and Uncertainty, 1,* 7–59.

Sarnoff, I. (1951). Identification with the aggressor: Some personality correlates of anti-Semitism among Jews. *Journal of Personality, 20,* 199–218.

Saunders, J. (1972). Class, color, and prejudice. A Brazilian counterpoint. In E. Q. Campbell (Ed.), *Racial tensions and national identity.* Nashville: Vanderbilt University Press.

Schachter, S., & Singer, J. E. (1962). Cognitive, social and physiological determinants of emotional state. *Psychological Review, 69,* 379–399.

Schaff, A. (1984). The pragmatic function of stereotypes. *International Journal of the Sociology of Language, 45,* 89–100.

Schlenker, B. R. (1980). *Impression management: The self-concept, social identity, and interpersonal relations.* Monterey, CA: Brooks/Cole.

Schwarz, N., & Clore, G. L. (1988). How do I feel about it? Informational function of affective states. In K. Fiedler & J. Forgas (Eds.), *Affect, cognition, and social behavior.* Toronto: Hogrefe International.

Scott, M. B. & Lyman, S. (1968). Accounts. *American Sociological Review, 33,* 46–62.

Scully, D. & Marolla, J. (1984). Convicted rapists' vocabulary of motive: Excuses and justifications. *Social Problems, 31,* 530–544.

Shavitt, S. (1989). Operationalizing functional theories of attitude. In A. R. Pratkanis, S. J. Breckler & A. G. Greenwald (Eds), *Attitude structure and function.* Hillsdale, NJ: Erlbaum.

Sherif, M. & Cantril, H. (1947/1966). *The psychology of ego-involvements.* New York: Wiley.

Sherif, M., & Sherif, C. W. (1956). *An outline of social psychology.* New York: Harper.

Sidanius, J. (1993). The psychology of group conflict and the dynamics of oppression: A social dominance perspective. In S. Iyengar & W. J. McGuire (Eds), *Explorations in Political Psychology.* Durham, NC: Duke University Press.

Sidanius, J., & Pratto, E. (1993). The inevitability of oppression and the dynamics of social dominance. In P. Sniderman & P. E. Tetlock (Eds.), *Prejudice, politics, and the American dilemma.* Stanford, CA: Stanford University Press.

Skrypnek, B. J., & Snyder, M. (1982). On the self-perpetuating nature of stereotypes about women and men. *Journal of Experimental Social Psychology, 18,* 277–291.

Smedley, J. W., & Bayton, J. A. (1978). Evaluative race-class stereotypes by race and perceived class of subjects. *Journal of Personality and Social Psychology, 36,* 530–535.

Smith, M. B., Bruner, J. S. & White, R. W. (1956/1964). *Opinions and personality.* New York: Wiley.

Snyder, M. (1981). On the self-perpetuating nature of social stereotypes. In D. L. Hamilton (Ed.), *Cognitive processes in stereotyping and intergroup behavior.* Hillsdale, NJ: Lawrence Erlbaum Associates.

Snyder, M., & DeBono, K. G. (1989). Understanding the functions of attitudes: Lessons from personality and social behavior. In A. R. Pratkanis, S. J. Breckler, & A. G. Greenwald (Eds.), *Attitude structure and function.* Hillsdale, NJ: Erlbaum.

Snyder, M., & Miene, P. (1994). On the functions of stereotypes and prejudice. In M. P. Zanna & J. M. Olson (Eds.), *The Psychology of Prejudice/The Ontario Symposium, vol. 7.* Hillsdale, NJ: Erlbaum.

Spears, R., & Manstead, A. S. R. (1989). The social context of stereotyping and differentiation. *European Journal of Social Psychology, 19,* 101–121.

Spence, J. T., Helmreich, R. L., & Holahan, C. K. (1979). Negative and positive components of psychological masculinity and femininity and their relationships to self-reports of neurotic and acting out behaviors. *Journal of Personality and Social Psychology, 37,* 1673–1682.

Staub, E. (1989). *The Roots of Evil: The Origins of Genocide and Other Group Violence.* Cambridge: Cambridge University Press.

Steele, C. M. (1988). The psychology of self-affirmation: Sustaining the integrity of the self. In L. Berkowitz (Ed.), *Advances in experimental social psychology, vol. 21.* New York: Academic Press.

Steele, C. M. (1992). Race and the schooling of Black Americans. *The Atlantic Monthly,* April, 68–78.

Stephan, W. G. (1985). Intergroup relations. In G. Lindzey & E. Aronson (Eds), *The handbook of social psychology, vol. 2.* New York: Random House.

Stotland, E. (1959). Peer groups and reactions to power figures. In D. Cartwright (Ed.), *Studies in social power.* Ann Arbor, MI: Institute for Social Research.

Struch, N. & Schwartz, S. H. (1989). Intergroup aggression: Its predictors and distinctness from in-group bias. *Journal of Personality and Social Psychology, 56,* 364–373.

Suls, J. & Wills, T. A. (1991). *Social comparison: Contemporary theory and research.* Hillsdale, NJ: Erlbaum.

Sunar, D. (1978). Stereotypes of the powerless: A social psychological analysis. *Psychological Reports, 43,* 511–528.

Swann, W. B. (1983). Self-verification: Bringing social reality into harmony with the self. In J. Suls & A. G. Greenwald (Eds), *Psychological Perspectives on the Self, vol. 2.* Hillsdale, NJ: Erlbaum.

Sykes, G. M. & Matza, D. (1957). Techniques of neutralization. *American Sociological Review, 22,* 664–670.

Tajfel, H. (1970). Aspects of national and ethnic loyalty. *Social Science Information, 9,* 119–144.

Tajfel, H. (1978). *Differentiation between social groups.* London: Academic Press.

Tajfel, H. (1981a). *Human groups and social categories.* Cambridge: Cambridge University Press.

Tajfel, H. (1981b). Social stereotypes and social groups. In J. C. Turner & H. Giles (Eds.), *Intergroup behavior.* Oxford: Basil Blackwell.

Tajfel, H. (1982). Social psychology of intergroup relations. *Annual Review of Psychology, 33,* 1–39.

Tajfel, H., & Turner, J. C. (1979). An integrative theory of intergroup conflict. In W. G. Austin & S. Worchel (Eds.), *The social psychology of intergroup relations.* Monterey, CA: Brooks/Cole.

Tajfel, H. & Turner, J. C. (1986). The social identity theory of intergroup behavior. In S. Worchel & W. G. Austin (Eds.), *The psychology of intergroup relations.* Chicago: Nelson-Hall.

Tetlock, P. E. (1992). The impact of accountability on judgment and choice: Toward a social contingency model. In L. Berkowitz (Ed.), *Advances in experimental social psychology (Vol. 25).* New York: Academic Press.

Triandis, H. C. (1977). *Interpersonal behavior.* Monterey, CA: Brooks/Cole.

Triandis, H. C., Lisansky, J., Setiadi, B., Chang, B., Marin, G., & Betancourt, H. (1982). Stereotyping among Hispanics and Anglos: The uniformity, intensity, direction, and quality of auto- and heterostereotypes. *Journal of Cross-Cultural Psychology, 13,* 409–426.

Turner, J. C. (1975). Social comparison and social identity: Some prospects for intergroup behavior. *European Journal of Social Psychology, 5,* 5–34.

Turner, J. C., & Brown, R. (1978). Social status, cognitive alternatives, and intergroup relations. In H. Tajfel (ed.) *Differentiation between social groups.* London: Academic Press.

Turner, J. C., Hogg, M. A., Oakes, P. J., Reicher, S., & Wetherell, M. S. (1987). *Re-discovering the social group: A self-categorization theory.* Oxford: Basil Blackwell.

Turner, J. C., Oakes, P. J., Haslam, S. A., & McGarty, C. (1992). Personal and social identity: Self and social context. Paper presented at the conference on 'The self and the collective.' Princeton University.

Tversky, A., & Kahneman, D. (1974). Judgment under uncertainty: Heuristics and biases. *Science, 185,* 1124–1131.

Tyler, T. R. (1990). *Why people obey the law.* New Haven, CT: Yale University Press.

Tyler, T. R., & McGraw, K. M. (1986). Ideology and the interpretation of personal experience: Procedural justice and political quiescence. *Journal of Social Issues, 42,* 115–128.

van Knippenberg, A. (1978). Status differences, comparative relevance and intergroup differentiation. In H. Tajfel (ed.) *Differentiation between social groups.* London: Academic Press.

van Knippenberg, A. (1984). Intergroup differences in group perceptions. In H. Tajfel (ed.) *The Social Dimension (Vol. 2).* Cambridge: Cambridge University Press.

Vaughan, G. M. (1978). Social change and intergroup preferences in New Zealand. *European Journal of Social Psychology, 8,* 297–314.

Wagner, U., Lampen, L., & Syllwasschy, J. (1986). In-group inferiority, social identity, and out-group devaluation in a modified minimal group study. *British Journal of Social Psychology, 25,* 15–23.

Ward, C. (1985). Sex trait stereotypes in Malaysian children. *Sex Roles, 12,* 35–45.

Wicklund, R. A., & Brehm, J. W. (1976). *Perspectives on cognitive dissonance.* Hillsdale, NJ: Erlbaum.

Widiger, T. A., & Settle, S. A. (1987). Broverman et al. revisited: An artifactual sex bias. *Journal of Personality and Social Psychology, 53,* 463–469.

Wilder, D. A. (1986). Social categorization: Implications for creation and reduction of intergroup bias. In L. Berkowitz (ed.). *Advances in experimental social psychology (Vol. 19).* New York: Academic Press.

Willhelm, S. M. (1980). Can Marxism explain America's racism? *Social Problems, 28,* 98–112.

Williams, J. E., & Best, D. L. (1982). *Measuring sex stereotypes: A thirty-nation study.* Beverly Hills, CA: Sage.

Williams, J. E., & Morland, J. K. (1979). Comment on Banks's 'white preference in blacks: A paradigm in search of a phenomenon'. *Psychological Bulletin, 86,* 28–32.

Wood, A. W. (1988). Ideology, false consciousness, and social illusion. In B. P. McLaughlin & A. O. Rorty (eds.) *Perspectives on self-deception.* Berkeley: University of California Press.

Worchel, S., & W. G. Austin (1986). *The psychology of intergroup relations.* Chicago: Nelson-Hall.

Word, C. O., Zanna, M. P., & Cooper, J. (1974). The nonverbal mediation of self-fulfilling prophecies in interracial interaction. *Journal of Experimental Social Psychology, 10,* 109–120.

Wortman, C. B. (1976). Causal attributions and personal control. In J. H. Harvey, W. J. Ickes, & R. F. Kidd (eds.) *New directions in attribution research (Vol. 2).* Hillsdale, NJ: Erlbaum.

Zanna, M. P., & Rempel, J. K. (1988). Attitudes: A new look at an old concept. In D. Bar-Tal & A. W. Kruglanski (eds.) *The social psychology of knowledge.* Cambridge: Cambridge University Press.

Zillman, D. (1978). Attribution and misattribution of excitatory reactions. In J. H. Harvey, W. J. Ickes, & R. F. Kidd (eds.) *New directions in attribution research (Vol. 2).* Hillsdale, NJ: Erlbaum.

Social Dominance Theory: A New Synthesis

Jim Sidanius • UCLA
Felicia Pratto • University of Connecticut

A number of classical and contemporary theories of social attitudes and intergroup relations have given us some important insights into the nature and dynamics of intergroup conflict, stereotyping, and group oppression. However, there has yet to be a serious effort to integrate these insights into one coherent and comprehensive theoretical model. While social dominance theory has been influenced by models within personality psychology, social psychology, and political sociology, it is neither strictly a psychological nor sociological theory, but rather an attempt to connect the worlds of individual personality and attitudes with the domains of institutional behavior and social structure. Thus, social dominance theory is an attempt to integrate several levels of analysis into one coherent theoretical framework.

Some Basic Observations

Social dominance theory (SDT) begins with the basic observation that all human societies tend to be structured as systems of *group-based social hierarchies*. At the very minimum, this hierarchical social structure consists of one or a small number of dominant and hegemonic groups at the top and one or a number of subordinate groups at the bottom of the hierarchical structure. Among other things, the dominant group is characterized by its possession of a disproportionately large share of *positive social value*, or all those material and symbolic things for which people strive. Examples of positive social value are things such as: political authority and power, good and plentiful food, splendid homes, the best available health care, wealth, and high social status. While dominant groups possess a disproportionately large share of positive social value, subordinate groups possess a disproportionately large share of *negative social value*, including such things as low power and social status, high-risk and low-status occupations, relatively poor health, poor food, modest or miserable homes, and severe negative sanctions (e.g., prison and death sentences).

After making the observation that human social systems are structured as group-based social hierarchies, social dominance theory then attempts to identify the various mechanisms that produce and maintain this group-based social hierarchy and how these various mechanisms interact with one another.

Group-Based Versus Individual-Based Social Hierarchies

By the term "group-based social hierarchy" we mean something quite distinct from an individual-based social hierarchy. In an individual-based social hierarchy, individuals might enjoy great power, prestige, or wealth by virtue of their own highly valued *individual* characteristics, such as great athletic or leadership ability, high intelligence, artistic, or political or scientific talent or achievement. Group-based social hierarchy, on the other hand, refers to that social power, prestige, and privilege that an individual possesses by virtue of their ascribed membership in a particular socially constructed group such as a "race," religion, clan, tribe, lineage, linguistic/ethnic group, or social class. This is not to imply that the power, prestige, and privilege of individuals in group-based social hierarchies are completely independent of the individual's personal characteristics and qualities. We only imply that the achievements and status of individuals are not completely independent of the status and power of the groups to which they belong. With ascribed or group-based hierarchies, on the other hand, one's social status, influence, and power are also a function of one's group membership and not simply of one's individual abilities or characteristics. Of course, in complex human social systems, individual- and group-based social hierarchies will not be completely independent. Access to the means of individual achievement (e.g., education, specialized skills) is differentially available to ascribed social groups. For example, two children may both have the same level of native talent, individual drive, and personal ambition. However, if one child is upper class, has ambitious, well-connected parents, and attends the "right" schools, the chances are that this child will do quite well in life. On the other hand, for the other child growing up in an impoverished, dangerous, and sociogenic neighborhood, and afflicted with inferior schools, chances are that child will not do quite as well in life, even if both children have equivalent talents and energies from birth. This, of course, is simply to state the obvious. Even in modern, "democratic," and multigroup societies, the "achieved" component of social status is, to a very significant degree, dependent upon one's the social status and power of one's ascribed group membership.

The Trimorphic Structure of Group-based Social Hierarchy

Pierre van den Berghe (1978) was among the first to observe that human group-based social hierarchies consist of distinctly different stratification systems. While he distinguished among four different stratification systems,[1] for our purposes, these can be collapsed into three: (a) an *age-system*, in which adults and middle-age people have disproportionate social power over children and younger adults,[2] (b) a *gender-system*, or *patriarchy* in which males have disproportionate social and political power compared to females, and (c) what we shall label an *arbitrary-set* system. The "arbitrary-set" system is filled with socially constructed, and highly salient groups based on characteristics such as clan, ethnicity, "estate," nation, "race," caste, social class, religious sect, regional grouping, or any other socially relevant group distinction which the human imagination is capable of constructing.

In such systems, one group is materially and/or politically dominant over the other. As we shall see below, while there are a number of similarities in the structural and functional characteristics of these different stratification systems, each of these three systems is unique, and each plays a different role in the overall construction and maintenance of group-based social hierarchy. For example, if a person lives long enough, he or she can occupy every level of the age-system, from the role of low-status small child, to the role of high-status "elder." This continually changing social role position is quite distinct from one's position in either the arbitrary-set or especially the gender-systems, in which one's position in the social hierarchy tends to be relatively fixed throughout life. This "fixedness" of status position is particularly dramatic with respect to the gender-system.

While the age and gender systems certainly have at least some degree of malleability in terms of who is defined as "young" or "old," "male" or "female," the arbitrary-set system is characterized by an unusually high degree of arbitrariness, plasticity, flexibility, and situational and contextual sensitivity in determining which group distinctions are socially salient and the manner in which ingroups and outgroups are defined. For example, the salient arbitrary-set ingroup/outgroup boundaries may be defined in terms of membership in street gangs (e.g., "Bloods" vs. "Crips"), nationality (e.g., American vs. Iraqi), "race" ("White" vs. "Black"), or a social class (e.g., "working-class" vs. "upper-class"). Furthermore, even using a particular arbitrary-set dimension (e.g., "race"), the criteria for membership in one category or another is highly dependent upon the cultural and situational context. For example, a given person would be classified as "Black" in early 19th century America (i.e., having at least 1/8 African heritage), classified as "mulatto" during the same period in the Caribbean or in South Africa, and "White" in late 20th century Sweden.

The arbitrary-set system is also, by far, associated with the greatest degree of violence, brutality, and oppression. While the age and gender systems are certainly no strangers to very brutal forms of social control, the brutality associated with arbitrary-set systems very often far exceeds that of the other two systems in terms of intensity and scope. For example, besides the infamous Holocaust, the 20th century alone has witnessed at least seven other major episodes of genocidal, arbitrary-set violence, including: (a) the episodic massacres of the Kurds by Turkey in 1924, Iran in 1979, and Iraq in 1988, (b) Stalin's wholesale slaughter of the Kulaks in 1929, (c) the widespread massacre of the inhabitants of East Timor in the late 1990s, (d) the Khmer Rouge terror in the late 1970s, (e) ethnic cleansing of Muslims in Bosnia and other regions of the former Yugoslavia in the late 1990s, (f) the widespread killings of Kasaians in Zaire, and (g) the most recent massacres of Tutsis and Hutus in Rwanda and Burundi in the late 1990s, just to name a few. Furthermore, Gurr and Harff catalogued some 63 ethnic and armed conflicts around the world in 1993 alone (Gurr & Harff, 1994). These conflicts were not restricted to any particular part of the world and could be found in Europe, the Middle East, North and Sub-Saharan Africa, Central, South and East Asia, the Pacific Islands, and the Americas. This level of barbarism and blood-lust is rarely, if ever, observed within the age and gender systems of social stratification.

Another difference between the arbitrary-set system and the age and gender stratification systems is that, with the exceptions of the social roles of headman and shaman, arbitrary-set stratification systems are generally not found among small hunter-gatherer societies (van den Berghe, 1978; Lenski, 1984). It is widely assumed that one major reason for the lack of arbitrary-set, group-based social hierarchy among hunter-gatherer societies is because such societies lack sufficient economic surplus. The technologies of food production and storage within hunter-gatherer societies do not permit long-term storage of food (Lenski, 1984).

Similarly, because hunter-gatherer societies tend to be nomadic, people within such societies are not able to accumulate large amounts of other, nonedible forms of economic surplus such as animal skins, weapons, armaments, etc. This lack of economic surplus does not allow for the development of highly specialized social roles, such as professional armies, police, and other bureaucracies facilitating the formation of expropriative political authority. Because of the absence of military and "coercive specialists," all adult males within hunter-gatherer societies are essentially the military equals of all other adult males. Therefore, the extent to which political authority among adult males exists, this authority tends to be based upon mutual agreement, persuasion, and consultation rather than coercion. Although hunter-gatherer societies are generally not *completely* egalitarian, when social and political hierarchy does exist among adult males, it tends to be based on the general skills and leadership capacities of particular *individuals*. As a result, this hierarchy tends not to be transgenerational or hereditary in nature.

In contrast, societies producing substantial and stable economic surplus (i.e., horticultural, agrarian, industrial, and post-industrial societies) are also those which have arbitrary-set systems of social hierarchy (Lenski, 1984). Because of economic surplus, not all adults need to devote most of their time to food procurement and survival. Certain males are then freed to specialize in the arts of coercion (e.g., war-lordism, policing) or spiritual and intellectual sophistry. These role specialists are used by political elites to establish and enforce expropriative economic and social relationships with other members of the society. Once these role specializations and expropriative relationships are in place, arbitrary-set, group-based hierarchies then emerge. Examples of societies containing systems of stable, arbitrary-set group-based hierarchies abound and can be found in both the ancient and modern worlds and on every continent, including nations and societies such as: Mexico, Japan, Sumeria, Nigeria, Germany, Israel, France, Canada, the United States, Taiwan, Zaire, Korea, the Zulu empire, the USSR, South Africa, the ancient societies of Rome, ancient and modern Egypt, Greece, China, Scandinavia, Benin, Persia, and the pre-Colombian societies of the Inca, Aztec, and Maya. Restricting our attention to nonsubsistence societies, one is truly hard pressed to find a society anywhere in the world which does *not* have an arbitrary-set stratification system.

Furthermore, every attempt to abolish arbitrary-set, group-based hierarchy within societies of economic surplus have, without exception, failed. These failures have ranged from attempts at massive, revolutionary transformation (e.g., the French, Russian, Mexican, Chinese, and American civil rights revolutions) to transformatory experiments within small and isolated utopian communities (e.g., New Harmony, Indiana; New Lanark, Scotland; the Oneida Community, New York). This apparently perfect correlation between the production of sustainable economic surplus and the emergence of arbitrary-set social hierarchy appears to imply that systems of arbitrary-set hierarchy will emerge *whenever the proper economic conditions allow.*

While arbitrary-set hierarchy tends to be restricted to those societies producing economic surplus, age and gender systems of social stratification appear to be completely universal. Adults generally have more power and privilege than children and younger people.

In both hunter-gatherer and early agricultural societies, while women contributed substantially to the subsistence of the group by frequently controlling and collecting the essentials for survival, there is no known society in which women, as a group, have had control over the political life of the community, the community's interaction with outgroups, or control over the technology and practice of warfare; arguably the ultimate arbiter of political power. While some scholars have argued that matriarchy is the foundation of human society (see e.g., Bachofen, Gimbutas), most anthropologists and social historians dispute this claim. Although there are several known examples of matrilineal societies (i.e., descent traced through the family of the mother), matrilocal or uxorilocal societies (i.e., newly married couples residing with the wife's kin), and societies in which women have near economic parity with men (Murdock, 1949), there are no known examples of matriarchal societies (i.e., where women, as a group, control the political and military authority within the society; see Busch, 1990; Collier & Yanagisako, 1987; Keegan, 1993).

We have evidence of women being excluded from significant political and military power as far back as 5,000 years. For example, by 3,000

BC, women in Sumer were excluded from almost all important political and military decisions. Similarly, approximately 3,700 years ago, the legal code of ancient Babylon (i.e., the Code of Hammurabi) built upon the patriarchal tendencies of Sumer and prescribed rather draconian punishments for women who challenged male dominance (Johns, 1947; Seagle, 1971). Even though some societies were occasionally ruled by very powerful individual queens, in the aggregate, the ultimate military power has always been in the hands of men. Furthermore, patriarchy in the ancient world was not restricted to Islamic societies and areas in and adjacent to the Near East, but also has been documented among the ancient and traditional cultures in Middle and South America, Africa, among the ancient Germanic tribes, and the ancient cultures in India, China and Japan (Abel & Nelson, 1990; Beck & Keddie, 1978).

In his discussion of the role of women in hunter-gatherer societies, Gerherd Lenski remarks:

> Women invariably occupy a position inferior to men, though in some societies, the differential is not great. Women are almost always excluded from the role of headman and usually are ineligible to become shamans or participate in council meetings. (Lenski, 1984, p. 111).

While not as stable as age and gender hierarchies, the evidence suggests that arbitrary-set stratification systems also display a remarkable degree of stability. One example of this stability is the Indian caste-system, which has remained relatively intact for at least 3,000 years. While caste is no longer part of the legal order of Indian society and "untouchability" was outlawed after Indian independence in 1947, caste remains an extremely important aspect of Indian social and political life. For example, most marriages are still made within castes, politicians rely on the "caste vote," castes continue to act as economic and political pressure groups, castes are still ranked in terms of "purity" and pollution, and intercaste violence continues to the present day.

While the United States is a more socially dynamic nation than India and is, of course, not nearly as old, the American version of the caste system shows every sign of being highly stable as well. Despite intense efforts to eliminate racism from American life, the relative dominance of Euro-

Americans over African-Americans has remained unchanged since the European occupation of the New World more than 400 years ago. Although not nearly as impressive as the Indian example above, some empirical evidence of the stability of the American ethnic hierarchy can be found in recent public opinion polling assembled by Tom Smith (1991). Using national probability samples, Smith tabulated the perceived social standing of a long array of American ethnic groups, once in 1964 and again a quarter of a century later in 1989. What makes this particular period of American history so interesting is that it embraces the era when the modern civil rights movement was at its height and America embarked on its most intense and ambitious efforts to eliminate racism and actualize the promise of American "democracy." Close inspection of these data discloses a very high degree of hierarchical stability. While the social status ranking of a number of ethnic groups increased during this period (e.g., Negroes: 2.75 in 1964 to 4.17 in 1989), the *relative* ethnic group rankings and thereby the hierarchical structure within this arbitrary-set system remained essentially unchanged.

Basic Assumptions of Social Dominance Theory

After observing the ubiquitousness and stability of group-based social hierarchy, and having identified the trimorphic nature of this social hierarchy, we can now introduce the three primary assumptions upon which social dominance theory is based:

1. *While age and gender based hierarchies will tend to exist within all social systems, arbitrary-set systems of social hierarchy will invariably emerge within social systems producing sustainable economic surplus.*

   This first assumption follows from our review of the anthropological literature on human social structure.

2. *Most forms of group conflict and oppression (e.g., racism, ethnocentrism, sexism, nationalism, classism, regionalism) can be regarded as different manifestations of the same basic human predisposition to form group-based social hierarchy.*

The second assumption touches upon a subtle yet extremely important distinction between social dominance theory and one of its intellectual parents, namely, social identity theory. While social identity theory clearly recognizes and in part, accommodates itself to the reality of social hierarchy and power differences between social groups, social dominance theory is centrally focused upon and built around the notion of group-based social hierarchy. In contrast to social identity theory, originally developed to explain ingroup favoritism within the context of essentially equal and arbitrarily defined social groups, social dominance theory was originally conceived as a model of social hierarchy. Because of this, SDT focuses on the way social discourse (e.g., ideology, attitudes and stereotypes) and individual and institutional behavior both contribute to and are affected by the nature and severity of group-based social hierarchy.

In situations in which hierarchical group relations cannot be identified, social dominance theory would, in principle, have little to explain, and one might be content to understand the nature of prejudice and discrimination in terms of some combination of earlier models such as authoritarian personality theory, realistic group conflict theory, and social identity theory. The social dominance synthesis not only states that group-based social hierarchy will tend to be ubiquitous, especially within social systems producing economic surplus, but more importantly, most if not all forms of group prejudices, stereotypes, ideologies of group superiority and inferiority, and forms of individual institutional discrimination both help produce and are reflections of this group-based social hierarchy. In other words phenomena such as prejudice, racism, stereotypes, and discrimination can simply not be understood outside of the conceptual framework of group-based social hierarchy, especially within social systems of economic surplus.

3. *Human social systems are subject to the counterbalancing influences of "hierarchy-enhancing" (HE) forces, producing and maintaining ever higher levels of group-based social inequality, and "hierarchy-attenuating" (HA) forces, producing greater levels of group-based social equality.*

A perusal of recorded history across all known non-hunter-gatherer societies testifies to clear and, sometimes, extreme levels of group-based social inequality. The relatively recent system of chattel slavery in the United States is perhaps one of the most brutal examples in human history. Group-based social inequality is often directly produced by the unequal distribution of social value (both positive and negative) to various groups within the social system. This unequal distribution of social value is, in turn, justified and defended by use of various social ideologies, beliefs, myths, and religious doctrines. At the same time, a fair reading of the historical record also reveals consistent attempts to create more egalitarian and inclusive social systems. Evidence of these hierarchy-attenuating forces can be seen in everything from early Christian discourse, to the widespread socio-political discourse emanating from social democratic, socialist, and Marxist movements of the 19th century, to the civil- and human-rights activists of the mid- and late 20th centuries. However, for the most part, these counterdominance or hierarchy-attenuating tendencies within post hunter-gatherer societies appear to function to moderate the degree of *inequality*.

Schematic Overview of Social Dominance Theory

Given these three basic assumptions of SDT, the body of social dominance theory concerns identifying and understanding the specific intrapersonal, interpersonal, intergroup, and institutional mechanisms that produce and maintain group-based social hierarchy, and how, in turn, this hierarchy affects these contributing mechanisms. In very broad terms, SDT argues that the general processes producing and maintaining group-based social hierarchy are those sketched out in Figure 18.1.

As shown in the extreme right-hand side of Figure 18.1, SDT argues that group-based social hierarchy is driven by three proximal processes: (a) *aggregated individual discrimination*, (b) *aggregated institutional discrimination,* and (c) *behavioral asymmetry*. These proximal processes are regulated, in part, by legitimizing myths. The extent to which an individual endorses legitimizing myths depends upon whether he or she generally endorses, desires, and supports a system of group-based social hierarchy or not. We call the generalized orientation towards group-based social hierarchy *social dominance orientation (SDO)*.

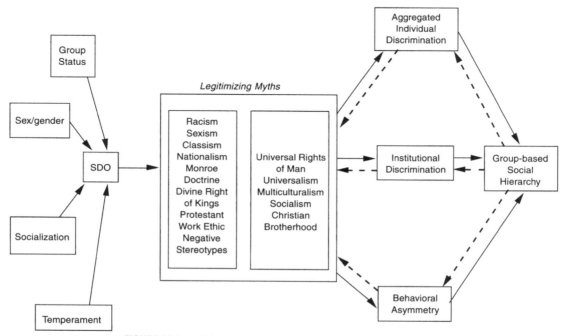

FIGURE 18.1 ■ Schematic overview of social dominance theory.

Aggregated Individual Discrimination

By the term *aggregated individual discrimination*, we are referring to the simple, daily, and sometimes quite inconspicuous individual acts of discrimination by one individual against another. Examples of such discrimination can be found in the decision of an employer not to hire or promote a person from a given minority group, or the decision of a voter not to vote for a given candidate because of race, ethnicity, or gender. When thousands of such individual acts of discrimination are aggregated over days, weeks, years, decades, and centuries, these individual actions contribute to the clear and salient differences in the power between social groups.

Aggregated Institutional Discrimination

Group-based social hierarchy is not only produced by individual and private acts of discrimination, but also by the rules, procedures, and actions of social institutions. These institutions may be public or private, including courts, lending institutions, hospitals, retail outlets, and schools. Sometimes this institutional discrimination is conscious, deliberate, and overt, and sometimes it is unconscious, unintended, and covert. Whatever form it takes, it can be identified by whether institutional decisions result in the disproportionate allocation of positive and negative social value across the social status hierarchy, all other factors being equal.

Systematic Terror

Besides the unequal distribution of social value, institutions also help maintain the integrity of the social hierarchy by the use of *systematic terror*. By systematic terror we refer to the use of violence or threats of violence disproportionately directed against subordinates. Systematic terror functions to maintain expropriative relationships between dominants (i.e., members of dominant groups) and subordinates (i.e., members of subordinate groups) and enforce the continued deference of subordinates toward dominants. Systematic terror is likely to be most ferocious when subordinates directly challenge and confront the hegemonic control of dominants. There are three basic forms of systematic terror: (a) *official terror*, (b) *semiofficial terror*, and (c) *unofficial terror*.

Official terror is the public and legally sanctioned violence and threat of violence perpetrated by organs of the state and disproportionately directed toward members of subordinate groups. The most contemporary examples of official terror are the disproportionate use of the death penalty against subordinates in nations such as apartheid South Africa and the United States, and the acts of collective punishment used against the Palestinians of Gaza and the West Bank by Israel. Rather than being a relatively uncommon occurrence in the modern world, the evidence suggests that official terror is quite widespread. For example, in a 1997 study of 151 countries, Amnesty International reported general, comprehensive, and widespread state violence against ethnic and racial minorities in the form of mass arrests, trials without due process of law, extended detention without trial, beatings, and the torture of children in front of their parents, etc.

Semiofficial terror is the violence or intimidation directed against subordinates, carried out by officials of the state (e.g., internal security forces, police, secret police, paramilitary organizations) but not publicly, overtly, officially, or legally sanctioned by the state. Examples of semiofficial terror can be seen in the death squad activities that have played such a prominent role in the politics of Asia, Central and South America, and Africa. Some of the most recent evidence of semiofficial terror can be found in the systematic and routine beatings, bombings, rapes, and murders perpetrated against opponents of the apartheid regime by members of the Vlakplass, or South African secret service (Koch, 1996). *Unofficial terror* is that violence or threat of violence perpetrated by *private individuals* from dominant groups against members of subordinate groups. While this terror does not enjoy the active approval or sanction of official government agencies, it usually does enjoy the tacit approval if not active participation of members of the security forces (e.g., lynchings by the Ku Klux Klan). This type of terror can be quite widespread in scope and comprehensive in its effects. For example, unofficial terror resulted in the deaths of at least 3,400 African Americans in the United States between 1882 and 1927 (Pomper, 1970).

One finding from the study of institutional discrimination and associated forms of terror is that the legal and criminal justice systems are among the major instruments used in establishing and maintaining the hierarchical structure of intergroup relations. Admittedly, the internal security and criminal justice systems are designed to maintain "law and order." However, from a social dominance perspective, in the aggregate, "law" is often written and enforced so as to favor the interests of dominants and "order" is often defined as those social conditions that disproportionately protect and maintain the interests of dominants. Therefore, contrary to the commonly held assumption that discrimination against subordinates within the criminal justice system is relatively rare, nonsystematic, and completely overshadowed by the everyday realities of basic fairness and equity, social dominance theory suggests that discrimination within the criminal justice system is quite systematic and comprehensive in its effects.

Social dominance theory expects that discrimination against subordinates is to be found in all societies with economic surplus, including societies with "democratic" and egalitarian pretensions. However, in general, the level of brutality and discrimination against subordinates within "democratic" societies will tend to be somewhat constrained, indirect, and covert due to the cultural ideals espousing equality before the law. As a consequence, although the criminal justice system will still behave in a discriminatory manner, the elites within these systems will be under some pains to justify the presence and extent of this discrimination. In other words, it is crucial that such "democratic" social systems maintain *plausible deniability*, or the ability to practice discrimination, while at the same time denying that any discrimination is actually taking place.

Behavioral Asymmetry

Group-based social hierarchy is also produced and maintained by a mechanism known as *behavioral asymmetry*. On average, there will be differences in the behavioral repertoires of individuals belonging to groups at different levels of the social power continuum. More importantly, however, these behavioral differences will both contribute to and be reinforced by the group-based hierarchical relationships within the social system. This behavioral asymmetry will also be affected by socialization patterns, stereotypes, legitimizing ideologies, temperamental predispositions, and the operation of systematic terror.

The construct of behavioral asymmetry highlights one of the major ways in which social dominance theory differs from other closely related structural models of group oppression such as classical Marxism, neo-classical elitism theory, or group positions theory. These latter models emphasize the manner in which people within elite, dominant, and ruling classes actively oppress, manipulate, and control people within subordinate groups. While social dominance theory does not dispute, and indeed incorporates many of these ideas, SDT places greater emphasis on the manner in which subordinates *actively* participate in and contribute to their own subordination. Within SD theory, we do not merely regard subordinates as *objects* of oppression, but also as people who usually retain some *agency* and actively participate in the oppressive exercise. In other words, within SD theory, *group oppression is very much a cooperative game.*

On the other hand, we do not mean to imply that subordinates do not resist their own oppression, for they most certainly do. At times, this resistance can be quite intense, leading to active rebellion and even social revolution. Nonetheless, successful social revolution is a rare event indeed, and most group-based systems of social hierarchy remain relatively stable over long swaths of time. Therefore, while we recognize that there always will be some element of resistance and resentment within subordinate groups (Scott, 1990), contrary to the arguments of more traditional elitism theorists, we suggest that within relatively stable group-based hierarchies, most of the activities of subordinates can be characterized as cooperative rather than subversive to the system of group-based domination. Furthermore, we suggest that it is subordinates' high level of both passive and active cooperation with their own oppression that provides systems of group-based social hierarchy with their remarkable degrees of resiliency, robustness, and stability. Therefore, seen from this perspective, social hierarchy is not primarily maintained by the oppressive behavior of dominants, but by the deferential and obsequious behavior of subordinates.

Thus far, we have been able to identify at least four varieties of behavioral asymmetry: (a) *asymmetrical in-group bias*, (b) *out-group favoritism* or *deference*, (c) *self-debilitation*, and (d) *ideological asymmetry*.

Asymmetrical ingroup bias. As Sumner (1906) remarked generations ago, and has been found to hold across most cultures, people generally tend to be *ethnocentric* and to favor their own ingroups over outgroups (e.g., Eibl-Eibesfeldt, 1989). However, within any given social system, not all groups will show ingroup bias to the same degree. Dominant groups will tend to display higher levels of ingroup favoritism or bias than will subordinate groups.

Deference or *out-group favoritism* can be regarded as a special case of asymmetrical ingroup bias, and can be said to occur when the degree of asymmetrical ingroup favoritism is so strong that subordinates actually favor dominants over their own ingroups. A well known example of such outgroup favoritism can be found in the "Uncle Toming" behavior of certain Afro-Americans towards Euro-Americans (e.g., Deane, 1968).

Self-debilitation occurs when subordinates show higher levels of self-destructive behaviors than dominants. These self-debilitating and self-destructive behaviors are often consistent with, but not exclusive to the negative stereotypes associated with subordinate groups. These lower expectations and stereotypes are consensually shared across the social status hierarchy and exist within the minds of both dominants and subordinates alike. From a social dominance perspective, the negative stereotypes of subordinates are important, not only because of the discriminatory behavior they induce among dominants, but perhaps even more importantly, because they also serve as behavioral scripts or schemas for subordinates. This is to say that the negative stereotypes subordinates carry in their heads about themselves induce them to behave in ways that reinforce these stereotypes. Stereotypes thus become *self-fulfilling prophecies* (Merton, 1972).

Not only should we expect to find asymmetry in the type and degree of ingroup-bias across the social status hierarchy, but the social dominance model also posits the existence of a much more subtle form of asymmetry, labeled *ideological asymmetry*. As we see in Figure 18.1, our theory assumes that a host of hierarchy-enhancing legitimizing ideologies, such as racism, sexism, classism, meritocracy, etc., are driven by one's acceptance of and desire for group-based social hierarchy. Not only is one's desire for group-based social dominance related to one's social ideologies, but both of these latter factors help drive group relevant social policies. Those holding hierarchy-enhancing social ideologies are also those who are most likely to support social policies perceived to increase the degree of group-based social inequality (e.g., punitive social welfare legislation). In addition, these are also the same individuals who are most likely to oppose those social policies perceived to decrease the degree of group-based social inequality (e.g., affirmative action). However, the ideological asymmetry hypothesis suggests that the degree to which hierarchy-enhancing and hierarchy-attenuating social ideologies and social policies are related to and driven by group dominance values will systematically vary as a function of one's position within the group-based, hierarchical social structure. Everything else being equal, the social attitudes and policy preferences of dominants are more strongly driven by social dominance values than is the case among subordinates.

Altogether, within SD theory these various forms of behavioral asymmetry are thought to be important because they illustrate the *cooperative* nature of intergroup oppression and group-based social hierarchies. Systems of group-based social hierarchy are not simply maintained by the oppressive activities of dominants, nor the *passive* compliance of subordinates, but rather the coordinated and collaborative activities of both dominants and subordinates.

Legitimizing Myths

Group-based social hierarchy is also affected by what we term *legitimizing myths*. Legitimizing myths (LMs) consist of attitudes, values, beliefs, stereotypes, or ideologies that provide moral and intellectual justification for the social practices that distribute social value within the social system. Our theory of legitimizing myths owes much to Marxist notions of "ideology," Mosca's concept of the "political formula," Pareto's notion of "derivations," Gramsci's idea of "ideological hegemony," Moscovici's notion of "social representations," and Durkheim's notion of "collective representations" (Gramsci, 1971; Durkheim, 1933;

Marx & Engels, 1846; Mosca, 1896; Moscovici, 1981, 1988). Within social dominance theory, legitimizing myths (LMs) can be distinguished by two independent characteristics: *functional type* and *potency*.

Functional type refers to whether a particular LM justifies either group-based social *inequality* or its exact opposite, social *equality*. LMs that justify and support group-based social inequality are referred to as *hierarchy-enhancing* (*HE*) LMs, while LMs that support and justify greater levels of group-based social equality are referred to as *hierarchy-attenuating* (*HA*) LMs.

There are many different examples of HE-LMs, including ideas and philosophies such as sexism, classical racism, the notion of the "White Man's burden," notions of "fate," the doctrine of meritorious karma, Confucianism, negative stereotypes of subordinate groups, traditional forms of classism, the thesis of Papal infallibility, nationalism, the Monroe Doctrine and the notion of manifest destiny, the thesis of the divine rights of kings, and "speciesism" (the idea that humans have the "right" to rule the planet and all living creatures on it).

While these are all fairly obvious examples of HE-LMs, there are also more subtle, yet no less powerful examples of HE-LMs. In contemporary American and Western cultures, among the most important of HE-LMs are the notions of "individual responsibility," the Protestant work ethic, internal attributions for the misfortunes of the poor, and the set of ideas and assumptions collectively referred to as "political conservatism." What all these ideas and doctrines have in common is the notion that each individual occupies that position along the social status continuum that she has earned and therefore deserves. From these perspectives then, the particular configuration of the hierarchical social system is fair, legitimate, natural and perhaps even inevitable.

While HE-LMs are often associated with what is regarded as "conservative" political beliefs, this need not always be the case. For example, there are also "left-wing" versions of HE-LMs. One such ideology is Lenin's theory of the leading and central role of the communist party. This theory asserted that since members of the communist party were the only individuals who truly understood the "real interests" of the working class, it was only right and just that they also exercise near complete monopolistic control of the state. This was the theoretical justification for the existence of the "Nomenklatura."

The set of beliefs, values, ideologies, and attitudes known as hierarchy-attenuating LMs have social functions directly contradicting HE-LMs. While HE-LMs serve to exacerbate and maintain group-based social inequality, HA-LMs serve to promote greater levels of group-based social egalitarianism. Examples of HA-LMs are as readily available as HE-LMs. They are political doctrines such as socialism, communism, feminism, the universal rights of man, and major themes in the American Declaration of Independence, and even portions of the New Testament.

The potency of an LM refers to the degree to which that LM will help promote, maintain, or overthrow a given group-based hierarchy. The degree to which an LM is potent is a function of at least four factors: (a) *consensuality*, (b) *embeddedness*, (c) *certainty*, and what we shall call (d) *mediational strength*.

Similar to arguments proposed by Gramsci, Durkheim, and Moscovici, by the term *consensuality* we are referring to the degree to which "social representations" and social ideologies are broadly shared within the social system. However, within SD-theory the notion of *consensuality* is given a much more precise and focused definition than has been generally provided in the past. Among other things, we argue that the notion of "consensuality" is particularly directed at the degree to which HE- and HA-LMs are shared across the continuum of social power and within both dominant and subordinate groups alike. For example, for most of American history, classical racism, or the belief that Blacks were inherently inferior to Whites, was not simply a belief held by most Whites, but arguably a belief shared by a substantial number of Blacks as well. Among other things, this implies that Blacks have endorsed anti-Black racism almost as intensively and thoroughly as Whites. This suggests that, from the point of view of system stability, the largest and most important component of anti-Black racism was not simply the beliefs held by Whites, but rather that anti-Black racism was shared by Blacks.

Everything else being equal, we postulate that the greater the degree to which dominants can induce subordinates to endorse self-demeaning ideologies such as anti-Black racism, the less physical force or threat of force (i.e., terror) will be necessary in order to keep the hierarchical group relationships in place. Similarly, within the contemporary United States and Western Europe, one of the reasons the Protestant work ethic is such a potent HE-LM is because it is widely embraced across broad swaths of the social power continuum, by rich and poor, Black and White, men and women (e.g., Kluegel & Smith, 1986).

By *embeddedness* we mean that the LM is strongly associated with and well-anchored to other parts of the ideological, religious, or aesthetic components of a culture. For example, classical racism against Blacks can be seen as rather well embedded within Western and American culture. While the color "black" is most often associated with implications of evil, filth, depravity, and fear, the color "white" is most often associated with notions of purity, truth, innocence, goodness, and righteousness. These two contrasting color symbols permeate a great deal of Western culture and can be discerned in everything from classical fairy tales, to popular film and literature.

By *certainty*, we are referring to whether a given LM appears to have a very high degree of moral, religious, or scientific certainty or "truth." For example, belief in inherent white superiority was a very robust LM in 19th century Western Europe in general, and the antebellum South in particular. One of the reasons this classical racism appeared to be so "obviously true" is that it was consistent with the emerging "scientific" literature of the time, including the new evolutionary thinking and its social Darwinist offshoots (e.g., Gobineau, see Biddiss, 1970). Furthermore, rather than having died out, this type of social Darwinist and "scientific racism" continues to be produced by American and Western European intellectuals such as Shockley, Rushton, Murray and Herrnstein, and Rasmussen (Herrnstein & Murray, 1994; Rushton, 1996; Shockley, 1972). Collectively, these intellectuals continue to exert significant influence on the direction and tenor of social discourse in the United States and Western Europe.

Finally, by *mediational strength* we refer to the degree with which a given LM serves as a link between the desire to establish and maintain group-based social hierarchy on the one hand, and endorsement of hierarchy-enhancing or hierarchy-attenuating social policies on the other hand. For example, those who strongly support the Protestant work ethic are also those most opposed to help for the poor and the less fortunate. According to SD theory, part of the reason people endorse the Protestant work ethic is because this ideology is an accessible and socially acceptable means of justifying group-based social inequality. The stronger an LM mediates the relationship between the desire for group-based hierarchy and a given social policy, the more potent the LM is said to be.

While the ideas of Marx, Gramsci, Pareto, Mosca, and Moscovici all suggest that ideology justifies group dominance, these ideas provide us with no empirical standard for testing whether any given ideology actually does so in any given situation. In contrast, the notion of mediation provides us with a relatively crisp empirical standard by which to judge whether a given ideology or belief is functioning as an LM. Namely, a given belief, attitude, opinion, or attribution can be classified as an LM if and only if it is found to have a mediational relationship between the desire for group-based social dominance, on the one hand, and support for hierarchy-enhancing or hierarchy-attenuating social policy on the other hand.

The Nature of Social Dominance Orientation

Perhaps the most "psychological" component of social dominance theory concerns the construct of *social dominance orientation* (SDO). SDO is defined as the degree to which individuals desire and support group-based hierarchy and the domination of "inferior" groups by "superior" groups. As a general orientation, SDO pertains to whatever group distinctions are salient within a given social context. These group distinctions may involve: sexes, genders, "races," social classes, nationalities, regions, religions, estates, linguistic groups, sports teams, or any of an essentially infinite number of potential distinctions between groups of human beings.

SDO is thought to have a widespread influence over the nature and intensity of group-based social hierarchy, not only because it influences a wide range of social ideologies and LMs, but also and perhaps most importantly because it influences the output of hierarchy-enhancing and hierarchy-attenuating public policies. The empirical and conceptual scope of SDO is expected to be extremely broad because it is related to attitudes toward *any* social ideology, attitude, belief, career path, or social policy with strong implications for the distribution of social value between social groups. This social value comes in a variety of forms, including wealth, power, status, jobs, health, and prestige.

SDO is significantly affected by at least four factors. First, SDO will be driven by one's membership in and identification with arbitrary, highly salient, and hierarchically organized arbitrary-set groups. In general and everything else being equal, one should expect that dominants and/or those who identify with dominants, will have higher levels of social dominance orientation than subordinates and/or those who identify with subordinates. Second, one's level of SDO is affected also by a series of background and socialization factors such as one's level of education, one's religious faith, traumatic life experiences, and a whole set of other socialization experiences (e.g., war, depression, natural disasters). Third, there is reason to believe that people are born with different "temperamental predispositions" and personalities (Bouchard, 1994; Loehlin, 1993). One such temperamental predisposition is empathy. There is reason to believe that the greater one's empathy, the lower one's level of SDO.

Fourth, one's level of SDO depends upon one's gender. Everything else being equal, males will have significantly higher average levels of social dominance orientation than females. This thesis is known as the *invariance hypothesis*. This greater level of SDO among males is not simply due to the fact that males occupy dominant social roles, but also due to factors that are largely independent of these social roles. For this and other reasons, the gender system of social hierarchy is related to yet quite distinct from the arbitrary-set system.

The Intersecting Psychologies of Gender and Arbitrary-Set Conflict

Since there is overwhelming evidence that intergroup aggression is primarily a male enterprise, there is also reason to expect that arbitrary-set aggression is primarily directed at outgroup males rather than outgroup females. If we regard normal forms of intergroup discrimination as mild forms of intergroup aggression, there is then also reason

to suspect that it will be primarily males rather than females who are the targets of this arbitrary-set discrimination. We label this thesis as the *subordinate-male target hypothesis*.

Note that the subordinate-male target hypothesis does *not* imply the absence of discrimination against women, for such discrimination clearly occurs and is part of the gender system of group-based social hierarchy (i.e., *patriarchy*). Rather, what we are suggesting is that, everything else being equal, subordinate males rather than subordinate females are the primary objects of *arbitrary-set discrimination*. In Figure 18.2, we ignore the absolute level of discrimination directed at any group and show the expected difference in discrimination directed against members of dominant and subordinate groups within each gender. Thus, for example, Figure 18.2 shows slightly more discrimination directed against dominant and subordinate women. However, the subordinate-male target hypothesis expects the difference in discrimination experienced by subordinate males as opposed to dominants males to be much greater. The subordinate-male target hypothesis is both counter-intuitive, and also stands in direct contradiction to the generally accepted "double-jeopardy" hypothesis. This hypothesis suggests that since both subordinate ethnic groups and women are discriminated against, women from subordinate ethnic groups are then at a double disadvantage (e.g., Beale, 1970; Almquist, 1975).

The subordinate-male-target thesis highlights another major difference between previous theories of intergroup relations and SD theory. Namely, SDT incorporates the political psychology of gender into the larger story of arbitrary-set conflict. Rather than regarding the psychology of intergroup conflict and the psychology of gender as being independent domains, we regard the psychology of the one as an important and fundamental component of the psychology of the other. Seen from the perspective of social dominance theory, the psychology of intergroup conflict is intimately connected to and bound up with the male predisposition for group boundary maintenance, territorial defense/acquisition, and the exercise of dominion. This implies that an understanding of the psychology of sex/gender is incomplete without an incorporation of the dynamics of intergroup relations, and an understanding of intergroup relations is incomplete without incorporating impor-

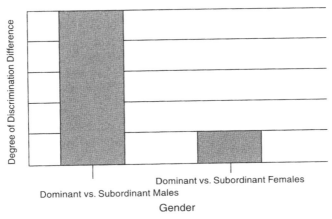

FIGURE 18.2 ■ Difference in level of discrimination between dominant and subordinate males versus dominant and subordinate females.

tant lessons of the psychology of male/female differences.

Hierarchical Equilibrium and Hierarchy Constraints

Given the historical record of both human and hominoid social structure, it seems most reasonable to assume that hominoid social systems are predisposed to organize themselves within some range of group-based inequality. Furthermore, the historical record also seems to suggest that, under "normal circumstances" and everything else being equal, the degree of this group-based social hierarchy will tend to stabilize around a given level that we can refer to as the "*point of hierarchical equilibrium.*" In broad terms, we suggest that this point is established at the fulcrum between: (a) *hierarchy-enhancing forces* and (b) *hierarchy-attenuating forces.*

Hierarchy-enhancing forces are the complete set of social ideologies, beliefs, attitudes, traditions, social institutions and social roles that promote and maintain group-based hierarchy within social systems. Besides the HE-LMs already mentioned above, these HE-forces also consist of important social institutions and social roles such as the internal security forces (e.g., local and secret police), major elements of the legal and criminal justice system (e.g., prosecutors) and major elements within the business community (e.g., banks, insurance companies). *Hierarchy-attenuating forces*

are those social institutions, traditions, and ideologies that tend to promote greater degrees of group-based social equality. Besides HA-LMs, other examples of HA-forces would be social roles and social institutions such as civil rights and social welfare organizations, charities, the public defender's office, and religious denominations such as the Society of Friends.

In sum, the counterbalancing and mutually constraining effects of hierarchy-enhancing and hierarchy-attenuating forces are thought to be among the factors helping to maintain hierarchical equilibrium in any society over time. Furthermore, we posit that within relatively stable social systems, hierarchical equilibrium is found at the point that simultaneously: (a) organizes the social system in a hierarchical and trimorphic fashion, and yet (b) does not allow the degree of group-based social hierarchy to become either "morally" offensive or structurally destabilizing.

Other Structural Implications of Social Dominance Theory

The mechanisms described above not only tend to make group-based social hierarchies ubiquitous and stable, but also provide these social hierarchies with a number of other common characteristics. Among the most important of these characteristics are features such as: *increasing disproportionality, consensuality,* and *resiliency.*

Increasing Disproportionality

One defining feature of group-based social hierarchies is what Robert Putnam (1976) has labeled the *law of increasing disproportion*. This law suggests that the more political authority exercised by a given political position, the greater the probability that this position will be occupied by a member of the dominant group (Putnam, 1976). In addition, the law of increasing disproportion operates within all three forms of group-based stratification (i.e., age-system, gender system, and arbitrary-set system).

For example, Putnam shows that the higher the post held by any given individual in the British government (e.g., Prime Minister vs. Member of Parliament), the greater the likelihood that this individual attended one of the two elite British universities (Oxford or Cambridge). Putnam presents evidence showing that this increasing disproportionality is not restricted to particular nations or cultures, but is found cross-culturally, and has been found to hold in countries such as the United States, the former Soviet Union, Israel, Italy, and Tunisia (Putnam, 1976).

Hierarchical Consensuality

Group-based social hierarchies are also characterized by a high degree of *hierarchical consensuality*. By this term we mean that there is a high degree of consensus within the social system as to which groups are "dominant" and which groups are "subordinate." This consensuality not only characterizes the beliefs of dominants, but more importantly, the beliefs of subordinates. This high degree of cross-group consensuality is critical for the orderly and relatively peaceful coordination of dominant and submissive behaviors and the maintenance of an ongoing system of group-based social inequality.

One example of this high degree of hierarchical consensuality can be found in our analysis of a sample of 723 UCLA undergraduates in 1989. We asked these students to rate the social status of five ethnic groups on a scale from "1-Very low status" to "7-Very high status." Results showed that the ethnic groups were perceived to have highly significant differences in social status. The average social status ratings were ordered: (1) Whites (M = 6.42), (2) Asians (M = 4.80), (3) Arabs (M =

3.59), (4) Blacks (M = 3.31) and (5) Latinos (M = 3.00). There was a very high level of consensus in the ethnic status ratings of these five groups across all respondents (intraclass r = .999). In addition, the degree of consensus among raters within each of the four ethnic groups was high: (Euro-Americans: intraclass r = .998; Asian-Americans: intraclass r = .997; Latino-Americans: intraclass r = .995; Afro-Americans intraclass r = .988. Most importantly, however, the consensuality in perceived social status of American ethnic groups was largely impervious of the ethnic group to which one belongs. Inspection of the mean status ratings of each of these five ethnic groups within each of four ethnic groups in Figure 18.3 shows a very high degree of cross-ethnic consistency in how American ethnic groups are perceived. The same basic results were found using a second sample of UCLA students and four ethnic groups four years later.

Resiliency

While group-based social hierarchies tend to be highly stable over time, this cross-temporal stability is not absolute. Not only does the *degree* of social hierarchy within any given social system vary across time, but at least within the arbitrary-set system, there are also rare yet dramatic occasions when a given group-based social hierarchy will be completely overthrown. While these "regime smashing" social revolutions are exceedingly rare, there have been at least seven such events within the last 300 years. These revolutionary

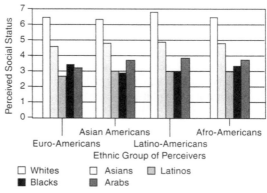

FIGURE 18.3 ■ Perceived social status of U.S. ethnic groups as a function of ethnic group membership.

events include: (a) the French revolution of 1789, (b) the Mexican revolution of 1910, (c) the Russian revolution of 1917, (d) The Chinese revolution of 1949, (e) the Vietnamese revolution (1954–1975), (f) the Cuban revolution of 1959, and (g) the Sandinista revolution of 1979. However, despite all these attempts at egalitarian social transformation, one is struck by the fact that there is not a single case in which an egalitarian transformation has actually succeeded. Even in the few cases in which the *ancien régime* was overthrown (e.g., the French, Russian, Mexican, and Chinese revolutions), like the myth of the phoenix, some new arbitrary-set order soon rose up to take its place. In other words, even though a given arbitrary-set stratification system might collapse or be overthrown, the phenomenon of arbitrary-set stratification itself appears to be extremely resilient.

Consistencies in Social Organization Across Primate Species

The evolutionary perspective suggests that not only will humans tend to live in group-based and hierarchically organized social systems, but that this form of social organization should also tend to be found among other species closely related to humans. Studies of other primate species tend to support this expectation (e.g., Bercovitch, 1991; Mazur, 1985; Sapolsky, 1993, 1995). Not only do all primates within the *hominoid clade* (i.e., chimpanzees, bonobos, gorillas, and baboons) have systems of social dominance, but there is a group-based nature to these systems. Several group-based primate systems outside of the hominoid clade also have a trimorphic structure not unlike that found among humans indicating that social status is a function of: (a) age – with older animals dominating younger animals (e.g., Kawanaka, 1989), (b) sex – with males dominating females (Kawanaka, 1982; Nadler, 1987; Strier, 1994; with the exception of bonobos), and (c) position in kinship and friendship groups, which might be considered rudimentary arbitrary-set systems (Rowell, 1974).

Among most primates, these kinship groups are most closely associated with mother-offspring lineage bonds. Besides age, sex, size, and intelligence, in certain primate species such as yellow baboons, the social rank of the offspring is influenced by the social rank of the mother (e.g., Lee & Oliver,

1979). Studies among olive baboons have shown that the death of the mother or the loss of social status of the mother affects the social status of her offspring (Johnson, 1987). Similarly, research has shown that when the social rank of rhesus monkey mothers was experimentally manipulated by the introduction or removal of higher ranking animals, the offspring showed changes in their level of aggressive behavior congruent with their changed social rank (Marsden, 1968). Another manifestation of the arbitrary-set system can be seen in the formation of political coalitions and alliances among high-status primate males. It is not uncommon for certain *alpha males* (i.e., dominant males) to achieve their dominant positions by forming and maintaining "ruling coalitions" with other high-status males (Leigh & Shea, 1995; Harcourt, 1988).

Considering only closely related primates in the hominoid clade, there are a number of other common and relevant features of social organization, including: (a) the existence of closed social networks or what might be called *ingroups*, (b) communal territoriality, (c) male domination of intergroup relations, (d) the male domination of hostile and antagonistic relations between groups, and (e) the male domination of stalking, attacking, and of killing outgroup males (Ghiglier, 1989; Wrangham, 1987). This list suggests that the hominoid clade appears to be predisposed towards an *ethnocentric* orientation in which boundary maintenance towards outgroups is largely enforced by males.

Summary

Social dominance theory begins with the observation that surplus-producing human social systems are structured as trimorphic, group-based social hierarchies. The three forms of group-based systems are: (a) an age system, (b) a gender system (i.e., patriarchy), and (c) an arbitrary-set system. The arbitrary-set system consists of socially constructed group distinctions that happen to be relevant within specific situational and historical contexts. Not only does this trimorphic structure appear to characterize human social systems that produce economic surplus, there are also rudimentary signs of this trimorphic structure within other groups of primates as well.

After noting the ubiquitousness of group-based social hierarchy, social dominance theory goes on to make three primary assumptions: (a) While age and gender based hierarchies tend to exist within all social systems, arbitrary-set systems of social hierarchy invariably emerge within social systems producing sustainable economic surplus; (b) Most forms of group conflict and oppression (e.g., racism, ethnocentrism, sexism, nationalism, classism, regionalism) are different manifestations of the same basic human predisposition toward group-based social hierarchy; (c) Human social systems are subject to the influences of "hierarchy-enhancing" (HE) forces, promoting group-based social inequality, and that are partially counterbalanced by opposing "hierarchy-attenuating" (HA) forces, group-based social equality.

Based on these assumptions, social dominance theory then goes on to explore the manner in which psychological, intergroup, and institutional processes interact with one another in the production and maintenance of group-based, hierarchical social structure.

Unlike most previous models of intergroup discrimination and prejudice, social dominance theory operates at several levels of analysis. While being influenced by many perspectives within evolutionary psychology and sociobiology, it does not make the assumption that the dynamics of intergroup conflict and oppression can be reduced to individual strategies of reproductive success or inclusive fitness maximization. Unlike classical "psychological" and individual differences theories such as authoritarian personality theory, social dominance theory does not restrict its explanation of discrimination and prejudice to the intrapsychic conflicts and mechanics of individual actors, but rather examines how psychological orientation and individuals act and are acted upon by group-based hierarchy. Unlike situational and cognitively oriented theories in social psychology, social dominance does not restrict itself to the nature and dynamics of the individual's self and social categorizations, but situates these processes in the context of motivational differences between individuals and the broader social context within which individuals find themselves. Finally, unlike classical "sociological" theories, SD-theory utilizes—but does not restrict itself to—the structural relations between groups or the operations of social institutions.

Therefore, as a general and synthetic perspective, social dominance theory attempts to take elements from the individual, group, institutional, and structural levels of analysis and to integrate these elements into a new, more comprehensive and more powerful theoretical framework. From evolutionary psychology come the notions that the ubiquitousness of social hierarchy and ethnocentrism are most parsimoniously understood in terms of survival strategies adopted by hominoids, including homo sapiens. From authoritarian personality theory and Rokeach's two-value theory of political ideology comes the notion that the importance that people place on the value of "equality," dominance, and submission is of fundamental importance to our understanding of a whole range of sociopolitical beliefs and behaviors. From realistic group conflict and group position theories comes the notion that the political choices and attitudes of individuals must often be seen within the context of group conflict over both real and symbolic resource allocation. From social identity theory come the important notions that the conflict between groups is not necessarily or even primarily designed to maximize the absolute material return to the ingroup but rather to maximize the *relative* return to the ingroup, sometimes even at the cost of substantial material loss to both the self and the ingroup. Finally, from classical and neoclassical elitism theories come the notion of the functional value of ideology in the dynamics of hierarchical social control.

To these basic ideas, we have constructed some new theoretical elements such as: (a) the notion of social dominance orientation as a ubiquitous motive driving most group-relevant social attitudes and allocative decisions, (b) the notion of behavioral asymmetry, or the different yet coordinated behavioral repertoires of dominants and subordinates that help maintain the stability of group-based hierarchy, (c) the notion that the dynamics of the political psychology of gender is an essential and universal element in the dynamics of hierarchical relationships among social groups in general, and (d) the notion that hierarchical stability is affected by the equilibrium-producing functions of hierarchy-enhancing and hierarchy-attenuating social forces. Among other things, we argue that this theoretical catholicism will allow us to get a firmer grip on the general dynamics of intergroup relations and to more clearly appreciate the underlying similarities in a wide array of social phenomena within one comprehensive theoretical framework. The phenomena of concern can range from simple acts of mobbing in the playground, to mild forms of prejudice and street-gang violence, to instances of genocide.

NOTES

1. Based on sex, age, descent, and marriage.
2. However, it should be noted that this age system is not completely linear. *Very* old people (i.e., aged 80 years or older) do not always dominate over somewhat younger people (e.g., 60 year olds).

REFERENCES

Abel, E., & Nelson, M. (1990). *Circles of care: Work and identity in women's lives*. Albany: State University of New York Press.

Almquist, E. M. (1975). Untagling the effects of race and sex: The disadvantaged status of Black women. *Social Science Quarterly*, *56*, 129–142.

Bachofen, J. J. (1861/1969). *Das Mutterrecht: Eine Untersuchung uber die Gynaikokratie der altern Welt nach ihrer religiosen und rechtlichen Natur*. Bruxelles: Culture et Civilisation.

Beale, F. (1970). Double jeopardy: To be black and female. In T. Cade (Ed.), *The Black woman*, (pp. 90–100). New York: New American Library.

Beck, L., & Keddie, N. (1978). *Women in the Muslim world*. Cambridge, MA: Harvard University Press.

Bercovitch, F. B. (1991). Social stratification, social strategies, and reproductive success in primates. *Ethology & Sociobiology*, *12*, 315–333.

Biddiss, M. D. (1970). *Father of racist ideology: The social and political thought of Count Gobineau*. London: Weidenfeld & Nicolson.

Bouchard, T. J. (1994). Genes, environment, and personality. *Science*, *264*, 1700–1701.

Busch, R. C. (1990). *Family systems: Comparative study of the family*. New York: P. Lang.

Collier, J. F., & Yanagisako, S. J. (Eds.). (1987). *Gender and kinship: Essays toward a unified analysis*. Stanford, CA: Stanford University Press.

Deane, P. C. (1968). The persistence of Uncle Tom: An examination of the image of the Negro in children's fiction series. *Journal of Negro Education*, *37*, 140–145.

Durkheim, E. (1933). *The division of labor in society* (G. Simpson, Trans.). New York: MacMillan. (Original work published 1893).

Eibl-Eibesfeldt, I. (1989). *Human Ethology*. New York: Aldine de Gruyter.

Ghiglieri, M. P. (1989). Hominoid sociobiology and hominid social evolution. In P. G. Heltne & L. A. Marquardt (Eds.), *Understanding Chimpanzees* (pp. 370–379). Cambridge, MA: Harvard University Press.

Gimbutas, M. A. (1989). *The language of the goddess: Unearthing the hidden symbols of Western civilization*. New York: Harper & Row.

Gramsci, A. (1971). *Selections from the prison notebooks*. London: Wishart.

Gurr, T. R., & Harff, B. (1994). *Ethnic conflict in world politics*. Boulder, CO: Westview Press.

Harcourt, A. H. (1988). Alliances in contests and social intelligence. In R. W. Byrne & A. Whiten (Eds), *Machiavellian intelligence: Social expertise and the evolution of intellect in monkeys, apes, and humans* (pp. 132–152). Oxford, England: Clarendon Press/Oxford University Press.

Herrnstein, R. J., & Murray, C. A. (1994). *The bell curve: Intelligence and class structure in American life*. New York, NY: Free Press.

Johns, C. H. W. (1947). *Babylonian and Assyrian laws, contracts, and letters*. New York: Scribner.

Johnson, J. A. (1987). Dominance rank in juvenile olive baboons, Papio anubis: The influence of gender, size, maternal rank and orphaning. *Animal Behaviour*, *35*, 1694–1708.

Kawanaka, K. (1982). Further studies on predation by chimpanzees of the Mahale mountains. *Primates*, *23*, 364–384.

Kawanaka, K. (1989). Age differences in social interactions of young males in a chimpanzee unit-group at the Mahale Mountains National Park, Tanzania. *Primates*, *30*, 285–305.

Keegan, J. (1993). *The history of warfare*. New York: Alfred A. Knopf.

Kluegel, J. R., & Smith, E. R. (1986). *Beliefs about inequality: Americans' views of what is and what ought to be*. New York: Aldine De Gruyter.

Koch, E. (1996). How murder became mere routine: De Kock trial. The Electronic Mail & Guardian. (*www.mg.co.za/mg/newss/96feb/27feb-dekock.html*).

Lee, P. C., & Oliver, J. I. (1979). Competition, dominance and the acquisition of rank in juvenile yellow baboons (Papio cynocephalus). *Animal Behaviour*, *27*, 576–585.

Leigh, S. R. & Shea, B. T. (1995). Ontogeny and the evolution of adult body size dimorphism in apes. *American Journal of Primatology*, *36*, 37–60.

Lenski, G. E. (1984). *Power and privilege: A theory of social stratification*. Chapel Hill: University of North Carolina Press.

Loehlin, J. C. (1993). What has behavioral genetics told us about the nature of personality? In T. J. Bouchard & P. Propping (Eds.), *Twins as a tool of behavioral genetics* (pp. 109–119). Chichester, England: John Wiley & Sons.

Marsden, H. M. (1968). Agonistic behaviour of young rhesus monkeys after changes induced in social rank of their mothers. *Animal Behaviour*, *16*, 38–44.

Marx, K., & Engels, F. (1846/1970). *The German ideology*. New York: International Publishers.

Mazur, A. (1985). A biosocial model of status in face-to-face primate groups. *Social Forces*, *64*, 377–402.

Merton, R. (1972). The self-fulfilling prophecy. In E. P. Hollander & R. G. Hunt (Eds.), *Classic contributions to social psychology* (pp. 260–266). New York: Oxford University Press.

Mosca, G. (1896/1939). *The ruling class: Elements of political science*. New York: McGraw-Hill.

Moscovici, S. (1981). On social representation. In J. P. Forgas (Ed.), *Social Cognition: Perspectives on Everyday Understanding*. London: Academic Press.

Moscovici, S. (1988). Notes towards a description of social representations. *European Journal of Social Psychology*, *18*, 211–250.

Murdock, G. P. (1949). *Social Structure*. New York: Macmillan.

Nadler, R. D. (1987). Sexual aggression in the great apes. Conference of the New York Academy of Sciences: Human sexual aggression: Current perspectives, New York, New York. *Annals of the New York Academy of Sciences*, 1988 Aug, 528, 154–162.

Pomper, G. N. (1970). *Elections in America*. New York: Dood, Mead.

Putnam, R. D. (1976). *The comparative study of political elites*. Englewood Cliffs, NJ: Prentice-Hall.

Rowell, T. E. (1974). The concept of social dominance. *Behavioral Biology*, *11*, 131–154.

Rushton, J. P. (1996). Race differences in brain size. *American Psychologist*, *51*, 556.

Sapolsky, R. M. (1993). The physiology of dominance in stable versus unstable social hierarchies. In W. A. Mason & S. P. Mendoza (Eds.), *Primate social conflict* (pp. 171–204). Albany, NY: State University of New York Press.

Sapolsky, R. M. (1995). Social subordinance as a marker of hypercortisolism: Some unexpected subtleties. In G. P. Chrousos, R. McCarty, K. Pacak, G. Cizza, E. Sternberg, P. W. Gold, & R. Kvetnansky (Eds.), *Stress: Basic mechanisms and clinical implications. Annals of the New York Academy of Sciences* (vol. 771). New York, NY: New York Academy of Sciences.

Scott, J. C. (1990). *Domination and the arts of resistance: Hidden transcripts*. New Haven: Yale University Press.

Seagle, W. (1971). *Men of Law, from Hammurabi to Holmes*. New York: Hafner Pub.

Shockley, W. (1972, January). Dysgenics, geneticity, raceology: A challenge to the intellectual responsibility of educators. *Phi Delta Kappan*, 297–307.

Strier, K. B. (1994). Brotherhoods among atelins: Kinship, affiliation, and competition. *Behaviour*, *130*, 151–167.

Wrangham, R. W. (1987). The significance of African apes for reconstructing human social evolution. In W. G. Kinsey (Ed.), *The evolution of human behavior: Primate models* (pp. 51–71). New York: Suny Press.

van den Berghe, P. L. (1978). *Man in society: A biosocial view*. New York: Elsevier North Holland.

Group Conflict, Prejudice, and the Paradox of Contemporary Racial Attitudes

Lawrence Bobo • University of Wisconsin, Madison

Introduction

The status of black Americans is the longest standing and most glaring exception to the American promise of freedom and equality. For this, as well as other reasons, social psychologists have long sought to shed light on the ways in which racial attitudes, beliefs, and values affect and are affected by patterns of black–white relations. Black–white relations now seem more complex and contradictory than ever before. From basic economic and demographic indicators to indicators of racial attitudes and beliefs, simultaneous patterns of progress, deterioration, and lack of change can be discerned.

I am concerned with the underlying meaning of race to white and black Americans (although, as in most of the literature in this area, disproportionate attention is given to white attitudes). This attempt to impose theoretical coherence on the complexities of racial attitudes and beliefs must begin, however, by recognizing a crucial shift in the character of black–white relations. The basic issues that define significant points of conflict and controversy in black-white relations have changed in many ways. Foremost among these changes has been a shift in focus from eliminating discrimination in access to public schools, facilities, employment, and the like, to a concern with mandatory school desegregation and the use of hiring goals

or quotas; a shift from removing formal exclusionary barriers to implementing the measures needed to ensure full inclusion and participation; a shift, that is, *from stuggles over acquiring basic civil rights to struggles over actually redistributing educational, economic, political, and social resources.*

For many social psychologists, these changes have signaled a need to modify their traditional conceptions of prejudice in order to understand the changes in attitudes associated with these more global shifts in black-white relations. Others have stressed the increasing importance of group conflict processes because these broader changes have pushed to the forefront of black–white relations explicit and increasing concern about the allocation of scarce resources and values, such as educational and job opportunities. Thus, this chapter is concerned with efforts to apply social-psychological theories of group conflict and of prejudice to an understanding of the nature and consequences of contemporary racial attitudes.

Many years ago, Gordon Allport (1954) noted that distinguishing the effects of prejudice from those of group conflict on intergroup relations would be a very difficult task. He suggested that, "Realistic conflict is like a note on an organ. It sets all prejudices that are attuned to it into simultaneous vibration. The listener can scarcely distinguish the pure note from the surrounding jangle"

(p. 233). Thus, it is with some trepidation that this chapter takes up the task of trying to clarify the distinctive social-psychological significance of group conflict and prejudice in the racial attitudes of white and, to a lesser degree, black Americans. Recent theoretical and empirical work has, however, raised this question anew and in the process has improved our conceptual leverage on these issues. As a result, an attempt to distinguish the "pure note" of group conflict from that of prejudice seems warranted.

The approach taken in this chapter is more that of a speculative essay than a traditional literature review. This approach is chosen, precarious though it may be, because there is a need for a discussion of broad theoretical issues raised by the controversy about the relative importance of group conflict and prejudice for contemporary racial attitudes. The departure from traditional literature reviews takes two forms. First, I propose and elaborate on a theoretical framework for understanding the place of group conflict in intergroup belief systems, and I attempt to specify ways of conceptualizing and measuring group conflict motives. Second, I take a quite catholic approach to the material as the research draws not only on the work of social psychologists, but also on that of historians, demographers, political scientists, and sociologists. The final outcome, I hope, is a better sense of the distinctive roles of prejudice and group conflict in racial attitudes as well as a sense of fruitful directions for future research.

Theoretical controversy of the kind examined here has occurred before within social psychology as well as in other disciplines. For example, Clark (1965), although not exclusively concerned with racial attitudes and relations, asserted that social psychology devoted too little attention to questions of power and political conflict. Rose (1956) argued that we shouldn't assume that prejudice underlies discrimination because "patterns of intergroup relations (including mainly discrimination and segregation) are quite distinct from attitudes of prejudice in that each has a separate and distinct history, cause, and process of change" (p. 173). Like Rose, Blumer (1958b) called for greater attention to the organization of society: to competing interests, differences in power, and situational contexts, which he saw as the underlying forces in intergroup relations. Allport (1962) took issue with these and similar assertions that social

structure was more important than individual prejudice. He argued that societal factors are "distal causal factors" in intergroup behavior, whereas individual personality is always the "proximal causal factor." Allport suggested an important link between the two, however: conformity to group norms. In a similar vein, Williams (1965), too, noted that social structure and personality are linked but added that we should be careful to distinguish "prejudice" as driven by feelings of competitive threat or the protection of vested interests from "prejudice" as driven by psychological affective or expressive needs.

A similar dialogue over societal versus personality factors in intergroup relations arose among historians with respect to attempts to explain the rise of slavery and racist ideology. In a controversial paper, the Handlins (1950) argued that black indentured servants were regarded and treated much the same as white servants when they first arrived in the American colonies in 1619. Over a period of roughly 40 years, they argued, the status of black servants deteriorated, whereas that of white servants improved. Thus, by around 1660, blacks had been reduced to a cheap, available, and easily exploited pool of servants whose bondage was viewed as lifelong. Importantly, this analysis suggested a gradual, not a rapid, degradation of blacks and transformation of the attitudes toward them. Such a pattern of events was more consistent with the view that antiblack prejudice resulted from the establishment of slavery, than with the claim that a deep psychological antipathy toward blacks preceded slavery. Instead, the rise of a new mode of organizing social life, a slave economy, led to the development of attitudes and beliefs justifying and reinforcing that new social form.

Degler (1959) challenged these claims, pointing to evidence that, from the earliest moment of their arrival, blacks had been treated differently— more harshly—than white servants (see also the exchange of letters of Degler, 1960, and Handlin & Handlin, 1960). In contradistinction to both positions, Jordan (1962) noted that the available information for the years in question, especially 1619–1640, was very sparse and at best inconclusive. He argued for a compromise position, which held that economic, political, and cultural factors conducive to the rise of slavery as an institution worked simultaneously with antiblack prejudice to foster the ultimate subjugation of blacks. The enslavement of blacks and the existence of individual-level prejudice, Jordan (1968) wrote, "may have been equally cause and effect, continuously reacting upon each other, dynamically joining hands to hustle the Negro down the road to complete degradation" (p. 80).

More recently, Fredrickson (1971b) questioned this conclusion and, indeed, the very terms of the debate that assumed that black slavery was a unique departure requiring special explanation. Although accepting Jordan's basic claim that prejudice played a role in the rise of slavery, Fredrickson argued that the real question was why not *all* black indentured servants were regarded as bound for a lifetime of servitude. Many were freed, just as their white counterparts were, when their term of service was completed. In Fredrickson's account, the forces that paved the way for black enslavement were the absence of any deep-seated cultural bias, at that time, against the institution of slavery and several societal factors (e.g., the political vulnerability of African blacks as compared to white European indentured servants, as well as the growing demand for a stable labor supply) that had, by the 1660s, led to the *de facto* (and later *de jure*) enslavement of a large number of blacks (see also Harris, 1964). From this point of view, it is as incorrect to claim that prejudice played no role in the rise of slavery as it is to assign prejudice the same causal weight as other societal factors. In particular, Fredrickson (1971b) argued

that "virulent prejudice," as compared to milder forms of ethnocentrism and stereotyping, followed in the wake of enslavement and probably did not take full possession of the white mind until slavery had become fully established as the basis of the economic and social order. (p. 246)

This argument is lent further support by the fact that a full articulation of theories of the permanent, innate inferiority of blacks followed the rise of the abolitionists' moral challenge to slavery and the Northern industrialists' challenge to economic policies conducive to plantation-based commodities and slave labor (Fredrickson, 1971a).

Several lessons are to be drawn from these earlier examinations of the role of societal versus personality—more loosely, group-conflict versus prejudice—approaches to intergroup relations. First, societal and personality approaches are not mutually exclusive frameworks of analysis. It sometimes seems that these approaches are irreconcilable because the former tends to assume that intergroup attitudes and behavior are guided by an interest-based, rational calculus, with interests being a function of position in the social structure. Personality or prejudice approaches, in contrast, tend to emphasize individual-level, psychological, and often irrational bases of intergroup relations. The present discussion seeks to avoid this constraining, and misleading, opposition by suggesting that certain types of attitudes and beliefs reflect group-based interests imposed by the social structure; that is, there are aspects of personality that reflect societal level processes and do so in a manner that should not be construed as "prejudice." Second, if this observation is to inform empirical research, then the relevant concepts need to be well defined, and appropriate measurement strategies must be outlined. Third, theory must be informed by an analysis of the sociohistorical context of group relations, as well as by the rules of cognitive functioning. The historically specific and socially relevant content of racial attitudes and beliefs cannot be derived from the psychological attributes of individuals alone. In particular, periods of substantial shift in the character of attitudes, such as the rise of sophisticated proslavery doctrines and, later, the scientific racism that accompanied the rise of Jim Crow, were inextricably linked to, and perhaps primarily driven by, larger economic, political, and cultural forces. Contemporary research on the growing complexity and subtlety of racial attitudes would benefit from a balanced concern with societal and personality factors (Pettigrew, 1985). Furthermore, research on racial attitudes and beliefs must be based on an analysis of the changes and continuities in the sociohistorical context of black-white relations. The relative economic and political status of blacks and whites, patterns of residential and school segregation, and enduring cultural beliefs are all important inputs to prevailing patterns of racial attitudes and beliefs.

The main question, then, is what role, if any, does group conflict play in racial attitudes in the contemporary United States? A full answer to this question requires a conception of group conflict and of group conflict motives, as well as a specification of the ways in which the latter differ from prejudice and other racial attitudes. Before addressing each of these matters, however, it would be instructive to consider why the question arises in the first place.

The Problem: Progress and Resistance

The attitudes of white Americans toward black people have undergone sweeping and dramatic change over the past several decades. In 1942, approximately 60% of whites believed that blacks were less intelligent than whites (Hyman & Sheatsley, 1956, p. 35). By 1964, that figure had declined to less than 25% (Hyman & Sheatsley, 1964; see also Schuman, 1971, p. 383). A substantial majority of white Americans in 1942 approved of the blatantly discriminatory proposition that "white people should have the first chance at any kind of job," whereas in 1972 nearly 100% of whites in a national survey rejected that statement. But just as survey research has chronicled such changes for the better, opposition to policies such as school busing (80%–90%; see Schuman, Steeh, & Bobo, 1985) and affirmative action (roughly 80%; see Lipset & Schneider, 1978) remain impediments to certain forms of racial change.

Research on racial attitudes thus increasingly presents a paradox: Although there is continuing improvement in whites' beliefs about blacks and support for the general principles of racial equality and integration (Taylor, Sheatsley, & Greeley, 1978), there is pronounced opposition to specific policies aimed at improving the social and economic position of blacks, as well as to participation in social settings where blacks are a substantial majority (Farley, Schuman, Bianchi, Colasanto, & Hatchett, 1978; Smith, 1981). Pettigrew (1979) described this paradox as follows: "white Americans increasingly reject racial injustice in principle, but are reluctant to accept the measures necessary to eliminate the injustice" (p. 119).

Students of democratic theory have also examined the extent to which abstract democratic principles are applied in more concrete situations (Prothro & Grigg, 1960). Jackman (1978), in particular, stressed this type of approach to the conceptualization of facial attitudes. Others have drawn on the distinction she made between racial principles and applied measures of racial policy preferences. Thus, recent research by Schuman, Steeh, and Bobo (1985) indicates that, across a number of important issues (access to public accommodations, discrimination in jobs, residential integration, and school integration), whites were more positive in attitude toward the principle of racial egalitarianism than toward policies to implement such principles. This disparity applied in terms of both lower absolute levels of support for implementation and less positive trends over time. In sum, this research demonstrated that one major characteristic of American racial attitudes is a gap between "principles and implementation."

The sustained positive movement on questions concerning the abstract goals of equal treatment and integration suggest that a fundamental change in racial norms has taken place (Schuman et al., 1985). This transformation in normative climate, however, has not eliminated race as a concern in American social and political life, nor has it resulted in support for strong efforts to equalize the opportunities afforded to blacks and whites. Research concerned with accounting for these patterns of "progress and resistance" has resulted in five broad approaches and answers.

First, a number of theories point to an underlying residue of prejudice and racism that is currently manifested in less overt ways (Crosby, Bromely, & Saxe, 1980; Donnerstein & Donnerstein, 1976; Gaertner & Dovidio, 1981; Kinder & Sears, 1981; Rogers & Prentice-Dunn, 1981). For example, Gaertner and Dovidio (1981) identified "aversive racists," people who have some degree of negative feelings toward blacks and yet are committed to a nonprejudiced self-image. A series of experiments suggests that the outcome, at least in situations involving ambiguous racial norms, is discriminatory treatment of blacks. Second, others have suggested that many contemporary proposals for racial change involve important value-violations. For instance, Lipset and Schneider (1978) noted that affirmative action programs, especially those involving quotas, are perceived as violating the values of individualism and meritocratic advancement. Others have argued that court orders for school desegregation and busing are viewed as violating the value of majority rule (Stinchcombe & Taylor, 1980) and the general cultural motif of noncoercive, voluntary compliance (Taylor, 1986). Third, some research (McClendon, 1985; McClendon & Pestello, 1982) points to pragmatic objections to racially neutral features of certain policies such as the cost, time, or safety considerations raised by school busing. Fourth, some researchers stress the importance of group-interested ideologies (Jackman & Muha 1984; Jackman & Senter, 1983) and realistic group-conflict motives (Bobo, 1983; Smith, 1981; Wellman, 1977). Finally, a number of researchers have alerted us to different cognitive processes that affect racial attitudes and perceptions. These processes include a tendency toward more extreme reactions, both positive and negative, to out-group members (Linville & Jones, 1980); the observation that ambivalent feelings can lead to "amplified" reactions of positive and negative valence (Katz, 1981); the differential consequences of distinct "modes" (e.g., genetic versus environmental) of explaining racial inequality (Apostle, Glock, Piazza, & Suelzle, 1983); and an examination of the impact of general and racially specific beliefs about social stratification on racial attitudes (Kluegel & Smith, 1982).

Despite critical differences in interpretation and analysis, these five strands of research share, to varying degrees, three assumptions about contemporary race relations. The first of these assumptions pertains to the far-reaching normative change in standards for interracial relations and conduct. In particular, it is assumed that this important transformation in racial norms does not easily extend to support for large-scale racial change or to fully color-blind behavior. Next, although this point is often treated more implicitly than explicitly, it is assumed that the character of the issues themselves has changed. Some have explicitly characterized the shift as being from equal rights or procedural issues to equal opportunity or redistributive issues (Kluegel & Smith, 1982). More generally, it is clear that, after 1965, there were key changes in law and politics pertaining to race, in the form and the articulated ideology of black political activism, in the status of many blacks, and in the questions that social researchers pursued (see Schuman et al., 1985). Finally, these two assumptions have resulted in a general concern about understanding the gap between "principles and implementation" or, more broadly, about explaining the apparent limitations on racial progress (blackwell, 1982; Rothbart, 1976).

For the present purposes, this problem is framed as the need to explain the emergence and charac-

ter of an ideology of "bounded" racial change. It is argued that there is a nascent view that, although blacks are entitled to full citizenship rights, moving beyond equal rights to ensuring equal opportunities, or to implementing policies that may impose substantial burdens on whites, is an illegitimate goal. In particular, the tendencies to attribute racial inequality to the shortcomings of blacks themselves (Kluegel, 1985; Schuman, 1971) and to view the opportunity structure as fair and open (Kluegel, 1985) are key elements of the ideology of bounded racial change. This emergent understanding of race relations is not adopted in a consistent and uniform fashion by all whites. But to the extent that many accept this view and to the extent that it is perceived as the current trend in opinion, it influences and constrains public dialogue and mass opinion (Noelle-Neumann, 1974, 1984). This view, then, becomes a cultural force that needs to be understood in its own right (Prager, 1982). Indeed, such a nascent ideology has the potential to crystallize into a politically potent set of attitudes and beliefs.

Although this problem can be addressed by means of different research methods and the ideas advanced by any (or all) of the five approaches outlined above, this chapter focuses on two theories that have grown primarily out of the recent survey research literature and that have a fairly direct concern with the gap between principles and implementation: realistic group conflict and symbolic racism. (This focus restricts concern to the dynamics of public opinion on race, leaving interpersonal attitudes and behavior largely untouched.) The latter theory, based in a prejudice tradition, contends that whites' attitudes have perhaps become more sophisticated but still reflect a basic nonrational antipathy toward blacks. Thus, whites may respond positively to survey questions about general racial principles, but they allow the depth of their antiblack prejudice to emerge when asked about issues such as school busing. The group conflict theory, as developed here, contends that white support for the principle of racial justice is a real but limited commitment. The commitment is limited in that it often fails to be translated into support for concrete policy change insofar as blacks are perceived as significantly competing for the resources that whites possess and value. These types of theories are not mutually exclusive (Allport, 1954; Williams, 1965), nor do they exhaust the possible factors shaping contemporary racial attitudes. For these reasons, this chapter concludes with a brief discussion of integrating the group-conflict-versus-prejudice debate into a more complex framework that recognizes the several approaches outlined above. I now turn to a discussion of group conflict and ideological processes in racial attitudes.

Group Conflict and Racial Ideology

Definitions

Social or group conflict involves—in a paraphrase and modification of Coser (1956)—a struggle over values or claims to status, power, and other scarce resources in which the aims of the conflict groups are not only to gain the desired values, but also to affect, change, or injure rivals. The specific tactics employed can range from efforts at influence or persuasion, to the use of positive inducements, to forms of constraint or coercive action (Gamson, 1968). Recent racial conflict in the United States has involved litigation and the pursuit of legal redress, conventional political action (voting and lobbying), and unconventional political action, such as nonviolent protest and mass demonstrations, as well as urban rioting (Himes, 1966, p. 3). All of these tactics have been used, to varying degrees, in the pursuit of (or to prevent) social change; all involve efforts to alter the distribution of power, wealth, and status between social groups (McAdam, 1982, p. 26) or to prevent such change from occurring (Taylor, 1986).

Realistic conflicts derive from incompatible—though not necessarily irreconcilable—group interests. According to Fireman and Gamson (1979), a "group can be assumed to have an objective interest in a collective good to the extent that the good promotes the long-run wealth and power of the group and the viability of its design for living (whether or not these consequences are known to group members)" (p. 24). Or more broadly, a group's objective interests involve the "shared advantages or disadvantages likely to accrue to" a group and its members as a result of interaction with other groups (Tilly, 1978, p. 54). Group interests are based in social structural conditions—in particular, long-standing patterns of inequality of power, wealth, and status that establish opposing interests (Jackman & Jackman, 1983, p. 6).

Three clarifications need to be made. First, objective group interests do not invariably become subjectively perceived interests, but they do, in the long-run, "exert an important influence on subjective ones" (Fireman & Gamson, 1979, p. 24). This point is especially pertinent to a discussion of intergroup ideologies where a more powerful or dominant group may promote ideas and interpretations that obscure a subordinate group's realization of its interests. Second, it is important to distinguish between personal interests and group interests. Outcomes that benefit (or injure) an individual may not benefit (or injure) a group and its position. But more important, part of what separates theories of social conflict from simple utilitarian logic is a concern with the solidary ties that exist among people with a shared group identity (Fireman & Gamson, 1979). Third, group interests have consequences for individuals. Insofar as individuals are socialized to identify with particular groups and their values, the group and its social position become part of the individual's social identity. More specifically, group members may develop a sense of investment in, or a felt need to challenge, some pattern of structural inequality on the basis of their group membership (Blumer, 1958a; Bobo, 1983; Tajfel & Turner, 1979; Wellman, 1977; Wilson, 1973).

In addition, realistic group conflict is distinguished from "nonrealistic" conflict in that it is directed toward achieving some group-interested outcome (Coser, 1956, pp. 48–55). It is goal-oriented, whereas nonrealistic conflict involves a nonspecific release of hostility or aggressive psychological impulses. Where dispute is focused on a delimited issue or set of issues concerned with the distribution of power, wealth, or status between social groups, and involves clearly defined groups with differing objectives, there is realistic conflict. Disputes lacking these features, especially those lacking a concern with the rival objectives of the conflict groups, are nonrealistic. Although cognitive processes and intergroup affective orientations enter into both types of conflict, nonrealistic conflict is largely reducible to nonrational psychological impulses.

The Current Social Context

Other than the fact of observable differences in skin color and the historically important identities of black and white Americans, the pivotal features of race relations in the United States are extensive residential segregation of the races, economic inequality, and inequality in political power. Although there has been real progress in each domain, most blacks still confront different chances in life than those that await most whites.

With respect to residential segregation, in 1965 the Taeubers documented extensive separation of blacks and whites. They concluded that, regardless of region, city size, economic base, local laws, and the extent of other forms of discrimination, there was "a very high degree of segregation of the residences of whites and Negroes" (Taeuber & Taeuber, 1965, p. 35). Van Valey, Roof, and Wilcox (1977) concluded that, between 1960 and 1970, the level of residential segregation by race had changed very little. Farley (1977) demonstrated that racial segregation was not only more extensive in absolute terms than the segregation of social classes, but that it occurred regardless of social class. For example, his analysis of 1970 Census data indicated that "whites who have more than a college education are more residentially segregated from similarly well educated blacks than they are from whites who have never completed a year of school" (p. 514). Although there is some evidence of increasing black suburbanization (Frey, 1985), a recent analysis of 1980 Census data indicated some, but far from striking, progress in reducing the overall residential segregation of blacks and whites in the nation's larger cities (Taueber, 1983a,b).

It should be noted that such segregation is inconsistent with the expressed desires of many blacks. As Farley et al. (1978) reported in their study of Detroit area residents that most blacks prefer to live in neighborhoods integrated 50–50. What is more, most whites have no absolute objection to residential integration (Farley et al., 1978; Schuman et al., 1985). Many whites do, however, express little enthusiasm for neighborhoods with substantial numbers of blacks. Farley and colleagues (1978, p. 335) found that, as the number of blacks mentioned in an integrated neighborhood setting neared one-third, 57% of the whites interviewed said they would feel uncomfortable, 41% said they would probably try to move out of such a neighborhood, and fully 73% said they would not consider moving into such a neighborhood. In addition, Schuman et al. (1985) reported that, when questions about possible degrees of neighborhood integration mentioned large numbers of blacks, education ceased to have a positive effect on such attitudes (see also Jackman & Muha, 1984; Smith, 1981). In sum, not only are blacks and whites separated as a matter of fact, but many whites prefer to live in neighborhoods that are clearly white in character.

One major consequence of residential segregation is the segregation of schools. Despite years of litigation, increasingly forceful court mandates, and heated debates, the public schools are still largely segregated. In 1974, more than 40% of black students attended schools with 90% or more minority enrollment (Orfield, 1978, p. 57). Segregation is especially clear-cut in large northern metropolitan areas. In the city of Los Angeles, for example, figures for 1974–1975 revealed that more than 60% of black students attended schools with 99%–100% minority enrollment (Orfield, 1978, p. 182). Although the mandate of the *Brown* decision has been considerably fulfilled in rural southern areas (Farley, 1984; Rodgers, 1975), the decision has had much less impact on the nation's larger cities. The level of school segregation may, in fact, be worsening because of white enrollment losses, court rulings disallowing "metropolitan plans" that consolidate city and suburban school districts, and the apparent effective end of pressure under the Reagan administration to use busing as a remedy for school segregation. Indeed, one recent investigation concluded that, after noteworthy progress in reducing isolation in the schools between 1968 and 1976, "Overall, segregation slightly increased between 1976 and 1980" (Hochschild, 1984, p. 31).

Blacks also lag behind whites economically. Even though substantial progress has been made, blacks still have lower levels of earnings, yearly income, and occupational attainment than whites (Farley, 1984). The level of unemployment among black adult males is roughly twice that among comparable whites and has been so for more than 30 years (Bonacich, 1976; Farley, 1984). Moreover, the percentage of blacks who have dropped out of the labor force entirely has risen to 13%, more than two and one-half times the rate (5%) among whites (Farley, 1984). Blacks are three times more likely than whites to have incomes below the poverty level (Farley, 1984), and roughly half of all black children can expect to spend some time below the poverty level (U.S. Bureau of the Census, 1983). There are indicators of vulnerable progress in other areas as well. Some reports suggest that the percentage of blacks entering college (*Wall Street Journal*, May 29, 1985, pp. 1, 24) and going on to graduate and professional schools (Berry, 1983) has begun to decline.

Even in the absence of direct personal experience with these problems, there is evidence suggesting that many whites have some awareness of black disadvantage. Survey data indicate that many whites acknowledge at least some degree of racial inequality and acknowledge the effects of past discrimination on blacks (Apostle et al., 1983; Kluegel & Smith, 1982; Lipset & Schneider, 1978). Because inequality may be explained in many different ways (Apostle et al., 1983), because the extent of the inequality may be misjudged (Robinson, 1983), and because the extent of ameliorative efforts may be exaggerated (Kluegel & Smith, 1982), white awareness of inequality and discrimination does not directly result in support for efforts to achieve equality.

Segregation and economic inequality notwithstanding, the basic rights of blacks as citizens have been given greater strength and efficacy by court rulings, by the actions of several presidents and the administrative agencies under their control, and by congressional enactment. As Wilson (1980) has pointed out, "Instead of reinforcing racial barriers created during the pre-industrial and industrial periods, the political system in recent years has tended to promote racial equality" (p. 17). In addition, organizations like the National Association for the Advancement of Colored People, the National Urban League, and the Leadership Conference on Civil Rights act as vigorous watchdogs. Such groups regularly press for the full implementation of civil rights policies and actively respond to efforts to weaken or reverse such policies. Two indicators of the continuing influence of these and similar organizations can be found in the recent strengthening and 25-year extension of the Voting Rights Act and, at a more symbolic level, in the establishment of a national holiday honoring the birthday of Martin Luther King, Jr.

blacks remain, however, a numerical minority in a democratic political system. According to figures compiled by the Joint Center for Political Studies, blacks still hold less than 2% of all elective offices (*Washington Post*, June 9, 1985, p. A5).

Thus, the ballot box and conventional politics generally have not always been the most effective means for blacks to achieve their political ends. Political gains have frequently required protest or "insurgent politics" (Eisinger, 1974; Lipsky, 1968; McAdam, 1983; Morris, 1984). Indeed, civil rights came to be viewed as the nation's most important problem during the height of nonviolent black protest and mass demonstration, roughly 1963 to 1965 (Smith, 1980), and for the entire decade from 1960 to 1970 concern about race issues ranked second in public concern and media coverage, following concern about the war in Vietnam (Funkhouser, 1973). Moreover, the passage of key legislation (the Civil Rights Act of 1964 and the Voting Rights Act of 1965) was closely linked to major protest efforts and the sense of crisis and urgency they created (Brauer, 1977; Burstein, 1979; Garrow, 1978; Lawson, 1976; McAdam, 1983; Zashin, 1978). In sum, many of the crucial gains that blacks have made came through the establishment of effective political networks and organizations of their own (Morris, 1984) and through protest politics. The historical record of black recourse to insurgent politics is underscored by blacks' tendency to feel alienated from white society (Schuman & Hatchett, 1974; Turner & Wilson, 1976), to express fairly high levels of power discontent and group consciousness (Gurin, Miller, & Gurin, 1980; Pitts, 1974; Shingles, 1980), and to endorse protest and demonstration as legitimate political tools (Bobo, 1985; Eisinger, 1974; Isaac, Mutran, & Stryker, 1980; Robinson, 1970).

One of the important changes that laid the cultural groundwork for the civil rights struggle of the 1950s and 1960s was the discrediting of theories of biological racism. A general shift away from notions of distinct "races" and theories of "social Darwinism" began in the 1920s (Gossett, 1963; Sitkoff, 1978). This trend accelerated in the 1930s and 1940s in response to Nazi Germany's racism. These changes in ideas were readily applied to the "Negro problem" in the United States (Sitkoff, 1978, p. 190). One of the clearest examples of the ultimate impact of this changing cultural attitude toward "prejudice" is the often hotly debated Footnote 11 to the *Brown* decision which cites the Clarks' doll selection studies (1947) and Myrdal's *An American Dilemma* (1944) as substantiation of the fact that discrimination and prejudice had damaged black children (Wilkinson, 1979).

Not only did academe turn against notions of biological racism, but much of the propaganda in the United States during World War II portrayed racism as inherently antidemocratic. As Woodward (1974) noted, "American war propaganda stressed above all else the abhorrence of the West for Hitler's brand of racism and its utter incompatibility with the democratic faith for which we fought" (p. 131). This ideological struggle bore clear relevance to the place of blacks at that time and became an important basis for appeals to end segregation (Woodward, 1974, pp. 130–134).

Any complete explanation of racial attitudes must attend to this backdrop of real social inequalities between the races, the presence of black political organization and activism, the existence of protective legislation, the disrepute accorded notions of biological racism, and the rhetoric of American democracy. The first of these considerations means that whites, on average, have a real stake in maintaining race relations as they are and no benefits to gain by implementing equal opportunity policies. Therefore, they remain ahead by resisting further change. The four latter considerations set limitations on the ways in which inequality can be culturally justified or defended. A belief system that tends to espouse only constrained or "bounded" racial change has resulted. In addition to racial prejudice, it is argued here that this set of beliefs reflects the operation of several specific group-conflict motives as well as a larger ideological process. In general, it is the expectation of group conflict theory that whites, as members of a dominant group, will tend to develop and adopt attitudes and beliefs that defend their privileged, hegemonic social position. Such an ideology, however, emerges and functions within the limitations set by the current social structure and cultural milieu.

Group Conflict Motives and Racial Attitudes

Group conflict is not an inevitable outcome of structural inequality. For this reason, study of the social-psychological processes through which conflict emerges is needed. In particular, empirical study of the role of group conflict in racial attitudes and ideology requires a specification of the attitudinal forms that group conflict motives assume.

Previous research has taken a variety of approaches. Sherif (1966) examined the effects of a competitive situation on perceptual processes and in-group cohesion and explored the effects of superordinate goals on the reduction of intergroup tensions. More recently, Tajfel and Turner (1979) provided an empirically grounded theoretical statement on the role of group identity and social comparison processes in group conflict. Yet, Blumer's observation (1958a) that racial attitudes involve a sense of group position provides the most direct starting point for the present argument. Blumer suggested that racial attitudes consist of a feeling of in-group superiority, a sense of a proprietary claim to certain resources, and a sense that the out-group poses a threat to the position of the in-group. Each of these attitudes is a social product, and taken together, they constitute a sense of group position.

A handful of empirical work has sought to document the effects of the sense of group position on racial attitudes. Drawing on in-depth interviews with several prototypical respondents from a survey of San Francisco Bay area residents, Wellman (1977) found that whites frequently objected to large-scale racial change. These objections, he concluded, were not grounded in a form of prejudice but appeared to serve as a defense of group privilege. Smith's analysis (1981) of national survey data for the period 1954–1978 showed that whites' willingness to send their children to integrated schools varied substantially with the number of blacks involved. He found that "whites of all regional, cohort, and educational attainment groups share a common self-interest in their unwillingness to accept minority dominance" (p. 569). Bobo's reanalysis (1983) of data used in two papers on symbolic racism showed that attitudes toward the black political movement were important determinants of whites' position on school busing. These effects were interpreted as evidence of group conflict because attitudes toward black activists involved a sense of political threat. Relatedly, Giles and Evans (1984) also treated attitudes toward the black political movement as a form of perceived racial threat. They cautioned, however, that such questions do not bear a simple relation to objective status characteristics. Other research points to an increasing element of status threat in white racial attitudes, especially among otherwise liberal whites (Caditz, 1976). There is also research indicating that economically vulnerable whites respond more negatively to black protest (Ransford, 1972), as well as to other racial attitude questions (Cummings, 1980), than do whites of higher economic status.

These investigations have not, however, aimed to provide a general definition of group conflict attitudes or to elaborate on the various forms that such attitudes may take. Toward this end, it is suggested that group conflict motives are attitudes directly concerned with the competitive aspects of group relations and attempts to alter those relations. They concern the distribution of scarce values and resources between social groups, as well as attempts to affect the process and pattern of their distribution. More specifically, three types of attitudes reflect group conflict motives: perceptions of incompatible group interests, perceptions and evaluations of relative group standing (fraternal deprivation), and perceived threats or challenges to group interests. Each type of attitude invokes a sense of in-group position vis-à-vis an out-group, and yet, these attitudes are not primarily expressions of intergroup affective orientations or trait beliefs about an out-group (stereotypes).

To elaborate, perceptions of incompatible group interests concern the extent to which groups are perceived as having conflicting interests and objectives. In addition, they concern beliefs about the group benefits (and consequences) of proposals for change. Very general questions of this type might take the following form: "As blacks move ahead economically, more and more whites fall behind." Kluegel and Smith (1983) provided evidence that a question concerning the zero-sum structure of economic opportunities is related to white attitudes toward affirmative action. More specific questions could concern the differing political objectives of blacks and whites, or beliefs about who is helped or hurt by policies like school busing or affirmative action.

Fraternal deprivation involves a sense that one's membership group is at a disadvantage with respect to a particular out-group (Runciman, 1966; Vanneman & Pettigrew, 1972; Williams, 1975). As treated here and elsewhere (Sears & Kinder 1985), this type of attitude involves a direct expression of satisfaction or dissatisfaction with the position of the in-group along some dimension (power, wealth, or status) relative to an out-group. This sort of attitudinal expression has also been termed a *group grievance* (Isaac et al., 1980; Useem, 1980, 1981) and a *form of power discontent* (Aberbach, 1977; Gurin et al., 1980). Considerable evidence suggests that such group-level discontents played an important role in the black urban unrest of the late 1960s (Abeles, 1976; Caplan & Paige, 1972), as well as in reactions to other social movements (Guimond & Dube-Simard, 1983), and in white voting for black candidates for political office (Vanneman & Pettigrew, 1972).

Perceptions of incompatible group interests and fraternal deprivation are attitudes focused on the structure of group relations; that is, they concern the conditions and characteristic features of group relations. Perceived threat, in contrast, concerns reactions to the primary sources or agents of pressure for social change. Attempts to alter the structural relations between groups may come from the actions of specific individuals or groups, or from broad and diverse social movements. To the degree that a social movement commands widespread, sustained media coverage, elite attention, and public salience, the response of the mass public becomes an indicator of perceived threat.

For example, blacks or Jews could be asked about their reactions to groups like the Ku Klux Klan or neo-Nazi organizations. Or to take a less extreme case, respondents could be asked to evaluate groups like ROAR or BUSTOP (antibusing groups that formed in Boston and Los Angeles, respectively). Importantly, there should be a group basis to such evaluations. As some have suggested, "The experience of threat is not entirely an individual matter. The self-conception is made up of group memberships, and the individual is threatened whenever an important membership group seems to be the object of threat" (Turner, 1969, p. 821). Groups or social movements seeking social change can be attitude objects. Indeed, social protest has been conceptualized as a communicative process that aims, among other things, not only to affect specific targets but to address and influence the larger bystander public (Lipsky, 1968; Turner, 1969). Insofar as the groups are real and seek concrete objectives, for some they may represent a voice for desired ends, whereas for others they constitute a threat to important values and interests. The extent to which reactions to such movements are realistic then becomes an empirical question.

Research on political tolerance has addressed

this point. Sullivan, Pierson, and Marcus (1982) found that blacks and Jews (and other liberal whites) tended to feel threatened by right-wing extremist groups such as the KKK, whereas more conservative whites tended to feel threatened by left-wing groups. Interestingly, Sullivan et al. found little differences between the correlates of perceived threat among blacks and Jews as compared to other whites, even though the two former groups presumably confronted more real-world external threats. The data do not rule out a purely psychological basis for feelings of threat; indeed, some of the open-ended comments reflect simple prejudice (Sullivan et al., 1982, pp. 165–175), but it appears that, on the whole, people are capable of realistically assessing threats to what they take as their values and interests. Shamir and Sullivan (1983) provided cross-national data (for the United States and Israel) that also indicate that expressions of perceived threat are based more in real-world politics than in psychological insecurity or projection.

Research by Bobo (1985) is more directly concerned with threat in the racial context. Using national survey data, he examined changes between 1964 and 1980 in the attitudes of blacks and whites toward the black political movement and the correlates of such attitudes. The trend analysis indicated significant differences between blacks and whites in patterns of change over time. Although both groups appeared to respond to the ebb and flow of actual black-protest activity, the trajectory of change suggested important group-interested differences. White attitudes moved from a clear rejection of black activism during the tumultuous 1960s to a more moderate stance by the late 1970s. For example, 51% of whites in 1980 said that blacks were pushing for change at "about the right speed," an increase of 26% from 1968. Fully 63% of blacks interviewed in 1964 felt civil rights leaders were pushing "at about the right speed." That figure had dropped to 49% by 1980, as more and more blacks expressed the feeling that things were moving "too slowly." In addition, the degree of

racial polarization on this item was quite striking. For example, in 1964, 74% of whites said blacks were moving "too fast," compared to only 9% of blacks, a difference of 65 percentage points. The trend analysis was supplemented with data on the correlates of a measure of perceived threat. Bobo found that general (nonracial) beliefs about social protest, along with indicators of the perceived incompatibility of group interests and fraternal deprivation, were strong predictors of the level of perceived threat. Indeed, these effects were substantially independent of intergroup affective orientations, political conservatism, and other background-control variables. The full set of results suggests that, to a considerable degree, attitudes toward the black political movement index concern with a real-world social-protest movement that attempted to affect the distribution of rights and resources between blacks and whites.

There is an implicit structure to the group conflict motives described above. This structure is depicted in Figure 19.1. As the model indicates, perceptions of the general structure of group relations (perceptions of incompatible group interests) precede a sense of fraternal deprivation. The latter, in turn, is related to the level of perceived threat. Perceived threat, among the group conflict motives, should be the most direct determinant of racial policy attitudes (attitudes toward policies like affirmative action or school busing). Indeed, Bobo (1985) found that, among the three types of group conflict motives, only perceived threat had a direct effect on attitudes toward government intervention on behalf of black interests. There should, however, be important feedback dynamics. Insofar as increased external threat serves to increase perceived threat, the latter should enhance feelings of fraternal deprivation, which, in turn, should exacerbate the perception that groups have incompatible group interests. This is not to argue that conflict invariably breeds greater conflict. Open dispute can activate a number of processes that facilitate negotiation and compromise (Williams, 1965, 1977).

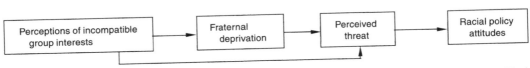

FIGURE 19.1 ■ Heuristic model of the structure of group conflict attitudes and their relation to racial policy attitudes.

Conflict and Positive Change

Open conflict and dispute can effectively dramatize a groups' grievances (see Morris, 1984, pp. 268–269, for a striking example). Himes (1966) argued that racial conflict can lead to greater recognition and more meaningful consideration of racial problems. Indeed, as Turner (1969) argued, without some form of protest or threat to the status quo, the grievances of a minority group might go unnoticed. Challenge and conflict can also create a bargaining atmosphere and can foster greater mutual respect among antagonists (Killian & Grigg, 1971).

With respect to attitudes and attitude change, Riley and Pettigrew (1976) found that dramatic political events led to a positive change in racial attitudes. They reported data on the attitudes of white Texans before and after Eisenhower's decision to send troops into Little Rock, Arkansas, in 1957. They also had data collected shortly before and after the assasination of Martin Luther King, Jr. Despite some countervailing movement among those with initially negative attitudes, both occurrences produced overall positive shifts on pertinent racial attitudes. In the case of the attitudinal impact of the assassination of Dr. King, Riley and Pettigrew were able to rule out the possibility of simply having captured a preexisting trend by comparing two preoccurrence surveys, separated by several months, that showed no change. Crain and Mahard (1982) found that open dispute and conflict preceding the implementation of school desegregation not only fostered more positive attitudes among black students, but generally improved the school racial climate. In terms of national survey data, Schuman et al. (1985) reported that change in the attitudes of individuals (as opposed to change resulting from cohort replacement) toward greater support of racial principles was more characteristic of the turbulent 1960s than of the quiescent 1970s.

Ideological Hegemony and Racial Attitudes

The ideas and research summarized above not only suggest ways in which group conflict enters into racial attitudes but also suggest that racial attitudes may serve ideological purposes. Recent sociological theories of ideology have made use of Gramsci's concept of ideological hegemony (Gitlin, 1980; Gramsci, 1971; Williams, 1973). Ideological hegemony is said to exist when the ideas of one group dominate or exert a predominant influence on the major cultural and social institutions (Fermia, 1975, p. 29; Williams, 1960, p. 587). These ideas explain social reality—in particular, inequalities between social groups—in a manner that defends and justifies such inequalities. A dominant group is truly hegemonic when people of all stations in life, dominant and subordinate, accept the vision of society as espoused by the dominant group. In this respect, Gramsci's notion of hegemony corresponds to Marx's dictum (1964) that "the ideas of the ruling class are, in every age, the ruling ideas" (p. 78). Gramsci, however, added an element of exchange and indeterminancy that elevates the role played by human subjectivity. For Gramsci, the economic base of society creates rough boundaries on ideas but does not predetermine or directly create ideological belief systems (the "superstructure").

In fact, Gramsci held that there may exist contradictory elements within an ideological belief system and that such contradictions often reflect the differing interests of social groups (Fermia, 1975, p. 37). Similarly, Jackman and Senter's work (1983) on group images in the race, gender, and class contexts emphasized that social groups are engaged in a process of exchanging ideas and interpretations. They are involved in efforts, within the existing social and cultural institutions, to influence and control one another.

On the basis of these observations, the present argument maintains that dominant group attitudes and beliefs involve a strain toward, or a pursuit of, hegemony. A dominant group seeks to articulate a set of beliefs that persuades themselves, as well as others, that their privileged status is for the general good. Within the context of racial relations, this tendency is aptly characterized as the pursuit of racial hegemony.

This ideological process is the product of the confluence of social structural conditions (inequality and segregation) and the effects of long-standing group identities; that is, the ideological element in racial attitudes is a product of the interaction of inequality and ethnocentrism. As used here, the term *ethnocentrism* refers to a sense of positive ingroup distinctiveness and commitment (Van den Berghe, 1967; Williams, Dean, &

Schuman, 1964) not emotional hostility toward an out-group. Together, these factors establish a set of group interests and motivate a particular direction for attitudes, beliefs, and interpretations.

Although dominant groups do attempt to propagate ideas that secure and advance their interests, such ideas seldom reign without some challenge from subordinates, difficulties introduced by unanticipated political or economic exigencies, or the influence of other internalized attitudes and values that might weaken or contradict the ideological commitment of dominant group members. As concerns an analysis of changing racial belief systems in the United States, blacks mounted a strong political challenge to their subordination in the 1950s and 1960s based on a direct appeal to the general values—what Myrdal (1944) termed the "democratic creed"—of the dominant group. They were facilitated in this effort by a number of changing conditions. A massive migration of blacks from the rural South to the North (Farley, 1968) enhanced their political influence (Lawson, 1976; Myrdal, 1944; Sitkoff, 1971, 1978) and increased their economic and social freedom. Also, by this time, many of the ideas used to justify black subordination were clearly on the defensive in academe and in the rhetoric of many prominent political figures. A unanimous U.S. Supreme Court authoritatively repudiated racial segregation. For a period of time, especially during the middle through the late 1960s, an era that some have characterized as a Second Reconstruction, the courts, Congress, and the executive branch appeared to be engaged in a coordinated effort to secure and protect the rights of blacks (Brauer, 1977). The high degree of unanimity at the level of national leadership provided legitimation for many of the changes blacks were demanding. As a practical political matter, moreover, many of the changes initially demanded by blacks had their focus on *de jure* segregation and discrimination in the South (Woodward, 1974; Zashin, 1978). The combination of these occurrences resulted in considerable external pressure, both political and cultural, and internal value-based pressure to support the ideals of racial equality and integration (see Katz, 1967, for a similar point).

At the same time, there was initially little reason for northern whites to believe that adherence to these principles would require any changes in their own position in society or that of their children. But as the issues shifted from largely southern problems of state-imposed segregation and voting hindrances, to economic and other redistributive issues of national scope (e.g., school busing, affirmative action, and the economic decline of urban areas), many whites no doubt came to sense a greater threat to their position in life. This sense of threat was probably amplified by the use of political slogans like Black Power (Aberbach & Walker, 1970) and the urban unrest of the late 1960s (Ashmore & Del Boca, 1976). Group conflict and ideological processes have thus contributed to the gap between support for racial principles and support for full implementation of such principles, that is, to the development of an ideology of bounded racial change.

The general process is summarized in Figure 19.2. To recapitulate, conditions of inequality and ethnocentrism establish conflicting group interests, which, in turn, translate into interpretive tendencies on the part of dominant and subordinate group members. These interpretive tendencies favor group interests. But as Figure 19.2 makes clear, the final outcome, the prevailing state of intergroup attitudes and beliefs, is influenced by exchanges between dominant and subordinate groups, by relevant cultural values and beliefs (e.g., equality and fairness), and by other aspects of the patterning of group relations (e.g., the extent and type of the contact between the group members, the past history of competition and conflict, and the clarity of group boundaries).

Progress and Resistance Revisited

At many points in U.S. racial history, those advocating more progressive racial attitudes did not necessarily express an overarching commitment to full racial equality (Turner & Singleton, 1978). For instance, many early opponents of slavery opposed it as a moral evil. All the same, they shared with their slave-owning contemporaries a belief that blacks and whites could not exist as equals in the same society. These people tended to become active participants in colonization movements (i.e., efforts to find a new homeland for blacks; see Fredrickson, 1971a). Similarly, there were liberal as well as conservative politicians in the South after the fall of Reconstruction who were not rabid "Negrophobes," but who nonetheless were committed to preserving white hegemony (Woodward,

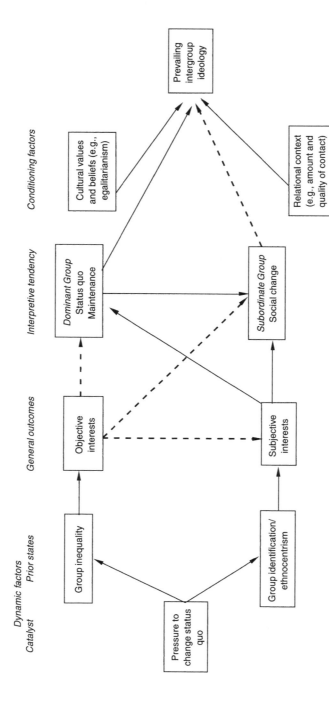

FIGURE 19.2 ■ Schematic representation of the ideological hegemony process.
――――― = Influences; – – – – = Strong Influences.

1974). Only the radical populists proposed anything near coequal partnership with blacks as part of their efforts to coalese the poor masses. Indeed, as Woodward (1974) suggested, the threat posed to economically and politically powerful whites by this potential coalition was a critical factor in the rise of Jim Crow laws and practices.

Two historically important examples of the admixture of positive and negative racial beliefs are to be found in the beliefs of Thomas Jefferson and Abraham Lincoln. Jefferson's writings indicate that he believed black enslavement to be at odds with the U.S. Constitution; yet, he personally owned many slaves. In a letter to a friend, Jefferson spoke about his own attitudes toward slavery: "You know that nobody wishes more ardently to see an abolition not only of the [African slave] trade but of the condition of slavery; and certainly nobody will be more willing to encounter every sacrifice for that object" (Takaki, 1979, p. 43). Although recognizing the contradiction and agonizing over it, Jefferson kept most of his slaves. In addition, there is evidence suggesting that he treated his slaves brutally (Takaki, 1979, p. 44), and Jefferson was perhaps the first American to venture the speculation that blacks were inherently less intelligent than whites (Jefferson, 1972; see also Takaki, 1979, pp. 47–50). As Fredrickson (1975) noted, Lincoln also held complex, contradictory views on race. He had been one of the strong advocates of colonization as a way to solve the race problem; in general, he felt that whites and blacks could not exist as civil equals in the same country. The motives of both men appear to have come from a combination of prejudice—in particular, a distaste for the mixing of black and white races—and an ideological commitment to the white control of major social and political institutions (Fredrickson, 1975; Takaki, 1979).

The acceptance of some progressive racial ideals—in the above examples, an objection to black slavery—did not guarantee a deep commitment to a racially equal and fully integrated society. In the past, such disjunctures or contradictions in belief have involved both prejudice and group-interested ideology. It seems likely that the inchoate ideology of bounded racial change evident in contemporary racial attitudes also involves such a combination of motives.

Prejudice and Racial Attitudes

Definitions

Prejudice is a term that is often used synonymously with simple "bias" (see the discussion in Ehrlich, 1973). But it is also invoked as a motive force in explaining such occurrences as the rise of black slavery in the United States (Degler, 1959; Jordan, 1968). In its more formal social-psychological use, prejudice has generally been "thought of as irrationally based, negative attitudes against certain ethnic groups and their members" (Pettigrew, 1982, p. 28). Or as others have put it, prejudice is "an emotional, rigid attitude . . . toward a group of people" (Simpson & Yinger, 1972, p. 24). Prejudice, then, is an emotional antipathy based on an inaccurate and rigidly held stereotype (see Allport, 1954, pp. 6–10).

Recent research has treated stereotyping as a cognitive process separable from affective orientations toward an out-group (see Ashmore & Del Boca, 1981; Brewer & Kramer, 1985; Miller, 1982). There is considerable evidence suggesting not only that stereotypes, or some simplified cognitive structure that aids information processing, are necessary, but that stereotypes can be fruitfully studied without a concern with prejudice (see essays in Hamilton, 1981). Yet, an affective orientation toward a group is to be regarded as a prejudice only to the degree that it is based on an underlying inaccurate stereotype that resists modification (Allport, 1954; Seeman, 1981). There may, in fact, be real differences between groups that inform the images people hold of one another and the evaluations they make (Campbell, 1967). For that reason, affective hostility alone, in the absence of an exaggerated or *faulty* stereotype, may not be a form of prejudice.

Symbolic Racism

A theory of prejudice labeled *symbolic racism* has been applied to the gap between principles and implementation. The theory and concept have been defined and elaborated upon on several occasions, and some important differences have emerged among its various advocates (compare Kinder & Sears, 1981, to McConahay, Hardee, & Batts,

1981). One central definition was provided by Kinder and Sears. (1981), who argued that symbolic racism involves

> a blend of antiblack affect and the kind of traditional American moral values embodied in the Protestant Ethic. Symbolic racism represents a form of resistance to change in the racial status quo based on moral feelings that blacks violate such traditional American values as individualism and self-reliance, the work ethic, obedience, and discipline. (p. 416)

It is argued that socialization to negative feelings toward blacks merges with other basic values to form psychological resistance to contemporary proposals beneficial to blacks as a group. Thus, the gap between principles and implementation is evidence of, or an aspect of, the emergence of a new form of prejudice. Older forms of antiblack sentiment (segregationist attitudes and beliefs) are being replaced by a new symbolic racism (opposition to school busing). The symbolic racism researchers assert that the amalgam of antiblack affect and traditional values is a new form of prejudice best understood from the perspective of a new "sociocultural theory" of prejudice. There are several reasons to question this account of the gap between principles and implementation and, more specifically, to note that, in a number of critical features, symbolic racism does not depart from more traditional conceptions of prejudice.

First, symbolic racism is a theory of prejudice (see also Brewer & Kramer, 1985). The proponents of the concept do not venture to explicitly differentiate the concept and/or theory of symbolic racism from the notion of prejudice as traditionally defined. Instead, it is argued that symbolic racism cannot be indexed by "old-fashioned" or passé racial beliefs (Kinder & Sears 1981; McConahay et al., 1981). The main point of differentiation from prejudice, then, is at the level of measurement, not at the level of theoretical development. In addition, the symbolic racism researchers also make frequent use of the terms *prejudice* and *intolerance*. Kinder and Sears (1981, p. 416) explicitly argued that symbolic racism is a variant of prejudice. McConahay et al. (1981, p. 577) contended that their "modern" or symbolic racism scale definitely measured an aspect of prejudice.

The main interpretive frame of the symbolic racism researchers also emphasizes the nonrational origins of opposition to implementing racial change. This is a distinctive feature of theories of prejudice (see Wellman, 1977, pp. 14–15). The main tests of symbolic racism have the aim of demonstrating two things: (a) that rational self-interest and group conflict do not influence attitudes toward school busing (McConahay, 1982; Sears, Hensler, & Speer, 1979; Sears, Lau, Tyler, & Allen, 1980) or voting against a black candidate for political office (Kinder & Sears, 1981); and (b) that some measure of racial attitudes and political conservatism does predict such attitudes.

As a result, it might be expected that the concept of symbolic racism would be operationalized with questions concerning clearly emotional and stereotyped orientations toward blacks. The general strategy, however, has been to rely on questions concerning a number of contemporary racial problems and disputes, especially attitudes toward black political activism and influence. From the present perspective, when attitude questions concerned with black protest and political influence are used to index symbolic racism, a theory of prejudice has incorporated elements of group conflict and group conflict motives (Bobo, 1983). Questions that explicitly invoke concern about real-world political actors and events, and that arguably tap a dominant groups' sense of political threat from a contentious subordinate group are being treated as indicators of prejudice.

Second, and more broadly, a strong case can be made that white racial attitudes have long involved some degree of less positive affect toward blacks than toward whites and a belief that blacks lack certain positively valued traits to be found in whites (e.g., industriousness, a capacity for hard work, and most of the qualities associated with the Protestant Ethic). Johnson (1949) pointed out that, after the Civil War, an ideology of laissez-faire individualism developed in the South as a way of justifying black subordination without the institution of slavery. These beliefs had clear origins in earlier proslavey doctrines. In particular, southern whites emphasized that blacks "would not work without compulsion" (Johnson, 1949, p. 130). This central claim had three subsidiary points:

> (1) The Negro needs the direction of the white man in order to be industrious and actually prefers it to supervision of another Negro; (2) without this supervision and compulsion the Negro

degenerates; and (3) the Negro is inherently *lazy, shiftless, and licentious.* (Johnson, 1949, p. 131; italics added).

Takaki (1970) noted that, during the 19th century, whites in the North and the South regarded blacks as lacking the Protestant qualities of hard work, obedience, and restraint that they (the whites) possessed. Whites in the nineteenth century viewed blacks, he argued, as a peculiar mixture of children, who needed paternal protection and guidance, and savages, who required constant monitoring because they might engage in violence, crime, or sexual debauchery. All in all, Takaki (1970) concluded:

> The image of the Negro served a need shared by whites, North and South; it performed an identity function for white Americans during a period when they were groping for self-definition. It is significant to note the way whites imagined the Negro in relation to themselves: the Negro was mentally inferior, naturally lazy, childlike, unwholesome, and given to vice. He was the antithesis of themselves and of what they valued: industriousness, intelligence, and moral restraint. (p. 42).

Takaki (1979) broadened and refined this point in his later work. There, he began with Gramsci's notion of hegemony and argued that whites have, since the American Revolution, striven to differentiate themselves from others. This differentiation has served to provide a source of identity and, crucially, played a part in the pursuit of various self- and group-interested ends (i.e., the taking of Indian lands, the enslavement of blacks, discrimination against Oriental laborers, and so on).

More concretely, the attitudes and beliefs of Thomas Jefferson provide a vivid example of how certain values became linked to a justification of white privilege. Jefferson argued that the United States should be a fundamentally new nation based on republican values. This ideology of republicanism held that the character and fate of a nation rest not so much on wealth and power, as was the case in Europe, as on the degree of value consensus and the public virtue of its citizenry. Virtue was a product of reason, self-reliance, industriousness, and moral restraint. These qualities, of course, were viewed as more characteristic of whites than of blacks (Takaki, 1979, p. 64). Although slavery,

with the enormous power it gave one person over the life of another, introduced temptations that might weaken adherence to these values, the gravest threat to republicanism came from the same forces that threatened the institution of slavery. For Jefferson, the increasing industrialization and commercialization of the North, along with the attendant pressures for a stronger federal government that would further facilitate these developments, would only undermine the Southern way of life and republican values. The pastoral character of the farm and the plantation were, in his view, most conducive to the maintenance of virtue. Thus, despite Jefferson's moral discomfort with slavery, many of his letters, speeches, and other writings would become a basis for certain secessionist, states' rights, and proslavery positions. Indeed, like many other Southern whites, according to historian Robert Shalhope (1976), "Jefferson clung to an ideology—to a way of life with identity and meaning in a changing world—which rested on slavery. The exploitation of the black was legitimized in terms of preserving higher values—a republican society" (p. 556).

Historians are not the only researchers to have pointed to whites' sense of themselves as a group endowed with valued traits that were absent or underdeveloped in blacks. A classic work in the empirical prejudice-stereotyping tradition (Katz & Braly, 1933) found laziness to be one of the primary traits attributed to blacks. Campbell (1967) noted that salient differences between groups, especially in highly valued traits (i.e., industriousness and moral restraint), are likely to be a central focus of group stereotypes. Additionally, concern with such perceived trait differences between groups continues to inform more contemporary research on group images (Jackman & Senter, 1983).

It is possible, however, that the distinguishing feature of contemporary prejudice, and hence of symbolic racism, is the concern with black "pushiness" expressed in white attitudes. This concern about the illegitimacy of blacks' demands may be what sets current prejudice apart from older manifestations of prejudice. Although the expressions of concern about black demands and their legitimacy are more widespread—perhaps for concrete historical reasons, namely, a nationally oriented civil rights movement covered by national news media—this type of racial attitude is by no means an entirely new occurrence (see Rudwick, 1967; Wilson, 1980). For example, Rudwick (1964) explained that, in the Chicago riot of 1919, the Detroit riot of 1943, and especially the East St. Louis riot of 1917,

> unskilled whites manifested tension after they considered their jobs threatened by Negroes. There was also concern because [recent black] migrants had overburdened the housing and transportation facilities. Everywhere, efforts of Negroes to improve their status were defined as arrogant assaults, and whites insisted on retaining competitive advantages enjoyed before the Negro migration. (p. 218)

The connection between the white public sentiment in these riot-torn cities of the early twentieth century and today's prevailing racial attitudes is the presence of some pressure or demand for change presented by blacks. The concern with black "pushiness," then, could plausibly be viewed as part of a dominant group's attempt to interpret subordinate group challenges as illegitimate, and yet to do so in a manner that offers an ostensibly principled defense of a privileged group position (Jackman & Muha, 1984).

The upshot of this is twofold. First, racial attitudes in the United States, at least for the past 150 years, have involved a blend of antiblack affect and traditional moral values. Indeed, theories of prejudice have been routinely concerned with intergroup affect and stereotyping, that is, with feelings and beliefs about the traits of group members. Second, the perception of some trait difference between blacks and whites can and has been used to rationalize a group advantage. As Jackman and Senter (1983) argued, perceived trait differences can serve the ideological needs of dominant groups.

Still, there remains the possibility that a substantial shift in the character of prejudice has taken place, thus creating a need for new measures of prejudice. The above comments suggest a different approach to explaining the changing content of racial attitudes. The major change between present-day attitudes and those characteristic of whites in the 19th century is that trait differences between blacks and whites are less likely to be viewed as inherent or of biological origin. As Schuman (1971) noted, "a considerable portion of the white urban population believes that the source

of Negro hardships lie within Negroes themselves, but denies that this source is inborn and unchangeable" (p. 386; see also Apostle et al., 1983). That is, the predominant interpretation holds that the problem is blacks' level of motivation and effort, not their genetic endowment.

Jackman and Senter (1983) added, on the basis of an analysis of national survey data on group images concerning the traits of intelligence, dependability, and laziness, that most whites do not posit the existence of large, categorical differences between themselves and blacks. Instead, they tend to express only small, qualified distinctions in those traits that favor whites. These small and qualified differences, however, are given a strong negative evaluation. This evaluative overlay is sufficient to justify a dominant group advantage. Jackman and Senter explained that "the perception of small but derogatory differences represents a hardening line of defense against challenge" (p. 332).

These sorts of changes—though certainly, in part, the result of prejudice, as the symbolic racism researchers have effectively argued—are also driven by alterations in the economic, political, and social context. The image of blacks as permanently and categorically inferior to whites has been shorn of its economic, political, and social underpinnings. blacks are no longer enslaved. Slave labor is not crucial to any aspect of the economy, and slavery is reviled throughout the world. blacks are no longer segregated and discriminated against under the majesty of law as was the case during the reign of Jim Crow; nor do they engage in the symbolically humbling behaviors (e.g., passivity and accommodation) required under Jim Crow. On the contrary, their legal right to full citizenship has been codified through legislation, legal interpretation, and the actions of administrative agencies. Moreover, blacks have more effective political power than they had in earlier periods. In view of these facts and the discrediting of notions of biological racism, it is understandably less common to find that the predominant mode of accounting for racial inequality involves genetic thinking and blatantly segregationist sentiments.

Insofar as important inequalities remain, it should be expected that new attitudes and beliefs, amenable to the current context, will begin to arise to explain and defend those inequalities. These new attitudes and beliefs emerge naturally from one group's "side" of social experience as they attempt to provide meaning and order in their lives. The bent of these emerging views will be such as to support a privileged group's hegemonic position. A key psychological basis for this tendency is the sense of group position. It has been suggested that the most persuasive argument for resistance to large-scale racial change in the present social context is an appeal to the value of individualism (Jackman & Muha, 1984). Policies that are premised on the recognition of group characteristics are resisted, ostensibly, because they violate the ideal of individualism.

At minimum, it seems unlikely that theories of prejudice alone can provide a full explanation of the contemporary paradox of racial attitudes. Indeed, the gap between principles and implementation suggests that racial attitudes have both positive and negative currents, a set of characteristics that on its face poses difficulties for a prejudice interpretation. The symbolic racism researchers have taken two slightly different positions on this problem. Kinder and Sears (1981) noted that "since the explicitly segregationist, white supremacist view has all but disappeared, it can no longer be a major political force" (p. 416). They asserted, however, that prejudice must still be operating, although in some new fashion. The task, then, is to conceptualize and measure the new manifestations of prejudice—hence, the notion of symbolic racism. As Kinder and Sears (1981) argued, "What has replaced [segregationist, white supremacist views], we suggest, is a new variant that might be called symbolic racism" (p. 416). From this point of view, support for racial principles is of little contemporary political consequence. McConahay et al. (1981) pressed this point further. They argued that whites can perceive the racist content of survey questions on racial principles and thus give the socially desirable response. New, modern racism items do not suffer from this contamination, McConahay et al. claimed, because people do not perceive the racist content of believing, for example, that blacks have too much political influence. In either treatment, the point is that prejudice has grown more sophisticated.

Although accurately describing an important change in the character of racial attitudes, both accounts are problematic. No sustained analysis of why this shift in attitudes has occurred is provided. If the root of the problem is a form of prejudice, then it is difficult to understand why there would be any pressure to change from segregationist attitudes to some newer, more relevant form of voicing an irrational hostility toward blacks. Furthermore, it is not entirely accurate to view segregationist beliefs and attitudes as merely a simpler, older form of prejudice (though many analysts have done so). The rise of white supremacist practices and ideology, especially the rise of segregation, although partially the result of prejudice, can also be traced to a combination of political exigencies (e.g., increased black voting and the Populist movement), cultural trends (e.g., social Darwinism), and the active protection of group interests (Cell, 1982; Fredrickson, 1971b; Woodward, 1974). According to Cell (1982), "Segregation is at the same time an interlocking system of economic institutions, social practices and customs, political power, law, and ideology, all of which function both as means and ends in one group's efforts to keep another (or others) in their place within a society that is actually becoming unified" (p. 14). Any new set of attitudes said to be derivative of segregationist attitudes may also reflect a group-interested ideology tailored to new circumstances. I suggest that a major contributor to the greater complexity of racial attitudes is the natural process of a dominant group's interpreting social events and proposals for change in a manner that allows the maintenance of its hegemony under very different structural (economic and political) and cultural conditions.

American historical experience and culture do make available, however, an unflattering image of blacks as lazy and dependent slaves, carefree minstrels, and potentially dangerous vagabonds. This image may even involve a deeply ingrained color complex that permeates Western society (Jordan, 1968). It must also be noted that this cultural baggage, though not as prominent or ubiquitous as it once was, is still dimly implicated in the racial attitudes of black and white Americans (Prager, 1982). In this more limited sense, the theory of symbolic racism rightly cautions us that prejudice has not vanished. Yet, the theory may exaggerate the importance of prejudice as such, especially insofar as attitudes toward black political activism are viewed as indicators of this concept.

If there had been no civil rights movement or urban riots, or if these events had gone without media coverage and sustained elite attention, then attitudes toward black activists and activism might well amount to an abstracted racial resentment. None of these conditions obtain. On the contrary, the mass media provided intensive coverage of black protest (Funkhouser, 1973; Garrow, 1978), the mass public developed fairly clear assessments of the aims of civil rights leaders (Sheatsley, 1966), and political leaders and institutions helped focus public attention on black grievances. Indeed, some have argued—and have provided data from national surveys that suggest—that the presidential elections of 1964 and 1968 served to make race one of the key features of conventional partisan political alignments and political thinking among the mass public (Carmines & Stimson, 1982). The designation of Martin Luther King's birthday as a national holiday has also served to embed more deeply in American culture an awareness of black protest as a vehicle for social change.

Empirical Assessments

The empirical research on symbolic racism has resulted in several consistent findings and contributions to our understanding of racial attitudes. First, indicators of objective, tangible personal threats from blacks (e.g., living in an area where a busing plan is being implemented) do not predict related racial-policy attitudes (Bobo, 1983; Sears, Hensler, & Speer, 1979, 1980) or a willingness to vote for black candidates for political office. Second, other types of racial attitudes, in particular those concerning contemporary race problems (e.g., welfare dependency and crime) and black political activism, are the strongest predictors of opposition to policies and candidates likely to improve the status of blacks relative to that of whites. In addition, neither the contemporary race problem nor the black political activism attitudes appear to be related to measures of tangible personal threat. Third, measures of political ideology (self-identification as a liberal or a conservative) are also important predictors of racial policy attitudes and a willingness to support black political candidates. Fourth, and more broadly, this line of speech has helped to focus attention on some real changes in the character of white racial attitudes.

These clear-cut findings and contributions do not, however, firmly substantiate the main theory. Early research on symbolic racism treated prejudice as a single unitary dimension (Sears, Hensler,

& Speer, 1979, 1980). Subsequent research has shown that racial attitudes have several reasonably distinct but correlated dimensions (Bobo, 1983). The most important of these dimensions for predicting school busing opposition is attitude toward black political activism.

This latter finding is congenial to a group conflict interpretation of racial attitudes once the conception of "interests" is broadened to include a sense of collective or group interest, with the latter indexed by measures of perceived threat. The symbolic racism researchers have typically conceptualized self-interest as a tangible personal risk. Yet, as others have noted (Bobo, 1983; Kluegel & Smith, 1983; Pettigrew, 1985), there are other viable conceptualizations of "interests" in an issue or outcome. The narrow definition preferred by the symbolic racism researchers is depoliticized and tends to overlook the potential for subjectively meaningful links between perceived collective and personal interests. Thus, the relationship between attitudes toward black political activism (perceived threat) and specific racial policy attitudes is plausibly interpreted as a manifestation of a group conflict. Indeed, research reviewed earlier—which showed substantial black–white polarization in attitudes toward the black political movement, racial differences in trends over time on such attitudes, and a clear relationship to other group-conflict and social-protest attitudes—argues in favor of a group conflict approach (Bobo, 1985).

Still, prejudice plays a role. In particular, there is evidence suggesting that "old-fashioned" prejudice retains contemporary political relevance. McClendon (1985) reported a connection between support for school busing and traditional segregationist attitudes net of the effect of modern racism. Jacobson (1985) found similar results for affirmative action attitudes. It is not the case, in sum, that prejudice needs new avenues of expression.

Conclusions

Recent research has rekindled a focused controversy over the relative importance of group conflict and prejudice in racial attitudes and relations. The case for either interpretation should not be pressed too far. Racial attitudes are complex, involving affective orientations, stereotypes, modes of explanation, group conflict motives, and several other types of attitudes, values, and concerns. This chapter has had the goal of clarifying the distinctive contribution of group conflict and group conflict motives while stressing that prejudice and group conflict approaches are not mutually exclusive. As others have noted, one process can readily feed into the other (Allport, 1954; Williams, 1965). For the present, if there is a general conclusion to be reached, it is that, alongside our traditional concern with individual prejudice, we should recognize the importance of group conflict. In short, racial attitudes can simultaneously involve group-interested ideology and irrational hostilities.

At the beginning of this chapter I suggested that a core problem touched on in a broad range of social-psychologically oriented research on race is the problem of resistance to more profound forms of racial change. A loosely coherent set of attitudes and beliefs that, among other things, attributes continuing patterns of black–white inequality to the dispositional shortcomings of blacks themselves and the otherwise fair operation of the economic and political system has developed and now characterizes much of the white population. I labeled this nascent set of beliefs an ideology of bounded racial change because although it involves support for the extension of basic citizenship rights to blacks the ideology also involves vigorous opposition to change that might impose substantial burdens on whites.

The growing complexity and subtlety of racial attitudes and beliefs, which the ideology of bounded racial change clearly reflects, derives from a social context still characterized by considerable black–white economic inequality, limited black political empowerment, extensive residential segregation by race, other historical trends, and the influence of enduring cultural values and beliefs. At the individual level, a number of social-psychological factors contribute to adherence to this ideology, especially a concern with group position that enters public opinion as perceptions of incompatible group interests, feelings of fraternal deprivation, and perceived threats posed by the black political actors who have pressured for social and political change.

REFERENCES

Abeles, R. P. (1976). Relative deprivation, rising expectations, and black militancy. *Journal of Social Issues, 32*, 119–137.

Aberbach, J. D. (1977). Power consciousness: A comparative analysis. *American Political Science Review, 71*, 1544–1560.

Aberbach, J. D., & Walker, J. L. (1970). The meanings of black power: A comparison of white and black interpretations of a political slogan. *American Political Science Review, 64*, 367–388.

Adorno, T. W., Frenkel-Brunswik, E., Levinson, D. J., & Sanford, R. N. (1950). *The authoritarian personality.* New York: W. W. Norton.

Allport, G. W. (1954). *The nature of prejudice.* Reading, MA: Addison-Wesley.

Allport, G. W. (1962). Prejudice: Is it societal or personal? *Journal of Social Issues, 18*, 120–134.

Apostle, R. A., Glock, C. Y., Piazza, T., & Suelzle, M. (1983). *The anatomy of racial attitudes.* Berkeley: University of California Press.

Ashmore, R. D., & Del Boca, F. K. (1976). Psychological approaches to understanding intergroup conflicts. In P. A. Katz (Ed.), *Towards the elimination of racism.* New York: Pergamon Press.

Ashmore, R. D. & Del Boca, F. K. (1981). Conceptual approaches to stereotypes and stereotyping. In D. L. Hamilton (Ed.), *Cognitive processes in stereotyping and intergroup behavior.* Hillsdale, NJ: Erlbaum.

Berry, M. F. (1983). Blacks in predominantly white institutions of higher learning. In J. D. Williams (Ed.), *The state of black America.* New York: National Urban League.

Blackwell, J. E. (1982). Persistence and change in intergroup relations: The crisis upon us. *Social Problems, 29*, 325–346.

Blumer, H. (1958a). Race prejudice as a sense of group position. *Pacific Sociological Review, 1*, 3–7.

Blumer, H. (1958b). Recent research on race relations: United States of America. *International Social Science Bulletin, 10*, 403–477.

Bobo, L. (1983). Whites' opposition to busing: Symbolic racism or realistic group conflict? *Journal of Personality and Social Psychology, 45*, 1196–1210.

Bobo, L. (1984). *Racial hegemony: Group conflict, prejudice, and the paradox of American racial attitudes.* Doctoral dissertation, University of Michigan, Ann Arbor.

Bobo, L. (1985, August). *Racial differences in response to the black political movement.* Paper presented at the 1985 Annual Meeting of the American Sociological Association, Washington, D.C.

Bonacich, E. (1976). Advanced capitalism and black/white relations in the United States. *American Sociological Review, 41*, 34–51.

Brauer, C. (1977). *John F. Kennedy and the Second Reconstruction.* New York: Columbia University Press.

Brewer, M. B., & Kramer, R. M. (1985). The psychology of intergroup attitudes and behavior. *Annual Review of Psychology, 36*, 219–243.

Burstein, P. (1979). Public opinion, demonstrations and the passage of antidiscrimination legislation. *Public Opinion Quarterly, 43*, 157–172.

Caditz, J. (1976). *White liberals in transition: Current dilemmas of ethnic integration.* New York: Spectrum Books.

Campbell, D. T. (1967). Stereotypes and the perception of group differences. *American Psychologist, 22*, 817–829.

Caplan, N., & Paige, J. M. (1971). A study of ghetto rioters.

Scientific American, 219, 15–21.

Carmines, E. G., & Stimson, J. A. (1982). Racial issues and the structure of mass belief systems. *Journal of Politics, 44,* 2–20.

Cell, J. W. (1982). *The highest stage of white supremacy: The origins of segregation in South Africa and the American South.* London: Cambridge University Press.

Clark, K. B. (1965). Problems of power and social change: Toward a relevant social psychology. *Journal of Social Issues, 21,* 4–20.

Clark, K. B., & Clark, M. (1947). Racial identification and preferences in Negro children. In T. M. Newcomb & E. L. Hartley (Eds.), *Readings in social psychology.* New York: Holt.

Coser, L. A. (1956). *The functions of social conflict.* New York: Free Press.

Crain, R. L., & Mahard, R. E. (1982). The consequences of controversy accompanying institutional change: The case of school desegregation. *American Sociological Review, 47,* 697–708.

Crosby, F., Bromely, S., & Saxe, L. (1980). Recent unobtrusive studies of black and white discrimination and prejudice: A literature review. *Psychological Bulletin, 87,* 546–563.

Cummings, S. (1980). White ethnics, racial prejudice, and labor market segmentation. *American Journal of Sociology, 85,* 938–958.

Degler, C. N. (1959). Slavery and the genesis of American race prejudice. *Comparative Studies in Society and History, 2,* 49–66.

Degler, C. N. (1960). Letters to the editor. *Comparative Studies in Society and History, 2,* 491–495.

Donnerstein, E., & Donnerstein, M. (1976). Research in the control of interracial aggression. In R. Green & E. O'Neal (Eds.), *Perspectives on aggression.* New York: Academic Press.

Ehrlich, H. J. (1973). *The social psychology of prejudice.* New York: Wiley.

Eisinger, P. K. (1974). Racial differences in protest participation. *American Political Science Review, 68,* 592–606.

Farley, R. (1968). The urbanization of Negroes in the United States. *Journal of Social History, 1,* 241–258.

Farley, R. (1977). Residential segregation in urbanized areas of the United States in 1970: An analysis of social class and racial differences. *Demography, 14,* 497–518.

Farley, R. (1984). *Blacks and whites: Narrowing the gap?* Cambridge: Harvard University Press.

Farley, R., Schuman, H., Bianchi, S., Colasanto, D., & Hatchett, S. (1978). Chocolate city, vanilla suburbs: Will the trend toward racially separate communities continue? *Social Science Quarterly, 7,* 319–344.

Farley, R., Bianchi, S., & Colasanto, D. (1979). Barriers to racial integration of neighborhoods: The Detroit case. *Annals of the American Academy of Political and Social Science, 441,* 97–113.

Fermia, J. (1975). Hegemony and consciousness in the thought of Antonio Gramsci. *Political Studies, 23,* 29–48.

Fireman, B., & Gamson, W. A. (1979). Utilitarian logic in the resource mobilization perspective. In M. N. Zald & J. D: McCarthy (Eds.), *The dynamics of social movements.* Cambridge, MA: Winthrop.

Fredrickson, G. M. (1971a). *The black image in the white mind: The debate on Afro-American character and destiny, 1817–1914.* New York: Harper & Row.

Fredrickson, G. M. (1971b). Toward a social interpretation of the development of American racism. In N. I. Huggins, M. Kilson, & D. M. Fox (Eds.), *Key issues in the Afro-American experience* (Vol. 1). San Francisco: Harcourt Brace Jovanovich.

Fredrickson, G. M. (1975). A man but not a brother: Abraham Lincoln and racial equality. *Journal of Southern History, 16,* 39–58.

Frey, W. H. (1985). Mover destination selectivity and the changing suburbanization of metropolitan whites and blacks. *Demography, 22,* 223–243.

Funkhouser, G. R. (1973). The issues of the sixties: An exploratory study in the dynamics of public opinion. *Public Opinion Quarterly, 37,* 62–75.

Gaertner, S. L., & Dovidio, J. F. (1981). Racism among the well-intentioned. In E. G. Clausen & J. Bermingham (Eds.), *Pluralism, racism, and public policy: The search for equality.* Boston: G. K. Hall.

Gamson, W. A. (1968). *Power and discontent.* Homewood, IL: Dorsey Press.

Garrow, D. J. (1978). *Protest at Selma: Martin Luther King, Jr., and the Voting Rights Act of 1965.* New Haven, CT: Yale University Press.

Giles, M. W., & Evans, A. S. (1984). External threat, perceived threat, and group identity. *Social Science Quarterly, 65,* 50–66.

Gitlin, T. (1980). *The whole world is watching: Mass media in the making and unmaking of the new left.* Berkeley: University of California Press.

Gossett, T. (1963). *Race: The history of an idea in America.* New York: Schocken.

Gramsci, A. (1971). *Selections from the prison notebooks* (ed. and trans. by Q. Hoare & G. N. Smith). New York: International Publishers.

Guimond, S., & Dube-Simard, L. (1983). Relative deprivation theory and the Quebec nationalist movement: The cognition-emotion distinction and the personal-group deprivation issue. *Journal of Personality and Social Psychology, 44,* 526–535.

Gurin, P., Miller, A. H., & Gurin, G. (1980). Stratum identification and consciousness. *Social Psychology Quarterly, 43,* 30–47.

Hamilton, D. L. (Ed.). (1981). *Cognitive process in stereotyping and intergroup behavior.* Hillsdale, NJ: Lawrence Erlbaum.

Handlin, O., & Handlin, M. F. (1950). Origins of the southern labor system. *William and Mary Quarterly, 7,* 199–222.

Handlin, O., & Handlin, M. F. (1960). Letters to the editor. *Comparative Studies in Society and History, 2,* 488–490.

Harris, M. (1964). *Patterns of race in the Americas.* New York: W. W. Norton.

Himes, J. S. (1966). The functions of racial conflict. *Social Forces, 45,* 1–10.

Hochschild, J. L. (1984). *The new American dilemma: Liberal democracy and school desegration.* New Haven, CT: Yale University Press.

Hyman, H. H., & Sheatsley, P. B. (1956). Attitudes toward desegregation. *Scientific American, 195,* 35–39.

Hyman, H. H., & Sheatsley, P. B. (1964). Attitudes toward desegregation. *Scientific American, 211,* 16–23.

Isaac, L., Mutran, E., & Stryker, S. (1980). Political protest orientations among black and white adults. *American Sociological Review, 45,* 191–213.

Jackman, M. R. (1978). General and applied tolerance: Does education increase commitment to racial integration? *American Journal of Political Science, 22,* 302–324.

Jackman, M. R., & Jackman, R. W. (1983). *Class awareness in the United States.* Berkeley: University of California Press.

Jackman, M. R., & Muha, M. J. (1984). Education and intergroup attitudes: Moral enlightenment, superficial democratic commitment, or ideological refinement? *American Sociological Review, 49,* 751–769.

Jackman, M. R., & Senter, M. S. (1983). Different, therefore unequal: Beliefs about trait differences between groups of unequal status. In D. J. Treiman & R. V. Robinson (Eds.), *Research in social stratification.* Greenwich, CT: JAI Press.

Jacobson, C. K. (1985). Resistance to affirmative action: Self-interest or racism? *Journal of Conflict Resolution, 29,* 306–329.

Jefferson, T. (1972). *Notes on the State of Virginia* (ed. by W. Peden). New York: W. W. Norton.

Johnson, G. (1949). The ideology of white supremacy, 1876–1910. In F. M. Green (Ed.), *The James Sprunt Studies in History and Political Science: Essays in southern history* (Vol. 31). Chapel Hill: University of North Carolina Press.

Jordan, W. D. (1962). Modern tensions and the origins of American slavery. *Journal of Southern History, 28,* 18–30.

Jordan, W. D. (1968). *White over black: American attitudes toward the Negro, 1550–1812.* New York: W. W. Norton.

Katz, D. (1960). The functional approach to the study of attitudes. *Public Opinion Quarterly, 24,* 163–204.

Katz, D. (1967). Group process and social integration: A system analysis of two movements of social protest. *Journal of Social Issues, 23,* 3–22.

Katz, D., & Braly, K. (1933). Racial stereotypes of one hundred college students. *Journal of Abnormal and Social Psychology, 28,* 280–290.

Katz, I. (1981). *Stigma: A social psychological analysis.* Hillsdale, NJ: Lawrence Erlbaum.

Killian, L., & Grigg, C. (1971). *Racial crisis in America: Leadership in conflict.* Englewood Cliffs, NJ: Prentice-Hall.

Kinder, D. R., & Sears, D. O. (1981). Prejudice and politics: Symbolic racism versus racial threats to the good life. *Journal of Personality and Social Psychology, 40,* 414–431.

King, M. L., Jr. (1967). *Where do we go from here? Chaos or community?* New York: Bantam.

Kluegel, J. R. (1985). If there isn't a problem, you don't need a solution: The bases of contemporary affirmative action attitudes. *American Behavioral Scientist, 28,* 761–787.

Kluegel, J. R., & Smith, E. R. (1982). Whites' beliefs about blacks' opportunity. *American Sociological Review, 47,* 518–532.

Kluegel, J. R., & Smith, E. R. (1983). Affirmative action attitudes: Effects of self-interest, racial affect, and stratification beliefs on whites' views. *Social Forces, 61,* 797–824.

Lawson, S. (1976). *black ballots: Voting rights in the South, 1944–1969.* New York: Columbia University Press.

Linville, P., & Jones, E. E. (1980). Polarized appraisals of out-group members. *Journal of Personality and Social Psychology, 38,* 689–703.

Lipset, S. M., & Schneider, W. (1978). The *Bakke* case: How would it be decided at the bar of public opinion? *Public Opinion, 1,* 38–44.

Lipsky, M. (1968). Protest as a political resource. *American Political Science Review, 62,* 1144–1158.

Marx, K. (1964). Existence and consciousness. In T. Bottomore (Ed.), *Karl Marx: Readings in sociology and social philosophy.* New York: McGraw-Hill.

McAdam, D. (1982). *Political process and the development of black insurgency, 1930–1970.* Chicago: University of Chicago Press.

McAdam, D. (1983). Tactical innovation and the pace of insurgency. *American Sociological Review, 48,* 735–754.

McClendon, M. J. (1985). Racism, rational choice, and white opposition to racial change: A case study of busing. *Public Opinion Quarterly, 49,* 214–233.

McClendon, M. J., & Pestello, F. P. (1982). White opposition: To busing or to desegregation? *Social Science Quarterly, 63,* 70–82.

McConahay, J. B. (1982). Self-interest versus racial attitudes as correlates of anti-busing attitudes in Louisville: Is it the buses or the blacks? *Journal of Politics, 44,* 692–720.

McConahay, J. B., Hardee, B. B., & Batts, V. (1981). Has racism declined in America? *Journal of Conflict Resolution, 25,* 563–580.

Miller, A. G. (1982). Historical and contemporary perspectives on stereotyping. In A. G. Miller (Ed.), *In the eye of the beholder: Contemporary issues in stereotyping.* New York: Praeger.

Morris, A. D. (1984). *The origins of the civil rights movement: black communities organizing for change.* New York: Free Press.

Myrdal, G. (1944). *An American dilemma: The Negro problem and modern democracy.* New York: Random House.

Noelle-Neumann, E. (1974). The spiral of silence: A theory of public opinion. *Journal of Communication, 24,* 43–51.

Noelle-Neumann, E. (1984). *The spiral of silence: Public opinion-our social skin.* Chicago: University of Chicago Press.

Orfield, G. (1978). *Must we bus? Segregated schools and national policy.* Washington, DC: Brookings Institution.

Pettigrew, T. F. (1979). Racial change and social policy. *Annals of the American Academy of Political and Social Science, 441,* 114–131.

Pettigrew, T. F. (1982). Prejudice. In S. Thernstrom, A. Orlov, & O. Handlin (Eds.), *Dimensions of ethnicity: Prejudice.* Cambridge: Belknap Press (Harvard University Press).

Pettigrew, T. F. (1985). New black-white patterns: How best to conceptualize them? *Annual Review of Sociology, 11,* 329–346.

Pitts, J. P. (1974). The study of race consciousness: Comments on new directions. *American Journal of Sociology, 80,* 665–687.

Prager, J. (1982). American racial ideology as collective representation. *Ethnic and Racial Studies, 5,* 99–119.

Prothro, J. W., & Grigg, C. M. (1960). Fundamental principles of democracy: Bases of agreement and disagreement. *Journal of Politics, 22,* 276–294.

Ransford, H. E. (1972). Blue collar anger: Reactions to student and black protest. *American Sociological Review, 37,* 333–346.

Riley, R. T., & Pettigrew, T. F. (1976). Dramatic events and attitude change. *Journal of Personality and Social Psychology, 34,* 1004–1015.

Robinson, J. P. (1970). Public reaction to political protest: Chicago, 1968. *Public Opinion Quarterly, 34,* 1–9.

Robinson, R. V. (1983). Explaining perceptions of class and racial inequality in England and the United States of America. *British Journal of Sociology, 34,* 344–366.

Rodgers, H. (1975). On integrating the public schools: An empirical and legal assessment. In H. Rodgers (Ed.), *Racism and inequality: The policy alternatives.* San Francisco: Freeman.

Rogers, R. W., & Prentice-Dunn, S. (1981). Deindividuation and anger-mediated interracial aggression: Unmasking regressive racism. *Journal of Personality and Social Psychology, 41,* 63–73.

Rose, A. M. (1956). Intergroup relations vs. prejudice. Pertinent theory for the study of social change. *Social Problems, 4,* 173–176.

Rothbart, Myron. (1976). Achieving radical equality: An analysis of resistance to social reform. In P. A. Katz (Ed.), *Towards the elimination of racism.* New York: Pergamon Press.

Rudwick, E. (1967). *Race riot at East St. Louis, July 2, 1917.* New York: World Publishing.

Runciman, W. G. (1966). *Relative deprivation and social justice.* Berkeley: University of California Press.

Scanzoni, J. (1972). *Sexual bargaining: Power politics in the American marriage.* Chicago: University of Chicago Press.

Schuman, H. (1971). Free will and determinism in beliefs about race. In N. C. Yetman & C. H. Steele (Eds.), *Majority and minority: The dynamics of racial and ethnic relations.* Boston: Allyn & Bacon.

Schuman, H., & Hatchett, S. (1974). *black racial attitudes: Trends and complexities.* Ann Arbor, MI: Institute for Social Research.

Schuman, H., Steeh, C., & Bobo, L. (1985). *Racial attitudes in America: Trends and interpretations.* Cambridge: Harvard University Press.

Sears, D. O., & Kinder, D. O. (1985). Whites' opposition to busing: On conceptualizing and operationalizing group conflict. *Journal of Personality and Social Psychology, 48,* 1141–1147.

Sears, D. O., Hensler, C. P. & Speer, L. K. (1979). Whites' opposition to busing: Self-interest or symbolic politics? *American Political Science Review, 73,* 369–384.

Sears, D. O., Lau, R. R., Tyler, T. R., & Allen, H. M. (1980). Self-interest or symbolic politics in policy attitudes and presidential voting. *American Political Science Review, 74,* 670–684.

Seeman, M. (1981). Intergroup relations. In M. Rosenberg & R. H. Turner (Eds.), *Social psychology: Sociological perspectives.* New York: Basic Books.

Shalhope, R. E. (1976). Thomas Jefferson's republicanism and antebellum southern thought. *Journal of Southern History, 42,* 529–556.

Shamir, M. & Sullivan, J. L. (1983). The political context of tolerance: The United States and Israel. *American Political Science Review, 77,* 911–928.

Sheatsley, P. B. (1966). White attitudes toward the Negro. *Daedalus, 95,* 217–238.

Sherif, M. (1966). *Group conflict and cooperation.* London: Routledge & Kegan Paul.

Shingles, R. D. (1980). Black consciousness and political participation: The missing link. *American Political Science Review, 75,* 76–91.

Simpson, G. E., & Yinger, J. M. (1972). *Racial and cultural minorities: An analysis of prejudice and discrimination.* (4th ed.). New York: Harper and Row.

Sitkoff, H. (1971). Harry Truman and the election of 1948: The coming of age of civil rights in American politics. *Journal of Southern History, 37,* 597–616.

Sitkoff, H. (1978). *A new deal for blacks: The emergence of civil rights as a national issue: Vol. 1. Depression decade.* New York: Oxford University Press.

Smith, A. W. (1981). Racial tolerance as a function of group position. *American Sociological Review, 46,* 558–573.

Smith, T. W. (1980). America's most important problem—A trend analysis. *Public Opinion Quarterly, 44,* 164–180.

Speigel, J. P. (1968). The resolution of the role conflict within the family. In N. W. Bell & E. F. Vogel (Eds.), *A modern introduction to the family.* New York: Free Press.

Stinchcombe, A., & Taylor. D. C. (1980). On democracy and school integration. In W. G. Stephan & J. R. Feagin (Eds.), *School desegregation: Past, present, and future.* New York: Plenum Press.

Sullivan, J. L., Piereson, J. E., & Marcus, G. E. (1982). *Political tolerance and American democracy.* Chicago: University of Chicago Press.

Taeuber, K. B. (1983a). *Racial residential segregation, 28 cities, 1970—1980* (Working Paper No. 83-12). Madison: University of Wisconsin, Center for Demography and Ecology.

Taeuber, K. E. (1983b). *Research issues concerning trends in residential segregation* (Working Paper No. 83-12). Madison: University of Wisconsin, Center for Demography and Ecology.

Taeuber, K. E., & Taeuber, A. F. (1965). *Negroes in cities: Residential segregation and neighborhood change.* Chicago: Aldine.

Tajfel, H., & Turner, J. C. (1979). An integrative theory of intergroup conflict. In W. S. Austin & S. Worchel (Eds.), *The social psychology of intergroup relations.* Monterey, CA: Wadsworth.

Takaki, R. T. (1970). The black child-savage in ante-bellum America. In G. B. Nash & R. Weiss (Eds.), *Race in the mind of America.* San Francisco: Holt, Rinehart, & Winston.

Takaki, R. T. (1979). *Iron cages: Race and culture in 19th century America.* Seattle: University of Washington Press.

Taylor, D. G. (1986). *Public opinion and collective action: The Boston school desegregation controversy.* Chicago: University of Chicago Press.

Taylor, D. G., Sheatsley, P. B., & Greeley, A. M. (1978). Attitudes toward racial integration. *Scientific American, 238,* 42–49.

Tilly, C. (1978). *From mobilization to revolution.* Reading, MA: Addison-Wesley.

Turner, C. B., & Wilson, W. J. (1976). Dimensions of racial ideology: A study of urban black attitudes. *Journal of Social Issues, 32,* 139–152.

Turner, J., & Singleton, R. (1978). A theory of ethnic oppression: Toward a reintegration of cultural and structural concepts in ethnic relations theory. *Social Forces, 56,* 1001–1018.

Turner, R. H. (1969). The public perception of protest. *American Sociological Review, 34,* 814–831.

U.S. Bureau of the Census. (1983). *Current population reports, Series P-60, No. 138, Characteristics of the population below the poverty level: 1981.* Washington, DC: U.S. Government Printing Office.

Useem, B. (1981). Solidarity model, breakdown model, and the Boston and-busing movement. *American Sociological Review, 45,* 357–369.

Van den Berghe, P. L. (1967). *Race and racism: A comparative perspective.* New York: Wiley.

Van Valey, T. L., Roof, W. C., & Wilcox, J. E. (1977). Trends in residential segregation: 1960–1970. *American Journal of Sociology, 87,* 826–844.

Vanneman, R. D., & Pettigrew, T. F. (1972). Race and relative deprivation in the urban United States. *Race, 13,* 461–486.

Wellman, D. T. (1977). *Portraits of white racism.* New York: Oxford University Press.

Wilkinson, J. H. (1979). *From* Brown *to* Bakke, *the Supreme Court and school integration: 1954–1978.* New York: Oxford University Press.

Williams, G. (1960, Oct.–Dec.). Egemonia in the thought of Antonio Gramsci: Some notes on interpretation. *Journal of the History of Ideas,* pp. 585–597.

Williams, R. (1973). Base and superstructure in Marxist cultural theory. *New Left Review* (82), pp. 3–16.

Williams, R. M., Jr. (1965). Social change and social conflict: Race relations in the United States, 1944–1964. *Sociological Inquiry, 35,* 8–25.

Williams. R. M., Jr. (1975). Relative deprivation. In L. A. Coser (Ed.), *The idea of social structure.* New York: Harcourt Brace Jovanovich.

Williams, R. M., Jr. (1977). *Mutual accommodation: Ethnic conflict and cooperation.* Minneapolis: University of Minnesota Press.

Williams, R. M., Jr., Dean, J. P., & Suchman, E. A. (1964). *Strangers next door: Ethnic relations in American communities.* Englewood Cliffs, NJ: Prentice-Hall.

Wilson, W. J. (1973). *Power, racism, and privilege: Race relations in theoretical and sociohistorical perspective.* New York: Free Press.

Wilson, W. J. (1980). *The declining significance of race* (2nd ed.). Chicago: University of Chicago Press.

Woodward, C. V. (1974). *The strange career of Jim Crow* (3rd rev. ed.). New York: Oxford University Press.

Zashin, E. (1978). The progress of black Americans in civil rights: The past two decades assessed. *Daedalus, 107,* 239–262.

Is it Really Racism?
The Origins of White Americans'
Opposition to Race-Targeted Policies

David O. Sears, Colette Van Laar, and Mary Carrillo • UCLA
Rick Kosterman • University of Washington

R ace relations in the United States have had a long history, but one that is marked by significant discontinuities over time. The period of slavery was followed by the brief but radically different window of Reconstruction. The Jim Crow system that developed over the following century legalized racial segregation and discrimination, especially but not exclusively in the South. The civil rights revolution effectively ended that two-caste system of race relations, replacing it with a universal system of formal legal equality. Nevertheless, considerable racial inequality remains in many areas of the society, such as in income, wealth, educational attainment, health, crime, and so forth.

The demise of Jim Crow was accompanied by a sharp decline in the prevalence of its supporting belief system. This has sometimes been described as "old-fashioned racism," incorporating both a biologically based theory of African racial inferiority and support for racial segregation and formal racial discrimination (McConahay, 1986). Old-fashioned racism has now largely been replaced by general support for the abstract principle of racial equality (Schuman, Steeh, & Bobo, 1985; Sears & Kinder, 1971). However, there is much evidence that whites do not fully support the implications of these general principles of equality. They have often strongly opposed policies implementing that general principle, such as busing or affirmative action, leading to what Schuman, Steeh, and Bobo (1985) have called the "principle-implementation gap." Similarly, black political candidates still seem to have unusual difficulty in attracting white support, despite some greater success in recent years. This seemingly paradoxical combination—widespread acceptance of the idea of racial equality mixed with continued resistance to change—is our starting point.

Is it Racism?

One possible explanation for this paradox is that racism did not disappear as a political force with the demise of Jim Crow. Rather, some political observers contend that racism continues to motivate much of the considerable white opposition to racial policies and black candidates, as in Edsall and Edsall's (1991) assertion that "when the official subject is presidential politics, taxes, welfare, crime, rights, or values . . . the real subject is race" (also see Edsall & Edsall, 1992; Greenberg, 1995). By contrast, conservatives tout "the end of racism" (D'Souza, 1995; also see Roth, 1994).

This controversy is mirrored in academic research, with some finding a continuing role of racism. Negative racial stereotypes have not disappeared (Bobo, Kluegel, & Smith, 1997; Devine & Elliot 1995; Kinder & Mendelberg, 1995; Sniderman & Piazza, 1993). Whites have been found to be significantly more opposed to racially targeted policies than to analogous policies targeted for the poor of all races (Bobo & Kluegel, 1993). Racial attitudes have been shown to have substantial effects on whites' opposition to busing, affirmative action, or welfare spending, and support for law and order or tax-reduction policies (Gilens, 1995; Kinder & Sanders, 1996; McConahay, 1982; Sears & Citrin, 1985; Sears, Hensler, & Speer, 1979; Sears et al., 1980; Sidanius, Pratto, & Bobo, 1996). Similar analyses have found a significant role of racial attitudes in whites' opposition to black candidates for mayor in large cities (Kinder & Sears, 1981; Pettigrew, 1972; Sears & Kinder, 1971), or Jesse Jackson's presidential candidacy (Abramowitz, 1994; Sears, Citrin, & Kosterman, 1987). There also is evidence that racism has played a role in campaigns in which white candidates have been accused of playing the "race card," such as those of David Duke (Kuzenski, Bullock, & Gaddie, 1995) or George Bush (Kinder & Sanders, 1996).

But others have been more skeptical about the continuing importance of racism. For example, Sniderman and Piazza (1993, p. 107) believe that "the central problem of racial politics is not the problem of prejudice," and that it no longer dominates whites' preferences about racial policies. Hagen (1995) reports a sharp decline in white Americans' mentioning race as one of America's most important problems, or as an explanation for their candidate or party preferences. Others note that opposition to race-targeted policies may lie instead in seemingly race-neutral attitudes, such as ideological conservatism (Sniderman & Piazza, 1993), opposition to the welfare state (Abramowitz, 1994), skepticism about failed liberal policies (Roth, 1994), or more general attitudes about individualism (Carmines & Merriman, 1993), equality (Miller & Shanks, 1996), or partisan interest groups (Miller, 1994). As a result, some argue that racial attitudes have little residual independent effect when nonracial attitudes are controlled for.

Our own general perspective is that of symbolic politics theory. This theory assumes that social-

ization leaves individuals with strong, long-standing attitudinal predispositions, which can be evoked by appropriate political symbols (Sears, 1993). We assume that for several centuries white Americans have grown up in a socializing culture marked by widespread negative attitudes toward African Americans, a socializing culture that seems unlikely to have been abruptly overturned within the relatively few years since the end of Jim Crow. Presenting whites with racially targeted policies or black candidates should evoke that common antiblack element.

Our first empirical goal is to provide some systematic data on how strong a role racism does play in white Americans' contemporary racial policy and candidate preferences. We attack this in four ways. Our primary analytic strategy is straightforward and reasonably standard: regressing policy attitudes on indicators of racism, imposing controls on the other plausible causal factors, especially ostensibly nonracial attitudes (such as party identification, ideology, social welfare attitudes, and traditional social values) and demographic variables. We proceed from that point with three further strategies. First, we test the contention (Sniderman & Piazza, 1993) that each racial policy issue elicits a different set of underlying attitudes and values appropriate to its unique content, rather than all tapping into a common substrate of racism. Second, we go beyond policy issues to test the effects of racial attitudes on whites' evaluations of black candidates and of fringe white candidates with a reputation for ethnocentrism. Third, we test whether or not higher education blocks the impact of racism. It has long been established that educational level is positively correlated with racial tolerance (see, e.g., Campbell, 1971; Schuman, Steeh, & Bobo, 1985). But does higher education, by teaching racial tolerance, also reduce the power of racial prejudices over policy and candidate preferences? Sniderman and Piazza (1993) argue that it should, and that higher education, by enlarging political sophistication, should instead enable individuals better to connect their own nonracial ideologies and values cognitively to ongoing policy debates. So higher education should reduce the power of racism and increase that of ideology. The symbolic politics perspective, in contrast, assumes that more education should increase the consistency of policy preferences with almost any long-standing predisposition, whether racial or nonracial (Sears, 1993). Available data concerning higher education as a moderator of the effects of racial antagonism are somewhat mixed (see Sidanius, Pratto, & Bobo, 1996; Sniderman & Piazza, 1993, pp. 117–126), so we examine whether or not higher education mitigates the power of racial antagonism over whites' racial policy preferences in favor of nonracial predispositions.

In pursuing these empirical goals, we by no means intend to suggest that racism is the only factor involved, or indeed that any single factor represents the whole story. But in view of the controversy over the role of racism, it seems to us important to provide a rigorous and focused test of its effects.

Forms of Racism in American Politics

Our second goal is to determine the most politically influential form of racism today. Our view is that each historical discontinuity described at the outset has significantly altered how ordinary citizens think about race in politics and so has changed the nature of racism in mass politics. Others might say that any racially based component of white resistance to change simply reflects familiar traditional prejudices or ethnocentrism that will always be with us (see, e.g., Sniderman & Piazza, 1993).

On this point, it is important to be clear about how we are defining "racism." Dictionaries commonly offer two definitions: the classic theory of biologically based racial superiority (e.g., "a belief that race is the primary determinant of human traits and capacities and that racial differences produce an inherent superiority of a particular race") and the more general "racial prejudice or discrimination" (see *Webster's Ninth New Collegiate Dictionary* [1989], p. 969). To avoid artificially narrowing the search for the most politically potent form of contemporary racism, we employ this second, more general definition. This describes a category-based affective response to attitude objects that have to do with race, in which racism is inferred if an individual responds systematically more negatively to attitude objects associated with blacks than to other comparable attitude objects (just as anti-Semitism is inferred when attitude objects associated with Jews are responded to especially negatively).

The contemporary empirical literature has distinguished five different ways of conceptualizing and operationalizing racial attitudes, all of which we will employ in our empirical comparisons.

1. The old-fashioned racism of Jim Crow days focused on the theory of biological superiority of the white race, and on the physical segregation of and legalized discrimination against African Americans. It has been variously referred to as "old-fashioned racism," "redneck racism" (McConahay, 1986; McConahay & Hough, 1976), "blatant racism" (Pettigrew & Meertens, 1995), or "classical racism" (Sidanius, Pratto, & Bobo, 1996).

2. Stereotypes of blacks as lazy, unintelligent, morally depraved, violent, loud, and ostentatious have long been common in American society (Devine & Elliot, 1995; Katz & Braly, 1933). Some of these traits invoke the theory of black genetic inferiority (which is also at the heart of old-fashioned racism), while others are widely assumed to be more culturally based. Both have frequently been used in survey studies of racial attitudes as predictors of policy and candidate preferences (see Bobo & Kluegel, 1993; Kinder & Mendelberg, 1995; Sniderman & Piazza, 1993; Tuch & Hughes, 1996).

3. Negative affect toward African Americans as a group has been measured most commonly with the National Election Studies (NES) "feeling thermometer" (Carmines & Merriman, 1993; Sears, 1988; Sears & Jessor, 1996; Sidanius, Pratto, & Bobo, 1996; Tuch & Hughes, 1996). This is usually treated as the simplest and most purely affective index of racial prejudice.

4. Old-fashioned racism, stereotypes, and negative affect have been familiar features of the racial landscape throughout the 20th century. However, evidence of continuing white resistance to change in an era that has generally renounced both biological theories of racial superiority and legalized racial inequality has generated a variety of descriptions of a "new racism." All share a component of negative attitudes toward African Americans; they differ in what is involved beyond that, and how they are measured. One family of concepts using very similar measurement includes "symbolic racism" (Kinder & Sears, 1981; Sears &

Kinder, 1971), "modern racism" (McConahay, 1986), "subtle racism" (Pettigrew & Meertens, 1995), and "racial resentments" (Kinder & Sanders, 1996). Other "new racisms," conceptualized and measured in other ways, include "ambivalent racism" (Katz, Wackenhut, & Hass, 1986), "aversive racism" (Gaertner & Dovidio, 1986), and "laissez-faire racism" (Bobo, Kluegel, & Smith, 1997).

Not everyone is persuaded that the notion of a "new" racism is required. Some say that the old racism is still quite common, and that the supposed decline in negative stereotyping has been exaggerated (Devine & Elliot, 1995; Sniderman & Piazza, 1993). Others say that any "new" racism is at bottom not very different from an "old" racial prejudice (Schuman, Steeh, & Bobo, 1985), ethnocentrism (Sniderman & Piazza, 1993), or authoritarianism (Raden, 1994). Still others say that a "new" racism may only look new because it merely confounds an underlying "old" racism with political conservatism (Fazio et al., 1995; Roth, 1994; Sniderman & Tetlock, 1986; Weigel & Howes, 1985). We will return to these points below.

5. Finally, group position theory (Bobo & Hutchings, 1996), realistic group conflict theory (Bobo 1988), social dominance theory (Sidanius, Pratto, & Bobo, 1996), and social identity theory (Tajfel & Turner, 1986) share the assumption that attachment to a hegemonic in-group is a key factor. According to this perspective, the underlying psychological motive is to protect a hegemonic in-group's privileged position and suppress less powerful groups that aspire to equality. The exact content of the myths or ideologies that promote that goal may be mostly opportunistic, if not epiphenomenal, but presumably normally includes attachment to the in-group. Operationally, positive affect toward whites as a group has most commonly (but minimally) been indexed with an NES feeling thermometer (Jessor, 1988; Sears & Jessor, 1996).

Symbolic Racism

Our view is that the distinctions among these five forms of racial attitudes are important, both to capture the essence of racism in today's mass poli-

tics, and for more fundamental psychological reasons. The symbolic politics argument would suggest that all four forms of antiblack racism draw in part on the residues of a common negative socialization about African Americans. But in addition to that, the content of political debate varies from era to era. To trigger the most potent available predispositions requires a political stimulus that is appropriate to the era in question. The older forms of antiblack antagonism draw on the wellsprings of underlying racial prejudice, but the content and form of contemporary racial resentments have changed markedly. Old-fashioned racism has disappeared as an effective political force, replaced by a societal consensus on general egalitarian principles; few want to go back to the old days of formal segregation and formal discrimination (Schuman, Steeh, & Bobo, 1985). Negative racial affect and stereotypes are essential components of contemporary racism, but only part of the story.

We argue that as a political force, symbolic racism has largely displaced the older forms of racial attitude. Symbolic racism can be conceptualized in three ways. First, it is described as "symbolic" because it is phrased in terms that are abstract and ideological; because it reflects whites' moral codes about how society should be organized rather than instrumental beliefs satisfying their own interests; and because it focuses on blacks as a group rather than on individual blacks (Sears & Kinder, 1971). Second, its cognitive content, as developed in earlier research, focuses explicitly on blacks in particular and includes the beliefs that racial discrimination is largely a thing of the past, that blacks should just work harder to overcome their disadvantages, and that blacks are making excessive demands for special treatment and get too much attention from elites, so their gains are often undeserved (Sears, 1988). Third, its attitudinal origins are hypothesized to lie in a blend of antiblack affect with the perception that blacks violate such traditional American values as the work ethic, traditional morality, and respect for traditional authority (Kinder & Sears, 1981).

Symbolic racism and the three older indicators of antiblack racism focus only on whites' derogation of the out-group. Does racism not also focus on attachment to the in-group? A symbolic politics theory would not assume that cultural socialization necessarily need embody both. To be sure, a culture may sometimes socialize both intense pride in the in-group, as in the Nazis' celebration of "the Aryan race," and intense derogation of the out-group, as in their vigorous anti-Semitism. But the two elements need not be highly correlated; indeed, they may often be socialized quite independently of each other. We would argue that the conventional socialization of American whites has inculcated negative attitudes toward African Americans without much explicit focus on whiteness or celebration of it. American white supremacy movements are still quite small and on the political fringe. So we would expect animosity toward blacks to play a major role in the politics of race, but attitudes toward whites to be quite peripheral.

The symbolic racism perspective has two empirical implications, then. First, it argues in favor of taking seriously the differences across types of racism, rather than assuming they are all merely different indicators of a common underlying racial antagonism. Indeed, there is persuasive evidence that the underlying factorial structure of these racial attitudes yields at least two correlated factors, old-fashioned and symbolic racism. Second, it would argue that symbolic racism should have strong political effects, while these older forms of racial antagonism are likely to have rather weak ones. There have been few rigorous comparisons between types of racism in previous research, but when assessed individually the older forms generally have not had very strong effects. These weak effects do not necessarily mean that racism is a weak force in American politics; they may just reflect looking in the wrong place for its effects, and so underestimating its effects on whites' political thinking.

We here repeat these assessments of the effects of older forms of racism, but adding an explicit comparison to symbolic racism, expecting that it resonates better with whites' contemporary political resentments of blacks. In doing so we also specifically respond to several prior critiques of research on symbolic racism (e.g., Colleau et al., 1990; Sniderman & Tetlock, 1986): that we do not distinguish sharply between measures of old-fashioned racism and symbolic racism, that symbolic racism is not internally homogeneous, that it is confounded with authoritarianism or nonracial conservatism, and that mere content overlap between measures of symbolic racism and those

of racial policy preferences largely explain any link between the two.

Goals and Hypotheses

The two major goals of this article, then, are to provide convincing data on the effects of racism on racial policy and candidate preferences, and on which form of racism is most central. It hopes to be more convincing than past research by providing extensive replication of the same basic test, using as independent variables (a) several different indicators of racism in each survey and (b) statistical controls on a comprehensive roster of the other usual suspects; as dependent variables (c) the full range of racial policies in debate today, including guarantees of equal opportunity, special aid to blacks, and affirmative action for blacks, and (d) a range of political candidates, including blacks, white liberals, and white conservatives; and as databases (e) four different surveys, conducted by three different survey houses for quite different purposes.

Our reasoning yields several hypotheses. Following from the assumptions that African Americans are a potent political symbol and that the overriding symbolism of racially targeted policies concerns race, (a) racial attitudes should be the single most important determinant of whites' opposition to racial policies, while ostensibly race-neutral predispositions should have minor effects. Concerning the various forms of racism; (b) symbolic racism should have stronger political effects than the older forms of racism; (c) the origins of symbolic racism should lie in both antiblack affect and such nonracial attitudes as ideology and traditional social values, but (d) symbolic racism should nevertheless have substantial independent effect above and beyond these antecedents. The generality of a role of racism should be demonstrated if (e) whites' responses to racial policies have a strong racial basis regardless of policy content; (f) racial attitudes have significant independent effects on whites' evaluations of black candidates and of fringe white candidates with a reputation for ethnocentrism, but evaluations of mainstream white candidates are overshadowed by nonracial partisan attitudes; (g) racial attitudes dominate nonracial attitudes in explaining even college-educated whites' racial policy preferences.

Method

This study uses four surveys: the 1986 (N = 2,176) and 1992 (N = 2,110) National Election Studies (NES), focused on the 1986 congressional and 1992 presidential elections; the 1994 General Social Survey (GSS; N = 2,992), focused principally on time-series measurement of sociological indicators; and the 1995 Los Angeles County Social Survey (LACSS; N = 595), focused on the politics of intergroup relations. These four surveys were chosen because they each contain measures of symbolic racism as well as measures of one or more other kinds of racial attitudes. The NES and GSS studies are based on large representative cross-sectional samples of American adults. The LACSS is a random digit dialing telephone survey conducted annually in Los Angeles County. For the analyses in all four surveys only white respondents were included.

Dependent Variables

Separate scales were developed for each of three areas of racial policy, which we describe as "equal opportunity," "federal assistance," and "affirmative action." Perceived obligation of the federal government to guarantee equal opportunity used (a) government assurance of fair treatment in jobs, (b) government-guaranteed school integration, and (c) government-guaranteed equal opportunity. All three items were used in 1986, and the first two in 1992. Preferences regarding the role of the government in delivering federal assistance to blacks were measured with (a) increased or decreased federal spending on programs benefiting blacks, and (b) the question, Should the government help blacks (and other minority groups) or should they help themselves? Affirmative action scales on extending special preferences to blacks in employment and education were available in all four surveys: (a) preferential hiring and promotion of blacks; (b) quotas for admitting black students in universities; (c) special treatment for blacks; (d) set-asides for black contractors.

Candidate evaluations were measured in the NES studies on a "feeling thermometer," where 0 is cold and 100 is warm. In 1986, the candidates were Ronald Reagan and Jesse Jackson; in 1992, the candidates were Jackson, Bill Clinton, George Bush, and Pat Buchanan.

Symbolic Racism

We rely on the measures of symbolic racism used most often in previous studies. All items refer explicitly to "blacks" (except in one case, to "civil rights leaders") as well as incorporating one of the following standard themes.

Denial of continuing racial discrimination. (a) Has there been a lot of real change in the position of black people in the past few years? (b) Generations of slavery and discrimination have created conditions that make it difficult for blacks to work their way out of the lower class.

Absence of positive emotions toward blacks. (c) How often have you felt sympathy for blacks? (d) How often have you felt admiration for blacks?

Blacks should work harder. (e) If blacks would only try harder they could be just as well off as whites. (f) Irish, Italians, Jewish, and many other minorities overcame prejudice and worked their way up. blacks should do the same without special favors. (g) Most blacks who receive money from welfare programs could get along without it if they tried.

Excessive demands. (h) Are civil rights leaders trying to push too fast, going too slowly, or are they moving at about the right speed? (i) blacks are getting too demanding in their push for equal rights.

Undeserved advantage. (j) Over the past few years, blacks have gotten less than they deserve. (k) Do blacks get much more attention from the government than they deserve, more attention, about the right amount, less attention, or much less attention from the government than they deserve? (l) Government officials usually pay less attention to a request or complaint from a black person than from a white person. Items a–d, j, and l were reverse-keyed.

Other Racial Attitudes

Racial affect toward "blacks" and "whites" were measured with the "feeling thermometer" cited above. The stereotype items involved ratings of blacks and whites on three 7-point scales whose endpoints were "hard-working/lazy," "violent/peaceful," and "unintelligent/intelligent." Scales were computed from the differences between ratings of blacks and whites, to control for individual differences in the use of the scale.

Old-fashioned racism was distinguished from symbolic racism both theoretically and empirically, according to factor analyses described later. In the 1986 NES only: (a) the races are different due to a divine plan, and (b) blacks come from a less able race. In the 1994 GSS only: (c) laws against marriages between blacks and whites; (d) blacks shouldn't push themselves where they are not wanted; (e) white people have a right to keep blacks out of their neighborhoods; (f) objections to sending your children to a school where half of the children are black; (g) voting for a black president; (h) blacks have worse jobs, income, and housing because they have less inborn ability to learn.

Nonracial Partisanship and Values

Party identification was measured with the standard 7-point summary variable running from "strong Democrat" to "strong Republican," combined, in the 1986 and 1992 NES only, with the difference score between the thermometer ratings of the two parties. In the 1992 NES, 1994 GSS, and 1995 LACSS *political ideology* was measured with the standard 7-point summary variable running from "strong liberal" to "strong conservative." In 1992 the difference between the thermometer ratings of conservatives and liberals was also included; in 1986, only the thermometer difference score was used because the standard self-rating was not asked of the split sample asked the racial items. *Social welfare policy* items (which did not mention blacks) were drawn from previous studies (Abramowitz, 1994; Miller, 1993, 1994; Miller & Shanks, 1996): (a) fewer versus more services and spending, (b) government-guaranteed jobs, and (c) government-guaranteed health insurance.

Nonracial values were also indexed with items that did not explicitly mention blacks. *Individualism* scales were developed from the 1986 NES and 1995 LACSS with items focused on the Protestant work ethic and on the role of effort in success. The 1994 GSS measure of individualism consisted of one item: getting ahead through hard work. *Morality/sexuality* scales focused on the tolerance of different lifestyles, the breakdown of moral standards, premarital sex, sexual education, and so on. *Authoritarianism* was measured in the 1992 NES with four items on childrearing values: (a) independence or respect for elders, (b) obedience or self-reliance, (c) curiosity or good manners, and (d) being considerate or well behaved. The 1994 GSS used: (a) necessary to discipline child with spanking, (b) obedience and respect for authority as virtues children should learn, and (c) the value of a child's learning "to obey," and (d) obedience or thinking for self more important. The 1995 LACSS repeated the first two GSS items.

The regression equations also included controls for the four demographic variables that are usually most highly correlated with white Americans' racial attitudes: age, gender, and education, and in the national surveys, a dummy variable for respondents' region of residence (South vs. non-South).

The Role of Racism

Is racism the most powerful contributor to whites' racial policy attitudes, as hypothesis 1 suggests? To test this, we present nine analyses that regress racial attitudes, partisanship, and nonracial values (along with relevant demographic controls) on attitudes toward policies providing blacks with equal opportunity (Table 20.1), federal assistance (Table 20.2), and affirmative action (Table 20.3). We present both the bivariate correlations (in parentheses) and the standardized regression coefficients, so we can compare the simple association of each predictor with policy attitudes against its power with all other predictors controlled.

It is clear that racial attitudes have consistent and powerful effects. Antiblack racial attitudes have an average correlation of .31 with these policy preferences. But nonracial predispositions have consistently positive bivariate associations with these policy preferences as well: the three partisan predispositions yield an average correlation of .25, while the three nonracial values average .16.

When we turn to the regression analyses, however, it becomes clear that racial attitudes consistently dominate. In every case, the strongest single predictor of these policy preferences is a racial attitude. All nine regression coefficients for symbolic racism are significant, averaging .39, and all six terms for antiblack affect are significant as well. The relationships of nonracial attitudes with these policy preferences are much reduced with racial attitudes considered. The strongest remaining nonracial effect is that of social welfare attitudes, yielding a mean regression coefficient of .16 (with five

TABLE 20.1. Origins of Whites' Opposition to Equal Opportunity for Blacks

	1986 NES		1992 NES	
	Beta	(r)	Beta	(r)
Racial attitudes:				
Symbolic racism	.40***	(.57)	.35***	(.49)
Black affect	.11*	(.28)	.17**	(.28)
Stereotypes	...		.04	(.25)
Old-fashioned racism	.06	(.21)	...	
White affect	...		.02	(.02)
Partisanship:				
Ideology	.12*	(.32)	.03	(.33)
Party identification	−.03	(.17)	.06	(.25)
Social welfare	.25***	(.41)	.15**	(.33)
Nonracial values:				
Individualism	.09*	(.27)	...	
Morality/sexuality	.02	(.25)	.09	(.30)
Authoritarianism	...		−.06	(.10)
Adjusted R^2 (%)	42.8		31.1	

Sources—1986 and 1992 National Election Studies.
Note—A positive entry means opposition to equal opportunity is associated with more negative racial attitudes and more conservative political attitudes and values. The full equations include age, education, gender, and region; those terms are not shown. Pairwise deletion is employed.
*$p < .05$.
**$p < .001$.
***$p < .0001$.

out of six terms significant). But the other nonracial predictors have little residual effect: the average regression coefficient for ideology is .03 (only three of nine significant); for party identification, .06; for individualism, .02; for morality, .04; and for authoritarianism, −.02. In short, in multivariate analyses, racial attitudes erase most of the original bivariate effects of nonracial predispositions.

A convenient way to summarize these effects is shown in Table 20.4. To start with, the racial attitudes were entered as the first stage of a three-stage regression analysis, the demographics were entered as the second stage, and the nonracial attitudes were entered as the third stage. In a parallel analysis, the nonracial attitudes were entered first, demographics second, and the racial attitudes last. The racial attitudes, when entered first, account for substantially more variance (25%, on average; see Table 20.4, col. 1) than do the nonracial attitudes (14%; col. 2). When entered last, the racial attitudes continue to add considerable incremental variance (15%, on average; col. 3), whereas the nonracial attitudes add rather little (5%; col. 4). In short, racial attitudes are consistently more powerful predictors of these racial policy preferences than are nonracial attitudes.

Which Form of Racism?

Hypothesis 2 suggested that symbolic racism would prove the strongest of the racial attitudes. And it does, quite handily. It has by far the strongest bivariate correlation with policy preferences, averaging .48 across the nine tests shown in Tables 20.1–20.3. The average correlations for the other racial attitudes are lower: antiblack affect, $r = .27$; antiblack stereotypes, $r = .23$; and old-fashioned racism, $r = .16$. In the regression analyses, the strength of symbolic racism emerges still more clearly. In all nine cases its effects are at least double the size of any other, with an average coefficient of .39. Antiblack affect also has significant effects in every case, though substantially weaker, averaging .13. Stereotypes and old-fashioned racism have virtually no residual effect, with significant effects in only two of 12 cases (and average coefficients of only .04 and -.01, respectively). All racial attitudes are not alike; symbolic racism has consistently more political power than do antiblack affect, stereotypes, or old-fashioned racism.

What about pro-white solidarity? Hypothesis 2 suggests that animosity toward blacks should play the central role in the politics of race, while atti-

TABLE 20.2. Origins of Whites' Opposition to Federal Assistance for Blacks

	1986 NES		1992 NES		1994 GSS	
	Beta	(r)	Beta	(r)	Beta	(r)
Racial attitudes:						
Symbolic racism	.41***	(.54)	.39***	(.54)	.38***	(.47)
Black affect	.19***	(.33)	.16***	(.31)	. . .	
Stereotypes	. . .		.08*	(.29)	.05	(.27)
Old-fashioned racism	−.04	(.12)	. . .		.15*	(.35)
White affect	. . .		−.01	(.00)	. . .	
Partisanship:						
Ideology	.09*	(.29)	.03	(.33)	−.08	(.12)
Party identification	.07*	(.23)	.02	(.23)	.10	(.14)
Social welfare	.21***	(.38)	.22***	(.35)	. . .	
Nonracial values:						
Individualism	−.03	(.17)	. . .		−.05	(.01)
Morality/sexuality	.01	(.19)	.03	(.26)	.02	(.22)
Authoritarianism	. . .		−.02	(.15)	.14*	(.30)
Adjusted R^2 (%)	40.4		37.7		26.0	

Sources—1986 and 1992 National Election Studies, 1994 General Social Survey.
Note—A positive entry means opposition to federal assistance for blacks is associated with more negative racial attitudes and more conservative political attitudes and values. The full equations include age, education, gender, and region; those terms are not shown. Pairwise deletion is employed.
*$p < .05$.
**$p < .001$.
***$p < .0001$.

tudes toward whites should be peripheral. This study does not claim to offer a thorough test of this hypothesis. But the evidence we have suggests that white affect is not a key factor. Tables 20.1–20.3 show that the "white thermometer," included in the 1992 NES, was essentially unrelated to whites' racial policy preferences, with a mean bivariate correlation of .01, and a mean regression coefficient of .00. These data suggest that animosity toward blacks has a great deal, and defense of the white in-group has rather little, to do with whites' racial policy preferences.

Content Overlap

The hypothesis that symbolic racism is a different and politically more powerful form of racism has attracted some criticism. One concern is that the indicators of symbolic racism themselves have too much conceptual overlap with the dependent variables in these analyses. If symbolic racism is merely a measure of opposition to the contemporary civil rights agenda concerning special, race-conscious government aid to blacks in the abstract, and the racial policy scales measure opposition to it in concrete form, any association between them

might reflect nothing more than that common content.

To check on this possibility, the basic analyses shown in Tables 20.1–20.3 were repeated on the 1986 and 1992 NES data after purging the symbolic racism scales of all items alluding to government (referring to "special favors," special attention from government, or dependency on government welfare payments) which would seem to be the most vulnerable to such conceptual overlap. The items that were retained did not allude to government at all, asking (a) whether there has been no real change for blacks, (b) whether generations of slavery and discrimination make it hard for blacks to work their way up, (c) whether blacks have gotten less than they deserve, (d) if blacks only tried harder they would be just as well off, and (e) civil rights people have been pushing too hard.

These scales of symbolic racism, purged of any reference to special government attention, had slightly lower reliabilities than did the originals (in 1986, the reliability drops from .78 to .65; in 1992, from .76 to .70). However, their associations with the policy preference scales hardly change at all. The average symbolic racism regression coef-

TABLE 20.3. Origins of Whites' Opposition to Affirmative Action for Blacks

	1986 NES		1992 NES		1994 GSS		1995 LACSS	
	Beta	(r)	Beta	(r)	Beta	(r)	Beta	(r)
Racial attitudes:								
Symbolic racism	.42***	(.43)	.44***	(.45)	.42***	(.44)	.34***	(.42)
Black affect	.08*	(.20)	.08*	(.21)	...		...	
Stereotypes	...		.01	(.17)	.04	(.18)	.04	(.22)
Old-fashioned racism	−.14**	(−.04)	...		−.10	(.15)	...	
White affect	...		−.01	(.00)	...		...	
Partisanship:								
Ideology	.02	(.22)	.08	(.28)	−.03	(.11)	−.01	(.28)
Party identification	.09*	(.16)	.03	(.20)	.04	(.11)	.20*	(.36)
Social welfare	.12*	(.27)	−.02	(.20)	...		...	
Nonracial values:								
Individualism	−.03	(.15)	...		.00	(.04)	.12	(−.01)
Morality/sexuality	.07	(.18)	.08*	(.24)	.08	(.19)	−.07	(−.12)
Authoritarianism	...		−.13**	(.00)	.01	(.19)	−.03	(.24)
Adjusted R^2 (%)	26.4		25.5		17.8		20.8	

Sources—1986 and 1992 National Election Studies, 1994 General Social Survey, and 1995 Los Angeles County Social Survey.
Note—A positive entry means opposition to affirmative action for blacks is associated with more negative racial attitudes and more conservative political attitudes and values. The full equations include age, education, gender, and, in the national surveys, region; those terms are not shown. Pairwise deletion is employed.
*$p < .05$.
**$p < .001$.
***$p < .0001$.

ficients drop only slightly, from .41 and .39 for the original scales, to .38 and .36 for the purged scales. These reductions are well within the bounds of what would be expected from the slightly lower scale reliabilities alone. Purging the symbolic racism scales of items that refer to government action does not alter the basic findings, so the central role of symbolic racism is not likely to be due merely to overlapping content of independent and dependent variables.

The Origins of Symbolic Racism

Hypothesis 3 suggests that symbolic racism originates in a blend of antiblack affect with the perception that blacks violate traditional nonracial values, which we measure here with scales of individualism, morality, and authoritarianism. In two respects the data are quite consistent with this hypothesis. The overall model accounts for a considerable amount of variance, ranging from 34% to 37% across the four studies, as shown in Table 20.5. This parallelism in r-square across the four studies is striking given the considerable differences in model specification, and in measurement of both the predictors and symbolic racism. Sec-

ond, antiblack affect has consistent effects throughout (whether measured directly through the black thermometer, or indirectly through antiblack stereotypes). Its bivariate correlations average .28, and its regression coefficients are significant in each study. So the racial affect piece of the puzzle appears to be in place.

The other presumed component of symbolic racism, nonracial values, has in the past proven a more elusive target (see, e.g., Sears, 1988). The original formulations cited earlier alluded in rather general terms to several traditional values, with the door also left open to the possibility that conservative political ideology might collect some of the variance that had originated in one or more of these values. The data in Table 20.5 are roughly consistent with these expectations, although it must be said that the expectations are rather general, and the fit quite variable across model specifications. The average bivariate correlation of traditional values with symbolic racism is .27, and 6 of the 10 regression coefficients are significant. The three partisanship predispositions yielded a similar average correlation (.26), with half of the ideology terms and both social welfare terms significant.

In sum, we can be confident that these variables

TABLE 20.4. Variance Accounted for by Racial and Nonracial Attitudes: Hierarchical Regressions

	First Stage		Last Stage			
	Racial Attitudes (1)	Nonracial Attitudes (2)	Racial Attitudes (3)	Nonracial Attitudes (4)	Symbolic Racism Alone (5)	All Variables (6)
Equal opportunity:						
1986 NES	33.8	24.8	14.4	9.6	9.9	44.8
1992 NES	26.4	16.3	15.1	5.2	7.5	32.7
Mean	30.1	20.6	14.8	7.4	8.7	38.8
Federal assistance:						
1986 NES	32.6	18.3	17.8	7.3	10.4	41.5
1992 NES	32.6	16.6	19.5	5.6	9.6	38.6
1994 GSS	23.8	9.1	16.9	2.2	15.1	29.4
Mean	29.7	14.7	18.1	5.0	11.7	36.5
Affirmative action:						
1986 NES	21.8	11.2	15.5	3.5	11.3	27.6
1992 NES	21.5	9.9	16.4	2.4	12.1	26.6
1994 GSS	18.6	3.9	13.1	.1	11.6	20.8
1995 LACSS	17.9	12.8	8.9	4.7	7.3	25.5
Mean	20.0	9.5	13.5	2.7	10.6	25.1

Note.—All data are percentages. Entries in columns 1 and 2 are the *r*-square for racial or nonracial attitudes considered alone; in column 3, the changes in *r*-square when racial attitudes are added as a final stage after demographics and nonracial attitudes are considered; in column 4, the change when nonracial attitudes are entered in the last stage; and in column 5, the increment in *r*-square when symbolic racism is added as a final stage after all other variables have been considered. The *r*-square for all variables shown in column 6 is not adjusted for the number of variables in each equation. For the adjusted *r*-squares, see Tables 20.1–20.3.

together consistently explain a satisfactory amount of variance in symbolic racism, and that symbolic racism has substantial origins in antiblack affect as well as some mixture of conservative partisan attitudes and nonracial traditional values. But we cannot attempt to be very precise here about the nature of that contribution. A more thorough analysis of the origins of symbolic racism would exceed the bounds of this article.

An Emergent Form of Racism

We have seen that there is a strong direct effect of symbolic racism on racial policy preferences, with rather weak effects of other attitudes. We also have seen that symbolic racism has origins in both antiblack affect and a mixture of conservative nonracial attitudes and values. These two findings by themselves might be consistent with the critique cited earlier that symbolic racism is nothing but an older form of racial prejudice confounded with ideological conservatism. From that view we would expect that traditional prejudice and conservative ideology would have strong indirect effects on racial policy preferences, with symbolic

racism simply serving as a convenient pass-through for these more fundamental attitudes, adding no explanatory power itself. Our view, in contrast, is that symbolic racism is a new and different form of racism, adding an independent note of its own. Accordingly, hypothesis 4 predicts that symbolic racism will have a substantial independent effect on racial policy preferences, above and beyond whatever it mediates on behalf of ideology and traditional prejudices.

The key statistic is the variance explained by symbolic racism when entered in a hierarchical regression equation after all other variables have been considered. It should explain no additional variance if it only mediates the indirect effects of other variables. However, it proves to have a substantial effect quite independent of any of the other variables. The increment to *r*-square that it adds as the last stage in the equation averages 10.5% across these nine tests and in every test is highly significant. The data are shown in Table 20.4 (col. 5). This consistently strong independent effect seems to us good evidence that symbolic racism is not merely a mediator of other conventional racial or nonracial attitudes, but that it represents a

TABLE 20.5. The Origins of Symbolic Racism

	1986 NES		1992 NES		1994 GSS		1995 LACSS	
	Beta	(r)	Beta	(r)	Beta	(r)	Beta	(r)
Racial attitudes:								
Black affect	.25***	(.31)	.21***	(.26)	...		...	
Stereotypes	...		.20***	(.40)	.21***	(.38)	.29***	(.41)
Old-fashioned racism	.00	(.25)	...		.26***	(.44)	...	
White affect	...		.09*	(.14)	...		...	
Partisanship:								
Ideology	.16***	(.26)	.18***	(.39)	.09	(.21)	.11	(.39)
Party identification	.00	(.11)	−.01	(.19)	.07	(.15)	.22**	(.44)
Social welfare	.07*	(.21)	.11**	(.25)	...		...	
Nonracial values:								
Individualism	.18***	(.23)	...		.03	(.08)	.05	(.14)
Morality/sexuality	.14***	(.30)	.14***	(.37)	.04	(.26)	−.11	(.16)
Authoritarianism	...		.07*	(.31)	.15*	(.38)	.25**	(.45)
Demographics:								
Age	.03	(.19)	.00	(.15)	−.21***	(−.04)	.13*	(.17)
Education	−.34***	(−.38)	−.18***	(−.28)	−.15**	(−.27)	.01	(−.14)
Gender	−.01	(.01)	.00	(.03)	−.10*	(−.17)	−.03	(−.14)
Region	.11**	(.19)	.07*	(.14)	.05	(.09)	...	
Adjusted R^2 (%)	35.7		36.8		33.9		35.2	

Sources.—1986 and 1992 National Election Studies, 1994 General Social Survey, and 1995 Los Angeles County Social Survey.
Note.—Entries are standardized regression coefficients, with bivariate correlations in parentheses. A positive entry means antiblack or conservative attitudes are associated with more symbolic racism. Years of age or education, male gender, and Southern region keyed as if they were conservative. Pairwise deletion is employed.
*$p < .05$.
**$p < .001$.
***$p < .0001$.

powerful and different form of white racial resentment.

The Generality of a Racial Response

Earlier we saw that racism is a dominant factor in whites' opposition to racially targeted policies. Next we take up three tests of the generality of those racially based responses.

Diverse Racial Policy Areas

Do whites respond similarly to quite different racial policies? Hypothesis 5 suggests that the common racial symbolism in these racial policies should dominate whites' responses to all of them, despite their unique features, indicating a central role of race. But if each policy issue were to be appraised quite independently, on its own merits, nonracial factors would seem to be more decisive (Sniderman & Piazza, 1993).

One approach to this question is to use factor analysis to determine whether or not whites' responses to all racial policies revolve around a single factor, presumably their common racial content. In contrast, a multiple-factor solution with uncorrelated factors would indicate that all these policies are evaluated on their own terms, irrespective of their common racial content. To begin with, we conducted exploratory (unconstrained) factor analyses on the two NES studies, using principal axis (principal factor) extraction with an oblique rotation. The 1986 data yielded two highly correlated factors, accounting for 41.9% of the variance (Table 20.6, cols. 1 and 2). The 1992 data yielded a single factor, accounting for 34.9% of the variance. Its loadings are also shown in Table 20.6 (col. 3).[1] An alternative test uses confirmatory factor analyses, constrained to either single-factor or three-factor solutions. In both years the single-factor solution fits well, with all items loading on a single factor (in 1986, the loadings ranged from .48 to .62; the results for 1992 are shown in

TABLE 20.6. Unconstrained Factor Analyses of Racial Policy Items

	1986 NES Factors		1992 NES Factors
	1	2	1
Equal opportunity:			
Fair treatment in jobs	.68	−.02	.56
Desegregated schools	.48	.16	.50
Equal opportunity	.65	−.11	...
Federal assistance:			
Aid to minorities	.46	.19	.65
Spending to assist blacks	.31	.30	.59
Affirmative action:			
Preferential treatment, jobs	.02	.71	.57
College quotas	−.02	.80	.66
Variance explained (%)	41.9	34.9	

Sources—1986 and 1992 National Election Studies.
Note—Entries are pattern matrix factor loadings, with oblique rotation in 1986 (the correlation between factors is .58).

Table 20.6). Constraining the analysis to a three-factor solution, with an oblique rotation, does yield three factors in both years, but they are highly correlated. In sum, the factor analytic evidence shows either a single factor on which all policy attitudes load, or a multiple-factor solution in which the obtained factors are very highly correlated. Either outcome suggests the power of the underlying racial basis of whites' responses to such policies.

Second, if whites are responding primarily to the common racial content of these policies, racial attitudes should play the strongest explanatory role in all three policy areas. They do. The standardized regression coefficients for symbolic racism average .38, .39, and .41 for the three issue areas (see Tables 20.1 to 20.3, respectively). Antiblack affect has weaker and more variable effects, but it is statistically significant in all cases. The weaker roles of nonracial attitudes are also quite similar across areas. Political ideology yielded average coefficients of .08, .01, and .02; party identification, .02, .06, and .09; social welfare, .20, .22, and .05; and morality/sexuality, .06, .02, and .04, to mention those with sufficient cases to make an average meaningful.

Perhaps the best summary statistic is the relative contribution of racial and nonracial attitudes to variance explained in the three policy areas. In each policy area, racial attitudes explain more variance than do nonracial attitudes, regardless of the stage at which either is entered in the equation. In

each area, the pooled racial attitudes contribute at least half again as much variance explained as do the pooled nonracial attitudes when entered at the first stage (cf. cols. 1 and 2 of Table 20.4), and they contribute over twice as much variance as nonracial attitudes when each is entered as the last stage of the equation (cf. cols. 3 and 4 in Table 20.4). The incremental effect of symbolic racism when added as the last stage of the regression is also very similar across policy areas, averaging 8.7%, 11.7%, and 10.6% in additional r-squared, respectively. The determinants of whites' racial policy attitudes are, therefore, very much the same across racial policy areas.

So the appropriate conclusion would seem to be that the racial content of these policies is the feature that captures much of whites' attention. There is little evidence of the kind of independence of white responses to the three policy areas hypothesized by Sniderman and Piazza (1993). To be sure, each policy also has its own idiosyncratic features to which whites respond, and which account for any differences in the frequency of opposition to each policy. But this indeterminacy should not blind us to the powerful evidence for a central role of racial attitudes in forming these preferences.

Candidate Evaluations

This literature has been concerned with the evaluation of political candidates as well as with racial policies. Hypothesis 6 suggests that racial attitudes are likely to have clear independent effects on the evaluations of black candidates, or of white candidates who engage in explicitly ethnocentric appeals, but less effect on those of more mainstream white major-party presidential candidates. To test this hypothesis, we examined evaluations of the most prominent candidates in the 1986 and 1992 National Election Studies (the 1994 GSS and 1995 LACSS had no items on candidates). The data are shown in Table 20.7.

This hypothesis receives substantial support. First, consider evaluations of Jesse Jackson, the most visible black candidate. In 1986 and 1992, both symbolic racism and antiblack affect have significant effects, of about equal magnitude. So does nonracial partisanship. Symbolic racism also contributes significantly to support for Pat Buchanan, the closest in these data sets to an ex-

TABLE 20.7. Origins of Whites' Evaluations of National Political Candidates: Regression Analysis

	Opposition to Democrats			Support for Republicans		
	Jackson 1986	Jackson 1992	Clinton 1992	Bush 1992	Reagan 1986	Buchanan 1992
Racial attitudes:						
Symbolic racism	.26***	.15***	.00	.01	.15***	.14**
Black affect	.22***	.22***	.14***	−.06	−.11**	−.07*
Stereotypes	...	.01	−.08*	.04	...	−.01
Old-fashioned racism	−.12*	...	...	...	.01	...
White affect	...	.04	−.06	.08*	...	.01
Partisanship:						
Ideology	.22***	.12*	.23***	.13*	.14**	.26***
Party identification	−.05	.14**	.41***	.03	.52***	.14**
Social welfare	.12*	.07	.03	.03	−.02	.04
Nonracial values:						
Individualism	−.11*	...	...	...	.09*	...
Morality/sexuality	−.03	.03	.08*	.09*	−.01	.07
Authoritarianism	...	-.04	−.02	.02	...	.15***
Adjusted R^2 (%)	24.0	22.8	43.1	41.6	43.6	31.3

Source—National Election Studies.
Note—Entries are standardized regression coefficients. A positive entry indicates an association of negative racial attitudes, conservative attitudes, or conservative values with anti-Democratic or pro-Republican candidate evaluations. All candidate evaluations were measured in postelection surveys except Jackson and Buchanan in 1992. The full equations include age, education, gender, and region; those terms are not shown. Pairwise deletion is employed.
*$p < .05$.
**$p < .001$.
***$p < .0001$.

plicitly ethnocentrically oriented white candidate, but not as much as do party identification and ideology. Racial attitudes have no systematic effect on evaluations of the more mainstream major-party white leaders, Reagan, Bush, and Clinton. Only two of the nine relevant coefficients are significant in the expected direction (and two in the opposite direction). Their evaluations are much more influenced by party identification and ideology. Racial attitudes in general, and symbolic racism in particular, are triggered first and foremost by candidates with a manifest connection to African Americans.

The Role of Higher Education

Finally, a more refined version of the emphasis on nonracial conservatism assumes a moderating effect of education. According to Sniderman and Piazza (1993), higher education, by teaching racial tolerance, should damp the political effects of racial prejudice and, by enlarging political sophistication, enhance one's ability to connect ongoing policy disputes to nonracial ideologies and values. In contrast, hypothesis 7, reflecting the symbolic politics perspective, assumes that more edu-

cation will increase the consistency of policy preferences with any long-standing predispositions, and therefore racial attitudes should remain dominant even among the college-educated.

To test these hypotheses, we have split the samples into those with college degrees and those with no college (conforming to Sniderman & Piazza's [1993] procedures). In fact, symbolic racism had substantially stronger bivariate correlations with racial policy preferences among the college-educated (average $r = .64$) than it did among the less educated (average $r = .44$). The regression coefficients for symbolic racism tend to be somewhat higher among the better-educated, but the differences between education groups are not large and none is significant, as shown in Table 20.8. Nor are the older and simpler forms of racial animosity more potent among those with no college education; neither the bivariate correlations nor the regression coefficients (see Table 20.8) differ much across the two education groups. On balance there is no evidence of any systematically stronger impact of racism among the less educated than among the college-educated.

As predicted from both theoretical perspectives, education strengthens the bivariate correlations of

TABLE 20.8. Origins of Whites' Opposition to Racial Policies among High and Low Educational Groups

	Equal Opportunity		Federal Assistance		Affirmative Action	
	College Graduates	No College	College Graduates	No College	College Graduates	No College
1986 NES:						
Racial attitudes:						
Symbolic racism	.64**	.73***	.50***	.60***	.84***	.60***
	(.18)	(.15)	(.10)	(.07)	(.14)	(.10)
Black affect	.41*	.21*	.22*	.22**	.10	.12
	(.15)	(.11)	(.08)	(.05)	(.11)	(.07)
Old-fashioned racism	.19	.02	−.09	−.04	−.06	−.18*
	(.14)	(.08)	(.08)	(.04)	(.11)	(.06)
Partisanship:						
Ideology	.10	.32*	.27*	.08	.12	−.07
	(.22)	(.18)	(.13)	(.09)	(.17)	(.12)
Party identification	.20	−.16	−.03	.06	.09	.11
	(.17)	(.10)	(.10)	(.05)	(.13)	(.07)
Social welfare	.28	.26*	.21*	.24***	.15	.11
	(.15)	(.11)	(.08)	(.06)	(.12)	(.08)
Adjusted R^2 (%)	53.1	28.4	49.4	35.1	43.3	22.4
N	105	153	158	327	160	327
1992 NES:						
Racial attitudes:						
Symbolic racism	.78***	.66***	.57***	.54***	.68***	.55***
	(.15)	(.15)	(.07)	(.08)	(.09)	(.09)
Black affect	.24	.44*	.26*	.27**	.12	.17
	(.19)	(.14)	(.09)	(.07)	(.11)	(.09)
Stereotypes	.15	.14	.05	.13	.04	−.02
	(.27)	(.17)	(.13)	(.09)	(.15)	(.11)
White affect	.22	.01	.09	-.01	.04	−.03
	(.18)	(.14)	(.09)	(.08)	(.11)	(.09)
Partisanship:						
Ideology	.26	.14	−.01	.04	.10	.03
	(.24)	(.20)	(.12)	(.10)	(.14)	(.12)
Party identification	.16	.10	.01	.01	.00	.04
	(.18)	(.13)	(.09)	(.07)	(.11)	(.08)
Social welfare	.13	.20	.36***	.25**	.12	−.07
	(.17)	(.13)	(.08)	(.07)	(.10)	(.08)
Adjusted R^2 (%)	38.7	24.7	51.3	28.9	40.6	21.6
N	169	247	260	335	260	335

Source—1986 and 1992 National Election Studies.
Note—Each column represents a separate equation. The values and demographics referred to in Table 20.1 were included in each equation, but the results are not shown here. Entries are unstandardized regression coefficients; those in parentheses are the standard errors.
*$p < .05$.
**$p < .001$.
***$p < .0001$.

ideology and the other partisan predispositions with policy preferences: the mean correlation of partisan attitudes with policy preferences is .47 among the college educated and .17 among the less educated. But there are no systematic differences between education groups in the regression coefficients, because of the strong effects of symbolic racism in both educational groups.

The data support hypothesis 7 quite well, then. The ordering of predictive power among these various predispositions is quite parallel among college-educated and non-college-educated whites: symbolic racism in particular, and racial attitudes in general, are considerably stronger than are nonracial predispositions even among the college-educated. Moreover, all these predispositions together account considerably better for policy preferences among the college-educated: as Table 20.8 shows, in each case the total r-squared is almost twice as high as it is for the less educated. There is no evidence that a college education leads to a replacement of racism by ideology as the key determinant of these policy preferences.

Discussion

The Role of Racism

The first goal of this study was to provide a systematic test of the hypothesis that racial attitudes make the pivotal contribution to whites' opposition to race-targeted policies. The data seem to us quite clear: racial predispositions dominate all other factors in terms of individual correlations or regression coefficients, and in their capacity for explaining variance in policy preferences. Nonracial attitudes (such as political ideology, party identification, social welfare policy attitudes, and such traditional social values as individualism, morality, and authoritarianism) have been as thoroughly controlled for as possible, and they do not have strong effects; they are overshadowed by the effects of racism.

Further evidence of the generality of a racially based response is the considerable commonality in whites' responses to these different racial policy areas. We have not attempted a systematic assessment of possible differences in level of white support across areas. But by two other criteria we find some striking similarities of response. The underlying structure of racial policy attitudes fits either a simple single-factor model or a multiple-factor model with highly correlated factors. This complements other findings that racial policy attitudes tend to load on a single factor distinct from nonracial attitudes (Abramowitz, 1994; Sears & Kosterman, 1991). Also, the determinants of policy preferences are quite similar across policy areas, even when measured in different surveys. These findings suggest that race is the dominant cue governing whites' responses to explicitly race-targeted policies, although other features of the policies clearly are visible as well.

Racial attitudes also influence evaluations of black and ethnocentric white candidates but do not have a clear independent influence on evaluations of the major-party presidential candidates. Finally, racial attitudes dominate racial policy preferences even among college graduates, contrary to the view that college education damps their effects.

These findings are quite consistent with the symbolic politics notion with which we began. Most of the racial and nonracial predictors had significant bivariate correlations with all our dependent variables. But when all factors were considered simultaneously, racial attitudes dominated preferences regarding racial policy (as well as of the black candidate, Jesse Jackson, and the ethnocentric white candidate, Pat Buchanan). Presumably, the explicit racial content of these attitude objects evoked racial predispositions. The mainstream white candidates, in contrast, seem to have evoked primarily nonracial predispositions. Moreover, higher education (as with higher information flows more generally) increased the constraint of all these predictor attitudes with policy and candidate evaluations—but did not influence the balance between racial and nonracial predictors.

This conclusion, that racism (in whatever form) is central to these political preferences, is contrary to that offered by some other researchers (e.g., Roth, 1994; Sniderman & Piazza, 1993). The difference, we believe, lies in our more comprehensive and systematic examination of antecedent racial attitudes, and our more thorough replication across policy areas and across surveys.

Symbolic Racism

Our second major goal was to test the hypothesis that symbolic racism is a considerably stronger political force in contemporary America than are other, more traditional indicators of racial prejudice. This case, too, we believe has been made quite strongly in our data. In bivariate correlations or in regression analyses, symbolic racism dominates while stereotypes and old-fashioned racism have little residual effect. Nor does prowhite loyalty play a significant role in opposition to racial policies. Other researchers' reports in the published literature of weak effects of racial attitudes have arisen, we believe, because they have been looking in the wrong place for them. This is not to say that anti-black affect and traditional racial stereotypes (or even pockets of old-fashioned racism) no longer exist. But they no longer have the political strength that symbolic racism has.

The hypothesis that symbolic racism is a different and politically more powerful form of racism has attracted several critiques that need to be addressed. One is that symbolic racism may not be very different from older forms of prejudice such as stereotypes or old-fashioned racism (Fazio et al., 1995; Miller, 1994; Raden, 1994; Sniderman & Tetlock, 1986; Weigel & Howes, 1985). Indeed, in our data they were correlated, but the consistently greater impact of symbolic racism compared with older forms of racial antagonism, across a number of different replications, would seem to indicate that it is a distinctive orientation. Moreover, symbolic racism contributes substantial independent variance of its own to racial policy preferences in addition to mediating some of the effects of its putative antecedents (antiblack affect and conservative nonracial values and attitudes). But to test directly for its independence, we conducted unconstrained factor analyses (with oblique rotation) of all racial independent variables in each survey. In brief, in every survey all symbolic racism items loaded on a factor separate from those on which the older forms of racial antagonism loaded.

A second critique is that symbolic racism may not be internally very homogeneous (Colleau et al., 1990; Sniderman & Tetlock, 1986). However, the factor analyses of racial attitudes just described, yielding a distinctive factor for symbolic racism in each survey, along with the quite reasonable levels of scale reliability for symbolic racism cited earlier, averaging about .70, sustain the view that symbolic racism is a reasonably internally homogenous construct.

A third critique is that symbolic racism is "confounded" with ideological conservatism and so does not cleanly assess the unique effects of racism. Ours would seem to be quite persuasive data against that view: controls on ideology do not weaken the effects of symbolic racism on policy preferences, and ideology itself has generally nonsignificant effects (Tables 20.1–20.3); symbolic racism adds substantial unique explanatory variance even after ideology and all other nonracial attitudes have been considered (Table 20.4); and ideology is not a strong determinant of symbolic racism (Table 20.5).

Fourth, others have suspected that symbolic racism might be just a minor variant of authoritarianism (Raden, 1994; Weigel & Howes, 1985), or that it might have lesser effects than authoritarianism (Sniderman & Piazza, 1993). Again, our evidence would seem persuasive against both views. The raw correlations between the two are substantial (averaging .38; see Table 20.5), but in the regression analyses authoritarianism is a modest contributor to either symbolic racism or racial policy preferences, having less effect than racial attitudes in each case. Authoritarianism and symbolic racism undoubtedly share some variance, but the explicitly racial character of symbolic racism is a critical distinction between them.

A fifth concern is that the impact of symbolic racism is just a result of conceptual overlap with our dependent variables. If symbolic racism merely measured opposition to special, race-conscious government aid to blacks in the abstract, and the racial policy scales, opposition to it in concrete form, any association between them might reflect nothing more than that common content. To begin with, it might be noted that abstract and concrete versions of sociopolitical attitudes are not invariably consistent with each other. Classic cases include the "principle-implementation" gap in racial attitudes (Schuman, Steeh, & Bobo, 1985), the gap in responses to abstract and concrete versions of civil liberties, or the common preference for both "smaller government" and increased spending on specific services (see, e.g., Sears & Citrin, 1985).

But we have more concrete evidence against this interpretation. (a) The effects of symbolic racism are not confined to contemporary race-conscious policies of special treatment for blacks but occur just as consistently concerning the equal opportunity policies dating from the 1950s (compare Table 20.1 with Table 20.3). Any policy issues with manifest racial content seem to evoke symbolic racism. (b) Symbolic racism has consistently significant effects on evaluations of Jesse Jackson and Pat Buchanan, neither of whom, as an attitude object, presumably suffers from this conceptual overlap. (c) We have imposed substantial controls on ideology, party identification, and social welfare attitudes, which bear directly on the magnitude of government action but make no explicit reference to blacks. They consistently have weaker effects than does symbolic racism, whose effects are not substantially reduced by such controls. And (d) we earlier presented analyses purging the symbolic racism scales of any items alluding to government action and "special favors," which reduced their reliability and predictive power very little. "Content overlap" does not seem to account for much of the link between symbolic racism and racial policy preferences.

Conclusions

The strengths of our analyses lie in the consistency of the findings across different tests, we believe. The basic findings are replicated in four different surveys spanning nearly a decade, and on three different policy areas. The basic independent and dependent variables were all operationalized somewhat differently across the four studies, giving some further confidence in the generality of the findings. And the findings are remarkably parallel across all these variations. We have not tried to squeeze a great deal of subtlety from the data; our goal in this article has been to ensure that the main findings are strong and replicable, and we have confidence that they are. Indeed, given the considerable replication of our core findings within this article, it seems likely that contrary reports based on single surveys may have overinterpreted possibly chance departures from the essential story.

Finally, we should take note of four important questions that we have not attempted to resolve in this article. As Bobo (1988; also Bobo, Kluegel, & Smith, 1997) has correctly observed, we have not here or elsewhere attempted to analyze the forces that gave rise to the shift from old-fashioned to symbolic racism; that probably requires a different form of analysis altogether. Second, we have indicated that an additive model involving both antiblack affect and conservative nonracial attitudes and values explains the origins of symbolic racism moderately well. However, we have not traveled far down the road of unraveling exactly which nonracial dispositions are involved, nor do we test nonadditive models, and both issues deserve more thorough analysis (see Sears & Kosterman, 1991; Wood, 1994). Third, we have not attempted to address in detail the numerous variants on a realistic group conflict model cited earlier. And, finally, there is work going forward on the assumption that indirect measures of prejudice will be more valid than the direct measures we have used (Banaji & Greenwald, 1994; Fazio et al., 1995; Gaertner & Dovidio, 1986). Our findings seem fairly robust, however, despite whatever weaknesses the direct approach entails (and recent findings suggest indirect and direct measures may in fact be producing very similar results, after all; see Wittenbrink, Judd, & Park, 1997).

In conclusion, we hope that the strength of the findings here will lay to rest the notion that white opposition to racially targeted policies is primarily motivated by nonracial considerations, or that any racially based motivation is limited to a few poorly educated ethnocentrics or believers in white supremacy. Racism is considerably more widespread in American society than that; it cannot be reduced to the older forms of prejudice familiar in the pre-civil rights era, and it continues to have quite pervasive effects. It is not a pleasant aspect of our society, but it is not one that should be swept under the carpet, either.

NOTE

1. The GSS and LACSS had insufficient policy items to permit this analysis.

REFERENCES

Abramowitz, A. I. 1994. "Issue Evolution Reconsidered: Racial Attitudes and Partisanship in the U.S. Electorate." *American Journal of Political Science* 38:1–24.

Banaji, M. R., and A. G. Greenwald. 1994. "Implicit Stereotyping and Prejudice." In *The Psychology of Prejudice: The Ontario Symposium*, vol. 7, ed. M. P. Zanna and J. M. Olson. Hillsdale, NJ: Erlbaum.

Bobo, L. 1988. "Group Conflict, Prejudice, and the Paradox of Contemporary Racial Attitudes." In *Eliminating Racism: Profiles in Controversy*, ed. P. Katz and D. Taylor. New York: Plenum.

Bobo, L., and V. L. Hutchings. 1996. "Perceptions of Racial Group Competition: Extending Blumer's Theory of Group Position to a Multiracial Social Context." *American Sociological Review* 61:951–73.

Bobo, L., and J. R. Kluegel. 1993. "Opposition to Race-Targeting: Self-Interest, Stratification Ideology, or Racial Attitudes?" *American Sociological Review* 58:443–64.

Bobo, L., J. R. Kluegel, and R. A. Smith. 1997. "Laissez Faire Racism: The Crystallization of a 'Kinder, Gentler' Antiblack Ideology." In *Racial Attitudes in the 1990s: Continuity and Change*, ed. S. A. Tuch and J. K. Martin. Westport, CT: Praeger.

Campbell, A. 1971. *White Attitudes toward Black People*. Ann Arbor, MI: Institute for Social Research.

Carmines, E. G., and W. R. Merriman, Jr. 1993. "The Changing American Dilemma: Liberal Values and Racial Policies." In *Prejudice, Politics, and the American Dilemma,* ed. P. M. Sniderman, P. E. Tetlock, and E. G. Carmines. Stanford, CA: Stanford University Press.

Citrin, J., D. P. Green, and D. O. Sears. 1990. "White Reactions to Black Candidates: When Does Race Matter?" *Public Opinion Quarterly* 54:74–96.

Colleau, S. M., K. Glynn, S. Lybrand, R. M. Merelman, P. Mohan, and J. E. Wall. 1990. "Symbolic Racism in Candidate Evaluation: An Experiment." *Political Behavior* 12:385–402.

Devine, P. G., and A. J. Elliot. 1995. "Are Racial Stereotypes Really Fading? The Princeton Trilogy Revisited." *Personality and Social Psychology Bulletin* 21:1139–50.

D'Souza, D. 1995. *The End of Racism.* New York: Free Press.

Edsall, T. B., and M. D. Edsall. 1991. "When the Official Subject Is Presidential Politics, Taxes, Welfare, Crime, Rights, or Values … the Real Subject Is Race." *Atlantic Monthly* (May), pp. 53–86.

———. 1992. *Chain Reaction: The Impact of Race, Rights, and Taxes on American Politics.* New York: Norton.

Fazio, R. H., J. R. Jackson, B. C. Dunton, and C. J. Williams. 1995. "Variability in Automatic Activation as an Unobtrusive Measure of Racial Attitudes: A Bona Fide Pipeline?" *Journal of Personality and Social Psychology* 69:1013–27.

Gaertner, S. L., and J. F. Dovidio. 1986. "The Aversive Form of Racism." In *Prejudice, Discrimination, and Racism,* ed. J. F. Dovidio and S. L. Gaertner, pp. 61–89. Orlando, FL: Academic Press.

Gilens, M. 1995. "Racial Attitudes and Opposition to Welfare." *Journal of Politics* 57:994–1014.

Greenberg, S. B. 1995. *Middle Class Dreams.* New York: New York Times Books.

Hagen, M. G. 1995. "References to Racial Issues." *Political Behavior* 17:49–88.

Jackman, M. R., and M. J. Muha. 1984. "Education and Intergroup Attitudes: Moral Enlightenment, Superficial Democratic Commitment, or Ideological Refinement?" *American Sociological Review* 49:751–69.

Jessor, T. 1988. "Personal Interest, Group Conflict, and Symbolic Group Affect: Explanations for whites' Opposition to Racial Equality." Doctoral dissertation, Department of Psychology, University of California, Los Angeles.

Katz, D., and K. W. Braly. 1933. "Racial Stereotypes of 100 College Students." *Journal of Abnormal and Social Psychology* 28:280–90.

Katz, I., J. Wackenhut, and R. G. Hass. 1986. "Racial Ambivalence, Value Duality, and Behavior." In *Prejudice, Discrimination, and Racism,* ed. J. F. Dovidio and S. L. Gaertner, pp. 35–60. New York: Academic Press.

Kinder, D. R., and T. Mendelberg. 1995. "Cracks in American Apartheid: The Political Impact of Prejudice among Desegregated whites." *Journal of Politics* 57:402–24.

Kinder, D. R., and L. M. Sanders. 1996. *Divided by Color: Racial Politics and Democratic Ideals.* Chicago: University of Chicago Press.

Kinder, D. R., and D. O. Sears. 1981. "Prejudice and Politics: Symbolic Racism versus Racial Threats to the Good Life." *Journal of Personality and Social Psychology* 40:414–31.

Kleinpenning, G., and L. Hagendoorn. 1993. "Forms of Racism and the Cumulative Dimension of Ethnic Attitudes." *Social Psychology Quarterly* 56:21–36.

Kuzenski, J. C., C. S. Bullock III, and R. K. Gaddie, eds. 1995. *David Duke and the Politics of Race in the South.* Nashville: Vanderbilt University Press.

McConahay, J. B. 1982. "Self-Interest versus Racial Attitudes as Correlates of Anti-busing Attitudes in Louisville: Is It the Buses or the blacks?" *Journal of Politics* 44:692–720.

———. 1986. "Modern Racism, Ambivalence, and the Modern Racism Scale." In *Prejudice, Discrimination, and Racism,* ed. J. F. Dovidio and S. L. Gaertner, pp. 91–126. Orlando, FL: Academic Press.

McConahay, J. B., and J. C. Hough, Jr. 1976. "Symbolic Racism." *Journal of Social Issues* 32:23–45.

Miller, A. H. 1993. "Economic, Character, and Social Issues in the 1992 Presidential Election." *American Behavioral Scientist* 37:315–27.

———. 1994. "Social Groups as Symbols in America's Sense of Democratic Consensus." In *Presidential Campaigns and American Self Images,* ed. A. H. Miller and B. E. Gronbeck. Boulder, CO: Westview.

Miller, W. E., and J. M. Shanks. 1996. *The New American Voter.* Cambridge, MA: Harvard University Press.

Monteith, M. J. 1996. "Contemporary Forms of Prejudice-Related Conflict: In Search of a Nutshell." *Personality and Social Psychology Bulletin* 22:461–73.

Pettigrew, T. F. 1972. "When a black Candidate Runs for Mayor: Race and Voting Behavior." In *Urban Affairs Annual Review,* 1972, ed. H. Hahn, pp. 95–117. Beverly Hills, CA: Sage.

Pettigrew, T. F., and R. W. Meertens. 1995. "Subtle and Blatant Prejudice in Western Europe." *European Journal of Social Psychology* 25:57–75.

Raden, D. 1994. "Are Symbolic Racism and Traditional Prejudice Part of a Contemporary Authoritarian Attitude Syndrome?" *Political Behavior* 16:365–84.

Roth, B. M. 1994. *Prescription for Failure: Race Relations in the Age of Social Science.* New Brunswick, NJ: Transaction.

Schuman, H., C. Steeh, and L. Bobo. 1985. *Racial Trends in America: Trends and Interpretations.* Cambridge, MA: Harvard University Press.

Sears, D. O. 1988. "Symbolic Racism." In *Eliminating Racism: Profiles in Controversy,* ed. P. A. Katz and D. A. Taylor, pp. 53–84. New York: Plenum.

———. 1993. "Symbolic Politics: A Socio-Psychological Theory." In *Explorations in Political Psychology,* ed. S. Iyengar and W. J. McGuire, pp. 113–49. Durham, NC: Duke University Press.

Sears, D. O., and J. Citrin. 1985. *Tax Revolt: Something for Nothing in California.* Enlarged edition. Cambridge, MA: Harvard University Press.

Sears, D. O., J. Citrin, and R. Kosterman, 1987. "Jesse Jackson and the Southern white Electorate in 1984." In *Blacks in Southern Politics,* ed. L. W. Moreland, R. P. Steed, and T. A. Baker, pp. 209–25. New York: Praeger.

Sears, D. O., J. Citrin, and C. van Laar. 1995. "Black Exceptionalism in a Multicultural Society." Paper presented at the annual meeting of the American Political Science Association, Chicago, September 1.

Sears, D. O., C. P. Hensler, and L. K. Speer. 1979. "Whites' Opposition to 'Busing': Self-Interest or Symbolic Politics?" *American Political Science Review* 73:369–84.

Sears, D. O., and T. Jessor. 1996. "Whites' Racial Policy Attitudes: The Role of white Racism." *Social Science Quarterly* 77:751–59.

Sears, D. O., and D. R. Kinder. 1971. "Racial Tensions and Voting in Los Angeles." In *Los Angeles: Viability and Prospects for Metropolitan Leadership*, ed. W. Z. Hirsch. New York: Praeger.

Sears, D. O., and R. Kosterman. 1991. "Is It Really Racism? The Origins and Dynamics of Symbolic Racism." Paper presented at the annual meeting of the Midwest Political Science Association, Chicago, April.

Sears, D. O., R. R. Lau, T. R. Tyler, and H. M. Allen, Jr. 1980. "Self-Interest vs. Symbolic Politics in Policy Attitudes and Presidential Voting." *American Political Science Review* 74:670–84.

Sidanius, J., F. Pratto, and L. Bobo. 1996. "Racism, Conservatism, Affirmative Action, and Intellectual Sophistication: A Matter of Principled Conservatism or Group Dominance?" *Journal of Personality and Social Psychology* 70:1–15.

Sniderman, P. M., and T. Piazza. 1993. *The Scar of Race.* Cambridge, MA: Harvard University Press.

Sniderman, P. M., and P. E. Tetlock. 1986. "Symbolic Racism: Problems of Motive Attribution in Political Debate." *Journal of Social Issues* 42:129–50.

Swim, J. K., K. J. Aikin, W. S. Hall, and B. A. Hunter. 1995. "Sexism and Racism: Old-Fashioned and Modern Prejudices." *Journal of Personality and Social Psychology* 68:199–214.

Tajfel, H., and J. C. Turner. 1986. "The Social Identity Theory of Intergroup Behavior." In *Psychology of Intergroup Relations*, ed. S. Worchel and W. G. Austin, 2d ed. Chicago: Nelson-Hall.

Tuch, S. A., and M. Hughes. 1996. "Whites' Racial Policy Attitudes." *Social Science Quarterly* 77:723–45.

Weigel, R. H., and P. W. Howes. 1985. "Conceptions of Racial Prejudice: Symbolic Racism Reconsidered." *Journal of Social Issues* 41:117–38.

Wittenbrink, B., C. M. Judd, and B. Park. 1997. "Evidence for Racial Prejudice at the Implicit Level and Its Relationship with Questionnaire Measures." *Journal of Personality and Social Psychology* 72:262–74.

Wood, J. 1994. "Is 'Symbolic Racism' Racism? A Review Informed by Intergroup Behavior." *Political Psychology* 15:673–86.

Prejudice, Diversity, and Social Contact

The readings in this section address two distinguishable but related topics. First, we cover contemporary political psychological approaches to intergroup relations. These general theories (social identity theory, system justification theory, and social dominance theory) can be applied to a wide 1998). Second, we turn our attention to issues of protest and revolution, recognizing that many forms of political transformation occur through violent means (Gurr, 1970; Martin, Scully, & Levitt, 1990; Muller, 1980; Rejai & Phillips, 1988; Tilly, 1975).

THE SOCIAL PSYCHOLOGY OF WRONGDOING AND HARM

We begin this section with John Darley's social psychological analysis of one of the most important and least systematically studied topics within the field of political psychology, namely the organization and production of evil. After exploring conceptual definitions of "evil," Darley distinguishes between two different forms of evil-doing: (a) the *kernel of evil* form of evil-doing, which results from the actions of truly malevolent individuals, and (b) *institutionalized evil*, which is the product of "normal" individuals working within the context of malevolent institutions or organizations. Darley points out that while "kernel of evil" malevolence is certainly a problem, it is neither as destructive nor as philosophically perplexing as the institutionalized evil perpetrated by ordinary citizens. At the heart of Darley's project is the drive to understand how malevolent organizations are created and sustained.

379

As the world-changing events of September 11, 2001 made brutally clear, no discussion of political violence would be complete without considering the subject of terrorism. Martha Crenshaw addresses this vexing topic in a paper she first published in 1986, almost a generation before the dramatic events of 9/11. The issues that she raises are perhaps more relevant today than when the paper was first written. Crenshaw underscores the extreme difficulty of studying terrorism because of social scientists' relatively poor access to those who are involved in terrorist activities. She also discusses several other challenges, among them the fact that precise definitions of "terrorism" are lacking, that there may be many different types of terrorism, and that the personalities of so-called terrorists may differ greatly depending upon the type of terrorism in question. Thus, rather than regarding Professor Crenshaw's essay as an exhaustive and definitive statement about the political psychology of terrorism, it is better regarded as a framework for generating profound questions about the psychological causes and consequences of terror and violence.

PROTEST AND REVOLUTION

The chapter by Harry Eckstein provides an insightful metatheoretical analysis of issues pertaining to collective political violence. After reviewing the voluminous research literature on political violence, Eckstein identifies two major classes of theoretical explanations of political violence: (a) *contingency theories*, which assume that individuals and groups are generally peaceful and only engage in political violence when their basic needs have been severely frustrated, and (b) *inherency models*, which assume that people are primarily interested in increasing their degree of power and privilege and that they will readily engage in political violence for the achievement of these ends whenever the potential gains of violence are seen as outweighing the costs. Eckstein summarizes the most well-known exemplars of these different approaches and concludes by finding fault with both types of theories.

The final essay by Simon and Klandermans is a good example of how modern theorists attempt to apply basic social psychological principles concerning social identification, self-categorization, and minority influence to understand how and when collective identities become politically mobilized for conflict and struggle. In defending what Eckstein would describe as an *inherency model*, Simon and Klandermans argue that political conflict should be viewed as a struggle for power within the framework of three politicized collective identities: (a) a politicized ingroup, (b) a politicized outgroup possessing a zero-sum relationship to the ingroup, and (c) a third party audience to whom both the ingroup and outgroup must appeal for political support. Briefly, the authors argue that collective identities become "politicized" to the extent that these identities become consciously engaged in a power struggle on behalf of their social groups. Political conflict becomes more likely as people become aware of additional grievances held by other members of the ingroup and as people begin to increasingly attribute the causes of their grievances to the actions of outgroup members and demand that corrective action be taken by society as a whole. Once politicized identities are formed, social and psychological consequences include increased conformity to ingroup norms, as well as increased stereotyping, discrimination, and even violence against outgroups.

Discussion Questions

1. What are the psychological processes by which people are socialized into committing acts of evil within institutional settings? Can you identify contemporary real-world cases in which these processes seem to be unfolding?
2. What are the most important considerations in deciding whether or not an action should be labeled "evil"?
3. It is often said that one person's "terrorist" is another's "freedom fighter." How would you go about trying to define "terrorism" in a politically objective way so that it could be studied scientifically?
4. There is some reason to believe that the personality types of terrorists might well depend upon the type of terrorist organization one is dealing with. How many different types of terrorist organizations can you identify, and how might the personalities of terrorists correspond to these different types of organizations?
5. Whether a terrorist maintains a favorable or unfavorable personal identity might well depend upon the specific social and historical context in which he or she is situated. Describe the nature of this context dependency and illustrate with the use of examples.
6. Which type of theoretical approach to understanding political violence (the contingency approach or the inherency approach) do you find most convincing and why?
7. List several examples of politicized collective identities from contemporary political life. How do you think that these collective identities might be "de-politicized?"

Suggested Readings

Arendt, H. (1951). *Origins of totalitarianism*. New York: Harcourt.

Bandura, A. (1999). Moral disengagement in the perpetration of inhumanities. *Personality and Social Psychology Review, 3*, 193–209.

Bar-Tal, D. (1989). Delegitimization: The extreme case of stereotyping and prejudice. In D. Bar-Tal, C. F. Graumann, A. W. Kruglanski, & W. Stroebe (Eds.) *Stereotyping and prejudice: Changing conceptions*. New York: Springer-Verlag.

Baumeister, R. (1997). *Evil: Inside human cruelty and violence*. New York: W.H. Freeman.

Berkowitz, L. (1999). Evil is more than banal: Situationism and the concept of evil. *Personality and Social Psychology Review, 3*, 246–253.

Blass, T. (1999). The Milgram paradigm after 35 years: Some things we now know about obedience to authority. *Journal of Applied Social Psychology, 29*, 955–978.

Davies, J. C. (1971). *When men revolt and why*. New York: Free Press.

Fanon, F. (1963). *The wretched of the earth*. New York: Grove Press.

Gurr, T. R. (1970). *Why men rebel*. Princeton University Press.

Gurr, T. R. (Ed.) (1980). *The handbook of political conflict: Theory and research.* New York: The Free Press.

Huntington, S. (1993). The clash of civilizations. *Foreign Affairs, 72,* 22–49.

Johnson, C. (2000). *The costs and consequences of American empire.* New York: Metropolitan Books.

Kelman, H. C., & Hamilton, V. L. (1988). *Crimes of obedience: Towards a social psychology of authority and responsibility.* New Haven, CT: Yale University Press.

Lewis, B. (1990, September). The roots of Muslim rage: Why so many Muslims deeply resent the West, and why their bitterness will not easily be mollified. *The Atlantic Monthly, 266,* 47–60.

Lifton, R. J. (1986). *The Nazi doctors: Medical killing and the psychology of genocide.* New York: Basic Books.

Martin, J., Scully, M., & Levitt, B. (1990). Injustice and the legitimation of revolution: Damning the past, excusing the present, and neglecting the future. *Journal of Personality and Social Psychology, 59,* 281–290.

Milgram, S. (1974). *Obedience to authority.* New York: Harper & Row.

Muller, E. N. (1980). The psychology of political protest and violence. In T. R. Gurr (Ed.), *The handbook of political conflict: Theory and research* (pp. 69-99). New York: Free Press.

Opotow, S. (1990). Moral exclusion and injustice: An introduction. *Journal of Social Issues, 46,* 1–20.

Pyszczynski, T., Solomon, S., & Greenberg, J. (2002). *In the wake of 9/11: The psychology of terror.* Washington, DC: American Psychological Association.

Reich, W. (Ed.) (1998). *Origins of terrorism: Psychologies, ideologies, theologies, states of mind.* Princeton: Woodrow Wilson Center.

Sabini, J. P., & Silver, M. (1993). Destroying the innocent with a clear conscience: A sociopsychology of the holocaust. In N. J. Kressel (Ed.), *Political psychology: Classic and contemporary readings* (pp. 192–217). New York: Paragon House.

Staub, E. (1989). *The roots of evil: The origins of genocide and other group violence.* New York: Cambridge University Press.

Tilly, C. (1975). Revolution and collective violence. In F. I. Greenstein & W. P. Nelson (Eds.), *Handbook of political science: Macropolitical theory: Vol. 7.* Reading, MA: Addison-Wesley.

Tyler, T. R. (1990). *Why people obey the law.* New Haven, CT: Yale University Press.

Waller, J. (2002). *Becoming evil: How ordinary people commit genocide and mass killing.* New York: Oxford University Press.

Zimbardo, P. G. (1998). The psychology of evil: A situationist perspective on recruiting good people to engage in anti-social acts. *Japanese Journal of Social Psychology, 11,* 125–133.

Social Organization for the Production of Evil

John M. Darley • Princeton University

I was born in 1938, into a cohort that was or-dained to think about evil—indeed to be haunted by it, given the events of the Nazi era. But that social psychology could come to grips with what this evil might mean I did not have the vision, or perhaps the courage, to see. Even now, having thought about the topic under the stimulus of three books, I would not want to say that my thinking has gone very far. In this essay, I attempt to present a social psychological perspective on evil, and contrast that perspective with two others: (a) the views of evil that we all hold at an unexamined level of everyday thought, and (b) the view of evil that I think might be drawn from the clinical per-spective. Finally, I suggest some conclusions we might draw about evil from the clash of these dif-ferent perspectives.

In recent years, we have seen the publication of Lifton's (1986) report of his interviews with phy-sicians who participated in the Nazi death camps, the long-awaited book by Herbert Kelman and Lee Hamilton (1989) containing their interpretations of survey data on My Lai and the related trial of Lt. Calley, and Ervin Staub's (1989) comparative study of several genocidal events. Reflecting on these books, I have been led back to Stanley Milgram's (1974) book detailing his obedience studies and his final interpretations of them, and to Hannah Arendt's (1963) seminal and contro-versial book *Eichmann in Jerusalem: Report on the Banality of Evil*. Each author has been willing to consider the events or people we label as *evil*. (Milgram does so somewhat implicitly, the others quite explicitly.) Each author deserves consider-able credit for this; evil is not a topic easily acces-sible within the confines of those psychological movements that are the inheritors of our earlier operationalist, positivist traditions. These people are working outside the mainstream of at least the sorts of psychological content customary within our academic enclaves.

They are not, however, always working outside the methodological traditions of modern social science. Milgram, famously and controversially, carried out social psychological experiments on harmdoing. Kelman and Hamilton (although their book is by no means confined to it) report survey results about the "Lt. Calley trial," the military court marshal of a platoon commander who pre-sided over the My Lai massacre. Lifton conducted interviews with doctors who had served in Nazi concentration camps. Only Staub does not present some form of new data, choosing instead to con-struct an account ranging across different fields of social science and different sources of social-science thinking.

Each book contributes to what becomes, at a general level, a consistent picture of the origins of many of the evil acts in the world. Reading and rereading them, I have come to see that they sharply contradict our ordinary ways of thinking about the origins of evil, and that this is one of the major messages to be extracted from them. The message they jointly present is a disconcerting one: Our everyday understandings of evil (to be sketched in my next section) are frequently incorrect or perhaps, more accurately, irrelevant to most acts of evil and therefore deeply misleading. Instead, the authors provide the material on which to form an alternate view, one that I have called the "social psychological perspective." Because that view clashes with views all of us hold, their message is an uncomfortable one, whose implications are not easily grasped.

Like most ordinary people, we psychologists are in the grip of another view. That other view exists at the level of our day-to-day, understood rather than examined, beliefs—the beliefs we hold as persons rather than as psychologists. To understand the social psychological view, it is useful to examine commonsensical views first, the ways that our culture currently thinks about the related notions of "moral wrong-doing" and "evil."

Everyday Thinking About 'Wrongdoing' and 'Evil'

Moral wrongdoing has proved to be a troubling concept to define. Uneasily recalling our exposure to philosophy courses, in which we discovered the difficulties in defining and defending our everyday concepts, we "ordinary persons" recognize at some level that we may not be able to clearly define and defend our particular concepts of "good" or "wrongdoing." Unlike some other cultures, or our own culture in the past, we do not have an agreed-on, authoritative list of actions that constitute wrongdoing. We used to have lists of sins, but because we no longer put much stock, as a culture, in the religious principles that generated these lists, we cannot much rely on them as defining the set of moral wrongs.[1] Thus, we have to generate such a list from some underlying philosophical principle.

Principle-Based Definitions of Wrongdoing

When we cast around for that agreed-on principle that might give us a tenable conceptualization of wrongdoing, we are not greatly helped. One prevailing theory of human motivation, the theory of

rational choice, does not easily justify the moral preferencing of certain desires over others, and thus does not give us any easy mechanism for designating certain actions as morally wrong. Contributing to the difficulties with the definition of "wrong," is our learned recognition, within our present society, that it is difficult to state our grounds for disagreeing with another individual's personal preference structure. One of us likes the paintings of Titian, another paintings of Elvis on black velvet; to each his own.[2]

As this hints, all these notions lead us to retreat to the culturally familiar stance of a last-resort utilitarianism. Within that system, we can all agree that causing harm or pain to others is the essence of wrongdoing. The definition of immorality that arises from utilitarian considerations centers around a notion of actions that inflict pain on others. As the old characterization went, "my freedom of action ends just a centimeter away from hitting your nose." We might say that, within a utilitarian perspective, my possibility of doing wrong begins about at your nose. Wrong actions, more formally, are those that impinge on the other, and cause that other pain or harm.

This definition needs qualification, but the moves to qualify it are well understood. Briefly, we need to rule out certain harmful actions, such as unforeseeable accidents, as necessarily morally wrong. So we add to the definition a qualification: a notion of a wrongdoing actor as somehow *intentionally*, *knowingly*, or *recklessly* harming or causing pain to another individual.

A few more qualifications bring us to a preliminary definition. We recognize that in certain times (such as wartime) or in certain places (such as prison death rows) actions that bring harm or even death to other individuals, are regarded by many not only as not evil, but as morally required actions, so we add a reference to "unjustified harmdoing" as the morally wrong sort of harmdoing. We also add qualifications pertaining to excused harmdoing incidents, or mitigated ones (Austin, 1956). What should count as justifications, mitigations, and excuses requires some elucidation, but we have generally agreed on examples to guide our judgments (Darley & Shultz, 1990; Darley & Zanna, 1982). Naturally, some tricky questions remain; we can be made uneasy by certain borderline cases.[3] Nonetheless, I want to suggest that this is how ordinary Americans resolve questions when they are pressed concerning their definitions of "morally wrong actions."

Staying at a self-conscious level of discourse, having struggled to arrive at this definition of "wrong," we seem to have very little left to say about evil. Evil is an even more difficult concept to define than "wrong." Uncharacteristically, *Webster's* flounders: "not good morally; causing or tending to cause harm; the antithesis of good; something that is injurious to moral or physical happiness or welfare" (*Webster's New Third International Dictionary*, 1963). Here evil is simply equated with moral wrongness. One gets the feeling that *evil* is a word falling out of use; it seems redundant with the notion of moral wrongness, bringing archaic baggage such as the notion of sin along with it.

Actually, I think we have difficulties with the notion of evil only when we take a certain analytic perspective. The perspective, or level of thought at which we have been analyzing wrongdoing thus far, is one that we might call *considered thought that one is prepared to defend against challenge*. The challenge might arise from an acquaintance with different values, a public opinion pollster, or a philosophy professor. We are all capable of functioning on that considered level of thought, and do so when we are facing definitional questions. At this level of thought, the notion of evil becomes difficult of definition or redundant. However, it is not always at this level of thought that ordinary people think about evil; in everyday thought, including that of psychologists, the notion of evil is alive and well. It may not be easy to define, but none of us have much trouble recognizing it.

Everyday Definitions of Evil

At the level of our everyday functioning, we operate on the basis of "naive psychology," which comprises the understandings we all carry around with us to analyze the events and actions of our everyday life. These are the sorts of understandings Heider (1958) most successfully called to our attention: those often unexamined understandings, frequently built into everyday vocabularies, that categorize our everyday world and enable us to function in it. At this level, we have both a conceptualization of evil acts that is generally shared and coherent and a theory of what causes these evil actions.

First, how do we conceive of evil acts? As follows: Evil actions are a subset of bad actions; all evil actions are bad, but not all bad actions are evil. A sports fan, provoked in a barroom by another who vilifies the losing performance of the fan's much-loved sports team, punches his tormenter. A morally bad action, but not one we would be prone to call evil.

This casting about does not yet give us a definition of evil actions, however. To be labeled as *evil*, the wrongdoing act often has to have a quality of egregious excess, such as a murder gratuitously committed in the course of a crime. A bank robber gratuitously shoots some elderly and disarmed bank guard as he exits the bank; the evil lies in the senselessness of the act. However, even if the elderly and disarmed guard was killed to demonstrate to the other victims the seriousness of the robber's threats to kill those who might pursue, we would still consider that act evil. The actor is seen to put such a low value on human life as to provide the moral outrage that triggers the label of evil.

At other times, the evil actor shows an equal disregard for humanity, but the evil act is not so much described as egregious excess as depraved excess. Those individuals who derive pleasure from the torture of children display this aspect of evil. One is struck by two things in this case: (a) the deviant and inhuman nature of the perverse impulse, and (b) the disproportion of the act in terms of the pleasure gained versus the pain inflicted. To inflict vast pain on the innocent to derive a fleeting and perverse pleasure is breathtakingly horrible.

The evil we have been describing contains elements of intention. The criminal intended to kill his hostage; the torturer intentionally chooses his victim. However, there is felt to be something bizarre about the intention. Sometimes the bizarre quality resides in the disparity between the intention and the grounds giving rise to that intention. A parent repeatedly batters an infant child because the child cries. We see from where the impetus to batter arises, but we simply cannot grant any sympathetic validity to the act arising out of the impetus. Again, a wildly disproportionate disregard for the humanity of the harmed individual seems indicated.[4]

At other times, we simply cannot fathom the sort of person who would intend to commit such terrible actions. We posit evildoing when we see that an individual is following our general societal template for the commission of an intentional action, and that the action is not only wrong but horribly wrong. The contrast between the apparent rationality of the sequence of behaviors that lead up to the action and the irrational character of the act is one cue we use to assign evil. To buy the instruments that will be used to torture another, or to dig the grave in which the kidnap victim will be buried alive, are evil acts. To plan to kidnap an individual for the purposes of deriving pleasure from torturing that individual is an act from which, among other things, an inference of evil is likely to arise. The buildup of the impulse in a serial killer to kill again, which I imagine to be experienced by the killer as an outside force, does not fit our usual definition of intentional action. Perhaps the imputation of evil arises because the killer deliberately organizes the acts to fulfill his "irresistible impulse."

In essence, then, an evil action occurs when an individual inflicts a highly negative state on another, without this negative state being balanced in any way in the perpetrator. I kill you to avoid being tortured. Terrible, but not evil. I kill you or torture you because it gives me some brief pleasure or avoids a slight annoyance to me. This is evil. Further, the evildoer knowingly violates society's norms. Thus, first, the actor puts his or her needs above the needs of those victimized, and, second, the actor puts his or her own judgments above others'. The imbalance here shows a chilling disregard for the humanity of the victim or the community; the other is given so little standing, as compared to the actor's pleasures and needs, as to be denied human existence.

An approach from another direction is possible. So far I have attempted to define evil as we use the concept in our everyday life. Now let me suggest a marker reaction that tells us when evil is present. Moral and jurisprudential philosophy typically identifies five reasons for incarcerating or otherwise punishing an individual who has committed wrongdoing, including (a) providing an opportunity for the correction or rehabilitation of the individual, (b) deterring that individual from future wrong acts, (c) deterring other individuals who witness the punishment, and (d) incapacitating the individual for a period to prevent the commission of other wrong actions, just as one would cage a dangerous animal. The last reason (e), which

seems to me to exist on a somewhat different plane, is called "just desserts," or closer to the bone, "retribution." The notion here is one of *lex talonis*—society must punish justly an individual who commits certain sorts of wrong actions. Evil actions invariably are seen by people as requiring this last sort of punishment; mere wrongdoing does not always elicit this requirement.

These are the ways that I think ordinary people in our culture come to identify acts as evil. I should admit that, armed with these definitional remarks, I do not think that it is possible to definitely, unequivocally categorize certain acts as evil, and certain others as merely "bad." That limitation is not fatal to the kind of psychological enterprise I am attempting. Instead I claim three things. First, a person who identifies an act as evil, when operating at the level of day-to-day understandings, does so with considerable personal certainty. Second, and again at this level, there is a considerable consensus among people about acts they will classify as evil. (Not surprisingly, this consensus contributes to the sense of certainty of classification that each individual feels.) Third, principles ordinary people say lie behind their intuitions about evil are the ones I have spelled out.[5] Of these three claims, the first—that people, in their day-to-day lives, make untroubled judgments of what actions are evil—is central to my argument.

Evil Actors and the Kernel of Evil

If we have an intuitive sense of an evil act, how do we pass from that to a recognition of the evilness of a person? Obviously, an evil person is one who has committed an evil action, and we are even more certain of our attribution of evilness if that individual has committed many evil actions, particularly if they all seem to point to some consistent origin of that evil, that is, to locate the evildoer in some particular corner of the linked set of domains that represents our conceptualization of evil. Saddam Hussein is a current candidate, as was Ted Bundy, the psychopathic serial killer of young women.[6]

Second, I suggest that we intuitively require that the evildoer will himself or herself be found to contain an element of evil, something with an almost physical characteristic (although, as in the suspense thriller, this evil may be hidden from outside scrutiny behind a mask of ordinariness and require unmasking). The evil person is expected to possess a "quality of evilness" having properties like the ones Allport (1937) attributed to central and cardinal traits. And intuitively, this internal quality of evil is matched in magnitude to the quantity of evil that we assess as having resided in his or her evil actions. As good crime novelists recognize, we require our evildoers to be major figures, with something of the demonic about them, rather than pathetic figures in the grip of impulse. Putting this in a related but somewhat different way, it is as if there is a naive assumption of an enduring kernel of evil which, once detected in the act, must be present in the actor. Behind evil actions must lie evil individuals.

At some day-to-day, "gut" level, we conceptualize evil actions as springing from the depraved minds of evil persons who will be found to contain a core quality of evil. I do not have what psychologists usually count as evidence for this assertion, but I offer two reasons for you to take it seriously. First, I think it probably accords with your intuitions, and remember that it is these intuitions, shared by members of our culture, that I am attempting to articulate. Second, take seriously the evidence presented by the existence of the suspense novels to which I have just alluded. Consider the enormous popularity of a rapidly growing genre of suspense novel, the "serial killer" novel. In it, a series of serial murders are committed, often in a bizarre and horrible fashion. At some point, the reader is led into the mind of the serial killer, and the pattern generating the sequence of killings is made intelligible, although no less horrible, to the reader. The detective's task is to intuit imaginatively the patterning in the sequence, predict the next crimes, and confront the evil killer in the act. The suspense is generated by the reader's knowledge of the true patterning, and the reader's necessarily passive watching, as the detective struggles toward understanding the pattern. Watching the killer rationally and logically set about preparations for the next killing act shows the discrepancy between the rationality of the plans and the horror of the contemplated act, and illustrates my earlier remarks about a depraved intention.

For those unacquainted with the terrain of the suspense novel, some examples may be useful. Thomas Harris seems to have an excellent sense of the genre. His first novel introduced a psychopath, a psychiatrist, which created the interesting possibility of the psychopath bringing to bear some very sophisticated interpretations of his own pathology. In two later novels, *The Red Dragon* (1981) and *The Silence of the Lambs* (1989), he has created other plausible serial killers and an interesting system of cross-referencing by having his original killer, now in solitary confinement, consulted by the detectives trying to enter the mind of their current quarry.

Harris's books succeed, others fail. One way in which suspense books fail is that they trivialize the evildoer, and the failure is on terms revealed by our analysis. He is portrayed by the author as pathetic rather than demonic; the killer, once discovered, does not have the chilling quality of evil that his actions signaled and that is required by our everyday conceptualizations of evil. (*His* is appropriate here. Both in suspense novels and real criminal statistics, the serial murderer is almost always a man.) The "quantum of evil" that we require to be preserved between the act and the actor is not present. To give an example of this in an otherwise quite well-conceived serial-murder novel, one might read Patricia Cornwell's (1990) *Postmortem*.

Psychological Functions of the Everyday Conceptualization of Evil

Sometimes, like the poor suspense novel, the real world fails us. That is, we cannot find the requisite quantum of evil when we examine the perpetrator of some particularly evil set of crimes. When this is so, I suggest, we fall back on some alternate models of explaining evil actions. A fellow named Whitman, who one day went up to the top of the University of Texas bell tower and shot and killed a number of his fellow students, had a rather wholesome, Boy-Scoutish, background. Rather fruitlessly, for several days after the incident, the newspapers scrabbled for "the story"—on my terms scrabbled for some prior evidence that Whitman was evil behind his amiable mask, and some further story that would account for the origins of that evil. None was found, but rumors of a brain tumor detected on autopsy provided an alternate, physical, source of causality for the acts that otherwise would require an evil individual to produce them. My point is this: These alternate explanations for evil actions have a particular function; they are the "licensed exceptions" to the quantum-of-evil view and thus protect the application of that view to other unexamined cases. For most of us, cerebral dysfunction whether by tumors, or involuntarily ingested mind-altering drugs, would explain acts we would otherwise ascribe to an evil actor. For some, other more psychological disturbances, such as posttraumatic stress syndrome or schizophrenia, also provide an alternative explanation for acts that would otherwise be taken as revealing the evil nature of the actor. Notice that these alternate explanations work best when the entities being postulated, such as tumors, are imagined to have a thinglike character, much like the quantum of evil I have suggested people imagine. In common-sense psychology, we conceive of the brain as occasionally intruding into the mind, so the more physical and palpable one can imagine the suggested intruder, the more comfortably it fits this model.

Here is where I think that clinical psychology and psychiatry fit in. I want to tread carefully here. More accurately, here is where I think that ordinary people's conceptualizations of psychology and psychiatry fit in. Although psychologists and psychiatrists sustain complex perspectives on these issues, I think that a frequent cultural use of the everyday equivalents of concepts in those fields is to provide alternate accounts of evil actions that attribute the act to other than an evil person. For instance, a culturally accepted form of the psychodynamic perspective, popularly thought to trace adult thought disorder to experiences inflicted on the person as a child, and inaccessible to current conscious control, removes the onus of evil from the individual who commits evil actions.

Sometimes, as I have already noted, the brain does intrude into the mind, and a tumor or hormonal dysfunction causes deviant and sometimes harmful behavior. As competent defense lawyers have long realized, sometimes a diagnostic label can be made to serve the same apparent explanatory function, although sometimes spuriously so to my mind. Much of the debate around certain diagnostic categories, such as posttraumatic stress disorder, stems from the fact that when they are used as legal defenses, lawyers can lead jurors to accept the "medical" metatheory underlying the particular diagnosis in question.

What are the psychological functions served by the view of evil that these exceptions serve to defend, the notion that behind evil actions lie evil-doers who can be identified as possessing an inherent and inward evilness? At first glance it seems to add an unnecessary component of terror to a world that is not short on other experiences of terror. Why do we imagine a world inhabited by evil-doers who could, for rationally unfathomable reasons, inflict horrors on ourselves and those we love, essentially at random?

Although this will be initially counterintuitive, I want to suggest that it preserves our belief in a just and ordered world. Just as the brain tumor functioned as the licensed exception to the requirement of an evil personality to lie behind the evil action, the notion of the evil individual is a licensed exception to, and thus protects our notion of, a just and ordered society. The problem is this; in this era, we cannot sustain a belief in a world in which only good things happen to good people. Television and the newspapers all too often remind us that joggers are beaten and raped by "wilding" teenagers, innocent passengers are blown up in airplanes or machine-gunned in airports, or good Samaritans are murdered in the course of their helping activities. So, to some degree, it is not a just and ordered world. But we do not want to relinquish the notion of the just world; it gives us the courage to go out into the world and to send our children out into the world. How can we maintain the notion of the just and ordered world, and yet recognize the undeniable occurrence of unjust actions?[7]

We recognize the unjust action but provide ourselves with a rule that at least partially restores order and justice and gives us some predictive power concerning those times when the order-and-justice rules are not in effect. They are not in effect when evil persons are around. And evil persons are generally recognizable; they contain the quantum or essence of evil that I have described. Of course, we cannot always perfectly identify evil people and we are sometimes taken in because their evilness is hidden behind a mask of normality. Thus, terrifyingly, evil actions happen to people because they did not discern the evil character of the perpetrator. However, and here we return to the suspense novels, the evil is recognizable in principle once we learn to "see it."[8] So, if the world is not a completely just and orderly place, we can know when it is not—when the general rules are in temporary abeyance. They are in abeyance when evil individuals enter the picture.[9] This, I submit, is a more tolerable exception to the principle of the just world than would be many other realizations about evil. Specifically, it is a more comfortable and containable exception to the principles of order and justice than are the views on the origins of evil jointly contained in a recently published and deeply disturbing set of books by social psychologists. It is to a consideration of those books that I now turn.

The Social Psychological Conceptualization of Evil

Consider a hypothetical experiment. By sampling newspaper accounts and other sources, we identify a large number of evil actions, and we set out to interview the actors who committed them, looking for this quantum or kernel of evilness. Next consider a possible but disturbing outcome: When one probes behind evil actions, one normally finds, not an evil individual viciously forwarding diabolical schemes, but instead ordinary individuals who have done acts of evil because they were caught up in complex social forces. The quantum of evil that we look for in the individual cannot be found. Instead we encounter again what Hannah Arendt found so striking about the Nazi mass murderer, Adolf Eichmann: the banality and ordinariness of an individual whom we expected to be demonic.

Surely, though, we can discover some such evil individuals and would expect to find them among the group of people Lifton studied. He, you will remember, studied the participation of medical doctors in horrendous acts of torture and murder in Nazi death camps. Surely, it is among Lifton's respondents, the medically trained upper-middle-class individuals who apparently chose to participate in horrible activities, that we would most expect to confront evil face to face. It is among them that we would expect to see the evil motives and evil hearts of the evildoing actors.

Sensing this agenda, this search, Lifton early on warns us that our search will fail. "The disturbing psychological truth [is] that participation in mass murder need not require emotions as extreme or demonic as would seem appropriate for such a malignant project. Or to put the matter another way, ordinary people can commit demonic acts" (p. 5). Staub remarks that "I believe that tragically

human beings have the capacity to come to experience killing other people as nothing extraordinary" (p. 13).

These, I want to assert, are examples of the major message arising from the books. Its validity is strengthened by the independent convergence of these books on this conclusion. The books examine a variety of evil acts. Lifton, using a close lens, examines the involvement of doctors in the Nazi death camps. Staub, using a longer lens, examines many episodes of genocide, mass killing, and torture. Milgram, as is well known, examined the behavior of individuals in a "psychological experiment" in which they were ordered to give what seemed to be painful and harmful electric shocks to others, thus giving us what may be regarded as the closest possible experimental analogue to evil. Kelman and Hamilton tell us a good deal, indeed sometimes as much as we can bear to read, about the circumstances leading U.S. Army units to the massacre of Vietnamese women and children at My Lai. As we will see, the proposition that arises from all these books is that many evil actions are not the volitional products of individual evildoers. Instead, they are in some sense societal products, in which a complex series of social forces interact to cause individuals to commit multiple acts of stunning evil.[10] In that process, the individuals committing the evil are themselves changed. They become evil although they still do not show the demonic properties suggested by our conventional views of evil.

The social psychological perspective suggests that generally organizations are required to produce sustained evil actions. The specific social forces that alter individuals are those produced in organizations. One needs a Nazi dictatorship, a Vietnam war, a Stalinesque gulag, or an Argentinean military dictatorship to train, reinforce, and sustain killing activities (although as shown later, it is not only these sorts of organizations that socialize their members into evildoing). This realization leads to several questions. What forces create these organizations and put their evil activities in motion? How do they alter the character of those individuals caught up in their activities? How do these organizations grow and change? Of these three questions, the second, involving the alteration of the individual by organizational and small-group processes, is the one most congenial to social psychologists, and I consider it first. But we need to consider the other two questions as well.

Organizations Socialize Individuals into Evildoing

How does an organization enlist individuals in harmdoing, and how are they altered by their involvement? This question recognizes that the output of these organizations is twofold; first and horribly, corpses, and second, and less commonly recognized, individuals who have been fundamentally altered by their participation in the harmdoing activities of the organization. Killing organizations produce those who are killed, and those who kill. Lifton, Milgram, Staub, and Kelman and Hamilton tell us how this is so; how organizations produce killers.

The Doubled Personality

As those of us who have read him over the years are well aware, Lifton's continuing concern has been with the darker issues of human existence: the meanings we attach to life when impersonal forces frequently threaten life, and the meanings we attach to deaths that we inflict on others. He has examined the collective forces that lead to these deaths, and the ways those collective forces act and interact with the perceptions and constructions of the individual to produce the actions that the individuals take. The wars of this century have furnished him with a rich set of materials, and brought out in him a correspondingly richly nuanced and intertwined analysis. In his recent book, *Nazi Doctors: Medical Killing and the Psychology of Genocide*, he continues this examination. Drawing on his work, we see how human beings adapted to participate in evil and were altered by it.

Lifton interviewed German doctors stationed in Auschwitz during World War II. He also interviewed prisoners who had been in the concentration camps, particularly those who had been both prisoners and somehow involved in the medical system set up within the camps—frequently those who were themselves doctors. My reconstruction of Lifton's analysis takes this path. When transferred to duty at Auschwitz, the doctor was confronted with the discovery that the machinery of state had certain aspects that were, on the face of them, morally terrible. The ideology of Nazism, and the resurgence of the German state, apparently required the incarceration and eventual killing of the "lesser" races. Still, as it always is, it was possible to see these terrible actions as somehow required to achieve generally good actions. The doctors perhaps had a feeling akin to what is called "dramatic inevitability" in the theater. Some entirely unexpected and perhaps violent outcome occurs, and yet the witnesses to it saw why that outcome was inevitably contained within the seeds of what had gone before. At Auschwitz, the Nazi doctors saw the inevitable unfolding of the meaning of the oath they took when they pledged allegiance to the state.

At the moment of confronting the horrible reality of Auschwitz, although the doctors' thinking was likely to be confused, nightmarish, and self-contradictory, certain bedrock truths would be confronted if the doctor reasoned far enough. First, the terrible machine would go on, whether or not the doctor participated in it. Auschwitz was, among other things, a vast complex of buildings and trains and medical wards and persons and schedules and procedures, an enterprise that would continue working regardless of the doctor's degree of participation. Second, although apparently the doctor could have declined to participate, that choice led at a minimum, to the dangers of the Russian Front. Doctors were in the military and were assigned to Auschwitz; that there was a choice about their participation was not necessarily apparent to them. (Of course, it was apparent to some, because they chose not to participate, an act of considerable courage in the circumstances.)

Meanwhile, old hands were available to socialize them, to help them in the process of conversion from outsider to insider. Let us examine that process. Apparently "selection" was one of the most frequent and taxing ordeals faced by the doctors. It was their task to select those who would be allowed to live and those who would immediately be sent to the gas chambers. The determination was supposed to be on the basis of those who remained fit to work, as against those who were exhausted by near starvation, were ill, or simply looked "unfit." Given the Nazi ideology, this killing of the lesser races was conceived of as a public health decision, somehow continuous with their previous program of euthanasia for the mentally inferior; thus, selection was fitted into a version of the medical ethic under the heading of the ruthless extirpation of germs, of loathsome diseases. Selection was a medical decision made by the SS doctors. And night and day they made it. When the prisoners left their boxcars to enter the camp, an SS doctor stationed on the arrival ramp selected those who would live and those who would die. When the prisoners went out to work for the day and when they came back at night, they passed a selection doctor—or failed to pass. Selection was incessant. In the medical wards, those too sick were "selected" for death: when new arrivals reached the camp, many of those already in the camp were selected to make room for the new arrivals.

Selection was by no means the most unambiguously morally wrong thing the doctors did. However, Lifton's interviews reveal that the doctors found it extremely stressful. They often did it drunk, or got drunk after it. Apparently, it caused them to face the moral implications of what they were doing, and did so in a particularly pointed way for the new doctors soon after their arrival in the camp.

The task for the new doctor was to fit into this machine. Other doctors provided whatever rationalizations were necessary to promote this "adaptation." This being the task, then it was in some sense better to still one's doubts about what one was doing, to develop a network of beliefs that stilled the moral doubts.

> Doctors became preoccupied with adapting themselves to that reality, and moral revulsion could be converted into feelings of discomfort, unhappiness, anxiety, and despair. Subjective struggles could replace moral questions. They became concerned not with the evil of the environment but with how to come to some terms with the place. (Lifton, 1986, p. 199)

What Lifton is suggesting is that human beings have the capacity to adapt to moral wrongdoing taking place within organizational settings and, although at some psychic cost, to blank out the implications of those actions and function as a cog within the terrible machine. He quotes one doctor as remarking "after a few weeks in that milieu, one thinks, 'Yes'" (p. 199).

Lifton's doctors found several ways of playing their roles. It is important to realize that the machine can tolerate different levels of commitment and even actions from its participants. An inmate, writing retrospectively, thought that the doctors seemed to fall into three categories:

> Zealots who participated eagerly in the extermination process and even did "extra work" on behalf of killing; those who went about the process more or less methodically and did no more and no less that they felt they had to do, and those who participated in the extermination process only reluctantly. (Langbein, paraphrased in Lifton, p. 194)

But, looking at it from an outside perspective, any level of participation was sufficient to keep the machine in motion. Organizations that kill do not need all individuals to participate in the most direct acts of killing; many individuals are needed to fill subsidiary and support roles.

Initially one suspects, the doctors stumbled through their dreadful activities, largely perceiving themselves as following orders, the implications of which they did not completely understand. Descriptively, however, their participation next began to be more voluntary, less well conceptualized as following orders, now functioning more independently and autonomously, and drawing on their skills and knowledge to increase the effectiveness of what they did within the camp. Famously, Lifton suggests that they adapted by the act of "doubling." Doubling is "the division of the self into two functioning wholes, so that a part-self acts as an entire self" (p. 418). Doubling created a self that would function within the Auschwitz walls, that still remained in contact with, and drew on the knowledge—and strength—of the pre-Auschwitz self. Doubling takes place largely outside of consciousness, and promotes the avoidance of guilt because it is the doubled self that commits actions, and the doubled self is the one that renders coherent the entire Auschwitz environment. The Auschwitz self avoids guilt because it is upholding the moral principles of the Auschwitz surroundings, promoting the values of the state, achieving racial purity, staying loyal to one's oath of obedience, and so on.

Lifton is offering us two propositions, or at least I have abstracted two from him. The first one is shocking, but I think in keeping with what many social psychologists would want to say. Situations can be created in which it is possible to enlist the ordinary participant in the commission of evil, and in the process the participant is transformed into a

creature capable of autonomously and knowledge-
ably committing evil actions. Importantly, this
conversion is, as most conversions are, a process.
Lifton's second proposition is that this conversion
process produces a doubled individual. (Putting
this another way, that it is useful to have the concept of doubling because all of the processes that
work on the inductee to the machine of terror converge to produce a personality that can only be
described as doubled.) Putting this yet another way,
those processes work in unison to produce a person whose personality is split in a particular way.
A personality is formed that is designed to cope
with the exigencies of the killing situation, but one
which can and does access the skills and knowledge of the prior personality.

Milgram's Contribution:
The Agentic State

The problem to assess now is whether we ought to
postulate that those who pass through experiences
such as the Nazi doctors had, are altered in a way
that requires concepts such as "the doubled individual." I waver about the necessity for the concept of doubling. In its favor, it makes clear that
the person in question has been altered in permanent ways. (But I am not sure that the evidence
points toward a unified conceptualization of the
altered individual, and if it does, that "doubled" is
the concept of choice for the resulting product.)
Seeking guidance on this, I returned to the Milgram
experiments, and looked again at Milgram's (1974)
Obedience to Authority: An Experimental View.

Recall the Milgram paradigm. A subject comes
to participate in an experiment on "teaching and
learning" and is randomly assigned to give electric shocks to the learner when the learner makes
mistakes in identifying the correct associate of a
stimulus word—this is an experiment about the
effects of punishment. Instructed to do so, and with
those instructions reiterated by an experimenter
who is present throughout the process, the subject
administers increasing levels of shock to the
learner, even when the marking on the shock apparatus reveal that these shock levels are dangerous and the learner calls out protests.

The copyright date, 1974, reminded me that the
book had been published more than a decade after
Milgram began his series of experiments, published by his own report, after he had spent some

years wrestling with what he wanted to say about
the meaning of his own work. Because the book
came such a long time after what the psychological community regarded as the completion of the
experimental program, I think that it has not played
the role it should in shaping our interpretations of
the Milgram findings. In fact, I suspect that it is
not much read. If so, this is a pity because it contains reports of many experimental variations in
the research paradigm that are reported nowhere
else, as well as Milgram's own interpretations of
his findings. These interpretations I often find
deeply insightful and, occasionally, deeply bizarre.

Milgram certainly agrees with Lifton that a concept like doubling is required. He postulates the
existence of an "agentic state" into which his subjects pass to administer shocks to the other individual. The assertion of the agentic state is one
that I find startling and bizarre, but we ought to
mark that two social scientists who have spent
many years examining individuals involved in the
commission of evil have both come to the conclusion that one commits evil in an altered state.

What is the "agentic state" according to
Milgram? He characterizes it in several ways, from
which an image of it gradually emerges. The first
characterization concerns its evolutionary nature.
Human beings must often function within organizations. Thus, evolutionarily, according to
Milgram, they have developed the potential for
obedience. That is, the standard workings of evolutionary selection pressures have brought about
an inherited propensity to obey.

> From an evolutionary standpoint each autono-
> mously functioning element must be regulated
> against the unrestrained pursuit of appetites, of
> which the individual element is the chief benefi-
> ciary. The superego, conscience, or some similar
> mechanism that pits moral ideals against the un-
> controlled expression of impulses fulfills this
> function. However, in the organizational mode,
> it is crucial for the operation of the system that
> these inhibitory mechanisms do not significantly
> conflict with directions from higher-level com-
> ponents. Therefore when the individual is work-
> ing on his own, conscience is brought into play.
> But when he functions in an organizational model,
> directions that come from the higher level com-
> ponent are not assessed against the internal stan-
> dards of moral judgment. Only impulses generated
> within the individual, in the autonomous mode,
> are so checked and regulated. (pp. 128–129)

Thus, we see the agentic state is one within which one is not governed by the operations of one's own conscience; instead, the conscience has been switched off in the individual.

Milgram's views about the physiological substratum of the agentic state, and the events that "trigger" an individual into that state, also require examination.

Where in a human being shall we find the switch that controls the transition from an autonomous to a systemic mode? No less than in the case of automata, there is certainly an alteration in the internal operations of the person, and these, no doubt, reduce to shifts in patterns of neural functioning. Chemical inhibitors and disinhibitors alter the probability of certain neural pathways and sequences being used. But it is totally beyond our technical skill to specify this event at the chemoneurological level. (p. 133)

Milgram also made clear how seriously he takes his concept. "The agentic state is the master attitude from which the observed behavior flows. The state of agency is more than a terminological burden imposed on the reader; it is the keystone of our analysis . . . " (p. 133). And further,

Since the agentic state is largely a state of mind, some will say that this shift in attitude is not a real alteration in the state of the person. I would argue, however, that these shifts in individuals are precisely equivalent to those major alterations in the logic system of the automata considered earlier. Of course, we do not have toggle switches emerging from our bodies, and the shifts are synaptically effected, but this makes them no less real. (p. 134)

The first time I read this, I was startled and appalled by what I took to be the odd and pseudoscientific/pseudophysiological concept of the agentic state, by the notion of the "trigger" that switches an individual between normal and agentic functioning, and by the dichotomous and all-or-nothing character of being in one state or another. And I continue to be. On rereading Milgram's work, however, I also see that he gives an inherently more social and less dichotomous account of the agentic state. Milgram wrote:

From a subjective standpoint, a person is in a state of agency when he defines himself in a social situation in a manner that renders him open to regulation by a person of higher status. In this condition the individual no longer views himself as responsible for his own actions but defines himself as an instrument for carrying out the wishes of others. . . .

An element of free choice determines whether the person defines himself in this way or not, but given the presence of certain critical releasers, the propensity to do so is exceedingly strong, and the shift is not freely reversible. (p. 134)[11]

Still I find this construction overly dichotomous, and by its reference to *releasers*, a term borrowed from a now somewhat outmoded notion of physiological reflexes, overly pseudobiological. However, this more phenomenological construction of the process, coupled with Milgram's later discussion of the situational events that enable an individual to construe himself or herself into obeying authorities, seems to me to contain many insights.

For instance, he pointed out the importance of the subject's perception that he has willingly entered into a transaction governed by an authority that is legitimate and has the scope to command the particular actions in question. Second, once the interaction starts, other forces bind the subject into the situation. The cues that somebody is possibly being harmed occur only later, after a "momentum" has been built up around the legitimate definition of the punishing actions, and the shock-giving participant has incurred all the obligations (that Goffman, 1961, has so convincingly pointed out) to continue an ongoing social activity and the definition of that activity. From these materials an account could be created of why the modal subject in many of the Milgram conditions gave the maximal level of shock.

Albert Bandura, in his 1986 book, *Social Foundations of Thought and Action*, gave us an account that addresses what is accomplished within the individual by the conversion process. He suggested that normal socialization processes produce what he called a "self-regulatory system," which functions to regulate and control the actions of the normally functioning individual. However, these control mechanisms do not operate in invariant ways. "Development of self-regulatory capabilities does not create an invariant control mechanism, as implied by theories of internalization that incorporate entities such as conscience and superego as continuous internal overseers of conduct" (p. 375).

He went on to remark that "self-evaluative influences do not operate unless activated" (p. 375), and it is also the case that they can be selectively disengaged as well. This might work as follows. Normally, people do not indulge in censurable behaviors because these will produce self-devaluative consequences as a result of the working of the self-regulatory system. However, "what is culpable can be made honorable through cognitive restructuring" (p. 376). One can morally justify harmdoing, find euphemistic labels for the action, minimize the harmful consequences, and dehumanize and blame the victim. There are also the usual possibilities of displacing responsibility for the detrimental actions elsewhere in the system. These are the family of processes that seem to me to be involved in creating individuals who willingly do evil. That they often occur together, and that many of them are frequently caused by the same circumstances, is undeniable. It is the fact that many of these processes are involved in the conversion process, and that the individual is in some unstable and dynamic state—now relying on one justification, now on another—that seems to me to become obscured when an altered state is postulated.

The Conversion Process

This returns us to the issue of the conversion process. Psychologists are, understandably, reluctant to write the "production of torturers" handbook, but social psychologists certainly have the knowledge to do so. The insights for it are there in such articles as Zimbardo (1969) on deindividuation, Gibson and Haritos-Fatouros (1986) on the recruitment of the Greek torturers during the reign of the colonels, and others. The essence of the process involves causing individuals, under pressure, to take small steps along a continuum that ends with evildoing. Each step is so small as to be essentially continuous with previous ones; after each step, the individual is positioned to take the next one. The individual's morality follows rather than leads. Morality is retrospectively fitted to previous acts by rationalizations involving "higher goods," "regrettable necessities," and other rationalizations mentioned by Bandura and others.

Other books under consideration here give alternate accounts of Lifton's conversion process, but do not contradict it. They draw on Milgram's experimental work to illuminate their accounts.

Without pausing here to sketch the account each gives, although that is a worthy task, I comment on what other elements of the process they call to our attention. Staub reminds us of the causal role of the bystander in the process—the interpreted meaning of the actions of those who stood by, not protesting, as harm was done to persecuted minorities. Their apparent indifference was certainly taken as tacit approval by others who also watched, and who might have been otherwise moved to protest. In a dynamic that Latané and I (1970) have described, this leads to a "contagion of inaction" among all bystanders. Thus, bystanders who fail to intervene, perhaps because they are stunned into passivity, are read by both perpetrator and victim as condoning the acts of the perpetrator and approving the victimization of the harmed. *Kristallnacht* was a signal to the Jews of what the Nazi regime would do. The general lack of protest by other Germans, whatever the reasons, was a signal to the Jews that they would not be protected by non-Nazi Germans.

Staub has thought deeply about the role of "bystanders" in the social processes we are describing, and he calls our attention to the occasionally absolutely critical importance of their actions—or more tragically their inactions. Often forces we are in the process of conceptualizing lead the "perpetrator" group to be constrained to continue along what Staub calls the "continuum of destructiveness." Justifying and rationalizing what they have done, they are led to do more and do worse. Given this, it frequently will be the responses of the other elements in the society that determine whether this appalling progress of the perpetrator group continues and enrolls other elements of society, or is checked. For instance, an independent judiciary, with powers enough to stand against the usurping actions of the executive branch, can block those actions. Watergate.

The Kelman and Hamilton book is the one I do the least justice to as I try to construct an account of the processes that socialize individuals toward evil, because they focused on how persons make moral judgments about crimes of obedience. (They did bring their thinking to bear on explaining how people pressed to commit those crimes chose or declined to participate.) In partial amends, later I sketch their general line of thinking, as they developed it in their study of people's reactions to the trial of Lt. Calley. Here I take up another of their points, which begins with Kelman's famous distinction of three modes of social influence: compliance, identification, and internalization. Each of those orientations, they suggested, can link individuals to the society in which they find themselves. Compliance considerations produce a rule orientation, in which a person is integrated into society via considerations of the rewards and punishments society delivers to those who follow or break its rules, and the social approval and disapproval that signal those rewards and punishments. Identification implies a commitment to a particular role within society as a part of the individual's self-definition. Generally, through the processes of socialization, a person comes to accept the values of a society, and thus can be said to internalize them. The society's values become his or her own, and naturally the person will act to further those values in the future. Given this, when a person violates some element of what society requires of him or her, he or she feels a mixture of fear of sanctions, distress for role failure, and regret for not living up to espoused values. All these are powerful enforcers of the person's tendency to do what society asks of him or her. If the society is asking that individuals obey orders resulting in evil outcomes, still these enforcing forces move the person toward obedience.

To the degree to which the nation-state, or any other organization, is viewed by the individuals within it as legitimate, it has these powers to induce obedience with its demands. Organizations are perceived by their members as legitimate insofar as they engage their sentiments, such as loyalties, and fulfill their instrumental needs, desires, and interests (Kelman & Hamilton, 1989, chap. 5, particularly pp. 112–119).

We are analyzing how it is that people are socialized through an organization to commit evil. Two relevant implications flow from Kelman and Hamilton's analysis of forces linking an individual to an organization. First (and the conclusion that we need here), within organizations that members perceive as legitimate, the forces leading to obedience are multiple, mutually reinforcing, and very strong. Obedience rather than disobedience to authority can be understood as the expected outcome. Second, as shown later, the different conditions binding an individual to an organization may produce different behavioral outcomes under certain kinds of pressures to obey.

The Product of the Process: The Evil Individual

Two intertwined issues are found in discussions of the individual who is the product of the perverse socialization process just described. First, how is the individual altered by the process, and second, are those alterations so great as to require the postulation of an discontinuous, dissociated state, such as an "agentic state" or "doubled personality"? Although we need to come to our own conclusions about those questions, let us first look at Milgram and Lifton's conclusions.

As we have seen, Milgram, like Lifton, concluded that the evidence requires the postulation of a different and basically discontinuous state created in the harmdoing individual. But the two sharply differ on how that state is created. Lifton made a comment on Arendt's thesis about the banality of evil, which can also be read as a comment on Milgram's concept of the agentic state:

> What I have noted about the ordinariness of Nazi doctors as men would seem to be further evidence of her thesis. [Recall that the thesis involved the banality of evil—in this context the ordinariness in the present of the individuals who had committed horrible acts of evil in the past.] But not quite. Nazi doctors were banal, but what they did was not. Repeatedly in this study, I describe banal men performing demonic acts. In doing so— or in order to do so—the men changed; and in carrying out their actions, they themselves were no longer banal. (p. 5)

Here Lifton reiterated his first point, that it is the individual's encounter with the killing machine that results in a conversion process altering that individual and creating a doubled personality. Although I have indicated my reservations about the concept of the doubled personality, I completely agree with Lifton that the encounter begins a process that morally alters the person who participates in that process. Although I am not sure that Lifton would agree with me, let me draw a line somewhere along the continuum of participation in the encounter, and suggest that people who go beyond that point are evil—more precisely, have become evil. The person who is induced into participation, and who goes far enough in the conversion process so that he or she autonomously and intelligently initiates evil actions, is an individual who has become evil. Examples may make this clearer. The soldiers who, yelled at by Lt. Calley, with tears in their eyes, fired into crowds of innocents were not evil. Those soldiers who coldly and knowingly killed innocents while operating independently, were evil. Staub reported a case of two young, rosy-cheeked *Hitlerjugend* whose frequent habit it was to "hunt" in the Warsaw ghetto. They simply wandered into the ghetto and shot whoever it captured their fancy to shoot.

As the reader will be aware, many have debated whether humankind is inherently good, inherently evil, or any of several other possibilities. Psychologists working within the academic and experimental traditions of modern psychology do not enter this debate willingly. Nonetheless, the previous analysis suggests an answer. The possibility of being evil is latent in all of us, and can be made actual and active, among other ways, by the conversion process. The person who goes a certain distance in the process has been fundamentally changed, and is now capable of doing harm in an autonomous way. He or she has "changed, changed utterly," has become evil.

But that is not at all what Milgram said. He argued that, as an inevitable condition of life, people come "prewired" as it were, with two possible states of functioning. Any person, therefore, could be put into the agentic state by the right combination of authoritative pressures. Milgram did not suggest that having once been thrown into that state, a person is fundamentally altered or that once a person has been through this process, it will be effected more easily in the future.

Not surprisingly, Milgram did not come to these conclusions. Were Milgram to have accepted Lifton's construction, that it was the obedience to the initial commands of authority that began the conversion-to-evil process, he would have found himself wearing a very uncomfortable shoe indeed. It would mean Milgram had begun the process of converting his innocent subjects to "doubled" individuals, capable, if they went further down that path, of independently acting to inflict harm on other individuals in the name of science, as did the Nazi doctors in the name of the state. To use Milgram's vocabulary, he took himself as showing that the agentic state already existed in his subjects, and his experimenter could rather easily "flip on" that state. But an uncomfortable alternate reading is possible: that Milgram had set up a terrible machine, and had begun to create (to again use the Lifton vocabulary) this doubled state in those unlucky individuals who were fed into the machine.

Why do I suggest this? For both theoretical and empirical reasons. Many of us still find considerable explanatory power in dissonance theory, particularly in the attitude-changing effects produced by the forced-compliance paradigm, of which Milgram's is one version. Thus the attitudes of the subjects about what they did can be predicted to have changed in directions favorable to repeating the actions. (Whether or not this is altered by the debriefing is unclear.) Nor is it only dissonance theory that would lead us to this conclusion. Any theory recognizing that the production of morally ambiguous actions can be rationalized after the fact by the actor would lead to these conclusions. Specifically, I would expect that Milgram's subjects, who were implicitly preselected to put a high value on "science," might have increased the value they placed on science as an important source of discoveries that would help humankind, and perhaps also derogated the intelligence of the individual who received the shocks. In both these ways, inflicting pain on the learner became justified.[12]

There is empirical evidence for the occurrence of these sorts of changes following the commission of a morally ambiguous act. In a set of studies involving an experimental cover story very similar to Milgram's, and in which subjects were led to give electric shocks to others, Brock and Buss (1962) demonstrated that the subjects' perceptions of the individual to whom they gave shocks altered in ways that justified their morally ambiguous actions; they derogated the victim, implying that the victim somehow deserved the punishment.

I have asserted that being "processed through a killing machine" can create an "evil individual." What exactly do I want to say about how that individual has been changed? And therefore, what do I want to assert that individual will think and, more to the point, do? What is the cash value of calling an individual "evil"? There are, I think, two answers to this, the first a partial perspective on the matter, the second a deeper perspective. First, in ways that the sociologist Weber initially conceptualized, the processes of doing evil have become routinized or alternately the person doing evil has become "a bureaucrat." Actions that initially were shocking have become routinized, habitual, and at the end of the day in the concentration camps, the executioner can go home and read his children bedtime stories. This, I think, best fits the case of the individual who has some fragmented role in producing the evil action. When death, like cars or chairs, is produced on assembly lines, each individual eventually concentrates on the micro-requirements of his or her part in the process; the eventual outcome is rarely thought of. A group of police in a city round up the Jews and take them to a stadium. Later an army contingent takes them to the boxcars. A railroad worker throws the switches that bring the train to one or another subdestination on the way to the concentration camp. The fact of the eventual deaths is so remote that no participant finds it salient. Each person doing a subtask does so in a routinized way; it is only the final assembly of those subtasks that is horrible, and no individual "sees" that final solution.

This explanation is good as far as it goes, but to my mind doesn't go far enough. As described earlier, many people participated in the direct acts of killing, and many others knew where the boxcars were going. More needs to be said about the mental alterations that took place in those individuals; Weber's "routinization of bureaucratic subroutines" is not enough. They normally have been permanently morally altered in ways that change their thinking and behavior. The continuing mark of their past experiences with the killing machine is mental, and consists of the structures of moral thought that they were led to use to rationalize their actions in the first place. Unless they have had some sort of moral epiphany, they continue to believe what the killing machine taught them: "regrettable necessities," "for the good of the state," "the alien communist ideology threatened the Argentine way of life." (This was the point of the banal conversations that Arendt had with Eichmann, in which he went on and on about "necessities of state." These statements reflected the moral rationalizations that he had formed to justify his conduct.)

Two consequences flow from these mental adjustments. Both these consequences go some way toward answering the question: In what ways should we conceptualize the alterations in the evil-doing individual? First, contained within these adjustments is a definition of the target groups toward whom harmdoing is deemed appropriate. In some ways this limits the operation of the forces that have been created. It is appropriate to execute the defined groups, but certainly not the groups on whose behalf one strives. One kills lesser races on behalf of the higher races, or one kills Communists to preserve the purity of Argentinean life. Of course, the target groups tend to grow larger. From our own history, not only "Communists" but also "fellow travelers" were seen as a threat to the "American way of life." And soon, "unknowing fellow travelers" or "Communist dupes" also needed to be ferreted out. To cite a particularly horrible example, some of the Argentinean military were unable to conceive children, and so the practice grew of identifying young women who had just had a child as "Communists" so they could be killed. The children were then given to the military families. The groups that this sort of evildoer feels justified in attacking are contained, but only partially.

The second consequence of the mental adjustments caused by participating in harmdoing organizations is straightforward: an increased readiness to participate in harmdoing activities again if any of a number of social conditions are recreated. The normal outcome of the kind of socialization process I have described is a permanent one. This is not to deny the possibilities of a moral reorganization taking place, in which the individual turns away from his or her previous actions, and painfully reconstitutes a morality in which those previous activities are seen as morally wrong. However, the guilt produced by this, certainly in the moral sense and possibly in the legal sense, is going to be high. Lifton's doctors had lived in a culture in which the wrongs of the Nazi era were about as thoroughly acknowledged as we can ever realistically expect, and I think that Lifton does not see many signs of a moral reorganization on their part. My sense is that the negative moral change caused by the perverse socialization that I describe generally persists, making the individual so socialized permanently susceptible to being caught up in harmdoing institutions in the future.

One way of characterizing these mental adjustments is as a neutralization or even a positive valuation of actions that are generally regarded as morally reprehensible. This tells us how the person will continue to act vis-à-vis those actions. That individual will autonomously and independently continue to harm others, but if and only if the harmdoing actions are rule-governed by the rationalizations of previous harms, and if the social conditions are generally supportive of harmdoing in the present. Those who have become evil in this fashion require cultural or small-group support for the rationalizations that supported their doings. (And in this fashion they are quite different from those, such as serial murderers, who fit the common-sense prototype of evildoers. They either are able to independently support whatever conceptual system justifies their acts or have no need for such a system.) If the Nazis had successfully invaded Britain, then Nazi doctors would have helped design and build concentration camps in Britain, brilliantly and logically adapting what they knew of selection ramps to the local conditions of Manchester or Liverpool. History turned out otherwise, and many of them returned to the conventional practice of medicine. Those who tortured in Argentina or Greece can now be encountered on the streets, going about mundane activities. All would commit evil again if social conditions altered.

The Creation of Killing Organizations

My argument thus far is simple. Most evildoers are produced by a process of socialization into doing evil, a process that makes them capable of doing evil autonomously and independently in the future.[13] If this argument is correct, then we come face-to-face with a question that we now recognize as urgent. How are the organizations that socialize an individual into doing harm created and sustained? If they are an important source of harmdoers, then how do they themselves come about? I do not think we have a complete account of how this happens, and what I have to suggest is tentative and incomplete. But I am sufficiently convinced of the importance of the task to make those suggestions, to advance the debate. First, let us look at the cultural and social conditions conducive to the development of such organizations, and next at the specific events that are the origins of such organizations.

The Cultural Preconditions for Destructive Organizations

Staub sets himself the task of describing the cultural conditions that lead to genocide. Specifically,

he has analyzed the Nazi Holocaust, the killings of the Armenians in Turkey from 1915 to 1916, the Cambodian massacre of their own countrymen during the 1970s, and the mass killings of "leftists" under the Argentinean dictators during the 1970s. His analysis deserves our attention for two reasons. First, genocidal movements are certainly evil ones, and therefore of direct interest. Second, as I have come to see, we can extract some generalizations from his conclusions, which can be applied to explain the origins of other destructive social organizations, in the interest of understanding these origins and the hope of preventing them.

Staub's story begins when a society or powerful groups within that society are subjected to difficult life conditions. The possible sources of these difficult life conditions are numerous and various; they can include economic hardship, political conflict between groups within a society (with the associated feelings of loss of control), perceived threats from criminal violence, as we currently experience in this country, and so on. As a psychologist is likely to do, Staub includes such things as threats to a sense of security, well-being, and even self-esteem as conditions that can be experienced as difficult life experiences. "The threat may be to life, to security, to well-being, to self-concept, or to world view" (p. 14). These difficult life circumstances bring about physical and psychological needs in people that are sometimes filled in positive ways, in ways we would regard as effective and morally appropriate. At other times though, the circumstances give rise to feelings of hostility directed at whomever can be made to seem responsible for the problems. Staub puts his case this way:

Blaming others, scapegoating, diminishes our own responsibility. By pointing to a cause of the problems, it offers understanding which, although false, has great psychological usefulness. It promises a solution to problems by action against the scapegoat. And it allows people to feel as they join to scapegoat others. Devaluation of a subgroup helps to raise low self-esteem. Adopting an ideology provides a new world view and a vision of a better society that gives hope. Joining a group enables people to give up a burdensome self, adopt a new social identity, and gain a connection to other people. This requires action, but it is frequently not constructive action.

Often all these tendencies work together. The

groups that are attractive in hard times often provide an ideological blueprint for a better world and an enemy who must be destroyed to fulfill the ideology. Sometimes having a scapegoat is the glue in the formation of the group. But even if the ideology does not begin by identifying an enemy, one is likely to appear when fulfillment of the ideological program proves difficult. Thus these psychological tendencies have violent potentials. (p. 17)

Certain cultural tendencies can make the forces unleashed during difficult times lead to scapegoating.

What motives arise and how they are fulfilled depend on the characteristics of the culture and society. For example, a society that has long devalued a group and discriminated against its members, has strong respect for authority and has an overly superior and/or vulnerable self-concept is more likely to turn against a subgroup. (p. 4)

Staub goes on to make another point, to which I have alluded earlier in this discussion. The scapegoating group is not capable of leaping immediately to genocide, to killing the members of the scapegoated group just because of their group membership. There is the familiar progression of acts. Open criticism of the scapegoated groups produces derogation, which licenses brutality; brutality is justified, and leads to further derogation and the discovery that the scapegoated group is somehow not included in humanity. Finally, killings, and then systematic killings. Genocide.

Initially, I found Staub's essential conceptualization of "difficult life conditions" too broad. It is a notion that, if defined narrowly, we can all understand and know when to apply. For example, the rampant economic inflation of Weimar Germany led many previously well-to-do people into poverty, and created the difficult life conditions he alludes to. However, Staub's notion of difficult life conditions is broader and less concrete. Essentially, he psychologizes it. Experiencing difficult life conditions is after all a psychological state, and may be caused not by obvious economic hardships or other deprivations such as those caused by famines, but by more symbolic and subjective disruptions. Threats to self-esteem, for instance, can cause the perception of difficult life circumstances. By psychologizing the concept, Staub has

made it potentially much more arguable in its application. It is relatively easy to determine when the material and economic conditions of an individual's life have declined. It is going to be much harder to determine when, historically, it makes sense to say that individuals were experiencing psychological feelings of deprivation. Some peasants in Cambodia were experiencing painful economic hardship but conditions for some were improving. Some Argentineans were doing more poorly, some were not. Staub makes the argument, particularly in the case of Argentina, that the feelings of decline were, at least considerably, psychological in nature, stemming from a perception that Argentina's hope of becoming a world power were fading. Although I do not think Staub stretches the application of his concept, I think it could be stretched by those who might use it in the future. (In fact, I am about to do so.) The core of my problem is this: I would be hard pressed to think of a time when one could not make the case that any population had reasons to feel psychological difficulties, either by comparing their status with that of past generations, individuals in other cultures, or some glorified notions of what they were entitled to; or alternatively, that some subgroups within a nation or culture had reasons to feel this way, given similar comparisons. Thus it seemed that Staub's "difficult life conditions" precondition for genocide could be found to exist in, if not all places at all times, then at least most places at most times.

The part of Staub's analysis that I have presented gives us the preconditions for a culture becoming "genocidal," more specifically, for the national leadership turning to killing members of an outgroup existing within or at the margins of that nation. But the analysis seems equally applicable at the organizational level. The cultural forces that he identifies must be the background conditions for the formation of organizations that actually carry out the genocide. With this as background, we can now (at last) turn to questions concerning the formation of those organizations. If it is a central claim of the social psychological analysis that evildoing is frequently a product of organizational processes, then it is necessary to delineate how the organizations that come to produce evil outcomes and evildoing individuals come into being and reproduce themselves.

The Origins of Destructive Organizations

It seems, though, that I am avoiding my own central question. How do killing organizations come into being in the first place? Is it not the case that I have just spent a great deal of time simply making minor shifts in the origins of evil? Are the people who put together the first killing machines not evil in the demonic sense that our commonsense analysis suggests? The answer, of course, is frequently "yes." Certainly Hitler was evil. Certainly too, the commanders of the Argentine forces who ordered the torture and killing of large segments of Argentinean society completely intended the killings they caused, and are evil.[14] However—and this is perhaps the most disturbing element of my case—I believe that organizations can lurch toward evil, in ways not intended by any of the participants in the organization.

Organizations of Social Control

First, however, consider the "yes" part of the story. Notice the organizations that we recognize as having a propensity for harm. As Kelman and Hamilton remark,

> The most obvious sources of crimes of obedience are military, paramilitary, and social-control hierarchies, in which soldiers, security agents, and police take on role obligations that explicitly include the use of forces. These hierarchies are the classic ones from which the term *chain of command* is borrowed; authority is bureaucratically stringent. The goals of these bureaucracies and the role definitions of actors within them in fact require harm to certain categories of others (such as an enemy or subversive). The sole question concerns the scope and definition of the target of harm rather than the existence of such a target. (p. 314)

In these organizations, coercive pressures are high. One "obeys orders," and often one's own life is in danger. Those to be controlled are the enemy and are often dehumanized. Criminals are called "scum"; Vietnamese are called "gooks." What one can do to the enemy or who counts as the enemy is rigidly rule-bound, but the reader will be well aware of the pressures to bend those rules and replace formal rules with informal rules that prescribe different and more lax standards. These in-

formal rules come to govern behavior, and are well understood at the level of the police officer on the beat or the soldier in the field. We do not have much difficulty seeing how those organizations can shift toward becoming illicitly destructive machines; they are destructive machines to begin with.

Of course, this does not imply that those who command such organizations are always evil, or that those organizations must necessarily shift in this fashion. The Argentine generals and Hitler were evil; I, at least, do not think that the Army high command in the Vietnam conflict was.

Yet large segments of the American Army did massacre civilians. So we face the fact that organizations can somehow be subverted or otherwise altered to turn persons within those organizations into evildoers, even when the apex of the organization does not direct this. Again, we do not have too much trouble understanding how this happens in an organization set up for purposes of social control. We will need to say something specific about this, and will do so shortly. Before exploring this specifically, let us consider a more disturbing possibility. The analysis we have constructed so far can be read in the following way. Organizations of a particular type, roughly those concerned with social control, have the unique capacity to turn their members into evildoers. We have a reasonably clear notion of which organizations those are. Our task, therefore, is to be particularly vigilant in monitoring them, so that they do not consciously stray or unconsciously slip into creating evil actions, and in the process, create evildoers. Success in this task, admittedly difficult to achieve, will protect us from this problem.

This analysis seems accurate as far as it goes, but it has one unfortunate implication. The truth is bleaker. Although I agree that organizations of social control are particularly vulnerable to this process, I disagree with the implicit contention that other kinds of organizations are not subject to similar problems. Normal organizations also bring their members to harm others.

Normal Organizations' Propensities for Harm

Many organizations exist that would not be conventionally regarded as organizations of social control: schools and universities, manufacturing firms, research organizations. Do they need to figure in this discussion in any way? What is their potential for socializing individuals into the harmdoing process? My answer is that their potential for the incubation of harm is high, and in many cases that we can cite, that potential has been actualized. Only one of the books we are examining answers this question directly. Kelman and Hamilton invite us to consider several examples in which corporations or other organizations have gone far down this road. Recall the design of the Ford Pinto, sold for years by a company in which many executives were aware that it had a gas tank likely to rupture in low-speed rear-end crashes, and thus incinerate its passengers. Recall Watergate or the Iran-Contra affair. Consider the silence of Morton Thiokol executives who were aware of the dangers to the space shuttle O-rings of a low-temperature launch. We could add to Kelman and Hamilton's list. Think about executives who continued to have shipyard employees work with asbestos long after its carcinogenic properties were known to them, or government bureaucrats who kept uranium miners at work long after the dangers of that occupation were known to them. Consider any number of defense contractors who have delivered military weapons systems to the defense department with faked safety and effectiveness tests and substandard internal electronic components.

A complicated set of issues are raised here. First, we have the case of an organization whose activities bring a great deal of harm to individuals, but in which it is hard to fix the responsibility for that harm within the organization. Second, we have the case of the organization in which evil individuals are produced but produced in a more complex way than they are produced in the concentration camp. Third, I argue that the division of organizations into those engaged in social control and related activities versus those engaged in, for instance, production or other purposes, is less useful for identifying organizations that may engage in harmdoing than we might think.

Let's look first at the case in which harm results from the unfortunate assembly of a set of innocent actions. When an organization does harm, that action can be the result of the interaction of many other actions, each of which is, on the face of it, innocent. Assume an organization has produced and marketed a drug that is later found to have terrible side-effects—thalidomide, or diethylstilbestrol (DES), for instance. One corporate

unit can develop a drug, and assume it will be tested for side-effects. Another unit can arrange for it to be marketed, assuming those safety checks have been completed. Those who actually carried out the drug tests may be aware that their tests were not the sort of tests that can determine side-effects with any sort of precision. (For instance, consider DES, a drug given to pregnant women to prevent miscarriages and reduce nausea during pregnancy. Only many years later could it be discovered that it produced various effects, including increased likelihood of cancer, among the young women who had been *in utero* when their mothers were taking the drug.) No individual intentionally brought about the horrid side-effects produced.[15] More to the point, it is difficult to identify exactly who within the organizations was negligent in allowing the mistake to happen. This becomes apparent in those few cases in which members of organizations are put on trial for the consequences of their actions. Rarely are any specific individuals found criminally liable.

As Kelman and Hamilton point out, this conclusion can be generalized to other cases in which, on first glance, there seem to be obvious wrongdoers to hold accountable. They report what they found in their survey of Americans' reactions to "the Lt. Calley trial." Recall the circumstances. During the Vietnam War, at the hamlet of My Lai, U.S. soldiers knowingly shot, clubbed, and bayoneted Vietnamese woman, children, old people, and babies. Once the cover-up was exposed, an investigation revealed that superior officers had ordered a "search and destroy" mission into a hamlet that intelligence indicated would be empty of civilians, and occupied only by enemy. Certainly nothing was said about the care to be taken if civilians were encountered in the hamlet. The company commander interpreted these orders to involve leveling the hamlet, and transmitted them to his subordinates, including Lt. Calley, who heard those orders as including the killing of the inhabitants.

Calley's platoon did so. They rounded up the inhabitants; saw that they were old people, women, and children; and massacred many of them. Calley both gave the orders to do so and shot many of them with his automatic weapon. Enlisted men also shot civilians.

Who was responsible for this? As Kelman and Hamilton analyze the situation, the answer depends on what kinds of responsibility we are considering. Clearly, Calley and the enlisted men had direct causal responsibility; they did it. They killed people and they did it knowingly. Yet we also hold the notion of role responsibility; in the military this is discussed under the notion of "command responsibility." Officers are responsible for the conduct of their subordinates whether they ordered the actions of those subordinates or only allowed them to happen. From that point of view, the higher-ups were responsible for the massacre. They certainly gave no orders concerning the protection of innocent life; some listeners read them as "saying" that they wanted the inhabitants killed.[16]

Calley, the only individual who had both role and direct causal responsibility, was the only individual tried and convicted for his actions. This makes intuitive sense. The enlisted men were seen as the physical cause of the killings, but it was recognized that they had a role responsibility to obey orders in general, which made them unattractive candidates for punishment. But looking at higher authorities, many felt that they had a plausible claim to deny that murder of innocents was what they meant. True, they in some sense allowed the murders to happen, because the murders *did* happen; but they were not present, perhaps couldn't conceive that anyone would murder innocents, and so on. Only Calley, having both kinds of responsibility, was convicted.

Kelman and Hamilton went on to discover another interesting fact. Their survey found that citizens had quite different reactions to Calley's conviction, and those reactions could be related to which view of responsibility they held. Some respondents held to the view that the individual actor is responsible for his actions, and that this responsibility is not canceled if those actions are committed under orders. A majority of them approved of the Calley trial. Interestingly, they were also likely to say that the higher-ups should be tried. Others believed that in the massacre situation they themselves would have obeyed orders, most people would have obeyed orders, and it was unfair to try Calley for "doing so." As people in this latter group also tended to disapprove of trying higher-up officers, they remind us of the way in which responsibility can be extraordinarily diminished when an organization commits an evil action. As Kelman and Hamilton remark,

individual responsibility and command responsibility together can add up to 200 percent responsibility, as they did for many (who asserted personal responsibility); or to 0 percent responsibility, as they did for many (who denied personal responsibility); or (presumably) to anything in between. With disturbingly high frequency, joint responsibility for the My Lai massacre added up to zero in the public's eye. (p. 223)

In sum then, sometimes in organizations an act harming others is innocently or unknowingly "assembled" from the actions of many individuals who are not aware that the consequence of the act to which their actions contribute will be destructive. Thus sometimes organizations perpetrate major evils, with no single individual having evil intentions, or being guilty of more than, arguably, negligence in not foreseeing the harmful consequences. Even when the organization acts through an individual who knowingly commits evil actions, if the individual's phenomenology is such that the individual may have regarded himself as acting at the behest or command of the organization, many people decrease the responsibility assigned to that person.

Consider now a second path by which organizations that are not military or social-control organizations can bring about harmdoing actions, which may in turn change the actors into autonomous sources of harm in the future. In many organizational settings in which an action that is going to result in harm to others is taken, at least initially, there is no overt target for the actions committed, no salient other human who is seen to be a victim of the actions. The individual who decides to let the assembly line use substandard cord in the fabrication of radial tires is not thinking of the accidents that decision could cause; he or she is simply keeping the assembly lines moving. Because a good many of the forces that cause people to avoid doing harm to others rely on the salient presence of specific or specifically imagined victims, if they are not present, then restraining forces are considerably weakened. "These opposing forces rest ultimately on the actor's awareness that he or she is connected to a victim," (p. 313) as Kelman and Hamilton remark.

What this creates is the possibility that individuals within organizations can lose sight of the fact that individuals may be harmed in the course of fulfilling the other goals of the corporation or bureaucracy. Then, let us assume that, suddenly and dramatically, it is discovered that the actions of the corporation have already harmed large classes of others. It is now realized that certain actions of the organization inevitably led to harmful outcomes. Pintos are actually rear-ended, gas tanks actually catch on fire, and actual passengers are actually, horribly killed. Memos are found to exist within the corporation in which design engineers warn about exactly these possibilities. To an outside observer, it seems apparent that those in the organization must have been aware of the harms risked, and thus, somewhere there must be evil individuals who have knowingly brought about those evils. Inside the organization, however, the phenomenology is very different. It is possible that the negative outcomes simply could not have been anticipated by any individual—an unanticipated drug side-effect might be an example of this. It is more likely, however, that some evidence existed calling attention to the negative outcomes, but that the evidence was not given sufficient attention or weight within the organization. The people within the organization were focusing on other organizational goals and missed the meanings of the danger signals because they were "negligent, hurried, sloppy, or overworked" (Kelman & Hamilton, p. 312). To this list could be added interpersonal processes involving breakdown of communication and diffusion of responsibility.

However it came about, harmful actions have been committed (in this scenario), and now the individuals who had some responsibility for those actions have become aware of those consequences. To my mind, this is a critical point at which those individuals can become evil actors. Notice that the question is not whether or not to commit an immoral act. It is what to do when such an act has been committed and is now recognized. To those "organizationally responsible" for the harmdoing act, there are several choices, none of which is comfortable. These choices all seem to me to take the system in the direction of rationalization and cover-up, rather than toward acknowledgement and amends. Again, the moral essence of the situation is this: An organization has unforeseeably, carelessly, or in some sense willfully harmed others. In the clear light of hindsight, to the organizational

higher-ups, it must seem, as it seems to the potential outside observers, that the negative outcomes were at least foreseeable and perhaps, in the complex sense that an organization can be said to intend something, "intended." There may be internal evidence that all the information was available within the organization to know that the effects would be harmful.[17] Thus, were they to publicly or privately admit to the existence of the outcomes, or their role in producing them, they would be publicly convicted of harmdoing and internally faced with feeling shame and guilt. These are negative outcomes, which do not fit in with the people's dim memories of the paths that led them to the present predicament. At this point, it must be extraordinarily tempting to "cover up" the evidence if it is possible to do so. Several mechanisms are available for doing so, depending on who has become aware of what. If the negative consequences are known only within the organization, then their existence can be minimized or denied. Apparently executives in cigarette companies to this day deny that cigarettes cause cancer. Thus the person denies the negativity of the consequences, or the responsibility for those consequences, and in so doing denies guilt, both to himself and to others. The second part of the motive—to avoid appearing immoral in the eyes of others—leads to concealment of the harms from the outside world. Individuals in corporations, when they discovered, for example, that asbestos used by workers was leading to high rates of lung cancer, sometimes chose to conceal that fact, perhaps because they were concerned with the liabilities they would incur if they revealed that information.

Concealment has a price. Covering up past evidence is also likely to lead to maintaining the current practices that bring about the harms; it is at this point that I think such an organizational actor becomes evil, becomes an independent perpetrator of further negative acts now knowingly done. Historically, it is clear that shipyard managers or nuclear-plant managers concealed increasing amounts of evidence that made clear to them that working with asbestos or mining uranium (or even living downwind from nuclear plants) caused cancer. But often the failure to acknowledge past harms is to continue to commit those harms in the present. On one hand, this may be exactly what those who conceal intend to accomplish; they can continue practices that they now know are unsafe. But the psychological dynamics can be more complex. Consider the plight of the manager who, although he wants to conceal evidence of past harms, also wants to change current practices. It may not be possible. How can a shipyard worker who has worked with asbestos for 20 years interpret a sudden request to put on a filter mask? Thus it is often the case that, driven by a desire to hide past inadvertent harms, managers continue to have their workers operate in what they now know are dangerous settings, or otherwise engage in dangerous activities. They now do intentionally what they had previously done unknowingly.

Concealment of harm within organizations is not easy. To maintain it, further concealments are likely to be necessary, even though these were perhaps not contemplated by the organizational actor at the moment of choice between acknowledging and denying the harms done. The evidence of previous harms had better disappear. Those in the organization who might discover the previous harms had better be hindered or muzzled. Computer memories had better be wiped clean. A chain of repugnant and evil actions are found to be required following the initial decision to conceal the initial harm. People who don't think of themselves as corrupt find themselves burning incriminating documents and paying out bribes to potential informers. (Needless to say, one thinks of Watergate here, and the Iran-Contra scandal.)

At some point the "face" or honor of the organization becomes committed to the concealment and the processes of denying that real harms were done or real wrongs perpetrated. For those versed in history, the Dreyfus affair comes to mind. An individual was falsely convicted of treason on rather flimsy evidence. This became apparent and when considerable new evidence pointing to Dreyfus's innocence had accumulated, a new trial was finally ordered. The original conviction was affirmed. A more likely candidate for the treasonous act was later tried, and although the evidence was better that he had committed the crime, he was acquitted. Why? Because those doing the retrospective reviewing feared that to reverse the verdict would be to dishonor the military or admit to national disgrace. And they were right. To do it would have dishonored the military justice system and the French government. So they chose a path that further dishonored and discredited the system.[18]

What we have discovered here, I claim, is a second way that an individual can be caught up in and altered by a harmdoing process. Whatever else might be said about the Nazi doctor who stood on the selection ramp, designating those who would live and those who would die, he knew what he was doing. But often an individual within an organization carries out what seem to be routine actions, and then discovers those actions had negative consequences that now seem to have been anticipatable. When he or she denies or conceals those consequences, and becomes enmeshed in a widening circle of actions necessary to maintain this denial and concealment, the person has moved to become an independent and autonomous perpetuator of the harms done. He or she has become evil. But the process here is an after-the-fact one, in which the person faces not the prospective choice to do harm, but the retrospective choice to acknowledge that his or her actions have already done harm. The more the person now sees that those harms should have been foreseen, the more guilt, shame, and blame is acquired if he or she chooses to acknowledge them.

"Normal" Organizations Sometimes Intend Harm

I suggest there is a third way that many organizations cause harm. Bluntly put, they set out to do it. That is, their corporate ideologies make it appropriate to harm others, and the conditions of life include elements Staub identified as important in facilitating the development of genocidal practices. Reading Staub, while reading several other similar books at the same time, caused, as the saying goes, the penny to drop. That is, it occurred to me that many elements of Staub's analysis could be used to analyze some otherwise puzzling things that occur within organizations, which may explain how those organizations come to initiate harmdoing acts and convert their members into evil individuals. In many organizations, the members are in fear of losing their positions; thus, even if they are well-to-do, they are experiencing difficult life conditions. Only if they perform up to a certain level will they keep their jobs. Or perhaps more interestingly, only if they perform up to very high levels will they advance within a corporation. Echoing Staub, to be deprived of opportunities is to be in danger in a competitive corporate environment. Second, within a good many corporate structures, there exist certain well-identified groups whose interests are in some zero-sum relationship with the interests of the corporate group. When one is in a zero-sum relationship with another group, it is easy to depersonalize members of that group and rationalize harming them. A few examples may clarify this point. Union management relations often take on this perspective. Corporations competing for the same markets tend to regard the others as the enemy and act accordingly. Political parties competing for votes certainly are in this relationship with one another, and we have recently seen cases that make the point. For instance, to justify to oneself launching the infamous Willie Horton campaign ads, one must have been convinced that the "other side" consisted of people who would so disastrously govern America that any means of stopping them was warranted. At the end of that path lies Richard Nixon, Watergate burglaries, and beating up demonstrators who might cause the electorate to vote against incumbents. In a similar vein, it is interesting to speculate about what certain corporations think of their customers—cigarette companies, for instance.

Michael Lewis (1989), who wrote *Liar's Poker*, provides a richly detailed case of how those joining a stock brokerage firm were socialized into regarding their customers as sheep to be fleeced. A good many customers' lives were destroyed in the process, as the book reveals. At one point the narrator, Michael Lewis, describes selling a bond to a customer that somebody within his brokerage house had advised him was a good bond to sell. It fell, taking the customer down with it, and Lewis discovered that it was indeed "a good bond to sell." It was one that the brokerage house held a large inventory on and had inside information of its impending fall. Thus, the brokers moved them out of inventory onto customers, letting the customers take the upcoming loss.

Considerably hilarity ensues within the brokerage house. Perhaps bent, although not morally broken by a similar set of experiences, Lewis leaves the firm, but the socialization process that he describes corrupts many of the participants.

Of course, it was intended to. That is, his book makes clear the willing participation of the firm's managers in the corruption, and their calculated efforts to corrupt lower-level staff. As an example, higher commissions were paid for moving poor-quality bonds off on unwary customers. One is reminded of the people who worked for the now-defunct Lincoln Savings and Loan Company, which sold a good many nongovernment-insured investments to elderly customers, allowing them to believe they were insured. Many lost their life savings.

Thus, in several complex ways, organizations that are not social-control organizations can still corrupt their members. In fact, they can do this in several complex ways and in one simple way. In the simple way, that is what they intend to do, to corrupt their members into dealing unethically with people that they regard as the enemy or their appropriately dehumanized "marks to be fleeced."

The Reproduction of Destructive Organizations

We now consider another aspect of the usually unthinkable. If one were to take on the task of duplicating a killing organization, how would one do so? The question of organizational reproduction is quite easy to answer. Implicit in our previous analysis is an account of how such organizations reproduce themselves and grow. Organizations such as those involved in the Nazi death camps have not one but two outputs. They produce not only death, but individuals who become autonomously capable of and committed to producing other deaths. They produce evil individuals who become available for the reproduction of the evil organization. Concretely, SS officers and soldiers who first murdered civilians on the eastern front could then be used to staff the concentration camps and initiate and socialize other individuals into the new organizations. Older soldiers in the U.S. Army in Vietnam made clear to the new inductees how the war was really to be fought. By using a single evil organization "intelligently," it can be made to produce a surplus of individuals who can be used to replicate the organization in other settings. Given that the individuals who have been "processed" by the evil organization have been brought to a point where they use their intelligence in the service of their evil actions, the replicated organizations can be counted on to transcend whatever local obstacles stand in the way of reproducing the results of the original organization. The staff of various concentration camps made numerous grisly procedural refinements that increased the efficiency of their activities.

The realization that evildoing organizations have the capacity for self-replication provides part of the explanation for one of the facts that so bewilders us about, for instance, the Nazi death camps: Why were so many individuals willing to participate in their immoral activities? One answer is that different individuals were "trained" (a horrible word, used in this context) at different times, and they in turn trained others, and so the camps were staffed.

Conclusions

The argument has been a long one and I am not so convinced of its validity that I will try to summarize it. Instead, to draw others into the discussion, it seems useful for me to suggest some of its implications. We now have in modern culture a well-developed psychology concerned with the origins of antisocial acts in the personality structures of those who originate those acts. The clinical investigation of "psychopaths," "sociopaths," "antisocial personalities," and other diagnostic categories into which we encode those who best fit our intuitive definition of the evil individual, while by no means concluded, has much to say about the origins of those individuals. This analysis is the sort we are all naturally drawn to because it fits with our everyday conceptualizations of evildoing, in which the person who does the evil contains the appropriate quantum of evil, which is ultimately recognizable even if it might not be apparent from casual scrutiny of the individual. But, the present argument goes, that individual-level psychology is largely irrelevant to the occurrence of a much more common source of evil actions—produced by what I call "organizational pathology." We now need to create—and the authors mentioned in this essay are creating—a psychology and sociology of how human institutions can purposively move or accidentally lurch toward causing these actions, somehow neutralizing, suspending, overriding, or replacing the moral scruples of their members. That

psychology will inevitably be a social and organizational one, rather than one centered on the individual acting alone, although, as all of them show, it will draw on the conceptualization of an individual-level psychology, particularly to explain how the individual participates in his or her training in the social movement and continues to access his or her own particular skills in the service of the pathological group projects.

A polemical message lies behind this scientific one, or at least I have extracted one. It is too easy to defuse conceptually the chilling implications of evil actions by psychologically distancing them. Reading about an evil action, we assume that it was committed by an evildoer, a person who, because of a psyche twisted by genetic mischance or developmental trauma, is abnormal and evil. We assume evil actions normally flow from the actions of individuals who contain the quantum of evil I described earlier. By doing this, I would argue, we preserve our belief in the essential justness of the world, by having a limited and contained generalization about when that justness will not prevail. We are assisted in this process in that we are led to commit what social psychologists call the *fundamental attribution error*, to attribute behavior to the internal dispositions of an individual rather than to recognize that it stems from situational pressure. Thinking about evil actions, we call to mind typical or modal representations ("prototypes" or exemplars) of such actions, and in examining those representations, we find that they include images of evil individuals. In our minds evil acts are committed by evil individuals.[19]

The point that the social psychologist wants to stress is this: Evildoing is not confined to individuals who are evil at the time of committing the act. Each of us has the capacity to do evil actions if our surroundings press us to do so. The wonderfulness of our upbringings and the goodness of our personalities do not protect us from doing so. What social psychologists generally call the forces of the situation, but what I have argued here is the recruitment into a killing organization, "socialize" us into committing evil actions.[20]

Many social psychologists, myself included, have made a good deal of intellectual and career yardage by demonstrating the complex and compelling nature of the forces of the contextual pressures on people, and the definitions of the situation that they engender in those people. We thus show how actions that seem from the outside to be apathetic, or inhuman, are actually very human responses to flawed social situations. Frequently, having shown this, we end our lecture with a second message, which goes something like this: "Students. I have now made you aware of the ways in which social forces bring about the social constructions of the actors in the situation, and lead them to participate in doing evil. By making you aware of those social forces, I intend to enable you to resist the apparent imperatives of the situations in which you find yourselves, so you can avoid doing evil or step forward to do good." It is a rare lecture on bystander responses to emergencies that I haven't ended with that ringing affirmation of individual powers.

I continue to believe in that message, but I find I cannot apply it with such conviction as I used to when I think about the cases discussed here. To resist the psychological forces characteristic of the organizations discussed herein, pressures which strike me as often highly coercive and reinforced by real physical threats, requires a rare degree of individual strength indeed. This plea for resistance at the individual level to the contrary, the real action in evil-prevention may lie elsewhere.

Where does it lie? What I suggest is that the prototypes we carry around about the sources of evil actions, which assign those actions to individuals who are themselves in some way intrinsically evil, causes us to ignore the more likely source of harmdoing actions, which is organizational in nature. If harmdoing actions are in the main committed by individuals caught up in organizations and their pathology, then prevention or amelioration of evil may be best done at the organizational level. How could we do this? We have a standard set of interventions designed to prevent the development of pathology in military and social-control organizations. What can we learn from these that could be applied in the context of conventional organizations? Given my comments about the somewhat different ways conventional organizations slip into wrongdoing, ways of preventing evildoing in these organizations may need to be tailored to their special characteristics. How, for instance, could we halt or limit the tendency of organizations to cover up past harms, and in the process inadvertently commit themselves to perpetrate future ones? Other writers who have contributed to what I have called the social psychological perspective on evil clearly direct us to these questions.

One last word about the banality of evil: One way of wording the insight that arises from considerations such as have been examined here, is that it is generally only possible for a person to do evil when that evil has been "banalized"—rendered routine and morally neutral. To analyze these processes to better understand them, we give phenomenological accounts of how ordinary people neutralize evil as they are caught up by forces urging them to commit it. By doing this, do we not banalize evil at second hand, as we render it understandable, and make its commission easier? I began with other discomforts; I end with that one.

NOTES

1. These remarks raise rather acutely the question of who the "ordinary person" I am talking about is taken to be, and just how many courses in moral philosophy I am assuming he or she has taken. One group that initially appears to be an exception includes those who hold fundamentalist Christian beliefs, and who do believe in sin. But I suggest that they are also prone to the utilitarian groundings of morality that seems to be the bedrock for the rest of us. As a test, ask a fundamentalist why some particular action is wrong. The initial answer may be some variant of "Because the Bible pronounced it a sin." However, if one continues to ask why God, Christ, or the Bible pronounced it a sin, answers will be forthcoming, and in my experience are based on causing harm to others or to self.

2. Not irrelevant here is the "deconstructionist" movement in literary analysis, which argues that those works of art we have characteristically regarded as masterpieces, and thus exemplars of the good, are in fact categorized as such because certain privileged elites have foisted this perspective on the rest of us. Thus, they too have been read as arguing for a relativistic world.

3. For instance, even if somebody consented to being tortured, would not it still be evil to torture him?

4. An individual who tortures animals is generally seen as evil. Thus, the inference of evil arises from crimes other than those directed against people. In fact, many feel mistreatment of animals is somehow particularly evil. I suspect that this is exactly because to hurt a creature who cannot have any reasoned role in the causal circumstances surrounding the incident seems particularly egregious. Still, this means that it is not the infliction of suffering on a human being that is necessary for evil, but the infliction of suffering on an organism capable of suffering—experiencing pain and perhaps anticipatory dread about that pain.

5. The reader is invited to explore this. Imagine a series of acts, some of which seem bad and others evil, and examine the differences. Ask others about these cases. If your

experience matches mine, the others will agree with your classifications of most of the acts. Some may be classified differently; this is because the individuals doing the classifying are emphasizing different aspects of the ways of thinking about evil that I have elucidated. Alternatively, they may be bringing to bear genuinely different perspectives.

6. Because Saddam Hussein has some possibility of playing the role for this generation that Hitler has played for earlier generations, a few remarks about him may be appropriate. It needs to be remembered that these remarks are made soon after the conclusion of the ground war in Iraq. Briefly, I have no difficulty asserting that he is evil, and that the commander of the Allied forces is not. This is so even though we assume for a moment that the Allied forces killed more civilians than did the Iraqi forces. The discussion to back that up would involve reference to Hussein's indiscriminate gassing of fleeing Iraqi Kurdish tribespeople, quasi-random launching of Scud missiles, and so on. Certainly Hussein will be enshrined within the institutional memories of those determining what sorts of conflicts American military must be prepared to fight. We will be, and probably should be, prepared to fight evil nations for years to come. It is also likely, however, that Hussein will not be as great a figure in the pantheon of demons as Hitler because he fought so ineptly. Perhaps complete evil needs to almost prevail.

7. Humanity has a long history of struggling with the problem posed by the existence of evil. For instance, it is obviously in conflict with the concept of an all-powerful God, and thus has generated various views that the early Christian church labeled *heretical*.

8. It is the task of the suspense novel's protagonist to discover which individual is evil by conceptually grasping the pattern of the serial killings. Here we use the notion of "protagonist" in the technically incorrect but usual sense of hero-protagonist—the detective who is tracking the killer. In the better-done suspense books, it is possible to make the case that the role of protagonist is shared equally between the villain-seeker and the villain.

9. It is as if the world fits a generic plot for science-fiction novels. Somehow living among us is a race of aliens, creatures from another planet, who commit evil. Under certain conditions, we can recognize the aliens for whom they are, and thus guard ourselves against their evil actions. However, terrifyingly, sometimes these aliens appear in the guise of humans, making it difficult to recognize them and guard against their actions.

10. Of course, the authors would not want to deny the existence of evil done by evil individuals, who do meet the specifications of our intuitive requirements for the evil actor. However, if we can extend their argument, surely they are showing us that the huge predominance of evil actions committed in the world are in keeping with their model rather than the intuitive individual-origins model. And surely they are correct here; surely this is one thing that the fate of the 6 million means.

11. Lifton (personal communication, 1991), I think, has the most revealing construction of what I am trying to say about Milgram's theory. Recall that Milgram's subjects completed their task of administering what they regarded as high-level shocks within 1 experimental hour. The acuteness of this shift, or rather Milgram's perceptions that this required an acutely abrupt shift, "made him think in terms of a sudden psychophysiological shift into an 'agentic state.' " Lifton gently continued: "In contrast, what I observed was a more gradual process, though it had an acute or transition element—the anxiety Nazi doctors felt during their first weeks in Auschwitz until they made their adaptation, which in my view took the form of developing an Auschwitz self."

12. Perhaps this is a useful place to discuss the importance of "individual differences" in the account of harmdoing that I am shaping here. In it, given my background as a social psychologist, I take what might be called the "strong" situationalist perspective—that the social forces acting on the individual are sufficient to convert any individual, regardless of the strength of his or her personality and character, to being a cog in a killing machine. I should acknowledge two difficulties with this view: First, in this extreme form, it is likely to be wrong—a fact I would argue is relatively unimportant to the argument; second, my unfolding of the process does not emphasize one more historical truth that contributes to the development of the killing machine. Individuals with certain personality characteristics are likely to be recruited into the harmdoing organization and to contribute to its progress. The group of malcontents that originally formed around Hitler was certainly violence prone. Certainly, as Staub reminds us, destructive organizations, particularly in the early stages of their development, have the chance to recruit individuals who are predisposed to fit in with their destructive purposes, and the timely recruitment of these cadres may contribute greatly to their later domination of the societies in which they exist.

Returning to the point about heroic individuals, in truth there are probably individuals who have the strength to "stand against" the forces that the present authors and I are conceptualizing. But my task in this essay is to elucidate the strengths of the forces that surround individuals caught up in these organizations, the forces that lead individuals along the continuum of destruction. I agree that there are some individuals who can stand against these pressures, but I do not accept the implication that is sometimes drawn from that—that the "real task" in resisting these atrocities is to produce more such heroes or martyrs. I see the central task of preventing these atrocities as existing at a different level, at the level of societal institutions.

13. Again Staub, who, most among the authors considered; has taken on the task of describing the many ways of coming to evildoing that a historical examination reveals, reminds us of an alternate path. The present account encases the individual in a social organization and shows how organizational pressure operates on that individual to turn him or her into an independent originator of evil actions. Staub points out that, in certain instances, an individual alone can move along this path. The husband who first strikes his wife, later with increasing frequency batters her to the point of injury, and finally kills her is one such example.

14. They are also free. As of the end of 1990, they were pardoned by the President of Argentina, Carlos Menem.

15. A science fiction reader reminded me of Asimov's fa-

mous laws governing the conduct of robots. Obviously, in a thoughtful society, one would build a prohibition against killing a human being into the governing program of a robot. In one disconcerting short story, I recall that the author figured out a way that robots could bring about the death of a human being. The programmer simply created a series of apparently innocent steps that brought about a human's death. For instance, one robot puts rat poison in a container in the tool shed, another robot is told to move the container from the shed to a kitchen shelf, the third robot is told to put a spoon of "sugar" from the container into the victim's coffee. To return from the fanciful, the general point is that a series of subroutines, each not morally outrageous, can sum to an outrageous act.

16. When uttered in different contexts, sentences sometimes "mean more than they say." This is the psycholinguistic notion of pragmatic implicatures. For instance, I am teaching a seminar. John the student comes late to the seminar and leaves the door to the hall open as he slinks to a seat near the door. If I say, "John, it is noisy out in the hall," I report a fact about noise, but surely mean that John should reach out and shut the door. It may go a step further; I may be telling John that his lateness is noticed and marked up against his name. This provides an interesting retrospective illumination of Milgram's experiments. At some points the experimenter said to the shock giver, "Please go on; the experiment requires that you go on." Because the shock giver knew that the experimenter had heard the victim's protests, he read the meaning of that sentence to be, roughly, "I am in charge here and I am sure that the learner is not getting harmed. He may be getting a little hurt, but he agreed to that in the beginning."

17. In the case of the Ford Motor Company, Kelman and Hamilton tell us that there were internal memos acknowledging the flaw, the danger it represented, and the cost of a redesign fix. The fix was about $11 per car, which was then cost-benefit compared to the costs of the estimated payouts to persons killed in rear-end accidents, estimated at about $200,000 per death (p. 311). It would have been rather difficult to deny corporate foreseeability or intentionality here.

18. Lest anyone think this is an isolated incident, let me remind them that the British justice system is currently seriously dishonored by exactly the same pattern of events in the case of the "Birmingham Six," a case where the initial conviction and subsequent denial of appeals of individuals accused of terrorist bombings were upheld. Initially, the system brought in a flawed verdict based on faked evidence. It dishonored itself by willfully blinding itself to this during the appeals process. In 1992, the Los Angeles police department brutally beat a Black speeder they stopped, then filed papers to cover this up. An amateur's videotape of the beating derailed that cover-up.

19. An example of this may make it concrete. Stanley Milgram made a film of his experiments (Milgram, 1965), in which he included several sequences of shock-giving individuals who "go all the way." That is, a person in the role of teacher was to give an ascending series of painful shocks to the learner if the learner made mistakes on an associative learning task. Several individuals shown in the film, under what appeared to be mild prodding from the experimenter, escalated to the maximum levels of shock, even in the face of the protests of the individual receiving the shocks. When this film is shown to introductory students, they invariably attribute a sadistic personality to the "teacher." The experienced lecturer sometimes allows this perception to be created, then dismantles it by showing that the degree of situational control of this behavior was so high as to preclude this explanatory possibility.

20. One needs to put this cautiously. Several social psychology studies including Zimbardo's (1969) on deindividuation, Latané's and my own on responding to emergencies, and Milgram's, have demonstrated a high degree of situational control over actions usually thought to be largely under dispositional control. Certainly, the Milgram (1974) findings of a high percentage of subjects behaving obediently defeats the attribution of sadistic personalities unless we want to make the rather improbable claim that a majority of New Haven dwellers are sadistic. However, as Funder and Ozer (1991) pointed out, there is still plenty of variance in those studies that potentially could be explained by individual-difference variables. True. Still, it may not be useful to conceive of these individual differences as trait-described dispositions acquired during childhood socialization.

REFERENCES

Allport, G. W. (1937). *Personality: A psychological interpretation*. New York: Holt.

Arendt, H. (1963). *Eichmann in Jerusalem: A report on the banality of evil* (rev. & enlrg. ed.). New York: Viking.

Austin, J. L. (1956). A plea for excuses. *Proceedings of the Aristotelian Society*.

Bandura, A. (1986). *Social foundations of thought and action: A social cognitive theory*. Englewood Cliffs, NJ: Prentice-Hall.

Brock, T., & Buss, A. (1962). Dissonance, aggression, and the evaluation of pain. *Journal of Abnormal and Social Psychology, 65*, 197–202.

Cornwell, P. (1990). *Postmortem*. New York: Macmillan.

Darley, J. M., & Shultz, T. R. (1990). Moral judgments: Their content and acquisition. *Annual Review of Psychology, 41*, 525–556.

Darley, J. M., & Zanna, M. P. (1982). Making moral judgments. *American Scientist, 70*, 512–521.

Erikson, K. (1989). *Big Daddy Lipscomb: A parable*. Unpublished manuscript, Yale University, New Haven, CT.

Funder, D. C., & Ozer, D. J. (1991). Behavior as a function of the situation. *Journal of Personality and Social Psychology, 44*, 107–112.

Gibson, J. T., & Haritos-Fatouros, M. (1986). The education of a torturer. *Psychology Today, 20*, 50–58.

Goffman, E. (1961). *Asylums: Essays on the social situation of mental patients*. Garden City, NY: Doubleday/Anchor.

Harris, T. (1981). *Red dragon*. New York: Dell.

Harris, T. (1989). *The silence of the lambs*. New York: St. Martin's.

Heider, F. (1958). *The psychology of interpersonal relations*. New York: Wiley.

Karski, J. (1944). *Story of a secret state*. Boston: Houghton Mifflin.

Kelman, H. C., & Hamilton, V. L. (1989). *Crimes of obedience: Towards a social psychology of authority and responsibility.* New Haven, CT: Yale University Press.

Latané, B., & Darley, J. M. (1970). *The unresponsive bystander: Why doesn't he help?* New York: Appleton–Century.

Lewis, M. (1989). *Liar's poker.* New York: Norton.

Lifton, R. J. (1986). *The Nazi doctors: Medical killing and the psychology of genocide.* New York: Basic.

Milgram, S. (1965). *Obedience* [A filmed experiment]. New York: New York University Film Library.

Milgram, S. (1974). *Obedience to authority: An experimental view.* New York: Harper & Row.

Rosenhan, D. (1973). On being sane in insane places. *Science, 179,* 250–258.

Ross, L. (1977). The intuitive psychologist and his shortcomings: Distortions in the attribution process. In L. Berkowitz (Ed.), *Advances in experimental social psychology* (Vol. 10, pp. 174–221). New York: Academic.

Staub, E. (1989). *The roots of evil: The origins of genocide and other group violence.* New York: Cambridge University Press.

Webster's New Third International Dictionary. (1963). Springfield, MA: Merriam.

Zimbardo, P. G. (1969). The human choice: Individuation, reason, and order versus deindividuation, impulse, and chaos. In W. J. Arnold & D. Levine (Eds.), *Nebraska Symposium on Motivation.* Lincoln: University of Nebraska Press.

The Psychology of Political Terrorism

Martha Crenshaw • Wesleyan University

Violence is a perennial problem of politics. Scholars and policy makers are rarely satisfied with their understanding of its sources or consequences—other than the manifest results of death and destruction, which only deepen frustration over being unable to prevent its occurrence. Terrorism used by underground organizations against state institutions and policies is a specific type of political violence, one that has attracted much attention in the past 15 years. As terrorism has affected Western liberal democracies, it has shaken their faith in the possibility of the eradication of civil strife through political and social reform or through the material benefits of the welfare state. Terrorism has shown that the end of colonialism does not bring an end to struggles for national liberation. Indeed, Third World violence has inspired imitation in the West, as ethnic minorities revive hopes of separatism and as radical political organizations, often growing out of the student movements of the 1960s, move to join what they perceive as a global struggle against imperialism. After 1968 in Western Europe terrorism seemed to replace riots and protest demonstrations as a dramatic and violent disruption of stability, often disturbing to the public because of its unexpectedness in societies hitherto thought immune to serious domestic violence. Ideology has also motivated terrorist resistance to regimes in Latin America and the Middle East. In the latter region, religious fundamentalism is now combined with secular opposition as a source of violence. Although terrorism

is not a historical novelty, changes in its form and scope have appeared in recent decades.

As Greenstein (1973, p. 464) has noted: "It would seem necessary to identify functionally discrete types of violence and aggression in order to identify reasonably stable and distinctive antecedents." This observation is equally appropriate to the analysis of the consequences of violence. Terrorism is one of these discrete types of violence. The purpose of this chapter is to use terrorism as the basis for a case study of the relationship between political violence and psychology. Terrorism, a rare and extreme form of political behavior, is dependent on the motivations of the small numbers who practice it. Because its effectiveness in influencing political events depends on arousing emotions, the psychological reactions of its target audiences are significant.

Before attempting to analyze the problem of terrorism from a psychological perspective, we must complete several preliminary tasks. First, the concept of terrorism must be defined. Second, a review of existing approaches to the subject of terrorism is needed to sketch the general state of theoretical advance in the area. Third, an explanation of the complexity of the phenomenon of terrorism suggests caution in generalization. Proceeding to the application of psychological theory to terrorism, a logical beginning is the question of individual motivation. Why do people resort to terrorism? A concept that serves to unify diverse interpretations of motivation is Erikson's (1963,

1968) theory of identity. An exclusive focus on the individual is, however, incomplete, since terrorism usually involves group activity. Patterns of small-group interaction are a significant part of the explanation of terrorism activity. The psychology of terrorism also concerns the effects of terrorism on audiences and victims. The fate of hostages, as the most intense experience of victimization, will be examined in some depth.

Definitions and Approaches

Defining the concept of terrorism has proved difficult, in part because judgments about what terrorism is frequently depend on the circumstances in which violence occurs. Most writers on this subject rely on one of the earliest definitions, that of Thornton (1964, p. 73), who proposed: "In an internal war situation, terror is a symbolic act designed to influence political behavior by extranormal means, entailing the use or threat of violence." The violence of terrorism is distinguished from other types of political violence by its extranormality (terrorism exceeds the bounds of socially acceptable violence) and by its symbolic nature (the targets of terrorism are symbols of the state or of social norms and structure) (see Thornton, 1964, pp. 73–78). Terrorism is based on systematic and purposive violence, designed to influence the political choices of other actors more than to inflict casualties or material destruction. To achieve political influence, terrorism depends on its power to arouse emotions in audiences, including the neutral, the supportive, and the antagonistic. The emotional reactions to terrorism (which, of course, may be unanticipated by the terrorists although they strive to control them) may thus range from terror or acute anxiety to enthusiasm (see Hutchinson, 1972).

Thornton's conception, as expanded here, is restricted to terrorism against the state; that is, terrorism from below rather than from above. Terrorism is also practiced by governments, and some characteristics of its processes, effects, and perpetrators are similar to the characteristics of insurgent or agitational terrorism. For example, insurgent terrorist organizations may use terrorism to control their supporters and to enforce obedience. There are, however, such critical differences in the power, authority, and status of governments as opposed to nongovernments that an undifferentiated analysis would be misleading. The potential magnitude of most government violence is incomparably greater than that of nongovernments.

The literature in the field of terrorism is unsystematic, despite great popular and governmental interest in terrorism and the promise that the social sciences and psychology hold for its theoretical development. There are numerous ahistorical or alarmist treatments, but few scholars have turned their attention to terrorism, and among them fewer are familiar with the literature and attempt to build on the work of others. Nevertheless, there are signs that terrorism is becoming an established subject for research in the mainstream of American political science, including both quantitative as well as conceptual studies (for the former approach, see Hamilton & Hamilton, 1983; Sandler, Tschirhart, & Cauley, 1983). Even so, few psychiatrists, psychologists, or social psychologists have worked in this area. The present analysis of the state of the field is as much a sketch of what needs to be accomplished as an overview of achievements. It attempts to synthesize existing findings, to point out the areas of psychology from which future theoretical contributions might come, and to define the directions that psychological approaches to the study of political terrorism might take.

Complexity of the Problem

In order to generalize about psychological influences on terrorism, one must take into account the diversity and variation of the phenomenon. One reason for the imprecision or bias of many definitions of terrorism is that the activity assumes different forms. For instance, terrorists claim to be inspired by ideological goals ranging from social revolution or national self-determination to reactionary or conservative defense of the status quo. Terrorist organizations range in structure from extremely hierarchical and centralized, with rigid role distinctions, to a decentralized or anarchical model. Terrorist strategies vary in degree of selectivity in targeting and in preferences for specific methods; some involve bargaining with governments by seizing hostages, while others are designed only for immediate effect. Some terrorists choose to operate on an international scale, while others restrict themselves to their domestic surroundings. Terrorist modes of operation change constantly, often as a result of technological opportunities or government pressures.

Furthermore, the situations in which terrorism occurs vary along a number of dimensions. Political contexts include democracies as well as authoritarian regimes and states ranging from strong to weak in coercive capability and political stability. Legal systems may be flexible or rigid in dealing with violent opposition. Target societies may be homogeneous or heterogeneous, and history and political culture may be tolerant or intolerant of violence against the state. The international environment can be permissive or discouraging. Several types of terrorism occur in this range of contexts. The organizational forms and capabilities of terrorist organizations and the environments they operate in are related to both motivations and psychological consequences. Any model of terrorism must take into account the varieties and the interactive dynamics of the process.

To illustrate briefly differences in motivation, context, and status among contemporary terrorist organizations, one can compare the Provisional Irish Republican Army (IRA) in the United Kingdom and Ireland to the Red Army Faction (RAF) and its successors in the Federal Republic of Germany. The Provisional IRA is the heir to a tradition of violent resistance to British rule, the "physical force" tradition that has its roots not only in Oliver Cromwell's depredations but in the mythology of the French Revolution. Although the majority of the citizens of Ireland and Northern Ireland do not actively support the IRA, belonging to the IRA in the divided society of Northern Ireland is more socially acceptable than belonging to the RAF in West Germany, where memories of violence against the regime derive primarily from the paramilitary extremists of both right and left under the Weimar Republic. In West Germany neither religious nor national divisions legitimize violence against the state. Most West German terrorists, whose organizations emerged from student protest movements, are from the middle or upper-middle classes; in contrast, members of the IRA are from working-class backgrounds. Whereas the aims of Irish Republicans focus sharply on creating a united and non-British Ireland, the vague and unrealistic goals of German terrorism center on the creation of an ill-defined socialist order. Many Irish, northern, southern, and American, sympa-

thize with the IRA's goals of national unity and British withdrawal if not its methods. Few Germans (despite the publicity over "sympathizers") want a revolution. The IRA generally restricts its activities to the traditional methods of terrorism and guerrilla warfare—selective assassinations, bombings, troop ambushes, sniper fire—that accord with its self-image as an army against the British. The RAF, on the contrary, progressed to kidnappings and hijackings in order to compel the government to release imprisoned fellow terrorists. This form of bargaining with governments has since 1968 represented a significant innovation in terrorist strategies.

Even this brief description indicates that psychological motivations, processes, and effects differ from case to case and that one should exercise caution in proposing generalizations. Answers to the questions of why individuals are attracted to terrorism, why terrorism finds supporters among the population, why a terrorist organization chooses particular strategies, and why terrorism has extreme effects in some cases but not in others depend on political and social context and type of terrorist organization as well as on psychological theory.

Another element in the complexity of modern terrorism is its transnational character. The fact that terrorism is a transnational phenomenon—one that in crossing national boundaries escapes the control of governments—blurs distinctions among different national groups and their contexts. As terrorists collaborate among themselves, imitate each other, and seek foreign support, it becomes difficult to isolate causes and effects. Furthermore, transnationalism (a product of modernization) means that terrorists can be both mobile and anonymous. Consequently, terrorists can be either close to or distant from the populations they target. Palestinian terrorism against Israelis in West Germany, for example, and Armenian terrorism against Turks in the United States will not have the same effects on its respective national audiences as indigenous terrorism would have.

Further complexities in analyzing terrorism arise from the widely held assumption that terrorism is intentional behavior, in which motivations of whatever sort, rational or irrational, lead to action that can be objectively identified as terrorism. However, the translation of intention into action is modified by chance and opportunity, neither of which can be satisfactorily predicted. Furthermore, in asking why terrorism happens, one must distinguish between the initiation of a campaign of terrorism and its continuation in the face of government reaction. One must also distinguish between why an individual becomes a terrorist and why an organization (already formed as a group) collectively turns to terrorism. Why terrorists persist despite the risks involved and the uncertainty of reward is an important question. Why terrorist organizations choose the particular strategies they do—bombings, kidnappings, or armed attacks, for example—is also significant.

Scholarly analysis should also be attentive to what is meant by becoming a "terrorist" or a member of a terrorist organization. Most people probably oversimplify the role of the "terrorist" into a mental picture of a wild-eyed 19th-century anarchist. Actually, complex role differentiation exists within terrorist organizations. First, there are significant differences between leaders and followers. The latter group is further divided into those who are active within the organization and those who are passive supporters, remaining outside the underground structure but providing needed services as well as channels for recruitment into the organization. Among active followers, one can distinguish a number of separate functions: public relations, propaganda, fund raising, forgery, weapons purchases, and logistics, as well as those related to planning and engaging in violence. A terrorist may be a sharpshooter, a builder of bombs, a specialist in armed attacks or kidnappings, or a guard for hostages. Terrorist violence need not involve physical interaction with victims.

Finally, constructing theories to explain the effects of terrorism on victims and on audiences is also hampered by the elusiveness of the phenomenon. It is difficult to separate the effects of terrorism from the effects of other social phenomena to which the public responds. It is somewhat easier to analyze the reactions of victims, especially former hostages. Yet even here, analysts are hard pressed to specify what it is about terrorism that accounts for its effects, or how much the strength of reaction lies in the predispositions of the victim or target audience.

Explanations of Individual Motivation

It would be simplistic to base an argument about motivation on the premise that terrorism is solely a result of specific personality patterns or traits. As with all forms of political behavior, terrorism cannot be studied in isolation from its political and social context. The analysis of terrorism clearly deals with the intersection of psychological predispositions (which may be derived as much from prior experience and socialization as from psychological traits emerging from early childhood and infancy) and the external environment. This interrelationship is the more compelling because the ostensible purpose of terrorist groups is to change that environment; terrorists invariably claim, in fact, that their behavior is the only logical response to external circumstances. Many indignantly reject psychological explanations. Terrorism, furthermore, is a result of group interactions as much as individual choice. Although isolated, individually motivated acts of terrorism can occur, the most important terrorist events are part of campaigns led by organizations.

Another problem with the study of individual motivation or predisposition toward terrorism is that it is difficult to go beyond a series of unrelated psychobiographies and focus on common themes. Most analysts agree that there is no common "terrorist personality." Terrorism is not purely expressive violence; it is also instrumental. We are thus dealing with individuals who are extremely goal oriented but whose goals and means of pursuing their goals are influenced (not determined) by psychological considerations in interaction with the situation.

Nor does terrorism in general appear to be a result of mental pathologies. Rasch (1979, p. 80), a psychiatrist who has analyzed several members of the West German terrorist organizations, warns that "no conclusive evidence has been found for the assumption that a significant number of them are disturbed or abnormal." In Rasch's (1979, p. 79) view, the argument that terrorism is pathological behavior is an attempt to avoid discussion of the political and social issues raised by terrorism. Rasch's position is reinforced by the studies performed under the aegis of the West German Ministry of the Interior, which include information on 227 leftist terrorists in West Germany (Jäger, Schmidtchen, & Süllwold, 1981, particularly Süllwold, pp. 101–102 and conclusions by Jäger & Böllinger, p. 235). Similarly, Ferracuti and Bruno (1981, p. 206), who studied Italian terrorists, note that "a general psychiatric explanation of terrorism is impossible. To define all terrorists as mentally ill would be an easy way to solve the problem, simply by invoking evil spirits in order to exclude from normality those from whom we want to be as different as possible." Heskin (1980, pp. 84–85), in a study of the psychology of Northern Ireland, similarly concludes that IRA members are not psychopaths, predisposed to violence, or mentally abnormal. Corrado (1981) has critically reviewed theories that regard terrorism in Western societies as rooted in sociopathy, narcissism, the death wish, or physiological impairment (such as neurological disorders leading to antisocial behavior). He found that the mental disorder approach lacks the systematic clinical observation and reliable diagnostic criteria necessary for its substantiation; furthermore, he suggests, terrorism is more likely to be a product of frustrated but rational idealism.

A possible reason for the apparently small numbers of pathologically ill individuals among the ranks of terrorists is that most terrorist organizations, as conspiratorial undergrounds, are careful about whom they recruit. Centralized, efficient organizations screen out potential members who could be dangerous to the survival of the group. This practical rule of organizational security and maintenance excludes the person of unpredictable or uncontrolled behavior. In less hierarchical organizations, those with a loose structure and relaxed central direction in the anarchist model, there is less control over membership. Hence, group exclusivity would be less of an obstacle to mentally ill persons who might be attracted to terrorism. Thus, according to Ferracuti and Bruno (1981, pp. 208–209), clinical analyses based on the few available case histories of individual left-wing Italian terrorists reveal that they rarely suffered from serious personality defects; in contrast, right-wing terrorists (who are more frequently examined by psychiatrists than are left-wing revolutionary terrorists because the insanity defense is more frequently employed at their trials) showed a much higher incidence of borderline or even psychotic personalities and of drug addiction. The glorification of violence in right-wing ideologies of terrorism may also explain their attraction for mentally disturbed individuals. The West German study, however, did not conclude that right-wing terrorists (of whom twenty-three cases were included) are more likely to be unbalanced, although

it noted several distinctive personality traits (see Süllwold, 1981, pp. 110–113).

To argue that terrorism does not result from a single personality constellation or from psychopathology is not to say that the political decision to join a terrorist organization is not influenced or, in some cases, even determined by subconscious or latent psychological motives. The problem is to find some commonality in a heterogeneous group of individuals, especially in considering cross-national terrorism. One facet of personality or one predisposition to which analysts have been drawn is the individual's attitudes toward and feelings about violence and aggression. The question is complex, since for most of its adherents terrorism does not necessarily involve direct participation in violent activities. An attraction to violence does not appear to be the dominant aspect of their personalities—unlike, for example, the most violent of the Nazi stormtroopers studied by Merkl (1980), who notes that these individuals showed an early, single-minded, and "awesome bent for violence" (p. 235). Terrorism involves reflective, not impulsive, violence and requires the ability to delay gratification through long and tedious planning stages.

Knutson (1981, p. 109) found that the terrorists she interviewed in American prisons were ambivalent in their attitudes toward the use of violence. Highly uncomfortable at being called "terrorists," they nevertheless admitted that a purpose of their action had been to cause fear. Yet they insisted that creating fear was less important than demonstrating their commitment to a cause through personal sacrifice. They also regarded terrorism as a last desperate alternative; it was almost an act of personal futility, used after all other options were exhausted, when there was nowhere else to go (Knutson, 1981, pp. 143–144). Certainly, the theme of "we had no choice" dominates terrorists' self-explanations, but it is difficult to distinguish motivation from rationalization.

Knutson (1981) also analyzed a single case in depth, that of Zvonko Busic, the Croatian hijacker of an American airliner to Paris in 1975, who in addition had placed a bomb in Grand Central Station that killed one policeman and injured three others. Busic had chosen hijacking precisely because he considered it "humane" violence, involving as it did the use of fake bombs. His attitude toward violence was conflicted; he looked forward not to frightening his hostages but to their relief, acceptance, and forgiveness when he exposed the reality that there were no explosive devices. He was unable to accept his own anger, felt remorse when he did have to face it, and thus denied it in order to preserve personality integration. Being unable to recognize or accept his own violent impulses, he separated the violent act from his own control and responsibility. Therefore, the bomb that Busic left at Grand Central was accompanied by instructions on how to dismantle it; Busic did not consciously mean to cause deaths. Someone else had to be blamed: in this case the police. A trace of sadism is also revealed in Busic's direction of violence toward "safe" targets—airline passengers—who were unable to respond in kind. Knutson's analysis leads us to suspect that psychological motives may influence the particular form that terrorism takes (for example, seizure of hostages as opposed to assassination) as much as the decision to become a terrorist.

Indeed, Knutson (1980, p. 197) maintains generally that "many terrorist events are carefully, painstakingly engineered to avoid ultimate responsibility for violent death." Many terrorists are "psychologically nonviolent" and spend much time trying to resolve the dilemma, devising ways to instill fear without assuming responsibility for deaths. Similar ambiguities in attitudes toward violence may lead other terrorists to adopt hostage taking as a mode of terrorism, a means by which the final responsibility for causing harm can be laid to the government that refuses to accommodate terrorist demands.

On the other hand, some evidence suggests that not all terrorists are ambivalent. Morf (1970), in an analysis of the early members of the Front de Libération de Québec (FLQ), found more explicit signs of an early interest in violence. Several FLQ members had already engaged in violent resistance to authority. As an adolescent, one had fought with the Belgian partisans in World War II. Another had lived through wartime air raids and subsequently fought with the French Foreign Legion in Vietnam and Algeria. Morf interprets the fascination with violence that he discovered in some individuals as compensation for feelings of inferiority.

Böllinger (1981), a member of the West German study team, also found that some of the terrorists he interviewed were attracted to violence—which he attributes to unconscious aggressive motives. Such motives, in his view, differentiate the terrorist from people with similar psychological features (resulting from early childhood traumas) who do not show the same behavioral outcome—some conforming to social norms and others choosing nonviolent yet nonconformist roles, such as membership in religious cults. The terrorist group represents an outlet for archaic aggressive tendencies, frequently rooted in youthful conflicts with stepfathers. Such aggressive tendencies reflect fantasies of omnipotence corresponding to the individual's own inner feelings of impotence and inferiority. The attraction to violence may also be a result of identification with the violent acts of father figures (a violence several individuals had actually experienced); that is, an identification with the aggressor (see especially Böllinger, 1981, pp. 222–224).

Jäger (1981, pp. 167–169), however, found no common pattern in attitudes toward violence, neither ambivalence nor attraction, among the West German terrorists. Some individuals reported a strong prior aversion to aggression. They were conscious of a need to justify their behavior and felt a sense of limitation. Others reported that violence was simply not a problem for them. Jäger concludes that these attitudes depend on individual socialization and are not particularly significant.

Possibly, rather than being attracted to the inherent violence of terrorism, some individuals are seduced by the lures of omnipotence and grandeur to compensate for feelings of inferiority or impotence. Kaplan (1981, pp. 41–42) contends that the self-righteousness of terrorism conceals the terrorists' insecurities and that "terrorism is a response to a lack of self-esteem." Süllwold (1981) believes that West German terrorists are people who have high aspiration levels but are internally conflicted and prone to failure because of unrealistic demands on themselves. They react to failure not by adapting to their realistic level of capability but by raising the level of their aspirations. Such neurotic behavior involves clinging to irrational goals regardless of outcomes, while refusing to engage in any activity that might test one's abilities. Failure leads to aimlessness and dissatisfaction, which make the individual susceptible to the appeal of terrorist organizations, whose goals are equally unrealistic. Such individuals are also prone to external attribution: to blame others for their failures and consequently to feel hostility toward the outside world (see Süllwold, 1981, pp. 89–96). Knutson (1981) noted a similar tendency to blame others. Böllinger (1981) observed in a limited number of West German terrorists the need to overcome feelings of inferiority.

Another possible psychological trait, which appears to have been neglected thus far by researchers, is stress seeking. Terrorism differs from other counterculture activity not only in its violence but also in its stress-producing character. The glamor and excitement of terrorism, perhaps the attraction for some individuals, lie partially in the physical danger it comports. Terrorists may be "stress seekers," who are attracted to "behavior designed to increase the intensity of emotion or level of activation of the organism" (Klausner, 1968, p. 139). Stress seekers carefully plan their behavior; they respond more to internal than to external imperatives; and they return repeatedly to stressful situations. Moreover, repetition of the stressful activity becomes not only obsessive but escalatory; the stress seeker is compelled to perform more and more difficult acts (see Klausner, 1968, pp. 143, 145). Not all stress seeking is socially destructive behavior; in fact, in many Western societies, the sort of adventurism it may produce is admired. Stress seeking would have to occur in conjunction with other predispositions to encourage violent defiance of government and society.

Stress seekers seem to fall into two types. The individualistic stress seeker is uncomfortable as a follower; he seeks attention to the point of being narcissistic. Such a person seeks self-affirmation in the face of danger. The group stress seeker, in contrast, wishes to abandon the self in the group. This type of stress seeker identifies with the group and merges himself completely in the collective personality (Klausner, 1968, pp. 143–145). This observation leads to an important distinction among terrorist roles between leaders and followers. Whereas leaders may be more likely to possess latent dispositions and traits (acquired through socialization) that make violent, stressful oppositional behavior attractive, followers may be attracted more to the group than to its activities. Followers exhibit strong affiliative needs. Süllwold (1981, pp. 103–106), for example, argues that a notable difference exists between leaders and followers. While there is no such thing as a typical terrorist, leaders are more likely to be people who combine a lack of scruples with extreme self-assurance. She found that leaders often lead by frightening or pressuring their followers.

Süllwold noted two types of personality traits among terrorist leaders. The first type is the extremely extroverted personality, whose behavior is unstable, uninhibited, inconsiderate, self-interested, and unemotional. (Although Süllwold does not suggest the concept of narcissism, these attributes resemble those of the narcissistic personality; see Rubins, 1983). Emotional deficiencies blind such individuals to the negative consequences of their actions. Such people also possess a high tolerance for stress. It is possible that this person is a stress seeker, for whom the excitement of danger compensates for the absence of feeling. Such persons, furthermore, do not accept responsibility for their actions and dislike boredom and inactivity. The second type of terrorist leader is neurotically hostile. Suspicious, aggressive, defensive, and intolerant, he rejects criticism and is extremely sensitive to external hostility. For this type of individual, the terrorist movement serves as a projection of inner hostility. Süllwold (1981) asserts, as does Pomper (1979) in his biography of the 19th-century Russian terrorist Sergei Nechaev, that terrorism is a field of action in which personality defects that would be punished in a normal social setting are rewarded. The psychology of terrorist leadership has otherwise been little studied, although several leaders—Boris Savinkov (1931) of the Combat Organization of the Socialist-Revolutionary Party in prerevolutionary Russia, Saadi Yacef (1962) of the Algerian FLN, and Menachem Begin (1977) of the Irgun zvai Leumi—have written autobiographies.

The available evidence strongly suggests that, for the majority of terrorists who are followers, to become a member of the group is a dominant motive. Terrorists, in contrast to assassins, are not usually comfortable acting alone; terrorism is a small-group activity. The path to joining a terrorist organization is often through other groups, such as in West German residential cooperatives, communes, and prisoners' help groups. The recruitment process of the Basque Euzkadi ta Askatasuna (ETA) is slow and gradual, moving like the West German organizations from legal to illegal assistance, and is based on groups in Basque youth culture (Clark, 1983). Kaplan (1981, p. 45) also emphasizes the importance of the "merged collective identity."

In West Germany the communal life from which terrorist groups emerged was extraordinarily homogeneous; it formed a counterculture dominated by leaders with extreme political views. Almost three quarters of the terrorists in Schmidtchen's (1981) sample lived in a commune or residential cooperative before their involvement in terrorism. Many were also individuals whose break with family and society and whose rejection of bourgeois culture and values preceded the politicization of their discontent and was intensified by association with like-minded individuals in closed communities (see Jäger, 1981, pp. 147–150). To many individuals the group substituted for family and filled needs for recognition, acceptance, warmth, and solidarity. Jäger (1981, pp. 151–153) argues that it was above all in this phase of entering a group that latent motives rather than the group's political goals influenced individual actions. The group itself becomes the aim of many people. Jäger also found that many terrorists expressed a need for the structure, discipline, and commitment they found in group life.

For West Germans entrance into the terrorist group was a gradual process—as it was for recruits into the Basque ETA—rather than an instantaneous conversion. As individuals joined groups that became more and more radical, they were drawn closer to the inner circles that espoused violence. Thus, the decision to use violence came only after association with the group; the choice was then between participating in violence or leaving the group. The individual who was already in need of the things a group could supply and who had over time become dependent on the group found it costly, in psychological terms, to go back.

Observers of terrorism in West Germany have also noted the importance of personal connections and relatives in the process of joining a group (Jäger, Schmidtchen, & Süllwold, 1981; Wasmund, 1982). Wasmund discovered a large number of couples and brothers and sisters participating in terrorism. This finding reinforces his argument that the terrorist group is a family substitute. Jäger (1981, pp. 156–157) noted that in some cases relationships with other influential persons were so significant that without them the terrorist's personal development would have taken a different course. Leaders of terrorist groups often fill the role of mentor, becoming substitute parents. Similarly, in the Basque resistance, young recruits frequently joined under the influence of older militants (Clark, 1983). Couples also are commonly found in Italian terrorist groups, and Japanese terrorist Kozo Okamoto followed the lead of his older brother.

A last issue that should be discussed in relation to individual psychological traits and the turn to terrorism concerns the role of women. Some authors believe that female participation in terrorism is unique in character or motivation. For example, Cooper (1979, pp. 151–155) describes the presence of women in terrorist organizations as shocking and their behavior as "vicious," "ferocious," and "intractable." Cooper refers to "fatal proclivities" and unusually intense and personal emotional involvement—the results of women's sexual nature—and to the low self-image, alienation, and bitterness of women terrorists. Knight (1979), in analyzing the significant female participation in the terrorist branch of the Russian Socialist Revolutionary party, contends that terrorism would not have developed as strongly as it did without the critical role of women. Although, Knight argues, the women terrorists whom she studied were more emotionally than rationally inspired, their emotional needs were derived less from inherently feminine traits than from their isolated and frustrated position in a society that offers few outlets for women. She found women terrorists distinctively ethical and moral in their approach to violence, determined and absolutely committed, and bent on self-sacrifice and martyrdom. Their view of terrorism was highly subjective and personal; women valued the sense of importance they gained from participation. The fact that several later showed signs of instability Knight attributes to the trauma of the experience rather than predisposition.

Süllwold (1981, pp. 106–110) does not regard the causes of female participation in terrorism as unusual. She views such assumptions as the result of social stereotyping rather than objective analysis. Süllwold suggests that the significant contribution of women to left-wing West German terrorism, especially to its leadership, was not the result of social frustration and attempts at emancipation. Instead, this participation stemmed from the same factors that drove men to terrorism, although the influence of personal contacts might have been somewhat greater. (An account that illustrates the role of emotional dependence in terrorism is found in Alpert's 1981 autobiography.)

Identity as an Organizing Concept

A theory is needed to integrate existing findings and link the psychological characteristics analysts have noted in individual terrorists to empirical observations. For example, take the fact that most terrorists are young. Many are students or recent students. Often they have already rejected society, choosing to live in a deviant subculture, or are members of ethnic minorities who reject the dominant culture and society. One attempt to link these factors is Feuer's (1969) theory of the "conflict of generations," which is based on a Freudian interpretation of terrorism as a psychological reaction of sons against fathers, a generational phenomenon rooted in the Oedipus complex and, thus, in maleness. Terrorism is seen as a universal and inevitable outgrowth of student movements, independent of political and social context. Authority figures are identified as fathers against whom adolescent sons inevitably rebel. With maturity, terrorism ceases. Liebert (1971, pp. 187–188) criticizes Feuer's monocausal explanation and his confusion of psychodynamics and psychopathology. He contends that Feuer fails to explain why some students do not become activists, although they share the same unconscious impulses as others, or why females are present in contemporary student and terrorist groups.

A more sophisticated theory connecting individual psychology to society is found in the developmental psychology of Erik Erikson (especially 1963 and 1968). Erikson's sensitivity to the interaction between psychoanalytic and social explanations of human behavior is highlighted in his concept of identity, which is a reflection of the individual in a setting, familial or social. To Erikson (1963, p. 242) identity is as central to today's world as sexuality was to Freud's. The successful development of personal identity is essential to the integrity and continuity of the personality. Identity enables the individual to experience the self as something that has continuity and sameness, to act accordingly, and to be confident that one's sense of self is matched by one's meaning for others. Erikson's theory has influenced at least two specific analyses of the personalities of terrorists.

To introduce and clarify these contributions, it is useful to review briefly the part of Erikson's work that pertains to the study of terrorism. Erikson based his concept of personality on the child's development through a series of cumulative developmental stages, each of which is a "crisis" (in the sense of a turning point rather than a catastrophe) that results either in matured integration of the personality or in the persistence of unresolved conflicts, which may torment the individual through later life (see Erikson, 1968, p. 96). Erikson considers the development of basic trust in the infant as the cornerstone of a vital personality. Early mistrust, accompanied by rage and fantasies of domination or destruction of the sources that give pleasure or provide sustenance, is revived when society fails to provide needed assurances. These conflicts of infanthood and early childhood resurface in later extreme circumstances, especially in adolescence, when the crisis facing the individual involves finding a stable identity. Earlier failures to establish trust, autonomy, initiative, or industry handicap the adolescent's search for positive identity, leading in some cases to extreme identity confusion and in others to the formation of a negative identity. Identity is something found not alone but in a collectivity and is rooted in one's ethnic, national, or family past. It cannot, therefore, be separated from historical circumstances.

At the stage of identity formation, individuals seek both meaning and a sense of wholeness or completeness as well as what Erikson (1968, especially p. 232) terms "fidelity," a need to have faith in something or someone outside oneself as well as to be trustworthy in its service. Ideologies, then, are guardians of identity. Erikson further suggests that political undergrounds utilize youth's need for fidelity as well as the "store of wrath" held by those deprived of something in which to have faith. A crisis of identity (when the individual who finds self-definition difficult is suffering from ambiguity, fragmentation, and contradiction) makes some adolescents susceptible to "totalism" or to totalistic collective identities that promise certainty. In such collectivities the troubled young find not only an identity but an explanation for their difficulties and a promise for the future.

Erikson's theories form the basis for Böllinger's (1981) psychoanalytic study of eight indicted or convicted members of West German terrorist groups. Böllinger found that his subjects had suffered serious traumas during critical stages of development, especially in failures to establish trust, autonomy, and initiative. Individuals who lacked the quality of basic trust failed to integrate excessive aggressive tendencies or maintain successful social relations. Böllinger believes that these disruptions at the stage where autonomy is developed were the fault of a nonsupportive environment. Failure to develop autonomy resulted in destructive tendencies, insecurity, and fear of personality disintegration. In Böllinger's subjects overcontrolling and unaffectionate parents had turned all relations with the child into a struggle for power, leading the child to clash repeatedly with outside authority. Upon reaching the formative identity period, these individuals found an ideology based on conflict between oppressed and oppressor highly attractive. Acquisition of weapons in an underground group made the "child" feel less small, weak, and helpless before the powerful authority. Böllinger found in these revivals of earlier power struggles an individual's need to control, to dominate, or even to inflict pain bound to feelings of childhood impotence, which were compensated for by illusions of grandeur and omnipotence.

According to Erikson, the rage that an individual feels at being helpless is projected onto the controlling figures; it may also engender guilt feelings, which lead to self-punitive actions. Thus, Erikson's theory can help explain the theme of self-sacrifice in terrorist behavior. Similarly, some individuals fail to surmount the crisis of initiative, so that on top of feelings of suspiciousness, self-doubt, powerlessness, and shame come inferiority and incompetence, feelings often resulting from social deficiencies and obstacles beyond the individual's control (such as weak educational background). Thus, for the individuals Böllinger studied, layer on layer of development and experience did not smooth over scars but reopened old wounds. Such individuals reached puberty and the crisis of identity formation already seriously impaired. They found themselves in social and political circumstances that for different reasons were not favorable to the acquisition of a positive identity.

Böllinger argues that joining a terrorist organization was the last of a series of attempts at identity formation. These potential terrorists were searching for meaning, structure, and a stable social role. They hoped to gain purpose and assurance from the terrorist organization. The group became the family that had never provided the warmth, protection, security, and support the individual had needed. The opportunity to join a terrorist organization allowed the individual to submerge himself in a collective identity and, thus, to lay down the burden of personal responsibility. The group met a need to idealize authority figures, to express aggressive tendencies, to feel omnipotent, and to belong. Its ideology of violent resistance to the state and to imperial domination allowed collective identification simultaneously with the victims of oppression and the aggressive authority figure, while neutralizing guilt through intellectual and emotional justifications. The group provided the structure and integration lacked by the isolated individual.

Knutson (1981) also used Erikson's conceptualization, especially his concept of negative identity. Erikson (1968, p. 174) defines negative identity as "an identity perversely based on all those identifications and roles which, at critical stages of development, had been presented to them [patients] as most undesirable or dangerous and yet also as most real." It involves what Erikson frequently terms a "vindictive" rejection of the roles considered desirable and proper by the individual's family and community; it may result from excessive normative ideals demanded by ambitious parents or actualized by superior ones. This interpretation accords with the findings of Schmidtchen (1981) that many terrorists come from families who exert strong pressure for achievement. If a positive identity is not possible, the individual prefers being a "bad" person to being nobody or partially somebody. If early steps toward the acquisition of a negative identity are interpreted and treated by society as final, individuals may be pushed into conformity with the worst that people expect of them (Erikson, 1968, p. 88). Not only may such confused individuals find refuge in radical groups where certainty is assured, but they may be forced into a choice by others' interpretations of their behavior.

Knutson (1981, p. 112) also emphasizes the theme of government actions narrowing choices and pushing an individual into the assumption of a negative identity. Croatian terrorist Zvonko Busic was a member of an oppressed minority in a dominant culture, a situation Erikson (1968, p. 303) considers likely to engender negative identities because minorities may fuse the negative image held of them by the majority with the negative self-image of the group. Knutson found that economic constraints prevented Busic from pursuing his early goal of a university education. This disappointment, which Knutson compares to life disappointments experienced by several other terrorists, blocked the path to a positive identity and led to his assuming negative roles. As a child in Yugoslavia, Busic was socialized into strong beliefs in the cause of Croatian separatism and had a nationalistic cousin who was a role model. Similarly, many German terrorists came from families where the parents were social activists. Knutson's contention is that the negative identity is not totally negative; although deviant in some ways, it is based on values acquired through early socialization. This fact seems to contradict Erikson's original theory of negative identity as the antithesis of what parents and society value.

In cases of nationalist or separatist terrorism, the concept of negative identity acquires a more subtle meaning. To become a violent revolutionary in the cause of Croatian, Basque, or Irish independence is not a totally negative identification. There is much more social approval within the minority community for such actions than there is for violent undergrounds in homogeneous Western societies or liberal states, where nonviolent means for expressing opposition exist. The choice of becoming a terrorist is extreme; but, for example, in the Basque region of Spain, the young man who becomes a member of the ETA receives strong social support from the Basque small-town milieu, although his family does not approve of the decision (mainly because of the dangers involved). After a period of under 3 years as an *etarra*, a young man usually returns to society (Clark, 1983). The opprobrium attached to violent dissent in Germany, Italy, or the United States is absent; the choice of joining the ETA would not represent an absolutely negative identity. Knutson argues that the negative identity actually reflects values instilled early in life and may reaffirm, albeit in a radical manner, ethnic roots and traditions. One should therefore be cautious about attributing all terrorist activity to the individual's rejection of, or inability to pursue, a positive identity. Furthermore, not all acquisitions of negative identities are politicized; many young people rebel socially—in clothes and manners—without political purpose. Such individuals may have neither the inner needs (which are impossible to ascertain from the outside observer's viewpoint) nor the opportunity to join violent undergrounds.

Both Böllinger and Knutson agree that the government often plays a critical role in pushing certain individuals into violent opposition. Government surveillance or persecution were factors in closing off the path to a positive identity for Busic, who encountered suspicious police in Yugoslavia, Austria, and the United States. In West Germany people who were only on the fringes of radical movements found their way back blocked by government records that marked them as sympathizers. Böllinger found, for example, that many of his interviewees had been harassed or, in one case, jailed for quite minor offenses. In the Basque region of Spain, in the Franco era, even cultural activities had to be clandestine because of government persecution. In the 19th century, the Russian government's repression of nonviolent reformist activities was a factor in convincing a minority of activists that terrorism was their only mode of self-expression.

To individuals already suffering from identity confusion, the attention paid them by the government not only confirms a negative identity but makes them feel like "somebody." They are gratified to be sufficiently important to be the object of excessive attention, even if that attention is negative. Harassment or surveillance is preferable to being ignored by society.

Another contribution of Erikson's, apparently unnoticed by students of terrorism, helps to confirm the relevance of his theory to an understanding of terrorism. Discussing the developmental stage of initiation, Erikson observes that, in addition to aggressive "ideals," the child develops a sense of guilt and, thus, a conscience. Individuals whose conscience (or superego) becomes too controlling and overinhibiting may become moralistic. If the parent who early served as a model for the conscience—that is, as the external authority imposing moral rules which are subsequently internalized in an inflexible way—subsequently proves unworthy of such a position, that parent can become the target of violent opposition and resentment. According to Erikson (1968, p. 119), the child becomes suspicious, vindictive, and prone to the suppression of others. Moreover, the assumption of a negative identity is rooted in a latent death wish against the parents and may result from overdemanding parents. Early feelings of moral betrayal by parents may be the basis for later acute sensitivity to perceived injustices by authorities, a trait noted in many terrorists. In West Germany, for example, children discovered that strict and puritanical fathers had been, if not Nazis, accomplices in the evil of the Hitler period. Such disillusionment, rooted in history and politics, can interact with excessive guilt or conscience to produce an individual disposed to violent action against a perfidious substitute for parental authority.

Erikson (1963, p. 189) also emphasizes a Freudian contribution that may explain an individual's choice of terrorism as a form of conflict with authority: "The individual unconsciously arranges for variations of an original theme which he has not learned either to overcome or to live with: he tries to master a situation which in its original form has been too much for him by meeting it repeatedly and of his own accord." The child who feared to mount a violent challenge to parents may later try to overcome that fear by attacking external authorities, such as political or social elites.

An interesting question is the relevance of the theories of Frantz Fanon (see McCulloch, 1983) to this framework. Fanon's conception of violence as a part of the self-liberation of the colonized person can be compared to Erikson's view of violence as reflecting unresolved childhood conflicts, the expression of which is not necessarily therapeutic. Certainly, Fanon's theory of the relationship between colonialism and personality links individual to social setting in a way compatible with Erikson's model. What Fanon saw as the psychopathology of the colonized could be the assumption of a negative identity.

The Social Psychology of the Group

The foregoing discussion indicates that the group is central to terrorist behavior. The individual's path to becoming an active terrorist is often through groups and through personal contacts who introduce him to the organization. Student political groups in the United States, West Germany, and Italy, as well as Basque cultural and political youth groups, often perform this initiatory function. Belonging to the group, as has been suggested, can

be critical to the integration of some personalities; the collective identity becomes the individual's identity. Therefore, the maintenance of this primary group or family substitute may become as important as political aims or events. Terrorist organizations are likely to be composed of people whose need is the group and others whose goals are to change their social and political environment. But both types are dependent on the organization.

The social psychological dynamics of terrorist organizations help determine not only why individuals join them but why they stay in and why they choose terrorism as a strategy. Some features are characteristic of all small groups; others are specific to underground conspiracies.

Terrorist organizations become countercultures, with their own values and norms, into which new recruits are indoctrinated (see Wolfgang & Ferracuti, 1982). They are in this respect similar to youth gangs or nonpolitical cults and sects (see Bainbridge & Stark, 1979; Balch, 1980; Levine, 1978; Stark & Bainbridge, 1980). They tend, as Erikson (1968) suspected, to be "totalistic," demanding the complete allegiance of members. Relations with "outsiders" are discouraged if not prohibited. (Security considerations also make this a rational precaution.) Clandestine organizations are isolated from the outside world, an isolation often reinforced by living "underground" with false identities. Even in more open situations, such as in Spain or Ireland, members of the terrorist organization tend to be exclusive and to trust only one another.

A similarity between terrorist organizations and religious cults underscores the group's dominance over individual members and the collective drive toward totalistic control. Both types of groups strictly regulate the sexual relations of their members. In some groups sexual contact with outsiders is banned. In others, such as the Weather Underground, monogamy is discouraged. Some exceedingly puritanical groups, such as the People's Will, encourage celibacy and asexual comradeship. It is impossible to know the meaning of these restrictions, beyond their implication of total control by the group. In puritanical groups the image of rigid morality (it is not clear that obedience to such precepts is absolute) may be a reflection of the overcontrolling superego and a rejection of society as immoral and inadequate.

The appearance of morality may also be an attempt to prove that the group's political stand is equally superior, despite its deviation from the social norm. The deliberate promiscuity of the Weathermen seems to have stemmed in part from a male drive to dominate the females in the organization (Stern, 1975). Terrorist groups are similar to other groups whose goal is to transform not only society but the individual (see Wilson, 1973).

All primary groups strive toward cohesion and uniformity (Cartwright, 1968; Verba, 1961), and terrorist organizations exhibit stronger than usual tendencies toward solidarity and conformity. Terrorist organizations are formed of like-minded individuals who build their association on prior homogeneity, at least in political attitude, and on explicit commitment to political goals. The terrorist group is an association whose members share a "common fate," in that their futures and the achievement of group goals—indeed, their lives—are bound together. Members must trust each other not to betray the group or endanger it in any way. Under these conditions of mutual interdependence, members of groups have been shown to develop the high interpersonal attraction that creates cohesiveness (Collins & Guetzkow, 1964, pp. 140–145). The group necessarily stands or falls together. In such circumstances members have more influence over each other; they feel more responsibility toward each other and more agreement with each other's views. Hence, the group's power over its members increases with cohesiveness.

A distinctive characteristic of terrorist groups is that they exist under conditions of extreme danger and corresponding stress. As Janis (1968, p. 80) observes, "When people are exposed to external danger, they show a remarkable increase in group solidarity. That is, they manifest increased motivation to retain affiliation with a face-to-face group and to avoid actions that deviate from its norms." Janis's (1968) studies of soldiers under combat conditions are relevant to this analysis of terrorist behavior. He notes, for example, that social isolation—something that terrorists choose—also increases dependence on the group. External danger stimulates needs for reassurance, which are satisfied through interaction with other members of the group, leading to a strong individual motivation to stay in the group and to avoid the risk of expulsion. The threat of group disapproval suppresses inclinations to deviate from group norms.

A further source of increased cohesion and ideological solidarity is the individual's reaction to the death of comrades. Survivors often try to adjust to death and to counteract group demoralization by unconsciously identifying with dead (or, as is often the case in terrorism, captured) comrades. Via a process of introjection, or internalization of the lost object, this reaction leads to a form of "postponed obedience," or strengthened adherence to the standards represented by the fallen comrade. This "blood price" contributes powerfully to group conformity (Janis, 1968, pp. 84–85).

Members of terrorist organizations are also well aware of the unattractiveness of alternatives to membership in the group. Their former life was sufficiently unsatisfactory that they abandoned it; in any event, for revolutionary terrorists in Western countries, the path back to the outside world is closed. In groups less isolated from society and for whom the option of return is open, one would expect less cohesiveness.

The consequences of strong cohesiveness and pressure to conform in terrorist groups are numerous. Naturally strong affective ties are formed among members, so that the dependence with which most members entered deepens. The rewards that members seek probably become more "interpersonal" than "task-environmental" (Collins & Guetzkow, 1964, pp. 74–80). That is, the approval of other group members becomes more important than the achievement of group goals. Approval is awarded not only for actions that move the group toward its political goals but also for conformity and correct ideological thinking. Under these conditions the goal of the terrorist organization may become self-maintenance more than the transformation of the political system (as happens with other political organizations; see Wilson, 1973). Members are now motivated by the desire to keep the group together. For example, terrorist organizations emerged from student movements in part because some activists were unwilling to see the group dissolved.

Another consequence of group cohesiveness is the tendency to encourage the pursuit of violence. As isolation deepens, most communication comes from within the group, and information about the outside world is filtered through the group. Growing misperceptions reinforce group beliefs and values. It becomes easier to depersonalize victims and to see the enemy as unmitigatingly hostile.

The need to deflect internal conflict that might disturb a vital harmony may lead to extreme aggressiveness toward outside enemies. Desperate attempts by terrorists to free imprisoned comrades are clearly related to the mutual interdependence of the group. They may also be related to survivor guilt, as well as to what Janis (1968, pp. 85–86) terms the "old sergeant" syndrome, in that the individual is unable to see new group members as acceptable emotional substitutes for former comrades and leaders.

Membership in a primary group may also help individuals cope with guilt. Research has not established that individual terrorists actually feel guilt over their behavior. The group both creates and imposes its own standards and norms and forms a counterculture in which violence against the enemy is morally acceptable and, indeed, may even be a duty. Degree of guilt probably varies with individual personality and the strength of group influence over members. Nevertheless, peer pressure can induce people to perform acts that they would ordinarily be prevented from doing by moral restraints. If guilt creates more stress for the individual, dependence on the group surely increases—with the result that group influence over the individual is strengthened, leading to the commission of more guilt-inducing acts. It then becomes difficult to leave the terrorist group, because the reformed terrorist would confront not only social opprobrium and legal sanctions but also remorse. Most individuals probably find it easier to continue to believe in the values and standards of the terrorist group. Some, however, do "repent," although their motivations remain obscure to researchers.

Other components of terrorist belief systems, common to most groups, may also provide means of coping with guilt. The often-encountered theme of self-sacrifice, for example, may be a form of atonement. Terrorists engage in what Bandura (1973, pp. 238–239) calls "slighting aggression by advantageous comparison"—that is, emphasizing the gross misdeeds of the government as justification for terrorism against it. Schmidtchen (1981, pp. 54–55) noted in West German terrorist groups a process of socialization resulting in a demarcation between friend and enemy that reserved all positive identifications for friends, all negative identifications for the enemy. The enemy was perceived as an abstraction, a structure rather than a group of individuals. Victims have no personal value to terrorists; they are merely representatives of institutions. In this regard it is useful to compare the process of dehumanization of the enemy in military combat units to that in terrorist organizations.

The image that terrorists often present of themselves—as soldiers acting only in the name of duty and a higher call—may also be a way of avoiding personal responsibility for acts of violence. This identification is a form of self-presentation as well as of self-perception. It is a method of coping with the prospect of physical danger as well as with the emotional consequences of harming others. Being a soldier means being part of a collective enterprise that is externally sanctioned. Ferracuti and Bruno (1983, pp. 308–310) have argued that Italian terrorists, by imagining themselves to be in a state of war with the government, are engaging in an important fantasy mechanism that makes their participation in violence possible.

A further consequence of group interaction, which may explain the escalation of terrorist violence, is the possibility of brutalization, or "graduated desensitization" (Bandura, 1973, p. 241), as the performance of acts of terrorism progressively extinguishes discomfort and self-censure. Dicks (1972, pp. 253–256) saw Nazi violence emerging over time from a triggering process shared by fellow Nazis in a facilitating group setting. This conditioning process, through which the individual comes to seek destructive power, is termed brutalization, a result of succumbing to group pressures and conforming to a new ethos. Even individuals who had at first shown anxiety and reluctance gave in to the group in the end.

In comparison, Liebert (1971) explains the shift in the Columbia University student movement from nonviolent protest to terrorism as a generational phenomenon; the second generation is recruited into a value system and socialized into a group that may be entirely different from the group that influenced the first generation. Value changes profoundly affect socialization: "When 'temporary' deviations from the humanistic tradition (such as terrorism) begin to characterize the tactics used to obtain the ends, these compromised values become internalized in the psychological organization of the members of the movement, particularly the younger ones who enter and are indoctrinated at that phase of the revolution. The corrupted values then are passed on through the generations" (Liebert, 1971, pp. 244–245). For example, whereas the initial decision to use terrorism is probably a topic of heated discussion in the early stage of the development of the organization, the more violence is used, the less controversial its value and acceptability become. The ends and means of actions are no longer separable; not only are values corrupted but the use of terrorism is tied irrevocably to the values it serves.

Another group characteristic that helps explain the conduct of a terrorist strategy concerns relationships between leaders and followers. Janis (1968, pp. 81–83) refers to the Freudian concept of transference to explain the motivation for group solidarity in military units. The individual's feelings of dependency, an unconscious need from childhood, are redirected to new objects. Janis describes in combat situations a "fear-ridden" dependency, based on the reactivation of early separation anxiety, which is likely to develop toward authority figures perceived as able to ward off danger. Social isolation is further likely to enhance such dependency. Transference also causes the follower to overestimate the power of the surrogate parent and to seek that parent's approval.

Verba (1961, p. 149) notes that while followers depend on their leaders, the reverse also holds: "The conflict between directing the group and maintaining one's acceptance by the group would seem to be the unique problem of the group leader." Leaders must spend as much time maintaining the group as in achieving instrumental goals. This balance is easier to attain when the leader is perceived as acting as an agent of impersonal forces and in the service of group norms (Verba, 1961, pp. 172–175). In terrorist as in revolutionary organizations, the ideological purity of the leader must be above question; the leader must be the chief interpreter and communicator of the group's beliefs and aims. Leaders are, thus, under great pressure to conform to group norms, making innovation or compromise difficult. Since the external power sources of terrorist leaders are surely few, their position depends on their interpretation of group goals and efficient direction of terrorist operations. In effect, the behavior of both leaders and followers is restricted by the terrorist group.

Another way the group facilitates terrorism is by creating an appropriate context for social learning. Bandura (1973) has argued that aggressive patterns of behavior are learned from observation or experience, rather than emerging from instinctual drives or frustration. His theory underscores the argument that participation in violent acts desensitizes the individual to guilt. Not only do individuals learn from their experiences in the organization, but they also are exposed to powerful external role models, whom they are encouraged to imitate. The narrow band of communication from the outside world, filtered through the perceptions of leaders, emphasizes the dramatic exploits of other terrorist groups. Terrorism, a symbolic action, is highly memorable; for this reason, as well as the ease with which it can be implemented, terrorism is almost ideally imitable (Bandura, 1973, p. 213; Midlarsky, Crenshaw, & Fumihiko, 1980). The terrorist subculture forms an environment in which violence is valued, and models such as the Tupamaros of Uruguay may be endowed with great prestige. The power of such models is not diluted by their objective failures. The 1960s revolutionary campaign of the Tupamaros, for example, culminated in a military dictatorship. The mass media, especially television, are often thought to be critical to the communication of information about models, but their actual influence remains undocumented. If members of terrorist groups receive most of their information from other sources in the group or from an underground press, the popular news media would not be a primary determinant of the social contagion of terrorism.

Bandura (1973, pp. 215–216) has suggested that symbolic modeling may help to explain the surge and decline of terrorist incidents: "Social contagion of new styles and tactics of aggression conforms to a pattern that characterizes the transitory changes of most other types of collective activities: New behavior is initiated by a salient example; it spreads rapidly in a contagious fashion; after it has been widely adopted, it is discarded, often in favor of a new form that follows a similar course." Decline is explained by the development of effective countermeasures, the discrepancy between anticipated and experienced consequences, and routinization of the activity. The decline of an activity, then, may depend on its not being rewarded.

The dynamics of reward and punishment in the case of terrorism are as yet poorly understood. Since the individual motivation for terrorism may be psychological, involving the acquisition of an identity or affiliation with a substitute family, the failure to achieve the organization's instrumental goals may not be a sufficient "aversive stimulation." Individuals who resort to terrorist behavior as part of the assumption of a negative identity expect and even seek social disapproval, which confirms their self-expectations. Some terrorists become disillusioned when anticipated social and political changes do not occur, but others continue despite the absence of positive external reinforcements. Given the small numbers of people required for the implementation of a terrorist strategy and a ready availability of recruits, terrorism can show remarkable persistence. A punitive government response may confirm terrorist expectations of coercive "enemy" behavior, provide a needed reward of attention and publicity, and generate resentment not only among terrorists but among the larger political or ethnic minorities from which they sprang. The government may wish, instead, to avoid creating obstacles to the reintegration of dissidents into society.

Psychological Effects of Terrorism

The political effectiveness of terrorism is importantly determined by the psychological effects of violence on audiences. The physical destructiveness of terrorism is in general minimal, despite the tragedy it may cause for individual victims. There is some feeling that the significance of terrorism has been exaggerated, perhaps as a result of the media's adoption of international terrorism as a news issue. Whether because of the intrinsic drama of terrorist violence or because of press and television hyperbole, hijackings, kidnappings, and other terrorist assaults have created large public concern (see de Boer, 1979).

In part because of public reaction, terrorism has become a salient policy issue for many governments. The general thrust of both public reaction and government response has been to resist giving in to terrorist demands or admitting the justice of their claims. The forceful reactions of the Israeli, West German, Egyptian, and American governments, respectively, in the crises of Entebbe, Mogadishu, Larnaca, and Iran were, in part, determined by the blow that terrorism dealt to domestic authority and international prestige. Terrorism is more a threat to image and reputation than to physical security.

Even Israel, surely the most directly endangered of all states affected by terrorism, is said to overreact (Alon, 1980). Although terrorism is perceived as a major threat by Israeli society, this assessment is based on subjective probabilities rather than a realistic estimate of the number of casualties caused by terrorism. Individuals feel both fearful and angry at the damage done to national prestige. Such perceptions are affected not only by the nature of terrorism but also by media portrayals and government countermeasures, which serve as a constant reminder of the threat. Alon (1980) concludes that the effect of terrorism should be downgraded; terrorism should be treated simply as one among many sources of casualties. Government resources should be allocated accordingly.

Despite the obvious importance of society's reactions to terrorism, there has been little research on general psychological and social effects. Gutmann (1979) argues that psychological studies neglect the audience for terrorism, although terrorists are shrewdly aware of the composition and attitudes of viewing groups. Even though the social arena—especially critical elites—is decisive to the success of terrorism, "liberals" have permitted the development of a terrorist mystique. Gutmann (1979) contends that academic elites are victims of a fatal fascination for terrorism, derived from their bourgeois midlife crises, the comfortable life they despise, and their idealization of the terrorist as a hero. In his opinion, those who study terrorism have made it respectable.

The practice of blaming intellectuals for the social ills they seek to explain, although common, is hardly conducive to the advancement of knowledge. Gutmann also reveals an ignorance of terrorism—placing the Tupamaros in Ecuador instead of Uruguay, for example—but his point that the study of audiences is neglected is obvious. However, neglect of the subject is due as much to the difficulties of studying audience reactions as to lack of recognition of their importance. Responses to terrorism are difficult to conceptualize and to measure.

Freedman (1983, pp. 399–400) has proposed a theoretical framework, a "model of terroristic resonance," to solve what he considers a significant puzzle. The reaction to terrorism depends on the audience's perception of the terrorist as single-minded, willful, fearless, and unremorseful. Terrorism must be seen as violence of human agency. Terrorist acts appear to the audience as anonymous, sudden, and random. The awareness of vulnerability undermines the victim's sense of autonomy and security. In this way terrorism arouses awe, anxiety, and a mystical dread. The id seems to be assaulting the superego, evoking infantile apprehensions.

The metaphor of resonance appropriately describes terrorism's effects, since acts of terrorism constitute a reasonably small stimulus that causes and intensifies an echo or vibration in the social system. This concept implies that the act of terrorism has to be properly attuned to its audience, to strike a chord, if it is to be effective. When the audience is responsive, the act of terrorism resonates or continues to sound beyond its immediate impact. However, a conceptual distinction must be drawn between direct and indirect audiences. The direct audience is composed of persons who identify with the victims of terrorism; they are potential victims because they belong to the same social category as the victims (such as judges, police, diplomats, airline passengers, foreign business executives). The indirect audience, in contrast, is not directly affiliated with the victims. Its members may be neutral or may even identify with the terrorists. The act of terrorism, if it seems a threat at all, is experienced only vicariously. The indirect audience is not a party to the struggle the terrorists have initiated. Most terrorists, of course, try to choose their audiences strategically. They may widen the scope of the conflict by incorporating new direct audiences. For example, Palestinian attacks on non-Israeli targets, such as foreign tourists or pilgrims, converted people who were uninvolved into direct audiences.

For the indirect audience, terrorism is a spectacle more than a personal experience. Terrorism shocks because its milieu and its specific victims are unpredictable. Terrorism attracts attention because it unexpectedly breaks social taboos. For most indirect audiences, terrorism is a geographically distant phenomenon. Information about it is communicated primarily by the news media, especially television. In these cases the manner of presentation of information about terrorism can significantly influence audience reactions. Furthermore, in order to maintain its psychological effectiveness, terrorism must become more dramatic as the distance, both geographical and psychological, between the act and the audience increases. Otherwise, competing with other newsworthy events and with more immediate personal concerns, terrorism may lose the salience upon which its influence over audiences depends. Most terrorists, aware of the risk of audience distraction, direct their actions accordingly and strive for innovativeness and timeliness.

The same factors that make terrorism a source of concern and interest for indirect audiences make it a source of personal anxiety for direct audiences, whose feelings of invulnerability are diminished. The reactions of direct audiences to terrorism can usefully be compared to those of the victims of aerial bombing (see Hutchinson, 1972; Janis, 1951). Extreme anxiety, disorientation, feelings of helplessness and defenselessness, and demoralization can characterize reactions to terrorism, which is the type of indefinite and unidentifiable threat that classical studies indicate as difficult to understand or to act against (see Lowenthal, 1946, pp. 2–5; May, 1940, pp. 191–195; Riezler, 1950, pp. 129, 131; Sullivan, 1941, p. 282).

Since fear of terrorism is the fear of death or mutilation, extremely powerful emotional drives direct the political behavior of potential victims. The fear of terrorism often leads to popular demands for protection and prevention. Democratic procedures can also be undermined. Judicial processes, for example, can be subverted. In April 1977 the assassination of the president of the Turin Bar Association was followed by a request to be excused for medical reasons by thirty-six of the forty-two jurors preliminarily selected for the trial of Renato Curcio and twelve other terrorist leaders of the Red Brigades. This postponement followed an earlier delay resulting from the June 1976 assassination of the attorney general of Genoa (Pisano, 1979, pp. 186–187).

Terrorism and reactions to it can also effect broad and diffuse social changes in the direction of decreased openness and trust. Officials in both czarist Russia and contemporary Italy hesitated to appear in public. Businessmen travel with bodyguards in bullet-proof limousines, altering their route for each journey. Diplomats live unostentatiously. The White House is ringed with concrete barriers. The long-term psychological effects of suspiciousness, isolation, and mistrust are largely unknown; they are surely destructive of political community.

Northern Ireland, an extreme case of the effects of terrorism, has been the subject of several studies (for example, Fields, 1980; Heskin, 1980). Researchers are divided on the question of how serious the psychological effects of terrorism have been in Northern Ireland. (This case is a reminder that it is difficult to isolate the effects of terrorism from those of other conflicts, social prejudice, and government countermeasures.) On the one hand, Fields (1980) and Fraser (1973) argue that terrorism has produced dramatic consequences, especially in the children of Northern Ireland. To Fraser children are being socialized into "a perpetual chaotic state of imminent violence" (p. 8). He notes the very high rate of youth involvement in the violence of Northern Ireland as a sign of how deeply children are affected. Although Fields is primarily concerned with the consequences of British repression more than of IRA or Protestant terrorism, she also foresees grave physical and mental harm and predicts a new generation of "militaristic automatons" who will require significant rehabilitation efforts if Northern Ireland is to survive as a society (p. 55).

Heskin (1980) is less pessimistic. He concludes, as have other observers of people living under conditions of pervasive insecurity, that life goes on as usual. Minor inconveniences no longer seem unusual; dramatic stress is seen in only a few places. He is cautious in interpreting the results of studies of the effects of violence on children; violence does seem to become more acceptable and normal, but this seems to come as much from watching it on television as from actually experiencing it. Violence also seems to have reinforced antisocial behavior, although to what extent is difficult to gauge. The data on the incidence of mental illness, most of which come from Belfast, are mixed and inconclusive. He agrees that increased psychiatric disturbance in the intermediate rather than the serious trouble spots may occur. These problems are more common in women than in men. There is less depression than usual, although attempted suicides (while still infrequent) increase (see Heskin, 1980, pp. 52–73). Heskin also warns, however, that the social and psychological resilience he observed may obscure hidden costs of adaptation to acute stress.

These studies point to a need to distinguish between different levels of terrorism as they affect audiences. In situations where the threat of terrorism is so constant as to be normal, it may be accepted as a fact of life. However, where the threat remains sufficiently random and unusual, its targets cannot adjust to uncertainty. For example, the "Document on Terror" (1952), purportedly a Communist instruction manual for the takeover of Eastern Europe after World War II, recommends that terrorism be applied scientifically in waves, in order to avoid producing the insensitivity that would diminish its effectiveness. The use of an analytical framework that distinguishes among levels of threat as well as among types of audience is essential to understanding the general psychological effects of terrorism.

Conclusion

Although uneven and sparsely developed, psychological studies of political terrorism against the state are important to understanding this extreme form of political behavior. Psychology helps answer questions of why the individual becomes a terrorist, how terrorist groups are formed and act, and why publics and governments react with alarm despite the minor physical menace of terrorism. Psychological findings dispute the assumption that personality abnormalities explain terrorism. Instead, they point to the significance of the small cohesive group in determining behavior. In many cases the purpose of the terrorist organization becomes the maintenance of the group as much as the achievement of its external political goals. Moreover, the psychological effects of terrorism are critical to its political effectiveness. Because terrorism is both frightening and dramatically symbolic, it influences distant as well as immediate audiences.

Existing psychological research on terrorism suffers from a lack of coherence. Some inconsistency is explained by the ambiguity of the central concept of terrorism. Terrorist activity is extraordinarily complex and varied; the very definition is disputed. For example, recommendations on how to handle negotiations with political terrorists who have seized hostages are not likely to be appropriate, and may even be harmful, if based on an analysis of what is actually criminal behavior. The field lacks systematic inquiry that builds on the work of other scholars and integrates psychology with what is known about the historical phenomenon of terrorism. More systematic and comprehensive theories are needed to develop cumulative knowledge and to fit the analysis of terrorism into larger theories of political behavior and social change. Definitive statements about the relationship between terrorism, psychological determinants, and sociopolitical change must be preceded by tentative and middle-range hypotheses closely linked to empirical data. Many puzzles remain to be solved.

These puzzles include questions related to both the causes and the consequences of terrorism. On the one hand, terrorist decision making is imperfectly understood. Studying this problem is difficult: Researchers usually have access to terrorists only after the fact, not while they are engaged in the activity, and there are impediments to conducting interviews, such as government reluctance and terrorist hostility. Research on the perceptions and beliefs of terrorists ultimately depends on government cooperation. Despite these complexities, comparative inquiry should work toward answering questions such as why terrorists exercise restraint. Apparently, some terrorist organizations have not taken advantage of the technological resources available to them, such as the possibility of exploiting nuclear capabilities. On the other hand, psychological factors may be at the root of the escalation of terrorism. Perhaps under pressure from the government, members of terrorist organizations grow desperate and lose control. What kinds of pressures and perceptions increase tendencies toward counterproductive violence? Innovation in terrorist strategies is another area of research to which psychology could contribute. Why, for example, did terrorist organizations shift to bargaining tactics after 1968? The answer to the question of why terrorism ends may also lie in the psychology of the terrorists rather than in the countervailing power of the government. Why some terrorists "repent" while others persist to their deaths is an important question. The role of terrorist leaders in restraint, escalation, and innovation may be critical. What are the bases of authority in violent undergrounds?

Understanding the psychology of the terrorist is also relevant to analysis of the government policy response. Appropriate countermeasures must be tailored to accurate assessment of terrorist behavior. How terrorists perceive the threat of government coercion may determine whether or not policies of deterrence will work. How terrorists interpret success and failure may be critical to policy effectiveness, since what the government regards as a threat of punishment may be considered by the terrorist as a reward. Policies intended to inhibit terrorism may instead lead to its escalation.

Surveys of the attitudinal reactions of different audiences could also help explain the consequences and effectiveness of strategies of violence. Is the seriousness with which governments take terrorism justified by the public insecurity it causes? Additionally, government decision making in terrorist crises is an important but neglected subject. Stress affects policy makers as well as terrorists. Are there similarities in government and terrorist reactions to each other, leading to conflict spiral syndromes? Do policy makers perceive foreign and domestic terrorist crises differently? Are terrorists considered to be unusual adversaries? The literature on crisis management could be useful in examining policies toward terrorism. It seems especially important in dealing with terrorism that political and military leaders learn to expect the unexpected and to cope with adversaries they perceive as irrational. Part of the explanation of why terrorist surprise succeeds lies in the mind-sets of government officials. Reliance on operational routine, inflexible doctrines, and narrow conceptions of the normal in politics may prevent policy makers from successfully anticipating terrorist innovations.

REFERENCES

Alon, H. *Countering Palestinian Terrorism in Israel: Toward a Policy Analysis of Countermeasures.* Santa Monica, CA: Rand, 1980.

Alpert, J. *Growing Up Underground.* New York: Morrow, 1981.

Bainbridge, W. S., and Stark, R. "Cult Formation: Three Compatible Models." *Sociological Analysis*, 1979, *40*, 283–295.

Balch, R. W. "Looking Behind the Scenes in a Religious Cult: Implications for the Study of Conversion." *Sociological Analysis*, 1980, *41*, 137–143.

Bandura, A. "Social Learning Theory of Aggression." In J. F. Knutson (ed.), *The Control of Aggression: Implications from Basic Research.* Hawthorne, N.Y.: Aldine, 1973.

Begin, M. *The Revolt.* (S. Katz, trans.) Los Angeles: Nash, 1977.

Bettelheim, B. *The Informed Heart*. New York: Free Press, 1960.

Böllinger, L. "Die Entwicklung zu terroristischem Handeln als psychosozialer Prozess: Begegnungen mit Beteiligten" [The development of terrorist actions as a psychosocial process: Encounters with participants]. In H. Jäger, G. Schmidtchen, and L. Süllwold, *Analysen zum Terrorismus* [Analysis of terrorism]. Vol. 2: *Lebenslauf-Analysen* [Biographical analysis]. Opladen: Westdeutscher Verlag, 1981.

Bourne, P. G. "Altered Adrenal Function in Two Combat Situations in Viet Nam." In B. E. Eleftheriou and J. P. Scott (eds.), *The Physiology of Aggression and Defeat*. New York: Plenum, 1971.

Brockman, R. "Notes While Being Hijacked." *Atlantic*, Dec. 1976, pp. 68–75.

Caplan, G. "Mastery of Stress: Psychosocial Aspects." *American Journal of Psychiatry*, 1981, *138*, 413–420.

Cartwright, D. "The Nature of Group Cohesiveness." In D. Cartwright and A. Zander (eds.), *Group Dynamics: Research and Theory*. (3rd ed.) New York: Harper & Row, 1968.

Clark, R. P. "Patterns in the Lives of ETA Members." *Terrorism: An International Journal*, 1983, *6*, 423–454.

Collins, B. E., and Guetzkow, H. *A Social Psychology of Group Processes for Decision-Making*. New York: Wiley, 1964.

Cooper, H. H. A. "Women as Terrorists." In F. Adler and R. J. Simon (eds.), *The Criminology of Deviant Women*. Boston: Houghton Mifflin, 1979.

Corrado, R. R. "A Critique of the Mental Disorder Perspective of Political Terrorism." *International Journal of Law and Psychiatry*, 1981, *4*, 293–310.

de Boer, C. "The Polls: Terrorism and Hijacking." *Public Opinion Quarterly*, 1979, *43*, 410–419.

Dicks, H. V. *Licensed Mass Murder: A Socio-Psychological Study of Some S.S. Killers*. New York: Basic Books, 1972.

"Document on Terror." *News from Behind the Iron Curtain*, 1952, *1*, 44–57.

Eitinger, L. "The Effects of Captivity." In F. M. Ochberg and D. A. Soskis (eds.), *Victims of Terrorism*. Boulder, Colo.: Westview Press, 1982.

Erikson, E. H. *Childhood and Society*. (2nd ed.) New York: Norton, 1963.

Erikson, E. H. *Identity: Youth and Crisis*. New York: Norton, 1968.

Ferracuti, F., and Bruno, F. "Psychiatric Aspects of Terrorism in Italy." In I. L. Barak-Glantz and C. R. Huff (eds.), *The Mad, the Bad and the Different: Essays in Honor of Simon Dinitz*. Lexington, Mass.: Heath, 1981.

Ferracuti, F., and Bruno, F. "Italy: A Systems Perspective." In A. P. Goldstein and M. H. Segall (eds.), *Aggression in Global Perspective*. Elmsford, N.Y.: Pergamon Press, 1983.

Feuer, L. *The Conflict of Generations: The Character and Significance of Student Movements*. New York: Basic Books, 1969.

Fields, R. M. *Northern Ireland: Society Under Siege*. New Brunswick, N.J.: Transaction Books, 1980.

Fields, R. M. "Psychological Sequelae of Terrorization." In Y. Alexander and J. M. Gleason (eds.), *Behavioral and Quantitative Perspectives on Terrorism*. Elmsford, N.Y.: Pergamon Press, 1981.

Fraser, M. *Children in Conflict: Growing Up in Northern Ireland*. New York: Basic Books, 1973.

Freedman, L. Z. "Why Does Terrorism Terrorize?" *Terrorism: An International Journal*, 1983, *6*, 389–402.

Greenstein, F. I. "Political Psychology: A Pluralistic Universe." In J. N. Knutson (ed.), *Handbook of Political Psychology*. San Francisco: Jossey-Bass, 1973.

Gutmann, D. "Killers and Consumers: The Terrorist and His Audience." *Social Research*, 1979, *46*, 517–526.

Hamburg, D. A. "Coping Behavior in Life-Threatening Circumstances." *Psychotherapy and Psychosomatics*, 1974, *23*, 13–25.

Hamilton, L. C., and Hamilton, J. D. "Dynamics of Terrorism." *International Studies Quarterly*, 1983, *27*, 39–54.

Heskin, K. *Northern Ireland: A Psychological Analysis*. New York: Columbia University Press, 1980.

Hutchinson, M. C. "The Concept of Revolutionary Terrorism." *Journal of Conflict Resolution*, 1972, *16*, 383–396.

Jackson, G. *Surviving the Long Night: An Autobiographical Account of a Political Kidnapping*. New York: Vanguard Press, 1974.

Jacobson, S. R. "Individual and Group Responses to Confinement in a Skyjacked Plane." *American Journal of Orthopsychiatry*, 1973, *43*, 459–469.

Jäger, H. "Die individuelle Dimension terroristischen Handelns: Annäherungen an Einzelfälle" [The individual dimension of terrorist actions: Approaches to individual cases]. In H. Jäger, G. Schmidtchen, and L. Süllwold, *Analysen zum Terrorismus* [Analysis of terrorism]. Vol. 2: *Lebenslauf-Analysen* [Biographical analysis]. Opladen: Westdeutscher Verlag, 1981.

Jäger, H., Schmidtchen, G., and Süllwold, L. *Analysen zum Terrorismus* [Analysis of terrorism]. Vol. 2: *Lebenslauf-Analysen* [Biographical analysis]. Opladen: Westdeutscher Verlag, 1981.

Janis, I. L. *Air War and Emotional Stress: Psychological Studies of Bombing and Civilian Defense*. New York: McGraw-Hill, 1951.

Janis, I. L. "Group Identification Under Conditions of External Danger." In D. Cartwright and A. Zander (eds.), *Group Dynamics: Research and Theory*. (3rd ed.) New York: Harper & Row, 1968.

Jenkins, B. G. "The Study of Terrorism: Definitional Problems." In Y. Alexander and J. M. Gleason (eds.), *Behavioral and Quantitative Perspectives on Terrorism*. Elmsford, N.Y.: Pergamon Press, 1981.

Kaplan, A. "The Psychodynamics of Terrorism." In Y. Alexander and J. M. Gleason (eds.), *Behavioral and Quantitative Perspectives on Terrorism*. Elmsford, N.Y.: Pergamon Press, 1981.

Klausner, S. Z. "The Intermingling of Pain and Pleasure: The Stress-Seeking Personality in Its Social Context." In S. Z. Klausner (ed.), *Why Man Takes Chances: Studies in Stress-Seeking*. New York: Doubleday, 1968.

Knight, A. "Female Terrorists in the Russian Socialist Revolutionary Party." *Russian Review*, 1979, *38*, 139–159.

Knutson, J. N. "The Terrorists' Dilemmas: Some Implicit Rules of the Game." *Terrorism: An International Journal*, 1980, *4*, 195–222.

Knutson, J. N. "Social and Psychodynamic Pressures Toward a Negative Identity: The Case of an American Revolutionary Terrorist." In Y. Alexander and J. M. Gleason (eds.), *Behavioral and Quantitative Perspectives on Terrorism*. Elmsford, N.Y.: Pergamon Press, 1981.

Lang, D. "A Reporter at Large: The Bank Drama." *New Yorker*, Nov. 25, 1974, pp. 56–126.

Levine, S. V. "Youth and Religious Cults: A Societal and Clinical Dilemma." *Adolescent Psychiatry*, 1978, *6*, 75–89.

Liebert, R. *Radical and Militant Youth: A Psychoanalytic Inquiry*. New York: Praeger, 1971.

Lowenthal, L. "Crisis of the Individual: Terror's Atomization of Man." *Commentary*, 1946, *1*, 1–8.

McCulloch, J. *Black Soul, White Artifact: Fanon's Clinical Psychology and Social Theory*. Cambridge, England: Cambridge University Press, 1983.

May, R. *The Meaning of Anxiety*. New York: Macmillan, 1940.

Merkl, P. *The Making of a Stormtrooper*. Princeton, N.J.: Princeton University Press, 1980.

Mickolus, E. F. *The Literature of Terrorism: A Selectively Annotated Bibliography*. Westport, Conn.: Greenwood Press, 1980.

Midlarsky, M. I., Crenshaw, M., and Fumihiko, Y. "Why Violence Spreads: The Contagion of International Terrorism." *International Studies Quarterly*, 1980, *24*, 262–298.

Miller, A. H. *Terrorism and Hostage Negotiations*. Boulder, Colo.: Westview Press, 1980.

Miron, M. S., and Goldstein, A. P. *Hostage*. Elmsford, N.Y.: Pergamon Press, 1979.

Morf, G. *Terror in Quebec: Case Studies of the FLQ*. Toronto: Clarke, Irwin, 1970.

Ochberg, F. M. "Preparing for Terrorist Victimization." In Y. Alexander and R. A. Kilmarx (eds.), *Political Terrorism and Business: The Threat and the Response*. New York: Praeger, 1979.

Ochberg, F. M. "A Case Study: Gerard Vaders." In F. M. Ochberg and D. A. Soskis (eds.), *Victims of Terrorism*. Boulder, Colo.: Westview Press, 1982.

Ochberg, F. M., and Soskis, D. A. (eds.). *Victims of Terrorism*. Boulder, Colo.: Westview Press, 1982.

Pisano, V. "A Survey of Terrorism of the Left in Italy: 1970–1978." *Terrorism: An International Journal*, 1979, *2*, 171–212.

Pomper, P. *Sergei Nechaev*. New Brunswick, N.J.: Rutgers University Press, 1979.

Rasch, W. "Psychological Dimensions of Political Terrorism in the Federal Republic of Germany." *International Journal of Law and Psychiatry*, 1979, *2*, 79–85.

Riezler, K. *Man: Mutable and Immutable*. Chicago: Contemporary Books, 1950.

Roth, W. T. "The Meaning of Stress." In F. M. Ochberg and D. A. Soskis (eds.), *Victims of Terrorism*. Boulder, Colo.: Westview Press, 1982.

Rubins, J. L. "Narcissism and the Narcissistic Personality: A Holistic Reappraisal." *American Journal of Psychoanalysis*, 1983, *43*, 3–20.

Sandler, T., Tschirhart, J. T., and Cauley, J. "A Theoretical Analysis of Transnational Terrorism." *American Political Science Review*, 1983, *77*, 36–54.

Savinkov, B. *Memoirs of a Terrorist*. (J. Shaplen, trans.) New York: A. and C. Boni, 1931.

Schmidtchen, G. "Terroristische Karrieren: Soziologische Analyse anhand von Fahndungsunterlagen und Prozessakten" [Terrorist careers: Sociological analysis based on investigation and trial documents]. In H. Jäger, G. Schmidtchen, and L. Süllwold, *Analysen zum Terrorismus* [Analysis of terrorism]. Vol. 2.: *Lebenslauf-Analysen* [Biographical analysis]. Opladen: Westdeutscher Verlag, 1981.

Silverstein, M. E. "Counterterrorist Medical Preparedness: A Necessity for the Corporate Executive." In Y. Alexander and R. A. Kilmarx (eds.), *Political Terrorism and Business: The Threat and the Response*. New York: Praeger, 1979.

Stark, R., and Bainbridge, W. S. "Networks of Faith: Interpersonal Bonds and Recruitment to Cults and Sects." *American Journal of Sociology*, 1980, *85*, 1376–1395.

Stein, M. R., and others (eds.). *Identity and Anxiety*. New York: Free Press, 1960.

Stern, S. *With the Weathermen: The Personal Journal of a Revolutionary Woman*. New York: Doubleday, 1975.

Strentz, T. "The Stockholm Syndrome: Law Enforcement Policy and Hostage Behavior." In F. M. Ochberg and D. A. Soskis (eds.), *Victims of Terrorism*. Boulder, Colo.: Westview Press, 1982.

Sullivan, H. S. "Psychiatric Aspects of Morale." *American Journal of Sociology*, 1941, *47*, 277–301.

Süllwold, L. "Stationen in der Entwicklung von Terroristen: Psychologische Aspekte biographischer Daten" [Stages in the development of terrorists: Psychological aspects of biographical data]. In H. Jäger, G. Schmidtchen, and L. Süllwold, *Analysen zum Terrorismus* [Analysis of terrorism]. Vol. 2.: *Lebenslauf-Analysen* [Biographical analysis]. Opladen: Westdeutscher Verlag, 1981.

Thornton, T. P. "Terror as a Weapon of Political Agitation." In H. Eckstein (ed.), *Internal War: Problems and Approaches*. New York: Free Press, 1964.

Tinklenberg, J. "Coping with Terrorist Victimization." In F. M. Ochberg and D. A. Soskis (eds.), *Victims of Terrorism*. Boulder, Colo.: Westview Press, 1982.

Verba, S. *Small Groups and Political Behavior: A Study of Leadership*. Princeton, N.J.: Princeton University Press, 1961.

Wasmund, K. "Political Socialization in Terrorist Groups—West Germany." Paper presented at Conference of Europeanists, Washington, D.C., May 1982.

Wilson, J. Q. *Political Organizations*. New York: Basic Books, 1973.

Wolfgang, M. E., and Ferracuti, F. *The Subculture of Violence: Towards an Integrated Theory in Criminology*. Beverly Hills, Calif.: Sage, 1982.

Yacef, S. *Souvenirs de la bataille d'Alger* [Memories of the battle of Algiers]. Paris: Julliard, 1962.

Theoretical Approaches to Explaining Collective Political Violence

Harry Eckstein • formerly of the University of California, Irvine

Large numbers of social scientists have studied political violence since the early 1960s, when the subject, after one of those long hiatuses that characterize its study, was back in vogue. Production of work has been anything but scant: Zimmerman's magisterial review of the literature (1980) lists about 2,400 items, most of them published since 1960 (though he includes some stones perhaps better left unturned). It might seem odd, then, that an essay should now be devoted to a discussion—not even, as readers will find at the end, a solution—of a "basic," a "primary" problem. But this is not at all odd. The discovery of primary problems usually culminates much work in positive study: it is a critical and difficult achievement. Before core problems can be defined with precision, there usually is much prior observation, speculation, debate, and, especially, diffuse dissatisfaction, a sense of growing mystery rather than of illumination. One gradually comes to see, through long groping, the basic puzzle that a subject presents: where to begin if a genuine unfolding of theory is to occur. Two decades seem a long time to get to that point, but it usually takes much longer (though afterwards progress is swift).

For my purpose here, I will assume that there will be no fundamental quarrels with the following definitional notions:

1. Collective political violence involves destructive attacks by groups within a political com-

munity against its regime, authorities, or policies (derived from Gurr, 1970b, pp. 3–4)
2. Revolutions are the extreme cases of collective political violence, in regard to (a) their magnitude (scope, intensity), (b) targets (the political community or "regime"), (c) goals (degree and rapidity of change desired), and (d) the extent to which there is conflict between elites and counterelites.[1]

Most important, I will emphasize one theoretical problem, that of "etiology": why does collective political violence, in general or in particular forms, occur, and why does it occur at different levels of magnitude and intensity? That problem has certainly held center-stage since about 1960, while the study of other phenomena (the "process" of revolution, issues of prudent action by authorities or rebels, determinants of outcomes, problems of postrevolutionary rule) have waxed and waned. Not least, the issue of etiology is the problem on which theoretical approaches now differ most, especially if we include in it the problem of why political violence takes different forms. And we may surmise that the solution of this problem will have important repercussions for all others.

'Contingency' Versus 'Inherency'

In a very early essay on the etiology of collective political violence—the label then used was "internal war," following French usage in the 18th and 19th centuries and the language of the Federalist Papers (H. Eckstein, 1965, p. 133)—I discussed a number of options in explaining its causes. Some of the choices to be made were between:

1. "preconditions" or "precipitants"—more remote or more proximate causes
2. "incumbents" or "insurgents"
3. "structural" or "behavioral" (cultural, attitudinal, psychological) factors
4. "specific occurrences" (say, economic depressions) or "general processes" (long-run patterns that may occur in numerous theoretically equivalent forms)
5. "obstacles" to collective political violence or "positive" factors that make for internal-war potential.

The result was a highly tentative eclectic model (not empirically grounded like that in Hibbs, 1973) in which internal wars are explained by complex balances of very different and logically heterogeneous factors.

The theme of such complex balances constantly recurs in the literature. Gurr's "simplified" model of the determinants of political violence lists seven factors that may act to enlarge or lessen its magnitude (Gurr, 1970b, p. 320). Another version of his model lists 3 proximate determinants, but also 19 factors that determine the values of the more general determinants (Gurr, 1970b, p. 332). In Hibbs's causal universe, positive and negative factors run amok. About 30 factors are directly or indirectly linked to coups, collective protests, and internal wars (Hibbs, 1973, p. 181). The occurrence of these events involves the interplay of all the factors, facilitative and obstructive.

The way to start, surely, is to find the most basic branch point for choice in theorizing. My thesis here can be put in a sentence: in studying collective political violence, the first and most fateful choice lies between regarding it as "contingent" or "inherent" in political life.

Nature of Contingency and Inherency

At the outset, I propose a broad thesis about basic branch points in building positive theories, regardless of subject. It seems historically true that primary branch points in theoretical inquiry are all alike: all involve a choice between contingency and inherency. Why so I will try to show momentarily. First, we must understand in a general way the nature of the two notions.

Something is *contingent* if its occurrence depends on the presence of unusual (we might say aberrant) conditions that occur accidentally—conditions that involve a large component of chance. An auto accident clearly is contingent in this sense. Drivers may or may not make mistakes, cars may fatefully malfunction. It is with reason then that we call such occurrences "accidents." Note immediately that contingency does not entail indeterminacy. We can specify that if a particular driver does something, an accident will probably occur. We can also determine general conditions that increase or decrease the probability of accidents. Contingencies thus are not random, and "may-may not" events can sometimes be controlled. Such events, though, do raise questions of explanation and theory in a special form: One wants to know what caused an accident where "normally" none was expected to occur. We are not mystified when a driver gets from here to there without malchance. We want to explain when the opposite occurs. Contingency implies "non-routine," something out of the ordinary, something not understood without special explanation.

Per contra, something is *inherent* either if it always will happen (e.g., entropy) or if the potentiality for it always exists and actuality can only be obstructed. Just when the inevitable occurs or hindrances are removed is decided by contingencies: chance occurrences that hinder or facilitate. As contingency does not entail randomness or inability to control, so inherency does not imply fully predictable determinacy. The decay of an automobile surely is inherent, even without any accidents. When or how it will fall apart, though, is not fully predictable. But basic questions of explanation differ in cases of inherency: we usually want to know why the inherent did not occur sooner, what obstructed or delayed decay and "termination." In contingencies, then, the puzzle is "why"; in inherency it is "why not?"

In the concrete world, contingency and inherency are almost always intertwined and hard to disentangle. What seems manifestly contingent to one observer may seem just as obviously inherent to another. This has been the case with studies of collective political violence. Occurrences, at bottom, must always be regarded as the one or the other. Consequently the issue of contingency versus inherency always arises. Both always occur in a mix hard to disentangle, but they cannot, logically, both be equally basic. Any theory that supposes the contrary, or avoids the issue, must end by making experience illogical, hence unintelligible.

Examples and Consequentiality of the Contingency-Inherency Distintion

Death (termination, entropy) is inexorable. But how should one regard illness and other disturbances of "normal" functioning? One possibility is the familiar "bacterial" explanation, and its extensions: diseases result from the invasion of organisms by virulent micro-organisms, and disabilities result from diseases, or from accidents, or from the consequences of other external matters (like dominant parents or competitive siblings). Diseases and disabilities are thus contingent—pathological. The alternative is to regard them as particular routine states of the living system: stress on systems is always present; the system defends and usually maintains itself through homeostatic devices, sometimes to avoid disturbance altogether, sometimes to recuperate; thus both illness and health essentially are intrinsic matters of the state of biological systems in interaction with their contexts. As one ages, of course, one becomes more vulnerable to stress, and homeostasis is more difficult to achieve. That does not resolve the fundamental problem: which version of disease and disability, the contingent or the inherent, is the better for all or some pathologies as the base of theory? There is no single, agreed upon view on this issue.[2]

The current debate in structural linguistics between adherents of "deep-structure" theory and "empiricism" furnishes another example. Its consequentiality lies, of course, in that it raises the fundamental issue of the very nature of speech.[3] In politics, as I have argued elsewhere (H. Eckstein, 1979), the analogous general branch point is between "culturalist" theories that explain political actions basically by (contingent) learned "orientations," and "rational-choice" theories which postulate an inherent tendency to maximize influence. In studies of social stability and integration, which is close to our subject here, there is a basic confrontation between considering the "normal" state of society to be harmonious or conflictual—for

instance, between functionalists and systems theorists, on the one hand, and class theorists, on the other.

Two Antithetical Explanation-Sketches for Collective Political Violence

How would a contingency theory about collective political violence compare with an inherency theory? At this point, we need broad "explanation-sketches" to illustrate the opposing approaches; in the next section I will summarize actual theories that fit the sketches.

Explanation-sketches (the term is from Hempel, 1965, p. 238) consist of an initial spelling out of laws and initial conditions—scientific *explanantia*—to be filled out and made into a full-fledged theory through research "for which this sketch suggests the direction." Explanation-sketches are more than the initial commitments of theoretical approaches, but much less than final statements of theories.

Contingency theory should conform to the following sketch:

1. The fundamental disposition of individuals (or groups) in politics is toward "peace": the resolution or avoidance of violent conflicts. There would be no governments otherwise (see "contract" theorists). Satisfaction of political values is normally sought through pacific competition (electoral, through interest groups, by petitions, et cetera). Violent conflict is not in the normal "repertoire" of political competition.
2. The disposition toward pacific politics may be blocked and diverted under specifiable and "special" (aberrant) conditions. Given the disposition toward peace, the conditions should not readily occur, least of all in extreme forms of conflict. Collective violence thus involves the blockage of inherent tendencies by peculiar causes.
3. The critical problem in studying collective political violence thus is why it occurs as often as it does.
4. As to "peculiar causes," the pacific disposition may be blocked when some other, discomfiting human disposition (which governments exist to suppress) is activated. This may be a disposition toward aggression or it may be a

disposition toward comparing one's condition in life with that of others.

5. It follows that choices of collective political violence are highly "affective" rather than coolly calculated.

6. The tendency to act violently in politics may be increased by cultural patterns—learned modes of action (these are always variable and "contingent," of course). Violent action may be a learned response; and to the extent that this is so, pacific dispositions are more readily diverted.

7. Given the affectivity of collective political violence, two factors should play a rather minor role in its explanation (though they may play some role as "mediating" variables that reduce or increase probability). These are coercive balances between incumbents and their opponents and other factors that facilitate the successful use of violence.

Readers can construct an explanation-sketch for inherency theory by inverting the contingency-sketch, but it will save effort if an equivalent framework is constructed explicitly here:

1. The fundamental disposition of individuals (groups) in politics is to maximize influence, or power, over decisions. This disposition may flow through numerous channels, of which collective violent action is one: extreme but "normal."

2. Since there are alternative channels for seeking power, the choice of violence must be activated, but activation readily occurs—though, of course, not as readily at the extreme of revolution. Collective political violence is a normal response to commonplace conditions.

3. The critical problem for inherency theory, given the normality of violence, is why collective political violence does not occur more often than it does.

4. The activation of the choice of violent channels is a matter of tactical considerations (not arousal of virulent affect).

5. Tactical choice involves cost-benefit calculation. Thus, the violent mode of political competition is chosen if lower-cost channels of influence-seeking are blocked, provided that violent means have a prospect of success that warrants their use. For extreme cases (revolu-

tions) the ideal combination is: blocked alternative channels, including those of lower-level violence; high valuation of goals; and perception of low capacity by opponents to inflict high costs.

6. Cultural patterns should play only a minor role; and to the extent that learning plays a role, it should inhibit violence at least as much as promote it, by teaching people that it is a high-cost resource.

7. More objective factors, like coercive balances or facilitating factors, should play a major and primary role in explaining collective political violence.

It should be evident that the two sketches intersect at some points, so that the allure of unparsimonious combination is, as always, considerable. But it should also be evident that what is primary, important, necessary in one case is secondary, minor, chancy in the other. Most important, the sketches lead in quite different directions in research (in logic and, as we will see, in practice): most patently, toward conditions that arouse exceptional types and degrees of affect (especially anger) versus conditions that influence calculations of cost-benefit ratios in choosing modes of political goal-seeking (especially intrinsically high-cost channels). Most fundamental, as in all political theorizing since ancient times, are two antithetical conceptions of political man: as a creature in search of either peace or power.

Major Illustrations from Studies of Collective Political Violence

We proceed to theorists that illustrate the opposed approaches. The theories will not add much to the explanation-sketches. We do not yet have "finished" theories of collective political violence but we do have "evolving" theories—unfortunately, they are becoming more and more complex and logically messy.

Contingency: The Relative Deprivation Family of Theories

Contingency theories of collective violence pivot on the notion of systemic breakdown where homeostatic devices normally provide negative entropy. It has been pointed out, correctly, that this implies sharp discontinuities between routine and nonroutine political activity, that the cause of violent action must be discontinuous (rapid, extensive) change in the context of politics, and that collective and individual behavioral pathologies should significantly covary, the former being a "version" of the latter (Tilly, 1978, pp. 23–24). Almost all such theories are subsumable under the notion of relative-deprivation theory, of which Gurr has been the leading exponent.

WHY MEN REBEL

Gurr's relative deprivation (RD) model can be summarized thus: (a) collective political violence is a form of aggression; (b) aggression results from anger, which is produced by frustration; (c) the fundamental cause of feeling frustration is an imbalance between what one gets and what one considers one's due: in Gurr's language, "discrepancy between men's value expectations and their value capabilities" (Gurr, 1970b, p. 24, also Gurr, 1968a, p. 1104). Obviously, the propensity to feel frustrated and its consequences are in a special sense "inherent." However, it is a dormant disposition until aroused by special extrinsic forces strong enough to overcome the tendency toward pacific acquiescence. The greater the scope and intensity of RD, of course, the more likely is violent behavior per se as well as at high "magnitudes" (see diagram in Gurr, 1970b, p. 320).

The above is only a first step. Aggression is not yet rebellion. It must be politicized if it is to appear as collective political violence, and latency must become actuality. Here, mediating (secondary) variables that do not themselves involve the frustration-anger-aggression nexus come into play. They include: (a) "normative justifications" for political violence or the lack of them, from Sorelian glorifications of violence (Gurr, 1970b, p. 193) to Gandhi's doctrine of nonviolence at the other extreme. Such justifications are themselves, of course, contingent, and unlikely to have consequences without prior frustration (Gurr, 1970b, pp. 197–210); (b) "utilitarian justifications," which are chiefly tactical considerations: estimations of the rational sense in collective violence. These involve calculations of numerous balances concerning the organizations of regimes and dissidents, their respective resources (actual and potential), and the availability of alternative channels of action; (c) a third mediating variable decides whether politicized aggression surfaces as fully actualized collective violence, and involves something obviously tactical (Gurr, 1970b, p. 232ff.): the balance of coercion between regimes and dissidents. The relation of that balance to magnitude of violent political conflict is curvilinear: strife will be greatest if there is an even balance of coercion. At the extremes, where coercion is highly unequal, regimes collapse virtually without being pushed or dissidents lie low out of fear or are quickly put down; (d) Gurr also has at times invoked still other factors, especially environmental conditions that facilitate strife (Gurr, 1968a, p. 1106): transportation networks, geographic traits, demographic characteristics—and, not least, the external support given dissidents.

In a contingency theory, such factors should themselves depend on rather fortuitous circumstances—as they do in Gurr. More important is an implication that must be read into relegating the factors to inferior status of mere mediating variables. Causal-path analysis aside, the implication is that the role of tactical variables diminishes as the more fundamental factor of frustration grows: desperate, impassioned people will not act coolly or be much governed by tactical calculations, even about coercive balances.[4] This is the only logical way to combine rationalistic with essentially arational motivation. Arationality also implies that a major role be assigned to cultural-variable learning. This too occurs in Gurr's theory, the cultural variable being the extent to which a culture of violence, rooted in the past, exists (Gurr, 1968a, p. 231).[5]

SIMILAR THEORIES

Gurr's theory belongs to a large family. Tilly traces its ancestry to Emile Durkheim—though Tilly's treatment of Durkheim (whose puzzle, after all, was solidarity in a differentiated society, not conflict) is debatable (Tilly, 1978, pp. 16–18). More obvious precursors among the great sociologists are Gaetano Mosca and Vilfredo Pareto. Pareto traces the decline of elites to the contingency of insufficient cooptation of dangerous, competent members of the nonelite, those in whom the deep-structural residues of combination (organizational skill) and force (ability and will to use coercion) coalesce. The exclusion of such men produces in them a kind of political RD. Mosca propounded Pareto's theory of elite-circulation earlier, though less elaborately. He also argued that the resort to violence is often a reaction to the estrangement of elites from masses: an elite's adoption of foreign ways—a kind of cultural deprivation. Whether or not such estrangement occurs is, of course, no more intrinsic to elitism than is the exclusion of a dangerous counterelite. In Pareto, especially, the most obviously symptomatic indication of contingency, blockage of a normal process, is central.

Among contemporary writers, the most influential member of the family, next to Gurr, probably is Huntington (1968). As in Pareto, the sense of deprivation in Huntington's theory is political, though less a matter of blocked channels than of their paucity or their insufficient capacity to handle "loads." In skeletal form: Huntington argues that revolutions and lesser forms of collective political violence are artifacts of rapid socioeconomic modernization. Such modernization "mobilizes" people and induces them to enter the arena of political conflict. No harm will be done if political channels can handle their demands and activities in pressing them. But if political development lags, blockage occurs and aggressive modes of action are generated. Note the incidence of extreme political violence in conditions of socioeconomic development, especially in centralized monarchies, narrow-based military dictatorships, and in new nations (Huntington, 1968, p. 275).[6]

The notions of overload and adaptation to stress belong to the world of systems theories. Since such theories are essentially concerned with negentropy as a normal state (see J. G. Miller, 1965 for a splendid summary), any theory of collective political violence derived from the systems perspective belongs to the universe of contingency (though entropy is inevitable in the very, very long run). C. Johnson (1966) has been perhaps the leading systems theorist of revolution, at any rate if we do not look far beneath his language. The causal chain in Johnson is quite similar to Huntington's, ignoring nominal differences: rapid change leads (sometimes) to system disequilibrium (the overload of mechanisms of homeostasis), which produces individual pathologies as well as collective movements. The sense of deprivation (Johnson actually avoids psychological concepts, and speaks of dysfunction) arises, of course, at the point of overload, or blockage. Similarly, Wolf's account of

peasant rebellions (1969), though making more of tactical considerations than Huntington or Johnson, rests on aberration: peasants—not capitalistic "cultivators"—resist the encroachment of market economies; but when traditional peasant life cannot be maintained and alternative arrangements are too ill-developed or restrictive, tensions arise and peasants rebel (Wolf, 1969, pp. xiv–xv). Here, aggression is unleashed by a combination of cultural and economic frustrations.[7]

We can perhaps best divide the members of the family of contingency theories according to whether their normal model is essentially macro-cosmic or micro-cosmic. In the first case, notions of systems and of their aberrations under conditions of extrinsically imposed strain are used to identify pathologies. In the latter case, apart from cultural learning, the micro-condition is more manifestly and explicitly a sense of deprivation, relative to others or to more abstract conceptions of what is justly due. Thus Gurr's theory is micro-cosmic (individual), and Huntington's and Johnson's, macro-cosmic (societal) in emphasis; but they converge at the explanandum, *collective* political violence.

Inherency: The Collective Action Family of Theories

Inherency theories of collective political violence at present are less common than contingency theories. They seem more numerous than they actually are because of a proliferation of labels for the same thing: resource-mobilization theory, political-process theory, theories of group dynamics, mobilization theory, strategic interaction models, and political contention theory. "Collective action (CA) theory" is used here because the postulate of the approach is that violent collective action is not aberrant but simply one of many alternative channels of group activity; like any other it is chosen by tactical calculation. Thus it belongs on a continuum or is part of a repertoire: different, sometimes extreme, but not off the normal scale.

FROM MOBILIZATION TO REVOLUTION'

Collective Action theory is chiefly the work of Charles Tilly and his associates; its *summa* is Tilly's *From Mobilization to Revolution* (1978).

Again, what I present here is a skeleton of a theory that, like Gurr's, has grown in complexity to accommodate data and objections, to the detriment of logical elegance.

Tilly begins with a simple conception of the polity. Polities have members, who have formal access to the political decision-making process, and challengers, who do not (Tilly, 1978, p. 53) All are contenders for power—with members, of course, enjoying privileges. Members use their resources in a game of continuous jockeying to enhance their power; challengers try, as a condition to all else, to get into the game. To be allowed to play, there are entrance fees. The higher the fees, the greater the pressure needed to become members; and at some point of cost-efficiency, violent action among contenders occurs, with revolution as the most extreme, but normal, form of such action.[8]

This is the barest précis. Some key points need to be added. Before any collective action (say, a strike, election, demonstration, riot) can occur, there must be a confluence of shared interests (Tilly, 1978, pp. 59–62)—though Tilly deliberately skirts the issue of how collective interests come to be perceived and pursued (1978, p. 62), perhaps wisely, given his purpose. The interests must possess organization: a combination of shared categoric traits and a pattern of frequent interaction, or network (1978, pp. 62–69). Beyond this, organized interests must be mobilized; by this Tilly means the possession and use of resources that may help achieve goals (1978, pp. 69–84).[9] Even at this point, collective action will not occur unless there is sufficient opportunity for it (1978, chapter 4). This is essentially a matter of power to repress (especially of credible threats) or, more generally, to make collective action costly. The obverse of repression is, of course, facilitation, not in the sense that Gurr usually employs the term, but with emphasis on political toleration of, or help to, the activities of groups in conflict.

There remains the question of what (if not contingent matters like anger or strain) activates violent collective action, particularly in the more extreme form of revolution rather than lower-cost actions. The answer is a process (1978, p. 201ff.): (a) Contenders (insiders or outsiders), organized around some specially motivated core group, make claims incompatible with a polity's survival in its existing form[10]; (b) the claims gain increasing acceptance, usually under conditions of alienation resulting from governmental malfunctioning: failures to meet obligations (provide benefits) or unexpected demands for resources (usually taxes); note here the intrusion of a glaring contingency— but only (as in Galilean motion) as an accelerator or as something that channels activity into a special path; (c) threatened authorities either cannot, or will not, or will not efficiently, block the potential for extreme action by suppression; hence (d) a condition of multiple sovereignty comes to exist. That condition never occurs after a short-run breakdown; it is always the result of a long-run chain of events. Multiple sovereignty involves mutually exclusive claims to legitimate governmental control, accepted by many (on both sides); often it is manifest in the establishment of parallel governments; and a struggle for partners in coalition occurs. Upon the reintegration of sovereignty, the process ends.

Apart from challengers' egregious "claims to resources," mysterious in origin, it seems plain that the crucial force that channels collective actions to violent political actions, once the (obvious) conditions of any such actions exist, is governmental inefficiency, timidity, and weakness. Revolutions thus occur when obstacles to strong pressures are unblocked; they are not, as typical contingency theorists believe, the very result of blockage. Hence the assertion in our explanation-sketches: for inherency theory, the pivotal problem is what *prevents* extreme conflict from taking place; in contingency theory, the issue is what *causes* it at all.

RELATIVES OF COLLECTIVE ACTION THEORY

Tilly himself locates the ancestry of his theory in John Stuart Mill (Tilly, 1978, pp. 24–25)—with a mandatory nod also to Marx and Marxists (1978, pp. 42–46), for whom inherency takes more the form of ineluctable historical process. Mill and the Utilitarians are aboriginal CA theorists in that they regard all action as based on the rational pursuit of self-interest (pleasure), in contrast to Durkheim's notion of aberrant phases in the unfolding of the division of labor, or Weber's notion of traumas in the unfolding of a disenchanted world.

Among contemporary writers, we find versions of CA theory in numerous strategic interaction models of behavior (for references, see Tilly, 1978, pp. 29–35). Such models treat forceful courses of action, such as strikes, not as releases for potent emotions but as moves in games—they involve bargains, coalitions, lying low or pouncing, to maximize one's take. Hirschman's elegant *Exit, Voice, and Loyalty* (1970) resembles Tilly's in that Hirschman accounts for "secession" from a social entity, protests (opposition) of various kinds within such entities, and acquiescence as a "repertoire" of responses to discontent; choice among them is considered a matter essentially of cost calculation. In an unfortunately discursive but fascinating work on violence by American Blacks during the Sixties, Nieburg (1969) argues at least implicitly in a similar vein. People prefer low-risk methods of resolving conflicts; the discovery of a method that offers a decent chance of success at low risk is a matter of trial and error (strategic interactions, in less plain words). In that process, violence may be used, usually under conditions of rapid social change, new group formations, and high levels of social uncertainty. In-groups and out-groups maneuver toward some new political balance, until a proper new low-risk mode of resolving conflicts is found; if not found, a life-and-death struggle for domination occurs. Violence here is, as in all CA theories, a "move" likely to be made if expected costs do not exceed expected benefits— more accurately, violence is used if it is the best available course of action. For manifest reasons, it often is for systematically disadvantaged groups. Nieburg's work represents a special form of rational choice: the choice of actions occurs not so much by hard calculation as by experience—trial-and-error among a set of (abstractly) equivalent actions.

Evaluation

We can now come to the crux. How can one make a reasoned choice at the branch point?

Unfortunately, there is no simple, workable way. One might simply reflect on the actual incidence of collective political violence. But that leads nowhere. One reason is logical. One might, superficially, expect something "inherent" to occur more often than something "contingent," but after a bit more thought it is clear that this is not necessarily so: contingencies can frequently occur (like physical "rest") and inherent tendencies may not generally be unblocked. (That is why people so often leap, like Aristotle, into obvious, but mistaken,

positions. Concrete nature is masterful at deceit.) In actuality, violent actions occur very often; but they do not occur as often as alternatives. Sorokin (1937, pp. 409–475) found, over two millennia, about one year of violent disturbance out of every four. From this it may follow that it does not take much to make violence occur contingently or that it does not take much to block the tendency toward it or make other actions more attractive.

It also goes without saying that studies by the theorists themselves fit whatever tack they choose—though sometimes in an eyebrow-raising way. Gurr, for instance, consistently does get good statistical results. But so does Tilly, when he confronts his models with data (which he does less well than Gurr). This is hardly surprising, since their models must come together at some point of explanation of concrete events, which, as stated, do nearly always have both contingent and inherent causes. At the same time, difficulties of research findings, even if manifest, are often glossed over or interpreted in a dubious way. To my knowledge, Tilly and collaborators have never succeeded in solving a crucial problem early recognized: finding "reliable procedures" for enumerating contenders, measuring mobilization, and specifying the relationship of groups to existing structures of power. Operationally, the theory is in limbo at all crucial points. Gurr, on the other hand, has been much criticized for his choice of "indicators" of RD. Deprivation is a "state of mind" that Cantril (1958) studies psychologically, but that is inferred in Gurr from objective (economic and political) indices. That begs many questions. One also wonders about: (a) the fact that Gurr and Duvall (1973) account for 75% of the variance in "civil conflict" across 86 countries in the early 1960s with five "causes" and eleven variables, in a simultaneous equation model—which could be worse, but hardly is conclusive; (b) the fact that mediating (secondary) variables in work by Gurr always account for a good deal of the variance in magnitude of civil strife, with social-structural facilitation always a significant variable—a result that CA theorists surely can turn to their own account.

At the very outset, then, we confront ambiguity. We should try to reduce it by inspecting available data bearing logically on one theory or the other. I will do so by discussing a number of selected issues, potentially helpful in choosing at the branch point.

Alternative Channels

If CA theory is the fruitful tack, a clear relationship should show up between the incidence of collective political violence and the availability of alternative channels for making and realizing "claims." We may thus posit that democracies ("open" polities) will rank low on the dependent variable. By extension, political violence should at least decline discernibly in cases of regular electoral competition. But since the less advantaged do not have equal access even in open polities one should find them playing a specially important role in political violence—following the cliché that violence is the resort of the weak: everyone's equal capacity, in Hobbes's state of nature.

The matter of alternative channels would seem immediately vital for anyone who considers all collective actions a set, or repertoire, of equivalent events. However, astonishingly little has been done with the subject by Tilly: some secondary analyses of lower-class actions such as strikes (see especially Tilly, 1978, p. 15ff.) and food riots (1978, pp. 185–187), and a study of the connection between elections, organized associations, and the occurrence of "demonstrations" (1978, pp. 167–171). We do have more direct evidence—though the subject cries for far more investigation by all inquirers into our subject.

In general, the data run counter to CA theory. Hibbs (1973, pp. 118–121) found virtually no statistical relationship between democratic polities and magnitude of political violence, either of the milder protest variety or with more virulent internal wars. To avoid the possibility that findings were distorted by including "ill-developed" democracies, a relationship was sought between levels of political violence and democratic development, in the well-known manner of McCrone and Cnudde (1967) and Neubauer (1967). Again, no significant relationship emerged with protest, and a weak negative association with internal war was convincingly explained away as spurious. Worse, a positive association turns up between elections and political violence (Hibbs, 1973; Snyder & Tilly, 1972), suggesting, perhaps, that electoral processes activate emotions appropriate also to other outlets. Hibbs also finds that effective exclusion from valued political positions due to ethnic, religious, or linguistic traits usually leads only to mild forms of protest—a finding that also turns up in Gurr (1966, p. 71).

In the most recent, and most persuasive, study of the subject by Gurr (Graham & Gurr, 1979), the results are more complex, but still of scant comfort to CA theorists. One critical finding is that democracies typically had more extensive "civil conflict" (a broad notion that ranges from demonstrations to guerrilla wars) than autocracies. (For simplicity's sake I ignore a third type that Gurr calls "elitist.") On the other hand, democratic civil conflicts were much less deadly. The first finding clearly impugns CA theory. However, the second provides CA theorists with a measure of comfort, since it must be due to a toleration in democracies of protests that, in repressive regimes, never surface, or else are forced to take virulent forms. RD theorists can rejoin that grievances in democracies are generally less serious (most obviously, because of lesser political deprivation per se). They can also sensibly hold that the greater deadliness of civil conflicts in autocracies may be a result of the actions of regimes, not of dissidents; this depends, obviously, on who is killed, and under what circumstances.

Two other relevant points: the old saw that violence is the political means of the impoverished—the basis of the McCone Report about the Los Angeles riots in the mid-1960s—simply does not stand up to close examination (e.g., Fogelson, 1971, p. 30; Caplan & Paige, 1968, pp. 19–20). There is also the much documented fact that revolutionary leaders do not much differ socioeconomically from other salient political figures, and that they differ more in regard to social marginality than in regard to resources at their disposal.

It seems evident—logically and empirically—that CA theorists must deflate many quantitative findings about the effects of alternative channels by stressing facilitation. Open polities do not block propensities to act of many, or any, kinds as much as closed polities. So they produce more collective political actions of all sorts. And the more advantaged and powerful have more means for deadly violence, no less than other actions: particularly military elites, who are more likely to act politically in closed polities. Our first test thus is one-sided in statistical results, but not hard to argue away.

Facilitation

It seems necessary then to look hard at the CA theorist's chief route of escape: facilitation—that is, how difficult or how easy pertinent circumstances make it to use collective violence in politics. Here, contingency theorists sometimes seem to turn the tables on themselves. Consider Gurr. In his early (now much modified) report (1968a, p. 1121), certain highly contextual factors presumed related to the possibility of violence (e.g., transportation networks, density of population, other geographic characteristics, and "external support of insurgents") account for more variance in magnitude of civil strife than anything else (twice as much as persistent deprivation!). Similarly, such facilitating factors as the distribution of value-stocks, complexity and cohesion of organization, number and scope of values (resources), are likely to decrease strife if regimes are better equipped and to increase it to the extent that dissidents possess them. In later work, facilitative matters still seem to have crucial effects on whether dissidence is peaceful or violent.

A picture begins to emerge. Having less costly channels available does seem to affect the choice of violent means: so, score a point for inherency. But the cost of violence does not much reduce deadly conflict in democracies, and still less in autocracies, where presumably it is likely to cost more: so, score a point for the other side. All would seem to depend then on what to regard as fundamental. I know no way to decide that issue yet, since CA theory incorporates facilitation (viz., opportunity), as does RD theory. The most we can say is that violence is more likely if easier to engage in and perceived to be more likely to succeed. Tactics play a role—but perhaps only for people afflicted by high RD. It seems necessary, then, to look at other issues that might break what, so far, appears to be a tie.

The Balance of Coercion

The most manifest "facility" for collective political violence is the ability and willingness of regimes to repress, relative to that of dissidents to be destructive. We should, of course, expect the balance of coercion to make a difference both in a contingency-sketch of political violence and in its opposite. For contingency theory, though, the tactical consideration involved is of lesser import: as stated earlier, very angry men are not likely to act coolly, even in the face of what Tilly calls "threat." For CA theories, *per contra*, little would seem

more important. What does the evidence suggest?

To begin with, we are handicapped by a flaw in method: the almost universal tendency to use the coercive capacities of regimes as measures of the coercive balance between authorities and dissidents. One exception is an article by Gurr (1970a). Gurr uses measures of loyalty and dissidence by military forces, and weighs familiar measures of the coercive potential of regimes against foreign support of dissidents and aspects of dissident groups, such as their size and organization, that may be assumed to have a bearing on coercive capacity (Gurr, 1970a, p. 138). The results Gurr obtains actually seem to offer some support to CA theorists, but not much. The coercive capacity of dissidents does "enhance the prospects for rebellion," the most extreme category of dissidence, whereas that of authorities reduces it. This is what CA theorists would expect. However, (a) regime coercion has "very little effect" on other forms of protest; (b) a different balance, concerning "institutional support" (support by "dense" and pervasive networks of organizations) consistently explains more; (c) throughout, the combined factor of institutional/coercive balance fares only a little better or worse in regard to different kinds of collective violence than a quite different explanatory variable, "justification," which includes both tactically relevant factors (e.g., success of past strife) and nontactical ones (legitimacy), but with the latter yielding better results than the former; (d) dissident coerciveness enhances the likelihood of rebellion much more than regime coercion inhibits it; (e) the latter has virtually no effect on lesser forms of strife.

What follows? Perhaps nothing, for operational reasons: leaving aside questions of data sources and scaling, Gurr's evidence comes from 21 Western countries over a mere 5-year span (1961–1965). However, the clear and strong result that CA theory would seem to call for manifestly fails to turn up. Also, CA theorists must make much of the capacity to inflict high costs (as pointed out in the explanation-sketch for inherency theory above); one therefore should not find that regime coercion is, as it seems to be, the least weighty explanatory factor in all types of strife. After an initial leaning toward CA theory, one thus is led to a contrary conclusion—though that, again, is offset by Gurr's conclusion that "variations in deprivation are not an important direct determinant of total strife, turmoil, or violent strife" (1970a, p. 142). Deprivation exists in the remote background, waiting to be "converted."

CA theory would be best supported by finding a strongly curvilinear relation between conflict and coercion. If one or another side greatly outweighs the other's capacity for coercion, rebellions should not start or regimes ought quickly to collapse, at low cost. The most intense conflicts ought to occur where coercive capacities are closely matched. Granted difficulties in the available data, the most recent study (by Gurr et al.) shows only slight curvilinearity. In addition, some other results that are very odd from the standpoint of CA theory turn up: In general, a positive relationship seems to exist between governmental coercion and conflict. This includes the finding that the cumulative application of sanctions increases conflict, even at the extreme of sanctions, and that the use of sanctions has no discernible time-lagged effect on conflict. These findings are contrary to Gurr's earlier position (1970b, p. 251) or that of the Feierabends (1971, p. 429). However, they are strongly supported by Hibbs (1973, pp. 86–87). And they are more consistent with contingency theory than the earlier position.

The unsatisfactory state of the available evidence does provide an escape hatch to CA theorists, at least for now. The tendency, though, has been for coercive balance to be of less importance as studies have improved. Most damaging, perhaps, has been the tendency of CA theorists themselves to argue away inconvenient findings by making fuzzy what should be especially clear in their theories. The problem is illustrated by Tilly's *magnum opus* (1978, pp. 106–115), in which repression is treated with unusual convolution—and by aphorism: for instance, "governments which repress also facilitate." Ultimately, Tilly resorts to a promising line of argument, one that involves historical patterns of repression. The special variable involves abrupt changes in such patterns. Unfortunately, the hypothetical relationship is either to "encourage" or "discourage" types of collective action (again, excepting only the obvious exception: very high levels of successful repression). That is simply not permissible—not, anyway, without a lot of added theory.

On the whole, contingency theory emerges healthier than inherency theory from our third test. But we cannot escape the problem of adequate data. For this reason, CA theorists need not throw in their towel yet. We need far more and better light on the issue. We want it especially from CA theorists themselves, the matter being critical for theories in which "causation" and "channeling" (or blockage) are the same thing. This is useful to know, but leaves our issue still undecided.

When Men Rebel

I referred above to Tilly's use of the historical pattern of repression as an explanatory factor. His doing so may be subsumed under a more general, widely followed line of assessment: To find out *why* men rebel we may be helped by studying *when* they do so. As we shall see, this involves a set of diverse tests that could also be invoked separately. Each, though, fits a general deduction from our two explanation-sketches:

1. For contingency theory, collective political violence, or such violence in its more extreme forms, should occur when, as the result of some temporal pattern, the specified contingency, such as RD, is or may be expected to be particularly great.
2. For inherence theory, collective political violence, or its more extreme forms, should occur when, as a result of a temporal pattern, (a) the costs of violent collective action are expected to be especially low, or (b) nonviolent actions in pursuit of highly valued goals have been shown to be unproductive.

There is much historical precedent for seeking explanations of political violence in the nature of historical moments of such violence. The classic source is Tocqueville. His basic argument in *The Ancient Regime* (1856) is familiar:

> Revolution does not always come when things are going from bad to worse. It occurs most often when a nation that has accepted, and indeed has given no sign of even having noticed the most crushing laws, rejects them at the very moment when their load is being lightened. . . . Usually the most dangerous time for a bad government is when it attempts to reform itself.

This argument is the theme for numerous variations. We will consider the most important.

RAPID CHANGE

There is a large family of theory that attributes extreme and destructive political behavior to an obviously "contingent" condition: unusually rapid, hence unusually unsettling, socioeconomic conditions. Frustrations are likely to arise under such conditions because of disorientation (anomie) per se, and because of the familiar occurrence of an excessive rise in expectations. At a minimum, the conditions of any contingency theory are more likely to be satisfied when change is rapid (and abrupt) than under more settled circumstances.

Olson's influential article on the consequences of rapid economic growth (1963) is prototypical of this view. A political, and otherwise modified, version of Olson's argument is Huntington's mobilization-institutionalization hypothesis. Both arguments are backed by persuasive reasoning, as well as the usual selectively chosen, *post hoc* illustrations. However, the evidence once again is surprisingly inconclusive; in general, only illustrations are used, and illustrations can be found of almost anything that is not wholly absurd.

Tilly and Johnson both have pointed out that contingency theorists should expect a high correlation, in cases of rapid change, between individual pathology (crime) and the collective variety (political violence). One can see why this should be so, the causes of individual and collective aberration (such as frustration) being presumably the same. But again, though the point seems crucial, evidence is strangely meager, and, for us, confusing. Gurr's work of 1970b cites a study that reports a decline in aggressive crimes (by Blacks and against Blacks) during periods of civil rights demonstrations (Gurr, 1970b, p. 310, note 92). That fact, though, can be interpreted almost any way one chooses—though, superficially, it runs against the expectations of contingency theory. By way of compensation, Tilly and Lodhi find a correlation of the two (1973, p. 296), but they emphasize that it is low. Perhaps, though, this is the correct expectation—anyway for them—since CA theorists regard different responses to similar conditions as alternatives in a repertoire of actions. If so, individual and group violence should be associated, but not very closely, for some people will choose the one response and others its alternative. Obviously, we need here both better data and better reasoning.

In any case, an impressive number of studies suggests that there is no simple, direct relationship between rates of socioeconomic change and political violence. The relationship, again, seems unusually ambiguous. Tanter and Midlarsky (1967) found a negative relationship between economic growth and, as they use the term, "revolutions" in Latin America, but a positive relationship in the Middle East and Asia. Bwy (1968b) confirms the Latin-American result, but argues that a different relationship among the variables holds for less developed countries. Flanigan and Fogelman (1970) find a negative relationship; Alker and Russett (1964) find the same. On the other hand, the Feierabends and Nesvold (1969) report a high association between rate of modernization and "instability." Hibbs (1973) finds different relations between rapid change and different types of political violence. And so it goes, in a very extensive set of works.

With enough ingenuity, one could probably trace this extreme confusion to different uses of concepts and measures. But if the relationships between the variables were very strong, mere differences in preferred measures ought not to produce such wildly divergent findings.

ADAPTATION TO CHANGE

The virulent potential effects of most stresses may, of course, be offset by the proper adaptation of "systems." If socioeconomic change is similar, differences in "adaptation" to it should be matched by differences in its consequences, including collective political violence. An example is the apparent relation (to be sure, small) between historical bourgeois radicalism and the relative lack of opportunities to become ennobled (see Shapiro & Dawson, 1972, p. 180)—a nice example of Pareto's hypothesis.

More to the point here is Barrington Moore's thesis that political outcomes (in Moore's case, the nature of regimes, but, by implication, also political processes more generally) depend chiefly on the adaptation of the traditional landed upper classes to "bourgeoisification"—economic modernization, as most of us think of it (Moore, 1966, p. 429ff.). That famous thesis fits, *post hoc*, eight widely assorted cases. But it has run into trouble when extended to other cases (or when examined more closely): by Tilton (Sweden) and Rokkan (the smaller countries in general); note also the crushing critique by Skocpol (1973). Moore's thesis can also be logically subsumed under either contingency theory, if change is emphasized, or inherency theory, if his argument is interpreted as hinging on choices of coalitions. Note, too, that despite the long vogue of "systems" theories in political science, operationally rigorous work on stress due to change, and adaptations to such stress, is just about nonexistent.

STRUCTURAL IMBALANCE

As implied earlier, Huntington's thesis rests on the notion of a "balance" of structures rather than on rapid mobilizing as such. This, in a sense, combines the variables of change and adaptation to change. Huntington's theory, of course, places the most inflammatory point in polities where the divergence between mobilization and institutionalization is greatest. As the space between the two narrows, collective political violence should decline. Like Moore, Huntington illustrates his argument. The evidence of other studies, however, runs strongly against him.

Schneider and Schneider (1971) accept Huntington's basic argument on the basis of a crossnational study, but their evidence leads them to reject the corollary that "mobilization" should be slow if it is to be balanced by "institutional" adaptations; this is damaging evidence, for one can easily show that the corollary is inherent in the postulate. Sanders (1973) concocts a resounding empirical refutation and also presents a strong critique of Huntington's conceptualization (which, of course, weakens the empirical refutation). Other important empirical rebuttals may be found in Yough and Sigelman (1976) and Duvall and Welfling (1973). Huntington himself distinguishes among "Western" and "Eastern" types of polities, to which his thesis (presumably) applies differently, and adds some very ill-fitting variables that confuse the nontactical character of his theory: the failure of elite-circulation and the effects of foreign wars and interventions (Huntington, 1968, pp. 273, 308).

Unfortunately, again, there seem to be no other theories of structural "imbalance" that have sufficient empirical support to allow a more definite verdict about this mode of theorizing; nor are other possibilities worked out as fully as is Huntington's theory (really, itself an "explanation-sketch").

THE J-CURVE

One major hope remains: that we can infer the conditions of collective political violence from some less simply wrought theory of change—some theory that finds the point of explosion at a particular point, or range, on a curve of change. The leading exposition of such a view is Davies's J-curve theory (1962).

The theory is that revolution is likely when periods of prolonged improvement, the historical pattern most likely to raise expectations, are interrupted by abrupt reversals; then frustrations due to unrequited expectations become intolerable. The J-curve theory, needless to say, involves contingency in its most pristine form, especially considering that it has never been diluted with logically confusing factors suggesting tactical choice—all honor to Davies for theoretical courage. What is the state of the evidence regarding the theory?

The supporting evidence should be very strong, for all contingency theory implies that the condition described by Davies frustrates and angers very deeply. In Davies's original formulation four cases were invoked—once again, as illustrations. Later, four other cases were added (see Davies in Graham and Gurr, 1969). In an impressive independent check, Grofman and Muller (1973) provide a clear measure of support, using data on individuals. But they also find strong evidence for a "relative gratification" theory of conflict behavior (drop-rise, or V-curve, theory). Still, their study manifestly remains within the realm of contingency theory, and rests on reasoning analogous to, though not wholly the same as, that of Gurr and Davies.

The chief problem with J-curve theory is the abundance of countercases. Consider, for example, the many countries in which the Great Depression of the 1930s did not increase political violence. Surely, the effects of sudden depression, following the orgiastic recovery of the 1920s were crucial—and no more in Germany than in all the countercases.

GROUP DYNAMICS

The question of when men rebel obviously has led, again, to puzzlement, if viewed from the standpoint of contingency theory. Does inherency theory, then, fare better with the question of timing? For RD theorists and their kin, the flashpoint of collective political violence should occur at a point of social process when rage or despair are most acute—when expectations and capabilities are most distant. For CA theorists, in contrast, violent action, being relatively high in cost in most circumstances, should generally be chosen after lower-cost channels are perceived as ineffectual, provided only that the balance of coercion does not manifestly rule out successful violence.

A tactical scenario that makes the resort to violence especially likely can readily be constructed. A group of contenders makes political claims cheaply, say, by petition. No response is made by authorities. Pressure is stepped up, perhaps through a stoppage of work; but still no response. A more dangerous organized demonstration is used next. The authorities remain intransigent and call out some squads of police to indicate determination. A more intense demonstration occurs; perhaps now some undisciplined elements or provocateurs throws rocks or do some looting. The authorities call on police and militia; heads are broken. At this point it will be clear that only violent collective action has any prospect of success at all. And, given some chance of success and intensity of claims, the high-cost method will be used. The moral is that negative sanctions precede collective political violence. On this point, CA theorists have differed from RD theorists almost from the beginning (see especially Tilly, 1971).[11]

WAR

A different argument for inherency involves the removal or weakening of coercive blockages, rather than gradual escalation as a forceful response to repression. A tendency may be present and emerge when resistance to it weakens, or actions may occur to overcome resistance when otherwise behavior would be more moderate.

When is coercion, as an obstacle to turbulent political action, likely to be unusually low? The most obvious answer is that the coercive potential of regimes will be exceptionally low when military forces have disintegrated, leaving the field free to less potent groups. This condition is likely after defeat in war, at least if occupation forces do not step in to help incumbent authorities (see, among others, Huntington, 1968, pp. 304–308; Arendt, 1963; Seton-Watson, 1951; and Hagopian, 1974).

Examples of revolutions after lost wars abound: France in 1871; Russia in 1905 and 1917; Turkey in 1918; China after World War II. Unfortunately, countercases can be invoked just as readily: Japan or Italy after the last great war, for instance. Perhaps these cases only show that losing a war is not a sufficient condition for revolution; but then, neither is it a necessary condition, or even a "normal" occurrence (e.g., France, 1789; Mexico, 1910; Cuba, 1959, et cetera). Anyway, the argument surely is more pertinent to the outcome of revolutionary conflicts than to their inception. This is Hammond's point about communist take-overs (1975, pp. 640–641) and, more broadly, that of D. E. H. Russell's study of 28 "mass rebellions" since 1906 (1974). Consider also Trotsky's familiar argument that the armed forces usually reflect popular conditions. If so, they would always facilitate violent action, if there is sufficient popular disposition to use it.

Learning: The 'Culture of Violence'

Contingency theories belong, in social analysis, to the same family as culturalist theories—theories based on learned orientations to action. Inherency theories are related to rationalist theories—based on the notion that actions are chosen by calculations of cost-efficiency.

There is much writing about the role of learning and culture in relation to political violence. Bandura (1973) is the leading exponent of the view that using violence individually is learned, and he makes a good case. On the macro-level, though, we should expect ambiguous findings about the relation of present to past violence. The use of violent action might, logically, become a learned response, but it might also teach people that its costs tend to be disproportionately large, even if successful. The problem here (as with violence by authorities, repression) is that any curve, or none, can support the cultural interpretation. Much, in other words, is made in the literature of "cultures" of violence, but nothing definitive for the debate between contingency and inherency theories is likely to emerge from studies linking past to present violence.

This point fits findings. At best, a moderate relationship tends to turn up, as in Gurr's work (1968a, p. 1121). Still, Gurr later (1970b, pp. 170, 176–177) strongly argues the "culture-of-violence" hypothesis on "varied evidence and arguments"—which, as I read them, support equally well utilitarian explanations of violence. Another recurrent theme in studies of the culture of violence, as we should expect, is that "it depends." For instance, statistical relations seem to vary, for some reason, with geographic areas. In Africa, past rebellions are associated with reduced "turmoil" (Welfling, 1975, p. 887); but Latin America is different, and Western Europe different again. Welfling (with Duvall) squares the circle on the basis of type of collective violence: Turmoil, it is argued, feeds on itself whereas "elitist" kinds of violence reduce the likelihood of later violence. But they do not do so through learning; rather, the cause seems to be the tactical factor of suppression (Duvall & Welfling, 1973, p. 692). Hibbs also reports quite contrary findings for "protest" and "internal war" (1973, pp. 159, 163); in his study, conflict akin to the "elitist" type in Welfling seems to be increased by the existence of a "culture" of violence.

As I argued, this contrariness can be accommodated to the premises of contingency theory. But to accommodate the evidence, we will have to specify when violence teaches violence or the imperative of peace. This will be difficult, at best. At present, the evidence may be regarded as typical of the too often ambiguous findings in the literature.

Conclusion

We began with an explication of a recurrent antithesis at the basic branch points of theorizing about any subject. We went on to a version of that branch point especially tailored to explaining collective political violence. We found that theories in the field do divide along the lines indicated. And we reviewed many empirical studies that bear on expectations deduced from the postulates of the antithetical approaches. No clear result emerged. Granted, conditions such as inequalities, unsatisfied demands, discrimination, and societal cleavages are related consistently to degrees of conflict. What remains mysterious, in the end, is the basic nature of the link between causes and effects—not least, therefore, understanding why similar conditions so often have dissimilar results.

The findings do not point strongly toward the superior fertility of a particular species of theorizing. "Fertility" in this connection is, first, the capacity of an approach to provide consistently superior explanations of many aspects of an independent variable—explanations that are themselves logically consistent, or entailed by a higher-order theory. Second, fertility is the ability of such higher-order theory deductively to yield new, and good, lower-order theoretical relations. On the whole, contingency theory probably has fared better than inherency theory. That may only be a byproduct of its more frequent use or it may result from a lesser empirical bent among inherency theorists. More important, we consistently found ambiguities in data bearing on the contingency perspective, no less than its antithesis—problems of interpreting correctly their implications; and often findings that were offset or made doubtful by other findings. Also, relationships that should have been clear and strong frequently were opaque and weak.

Surely, the difficulty is not any lack of studies or data. We are inundated with both, and the data cover a vast range of variables, history, geography, and types of polities.

Somewhat more likely (though I doubt it) is that we arrived at a confusing result because the empirical studies cited were an inadequate sample. They certainly do not exhaust the literature and are a mix of methodologically good, bad, and indifferent studies. This implies a challenge to specialists in the field: Before embarking on new empirical studies, identify the high-quality works in both approaches and analyze their procedures and results from the perspective sketched here.

Another strong possibility is that confusion has emerged because of a taxonomic error. We have treated cases of collective political violence as a single class—as Tilly treats a still much larger universe: all collective actions. Even if this is typologically plausible, doing so may be theoretically confusing: as suggested early in this essay, certain kinds of political violence might better be treated as "contingent," others as "inherent." We did frequently find such results in the literature, especially between lesser and greater types of strife. For reasons of parsimony, we ought perhaps to resist using this possibility, but evidence might compel resorting to it. In any case, here is another challenge for analysis.

A third likely difficulty—one common in the social sciences, and one that may well condemn to futility exercises like those just suggested—is method: an overdose of induction. One doubts that underlying determinants can ever be mechanically teased out of the complexity of highly disparate events, no matter how sophisticated the quantitative methods used. A related problem is deliberate eclecticism. Choosing eclecticism at the outset virtually guarantees confusion in the end, and thus seems self-defeating—even perverse.

Although we have not found a hero, we have surely found a villain: prehedged models, or models ground out mechanically from motley data. The resulting "modeled" world appears about as complex (and thus mystifying) as the concrete world it models. In Hibbs (1973, p. 181), we find no illuminating simplification: We find only a complex world of variables, vertiginous with arrows and proportions. The artfulness of nature wins out over that of theory because, *contra* Bacon, nature is not "put to the test." One should not be too censorious about this, since Hibbs's deliberate aim is eclecticism. Gurr's "model,"—more surprisingly, because based on an elegantly parsimonious theory—is not much less complex. Is not the reason fear of potential disconfirmation, even at the cost of mixing up a highly plausible line of analysis with its antithesis?

The result always is a realized intention: a model that "fits" the data. But if such a model is irrefutable in principle, it will fit only without really illuminating experience. That, I suggest, is inadvertently the case in Gurr's work, however tenacious and ingenious the work has been. Try to refute the following, which is essential RD theory, à la Gurr:

1. No political violence can occur without politicized discontent (satisfied people do not rebel).
2. No discontent will exist unless somebody feels deprived.
3. Politicization involves both normative and utilitarian (tactical) considerations.
4. Even so, little or nothing will happen when facilitative and coercive resources available to dissidents and authorities are distributed onesidedly.

Admittedly, this is a great simplification. But it surely shows, by omitting inessentials, how RD theory has been insulated against tactical accounts of collective political violence by incorporating them.

Tilly, too, has increasingly complicated his theoretical model, as well as swallowed up inconvenient data by reinterpretations. A still greater difficulty that emerges in his work, and also disarms invalidation, is a kind of clever triviality (in the philosophic sense). Something *seems* to be said to explain a mystifying set of events. But except for labels (members, challengers, et cetera) we know it already, and so remain mystified. No substantial violent action will occur unless:

1. Some group wants something it does not have.
2. A fair number of people agree that their claim is justified.
3. The group is not successfully suppressed to begin with.
4. The group controls some suitable resources (and wants to control more).

And who does not know that extreme rebels lay claim to nothing less than sovereign authority, against the claims of incumbent authorities? I do not mean to be sardonic. The point of the argument is that the "interesting" issues (those that really need explaining) always are a step removed from those Tilly faces: Why do "outgroups" actually (not latently) come to want "in," where before they acquiesced? Under what conditions do people come to perceive the illegitimacy of a pattern of governmental authority, rather than continue to acquiesce?

A conclusion seems to emerge. The literature, even if differently surveyed, will probably be inconclusive for us, because a well-defined choice among theoretical approaches has not been faced at all by the many scholars of collective political violence. Perhaps this is due to failure to recognize that such a choice exists. If so, this essay, though it has no "result," should help. More immediate reasons are the understandable desire to be "right," which, in a messy world, is easier to achieve with messy theory than with parsimonious theory. If not tautological, our explanations of collective political violence thus far have been too close to descriptions: too close, that is, to being depictions of the concrete, in the jargon of either contingency or inherency theory. On that basis, explanation hardly can fail; but it also cannot succeed in getting to, or even near, essentials. The remedy is to regard theory as what it is: a tool of explanation, not something that models all facets of the concrete. We want deliberate one-sidedness that may fall in clean, competitive tests, not deliberate, or face-saving, eclecticism. If the choice of a theoretical approach is a choice among conceptions of the essential nature of a set of phenomena, studies that circumnavigate that issue can only defeat us.

We *can* choose between the two most basic models of political man: peace-seeking man versus power-seeking man.[12] But in my view we cannot do it effectively by incorporating both in our initial models. If we do that, results pointing to both assuredly will turn up, both being at work—as they are also in physical motion, language, or the malfunctioning of organisms. Nor can we do it by largely arbitrary commitments. Political "theorists" have always dealt with basic branch points in one way or the other. Thus they have come to no resolution at the foundations of theory; rather, they simply have divided "members" and "challengers" into disciplinary factions, always for suspect reasons—the worst of which is not facing up thoughtfully, with open minds, to the problem of primary theoretical choice.

One way to do so would be to work along a given line to see how far it leads. All considered, I would at present choose contingency theory in the RD version—but in a much more simplified form than Gurr and his associates have used, recognizing that the goal is to construct good "theory," which is an abstract tool of understanding, not to reconstruct concrete reality in all its nuances and complexities. Once the essentials are known, the nagging complexities will (on past scientific evidence) fall into place more persuasively.

NOTES

1. No doubt this leaves loose ends: e.g., should political "violence" really be distinguished from nonviolent actions? What about violent coercion by authorities? How does one measure "extreme" collective political violence? Let us leave the ends loose. If they affect our discussion, they will be confronted when required.

2. At issue, of course, is general theory, not accounts of particular cases. No one could explain a cut finger or a cold through "normal" entropy. It is distinctly likely, though, that many diseases resist understanding because we proceed from basic premises bound to be fruitless—usually those of exogenous, contingent causation.

3. The fatefulness of the question is reflected, as earlier in physics, by extreme acrimony and the extension of the argument into the realm of political morality.

4. There is internal evidence in Gurr's work that the "tactical" variables were in fact rather late concessions to the counterarguments of rational-choice theorists (see, for instance, Gurr, 1970b, p. 210, note 54).

5. This summary omits most of the nuances of a still evolving set of empirical and theoretical works. But I suspect that a fuller summary would serve my purpose of displaying contingency theory less well; for Gurr has not resisted the temptation to increase explanatory power (and disarm objections) by incorporating others' models, even if antithetical. I will try to show in the Conclusion, below, that the reasons for doing so are not overwhelming—logic aside.

6. Huntington sometimes writes as if blockage were "normal" if modernization is rapid. However, modernization itself may be gradual and can be coped with politically. His theoretical account thus remains fundamentally contingent.

7. Other important members of the family, omitted here only because of space, are Galtung, 1964 (rank-disequilibrium theory), and D. C. Schwartz, 1972 (cognitive-inconsistency theory applied to revolution).

8. Political violence, in Tilly, may take three forms (1975, pp. 506–507): competitive (two groups attack each others' resources), reactive (a group responds to attack), or proactive (a group attacks to obtain resources). Each of these types comes in modern (associational) and nonmodern (communal) versions; therefore, types of political violence can be distinguished historically and associated with social development—but not at all in the manner of Huntington or Johnson.

9. Tilly uses the terms "organization" and "mobilization" largely in his own way, only loosely related to more familiar ways. Readers should not assume that Tilly can be fully understood without going into terminological (and other nuances) at the source.

10. We would, of course, like to know what makes claims indigestible, but are told almost nothing about this—no doubt because the emphasis remains on process, not content.

11. The use of negative sanctions should not invariably lead to escalation by dissidents: the sanctions may succeed.

12. Here, let me make a very brief proposal. To choose among theoretical approaches we need deliberately simple, antithetical models, and to test them in fair competition, in well-selected cases, and in ways precluding ambivalent results. How this might be done I have described in a separate essay (H. Eckstein, 1979), which is also the design of a (potential) project. It happens that the issue of that essay is support for regimes—"legitimacy." But that is simply the obverse of dissidence. It also happens that the essay constructs a clean (and, I think, compelling) contingency model and, as its antithesis, a clean (also compelling) inherency model; it also tries to show how to go about resolving the theoretical antithesis by "strong" tests. If the work is done (which is at present contingent) the choice at the branch point discussed here will follow from it—for Tilly is right: a theory of violent politics must also, *mutatis mutandis*, be a theory of peaceful politics. (The proposal may smack of self-advertisement but should need no apology, for the essay cited resulted from reflections on my own failures.)

Politicized Collective Identity: A Social Psychological Analysis

Bernd Simon • Christian-Albrechts University, Kiel, Germany
Bert Klandermans • Free University, Amsterdam, the Netherlands

This article develops a social psychological model of politicized collective identity that revolves around 3 conceptual triads. The 1st triad consists of collective identity, the struggle between groups for power, and the wider societal context. It is proposed that people evince politicized collective identity to the extent that they engage as self-conscious group members in a power struggle on behalf of their group knowing that it is the more inclusive societal context in which this struggle has to be fought out. Next, 3 antecedent stages leading to politicized collective identity are distinguished: awareness of shared grievances, adversarial attributions, and involvement of society at large. This sequence culminates in the final triad because the intergroup power struggle is eventually triangulated by involving society at large or representatives thereof. Consequences of politicized collective identity are discussed.

When President de Klerk of South Africa announced in 1990 that the government was prepared to negotiate with the African National Congress about a peaceful transition to a nonracial, democratic society, quite a few White South Africans were shocked, especially among the Afrikaner population. They felt besieged, and some even threatened violent action to halt the transition process. Indeed, some violent attacks took place, but as the transition proceeded, Afrikaner violence ceased. The opponents of the transition among the Afrikaners eventually flocked together to form what became the Freedom Front. They felt that the interests of the Afrikaners were threatened in the new South Africa and therefore engaged collectively in the political struggle at the national level (see Klandermans, Roefs, & Olivier, 1998; Roefs, Klandermans, & Olivier, 1998).

On April 2, 1995, thousands of farmers marched through the ancient streets of Santiago de Compostela, the provincial capital of Galicia, Spain's most northern province. They were protesting on the doorstep of the provincial government. They demanded that the provincial and national government raise the milk quota given to Galician farmers and that the government, rather than the farmers, pay the fines for overproduction of milk. At about the same time, Dutch farmers were dumping dung on the doorstep of the Ministry of Agriculture in The Hague. Later that year, they occupied a provincial magistrate where the so-called manure rights were registered. Their protests were aimed at the government's manure regulations that, in effect, forced farmers to reduce their stocks or to invest in alternative means of manure processing. In both Spain and the Netherlands, farmers were fighting provincial and national authorities because they felt that their interests had not been represented properly by their governments. In fact, over the past decades, farmers all over Europe have engaged in similar collective action.

In 2000, the cities of Amsterdam in the Netherlands and Frankfurt in Germany were witnessing collective action by people opposing the expansion of the Schiphol airport and the Rhein-Main airport, respectively. The battle was between the environmental movement and the people living beside the airport on the one hand and airport and civic authorities on the other hand. The conflicts oscillated between escalation and de-escalation, and the people involved were mobilized and demobilized time and again. One moment airport and civic authorities were confronted with activists occupying a runway or talking to travelers at the airport, and the next moment these authorities were confronted with activists appealing to members of parliament or the minister of transportation. One moment activist organizations or their representatives were confronted with the police attempting to evacuate and arrest them, and the next moment they sat in consultative meetings with airport and civic authorities.

These examples are drawn from very different cultural, national, and political contexts, but they all share three critical themes. First, the protagonists in these scenarios acted not as single individuals but as members of social groups. Second, these groups and their members were involved in power struggles. Third, the power struggles were about control in the wider societal context so that besides the immediate antagonists, these struggles also involved third parties such as societal authorities or the general public. We suggest that it is possible to derive from these themes the critical constituents of a social psychological conceptualization of politicized collective identity.

The remainder of this article is divided into four major sections. In the first section, we explore in more detail the three themes indicated above and thus provide a conceptual backdrop against which we then suggest a social psychological definition of politicized collective identity. In the second section, we turn to the antecedents of politicized collective identity and try to answer the question, How is collective identity politicized? In the third section, we show that politicized collective identity

has important and unique consequences that differentiate this form of collective identity from other forms. In the final section, we summarize our main conclusions and suggest novel and promising directions for future research.

Conceptualizing Politicized Collective Identity

Collective Identity

Most, if not all, social behavior takes place in the context of social groups or structured systems of social groups. Accordingly, scholars stress the role of people's group memberships in social behavior (Tajfel & Turner, 1979, 1986; Turner & Onorato, 1999). In particular, it is suggested that salient group memberships direct people's attention to their collective (or social) as opposed to their individual (or personal) identities, which then regulate their social behavior. There is much empirical evidence corroborating the role of collective identity as an important explanatory variable. For example, the concept of collective identity helps researchers to better understand when and why people stereotype themselves and others, discriminate against out-groups in favor of in-groups, and accept influence from in-group members but reject influence from out-group members (for reviews, see Brown & Gaertner, 2001). It has also been shown that collective identity influences people's justice concerns (Tyler & Smith, 1999) and their willingness to engage in social protest as well as other collective activities that aim at social change (De Weerd & Klandermans, 1999; Klandermans, 2000; Simon et al., 1998). Collective identity thus plays an important role as an "intervening causal mechanism in situations of 'objective' social change" (Tajfel, 1978, p. 86). In short, it affects the struggles within society.

Before we elaborate on the concept of collective identity, a few comments on our terminology are in order. First social psychologists, especially European social psychologists (cf. Luhtanen & Crocker, 1992, p. 302), have traditionally used the term *social identity* to refer to the identity that people derive from their memberships in social groups (Tajfel & Turner, 1979, 1986). However, we prefer the attribute *collective* to the attribute *social* in this expression to preclude the misinterpretation that, by implication, any other form of identity (e.g., individual identity) would necessarily be *asocial*. As has been shown elsewhere (Simon, 1999), such an implication would be false and was certainly never intended by the original social identity theorists (see Turner, Hogg, Oakes, Reicher, & Wetherell, 1987, p. 46). Second, especially in the social cognition literature, the term *self* is typically preferred to the term *identity*. This is so because the former term seems to better connote the plasticity and malleability of the "working self" as a context-dependent cognitive representation or process (Markus & Kunda, 1986; McAdams, 1997; Sherman, Judd, & Park, 1989; Simon, 1997). In the present analysis, however, we focus on relatively enduring memberships in real-life social groups, which are in turn typically embedded in structured and rather stable systems of intergroup relations. As a consequence, those group memberships tend to provide a fair degree of social–contextual invariance and thus a rather stable and comprehensive sense of who one is. To indicate this shift in emphasis, we use the term *identity* instead of *self*. Finally, we want to clarify that *collective identity* is used in this analysis as a (*social*) *psychological* concept and not as a sociological concept in a Durkheimian sense (Durkheim, 1895/1976; Rucht, 1995). That is, collective identity in the present sense is the identity of a person as a group member and not the identity of a group as a sui generis entity. It is collective in the sense that the person shares the source of his or her identity (i.e., the relevant group membership), and therefore also the ensuing identity, with other people. After these terminological clarifications, we can now elaborate on the definition of collective identity.

In the most basic social psychological sense, identity is a place in the social world. A place is a metaphorical expression and stands for any position on any socially relevant dimension, such as gender, age, ethnicity, trait, attitude, and so forth (Simon, 1998b, 1999). In contrast to individual identity (I or me), collective identity (we or us) is a place that is shared with a group of other people. It is thus a more inclusive identity (Turner et al., 1987). Especially in modern society, people have access to multiple shared places in the social world. Although they are shared with other people, not all of these multiple places are necessarily shared with exactly the same group of other people. As a

consequence, there is a potential for multiple, partly overlapping, or crosscutting and even conflicting collective identities.

However, not all collective identities of a person are salient at the same time. Which specific collective identity becomes salient while others remain dormant depends on which socially shared place or group membership moves into the psychological foreground, which is in turn a joint function of person variables ("readiness") and more immediate social context variables ("fit"; Turner et al., 1987). For example, depending on people's unique prior experiences or life histories, they are likely to attach differentially strong emotional or value significance to a particular group membership (e.g., ethnicity) so that they are differentially predisposed or ready to define themselves in terms of the respective collective identity (Simon, 1999). In addition to such interindividual variation, there may also be intraindividual variation over the life span to the extent that people go through different stages of collective identity development (e.g., see Cross, 1995, for a model of Black identity change). Moreover, group membership or collective identity salience also depends on the immediate social context because a particular in-group/out-group categorization is more meaningful in some social contexts than in others (Oakes, Haslam, & Turner, 1994). For example, in all likelihood, a male-female categorization is more meaningful or fits better in a situation in which male and female students discuss issues of abortion or rape than in a situation in which they discuss issues of drug abuse. In the former case, the students should be particularly likely to define themselves in terms of their collective male or female identity, and this tendency should further intensify if their in-group is outnumbered by the out-group so that the in-group is particularly distinctive in the immediate social context (Simon, 1998b).

Collective identity, like identity in general, serves important psychological functions for the person, and satisfaction with one's collective identity critically depends on the extent to which it successfully fulfills these functions. Five collective identity functions seem particularly important. They relate to basic psychological needs, namely, belongingness, distinctiveness, respect, understanding (or meaning), and agency (Baumeister & Leary, 1995; Brewer, 1991; Fiske, 2000; Maslow,

1970; E. R. Smith & Mackie, 1995; Tajfel & Turner, 1979, 1986). For instance, collective identity confirms that one belongs to a particular place in the social world. At the same time, it also affords distinctiveness from those other social places (or people) to which one does not belong. It further signals that one is like other people, though not necessarily like all other people, so that one can expect respect, at least from these similar others (which in turn is a necessary precondition for self-respect or self-esteem). Moreover, collective identity provides a meaningful perspective on the social world from which this world can be interpreted and understood. Finally, collective identity signals that one is not alone but can count on the social support and solidarity of other in-group members so that, as a group, one is a much more efficacious social agent ("Together we are strong!").

Several social psychological processes operate in the service of these collective identity functions. For instance, stereotyping and self-stereotyping processes at the cognitive level and conformity processes at the behavioral level accentuate intragroup similarities and intergroup differences (Oakes et al., 1994; Turner et al., 1987). In addition, prejudice processes at the affective level and discrimination processes at the behavioral level induce group members to see their in-group in a positive light vis-à-vis relevant out-groups and to secure a privileged position for their in-group (Brown, 1995). As a consequence, these processes strengthen group members' sense that they belong to a distinct, cohesive, and superior social group that provides them with mutual respect, a meaningful understanding of the social world, and the collective strength to act efficaciously.

To summarize, collective identity is a more inclusive self-definition that is focused on a particular group membership. In combination with several mediating social psychological processes (e.g., stereotyping, conformity, prejudice, and discrimination), it serves important functions related to basic psychological needs (e.g., belongingness, distinctiveness, respect, understanding, and agency) and thus contributes ultimately to a meaningful social existence.

The Struggle for Power

Groups do not exist in a social vacuum. They are embedded in intergroup relations or systems of intergroup relations, which are in turn characterized by differentials or asymmetries on sociostructural dimensions (Farley, 1982). One important sociostructural dimension is power, and power asymmetries are a typical characteristic of many, if not most, intergroup relations (Ng, 1982; Sachdev & Bourhis, 1985, 1991). From a social psychological perspective, power is generally viewed as a relational construct that describes a social relationship in which one party has, or is perceived to have, the ability to impose its will on another to achieve desired outcomes (Haslam, 2001, p. 210). Power can be based not only on the ability to allocate material rewards or punishments but also on the possession of immaterial resources such as information, expert knowledge, and status or reputation (French & Raven, 1959). In short, someone has power to the extent that he or she can control his or her own and other people's outcomes (Dépret & Fiske, 1993; Fiske, 1993; Jones, 1972; see also Moscovici, 1976; for a comprehensive, multidisciplinary review, see Ng, 1980). By the same token, the power of a social group has typically been defined as the degree of control the group has over its own fate and that of out-groups (Sachdev & Bourhis, 1985).

As we indicated above, intergroup power relations, like all power relations, are rarely symmetrical. Instead, social groups often differ in the degree of control they have over their own outcomes, the outcomes of relevant outgroups, or both. They have differential power. These power differentials or asymmetries can be more or less explicit (Ng, 1980) and are often, but not necessarily, linked to intergroup asymmetries on other important sociostructural dimensions such as group size or social status (Simon, Aufderheide, & Kampmeier, 2001). More important for the present discussion, power asymmetries are a frequent source of intense intergroup conflict. For instance, the more powerful group, by virtue of its superior outcome control, is in a better position to achieve desirable outcomes and to avoid undesirable ones than is the less powerful group. The likely result is an outcome distribution that favors the more powerful group. This should be so even if that group does not engage in active discrimination against the less powerful group but simply follows its own self-interests. However, this may in fact be too optimistic because research indicates that more powerful groups are quite willing to use the power asymmetry to actively discriminate against less powerful groups (Ng, 1982; Sachdev & Bourhis, 1985, 1991). In any case, less powerful groups should be dissatisfied with the unfavorable outcome distribution and thus should be motivated to work or even fight for a redistribution of the specific outcomes and ultimately for a redistribution of intergroup power unless easy individual exit or legitimizing ideologies undermine their members' collective identity (Ellemers, 1993; Sidanius & Pratto, 1999; Tajfel & Turner, 1979, 1986). But the struggle for power is not limited to intergroup relations with an established power asymmetry. On the contrary, when the power structure is unclear or unstable, the struggle for power and the ensuing conflict may be particularly fierce because each group is tempted to secure for itself the lion's share or at least to prevent the other group from getting it. Finally, the struggle for power may intensify for yet another reason. In addition to, and on the basis of, its primary instrumental value related to direct outcome control, power is likely to acquire a secondary psychological value in that powerful groups typically enjoy more respect and are (perceived as more efficacious social agents than powerless [or less powerful] groups. Consequently, the respect and agency functions of collective identity are likely to additionally spur the intergroup competition for power.

All this is not to say that the struggle for power excludes the possibility of intergroup cooperation. On the contrary, opponents may realize that neither party is strong enough to defeat the other and conclude that a power sharing arrangement might therefore be the best solution. This was, for example, the case in South Africa when in 1990 the African National Congress and the government of President de Klerk agreed to collaborate on a peaceful transition to a nonracial, democratic society. It should be noted, however, that this agreement was already the result of a power struggle during which the African National Congress had empowered itself to the point where the government was no longer able to oppress it.

The Societal Context

We have argued that social groups are often involved in power struggles in that they try to establish, change, or defend a power structure. We now need to make explicit an important, but often ne-

glected, aspect of power struggles between social groups. That aspect is the societal embeddedness of intergroup power struggles and of their immediate protagonists. As a consequence, such power struggles also have repercussions for the overall power structure of the more inclusive societal context. By the same token, they are not merely bipolar conflicts between two opposing groups, but additional groups or segments of the wider society are involved as well. This calls for (at least) a triangulated or tripolar approach to power struggles. Typically, the following three parties are likely be involved: two antagonistic parties or groups, one of which may be an elite or authority, and the general public (or representatives thereof) as the third party, which each of the two antagonistic groups tries to control or otherwise enlist for its own particularistic interests. These three social entities need not be conceived of as mutually exclusive. On the contrary, each of the two antagonistic groups (e.g., a particular social movement and its countermovement) should be anxious to stress that it is an important part of the more inclusive general public or population so that its own interests appear to be compatible with, if not identical to, the "common" interest. By the same token, each group can be expected to strive for hegemony, claiming that their own position is or should be prototypical or normative for that more inclusive "in-group," whereas the position of the other group is discredited as beyond the latitude of general acceptance (Mummendey & Wenzel, 1999).

Until now, this tripolar approach has had little direct impact on social psychological research. Especially the laboratory and field work prompted by social identity theory (Tajfel & Turner, 1979, 1986) has traditionally focused on bipolar intergroup relationships (for an exception, see, e.g., Wagner, Lampen, & Syllwasschy, 1986). However, two other influential theoretical frameworks are directly compatible with such a tripolar approach. In fact, they inspired the analysis presented in this article in important ways. The first framework is Mugny's (1982) theory of "the power of minorities." Mugny argued that the social context in which the diffusion of minority influence takes place consists of (at least) three social entities. These are the (numerical) minority, the population that the minority tries to influence, and a powerful third group that tries to counteract the minority influence. This latter group may itself be a numerical minority but one that enjoys an institutionalized power advantage vis-à-vis the (counternormative) minority and the population ("the silent majority"). Any attempt by the minority to influence the population operates against the backdrop of an antagonistic relationship between the minority and the powerful group and a relationship of domination of the population by the powerful group. It is impossible to review all pertinent empirical evidence here, but this tripolar approach to minority influence has certainly made an important contribution to overcoming the reductionism that characterized the traditional study of social influence processes (see Moscovici, Mucchi-Faina, & Maass, 1994; Turner, 1991).

The second framework that goes beyond an analysis of simple bipolar intergroup relations is Turner et al.'s (1987) self-categorization theory. It is an extension of social identity theory in that it makes use of, and further develops, key assumptions of that theory so as to provide a comprehensive explanation of how individuals are able to act as a group. Two assumptions are of particular relevance to the present discussion. One states that self-representation or identity can be construed at different levels of abstraction related by means of class inclusion. For example, one's identity as a resident of the city of Berlin is more abstract than, and thus includes, one's identity as a resident of a specific neighborhood in Berlin. At the same time, one's identity as a German citizen is even more abstract and includes both the city identity and the neighborhood identity. The other relevant assumption postulates that groups are compared and evaluated in terms of the next more inclusive group or social category that includes both. For instance, residents of different neighborhoods in Berlin would thus be compared and evaluated with respect to attributes that characterize residents of Berlin in general (e.g., witty). By the same token, residents of Berlin would be compared with, and evaluated relative to, say residents of Cologne or Munich with respect to attributes that characterize German citizens in general (e.g., efficient). The important point is that intergroup relations are embedded in the context of even more inclusive or shared group memberships, and this is likely to bring into play third parties such as representatives of the more inclusive in-groups.

In conclusion, both the minority influence and the self-categorization frameworks recommend an extension of the conceptual arena to also take into account the role of third parties. With respect to power struggles between social groups, we can then derive from both frameworks that the general public, its institutions, or its representatives are likely to be involved as a third party. In short, these struggles are struggles between social groups for power within society, which brings us to the political dimension of group behavior or, for that matter, of collective identity (Reicher, 1995).

Politicized Collective Identity

Politics is typically defined as the constrained use of power by people over other people (Goodin & Klingemann, 1996, p. 7; see also M. Weber, 1919). The struggle between social groups for power within society can therefore be understood as political group activity. Accordingly, we suggest that politicized collective identity can be understood as a form of collective identity that underlies group members' explicit motivations to engage in such a power struggle. At this point, it may be helpful to distinguish between political repercussions of collective identity and politicized collective identity proper. In many cases, behavior or action in terms of collective identity might have political repercussions in that it also affects the power structure within society. However, these political repercussions may or may not be intended by the collective actors. Take, for example, a religious group that "simply" wants its children to be taught in its own schools. It is not difficult to imagine that this acting out of a specific collective identity may have wider political repercussions in that it may challenge the educational system of society at large and, more generally, the power relations between church and state, although such challenges were not intended by the religious group in the first place.

In the case of a politicized collective identity, however, group members should intentionally engage, as a mindful and self-conscious collective (or as representatives thereof), in such a power struggle knowing that it is the wider, more inclusive societal context in which this struggle takes place and needs to be orchestrated accordingly. To borrow from Marxian terminology, it is politicized collective identity that turns the social group from "a group of itself" ("Klasse an sich") into "a group of and for itself" ("Klasse an und für sich") in the political arena (see Esser, 1993, p. 116).

Antecedents of Politicized Collective Identity

Our central thesis in this article is that the collective identity of members of a particular group is politicized to the extent that those group members (self-)consciously engage in a power struggle on behalf of their group. We argue that group members need to be mindful of their shared group membership, their common enemy or opponent, and especially the wider societal context that is affected by and affects this power struggle. Awareness of the wider societal context of the power struggle in turn implies the acknowledgment of the role of third parties such as the general public or authorities that politicized group members should try to control, influence, or otherwise enlist for their collective interests.

Politicized collective identity is not an all-or-nothing or on-off phenomenon. Instead, politicization of collective identity and the underlying power struggle unfold as a sequence of politicizing events that gradually transform the group's relationship to its social environment. Typically, this process begins with the awareness of shared grievances. Next, an external enemy is blamed for the group's predicament, and claims for compensation are leveled against this enemy. Unless appropriate compensation is granted, the power struggle continues. If in the course of this struggle the group seeks to win the support of third parties such as more powerful authorities (e.g., the national government) or the general public, collective identity fully politicizes. The attempt to involve these parties in the power struggle inevitably turns the issue into a matter of public or general interest. This final step also results in a transformation of the group's relationship to its social environment because involving a third party implies recognition of society or the larger community (e.g., the city, region, country, or European Union) as a more inclusive in-group membership.

Awareness of shared grievances, adversarial attributions to blame opponents, and the involvement of society by triangulation are, in our view, the three critical ingredients of the process of politicization of collective identity. Accordingly,

we propose that it is possible to capture and organize the most important social psychological antecedents of politicized collective identity in a sequence of three broad consecutive steps or stages proceeding from awareness of shared grievances, through adversarial attributions, to the involvement of society by triangulation. As depicted in Figure 24.1, the conceptual triad of collective identity, power struggle, and societal context discussed in the preceding section provides the theoretical platform on which this sequence unfolds. In the next three subsections, we examine in more detail each of the three steps and how they build on each other. Although we concede that this is an idealized or ideal-typical sequence and that in reality the three stages and the associated processes may often overlap, interact, and feed back on each other, we demonstrate that the suggested succession and the resulting triangular model are of high heuristic value for a systematic understanding of the antecedents of politicized collective identity.

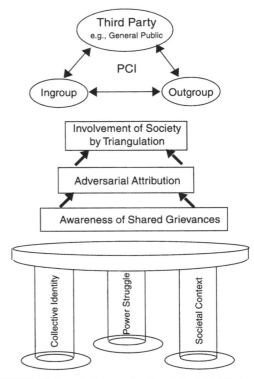

FIGURE 24.1 ■ A Triangular Model of Politicized Collective Identity (PCI)

Awareness of Shared Grievances

A solid body of social psychological theorizing and research suggests that feeling aggrieved as a group is a necessary first step for people to engage in a power struggle on behalf of their group and thus a necessary step toward politicized collective identity (Klandermans, 1997; Lalonde & Cameron, 1994; H. Smith, Spears, & Oyen, 1994; Tajfel & Turner, 1979, 1986; Walker & Pettigrew, 1984; Wright, Taylor, & Moghaddam, 1990). Shared grievances can take on different forms. Klandermans (1997) identified illegitimate inequality, suddenly imposed grievances, and violated principles as important grievances, to which threatened privileges could be added as a fourth type.

Feelings of illegitimate inequality or injustice typically result when social comparisons reveal that one's in-group is worse off than relevant out-groups. In keeping with self-categorization theory (Turner et al., 1987), relevant out-groups are out-groups that are construed at the same level of abstraction as the in-group and nested in the same more inclusive social entity that defines the current frame of reference. This shared higher order group membership (e.g., shared nationality in the case of East and West Germans) not only ensures the comparability of the lower order in-group and out-group but also implies that, by virtue of this commonality, both groups are entitled to equal treatment so that any inequality is likely to be perceived as injustice, at least as long as group members do not embrace legitimizing myths or ideologies (Gamson, 1992; Major, 1994; Sidanius & Pratto, 1999; Wenzel, 2000). The concept of suddenly imposed grievances was proposed by Walsh (1988) in his study of protest in response to the accident in the Three Mile Island nuclear reactor. The discovery of toxic waste in a neighborhood, the announced establishment of an unwanted industry, or the closure of a company can also suddenly impose serious grievances on a group of people (Aarts, 1990; Boender, 1985; Szasz, 1994). Moreover, Kriesi's (1993) work on new social movements in the Netherlands points to the violation of principles or values as an important source of shared grievances. He described how in the Netherlands cultural transformations resulted in the emergence of a new middle class with its specific principles and values (e.g., nonviolent con-flict resolution, egalitarianism, ecological consciousness) and how these changes have fostered the emergence of new social movements, such as the peace movement, the antiapartheid movement, and the environmental movement. It seems reasonable to assume that it was the violation of these "new" principles that led to shared grievances in the form of moral indignation and ultimately to collective protest on the part of many members of the new middle class. Although they are defending very different principles, supporters of the antiabortion movement may in this sense be similar to the supporters of the new social movements because both seem to be aggrieved by a violation of their specific principles. Finally, members of a group can feel aggrieved because they feel their privileges are threatened. The extreme-right Whites in South Africa may be a case in point.

It is important to reiterate that, for collective identity to politicize, these grievances must be experienced as widely shared among in-group members. Collective identity itself should be a facilitating factor here because it fosters homogenization and (self-)stereotyping processes that in turn transform "your" and "my" experiences into "our" experiences (Simon & Hamilton, 1994; Turner et al., 1987). Collective identity thus heightens the awareness of shared grievances. Conversely, shared grievances also reinforce collective identity in that special treatment or events affecting primarily the in-group (e.g., its material living conditions, values, principles, or privileges), but not other groups, enhance the social-contextual fit or salience of "us-them" distinctions (Simon, Pantaleo, & Mummendey, 1995; Turner et al., 1987). The causal relationship between collective identity and awareness of shared grievances is therefore bidirectional.

Adversarial Attributions

Awareness of shared grievances or suffering is not enough to become politicized as a group. As a next step, an external opponent or enemy, such as a specific out-group, an authority, or "the system," must be blamed for the group's predicament (Ferree & Miller, 1985; Major, 1994). Internal attributions of blame (i.e., blaming oneself or the in-group) generate feelings of shame or guilt that may spur individual or collective action to redress the adverse situation (Frijda, Kuipers, & Ter

Schure, 1989; Landman, 1993; Weiner, 1995), but they do not politicize. On the contrary, they usually depoliticize because individual or collective deficiencies are made responsible for one's grievances. Adversarial attributions, however, are a further step on the way to politicization because group members then hold an external opponent responsible and become angry at "them" for what they are doing to "us."

Gupta's (1998) analysis of the predicament of the African American community supports the proposed role of adversarial attributions. He argued that despite widespread grievances among African Americans, the notion of a "common enemy" has been diluted in the post-civil rights era, which in turn undermined collective rebellion. He noted that even the Million Men March of 1995 contributed to this dilution because its main message was not the struggle against the dominant White group as the enemy. Instead, it focused on African Americans' personal responsibilities and thus fostered internal attributions.

As with shared grievances, a bidirectional causal relationship can be assumed between collective identity and adversarial attributions because they tend to reinforce each other. Collective identity fosters (self-)stereotyping processes, and stereotypes provide easy and simple explanations for complex social events (e.g., "Jews are greedy and responsible for our nation's economic problems"; Tajfel, 1981). Thus, stereotypes lend themselves to group-based attributions in general and to in-group-serving attributions in particular, resulting in adversarial attributions from which "we" emerge as the innocent victims or good guys and "they" as the perpetrators or bad guys (Hewstone, 1990; Pettigrew, 1979). Conversely, adversarial attributions to an external enemy or opponent enhance the salience of "us-them" distinctions and thus the salience of collective identity.

Involving Society by Triangulation

A group that shares grievances and holds an external enemy or opponent responsible is likely to demand corrective action or compensation from that opponent. If the opponent complies with such claims, no politicization of collective identity takes place. However, if the claims are refused and the aggrieved group does not give in, the interaction becomes more confrontational, and politicization

continues. This is not to say that increased confrontation as such is responsible for a politicized collective identity. Many fierce intergroup confrontations exist that do not provide the members of the antagonistic groups with a politicized collective identity (e.g., confrontations between fans of competing soccer teams or confrontations between members of different street gangs). Instead, we hold that the collective identity of the members of an aggrieved group who engage in adversarial attributions finally politicizes to the extent that these group members try to transform the confrontation into a more comprehensive power struggle forcing society at large to take sides either with their in-group or with their opponent. This implies that they acknowledge or even stress their identity as a member of that society because only by virtue of their membership in this more inclusive group or community are they entitled to societal support for their claims (Wenzel, 2000). This insight is nicely captured in a recent statement made by the then leader of the parliamentary faction of the German socialist party, Gregor Gysi, who, shortly before his resignation, admonished his party that "[we] have to become part of society—if we want to change it" ("Words of the Week," 2000, p. 2). In a similar manner, Klandermans et al. (1998; see also Roefs et al., 1998) observed that, while their ethnic identity as Afrikaners politicized, supporters of the Freedom Front in South Africa also maintained a strong national identity. In more general terms, politicized collective identity is always also nested identity in that it presupposes identification with the more inclusive social entity that provides the context for shared grievances, adversarial attributions, and the ensuing power struggles for social change (or resistance to such change).

Two less abstract scenarios shall help to illustrate this final step to a politicized collective identity. For instance, university students may become aware of their shared grievances (e.g., high study load for students but insufficient tutoring by professors). They make adversarial attributions for their grievances by blaming professors' selfish preferences for research over teaching. They make claims demanding that their professors devote more time to tutoring them than to doing research or writing books and articles. The interaction between students and professors becomes more confrontational as the latter refuse to comply with their students' claims. The conflict escalates, and the students engage in an open power struggle with their professors in which the students finally organize exam boycotts and public demonstrations. They thus involve society at large. More specifically, they triangulate the conflict by forcing third parties such as the ministry of education, the media, or the general public to take sides.

In another scenario, a conservative group of indigenous inhabitants of a particular country may realize that because of immigration their own values and principles are increasingly questioned as absolute truths and construe this loss of cultural hegemony as shared grievances. They make adversarial attributions by blaming "uncultured aliens" for their grievances and demand that immigrants assimilate "our" culture or stay away from "us." Finally, they triangulate the power struggle by collecting signatures from the general public for a petition against any legislation that would give immigrants equal rights. They thus involve society or the general public as a third party and force it to take sides.

For both scenarios, we would argue that collective identity is not fully politicized until after the last step that triangulates the power struggle by involving society at large, or representatives thereof, as a third party. Moreover, in this last politicizing step, both groups of protagonists acknowledge that their specific collective identity (i.e., as students or conservatives) is part of a more inclusive societal identity, which simultaneously allows and constrains the politicization of their more specific collective identity.

Additional Variables and Possible Extensions

It is important to note that we do not wish to maintain that beyond the variables discussed so far, no other variable may play a (facilitating or inhibitory) role in the politicizing process. On the contrary, we would like to argue that it is a distinctive strength of our ideal-typical model that it enables us to incorporate such additional variables to gain a more systematic understanding of their role in the politicizing process. The role of leaders may be a case in point. Following Reicher and Hopkins (1996a, 1996b), leaders can be understood as "entrepreneurs of identity" that facilitate the various steps of the politicizing process. To the extent that they epitomize the collective "we," they are able to facilitate the propagation of collective frames that help group members to interpret shared grievances, to identify an external enemy, and to define the wider societal context including the third party. This should be so because, by virtue of the shared group membership, the attitudes and actions of the leader are rendered normative for ordinary group members who should feel compelled to follow the leader's example to verify their collective identity (Haslam, 2001).

Group members' social dominance orientation (Sidanius & Pratto, 1999) may be another variable the influence of which can systematically be examined in light of our model of politicized collective identity. We have already indicated that legitimizing myths or ideologies could obstruct, or at least inhibit, the politicizing process. Specifically, hierarchy-enhancing myths can undermine the awareness of shared grievances, foster internal attributions as opposed to external or adversarial attributions, or discourage group members from transforming the in-group/out-group confrontation into a more comprehensive power struggle involving society at large. Research suggests that people high on social dominance orientation are more likely to endorse (hierarchy-enhancing) legitimizing myths than people low on social dominance orientation so that social dominance orientation could play an inhibitory role in the politicizing process. However, research also demonstrates that members of low-status groups are generally lower on social dominance orientation than members of high-status groups (Sidanius & Pratto, 1999). At the same time, given their relatively disadvantaged social position, members of low-status groups typically have more reason to politicize than members of high-status groups. Taken together, it follows that social dominance orientation and legitimizing myths should not be insurmountable obstacles to a politicized collective identity for those who need it most. This is not to say that high-status or privileged groups cannot develop a politicized collective identity. Extreme-right Whites in South Africa are a case in point. As for all groups, the first step to politicized collective identity is awareness of shared grievances, which, for high-status groups, most likely means awareness that their status and the associated privileges are threatened. For high-status groups, the reappraisal of relative status and associated beliefs (including legitimizing myths) should therefore be part and parcel of this politicizing step.

In addition to incorporating other potentially relevant variables, the present model also lends itself to an analysis of politicizing processes that transcend national boundaries. The model was developed primarily with a focus on politicized collective identities that are nested in a more inclusive national identity. In other words, it is the nation that provides the major societal context and thus the arena for the triangulated power struggle. Typical examples are peace activists who confront the federal government and seek the support of the churches in their struggle against nuclear arms or environmental activists who struggle against local airport authorities and try to persuade the federal government to limit the growth of an airport. Other struggles, however, although they also involve politicized collective identities, increasingly transcend national boundaries. The Palestinian–Israeli conflict can serve as an instructive example. In fact, two levels of that conflict may be distinguished, but in each case, our model of politicized collective identity can guide the analysis. First, there is the intergroup relation between the minority of Arab Israelis and the Jewish majority within Israel. Here, the collective identity of the minority politicizes to the extent that Arab Israelis feel oppressed, blame the Jewish majority for it, and attempt to achieve equal treatment as Israeli citizens by involving Israeli society at large (e.g., the general public, the media, the government). Analogously, the collective identity of the Jewish majority begins to politicize when its members feel that their privileges are threatened by the attempted social change. In any case, the state of Israel is the critical political arena, and it is this state, albeit not its Zionist version, in which even the minority claims membership and in which its politicized collective identity is nested. The second level of the conflict involves the larger body of the Palestinian people, and here the power struggle is situated in the international arena. Nevertheless, analogous steps to politicized collective identity can be identified in line with the model presented in this article. Grievances shared by the Palestinian people as a nation are blamed on Israel as the occupying power or external enemy, and the power struggle for or against a Palestinian state is triangulated by involving a third nation as an ally or mediator (e.g., the United States). At the same time, the international community represented, for example, by the United Nations serves as the most inclusive polity in which all protagonists claim membership and in which their respective politicized collective identities (as Palestinians or Israelis) are nested.

Consequences of Politicized Collective Identity

Like all forms of identity, politicized collective identity affects how people perceive the social world and act on and in it. As a specific form of collective identity, politicized collective identity obviously entails many of the consequences identified in social psychological analyses of collective identity in general (for reviews, see Brown & Gaertner, 2001; Oakes et al., 1994). Thus, it should foster (self-) stereotyping processes at the cognitive level, prejudice processes at the affective level, and conformity and discrimination processes at the behavioral level. As many of the politicizing steps or processes discussed above feed back positively on collective identity and strengthen it, the politicization of collective identity should intensify these consequences. For example, when out-groups turn into opponents during the politicization process, group members may be more willing to act on their biased perceptions and evaluations and engage in hostile behavior with the explicit objective of causing their opponents to incur costs (Klandermans, 1997, pp. 156–158; Mummendey & Otten, 1998; H. Weber, 1989). By the same token, politicized collective identity should be particularly well equipped to fulfill the various collective identity functions (i.e., the belongingness, distinctiveness, respect, understanding, and agency functions).[1] In many respects, politicized collective identity is therefore intensified collective identity with quantitatively stronger effects than its nonpoliticized counterpart.

In addition to such general intensification effects, however, we propose that there are also more specific consequences of politicized collective identity. In particular, our conceptualization of politicized collective identity suggests two additional categories of consequences. One category concerns the psychological functions of politicized collective identity. Although, as we noted above, politicized collective identity may generally be superior to other forms of collective identity in fulfilling important psychological functions, more specific predictions can be derived as well. Thus, we hypothesize that this superiority is most marked with respect to the understanding and agency functions. This should be so because the politicization process furthers both reasoning about and acting in and on the social world. Reasoning about the social world is most apparent when group members make adversarial attributions concerning their shared grievances. At that stage, group members' collective self-understanding is sharpened in relation to other groups, and meaning is given to group members' common fate in terms of a shared explanation or ideology (e.g., "We, females, are victims of sexist oppression."). In the social movement literature, this process is often described as consciousness raising (Johnston & Klandermans, 1995). The growing awareness of shared grievances and a clearer idea of who or what is responsible for those grievances reflect a distinct cognitive elaboration of one's worldview providing group members with a meaningful perspective on the social world and their place in it. Further along the politicization process, the agency function is served particularly well by group members' active struggle for social change (or resistance to such change). Even if ultimately unsuccessful or defeated in the triangulated power struggle, having forced society or its representatives to take sides confers recognition as a social agent on group members (e.g., "We made a difference—or at least we tried."). At the same time, their collective self-understanding is further promoted during the power struggle as group members can construe a meaningful role for themselves in the wider societal and historical context, be it as heroes or martyrs.

So far, the understanding and agency functions are underresearched functions of collective identity because social psychological research on intergroup relations has focused more on the role of the belongingness, distinctiveness, and respect functions of collective identity (Brewer & Pickett, 1999; Ellemers, Kortekaas, & Ouwerkerk, 1999; Hogg & Abrams, 1993; Simon, 1999; Tyler & Smith, 1999). This asymmetry directly parallels the relative neglect of politicized collective identity by social psychologists. Both lacunae in the literature thus seem related, and there is therefore hope that an increased interest in politicized collective identity will also shed more light on the understanding and agency functions of collective identity.

The second category of more specific consequences concerns the unique behavioral consequences of politicized collective identity. These behavioral consequences are linked to the role of third parties in our conceptualization of politicized collective identity. We argued that the politicization of collective identity implies that bipolar power struggles between in-group and out-group are triangulated by involving society at large, or representatives thereof, as a third party. Politicized collective identity thus implies a cognitive restructuring of the social environment that is no longer defined exclusively in terms of a bipolar in-group/out-group confrontation. Instead, the social environment is further differentiated into opponents and (potential) allies, which also involves strategic reformulation of the conflict issue such that it also appeals to potential allies (Gerhards & Rucht, 1992; Snow, Rochford, Worden, & Benford, 1986). Politicized collective identity should therefore motivate not only collective action that is aimed at opponents but also attempts to directly or indirectly enlist third parties as allies. For example, politicized group members should be likely to engage in collective action directed at the government or the general public to force them to intervene or to take sides.

Although not specifically designed to test the validity of the conceptualization of politicized collective identity developed in this article, recent research on social movement participation indeed points to the unique explanatory power of politicized collective identity with respect to collective action (Simon et al., 1998; Stürmer & Simon, 2001; Stürmer, Simon, Loewy, Duhme, & Jörger, 2001). This research was conducted in several different social movement contexts, such as the older people's movement in Germany; the fat acceptance movement in Germany and the United States; and the gay movement, again both in the United States and Germany. In addition to the predictor variables typically examined in traditional social movement research (i.e., perceived individual and collective costs and benefits of participation), indicators of collective identification processes were also included as predictor variables. More specifically, two levels of collective identity were considered. One concerned the broader social categories from which the social movements in question typically recruit their members (i.e., older people, fat people, and gay people), whereas the other targeted the more politicized social movements themselves or their specific organizations (i.e., the Gray Panthers, the fat acceptance movement, and the gay movement). Intention to participate as well as actual participation in collective action directed primarily at the general public or the government (e.g., public campaigns and demonstrations, sit-ins, and other forms of civil disobedience) served as the main dependent variable or criterion. Multiple regression analyses revealed that identification with the broader recruitment category made no unique contribution to the prediction of behavioral intentions or actual participation, whereas identification with the more politicized social movement organization had a reliable and unique (positive) effect in all cases (with one exception discussed below). In addition to correlational data from cross-sectional designs, data from experimental and longitudinal designs further corroborated the causal role in social movement participation of the more politicized form of collective identity (Simon et al., 1998; Stürmer & Simon, 2001).

However, this longitudinal research also demonstrated that collective identity at the level of the broader recruitment category, which was ineffective as a unique predictor of collective action in prior research, can politicize under the appropriate conditions to such an extent that it also reliably predicts collective action (Stürmer & Simon, 2001). More specifically, gay respondents' identification with gay people in general did not predict (self-reported) participation in collective action organized by the German gay and lesbian movement in the following year. Interestingly, more than 2 years after the identification measurement, the German gay and lesbian movement started an initiative requesting legislation to allow same-sex marriage. As this initiative encountered fierce opposition from the conservative political parties in Germany, the movement launched a public campaign in support of same-sex marriage. Stürmer and Simon (2001) reasoned that this climate would promote a general politicization of gay identity and therefore conducted follow-up telephone interviews with former respondents and recorded their (self-reported) participation in collective action organized in support of the campaign for same-sex marriage. As expected, identification with gay people measured almost 3 years before

the telephone interviews now reliably predicted movement participation.

In addition to action aimed directly at a third party such as the general public or the government, politicized collective identity should also motivate strategic action that appears to target an immediate out-group or antagonist but that can meaningfully be understood only if its intended indirect effect on the third party is taken into account. Many social movement activities provide illustrative examples. Although militant civil rights activists have often selected their segregationist or racist opponents (e.g., all-White schools or companies) as immediate targets of their disruptive collective actions, the strategic or ultimate goal of such actions was obviously to provoke the attention of and intervention by third parties such as the general public, the media, or the federal government (McAdam, 1982). Moreover, in such scenarios, politicized group members not only plan and strategically implement their own behavior to involve a third party and to force it to take sides, they may also intentionally provoke and instrumentalize the reaction of the immediate target for the same purposes. Thus, striking workers can deliberately provoke an overreaction from their employers to induce the government to intervene or the general public to take sides with the workers. In a similar manner, protesters can provoke police brutality to win the support of the general public. In more extreme cases such as terrorism, activists have even tried to provoke authorities (e.g., the police or the government) to engage in oppressive action or legislation, hoping that such oppression will generate anger and solidarity on the part of potential allies or the general public.

In conclusion, the important point is that politicized collective identity is likely to motivate actions aimed both directly and indirectly at a third party that easily evade our analysis if we rely exclusively on a nonpoliticized conceptualization of collective identity limited to bipolar in-group/out-group relations. As the above examples illustrate, we would even be unable to adequately understand many seemingly simple in-group/out-group interactions because they often contain a critical strategic component, the meaning of which becomes accessible only if the analytical context is extended to include third parties. Finally, the reactions of third parties must remain a conundrum as long as we do not analyze their antecedents in the context of politicized collective identity. It is therefore the concept of politicized collective identity that directs intergroup researchers' attention to a number of unique behavioral phenomena and that provides a refined perspective for a better understanding of the complexities of intergroup behavior.

Conclusion and Future Directions

The aim of this article was to contribute to a social psychological analysis of politicized collective identity. We suggested that a stable theoretical platform on which such an analysis can be erected rests on three critical pillars (see Figure 24.1). These are collective identity, the struggle for power, and the wider societal context of that power struggle. On the basis of that platform, we proposed that people evince politicized collective identity to the extent that they engage as self-conscious group members in a power struggle on behalf of their group knowing that it is the wider, more inclusive societal context in which this struggle has to be fought out. We further suggested that politicized collective identity unfolds through a sequence of antecedent processes or stages. In an attempt to sketch an ideal-typical sequence, we distinguished and elaborated on three stages of the politicization process, namely, awareness of shared grievances; adversarial attributions; and involvement of society at large, or representatives thereof, as a third party in addition to the immediate outgroup or opponent. The politicization sequence thus culminates in a triangulation of the power struggle, and it is this stage in which politicized collective identity is expected to be in full blossom.

Finally, we pointed out that this triangular model immediately lends itself to the prediction of important consequences of politicized collective identity. For example, because the politicization process tends to reinforce collective identity, politicized collective identity often has qualitatively similar, but more intense, effects than collective identity in general. Moreover, our model led us to predict that politicized collective identity should be particularly well equipped to fulfill certain psychological functions for the group member, namely, to provide him or her with a meaningful framework to understand his or her social world as well as with the feeling of being an efficacious social agent. Perhaps most interesting, we

were also able to deduce predictions concerning unique behavioral consequences that most clearly differentiate politicized collective identity from other forms of collective identity. These predictions revolve around the actions directly or indirectly (strategically) aimed at the third party that becomes involved in the power struggle during the politicization process (as well as around the reactions of that third party).

In concluding this article, we need to emphasize again that it is not, nor was it intended to be, a review of the extant theoretical and empirical work on collective identity as it relates to political behavior. Such attempts are equally worthwhile and have appeared elsewhere (e.g., Huddy, 2001; Stryker, Owens, & White, 2000). They are an important complement to the present article that puts forward a new theoretical perspective on politicized collective identity in general and on the process of its politicization in particular. This perspective is rooted in, and grew out of, an articulation of our work on the social psychology of self and identity, intergroup relations, and social movements (Klandermans, 1997; Simon, 1998a, 1999). It draws explicitly and often also implicitly on other scholars' work on social psychological processes and phenomena that play an important role as antecedents or constituents of politicized collective identity (e.g., identity, self-categorization, perceived justice, causal attribution, power). Naturally, we have not been able to fully discuss the intricacies of these processes or phenomena, which are all highly interesting and important social psychological topics in their own right. Such a heroic deed was fortunately not necessary in the present context because excellent discussions of those topics already exist elsewhere (e.g., Hewstone, 1989; Ng, 1980; Oakes et al., 1994; Turner et al., 1987; Tyler & Smith, 1999).

We thus hope that the model of politicized collective identity presented in this article proves useful in generating a fruitful scientific debate about the conceptualization, antecedents, and consequences of politicized collective identity. We are especially confident that it will help to explore several promising new directions of empirical research. In particular, we hope that future empirical research will be devoted to a careful scrutiny of the hypothesized process of politicization, its various stages and the suggested sequence, the specific psychological functions of politicized collective identity for the individual group member, and the unique behavioral consequences of politicized collective identity with particular emphasis on strategic collective action in triangulated social contexts.

NOTE

1. This assumption does not imply that politicized collective identity necessarily is a very prevalent form of collective identity. Politicization is an effortful process that also entails numerous costs for the individual group member (e.g., opportunity costs, victimization by discrimination and oppression) so that, overall, politicized collective identity may often not be the most attractive option.

REFERENCES

Aarts, C. W. M. A. (1990). *Bodemverontreiniging en collectieve actie* [Soil pollution and collective action]. Unpublished doctoral dissertation, University of Twente, Enschede, the Netherlands.

Baumeister, R. F., & Leary, M. R. (1995). The need to belong: Desire for interpersonal attachments as a fundamental human motivation. *Psychological Bulletin, 117,* 497–529.

Boender, K. (1985). *Sociologische Analyse van Milieusolidariteit onder Elites en Publiek* [Sociological analysis of environmental solidarity among elites and the general public]. Rijswijk, the Netherlands: Sythoff Pers.

Brewer, M. B. (1991). The social self: On being the same and different at the same time. *Personality and Social Psychology Bulletin, 17,* 475–482.

Brewer, M. B., & Pickett, C. L. (1999). Distinctiveness motives as a source of the social self. In T. R. Tyler, R. M. Kramer, & O. P. John (Eds.), *The psychology of the social self* (pp. 71–87). Mahwah, NJ: Erlbaum.

Brown, R. (1995). *Prejudice: its social psychology.* Oxford, England: Blackwell.

Brown, R., & Gaertner, S. (Eds.). (2001). *Blackwell handbook in social psychology: Intergroup processes* (Vol. 4). Oxford, England: Blackwell.

Cross, W. E. (1995). In search of Blackness and Afrocentricity: The psychology of Black identity change. In H. W. Harris, H. C. Blue, & E. E. H. Griffith (Eds.), *Racial and ethnic identity: Psychological development and creative expression* (pp. 53–72). New York: Routledge.

Dépret, E. F., & Fiske, S. T. (1993). Social cognition and power: Some cognitive consequences of social structure as a source of control deprivation. In G. Weary, F. Gleicher, & K. Marsh (Eds.), *Control motivation and social cognition* (pp. 176–202). New York: Springer-Verlag.

De Weerd, M., & Klandermans, B. (1999). Group identification and social protest: Farmers' protest in the Netherlands. *European Journal of Social Psychology, 29,* 1073–1095.

Durkheim, E. (1976). *Die Regeln der soziologischen Methode* [The rule of the sociological method] (5th ed.). Darmstadt, Germany: Luchterhand. (Original work published 1895)

Ellemers, N. (1993). The influence of socio-structural variables on identity management strategies. In W. Stroebe & M. Hewstone (Eds.), *European review of social psychology* (Vol. 4, pp. 27–57). Chichester, England: Wiley.

Ellemers, N., Kortekaas, P., & Ouwerkerk, J. W. (1999). Self-categorization, commitment to the group and group self-esteem as related but distinct aspects of social identity. *European Journal of Social Psychology, 29,* 371–389.

Esser, H. (1993). *Soziologie—Allgemeine Grundlagen* [Sociology—General foundations]. Frankfurt/Main, Germany: Campus.

Farley, J. (1982). *Majority–minority relations.* Englewood, NJ: Prentice Hall.

Ferree, M. M., & Miller, F. D. (1985). Mobilization and meaning: Toward an integration of social psychological and resource perspectives on social movements. *Sociology Inquiry, 55,* 38–61.

Fiske, S. T. (1993). Controlling other people: The impact of power on stereotyping. *American Psychologist, 48,* 621–628.

Fiske, S. T. (2000). Stereotyping, prejudice, and discrimination at the seam between the centuries: Evolution, culture, mind, and brain. *European Journal of Social Psychology, 30,* 299–322.

French, J. R. P., & Raven, B. (1959). The bases of social power. In D. Cartwright (Ed.), *Studies in social power* (pp. 150–167). Ann Arbor, MI: Institute for Social Research.

Frijda, N. H., Kuipers, P., & Ter Schure, E. (1989). Relations among emotions, appraisal, and emotional readiness. *Journal of Personality and Social Psychology, 57,* 212–228.

Gamson, W. A. (1992). *Talking politics.* Cambridge, England: Cambridge University Press.

Gerhards, J., & Rucht, D. (1992). Mesomobilization: Organizing and framing in two protest campaigns in West Germany. *American Journal of Sociology, 98,* 555–596.

Goodin, R. E., & Klingemann, H.-D. (1996). Political science: The discipline. In R. E. Goodin & H.-D. Klingemann (Eds.), *A new handbook of political science* (pp. 3–49). Oxford, England: Oxford University Press.

Gupta, D. K. (1998). Ethnicity and politics in the US: The predicament of the African-American minority. *Ethnic Studies Report, 16,* 215–254.

Haslam, S. A. (2001). *Psychology in organizations: The social identity approach.* London: Sage.

Hewstone, M. (1989). *Causal attribution: From cognitive processes to collective beliefs.* Oxford, England: Blackwell.

Hewstone, M. (1990). The "ultimate attribution error." A review of the literature on intergroup causal attribution. *European Journal of Social Psychology, 20,* 311–335.

Hogg, M. A., & Abrams, D. (Eds.). (1993). *Group motivation: Social psychology perspectives.* Hemel Hempstead, England: Harvester Wheatsheaf.

Huddy, L. (2001). From social to political identity: A critical examination of social identity theory. *Political Psychology, 22,* 127–156.

Johnston, H., & Klandermans, B. (1995). The cultural analysis of social movements. In H. Johnston & B. Klandermans (Eds.), *Social movement and culture* (pp. 3–24). Minneapolis: University of Minnesota Press.

Jones, J. R. (1972). *Prejudice and racism.* Reading, MA: Addison-Wesley.

Klandermans, B. (1997). *The social psychology of protest.* Oxford. England: Basil Blackwell.

Klandermans, B. (2000). Identity and protest: How group identification helps to overcome collective action dilemmas. In M. van Vugt, M. Snyder, T. Tyler, & A. Biehl (Eds.), *Col-*

lective helping in modern society (pp. 162–183). London: Routledge.

Klandermans, B., Roefs, M., & Olivier, J. (1998). A movement takes office. In D. S. Meyer & S. Tarrow (Eds.), *The social movement society: Contentious politics for a century* (pp. 173–194). Lanham, MD: Rowman & Littlefield.

Kriesi, H. (1993). *Political mobilization and social change: The Dutch case in comparative perspective.* Aldershot, England: Avebury.

Lalonde, R. N., & Cameron, J. E. (1994). Behavioral responses to discrimination: A focus on action. In M. P. Zanna & J. M. Olson (Eds.). *The psychology of prejudice: The Ontario symposium* (Vol. 7, pp. 257–288). Hillsdale, NJ: Erlbaum.

Landman, J. (1993). *Regret: The persistence of the possible.* New York: Oxford University Press.

Luhtanen, R., & Crocker, J. (1992). A collective self-esteem scale: Self-evaluation of one's social identity. *Personality and Social Psychology Bulletin, 18,* 302–318.

Major, B. (1994). From social inequality to personal entitlement: The role of social comparisons, legitimacy appraisals, and group membership. In M. P. Zanna (Ed.), *Advances in experimental social psychology* (Vol. 26, pp. 293–355). San Diego, CA: Academic Press.

Markus, H., & Kunda, Z. (1986). Stability and malleability of the self-concept. *Journal of Personality and Social Psychology, 51,* 858–866.

Maslow, A. H. (1970). *Motivation and personality.* New York: Harper & Row.

McAdam, D. (1982). *Political process and the development of Black insurgency.* Chicago: University of Chicago Press.

McAdams, D. P. (1997). The case for unity in the (post)modern self. In R. D. Ashmore & L. Jussim (Eds.), *Self and identity* (pp. 46–78). Oxford, England: Oxford University Press.

Moscovici, S. (1976). *Social influence and social change.* London: Academic Press.

Moscovici, S., Mucchi-Faina, A., & Maass, A. (Eds.). (1994). *Minority influence.* Chicago: Nelson-Hall.

Mugny, G. (1982). *The power of minorities.* London: Academic Press.

Mummendey, A., & Otten, S. (1998). Positive-negative asymmetry in social discrimination. In W. Stroebe & M. Hewstone (Eds.), *European review of social psychology* (Vol. 9, pp. 107–143). Chichester, England: Wiley.

Mummendey, A., & Wenzel, M. (1999). Social discrimination and tolerance in intergroup relations: Reactions to intergroup difference. *Personality and Social Psychology Review, 3,* 158–174.

Ng. S. H. (1980). *The social psychology of power.* London: Academic Press.

Ng. S. H. (1982). Power and intergroup discrimination. In H. Tajfel (Ed.), *Social identity and intergroup relations* (pp. 179–206). Cambridge, England: Cambridge University Press.

Oakes, P. J., Haslam, S. A., & Turner, J. C. (1994). *Stereotyping and social reality.* Oxford, England: Blackwell.

Pettigrew, T. F. (1979). The ultimate attribution error: Extending Allport's cognitive analysis of prejudice. *Personality and Social Psychology Bulletin, 5,* 461–476.

Reicher, S. D. (1995). Three dimensions of the social self. In A. Oosterwegel & R. A. Wicklund (Eds.), *The self in European and North American culture: Development and processes* (pp. 277–290). Dordrecht, the Netherlands: Kluwer Academic.

Reicher, S. D., & Hopkins, N. (1996a). Seeking influence through characterising self-categories: An analysis of anti-abortionist rhetoric. *British Journal of Social Psychology, 35,* 297–311.

Reicher, S. D., & Hopkins, N. (1996b). Self-category constructions in political rhetoric: An analysis of Thatcher's and Kinnock's speeches concerning the British miners' strike (1984–5). *European Journal of Social Psychology, 26,* 353–372.

Roefs, M., Klandermans, B., & Olivier, J. (1998). Protest intentions on the eve of South Africa's first nonracial elections: Optimists look beyond injustice. *Mobilization, 3,* 51–68.

Rucht, D. (1995). Kollektive Identität: Konzeptuelle Überlegungen zu einem Desiderat der Bewegungsforschung [Collective identity: Some conceptual considerations on a lacuna of social movement research]. *Forschungsjournal Neue Soziale Bewegungen, 8*(1), 9–23.

Sachdev, I., & Bourhis, R. Y. (1985). Social categorization and power differentials in group relations. *European Journal of Social Psychology, 15,* 415–434.

Sachdev, I., & Bourhis, R. Y. (1991). Power and status differentials in minority and majority group relations. *European Journal of Social Psychology, 21,* 1–24.

Sherman, J. S., Judd, C. M., & Park, B. (1989). Social cognition. *Annual Review of Psychology, 40,* 281–326.

Sidanius, J., & Pratto, F. (1999). *An intergroup theory of social hierarchy and oppression.* New York: Cambridge University Press.

Simon, B. (1997). Self and group in modern society: Ten theses on the individual self and the collective self. In R. Spears, P. J. Oakes, N. Ellemers, & S. A. Haslam (Eds.), *The social psychology of stereotyping and group life* (pp. 318–335). Oxford, England: Blackwell.

Simon, B. (1998a). Individuals, groups, and social change: On the relationship between individual and collective self-interpretations and collective action. In C. Sedikides, J. Schopler, & C. Insko (Eds.), *Intergroup cognition and intergroup behavior* (pp. 257–282). Mahwah, NJ: Erlbaum.

Simon, B. (1998b). The self in minority–majority contexts. In W. Stroebe & M. Hewstone (Eds.), *European review of social psychology* (Vol. 9, pp. 1–31). Chichester, England: Wiley.

Simon, B. (1999). A place in the world: Self and social categorization. In T. R. Tyler, R. M. Kramer, & O. P. John (Eds.), *The psychology of the social self* (pp. 47–69). Mahwah, NJ: Erlbaum.

Simon, B., Aufderheide, B., & Kampmeier, C. (2001). The social psychology of minority-majority relations. In R. Brown & S. Gaertner (Eds.), *Blackwell handbook in social psychology: Intergroup processes* (Vol. 4, pp. 303–323). Oxford, England: Blackwell.

Simon, B., & Hamilton, D. L. (1994). Self-stereotyping and social context: The effects of relative in-group size and in-group status. *Journal of Personality and Social Psychology, 66,* 699–711.

Simon, B., Loewy, M., Stürmer, S., Weber, U., Freytag, P., Habig, C., Kampmeier, C., & Spahlinger, P. (1998). Collective identification and social movement participation. *Journal of Personality and Social Psychology, 74,* 646–658.

Simon, B., Pantaleo, G., & Mummendey, A. (1995). Unique individual or interchangeable group member? The accentuation of intragroup differences versus similarities as an indicator of the individual self versus the collective self. *Journal of Personality and Social Psychology, 69,* 106–119.

Smith, E. R., & Mackie, D. M. (1995). *Social psychology.* New York: Worth.

Smith, H., Spears, R., & Oyen, M. (1994). "People like us": The influence of personal deprivation and group membership salience on justice evaluations. *Journal of Experimental Social Psychology, 30,* 277–299.

Snow, D. A., Rochford, B. E., Worden, S. K., & Benford, R. D. (1986). Frame alignment processes, micromobilization, and movement participation. *American Sociological Review, 51,* 464–481.

Stryker, S., Owens, T., & White, R. (Eds.). (2000). *Self, identity, and social movements.* Minneapolis: University of Minnesota Press.

Stürmer, S., & Simon, B. (2001). *Collective identity and social movement participation: A longitudinal test of the dual-pathway model.* Manuscript in preparation.

Stürmer, S., Simon, B., Loewy, M., Duhme, M., & Jörger, H. (2001). *The dual-pathway model of social movement participation: The case of the fat acceptance movement.* Unpublished manuscript, University of Kiel, Kiel, Germany.

Szasz, A. (1994). *EcoPopulism: Toxic waste and the movement for environmental justice.* Minneapolis: University of Minnesota Press.

Tajfel, H. (Ed.). (1978). *Differentiation between social groups.* London: Academic Press.

Tajfel, H. (1981). *Human groups and social categories: Studies in social psychology.* Cambridge, England: Cambridge University Press.

Tajfel, H., & Turner, J. C. (1979). An integrative theory of intergroup conflict. In W. G. Austin & S. Worchel (Eds.), *The social psychology of intergroup relations* (pp. 33–47). Monterey, CA: Brooks/Cole.

Tajfel, H., & Turner, J. C. (1986). The social identity theory of intergroup behavior. In S. Worchel & W. G. Austin (Eds.), *Psychology of intergroup relations* (pp. 7–24). Chicago: Nelson-Hall.

Turner, J. C. (1991). *Social influence.* Pacific Grove, CA: Brooks/Cole.

Turner, J. C., Hogg, M. A., Oakes, P. J., Reicher, S. D., & Wetherell, M. S. (1987). *Rediscovering the social group: A self-categorization theory.* Oxford, England: Basil Blackwell.

Turner, J. C., & Onorato, R. S. (1999). Social identity, personality, and the self-concept: A self-categorization perspective. In T. R. Tyler, R. M. Kramer, & O. P. John (Eds.), *The psychology of the social self* (pp. 11–46). Mahwah, NJ: Erlbaum.

Tyler, T. R., & Smith, H. J. (1999). Justice, social identity, and group processes. In T. R. Tyler, R. M. Kramer, & O. P. John (Eds.), *The psychology of the social self* (pp. 223–264). Mahwah, NJ: Erlbaum.

Wagner, U., Lampen, L., & Syllwasschy, J. (1986). Ingroup inferiority, social identity and outgroup devaluation in a modified minimal group. *British Journal of Social Psychology, 25,* 15–24.

Walker, I., & Pettigrew, T. F. (1984). Relative deprivation theory: An overview and conceptual critique. *British Journal of Social Psychology, 23,* 303–310.

Walsh, E. J. (1988). *Democracy in the shadows: Citizen mobilization in the wake of the accident at Three Mile Island.* Westport, CT: Greenwood Press.

Weber, H. (1989). Conflict in interorganizational systems: On the logic of conflict of trade unions and employers' associations in the 1984 metal strike in West Germany. In B. Klandermans (Ed.), *International social movement research: Vol. 2. Organizing for change: Social movement organizations in Europe and the United States* (pp. 363–382). Greenwich, CT: JAI Press.

Weber, M. (1919). Politik als Beruf [Politics as profession]. In H. Baier, M. R. Lepsius, W. J. Mommsen, W. Schluchter, & J. Winckelmann (Eds.), *Max Weber Gesamtausgabe* (pp. 113–252). Tübingen, Germany: Mohr.

Weiner, B. (1995). *Judgements of responsibility: A foundation for a theory of shame, guilt, embarrassment, and pride.* New York: Guilford Press.

Wenzel, M. (2000). Justice and identity: The significance of inclusion for perceptions of entitlement and the justice motive. *Personality and Social Psychology Bulletin, 26,* 157–176.

Words of the Week. (2000, April 13). *Die Zeit,* p. 2.

Wright, S. C., Taylor, D. M., & Moghaddam, F. M. (1990). Responding to membership in a disadvantaged group: From acceptance to collective protest. *Journal of Personality and Social Psychology, 58,* 994–1003.

Appendix: How to Read a Journal Article in Social Psychology

Christian H. Jordan and Mark P. Zanna • University of Waterloo

When approaching a journal article for the first time, and often on subsequent occasions, most people try to digest it as they would any piece of prose. They start at the beginning and read word for word, until eventually they arrive at the end, perhaps a little bewildered, but with a vague sense of relief. This is not an altogether terrible strategy; journal articles do have a logical structure that lends itself to this sort of reading. There are, however, more efficient approaches—approaches that enable you, a student of social psychology, to cut through peripheral details, avoid sophisticated statistics with which you may not be familiar, and focus on the central ideas in an article. Arming yourself with a little foreknowledge of what is contained in journal articles, as well as some practical advice on how to read them, should help you read journal articles more effectively. If this sounds tempting, read on.

Journal articles offer a window into the inner workings of social psychology. They document how social psychologists formulate hypotheses, design empirical studies, analyze the observations they collect, and interpret their results. Journal articles also serve an invaluable archival function: They contain the full store of common and cumulative knowledge of social psychology. Having documentation of past research allows researchers to build on past findings and advance our understanding of social behavior, without pursuing avenues of investigation that have already been explored. Perhaps most importantly, a research study is never complete until its results have been shared with others, colleagues and students alike. Journal articles are a primary means of communicating research findings. As such, they can be genuinely exciting and interesting to read.

That last claim may have caught you off guard. For beginning readers, journal articles may seem anything but interesting and exciting. They may, on the contrary, appear daunting and esoteric, laden with jargon and obscured by menacing statistics. Recognizing this fact, we hope to arm you, through this chapter, with the basic information you will need to read journal articles with a greater sense of comfort and perspective.

Social psychologists study many fascinating topics, ranging from prejudice and discrimination, to culture, persuasion, liking and love, conformity and obedience, aggression, and the self. In our daily lives, these are issues we often struggle to understand. Social psychologists present systematic observations of, as well as a wealth of ideas about, such issues in journal articles. It would be a shame if the fascination and intrigue these topics have were lost in their translation into journal publications. We don't think they are, and by the end of this chapter, we hope, you won't either.

Journal articles come in a variety of forms, including research reports, review articles, and theoretical articles. Put briefly, a *research report* is a formal presentation of an original research study, or series of studies. A *review article* is an evaluative survey of previously published work, usually organized by a guiding theory or point of view. The author of a review article summarizes previous investigations of a circumscribed problem, comments on what progress has been made toward its resolution, and suggests areas of the problem that require further study. A *theoretical article* also evaluates past research, but focuses on the development of theories used to explain empirical findings. Here, the author may present a new theory to explain a set of findings, or may compare and contrast a set of competing theories, suggesting why one theory might be the superior one.

This chapter focuses primarily on how to read research reports, for several reasons. First, the bulk of published literature in social psychology consists of research reports. Second, the summaries presented in review articles, and the ideas set forth in theoretical articles, are built on findings presented in research reports. To get a deep understanding of how research is done in social psychology, fluency in reading original research reports is essential. Moreover, theoretical articles frequently report new studies that pit one theory against another, or test a novel prediction derived from a new theory. In order to appraise the validity of such theoretical contentions, a grounded understanding of basic findings is invaluable. Finally, most research reports are written in a standard format that is likely unfamiliar to new readers. The format of review and theoretical articles is less standardized, and more like that of textbooks and other scholarly writings, with which most readers are familiar. This is not to suggest that such articles are easier to read and comprehend than research reports; they can be quite challenging indeed. It is simply the case that because more rules apply to the writing of research reports, more guidelines can be offered on how to read them.

The Anatomy of Research Reports

Most research reports in social psychology, and in psychology in general, are written in a standard format prescribed by the American Psychological Association (1994). This is a great boon to both readers and writers. It allows writers to present their ideas and findings in a clear, systematic manner. Consequently, as a reader, once you understand this format, you will not be on completely foreign ground when you approach a new research report— regardless of its specific content. You will know where in the paper particular information is found, making it easier to locate. No matter what your reasons for reading a research report, a firm understanding of the format in which they are written will ease your task. We discuss the format of research reports next, with some practical suggestions on how to read them. Later, we discuss how this format reflects the process of scientific investigation, illustrating how research reports have a coherent narrative structure.

TITLE AND ABSTRACT

Alhough you can't judge a book by its cover, you can learn a lot about a research report simply by reading its title. The title presents a concise statement of the theoretical issues investigated and/or the variables that were studied. For example, the following title was taken almost at random from a prestigious journal in social psychology: "Sad and Guilty? Affective Influences on the Explanation of Conflict in Close Relationships" (Forgas, 1994, p. 56). Just by reading the title, it can be inferred that the study investigated how emotional states change the way people explain conflict in close relationships. The title also suggests that when feeling sad, people accept more personal blame for such conflicts (i.e., feel more guilty).

The abstract is also an invaluable source of information. It is a brief synopsis of the study and packs a lot of information into 150 words or less. The abstract contains information about the problem that was investigated, how it was investigated, and the major findings of the study, and hints at the theoretical and practical implications of the findings. Thus, the abstract is a useful summary of the research that provides the gist of the investigation. Reading this outline first can be very helpful, because it tells you where the report is going and gives you a useful framework for organizing information contained in the article.

The title and abstract of a research report are like a movie preview. A movie preview highlights the important aspects of a movie's plot, and provides just enough information for one to decide whether to watch the whole movie. Just so with titles and abstracts: They highlight the key features of a research report to allow you to decide if you want to read the whole paper. And just as with movie previews, they do not give the whole story. Reading just the title and abstract is never enough to fully understand a research report.

INTRODUCTION

A research report has four main sections: Introduction, Method, Results, and Discussion. Though it is not explicitly labeled, the introduction begins the main body of a research report. Here, the researchers set the stage for the study. They present the problem under investigation, and state why it was important to study. By providing a brief review of past research and theory relevant to the central issue of investigation, the researchers place the study in an historical context and suggest how the study advances knowledge of the problem. Beginning with broad theoretical and practical considerations, the researchers delineate the rationale that led them to the specific set of hypotheses tested in the study. They also describe how they decided on their research strategy (e.g., why they chose an experiment or a correlational study).

The introduction generally begins with a broad consideration of the problem investigated. Here, the researchers want to illustrate that the problem they studied is a real problem about which people should care. If the researchers are studying prejudice, they may cite statistics that suggest discrimination is prevalent, or describe specific cases of discrimination. Such information helps illustrate why the research is both practically and theoretically meaningful, and why you should bother reading about it. Such discussions are often quite interesting and useful. They can help you decide for yourself if the research has merit. But they may not be essential for understanding the study at hand. Read the introduction carefully, but choose judiciously what to focus on and remember. To understand a study, what you really need to understand is what the researchers' hypotheses were, and how they were derived from theory, informal observation, or intuition. Other background information may be intriguing, but may not be critical to understand what the researchers did and why they did it.

While reading the introduction, try answering these questions: What problem was studied, and why? How does this study relate to, and go beyond, past investigations of the problem? How did the researchers derive their hypotheses? What questions do the researchers hope to answer with this study?

METHOD

In the Method section, the researchers translate their hypotheses into a set of specific, testable questions. Here, the researchers introduce the main characters of the study—the subjects or participants—describing their characteristics (gender, age, etc.) and how many of them were involved. Then they describe the materials (or apparatus), such as any questionnaires or special equipment, used in the study. Finally, they describe chronologically the procedures of the study—that is, how the study was conducted. Often, an overview of the research design will begin the Method section. This overview provides a broad outline of the design, alerting you to what you should attend.

The method is presented in great detail so that other researchers can recreate the study to confirm (or question) its results. This degree of detail is normally not necessary to understand a study, so don't get bogged down trying to memorize the particulars of the procedures. Focus on how the independent variables were manipulated (or measured) and how the dependent variables were measured.

Measuring variables adequately is not always an easy matter. Many of the variables psychologists are interested in cannot be directly observed, so they must be inferred from participants' behavior. Happiness, for example, cannot be directly observed. Thus, researchers interested in how being happy influences people's judgments must infer happiness (or its absence) from their behavior—perhaps by asking people how happy they are, and judging their degree of happiness from their responses; perhaps by studying people's facial expressions for signs of happiness, such as smiling. Think about the measures researchers use while reading the Method section. Do they adequately reflect or capture the concepts they are meant to measure? If a measure seems odd, consider carefully how the researchers justify its use.

Often in social psychology, getting there is half the fun. In other words, how a result is obtained can be just as interesting as the result itself. Social psychologists often strive to have participants behave in a natural, spontaneous manner, while controlling enough of their environment to pinpoint the causes of their behavior. Sometimes the major contribution of a research report is its presentation of a novel method of investigation. When this is the case, the method will be discussed in some detail in the introduction.

Participants in social psychology studies are intelligent and inquisitive people who are responsive to what happens around them. Because of this, they are not always initially told the true purpose of a study. If they were told, they might not act naturally. Thus, researchers frequently need to be creative, presenting a credible rationale for complying with procedures, without revealing the study's purpose. This rationale is known as a *cover story,* and is often an elaborate scenario. While reading the method section, try putting yourself in the shoes of a participant in the study, and ask yourself if the instructions given to participants seem sensible, realistic, and engaging. Imagining what it was like to be in the study will also help you remember the study's procedure and will aid you in interpreting the study's results.

While reading the method section, try answering these questions: How were the hypotheses translated into testable questions? How were the variables of interest manipulated and/or measured? Did the measures used adequately reflect the variables of interest? For example, is self-reported income an adequate measure of social class? Why or why not?

RESULTS

The results section describes how the observations collected were analyzed to determine whether the original hypotheses were supported. Here, the data (observations of behavior) are described, and statistical tests are presented. Because of this, the Results section is often intimidating to readers who have little or no training in statistics. Wading through complex and unfamiliar statistical analyses is understandably confusing and frustrating. As a result, many students are tempted to skip over reading this section. We advise you not to do so. Empirical findings are the foundation of any science and Results sections are where such findings are presented.

Take heart. Even the most prestigious researchers were once in your shoes and sympathize with you. Though space in psychology journals is limited, researchers try to strike a balance between the need to be clear and the need to be brief in describing their results. In an influential paper on how to write good research reports, Bem (1987) offered this advice to researchers:

> No matter how technical or abstruse your article is in its particulars, intelligent nonpsychologists with no expertise in statistics or experimental design should be able to comprehend the broad outlines of what you did and why. They should understand in general terms what was learned. (p. 74)

Generally speaking, social psychologists try to practice this advice.

Most statistical analyses presented in research reports test specific hypotheses. Often, each analysis presented is preceded by a reminder of the hypothesis it is meant to test. After an analysis is presented, researchers usually provide a narrative description of the result in plain English. When the hypothesis tested by a statistical analysis is not explicitly stated, you can usually determine the hypothesis that was tested by reading this narrative description of the result, and referring back to the introduction to locate an hypothesis that corresponds to that result. After even the most complex statistical analysis, there will be a written description of what the result means conceptually. Turn your attention to these descriptions. Focus on the conceptual meaning of research findings, not on the mechanics of how they were obtained (unless you're comfortable with statistics).

Aside from statistical tests and narrative descriptions of results, Results sections also frequently contain tables and graphs. These are efficient summaries of data. Even if you are not familiar with statistics, look closely at tables and graphs, and pay attention to the means or correlations presented in them. Researchers always include written descriptions of the pertinent aspects of tables and graphs. While reading these descriptions, check the tables and graphs to make sure what the researchers say accurately reflects their data. If they say there was a difference between two groups on a particular dependent measure, look at the means in the table that correspond to those two groups, and see if the means do differ as described. Occasionally, results seem to become stronger in their narrative description than an examination of the data would warrant.

Statistics *can* be misused. When they are, results are difficult to interpret. Having said this, a lack of statistical knowledge should not make you overly cautious while reading results sections. Though not a perfect antidote, journal articles undergo extensive review by professional researchers before publication. Thus, most misapplications of statistics are caught and corrected before an article is published. So, if you are unfamiliar with statistics, you can be reasonably confident that findings are accurately reported.

While reading the results section, try answering these questions: Did the researchers provide evidence that any independent variable manipulations were effective? For example, if testing for behavioral differences between happy and sad participants, did the researchers demonstrate that one group was in fact happier than the other? What were the major findings of the study? Were the researchers' original hypotheses supported by their observations? If not, look in the discussion section for how the researchers explain the findings that were obtained.

DISCUSSION

The discussion section frequently opens with a summary of what the study found, and an evaluation of whether the findings supported the original hypotheses. Here, the researchers evaluate the theoretical and practical implications of their results. This can be particularly interesting when the results did not work out exactly as the researchers anticipated. When such is the case, consider the researchers' explanations carefully, and see if they seem plausible to you. Often, researchers will also report any aspects of their study that limit their interpretation of its results, and suggest further research that could overcome these limitations to provide a better understanding of the problem under investigation.

Some readers find it useful to read the first few paragraphs of the discussion section before reading any other part of a research report. Like the abstract, these few paragraphs usually contain all of the main ideas of a research report: what the hypotheses were, the major findings and whether they supported the original hypotheses, and how the findings relate to past research and theory. Having this information before reading a research report can guide your reading, allowing you to focus on the specific details you need to complete your understanding of a study. The description of the results, for example, will alert you to the major variables that were studied. If they are unfamiliar to you, you can pay special attention to how they are defined in the introduction, and how they are operationalized in the Method section.

After you have finished reading an article, it can also be helpful to reread the first few paragraphs of the discussion and the abstract. As noted, these two passages present highly distilled summaries of the major ideas in a research report. Just as they can help guide your reading of a report, they can also help you consolidate your understanding of a report once you have finished reading it. They provide a check on whether you have understood the main points of a report, and offer a succinct digest of the research in the authors' own words.

While reading the discussion section, try answering these questions: What conclusions can be drawn from the study? What new information does the study provide about the problem under investigation? Does the study help resolve the problem? What are the practical and theoretical implications of the study's findings? Did the results contradict past research findings? If so, how do the researchers explain this discrepancy?

Some Notes on Reports of Multiple Studies

Up to this point, we have implicitly assumed that a research report describes just one study. It is also quite common, however, for a research report to describe a series of studies of the same problem in a single article. When such is the case, each study reported will have the same basic structure (Introduction, Method, Results, and Discussion sections) that we have outlined, with the notable exception that sometimes the results and discussion section for each study are combined. Combined "results and discussion" sections contain the same information that separate Results and Discussion sections normally contain. Sometimes the authors present all their results first, and only then discuss the implications of these results, just as they would in separate results and discussion sections. At other times, however, the authors alternate between describing Results and Discussing their implications, as each result is presented. In either case, you should be on the lookout for the same information, as already outlined in our consideration of separate Results and Discussion sections.

Reports including multiple studies also differ from single study reports in that they include more general Introduction and Discussion sections. The general Introduction, which begins the main body of a research report, is similar in essence to the introduction of a single study report. In both cases, the researchers describe the problem investigated and its practical and theoretical significance. They also demonstrate how they derived their hypotheses, and explain how their research relates to past investigations of the problem. In contrast, the separate Introductions to each individual study in reports of multiple studies are usually quite brief, and focus more specifically on the logic and rationale of each particular study presented. Such Introductions generally describe the methods used in the particular study, outlining how they answer questions that have not been adequately addressed by past research, including studies reported earlier in the same article.

General Discussion sections parallel discussions of single studies, except on a somewhat grander scale. They present all of the information contained in discussions of single studies, but consider the implications of all the studies presented together. A general Discussion section brings the main ideas of a research program into bold relief. It typically begins with a concise summary of a research program's main findings, their relation to the original hypotheses, and their practical and theoretical implications. Thus, the summaries that begin general Discussion sections are counterparts of the summaries that begin Discussion sections of single study reports. Each presents a digest of the research presented in an article that can serve as both an organizing framework (when read first), and as a check on how well you have understood the main points of an article (when read last).

Research Reporting as Storytelling

A research report tells the story of how a researcher or group of researchers investigated a specific problem. Thus, a research report has a linear, narrative structure with a beginning, middle, and end. In his paper on writing research reports, Bem (1987) noted that a research report:

> . . . is shaped like an hourglass. It begins with broad general statements, progressively narrows down to the specifics of [the] study, and then broadens out again to more general considerations. (p. 175)

This format roughly mirrors the process of scientific investigation, wherein researchers do the following: (1) start with a broad idea from which they formulate a narrower set of hypotheses, informed by past empirical findings (Introduction); (2) design a specific set of concrete operations to test these hypotheses (Method); (3) analyze the observations collected in this way, and decide if they support the original hypotheses (Results); and (4) explore the broader theoretical and practical implications of the findings, and consider how they contribute to an understanding of the problem under investigation (Discussion). Although these stages are somewhat arbitrary distinctions—research actually proceeds in a number of different ways—they help elucidate the inner logic of research reports.

While reading a research report, keep this linear structure in mind. Although it is difficult to remember a series of seemingly disjointed facts, when these facts are joined together in a logical, narrative structure, they become easier to comprehend and recall. Thus, always remember that a research report tells a story. It will help you to organize the information you read and to remember it later.

Describing research reports as stories is not just a convenient metaphor. Research reports *are* stories. Stories can be said to consist of two components: a telling of what happened, and an explanation of why it happened. It is tempting to view science as an endeavor that simply catalogues facts, but nothing is further from the truth. The goal of science, social psychology included, is to *explain* facts, to explain *why* what happened happened. Social psychology is built on the dynamic interplay of discovery and justification, the dialogue between systematic observation of relations and their theoretical explanation. Although research reports do present novel facts based on systematic observation, these facts are presented in the service of ideas. Facts in isolation are trivia. Facts tied together by an explanatory theory are science. Therein lies the story. To really understand what researchers have to say, you need consider how their explanations relate to their findings.

The Rest of the Story

> There is really no such thing as research. There is only search, more search, keep on searching. (Bowering, 1988, p. 95)

Once you have read through a research report, and understand the researchers' findings and their explanations of them, the story does not end there. There is more than one interpretation for any set of findings. Different researchers often explain the same set of facts in different ways.

Let's take a moment to dispel a nasty rumor. The rumor is this: Researchers present their studies in a dispassionate manner, intending only to inform readers of their findings and their interpretation of those findings. In truth, researchers aim not only to inform readers, but also to *persuade* them (Sternberg, 1995). Researchers want to convince you their ideas are right. There is never only one explanation for a set of findings. Certainly, some explanations are better than others; some fit the available data better, are more parsimonious, or require fewer questionable assumptions. The point here is that researchers are very passionate about their ideas, and want you to believe them. It is up to you to decide if you want to buy their ideas or not.

Let's compare social psychologists to sales clerks. Both social psychologists and sales clerks want to sell you something: either their ideas: or their wares. You need to decide if you want to buy what they're selling or not—and there are potentially negative consequences for either decision. If you let a sales clerk dazzle you with a sales pitch, without thinking about it carefully, you might end up buying a substandard product that you don't really need. After having done this a few times, people tend to become cynical, steeling themselves against any and all sales pitches. This too is dangerous. If you are overly critical of sales pitches, you could end up foregoing genuinely useful products. Thus, by analogy, when you are too critical in your reading of research reports, you might dismiss, out of hand, some genuinely useful ideas—ideas that can help shed light on why people behave the way they do.

This discussion raises the important question of how critical one should be while reading a research report. In part, this will depend on why one is reading the report. If you are reading it simply to learn what the researchers have to say about a particular issue, for example, then there is usually no need to be overly critical. If you want to use the research as a basis for planning a new study, then you should be more critical. As you develop an understanding of psychological theory and research methods, you will also develop an ability to criticize research on many different levels. And *any* piece of research can be criticized at some level. As Jacob Cohen (1990) put it, "A successful piece of research doesn't conclusively settle an issue, it just makes some theoretical proposition to some degree more likely" (p. 1311). Thus, as a consumer of research reports, you have to strike a delicate balance between being overly critical and overly accepting.

While reading a research report, at least initially, try to suspend your disbelief. Try to understand the researchers' story; that is, try to understand the facts—the findings and how they were obtained—and the suggested explanation of those facts—the researchers' interpretation of the findings and what they mean. Take the research to task only after you feel you understand what the authors are trying to say.

Research reports serve not only an important archival function, documenting research and its findings, but also an invaluable stimulus function. They can excite other researchers to join the investigation of a particular issue, or to apply new methods or theory to a different, perhaps novel, issue. It is this stimulus function that Elliot Aronson, an eminent social psychologist, referred to when he admitted that in publishing a study he hopes his colleagues will "look at it, be stimulated by it, be provoked by it, annoyed by it, and then go ahead and do it better. . . . That's the exciting thing about science; it progresses by people taking off on one another's work" (1995, p. 5). Science is indeed a cumulative enterprise, and each new study builds on what has (or, sometimes, has not) gone before it. In this way, research articles keep social psychology vibrant.

A study can inspire new research in a number of different ways, such as: (a) It can lead one to conduct a better test of the hypotheses, trying to rule out alternative explanations of the findings; (b) it can lead one to explore the limits of the findings, to see how widely applicable they are, perhaps exploring situations to which they do not apply; (c) it can lead one to test the implications of the findings, furthering scientific investigation of the phenomenon; (d) it can inspire one to apply the findings, or a novel methodology, to a different area of investigation; and (e) it can provoke one to test the findings in the context of a specific real-world problem, to see if they can shed light on it. All of these are excellent extensions of the original research, and there are, undoubtedly, other ways that research findings can spur new investigations.

The problem with being too critical, too soon, while reading research reports is that the only further research one may be willing to attempt is research of the first type: redoing a study better. Sometimes this is desirable, particularly in the early stages of investigating a particular issue, when the findings are novel and perhaps unexpected. But redoing a reasonably compelling study, without extending it in any way, does little to advance our understanding of human behavior. Although the new study might be "better," it will not be "perfect," so *it* would have to be run again, and again, likely never reaching a stage where it is beyond criticism. At some point, researchers have to decide that the evidence is compelling enough to warrant investigation of types (b) through (e). It is these types of studies that most advance our knowledge of social behavior. As you read more research reports, you will become more comfortable deciding when a study is "good enough" to move beyond it. This is a somewhat subjective judgment and should be made carefully.

When social psychologists write up a research report for publication, it is because they believe they have something new and exciting to communicate about social behavior. Most research reports that are submitted for publication are rejected. Thus, the reports that are eventually published are deemed pertinent not only by the researchers who wrote them, but also by the reviewers and editors of the journals in which they are published. These people, at least, believe the research reports they write and publish have something important and interesting to say. Sometimes, you'll disagree; not all journal articles are created equal, after all. But we recommend that you, at least initially, give these well-meaning social psychologists the benefit of the doubt. Look for what they're excited about. Try to understand the authors' story, and see where it leads you.

NOTE

Preparation of this paper was facilitated by a Natural Sciences and Engineering Research Council of Canada doctoral fellowship to Christian H. Jordan. Thanks to Roy Baumeister, Arie Kruglanski, Ziva Kunda, John Levine, Geoff MacDonald, Richard Moreland, Ian Newby-Clark, Steve Spencer, and Adam Zanna for their insightful comments on, and appraisals of, various drafts of this chapter. Thanks also to Arie Kruglanski and four anonymous editors of volumes in the series Key Readings in Social Psychology, for their helpful critiques of an initial outline of this paper. Correspondence concerning this article should be addressed to Christian H. Jordan, Department of Psychology, University of Waterloo, Waterloo, Ontario, Canada N2L 3G1. Electronic mail can be sent to chjordan@watarts. uwaterloo.ca.

REFERENCES

American Psychological Association. (1994). *Publication manual* (4th ed.). Washington, DC: Author.

Aronson, E. (1995). Research in social psychology as a leap of faith. In E. Aronson (Ed.), *Readings about the social animal* (7th ed., pp. 3–9). New York: W. H. Freeman and Company.

Bem, D. J. (1987). Writing the empirical journal article. In M. P. Zanna & J. M. Darley (Eds.), *The compleat academic: A practical guide for the beginning social scientist* (pp. 171–201). New York: Random House.

Bowering, G. (1988). *Errata*. Red Deer, Alberta.: Red Deer College Press.

Cohen, J. (1990). Things I have learned (so far). *American Psychologist, 45*, 1304–1312.

Forgas, J. P. (1994). Sad and guilty? Affective influences on the explanation of conflict in close relationships. *Journal of Personality and Social Psychology, 66*, 56–68.

Sternberg, R. J. (1995). *The psychologist's companion: A guide to scientific writing for students and researchers* (3rd ed.). Cambridge: Cambridge University Press.

Author Index

Aarts, C.W.M.A., 456
ABC, 142, 148, 149, 152
Abel, E., 318
Abeles, R.P., 342
Abelson, R.P., 7, 136, 164, 165, 172, 232, 245
Aberbach, J.D., 342, 345
Aboud, F.E., 297
Abramowitz, A.I., 359, 364, 373
Abrams, D., 294, 295, 298, 299, 460
Adams, Gordon S., 156
Adams, Henry, 27
Adams, John, 6, 128
Adams, John Quincy, 128
Adelson, Sherman, 89–90, 103, 106
Adorno, T.W., 3, 4, 6, 19, 33–36, 39, 41, 46, 57, 69, 70, 74, 75, 77–78, 78, 85, 118, 230, 257, 271, 276, 295, 296, 297
African National Congress, 449, 453
Ahlfinger, N.R., 9
Aldrich, J., 7
Allais, Maurice, 255
Allen, H.M., 348
Allen, V.L., 111
Allport, Gordon, 5, 102, 111, 116, 126, 294, 296, 297, 298, 308, 333–334, 334, 337, 347, 353, 387
Almquist, E.M., 326
Alon, H., 426
Alpert, J., 419
Altemeyer, Robert, 5, 35, 69, 85, 90, 94, 97, 118
Amabile, T.M., 295
American Anti-Slavery Society, 197
American Jewish Committee, 33, 40, 59
American Library Association, 76
American Psychological Association, 76, 468
Americans for Constitutional Action (ACA), 78
Americans for Democratic Action (ADA), 78
Andrews, F.M., 295
Anti-Defamation League of B'Nai B'rith, 78
Apfelbaum, E., 299, 302
Apostle, R.A., 337, 340, 350
Archibald, W.P., 306
Arendt, Hannah, 12, 383, 389, 395, 397
Argentina, 398, 399
Aristotle, 163

Armenians, 398
Aronson, E., 135, 295, 306, 474–475
Arrow, K.J., 241, 257
Arthur, Chester, 127
Asch, S.E., 111
Aschenbrenner, K.M., 281
Asher, Herbert B., 201
Ashmore, R.D., 295, 296–297, 298, 302, 345, 347
Ataturk, Kemal, 117
Aufderheide, B., 452
Austin, J.L., 384
Austin, W., 298
Ax, Albert, 164
Ayres, I., 11

B'Nai B'rith, 78
Bachman, J.G., 74–75, 79, 80
Bachofen, J.J., 318
Bachrach, H., 89
Bainbridge, W.S., 422
Balch, P., 297
Balch, R.W., 422
Bales, R.F., 127
Balfour, Lord, 264
Banaji, Mahzarin, 8, 11, 272, 296, 298, 305, 305=306, 307
Bandura, Albert, 104, 295, 393, 394, 424, 425
Banks, W.C., 297
Bar-Tal, D., 295, 297, 298
Barber, J.D., 6, 118, 125, 128, 130
Barker, E.N., 231
Barkow, J.H., 11
Barone, M., 78
Basow, S.A., 299
Basque Euzkadi ta Askatasuna (ETA), 417, 421
Bass, B.M., 55, 126, 276, 285
Batts, V., 347–348
Baumeister, R.F., 451–452
Baxter, G.W., 289
Bayton, J.A., 298, 302, 303
Bazerman, Max H., 250
Beale, F., 326
Beck, L., 318
Begin, Menachem, 417

Bell, D., 177
Bem, D.J., 125, 295
Bem, S.L., 294, 295
Bendix, Reinhard, 197–198, 198
Benford, R.D., 460
Benjamin, L., 111
Bercovitch, F.B., 329
Berelson, B., 139
Berkowitz, L., 276
Bernat, G., 297
Bernoulli, Daniel, 245
Bernzweig, J., 179
Berry, J.W., 280, 288
Berry, M.F., 340
Best, D.L., 299
Betancourt, H., 297
Bettelheim, B., 6, 296, 297
Bhatt, S., 297
Bianchi, S., 336
Biddiss, M.D., 325
Billig, M., 282, 289, 298, 304
Bilorusky, J.A., 114
Bishop, G.F., 7
Blackwell, J.E., 337
Blake, R.R., 10, 276
Blessing, T.H., 126
Block, J.H., 114
Blumenthal, M.D., 295
Blumer, H., 334, 338, 341
Bobo, Lawrence, 11, 12, 272, 337, 338, 340, 341, 348, 352, 358, 359, 360, 361, 374
Boender, K., 456
Böllinger, L., 414, 416, 417, 419–420, 421
Bonacich, E., 339
Borgida, E., 7
Bornstein, G., 281
Bouchard, T.J., 326
Bourhis, R.Y., 280, 452, 453
Bowering, G., 474
Bowers, C., 297
Boyatzis, R.E., 127
Boyd, C., 90
Brady, Henry, 171
Braly, K., 295, 296, 297, 298, 299, 308, 349, 360
Branthwaite, A., 281
Brauer, C., 340, 345
Braun, J.R., 280
Brehm, J.W., 294
Brent, E., 172
Brewer, M.B., 280, 281, 298, 347, 348, 451–452, 460
Brickman, P., 295
Brigham, J.C., 280, 296, 308
British House of Commons, 230–239
Brock, T.C., 145, 295
Brody, R.A., 241
Bromley, S., 305, 336
Brooks, T., 74
Broverman, I., 297, 298, 299, 308
Brown, Norman O., 117
Brown, Roger, 4, 10, 34–35, 126, 277, 281, 285, 289, 297, 298, 299, 302, 450, 452, 459
Brown, Steven R., 202
Browning, R.P., 109

Brownmiller, S., 77
Bruner, Jerome, 6, 109, 296, 298
Bruno, F., 414–415
Brunswik, Egon, 40
Buchanan, James, 128, 132
Buchanan, Pat, 363, 370–371, 373, 374
Budner, S., 111
Bullock, A., 85
Bullock, C.S., III, 359
Bundy, Ted, 386
Burke, J.P., 116, 120
Burnham, D., 127
Burns, J.M., 115, 124
Burstein, P., 340
Burt, M.R., 95
Busch, R.C., 318
Bush, George H.W., 158, 167, 168, 359, 363
Busic, Zvonko, 415–416, 420–421
Buss, A.H., 295

Cacioppo, J.T., 135, 165
Caddick, B., 285, 289
Caditz, J., 341
Calley, Lt., 383, 394–395, 396, 401–402
Cambodia, 398
Cameron, J.E., 456
Campbell, A., 10, 29, 359
Campbell, Donald, 110, 140, 276, 307, 347
Campbell, R.T., 295
Canada, 416
Cantril, H., 296
Caplan, N., 342
Carlsmith, J.M., 295
Carlyle, Thomas, 115
Carmines, Edward G., 214, 352, 359, 360
Carsch, H., 62, 64
Carter, Jimmy, 72, 128, 143–145, 147, 166–175, 213
Cartwright, D., 423
Cauley, J., 412
Cederblom, D., 289
Cell, J.W., 351
Center for Political Studies, Institute for Social Research, University of Michigan, 154, 205
Central America, 156–161. *see also* Nicaragua
Chaffee, S.H., 139
Chaiken, S., 135
Chaikin, A.L., 295
Chamberlain, Neville, 266
Chang, B., 297
China, 265–266
Choi, J.N., 9
Chong, D., 177
Christian Beacon, 75
Christie, R., 4, 6, 54, 55, 56, 60, 62, 64, 65, 98, 105, 118, 119
Churchill, Winston, 135, 266, 268
Cialdini, R.B., 7, 135, 241, 295
Citrin, J., 359, 374
Clark, K.B., 297, 334, 340
Clark, Lee Anna, 167
Clark, M.P., 297
Clark, R.P., 418, 421
Clarkson, F.E., 297
Cleveland, Grover, 128

Clinton, Bill, 363
Clore, G.L., 295
Cobb, Roger W., 203
Cody, M.J., 295
Cohen, B., 139
Cohen, Jacob, 474
Cohn, T.S., 55, 62, 64
Colasanto, D., 336
Coleman, J.S., 241
Coleman, L.M., 298
Colleau, S.M., 12, 362
Collier, J.F., 318
Collins, A.M., 146–147
Collins, B.E., 423
Combs, S.L., 146
Commins, B., 285
Condor, S., 298, 299, 302
Connell, R.W., 5
Conover, Pamela Johnston, 8, 10, 178, 202
Conte, H.R., 126
Converse, P.E., 7–8, 119, 147, 174, 177–178, 207, 257
Cook, Peggy, 62
Cook, T.D., 140
Coolidge, Calvin, 128, 129, 132
Coombs, S.L., 140
Cooper, H.H.A., 418
Cooper, J., 307
Cornwell, Patricia, 387
Corrado, R.R., 415
Coser, L.A., 338
Cosmides, L., 11
Couch, A., 56–57
Coulter, Thelma, 64, 237
Coveyou, Michael R., 202
Cox, O.C., 297
Crain, R.L., 344
Crenshaw, Martha, 13, 380, 425
Crocker, J., 90, 297, 304, 305, 450–451
Cronbach, L.J., 55
Cropanzano, Russell, 167
Crosby, F., 305, 336
Crosby, G.C., 12
Cross, W.E., 451
Crowne, D.P., 102
Cummings, S., 342
Cunningham, F., 295, 297, 301, 302, 304

D'Souza, D., 358
Da Vinci, Leonardo, 25
Daniloff, Nicholas, 261–262
Danilovacs, P., 90
Darley, John, 12, 295, 302, 380, 384
Dawes, R.M., 241, 242, 245
De Boer, C., 426
De Klerk, F.W., 449, 453
De Weerd, M., 450
Deam, J.P., 344–345
Deane, P.C., 323
DeBono, K.G., 296
Degler, C.N., 334, 347
Degoey, P., 10
Del Boca, F.K., 295, 296, 298, 302, 345, 347
Dennis, J., 5

Dépret, E.F., 452
Derryberry, Douglas, 165
Deutsch, M., 2, 276
Devine, P.G., 11, 305, 306, 359, 360
Di Palma, G., 117
Diab, L., 276, 297, 299
Dicks, H.V., 64
Diener, Ed, 164, 167
Diers, C.J., 289
Dillehay, J.P., 118
Dittmarr, H., 299, 302
Dizard, J.E., 280
Dod, A.W., 6
Doise, W., 284
Dole, Robert, 158
Donley, R.E., 127, 132
Donnerstein, E., 336
Donnerstein, M., 336
Donohue, G.A., 171
Donovan, R.L., 77
Doty, Richard, 35
Dovidio, J.F., 11, 298, 308, 336, 361
Downs, A., 9, 140, 174, 184, 241, 255
Doyle, S., 281
Driver, M., 231
Dube-Simard, L., 342
Duckitt, John, 102
Duhme, M., 460
Dukakis, Michael, 167, 168
Duke, David, 359
Duncan, Otis D., 209, 210
Dunlap, R., 114
Dunteman, G., 276, 285
Durkheim, E., 323, 436, 451

Eagleton, T., 295
Eagly, A.H., 135, 295, 299, 302–303, 307, 308
Easton, D., 5
Eccles, John C., 164
Eckstein, Harry, 13, 380, 433, 434
Edelman, Murray, 165
Edsall, M.D., 358
Edsall, T.B., 358
Edwards, A.L., 65
Ehrlich, H.J., 297, 347
Eibl-Eibesfeldt, I., 323
Eichmann, Adolf, 383, 389, 397
Eisenhower, Dwight, 128, 186, 188, 344
Eisinger, P.K., 340
Ekehammar, B., 5
Elder, Charles D., 203
Ellemers, N., 453, 460
Elliot, A.J., 359, 360
Elster, J., 295
Emmons, Robert A., 164
Endler, N.S., 111, 126
Enelow, James M., 174
Engels, F., 301, 307, 324
England, 230–239, 264–270
Epstein, E.J., 146
Erbring, L., 140
Erikson, E.H., 6, 117, 125–126, 130, 411–412, 419, 421, 422
Erikson, Robert S., 201

Esser, H., 9, 454
Evans, A.S., 341
Eysenck, H.J., 4, 45, 64, 65, 90, 177, 231, 237, 238
Eysenck, S.B., 90

Falger, V., 11
Fanon, Frantz, 422
Fararo, T.J., 241
Farley, J., 452
Farley, R., 336, 339, 345
Farrow, D.L., 127
Fazio, R.H., 12, 361, 374
FBI, 253
Federico, C.M., 12
Feldman, J., 8, 139, 302
Feldman, Stanley, 178, 202
Ferguson, C.K., 284
Fermia J., 344
Fernandez, G., 90
Ferracuti, F., 414–415, 422
Ferree, M.M., 456
Festinger, L., 280, 288, 294, 295
Feuer, L., 419
Fiedler, F.E., 276
Fields, R.M., 428
Fillenbaum, S., 297297
Fillmore, Millard, 127
Fine, M., 297
Fiorina, Morris, 156
Fireman, B., 338
Fischhoff, Baruch, 152
Fishman, J.A., 296, 297, 308
Fiske, S.T., 7, 136, 146, 153, 242, 305, 451–452, 452
Flacks, R., 114
Fletcher, G.J.O., 90
Fodor, E.M., 127
Fonberg, Elzbieta, 164
Forbes, H.A., 69
Ford Motor Company, 401
Ford, Gerald, 213
Forgas, J.P., 468
France, 265
Fraser, M., 428
Fredrickson, G.M., 335, 345, 347, 351
Freedman, L.Z., 426–427
Freedom Front, 449
French, J.R.P., 452
Frenkel-Brunswik, E., 33, 40, 61, 69, 85, 230, 295
Freud, Sigmund, 2, 3, 24, 25, 50, 51, 116, 117, 127, 294, 296, 419
Frey, W.H., 339
Friedman, N., 280
Friend, K.E., 69
Frijda, N.H., 456–457
Fromm, Erich, 3, 19, 34, 35, 69, 79–80, 85, 105, 117, 271
Front de Libération de Québec (FLQ), 416
Fumihiko, Y., 425
Funder, D.C., 125
Funkhouser, G.R., 140, 340, 352

Gaddie, R.K., 359
Gaertner, S.L., 11, 298, 305, 308, 336, 361, 450, 459
Gallant, J.L., 179

Gallup International, 71, 75, 77, 152
Gallup, George, 3
Gamson, W.A., 338, 456
Gandhi, Mohatma, 6, 13, 125–126, 436
Garfield, James, 128
Garrison, William Lloyd, 197
Garrow, D.J., 340, 352
Gaudet, H., 139
Geis, F., 6, 98, 118, 119, 303, 304, 307, 308
George, A.L., 6, 117, 118, 120
George, J.L., 6, 117, 120
Gerard, H.B., 295, 306
Gergen, K.J., 297, 298, 299
Germany, 261–270, 413, 450
Ghiglier, M.P., 329
Gibb, C.A., 126
Gibson, J.L., 10
Gibson, J.T., 394
Gilbert, D.T., 305
Gilens, M., 359
Giles, H., 278, 279, 280, 284, 286, 297, 298
Giles, M.W., 341
Gilovich, T., 242
Gimbutas, M.A., 318
Gitlin, T., 344
Glaser, J., 7, 9, 34, 136, 177
Glazer, N., 117
Glock, C.Y., 337
Goel, M.L., 174
Goffman, E., 393
Goldenberg, E.N., 140
Goldwater, Barry, 190
Goodin, R.E., 454
Goodman, Leo A., 191
Gorbachev, Mikhail, 108, 109, 111, 116
Gossett, T., 340
Gough, H., 88
Gouws, A., 10
Graber, D.A., 7, 136
Gramsci, A., 306, 323, 325, 344
Granberg, D., 172
Grant, G., 280, 297
Grant, Ulysses, 128, 130, 132
Graumann, C., 298
Gray, Jeffrey A., 164, 165
Greeley, A.M., 336
Green, D.P., 9, 20, 241
Greenberg, J., 177
Greenberg, S.B., 358
Greenstein, F.I., 6, 36, 109, 110, 111, 116, 120, 411
Greenwald, A.G., 11, 295, 296, 297, 298, 305–306, 306, 307
Gregor, A.J., 280, 297
Griffin, D., 242
Grigg, C.M., 336, 344
Gronke, Paul W., 156
Gross, R.H., 295, 302
Gruenfeld, D.H., 9
Guetzkow, H., 423
Guimond, S., 342
Gupta, D.K., 457
Gurin, G., 306, 340
Gurin, P., 299, 306, 340, 342
Gurr, T.R., 317, 380

Gutmann, D., 426
Gynther, M., 118
Gysi, Gregor, 457

Hagen, M.G., 359
Haley, J., 124
Hall, C.S., 112, 116
Hamer, J., 298
Hamilton, David L., 11, 204, 298, 347, 456
Hamilton, J.D., 412
Hamilton, Lee, 383, 412
Hamilton, V.L., 12, 380, 389, 390, 394–395, 400, 401–402
Handlins, O., 334
Hannum, K.A., 179, 238
Harcourt, A.H., 329
Hardee, B.B., 347–348
Hardin, C.D., 305
Harding, Warren, 128, 130, 132
Harff, B., 317
Haritos-Fatouros, M., 394
Harris (poll), 201
Harris, M., 335
Harris, S., 280
Harris, Thomas, 387
Harrison, Benjamin, 128
Harrison, William Henry, 128
Hart, P., 9
Harvey, O.J., 276
Haslam, S.A., 307, 451, 452, 458
Hass, R.G., 11, 361
Hastie, R., 295
Hatchett, S., 336, 340
Havel, Vaclav, 13
Hayes, B.K., 307
Hayes, Rutherford, 128
Head, K.B., 295
Heberle, Rudolf, 198
Heider, Fritz, 172, 294, 385
Helmreich, R.L., 100, 308
Hensler, Carl, 174, 348, 352, 359
Herek, G., 296, 297
Hermann, M.G., 13, 120, 126, 130, 231
Herring, M.H., 10
Herrnstein, R.J., 325
Herzon, Frederick D., 202
Heskin, K., 415, 428
Hess, R.D., 5
Hewstone, M., 295, 298, 299, 457, 462
Hibbs, Douglas A., Jr., 150
Higgins, E. T., 152
Higgins, E.T., 146
Himes, J.S., 338, 344
Hinckley, John, Jr., 113
Hinich, Melvin J., 174
Hinkle, S., 299, 302
Hirsch, P.M., 146
Hirschman, A.O., 278
Hitler, Adolf, 25, 39, 85, 101, 105, 125–126, 341
Hixon, J.G., 305
Hobbes, Thomas, 2
Hochschild, J.L., 339
Hodgson, R.C., 297
Hoerig, J., 295

Hoffman, C., 295, 303, 307, 308
Hogg, M.A., 288, 294, 295, 298, 299, 451, 460
Holahan, C.K., 308
Hollander, E.P., 126
Holm, John D., 200, 202, 213, 214
Hoover, Herbert, 128
Hopkins, N., 458
Horkheimer, 19
Hough, J.C., Jr., 360
House, Edward, 117
Hovland, C.I., 139, 147
Howard, J.A., 295, 298, 302, 304
Howell, W.G., 12
Howes, P.W., 12, 361, 374
Hraba, J., 280, 297
Huddy, L., 13, 462
Hughes, M., 360
Huici, C., 295, 298
Hull, Clark, 24
Hunsberger, B., 90
Hurst, N., 295, 303, 307, 308
Hussein, Saddam, 386
Hutchings, V.L., 361
Hutchinson, M.C., 412, 427
Hyman, H.H., 5, 54, 59–62, 62–63, 336

India, 318
Inglehart, R., 75
Inkeles, I., 119
Institute for Social Research, University of Michigan, 74, 154, 205
International Society of Political Psychology (ISPP), 3
Iran, 151–161
Ireland, 413, 428
Irish Republican Army (IRA), 413, 428
Isaac, L., 340, 342
Israel, 413, 426–427, 459
Itzkowitz, N., 6, 117
Iyengar, S., 7, 13, 136, 153

Jackman, M.R., 336, 337, 338, 339, 344, 349, 350, 351
Jackman, R.W., 338
Jackson, Andrew, 128, 130
Jackson, D.N., 55, 88
Jackson, Jesse, 359, 363, 370–371, 373, 374
Jackson, Thomas H., 202
Jacobs, H., 109
Jacobson, C.K., 352
Jacoby, L.L., 305
Jaensch, Ernst R., 34, 39–40
Jäger, H., 414, 416, 418
Jahoda, G., 286, 297
Jahoda, Marie, 54, 60
Janis, I.L., 9, 111, 120, 241, 423, 425, 427
Jankowski, T.B., 10
Janoff-Bulman, R., 295, 304, 305
Janowitz, M., 296, 297
Japan, 262–263, 265–266
Jaspars, J., 298, 299
Jefferson, Thomas, 128, 130, 347, 349
Jennings, K.M., 5
Jennings, Peter, 7
Jervis, R., 9, 13, 112, 241, 242

Jessor, T., 360, 361
John, Oliver P., 165
Johns, C.H.W., 318
Johnson, Andrew, 127
Johnson, C., 437
Johnson, D.W., 276
Johnson, G., 348, 349
Johnson, J.A., 329
Johnson, Lyndon, 120, 128, 129
Johnson, P., 278, 284
Johnston, H., 460
Johnston, L.D., 74, 79, 80
Joint Center for Political Studies, 340
Jonas, E., 177
Jones, E.E., 337
Jones, J.R., 452
Jones, M., 294, 302
Jordan, W.D., 334–335, 351
Jorgenson, D.O., 70, 72
Jörger, H., 460
Jost, J.T., 8, 9, 10, 11, 34, 177, 178, 272, 299
Journal of the American Statistical Association, 191
Judd, C.M., 8, 451
Julian, J.W., 276
Jung, Carl, 116
Jussim, L., 298, 302

Kahn, Herman, 266
Kahn, R.L., 238, 295
Kahneman, Daniel, 152, 242, 245, 247, 249, 250, 294
Kalin, R., 276, 280
Kalmuss, D., 299, 306
Kampmeier, C., 452
Kane, J.N., 129
Kanouse, D.E., 294
Kaplan, A., 110, 120, 416
Katz, D., 113, 238, 295, 296, 297, 298, 299, 308, 337, 345, 349, 360
Katz, E., 139
Katz, I., 11, 111, 287
Kawanaka, K., 329
Kay, A.C., 8, 178
Keddie, N., 318
Kellerman, B., 115
Kelley, H.H., 284, 294
Kelley, S.K., Jr., 119
Kelman, H.C., 12, 380, 383, 389, 390, 394–395, 400, 401–402
Kendrick, A., 12, 273
Keniston, K., 56–57
Kennedy, John, 7, 128, 132, 241, 261
Kenny, D.A., 146
Kenrick, R.B., 295
Kerlinger, F.M., 177, 202
Kernell, Samuel, 150, 161
Kessler, R., 142
Kidder, L.H., 280, 288
Kiewiet, D.R., 174, 250
Kihlstrom, J.F., 305, 306
Killian, L., 344
Kinder, D., 7, 11, 13, 136, 153, 156, 172, 174, 261, 336, 342, 347, 348, 351, 358, 359, 360, 361
King, G., 146

King, Gary, 152
King, Martin Luther, Jr., 13, 340, 344, 352
Kinnvall, C., 2
Kipnis, D., 295
Kirscht, J.P., 118
Kissinger, Henry, 268
Klanderman, Bert, 381
Klandermans, B., 13, 449, 450, 456, 457, 459, 460, 462
Klausner, S.Z., 417
Klineberg, O., 286
Klingemann, Hans D., 200, 202, 207, 454
Kluckhohn, C., 116–117, 117
Kluegel, J.R., 295, 301, 325, 337, 340, 342, 352, 359, 360, 361
Knight, A., 418
Knutson, J.N., 120, 415, 416, 417, 420–421
Koch, E., 319
Kornhauser, A., 62
Kortekaas, P., 460
Kosterman, R., 359, 373
Kozo Okamoto, 418
Kramer, Gerald H., 248
Kramer, R.M., 298, 347, 348
Kressel, N.J., 13
Kriesi, H., 456
Kroeber, A.L., 116–117
Krosnick, J.A., 7, 8, 177
Kruglanski, A.W., 9, 34, 177, 298
Kruskal, William H., 191
Ku Klux Klan, 79
Kuipers, P., 456–457
Kull, S., 117
Kunda, Z., 451
Kurzban, R., 11
Kuzenski, J.C., 359

Ladwig, G., 287
Lalljee, M., 298
Lalonde, R.N., 456
Lambert, W.E., 297
Lampen, L., 298, 453
Landis, M., 119
Landman, J., 457
Lane, Robert, 6, 8, 117, 178, 202
Langton, K.P., 5
LaPiere, R.T., 295, 297
Larsen, Randy, 167
Larson, D.W., 241
Larter, W. Michael, 153
Lasswell, Harold, 3, 6, 24, 67, 109, 110, 118, 230
Lau, R.R., 7, 13, 112, 348
LaViolette, F., 295, 296, 297
Lawson, S., 340
Lazarsfeld, Paul, 3, 139
Leary, M.R., 451–452
Lebow, Richard N., 250
Lederer, G., 33
Lee, P.C., 329
Lefcourt, H.M., 287
Leigh, S.R., 329
Lemaine, G., 287
Lenin, V., 6
Lenski, G.E., 317, 318

Lepper, M., 7
Lerch, L., 298
Lerner, M., 120, 294, 295, 301, 304
Levi, A., 231, 245
Levin, S., 89
LeVine, R.A., 295, 307
Levine, S.V., 422
Levinson, D.J., 33, 69, 85, 116, 119, 230, 295
Levitin, Teresa E., 200, 202, 204, 207, 208, 213, 214
Levitt, B., 12, 380
Lewin, Kurt, 110, 297
Lewis, M., 111, 405
Lewis, Oscar, 25
Liberty Federation, 75
Lichtenstein, Sarah, 152
Liebert, R., 419, 424
Lifton, R.J., 295, 380, 383, 389, 390, 391, 394, 395, 397
Lightbown, B., 281
Lincoln Savings and Loan Company, 405
Lincoln, Abraham, 124, 128, 130, 132, 347
Lind, E.A., 304
Lindsay, D.S., 305
Lindzey, G., 112, 116
Linville, P., 337
Lippmann, W., 145, 295, 296, 298
Lipset, S.M., 69, 114–115, 336, 340
Lipsky, M., 340, 342
Lisansky, J., 297
Liu, J.H., 89
Locke, John, 2
Lockwood, J., 285
Lodge, M., 7, 13
Loehlin, J.C., 326
Loewy, M., 460
Loftus, E.F., 146–147
Lord, C.G., 7, 125
Lorenzi-Cioldi. F/, 299
Louis XII, 117
Lowenthal, L., 427
Luhtanen, R., 90, 450–451
Lukács, G., 306
Lumsdaine, A., 139
Luskin, Robert C., 174
Luther, Martin, 6, 25, 117, 125–126
Lyman, S., 295

Maass, A., 298, 454
MacDonald, Stuart Elaine, 174
Machiavelli, Niccolo, 2
Mackie, D.M., 298, 452
MacKinnon, C.A., 301, 307
MacKuen, M.J., 7, 136, 140, 146, 150, 167
Madison, James, 128
Maggiotto, Michael A., 207
Magnusson, D., 126
Mahard, R.E., 344
Major, B., 10, 297, 304, 456
Malle, B.F., 5, 88
Mandela, Nelson, 13
Mannheim, Karl, 181
Manstead, A.S.R., 298, 299, 302
Maranell, G., 126, 130, 132
Marcus, George E., 7, 136, 164, 165, 169, 174, 202, 343

Marcuse, Herbert, 117, 295–296, 301
Marin, G., 297
Markus, Gregory B., 170, 174
Markus, H., 451
Marlowe, D., 102, 276
Marolla, J., 295
Marsden, H.M., 329
Marsh, E., 74
Marshall, G.D., 295
Martin, J., 12, 295, 380
Marvick, E.W., 117
Marx, Karl, 3, 183, 217, 234, 301, 307, 324, 325, 344
Maslow, A.H., 451–452
Mason, P., 301, 302
Masters, Roger D., 112, 164
Mathewson, G.C., 306
Matza, D., 295
May, R., 427
Mayer, A.J., 62
Mayhew, Henry, 28
Mazer, D.B., 100
Mazur, A., 329
McAdam, D., 338, 340, 461
McAdams, D.P., 126, 451
McAlister, L.B., 298
McCann, S.J.H., 70, 72
McCarthy, C., 299
McCarthy, Joseph, 119
McClelland, D.C., 126, 127
McClendon, M.J., 336, 352
McClosky, H., 118, 119, 177, 231
McClure, R.D., 139, 295
McCombs, M.C., 140
McConahay, J.B., 11, 296–297, 302, 347–348, 348, 351, 359, 360, 361
McCullough, D., 6
McFarland, Sam, 89–90, 103, 106
McFarlane, Robert C., 151
McGarty, C., 307
McGraw, K.M., 7, 13, 295, 304
McGuire, William J., 4, 7, 8, 13, 19, 135, 177, 183
McKee, J.P., 298, 308
McKinley, William, 128, 129
McLaughlin, M.L., 295, 305
McMurtry, J., 296
McNaught, B.R., 297
McPherson, D.A., 280, 297
Meehl, Paul, 257
Meertens, R.W., 11, 360, 361
Meese, Edwin, 151
Melvin, D., 45
Mendelberg, T., 359, 360
Merelman, R.M., 117
Merkl, P., 415
Merriman, W.R., Jr., 359, 360
Merton, R., 323
Messick, S.J., 55, 298
Mészáros, I., 306
Meyerson, D., 295, 306
Micheletti, P.M., 179, 238
Michigan Department of Corrections, 77
Midlarsky, M.I., 425
Miene, P., 296, 297

Milbrath, Lester W., 174
Milburn, M.A., 7, 8, 136, 177
Milgram, S., 12, 380, 383, 389, 390, 392–394, 395
Mill, John Stuart, 438
Miller, A.G., 340, 347
Miller, A.H., 12, 140, 174, 200, 306, 364
Miller, Arthur B., 201, 204, 207, 208
Miller, D.T., 295, 304
Miller, F.D., 456
Miller, J.G., 437
Miller, N., 285
Miller, W.E., 75, 170, 201, 202, 213, 214, 359, 364
Millet, K., 297, 307
Mills, J., 295, 306
Milner, D., 279, 280, 289, 297
Ming, M.U., 9
Mingst, K.A., 10
Mischel, W., 4, 126
Missouri, 165–166, 167, 169, 170
Mladinic, A., 299, 308
Moghaddam, F.M., 456
Mondale, Walter, 7
Monroe, James, 128
Monroe, K.R., 13, 241
Monson, T.C., 295
Moore, Barrington, 443–444
Moral Majority, 75, 86
Morf, G., 416
Morgenstern, Oskar, 245
Morland, J.K., 280, 284, 297
Morrett, D.C., 77
Morris, A.D., 340, 344
Morris, R.B., 130
Mosca, G., 323, 436–437
Moscovici, S., 323, 452, 454
Mouto, J.S., 276
Mouton, J.S., 10
Mucchi-Faina, A., 454
Mugny, G., 453
Muha, M.J., 337, 339, 350, 351
Mullen, B., 7, 136, 298, 299
Muller, E.N., 380
Mummendey, A., 453, 456, 459
Murdock, G.P., 318
Murray, C.A., 325
Murray, Henry, 109, 111, 116, 117
Murray, R.K., 126
Mutran, E., 340
Myrdal, G., 296, 308, 340, 345

Nadler, R.D., 329
National Commission on Libraries and Information Science, 75–76
National Security Council (NSC), 151–152
NBC, 142, 148, 149
Nechaev, Sergei, 417
Nelson, M., 318
Netherlands, 450, 456
Neuman, Russell, 171, 174, 237
Neuman, W.R., 231
Neustadt, Richard E., 150
New York Times, 151, 152
New York Times Index, 79

Newcomb, T.M., 86
Newhill, C.E., 118
Ng, S.H., 452, 453, 462
Nicaragua, 150–161
Nie, N.H., 124, 174
Niemi, R.G., 5, 119
Nisbett, R.E., 5, 146, 242, 294
Nixon, Richard, 6, 7, 25, 114, 128, 241, 268
Noelle-Neumann, E., 337
North, Oliver, 152

O'Brien, M., 90
O'Mahoney, Joseph, 259
O'Malley, P.M., 74, 79, 80
O'Neill, Thomas (Tip), 158
Oakes, P.J., 286, 299, 301, 307, 451, 452, 459, 462
Oberschall, A., 279
Oewerkerk, J.W., 460
Oldendick, R.W., 7
Olien, C.N., 171
Oliver, J.I., 329
Olivier, J.I., 449
Olson, M., 241
Onorato, R.C., 450
Oppenheim, A.N., 5
Oppenheim, D.B., 297
Ordeshook, Peter, 255
Orfield, G., 339
Orne, M.T., 142
Osgood, C.E., 127
Ostrom, Charles W., 150
Ostrum, T.M., 145
Otten, S., 459
Otto, S., 308
Owens, T., 462
Oyen, M., 456

Padgett, V.R., 70, 72
Page, Benjamin I., 213, 214
Paige, J.M., 342
Pantaleo, G., 456
Pareto, Vilfredo, 323, 436–437
Park, B.E., 112, 451
Parkin, F., 295
Patterson, T.E., 139
Paulhus, D.L., 102
Peabody, D., 64, 287
Pepitone, A., 295
Peplau, A., 90
Percival, E.F., 100
Pervin, L.A., 111
Pestello, F.P., 336
Peters, M.D., 7, 136, 153
Peterson, Bill, 35, 297
Peterson, D., 90
Peterson, G., 90
Peterson, R.E., 114
Peterson, S.A., 11
Petrocik, J.R., 124
Pettigrew, T.F., 4, 11, 297, 335, 336, 342, 344, 347, 352, 360, 361, 456, 457
Petty, R.E., 135, 145
Phillips, K., 12

Piazza, T., 12, 273, 337, 359, 360, 369, 370, 371, 373, 374
Picasso, Pablo, 1
Pickett, C.L., 460
Pierce, Franklin, 128
Pierce, R., 119
Piereson, James, 202, 207, 343
Pike, K.C., 302
Pisano, V., 427
Pitts, J.P., 340
Plato, 118
Plutchik, R., 126, 164
Poindexter, John, 152
Polk, James, 128
Pomper, G.N., 319
Pomper, P., 417
Popkin, S.L., 7, 136
Porter, C.A., 295, 304
Porter, J.R., 297
Powesland, P.E., 279, 280, 284, 297
Prager, J., 351
Pratkanis, A., 112, 135
Pratto, F., 5, 10, 11, 88, 89, 92, 165, 272, 295, 299, 301, 302, 359, 360, 361, 453, 456, 458
Prentice-Dunn, S., 336
Prothro, J.W., 297, 299, 336
Putnam, R., 230–239, 328

Quattrone, George A., 9, 242, 253, 256
Quinsey, V.L., 87

Rabbie, J.M., 284
Rabinowitz, George, 174
Raden, D., 12, 374
Rahn, W.M., 7
Raiffa, Howard, 245
Ramirez, M., 297
Rank, A.D., 230, 231
Ransford, H.E., 342
Rasch, W., 414
Raven, B., 452
Read, S., 295
Reagan, Ronald, 6, 7, 72, 82, 113, 128, 150–161, 166–175, 339, 363
Red Army Faction (RAF), 413
Reeder, G.D., 90
Regents of the University of California, 40
Rehnquist, William, 158
Reich, Wilhelm, 3
Reicher, N., 299, 451
Reicher, S.D., 44, 458
Reid, D.B., 102
Rejai, M., 12, 177
Rempel, J.K., 295
Renshon, S.A., 241
Reynolds, V., 11
Richardson, L., 129
Riesman, D., 117
Riezler, K., 427
Riker, William, 255
Riley, R.T., 344
Rimmer, R.H., 77
Rivers, Douglas, 150, 161
Robinson, John P., 200, 202, 213, 214, 340

Rochford, B.E., 460
Rodgers, H., 339
Roefs, M., 449, 457
Rogers, R.W., 336
Rokeach, M., 4, 6, 7, 65, 66, 69, 177, 230, 231, 232, 233, 237
Roman Catholic Church, 69
Roof, W.C., 339
Roosevelt, Franklin D., 108, 109, 116, 124, 128, 130, 132
Roosevelt, Theodore, 128, 129, 132
Rose, Nancy L., 150, 161
Rosenberg, M., 90, 172, 287
Rosenkrantz, P.S., 297
Rosenstone, Steven J., 156
Ross, D., 104
Ross, G.F., 286
Ross, L., 5, 7, 146, 242, 250, 294, 302, 303
Ross, M., 295, 305
Ross, S., 104
Roth, B.M., 358, 359, 361, 373
Rothbart, Myron, 298, 337
Rothman, A.J., 305
Rousseau, Jean Jacques, 2
Rowe, R.C., 87
Rowell, T.E., 329
Rubin, Z., 90
Rucht, D., 451
Rudwick, E., 350
Rummel, R.J., 12
Runciman, W.G., 288, 289, 342
Rushton, J.P., 325
Rusk, Jerrold G., 201
Russell, E.H., 445
Russell, James A., 164, 167
Ryan, W., 295

Sabini, J.P., 380
Sachdev, I., 288, 452, 453
Sagar, H.A., 298
Sales, S.M., 5, 69, 70, 73, 74, 75, 77, 78, 80, 81
Salovey, P., 7, 136
Sampson, E.E., 295
Samuelsen, W., 295, 305
Sanders, L.M., 11, 359, 361
Sandler, T., 412
Sanford, R.N., 33, 69, 85, 230, 295
Sapolsky, R.M., 329
Sarnoff, I., 297
Saunders, J., 308
Savage, Leonard, 245
Savinkov, Boris, 417
Saxe, L., 305, 336
Schacter, S., 295
Schaefer, R.E., 281
Schaff, A., 295, 298
Schaffner, P.E., 8, 13
Schaller, M., 90, 298
Schattschneider, E.E., 164
Schelling, Thomas, 262
Schlenker, B.R., 294
Schmidtchen, G., 414, 418, 420, 424
Schneider, W., 336, 340
Schofield, J.W., 298
Schroder, H.M., 231, 233

Schuman, E.A., 344–345, 350, 358, 359, 361, 374
Schuman, H., 336, 337, 339, 340, 344
Schwartz, S.H., 90, 295
Schwarz, N., 295
Scott, J.C., 319
Scott, M.B., 295
Scully, D., 295
Scully, M., 12, 380
Seagle, W., 318
Sears, D.O., 2, 7, 11, 13, 112, 124, 139, 174, 203, 227, 273, 336, 342, 347, 348, 351, 352, 358, 360, 361, 367, 373
Seeman, M., 347
Senter, M.S., 337, 344, 349
Setiadi, B., 297
Settle, S.A., 299, 308
Shalhope, Robert, 349
Shamir, M., 343
Shanks, J. Merrill, 170, 359, 364
Shapiro, I., 9, 20, 241
Shavitt, S., 296
Shaw, D., 140
Shea, B.T., 329
Sheatsley, P.B., 54, 59–62, 62–63, 336
Sheffield, F., 139
Sheppard, H.L., 62
Shepsle, Kenneth, 248
Sherif, C.W., 276, 283, 298
Sherif, M., 10, 276, 277, 279, 289, 290, 296, 298, 341
Sherman, J.S., 451
Sherriffs, A.C., 298, 308
Shih, M., 89
Shils, E.A., 4, 66, 97, 177, 231
Shingles, R.D., 340
Shockley, W., 325
Shulman, Marshall, 264
Shultz, T.R., 384
Sidanius, J., 5, 9, 10, 11, 12, 88, 89, 177, 230, 272, 295, 299, 301, 302, 359, 360, 361, 453, 456, 458
Siers, B., 89
Sievert, K.H., 295, 297
Sigelman, L., 10
Silver, M., 380
Silvert, K.H., 296
Simmons, R.G., 287
Simon, B., 13, 381, 450, 451, 452, 456, 460, 461, 462
Simon, Dennis M., 150
Simon, H.A., 9, 109, 164, 241, 244–245
Simonton, Dean Keith, 6, 30, 120, 126, 132
Simpson, G.E., 347
Singer, J.E., 295
Singleton, R., 345
Sitkoff, H., 340, 345
Skevington, S.M., 289
Skrypnek, B.J., 303, 304, 307
Slade, J.W., 77
Slovic, Paul, 152, 242, 245
Smedley, J.W., 302
Smith, A.W., 336, 337, 339, 341
Smith, Adam, 234
Smith, C., 298
Smith, E.R., 295, 301, 325, 337, 340, 342, 352, 452
Smith, H.J., 450, 456, 460, 462
Smith, M. Brewster, 6, 109, 112, 117, 296, 298

Smith, R.A., 358, 361
Smith, T.W., 340
Smith, Tom, 319
Snider, J.G., 127
Sniderman, P.M., 12, 118, 241, 273, 359, 360, 362, 369, 370, 371, 373, 374
Sniderman, Paul, 171
Snow, D.A., 460
Snyder, M., 295, 297, 304, 307
Sober, E., 11
Somit, A., 11
South Africa, 449, 456, 458
Soviet Union, 262–269
Spain, 417, 421
Spears, R., 298, 299, 302, 456
Speer, Leslie, 174, 348, 352, 359
Spence, J.T., 100, 308
Spencer, Herbert, 115
Srole, L., 90
St. Claire, L., 282
Stagner, R., 64
Stalin, Josef, 117
Stallworth, L.M., 5, 88, 89
Stankiewicz, J.F., 5
Stark, R., 422
Staub, E., 12, 295, 380, 383, 389, 390, 394, 396, 398, 404
Steeh, C., 358, 359, 361, 374
Steele, C.M., 294, 304
Steele, R.S., 127
Steffen, V.J., 295, 302–303, 307
Stein, J.G., 241, 250
Steinmetz, J.L., 295
Stephan, W.G., 298
Stephenson, G.M., 280
Stern, E.K., 9
Sternberg, R.J., 474
Stewart, A.J., 126, 127, 231
Stewart, V.M., 280, 288
Stewin, L.L., 70, 72
Stimson, James A., 214, 352
Stinchcombe, A., 336
Stires, L.K., 77
Stone, W.F., 2, 8, 13, 33, 109, 120, 177, 231, 237
Storm, Christine, 164
Storm, Tom, 164
Stotland, E., 295
Stouffer, S.A., 197
Streufert, S. and S., 231
Stroebe, W., 298
Struch, N., 295
Stryker, S., 340, 462
Stürmer, S., 460, 461
Suedfeld, P., 230, 231
Suelzle, M., 337
Sullivan, Denis G., 164
Sullivan, H.S., 427
Sullivan, J.L., 7, 343
Sulloway, F., 9, 34, 177
Süllwold, L., 414, 415, 416, 417, 418–419
Suls, J., 294
Sumner, William Graham, 42
Sunar, D., 295, 297, 298, 307
Sundelius, B., 9

Survey Research Center, 153
Swann, W.B., 304
Sykes, G.M., 295
Syllwasschy, J., 298, 453
Szasz, A., 456

Taeuber, A.F., 339
Taeuber, K.E., 339
Taft, William Howard, 128, 132
Tajfel, H., 10, 276, 278, 280, 281, 283, 284, 285, 286, 288–289, 289, 294, 295, 297, 298, 302, 306, 307, 338, 341, 361, 450, 452, 453, 456, 457
Takaki, R.T., 347, 349
Taylor, D.C., 336
Taylor, D.G., 336, 338
Taylor, D.M., 280, 456
Taylor, I.A., 230, 231
Taylor, Richard W., 202
Taylor, S.E., 136, 146, 152, 242
Taylor, Zachary, 128
Tellegen, Auke, 164, 167
Ter Schure, E., 457
Tetlock, P.E., 2, 8–9, 9, 12, 177, 178, 179, 230, 231, 232, 234, 237, 238, 241, 242, 273, 295, 305, 361, 362, 374
Thaler, R.H., 242
Thibaut, J., 280
Thomas, L.E., 5
Thompson, S.S., 297
Thornton, T.P., 412
Tichenor, P.J., 171
Tilly, C., 12, 338, 380, 436, 437–439, 440, 441, 443, 446–447
Tocqueville, Alexis de, 442
Tomlinson, T.M., 280
Tooby, J., 11
Torney, J.V., 5
Toth, J.P., 305
Townsend, A.L., 299, 306
Triandis, H.C., 297, 298, 302
Trivers, R.L., 11
Trolier, T.K., 298
Trotsky, L., 6, 445
Truman, Harry, 128, 129, 132, 186
Tshirhart, J.T., 412
Tuch, S.A., 360
Tuchfarber, J.J., 7
Tucker, R.C., 111, 115, 117
Turner, C.B., 340
Turner, Frederick Jackson, 27
Turner, J.C., 10, 271, 277, 280, 281, 282, 284, 285, 286, 288, 289, 290, 294, 297, 298, 299, 301, 302, 306, 307, 338, 341, 345, 361, 450, 451, 452, 453, 454, 456, 462
Turner, R.H., 342, 344
Tursky, Bernard, 252
Tversky, Amos, 9, 152, 242, 245, 247, 249, 250, 256, 294
Tyler, John, 127
Tyler, T.R., 10, 241, 295, 304, 348, 460, 462

U.S. Army, 389, 401, 405
U.S. Bureau of the Census, 76–77, 129, 340
U.S. Congress, 129, 186. *see also* U.S. House of Representatives; U.S. Senate
U.S. Department of Justice, 74

U.S. House of Representatives, 78, 129
U.S. Senate, 231, 232
U.S. Senate Library, 129
Ujifusa, G., 78
University of California at Berkeley, 40
University of Michigan, 29, 74, 154, 205
Useem, B., 342

Valentino, N.A., 7
Valins, S., 294
Van Buren, Martin, 128
Van den Berghe, Pierre, 289, 316, 317, 344–345
Van Ginneken, J., 2
Van Knippenberg, A., 302, 308
Van Valey, T.L., 339
Vance, Cyrus, 264
Vanderbilt Television News Archive, 140, 142
Vanneman, R.D., 342
Vasilatos, Nicholas, 150
Vaughan, G.M., 280, 289, 297, 306
Verba, S., 124, 174
Vertzberger, Y.Y.I., 112
Vidal, G., 124
Vietnam, 262, 269, 389, 394–395, 400, 401–402, 405
Vinacke, W.E., 276
Vine, I., 11
Volkan, V.D., 6, 117
Volker, Paul, 158
Von Neumann, John, 245

Wackenhut, J., 361
Wagner, U., 298, 453
Walker, I., 456
Walker, J.L., 345
Walker, W.D., 87
Wall Street Journal, 340
Wallace, Henry, 40
Wallas, Graham, 3, 117
Walter, J., 119
Ward, C., 299
Ward, D., 2
Warr, Peter B., 202
Warren, Diann, 253
Washington Post, 152, 340
Washington, George, 6, 128, 130, 132
Washington, R.E., 297
Wasmund, K., 418
Watson, David, 164, 167
Watson, J.B., 2
Watts, M.W., 5
Waxman, C.I., 177
Weber, H., 459
Weber, Max, 125, 127, 397, 454
Weigel, R.H., 12, 361, 374
Weinberger, Caspar, 158
Weinberger, M., 284
Weiner, B., 294, 457
Weisberg, Herbert F., 119, 201, 207
Wellman, D.T., 337, 338, 341, 348
Wenzel, M., 453, 456, 457
Westholm, A., 5
Wetherell, M.S., 299, 451
White, R., 6, 298, 462

White, R.W., 296
White, Robert, 109
Whitlam, Gough, 119
Wicklund, R.A., 294
Widiger, T.A., 299, 308
Wiegele, T., 11
Wiggins, J.S., 126
Wilcox, J.E., 339
Wilder, D.A., 298
Wilkens, C., 284
Wilkinson, J.H., 340
Willhelm, S.M., 297
Williams, C., 334, 337, 344
Williams, G.C., 11
Williams, J.E., 297, 299
Williams, R.M., Jr., 342, 343, 344–345, 353
Wills, T.A., 294
Wilson, D.S., 11
Wilson, E.O., 11
Wilson, G.D., 9, 177, 231, 237, 238
Wilson, J.Q., 423
Wilson, W.J., 338, 340, 350
Wilson, Woodrow, 6, 25, 117, 128
Winter, David, 6, 35, 36, 105, 126, 127, 130, 132, 231
Wolfgang, M.E., 422
Wood, A.W., 296

Wood, W., 302
Worchel, S., 298
Word, C.O., 307
Worden, S.K., 460
Wortman, C.B., 304
Wrangham, R.W., 329
Wright, S.C., 456

Yacef, Saadi, 417
Yale University, 141
Yanagisako, S.J., 318
Yinger, J.M., 347
Yohannes, J., 90
York, Herbert, 261
Yugoslavia, 421

Zalk, S.R., 297
Zaller, J.R., 8, 118, 177
Zanna, M.P., 295, 307, 384
Zashin, E., 340, 345
Zavalloni, M., 286
Zeckhauser, R., 295, 305
Zevon, Michael, 164
Zillman, D., 295
Zimbardo, P.G., 295, 380, 394
Znaniecki, Florian, 192

Subject Index

abolition, 196–197. *see also* slavery
abstracts, of journal articles, 468–469
acquiescence, 55–57
action dispensability, 116, 120
actor dispensability, 116, 120
adaptation, 443
adolescents, prejudice in, 61, 63, 80
affirmative action, 338
African Americans, 280. *see also* prejudice; racism
    black political activism, 352
    legitimizing myths and, 323–325
    projection and, 51
age, belief systems and, 198
agenda setting, 7, 136, 142–143, 145
agentic state, 392–394, 396
age-system, of group-based social hierarchies, 316–320
aggregated individual discrimination, 320, 321
aggregated institutional discrimination, 320, 321
aggregation, 117
aggression. *see also* authoritarian aggression
    authoritarian, 76–77
    rebellion and, 436
    "slighting aggression by advantageous comparison," 424
    terrorism and, 425
ambiguity, 116–117, 439
ambivalence, 49–50, 53–54
ambivalent racism, 273
American Dilemma, An (Myrdal), 340
American National Election Studies, 75
    1976, 205
    1978, 200
    1980, 165–166, 172
    1986, 150, 153, 154, 157–158, 363, 366, 367, 369–372
    1992, 363, 366, 367, 369–372
American presidents. *see* presidents, American
Ancient Regime, The (Tocqueville), 442
anti-intraception, 44, 46, 48–49, 76
anti-Semitism, 33–34, 45. *see also* authoritarian personality syndrome
    Anti-Semitism (A-S) Scale, 41–42, 54–57
    attitudes and, 360
    covariation of attitudes, 39–49
    incidents of, 78–79

Kristallnacht, 394
Militia Attitudes Scale, 95, 100–101
Wild-Card Authoritarians, 98
Anti-Type, The (Jaensch), 34, 39
anxiety, 136, 164–165. *see also* emotions
    learning stimulated by, 170–174
    voting decision and, 169–170
APA Membership Register (American Psychological Association), 76
arbitrary-set system, of group-based social hierarchies, 316–319, 326–327
assumption of invariance, 251–253
astrology, 75
asymmetrical in-group bias, 322–323
attitude, 119. *see also* racism
    organization of, 39–62, 66–67
    racial, prejudice and, 347–352
attitudes and voting behavior era, 19–20, 22, 27–29
    connotative characteristics of, 27
    denotative mapping of, 28
    macrohumanistic studies, 28
    macroscientific studies, 29
    methodology, 28
    microhumanistic studies, 28
    microscientific studies, 28–29
    preferred topics in, 27–28
authoritarian aggression, 35, 44
Authoritarian Personality, The (Adorno, Frenkel-Brunswik, Levinson, Sanford), 3, 33–36, 39, 59, 177. *see also* authoritarian personality syndrome
    criminal interviews in, 47
    criticism of, 238–239, 257 (*see also* ideology)
    Further Explorations by a Contributor to ... (Frenkel-Brunswik), 61
    left-wing authoritarianism, 66
    status anxiety and, 53
    Studies in the Scope and Method of ... (Christie, Jahoda), 54
authoritarian personality syndrome
    education and, 59–62
    intergroup conflict and, 271
    mass psychology and, 33–36
    measures of behavior, 72–73

489

authoritarian personality syndrome (*continued*)
  microscientific study of, 26
  organization of attitudes and, 39–40, 66–67
    cognitive style, 53–62
    covariation, 40–49
    personality construction, 49–53
  political elites and leadership, 36
  social dominance orientation and, 104–105
    dominant personality, 88–89
    identifying social dominators, 92–93, 102–103
    improving SDO scale, 105–106
    McFarland/Adelson study (1996), 89–90
    origins of, 104
    parent studies, 94–98, 98–100
    student studies, 90–92, 93–94, 98–100, 100–102
    submissive personality, 85–88
  threat and, 69, 79–82
    aggression, 76–77
    anti-intraception, 76
    archival studies, 70
    conventionalism, 77–78
    cynicism, 74–75
    future research, 82–83
    identifying periods of high and low threat, 70–73
    power and toughness, 73–74
    prejudice, 78–79
    sex, 77
    submission, 75–76
    superstition, 75
authoritarian submission, 35, 44, 75–76, 85–88
autonomy, 420
aversive racism, 273, 338

behavioral approach system, 165
behavioral asymmetry, 320, 322–323
behavioral inhibition system, 164–165, 173
belief systems, 181. *see also* ideology
  abolition and Republican Party, 196–197
  active use of ideological dimensions of judgment, 185–188
  contraints among idea-elements, 190–191
  declining information for, 185
  definitions, 181–182
  issue publics, 195
  recognition of ideological dimensions of judgment, 188–190
  social groupings as central objects in, 191–192
  stability of belief elements, 192–195
  turnover correlations between time points, 194
Berkeley study, 85. *see also* authoritarian personality syndrome
biology, personality and, 104, 116, 337
black political activism, 352
boxing, threat and, 73
Brown decision, 339, 340
bureaucratic subroutines, 397

California Personality Inventory, 88
candidate perception. *see* mass media/candidate perception
capitalism, meaning of, 206–211
capital punishment, 77
caste system, 318
Catholic Church, 69

causal contingencies, 255–257
censorship, 75–76
certainty effect, 254–255, 260–261, 324, 325
chance events, 253–254
change, political, 160–161, 443–444
charisma, 125
children, prejudice in, 61, 63
circumplex, 164
citizen's duty, 255–256
civil conflict, 440
Civilization and its Discontents (Freud), 2, 117
civil rights movement, 273, 340. *see also* racism
class consciousness, 306
class structure, 217, 219. *see also* equality, fear of
"coattails effect," 129
coercion, 440–441, 445
cognition. *see also* decision-making
  authoritarian personality and, 53–55
  decreasing burden of, 259–264
  liberal/conservative ideology and, 177
  political cognition and decision era, 29–30
cognitive conservatism, 305
cognitive factors, meaning and, 204
cognitive heuristics, 30
cognitive psychology, rationality and, 244–245
cognitive unconscious, 305
collective action (CA) theory, 437–439
collective identity, 380–381, 450–452, 455. *see also* politicized collective identity
collective political violence. *see* political violence
comic strips, threat and, 73–74
communism, 97, 197. *see also* ideology; left-wing authoritarianism
  in Argentina, 397, 398
  cognitive style and ideology, 232–239
  "Document on Terror," 428
  F-Scale scores for, 64–66
  phobia, 40
conflict theory, 12, 298, 344. *see also* political violence
consciousness, 306
consensuality, 280, 324, 327, 328
conservatism, 8, 43, 171. *see also* ideology
  cognitive conservatism, 305
  cognitive style and ideology, 232–239
  defining, 178
  ego-defensive functions, 230–231
  judgment and, 185
  meaning and, 202
  self-identification, 200–201
conspiracy theories, 260
constraint, 182
  among idea-elements, 190–191
  of idea-elements, 182–185
  social sources of, 184–185
consumption, 228
"contextual knowledge," 184
contingency theory, 380, 432–435
  rebellion and, 442–445
  relative deprivation family of, 435–436
conventionalism, 35, 44, 77–78
conversion process, 394–395
counterarguing, 145, 146
counter-factual reasoning, 108, 120

crime, 252–253
criminal authoritarianism, 47
criticism, prejudice and, 50
culture of poverty concept, 25
culture of violence, 445–446
Cumulative Book Index (Wilson), 75, 76
cyclical model of elections, 125
cynicism, 44, 74–75

death penalty, 77
decision-making, 9, 241–242
    inadequate information, 259, 266–270
        benchmarks and analogies, 261–262
        certainty, 260–261
        common dimensions for, 262–263
        consequences of, 264–266
        readily available information and, 263–264
        simple models, 259–260
    rational/psychological analyses of political choice, 27,
        244–245
        causal *vs.* diagnostic contingencies, 255–257
        certainty and pseudocertainty, 254–255
        framing, 242, 253
        invariance, 251–253
        loss aversion, 249–251
        ratio-difference principle, 251–253
        reference effects, 245–246
        risk, 242, 244, 246–248
        weighting of chance events, 253–254
deference, 323
democracy, social dominators and, 102–103
"democratic creed," 345
deprivation, 439
destructiveness, 44, 74–75
diagnostic contingencies, 255–257
Directory of the APA (American Psychological
        Association), 76
disadvantaged, meaning of, 206–211
Discussion section, in journal articles, 469, 471–472
displacement, 52–53
dissonance theory, 396
diversity, 9–12. *see also* prejudice
divisions of labor, 302–303
"Document on Terror," 428
dog breeds, threat and, 73
dogmatism, 6, 66, 69
dominance, 44
    identifying high social dominators, 92–93
    RWA Scale, 88–89
    stereotyping and, 301
doubled personality, 390–392
"dramatic inevitability," 390
Dreyfus affair, 404
"Drunkard's Search" analogy, 259, 269–270

East Timor massacres, 317
Economic Philosophy Scale, 9, 94, 95, 103
economics. *see* decision-making; economy
economy
    arbitary-set, group-based social hierarchies and, 317–318
    economic threat, 69
    emotions and, 174
    equality and, 221

rapid growth of, 443
    social, economic, and political threat (SEPT), 71–72
education, 371–373
    authoritarianism and, 59–62
    belief systems and, 198
    class, status and, 223
    political knowledge and, 171
ego-alien, 50
ego-defense motivation, 112
ego-justification, 11, 272, 296–297. *see also* system
        justification theory
Eichmann in Jerusalem (Arendt), 383, 389
elections. *see also* leadership
    leader appeal and, 124–133
    political violence and, 440
elite decisions, 198
embeddedness, 324, 325
emotions, 163–165, 173–175
    dynamics of response, 168–169
    political knowledge and, 170–174
    types of response, 165–168
    voting decision and, 169–170
enthusiasm, 136. *see also* emotions
    political involvement and, 164
    political learning and, 172
    voting decision and, 169–170
environment
    E®P®R (human response/environment/predispositions)
        formula, 110–112
    personality and, 104, 110–112, 116, 337
environmental determinism, 19, 23–24
environmental stimuli, 136
E®P®R (human response/environment/predispositions)
        formula, 110–111
equality, fear of, 217. *see also* racism
    income and opportunity, 224–227
    status accountability, 218–219
    status and, 222–224
    status struggle, 219–220
    study subjects, 217–218
Equal Rights Amendment (ERA), 250–251
Eros and Civilization (Marcuse), 117
Escape from Freedom (Fromm), 3, 117
ethnic cleansing, 317
ethnocentrism, 45. *see also* authoritarian personality
        syndrome; racism
    defined, 344–345
    education and, 59–62
    Ethnocentrism (E) Scale, 41–43, 54–57
    Manitoba Ethnocentrism Scale (1996), 90, 98
    Manitoba Ethnocentrism Scale (1997), 89
European Americans, 273, 319
evil, 383–384
    actors and kernel of evil, 386–387
    agentic state, 392–394, 396
    conversion process, 394–395
    doubled personality, 390–392
    everyday thinking about, 384–389
    individuals, 395–398
    killing organizations
        creation of, 398–400
        origins of, 400–405
        reproduction of, 405–406

evil (*continued*)
  organizations socialize individuals into, 390–398
  psychological functions of everyday conceptualization
      of, 387–389
  social psychological conceptualization of, 387–389
evolution, 329
Exit, Voice, and Loyalty (Hirschman), 439
expectation principle, 253–254
expected utility theory, 245, 246–248
expertise, priming and, 153, 158–159
Exploitive Manipulative Amoral Dishonesty (E-MAD)
      Scale, 100–101

false consciousness, 305–306. *see also* stereotyping
fascism, 43. *see also* F-Scale (Fascism Scale); ideology
  cognitive style and ideology, 232–239
  F-Scale scores, 64–66
  potentiality for, 45
  rise of, 69
fear of equality. *see* equality, fear of
"feeling thermometer," 360, 363
fertility, 446
fictional characters, threat and, 73–74
fidelity, 419
fixed-alternative questionnaire, 40–41
Folkways (Sumner), 42
foreign affairs, 155–159. *see also* decision-making; Iran-
      Contra affair
framing, 242, 253
French Canadians, 280, 288. *see also* racism
From Mobilization to Revolution (Tilly), 437–438
F-Scale (Fascism Scale), 34, 78
  dogmatism and, 66
  education and, 59–62
  left-wing authoritarianism and, 63–64
  organization of attitudes study, 41, 43–45, 54–57
  submission and domination, 85
  superstition and, 75
"functional bases of conscious orientations," 113
fundamental attribution error, 406
*Further Explorations by a Contributor to "The
      Authoritarian Personality"* (Frenkel-Brunswik), 61

Gallup Report (Gallup International), 75
gangs, 316–317
gay and lesbian movement, 460–461
Gegentypus, Der (Jaensch), 34, 39
gender
  group-based social hierarchies and, 318
  prejudice and, 90
  social dominance and, 96, 98
  stereotypes, 302–303
gender-system, of group-based social hierarchies, 316–320,
      326–327
General Social Survey (1994), 363, 366, 367, 369
genocide, 317, 389, 398. *see also* arbitrary-set system, of
      group-based social hierarchies; evil; Holocaust
"gift of grace," 125
goals, 226
great-person theory of leadership, 125
group-based social hierarchies, 315–319
group conflict, 333–336
  motives, 341–343

racial ideology and, 338
group dynamics, leadership and, 125, 444–445
group-justification, 11, 272, 297–300. *see also* system
      justification theory
groups
  as central objects in belief systems, 191–192
  social psychology of, 422–426
  visibility 6f, 192
groupthink, 120
Guernica (Picasso), 1

happiness, equality and, 220
harm, 12, 404. *see also* evil
hierarchical consensuality, 280, 324, 327, 328
hierarchical equilibrium, 327
hierarchy-attenuating (HA) forces, 319–320, 324–325, 327,
      330
hierarchy-enhancing (HE) forces, 319–320, 324–325, 327,
      330
higher education, 371–373
high school seniors, survey about friendships/race, 80
Historical Statistics of the United States (U.S. Bureau of the
      Census), 129
Holocaust, 33–34, 317. *see also* authoritarian personality
      syndrome
homosexuals, 95, 96–97, 103
humanistic research, 22, 23
humanistic studies, 25–26
Human Nature in Politics (Wallas), 3, 117
human response (H), 110–112
hunter-gatherer societies, 317–318
Hutus, massacres of, 317

"idealogues," 178, 186–187
identity, 419–422. *see also* collective identity; social
      identity theory
ideological asymmetry, 323
ideological hegemony, 344–345, 346
ideologue hypothesis, 230–235, 237
ideology, 177–179. *see also* belief systems; legitimizing
      myths (LMs)
  cognitive style/political belief systems in British House
      of Commons, 230–233, 236–239
    study methodology, 233–235
    study results, 235–236
  equality
    fear of, 217
    income and opportunity, 224–227
    moral equality, 221–222
    status, 218–219, 222–224
    struggle for, 219–220
    study subjects, 226–227
    theoretical implications of, 227–228
    working class, 220–221
  ideology and decision era, 20, 22
  liberal/conservative self-identification, 200–201, 213–
      215
    cognitive and symbolic sources of meaning, 205–206
    content of meaning, 202–203
    evaluation of labels, 205
    meaning of labels, 201, 211–213
    model of self-identification, 203–205
    self-identification, 205

sources of evaluation of labels, 210–211
  structure of meaning, 201–202
political cognition and decision era, 29–30
public opinion and, 7–8
stereotyping and, 301
"ideology by proxy," 187
inaugural addresses, of American presidents, 127–130
income, opportunity and, 224–227
individuals
  individual-based social hierarchies, 315–319
  individual mobility, 286–287
  motivation for terrorism, 414–419
  in political roles, 110
inertia, inadequate information and, 264–265
"inferiority," consensual, 280, 324, 327, 328
information recall, 145
inherency theory, 380, 432–435
  collective action family of theories, 437–438
  rebellion and, 442–445
insecure intergroup comparisons, 288–289
institutional evil, 379
instrumental category, of discrimination, 290
integrative complexity coding system, 231, 233–235, 236–239
interaction effects, ignoring, 265–266
interdependence, 182
intergroup relations, 10, 271–272. see also racism
  group conflict, 333–336
  social categorization and, 281–283
  social context of, 277–281
interpersonal behavior, intergroup behavior vs., 277–281
interpersonal/intergroup processes, 31
intolerance, defined, 348
Introduction, to journal articles, 469, 472–473
invariance, 251–253, 326
IQ (intelligence quotient), authoritarianism and, 59–62
Iran-Contra affair, 151–161

Jackson Personality Research Form, 88
J-curve theory, 444
Jews, as student activists, 114–115. see also anti-Semitism
Jim Crow laws. see racism
journal articles, how to read, 467–475
J-type personality, 34, 39
justification, 294. see also system justification theory
just-world theory, 304, 389

Kasaians, massacres of, 317
kernel of evil, 379, 386–387
Khmer Rouge massacres, 317, 398
killing organizations, 398–406
Kristallnacht, 394
Kulaks, massacres of, 317
Kurds, massacres of, 317

law of increasing disproportionality, 327, 328
leadership, 124–125
  characteristics of, 36, 125
  empirical studies of presidents and elections
    methodology, 127–130
    results, 130–133
  inaugural addresses by presidents, 127–130
  leader appeal, 132

leader-follower match, 36, 125–126
leader performance, 132
leader-situation match, 36, 125, 131
political elites and, 36
presidential appeal, 131
learning (reinforcement) theory, 24
"left," as ideological label, 200–201
left-wing authoritarianism, 63–66, 96
  ideologue hypothesis and, 231
  LWA Scale, 97–98
legitimizing myths (LMs), 272, 323–325, 458–459
Leviathan, The (Hobbes), 2
Liar's Poker (Lewis), 405
liberalism, 8, 43, 171
  defining, 178
  judgment and, 185
  meaning and, 202
  self-identification, 200–201
Life Against Death (Brown), 117
limbic system, 164
Los Angeles County Social Survey (1995), 363, 367, 369
loss aversion, 249–251
lower classes, 223–224. see also equality, fear of; working class

Machiavellianism, 119
Machiavellianism (Mach IV) scale, 98–99
Manitoba Ethnocentrism Scale
  1996, 90, 98
  1997, 89
Manitoba parent studies, 94–100
Manitoba student studies, 90–94, 98–102
"map for study of personality/politics," 110
Marlowe-Crowne scale, 102
Marxism, 183, 323, 454
mass media/candidate perception, 6–7, 135–136. see also priming; television news programs
Mass Psychology of Fascism, The (Reich), 3
matriarchy, 318
maximization doctrine, 244–245
McCone Report, 440
McFarland/Adelson Study (1996), 89–90
meaning, 201–203
"Measures of Association for Cross Classifications" (Journal of the American Statistical Association), 191
mediational strength, 325
membership, in groups, 316–317. see also group-based social hierarchies
  evil and, 390–398
  personality and, 115
  shared grievances and, 455, 456, 459
  terrorism and, 424
Militia Attitudes Scale, 95, 97, 100–101
Minnesota Multiphasic Personality Inventory (MMPI), 118
minority groups, 252–253. see also racism; individual names of groups
Minuteman missiles, 261
modern racism, 273
Monitoring the Future (Bachman, Johnston, O'Malley), 74, 79
moods, 164, 165–168
moral equality, 221–222

moral judgement, 394–395
moral wrongdoing, 384–389. *see also* evil
motivation
    environment and, 116
    liberal/conservative ideology and, 177
    psychopathology, 112–114
    terrorism and, 411–412, 414–419
multiple studies, reports of, 472–473
Muslims, Bosnian, 317
My Lai massacre, 389, 394–395, 401–402, 405

nature *vs.* nurture, social dominance and, 104, 110–112, 116, 337
naysayers, 56
Nazis, 39, 67, 85. *see also* authoritarian personality syndrome
    agentic state and, 392–394
    Eichmann in Jerusalem (Arendt), 383, 389
    evil individuals, 395–398
    ideology of, 390
    mass base of Nazi Party, 197–198
    personality characteristics of, 64
    symbolic racism of, 362
"near-idealogues," 178, 186–187
neurophysiology, 165–168
New Age lifestyle, 75
Newsletter on Intellectual Freedom (American Library Association), 76
New Zealand Maoris, 280. *see also* racism
non-aligned voter's theory, 256
noninstrumental category, of discrimination, 290
"normative justifications," for political violence, 436
Nuremberg rallies, 85

Obedience to Authority (Milgram), 392
objective conflicts, 290–291
official terror, 321–322
Opinions and Personality (Smith, Bruner, White), 109
organizations, membership in, 54–55
outcome framing, 242, 253
out-group favoritism, 299–300, 322–323
overload, 437

parents
    Manitoba parent studies, 94–100
    power relations with, 46, 49–53
    terrorism and, 421
partisanship, 5, 170, 171–172
    ideological identification and voting behavior, 200–201
    nonracial, 364
party supporter's theory, 256
patriarchy, 318
perception
    group conflict, 342
    perceived threat, 343
    perceptual satisficing, 265
personality, 5. *see also* authoritarian personality syndrome
    construction of, 49–53
    defined, 24
    doubled, 390–392
    Nazis, characteristics of, 64
    politics and, 4
    social factors *vs.*, 334

personality and culture era, 19, 22
    connotative definitions of, 23–24
    denotative definition, 23, 25
    macrohumanistic national character studies, 25–26
    macroscientific studies, 26–27
    methodology, 24–25
    microhumanistic studies, 25
    microscientific studies, 26
    preferred topics in, 24
personality and politics, systematic study of, 22–23, 108–109, 120–121
    attitudes and voting behavior era, 19–20, 22, 27–29
    definitions, 109–110
    distribution of individuals in roles, 110
    environment and, 110–112
    future directions in, 30–31
    historical context and social background, 114–115
    ideology and decision era, 20, 22
    impact of personality of events, 115–116
    kinds of analysis, 117–120
    personality and culture era, 19, 22–27
    political cognition and decision era, 29–30
    psychopathology and, 112–114
    theory, role, and culture, 116–117
Personal Power, Meanness, and Dominance (PP-MAD) Scale, 99
persuasion, 6–7
plausible deniability, 322
policy evaluation, 187–188
Political and Economic Conservatism (PEC) Scale, 41, 42, 43, 54–57
political change, 160–161
political cognition and decision era, 29–30
political elites/leadership, 5–6, 36
political knowledge, 170–174
political leaders. *see individual names*
political psychology
    defined, 1–2
    history of, 2–3, 19–20
Political Psychology (journal), 3, 108
political style, 119
political symbols, 204, 213–215
political violence, 12, 379–381. *see also* politicized collective identity
    collective, 432, 446–448
        alternative channels, 440
        coercion, 440–441, 445
        conceptualizing, 450–452
        contingency *vs.* inherency, 432–435
        evaluation of, 439–446
        facilitation, 440–441
        inherency models, 437–438
        studies of, 435–439
    evil, 383–384
        actors and kernel of evil, 386–387
        everyday thinking about, 384–389
        individuals, 395–398
        killing organizations, 398–406
        organizations socialize individuals into, 390–398
        psychological functions of everyday conceptualization of, 387–389
        social psychological conceptualization of, 387–389
    terrorism, 411–412, 428–429